KARL MARX
FREDERICK ENGELS

Volume
37

KARL MARX: *CAPITAL*, Vol. III

LAWRENCE & WISHART

LONDON

This volume has been prepared jointly by Lawrence & Wishart Ltd., London, International Publishers Co. Inc., New York, and Progress Publishing Group Corporation, Moscow, in collaboration with the Russian Independent Institute of Social and National Problems (former Institute of Marxism-Leninism), Moscow.

Editorial commissions:
GREAT BRITAIN: Eric Hobsbawm, John Hoffman, Nicholas Jacobs, Monty Johnstone, Jeff Skelley, Ernst Wangermann, Ben Fowkes.
USA: James E. Jackson, Victor Perlo, Betty Smith, Dirk J. Struik.
RUSSIA: for Progress Publishing Group Corporation — Yu. V. Semyonov, Ye. N. Vladimirova; for the Russian Independent Institute of Social and National Problems — L. I. Golman, M. P. Mchedlov, V. N. Pospelova, G. S. Smirnov.

ISBN 0-85315-458-9

Printed in the USA

Contents

KARL MARX
CAPITAL
A CRITIQUE OF POLITICAL ECONOMY
Volume III

BOOK III
THE PROCESS OF CAPITALIST PRODUCTION
AS A WHOLE

I

PART I

THE CONVERSION OF SURPLUS VALUE
INTO PROFIT AND OF THE RATE OF SURPLUS VALUE
INTO THE RATE OF PROFIT

PART II

CONVERSION OF PROFIT INTO AVERAGE PROFIT

PART III

THE LAW OF THE TENDENCY
OF THE RATE OF PROFIT TO FALL

PART IV

CONVERSION OF COMMODITY CAPITAL AND MONEY CAPITAL INTO COMMERCIAL CAPITAL AND MONEY-DEALING CAPITAL (MERCHANT'S CAPITAL)

PART V

DIVISION OF PROFIT INTO INTEREST AND PROFIT OF ENTERPRISE. INTEREST-BEARING CAPITAL

BOOK III

THE PROCESS OF CAPITALIST PRODUCTION AS A WHOLE

II

PART V

DIVISION OF PROFIT INTO INTEREST AND PROFIT OF ENTERPRISE. INTEREST-BEARING CAPITAL *(CONTINUED)*

PART VI

TRANSFORMATION OF SURPLUS PROFIT INTO GROUND RENT

PART VII
REVENUES AND THEIR SOURCES

NOTES AND INDEXES

ILLUSTRATIONS

Illustrations on p.29 and p.36 with blank versos were consolidated to pp. 29-30 to meet U.S. production requirements.

Preface

Volume 37 of the *Collected Works* of Marx and Engels contains Volume III of *Capital*, and Preface and Supplement to *Capital*, Volume Three, by Engels.

Volume III deals with the process of capitalist production as a whole.

The present English edition follows the first German edition of 1894 edited by Engels. Errors and misprints found in the first German edition have been corrected. Figures and other data have been checked and set right where necessary. Quotations from different sources have been ascertained; those from English and American authors were checked with the original publications and given according to the 1894 German edition. Quotations in French, Latin and Greek are given in English translation. Bibliographical footnotes are based on Marx's excerpts and preparatory material.

The author's footnotes are marked by superior numbers with a round bracket, as distinct from editors' notes marked merely by numbers and footnotes indicated by index letters. Engels' insertions and footnotes are, as a rule, marked by his initials and placed into double oblique lines.

Foreign words and expressions are italicised and retained in the form used in the original with translation in the footnote where necessary. English words and expressions used by Marx and Engels are set in small caps, longer passages are placed in asterisks.

The volume was compiled and the preface, notes and indexes written by Tatyana Andrushchenko and Izora Kazmina; Mikhail Ter-

novsky took part in editing the volume (Russian Independent Institute of Social and National Problems).

The present English edition is based on the 1958 publication of
Capital by the Foreign Languages Publishing House, Moscow, in
which extensive use was made of the English translation by Ernest
Untermann printed by Charles H. Kerr & Co., Chicago, 1909.

The volume was prepared for the press by Yelena Chistyakova,
Margarita Lopukhina and Maria Shcheglova (Progress Publishing
Group Corporation).

KARL MARX

CAPITAL

A CRITIQUE OF POLITICAL ECONOMY

VOLUME III

BOOK THREE

THE PROCESS
OF CAPITALIST PRODUCTION AS A WHOLE

Edited by Frederick Engels

Das Kapital.

Kritik der politischen Oekonomie.

Von

Karl Marx.

Dritter Band, erster Theil.

Buch III:
Der Gesammtprocess der kapitalistischen Produktion.
Kapitel I bis XXVIII.

Herausgegeben von Friedrich Engels.

Hamburg
Verlag von Otto Meissner.
1894.

Title page of the first German edition
of Vol. III, I, of *Capital*

Frederick Engels

PREFACE

At last I have the privilege of making public this third book of Marx's main work, the conclusion of the theoretical part.[1] When I published the second volume, in 1885, I thought that except for a few, certainly very important, sections the third volume would probably offer only technical difficulties. This was indeed the case. But I had no idea at the time that these sections, the most important parts of the entire work, would give me as much trouble as they did, just as I did not anticipate the other obstacles, which were to retard completion of the work to such an extent.

Next and most important of all, it was my eye weakness which for years restricted my writing time to a minimum, and which, even now, permits me to write by artificial light only in exceptional cases. Furthermore, there were other pressing labours which could not be turned down, such as new editions and translations of Marx's and my own earlier works, hence reviews, prefaces, and supplements, often impossible without fresh study, etc. Above all, there was the English edition of the first volume of this work, for whose text I am ultimately responsible and which consequently consumed much of my time.[2] Whoever has in any way followed the colossal growth of international socialist literature during the last ten years, particularly the great number of translations of Marx's and my own earlier works, will agree with me that I have been lucky that the number of languages in which I could be of help to the translators, and therefore could not refuse in all conscience to review their work, is very limited. But the growth of literature was merely indicative of a corresponding growth of the international working-class movement itself. And this imposed new obligations upon me. From the first days of our public activity it was Marx and I who shouldered the main burden of the work as go-betweens for the national movements of socialists and workers in the various countries. This work expanded in proportion to the expansion of the movement as a whole. Up to the time of his death, Marx had borne the brunt of the burden in this as well. But after his death the ever-increasing bulk of work had to be done by myself alone. Since then it has become the rule for the various national workers' parties to establish direct contacts, and this is fortunately ever more the case. Yet requests for my assistance are still far more frequent than I would wish in view of my theoretical work. But if a man has been active in the movement for more than fifty years, as I have been, he regards the work connected with it as a bounden duty that brooks no delay. In our eventful time, just as in the 16th century, pure theorists on social affairs are found only on the side of reaction and for this reason these gentlemen are not even theorists in the full sense of the word, but simply apologists of reaction.

In view of the fact that I live in London my party contacts are limited to correspondence in winter, while in summer they are largely personal. This fact, and the necessity of following the movement in a steadily growing number of countries and a still more rapidly growing number of press organs, have compelled me to reserve matters which permit no interruption for completion during the winter months, and primarily the first three months of the year. When a man is past seventy his Meynert's association fibres of the brain function with a certain annoying prudence. He no longer surmounts interruptions in difficult theoretical problems as easily and quickly as before. It came about therefore that the work of one winter, if it was not completed, had to be largely begun anew the following winter. This was the case with the most difficult fifth part.

As the reader will observe from the following, the work of editing the third volume was essentially different from that of editing the second. In the case of the third volume there was nothing to go by outside a first extremely incomplete draft. The beginnings of the various parts were, as a rule, pretty carefully done and even stylistically polished. But the farther one went, the more sketchy and incomplete was the analysis, the more excursions it contained into arising side-issues whose proper place in the argument was left for later decision, and the longer and more complex the sentences, in which thoughts

were recorded *in statu nascendi*.[a] In some places handwriting and presentation betrayed all too clearly the outbreak and gradual progress
of the attacks of ill health, caused by overwork, which at the outset rendered the author's work increasingly difficult and finally compelled
him periodically to stop work altogether. And no wonder. Between
1863 and 1867, Marx not only completed the first draft of the two last
volumes of *Capital* and prepared the first volume for the printer, but
also performed the enormous work connected with the founding and
expansion of the International Workingmen's Association. As a result, already in 1864 and 1865 ominous signs of ill health appeared
which prevented Marx from personally putting the finishing touches
to the second and third volumes.

I began my work by dictating into readable copy the entire manuscript, which was often hard to decipher even for me. This alone required considerable time. It was only then that I could start on the
actual editing. I limited this to the essential. I tried my best to preserve the character of the first draft wherever it was sufficiently clear.
I did not even eliminate repetitions, wherever they, as was Marx's
custom, viewed the subject from another standpoint or at least expressed the same thought in different words. Wherever my alterations
or additions exceeded the bounds of editing, or where I had to apply
Marx's factual material to independent conclusions of my own, if
even as faithful as possible to the spirit of Marx, I have enclosed the
entire passage in brackets and affixed my initials. Some of my footnotes are not enclosed in brackets; but wherever I have initialled
them I am responsible for the entire note.

As is only to be expected in a first draft, there are numerous allu-
sions in the manuscript to points which were to have been expanded
upon later, without these promises always having been kept. I have
left them, because they reveal the author's intentions relative to future elaboration.

Now as to details.

As regards the first part, the main manuscript was serviceable only
with substantial limitations. The entire mathematical calculation of
the relation between the rate of surplus value and the rate of profit
(which makes up our Chapter III) is introduced in the very beginning, while the subject treated in our Chapter I is considered later
and as the occasion arises. Two attempts at revising, each of them

---

[a] at the moment of formation

eight pages *in folio*, were useful here. But even these did not possess
the desired continuity throughout. They furnished the substance for
what is now Chapter I. Chapter II is taken from the main manuscript. There was a series of uncompleted mathematical calculations
for Chapter III, as well as a whole, almost complete, notebook dating
from the seventies, which presents the relation of the rate of surplus
value to the rate of profit in the form of equations. My friend Samuel
Moore, who has also translated the greater portion of the first volume
into English, undertook to edit this notebook for me, a work for which
he was far better equipped, being an old Cambridge mathematician.
It was from his summary, with occasional use of the main manuscript, that I then compiled Chapter III. Nothing but the title was
available for Chapter IV. But since its subject-matter, the influence of
turnover on the rate of profit, is of vital importance, I have written it
myself, for which reason the whole chapter has been placed in brackets. It developed in the course of this work that the formula for the
rate of profit given in Chapter III required modification to be generally valid. Beginning with Chapter V, the main manuscript is the sole
source for the remainder of the part, although many transpositions
and supplements were also essential.

As for the following three parts, aside from stylistic editing I was
able to follow the original manuscript almost throughout. A few passages dealing mostly with the influence of turnover had to be brought
into agreement with Chapter IV, which I had inserted, and are likewise placed in brackets [a] and marked by my initials.

The greatest difficulty was presented by Part V which dealt with
the most complicated subject in the entire volume. And it was just at
this point that Marx was overtaken by one of the above-mentioned
serious attacks of illness. Here, then, was no finished draft, not even
a scheme whose outlines might have been filled out, but only the beginning of an elaboration — often just a disorderly mass of notes, comments and extracts. I tried at first to complete this part, as I had done
to a certain extent with the first one, by filling in the gaps and expanding upon passages that were only indicated, so that it would at
least approximately contain everything the author had intended.
I tried this no less than three times, but failed in every attempt, and
the time lost in this is one of the chief causes that held up this volume.
At last I realised that I was on the wrong track. I should have had to

---

[a] In this volume they are replaced by two oblique lines.

go through the entire voluminous literature in this field, and would in the end have produced something that would nevertheless not have been a book by Marx. I had no other choice but to more or less cut the Gordian knot by confining myself to as orderly an arrangement of available matter as possible, and to making only the most indispensable additions. And so it was that I succeeded in completing the principal labours for this part in the spring of 1893.

As for the various chapters, chapters XXI to XXIV were, in the main, complete. Chapters XXV and XXVI required a sifting of the references and an interpolation of material found elsewhere. Chapters XXVII and XXIX could be taken almost completely from the original manuscript, but Chapter XXVIII had to be re-arranged in places. The real difficulty, however, began with Chapter XXX. From here on it was not only a matter of properly arranging the references, but of putting the train of thought into proper order, interrupted as it was at every point by intervening clauses and deviations, etc., and resumed elsewhere, often just casually. Thus, Chapter XXX was put together by means of transpositions and excisions which were utilised, however, in other places. Chapter XXXI, again, possessed greater continuity. But then follows a long section in the manuscript, entitled "The Confusion", containing nothing but extracts from parliamentary reports on the crises of 1847 and 1857, in which are compiled statements of twenty-three businessmen and economists, largely on money and capital, gold drain, over-speculation, etc., and supplied here and there with short facetious comments. Practically all the then current views concerning the relation of money to capital are represented therein, either in the answers or in the questions, and it was the "confusion" revealed in identifying money and capital in the money market that Marx meant to treat with criticism and sarcasm. After many attempts I convinced myself that this chapter could not be put into shape. Its material, particularly that supplied with Marx's comments, was used wherever I found an opportune place for it.

Next, in tolerable order, comes what I placed in Chapter XXXII. But this is immediately followed by a new batch of extracts from parliamentary reports on every conceivable thing pertinent to this part, intermingled with the author's comments. Toward the end these extracts and comments are focussed more and more on the movement of monetary metals and on exchange rates, and close with all kinds of miscellaneous remarks. On the other hand, the "Precapitalist" chapter (Chap. XXXVI) was quite complete.

Of all this material beginning with the "Confusion", save that which had been previously inserted, I made up chapters XXXIII to XXXV. This could not, of course, be done without considerable interpolations on my part for the sake of continuity. Unless they are merely formal in nature, the interpolations are expressly indicated as belonging to me. In this way I have finally succeeded in working into the text *all* the author's relevant statements. Nothing has been left out but a small portion of the extracts, which either repeated what had already been said, or touched on points which the manuscript did not treat any further.

The part on ground rent was much more fully treated, although by no means properly arranged, if only for the fact that Marx found it necessary to recapitulate the plan of the entire part in Chapter XLIII (the last portion of the part on rent in the manuscript). This was all the more desirable, since the manuscript opens with Chapter XXXVII, followed by chapters XLV to XLVII, and only thereafter chapters XXXVIII to XLIV. The tables for the differential rent II involved the greatest amount of work and so did the discovery that the third case of this class of rent had not at all been analysed in Chapter XLIII, where it belonged.

In the seventies Marx engaged in entirely new special studies for this part on ground rent. For years he had studied the Russian originals of statistical reports inevitable after the "reform" of 1861 in Russia and other publications on landownership, had taken extracts from these originals, placed at his disposal in admirably complete form by his Russian friends, and had intended to use them for a new version of this part. Owing to the variety of forms both of landownership and of exploitation of agricultural producers in Russia, this country was to play the same role in the part dealing with ground rent that England played in Book I in connection with industrial wage labour.[3] He was unfortunately denied the opportunity of carrying out this plan.

Lastly, the seventh part was available complete, but only as a first draft, whose endlessly involved periods had first to be dissected to be made printable. There exists only the beginning of the final chapter. It was to treat of the three major classes of developed capitalist society — the landowners, capitalists and wage labourers — corresponding to the three great forms of revenue, ground rent, profit and wages, and the class struggle, an inevitable concomitant of their existence, as the actual consequence of the capitalist period.[4] Marx used to leave such concluding summaries until the final editing, just before going to press, when the latest historical developments furnished him with unfailing regularity with proofs of the most laudable timeliness for his theoretical propositions.

Citations and proofs illustrating his statements are, as in the second volume, considerably less numerous than in the first. Quotations from Book I refer to pages in the 2nd and 3rd editions. Wherever the manuscript refers to theoretical statements of earlier economists, the name alone is given as a rule, and the quotations were to be added during the final editing. Of course, I had to leave this as it was. There are only four parliamentary reports, but these are abundantly used. They are the following:

1) Reports from Committees (of the Lower House), Volume VIII, Commercial Distress, Volume II, Part I, 1847-48. Minutes of Evidence.— Quoted as Commercial Distress, 1847-48.

2) Secret Committee of the House of Lords on Commercial Distress 1847. Report printed in 1848. Evidence printed in 1857 (because considered too compromising in 1848).— Quoted as C. D. 1848/57.[5]

3) Report: Bank Acts, 1857.— Ditto, 1858.— Reports of the Committee of the Lower House on the Effect of the Bank Acts of 1844 and 1845. With evidence.— Quoted as: B. A. (also as B. C.) 1857 or 1858.[6]

I am going to start on the fourth volume — the history of the theory of surplus value — as soon as it is in any way possible.[7]

———

In the preface to the second volume of *Capital* I had to square accounts with the gentlemen who raised a hue and cry at the time because they fancied to have discovered "in Rodbertus the secret source and a superior predecessor of Marx". I offered them an opportunity to show "what the economics of a Rodbertus can accomplish"; I defied them to show "how an equal average rate of profit can and must come about, not only without a violation of the law of value, but rather on the very basis of it".[a] These same gentlemen who for either subjective or objective, but as a rule anything but scientific reasons were then lionising the brave Rodbertus as an economic star of the first magnitude, have without exception failed to furnish an answer.

---

[a] See present edition, Vol. 36, p. 23.

However, other people have thought it worth their while to occupy
themselves with the problem.

In his critique of the second volume (*Conrads Jahrbücher*, XI, 5,
1885, S. 452-65), Professor *W. Lexis* took up the question, although
he did not care to offer a direct solution.[a] He says:

> "The solution of the contradiction" (between the Ricardo-Marxian law of value
> and an equal average rate of profit) "is impossible if the various classes of commodities
> are considered *individually* and if their value is to be equal to their exchange value,
> and the latter equal or proportional to their price."

According to him, the solution is only possible if

> "we cease measuring the value of individual commodities according to labour, and
> consider only the production of commodities *as a whole* and their distribution among
> the aggregate classes of capitalists and workers.... The working class receives but a cer-
> tain portion of the total product,... the other portion, which falls to the share of the cap-
> italist class, represents the surplus product in Marxian sense, and accordingly ... the
> surplus value. Then the members of the capitalist class divide this total surplus value
> among themselves *not* in accordance with the number of workers employed by them,
> but in proportion to the capital invested by each, the land also being accounted for as
> capital value."

The Marxian ideal values determined by units of labour incorporated in the commodities do not correspond to prices but may be

> "regarded as points of departure of a shift which leads to the actual prices. The lat-
> ter depend on the fact that equal sums of capital demand equal profits."

For this reason some capitalists will secure prices higher than the
ideal values for their commodities, and others will secure lower prices.

> "But since the losses and gains of surplus value balance one another within the cap-
> italist class, the total amount of the surplus value is the same as it would be if all prices
> were proportional to the ideal values."

It is evident that the problem has not in any way been solved here,
but has, though somewhat loosely and shallowly, been on the whole
correctly *formulated*. And this is, indeed, more than we could have
expected from a man who, like the above author, takes a certain
pride in being a "vulgar economist". It is really surprising when compared with the handiwork of other vulgar economists, which we shall
later discuss. Lexis' vulgar economy is, anyhow, in a class of its own.
He says that capital gains *might*, at any rate, be derived in the way indicated by Marx, but that nothing *compels* one to accept this view.

---

[a] W. Lexis, "Die Marx'sche Kapitaltheorie".

On the contrary. Vulgar economy, he says, has at least a more plausible explanation, namely:

> "The capitalist sellers, such as the producer of raw materials, the manufacturer, the wholesale dealer, and the retail dealer, all make a gain on their transactions by selling at a price higher than the purchase price, thus adding a certain percentage to the price they themselves pay for the commodity. The worker alone is unable to obtain a similar additional value for his commodity; he is compelled by reason of his unfavourable condition vis-à-vis the capitalist to sell his labour at the price it costs him, that is to say, for the essential means of his subsistence.... Thus, these additions to prices retain their full impact with regard to the buying wage-worker, and cause the transfer of a part of the value of the total product to the capitalist class."

One need not strain his thinking powers to see that this explanation for the profits of capital, as advanced by "vulgar economy", amounts in practice to the same thing as the Marxian theory of surplus value; that the workers are in just the same "unfavourable condition" according to Lexis as according to Marx; that they are just as much the victims of swindle because every non-worker can sell commodities above price, while the worker cannot do so; and that it is just as easy to build up an at least equally plausible vulgar socialism on the basis of this theory, as that built in England on the foundation of Jevons's and Menger's theory of use value and marginal utility.[8] I even suspect that if Mr. George Bernard Shaw had been familiar with this theory of profit, he would have likely fallen to with both hands, discarding Jevons and Karl Menger, to build anew the Fabian church of the future[9] upon this rock.

In reality, however, this theory is merely a paraphrase of the Marxian. What defrays all the price additions? It is the workers' "total product". And this is due to the fact that the commodity "labour", or, as Marx has it, labour power, has to be sold below its price. For if it is a common property of all commodities to be sold at a price higher than their cost of production, with labour being the sole exception since it is always sold at the cost of production, then labour is simply sold below the price that rules in this world of vulgar economy. Hence the resultant extra profit accruing to the capitalist, or capitalist class, arises, and can only arise, in the last analysis, from the fact that the worker, after reproducing the equivalent for the price of his labour power, must produce an additional product for which he is not paid — i. e., a surplus product, a product of unpaid labour, or surplus value. Lexis is an extremely cautious man in the choice of his terms. He does not say anywhere outright that the above is his own conception. But if it is, it is plain as day that we are not dealing with one of those ordinary vulgar economists, of whom he says himself that every one of them is "at best only a hopeless idiot" in Marx's eyes, but with a Marxist disguised as a vulgar economist. Whether this disguise has occurred consciously or unconsciously is a psychological question which does not interest us at this point. Whoever would care to investigate this, might also probe how a man as shrewd as Lexis undoubtedly is, could at one time defend such nonsense as bimetallism.[10]

The first to really attempt an answer to the question was Dr. Conrad Schmidt in his pamphlet entitled *Die Durchschnittsprofitrate auf Grundlage des Marx'schen Werthgesetzes*, Stuttgart, Dietz, 1889. Schmidt seeks to reconcile the details of the formation of market prices with both the law of value and with the average rate of profit. The industrial capitalist receives in his product, first, an equivalent of the capital he has advanced, and, second, a surplus product for which he has paid nothing. But to obtain a surplus product he must advance capital to production. That is, he must apply a certain quantity of objectified labour to be able to appropriate this surplus product. For the capitalist, therefore, the capital he advances represents the quantity of objectified labour socially necessary for him to obtain this surplus product. This applies to every industrial capitalist. Now, since products are mutually exchanged, according to the law of value, in proportion to the labour socially necessary for their production, and since, as far as the capitalist is concerned, the labour necessary for the manufacture of the surplus product happens to be past labour accumulated in his capital, it follows that surplus products are exchanged in proportion to the sums of capital required for their production, and not in proportion to the labour *actually* incorporated in them. Hence the share of each unit of capital is equal to the sum of all produced surplus values divided by the sum of the capitals expended in production. Accordingly, equal sums of capital yield equal profits in equal time spans, and this is accomplished by adding the cost price of the surplus product so calculated, i. e., the average profit, to the cost price of the paid product and by selling both the paid and unpaid product at this increased price. The average rate of profit takes shape in spite of average commodity prices being determined, as Schmidt holds, by the law of value.

The construction is extremely ingenious. It is completely patterned after the Hegelian model, but like the majority of Hegelian constructions it is not correct. Surplus product or paid product, makes no difference. If the law of value is also to be *directly* valid for the average prices, both of them must be sold at prices proportionate to the socially necessary labour required and expended in producing them. The law of value is aimed from the first against the idea derived from the capitalist mode of thought that accumulated labour of the past, which comprises capital, is not merely a certain sum of finished value, but that, because a factor in production and the formation of profit, it also produces value and is hence a source of more value than it has itself; it establishes that living labour alone possesses this faculty. It is well known that capitalists expect equal profits proportionate to their capitals and regard their advances of capital as a sort of cost price of their profits. But if Schmidt utilises this conception as a means of reconciling prices based on the average rate of profit with the law of value, repudiates the law of value itself by attributing to it as one of its co-determinative factors a conception with which the law is wholly at variance.

Either accumulated labour creates value the same as living labour. In that case the law of value does not apply.

Or, it does not create value. In that case Schmidt's demonstration is incompatible with the law of value.

Schmidt strayed into this bypath when quite close to the solution, because he believed that he needed nothing short of a mathematical formula to demonstrate the conformance of the average price of every individual commodity with the law of value. But while on the wrong track in this instance, in the immediate proximity of the goal, the rest of his booklet is evidence of the understanding with which he drew further conclusions from the first two volumes of *Capital*. His is the honour of independently finding the correct explanation developed by Marx in the third part of the third volume for the hitherto inexplicable sinking tendency of the rate of profit, and, similarly, of explaining the derivation of commercial profit out of industrial surplus value, and of making a great number of observations concerning interest and ground rent, in which he anticipates ideas developed by Marx in the fourth and fifth parts of the third volume.

In a subsequent article (*Neue Zeit*, 1892-93, Nos. 3 and 4), Schmidt takes a different tack in his effort to solve the problem.[a] He contends that it is competition which produces the average rate of profit by causing the transfer of capital from branches of production with under-average profit to branches with above-average profit. It is not a

---

[a] C. Schmidt, "Die Durchschnittsprofitrate und das Marx'sche Werthgesetz".

revelation that competition is the great equaliser of profits. But now Schmidt tries to prove that this levelling of profits is identical with a reduction of the selling price of commodities in excess supply to a magnitude of value which society can pay for them according to the law of value. Marx's analyses in the book itself are ample evidence why this way, too, could not lead to the goal.

After Schmidt P. Fireman tackled the problem (*Conrads Jahrbücher*, dritte Folge, III, 1891, S. 793).[a] I shall not go into his remarks on other aspects of the Marxian analysis. They rest upon the false assumption that Marx wishes to define where he only investigates, and that in general one might expect fixed, cut-to-measure, once and for all applicable definitions in Marx's works. It is self-evident that where things and their interrelations are conceived, not as fixed, but as changing, their mental images, the ideas, are likewise subject to change and transformation; and they are not encapsulated in rigid definitions, but are developed in their historical or logical process of formation. This makes clear, of course, why in the beginning of his first book Marx proceeds from the simple production of commodities as the historical premise, ultimately to arrive from this basis to capital — why he proceeds from the simple commodity instead of a logically and historically secondary form — from an already capitalistically modified commodity. To be sure, Fireman positively fails to see this. These and other side-issues, which could give rise to still other diverse objections, are better left by the wayside, while we go on forthwith to the gist of the matter.[b] While theory teaches Fireman that at a given rate of surplus value the latter is proportional to the labour power employed, he learns from experience that at a given average rate of profit, profit is proportional to the total capital employed. He explains this by saying that profit is merely a conventional phenomenon (which means in his language that it belongs to a definite social formation with which it stands and falls). Its existence is simply tied up with capital. The latter, provided it is strong enough to secure a profit for itself, is compelled by competition also to secure for itself a rate of profit equal for all sums of capital. Capitalist production is simply impossible without an equal rate of profit. Given this mode of production, the quantity of profit for the individual capitalist can, at

---

[a] P. Fireman, "Kritik der Marx'schen Werttheorie".- [b] See also F. Engels, Supplement to *Capital*, Volume Three, 1. Law of Value and Rate of Profit (this volume, pp. 876-94).

a certain rate of profit, depend only on the magnitude of his capital. On the other hand, profit consists of surplus value, of unpaid labour. But how is surplus value, whose magnitude hinges upon the degree of labour exploitation, transformed into profit, whose magnitude depends upon the amount of the capital employed?

"Simply by selling commodities above their value in all branches of production in which the ratio between ... constant and variable capital is greatest; but this also implies that commodities are sold below their value in those branches of production in which the ratio between constant and variable capital = c:v is smallest, and that commodities are sold at their true value only in branches in which the ratio of c:v represents a certain mean figure.... Is this discrepancy between individual prices and their respective values a refutation of the value principle? By no means. For since the prices of some commodities rise above their value as much as the prices of others fall below it, the total sum of prices remains equal to the total sum of values ... in the end this incongruity disappears." This incongruity is a "disturbance"; "however, in the exact sciences it is not customary to regard a predictable disturbance as a refutation of a law".

On comparing the relevant passages in Chapter IX with the above, it will be seen that Fireman has indeed placed his finger on the salient point. But the undeservedly cool reception of his able article shows how many interconnecting links would still be needed even after this discovery to enable Fireman to work out a full and comprehensive solution. Although many were interested in this problem, they were all still fearful of getting their fingers burnt. And this is explained not only by the incomplete form in which Fireman left his discovery, but also by the undeniable faultiness of both his conception of the Marxian analysis and of his own general critique of the latter, based as it was on his misconception.

Whenever there is a chance of making a fool of himself over some difficult matter, Herr Professor Julius Wolf, of Zurich, never fails to do so. He tells us (*Conrads Jahrbücher*, dritte Folge, II, S. 352 and following)[a] that the entire problem is resolved in relative surplus value. The production of relative surplus value rests on the increase of constant capital vis-à-vis variable capital.

"A plus in constant capital presupposes a plus in the productive power of the labourers. Since this plus in productive power (by way of lowering the worker's cost of living) produces a plus in surplus value, a direct relation is established between the increasing surplus value and the increasing share of constant capital in total capital. A plus in constant capital indicates a plus in the productive power of labour. With variable capital remaining the same and constant capital increasing, surplus value must therefore, in accordance with Marx, increase as well. This was the problem presented to us."

---

[a] J. Wolf, "Das Rätsel der Durchschnittsprofitrate bei Marx".

True, Marx says the very opposite in a hundred places in the first book; true, the assertion that, according to Marx, when variable capital shrinks, relative surplus value increases in proportion to the increase in constant capital, is so astounding that it puts to shame all parliamentary declamation; true, Herr Julius Wolf demonstrates in his every line that he does not in the least understand, be it relatively or absolutely, the concepts of relative or absolute surplus value; to be sure he says himself that

"at first glance one seems really to be in a nest of incongruities",

which, by the way, is the only true statement in his entire article. But what does all that matter? Herr Julius Wolf is so proud of his brilliant discovery that he cannot refrain from bestowing posthumous praise on Marx for it and from extolling his own fathomless nonsense as a

"new proof of the keen and far-sighted way his" (Marx's) "system of criticism of capitalist economy is set forth".

But now comes the choicest bit of all. Herr Wolf says:

"Ricardo has likewise claimed that an equal investment of capital yielded equal surplus value (profit), just as the same expenditure of labour created the same surplus value (as regards its quantity). And the question now was how the one agreed with the other. But Marx has refused to accept this way of putting the problem. *He has proved beyond a doubt (in the third volume)* that the second statement was not necessarily a consequence of the law of value, that it even contradicted his law of value and should therefore ... be forthwith repudiated."

And thereupon Wolf probes who of us two, Marx or I, had made a mistake. It does not occur to him, naturally, that it is he who is groping in the dark.

I should offend my readers and fail to see the humour of the situation if I were to waste a single word on this choice morsel. I shall only add that his audacity in using the opportunity to report the ostensible gossip among professors that Conrad Schmidt's above-named work was "directly inspired by Engels" matches the audacity with which he dared to say at one time what "Marx has proved beyond a doubt in the third volume". Herr Julius Wolf! It may be customary in the world in which you live and strive for the man who publicly poses a problem to others to acquaint his close friends on the sly with its solution. I am quite prepared to believe that you are capable of this sort of thing. But that a man need not stoop to such shabby tricks in my world is proved by the present preface.

No sooner had Marx died than Mr. Achille Loria hastened to publish an article about him in the *Nuova Antologia* (April 1883).[a] To begin with, a biography brimming with misinformation, followed by a
critique of public, political and literary work. He falsifies Marx's materialist conception of history and distorts it with an assurance that
bespeaks a great purpose. And this purpose was eventually carried
out. In 1886, the same Mr. Loria published a book, *La teoria economica
della constituzione politica*, in which he announced to his astounded
contemporaries that Marx's conception of history, so completely and
purposefully misrepresented by him in 1883, was his own discovery.
To be sure, the Marxian theory is reduced in this book to a rather
philistine level, and the historical illustrations and proofs abound in
blunders which would never be tolerated in a fourth-form boy. But
what does that matter? The discovery that political conditions and
events are everywhere invariably explained by corresponding economic conditions was, as is herewith demonstrated, not made by Marx
in 1845, but by Mr. Loria in 1886. At least he has happily convinced
his countrymen of this, and, after his book appeared in French,[b] also
some Frenchmen, and can now pose in Italy as the author of a new
epoch-making theory of history until the Italian socialists find time to
strip the *illustre* Loria of his stolen peacock feathers.

But this is just a sample of Mr. Loria's style. He assures us that all
Marx's theories rest on *conscious* sophistry (*un consaputo sofisma*); that
Marx did not stop at paralogisms even when he *knew them to be paralogisms* (*sapendoli tali*), etc. And after thus impressing the necessary
upon his readers with a series of similar contemptible insinuations, so
that they should regard Marx as an unprincipled upstart *à la* Loria
who achieves his little effects by the same wretched humbug as our
professor from Padua, he reveals an important secret to them, and
thereby takes us back to the rate of profit.

Mr. Loria says: According to Marx, the amount of surplus value
(which Mr. Loria here identifies with profit) produced in a capitalist
industrial establishment should depend on the variable capital employed in it, since constant capital does not yield profit. But this is
contrary to fact. For in practice profit does not depend on variable,
but on total capital. And Marx himself recognises this (Buch I, Kap.
XI[11]) and admits that on the surface facts appear to contradict his

[a] A. Loria, "Karl Marx". - [b] A. Loria, *Les Bases économiques de la constitution soziale*, Paris, 1893.

theory. But how does he get around this contradiction? He refers his readers to an as yet unpublished subsequent volume. Loria has already told *his* readers about this volume that he did not believe Marx had ever entertained the thought of writing it, and now exclaims triumphantly:

"I have not been wrong in contending that this second volume, which Marx always flings at his adversaries without it ever appearing, might very well have been a shrewd expedient applied by Marx whenever scientific arguments failed him (*un ingegnoso spediente ideato dal Marx a sostituzione degli argomenti scientifici*)."

And whosoever is not convinced after this that Marx stands in the same class of scientific swindlers as *l'illustre* Loria, is past all redemption.

We have at least learned this much: According to Mr. Loria, the Marxian theory of surplus value is absolutely incompatible with the existence of a general equal rate of profit. Then, there appeared the second volume and therewith my public challenge precisely on this very point.[a] If Mr. Loria had been one of us diffident Germans, he would have experienced a certain degree of embarrassment. But he is a cocky southerner, coming from a hot climate, where, as he can testify, cool nerve is a natural requirement. The question of the rate of profit has been publicly put. Mr. Loria has publicly declared it insoluble. And for this very reason he is now going to outdo himself by publicly solving it.

This miracle is accomplished in *Conrads Jahrbücher*, neue Folge, Buch XX, S. 272 and following, in an article dealing with Conrad Schmidt's already cited pamphlet.[b] After Loria learned from Schmidt how commercial profit was made, he suddenly saw daylight.

"Since determining value by means of labour time is to the advantage of those capitalists who invest a greater portion of their capital in wages, the unproductive" (read commercial) "capital can derive a higher interest" (read profit) "from these privileged capitalists and thus bring about an equalisation between the individual industrial capitalists... For instance, if each of the industrial capitalists A, B, C uses 100 working days and 0, 100, 200 constant capital respectively in production, and if the wages for 100 working days amount to 50 working days, then each receives a surplus value of 50 working days, and the rate of profit is 100% for the first, 33.3% for the second, and 20% for the third capitalist. But if a fourth capitalist D accumulates an unproductive capital of 300, which claims an interest" (profit) "equal in value to 40 working days from A, and an interest of 20 working days from B, then the rate of profit of capitalists A and B

---

[a] See present edition, Vol. 36, p. 23. - [b] A. Loria, *Die Durchschnittsprofitrate auf Grundlage des Marx'schen Wertgesetzes.*

will sink to 20%, just as that of C, while D with his capital of 300 receives profit of 60, or a rate of profit of 20%, the same as the other capitalists."

With such astonishing dexterity, *l'illustre* Loria solves by sleight of hand the question which he had declared insoluble ten years previously. Unfortunately, he did not let us into the secret wherefrom the "unproductive capital" obtained the power to squeeze out of the industrialists their extra profit in excess of the average rate of profit, and to retain it in its own pocket, just as the landlord pockets the tenant's surplus profit as ground rent. Indeed, according to him it would be the merchants who would raise a tribute analogous to ground rent from the industrialists, and would thereby bring about an average rate of profit. Commercial capital is indeed a very essential factor in producing the general rate of profit, as nearly everybody knows. But only a literary adventurer who in his heart sneezes at political economy, can venture the assertion that it has the magic power to absorb all surplus value in excess of the general rate of profit even before this general rate has taken shape, and to convert it into ground rent for itself without, moreover, even having need to do with any real estate. No less astonishing is the assertion that commercial capital manages to discover the particular industrialists, whose surplus value just covers the average rate of profit, and that it considers it a privilege to mitigate the lot of these luckless victims of the Marxian law of value to a certain extent by selling their products gratis for them, without asking as much as a commission for it. What a mountebank one must be to imagine that Marx had need to resort to such miserable tricks!

But it is not until we compare him with his northern competitors, for instance with Herr Julius Wolf, who was not born yesterday either, that *l'illustre* Loria shines in his full glory. What a yelping pup Herr Wolf appears even in his big volume on *Sozialismus und kapitalistische Gesellschaftsordnung*, alongside the Italian! How awkward, I am almost tempted to say modest, he appears beside the noble audacity of the *maestro* who takes it for granted that Marx, neither more nor less than other people, was as much a conscious sophist, paralogist, humbug and mountebank as Mr. Loria himself— that Marx took in the public with the promise of rounding out his theory in a subsequent volume whenever he was in a difficult position, knowing full well that he neither could nor ever would write it. Boundless nerve coupled with a flair for slipping like an eel through impossible situations, a heroic contempt for pummellings received, hasty plagia-

rism of other people's accomplishments, importunate and fanfa-
ronading advertising, spreading his fame by means of a chorus of
friends — who can equal him in all this?

Italy is the land of classicism. Ever since the great era when the
dawn of modern times rose there, it has produced magnificent characters of unequalled classic perfection, from Dante to Garibaldi. But
the period of its degradation and foreign domination also bequeathed
it classic character-masks, among them two particularly clear-cut
types, that of Sganarelle and Dulcamara. The classic unity of both is
embodied in our *illustre* Loria.

In conclusion I must take my readers across the Atlantic. Dr.
(Med.) George C. Stiebeling, of New York, has also found a solution
to the problem, and a very simple one. So simple, indeed, that no one
either here, or there, took him seriously. This aroused his ire, and he
complained bitterly about the injustice of it in an endless stream of
pamphlets and newspaper articles appearing on both sides of the
great water. He was told in the *Neue Zeit*[a] that his entire solution
rested on a mathematical error. But this could scarcely disturb him.
Marx had also made mathematical errors, and was yet right in many
things. Let us then take a look at Dr. Stiebeling's solution.

"I take two factories working with equal capitals for an equal length of time, but
with a different ratio of constant and variable capitals. I make the total capital
$(c + v) = y$, and the difference in the ratio of the constant and variable capital $= x$.
For factory I, $y = c + v$, for factory II, $y = (c - x) + (v + x)$. Therefore the rate of
surplus value for factory $I = \frac{s}{v}$, and for factory $II = \frac{s}{v+x}$. Profit (p) is what I call
the total surplus value (s) by which the total capital y, or $c + v$, is augmented in the
given time; thus, $p = s$. Hence, the rate of profit for factory $I = \frac{p}{y}$, or $\frac{s}{c+v}$, and
for factory II it is also $\frac{p}{y}$, or $\frac{s}{(c-x)+(v+x)}$, i. e. it is also $= \frac{s}{c+v}$. The... problem
thus resolves itself in such a way that, on the basis of the law of value, with equal capi-
tal and equal time, but unequal quantities of living labour, a change in the rate of surplus value causes the equalisation of an average rate of profit" (G. C. Stiebeling, *Das
Werthgesetz und die Profitrate*, New York, John Heinrich).

However pretty and revealing the above calculation may be, we
are compelled to ask Dr. Stiebeling *one* question: How does he know
that the sum of surplus value produced by factory I is exactly equal to
the sum of the surplus value produced by factory II? He states explic-

---

[a] [A. Luxenberg,] "Bemerkung zu dem Aufsatze des Herrn Stiebeling", *Die Neue Zeit*,
No. 3, 1887, S. 123-27.

itly that c, v, y and x, that is, all the other factors in the calculation, are the same for both factories, but makes no mention of s. It does not by any means follow from the fact that he designated both of the above-mentioned quantities of surplus value algebraically with s. Rather, it is just the thing that has to be proved, since Mr. Stiebeling without further ado also identifies profit p with the surplus value. Now there are just two possible alternatives. Either the two s's are equal, both factories produce equal quantities of surplus value, and therefore also equal quantities of profit, since both capitals are equal. In that case Mr. Stiebeling has from the start taken for granted what he was really called upon to prove. Or, one factory produces more surplus value than the other, in which case his entire calculation tumbles about his ears.

Mr. Stiebeling spared neither pains nor money to build mountains of calculations upon this mathematical error, and to exhibit them to the public. I can assure him, for his own peace of mind, that they are nearly all equally wrong, and that in the exceptional cases when this is not so, they prove something entirely different from what he set out to prove. He proves, for instance, by comparing U. S. census figures for 1870 and 1880 that the rate of profit has actually fallen, but interprets it wrongly and assumes that Marx's theory of a constantly stable rate of profit should be corrected on the basis of experience. Yet it follows from the third part of the present third book that this Marxian "stable rate of profit" is purely a figment of Mr. Stiebeling's imagination, and that the tendency for the rate of profit to fall is due to circumstances which are just the reverse of those indicated by Dr. Stiebeling. No doubt Dr. Stiebeling has the best intentions, but when a man wants to deal with scientific questions he should above all learn to read the works he wishes to use just as the author had written them, and above all without reading anything into them that they do not contain.

The outcome of the entire investigation shows again with reference to this question as well that it is the Marxian school alone which has accomplished something. If Fireman and Conrad Schmidt read this third book, each one, for his part, may well be satisfied with his own work.

London, October 4, 1894   *Fr. Engels*

BOOK III

THE PROCESS
OF CAPITALIST PRODUCTION
AS A WHOLE

I

Part I

THE CONVERSION OF SURPLUS VALUE INTO PROFIT AND OF THE RATE OF SURPLUS VALUE INTO THE RATE OF PROFIT

Chapter I

COST PRICE AND PROFIT

In Book I we analysed the phenomena which constitute the capitalist *process of production* as such, as the immediate production process, with no regard for any of the secondary effects of outside influences. But this immediate process of production does not exhaust the life span of capital. It is supplemented in the actual world by the *process of circulation*, which was the object of study in Book II. In the latter, namely in Part III, which treated the process of circulation as a medium for the social process of reproduction, it developed that the capitalist process of production taken as a whole represents a synthesis of the processes of production and circulation. Considering what this third book treats, it cannot confine itself to general reflection relative to this synthesis. On the contrary, it must locate and describe the concrete forms which grow out of the *movements of capital as a whole*. In their actual movement capitals confront each other in such concrete shape, for which the form of capital in the immediate process of production, just as its form in the process of circulation, appear only as special instances. The various forms of capital, as evolved in this book, thus approach step by step the form which they assume on the surface of society, in the action of different capitals upon one another, in competition, and in the ordinary consciousness of the agents of production themselves.

The value of every commodity (C) produced in the capitalist way is represented in the formula: $C = c + v + s$. If we subtract surplus

value s from this value of the product there remains a bare equivalent
or a substitute value in goods, for the capital value c + v expended in
the elements of production.

For example, if the production of a certain article requires a capital
outlay of £500, of which £20 are for the wear and tear of means of labour, £380 for the materials of production, and £100 for labour power, and if the rate of surplus value is 100%, then the value of the
product = $400_c + 100_v + 100_s = £600$.

After deducting the surplus value of £100, there remains a commodity value of £500 which only replaces the expended capital of £500.
This portion of the value of the commodity, which replaces the price
of the consumed means of production and labour power, only replaces what the commodity costs the capitalist himself. For him it,
therefore, represents the cost price of the commodity.

What the commodity costs the capitalist and its actual production
cost are two quite different magnitudes. The portion of the commodity value making up the surplus value does not cost the capitalist
anything simply because it costs the labourer unpaid labour. Yet, on
the basis of capitalist production, after the labourer enters the production process he himself constitutes an ingredient of operating productive capital, which belongs to the capitalist. Therefore, the capitalist is the actual producer of the commodity. For this reason the cost
price of the commodity necessarily appears to the capitalist as the actual cost of the commodity. If we take k to be the cost price, the formula C = c + v + s turns into the formula C = k + s, that is, the
commodity value = cost price + surplus value.

The grouping of the various value portions of a commodity which
only replace the value of the capital expended in its production under
the head of cost price expresses, on the one hand, the specific character of capitalist production. The capitalist cost of the commodity is
measured by the expenditure of *capital*, while the actual cost of the
commodity is measured by the expenditure of *labour*. Thus, the capitalist cost price of the commodity differs in quantity from its value, or
its actual cost price. It is smaller than the value of the commodity, because, with C = k + s, it is evident that k = C − s. On the other
hand, the cost price of a commodity is by no means simply a category
which exists only in capitalist bookkeeping. The individualisation of
this portion of value is continually manifest in practice in the actual
production of the commodity, because it has ever to be reconverted
from its commodity form by way of the process of circulation into the

First page of Marx's manuscript of the third volume of *Capital*,
marked by Engels as "Ms. I"

A page of Vol. III of *Capital*, copied by a secretary, with alterations by Engels. The insertion at the top of the page is by Engels

(Reduced)

form of productive capital, so that the cost price of the commodity always must repurchase the elements of production consumed in its manufacture.

The category of cost price, on the other hand, has nothing to do with the formation of commodity value, or with the process of self-expansion of capital. When I know that of the value of a commodity worth £600, $\frac{5}{6}$, or £500, represent no more than an equivalent of the capital of £500 consumed in its production and that it can therefore suffice only to repurchase the material elements of this capital, I know nothing as yet either of the way in which these $\frac{5}{6}$ of the value of the commodity, which represent its cost price, are produced, or about the way in which the last sixth, which constitutes its surplus value, was produced. The investigation will show, however, that in capitalist economics the cost price assumes the false appearance of a category of value production itself.

To return to our example. Suppose the value produced by one labourer during an average social working day is represented by a money sum of 6s. = 6M. Then the advanced capital of £500 = $400_c + 100_v$ represents a value produced in $1,666\frac{2}{3}$ ten-hour working days, of which $1,333\frac{1}{3}$ working days are crystallised in the value of the means of production = 400_c, and $333\frac{1}{3}$ working days are crystallised in the value of labour power = 100_v. Having assumed a rate of surplus value of 100%, the production of the commodity to be newly formed entails a labour expenditure = $100_v + 100_s = 666\frac{2}{3}$ ten-hour working days.

We know, then (see Buch I, Kap. VII, S. 201/193 [a]) that the value of the newly created product of £600 is composed of 1) the reappearing value of the constant capital of £400 expended for means of production, and 2) a newly produced value of £200. The cost price of the commodity = £500 comprises the reappearing 400_c and one-half of the newly produced value of £200 (= 100_v), that is, two elements of the commodity value which are of entirely different origin.

Owing to the purposive nature of the labour expended during $666\frac{2}{3}$ ten-hour working days, the value of the consumed means of production amounting to £400 is transferred from these means of production to the product. This previously existing value thus reap-

---

[a] English edition: Ch. IX (see present edition, Vol. 35, pp. 221-22).

pears as a component part of the value of the product, but is not created in the process of production of *this* commodity. It exists as a component of the value of the commodity only because it previously existed as an element of the advanced capital. The expended constant capital is therefore replaced by that portion of the value of the commodity which this capital itself adds to that value. This element of the cost price, therefore, has a double meaning. On the one hand, it goes into the cost price of the commodity, because it is part of the commodity value which replaces consumed capital. And on the other hand, it forms an element of the commodity value only because it is the value of expended capital or because the means of production cost so and so much.

It is quite the reverse in the case of the other element of the cost price. The $666\frac{2}{3}$ working days expended in the production of the commodity create a new value of £200. One portion of this new value merely replaces the advanced variable capital of £100, or the price of the labour power employed. But this advanced capital value does not in any way go into the creation of the new value. So far as the advance of capital is concerned, labour power counts as a *value*. But in the process of production it acts as the *creator of value*. The place of the value of the labour power that obtains within the advanced capital is taken in the actually *functioning* productive capital by living value-creating labour power itself.

The difference between these various elements of the commodity value, which together make up the cost price, leaps to the eye whenever a change takes place in the size of the value of either the expended constant, or the expended variable, part of the capital. Let the price of the same means of production, or of the constant part of capital, rise from £400 to £600, or, conversely, let it fall to £200. In the first case it is not only the cost price of the commodity which rises from £500 to $600_c + 100_v = £700$, but also the value of the commodity which rises from £600 to $600_c + 100_v + 100_s = £800$. In the second case, it is not only the cost price which falls from £500 to $200_c + 100_v = £300$, but also the value of the commodity which falls from £600 to $200_c + 100_v + 100_s = £400$. Since the expended constant capital transfers its own value to the product, the value of the product rises or falls with the absolute magnitude of that capital value, other conditions remaining equal. Assume, on the other hand, that, other circumstances remaining unchanged, the price of the same amount of labour power rises from £100 to £150, or, conversely, that it falls from £100 to £50. In the first case, the cost price rises from £500 to $400_c + 150_v = £550$, and falls in the second case from £500 to $400_c + 50_v = £450$. But in either case the commodity value remains unchanged $= £600$; one time it is $400_c + 150_v + 50_s$, and the other time, $400_c + 50_v + 150_s$. The advanced variable capital does not add its own value to the product. The place of its value is taken in the product rather by a new value created by labour. Therefore, a change in the absolute magnitude of the variable capital, so far as it expresses merely a change in the price of labour power, does not in the least alter the absolute magnitude of the commodity value, because it does not alter anything in the absolute magnitude of the new value created by living labour power. Such a change rather affects only the relative proportion of the two component parts of the new value, of which one forms surplus value and the other makes good the variable capital and therefore passes into the cost price of the commodity.

The two elements of the cost price, in the present case $400_c + 100_v$, have only this in common that they are both parts of the commodity value that replace advanced capital.

But this true state of affairs necessarily appears reversed from the standpoint of capitalist production.

The capitalist mode of production differs from the mode of production based on slavery, among other things, by the fact that in it the value, and accordingly the price, of labour power appears as the value, or price, of labour itself, or as wages (Buch I, Kap. XVII[a]). The variable part of the advanced capital, therefore, appears as capital expended in wages, as a capital value which pays for the value, and accordingly the price, of all the labour expended in production. Let us assume, for instance, that an average ten-hour social working day is incorporated in a sum of money amounting to 6 shillings. In that case the advance of a variable capital of £100 represents the money expression of a value produced in $333\frac{1}{3}$ ten-hour working days. But this value, representing purchased labour power in the capital advanced, does not, however, form a part of the actually functioning capital. Its place in the process of production is taken by living labour power. If, as in our illustration, the degree of exploitation of the latter is 100%, then it is expended during $666\frac{2}{3}$ ten-hour working days, and thereby adds to the product a new value of £200. But in the capi-

---

[a] English edition: Ch. XIX (see present edition, Vol. 35, p. 535-42).

tal advanced the variable capital of £100 figures as capital invested in wages, or as the price of labour performed during $666\frac{2}{3}$ ten-hour days. The sum of £100 divided by $666\frac{2}{3}$ gives us 3 shillings as the price of a ten-hour working day, which is equal in value to the product of five hours' labour.

Now, if we compare the capital advanced on the one hand with the commodity value on the other, we find:

    I. Capital advanced £500 = £400 of capital expended in means of production (price of means of production) + £100 of capital expended in labour (price of $666\frac{2}{3}$ working days, or wages for same).

   II. Value of commodities £600 = £500 representing the cost price (£400 price of expended means of production + £100 price of expended $666\frac{2}{3}$ working days) + £100 surplus value.

In this formula, the portion of capital invested in labour differs from that invested in means of production, such as cotton or coal, only by serving as payment for a materially different element of production, but not by any means because it serves a functionally different purpose in the process of creating commodity value, and thereby also in the process of the self-expansion of capital. The price of the means of production reappears in the cost price of the commodities, just as it figured in the capital advanced, and it does so because these means of production have been purposively consumed. The price, or wages, for the $666\frac{2}{3}$ working days consumed in the production of these commodities likewise reappears in the cost price of the commodities just as it has figured in the capital advanced, and also because this amount of labour has been purposively expended. We see only finished and existing values — the portions of the value of the advanced capital which go into the making of the value of the product — but not the element creating new values. The distinction between constant and variable capital has disappeared. The entire cost price of £500 now has the double meaning that, first, it is that portion of the commodity value of £600 which replaces the capital of £500 expended in the production of the commodity; and that, secondly, this component of the commodity value exists only because it existed previously as the cost price of the elements of production employed, namely means of production and labour, i. e., as advanced capital. The capital value reappears as the cost price of a commodity because, and in so far as, it has been expended as a capital value.

The next text page is 37. See note on p. X

The fact that the various components of the value of the advanced capital have been expended for materially different elements of production, namely for means of labour, raw materials, auxiliary materials, and labour, requires only that the cost price of the commodity must buy back these materially different elements of production. So far as the formation of the cost price is concerned, however, only one distinction is appreciable, namely that between fixed and circulating capital. In our example we have set down £20 for wear and tear of means of labour (400$_c$ = £20 for depreciation of means of labour + £380 for materials of production). Before the production process the value of these means of labour was, say, £1,200. After the commodities have been produced it exists in two forms, the £20 as part of the value of the commodity, and 1,200—20, or £1,180, as the remaining value of the means of labour which, as before, are in the possession of the capitalist; in other words, as an element of his productive, not of his commodity capital. Materials of production and wages, as distinct from means of labour, are entirely consumed in the production of the commodity and thus their entire value goes into that of the produced commodity. We have seen how these various components of the advanced capital assume the forms of fixed and circulating capital in relation to the turnover.[a]

Accordingly, the capital advanced = £1,680: fixed capital = = £1,200 plus circulating capital = £480 (= £380 in materials of production plus £100 in wages).

But the cost price of the commodity only = £500 (£20 for the wear and tear of the fixed capital, and £480 for circulating capital).

This difference between the cost price of the commodity and the capital advanced merely proves, however, that the cost price of the commodity is formed exclusively by the capital actually consumed in its production.

Means of labour valued at £1,200 are employed in producing the commodity, but only £20 of this advanced capital value are lost in production. Thus, the employed fixed capital goes only partially into the cost price of the commodity, because it is only partially consumed in its production. The employed circulating capital goes entirely into the cost price of the commodity, because it is entirely consumed in its production. But does not this only prove that the consumed portions of the fixed and circulating capital pass uniformly, *pro rata* to the mag-

---

[a] See present edition, Vol. 36, pp. 159-84.

nitude of their values, into the cost price of the commodity and that this component of the value of the commodity originates solely with the capital expended in its production? If this were not so, it would be inexplicable why the advanced fixed capital of £1,200 should not, aside from the £20 which it loses in the production process, also contribute the other £1,180 which it does not lose.

This difference between fixed and circulating capital with reference to the calculation of the cost price, therefore, only confirms the seeming origination of the cost price from the expended capital value, or the price paid by the capitalist himself for the expended elements of production, including labour. On the other hand, so far as the formation of value is concerned, the variable portion of capital invested in labour power is here emphatically identified under the head of circulating capital with constant capital (that part of capital which consists of materials of production), and this completes the mystification of the self-expansion process of capital.[1]

So far we have considered just one element of the value of commodities, namely the cost price. We must now turn also to the other component of the value of commodities, namely the excess over the cost price, or the surplus value. In the first place, then, surplus value is the excess value of a commodity over and above its cost price. But since the cost price equals the value of the consumed capital, into whose material elements it is continually reconverted, this excess value is an accretion in the value of the capital expended in the production of the commodity and returning by way of its circulation.

We have already seen earlier that, though s, the surplus value, springs merely from a change in the value of the variable capital v and is, therefore, originally but an increment of variable capital, after the process of production is over it nevertheless also forms a value increment of c + v, the expended total capital. The formula c + (v + s), which indicates that s is produced through the conversion of a definite capital value v advanced for labour power into a fluctuating magnitude, i. e., of a constant magnitude into a variable one, may also be represented as (c + v) + s. Before production took place we had a capital of £500. After production

---

[1] In Book I (Kap. VII, 3, S. 216/206 ff.) [a] we have given the example of N. W. Senior to show what confusion this may create in the mind of the economist.

---

[a] English edition: Ch. IX, 3 (present edition, Vol. 35, p. 233).

is completed we have the capital of £500 plus a value increment of £100.[2]

However, surplus value forms an increment not only of the portion of the advanced capital which goes into the self-expansion process, but also of the portion which does not go into it. In other words, it is an accretion not only to the consumed capital made good out of the cost price of the commodity, but to all the capital invested in production. Before the production process we had a capital valued at £1,680, namely £1,200 of fixed capital invested in means of labour, only £20 of which go into the value of the commodity for wear and tear, plus £480 of circulating capital in materials of production and wages. After the production process we have £1,180 as the constituent element of the value of the productive capital plus a commodity capital of £600. By adding these two sums of value we find that the capitalist now has a value of £1,780. After deducting his advanced total capital of £1,680 there remains a value increment of £100. The £100 of surplus value thus form as much of a value increment in relation to the invested £1,680 as to its fraction of £500 expended during production.

It is now clear to the capitalist that this increment of value springs from the productive processes undertaken with the capital, that it therefore springs from the capital itself, because it is there after the production process, while it is not there before it. As for the capital consumed in production, the surplus value seems to spring equally from all its different elements of value consisting of means of production and labour. For all these elements contribute equally to the formation of the cost price. All of them add their values, obtaining as advanced capital, to the value of the product, and are not differentiated as constant and variable magnitudes of value. This becomes obvious if we assume for a moment that all the expended capital consisted either exclusively of wages, or exclusively of the value of

---

[2] "From what has gone before, we know that surplus value is purely the result of a variation in the value of v, of that portion of the capital which is transformed into labour power; consequently, v + s = Δv (or v plus an increment of v). But the fact that it is v alone that varies, and the conditions of that variation, are obscured by the circumstance that in consequence of the increase in the variable component of the capital, there is also an increase in the sum total of the advanced capital. It was originally £500, and becomes £590" (Buch I, Kap. VII, 1, S. 203/195).[a]

[a] English edition: Ch. IX, 1 (ibid., p. 221).

the means of production. In the first case, we should then have the commodity value of $500_v + 100_s$ instead of the commodity value of $400_c + 100_v + 100_s$. The capital of £500 laid out in wages represents the value of all the labour expended in the production of the commodity value of £600, and for just this reason forms the cost price of the entire product. But the formation of this cost price, whereby the value of the expended capital is reproduced as a constituent part of the value of the product, is the only process in the formation of this commodity value that is known to us. We do not know how its surplus value portion of £100 is formed. The same is true in the second case, in which the commodity value $= 500_c + 100_s$. We know in both cases that surplus value is derived from a given value, because this value was advanced in the form of productive capital, be it in the form of labour or of means of production. On the other hand, this advanced capital value cannot form surplus value for the reason that it has been expended and therefore constitutes the cost price of the commodity. Precisely because it forms the cost price of the commodity, it does not form any surplus value, but merely an equivalent, a value replacing the expended capital. So far, therefore, as it forms surplus value, it does so not in its specific capacity as expended, but rather as advanced, and hence utilised, capital. For this reason, the surplus value arises as much out of the portion of the advanced capital which goes into the cost price of the commodity as out of the portion which does not. In short, it arises equally out of the fixed and the circulating components of the utilised capital. The aggregate capital serves materially as the creator of products, the means of labour as well as the materials of production, and the labour. The total capital materially enters into the actual labour process, even though only a portion of it enters the process of self-expansion. This is, perhaps, the very reason why it contributes only in part to the formation of the cost price, but totally to the formation of surplus value. However that may be, the outcome is that surplus value springs simultaneously from all portions of the invested capital. This deduction may be substantially abbreviated, by saying pointedly and concisely in the words of Malthus:

"The capitalist ... *expects* an equal profit upon all the parts of the capital which he advances." [3]

In its assumed capacity of offspring of the aggregate advanced

[3] Malthus, *Principles of Political Economy*, 2nd ed., London, 1836, p. 268.

capital, surplus value takes the converted form of *profit*. Hence, a certain value is capital when it is invested with a view to producing profit,[4] or, there is profit because a certain value was employed as capital. Suppose profit is p. Then the formula $C = c + v + s = k + s$ turns into the formula $C = k + p$, or the *value of a commodity = cost price + profit*.

The profit, such as it is represented here, is thus the same as surplus value, only in a mystified form that is nonetheless a necessary outgrowth of the capitalist mode of production. The genesis of the mutation of values that occurs in the course of the production process must be transferred from the variable portion of the capital to the total capital, because there is no apparent distinction between constant and variable capital in the assumed formation of the cost price. Because at one pole the price of labour power assumes the converted form of wages, surplus value appears at the opposite pole in the converted form of profit.

We have seen that the cost price of a commodity is smaller than its value. Since $C = k + s$, it follows that $k = C - s$. The formula $C = k + s$ reduces itself to $C = k$, or commodity value = commodity cost price only if $s = 0$, a case which never occurs on the basis of capitalist production, although peculiar market conditions may reduce the selling price of commodities to the level of, or even below, their cost price.

Hence, if a commodity is sold at its value, a profit is realised which is equal to the excess of its value over its cost price, and therefore equal to the entire surplus value incorporated in the value of the commodity. But the capitalist may sell a commodity at a profit even when he sells it below its value. So long as its selling price is higher than its cost price, though it may be lower than its value, a portion of the surplus value incorporated in it is always realised, thus always yielding a profit. In our illustration the value of the commodity is £600, and the cost price £500. If the commodity is sold at £510, 520, 530, 560 or 590, it is sold respectively £90, 80, 70, 40, or 10 below its value. Yet a profit of £10, 20, 30, 60, or 90 respectively is realised in its sale. There is obviously an indefinite number of selling prices possible between the value of a commodity and its cost price. The greater the surplus-value element of the value of a commodity, the greater the practical range of these intermediate prices.

[4] "CAPITAL IS THAT WHICH IS EXPENDED WITH A VIEW TO PROFIT." Malthus, *Definitions in Political Economy*, London, 1827, p. 86.

This explains more than just the everyday phenomena of competition, such as certain cases of UNDERSELLING,[a] abnormally low commodity prices in certain lines of industry,[5] etc. The fundamental law of capitalist competition, which political economy had not hitherto grasped, the law which regulates the general rate of profit and the so-called prices of production determined by it, rests, as we shall later see, on this difference between the value and the cost price of commodities, and on the resulting possibility of selling a commodity at a profit under its value.

The minimal limit of the selling price of a commodity is its cost price. If it is sold under its cost price, the expended constituent elements of productive capital cannot be fully replaced out of the selling price. If this process continues, the value of the advanced capital disappears. From this point of view alone, the capitalist is inclined to regard the cost price as the true *inner* value of the commodity, because it is the price required for the bare conservation of his capital. But there is also this, that the cost price of a commodity is the purchase price paid by the capitalist himself for its production, therefore the purchase price determined by the production process itself. For this reason, the excess value, or the surplus value, realised in the sale of a commodity appears to the capitalist as an excess of its selling price over its value, instead of an excess of its value over its cost price, so that accordingly the surplus value incorporated in a commodity is not realised through its sale, but springs out of the sale itself. We have given this illusion closer consideration in Book I (Kap. IV, 2) ("Contradictions in the General Formula of Capital"),[c] but revert here for a moment to the form in which it was reaffirmed by Torrens, among others, as an advance of political economy beyond Ricardo.

"The natural price, consisting of the cost of production, or, in other words, of the capital expended in raising or fabricating commodities, cannot include the profit.... The farmer, we will suppose, expends one hundred quarters of corn in cultivating his fields, and obtains in return one hundred and twenty quarters. In this case, twenty quarters, being the excess of produce above expenditure, constitute the farmer's profit; but it would be absurd to call this excess, or profit, a part of the expenditure.... The

[5] Cf. Buch I, Kap. XVIII, S. 571/561 ff.[b]

---

[a] In the 1894 German edition this English word is given in parentheses after its German equivalent. - [b] English edition: Ch. XX, (see present edition, Vol. 35, pp. 542-50). - [c] English edition: Ch. V, (see present edition, Vol. 35, pp. 166-77).

master manufacturer expends a certain quantity of raw material, of tools and implements of trade, and of subsistence for labour, and obtains in return a quantity of finished work. This finished work must possess a higher exchangeable value than the
materials, tools, and subsistence, by the advance of which it was obtained."

Torrens concludes therefrom that the excess of the selling price
over the cost price, or profit, is derived from the fact that the consumers,

"either by immediate or CIRCUITOUS [a] barter give some greater portion of all the
ingredients of capital than their production costs".[6]

Indeed, the excess over a given magnitude cannot form a part of
this magnitude, and therefore the profit, the excess value of a commodity over the capitalist's expenditures, cannot form a part of these expenditures. Hence, if no other element than the value advance of the
capitalist enters into the formation of the value of a commodity, it is
inexplicable how more value should come out of production than
went into it, for something cannot come out of nothing. But Torrens
only evades this creation out of nothing by transferring it from the
sphere of commodity production to that of commodity circulation.
Profit cannot come out of production, says Torrens, for otherwise it
would already be contained in the cost of production, and there
would not be a surplus over this cost. Profit cannot come out of the
exchange of commodities, replies Ramsay,[b] unless it already existed
before this exchange. The sum of the value of the exchanged products
is evidently not altered in the exchange of these products, whose sum
of value it is. It is the same before and after the exchange. It should be
noted here that Malthus refers expressly to the authority of Torrens,[7] although he himself has a different explanation for the sale of
commodities above their value, or rather has no explanation at all,
since all arguments of this sort never, in effect, fail to be reduced to
the same thing as the once-famed negative weight of phlogiston.[12]

In a social order dominated by capitalist production even the non-
capitalist producer is gripped by capitalist conceptions. Balzac, who

---

[6] R. Torrens, *An Essay on the Production of Wealth*, London, 1821, pp. 51-53, and
349.

[7] Malthus, *Definitions in Political Economy*, London, 1853, pp. 70, 71.

---

[a] In the 1894 German edition this English word is given in parentheses after its
German equivalent. - [b] G. Ramsay, *An Essay on the Distribution of Wealth*, Edinburgh,
London, 1836, pp. 183-84.

is generally remarkable for his profound grasp of reality, aptly describes in his last novel, *Les Paysans*, how a petty peasant performs many small tasks gratuitously for his usurer, whose goodwill he is eager to retain, and how he fancies that he does not give the latter something for nothing because his own labour does not cost him any cash outlay. As for the usurer, he thus fells two dogs with one stone. He saves the cash outlay for wages and enmeshes the peasant, who is gradually ruined by depriving his own field of labour, deeper and deeper in the spider-web of usury.

The thoughtless conception that the cost price of a commodity constitutes its actual value, and that surplus value springs from selling the product above its value, so that commodities would be sold at their value if their selling price were to equal their cost price, i. e., if it were to equal the price of the consumed means of production plus wages, has been heralded to the world as a newly discovered secret of socialism by Proudhon with his customary quasi-scientific chicanery. Indeed, this reduction of the value of commodities to their cost price is the basis of his People's Bank.[13] It was earlier shown that the various constituent elements of the value of a product may be represented in proportional parts of the product itself. For instance (Buch I, Kap. VII, 2, S. 211/203[a]), if the value of 20 lbs of yarn is 30 shillings — namely 24 shillings of means of production, 3 shillings of labour power, and 3 shillings of surplus value — then this surplus value may be represented as $\frac{1}{10}$ of the product = 2 lbs of yarn. Should these 20 lbs of yarn now be sold at their cost price, at 27 shillings, then the purchaser receives 2 lbs of yarn for nothing, or the article is sold $\frac{1}{10}$ below its value. But the labourer has, as before, performed his surplus labour, only this time for the purchaser of the yarn instead of the capitalist yarn producer. It would be altogether wrong to assume that if all commodities were sold at their cost price, the result would really be the same as if they had all been sold above their cost price, but at their value. For even if the value of the labour power, the length of the working day, and the degree of exploitation of labour were the same everywhere, the quantities of surplus value contained in the values of the various kinds of commodities would be unequal, depending on the different organic composition of the capitals advanced for their production.[8]

[8] "The masses of value and of surplus value produced by different capitals — the

---

[a] English edition: Ch. IX, 2 (see present edition, Vol. 35, p. 230).

Chapter II

THE RATE OF PROFIT

The general formula of capital is M — C — M '. In other words, a sum of value is thrown into circulation to extract a larger sum out of it. The process which produces this larger sum is capitalist production. The process that realises it is circulation of capital. The capitalist does not produce a commodity for its own sake, nor for the sake of its use value, or his personal consumption. The product in which the capitalist is really interested is not the palpable product itself, but the excess value of the product over the value of the capital consumed by it. The capitalist advances the total capital without regard to the different roles played by its components in the production of surplus value. He advances all these components uniformly, not just to reproduce the advanced capital, but rather to produce value in excess of it. The only way in which he can convert the value of his advanced variable capital into a greater value is by exchanging it for living labour and exploiting living labour. But he cannot exploit this labour unless he makes a simultaneous advance of the conditions for performing this labour, namely means of labour and subjects of labour, machinery and raw materials, i. e., unless he converts a certain amount of value in his possession into the form of conditions of production; for he is a capitalist and can undertake the process of exploiting labour only because, being the owner of the conditions of labour, he confronts the labourer as the owner of only labour power. [b] As already shown in the first book, [c] it is precisely the fact that nonworkers own the means of production which turns labourers into wage workers and nonworkers into capitalists.

The capitalist does not care whether it is considered that he advances constant capital to make a profit out of his variable capital, or that he advances variable capital to enhance the value of the constant capital; that he invests money in wages to raise the value of his machinery and raw materials, or that he invests money in machinery and raw materials to be able to exploit labour. Although it is only the var-

value of labour power being given and its degree of exploitation being equal—vary directly as the amounts of the variable constituents of these capitals, i. e., as their constituents transformed into living labour power" (Buch I, Kap. IX, S. 312/303). [a]

---

[a] English edition: Ch. XI (ibid., p. 311). - [b] Cf. *Economic Manuscript of 1861-63* (present edition, Vol. 33, pp. 78-79). - [c] Ibid., Vol. 35, p. 179.

riable portion of capital which creates surplus value, it does so only if the other portions, the conditions of production, are likewise advanced. Seeing that the capitalist can exploit labour only by advancing constant capital and that he can turn his constant capital to good account only by advancing variable capital, he lumps them all together in his imagination, and much more so since the actual rate of his gain is not determined by its proportion to the variable, but to the total capital, not by the rate of surplus value, but by the rate of profit. And the latter, as we shall see, may remain the same and yet express different rates of surplus value.[a]

The costs of the product include all the elements of its value paid by the capitalist or for which he has thrown an equivalent into production. These costs must be made good to preserve the capital or to reproduce it in its original magnitude.

The value contained in a commodity is equal to the labour time expended in its production, and the sum of this labour consists of paid and unpaid portions. But for the capitalist the costs of the commodity consist only of that portion of the labour objectified in it for which he has paid. The surplus labour contained in the commodity costs the capitalist nothing, although, like the paid portion, it costs the labourer his labour, and although it creates value and enters into the commodity as a value-creating element quite like paid labour. The capitalist's profit is derived from the fact that he has something to sell for which he has paid nothing. The surplus value, or profit, consists precisely in the excess value of a commodity over its cost price, i. e., the excess of the total labour embodied in the commodity over the paid labour embodied in it. The surplus value, whatever its origin, is thus a surplus over the advanced total capital. The proportion of this surplus to the total capital is therefore expressed by the fraction $\frac{s}{C}$, in which C stands for total capital. We thus obtain the *rate of profit* $\frac{s}{C} = \frac{s}{c+v}$, as distinct from the rate of surplus value $\frac{s}{v}$.

The rate of surplus value measured against the variable capital is called rate of surplus value. The rate of surplus value measured against the total capital is called rate of profit. These are two different measurements of the same entity, and owing to the difference of the two standards of measurement they express different proportions or relations of this entity.

---

[a] Ibid., Vol. 33, pp. 79-80.

The transformation of surplus value into profit must be deduced from the transformation of the rate of surplus value into the rate of profit, not vice versa. And in fact it was rate of profit which was the historical point of departure. Surplus value and rate of surplus value are, relatively, the invisible and unknown essence that wants investigating, while rate of profit and therefore the appearance of surplus value in the form of profit are revealed on the surface of the phenomenon.

So far as the individual capitalist is concerned, it is evident that he is only interested in the relation of the surplus value, or the excess value at which he sells his commodities, to the total capital advanced for the production of the commodities, while the specific relationship and inner connection of this surplus with the various components of capital fail to interest him, and it is, moreover, rather in his interests to draw the veil over this specific relationship and this intrinsic connection.

Although the excess value of a commodity over its cost price is shaped in the immediate process of production, it is realised only in the process of circulation, and appears all the more readily to have arisen from the process of circulation, since in reality, under competition, in the actual market, it depends on market conditions whether or not and to what extent this surplus is realised. There is no need to waste words at this point about the fact that if a commodity is sold above or below its value, there is merely another kind of division of surplus value, and that this different division, this changed proportion in which various persons share in the surplus value, does not in any way alter either the magnitude or the nature of that surplus value. It is not alone the metamorphoses discussed by us in Book II that take place in the process of circulation; they fall in with actual competition, the sale and purchase of commodities above or below their value, so that the surplus value realised by the individual capitalist depends as much on the sharpness of his business wits as on the direct exploitation of labour.[a]

In the process of circulation the time of circulation comes to exert its influence alongside the working time, thereby limiting the amount of surplus value realisable within a given time span. Still other elements derived from circulation intrude decisively into the actual production process. The actual process of production and the process of

---

[a] Ibid., p. 75.

circulation intertwine and intermingle continually, and thereby invariably adulterate their typical distinctive features. The production of surplus value, and of value in general, receives new definition in the process of circulation, as previously shown. Capital passes through the circuit of its metamorphoses. Finally, stepping beyond its inner organic life, so to say, it enters into relations with outer life, into relations in which it is not capital and labour which confront one another, but capital and capital in one case, and individuals, again simply as buyers and sellers, in the other. The time of circulation and working time cross paths and thus both seem to determine the surplus value. The original form in which capital and wage labour confront one another is disguised through the intervention of relationships seemingly independent of it. Surplus value itself does not appear as the product of the appropriation of labour time, but as an excess of the selling price of commodities over their cost price, the latter thus being easily represented as their actual value (*valeur intrinsèque*), while profit appears as an excess of the selling price of commodities over their immanent value.[a]

True, the nature of surplus value impresses itself constantly upon the consciousness of the capitalist during the direct process of production, as his greed for the labour time of others, etc., has revealed in our analysis of surplus value. But: 1) The direct process of production is only a fleeting stage which continually merges with the process of circulation, just as the latter merges with the former, so that in the process of production, the more or less clearly dawning notion of the source of the gain made in it, i. e., the inkling of the nature of surplus value, stands at best as a factor equally valid as the idea that the realised surplus originates in a movement that is independent of the production process, that it arises in circulation, and that it belongs to capital irrespective of the latter's relation to labour. Even such modern economists as Ramsay, Malthus, Senior, Torrens, etc., identify these phenomena of circulation directly as proofs that capital in its bare material existence, independent of its social relation to labour which makes capital of it, is, as it were, an independent source of surplus value alongside labour and independent of labour.[14] —2) Under the item of expenses, which embrace wages as well as the price of raw materials, wear and tear of machinery, etc., the extortion of unpaid labour figures only as a saving in paying for

---

[a] Ibid., Vol. 33, pp. 72-73.

an article which is included in expenses, only as a smaller payment for a certain quantity of labour, similar to the saving when raw materials are bought more cheaply, or the depreciation of machinery decreases. In this way the extortion of surplus labour loses its specific character. Its specific relationship to surplus value is obscured. This is greatly furthered and facilitated, as shown in Book I (Abschn. VI),[a] by representing the value of labour power in the form of wages.

The relationships of capital are obscured by the fact that all parts of capital appear equally as the source of excess value (profit).

The way in which surplus value is transformed into the form of profit by means of the rate of profit is, however, a further development of the inversion of subject and object that takes place already in the process of production. In the latter, we have seen, the subjective productive forces of labour appear as productive forces of capital.[b] On the one hand, the value, or the past labour, which dominates living labour, is incarnated in the capitalist. On the other hand, the labourer appears as bare material labour power, as a commodity. Even in the simple relations of production this inverted relationship necessarily produces certain correspondingly inverted conceptions, a transposed consciousness which is further developed by the metamorphoses and modifications of the actual circulation process.

It is altogether erroneous, as a study of the Ricardian school shows, to try to identify the laws of the rate of profit with the laws of the rate of surplus value, or vice versa. [c] The capitalist naturally does not see the difference between them. In the formula $\frac{s}{C}$ the surplus value is measured by the value of the total capital advanced for its production, of which a part was totally consumed in this production and a part was merely employed in it. In fact, the formula $\frac{s}{C}$ expresses the degree of self-expansion of the total capital advanced, or, taken in conformity with inner conceptual connections and the nature of surplus value, it indicates the ratio of the amount of variation of variable capital to the magnitude of the advanced total capital.

In itself, the magnitude of value of total capital has no inner relationship to the magnitude of surplus value, at least not directly. So far as its material elements are concerned, the total capital minus the variable capital, that is, the constant capital, consists of the material

---

a English edition: Part VI (see present edition, Vol. 35, pp. 535-42). - b Ibid., pp. 338-39. - c Ibid., Vol. 32, pp. 60-72.

requisites — the means of labour and materials of labour — needed to materialise labour. It is necessary to have a certain quantity of means and materials of labour for a specific quantity of labour to materialise in commodities and thereby to produce value. A definite technical relation depending on the special nature of the labour added is established between the quantity of labour and the quantity of means of production to which this living labour is to be added. Hence there is also to that extent a definite relation between the quantity of surplus value, or surplus labour, and the quantity of means of production. For instance, if the labour necessary for the production of the wage amounts to a daily 6 hours, the labourer must work 12 hours to do 6 hours of surplus labour, or produce a surplus value of 100%. He uses up twice as much of the means of production in 12 hours as he does in 6. Yet this is no reason for the surplus value added by him in 6 hours to be directly related to the value of the means of production used up in those 6, or in 12 hours. This value is here altogether immaterial; it is only a matter of the technically required quantity. It does not matter whether the raw materials or means of labour are cheap or dear, as long as they have the required use value and are available in technically prescribed proportion to the living labour to be absorbed. If I know that x lbs of cotton are consumed in an hour of spinning and that they cost a shillings, then, of course, I also know that 12 hours' spinning consumes 12x lbs of cotton = 12a shillings, and can then calculate the proportion of the surplus value to the value of the 12 as well as to that of the 6. But the relation of living labour to the *value* of means of production obtains here only to the extent that a shillings serve as a name for x lbs of cotton; because a definite quantity of cotton has a definite price, and therefore, conversely, a definite price may also serve as an index for a definite quantity of cotton, so long as the price of cotton does not change. If I know that the labourer must work 12 hours for me to appropriate 6 hours of surplus labour, that therefore I must have a 12-hour supply of cotton ready for use, and if I know the price of this quantity of cotton needed for 12 hours, then I have an indirect relation between the price of cotton (as an index of the required quantity) and the surplus value. But, conversely, I can never conclude the quantity of the raw material that may be consumed in, say, one hour, and not 6, of spinning from the price of the raw material. There is, then, no necessary inner relation between the value of the constant capital, nor, therefore, between the value of the total capital ($= c + v$) and the surplus value.

If the rate of surplus value is known and its magnitude given, the rate of profit expresses nothing but what it actually is, namely a different way of measuring surplus value, its measurement according to the value of the total capital instead of the value of the portion of capital from which surplus value directly originates by way of its exchange for labour. But in reality (i. e., in the world of phenomena) the matter is reversed. Surplus value is given, but given as an excess of the selling price of the commodity over its cost price; and it remains a mystery where this excess originated — from the exploitation of labour in the process of production, or from outwitting the purchaser in the process of circulation, or from both. What is also given is the proportion of this excess to the value of the total capital, or the rate of profit. The calculation of this excess of the selling price over the cost price in relation to the value of the advanced total capital is very important and natural, because in effect it yields the ratio in which total capital has been expanded, i. e., the degree of its self-expansion. If we proceed from this rate of profit, we cannot therefore conclude the specific relations between the surplus and the portion of capital invested in wages. We shall see in a subsequent chapter what amusing somersaults Malthus makes when he tries in this way to get at the secret of the surplus value and of its specific relation to the variable part of the capital. [15] What the rate of profit actually shows is rather a uniform relation of the excess to equal portions of the capital, which, from this point of view, does not show any inner difference at all, unless it be between the fixed and circulating capital. And it shows this difference, too, only because the excess is calculated in two ways; namely, first, as a simple magnitude — as excess over the cost price. In this, its initial, form, the entire circulating capital goes into the cost price, while of the fixed capital only the wear and tear goes into it. Second, the relation of this excess in value to the total value of the advanced capital. In this case, the value of the total fixed capital enters into the calculation, quite the same as the circulating capital. Therefore, the circulating capital goes in both times in the same way, while the fixed capital goes in differently the first time, and in the same way as circulating capital the second time. Under the circumstances the difference between fixed and circulating capital is the only one which obtrudes itself.

If, as Hegel would put it, the excess therefore re-reflects itself in itself out of the rate of profit, or, put differently, the excess is more closely characterised by the rate of profit, it appears as an excess produced by capital above its own value over a year, or in a given period of circulation.

Although the rate of profit thus differs numerically from the rate of surplus value, while surplus value and profit are actually the same thing and numerically equal, profit is nevertheless a converted form of surplus value, a form in which its origin and the secret of its existence are obscured and extinguished. In effect, profit is the form in which surplus value presents itself to the view, and must initially be stripped by analysis to disclose the latter. In surplus value, the relation between capital and labour is laid bare; in the relation of capital to profit, i. e., of capital to surplus value that appears on the one hand as an excess over the cost price of commodities realised in the process of circulation and, on the other, as an excess more closely determined by its relation to the total capital, *the capital* appears *as a relation to itself*, a relation in which it, as the original sum of value, is distinguished from a new value which it generated. One is conscious that capital generates this new value by its movement in the processes of production and circulation. But the way in which this occurs is cloaked in mystery and appears to originate from hidden qualities inherent in capital itself.[a]

The further we follow the process of the self-expansion of capital, the more mysterious the relations of capital will become, and the less the secret of its internal organism will be revealed.

In this part, the rate of profit is numerically different from the rate of surplus value; while profit and surplus value are treated as having the same numerical magnitude but only a different form. In the next part we shall see how the alienation goes further, and how profit represents a magnitude differing also numerically from surplus value.

Chapter III

THE RELATION OF THE RATE OF PROFIT
TO THE RATE OF SURPLUS VALUE

Here, as at the close of the preceding chapter, and generally in this entire first part, we presume the amount of profit falling to a given capital to be equal to the total amount of surplus value produced by

---

[a] Cf. present edition, Vol. 33, pp. 70-71.

means of this capital during a certain period of circulation. We thus leave aside for the present the fact that, on the one hand, this surplus value may be broken up into various subforms, such as interest on capital, ground rent, taxes, etc., and that, on the other, it is not, as a rule, identical with profit as appropriated by virtue of a general average rate of profit, which will be discussed in the second part.

So far as the quantity of profit is assumed to be equal to that of surplus value, its magnitude, and that of the rate of profit, is determined by ratios of simple figures given or ascertainable in every individual case. The analysis, therefore, first is carried on purely in the mathematical field.

We retain the designations used in Books I and II. Total capital C consists of constant capital c and variable capital v, and produces a surplus value s. The ratio of this surplus value to the advanced variable capital, or $\frac{s}{v}$, is called the rate of surplus value and designated s'. Therefore $\frac{s}{v} = s'$, and consequently $s = s'v$. If this surplus value is related to the total capital instead of the variable capital, it is called profit, p, and the ratio of the surplus value s to the total capital C, or $\frac{s}{C}$, is called the rate of profit, p'. Accordingly,

$$p' = \frac{s}{C} = \frac{s}{c+v}.$$

Now, substituting for s its equivalent $s'v$, we find

$$p' = s'\frac{v}{C} = s'\frac{v}{c+v}$$

which equation may also be expressed by the proportion

$$p' : s' = v : C;$$

the rate of profit is related to the rate of surplus value as the variable capital is to the total capital.

It follows from this proportion that the rate of profit, p', is always smaller than s', the rate of surplus value, because v, the variable capital, is always smaller than C, the sum of v + c, or the variable plus the constant capital; the only, practically impossible case excepted, in which v = C, that is, no constant capital at all, no means of production, but only wages are advanced by the capitalist.

However, our analysis also considers a number of other factors which have a determining influence on the magnitude of c, v, and s, and must therefore be briefly examined.

First, the *value of money*. We may assume this to be constant throughout.

Second, the *turnover*. We shall leave this factor entirely out of consideration for the present, since its influence on the rate of profit will be treated specially in a later chapter. //Here we anticipate just one point, that the formula $p' = s'\dfrac{v}{C}$ is strictly correct only for *one* period of turnover of the variable capital. But we may correct it for an annual turnover by substituting for the simple rate of surplus value, s', the annual rate of surplus value, s'n. In this, n is the number of turnovers of the variable capital within one year. (Cf. Book II, Chapter XVI, 1.) — *F. E.*//[a]

Third, due consideration must be given to *productivity of labour*, whose influence on the rate of surplus value has been thoroughly discussed in Book I (Abschn. IV).[b] Productivity of labour may also exert a direct influence on the rate of profit, at least of an individual capital, if, as has been demonstrated in Book I (Kap. X, S. 323/314),[c] this individual capital operates with a higher than the average social productivity and produces commodities at a lower value than their average social value, thereby realising an extra profit. However, this case will not be considered for the present, since in this part of the work we also proceed from the premiss that commodities are produced under normal social conditions and are sold at their values. Hence, we assume in each case that the productivity of labour remains constant. In effect, the value composition of a capital invested in a branch of industry, that is, a certain proportion between the variable and constant capital, always expresses a definite degree of labour productivity. As soon, therefore, as this proportion is altered by means other than a mere change in the value of the material elements of the constant capital, or a change in wages, the productivity of labour must likewise undergo a corresponding change, and we shall often enough see, for this reason, that changes in the factors c, v, and s also imply changes in the productivity of labour.

The same applies to the three remaining factors — the *length of the working day, intensity of labour, and wages*. Their influence on the quantity and rate of surplus value has been exhaustively discussed in Book I.[d] It will be understood, therefore, that notwithstanding the assump-

---

[a] See present edition, Vol. 36. - [b] English edition: Part IV (ibid., Vol. 35). - [c] English edition: Ch. XII (ibid., pp. 321-24). - [d] Ibid., pp. 519-31.

tion, which we make for the sake of simplicity, that these three factors remain constant, the changes that occur in v and s may nevertheless imply changes in the magnitude of these, their determining elements. In this respect we must briefly recall that the wage influences the quantity of surplus value and the rate of surplus value in inverse proportion to the length of the working day and the intensity of labour; that an increase in wages reduces the surplus value, while a lengthening of the working day and an increase in the intensity of labour add to it.

Suppose a capital of 100 produces a surplus value of 20 employing 20 labourers working a 10-hour day for a total weekly wage of 20. Then we have:

$$80_c + 20_v + 20_s; \; s' = 100\%, \; p' = 20\%.$$

Now the working day is lengthened to 15 hours without raising the wages. The total value produced by the 20 labourers will thereby increase from 40 to 60 $(10:15 = 40:60)$. Since v, the wages paid to the labourers, remains the same, the surplus value rises from 20 to 40, and we have:

$$80_c + 20_v + 40_s; \; s' = 200\%, \; p' = 40\%.$$

If, conversely, the ten-hour working day remains unchanged, while wages fall from 20 to 12, the total value product amounts to 40 as before, but is differently distributed; v falls to 12, leaving a remainder of 28 for s. Then we have:

$$80_c + 12_v + 28_s; \; s' = 233\tfrac{1}{3}\%, \; p' = \tfrac{28}{92} = 30\tfrac{10}{23}\%.$$

Hence, we see that a prolonged working day (or a corresponding increase in the intensity of labour) and a fall in wages both increase the amount, and thus the rate, of surplus value. Conversely, a rise in wages, other things being equal, would lower the rate of surplus value. Hence, if v rises through a rise in wages, it does not express a greater, but only a dearer quantity of labour, in which case s' and p' do not rise, but fall.

This indicates that changes in the working day, intensity of labour and wages cannot take place without a simultaneous change in v and s and their ratio, and therefore also p', which is the ratio of s to the total capital c + v. And it is also evident that changes in the ratio of s to v also imply corresponding changes in at least one of the three above-mentioned labour conditions.

Precisely this reveals the specific organic relationship of variable capital to the movement of the total capital and to its self-expansion, and also its difference from constant capital. So far as generation of value is concerned, the constant capital is important only for the value it has. And it is immaterial to the generation of value whether a constant capital of £1,500 represents 1,500 tons of iron at, say, £1, or 500 tons of iron at £3. The quantity of actual material, in which the value of the constant capital is incorporated, is altogether irrelevant to the formation of value and the rate of profit, which varies inversely to this value no matter what the ratio of the increase or decrease of the value of constant capital to the mass of material use value which it represents.

It is different with variable capital. It is not the value it has, not the labour objectified in it, that matter at this point, but this value as a mere index of the total labour that it sets in motion and which is not expressed in it — the total labour, whose difference from the labour expressed in the value of the variable capital, hence the paid labour, i. e., that portion of the total labour which produces surplus value, is all the greater, the less labour is contained in that variable capital itself. Suppose, a 10-hour working day is equal to ten shillings = ten marks. If the labour necessary to replace the wages, and thus the variable capital = 5 hours = 5 shillings, then the surplus labour = 5 hours and the surplus value = 5 shillings. Should the necessary labour = 4 hours = 4 shillings, then the surplus labour = 6 hours and the surplus value = 6 shillings.

Hence, as soon as the value of the variable capital ceases to be an index of the quantity of labour set in motion by it, and, moreover, the measure of this index is altered, the rate of surplus value will change in the opposite direction and inversely.

Let us now go on to apply the above-mentioned equation of the rate of profit, $p' = s'\frac{v}{C}$, to the various possible cases. We shall successively change the value of the individual factors of $s'\frac{v}{C}$ and determine the effect of these changes on the rate of profit. In this way we shall obtain different series of cases, which we may regard either as successive altered conditions of operation for one and the same capital, or as different capitals existing side by side and introduced for the sake of comparison, taken, as it were, from different branches of industry or different countries. In cases, therefore, where the conception of some of our examples as successive conditions for one and the same capital appears to be forced or impracticable, this objection falls away the moment they are regarded as comparisons of independent capitals.

Hence, we now separate the product $s'\frac{v}{C}$ into its two factors s' and $\frac{v}{C}$. At first we shall treat s' as constant and analyse the effect of the possible variations of $\frac{v}{C}$. After that we shall treat the fraction $\frac{v}{C}$ as constant and let s' pass through its possible variations. Finally we shall treat all factors as variable magnitudes and thereby exhaust all the cases from which laws concerning the rate of profit may be derived.

I. S' CONSTANT, $\frac{v}{C}$ VARIABLE

This case, which embraces a number of subordinate cases, may be covered by a general formula. Take two capitals, C and C_1, with their respective variable components, v and v_1, with a common rate of surplus value s', and rates of profit p' and p'_1. Then:

$$p' = s'\frac{v}{C} ; \; p'_1 = s'\frac{v_1}{C_1} .$$

Now let us make a proportion of C and C_1, and of v and v_1. For instance, let the value of the fraction $\frac{C_1}{C} = E$, and that of $\frac{v_1}{v} = e$. Then $C_1 = EC$, and $v_1 = ev$. Substituting in the above equation these values for p'_1, C_1 and v_1, we obtain

$$p'_1 = s'\frac{ev}{EC} .$$

Again, we may derive a second formula from the above two equations by transforming them into the proportion:

$$p' : p'_1 = s'\frac{v}{C} : s'\frac{v_1}{C_1} = \frac{v}{C} : \frac{v_1}{C_1} .$$

Since the value of a fraction is not changed if we multiply or divide its numerator and denominator by the same number, we may reduce $\frac{v}{C}$ and $\frac{v_1}{C_1}$ to percentages, that is, we may make C and C_1 both = 100. Then we have $\frac{v}{C} = \frac{v}{100}$ and $\frac{v_1}{C_1} = \frac{v_1}{100}$, and may then drop the denominators in the above proportion, obtaining:

$$p' : p'_1 = v : v_1, \text{ or:}$$

Taking any two capitals operating with the same rate of surplus value, the rates of profit are to each other as the variable portions of the capitals calculated as percentages of their respective total capitals.

These two formulas embrace all the possible variations of $\frac{v}{C}$.

One more remark before we analyse these various cases singly. Since C is the sum of c and v, of the constant and variable capitals, and since the rates of surplus value, as of profit, are usually expressed in percentages, it is convenient to assume that the sum of c + v is also equal to 100, i. e., to express c and v in percentages. For the determination of the rate of profit, if not of the amount, it is immaterial whether we say that a capital of 15,000, of which 12,000 is constant and 3,000 is variable, produces a surplus value of 3,000, or whether we reduce this capital to percentages.

$$15,000 \ C = 12,000_c + 3,000_v \ (+ \ 3,000_s)$$
$$100 \ C = 80_c + 20_v \ (+ \ 20_s).$$

In either case the rate of surplus value $s' = 100\%$, and the rate of profit $= 20\%$.

The same is true when we compare two capitals, say, the foregoing capital with another, such as

$$12,000 \ C = 10,800_c + 1,200_v \ (+1,200_s)$$
$$100 \ C = 90_c + 10_v \ (+10_s)$$

in both of which $s' = 100\%$, $p' = 10\%$, and in which the comparison with the foregoing capital is clearer in percentage form.

On the other hand, if it is a matter of changes taking place in one and the same capital, the form of percentages is rarely to be used, because it almost always obscures these changes. If a capital expressed in the form of percentages:

$$80_c + 20_v + 20_s$$

assumes the form of percentages:

$$90_c + 10_v + 10_s,$$

we cannot tell whether the changed composition in percentages, $90_c + 10_v$, is due to an absolute decrease of v or an absolute increase of c, or to both. We would need the absolute magnitudes in figures to ascertain this. In the analysis of the following individual cases of variation, however, everything depends on how these changes have come about; whether $80_c + 20_v$ changed into $90_c + 10_v$ through an increase of the constant capital without any change in the variable capital, for instance through $12,000_c + 3,000_v$ changing into

$27,000_c + 3,000_v$ (corresponding to a percentage of $90_c + 10_v$); or whether they took this form through a reduction of the variable capital, with the constant capital remaining unchanged, that is, through a change into $12,000_c + 1,333\frac{1}{3}_v$ (also corresponding to a percentage of $90_c + 10_v$); or, lastly, whether both of the terms changed into $13,500_c + 1,500_v$ (corresponding once more to a percentage of $90_c + + 10_v$). But it is precisely these cases which we shall have to successively analyse, and in so doing dispense with the convenient form of percentages, or at least employ these only as a secondary alternative.

1) s' and C constant, v variable

If v changes in magnitude, C can remain unaltered only if c, the other component of C, that is, the constant capital, changes by the same amount as v, but in the opposite direction. If C originally $= 80_c + 20_v = 100$, and if v is then reduced to 10, then C can $= 100$ only if c is increased to 90; $90_c + 10_v = 100$. Generally speaking, if v is transformed into $v \pm d$, into v increased or decreased by d, then c must be transformed into $c \mp d$, into c varying by the same amount, but in the opposite direction, so that the conditions of the present case are satisfied.

Similarly, if the rate of surplus value s' remains the same, while the variable capital v changes, the amount of surplus value s must change, since $s = s'v$, and since one of the factors of $s'v$, namely v, is given another value.

The assumptions of the present case produce, alongside the original equation,

$$p' = s'\frac{v}{C},$$

still another equation through the variation of v:

$$p'_1 = s'\frac{v_1}{C},$$

in which v has become v_1 and p'_1, the resultant changed rate of profit, is to be found.

It is determined by the following proportion:

$$p' : p'_1 = s'\frac{v}{C} : s'\frac{v_1}{C}, = v : v_1$$

Or: with the rate of surplus value and total capital remaining the same, the original rate of profit is to the new rate of profit produced by a change in the variable capital as the original variable capital is to the changed variable capital.

If the original capital was, as above:

I. $15,000 \; C = 12,000_c + 3,000_v \; (+3,000_s)$, and if it is now:

II. $15,000 \; C = 13,000_c + 2,000_v \; (+2,000_s)$, then $C = 15,000$ and $s' = 100\%$ in either case, and the rate of profit of I, 20%, is to that of II, $13\frac{1}{3}\%$, as the variable capital of I, 3,000, is to that of II, 2,000, i. e., $20\% : 13\frac{1}{3}\% = 3,000 : 2,000$.

Now, the variable capital may either rise or fall. Let us first take an example in which it rises. Let a certain capital be originally constituted and employed as follows:

$$\text{I. } 100_c + 20_v + 10_s; \; C = 120, \; s' = 50\%, \; p' = 8\tfrac{1}{3}\%.$$

Now let the variable capital rise to 30. In that case, according to our assumption, the constant capital must fall from 100 to 90 so that total capital remains unchanged at 120. The rate of surplus value remaining constant at 50%, the surplus value produced will then rise from 10 to 15. We shall then have:

$$\text{II. } 90_c + 30_v + 15_s; \; C = 120, \; s' = 50\%, \; p' = 12\tfrac{1}{2}\%.$$

Let us first proceed from the assumption that wages remain unchanged. Then the other factors of the rate of surplus value, i e., the working day and the intensity of labour, must also remain unchanged. In that event the rise of v (from 20 to 30) can signify only that another half as many labourers are employed. Then the total value produced also rises one-half, from 30 to 45, and is distributed, just as before, $\frac{2}{3}$ for wages and $\frac{1}{3}$ for surplus value. But at the same time, with the increase in the number of labourers, the constant capital, the value of the means of production, has fallen from 100 to 90. We have, then, a case of decreasing productivity of labour combined with a simultaneous shrinkage of constant capital. Is such a case economically possible?

In agriculture and the extractive industries, in which a decrease in labour productivity and, therefore, an increase in the number of employed labourers is quite comprehensible, this process is — on the basis and within the scope of capitalist production — attended by an increase, instead of a decrease, of constant capital. Even if the above fall of c were due merely to a fall in prices, an individual capital would be able to accomplish the transition from I to II only under very exceptional circumstances. But in the case of two independent capitals invested in different countries, or in different branches of agriculture or extractive industry, it would be nothing out of the ordinary if in one of the cases more labourers (and therefore more variable capital) were employed and worked with less valuable or scantier means of production than in the other case.

But let us drop the assumption that the wage remains the same, and let us explain the rise of the variable capital from 20 to 30 through a rise of wages by one-half. Then we shall have an entirely different case. The same number of labourers — say, 20 — continue to work with the same or only slightly reduced means of production. If the working day remains unchanged — say, 10 hours — then the total value produced also remains unchanged. It was and remains = 30. But all of this 30 is now required to make good the advanced variable capital of 30; the surplus value would disappear. We have assumed, however, that the rate of surplus value should remain constant, that is, the same as in I, at 50%. This is possible only if the working day is prolonged by one-half, to 15 hours. Then the 20 labourers would produce a total value of 45 in 15 hours, and all conditions would be satisfied:

$$\text{II. } 90_c + 30_v + 15_s; \text{ C} = 120, \text{ s}' = 50\%, \text{ p}' = 12\tfrac{1}{2}\%.$$

In this case, the 20 labourers do not require any more means of labour, tools, machines, etc., than in case I. Only the raw materials or auxiliary materials would have to be increased by one-half. In the event of a fall in the prices of these materials, the transition from I to II might be more possible economically, even for an individual capital in keeping with our assumption. And the capitalist would be somewhat compensated by increased profits for any loss incurred through the depreciation of his constant capital.

Now let us assume that the variable capital falls, instead of rising. Then we have but to reverse our example, taking II as the original capital, and passing from II to I.

II. $90_c + 30_v + 15_s$ then changes into

I. $100_c + 20_v + 10_s$, and it is evident that this transposition does not in the least alter any of the conditions regulating the respective rates of profit and their mutual relation.

If v falls from 30 to 20 because $\tfrac{1}{3}$ fewer labourers are employed with the growing constant capital, then we have before us the normal case of modern industry, namely, an increasing productivity of labour, and the operation of a larger quantity of means of production by fewer labourers. That this movement is necessarily connected with a simultaneous drop in the rate of profit will be developed in the third part of this book.

If, on the other hand, v falls from 30 to 20, because the same number of labourers is employed at lower wages, the total value produced would, with the working day unchanged, as before $= 30_v + 15_s = 45$. Since v fell to 20, the surplus value would rise to 25, the rate of surplus value from 50% to 125%, which would be contrary to our assumption. To comply with the conditions of our case, the surplus value, with its rate at 50%, must rather fall to 10, and the total value produced must, therefore, fall from 45 to 30, and this is possible only if the working day is reduced by $\frac{1}{3}$. Then, as before, we have:

$$100_c + 20_v + 10_s; \ s' = 50\%, \ p' = 8\tfrac{1}{3}\%.$$

It need hardly be said that this reduction of the working time, in the case of a fall in wages, would not occur in practice. But that is immaterial. The rate of profit is a function of several variable magnitudes, and if we wish to know how these variables influence the rate of profit, we must analyse the individual effect of each in turn, regardless of whether such an isolated effect is economically practicable with one and the same capital.

2) *s' constant, v variable, C changes through the variation of v*

This case differs from the preceding one only in degree. Instead of decreasing or increasing by as much as v increases or decreases, c remains constant. Under present-day conditions in the major industries and agriculture the variable capital is only a relatively small part of the total capital. For this reason, its increase or decrease, so far as either is due to changes in the variable capital, are likewise relatively small. Let us again proceed with a capital:

$$\text{I. } 100_c + 20_v + 10_s; \ C = 120, \ s' = 50\%, \ p' = 8\tfrac{1}{3}\%,$$

which would then change, say, into:

$$\text{II. } 100_c + 30_v + 15_s; \ C = 130, \ s' = 50\%, \ p' = 11\tfrac{7}{13}\%.$$

The opposite case, in which the variable capital decreases, would again be illustrated by the reverse transition from II to I.

The economic conditions would be essentially the same as in

the preceding case, and therefore they need not be discussed again. The transition from I to II implies a decrease in the productivity of labour by one-half; for II the utilisation of 100_c requires an increase of labour by one-half over that of I. This case may occur in agriculture.[9]

But while the total capital remains constant in the preceding case, owing to the conversion of constant into variable capital, or vice versa, there is in this case a tie-up of additional capital if the variable capital increases, and a release of previously employed capital if the variable capital decreases.

3) s' and v constant, c and therefore C variable

In this case the equation changes from:

$$p' = s'\frac{v}{C} \text{ into } p'_1 = s'\frac{v}{C_1}$$

and after reducing the same factors on both sides, we have:

$$p'_1 : p' = C : C_1;$$

with the same rate of surplus value and equal variable capitals, the rates of profit are inversely proportional to the total capitals.

Should we, for example, have three capitals, or three different conditions of the same capital:

I. $80_c + 20_v + 20_s$; $C = 100$, $s' = 100\%$, $p' = 20\%$;
II. $100_c + 20_v + 20_s$; $C = 120$, $s' = 100\%$, $p' = 16\frac{2}{3}\%$;
III. $60_c + 20_v + 20_s$; $C = 80$, $s' = 100\%$, $p' = 25\%$.

Then we obtain the proportions:

$$20\% : 16\frac{2}{3}\% = 120 : 100 \text{ and } 20\% : 25\% = 80 : 100.$$

The previously given general formula for variations of $\frac{v}{C}$ with a constant s' was:

$$p'_1 = s'\frac{ev}{EC}; \text{ now it becomes: } p'_1 = s'\frac{v}{EC},$$

since v does not change, the factor $e = \frac{v_1}{v}$ becomes $= 1$.

Since $s'v = s$, the quantity of surplus value, and since both s' and v remain constant, it follows that s, too, is not affected by

---

[9] The manuscript has the following note at this point: "Investigate later in what manner this case is connected with ground rent." [F. E.]

any variation of C. The amount of surplus value is the same after the change as it was before it.

If c were to fall to zero, p′ would = s′, i.e., the rate of profit would equal the rate of surplus value.

The alteration of c may be due either to a mere change in the value of the material elements of constant capital, or to a change in the technical composition of the total capital, that is, a change in the productivity of labour in the given branch of industry. In the latter case, the productivity of social labour mounting due to the development of industry and agriculture on a large scale would bring about a transition (in the above illustration) in the sequence from III to I and from I to II. A quantity of labour which is paid with 20 and produces a value of 40 would first utilise means of labour to a value of 60; if productivity mounted and the value remained the same, the used up means of labour would rise first to 80, and then to 100. An inversion of this sequence would imply a decrease in productivity. The same quantity of labour would put a smaller quantity of means of production into motion and the operation would be curtailed, as may occur in agriculture, mining, etc.

A saving in constant capital increases the rate of profit on the one hand, and, on the other, sets free capital, for which reason it is of importance to the capitalist. We shall make a closer study of this, and likewise of the influence of a change in the prices of the elements of constant capital, particularly of raw materials, at a later point.[a]

It is again evident here that a variation of the constant capital equally affects the rate of profit, regardless of whether this variation is due to an increase or decrease of the material elements of c, or merely to a change in their value.

4) s' constant, v, c, and C all variable

In this case, the general formula for the changed rate of profit, given at the outset, remains in force:

$$p'_1 = s'\frac{ev}{EC}.$$

---

[a] See this volume, chapters V and VI.

It follows from this that with the rate of surplus value remaining the same:

a) The rate of profit falls if E is greater than e, that is, if the constant capital is augmented to such an extent that the total capital grows at a faster rate than the variable capital. If a capital of $80_c + 20_v + 20_s$ changes into $170_c + 30_v + 30_s$, then s' remains $= 100\%$, but $\frac{v}{C}$ falls from $\frac{20}{100}$ to $\frac{30}{200}$, in spite of the fact that both v and C have grown, and the rate of profit falls correspondingly from 20% to 15%.

b) The rate of profit remains unchanged only if e = E, that is, if the fraction $\frac{v}{C}$ retains the same value in spite of a seeming change, i. e., if its numerator and denominator are multiplied or divided by the same factor. The capitals $80_c + 20_v + 20_s$ and $160_c + 40_v + 40_s$ obviously have the same rate of profit of 20%, because s' remains $= 100\%$ and $\frac{v}{C} = \frac{20}{100} = \frac{40}{200}$ represents the same value in both examples.

c) The rate of profit rises when e is greater than E, that is, when the variable capital grows at a faster rate than the total capital. If $80_c + 20_v + 20_s$ turns into $120_c + 40_v + 40_s$, the rate of profit rises from 20% to 25%, because with an unchanged s' $\frac{v}{C} = \frac{20}{100}$ rises to $\frac{40}{160}$, or from $^1/_5$ to $^1/_4$.

If the changes of v and C are in the same direction, we may view this change of magnitude as though, to a certain extent, both of them varied in the same proportion, so that $\frac{v}{C}$ remained unchanged up to that point. Beyond this point, only one of them would vary, and we shall have thereby reduced this complicated case to one of the preceding simpler ones.

Should, for instance, $80_c + 20_v + 20_s$ become $100_c + 30_v + 30_s$, then the proportion of v to c, and also to C, remains the same in this variation up to: $100_c + 25_v + 25_s$. Up to that point, therefore, the rate of profit likewise remains unchanged. We may then take $100_c + 25_v + 25_s$ as our point of departure; we find that v increased by 5 to become 30_v, so that C rose from 125 to 130, thus giving us the second case, that of the simple variation of v and the consequent variation of C. The rate of profit, which was originally 20%, rises through this addition of 5_v to $23^1/_{13}\%$, provided the rate of surplus value remains the same.

The same reduction to a simpler case can also take place if

v and C change their magnitudes in opposite directions. For instance, let us again start with $80_c + 20_v + 20_s$, and let this become: $110_c + 10_v + 10_s$. In that case, with the change going as far as $40_c + 10_v + 10_s$, the rate of profit would remain the same 20%. By adding 70_c to this intermediate form, it will drop to $8\frac{1}{3}\%$. Thus, we have again reduced the case to an instance of change of one variable, namely of c.

Simultaneous variation of v, c, and C, does not, therefore, offer any new aspects and in the final analysis leads back to a case in which only one factor is a variable.

Even the sole remaining case has actually been exhausted, namely that in which v and C remain numerically the same, while their material elements undergo a change of value, so that v stands for a changed quantity of labour put in motion and c for a changed quantity of means of production put in motion.

In $80_c + 20_v + 20_s$, let 20_v originally represent the wages of 20 labourers working 10 hours daily. Then let the wages of each rise from 1 to $1\frac{1}{4}$. In that case the 20_v will pay only 16 labourers instead of 20. But if 20 labourers produce a value of 40 in 200 working hours, 16 labourers working 10 hours daily will in 160 working hours produce a value of only 32. After deducting 20_v for wages, only 12 of the 32 would then remain for surplus value. The rate of surplus value would have fallen from 100% to 60%. But since we have assumed the rate of surplus value to be constant, the working day would have to be prolonged by one-quarter, from 10 to $12\frac{1}{2}$ hours. If 20 labourers working 10 hours daily = 200 working hours produce a value of 40,[a] then 16 labourers working $12\frac{1}{2}$ hours daily = 200 hours will produce the same value, and the capital of $80_c + 20_v$ would as before yield the same surplus value of 20.

Conversely, if wages were to fall to such an extent that 20_v would represent the wages of 30 labourers, then s′ would remain constant only if the working day were reduced from 10 to $6\frac{2}{3}$ hours. For $20 \times 10 = 30 \times 6\frac{2}{3} = 200$ working hours.

We have already in the main discussed to what extent c may in these divergent examples remain unchanged in terms of value expressed in money and yet represent different quantities of means of production changed in accordance with changing conditions. In its pure form this case would be possible only by way of an exception.

---

[a] In Marx's manuscript: 80.

As for a change in the value of the elements of c which increases or decreases their mass but leaves the sum of the value of c unchanged, it does not affect either the rate of profit or the rate of surplus value, so long as it does not lead to a change in the magnitude of v.

We have herewith exhausted all the possible cases of variation of v, c, and C in our equation. We have seen that the rate of profit may fall, remain unchanged, or rise, while the rate of surplus value remains the same, with the least change in the proportion of v to c, or to C, being sufficient to change the rate of profit as well.

We have seen, furthermore, that in variations of v there is a certain limit everywhere beyond which it is economically impossible for s′ to remain constant. Since every one-sided variation of c must also reach a certain limit where v can no longer remain unchanged, we find that there are limits for every possible variation of $\frac{v}{C}$, beyond which s′ must likewise become variable. In the variations of s′ which we shall now discuss, this interaction of the different variables of our equation will stand out still clearer.

II. S′ VARIABLE

We obtain a general formula for the rates of profit with different rates of surplus value, no matter whether $\frac{v}{C}$ remains constant or not, by converting the equation:

$$p' = s'\frac{v}{C}$$

into

$$p'_1 = s'_1\frac{v_1}{C_1},$$

in which p'_1, s'_1, v_1 and C_1 denote the changed values of p′, s′, v and C. Then we have:

$$p' : p'_1 = s'\frac{v}{C} : s'_1\frac{v_1}{C_1},$$

and hence:

$$p'_1 = \frac{s'_1}{s'} \times \frac{v_1}{v} \times \frac{C}{C_1} \times p'.$$

$$1)\ s'\ variable,\ \frac{v}{C}\ constant$$

In this case we have the equations:

$$p' = s'\frac{v}{C}\ ;\ p'_1 = s'_1\frac{v}{C},$$

in both of which $\frac{v}{C}$ is equal. Therefore:

$$p' : p'_1 = s' : s'_1.$$

The rates of profit of two capitals of the same composition are to each other as the two corresponding rates of surplus value. Since in the fraction $\frac{v}{C}$ it is not a question of the absolute magnitudes of v and C, but only of their ratio, this applies to all capitals of equal composition whatever their absolute magnitude.

$$80_c + 20_v + 20_s;\ C = 100,\ s' = 100\%,\ p' = 20\%$$
$$160_c + 40_v + 20_s;\ C = 200,\ s' = 50\%,\ p' = 10\%$$
$$100\% : 50\% = 20\% : 10\%.$$

If the absolute magnitudes of v and C are the same in both cases, the rates of profit are moreover also related to one another as the amounts of surplus value:

$$p' : p'_1 = s'v : s'_1v = s : s_1.$$

For instance:

$$80_c + 20_v + 20_s;\ s' = 100\%,\ p' = 20\%$$
$$80_c + 20_v + 10_s;\ s' = 50\%,\ p' = 10\%$$
$$20\% : 10\% = 100 \times 20 : 50 \times 20 = 20_s : 10_s.$$

It is now clear that with capitals of equal absolute or percentage composition the rate of surplus value can differ only if either the wages, or the length of the working day, or the intensity of labour, differ. In the following three cases:

$$\text{I.}\ \ 80_c + 20_v + 10_s;\ s' = 50\%,\ p' = 10\%$$
$$\text{II.}\ \ 80_c + 20_v + 20_s;\ s' = 100\%,\ p' = 20\%$$
$$\text{III.}\ \ 80_c + 20_v + 40_s;\ s' = 200\%,\ p' = 40\%$$

the total value produced in I is 30 ($20_v + 10_s$); in II it is 40; in III it is 60. This may come about in three different ways.

First, if the wages are different, and 20_v stands for a different number of labourers in every individual case. Suppose capital I employs 15 labourers 10 hours daily at a wage of £$1\frac{1}{3}$, who produce a value of £30, of which £20 replace the wages and £10 are surplus value. If wages fall to £1, then 20 labourers may be employed for 10 hours; they will produce a value of £40, of which £20 will replace the wages and £20 will be surplus value. Should wages fall still more, to £$^2/_3$, thirty labourers may be employed for 10 hours. They will produce a value of £60, of which £20 will be deducted for wages and £40 will represent surplus value.

This case — a constant composition of capital in per cent, a constant working day and constant intensity of labour, and the rate of surplus value varying because of variation in wages — is the only one in which Ricardo's assumption is correct:

*"Profit would be high or low, *exactly in proportion* as wages were low or high"* (*Principles*, Ch. I, Sect. III, p. 18 of the *Works* of D. Ricardo, ed. by MacCulloch, 1852).

Or *second*, if the intensity of labour varies. In that case, say, 20 labourers working 10 hours daily with the same means of labour produce 30 pieces of a certain commodity in I, 40 in II, and 60 in III, of which every piece, aside from the value of the means of production incorporated in it, represents a new value of £1. Since every 20 pieces = £20 make good the wages, there remain 10 pieces = £10 for surplus value in I, 20 pieces = £20 in II, and 40 pieces = £40 in III.

Or *third*, the working day differs in length. If 20 labourers work with the same intensity for 9 hours in I, 12 hours in II, and 18 hours in III, their total products, 30:40:60 vary as 9:12:18. And since wages = 20 in every case, 10, 20, and 40 respectively again remain as surplus value.

A rise or fall in wages, therefore, influences the rate of surplus value inversely, and a rise or fall in the intensity of labour, and a lengthening or shortening of the working day, act the same way on the rate of surplus value and thereby, with $\frac{v}{C}$ constant, on the rate of profit.

2) s' and v variable, C constant

The following proportion applies in this case:

$$p' : p'_1 = s'\frac{v}{C} : s'_1\frac{v_1}{C} = s'v : s'_1v_1 = s : s_1.$$

The rates of profit are related to one another as the respective amounts of surplus value.

Changes in the rate of surplus value with the variable capital remaining constant meant a change in the magnitude and distribution of the produced value. A simultaneous variation of v and s' also always implies a different distribution, but not always a change in the magnitude of the produced value. Three cases are possible:

a) Variation of v and s' takes place in opposite directions, but by the same amount; for instance:

$$80_c + 20_v + 10_s;\ s' = 50\%,\ p' = 10\%$$
$$90_c + 10_v + 20_s;\ s' = 200\%,\ p' = 20\%.$$

The produced value is equal in both cases, hence also the quantity of labour performed; $20_v + 10_s = 10_v + 20_s = 30$. The only difference is that in the first case 20 is paid out for wages and 10 remains as surplus value, while in the second case wages are only 10 and surplus value is therefore 20. This is the only case in which the number of labourers, the intensity of labour, and the length of the working day remain unchanged, while v and s' vary simultaneously.

b) Variation of s' and v also takes place in opposite directions, but not by the same amount. In that case the variation of either v or s' outweighs the other.

$$\text{I. } 80_c + 20_v + 20_s;\ s' = 100\%,\quad p' = 20\%$$
$$\text{II. } 72_c + 28_v + 20_s;\ s' = 71^3/_7\%,\ p' = 20\%$$
$$\text{III. } 84_c + 16_v + 20_s;\ s' = 125\%,\quad p' = 20\%.$$

Capital I pays for produced value amounting to 40 with 20_v, II a value of 48 with 28_v, and III a value of 36 with 16_v. Both the produced value and the wages have changed. But a change in the produced value means a change in the amount of labour performed, hence a change either in the number of labourers, the hours of labour, the intensity of labour, or in more than one of these.

c) Variation of s' and v takes place in the same direction. In that case the one intensifies the effect of the other.

$$90_c + 10_v + 10_s;\ s' = 100\%,\ p' = 10\%$$
$$80_c + 20_v + 30_s;\ s' = 150\%,\ p' = 30\%$$
$$92_c + 8_v + 6_s;\ s' = 75\%,\ p' = 6\%.$$

Here too the three values produced are different, namely 20, 50, and 14. And this difference in the magnitude of the respective quantities of labour reduces itself once more to a difference in the number of labourers, the hours of labour, and the intensity of labour, or several or all of these factors.

3) s', v and C variable

This case offers no new aspects and is solved by the general formula given under II, in which s' is variable.

––––––––––

The effect of a change in the magnitude of the rate of surplus value on the rate of profit hence yields the following cases:

1) p' increases or decreases in the same proportion as s' if $\frac{v}{C}$ remains constant.

$$80_c + 20_v + 20_s;\ s' = 100\%,\ p' = 20\%$$
$$80_c + 20_v + 10_s;\ s' = 50\%,\ p' = 10\%$$
$$100\% : 50\% = 20\% : 10\%.$$

2) p' rises or falls at a faster rate than s' if $\frac{v}{C}$ moves in the same direction as s', that is, if it increases or decreases when s' increases or decreases.

$$80_c + 20_v + 10_s;\ s' = 50\%,\ p' = 10\%$$
$$70_c + 30_v + 20_s;\ s' = 66\tfrac{2}{3}\%,\ p' = 20\%$$
$$50\% : 66\tfrac{2}{3}\% < 10\% : 20\%.$$

3) p' rises or falls at a slower rate than s' if $\frac{v}{C}$ changes inversely to s', but at a slower rate.

$$80_c + 20_v + 10_s;\ s' = 50\%,\ p' = 10\%$$
$$90_c + 10_v + 15_s;\ s' = 150\%,\ p' = 15\%$$
$$50\% : 150\% > 10\% : 15\%.$$

4) p' rises while s' falls, or falls while s' rises if $\frac{v}{C}$ changes inversely to, and at a faster rate than, s'.

$$80_c + 20_v + 20_s;\ s' = 100\%,\ p' = 20\%$$
$$90_c + 10_v + 15_s;\ s' = 150\%,\ p' = 15\%.$$

s' has risen from 100% to 150%, p' has fallen from 20% to 15%.

5) Finally, p' remains constant whereas s' rises or falls, while $\frac{v}{C}$ changes inversely to, but in exactly the same proportion as, s'.

It is only this last case which still requires some explanation. We have observed earlier in the variations of $\frac{v}{C}$ that one and the same rate of surplus value may be expressed in very much different rates of profit. Now we see that one and the same rate of profit may be based on very much different rates of surplus value. But while any change in the proportion of v to C is sufficient to produce a difference in the rate of profit so long as s′ is constant, a change in the magnitude of s′ must lead to a corresponding inverse change of $\frac{v}{C}$ in order that the rate of profit remain the same. In the case of one and the same capital, or in that of two capitals in one and the same country this is possible but in exceptional cases. Assume, for example, that we have a capital of

$$80_c + 20_v + 20_s; \; C = 100, \; s' = 100\%, \; p' = 20\%;$$

and let us suppose that wages fall to such an extent that the same number of labourers is obtainable for 16_v instead of 20_v. Then, other things being equal, and 4_v being released, we shall have:

$$80_c + 16_v + 24_s; \; C = 96, \; s' = 150\%, \; p' = 25\%.$$

In order that p′ may now $= 20\%$ as before, the total capital would have to increase to 120, the constant capital therefore rising to 104:

$$104_c + 16_v + 24_s; \; C = 120, \; s' = 150\%, \; p' = 20\%.$$

This would only be possible if the fall in wages were attended simultaneously by a change in the productivity of labour which required such a change in the composition of capital. Or, if the value in money of the constant capital increased from 80 to 104. In short, it would require an accidental coincidence of conditions such as occurs in exceptional cases. In fact, a variation of s′ that does not call for the simultaneous variation of v, and thus of $\frac{v}{C}$ is conceivable only under very definite conditions, namely in such branches of industry in which only fixed capital and labour are employed, while the materials of labour are supplied by Nature.

But this is not so when the rates of profit of two different countries are compared. For in that case the same rate of profit is, in effect, based largely on different rates of surplus value.

It follows from all these five cases, therefore, that a rising rate of profit may correspond to a falling or rising rate of surplus value, a falling rate of profit to a rising or falling rate of surplus value, and a constant rate of profit to a rising or falling rate of surplus value. And we have seen in I that a rising, falling, or constant rate of profit may also accord with a constant rate of surplus value.

———

The rate of profit, therefore, depends on two main factors — the rate of surplus value and the value composition of capital. The effects of these two factors may be briefly summed up as follows, by giving the composition in per cent, for it is immaterial which of the two portions of the capital causes the variation:

The rates of profit of two different capitals, or of one and the same capital in two successive different conditions,

are equal

1) if the per cent composition of the capitals is the same and their rates of surplus value are equal;

2) if their per cent composition is not the same, and the rates of surplus value are unequal, provided the products of the rates of surplus value by the percentages of the variable portions of capitals (s′ by v) are the same, i. e., if the *masses* of surplus value (s = s′v) calculated in per cent of the total capital are equal; in other words, if the factors s′ and v are inversely proportional to one another in both cases.

They are unequal

1) if the per cent composition is equal and the rates of surplus value are unequal, in which case they are related as the rates of surplus value;

2) if the rates of surplus value are the same and the per cent composition is unequal, in which case they are related as the variable portions of the capitals;

3) if the rates of surplus value are unequal and the per cent composition not the same, in which case they are related as the products s′v, i. e., as the quantities of surplus value calculated in per cent of the total capital.[10]

Chapter IV

THE EFFECT OF THE TURNOVER
ON THE RATE OF PROFIT

//The effect of the turnover on the production of surplus value, and

[10] The manuscript contains also very detailed calculations of the difference between the rate of surplus value and the rate of profit (s′ — p′), which has very interesting peculiarities, and whose movement indicates where the two rates draw apart or approach one another. These movements may also be represented by curves. I am not reproducing this material because it is of less importance to the immediate purposes of this work, and because it is enough here to call attention to this fact for readers who wish to pursue this point further. — *F. E.*

consequently of profit, has been discussed in Book II.[a] Briefly summarised it signifies that owing to the time span required for turnover, not all the capital can be employed all at once in production; some of the capital always lies idle, either in the form of money capital, of raw material supplies, of finished but still unsold commodity capital, or of outstanding claims; that the capital in active production, i. e., in the production and appropriation of surplus value, is always short by this amount, and that the produced and appropriated surplus value is always curtailed to the same extent. The shorter the period of turnover, the smaller this idle portion of capital as compared with the whole, and the larger, therefore, the appropriated surplus value, provided other conditions remain the same.

It has already been shown in detail in Book II how the quantity of produced surplus value is augmented by reductions in the period of turnover, or of one of its two sections, in the time of production and the time of circulation.[b] But since the rate of profit only expresses the relation of the produced quantity of surplus value to the total capital employed in its production, it is evident that any such reduction increases the rate of profit. Whatever has been said earlier in Part II of Book II in regard to surplus value, applies equally to profit and the rate of profit and needs no repetition here. We wish only to stress a few of the principal points.

The chief means of reducing the time of production is higher labour productivity, which is commonly called industrial progress. If this does not involve a simultaneous considerable increase in the outlay of total capital resulting from the installation of expensive machinery, etc., and thus a reduction of the rate of profit, which is calculated on the total capital, this rate must rise. And this is decidedly true in the case of many of the latest improvements in metallurgy and in the chemical industry. The recently discovered methods of producing iron and steel, such as the processes of Bessemer, Siemens, Gilchrist-Thomas, etc., cut to a minimum at relatively small costs the formerly arduous processes. The making of alizarin, a red dye-stuff extracted from coal-tar, requires but a few weeks, and this by means of already existing coal-tar dye-producing installations, to yield the same results which formerly required years. It took a year for the madder to mature, and it was customary to let the roots grow a few years more before they were processed.

---

[a] See present edition, Vol. 36, pp. 293-98. - [b] Ibid., chapters XIII and XIV.

The chief means of reducing the time of circulation is improved communications. The last fifty years have brought about a revolution in this field, comparable only with the industrial revolution of the latter half of the 18th century. On land the macadamised road has been displaced by the railway, on sea the slow and irregular sailing vessel has been pushed into the background by the rapid and regular steamboat line, and the entire globe is being girdled by telegraph wires. The Suez Canal has fully opened East Asia and Australia to steamer traffic. The time of circulation of a shipment of commodities to East Asia, at least twelve months in 1847 (cf. Buch II, S. 235[a]), has now been reduced to almost as many weeks. The two large centres of the crises of 1825-57, America and India, have been brought from 70 to 90% nearer to the European industrial countries by this revolution in transport, and have thereby lost a good deal of their explosive nature. The period of turnover of the total world commerce has been reduced to the same extent, and the efficacy of the capital involved in it has been more than doubled or trebled. It goes without saying that this has not been without effect on the rate of profit.

To single out the effect of the turnover of total capital on the rate of profit we must assume all other conditions of two capitals to be compared as equal. Aside from the rate of surplus value and the working day it is also notably the per cent composition which we must assume to be the same. Now let us take a capital A composed of $80_c + 20_v = 100$ C, which makes two turnovers yearly at a rate of surplus value of 100%. The annual product is then:

$160_c + 40_v + 40_s$. However, to determine the rate of profit we do not calculate the 40_s on the turned-over capital value of 200, but on the advanced capital of 100, and thus obtain $p' = 40\%$.

Now let us compare this with a capital $B = 160_c + 40_v = 200$ C, which has the same rate of surplus value of 100%, but which is turned over only once a year. The annual product of this capital is, therefore, the same as that of A:

$160_c + 40_v + 40_s$. But this time the 40_s are to be calculated on an advance of capital amounting to 200, which yields a rate of profit of only 20%, or one-half that of A.

We find, then, that for capitals with an equal per cent composition, with equal rates of surplus value and equal working days, the rates of profit of the two capitals are related inversely as their periods of

---

[a] Ibid., pp. 251-52.

turnover. If either the composition, the rates of surplus value, the working day, or the wages, are unequal in the two compared cases, this would naturally produce further differences in the rates of profit; but these are independent of the turnover and, for this reason, do not concern us at this point. They have already been discussed in Chapter III.

The direct effect of a reduced period of turnover on the production of surplus value, and consequently of profit, consists of an increased efficiency imparted thereby to the variable portion of capital, as shown in Book II, Chapter XVI, "The Turnover of Variable Capital". This chapter demonstrated that a variable capital of 500 turned over ten times a year produces as much surplus value in this time as a variable capital of 5,000 with the same rate of surplus value and the same wages, turned over just once a year.

Take capital I, consisting of 10,000 fixed capital whose annual depreciation is $10\% = 1,000$, of 500 circulating constant and 500 variable capital. Let the variable capital turn over ten times per year at a 100% rate of surplus value. For the sake of simplicity we assume in all the following examples that the circulating constant capital is turned over in the same time as the variable, which is generally the case in practice. Then the product of one such period of turnover will be:

$$100_c \text{ (depreciation)} + 500_c + 500_v + 500_s = 1,600$$

and the product of one entire year, with ten such turnovers, will be

$$1,000_c \text{ (depreciation)} + 5,000_c + 5,000_v + 5,000_s = 16,000,$$
$$C = 11,000, \ s = 5,000, \ p' = \frac{5,000}{11,000} = 45\tfrac{5}{11}\%.$$

Now let us take capital II: 9,000 fixed capital, 1,000 annual wear and tear, 1,000 circulating constant capital, 1,000 variable capital, 100% rate of surplus value, 5 turnovers of variable capital per year. Then the product of each of the turnovers of the variable capital will be:

$$200_c \text{ (depreciation)} + 1,000_c + 1,000_v + 1,000_s = 3,200,$$

and the total annual product after five turnovers:

$$1,000_c \text{ (depreciation)} + 5,000_c + 5,000_v + 5,000_s = 16,000,$$
$$C = 11,000, \ s = 5,000, \ p' = \frac{5,000}{11,000} = 45\tfrac{5}{11}\%.$$

Further, take capital III with no fixed capital, 6,000 circulating constant capital and 5,000 variable capital. Let there be one turnover per year at a 100% rate of surplus value. Then the total annual product is:

$$6,000_c + 5,000_v + 5,000_s = 16,000,$$
$$C = 11,000, \ s = 5,000, \ p' = \frac{5,000}{11,000} = 45 \tfrac{5}{11} \%.$$

In all the three cases we therefore have the same annual quantity of surplus value = 5,000, and, since the total capital is likewise equal in all three cases, namely = 11,000, also the same rate of profit of $45 \tfrac{5}{11} \%$.

But should capital I have only 5 instead of 10 turnovers of its variable part per year, the result would be different. The product of one turnover would then be:

$$200_c \ \text{(depreciation)} + 500_c + 500_v + 500_s = 1,700.$$

And the annual product:

$$1,000_c \ \text{(depreciation)} + 2,500_c + 2,500_v + 2,500_s = 8,500,$$
$$C = 11,000, \ s = 2,500, \ p' = \frac{2,500}{11,000} = 22 \tfrac{8}{11} \%.$$

The rate of profit has fallen one-half, because the period of turnover has doubled.

The quantity of surplus value appropriated in one year is therefore equal to the quantity of surplus value appropriated in one turnover of the *variable* capital multiplied by the number of such turnovers per year. Suppose we call the surplus value, or profit, appropriated in one year S, the surplus value appropriated in one period of turnover s, the number of turnovers of the variable capital in one year n, then $S = sn$, and the annual rate of surplus value $S' = s'n$, as already demonstrated in Book II, Chapter XVI, I.[a]

It goes without saying that the formula $p' = s' \frac{v}{C} = s' \frac{v}{c+v}$, is correct only so long as the v in the numerator is the same as that in the denominator. In the denominator v stands for the entire portion of the total capital used on an average as variable capital for the payment of wages. The v of the numerator is primarily only determined by the fact that a certain quantity of surplus value = s is produced and appropriated by it, whose relation to it $\frac{s}{v}$ is s', the rate of surplus value. It is only along these lines that the formula $p' = \frac{s}{c+v}$ is transformed into the other: $p' = s' \frac{v}{c+v}$. The v of the numerator will now

---

[a] See present edition, Vol. 36, pp. 293-307.

be more accurately determined by the fact that it must equal the v of the denominator, that is, entire variable portion of capital C. In other words, the equation $p' = \frac{s}{C}$ may be correctly transformed into the equation $p' = s'\frac{v}{c+v}$ only if s stands for surplus value produced in *one* turnover of the variable capital. Should s be only a portion of this surplus value, then $s = s'v$ is still correct, but this v is then smaller than the v in $C = c + v$, because it is smaller than the entire variable capital expended for wages. But should s stand for more than the surplus value of one turnover of v, then a portion of this v, or perhaps the whole of it, serves twice, namely in the first and in the second turnover, and eventually in subsequent turnovers. The v which produces the surplus value and represents the sum of all paid wages, is therefore greater than the v in $c + v$ and the calculation falls into error.

To make the formula precise for the annual rate of profit, we must substitute the annual rate of surplus value for the simple rate of surplus value, that is, substitute S' or $s'n$ for s'. In other words, we must multiply the rate of surplus value s', or, what amounts to the same thing, the variable capital v contained in C, by n, the number of turnovers of this variable capital in one year. Thus we obtain $p' = s'n\frac{v}{C}$, which is the formula for calculating the annual rate of profit.

The amount of variable capital invested in his business is something the capitalist himself does not know in most cases. We have seen in Chapter VIII of Book II, and shall see further along, that the only essential distinction within his capital which impresses itself upon the capitalist is that of fixed and circulating capital. He takes money to pay wages from his cash-box containing the part of the circulating capital he has on hand in the form of money, so far as it is not deposited in a bank; he takes money from the same cash-box for raw and auxiliary materials, and credits both items to the same cash account. And even if he should keep a separate account for wages, at the close of the year this would only show the sum paid out for this item, hence vn, but not the variable capital v itself. In order to ascertain this, he would have to make a special calculation, of which we propose here to give an illustration.

For this purpose we select the cotton spinnery of 10,000 mule spindles described in Book I (S. 209/201)[a] and assume that the data given

---

[a] Ibid., Vol. 35, pp. 228-29.

there for one week of April 1871, are in force during the whole year. The fixed capital incorporated in the machinery was £10,000. The circulating capital was not given. We assume it to have been £2,500. This is a rather high estimate, but justified by the assumption, which we must always make here, that no credit operations were effected, hence no permanent or temporary employment of other people's capital. The value of the weekly product was composed of £20 for depreciation of machinery, £358 circulating constant advanced capital (rent £6; cotton £342; coal, gas, oil, £10), £52 variable capital paid out for wages, and £80 surplus value. Therefore,

$$20_c \text{ (depreciation)} + 358_c + 52_v + 80_s = 510.$$

The weekly advance of circulating capital therefore was $358_c + 52_v = 410$. In terms of per cent this was $87.3_c + 12.7_v$. For the entire circulating capital of £2,500 this would be £2,182 constant and £318 variable capital. Since the total expenditure for wages in one year was 52 times £52, or £2,704, it follows that in a year the variable capital of £318 was turned over almost exactly $8\frac{1}{2}$ times. The rate of surplus value was $\frac{80}{52} = 153\frac{11}{13}$. We calculate the rate of profit on the basis of these elements by inserting the above values in the formula $p' = s'n\frac{v}{C}$: $s' = 153\frac{11}{13}$, $n = 8\frac{1}{2}$, $v = 318$, $C = 12,500$; hence:

$$p' = 153\frac{11}{13} \times 8\frac{1}{2} \times \frac{318}{12,500} = 33.27\%.$$

We test this by means of the simple formula $p' = \frac{s}{C}$. The total annual surplus value or profit amounts to 52 times £80, or £4,160, and this divided by the total capital of £12,500 gives us 33.28%, or almost an identical result. This is an abnormally high rate of profit, which may only be explained by extraordinarily favourable conditions of the moment (very low prices of cotton along with very high prices of yarn), and could certainly not have obtained throughout the year.

The s'n in the formula $p' = s'n\frac{v}{C}$ stands, as has been said, for the thing called in Book II[a] the annual rate of surplus value. In the above case it is $153\frac{11}{13}\%$ multiplied by $8\frac{1}{2}$, or in exact figures, $1,307\frac{9}{13}\%$. Thus, if a certain philistine was shocked by the abnormity of an annual rate of surplus value of 1,000% used as an illustration in

---

[a] Ibid., Vol. 36, p. 295.

Book II, he will now perhaps be pacified by this annual rate of surplus value of more than 1,300% taken from the living experience of Manchester.[16] In times of greatest prosperity, such as we have not indeed seen for a long time, such a rate is by no means a rarity.

For that matter we have here an illustration of the actual composition of capital in modern large-scale industry. The total capital is broken up into £12,182 constant and £318 variable capital, a sum of £12,500. In terms of per cent this is $97\frac{1}{2}\,c + 2\frac{1}{2}\,v = 100\ C$. Only one-fortieth of the total, but in more than an eightfold annual turnover, serves for the payment of wages.

Since very few capitalists ever think of making calculations of this sort with reference to their own business, statistics is almost completely silent about the relation of the constant portion of the total social capital to its variable portion. Only the American census gives what is possible under modern conditions, namely the sum of wages paid in each line of business and the profits realised. Questionable as they may be, being based on the industrialist's own uncontrolled statements, they are nevertheless very valuable and the only records available to us on this subject. In Europe we are far too delicate to expect such revelations from our major industrialists.— *F. E.*//

Chapter V

ECONOMY IN THE EMPLOYMENT OF CONSTANT CAPITAL

I. IN GENERAL

The increase of absolute surplus value, or the prolongation of surplus labour, and thus of the working day, while the variable capital remains the same and thus employs the same number of labourers at the same nominal wages, regardless of whether overtime is paid or not, reduces relatively the value of the constant capital as compared to the total and the variable capital, and thereby increases the rate of profit, again irrespective of the growth of the quantity of surplus value and a possibly rising rate of surplus value. The volume of the fixed portion of constant capital, such as factory buildings, machinery, etc., remains the same, no matter whether these serve the labour process 16 or 12 hours. A prolongation of the working day does not entail any fresh expenditures in this, the most expensive portion of constant

capital. Furthermore, the value of the fixed capital is thereby reproduced in a smaller number of turnover periods, so that the time for
which it must be advanced to make a certain profit is abbreviated.
A prolongation of the working day therefore increases the profit, even
if overtime is paid, or even if, up to a certain point, it is better paid
than the normal hours of labour. The ever-mounting need to increase
fixed capital in modern industry was therefore one of the main reasons prompting profit-mad capitalists to lengthen the working day.[11]

The same conditions do not obtain if the working day is constant.
Then it is necessary either to increase the number of labourers, and
with them to a certain extent the amount of fixed capital, the buildings, machinery, etc., in order to exploit a greater quantity of labour
(for we leave aside deductions from wages or the depression of wages
below their normal level), or, if the intensity and, consequently, the
productive power, of labour increase and, generally, more relative
surplus value is produced, the magnitude of the circulating portion
of constant capital increases in such industrial branches which use
raw materials, since more raw material, etc., is processed in a given
time; and, secondly, the amount of machinery set in motion by the
same number of labourers, therefore also this part of constant capital,
increases as well. Hence, an increase in surplus value is accompanied
by an increase in constant capital, and the growing exploitation of labour by greater outlays in the conditions of production through
which labour is exploited, i. e., by a greater investment of capital.
Therefore, the rate of profit is thereby reduced on the one hand while
it increases on the other.

Quite a number of current expenses remain almost or entirely the
same whether the working day is longer or shorter. The cost of supervision is less for 500 working men during 18 working hours than for
750 working men during 12 working hours.

"The expense of working a factory 10 hours almost equals that of working it 12"
(Reports of Insp. of Fact., October 1848, p. 37).

State and municipal taxes, fire insurance, wages of various permanent employees, depreciation of machinery, and various other
expenses of a factory, remain unchanged whether the working time
is long or short. To the extent to which production decreases, these

[11] "Since in all factories there is a very large amount of fixed capital in buildings
and machinery, the greater the number of hours that machinery can be kept at work
the greater will be the return" (Reports of Insp. of Fact., 31st October, 1858, p. 8).

expenses rise as compared to the profit (Reports of Insp. of Fact., October 1862, p. 19).

The period in which the value of the machinery and of the other components of fixed capital is reproduced is determined in practice not by their mere lifetime, but by the duration of the entire labour process during which they serve and wear out. If the labourers must work 18 instead of 12 hours, this makes a difference of three days more per week, so that one week is stretched into one and a half, and two years into three. If this overtime is unpaid the labourers give away gratis a week out of every three and a year out of every three on top of the normal surplus labour time. In this way, the reproduction of the value of the machinery is speeded up 50% and accomplished in $\frac{2}{3}$ of the usually required time.

To avoid useless complications, we proceed in this analysis, and in that of price fluctuations for raw materials (Chap. VI), from the assumption that the mass and rate of surplus value are given.

As already shown in the presentation of co-operation, division of labour and machinery,[a] the economy of production conditions found in large-scale production is essentially due to the fact that these conditions prevail as conditions of social, or socially combined, labour, and therefore as social conditions of labour. They are commonly consumed in the process of production by the aggregate labourer, instead of being consumed in small fractions by a mass of labourers operating disconnectedly or, at best, directly co-operating on a small scale. In a large factory with one or two central motors the cost of these motors does not increase in the same ratio as their horse-power and, hence, their possible sphere of activity. The cost of the transmission equipment does not grow in the same ratio as the number of working machines which it sets in motion. The frame of a machine does not become dearer in the same ratio as the mounting number of tools which it employs as its organs, etc. Furthermore, the concentration of means of production yields a saving on buildings of various kinds not only for the actual workshops, but also for storage, etc. The same applies to expenditures for fuel, lighting, etc. Other conditions of production remain the same, whether used by many or by few.

This total economy, arising as it does from the concentration of means of production and their use *en masse*, imperatively requires, however, the accumulation and co-operation of labourers, i. e., a social

---

[a] See present edition, Vol. 35, pp. 329-30.

combination of labour. Hence, it originates quite as much from the social nature of labour, just as surplus value originates from the surplus labour of the individual labourer considered singly. Even the continual improvements, which are here possible and necessary, are due solely to the social experience and observation ensured and made possible by production of aggregate labour combined on a large scale.

The same is true of the second big source of economy in the conditions of production. We refer to the reconversion of the excretions of production, the so-called waste, into new elements of production, either of the same, or of some other line of industry; to the processes by which this so-called excretion is thrown back into the cycle of production and, consequently, consumption, whether productive or individual. This line of savings, which we shall later examine more closely, is likewise the result of large-scale social labour. It is the attendant abundance of this waste which renders it available again for commerce and thereby turns it into new elements of production. It is only as waste of combined production, therefore of large-scale production, that it becomes important to the production process and remains a bearer of exchange value. This waste, aside from the services which it performs as a new element of production, reduces the cost of the raw material to the extent to which it is again saleable, for this cost always includes the normal waste, namely the quantity ordinarily lost in processing. The reduction of the cost of this portion of constant capital increases *pro tanto*[a] the rate of profit, assuming the magnitude of the variable capital and the rate of surplus value to be given.

If the surplus value is given, the rate of profit can be increased only by reducing the value of the constant capital required for commodity production. So far as constant capital enters into the production of commodities, it is not its exchange value, but its use value alone, which matters. The quantity of labour which flax can absorb in a spinnery does not depend on its value, but on its quantity, assuming the productivity of labour, i. e., the level of technical development, to be given. In like manner the assistance rendered by a machine to, say, three labourers does not depend on its value, but on its use value as a machine. On one level of technical development a bad machine may be expensive and on another a good machine may be cheap.

The increased profit received by a capitalist through the cheapening of, say, cotton and spinning machinery, is the result of higher

---

[a] for so much

labour productivity, not in the spinnery, to be sure, but in cotton cultivation and construction of machinery. It requires smaller outlays of
the conditions of labour to objectify a given quantity of labour, and
hence to appropriate a given quantity of surplus labour. The costs required to appropriate a certain quantity of surplus labour diminish.[a]

We have already mentioned savings yielded in the production process through co-operative use of means of production by the aggregate, or socially combined, labour. Other savings of constant capital
arising from the shortening of the time of circulation in which the development of means of communication is a dominant material factor
will be discussed later. At this point we shall deal with the savings
yielded by continuous improvements of machinery, namely 1) of its
material, e. g., the substitution of iron for wood; 2) the cheapening of
machinery due to the general improvement of machine-building; so
that, although the value of the fixed portion of constant capital
increases continually with the development of labour on a large scale,
it does not increase at the same rate[12]; 3) special improvements
enabling existing machinery to work more cheaply and effectively; for
instance, improvements of steam-boilers, etc., which will be discussed
later on in greater detail; 4) reduction of waste through better machinery.

Whatever reduces the wear of machinery, and of fixed capital in
general, for any given period of production, cheapens not only the individual commodity, in view of the fact that in its price every individual commodity reproduces its aliquot share of this depreciation, but
reduces also the aliquot portion of the invested capital for this period.
Repair work, etc., to the extent that it becomes necessary, is added to
the original cost of the machinery. A reduction in repair costs, due to
greater durability of the machinery, lowers *pro tanto* the price of this
machinery.

It may again be said of all these savings that they are largely possible only for combined labour, and are often not realised until production is carried forward on a still larger scale, so that they require an
even greater combination of labour in the immediate process of production.

[12] Cf. Ure on the progress in factory construction.[b]

---

[a] Cf. present edition, Vol. 33, p. 84. - [b] A. Ure, *Philosophie des manufactures...*, Vol. 1,
Paris, 1836, pp. 61-63 (Cf. present edition, Vol. 33, pp. 363-64).

However, on the other hand, the development of the productive power of labour in any *one* line of production, e. g., the production of iron, coal, machinery, in architecture, etc., which may again be partly connected with progress in the field of intellectual production, notably natural science and its practical application, appears to be the premiss for a reduction of the value, and consequently of the cost, of means of production in *other* lines of industry, e. g., the textile industry, or agriculture. This is self-evident, since a commodity which is the product of a certain branch of industry enters another as a means of production. Its greater or lesser price depends on the productivity of labour in the line of production from which it issues as a product, and is at the same time a factor that not only cheapens the commodities into whose production it goes as a means of production, but also reduces the value of the constant capital whose element it here becomes, and thereby one that increases the rate of profit.

The characteristic feature of this kind of saving of constant capital arising from the progressive development of industry is that the rise in the rate of profit in *one* line of industry depends on the development of the productive power of labour in *another*. Whatever falls to the capitalist's advantage in this case is once more a gain produced by social labour, if not a product of the labourers he himself exploits. Such a development of productive power is again traceable in the final analysis to the social nature of the labour engaged in production; to the division of labour in society; and to the development of intellectual labour, especially in the natural sciences. What the capitalist thus utilises are the advantages of the entire system of the social division of labour. It is the development of the productive power of labour in its exterior department, in that department which supplies it with means of production, whereby the value of the constant capital employed by the capitalist is relatively lowered and consequently the rate of profit is raised.

Another rise in the rate of profit is produced, not by savings in the labour creating the constant capital, but by savings in the application of this capital itself. On the one hand, the concentration of labourers, and their large-scale co-operation, saves constant capital. The same buildings, and heating and lighting appliances, etc., cost relatively less for the large-scale than for small-scale production. The same is true of power and working machinery. Although their absolute value increases, it falls in comparison to the increasing extension of production and the magnitude of the variable capital, or the quantity of labour power set in motion. The economy realised by a certain capital within its own line of production is first and foremost an economy in labour, i. e., a reduction of the paid labour of its own labourers. The previously mentioned economy, on the other hand, is distinguished from this one by the fact that it accomplishes the greatest possible appropriation of other people's unpaid labour in the most economical way, i. e., with as little expense as the given scale of production will permit. Inasmuch as this economy does not rest with the previously mentioned exploitation of the productivity of the social labour employed in the production of constant capital, but with the economy in the constant capital itself, it springs either directly from the co-operation and social form of labour within a certain branch of production, or from the production of machinery, etc., on a scale in which its value does not grow at the same rate as its use value.[a]

Two points must be borne in mind here: If the value of c = zero, then $p' = s'$, and the rate of profit would be at its maximum. Second, however, the most important thing for the direct exploitation of labour itself is not the value of the employed means of exploitation, be they fixed capital, raw or auxiliary materials. In so far as they serve as means of absorbing labour, as media in or by which labour and, hence, surplus labour are objectified, the exchange value of machinery, buildings, raw materials, etc., is quite immaterial. What is ultimately essential is, on the one hand, the quantity of them technically required for combination with a certain quantity of living labour, and, on the other, their suitability, i e., not only good machinery, but also good raw and auxiliary materials. The rate of profit depends partly on the good quality of the raw material. Good material produces less waste. Less raw materials are then needed to absorb the same quantity of labour. Furthermore, the resistance to be overcome by the working machine is also less. This partly affects even the surplus value and the rate of surplus value. The labourer needs more time when using bad raw materials to process the same quantity. Assuming wages remain the same, this causes a reduction in surplus labour. This also substantially affects the reproduction and accumulation of capital, which depend more on the productivity than on the amount of labour employed, as shown in Book I (S. 627/619 ff.).[b]

The capitalist's fanatical insistence on economy in means of production is therefore quite understandable. That nothing is lost or

---

[a] Cf. present edition, Vol. 33, p. 89. - [b] Ibid., Vol. 35, pp. 599-600.

wasted and the means of production are consumed only in the manner required by production itself, depends partly on the skill and intelligence of the labourers and partly on the discipline enforced by the capitalist for the combined labour. This discipline will become superfluous under a social system in which the labourers work for their own account, as it has already become practically superfluous in piece-work. This fanatical insistence comes to the surface also conversely in the adulteration of the elements of production, which is one of the principal means of lowering the relation of the value of the constant capital to the variable capital, and thus of raising the rate of profit. Whereby the sale of these elements of production above their value, so far as this reappears in the product, acquires a marked element of cheating. This practice plays an essential part particularly in German industry, whose maxim is: People will surely appreciate if we send them good samples at first, and then inferior goods afterward. However, as these matters belong to the sphere of competition they do not concern us here.

It should be noted that this raising of the rate of profit by means of lowering the value of the constant capital, i. e., by reducing its expensiveness, does not in any way depend on whether the branch of industry in which it takes place produces luxuries, or necessities for the consumption of labourers, or means of production generally. This last circumstance would only be of material importance if it were a question of the rate of surplus value, which depends essentially on the value of labour power, i. e., on the value of the customary necessities of the labourer. But in the present case the surplus value and the rate of surplus value have been assumed as given. The relation of surplus value to total capital — and this determines the rate of profit — depends under these circumstances exclusively on the value of the constant capital, and in no way on the use value of the elements of which it is composed.

A relative cheapening of the means of production does not, of course, exclude the possible increase of their absolute aggregate value, for the absolute volume in which they are employed grows tremendously with the development of the productive power of labour and the attendant growth of the level of production. Economy in the use of constant capital, from whatever angle it may be viewed, is, in part, the exclusive result of the fact that the means of production function and are consumed as joint means of production of the combined labourer, so that the resulting saving appears as a product of the social nature of directly productive labour; in part, however, it is the result of developing productivity of labour in spheres which supply capital with its means of production, so that if we view the total labour in relation to total capital, and not simply the labourers employed by capitalist X in relation to capitalist X, this economy presents itself once more as a product of the development of the productive forces of social labour, with the only difference that capitalist X enjoys the advantage not only of the productivity of labour in his own establishment, but also of that in other establishments. Yet the capitalist views economy of his constant capital as a condition wholly independent of, and entirely alien to, his labourers. He is always well aware, however, that the labourer has something to do with the employer buying much or little labour with the same amount of money (for this is how the transaction between the capitalist and labourer appears in his mind). This economy in the application of the means of production, this method of obtaining a certain result with a minimum outlay appears more than any other inner power of labour as an inherent power of capital and a method peculiar and characteristic of the capitalist mode of production.

This conception is so much the less surprising since it appears to accord with fact, and since the relationship of capital actually conceals the inner connection behind the utter indifference, isolation, and estrangement in which they place the labourer vis-à-vis the conditions of realising his labour.

First, the means of production that make up the constant capital represent only the money belonging to the capitalist (just as the body of the Roman debtor represented the money of his creditor, according to Linguet[a]) and are related to him alone, while the labourer, who comes in contact with them only in the direct process of production, deals with them as use values of production only, as means of labour and materials of labour. Increase or decrease of their value, therefore, has as little bearing on his relations to the capitalist as the circumstance whether he may be working with copper or iron. For that matter, the capitalist likes to view this point differently, as we shall later indicate, whenever the means of production gain in value and thereby reduce his rate of profit.

Second, in so far as these means of production in the capitalist production process are at the same time means of exploiting labour, the

---

a [S. N. H. Linguet,] *Théorie des loix civiles...*, Vol. II, London, 1767, Book V, Ch. XX.

labourer is no more concerned with their relative dearness or cheapness than a horse is concerned with the dearness or cheapness of its bit and bridle.

Finally, we have earlier seen[a] that, in fact, the labourer looks at the social nature of his labour, at its combination with the labour of others for a common purpose, as he would at an alien power; the condition of realising this combination is alien property, whose dissipation would be totally indifferent to him if he were not compelled to economise with it. The situation is quite different in factories owned by the labourers themselves, as in Rochdale, for instance.[17]

It scarcely needs to be mentioned, then, that as far as concerns the productivity of labour in one branch of industry as a lever for cheapening and improving the means of production in another, and thereby raising the rate of profit, the general interconnection of social labour affects the labourers as a matter alien to them, a matter that actually concerns the capitalist alone, since it is he who buys and appropriates these means of production. The fact that he buys the product of labourers in another branch of industry with the product of labourers in his own, and that he therefore disposes of the product of the labourers of another capitalist only by gratuitously appropriating that of his own, is a development that is fortunately concealed by the process of circulation, etc.

Moreover, since production on a large scale develops for the first time in its capitalist form, the thirst for profits on the one hand, and competition on the other, which compels the cheapest possible production of commodities, make this economy in the employment of constant capital appear as something peculiar to the capitalist mode of production and therefore as a function of the capitalist.

Just as the capitalist mode of production promotes the development of the productive powers of social labour, on the one hand, so does it whip on to economy in the employment of constant capital on the other.

However, it is not only the estrangement and indifference that arise between the labourer, the bearer of living labour, and the economical, i. e., rational and thrifty, use of the material conditions of his labour. In line with its contradictory and antagonistic nature, the capitalist mode of production proceeds to count the prodigious dissipation of the labourer's life and health, and the lowering of his

---

[a] See present edition, Vol. 35, p. 330.

living conditions, as an economy in the use of constant capital and thereby as a means of raising the rate of profit.

Since the labourer passes the greater portion of his life in the process of production, the conditions of the production process are largely the conditions of his active life process, or his living conditions, and economy in these living conditions is a method of raising the rate of profit; just as we saw earlier[a] that overwork, the transformation of the labourer into a work horse, is a means of increasing capital, or speeding up the production of surplus value. Such economy extends to overcrowding close and unsanitary premises with labourers, or, as capitalists put it, to space saving; to crowding dangerous machinery into close quarters without using safety devices, to neglecting safety rules in production processes pernicious to health, or, as in mining, bound up with danger, etc. Not to mention the absence of all provisions to render the production process human, agreeable, or at least bearable. From the capitalist point of view this would be quite a useless and senseless waste. The capitalist mode of production is generally, despite all its niggardliness, altogether too prodigal with its human material, just as, conversely, thanks to its method of distribution of products through commerce and manner of competition, it is very prodigal with its material means, and loses for society what it gains for the individual capitalist.

Just as capital has the tendency to reduce the direct employment of living labour to no more than the necessary labour, and always to cut down the labour required to produce a commodity by exploiting the social productive power of labour and thus to save a maximum of directly applied living labour, so it has also the tendency to employ this labour, reduced to a minimum, under the most economical conditions, i. e., to reduce to its minimum the value of the employed constant capital. If it is the necessary labour which determines the value of commodities, instead of all the labour time contained in them, so it is the capital which realises this determination and, at the same time, continually reduces the labour time socially necessary to produce a given commodity. The price of the commodity is thereby lowered to its minimum since every portion of the labour required for its production is reduced to its minimum.[b]

We must make a distinction in economy as regards use of constant capital. If the quantity, and consequently the sum of the value of

---

[a] Ibid., pp. 239-307. - [b] Cf. present edition, Vol. 33, p. 90.

employed capital, increases, this is primarily only a concentration of more capital in a single hand. Yet it is precisely this greater quantity applied by a single source — attended, as a rule, by an absolutely greater but relatively smaller amount of employed labour — which permits economy of constant capital. To take an individual capitalist, the volume of the necessary investment of capital, especially of its fixed portion, increases. But its value decreases relative to the mass of worked-up materials and exploited labour.

This is now to be briefly illustrated by a few examples. We shall begin at the end — the economy in the conditions of production, in so far as these also constitute the living conditions of the labourer.

II. SAVINGS IN LABOUR CONDITIONS
AT THE EXPENSE OF THE LABOURERS

Coal mines. Neglect of indispensable outlays.

"Under the competition which exists among the coal-owners and coal-proprietors ... no more outlay is incurred than is sufficient to overcome the most obvious physical difficulties; and under that which prevails among the labouring colliers, who are ordinarily more numerous than the work to be done requires, a large amount of danger and exposure to the most noxious influences will gladly be encountered for wages a little in advance of the agricultural population round them, in an occupation, in which they can moreover make a profitable use of their children. This double competition is quite sufficient ... to cause a large proportion of the pits to be worked with the most imperfect drainage and ventilation; often with ill-constructed shafts, bad gearing, incompetent engineers; and ill-constructed and ill-prepared bays and roadways; causing a destruction of life, and limb, and health, the statistics of which would present an appalling picture" (First Report on Children's Employment in Mines and Collieries, etc., April 21, 1829, p. 102).[18]

About 1860, a weekly average of 15 men lost their lives in the English collieries. According to the report on Coal Mines Accidents (February 6, 1862), a total of 8,466 were killed in the ten years 1852-61.[a] But the report admits that this number is far too low, because in the first few years, when the inspectors had just been installed and their districts were far too large, a great many accidents and deaths were not reported. The very fact that the number of accidents, though still very high, has decreased markedly since the inspection system was established, and this in spite of the limited powers and insufficient numbers of the inspectors, demonstrates the natural tendency of capi-

---

[a] Cf. present edition, Vol. 30, p. 168.

talist exploitation.— These human sacrifices are mostly due to the inordinate avarice of the mine owners. Very often they had only one shaft sunk, so that apart from the lack of effective ventilation there was no escape were this shaft to become obstructed.

Capitalist production, when considered in isolation from the process of circulation and the excesses of competition, is very economical with the materialised labour objectified in commodities. Yet, more than any other mode of production, it squanders human lives, or living labour, and not only blood and flesh, but also nerve and brain. Indeed, it is only by dint of the most extravagant waste of individual development that the development of the human race is at all safeguarded and maintained in the epoch of history immediately preceding the conscious reorganisation of society. Since all of the economising here discussed arises from the social nature of labour, it is indeed just this directly social nature of labour which causes the waste of life and health. The following question suggested by factory inspector R. Baker is characteristic in this respect:

*"The whole question is one for serious consideration, and in what way *this sacrifice of infant life occasioned by congregational labour* can be best averted?"* (Reports of Insp. of Fact., October 1863, p. 157).

Factories. Here we have to deal with the disregard for every measure aimed at ensuring the safety, convenience, and health of labourers also in the actual factories. It is to blame for a large portion of the casualty lists containing the wounded and killed of the industrial army (cf. the annual factory reports). Similarly, lack of space, ventilation, etc.[a]

As far back as October 1855, Leonard Horner complained about the resistance of very many manufacturers to the legal requirements concerning safety devices on horizontal shafts, although the danger was continually emphasised by accidents, many of them fatal, and although these safety devices did not cost much and did not interfere with production (Reports of Insp. of Fact., October 1855, p. 6).[b] In their resistance against these and other legal requirements the manufacturers were openly seconded by the unpaid justices of the peace, who were themselves mostly manufacturers or friends of manufacturers, and handed down their decisions accordingly. What sort of verdicts these gentlemen handed down was revealed by Superior Judge

---

[a] Ibid., Vol. 33, pp. 152-53. - [b] Cf. present edition, Vol. 35, p. 430.

Campbell, who said with reference to one of them, against which an appeal had been made to him:

"It is not an interpretation of the Act of Parliament, it is a repeal of the Act of Parliament" (l. c., p. 11).

Horner states in the same report that in many factories labourers are not warned when machinery is about to be started up. Since there is always something to be done about machinery even when it is not operating, fingers and hands are always occupied with it, and accidents happen continually due to the mere omission of a warning signal (l. c., p. 44). The manufacturers had formed a TRADES-UNION at the time to oppose factory legislation, the so-called NATIONAL ASSOCIATION FOR THE AMENDMENT OF THE FACTORY LAWS in Manchester, which in March 1855 collected more than £50,000 by assessing 2 shillings per horse-power, to pay for the court proceedings against its members started by factory inspectors, and to conduct the cases in the name of the union. It was a matter of proving that KILLING WAS NO MURDER [19] when it occurred for the sake of profit. A factory inspector for Scotland, Sir John Kincaid, tells about a certain firm in Glasgow which used the iron scrap at its factory to make protective shields for all its machinery, the cost amounting to £9 ls. Joining the manufacturers' union would have cost it an assessment of £11 for its 110 horse-power, which was more than the cost of all its protective appliances. But the NATIONAL ASSOCIATION had been organised in 1854 for the express purpose of opposing the law which prescribed such protection. The manufacturers had not paid the least heed to it during the whole period from 1844 to 1854. When the factory inspectors, at instructions from Palmerston, then informed the manufacturers that the law would be enforced in earnest, the manufacturers instantly founded their association, many of whose most prominent members were themselves justices of the peace and in this capacity were supposed to enforce the law. When in April 1855 the new Home Secretary, Sir George Grey, offered a compromise under which the government would be content with practically nominal safety appliances the Association indignantly rejected even this. In various lawsuits the famous engineer William Fairbairn threw the weight of his reputation behind the principle of economy and in defence of the freedom of capital which had been violated. The head of factory inspection, Leonard Horner, was persecuted and maligned by the manufacturers in every conceivable manner.

But the manufacturers did not rest until they obtained a writ of the COURT OF QUEEN'S BENCH, [20] according to which the Law of 1844 did not prescribe protective devices for horizontal shafts installed more than 7 feet above the ground and, finally, in 1856 they succeeded in securing an Act of Parliament [21] entirely satisfactory to them in the circumstances, through the services of the bigot Wilson Patten, one of those pious souls whose display of religion is always ready to do the dirty work for the knights of the money-bag. This Act practically deprived the labourers of all special protection and referred them to the common courts for compensation in the event of industrial accidents (sheer mockery in view of the excessive cost of English lawsuits), while it made it almost impossible for the manufacturer to lose the lawsuit by providing in a finely-worded clause for expert testimony. The result was a rapid increase of accidents. In the six months from May to October 1858, Inspector Baker reported that accidents increased by 21% compared with the preceding half-year. In his opinion 36.7% of these accidents might have been avoided. It is true that the number of accidents in 1858 and 1859 was considerably below that of 1845 and 1846. It was actually 29% less although the number of labourers in the industries subject to inspection had increased 20%. But what was the reason for this? In so far as this issue has been settled now (1865), it was mainly accomplished through the introduction of new machinery already provided with safety devices to which the manufacturer did not object because they cost him no extra expense. Furthermore, a few labourers succeeded in securing heavy damages for their lost arms, and had this judgment upheld even by the highest courts (Reports of Insp. of Fact., April 30, 1861, p. 31, ditto April 1862, p. 17).

So much for economy in devices protecting the life and limbs of labourers (among whom many children) against the dangers of handling and operating machinery.

Work in enclosed places generally. It is well known to what extent economy of space, and thus of buildings, crowds labourers into close quarters. In addition, there is also economy in means of ventilation. Coupled with the long working hours, the two cause a large increase in diseases of the respiratory organs, and an attendant increase in mortality. The following illustrations have been taken from Reports on Public Health, 6th report, 1863. This report was compiled by Dr. John Simon, well known from our Book I.[a]

Just as combination and co-operation of labour permits large-scale employment of machinery, concentration of means of production,

---

[a] See present edition, Vol. 35, p. 468.

and economy in their use, it is this very working together *en masse* in enclosed places and under conditions rather determined by ease of manufacture than by health requirements — it is this mass concentration in one and the same workshop that acts, on the one hand, as a source of greater profits for the capitalist and, on the other, unless counteracted by a reduced number of hours and special precautions, as the cause of the squandering of the lives and health of the labourers.

Dr. Simon formulates the following rule and backs it up with abundant statistics:

"In proportion as the people of a district are attracted to any collective indoor occupation, in such proportion, other things being equal, the district death rate by lung diseases will be increased" (p. 23). The cause is bad ventilation. "And probably in all England there is no exception to the rule, that, in every district which has a large indoor industry, the increased mortality of the workpeople is such as to colour the death return of the whole district with a marked excess of lung disease" (p. 23).

Mortality figures for industries carried on in enclosed places, collected by the Board of Health in 1860 and 1861, indicate that for the same number of men between the ages of 15 and 55, for which the death rate from consumption and other pulmonary diseases in English agricultural districts is 100, the death rate in Coventry is 163, in Blackburn and Skipton 167, Congleton and Bradford 168, Leicester 171, Leek 182, Macclesfield 184, Bolton 190, Nottingham 192, Rochdale 193, Derby 198, Salford and Ashton-under-Lyne 203, Leeds 218, Preston 220, and Manchester 263 (p. 24). The following table presents a still more striking illustration.

District	Chief industry	Deaths from pulmonary diseases between the ages of 15 and 25, per 100,000 population	
		Men	Women
Berkhampstead	Straw plaiting (women)	219	578
Leighton Buzzard	Straw plaiting (women)	309	554
Newport Pagnell	Lace manufacture (women)	301	617
Towcester	Lace manufacture (women)	239	577
Yeovil	Manufacture of gloves (mainly women)	280	409
Leek	Silk industry (predominantly women) .	437	856
Congleton	Silk industry (predominantly women) .	566	790
Macclesfield	Silk industry (predominantly women) .	593	890
Healthy country district	Agriculture	331	333

It shows the death rate for pulmonary diseases separately for both sexes between the ages of 15 and 25 computed for every 100,000 population. In the districts selected only women are employed in industries carried on in enclosed places, while men work in all other possible lines.[a]

In the silk districts, where more men are employed in the factory, their mortality is also higher. The death rate from consumption, etc., for both sexes, reveals, as the report says,

"the ATROCIOUS [b] sanitary circumstances under which much of our silk industry is conducted".

And it is in this same silk industry that the manufacturers, pleading exceptionally favourable and sanitary conditions in their establishments, demanded by way of an exception, and partially obtained, long working hours for children under 13 years of age (Buch I, Kap. VIII, 6, S. 296/286 [c]).

"Probably no industry which has yet been investigated has afforded a worse picture than that which Dr. Smith gives of tailoring:—'Shops vary much in their sanitary conditions, but almost universally are overcrowded and ill-ventilated, and in a high degree unfavourable to health.... Such rooms are necessarily warm; but when the gas is lit, as during the day-time on foggy days, and at night during the winter, the heat increases to 80° and even to upwards of 90°" (Fahrenheit, = 27-33° C), 'causing profuse perspiration, and condensation of vapour upon the panes of glass, so that it runs down in streams or drops from the roof, and the operatives are compelled to keep some windows open, at whatever risk to themselves of taking cold.' And he gives the following account of what he found in 16 of the most important West End shops.— 'The largest cubic space in these ill-ventilated rooms allowed to each operative is 270 feet, and the least 105 feet, and in the whole averages only 156 feet per man. In one room, with a gallery running round it, and lighted only from the roof, from 92 to upwards of 100 men are employed, where a large number of gaslights burn, and where the urinals are in the closest proximity, the cubic space does not exceed 150 feet per man. In another room, which can only be called a kennel in a yard, lighted from the roof, and ventilated by a small skylight opening, five to six men work in a space of 112 cubic feet per man.' ... Tailors, in those ATROCIOUS [d] workshops which Dr. Smith describes, work generally for about 12 or 13 hours a day, and at some times the work will be continued for 15 or 16 hours" (pp. 25, 26, 28).

---

[a] Cf. present edition, Vol. 33, pp. 475-76. - [b] In the 1894 German edition this English word is given in parentheses after its German equivalent. - [c] English edition: Ch. X, 6 (see present edition, Vol. 35, pp. 297-98). - [d] In the 1894 German edition this English word is given in parentheses after its German equivalent.

Number of persons employed	Branches of industry and locality	Death rate per 100,000 between the ages of		
		25-35	35-45	45-55
958,265	Agriculture, England and Wales	743	805	1,145
22,301 men and 12,377 women }	Tailoring, London	958	1,262	2,093
13,803	Type-setters and printers, London	894	1,747	2,367

(p. 30). It must be noted, and has in fact been remarked by John Simon, chief of the Medical Department and author of the report, that the mortality rate for tailors, type-setters, and printers of London between the ages of 25 and 35 was cited lower than the real figure, because London employers in both lines of business have a large number of young people (probably up to 30 years of age) from the country engaged as apprentices and "IMPROVERS", i. e., men getting additional training. These swell the number of hands for which the London industrial death rates are computed. But they do not proportionally contribute to the number of deaths in London because their stay there is only temporary. If they fall ill during this period, they return to their homes in the country, where their death is registered if they die. This circumstance affects the earlier ages still more and renders the London death rates for these age groups completely valueless as indexes of the ill-effects of industry on health (p. 30).

The case of the type-setters is similar to that of the tailors. In addition to lack of ventilation, to poisoned air, etc., there is still nightwork to be mentioned. Their regular working time is 12 to 13 hours, sometimes 15 to 16.

"Great heat and foulness which begin when the gas-jets are lit. ... It not infrequently happens that fumes from a foundry, or foul odours from machinery or sinks, rise from the lower room, and aggravate the evils of the upper one. The heated air of the lower rooms always tends to heat the upper by warming the floor, and when the rooms are low, and the consumption of gas great, this is a serious evil, and one only surpassed in the case where the steam-boilers are placed in the lower room, and supply unwished-for heat to the whole house.... As a general expression, it may be stated that universally the ventilation is defective, and quite insufficient to remove the heat and the products of the combustion of gas in the evening and during the night, and that in many offices, and particularly in those made from dwelling-houses, the condition is most deplorable. ... And in some offices (especially those of weekly newspapers) there will be work — work too, in which boys between 12 and 16 years of age take equal part — for almost uninterrupted periods of two days and a night at a time; — while, in other printing-offices which lay themselves out for the doing of 'urgent' business, Sunday gives no relaxation to the workman, and his working days become seven instead of six in every week" (pp. 26, 28).

The MILLINERS and DRESSMAKERS[a] have already attracted our attention in Book I (Kap. VIII, 3, S. 249/241)[b] in respect to overwork. Their workshops are described in our report by Dr. Ord. Even if better during the day, they become overheated, FOUL,[c] and unhealthy during the hours in which gas is burned. Dr. Ord found in 34 shops of the better sort that the average number of cubic feet per worker was as follows:

"... In four cases more than 500, in four other cases from 400 to 500, ... in seven others from 200 to 250, in four others from 150 to 200, and in nine others only from 100 to 150. The largest of these allowances would but be scanty for continuous work, unless the space were thoroughly well ventilated; and, except with extraordinary ventilation, its atmosphere could not be tolerably wholesome during gas-light."

And here is Dr. Ord's remark about one of the minor workshops which he visited, operated for the account of a MIDDLEMAN[c]:

"One room, area in cubical feet, 1,280; persons present, 14; area to each, in cubical feet, 91.5. The women here were weary-looking and squalid; their earnings were stated to be 7s. to 15s. a week, and their tea. ... Hours 8 a. m. to 8 p. m. The small room into which these 14 persons were crowded was ill-ventilated. There were two movable windows and a fire-place, but the latter was blocked up, and there was no special ventilation of any kind" (p. 27).

The same report states with reference to the overwork of milliners and dressmakers:

"... The overwork of the young women in fashionable dressmaking establishments does not, for more than about four months of the year, prevail in that monstrous degree which has on many occasions excited momentary public surprise and indignation; but for the indoor hands during these months it will, as a rule, be of full 14 hours a day, and will, when there is pressure, be, for days together, of 17 or even 18 hours. At other times of the year the work of the indoor hands ranges probably from 10 to 14 hours; and uniformly the hours for outdoor hands are 12 or 13. For mantle-makers, collar-makers, shirt-makers, and various other classes of needleworkers (including persons who work at the sewing-machine) the hours spent in the common workroom are fewer — generally not more than 10 to 12 hours; but, says Dr. Ord, the regular hours of work are subject to considerable extension in certain houses at certain times, by the practice of working extra hours for extra pay, and in other houses by the practice of taking work away

---

[a] In the 1894 German edition these English words are given in parentheses after their German equivalents. - [b] English edition: Ch. X, 3 (see present edition, Vol. 35, pp. 261-62). - [c] In the 1894 German edition this English word is given in parentheses after its German equivalent.

from houses of business, to be done after hours at home, both practices being, it may be added, often compulsory" (p. 28).

John Simon remarks in a footnote to this page:

"Mr. Radcliffe, ... the Honorary Secretary of the EPIDEMIOLOGICAL SOCIETY, ... happening to have unusual opportunities for questioning the young women employed in first-class houses of business ... has found that in only one out of twenty girls examined who called themselves 'quite well' could the state of health be pronounced good; the rest exhibiting in various degrees evidences of depressed physical power, nervous exhaustion, and numerous functional disorders thereupon dependent. He attributes these conditions in the first place to the length of the hours of work — the minimum of which he estimates at 12 hours a day out of the season; and secondarily to ... crowding and bad ventilation of workrooms, gas-vapours, insufficiency or bad quality of food, and inattention to domestic comfort."

The conclusion arrived at by the chief of the English Board of Health is that

"it is practically impossible for workpeople to insist upon that which in theory is their first sanitary right — the right that whatever work their employer assembles them to do, shall, so far as depends upon him, be, at his cost, divested of all needlessly unwholesome circumstances; ... while workpeople are practically unable to exact that sanitary justice for themselves, they also (notwithstanding the presumed intentions of the law) cannot expect any effectual assistance from the appointed administrators of the NUISANCES REMOVAL ACTS" (p. 29).— "Doubtless there may be some small technical difficulty in defining the exact line at which employers shall become subject to regulation. But ... in principle, the sanitary claim is universal. And in the interest of myriads of labouring men and women, whose lives are now needlessly afflicted and shortened by the infinite physical suffering which their mere employment engenders, I would venture to express my hope, that universally the sanitary circumstances of labour may, at least so far, be brought within appropriate provisions of law, that the effective ventilation of all indoor workplaces may be ensured, and that in every naturally insalubrious occupation the specific health-endangering influence may as far as practicable be reduced" (p. 31).

III. ECONOMY IN THE GENERATION AND TRANSMISSION
OF POWER, AND IN BUILDINGS

In his October 1852 report L. Horner quotes a letter of the famous engineer James Nasmyth of Patricroft, the inventor of the steam-hammer, which, among other things, contains the following [a]:

"... The public are little aware of the vast increase in driving power which has been obtained by such changes of system and improvements" (of steam-engines) "as I allude

---

[a] Cf. present edition, Vol. 33, p. 470.

to. The engine power of this district" (Lancashire) "lay under the incubus of timid and prejudiced traditions for nearly forty years, but now we are happily emancipated. During the last fifteen years, but more especially in the course of the last four years" (since 1848), "some very important changes have taken place in the system of working condensing steam-engines. ... The result ... has been to realise a much greater amount of duty or work performed by the identical engines, and that again at a very considerable reduction of the expenditure of fuel. ... For a great many years after the introduction of steam-power into the mills and manufactories of the above-named districts, the velocity of which it was considered proper to work condensing steam-engines was about 220 feet per minute of the piston; that is to say, an engine with a 5-feet stroke was restricted by 'rule' to make 22 revolutions of the crankshaft per minute. Beyond this speed it was not considered prudent or desirable to work the engine; and as all the mill gearing ... were made suitable to this 220 feet per minute speed of piston, this slow and absurdly restricted velocity ruled the working of such engines for many years. However, at length, either through fortunate ignorance of the 'rule', or by better reasons on the part of some bold innovator, a greater speed was tried, and as the result was highly favourable, others followed the example, by, as it is termed, 'letting the engine away', namely, by so modifying the proportions of the first motion wheels of the mill gearing as to permit the engine to run at 300 feet and upwards per minute, while the mill gearing generally was kept at its former speed.... This 'letting the engine away'... has led to the almost universal 'speeding' of engines, because it was proved that not only was there available power gained from the identical engines, but also as the higher velocity of the engine yielded a greater momentum in the fly-wheel the motion was found to be much more regular.... We ... obtain more power from a steam-engine by simply permitting its piston to move at a higher velocity (pressure of steam and vacuum in the condenser remaining the same).... Thus, for example, suppose any given engine yields 40 horse-power when its piston is travelling at 200 feet per minute, if by suitable arrangement or modification we can permit this same engine to run at such a speed as that its piston will travel through space at 400 feet per minute (pressure of steam and vacuum, as before said, remaining the same), we shall then have just double the power ... and as the pressure by steam and vacuum is the same in both cases, the strain upon the parts of this engine will be no greater at 400 than at 200 feet speed of piston, so that the risk of 'break-down' does not materially increase with the increase of speed. All the difference is, that we shall in such case consume steam at a rate proportional to the speed of piston, or nearly so; and there will be some small increase in the wear and tear of 'the brasses' or rubbing-parts, but so slight as to be scarcely worth notice.... But in order to obtain increase of power from the same engine by permitting its piston to travel at a higher velocity it is requisite ... to burn more coal per hour under the same boiler, or employ boilers of greater evaporating capabilities, i. e., greater steam-generating powers. This accordingly was done, and boilers of greater steam-generating or water-evaporating powers were supplied to the old 'speeded' engines, and in many cases near 100 per cent more work was got out of the identical engines by means of such changes as above named. About ten years ago the extraordinary economical production of power as realised by the engines employed in the mining operations of Cornwall began to attract attention; and as competition in the spinning trade forced manufacturers to look to 'savings' as the chief source of profits, the remarkable difference in the consumption of coal per horse-power per hour, as indicated by the performance of the Cornish engines, as also the extraordinary economical performance of Woolf's double-cylinder engines, began to attract increased attention to the subject of economy of fuel in this district, and as the Cornish and double-cylinder engines gave a horse-power for every $3\frac{1}{2}$ to 4 pounds of coal per hour, while the generality of cotton-mill engines were consuming 8 or 12 pounds per horse per hour, so remarkable a difference induced mill-owners and engine-makers in this district to endeavour to realise, by the adoption of similar means, such extraordinary economical results as were proved to be common in Cornwall and France, where the high price of coal had compelled manufacturers to look more sharply to such costly departments of their establishments. The result of this increased attention to economy of fuel has been most important in many respects. In the first place, many boilers, the half of whose surface had been in the good old times of high profits left exposed quite naked to the cold air, began to get covered with thick blankets of felt, and brick and plaster, and other modes and means whereby to prevent the escape of that heat from their exposed surface which had cost so much fuel to maintain. Steam-pipes began to be 'protected' in the same manner, and the outside of the cylinder of the engine felted and cased in with wood in like manner. Next came the use of 'high steam', namely, instead of having the safety-valve loaded so as to blow off at 4, 6, or 8 lbs to the square inch, it was found that by raising the pressure to 14 or 20 lbs ... a very decided economy of fuel resulted; in other words, the work of the mill was performed by a very notable reduced consumption of coals, ... and those who had the means and the boldness carried the increased pressure and 'expansion system' of working to the full extent, by employing properly constructed boilers to supply steam of 30, 40, 50, 60, and 70 lbs to the square inch; pressures which would have frightened an engineer of the old school out of his wits. But as the economic results of so increasing the pressure of steam ... soon appeared in most unmistakable £ s. d. forms, the use of high-pressure steam-boilers for working condensing engines became almost general. And those who desired to go to the full extent ... soon adopted the employment of the Woolf engine in its full integrity, and most of our mills lately built are worked by the Woolf engines, namely, those on which there are two cylinders to each engine, in one of which the high-pressure steam from the boiler exerts or yields power by its excess of pressure over that of the atmosphere, which, instead of the said high-pressure steam being let pass off at the end of each stroke free into the atmosphere, is caused to pass into a low-pressure cylinder of about four times the area of the former, and after due expansion passes to the condenser, the economic result obtained from engines of this class is such that the consumption of fuel is at the rate of from $3\frac{1}{2}$ to 4 lbs of coal per horse per hour; while in the engines of the old system the consumption used to be on the average from 12 to 14 lbs per horse per hour. By an ingenious arrangement, the Woolf system of double cylinder or combined low- and high-pressure engine has been introduced extensively to already existing engines, whereby their performance has been increased both as to power and economy of fuel. The same result ... has been in use these eight or ten years, by having a high-pressure engine so connected with a condensing engine as to enable the waste steam of the former to pass on to and work the latter. This system is in many cases very convenient.

"It would not be very easy to get an exact return as to the increase of performance or work done by the identical engines to which some or all of these improvements have been applied; I am confident, however, ... that from the same weight of steam-engine machinery we are now obtaining at least 50 per cent more duty or work performed on the average, and that ... in many cases, the identical steam-engines which, in the days of the restricted speed of 220 feet per minute, yielded 50 horse-power, are now yielding upwards of 100. The very economical results derived from the employment of high-pressure steam in working condensing steam-engines, together with the much higher power required by mill extensions from the same engines, has within the last three years led to the adoption of tubular boilers, yielding a much more economical result than those formerly employed in generating steam for mill engines" (Reports of Insp. of Fact., October 1852, pp. 23-27).

What applies to power generation also applies to power transmission and working machinery.

"The rapid strides with which improvement in machinery has advanced within these few years have enabled manufacturers to increase production without additional moving power. The more economical application of labour has been rendered necessary by the diminished length of the working day, and in most well-regulated mills an intelligent mind is always considering in what manner production can be increased with decreased expenditure. I have before me a statement, kindly prepared by a very intelligent gentleman in my district, showing the number of hands employed, their ages, the machines at work, and the wages paid from 1840 to the present time. In October 1840, his firm employed 600 hands, of whom 200 were under 13 years of age. In October last, 350 hands were employed, of whom 60 only were under 13; the same number of machines, within very few, were at work, and the same sum in wages was paid at both periods" (Redgrave's Report in Reports of Insp. of Fact., Oct. 1852, pp. 58-59).

These improvements of the machinery do not show their full effect until they are used in new, appropriately arranged factories.

"As regards the improvement made in machinery, I may say in the first place that a great advance has been made in the construction of mills adapted to receive improved machinery.... In the bottom room I double all my yarn, and upon that single floor I shall put 29,000 doubling spindles. I effect a saving of labour in the room and shed of at least 10%, not so much from any improvement in the principle of doubling yarn, but from a concentration of machinery under a single management; and I am enabled to drive the said number of spindles by one single shaft, a saving in shafting, compared with what other firms have to use to work the same number of spindles, of 60%, in some cases 80%. There is a large saving in oil, and shafting, and in grease.... With superior mill arrangements and improved machinery, at the lowest estimate I have effected a saving in labour of 10%, a great saving in power, coal, oil, tallow, shafting and strapping" (Evidence of a cotton spinner, Reports of Insp. of Fact., Oct. 1863, pp. 109, 110).

IV. UTILISATION OF THE EXCRETIONS OF PRODUCTION

The capitalist mode of production extends the utilisation of the excretions of production and consumption. By the former we mean the waste of industry and agriculture, and by the latter partly the excretions produced by the natural exchange of matter in the human body and partly the form of objects that remains after their consumption. In the chemical industry, for instance, excretions of production are such by-products as are wasted in production on a smaller scale; iron filings accumulating in the manufacture of machinery and returning into the production of iron as raw material, etc. Excretions of consumption are the natural waste matter discharged by the human body, remains of clothing in the form of rags, etc. Excretions of consumption are of the greatest importance for agriculture.[a] So far as their utilisation is concerned, there is an enormous waste of them in the capitalist economy. In London, for instance, they find no better use for the excretion of $4\frac{1}{2}$ million human beings than to contaminate the Thames with it at heavy expense.

Rising prices of raw materials naturally stimulate the utilisation of waste products.

The general requirements for the re-employment of these excretions are: large quantities of such waste, such as are available only in large-scale production; improved machinery whereby materials, formerly useless in their prevailing form, are put into a state fit for new production; scientific progress, particularly of chemistry, which reveals the useful properties of such waste. It is true that great savings of this sort are also observed in small-scale agriculture, as prevails in, say, Lombardy, southern China, and Japan. But on the whole, the productivity of agriculture under this system obtains from the prodigal use of human labour power, which is withheld from other spheres of production.

The so-called waste plays an important role in almost every industry. Thus, the Factory Report for December 1863 mentions as one of the principal reasons why the English and many of the Irish farmers do not like to grow flax, or do so but rarely,

"the great waste ... which has taken place at the little water SCUTCH MILLS[b] ... the waste in cotton is comparatively small, but in flax very large. The efficiency of water steeping and of good machine scutching will reduce this disadvantage very considerably.... Flax, scutched in Ireland in a most shameful way, and a large percentage actually lost by it, equal to 28 or 30%" (Reports of Insp. of Fact., Dec. 1863, pp. 139, 142),

whereas all this might be avoided through the use of better machinery. So much tow fell by the wayside that the factory inspector reports:

---

[a] Cf. present edition, Vol. 34, pp. 218-19. - [b] In the 1894 German edition these English words are given in parentheses after their German equivalents.

"I have been informed with respect to some of the scutch mills in Ireland, that the waste made at them has often been used by the scutchers to burn on their fires at home, and yet it is very valuable" (l. c., p. 140).

We shall speak of cotton waste later, when we deal with the price fluctuations of raw materials.

The wool industry was shrewder than the flax manufacturers.

"It was once the common practice to decry the preparation of waste and woollen rags for re-manufacture, but the prejudice has entirely subsided as regards the SHODDY TRADE,[a] which has become an important branch of the woollen trade of Yorkshire, and doubtless the cotton waste trade will be recognised in the same manner as supplying an admitted want. Thirty years since, woollen rags, i. e., pieces of cloth, old clothes, etc., of nothing but wool, would average about £4 4s. per ton in price: within the last few years they have become worth £44 per ton, and the demand for them has so increased that means have been found for utilising the rags of fabrics of cotton and wool mixed by destroying the cotton and leaving the wool intact, and now thousands of operatives are engaged in the manufacture of shoddy, from which the consumer has greatly benefited in being able to purchase cloth of a fair and average quality at a very moderate price" (Reports of Insp. of Fact., Oct. 1863, p. 107).

By the end of 1862 the rejuvenated shoddy made up as much as one-third of the entire consumption of wool in English industry (Reports of Insp. of Fact., October 1862, p. 81). The "big benefit" for the "consumer" is that his shoddy clothes wear out in just one-third of the previous time and turn threadbare in one-sixth of this time.

The English silk industry moved along the same downward path. The consumption of genuine raw silk decreased somewhat between 1839 and 1862, while that of silk waste doubled. Improved machinery helped to manufacture a silk useful for many purposes from this otherwise rather worthless stuff.

The most striking example of utilising waste is furnished by the chemical industry. It utilises not only its own waste, for which it finds new uses, but also that of many other industries. For instance, it converts the formerly almost useless gas-tar into aniline dyes, alizarin, and, more recently, even into drugs.

This economy of the excretions of production through their re-employment is to be distinguished from economy through the prevention of waste, that is to say, the reduction of excretions of production to a minimum, and the immediate utilisation to a maximum of all raw and auxiliary materials required in production.

---

[a] In the 1894 German edition these English words are given in parentheses after their German equivalents.

Reduction of waste depends in part on the quality of the machinery in use. Economy in oil, soap, etc., depends on how well the mechanical parts are machined and polished. This refers to the auxiliary materials. In part, however, and this is most important, it depends on the quality of the employed machines and tools whether a larger or smaller portion of the raw materials is turned into waste in the production process. Finally, this depends on the quality of the raw material itself. This, in turn, depends partly on the development of the extractive industry and agriculture which produce the raw material (strictly speaking on the progress of civilisation), and partly on the improvement of processes through which raw materials pass before they enter into manufacture.

"Parmentier has demonstrated that the art of grinding grain has improved very materially in France since a none too distant epoch, for instance the time of Louis XIV, so that the new mills, compared to the old, can make up to half as much more bread from the same amount of grain. The annual consumption of a Parisian, indeed, has first been estimated at 4 *setiers* of grain, then at 3, finally at 2, while nowadays it is only $1\frac{1}{3}$ *setiers*, or about 342 lbs per capita.... In the Perche, where I have lived for a long time, the crude mills of granite and trap rock millstones have been mostly rebuilt according to the rules of mechanics which has made such rapid progress in the last 30 years. They have been provided with good millstones from La Ferté, have ground the grain twice, the milling sack has been given a circular motion, and the output of flour from the same amount of grain has increased $\frac{1}{6}$. The enormous discrepancy between the daily grain consumption of the Romans and ourselves is therefore easily explained. It is due simply to imperfect methods of milling and bread-making. This is the way I feel I must explain a remarkable observation made by Pliny, XVIII, Ch. 20, 2: ...'The flour was sold in Rome, depending on its quality, at 40, 48 or 96 *as* per modius. These prices, so high in proportion to the contemporaneous grain prices, are due to the imperfect state of the mills of that period, which were still in their infancy, and the resultant heavy cost of milling'" (Dureau de la Malle, *Économie politique des Romains*, Paris, 1840, I, pp. 280-81).

V. ECONOMY THROUGH INVENTIONS

These savings in the application of fixed capital are, we repeat, due to the employment of the conditions of labour on a large scale; in short, are due to the fact that these serve as conditions of directly social, socialised labour or direct co-operation within the process of production. On the one hand, this is the indispensable requirement for the utilisation of mechanical and chemical inventions without increasing the price of the commodity, and this is always the *conditio sine qua non*. On the other hand, only production on a large scale permits the savings derived from co-operative productive consumption. Finally, it is only the experience of the combined labourer which discovers and reveals the where and how of saving, the simplest methods of applying the discoveries, and the ways to overcome the practical frictions arising from carrying out the theory—in its application to the production process—etc.

Incidentally, a distinction should be made between universal labour and co-operative labour. Both kinds play their role in the process of production, both flow one into the other, but both are also differentiated. Universal labour is all scientific labour, all discovery and all invention. This labour depends partly on the co-operation of the living, and partly on the utilisation of the labours of those who have gone before. Co-operative labour, on the other hand, is the direct co-operation of individuals.

The foregoing is corroborated by frequent observation, to wit:

1) The great difference in the cost of the first model of a new machine and that of its reproduction (regarding which, see Ure[a] and Babbage[b]).

2) The far greater cost of operating an ESTABLISHMENT based on a new invention as compared to later ESTABLISHMENTS arising out of their ruins, *ex suis ossibus*. This is so very true that the trail-blazers generally go bankrupt, and only those who later buy the buildings, machinery, etc., at a cheaper price, make money out of it. It is, therefore, generally the most worthless and miserable sort of money capitalists who draw the greatest profit out of all new developments of the universal labour of the human spirit and their social application through combined labour.

Chapter VI

THE EFFECT OF PRICE FLUCTUATIONS

I. FLUCTUATIONS IN THE PRICE OF RAW MATERIALS, AND THEIR DIRECT EFFECTS ON THE RATE OF PROFIT

The assumption in this case, as in previous ones, is that no change takes place in the rate of surplus value. It is necessary to analyse

---

[a] See this volume, p.84. - [b] Ch. Babbage, *Traité sur l'economie des machines et des manufactures*, Paris, 1833, pp. 377-78 (cf. present edition, Vol. 33, p. 350 and Vol. 35, p. 408).

the case in its pure form. However, it might be possible for a specific capital, whose rate of surplus value remains unchanged, to employ an increasing or decreasing number of labourers, in consequence of contraction or EXPANSION caused by such fluctuations in the price of raw materials as we are to analyse here. In that case the quantity of surplus value might vary, while the rate of surplus value remains the same. Yet this should also be disregarded here as a side-issue. If improvements of machinery and changes in the price of raw materials simultaneously influence either the number of labourers employed by a definite capital, or the level of wages, one has but to put together 1) the effect caused by the variations of constant capital on the rate of profit, and 2) the effect caused by variations in wages on the rate of profit. The result is then obtained of itself.

But in general, it should be noted here, as in the previous case, that if variations take place, either due to savings in constant capital, or due to fluctuations in the price of raw materials, they always affect the rate of profit, even if they leave the wage, hence the rate and amount of surplus value, untouched. They change the magnitude of C in $s'\frac{v}{C}$, and thus the value of the whole fraction. It is therefore immaterial, in this case as well — in contrast to what we found in our analysis of surplus value — in which sphere of production these variations occur; whether or not the production branches affected by them produce necessities for labourers, or constant capital for the production of such necessities. The deductions made here are equally valid for variations occurring in the production of luxury articles, and by luxury articles we here mean all production that does not serve the reproduction of labour power.

The raw materials here include auxiliary materials as well, such as indigo, coal, gas, etc. Furthermore, so far as machinery is concerned under this head, its own raw material consists of iron, wood, leather, etc. Its own price is therefore affected by fluctuations in the price of raw materials used in its construction. To the extent that its price is raised through fluctuations, either in the price of the raw materials of which it consists, or of the auxiliary materials consumed in its operation, the rate of profit falls *pro tanto*. And vice versa.

In the following analysis we shall confine ourselves to fluctuations in the price of raw materials, not so far as they go to make up the raw materials of machinery serving as means of labour or as auxiliary materials applied in its operation, but in so far as they are raw materials entering the process in which commodities are produced. There is just one thing to be noted here: the natural wealth in iron, coal, wood, etc., which are the principal elements used in the construction and operation of machinery, presents itself here as a natural fertility of capital and is a factor determining the rate of profit irrespective of the high or low level of wages.

Since the rate of profit is $\frac{s}{C}$, or $\frac{s}{c+v}$, it is evident that everything causing a variation in the magnitude of c, and thereby of C, must also bring about a variation in the rate of profit, even if s and v, and their mutual relation, remain unaltered. Now, raw materials are one of the principal components of constant capital. Even in industries which consume no actual raw materials, these enter the picture as auxiliary materials or components of machinery, etc., and their price fluctuations thus *pro tanto* influence the rate of profit. Should the price of raw material fall by an amount = d, then $\frac{s}{C}$, or $\frac{s}{c+v}$, becomes $\frac{s}{C-d}$, or $\frac{s}{(c-d)+v}$. Thus, the rate of profit rises. Conversely, if the price of raw material rises, then $\frac{s}{C}$, or $\frac{s}{c+v}$, becomes $\frac{s}{C+d}$, or $\frac{s}{(c+d)+v}$, and the rate of profit falls. Other conditions being equal, the rate of profit, therefore, falls and rises inversely to the price of raw material. This shows, among other things, how important the low price of raw material is for industrial countries, even if fluctuations in the price of raw materials are not accompanied by variations in the sales sphere of the product, and thus quite aside from the relation of demand to supply. It follows furthermore that foreign trade influences the rate of profit, regardless of its influence on wages through the cheapening of the necessities of life. The point is that it affects the prices of raw or auxiliary materials consumed in industry and agriculture. It is due to an as yet imperfect understanding of the nature of the rate of profit and of its specific difference from the rate of surplus value that, on the one hand, economists (like Torrens[a]) wrongly explain the marked influence of the prices of raw material on the rate of profit, which they note through practical experience, and that, on the other, economists like Ricardo,[b] who cling to general principles, do not recognise the influence of, say, world trade on the rate of profit.

---

[a] R. Torrens, *An Essay on the Production of Wealth*, London, 1821, p. 28 et seq. Cf. present edition, Vol. 32, pp. 262-63. - [b] D. Ricardo, *On the Principles of Political Economy, and Taxation*, Third edition, London, 1821, pp. 131-38. Cf. present edition, Vol. 32, pp. 71-72.

This makes clear the great importance to industry of the elimination or reduction of customs duties on raw materials. The rational development of the protective tariff system made the utmost reduction of import duties on raw materials one of its cardinal principles. This, and the abolition of the duty on corn,[22] was the main object of the English FREE-TRADERS, who were primarily concerned with having the duty on cotton lifted as well.

The use of flour in the cotton industry may serve as an illustration of the importance of a price reduction for an article which is not strictly a raw material but an auxiliary and at the same time one of the principal elements of nourishment. As far back as 1837, R. H. Greg [13] calculated that the 100,000 power-looms and 250,000 hand-looms then operating in the cotton-mills of Great Britain annually consumed 41 million lbs of flour to smooth the warp. He added a third of this quantity for bleaching and other processes, and estimated the total annual value of the flour so consumed at £342,000 for the preceding 10 years. A comparison with flour prices on the continent showed that the higher flour price forced upon manufacturers by corn tariffs alone amounted to £170,000 per year. Greg estimated the sum at a minimum of £200,000 for 1837 and cited a firm for which the flour price difference amounted to £1,000 annually. As a result,

"great manufacturers, thoughtful, calculating men of business, have said that ten hours' labour would be quite sufficient, if the Corn Laws were repealed" (Reports of Insp. of Fact., Oct. 1848, p. 98).

The Corn Laws were repealed. So were the duties on cotton and other raw materials. But no sooner had this been accomplished than the opposition of the manufacturers to the Ten Hours' Bill [23] became more violent than ever. And when the ten-hour factory day nevertheless became a law soon after, the first result was a general attempt to reduce wages.

The value of raw and auxiliary materials passes entirely and all at one time into the value of the product in the manufacture of which they are consumed, while the elements of fixed capital transfer their value to the product only gradually in proportion to their wear and tear. It follows that the price of the product is influenced far more by the price of raw materials than by that of fixed capital, although the

---

[13] *The Factory Question and the Ten Hours' Bill* by R. H. Greg, London, 1837, p. 115.

rate of profit is determined by the total value of the capital applied no matter how much of it is consumed in the making of the product. But it is evident — although we merely mention it in passing, since we here still assume that commodities are sold at their values, so that price fluctuations caused by competition do not as yet concern us — that the expansion or contraction of the market depends on the price of the individual commodity and is inversely proportional to the rise or fall of this price. It actually develops, therefore, that the price of the finished product does not rise in proportion to that of the raw material, and that it does not fall in proportion to that of raw material. Consequently, the rate of profit falls lower in one instance, and rises higher in the other than would have been the case if commodities were sold at their value.

Further, the quantity and value of the employed machinery grows with the development of the productive power of labour but not in the same proportion as this productive power, i. e., not in the proportion in which this machinery increases its output. In those branches of industry, therefore, which do consume raw materials, i. e., in which the subject of labour is itself a product of previous labour, the growing productive power of labour is expressed precisely in the proportion in which a larger quantity of raw material absorbs a definite quantity of labour, hence in the increasing amount of raw material converted in, say, one hour into products, or processed into commodities. The value of raw material, therefore, forms an ever-growing component of the value of the commodity product in proportion to the development of the productive power of labour, not only because it passes wholly into this latter value, but also because in every aliquot part of the aggregate product the portion representing depreciation of machinery and the portion formed by the newly added labour — both continually decrease. Owing to this falling tendency, the other portion of the value representing raw material increases proportionally, unless this increase is counterbalanced by a proportionate decrease in the value of the raw material arising from the growing productivity of the labour employed in its own production.

Further, raw and auxiliary materials, just like wages, form parts of the circulating capital and must, therefore, be continually replaced in their entirety through the sale of the product, while only the depreciation is to be renewed in the case of machinery, and first of all in the form of a reserve fund. It is, moreover, in no way essential for each individual sale to contribute its share to this reserve fund, so long as the total annual sales contribute their annual share. This shows again how a rise in the price of raw material can curtail or arrest the entire process of reproduction if the price realised by the sale of the commodities should not suffice to replace all the elements of these commodities. Or, it may make it impossible to continue the process on the scale required by its technical basis, so that only a part of the machinery will remain in operation, or all the machinery will work for only a fraction of the usual time.

Finally, the expense incurred through waste varies in direct proportion to the price fluctuations of the raw material, rising when they rise and falling when they fall. But there is a limit here as well. In 1850 it was still maintained:

"One source of considerable loss arising from an advance in the price of the raw material would hardly occur to any one but a practical spinner, viz., that from waste. I am informed that when cotton advances, the cost to the spinner, of the lower qualities especially, is increased in a ratio beyond the advance actually paid, because the waste made in spinning coarse yarns is fully 15 per cent; and this rate, while it causes a loss of $\frac{1}{2}$ d. per lb. on cotton at $3\frac{1}{2}$ d. per lb., brings up the loss to ld. per lb. when cotton advances to 7d" (Reports of Insp. of Fact., April 1850, p. 17).

But when, as a result of the American Civil War, the price of cotton rose to a level unequalled in almost 100 years, the report read differently:

"The price now given for waste, and its re-introduction in the factory in the share of cotton waste, go some way to compensate for the difference in the loss by waste, between Surat cotton and American cotton, about $12\frac{1}{2}$ per cent.

"The waste in working Surat cotton being 25 per cent, the cost of the cotton to the spinner is enhanced one-fourth before he has manufactured it. The loss by waste used not to be of much moment when American cotton was 5d. or 6d. per lb., for it did not exceed $\frac{3}{4}$ d. per lb., but it is now of great importance when upon every lb. of cotton which costs 2s. there is a loss by waste equal to 6d." [14] (Reports of Insp. of Fact., Oct. 1863, p. 106).

[14] The report errs in the final sentence. Instead of 6d. it should be 3d. for loss through waste. This loss amounts to 25% in the case of Surat, and only $12\frac{1}{2}$ to 15% in the case of American cotton, and this latter is meant, the same percentage having been correctly calculated for the price of 5 to 6d. It is true, however, that also in the case of American cotton brought to Europe during the latter years of the Civil War the proportion of waste often rose considerably higher than before.— *F. E.*

II. APPRECIATION, DEPRECIATION, RELEASE
AND TIE-UP OF CAPITAL

The phenomena analysed in this chapter require for their full development the credit system and competition on the world market, the latter being the basis and the vital element of capitalist production. These more definite forms of capitalist production can only be comprehensively presented, however, after the general nature of capital is understood. Furthermore, they do not come within the scope of this work and belong to its eventual continuation.[1] Nevertheless the phenomena listed in the above title may be discussed in a general way at this stage. They are interrelated, first with one another and, secondly, also with the rate and amount of profit. They are to be briefly discussed here if only because they create the impression that not only the rate, but also the amount of profit — which is actually identical with the amount of surplus value — could increase or decrease independently of the movements of the quantity or rate of surplus value.

Are we to consider release and tie-up of capital, on the one hand, and its appreciation and depreciation, on the other, as different phenomena?

The question is what we mean by release and tie-up of capital? Appreciation and depreciation are self-explanatory. All they mean is that a given capital increases or decreases in value as a result of certain general economic conditions, for we are not discussing the particular fate of an individual capital. All they mean, therefore, is that the value of a capital invested in production rises or falls, irrespective of its self-expansion by virtue of the surplus labour employed by it.

By tie-up of capital we mean that certain portions of the total value of the product must be reconverted into elements of constant and variable capital if production is to proceed on the same scale. By release of capital we mean that a portion of the total value of the product which had to be reconverted into constant or variable capital up to a certain time, becomes disposable and superfluous, should production continue on the previous scale. This release or tie-up of capital is different from the release or tie-up of revenue. If the annual surplus value of an individual capital C is, let us say, equal to x, then a reduction in the price of commodities consumed by the capitalists would make x — a sufficient to procure the same enjoyments, etc., as before. A portion of the revenue = a is released, therefore, and may serve either to increase consumption or to be reconverted into capital (for the purpose of accumulation). Conversely, if x + a is needed to continue to live as before, then this standard of living must either be reduced or a portion of the previously accumulated income = a, expended as revenue.

Appreciation and depreciation may affect either constant or variable capital, or both, and in the case of constant capital it may, in turn, affect either the fixed, or the circulating portion, or both.

Under constant capital we must consider the raw and auxiliary materials, including semi-finished products, all of which we here include under the term of raw materials, machinery, and other fixed capital.

In the preceding analysis we referred especially to VARIATIONS in the price, or the value, of raw materials in respect to their influence on the rate of profit, and determined the general law that with other conditions being equal, the rate of profit is inversely proportional to the value of the raw materials. This is absolutely true for capital newly invested in a business enterprise, in which the investment, i. e., the conversion of money into productive capital, is only just taking place.

But aside from this capital, which is being newly invested, a large portion of the already functioning capital is in the sphere of circulation, while another portion is in the sphere of production. One portion is in the market in the shape of commodities waiting to be converted into money; another is on hand as money, in whatever form, waiting to be reconverted into elements of production; finally, a third portion is in the sphere of production, partly in its original form of means of production such as raw and auxiliary materials, semi-finished products purchased in the market, machinery and other fixed capital, and partly in the form of products which are in the process of manufacture. The effect of appreciation or depreciation depends here to a great extent on the relative proportion of these component parts. Let us, for the sake of simplicity, leave aside all fixed capital and consider only that portion of constant capital which consists of raw and auxiliary materials, and semi-finished products, and both finished commodities in the market and commodities still in the process of production.

If the price of raw material, for instance of cotton, rises, then the price of cotton goods — both semi-finished goods like yarn and finished goods like cotton fabrics — manufactured while cotton was cheaper, rises also. So does the value of the unprocessed cotton held in stock and of the cotton in the process of manufacture. The latter because it comes to represent more labour time in retrospect and thus adds more than its original value to the product which it enters, and more than the capitalist paid for it.

Hence, if the price of raw materials rises, and there is a considerable quantity of available finished commodities in the market, no matter what the stage of their manufacture, the value of these commodities rises, thereby enhancing the value of the existing capital. The same is true for the supply of raw materials, etc., in the hands of the producer. This appreciation of value may compensate, or more than compensate, the individual capitalist, or even an entire separate sphere of capitalist production, for the drop in the rate of profit attending a rise in the price of raw materials. Without entering into the detailed effects of competition, we might state for the sake of thoroughness that 1) if available supplies of raw material are considerable, they tend to counteract the price increase which occurred at the place of their origin; 2) if the semi-finished and finished goods press very heavily upon the market, their price is thereby prevented from rising proportionately to the price of their raw materials.

The reverse takes place when the price of raw materials falls. Other circumstances remaining the same, this increases the rate of profit. The commodities in the market, the articles in the process of production, and the available supplies of raw material, depreciate in value and thereby counteract the attendant rise in the rate of profit.

The effect of price variations for raw materials is the more pronounced, the smaller the supplies available in the sphere of production and in the market at, say, the close of a business year, i. e., after the harvest in agriculture, when great quantities of raw materials are delivered anew.

We proceed in this entire analysis from the assumption that the rise or fall in prices expresses actual fluctuations in value. But since we are here concerned with the effects such price variations have on the rate of profit, it matters little what is at the bottom of them. The present statements apply equally if prices rise or fall under the influence of the credit system, competition, etc., and not on account of fluctuations in value.

Since the rate of profit equals the ratio of the excess over the value of the product to the value of the total capital advanced, a rise caused in the rate of profit by a depreciation of the advanced capital would be associated with a loss in the value of capital. Similarly, a drop caused in the rate of profit by an appreciation of the advanced capital might possibly be associated with a gain.

As for the other portion of constant capital, such as machinery and fixed capital in general, the appreciation of value taking place in it with respect mainly to buildings, real estate, etc., cannot be discussed without the theory of ground rent, and does not therefore belong in this chapter. But of a general importance to the question of depreciation are:

The continual improvements which lower the use value, and therefore the value, of existing machinery, factory equipment, etc. This process has a particularly dire effect during the first period of newly introduced machinery, before it attains a certain stage of maturity, when it continually becomes antiquated before it has time to reproduce its own value. This is one of the reasons for the flagrant prolongation of the working time usual in such periods, for alternating day and night shifts, so that the value of the machinery may be reproduced in a shorter time without having to place the figures for wear and tear too high. If, on the other hand, the short period in which the machinery is effective (its short life vis-à-vis the anticipated improvements) is not compensated in this manner, it gives up so much of its value to the product through moral depreciation that it cannot compete even with hand labour. [15]

After machinery, equipment of buildings, and fixed capital in general, attain a certain maturity, so that they remain unaltered for some length of time at least in their basic construction, there arises a similar depreciation due to improvements in the methods of reproducing this fixed capital. The value of the machinery, etc., falls in this case not so much because the machinery is rapidly crowded out or depreciated to a certain degree by new and more productive machinery, etc., but because it can be reproduced more cheaply. This is one of the reasons why large enterprises frequently do not flourish until they pass into other hands, i. e., after their first proprietors have been bankrupted, and their successors, who buy them cheaply, therefore begin from the outset with a smaller outlay of capital.

It leaps to the eye, particularly in the case of agriculture, that the

---

[15] For examples see Babbage,[24] among others. The usual expedient — a reduction of wages — is also employed in this instance, so that this continual depreciation acts quite contrary to the dreams of Mr. Carey's "harmonious brain".[25]

causes which raise or lower the price of a product, also raise or lower the value of capital, since the latter consists to a large degree of this product, whether as grain, cattle, etc. (Ricardo[a]).

There is still variable capital to be considered.

Inasmuch as the value of labour power rises because there is a rise in the value of the means of subsistence required for its reproduction, or falls because there is a reduction in their value — and the appreciation and depreciation of variable capital are really nothing more than expressions of these two cases — a drop in surplus value corresponds to such appreciation and an increase in surplus value to such depreciation, provided the length of the working day remains the same. But other circumstances — the release and tie-up of capital — may also be associated with such cases, and since we have not analysed them so far, we shall briefly mention them now.

If wages fall in consequence of a depreciation in the value of labour power (which may even be attended by a rise in the real price of labour), a portion of the capital hitherto invested in wages is released. Variable capital is set free. In the case of new investments of capital, this has simply the effect of its operating with a higher rate of surplus value. It takes less money than before to set in motion the same amount of labour, and in this way the unpaid portion of labour increases at the expense of the paid portion. But in the case of already invested capital, not only does the rate of surplus value rise but a portion of the capital previously invested in wages is also released. Until this time it was tied up and formed a regular portion which had to be deducted from the proceeds for the product and advanced for wages, acting as variable capital if the business were to continue on its former scale. Now this portion becomes disposable and may be used as a new investment, be it to extend the same business or to operate in some other sphere of production.

Let us assume, for instance, that £500 per week were required at first to employ 500 labourers, and that now only £400 are needed for the same purpose. If the quantity of value produced in either case = £1,000, the amount of weekly surplus value in the first case = £500 and the rate of surplus value $\frac{500}{500}$ = 100%. But after the

---

[a] D. Ricardo, *On the Principles of Political Economy, and Taxation*, Third edition, London, 1821, pp. 123-24. Cf. present edition, Vol. 32, pp. 172-73.

wage reduction the quantity of surplus value $£1,000 - £400 = £600$, and its rate $\frac{600}{400} = 150\%$. And this increase in the rate of surplus value is the only effect for one who starts a new enterprise in this sphere of production with a variable capital of $£400$ and a corresponding constant capital. But when this takes place in a business already in operation, the depreciation of the variable capital does not only increase the quantity of surplus value from $£500$ to $£600$, and the rate of surplus value from 100 to 150%, but releases $£100$ of the variable capital for the further exploitation of labour. Hence, the same amount of labour is exploited to greater advantage, and, what is more, the release of $£100$ makes it possible to exploit more labourers than before at the higher rate with the same variable capital of $£500$.

Now the reverse situation. Suppose, with 500 employed labourers, the original proportion in which the product is divided $= 400_v + 600_s = 1,000$, making the rate of surplus value $= 150\%$. In that case, the labourer receives $£^4/_5$, or 16 shillings per week. Should 500 labourers cost $£500$ per week, due to an appreciation of variable capital, each one of them will receive a weekly wage $= £1$, and $£400$ can employ only 400 labourers. If the same number of labourers as before is put to work, therefore, we have $500_v + 500_s = 1,000$. The rate of surplus value would fall from 150 to 100%, which is $\frac{1}{3}$. In the case of new capital the only effect would be this lower rate of surplus value. Other conditions being equal, the rate of profit would also have fallen accordingly, although not in the same proportion. For instance, if $c = 2,000$, we have in the one case $2,000_c + 400_v + 600_s = 3,000$; $s' = 150\%$, $p' = \frac{600}{2,400} = 25\%$. In the second case, $2,000_c + 500_v + 500_s = 3,000$; $s' = 100\%$, $p' = \frac{500}{2,500} = 20\%$. In the case of already engaged capital, however, there would be a dual effect. Only 400 labourers could be employed with a $£400$ variable capital, and that at a rate of surplus value of 100%. They would therefore produce an aggregate surplus value of only $£400$. Furthermore, since a constant capital of $£2,000$ requires 500 labourers for its operation, 400 labourers can put into motion only a constant capital of $£1,600$. For production to continue on the same scale, so that $\frac{1}{5}$ of the machinery does not stand idle, $£100$ must be added to the variable capital in order to employ 500 labourers as before. And this can be accomplished only by tying up hitherto disposable capital, so that part of the accumulation intended to extend production serves merely to stop a gap, or a portion reserved for revenue is added to the old capital. Then a variable capital increased by £100 produces £100 less surplus value. More capital is required to employ the same number of labourers, and at the same time the surplus value produced by each labourer is reduced.

The advantages resulting from a release and the disadvantages resulting from a tie-up of variable capital both exist only for capital already engaged and reproducing itself under certain given conditions. For newly invested capital the advantages on the one hand, and the disadvantages on the other, are confined to an increase or drop in the rate of surplus value, and to a corresponding, if in no way proportionate, change in the rate of profit.

————

The release and tie-up of variable capital, just analysed, is the result of a depreciation or appreciation of the elements of variable capital, that is, of the cost of reproducing labour power. But variable capital could also be released if, with the wage rate unchanged, fewer labourers were required due to the development of the productive power of labour to set in motion the same amount of constant capital. In like manner, there may reversely be a tie-up of additional variable capital if more labourers are required for the same quantity of constant capital due to a drop in productivity. If, on the other hand, a portion of capital formerly employed as variable capital is employed in the form of constant capital, so that merely a different distribution exists between the components of the same capital, this has an influence on both the rate of surplus value and the rate of profit, but does not belong under the heading of tie-up and release of capital, which is here being discussed.

We have already seen that constant capital may also be tied up or released by the appreciation or depreciation of its component elements. Aside from this, it can be tied up only if the productive power of labour increases (provided a portion of the variable is not converted into constant capital), so that the same amount of labour creates a greater product and therefore sets in motion a larger constant capital. The same may occur under certain circumstances if productive power decreases, for instance in agriculture, so that the same quantity of labour requires more means of production, such as seeds or manure, drainage, etc., in order to produce the same output. Constant capital may be released without depreciation if improvements, utilisation of the forces of Nature, etc., enable a constant capital of smaller value to technically perform the same services as were formerly performed by a constant capital of greater value.

We have seen in Book II[a] that once commodities have been converted into money, or sold, a certain portion of this money must be reconverted into the material elements of constant capital, and in the proportions required by the technical nature of the particular sphere of production. In this respect, the most important element in all branches — aside from wages, i. e., variable capital — is raw material, including auxiliary material, which is particularly important in such lines of production as do not involve raw materials in the strict sense of the term, for instance in mining and the extractive industries in general. That portion of the price which is to make good the wear and tear of machinery enters the accounts chiefly nominally so long as the machinery is at all in an operating condition. It does not greatly matter whether it is paid for and replaced by money one day or the next, or at any other stage of the period of turnover of the capital. It is quite different in the case of the raw material. If the price of raw material rises, it may be impossible to make it good fully out of the price of the commodities after wages are deducted. Violent price fluctuations therefore cause interruptions, great collisions, even catastrophes, in the process of reproduction. It is especially agricultural produce proper, i. e., raw materials taken from organic nature, which — leaving aside the credit system for the present [1] — is subject to such fluctuations of value in consequence of changing yields, etc. Due to uncontrollable natural conditions, favourable or unfavourable seasons, etc., the same quantity of labour may be represented in very different quantities of use values, and a definite quantity of these use values may therefore have very different prices. If the value x is represented by 100 lbs of the commodity a, then the price of one lb. of $a = \frac{x}{100}$; if it is represented by 1,000 lbs of a, the price of one lb. of $a = \frac{x}{1,000}$, etc. This is therefore one of the elements of these fluctuations in the price of raw materials. A second element, mentioned at this point only for the sake of completeness — since competition and the credit system are still outside the scope of our analysis — is this: It is the nature of things that vegetable and

---

animal substances whose growth and production are subject to certain organic laws and bound up with definite natural time periods, cannot be suddenly augmented in the same degree as, for instance, machines and other fixed capital, or coal, ore, etc., whose augmentation can, provided the natural conditions do not change, be rapidly accomplished in an industrially developed country. It is therefore quite possible, and under a developed system of capitalist production even inevitable, that the production and increase of the portion of constant capital consisting of fixed capital, machinery, etc., should considerably outstrip the portion consisting of organic raw materials, so that demand for the latter grows more rapidly than their supply, causing their price to rise. Rising prices actually cause 1) these raw materials to be shipped from greater distances, since the mounting prices suffice to cover greater freight rates; 2) an increase in their production, which circumstance, however, will probably not, for natural reasons, multiply the quantity of products until the following year; 3) the use of various previously unused substitutes and greater utilisation of waste. When this rise of prices begins to exert a marked influence on production and supply it indicates in most cases that the turning-point has been reached at which demand drops on account of the protracted rise in the price of the raw material and of all commodities of which it is an element, causing a reaction in the price of raw material. Aside from the convulsions which this causes in various forms through depreciation of capital, there are also other circumstances, which we shall mention shortly.

But so much is already evident from the foregoing: The greater the development of capitalist production, and, consequently, the greater the means of suddenly and permanently increasing that portion of constant capital consisting of machinery, etc., and the more rapid the accumulation (particularly in times of prosperity), so much greater the relative overproduction of machinery and other fixed capital, so much more frequent the relative underproduction of vegetable and animal raw materials, and so much more pronounced the previously described rise of their prices and the attendant reaction. And so much more frequent are the convulsions caused as they are by the violent price fluctuations of one of the main elements in the process of reproduction.

If, however, a collapse of these high prices occurs because their rise caused a drop in demand on the one hand, and, on the other, an expansion of production in one place and in another importation from remote and previously less resorted to, or entirely ignored, production areas, and, in both cases, a supply of raw materials exceeding the demand — particularly at the old high prices — then the result may be considered from different points of view. The sudden collapse of the price of raw materials checks their reproduction, and the monopoly of the original producing countries, which enjoy the most favourable conditions of production, is thereby restored — possibly with certain limitations, but restored nevertheless. True, due to the impetus it has had, reproduction of raw material proceeds on an extended scale, especially in those countries which more or less possess a monopoly of this production. But the basis on which production carries on after the extension of machinery, etc., and which, after some fluctuations, is to serve as the new normal basis, the new point of departure, is very much extended by the developments in the preceding cycle of turnover. In the meantime, the barely increased reproduction again experiences considerable impediments in some of the secondary sources of supply. For instance, it is easily demonstrated on the basis of the export tables that in the last 30 years (up to 1865) the production of cotton in India increases whenever there has been a drop in American production, and subsequently it drops again more or less permanently. During the period in which raw materials become dear, industrial capitalists join hands and form associations to regulate production. They did so after the rise of cotton prices in 1848 in Manchester, for example, and similarly in the case of flax production in Ireland. But as soon as the immediate impulse is over and the general principle of competition to "buy in the cheapest market" (instead of stimulating production in the countries of origin, as the associations attempt to do, without regard to the immediate price at which these may happen at that time to be able to supply their product) — as soon as the principle of competition again reigns supreme, the regulation of the supply is left once again to "prices". All thought of a common, all-embracing and far-sighted control of the production of raw materials gives way once more to the faith that demand and supply will mutually regulate one another. And it must be admitted that such control is on the whole irreconcilable with the laws of capitalist production, and remains for ever a pious wish, or is limited to exceptional co-operation in times of great stress and confusion.[16] The superstition of the capitalists in this

[16] Since the above was written (1865), competition on the world market has been considerably intensified by the rapid development of industry in all civilised countries,

respect is so deep that in their reports even factory inspectors again and again throw up their hands in astonishment. The alternation of good and bad years naturally also provides for cheaper raw materials. Aside from the direct effect this has on raising the demand, there is also the added stimulus of the previously mentioned influence on the rate of profit. The aforesaid process of production of raw materials being gradually overtaken by the production of machinery, etc., is then repeated on a larger scale. An actual improvement of raw materials satisfying not only the desired quantity, but also the quality desired, such as cotton from India of American quality, would require a prolonged, regularly growing and steady European demand (regardless of the economic conditions under which the Indian producer labours in his country). As it is, however, the sphere of production of raw materials is, by fits, first suddenly enlarged, and then again violently curtailed. All this, and the spirit of capitalist production in general, may be very well studied in the cotton shortage of 1861-65, [26] further characterised as it was by the fact that a raw material, one of the principal elements of reproduction, was for a time entirely unavailable. To be sure, the price may also rise in the event of an abundant supply, provided the conditions for this abundance are more knotty. Or, there may be an actual shortage of raw material. It was this last situation which originally prevailed in the cotton crisis.

The closer we approach our own time in the history of production, the more regularly do we find, especially in the essential lines of industry, the ever-recurring alternation between relative appreciation and the subsequent resulting depreciation of raw materials obtained from organic nature. What we have just

especially in America and Germany. The fact that the rapidly and enormously expanding productive forces today outgrow the control of the laws of the capitalist mode of commodity exchange, within which they are supposed to operate, impresses itself more and more even on the minds of the capitalists. This is disclosed especially by two symptoms. First, by the new and general mania for a protective tariff, which differs from the old protectionism in that now articles fit for export are those best protected. And secondly, by the trusts of manufacturers of whole spheres of production which regulate production, and thus prices and profits. It goes without saying that these experiments are practicable only so long as the economic climate is relatively favourable. The first storm must upset them and prove that, although production assuredly needs regulation, it is certainly not the capitalist class which is fitted for that task. Meanwhile, the trusts have no other mission but to see to it that the little fish are swallowed by the big fish still more rapidly than before.—*F. E.*

analysed will be illustrated by the following examples taken from reports of factory inspectors.

The moral of history, also to be deduced from other observations concerning agriculture, is that the capitalist system works against a rational agriculture, or that a rational agriculture is incompatible with the capitalist system (although the latter promotes technical improvements in agriculture), and needs either the hand of the small farmer living by his own labour or the control of associated producers.

———

Herewith follow the illustrations referred to above, taken from the English Factory Reports.

"The state of trade is better; but the cycle of good and bad times diminishes as machinery increases, and the changes from the one to the other happen oftener, as the demand for raw materials increases with it.... At present, confidence is not only restored after the panic of 1857, but the panic itself seems to be almost forgotten. Whether this improvement will continue or not depends greatly upon the price of raw materials. There appear to me evidences already, that in some instances the maximum has been reached, beyond which their manufacture becomes gradually less and less profitable, till it ceases to be so altogether. If we take, for instance, the lucrative years in the WORSTED trade of 1849 and 1850, we see that the price of Englsh combing wool stood at 1s.1d., and of Australian at between 1s. 2d. and 1s. 5d. per lb., and that on the average of the ten years from 1841 to 1850, both inclusive, the average price of English wool never exceeded 1s. 2d. and of Australian wool 1s. 5d. per lb. But that in the commencement of the disastrous year of 1857, the price of Australian wool began with 1s. 11d., falling to 1s. 6d. in December, when the panic was at its height, but has gradually risen again to 1s. 9d. through 1858, at which it now stands; whilst that of English wool, commencing with 1s. 8d., and rising in April and September 1857 to 1s. 9d., falling in January 1858 to 1s. 2d., has since risen to 1s. 5d., which is 3d. per lb. higher than the average of the ten years to which I have referred.... This shows, I think, ... either that the bankruptcies which similar prices occasioned in 1857 are forgotten; or that there is barely the wool grown which the existing spindles are capable of consuming; or else, that the prices of manufactured articles are about to be permanently higher.... And as in past experience I have seen spindles and looms multiply both in numbers and speed in an incredibly short space of time, and our exports of wool to France increase in an almost equal ratio, and as both at home and abroad the average age of sheep seems to be getting less and less, owing to rapidly increasing populations and to what the agriculturalists call 'a quick return in stock', so I have often felt anxious for persons whom, without this knowledge, I have seen embarking skill and capital in undertakings, wholly reliant for their success on a product which can only be increased according to organic laws. ... The ... state of supply and demand of all raw materials ... seems to account for many of the fluctuations in the cotton trade ..., as well as for the condition of the English wool market in the autumn of 1857, and the subsequent commercial crisis[a][17) (R. Baker in Reports of Insp. of Fact., Oct. 1858, pp. 56-61).

The halcyon days of the West-Riding WORSTED industry, of Yorkshire, were 1849-50. This industry employed 29,246 persons in 1838; 37,000 persons in 1843; 48,097 in 1845; and 74,891 in 1850. The same district had 2,768 mechanical looms in 1838[b]; 11,458 in 1841; 16,870 in 1843; 19,121 in 1845 and 29,539 in 1850 (Reports of Insp. of Fact., 1850, p. 60). This prosperity of the carded wool industry excited certain forebodings as early as October 1850. In his report of April 1851, Sub-Inspector Baker said in regard to Leeds and Bradford:

"The state of trade is, and has been for some time, very unsatisfactory. The worsted spinners are fast losing the profits of 1850, and, in the majority of cases, the manufacturers are not doing much good. I believe, at this moment, there is more woollen machinery standing than I have almost ever known at one time, and the flax spinners are also turning off hands and stopping frames. The cycles of trade, in fact, in the textile fabrics, are now extremely uncertain, and I think we shall shortly find to be true ... that there is no comparison made between the producing power of the spindles, the quantity of raw material, and the growth of the population" (p. 52).

The same is true of the cotton industry. In the cited report for October 1858, we read:

"Since the hours of labour in factories have been fixed, the amounts of consumption, produce, and wages in all textile fabrics have been reduced to a rule of three. ... I quote from a recent lecture delivered by ... the present Mayor of Blackburn, Mr. Baynes, on the cotton trade, who by such means has reduced the cotton statistics of his own neighbourhood to the closest approximation[c]:—

"'Each real and mechanical horse-power will drive 450 self-acting mule spindles with preparation, or 200 THROSTLE spindles, or 15 looms for 40 inches cloth, with winding, warping, and sizing. Each horse-power in spinning will give employment to $2^1/_2$ operatives, but in weaving to 10 persons, at wages averaging full 10s. 6d. a week to each person. ... The average counts of yarn spun and woven are from 30s. to 32s. twist, and 34s. to 36s. weft yarns; and taking the spinning production at 13 ounces per spindle per week, will give 824,700 lbs yarn spun per week, requiring 970,000 lbs or 2,300 bales of cotton, at a cost of £28,300. ... The total cotton consumed in this district (within a five-mile radius round Blackburn) per week is 1,530,000 lbs, or 3,650 bales, at a cost of £44,625.... This is one-eighteenth of the whole cotton spinning of the United Kingdom, and one-sixth of the whole power-loom weaving.'

[17) It goes without saying that we do not, like Mr. Baker, *explain* the wool crisis of 1857 on the basis of the disproportion between the prices of raw material and finished product. This disproportion was itself but a symptom, and the crisis was a general one.— *F. E.*

---

[a] The Report has: "with its overwhelming consequences". - [b] The Report has: "1836". - [c] [J.] Baynes, *The Cotton Trade...*, Blackburn, London, 1857, pp. 48-49.

"Thus we see that, according to Mr. Baynes's calculations, the total number of cotton spindles in the United Kingdom is 28,800,000, and supposing these to be always working full time, that the annual consumption of cotton ought to be 1,432,080,000 lbs. But as the import of cotton, less the export in 1856 and 1857, was only 1,022,576,832 lbs, there must necessarily be a deficiency of supply equal to 409,503,168 lbs. Mr. Baynes, however, who has been good enough to communicate with me on this subject, thinks that an annual consumption of cotton based upon the quantity used in the Blackburn district would be liable to be overcharged, owing to the difference, not only in the counts spun, but in the excellence of the machinery. He estimates the total annual consumption of cotton in the United Kingdom at 1,000,000,000 lbs. But if he is right, and there really is an excess of supply equal to 22,576,832 lbs, supply and demand seem to be nearly balanced already, without taking into consideration those additional spindles and looms which Mr. Baynes speaks of as getting ready for work in his own district, and, by parity of reasoning, probably in other districts also" (pp. 59, 60, 61).

III. GENERAL ILLUSTRATION. THE COTTON CRISIS OF 1861-65

Preliminary History. 1845-60

1845. The golden age of cotton industry. Price of cotton very low. L. Horner says on this point:

"For the last eight years I have not known so active a state of trade as has prevailed during the last summer and autumn, particularly in cotton spinning. Throughout the half-year I have been receiving notices every week of new investments of capital in factories, either in the form of new mills being built, of the few that were untenanted finding occupiers, of enlargements of existing mills, of new engines of increased power, and of manufacturing machinery" (Reports of Insp. of Fact., Oct. 1845, p. 13).

1846. The complaints begin:

"For a considerable time past I have heard from the occupiers of cotton mills very general complaints of the depressed state of their trade ... for within the last six weeks several mills have begun to work short time, usually eight hours a day instead of twelve; this appears to be on the increase.... There has been a great advance in the price of the raw material,... there has been not only no advance in the manufactured articles, but ... prices are lower than they were before the rise in cotton began. From the great increase in the number of cotton mills within the last four years, there must have been, on the one hand, a greatly increased demand for the raw material, and, on the other, a greatly increased supply in the market of the manufactured articles; causes that must concurrently have operated against profits, supposing the supply of the raw material and the consumption of the manufactured article to have remained unaltered; but, of course, in the greater ratio by the late short supply of cotton, and the falling off in the demand for the manufactured articles in several markets, both home and foreign" (Reports of Insp. of Fact., Oct. 1846, p. 10).

The rising demand for raw materials naturally went hand in hand with a market flooded with manufactures.— By the way, the expansion of industry at that time and the subsequent stagnation were not confined to the cotton districts. The carded wool district of Bradford had only 318 factories in 1836 and 490 in 1846. These figures do not by any means express the actual growth of production, since the existing factories were also considerably enlarged. This was particularly true of the flax spinning-mills.

"All have contributed more or less, during the last ten years, to the over-stocking of the market, to which a great part of the present stagnation of trade must be attributed.... The depression ... naturally results from such rapid increase of mills and machinery" (Reports of Insp. of Fact., Oct. 1846, p. 30).

1847. In October, a money panic. Discount 8%. This was preceded by the debacle of the railway swindle and the East Indian speculation in accommodation bills. But:

"Mr. Baker enters into very interesting details respecting the increased demand, in the last few years, for cotton, wool, and flax, owing to the great extension of these trades. He considers the increased demand for these raw materials, occurring, as it has, at a period when the produce has fallen much below an average supply, as almost sufficient, even without reference to the monetary derangement, to account for the present state of these branches. This opinion is fully confirmed, by my own observations, and conversation with persons well acquainted with trade. Those several branches were all in a very depressed state, while discounts were readily obtained at and under 5 per cent. The supply of raw silk has, on the contrary, been abundant, the prices moderate, and the trade, consequently, very active, till ... the last two or three weeks, when there is no doubt the monetary derangement has affected not only the persons actually engaged in the manufacture, but more extensively still, the manufacturers of fancy goods, who were great customers to the throwster. A reference to published returns shows that the cotton trade had increased nearly 27 per cent in the last three years. Cotton has consequently increased, in round numbers, from 4d. to 6d. per lb., while twist, in consequence of the increased supply, is yet only a fraction above its former price. The woollen trade began its increase in 1836, since which Yorkshire has increased its manufacture of this article 40 per cent, but Scotland exhibits a yet greater increase. The increase of the worsted trade [18] is still larger. Calculations give a result of upwards of 74 per cent increase within the same period. The consumption of raw wool has therefore been immense. Flax has increased since 1839 about 25 per cent in England, 22 per cent in Scotland, and nearly 90 per cent in Ireland [19]; the consequence of this,

[18] A sharp distinction is made in England between woollen manufacture, which spins carded yarn from short wool and weaves it (main centre Leeds), and worsted manufacture, which makes worsted yarn from long wool and weaves it (main seat Bradford, in Yorkshire).— *F. E.*

[19] This rapid expansion of output of machine-made linen yarn in Ireland dealt a death-blow to exports of linen made of hand-made yarn in Germany (Silesia, Lusatia, and Westphalia).— *F. E.*

in connexion with bad crops, has been that the raw material has gone up £10 per ton, while the price of yarn has fallen 6d. a bundle" (Reports of Insp. of Fact., Oct. 1847, pp. 30-31).

1849. Since late in 1848 business revived.

"The price of flax which has been so low as to almost guarantee a reasonable profit under any future circumstances, has induced the manufacturers to carry on their work very steadily.... The woollen manufacturers were exceedingly busy for a while in the early part of the year.... I fear that consignments of woollen goods often take the place of real demand, and that periods of apparent prosperity, i. e., of full work, are not always periods of legitimate demand. In some months the WORSTED has been exceedingly good, in fact flourishing.... At the commencement of the period referred to, wool was exceedingly low; what was bought by the spinners was well bought, and no doubt in considerable quantities. When the price of wool rose with the spring wool sales, the spinner had the advantage, and the demand for manufactured goods becoming considerable and imperative, they kept it" (Reports of Insp. of Fact., [April] 1849, p. 42).

"If we look at the variations in the state of trade, which have occurred in the manufacturing districts ... for a period now of between three and four years, I think we must admit the existence of a great disturbing cause somewhere ... but may not the immensely productive power of increased machinery have added another element to the same cause?" (Reports of Insp. of Fact., April 1849, pp. 42, 43).

In November 1848, and in May and summer of 1849, right up to October, business flourished.

"The worsted stuff trade, of which Bradford and Halifax are the great hives of industry, has been the one most active; this trade has never before reached anything like the extent, to which it has now attained.... Speculation, and uncertainty as to the probable supply of cotton wool, have ever had the effect of causing greater excitement, and more frequent alterations in the state of that branch of manufacture, than any other. There is ... at present an accumulation in stock of the coarser kinds of cotton goods, which creates anxiety on the part of the smaller spinners, and is already acting to their detriment, having caused several of them to work their mills short time" (Reports of Insp. of Fact., Oct. 1849, pp. 64-65).

1850. April. Business continued brisk. The exception:

"The great depression in a part of the cotton trade ... attributable to the scarcity in the supply of the raw material more especially adapted to the branch engaged in spinning low numbers of cotton yarns, or manufacturing heavy cotton goods. A fear is entertained that the increased machinery built recently for the WORSTED trade, may be followed with a similar reaction. Mr. Baker computes that in the year 1849 alone the worsted looms have increased their produce 40 per cent, and the spindles 25 or 30 per cent, and they are still increasing at the same rate" (Reports of Insp. of Fact., April 1850, p. 54).

1850. October.

"The high price of raw cotton continues ... to cause a considerable depression in this branch of manufacture, especially in those descriptions of goods in which the raw material constitutes a considerable part of the cost of production.... The great advance in the price of raw silk has likewise caused a depression in many branches of that manufacture" (Reports of Insp. of Fact., Oct. 1850, p. 14).

From the same report we learn that the Committee of the Royal Society for the Promotion and Improvement of the Growth of Flax in Ireland predicted that the high price of flax, together with the low level of prices for other agricultural products, ensured a considerable increase in flax production in the ensuing year (p. 33).

1853. April. Great prosperity. L. Horner says in his report:

"At no period during the last seventeen years that I have been officially acquainted with the manufacturing districts in Lancashire have I known such general prosperity; the activity in every branch is extraordinary" (Reports of Insp. of Fact., April 1853, p. 19).

1853. October. Depression in the cotton industry."Over-production" (Reports of Insp. of Fact., Oct. 1853, p. 15).

1854. April.

"The woollen trade, although not brisk, has given full employment to all the factories engaged upon that fabric, and a similar remark applies to the cotton factories. The WORSTED trade generally has been in an uncertain and unsatisfactory condition during the whole of the last half-year.... The manufacture of flax and hemp are ... seriously impeded, by reason of the diminished supplies of the raw materials from Russia due to the Crimean war" (Reports of Insp. of Fact., [April] 1854, p. 37).

1859.

"The trade in the Scottish flax districts still continues depressed — the raw material being scarce, as well as high in price; and the inferior quality of the last year's crop in the Baltic, from whence come our principal supplies, will have an injurious effect on the trade of the district; jute, however, which is gradually superseding flax in many of the coarser fabrics, is neither unusually high in price, nor scarce in quantity ... about one-half of the machinery in Dundee is now employed in jute spinning" (Reports of Insp. of Fact., April 1859, p. 19).— "Owing to the high price of the raw material, flax spinning is still far from remunerating, and while all the other mills are going full time, there are several instances of the stoppage of flax machinery.... Jute spinning is ... in a rather more satisfactory state, owing to ·the recent decline in the price of material, which has now fallen to a very moderate point" (Reports of Insp. of Fact., Oct. 1859, p. 20).

1861-64. American Civil War. Cotton Famine. The Greatest Example of an Interruption in the Production Process through Scarcity and Dearness of Raw Material

1860. April.

"With respect to the state of trade, I am happy to be able to inform you that, notwithstanding the high price of raw material, all the textile manufactures, with the exception of silk, have been fairly busy during the past half-year.... In some of the cotton districts hands have been advertised for, and have migrated thither from Norfolk and other rural counties.... There appears to be, in every branch of trade, a great scarcity of raw material. It is ... the want of it alone, which keeps us within bounds. In the cotton trade, the erection of new mills, the formation of new systems of extension, and the demand for hands, can scarcely, I think, have been at any time exceeded. Everywhere there are new movements in search of raw material" (Reports of Insp. of Fact., April 1860 [p.57]).

1860. October.

"The state of trade in the cotton, woollen, and flax districts has been good; indeed in Ireland, it is stated to have been 'very good' for now more than a year; and that it would have been still better, but for the high price of raw material. The flax spinners appear to be looking with more anxiety than ever to the opening out of India by railways, and to the development of its agriculture, for a supply of flax which may be commensurate with their wants" (Reports of Insp. of Fact., Oct. 1860, p. 37).

1861. April.

"The state of trade is at present depressed.... A few cotton mills are running short time, and many silk mills are only partially employed. Raw material is high. In almost every branch of textile manufacture it is above the price at which it can be manufactured for the masses of the consumers" (Reports of Insp. of Fact., April 1861, p. 33).

It had become evident that in 1860 the cotton industry had over-produced. The effect of this made itself felt during the next few years.

"It has taken between two and three years to absorb the overproduction of 1860 in the markets of the world" (Reports of Insp. of Fact., December 1863, p. 127). "The depressed state of the markets for cotton manufactures in the East, early in 1860, had a corresponding effect upon the trade of Blackburn, in which 30,000 power-looms are usually employed almost exclusively in the production of cloth to be consumed in the East. There was consequently but a limited demand for labour for many months prior to the effects of the cotton blockade being felt.... Fortunately this preserved many of the spinners and manufacturers from being involved in the common ruin. Stocks increased in value so long as they were held, and there had been consequently nothing like that alarming depreciation in the value of property which might not unreasonably have been looked for in such a crisis" (Reports of Insp. of Fact., Oct. 1862, pp. 28-29, 30).

1861. October.

"Trade has been for some time in a very depressed state.... It is not improbable indeed that during the winter months many establishments will be found to work very short time. This might, however, have been anticipated ... irrespective of the causes which have interrupted our usual supplies of cotton from America and our exports, short time must have been kept during the ensuing winter in consequence of the great increase of production during the last three years, and the unsettled state of the Indian and Chinese markets" (Reports of Insp. of Fact., Oct. 1861, p. 19).

Cotton Waste. East Indian Cotton (SURAT). *Influence on the Wages of Labourers. Improvement of Machinery. Adding Starch Flour and Mineral Substitutes to Cotton. Effect of Starch Flour Sizing on Labourers. Manufacturers of Finer Yarn Grades. Manufacturers' Fraud*

"A manufacturer writes to me thus: 'As to estimates of consumption per spindle, I doubt if you take sufficiently into calculation the fact that when cotton is high in price, every spinner of ordinary yarns (say up to 40s.) (principally 12s. to 32s.) will raise his counts as much as he can, that is, will spin 16s. where he used to spin 12s., or 22s.in the place of 16s., and so on; and the manufacturer using these fine yarns will make his cloth the usual weight by the addition of so much more size. The trade is availing itself of this resource at present to an extent which is even discreditable. I have heard on good authority of ordinary export SHIRTING weighing 8 lbs of which $2\frac{3}{4}$ lbs were size.... In cloths of other descriptions as much as 50 per cent size is sometimes added; so that a manufacturer may and does truly boast that he is getting rich by selling cloth for less money per pound than he paid for the mere yarn of which they are composed' " (Reports of Insp. of Fact., April 1864, p. 27).

"I have also received statements that the weavers attribute increased sickness to the size which is used in dressing the warps of Surat cotton, and which is not made of the same material as formerly, viz., flour. This substitute for flour is said, however, to have the very important advantage of increasing greatly the weight of the cloth manufactured, making 15 lbs of the raw material to weigh 20 lbs, when woven into cloth." (Reports of Insp. of Fact., Oct. 1863, p. 63. This substitute was ground talcum, called CHINA CLAY, or gypsum, called FRENCH CHALK.) — "The earnings of the weavers" (meaning the operatives) "are much reduced from the employment of substitutes for flour as sizing for warps. This sizing, which gives weight to the yarn, renders it hard and brittle. Each thread of the warp in the loom passes through a part of the loom called 'a heald', which consists of strong threads to keep the warp in its proper place, and the hard state of the warp causes the threads of the heald to break frequently; and it is said to take a weaver five minutes to tie up the threads every time they break; and a weaver has to piece these ends at least ten times as often as formerly, thus reducing the productive powers of the loom in the working-hours" (ibid., pp. 42-43).

"In Ashton, Stalybridge, Mossley, Oldham, etc., the reduction of time has been fully one-third, and the hours are lessening every week.... Simultaneously with this diminution of time there is also a reduction of wages in many departments" (Reports of Insp. of Fact., Oct. 1861, pp. 12-13).

Early in 1861 there was a strike among the mechanical weavers
in some parts of Lancashire. Several manufacturers had announced
a wage reduction of 5 to 7.5%. The operatives insisted that the wage
scale remain the same while working hours were reduced. This was
not granted, and a strike was called. A month later, the operatives
had to give in. But then they got both.

"In addition to the reduction of wages to which the operatives at last consented,
many mills are now running short time" (Reports of Insp. of Fact., April 1861, p. 23).

1862. April.

"The sufferings of the operatives since the date of my last report have greatly
increased; but at no period of the history of manufactures, have sufferings so sudden and
so severe been borne with so much silent resignation and so much patient self-respect"
(Reports of Insp. of Fact., April 1862, p. 10). "The proportionate number of operatives
wholly out of employment at this date appears not to be much larger than it was in
1848, when there was an ordinary panic of sufficient consequences to excite alarm
amongst the manufacturers, so much so as to warrant the collection of similar statistics
of the state of the cotton trade as are now issued weekly.... In May 1848, the proportion
of cotton operatives out of work in Manchester out of the whole number usually
employed was 15 per cent, on short time 12 per cent, whilst 70 per cent were in full
work. On the 28th of May of the present year, of the whole number of persons usually
employed 15 per cent were out of work, 35 per cent were on short time, and 49 per cent
were working full time.... In some other places, Stockport for example, the averages of
short time and of non-employment are higher, whilst those of full time are less", because
coarser numbers are spun there than in Manchester (p. 16).

1862. October.

"I find by the last return to Parliament that there were 2,887 cotton factories in
the United Kingdom in 1861, 2,109 of them being in my district" (Lancashire and
Cheshire). "I was aware that a very large proportion of the 2,109 factories in my
district were small establishments, giving employment to few persons, but I have been
surprised to find how large that proportion is. In 392, or 19 per cent, the steam-engine
or water-wheel is under 10 horse-power; in 345, or 16 per cent, the horse-power is
above 10 and under 20; and in 1,372 the power is 20 horses and more.... A very large
proportion of these small manufacturers — being more than a third of the whole number — were operatives themselves at no distant period; they are men without command
of capital.... The brunt of the burden then would have to be borne by the remaining
two-thirds" (Reports of Insp. of Fact., Oct. 1862, pp. 18, 19).

According to the same report, 40,146, or 11.3%, of the cotton
operatives in Lancashire and Cheshire were then working full time;
134,767, or 38%, were working short time; and 179,721, or 50.7%,
were unemployed. After deducting the returns from Manchester
and Bolton, where mainly fine grades were spun, a line relatively little
affected by the cotton famine, the matter looks still more unfavourable;

namely, fully employed 8.5%, partly employed 38%, and unemployed 53.5% (pp. 19 and 20).

"Working up good or bad cotton makes a material difference to the operatives. In the earlier part of the year, when manufacturers were endeavouring to keep their mills at work by using up all the moderately priced cotton they could obtain, much bad cotton was brought into mills in which good cotton was ordinarily used, and the difference to the operatives in wages was so great that many strikes took place on the ground that they could not make a fair day's wages at the old rates.... In some cases, although working full time, the difference in wages from working bad cotton was as much as one-half" (p. 27).

1863. April.

"During the present year there will not be full employment for much more than one-half of the cotton operatives in the country" (Reports of Insp. of Fact., April 1863, p. 14).

"A very serious objection to the use of Surat cotton, as manufacturers are now compelled to use it, is that the speed of the machinery must be greatly reduced in the processes of manufacture. For some years past every effort has been made to increase the speed of machinery, in order to make the same machinery produce more work; and the reduction of the speed becomes therefore a question which affects the operative as well as the manufacturer; for the chief part of the operatives are paid by the work done; for instance, spinners are paid per lb. for the yarn spun, weavers per piece for the number of pieces woven; and even with the other classes of operatives paid by the week there would be a diminution of wages in consideration of the less amount of goods produced. From inquiries I have made, and statements placed in my hands, of the earnings of cotton operatives during the present year, I find there is a diminution averaging 20 per cent upon their former earnings, in some instances the diminution has been as much as 50 per cent, calculated upon the same rate of wages as prevailed in 1861" (p. 13). "...The sum earned depends upon ... the nature of the material operated upon.... The position of the operatives in regard to the amount of their earnings is very much better now" (October 1863) "than it was this time last year. Machinery has improved, the material is better understood, and the operatives are able better to overcome the difficulties they had to contend with at first. I remember being in a sewing school" (a charity institution for unemployed) "at Preston last spring, when two young women, who had been sent to work at a weaving shed the day before, upon the representation of the manufacturer that they could earn 4s. per week, returned to the school to be readmitted, complaining that they could not have earned 1s. per week. I have been informed of 'SELF-ACTING MINDERS', ... men who manage a pair of self-acting mules, earning at the end of a fortnight's full work 8s. 11d., and that from this sum was deducted the rent of the house, the manufacturer, however, returning half the rent as a gift." (How generous!) "The MINDERS took away the sum of 6s. 11d. In many places the SELF-ACTING MINDERS ranged from 5s. to 9s. per week, and the weavers from 2s. to 6s. per week in the last months of 1862.... At the present time a much more healthy state of things exists, although there is still a great decrease in the earnings in most districts.... There are several causes which have tended to the reduction of earnings, besides the shorter staple of the Surat cotton and its dirty condition; for instance, it is now the practice to mix 'waste' largely with Surat, which consequently increases the difficulties of the spinner or minder. The threads, from their shortness of fibre, are more liable to break in the drawing out of the mule and in the twisting of the yarn, and the mule cannot be kept so continuously in motion.... Then, from the great attention required in watching the threads in weaving, many weavers can only mind one loom, and very few can mind more than two looms.... There has been a direct reduction of 5, $7\frac{1}{2}$ and 10 per cent upon the wages of the operatives.... In the majority of cases the operative has to make the best of his material, and to earn the best wages he can at the ordinary rates.... Another difficulty the weavers have sometimes to contend with is, that they are expected to produce well-finished cloth from inferior materials, and are subject to fine for the flaws in their work" (Reports of Insp. of Fact., Oct. 1863, pp. 41-43).

Wages were miserable, even where work was full time. The cotton workers willingly offered themselves for all public works such as drainage, road-building, stone-breaking and street-paving, in which they were employed, to get their keep from the local authorities (although this practically amounted to assistance to the manufacturer. See Book I, S. 598/589[a]). The whole bourgeoisie stood guard over the labourers. Were the worst dog's wages offered, and a labourer refused to accept them, the Relief Committee[27] would strike him from its lists. It was in a way a golden age for the manufacturers, for the labourers had either to starve or work at a price most profitable for the bourgeois. The Relief Committees acted as watchdogs. At the same time, the manufacturers acted in secret agreement with the government to hinder emigration as much as possible, partly to retain in readiness the capital invested in the flesh and blood of the labourers, and partly to safeguard the house rent squeezed out of the labourers.

"The Relief Committees acted with great strictness upon this point. If work was offered, the operatives to whom it was proposed were struck off the lists, and thus compelled to accept the offer. When they objected to accept work... the cause has been that their earnings would have been merely nominal, and the work exceedingly severe" (Reports of Insp. of Fact., Oct. 1863, p. 97).

The operatives were willing to perform any work given to them under the PUBLIC WORKS ACT.

"The principle upon which industrial employments were organised varied considerably in different towns, but in those places even in which the outdoor work was not absolutely a LABOUR TEST[b] the manner in which labour was remunerated by its being paid for either at the exact rate of relief, or closely approximating the rate, it became in fact a labour test" (p. 69). "The PUBLIC WORKS ACT of 1863 was intended to remedy this inconvenience, and to enable the operative to earn his day's wages as an independent labourer. The purpose of this Act was three-fold: firstly, to enable local authorities

---

[a] See present edition, Vol. 35, pp. 574-77. - [b] In the 1894 German edition this English term is given in parentheses after its German equivalent.

to borrow money of the Exchequer Loan Commissioners" (with consent of the President of the Central Relief Committee); "secondly, to facilitate the improvement of the towns of the cotton districts; thirdly, to provide work and REMUNERATIVE WAGES[a] to the unemployed operatives." Loans to the amount of £883,700 had been granted under this Act up to the end of October 1863 (p. 70).

The works undertaken were mainly canalisation, road-building, street-paving, water-works reservoirs, etc.

Mr. Henderson, Chairman of the committee in Blackburn, wrote with reference to this to factory inspector Redgrave:

"Nothing in my experience, during the present period of suffering and distress, has struck me more forcibly or given me more satisfaction, than the cheerful alacrity with which the unemployed operatives of this district have accepted of the work offered to them through the adoption of the Public Works Act, by the Corporation of Blackburn. A greater contrast than that presented between the cotton spinner as a skilled workman in a factory, and as a labourer in a sewer 14 or 18 feet deep, can scarcely be conceived."

(Depending on the size of his family, he earned 4 to 12s. per week, this enormous amount providing sometimes for a family of eight. The townsmen derived a double profit from this. In the first place, they secured money to improve their smoky and neglected cities at exceptionally low interest. In the second place, they paid the labourers far less than the regular wage.)

"Accustomed as he had been to a temperature all but tropical, to work at which agility and delicacy of manipulation availed him infinitely more than muscular strength and to double and sometimes treble the remuneration which it is possible for him now to obtain, his ready acceptance of the proffered employment involved an amount of self-denial and consideration the exercise of which is most creditable. In Blackburn the men have been tested at almost every variety of outdoor work; in excavating a stiff heavy clay soil to a considerable depth, in draining, in stone-breaking, in road-making, and in excavating for street sewers to a depth of 14, 16, and sometimes 20 feet. In many cases while thus employed they are standing in mud and water to the depth of 10 or 12 inches, and in all they are exposed to a climate which, for chilly humidity is not surpassed I suppose, even if it is equalled, by that of any district in England" (pp. 91-92).— "The conduct of the operatives has been almost blameless, and their readiness to accept and make the best of outdoor labour" (p. 69).

1864. April.

"Complaints are occasionally made in different districts of the scarcity of hands, but this deficiency is chiefly felt in particular departments, as, for instance, of weavers.... These complaints have their origin as much from the low rate of wages which

---

[a] In the 1894 German edition this English term is given in parentheses after its German equivalent.

the hands can earn owing to the inferior qualities of yarn used, as from any positive scarcity of workpeople even in that particular department. Numerous differences have taken place during the past month between the masters of particular mills and their operatives in respect of the wages. Strikes, I am sorry to say, are but too frequently resorted to. ... The effect of the PUBLIC WORKS ACT is felt as a competition by the mill-owners. The local committee at Bacup has suspended operations, for although all the mills are not running, yet a scarcity of hands has been experienced" (Reports of Insp. of Fact., April 1864, p. 9).

It was indeed high time for the manufacturers. Due to the PUBLIC WORKS ACT the demand for labour grew so strong that many a factory hand was earning 4 to 5 shillings daily in the quarries of Bacup. And so the public works were gradually suspended — this new edition of the *Ateliers nationaux* of 1848,[28] but this time instituted in the interests of the bourgeoisie.

Experiments in corpore vili[a]

"Although I have given the very reduced wages" (of the fully employed), "the actual earnings of the operatives in several mills, it does not follow that they earn the same amount week by week. The operatives are subject to great fluctuation, from the constant experimentalising of the manufacturers upon different kinds and proportions of cotton and waste in the same mill, the 'mixings' as it is called, being frequently changed; and the earnings of the operatives rise and fall with the quality of the cotton mixings; sometimes they have been within 15 per cent of former earnings, and then in a week or two, they have fallen from 50 to 60 per cent."

Inspector Redgrave, who makes this report, then proceeds to cite wage figures taken from actual practice, of which the following examples may suffice:

A, weaver, family of 6, employed 4 days a week, 6s. 8.5d.; B, TWISTER, employed 4.5 days a week, 6s.; C, weaver, family of 4, employed 5 days a week, 5s. 1d.; D, SLUBBER, family of 6, employed 4 days a week, 7s. 10d.; E, weaver, family of 7, employed 3 days a week, 5s., etc. Redgrave continues:

"The above returns are deserving of consideration, for they show that work would become a misfortune in many a family, as it not merely reduces the income, but brings it so low as to be utterly insufficient to provide more than a small portion of the absolute wants, were it not that supplemental relief is granted to operatives when the wages of the family do not reach the sum that would be given to them as relief, if they were all unemployed" (Reports of Insp. of Fact., Oct.1863, pp. 50, 53).

"In no week since the 5th of June last was there more than two days seven hours and a few minutes employment for all the workers" (ibid., p. 121).

---

[a] on a useless thing

From the beginning of the crisis to March 25, 1863, nearly three million pounds sterling were expended by the guardians, the Central Relief Committee, and the London Mansion House Committee (ibid., p. 13).

"In a district in which the finest yarn is spun ... the spinners suffer an indirect reduction of 15 per cent in consequence of the change from South SEA ISLAND to Egyptian cotton.... In an extensive district, in many parts of which waste is largely used as a mixture with Surat ... the spinners have had a reduction of 5 per cent, and have lost from 20 to 30 per cent in addition, through working SURAT and waste. The weavers are reduced from 4 looms to 2 looms. In 1860, they averaged 5s. 7d. per loom, in 1863, only 3s. 4d. The fines, which formerly varied from 3d. to 6d." (for the weaver) "on American, now run up to from 1s. to 3s. 6d."

In one district, where Egyptian cotton was used with an admixture of East Indian

"the average of the MULE SPINNERS, which was in 1860 18s. to 25s., now averages from 10s. to 18s. per week, caused, in addition to inferior cotton, by the reduction of the speed of the mule to put an extra amount of twist in the yarn, which in ordinary times would be paid for according to list" (pp. 43, 44). "Although the Indian cotton may have been worked to profit by the manufacturer, it will be seen" (see the wage list on pp. 51-52) "that the operatives are sufferers compared with 1861, and if the use of SURAT be confirmed, the operatives will want to earn the wages of 1861, which would seriously affect the profits of the manufacturer, unless he obtain compensation either in the price of the raw cotton or of his products" (p. 105).

House Rent.

"The rent is frequently deducted from the wages of operatives, even when working short time, by the manufacturers whose COTTAGES they may be occupying. Nevertheless the value of this class of property has diminished, and houses may be obtained at a reduction of from 25 to 50 per cent upon the rent of the houses in ordinary times; for instance, a COTTAGE which would have cost 3s. 6d. per week can now be had for 2s. 4d. per week, and sometimes even for less" (p. 57).

Emigration. The manufacturers were naturally opposed to emigration of labourers, because, on the one hand,

"looking forward to the recovery of the cotton trade from its present depression, they keep within their reach the means whereby their mills can be worked in the most advantageous manner". On the other hand, "many manufacturers are owners of the houses in which operatives employed in their mills reside, and some unquestionably expect to obtain a portion of the back rent owing" (p. 96).

Mr. Bernall Osborne said in a speech to his parliamentary constituents on October 22, 1864, that the labourers of Lancashire had behaved like the ancient philosophers (Stoics).[a] Not like sheep?

---

[a] See *The Times*, No. 25011, October 24, 1864, p. 8.

Chapter VII

SUPPLEMENTARY REMARKS

Suppose, as is assumed in this part, the amount of profit in any particular sphere of production equals the sum of the surplus value produced by the total capital invested in that sphere. Even then the bourgeois will not consider his profit as identical with surplus value, i. e., with unpaid surplus labour, and, to be sure, for the following reasons:

1) In the process of circulation he forgets the process of production. He thinks that surplus value is made when he realises the value of commodities, which includes realisation of their surplus value. //A blank space which follows in the manuscript, indicates that Marx intended to dwell in greater detail on this point.— *F. E.*//

2) Assuming a uniform degree of exploitation, we have seen that regardless of all modifications originating in the credit system, regardless of the capitalists' efforts to outwit and cheat one another, and, lastly, regardless of any favourable choice of the market — the rate of profit may differ considerably, depending on the low or high prices of raw materials and the experience of the buyer, on the relative productivity, efficiency and cheapness of the machinery, on the greater or lesser efficiency of the aggregate arrangement in the various stages of the productive process, elimination of waste, the simplicity and efficiency of management and supervision, etc. In short, given the surplus value for a certain variable capital, it still depends very much on the individual business acumen of the capitalist, or of his managers and salesmen, whether this same surplus value is expressed in a greater or smaller rate of profit, and accordingly yields a greater or smaller amount of profit. Let the same surplus value of £1,000, the product of £1,000 in wages, obtain in enterprise A for a constant capital of £9,000, and in enterprise B for £11,000. In case A we have $p' = \frac{1,000}{10,000}$, or 10%. In case B we have $p' = \frac{1,000}{12,000}$, or $8\frac{1}{3}$ %. The total capital produces relatively more profit in enterprise A than in B, because of a higher rate of profit, although the variable capital advanced in both cases = 1,000 and the surplus value produced by each likewise = 1,000, so that in both cases there exists the same degree of exploitation of the same number of labourers. This difference in the presentation of the same mass of surplus value, or the difference in the rates of profit, and therefore in the profit itself, while

the exploitation of labour is the same, may also be due to other causes. Still, it may also be due wholly to a difference in the business acumen with which both establishments are run. And this circumstance misleads the capitalist, convinces him that his profits are not due to exploiting labour, but, at least in part, to other independent circumstances, and particularly his individual activity.

————

The analyses in this first part demonstrate the incorrectness of the view (Rodbertus [a]) according to which (as distinct from ground rent, in which case, for example, the area of real estate remains the same and yet the rent rises) a change in the magnitude of an individual capital is supposed to have no influence on the ratio of profit to capital, and thus on the rate of profit, because if the mass of profit should grow, so does the mass of capital upon which it is calculated, and vice versa.

This is true only in two cases. First, when — assuming that all other circumstances, especially the rate of surplus value, remain unchanged — there is a change in the value of that commodity which is a money commodity. (The same occurs in a merely nominal change of value, the rise or fall of mere tokens of value, other conditions being equal.) Let the total capital = £100, and the profit = £20, the rate of profit being = 20%. Should gold fall by half, or double, the same capital previously worth only £100, will be worth £200 if it falls and the profit will be worth £40, i. e., it will be expressed in so much money instead of the former £20; if it rises, the capital of £100 will be worth only £50, and the profit will be represented by a product, whose value will be £10. But in either case 200:40 = 50:10 = 100:20 = 20%. In all these examples there would, however, have been no actual change in the magnitude of capital value, and only in the money expression of the same value and the same surplus value. For this reason $\frac{s}{C}$, or the rate of profit, could not be affected.

In the second case there is an actual change of magnitude in the value, but unaccompanied by a change in the ratio of v to c; in other words, with a constant rate of surplus value the relation of capital invested in labour power (variable capital considered as an index of

————

[a] [J. K.] Rodbertus, *Sociale Briefe an von Kirchmann*, Dritter Brief, Berlin, 1851, p. 125. Cf. present edition, Vol. 31, p. 320.

the amount of labour power set in motion) to the capital invested in means of production remains the same. Under these circumstances, no matter whether we have C, or nC, or$\frac{C}{n}$, e. g., 1,000, or 2,000, or 500, and the rate of profit being 20%, the profit = 200 in the first case, = 400 in the second, and = 100 in the third. But 200:1,000 = 400:2,000 = 100:500 = 20%. That is to say, the rate of profit is unchanged, because the composition of capital remains the same and is not affected by the change in magnitude. Therefore, an increase or decrease in the amount of profit shows merely an increase or decrease in the magnitude of the applied capital.

In the first case there is, therefore, but the appearance of a change in the magnitude of the employed capital, while in the second case there is an actual change in magnitude, but no change in the organic composition of the capital, i. e., in the relative proportions of its variable and constant portions. But with the exception of these two cases, a change in the magnitude of the employed capital is either the *result* of a preceding change in the value of one of its components, and therefore of a change in the relative magnitude of these components (as long as the surplus value itself does not change with the variable capital); or, this change of magnitude (as in labour processes on a large scale, introduction of new machinery, etc.) is the *cause* of a change in the relative magnitude of its two organic components. In all these cases, other circumstances remaining the same, a change in the magnitude of the employed capital must therefore be accompanied simultaneously by a change in the rate of profit.

A rise in the rate of profit is always due to a relative or absolute increase of the surplus value in relation to its cost of production, i. e., to the advanced total capital, or to a decrease in the difference between the rate of profit and the rate of surplus value.

Fluctuations in the rate of profit may occur irrespective of changes in the organic components of the capital, or of the absolute magnitude of the capital, through a rise or fall in the value of the fixed or circulating advanced capital caused by an increase or a reduction of the working time required for its reproduction, this increase or reduction taking place independently of the already existing capital. The value of every commodity—thus also of the commodities making up the capital—is determined not by the necessary labour time

contained in it, but by the *social* labour time required for its reproduction. This reproduction may take place under unfavourable or
under propitious circumstances, distinct from the conditions of original production. If, under altered conditions, it takes double or, conversely, half the time, to reproduce the same material capital, and if
the value of money remains unchanged, a capital formerly worth
£100 would be worth £200, or £50 respectively. Should this appreciation or depreciation affect all parts of capital uniformly, then the
profit would also be accordingly expressed in double, or half, the
amount of money. But if it involves a change in the organic composition of the capital, if the ratio of the variable to the constant portion
of capital rises or falls, then, other circumstances remaining the same,
the rate of profit will rise with a relatively rising variable capital and
fall with a relatively falling one. If only the money value of the advanced capital rises or falls (in consequence of a change in the value
of money), then the money expression of the surplus value rises, or
falls, in the same proportion. The rate of profit remains unchanged.[a]

---

[a] Cf. present edition, Vol. 33, pp. 105-06.

Part II

CONVERSION OF PROFIT
INTO AVERAGE PROFIT

Chapter VIII

DIFFERENT COMPOSITIONS OF CAPITALS
IN DIFFERENT BRANCHES OF PRODUCTION
AND RESULTING DIFFERENCES IN RATES OF PROFIT

In the preceding part we demonstrated, among other things, that the rate of profit may vary — rise or fall — while the rate of surplus value remains the same. In the present chapter we assume that the intensity of labour exploitation, and therefore the rate of surplus value and the length of the working day, are the same in all the spheres of production into which the social labour of a given country is divided. Adam Smith has already comprehensively shown[a] that the numerous differences in the exploitation of labour in various spheres of production balance one another by means of all kinds of existing compensations, or compensations accepted as such on the basis of current prejudice, so that they are merely evanescent distinctions and are of no moment in a study of the general relations. Other differences, for instance those in the wage scale, rest largely on the difference between simple and complicated labour mentioned in the beginning of Book I (S. 19),[b] and have nothing to do with the intensity of exploitation in the different spheres of production, although they render the lot of the labourer in those spheres very unequal. For instance, if the labour of a goldsmith is better paid than that of a day labourer, the former's surplus labour produces proportionately more surplus value than the latter's. And although the equalising of wages and working days, and thereby of the rates of surplus value, among different spheres of production, and even among different investments of capital in the same

---

[a] A. Smith, *Recherches sur la nature et les causes de la richesse des nations*, Vol. I, Paris, 1802. Cf. present edition, Vol. 31, pp. 451-57. - [b] See present edition, Vol. 35, p. 54.

sphere of production, is checked by all kinds of local obstacles, it is nevertheless taking place more and more with the advance of capitalist production and the subordination of all economic conditions to this mode of production. The study of such frictions, while important to any special work on wages, may be dispensed with as incidental and irrelevant in a general analysis of capitalist production. In a general analysis of this kind it is usually always assumed that the actual conditions correspond to their conception, or, what is the same, that actual conditions are represented only to the extent that they are typical of their own general case.

The difference in the rates of surplus value in different countries, and consequently the national differences in the degree of exploitation of labour, are immaterial for our present analysis. What we want to show in this part is precisely the way in which a general rate of profit takes shape in any given country. It is evident, however, that a comparison of the various national rates of profit requires only a collation of the previously studied with that which is here to be studied. First one should consider the differences in the national rates of surplus value, and then, on the basis of these given rates, a comparison should be made of the differences in the national rates of profit. In so far as those differences are not due to differences in the national rates of surplus value, they must be due to circumstances in which the surplus value is assumed, just as in the analysis of this chapter, to be universally the same, i. e., constant.

We demonstrated in the preceding chapter that, assuming the rate of surplus value to be constant, the rate of profit obtaining for a given capital may rise or fall in consequence of circumstances which raise or lower the value of one or the other portion of constant capital, and so affect the proportion between the constant and variable components of capital in general. We further observed that circumstances which prolong or reduce the time of turnover of an individual capital may similarly influence the rate of profit. Since the mass of the profit is identical with the mass of the surplus value, and with the surplus value itself, it was also seen that the *mass* of the profit — as distinct from the *rate* of profit — is not affected by the aforementioned fluctuations of value. They only modify the rate in which a given surplus value, and therefore a profit of a given magnitude, express themselves; in other words, they modify only the relative magnitude of profit, i. e., its magnitude compared with the magnitude of the advanced capital. Inasmuch as capital was tied up or released by such fluctuations of value, it was not only the rate of profit, but the profit itself, which was likely to be affected in this indirect manner. However, this has then always applied only to such capital as was already used, and not to new investments. Besides, the increase or reduction of profit always depended on the extent to which the same capital could, in consequence of such fluctuation of value, set in motion more or less labour; in other words, it depended on the extent to which the same capital could, with the rate of surplus value remaining the same, obtain a larger or smaller amount of surplus value. Far from contradicting the general rule, or from being an exception to it, this seeming exception was really but a special case in the application of the general rule.

It was seen in the preceding part that, the degree of exploitation remaining constant, changes in the value of the component parts of constant capital and in the time of turnover of capital are attended by changes in the rate of profit. The obvious conclusion is that the rates of profit in different spheres of production existing side by side have to differ when, other circumstances remaining unchanged, the time of turnover of capitals employed in the different spheres differs, or when the value relation of the organic components of these capitals differs in the various branches of production. What we previously regarded as changes occurring successively with one and the same capital is now to be regarded as simultaneous differences among capital investments existing side by side in different spheres of production.

In these circumstances we shall have to analyse: 1) the difference in the *organic composition* of capitals, and 2) the difference in their period of turnover.

The premiss in this entire analysis is naturally that by speaking of the composition or turnover of a capital in a certain line of production we always mean the average normal proportions of capital invested in this sphere, and generally the average in the total capital employed in that particular sphere, and not the accidental differences of the individual capitals in it.

Since it is further assumed that the rate of surplus value and the working day are constant, and since this assumption also implies constant wages, a certain quantity of variable capital represents a definite quantity of labour power set in motion, and therefore a definite quantity of objectified labour. If, therefore, £100 represent the weekly wage of 100 labourers, indicating 100 actual labour powers, then n times £100 indicate the labour powers of n times 100 labourers, and $\frac{£100}{n}$ those of $\frac{100}{n}$ labourers. The variable capital thus serves here (as is always the case when the wage is given) as an index of the amount of labour set in motion by a definite total capital. Differences in the magnitude of the employed variable capitals serve, therefore, as indexes of the difference in the amount of employed labour power. If £100 indicate 100 labourers per week, and represent 6,000 working hours at 60 working hours per week, then £200 represent 12,000, and £50 only 3,000 working hours.

By composition of capital we mean, as stated in Book I, the proportion of its active and passive components, i. e., of variable and constant capital. Two proportions enter into consideration under this heading. They are not equally important, although they may produce similar effects under certain circumstances.

The first proportion rests on a technical basis, and must be regarded as given at a certain stage of development of the productive forces. A definite quantity of labour power represented by a definite number of labourers is required to produce a definite quantity of products in, say, one day, and — what is self-evident — thereby to consume productively, i. e., to set in motion, a definite quantity of means of production, machinery, raw materials, etc. A definite number of labourers corresponds to a difinite quantity of means of production, and hence a definite quantity of living labour to a definite quantity of labour already objectified in means of production. This proportion differs greatly in different spheres of production, and frequently even in different branches of one and the same industry, although it may by coincidence be entirely or approximately the same in entirely separate lines of industry.

This proportion forms the technical composition of capital and is the real basis of its organic composition.

However, it is also possible that this first proportion may be the same in different lines of industry, provided variable capital is merely an index of labour power and constant capital merely an index of the mass of means of production set in motion by this labour power. For instance, certain work in copper and iron may require the same ratio of labour power to mass of means of production. But since copper is more expensive than iron, the value relation between variable and constant capital is different in each case, and hence also the value composition of the two total capitals. The difference between the technical composition and the value composition is manifested in each branch of industry in that the value relation of the two portions of capital may vary while the technical composition is constant, and the value relation may remain the same while the technical composition varies. The latter case will, of course, be possible only if the change in the ratio of the employed masses of means of production and labour power is compensated by a reverse change in their values.

The value composition of capital, inasmuch as it is determined by, and reflects, its technical composition, is called the *organic* composition of capital. [20]

In the case of variable capital, therefore, we assume that it is the index of a definite quantity of labour power, or of a definite number of labourers, or a definite quantity of living labour set in motion. We have seen in the preceding part that a change in the magnitude of the value of variable capital might eventually indicate nothing but a higher or lower price of the same mass of labour. But here, where the rate of surplus value and the working day are taken to be constant, and the wages for a definite working period are given, this is out of the question. On the other hand, a difference in the magnitude of the constant capital may likewise be an index of a change in the mass of means of production set in motion by a definite quantity of labour power. But it may also stem from a difference in value between the means of production set in motion in one sphere and those of another. Both points of view must therefore be examined here.

Finally, we must take note of the following essential facts:

Let £100 be the weekly wage of 100 labourers. Let the weekly working hours = 60. Furthermore, let the rate of surplus value = 100%. In this case, the labourers work 30 of the 60 hours for themselves and 30 hours gratis for the capitalist. In fact, the £100 of wages represent just the 30 working hours of 100 labourers, or altogether 3,000 working hours, while the other 3,000 hours worked by the labourers are incorporated in the £100 of surplus value, or in the profit pocketed by the capitalist. Although the wage of £100 does not, therefore, express the value in which the weekly labour of the 100 labourers is incorporated it indicates nevertheless (since the length of the working day and the rate of surplus value are given) that this capital sets

---

[20] The above has already been briefly developed in the third edition of Book I in the beginning of Kap. XXIII, S. 628. [a] Since the two first editions do not contain that passage, its repetition here is all the more desirable.— *F. E.*

---

[a] English edition: Ch. XXV (see present edition, Vol. 35, p. 607).

in motion 100 labourers for 6,000 working hours. The capital of £100 indicates this, first, because it indicates the number of labourers set in motion, with £1 = 1 labourer per week, hence £100 = 100 labourers; and, secondly, because, since the rate of surplus value is given as 100%, each of these labourers performs twice as much work as is contained in his wages, so that £1, i. e., his wage, which is the expression of half a week of labour, actuates a whole week's labour, just as £100 sets in motion 100 weeks of labour, although it contains only 50. A very essential distinction is thus to be made in regard to variable capital laid out in wages. Its value as the sum of wages, i. e., as a certain amount of objectified labour, is to be distinguished from its value as a mere index of the mass of living labour which it sets in motion. The latter is always greater than the labour which it incorporates, and is, therefore, represented by a greater value than that of the variable capital. This greater value is determined, on the one hand, by the number of labourers set in motion by the variable capital and, on the other, by the quantity of surplus labour performed by them.

It follows from this manner of looking upon variable capital that:

When a capital invested in production sphere A expends only 100 in variable capital for each 700 of total capital, leaving 600 for constant capital, while a capital invested in production sphere B expends 600 for variable and only 100 for constant capital, then capital A of 700 sets in motion only 100 of labour power, or, in the terms of our previous assumption, 100 weeks of labour, or 6,000 hours of living labour, while the same amount of capital B will set in motion 600 weeks of labour, or 36,000 hours of living labour. The capital in A would then appropriate only 50 weeks of labour, or 3,000 hours of surplus labour, while the same amount of capital in B would appropriate 300 weeks of labour, or 18,000 hours. Variable capital is not only the index of the labour embodied in it. When the rate of surplus value is known it is also an index of the amount of labour set in motion over and above that embodied in itself, i. e., of surplus labour. Assuming the same intensity of exploitation, the profit in the first case would be $\frac{100}{700} = \frac{1}{7} = 14\frac{2}{7}\%$, and in the second case, $\frac{600}{700} = 85\frac{5}{7}\%$, or a sixfold rate of profit. In this case, the profit itself would actually be six times as great, 600 in B as against 100 in A, because the same capital set in motion six times as much living labour, which at the same level of exploitation means six times as much surplus value, and thus six times as much profit.

But if the capital invested in A were not 700 but £7,000, while that invested in B were only £700, and the organic composition of both were to remain the same, then the capital in A would employ £1,000 of the £7,000 as variable capital, that is, 1,000 labourers per week = 60,000 hours of living labour, of which 30,000 would be surplus labour. Yet each £700 of the capital in A would continue to set in motion only $\frac{1}{6}$ as much living labour, and hence only $\frac{1}{6}$ as much surplus labour, as the capital in B, and would produce only $\frac{1}{6}$ as much profit. If we consider the rate of profit, then in A $\frac{1,000}{7,000} = \frac{100}{700} = 14\frac{2}{7}\%$, as compared with $\frac{600}{700}$, or $85\frac{5}{7}\%$, in B. Taking equal amounts of capital, the rates of profit differ because, owing to the different masses of living labour set in motion, the masses of surplus value, and thus of profit, differ, although the rates of surplus value are the same.

We get practically the same result if the technical conditions are the same in both spheres of production, but the value of the elements of the employed constant capital is greater or smaller in the one than in the other. Let us assume that both invest £100 as variable capital and therefore employ 100 labourers per week to set in motion the same quantity of machinery and raw materials. But let the latter be more expensive in B than in A. For instance, let the £100 of variable capital set in motion £200 of constant capital in A, and £400 in B. With the same rate of surplus value, of 100%, the surplus value produced is in either case equal to £100. Hence, the profit is also equal to £100 in both. But the rate of profit in A is $\frac{100}{200_c + 100_v} = \frac{1}{3} = 33\frac{1}{3}\%$, while in B it is $\frac{100}{400_c + 100_v} = \frac{1}{5} = 20\%$. In fact, if we select a certain aliquot part of the total capital in either case, we find that in every £100 of B only £20, or $\frac{1}{5}$, constitute variable capital, while in every £100 of A £33$\frac{1}{3}$, or $\frac{1}{3}$, form variable capital. B produces less profit for each £100, because it sets in motion less living labour than A. The difference in the rates of profit thus resolves itself once more, in this case, into a difference of the masses of profit, i.e., in effect, the masses of surplus value, produced by each 100 of invested capital.

The difference between this second example and the first is just this: The equalisation between A and B in the second case would require only a change in the value of the constant capital of either A or B, provided the technical basis remained the same. But in the first case the technical composition itself is different in the two spheres of production and would have to be completely changed to achieve an equalisation.

The different organic composition of various capitals is thus independent of their absolute magnitude. It is always but a question of how much of every 100 is variable and how much constant capital.

Capitals of different magnitude, calculated in percentages, or, what amounts to the same in this case, capitals of the same magnitude operating for the same working time and with the same degree of exploitation may produce very much different amounts of profit, because of surplus value, for the reason that a difference in the organic composition of capital in different spheres of production implies a difference in their variable part, thus a difference in the quantities of living labour set in motion by them, and therefore also a difference in the quantities of surplus labour appropriated by them. And this surplus labour is the substance of surplus value, and thus of profit. In different spheres of production equal portions of the total capital comprise unequal sources of surplus value, and the sole source of surplus value is living labour. Assuming the same degree of labour exploitation, the mass of labour set in motion by a capital of 100, and consequently the mass of surplus labour appropriated by it, depend on the magnitude of its variable component. If a capital, consisting in per cent of $90_c + 10_v$, produced as much surplus value, or profit, at the same degree of exploitation as a capital consisting of $10_c + 90_v$, it would be as plain as day that the surplus value, and thus value in general, must have an entirely different source than labour, and that political economy would then be deprived of every rational basis. If we are to assume all the time that £1 stands for the weekly wage of a labourer working 60 hours, and that the rate of surplus value $= 100\%$, then it is evident that the total value product of one labourer in a week $= £2$. Ten labourers would then produce no more than £20. And since £10 of the £20 replace the wages, the ten labourers cannot produce more surplus value than £10. On the other hand, 90 labourers, whose total product $= £180$, and whose wages $= £90$, would produce a surplus value of £90. The rate of profit in the first case would thus be 10%, and in the other 90%. If this were not so, then value and surplus value would be something else than objectified labour. Since capitals in different spheres of production viewed in percentages—or as capitals of equal magnitude—are divided differently into variable and constant capital, setting in motion unequal quantities of living labour and producing different surplus values, and therefore profits, it follows that the rate of profit, which consists precisely of the ratio of surplus value to total capital in per cent, must also differ.

Now, if capitals in different spheres of production, calculated in per cent, i. e., capitals of equal magnitude, produce unequal profits in consequence of their different organic composition, then it follows that the profits of unequal capitals in different spheres of production cannot be proportional to their respective magnitudes, or that profits in different spheres of production are not proportional to the magnitude of the respective capitals invested in them. For if profits were to grow *pro rata* to the magnitude of invested capital, it would mean that in per cent the profits would be the same, so that in different spheres of production capitals of equal magnitude would have equal rates of profit, in spite of their different organic composition. It is only in the same sphere of production, where we have a given organic composition of capital, or in different spheres with the same organic composition of capital, that the amounts of profits are directly proportional to the amounts of invested capitals. To say that the profits of unequal capitals are proportional to their magnitudes would only mean that capitals of equal magnitude yield equal profits, or that the rate of profit is the same for all capitals, whatever their magnitude and organic composition.

These statements hold good on the assumption that the commodities are sold at their values. The value of a commodity is equal to the value of the constant capital contained in it, plus the value of the variable capital reproduced in it, plus the increment — the surplus value produced — of this variable capital. At the same rate of surplus value, its quantity evidently depends on the quantity of the variable capital. The value of the product of an individual capital of 100 is, in one case, $90_c + 10_v + 10_s = 110$; and in the other, $10_c + 90_v + 90_s = 190$. If the commodities go at their values, the first product is sold at 110, of which 10 represent surplus value, or unpaid labour, and the second at 190, of which 90 represent surplus value, or unpaid labour.

This is particularly important in comparing rates of profit in different countries. Let us assume that the rate of surplus value in one European country = 100%, so that the labourer works half of the working day for himself and the other half for his employer. Let us further assume that the rate of surplus value in an Asian country = 25%, so that the labourer works $\frac{4}{5}$ of the working day for himself, and $\frac{1}{5}$ for his employer. Let $84_c + 16_v$ be the composition of the national capital in the European country, and $16_c + 84_v$ in the Asian country, where little machinery, etc., is used, and where a given quantity of labour power consumes relatively little raw material productively in a given time. Then we have the following calculation:

In the European country the value of the product = $84_c + 16_v +$ $+ 16_s = 116$; rate of profit $= \frac{16}{100} = 16\%$.

In the Asian country the value of the product = $16_c + 84_v +$ $+ 21_s = 121$; rate of profit $= \frac{21}{100} = 21\%$.

The rate of profit in the Asian country is thus more than 25% higher than in the European country although the rate of surplus value in the former is one-fourth that of the latter. Men like Carey, Bastiat, and *tutti quanti*,[a] would arrive at the very opposite conclusion.[b]

By the way, different national rates of profit are mostly based on different national rates of surplus value. But in this chapter we compare unequal rates of profit derived from the same rate of surplus value.

Aside from differences in the organic composition of capitals, and therefore aside from the different masses of labour — and consequently, other circumstances remaining the same, from different masses of surplus labour set in motion by capitals of the same magnitude in different spheres of production, there is yet another source of inequality in rates of profit. This is the different period of turnover of capital in different spheres of production. We have seen in Chapter IV that, other conditions being equal, the rates of profit of capitals of the same organic composition are inversely proportional to their periods of turnover. We have also seen that the same variable capital turned over in different periods of time produces different quantities of annual surplus value. The difference in the periods of turnover is therefore another reason why capitals of equal magnitude in different spheres of production do not produce equal profits in equal periods, and why, consequently, the rates of profit in these different spheres differ.

As far as the ratio of the fixed and circulating capital in the composition of capitals is concerned, however, it does not in itself affect the rate of profit in the least. It can affect the rate of profit only if, in one case, this difference in composition coincides with a different ratio of

---

[a] all the rest - [b] Cf. present edition, Vol. 33, p. 107.

the variable and constant parts, so that the difference in the rate of profit is due to this latter difference, and not to the different ratio of fixed and circulating capital; and, in the other case, if the difference in the ratio of the fixed and circulating parts of capital is responsible for a difference in the period of turnover in which a certain profit is realised. If capitals are divided into fixed and circulating capital in different proportions, this will naturally always influence the period of turnover and cause differences in it. But this does not imply that the period of turnover, in which the same capitals realise certain profits, is different. For instance, A may continually have to convert the greater part of its product into raw materials, etc., while B may use the same machinery, etc., for a longer time, and may need less raw material, but both A and B, being occupied in production, always have a part of their capital engaged, the one in raw materials, i. e., in circulating capital, and the other in machinery, etc., or in fixed capital. A continually converts a portion of its capital from the form of commodities into that of money, and the latter again into the form of raw material, while B employs a portion of its capital for a longer time as an instrument of labour without any such conversions. If both of them employ the same amount of labour, they will indeed sell quantities of products of unequal value in the course of the year, but both quantities of products will contain equal amounts of surplus value, and their rates of profit, calculated on the entire capital advanced, will be the same, although their composition of fixed and circulating capital, and their periods of turnover, are different. Both capitals realise equal profits in equal periods, although their periods of turnover are different.[21] The difference in the period of turnover is in itself of no importance, except so far as it affects the mass of surplus labour appropriated and realised by the same capital in a given time. If, therefore, a different division into fixed and circulating capital does

[21] //It follows from Chapter IV that the above statement correctly applies only when capitals A and B are differently composed in respect to their values, but that the percentages of their variable parts are proportionate to their periods of turnover, i. e., inversely proportionate to their number of turnovers. Let capital A have the following percentages of composition: 20_c fixed $+ 70_c$ circulating, and thus $90_c + 10_v = 100$. At a rate of surplus value of 100% the 10_v produce 10_s in one turnover, yielding a rate of profit for one turnover $= 10\%$. Let capital B $= 60_c$ fixed $+ 20_c$ circulating, and thus $80_c + 20_v = 100$. The 20_v produce 20_s in one turnover at the above rate of surplus value, yielding a rate of profit for one turnover $= 20\%$, which is double that of A. But if A is turned over twice per year, and B only once, then 2×10 also make 20_s per year, and the annual rate of profit is the same for both, namely 20%.— F. E.//

not necessarily imply a different period of turnover, which would in its turn imply a different rate of profit, it is evident that if there is any such difference in the rates of profit, it is not due to a different ratio of fixed to circulating capital as such, but rather to the fact that this different ratio indicates an inequality in the periods of turnover affecting the rate of profit.

It follows, therefore, that the different composition of constant capital in respect to its fixed and circulating portions in various branches of production has in itself no bearing on the rate of profit, since it is the ratio of variable to constant capital which decides this question, while the value of the constant capital, and therefore also its magnitude in relation to the variable is entirely unrelated to the fixed or circulating nature of its components. Yet it may be found — and this often leads to incorrect conclusions — that wherever fixed capital is considerably advanced this but expresses the fact that production is on a large scale, so that constant capital greatly outweighs the variable, or that the living labour power it employs is small compared to the mass of the means of production which it operates.

We have thus demonstrated that different lines of industry have different rates of profit, which correspond to differences in the organic composition of their capitals and, within indicated limits, also to their different periods of turnover; given the same time of turnover, the law (as a general tendency) that profits are related to one another as the magnitudes of the capitals, and that, consequently, capitals of equal magnitude yield equal profits in equal periods, applies only to capitals of the same organic composition, even with the same rate of surplus value. These statements hold good on the assumption which has been the basis of all our analyses so far, namely that the commodities are sold at their values. There is no doubt, on the other hand, that aside from unessential, incidental and mutually compensating distinctions, differences in the average rate of profit in the various branches of industry do not exist in reality, and could not exist without abolishing the entire system of capitalist production. It would seem, therefore, that here the theory of value is incompatible with the actual process, incompatible with the real phenomena of production, and that for this reason any attempt to understand these phenomena should be given up.

It follows from the first part of this volume that the cost prices of products in different spheres of production are equal if equal portions of capital have been advanced for their production, however different the organic composition of such capitals. The distinction between variable and constant capital escapes the capitalist in the cost price. A commodity for whose production he must advance £100 costs him just as much, whether he invests $90_c + 10_v$, or $10_c + 90_v$. It costs him £100 in either case—no more and no less. The cost prices are the same for equal invested capitals in different spheres, no matter how much the produced values and surplus values may differ. The equality of cost prices is the basis for competition among invested capitals whereby an average profit is brought about.

Chapter IX

FORMATION OF A GENERAL RATE OF PROFIT (AVERAGE RATE OF PROFIT) AND TRANSFORMATION OF THE VALUES OF COMMODITIES INTO PRICES OF PRODUCTION

The organic composition of capital depends at any given time on two circumstances: first, on the technical relation of labour power employed to the mass of the means of production employed; secondly, on the price of these means of production. This composition, as we have seen, must be examined on the basis of percentage ratios. We express the organic composition of a certain capital consisting $\frac{4}{5}$ of constant and $\frac{1}{5}$ of variable capital, by the formula $80_c + 20_v$. It is furthermore assumed in this comparison that the rate of surplus value is unchangeable. Let it be any rate picked at random; say, 100%. The capital of $80_c + 20_v$ then produces a surplus value of 20_s, and this yields a rate of profit of 20% on the total capital. The magnitude of the actual value of its product depends on the magnitude of the fixed part of the constant capital, and on the portion which passes from it through wear and tear into the product. But since this circumstance has absolutely no bearing on the rate of profit, and hence, in the present analysis, we shall assume, for the sake of simplicity, that the constant capital is everywhere uniformly and entirely transferred to the annual product of the capitals. It is further assumed that the capitals in the different spheres of production annually realise the same quantities of surplus value proportionate to the magnitude of their variable parts. For the present, therefore, we disregard the difference which may be produced in this respect by variations in the duration of turnovers. This point will be discussed later.

Let us take five different spheres of production, and let the capital in each have a different organic composition as follows:

Capitals	Rate of Surplus Value	Surplus Value	Value of Product	Rate of Profit
I. $80_c + 20_v$	100%	20	120	20%
II. $70_c + 30_v$	100%	30	130	30%
III. $60_c + 40_v$	100%	40	140	40%
IV. $85_c + 15_v$	100%	15	115	15%
V. $95_c + 5_v$	100%	5	105	5%

Here, in different spheres of production with the same degree of exploitation of labour, we find considerably different rates of profit corresponding to the different organic composition of these capitals.

The sum total of the capitals invested in these five spheres of production = 500; the sum total of the surplus value produced by them = 110; the aggregate value of the commodities produced by them = 610. If we consider the 500 as a single capital, and capitals I to V merely as its component parts (as, say, different departments of a cotton mill, which has different ratios of constant to variable capital in its carding, preparatory spinning, spinning, and weaving shops, and in which the average ratio for the factory as a whole has still to be calculated), the mean composition of this capital of 500 would = $390_c + 110_v$, or, in per cent, = $78_c + 22_v$. Should each of the capitals of 100 be regarded as $\frac{1}{5}$ of the total capital, its composition would equal this average of $78_c + 22_v$; for every 100 there would be an average surplus value of 22; thus, the average rate of profit would = 22%, and, finally, the price of every fifth of the total product produced by the 500 would = 122. The product of each fifth of the advanced total capital would then have to be sold at 122.

But to avoid entirely erroneous conclusions it must not be assumed that all cost prices = 100.

With $80_c + 20_v$ and a rate of surplus value = 100%, the total value of commodities produced by capital I = 100 would be $80_c + 20_v + 20_s = 120$, provided the entire constant capital went into the annual product. Now, this may under certain circumstances be the case in some spheres of production. But hardly in cases where the proportion of $c : v = 4 : 1$. We must, therefore, remember in comparing the values produced by each 100 of the different capitals, that they will differ in accordance with the different composition of c as to its fixed and circulating parts, and that, in turn, the fixed portions of each of the different capitals depreciate slowly or rapidly as the case may be, thus transferring unequal quantities of their value to the product in equal periods of time. But this is immaterial to the rate of profit. No matter whether the 80_c give up a value of 80, or 50, or 5, to the annual product, and the annual product consequently $= 80_c + 20_v + 20_s = 120$, or $50_c + 20_v + 20_s = 90$, or $5_c + 20_v + 20_s = 45$; in all these cases the excess of the product's value over its cost price $= 20$, and in calculating the rate of profit these 20 are related to the capital of 100 in all of them. The rate of profit of capital I, therefore, is 20% in every case. To make this still plainer, we let different portions of constant capital go into the value of the product of the same five capitals in the following table:

Capitals	Rate of Surplus Value	Surplus Value	Rate of Profit	Used up c	Value of Com-modities	Cost Price	
I. $80_c + 20_v$	100%	20	20%	50	90	70	
II. $70_c + 30_v$	100%	30	30%	51	111	81	
III. $60_c + 40_v$	100%	40	40%	51	131	91	
IV. $85_c + 15_v$	100%	15	15%	40	70	55	
V. $95_c + 5_v$	100%	5	5%	10	20	15	
$390_c + 110_v$	—	110	—	—	—	—	Total
$78_c + 22_v$	—	22	22%	—	—	—	Average

If we now again consider capitals I to V as a single total capital, we shall see that, in this case as well, the composition of the sums of these five capitals $= 500 = 390_c + 110_v$, so that we get the same average composition $= 78_c + 22_v$, and, similarly, the average surplus value remains 22.[a] If we divide this surplus value uniformly among capitals I to V, we get the following commodity prices:

---

[a] In the 1894 German edition "22%"; corrected after Marx's manuscript.

Capitals	Surplus Value	Value of Commodities	Cost Price of Commodities	Price of Commodities	Rate of Profit	Deviation of Price from Value
I. $80_c + 20_v$	20	90	70	92	22%	+ 2
II. $70_c + 30_v$	30	111	81	103	22%	− 8
III. $60_c + 40_v$	40	131	91	113	22%	− 18
IV. $85_c + 15_v$	15	70[a]	55	77	22%	+ 7
V. $95_c + 5_v$	5	20	15	37	22%	+ 17

Taken together, the commodities are sold at 2 + 7 + 17 = 26 above, and 8 + 18 = 26 below their value, so that the deviations of price from value balance out one another through the uniform distribution of surplus value, or through addition of the average profit of 22 per 100 units of advanced capital to the respective cost prices of the commodities I to V. One portion of the commodities is sold above its value in the same proportion in which the other is sold below it. And it is only the sale of the commodities at such prices that enables the rate of profit for capitals I to V to be uniformly 22%, regardless of their different organic composition. The prices which obtain as the average of the various rates of profit in the different spheres of production added to the cost prices of the different spheres of production, constitute the *prices of production*. They have as their prerequisite the existence of a general rate of profit, and this, again, presupposes that the rates of profit in every individual sphere of production taken by itself have previously been reduced to just as many average rates. These particular rates of profit = $\frac{s}{C}$ in every sphere of production, and must, as occurs in Part I of this book, be deduced out of the values of the commodities. Without such deduction the general rate of profit (and consequently the price of production of commodities) remains a vague and senseless conception. Hence, the price of production of a commodity is equal to its cost price plus the profit, added to it in per cent, in accordance with the general rate of profit, or, in other words, to its cost price plus the average profit.

Owing to the different organic compositions of capitals invested in different lines of production, and, hence, owing to the circumstance that — depending on the different percentage which the variable part makes up in a total capital of a given magnitude — capitals of equal

---

[a] In the 1894 German edition "40"; corrected after Marx's manuscript.

magnitude put into motion very different quantities of labour, they also appropriate very different quantities of surplus labour or produce very different quantities of surplus value. Accordingly, the rates of profit prevailing in the various branches of production are originally very different. These different rates of profit are equalised by competition to a single general rate of profit, which is the average of all these different rates of profit. The profit accruing in accordance with this general rate of profit to any capital of a given magnitude, whatever its organic composition, is called the average profit. The price of a commodity, which is equal to its cost price plus the share of the annual average profit on the capital advanced (not merely consumed) in its production that falls to it in accordance with the conditions of turnover, is called its price of production. Take, for example, a capital of 500, of which 100 is fixed capital, and let 10% of this wear out during one turnover of the circulating capital of 400. Let the average profit for the period of turnover be 10%. In that case the cost price of the product created during this turnover will be 10_c for wear plus 400 (c + v) circulating capital = 410, and its price of production will be 410 cost price plus (10% profit on 500) 50 = 460.

Thus, although in selling their commodities the capitalists of the various spheres of production recover the value of the capital consumed in their production, they do not secure the surplus value, and consequently the profit, created in their own sphere by the production of these commodities. What they secure is only as much surplus value, and hence profit, as falls, when uniformly distributed, to the share of every aliquot part of the total capital from the total surplus value, or total profit, produced in a given time by the total social capital in all spheres of production. Every 100 of an advanced capital, whatever its composition, draws as much profit in a year, or any other period of time, as falls to the share of every 100, the n'th part of the total capital, during the same period. So far as profits are concerned, the various capitalists are just so many stockholders in a stock company in which the shares of profit are uniformly divided per 100, so that profits differ in the case of the individual capitalists only in accordance with the amount of capital invested by each in the aggregate enterprise, i. e., according to his investment in social production as a whole, according to the number of his shares. Therefore, the portion of the price of commodities which replaces the elements of capital consumed in the production of these commodities, the portion, therefore, which will have to be used to buy back these consumed capital values, i. e., their cost price, depends entirely on the outlay of capital within the respective spheres of production. But the other element of the price of commodities, the profit added to this cost price, does not depend on the amount of profit produced in a given sphere of production by a given capital in a given period of time. It depends on the mass of profit which falls as an average for any given period to each individual capital as an aliquot part of the total social capital invested in social production. [22]

When a capitalist sells his commodities at their price of production, therefore, he recovers money in proportion to the value of the capital consumed in their production and secures profit in proportion to his advanced capital as the aliquot part in the total social capital. His cost prices are specific. But the profit added to them is independent of his particular sphere of production, being a simple average per 100 units of invested capital.

Let us assume that the five different investments I to V of the foregoing illustration belong to one man. The quantity of variable and constant capital consumed per 100 of the invested capital in each of the departments I to V in the production of commodities would be known, and this portion of the value of the commodities I to V would, needless to say, make up a part of their price, since at least this price is required to recover the advanced and consumed portions of the capital. These cost prices would therefore be different for each class of the commodities I to V, and would as such be set differently by the owner. But as regards the different quantities of surplus value, or profit, produced by I to V, they might easily be regarded by capitalist as profit on his advanced aggregate capital, so that each 100 units would get their definite aliquot part. Hence, the cost prices of the commodities produced in the various departments I to V would be different; but that portion of their selling price derived from the profit added per 100 capital would be the same for all these commodities. The aggregate price of the commodities I to V would therefore equal their aggregate value, i. e., the sum of the cost prices I to V plus the sum of the surplus values, or profits, produced in I to V. It would hence actually be the money expression of the total quantity of past

[22] Cherbuliez.[a]

---

[a] *Richesse ou pauvreté*, 2nd ed., Paris, 1841, pp. 71-72. See also present edition, Vol. 33, pp. 292-99.

and newly added labour incorporated in commodities I to V. And in the same way the sum of the prices of production of all commodities produced in society — the totality of all branches of production — is equal to the sum of their values.

This statement seems to conflict with the fact that under capitalist production the elements of productive capital are, as a rule, bought on the market, and that for this reason their prices include profit which has already been realised, hence, include the price of production of the respective branch of industry together with the profit contained in it, so that the profit of one branch of industry goes into the cost price of another. But if we place the sum of the cost prices of the commodities of an entire country on one side, and the sum of its surplus values, or profits, on the other, the calculation must evidently be right. For instance, take a certain commodity A. Its cost price may contain the profits of B, C, D, etc., just as the cost prices of B, C, D, etc., may contain the profits of A. Now, as we make our calculation the profit of A will not be included in its cost price, nor will the profits of B, C, D, etc., be included in theirs. Nobody ever includes his own profit in his cost price. If there are, therefore, n spheres of production, and if each makes a profit amounting to p, then their aggregate cost price = k — np. Considering the calculation as a whole we see that since the profits of one sphere of production pass into the cost price of another, they are therefore included in the calculation as constituents of the total price of the end product, and so cannot appear a second time on the profit side. If any do appear on this side, however, then only because the commodity in question is itself an ultimate product, whose price of production does not pass into the cost price of some other commodity.

If the cost price of a commodity includes a sum = p, which stands for the profits of the producers of the means of production, and if a profit = p_1 is added to this cost price, the aggregate profit $P = p + p_1$. The aggregate cost price of the commodity, considered without the profit portions, is then its own cost price minus P. Let this cost price be k. Then, obviously, $k + P = k + p + p_1$. In dealing with surplus values, we have seen in Book I (Kap. VII, 2, S. 211/203)[a] that the product of every capital may be so treated, as though a part of it replaces only capital, while the other part represents only surplus

---

value. In applying this approach to the aggregate product of society, we must make some rectifications. Looking upon society as a whole, the profit contained in, say, the price of flax cannot appear twice —not both as a portion of the linen price and as the profit of the flax.

There is no difference between surplus value and profit, as long as, e. g., A's surplus value passes into B's constant capital. It is, after all, quite immaterial to the value of the commodities, whether the labour contained in them is paid or unpaid. This merely shows that B pays for A's surplus value. A's surplus value cannot be entered twice in the total calculation.

But the difference is this: Aside from the fact that the price of a particular product, let us say that of capital B, differs from its value because the surplus value realised in B may be greater or smaller than the profit added to the price of the products of B, the same circumstance applies also to those commodities which form the constant part of capital B, and indirectly also its variable part, as the labourers' necessities of life. So far as the constant portion is concerned, it is itself equal to the cost price plus the surplus value, here therefore equal to cost price plus profit, and this profit may again be greater or smaller than the surplus value for which it stands. As for the variable capital, the average daily wage is indeed always equal to the value produced in the number of hours the labourer must work to produce the necessities of life. But this number of hours is in its turn obscured by the deviation of the prices of production of the necessities of life from their values. However, this always resolves itself to one commodity receiving too little of the surplus value while another receives too much, so that the deviations from the value which are embodied in the prices of production compensate one another. Under capitalist production, the general law acts as the prevailing tendency only in a very complicated and approximate manner, as a never ascertainable average of ceaseless fluctuations.

Since the general rate of profit is formed by taking the average of the various rates of profit for each 100 of capital advanced in a definite period, e. g., a year, it follows that in it the difference brought about by different periods of turnover of different capitals is also effaced. But these differences have a decisive bearing on the different rates of profit in the various spheres of production whose average forms the general rate of profit.

In the preceding illustration concerning the formation of the general rate of profit we assumed each capital in each sphere of production = 100, and we did so to show the difference in the rates of profit in per cent, and thus also the difference in the values of commodities produced by equal amounts of capital. But it goes without saying that the actual amounts of surplus value produced in each sphere of production depend on the magnitude of the employed capitals, since the composition of capital is given in each sphere of production. Yet the actual *rate* of profit in any particular sphere of production is not affected by the fact that the capital invested is 100, or m times 100, or xm times 100. The rate of profit remains 10%, whether the total profit is 10:100, or 1,000:10,000.

However, since the rates of profit differ in the various spheres of production, with very much different quantities of surplus value, or profit, being produced in them, depending on the proportion of the variable to the total capital, it is evident that the average profit per 100 of the social capital, and hence the average, or general, rate of profit, will differ considerably in accordance with the respective magnitudes of the capitals invested in the various spheres. Let us take four capitals A, B, C, D. Let the rate of surplus value for all = 100%. Let the variable capital for each 100 of the total be 25 in A, 40 in B, 15 in C, and 10 in D. Then each 100 of the total capital would yield a surplus value, or profit, of 25 in A, 40 in B, 15 in C, and 10 in D. This would total 90, and if these four capitals are of the same magnitude, the average rate of profit would then be $\frac{90}{4}$ or 22 $^1/_2$%.

Suppose, however, the total capitals are as follows: A = 200, B = 300, C = 1,000, D = 4,000. The profits produced would then respectively = 50, 120, 150, and 400. This makes a profit of 720, and an average rate of profit of 13 $^1/_{11}$% for 5,500, the sum of the four capitals.

The masses of the total value produced differ in accordance with the magnitudes of the total capitals invested in A, B, C, D, respectively. The formation of the general rate of profit is, therefore, not merely a matter of obtaining the simple average of the different *rates* of profit in the various spheres of production, but rather one of the relative weight which these different rates of profit have in forming this average. This, however, depends on the relative magnitude of the capital invested in each particular sphere, or on the aliquot part which the capital invested in each particular sphere forms in the aggregate social capital. There will naturally be a very great difference, depending on whether a greater or smaller part of the total capital produces a higher or lower rate of profit. And this, again, depends on how much capital is invested in spheres, in which the variable capital is relatively small or large compared to the total capital. It is just like the average interest obtained by a usurer who lends various quantities of capital at different interest rates; for instance, at 4, 5, 6, 7%, etc. The average rate will depend entirely on how much of his capital he has loaned out at each of the different rates of interest.

The general rate of profit is, therefore, determined by two factors:

1) The organic composition of the capitals in the different spheres of production, and thus, the different rates of profit in the individual spheres.

2) The distribution of the total social capital in these different spheres, and thus, the relative magnitude of the capital invested in each particular sphere at the specific rate of profit prevailing in it; i.e., the relative share of the total social capital absorbed by each individual sphere of production.

In Books I and II we dealt only with the *value* of commodities. On the one hand, the *cost price* has now been singled out as a part of this value, and, on the other, the *price of production* of commodities has been developed as its converted form.

Suppose the composition of the average social capital is $80_c + 20_v$, and the annual rate of surplus value, s', $= 100\%$. In that case the average annual profit for a capital of $100 = 20$, and the general annual rate of profit $= 20\%$. Whatever the cost price, k, of the commodities annually produced by a capital of 100, their price of production would then $= k + 20$. In those spheres of production in which the composition of capital would $= (80 - x)_c + (20 + x)_v$, the actually produced surplus value, or the annual profit produced in that particular sphere, would $= 20 + x$, that is, greater than 20, and the value of the produced commodities $= k + 20 + x$, that is, greater than $k + 20$, or greater than their price of production. In those spheres, in which the composition of the capital $= (80 + x)_c + (20 - x)_v$, the annually produced surplus value, or profit, would $= 20 - x$, or less than 20, and consequently the value of the commodities $k + 20 - x$ less than the price of production, which $= k + 20$. Aside from possible differences in the periods of turnover, the price of production of the commodities would then equal their value only in spheres, in which the composition of capital would happen to be $80_c + 20_v$.

The specific development of the social productive power of labour in each particular sphere of production varies in degree, higher or lower, depending on how large a quantity of means of production are set in motion by a definite quantity of labour, hence in a given working day by a definite number of labourers, and, consequently, on how small a quantity of labour is required for a given quantity of means of production. Such capitals as contain a larger percentage of constant and a smaller percentage of variable capital than the average social capital are, therefore, called capitals of *higher* composition, and, conversely, those capitals in which the constant is relatively smaller, and the variable relatively greater than in the average social capital, are called capitals of *lower* composition. Finally, we call those capitals whose composition coincides with the average, capitals of average composition. Should the average social capital be composed in per cent of $80_c + 20_v$, then a capital of $90_c + 10_v$ is *higher*, and a capital of $70_c + 30_v$ *lower* than the social average. Generally speaking, if the composition of the average social capital $= m_c + n_v$, in which m and n are constant magnitudes and $m + n = 100$, the formula $(m + x)_c + (n - x)_v$ represents the higher composition, and $(m - x)_c + (n + x)_v$ the lower composition of an individual capital or group of capitals. The way in which these capitals perform their functions after establishment of an average rate of profit and assuming one turnover per year, is shown in the following tabulation, in which I represents the average composition with an average rate of profit of 20%.

I) $80_c + 20_v + 20_s$. Rate of profit = 20%.
Price of product = 120. Value = 120.

II) $90_c + 10_v + 10_s$. Rate of profit = 20%.
Price of product = 120. Value = 110.

III) $70_c + 30_v + 30_s$. Rate of profit = 20%.
Price of product = 120. Value = 130.

The value of the commodities produced by capital II would, therefore, be smaller than their price of production, the price of production of the commodities of III smaller than their value, and only in the case of capital I in branches of production in which the composition happens to coincide with the social average, would value and price of production be equal. In applying these terms to any particular cases note must, however, be taken whether a deviation of the ratio between c and v from the general average is simply due to a change in the value of the elements of constant capital, rather than to a difference in the technical composition.

The foregoing statements have at any rate modified the original assumption concerning the determination of the cost price of commodities. We had originally assumed that the cost price of a commodity equalled the *value* of the commodities consumed in its production.But for the buyer the price of production of a specific commodity is its cost price, and may thus pass as cost price into the prices of other commodities. Since the price of production may differ from the value of a commodity, it follows that the cost price of a commodity containing this price of production of another commodity may also stand above or below that portion of its total value derived from the value of the means of production consumed by it. It is necessary to remember this modified significance of the cost price, and to bear in mind that there is always the possibility of an error if the cost price of a commodity in any particular sphere is identified with the value of the means of production consumed by it. Our present analysis does not necessitate a closer examination of this point. It remains true, nevertheless, that the cost price of a commodity is always smaller than its value. For no matter how much the cost price of a commodity may differ from the value of the means of production consumed by it, this past mistake is immaterial to the capitalist. The cost price of a particular commodity is a definite condition which is given, and independent of the production of our capitalist, while the result of his production is a commodity containing surplus value, therefore an excess of value over and above its cost price. For all other purposes, the statement that the cost price is smaller than the value of a commodity has now changed practically into the statement that the cost price is smaller than the price of production. As concerns the total social capital, in which the price of production is equal to the value, this statement is identical with the former, namely that the cost price is smaller than the value. And while it is modified in the individual spheres of production, the fundamental fact always remains that in the case of the total social capital the cost price of the commodities produced by it is smaller than their value, or, in the case of the total mass of social commodities, smaller than their price of production, which is identical with their value. The cost price of a commodity refers only to the quantity of paid labour contained in it, while its value refers to all the paid and unpaid labour contained in it. The price of production refers to the sum of the paid labour plus a certain quantity of unpaid labour determined for any particular sphere of production by conditions over which it has no control.

The formula that the price of production of a commodity $= k + p$, i. e., equals its cost price plus profit, is now more precisely defined with $p = kp'$ (p' being the general rate of profit). Hence the price of production $= k + kp'$. If $k = 300$ and $p' = 15\%$, then the price of production is $k + kp' = 300 + 300 \times \frac{15}{100}$, or 345.

The price of production of the commodities in any particular sphere may change in magnitude:

1) If the general rate of profit changes independently of this particular sphere, while the value of the commodities remains the same (the same quantities of congealed and living labour being consumed in their production as before).

2) If there is a change of value, either in this particular sphere in consequence of technical changes, or in consequence of a change in the value of those commodities which form the elements of its constant capital, while the general rate of profit remains unchanged.

3) Finally, if a combination of the two aforementioned circumstances takes place.

In spite of the great changes occurring continually, as we shall see, in the actual rates of profit within the individual spheres of production, any real change in the general rate of profit, unless brought about by way of an exception by extraordinary economic events, is the belated effect of a series of fluctuations extending over very long periods, fluctuations which require much time before consolidating and equalising one another to bring about a change in the general rate of profit. In all shorter periods (quite aside from fluctuations of market prices), a change in the prices of production is, therefore, always traceable *prima facie* to actual changes in the value of commodities, i. e., to changes in the total amount of labour time required for their production. Mere changes in the money expression of the same values are, naturally, not at all considered here. [23]

On the other hand, it is evident that from the point of view of the total social capital the value of the commodities produced by it (or, expressed in money, their price) = value of constant capital + value of variable capital + surplus value. Assuming the degree of labour exploitation to be constant, the rate of profit cannot change so long as

---

[23] Corbet, p. 174.[a]

---

[a] *An Inquiry into the Causes and Modes of the Wealth of Individuals...*, London, 1841. Cf. present edition, Vol. 33, p. 250.

the mass of surplus value remains the same, unless there is a change in either the value of the constant capital, the value of the variable capital, or the value of both, so that C changes, and thereby $\frac{s}{C}$, which represents the general rate of profit. In each case, therefore, a change in the general rate of profit implies a change in the value of commodities which form the elements of the constant or variable capital, or of both.

Or, the general rate of profit may change, while the value of the commodities remains the same, when the degree of labour exploitation changes.

Or, if the degree of labour exploitation remains the same, the general rate of profit may change through a change in the amount of labour employed relative to the constant capital as a result of technical changes in the labour process. But such technical changes must always show themselves in, and be attended by, a change in the value of the commodities, whose production would then require more or less labour than before.

We saw in Part I that surplus value and profit are identical from the standpoint of their mass. But the rate of profit is from the very outset distinct from the rate of surplus value, which appears at first sight as merely a different form of calculating. But at the same time this serves, also from the outset, to obscure and mystify the actual origin of surplus value, since the rate of profit can rise or fall while the rate of surplus value remains the same, and vice versa, and since the capitalist is in practice solely interested in the rate of profit. Yet there was difference of magnitude only between the rate of surplus value and the rate of profit and not between the surplus value itself and profit. Since in the rate of profit the surplus value is calculated in relation to the total capital and the latter is taken as its standard of measurement, the surplus value itself appears to originate from the total capital, uniformly derived from all its parts, so that the organic difference between constant and variable capital is obliterated in the conception of profit. Disguised as profit, surplus value actually denies its origin, loses its character, and becomes unrecognisable. However, hitherto the distinction between profit and surplus value applied solely to a qualitative change, or change of form, while there was no real difference of magnitude in this first stage of the change between profit and surplus value, but only between the rate of profit and the rate of surplus value.

But it is different, as soon as a general rate of profit, and thereby an average profit corresponding to the magnitude of employed capital given in the various spheres of production, have been established.

It is then only an accident if the surpuls value, and thus the profit, actually produced in any particular sphere of production, coincides with the profit contained in the selling price of a commodity. As a rule, surplus value and profit and not their rates alone, are then different magnitudes. At a given degree of exploitation, the mass of surplus value produced in a particular sphere of production is then more important for the aggregate average profit of social capital, and thus for the capitalist class in general, than for the individual capitalist in any specific branch of production. It is of importance to the latter [24] only in so far as the quantity of surplus value produced in his branch helps to regulate the average profit. But this is a process which occurs behind his back, one he does not see, nor understand, and which indeed does not interest him. The actual difference of magnitude between profit and surplus value — not merely between the rate of profit and the rate of surplus value — in the various spheres of production now completely conceals the true nature and origin of profit not only from the capitalist, who has a special interest in deceiving himself on this score, but also from the labourer. The transformation of values into prices of production serves to obscure the basis for determining value itself. Finally, since the mere transformation of surplus value into profit distinguishes the portion of the value of a commodity forming the profit from the portion forming its cost price, it is natural that the conception of value should elude the capitalist at this juncture, for he does not see the total labour put into the commodity, but only that portion of the total labour for which he has paid in the shape of means of production, be they living or not, so that his profit appears to him as something outside the immanent value of the commodity. Now this idea is fully confirmed, fortified, and ossified in that, from the standpoint of his particular sphere of production, the profit added to the cost price is not actually determined by the limits of the formation of value within his own sphere, but through completely outside influences.

The fact that this intrinsic connection is here revealed for the first time; that up to the present time political economy, as we shall see in

---

[24] We naturally leave aside for the moment the possibility of securing a temporary extra profit through wage reductions, monopoly prices, etc. [F. E.]

the following and in Book IV,[7] either forcibly abstracted itself from
the distinctions between surplus value and profit, and their rates, so it
could retain value determination as a basis, or else abandoned this
value determination and with it all vestiges of a scientific approach,
in order to cling to the differences that strike the eye in this phenomenon — this confusion of the theorists best illustrates the utter incapa-
city of the practical capitalist, blinded by competition as he is, and incapable of penetrating its phenomena, to recognise the inner essence
and inner structure of this process behind its outer appearance.

In fact, all the laws evolved in Part I concerning the rise and fall of
the rate of profit have the following twofold meaning:

1) On the one hand, they are the laws of the general rate of profit.
In view of the many different causes which make the rate of profit
rise or fall one would think, after everything that has been said and
done, that the general rate of profit must change every day. But a
trend in one sphere of production compensates for that in another,
their effects cross and paralyse one another. We shall later examine to
which side these fluctuations ultimately gravitate. But they are slow.
The suddenness, multiplicity, and different duration of the fluctuations
in the individual spheres of production make them compensate for
one another in the order of their succession in time, a fall in prices following a rise, and vice versa, so that they remain limited to local, i. e.,
individual, spheres. Finally, the various local fluctuations neutralise
one another. Within each individual sphere of production, there take
place changes, i. e., deviations from the general rate of profit, which
counterbalance one another in a difinite time on the one hand, and
thus have no influence upon the general rate of profit, and which, on
the other, do not react upon it, because they are balanced by other
simultaneous local fluctuations. Since the general rate of profit is not
only determined by the average rate of profit in each sphere, but also
by the distribution of the total capital among the different individual
spheres, and since this distribution is continually changing, it becomes another constant cause of change in the general rate of profit.
But it is a cause of change which mostly paralyses itself, owing to the
uninterrupted[a] and many-sided nature of this movement.

2) Within each sphere, there is some room for play for a longer or
shorter space of time, in which the rate of profit of this sphere may
fluctuate, before this fluctuation consolidates sufficiently after rising

---

[a] In the 1894 German edition "interrupted"; corrected after Marx's manuscript.

or falling to gain time for influencing the general rate of profit and therefore assuming more than local importance. The laws of the rate of profit, as developed in Part I of this book, likewise remain applicable within these limits of space and time.

The theoretical conception concerning the first transformation of surplus value into profit, that every part of a capital yields a uniform profit, [25] expresses a practical fact. Whatever the composition of an industrial capital, whether it sets in motion one-quarter of congealed labour and three-quarters of living labour, or three-quarters of congealed labour and one-quarter of living labour, whether in one case it absorbs three times as much surplus labour, or produces three times as much surplus value than in another—in either case it yields the same profit, given the same degree of labour exploitation and leaving aside individual differences, which, incidentally, disappear because we are dealing in both cases with the average composition of the entire sphere of production. The individual capitalist (or all the capitalists in each individual sphere of production), whose outlook is limited, rightly believes that his profit is not derived solely from the labour employed by him, or in his line of production. This is quite true, as far as his average profit is concerned. To what extent this profit is due to the aggregate exploitation of labour on the part of the total capital, i. e., by all his capitalist colleagues — this interrelation is a complete mystery to the individual capitalist; all the more so, since no bourgeois theorists, the political economists, have so far revealed it. A saving of labour — not only labour necessary to produce a certain product, but also the number of employed labourers — and the employment of more congealed labour (constant capital), appear to be very sound operations from the economic standpoint and do not seem to exert the least influence on the general rate of profit and the average profit. How could living labour be the sole source of profit, in view of the fact that a reduction in the quantity of labour required for production appears not to exert any influence on profit? Moreover, it even seems in certain circumstances to be the nearest source of an increase of profits, at least for the individual capitalist.

If in any particular sphere of production there is a rise or fall of the

---

[25] Malthus.[a]

---

[a] *Principles of Political Economy*, 2nd ed., London, 1836, p. 268. Cf. present edition, Vol. 33, p. 71.

portion of the cost price which represents the value of constant capital, this portion comes from the circulation and, either enlarged or reduced, passes from the very outset into the process of production of the commodity. If, on the other hand, the same number of labourers produces more or less in the same time, so that the quantity of labour required for the production of a definite quantity of commodities varies while the number of labourers remains the same, that portion of the cost price which represents the value of the variable capital may remain the same, i. e., contribute the same amount to the cost price of the total product. But every one of the individual commodities whose sum makes up the total product, shares in more or less labour (paid and therefore also unpaid), and shares consequently in the greater or smaller outlay for this labour, i. e., a larger or smaller portion of the wage. The total wages paid by the capitalist remain the same, but wages differ if calculated per piece of the commodity. Thus, there is a change in this portion of the cost price of the commodity. But no matter whether the cost price of the individual commodity (or, perhaps, the cost price of the sum of commodities produced by a capital of a given magnitude) rises or falls, be it due to such changes in its own value, or in that of its elements, the average profit of, e. g., 10% remains 10%. Still, 10% of an individual commodity may represent very different amounts, depending on the change of magnitude caused in the cost price of the individual commodity by such changes of value as we have assumed.[26]

So far as the variable capital is concerned — and this is most important, because it is the source of surplus value, and because anything which conceals its relation to the enrichment of the capitalist serves to mystify the entire system — matters get cruder or appear to the capitalist in the following light: A variable capital of £100 represents the weekly wage of, say, 100 labourers. If these 100 labourers weekly produce 200 pieces of a commodity = 200C in a given working time, then 1C — abstracted from that portion of its cost price which is added by the constant capital, costs $\frac{£100}{200}$ = 10 shillings, since £100 = 200C. Now suppose that a change occurs in the productive power of labour. Suppose it doubles, so that the same number of

---

[26] Corbet.[a]

---

[a] An Inquiry into the Causes and Modes of the Wealth of Individuals..., London, 1841, p. 20. Cf. present edition, Vol. 33, pp. 241-42.

labourers now produces twice 200C in the time which it previously took to produce 200C. In that case (considering only that part of the cost price which consists of wages) $1C = \frac{\pounds 100}{400} = 5$ shillings, since now $\pounds 100 = 400C$. Should the productive power decrease one-half, the same labour would produce only $\frac{200C}{2}$ and since $\pounds 100 = \frac{200C}{2}$, $1C = \frac{\pounds 200}{200} = \pounds 1$. The changes in the labour time required for the production of the commodities, and hence the changes in their value, thus appear in regard to the cost price, and hence to the price of production, as a different distribution of the same wage for more or fewer commodities, depending on the greater or smaller quantity of commodities produced in the same working time for the same wage. What the capitalist, and consequently also the political economist, see is that the part of the paid labour per piece of commodity changes with the productivity of labour, and that the value of each piece also changes accordingly. What they do not see is that the same applies to unpaid labour contained in every piece of the commodity, and this is perceived so much less since the average profit actually is only accidentally determined by the unpaid labour absorbed in the sphere of the individual capitalist. It is only in such crude and meaningless form that we can glimpse that the value of commodities is determined by the labour contained in them.

Chapter X

EQUALISATION OF THE GENERAL RATE OF PROFIT THROUGH COMPETITION. MARKET PRICES AND MARKET VALUES. SURPLUS PROFIT

The capital employed in some spheres of production has a mean, or average, composition, that is, it has the same, or almost the same composition as the average social capital.

In these spheres the price of production of the produced commodities is exactly or almost the same as their value expressed in money. If there were no other way of reaching a mathematical limit, this would be the one. Competition so distributes the social capital among the various spheres of production that the prices of production in each sphere take shape according to the model of the prices of production in these spheres of average composition, i.e., they = k + kp' (cost price plus the average rate of profit multiplied by the cost price). This average rate of profit, however, is the percentage of profit in that sphere of average composition in which profit, therefore, coincides with surplus value. Hence, the rate of profit is the same in all spheres of production, for it is equalised on the basis of those average spheres of production which has the average composition of capital. Consequently, the sum of the profits in all spheres of production must equal the sum of the surplus values, and the sum of the prices of production of the total social product equal the sum of its value. But it is evident that the balance among spheres of production of different composition must tend to equalise them with the spheres of average composition, be it exactly or only approximately the same as the social average. Between the spheres more or less approximating the average there is again a tendency toward equalisation, seeking the ideal average, i.e., an average that does not really exist, i.e., a tendency to take this ideal as a standard. In this way the tendency necessarily prevails to make the prices of production merely converted forms of value, or to turn profits into mere portions of surplus value. However, these are not distributed in proportion to the surplus value produced in each special sphere of production, but rather in proportion to the mass of capital employed in each sphere, so that equal masses of capital, whatever their composition, receive equal aliquot shares of the total surplus value produced by the total social capital.

In the case of capitals of average, or approximately average, composition, the price of production is thus the same or almost the same as the value, and the profit the same as the surplus value produced by them. All other capitals, of whatever composition, tend toward this average under pressure of competition. But since the capitals of average composition are of the same, or approximately the same, structure as the average social capital, all capitals have the tendency, regardless of the surplus value produced by them, to realise the average profit, rather than their own surplus value in the price of their commodity, i.e., to realise the prices of production.

On the other hand, it may be said that wherever an average profit, and therefore a general rate of profit, are produced—no matter by what means—such an average profit cannot be anything but the profit on the average social capital, whose sum is equal to the sum of surplus value. Moreover, the prices obtained by adding this average profit to the cost prices cannot be anything but the values converted into prices of production. Nothing would be altered if capitals in certain spheres of production would not, for some reason, be subject to the process of equalisation. The average profit would then be computed on that portion of the social capital which enters the equalisation process. It is evident that the average profit can be nothing but the total mass of surplus values allotted to the various quantities of capital proportionally to their magnitudes in the different spheres of production. It is the total realised unpaid labour, and this total mass, like the paid, congealed or living, labour, obtains in the total mass of commodities and money that falls to the capitalists.

The really difficult question is this: how is this equalisation of profits into a general rate of profit brought about, since it is obviously a result rather than a point of departure?

To begin with, an estimate of the values of commodities, for instance in terms of money, can obviously only be the result of their exchange. If, therefore, we assume such an estimate, we must regard it as the outcome of an actual exchange of commodity value for commodity value. But how does this exchange of commodities at their real values come about?

Let us first assume that all commodities in the different branches of production are sold at their real values. What would then be the outcome? According to the foregoing, very different rates of profit would then reign in the various spheres of production. It is *prima facie* two entirely different matters whether commodities are sold at their values (i. e., exchanged in proportion to the value contained in them at prices corresponding to their value), or whether they are sold at such prices that their sale yields equal profits for equal masses of the capitals advanced for their respective production.

The fact that capitals employing unequal amounts of living labour produce unequal amounts of surplus value, presupposes at least to a certain extent that the degree of exploitation or the rate of surplus value are the same, or that any existing differences in them are equalised by real or imaginary (conventional) grounds of compensation. This would assume competition among labourers and equalisation through their continual migration from one sphere of production to another. Such a general rate of surplus value — viewed as a tendency, like all other economic laws — has been assumed by us for the sake of theoretical simplification. But in reality it is an actual premiss of the capitalist mode of production, although it is more or less obstructed by practical frictions causing more or less considerable local differences, such as the SETTLEMENT LAWS[a] [29] for farm labourers in Britain. But in theory it is assumed that the laws of capitalist mode of production operate in their pure form. In reality there exists only approximation; but, this approximation is the greater, the more developed the capitalist mode of production and the less it is adulterated and amalgamated with survivals of former economic conditions.

The whole difficulty arises from the fact that commodities are not exchanged simply as *commodities*, but as *products of capitals*, which claim participation in the total amount of surplus value, proportional to their magnitude, or equal if they are of equal magnitude. And this claim is to be satisfied by the total price for commodities produced by a given capital in a certain space of time. This total price is, however, only the sum of the prices of the individual commodities produced by this capital.

The *punctum saliens*[b] will be best brought out if we approach the matter as follows: Suppose, the labourers themselves are in possession of their respective means of production and exchange their commodities with one another. In that case these commodities would not be products of capital. The value of the various means of labour and raw materials would differ in accordance with the technical nature of the labours performed in the different branches of production. Furthermore, aside from the unequal value of the means of production employed by them, they would require different quantities of means of production for given quantities of labour, depending on whether a certain commodity can be finished in one hour, another in one day, and so forth. Also suppose the labourers work an equal average length of time, allowing for compensations that arise from the different labour intensities, etc. In such a case, two labourers would, first, both have replaced their outlays, the cost prices of the consumed means of production, in the commodities which make up the product of their day's work. These outlays would differ, depending on the technical nature of their labour. Secondly, both of them would have created equal amounts of new value, namely the working day added by them to the means of production. This would comprise their wages plus the surplus value, the latter representing surplus labour over and above their necessary wants, the product of which would however belong to them. To put it the capitalist way, both of them receive the same

---

a In the 1894 German edition this English term is given in parentheses after its German equivalent. - b the essential point

wages plus the same profit, = the value, expressed, say, by the product of a ten-hour working day. But in the first place, the values of their commodities would have to differ. In commodity I, for instance, the portion of value corresponding to the consumed means of production might be higher than in commodity II. And, to introduce all possible differences, we might assume right now that commodity I absorbs more living labour, and consequently requires more labour time to be produced, than commodity II. The values of commodities I and II are, therefore, very different. So are the sums of the values of the commodities, which represent the product of the labour performed by labourers I and II in a given time. The rates of profit would also differ considerably for I and II if we take the rate of profit to be the proportion of the surplus value to the total value of the invested means of production. The means of subsistence daily consumed by I and II during production, which take the place of wages, here form the part of the invested means of production ordinarily called variable capital. But for equal working periods the surplus values would be the same for I and II, or, more precisely, since I and II each receive the value of the product of a day's work, both of them receive equal values after the value of the invested "constant" elements has been deducted, and one portion of these equal values may be regarded as a substitute for the means of subsistence consumed in production, and the other as surplus value in excess of it. If labourer I has greater expenses, they are made good by a greater portion of the value of his commodity, which replaces this "constant" part, and he therefore has to reconvert a larger portion of the total value of his product into the material elements of this constant part, while labourer II, if he receives less for this, has so much less to reconvert. In these circumstances, a difference in the rates of profit would therefore be immaterial, just as it is immaterial to the wage labourer today what rate of profit may express the amount of surplus value filched from him, and just as in international commerce the difference in the various national rates of profit is immaterial to commodity exchange.

The exchange of commodities at their values, or approximately at their values, thus requires a much lower stage than their exchange at their prices of production, which requires a definite level of capitalist development.

Whatever the manner in which the prices of various commodities are first mutually fixed or regulated, their movements are always governed by the law of value. If the labour time required for their production happens to shrink, prices fall; if it increases, prices rise, provided other conditions remain the same.

Apart from the domination of prices and price movement by the law of value, it is quite appropriate to regard the values of commodities as not only theoretically but also historically *prius* [a] to the prices of production. This applies to conditions in which the labourer owns his means of production, and this is the condition of the land-owning farmer living off his own labour and the craftsman, in the ancient as well as in the modern world. This agrees also with the view [27] we expressed previously, that the evolution of products into commodities arises through exchange between different communities, not between the members of the same community.[b] It holds not only for this primitive condition, but also for subsequent conditions, based on slavery and serfdom, and for the guild organisation of handicrafts, so long as the means of production involved in each branch of production can be transferred from one sphere to another only with difficulty and therefore the various spheres of production are related to one another, within certain limits, as foreign countries or communist communities.

For prices at which commodities are exchanged to approximately correspond to their values, nothing more is necessary than 1) for the exchange of the various commodities to cease being purely accidental or only occasional; 2) so far as direct exchange of commodities is concerned, for these commodities to be produced on both sides in approximately sufficient quantities to meet mutual requirements, something learned from mutual experience in trading and therefore a natural outgrowth of continued trading; and 3) so far as selling is concerned, for no natural or artificial monopoly to enable either of the contracting sides to sell commodities above their value or to compel them to undersell. By accidental monopoly we mean a monopoly which a buyer or seller acquires through an accidental state of supply and demand.

The assumption that the commodities of the various spheres of production are sold at their value merely implies, of course, that their

---

[27] In 1865, this was merely Marx's "view". Today, after the extensive research ranging from Maurer to Morgan into the nature of primitive communities, it is an accepted fact which is hardly anywhere denied.— *F. E.*

---

[a] prior - [b] See present edition, Vol. 29, p. 290 and Vol. 35, p. 98.

value is the centre of gravity around which their prices fluctuate, and their continual rises and drops tend to equalise. There is also the *market value* — of which later — to be distinguished from the individual value of particular commodities produced by different producers. The individual value of some of these commodities will be below their market value (that is, less labour time is required for their production than expressed in the market value) while that of others will exceed the market value. On the one hand, market value is to be viewed as the average value of commodities produced in a single sphere, and, on the other, as the individual value of the commodities produced under average conditions of their respective sphere and forming the bulk of the products of that sphere. It is only in extraordinary combinations that commodities produced under the worst, or the most favourable, conditions regulate the market value, which, in turn, forms the centre of fluctuation for market prices. The latter, however, are the same for commodities of the same kind. If the ordinary demand is satisfied by the supply of commodities of average value, hence of a value midway between the two extremes, then the commodities whose individual value is below the market value realise an extra surplus value, or surplus profit, while those, whose individual value exceeds the market value, are unable to realise a portion of the surplus value contained in them.

It does no good to say that the sale of commodities produced under the least favourable conditions proves that they are required to satisfy the demand.[a] If in the assumed case the price were higher than the average market value, the demand would be smaller.[b] At a certain price, a commodity occupies just so much place on the market. This place remains the same in case of a price change only if the higher price is accompanied by a drop in the supply of the commodity, and a lower price by an increase of supply. And if the demand is so great that it does not contract when the price is regulated by the value of commodities produced under the least favourable conditions, then these determine the market value. This is not possible unless demand is greater than usual, or if supply drops below the usual level. Finally, if the mass of the produced commodities exceeds the quantity disposed of at average market values, the commodities produced under the most favourable conditions regulate the market value. They may, for

---

a In the 1894 German edition "supply"; corrected after Marx's manuscript. - b In the 1894 German edition "greater"; corrected after Marx's manuscript.

example, be sold exactly or approximately at their individual value, in which case the commodities produced under the least favourable conditions may not even realise their cost price, while those produced under average conditions realise only a portion of the surplus value contained in them. What has been said here of market value applies to the price of production as soon as it takes the place of market value. The price of production is regulated in each sphere, and likewise regulated by special circumstances. And this price of production is, in its turn, the centre around which the daily market prices fluctuate and tend to equalise one another within definite periods. (See Ricardo on determining the price of production through those working under the least favourable conditions.[a])

No matter how the prices are regulated, we arrive at the following:

1) The law of value dominates price movements since reduction or increase in the labour time required for production makes prices of production fall or rise. It is in this sense that Ricardo (who doubtlessly realised that his prices of production deviated from the value of commodities) says that

     * "the inquiry to which I wish to draw the reader's attention relates to the effect of the variations in the relative value of commodities, and not in their absolute value".* [b]

2) The average profit determining the prices of production must always be approximately equal to that quantity of surplus value which falls to the share of individual capital in its capacity of an aliquot part of the total social capital. Suppose that the general rate of profit, and therefore the average profit, are expressed by money value greater than the money value of the actual average surplus value. So far as the capitalists are concerned, it is then immaterial whether they reciprocally charge 10 or 15% profit. Neither of these percentages covers more actual commodity value than the other, since the overcharge in money is mutual. As for the labourer (the assumption being that he receives his normal wage and the rise in the average profit does not therefore imply an actual deduction from his wage, i. e., something entirely different from the normal surplus value of the capitalist), the rise in commodity prices caused by an increase of the

---

a D. Ricardo, *On the Principles of Political Economy, and Taxation*, 3rd ed., London, 1821, pp. 60-61. Cf. present edition, Vol. 31, p. 428. - b D. Ricardo, op. cit., p. 15. Cf. present edition, Vol. 31, pp. 394-400.

average profit must correspond to the rise of the money expression of the variable capital. Such a general nominal increase in the rate of profit and the average profit above the limit provided by the ratio of the actual surplus value to the total invested capital is not, in effect, possible without causing an increase in wages, and also an increase in the prices of commodities forming the constant capital. The reverse is true in case of a reduction. Since the total value of the commodities regulates the total surplus value, and this in turn regulates the level of average profit and thereby the general rate of profit — as a general law or a law governing fluctuations — it follows that the law of value regulates the prices of production.

What competition, first in a single sphere, achieves is a single market value and market price derived from the various individual values of commodities. And it is competition of capitals in different spheres, which first brings out the price of production equalising the rates of profit in the different spheres. The latter process requires a higher development of capitalist production than the previous one.

For commodities of the same sphere of production, the same kind, and approximately the same quality, to be sold at their values, the following two requirements are necessary:

First, the different individual values must be equalised at *one* social value, the above-named market value, and this implies competition among producers of the same kind of commodities and, likewise, the existence of a common market in which they offer their articles for sale. For the market price of identical commodities, each, however, produced under different individual circumstances, to correspond to the market value and not to deviate from it either by rising above or falling below it, it is necessary that the pressure exerted by different sellers upon one another be sufficient to bring enough commodities to market to fill the social requirements, i. e., a quantity for which society is capable of paying the market value. Should the mass of products exceed this demand, the commodities would have to be sold below their market value; and conversely, above their market value if the mass of products were not large enough to meet the demand, or, what amounts to the same, if the pressure of competition among sellers were not strong enough to bring this mass of commodities to market. Should the market value change, this would also entail a change in the conditions on which the total mass of commodities could be sold. Should the market value fall, this would entail a rise in the average social demand (this always taken to mean the effective demand), which could, within certain limits, absorb larger masses of commodities. Should the market value rise, this would entail a drop in the social demand, and a smaller mass of commodities would be absorbed. Hence, if supply and demand regulate the market price, or rather the deviations of the market price from the market value, then, in turn, the market value regulates the ratio of supply to demand, or the centre round which fluctuations of supply and demand cause market prices to oscillate.

Looking closer, we find that the conditions applicable to the value of an individual commodity are here reproduced as conditions governing the value of the aggregate of a certain kind of commodity. Capitalist production is mass production from the very outset. But even in other, less developed, modes of production that which is produced in relatively small quantities as a common product by small-scale, even if numerous, producers, is concentrated in the market in large quantities — at least in the case of the vital commodities — in the hands of relatively few merchants. The latter accumulate them and sell them as the common product of an entire branch of production, or of a more or less considerable contingent of it.

It should be here noted in passing that the "social demand", i. e., the factor which regulates the principle of demand, is essentially subject to the mutual relationship of the different classes and their respective economic position, notably therefore to, firstly, the ratio of total surplus value to wages, and, secondly, to the relation of the various parts into which surplus value is split up (profit, interest, ground rent, taxes, etc.). And this thus again shows how absolutely nothing can be explained by the relation of supply to demand before ascertaining the basis on which this relation rests.

Although both commodity and money represent a unity of exchange value and use value, we have already seen (Buch I, Kap. I, 3) that in buying and selling both of these functions are polarised at the two extremes, the commodity (seller) representing the use value, and the money (buyer) representing the exchange value. One of the first premisses of selling was that a commodity should have use value and should therefore satisfy a social need. The other premiss was that the quantity of labour contained in the commodity should represent socially necessary labour, i. e., its individual value (and, what amounts to the same under the present assumption, its selling price) should coincide with its social value. [28]

Let us apply this to the mass of commodities available in the market, which represents the product of a whole sphere.

The matter will be most readily pictured by regarding this whole mass of commodities, produced by *one* branch of industry, as *one* commodity, and the sum of the prices of the many identical commodities as *one* price. Then, whatever has been said of a single commodity applies literally to the mass of commodities of an entire branch of production available in the market. The requirement that the individual value of a commodity should correspond to its social value is now realised, or further determined, in that the mass contains social labour necessary for its production, and that the value of this mass = its market value.

Now suppose that the bulk of these commodities is produced under approximately similar normal social conditions, so that this value is at the same time the individual value of the individual commodities which make up this mass. If a relatively small portion of these commodities may now have been produced below, and another above, these conditions, so that the individual value of one portion is greater, and that of the other smaller, than the average value of the bulk of the commodities, but in such proportions that these extremes balance one another, so that the average value of the commodities at these extremes is equal to the value of commodities in the centre, then the market value is determined by the value of the commodities produced under average conditions. [29] The value of the entire mass of commodities is equal to the actual sum of the values of all individual commodities taken together, whether produced under average conditions, or under conditions above or below the average. In that case, the market value, or social value, of the mass of commodities — the necessary labour time contained in them — is determined by the value of the preponderant mean mass.

Suppose, on the contrary, that the total mass of the commodities in question brought to market remains the same, while the value of the commodities produced under less favourable conditions fails

---

[28] K. Marx, *Zur Kritik der pol. Oek.*, Berlin, 1859. [a]
[29] K. Marx, *Zur Kritik etc.*[b]

---

[a] See present edition, Vol. 29, pp. 273-74. - [b] Ibid., p. 302.

to balance out the value of commodities produced under more favourable conditions, so that the part of the mass produced under less favourable conditions forms a relatively weighty quantity as compared with the average mass and with the other extreme. In that case, the mass produced under less favourable conditions regulates the market, or social, value.

Suppose, finally, that the mass of commodities produced under better than average conditions considerably exceeds that produced under worse conditions, and is large even compared with that produced under average conditions. In that case, the part produced under the most favourable conditions determines the market value. We ignore here the overstocked market, in which the part produced under most favourable conditions always regulates the market price. We are not dealing here with the market price, in so far as it differs from the market value, but with the various determinations of the market value itself. [30]

In fact, strictly speaking (which, of course, occurs in reality only in approximation and with a thousand modifications) the market value of the entire mass, regulated as it is by the average values, is in case I equal to the sum of their individual values; although in the case of the commodities produced at the extremes, this value is represented as an average value which is forced upon them. Those who produce at the worst extreme must then sell their commodities below the individual value; those producing at the best extreme sell them above it.

In case II the individual lots of commodity values produced at the

---

[30] The controversy between Storch and Ricardo with regard to ground rent (a controversy pertaining only to the subject; in fact, the two opponents pay no attention to one another), whether the market value (or rather what they call market price and price of production respectively) was regulated by the commodities produced under unfavourable conditions (Ricardo), or by those produced under favourable conditions (Storch), [30] resolves itself in the final analysis in that both are right and both wrong, and that both of them have failed to consider the average case. Compare Corbet on the cases in which the price is regulated by commodities produced under the most favourable conditions [31] — "It is not meant to be asserted by him" (Ricardo) "that two particular lots of two different articles, as a hat and a pair of shoes, exchange with one another when those two particular lots were produced by equal quantities of labour. By 'commodity' we must here understand the 'description of commodity', not a particular individual hat, pair of shoes, etc. The whole labour which produces all the hats in England is to be considered, to this purpose, as divided among all the hats. This seems to me not to have been expressed at first, and in the general statements of this doctrine." (Observations on Certain Verbal Disputes in Pol. Econ., etc., London, 1821, pp. 53-54.)

two extremes do not balance one another. Rather, the lot produced under the worse conditions decides the issue. Strictly speaking, the average price, or the market value, of each individual commodity, or each aliquot part of the total mass, would now be determined by the total value of the mass as obtained by adding up the values of the commodities produced under different conditions, and in accordance with the aliquot part of this total value falling to the share of each individual commodity. The market value thus obtained would exceed the individual value not only of the commodities belonging to the favourable extreme, but also of those belonging to the average lot. Yet it would still be below the individual value of those commodities produced at the unfavourable extreme. How close the market value approaches, or finally coincides with, the latter would depend entirely on the volume occupied by commodities produced at the unfavourable extreme of the commodity sphere in question. If demand is only slightly greater than supply, the individual value of the unfavourably produced commodities regulates the market price.

Finally, if the lot of commodities produced at the favourable extreme occupies greater place than the other extreme, and also than the average lot, as it does in case III, then the market value falls below the average value. The average value, computed by adding the sums of values at the two extremes and at the middle, stands here below the value of the middle, which it approaches, or vice versa, depending on the relative place occupied by the favourable extreme. Should demand be weaker than supply, the favourably situated part, whatever its size, makes room for itself forcibly by contracting its price down to its individual value. The market value cannot ever coincide with this individual value of the commodities produced under the most favourable conditions, except when supply far exceeds demand.

This mode of determining market values, which we have here outlined *abstractly*, is promoted in the real market by competition among the buyers, provided the demand is large enough to absorb the mass of commodities at values so fixed. And this brings us to the other point.

Second, to say that a commodity has a use value is merely to say that it satisfies some social want. So long as we dealt with individual commodities only, we could assume that there was a need for a particular commodity — its quantity already implied by its price — without inquiring further into the quantity required to satisfy this want. This quantity is, however, of essential importance, as soon as the product of an entire branch of production is placed on one side, and the social need for it on the other. It then becomes necessary to consider the extent, i. e., the amount of this social want.

In the foregoing determinations of market value it was assumed that the mass of the produced commodities is given, i. e., remains the same, and that there is a change only in the proportions of its constituent elements, which are produced under different conditions, and that, hence, the market value of the same mass of commodities is differently regulated. Suppose, this mass corresponds in size to the usual supply, leaving aside the possibility that a portion of the produced commodities may be temporarily withdrawn from the market. Should demand for this mass now also remain the same, this commodity will be sold at its market value, no matter which of the three aforementioned cases regulates this market value. This mass of commodities does not merely satisfy a need, but satisfies it to its full social extent. Should their quantity be smaller or greater, however, than the demand for them, there will be deviations of the market price from the market value. And the first deviation is that if the supply is too small, the market value is always regulated by the commodities produced under the least favourable circumstances and, if the supply is too large, always by the commodities produced under the most favourable conditions; that therefore it is one of the extremes which determines the market value, in spite of the fact that in accordance with the mere proportion of the commodity masses produced under different conditions, a different result should obtain. If the difference between demand and the available quantity of the product is more considerable, the market price will likewise be considerably above or below the market value. Now, the difference between the quantity of the produced commodities and that quantity of them at which they are sold at market value may be due to two reasons. Either the quantity itself changes, becoming too small or too large, so that reproduction would have taken place on a different scale than that which regulated the given market value. In that case the supply changed, although demand remained the same, and there was, therefore, relative overproduction or underproduction. Or else reproduction, and thus supply, remained the same, while demand shrank or increased, which may be due to several reasons. Although the absolute magnitude of the supply was the same, its relative magnitude, its magnitude relative to, or measured by, the demand, had changed. The effect is the same as in the first case, but in the reverse direction. Finally, if changes take place on both sides, but either in reverse directions, or, if in the same direction, then not to the same extent, if therefore there are changes on both sides, but these alter the former proportion between the two sides, then the final result must always lead to one of the two above-mentioned cases.

The real difficulty in formulating the general definition of supply and demand is that it seems to take on the appearance of a tautology. First consider the supply — the product available in the market, or that which can be delivered to it. To avoid dwelling upon useless detail, we shall here consider only the mass annually reproduced in every given branch of production and ignore the greater or lesser faculty possessed by the different commodities to be withdrawn from the market and stored away for consumption, say, until next year. This annual reproduction is expressed by a certain quantity — in weight or numbers — depending on whether this mass of commodities is measured in discrete elements or continuously. They are not only use values satisfying human wants, but these use values are available in the market in definite quantities. Secondly, however, this quantity of commodities has a specific market value, which may be expressed by a multiple of the market value of the commodity, or of its measure, which serves as unit. Thus, there is no necessary connection between the quantitative volume of the commodities in the market and their market value, since, for instance, many commodities have a specifically high value, and others a specifically low value, so that a given sum of values may be represented by a very large quantity of one commodity, and a very small quantity of another. There is only the following connection between the quantity of the articles available in the market and the market value of these articles: On a given basis of labour productivity the production of a certain quantity of articles in every particular sphere of production requires a definite quantity of social labour time; although this proportion varies in different spheres of production and has no inner relation to the usefulness of these articles or the special nature of their use values. Assuming all other circumstances to be equal, and a certain quantity a of some commodity to cost b labour time, a quantity na of the same commodity will cost nb labour time. Further, if society wants to satisfy some want and have an article produced for this purpose, it must pay for it. Indeed, since commodity production necessitates a division of labour, society buys this article by devoting a portion of the available labour time to its production. Therefore, society buys it with a definite quantity of its disposable labour time. That part of society which through the division of labour happens to employ its labour in producing this particular article, must receive an equivalent in social labour incorporated in articles which satisfy its own wants. However, there exists an accidental rather than a necessary connection between the total amount of social labour applied to a social article, i. e., between the aliquot part of society's total labour power allocated to producing this article, or between the volume which the production of this article occupies in total production, on the one hand, and the volume whereby society seeks to satisfy the want gratified by the article in question, on the other. Every individual article, or every definite quantity of a commodity may, indeed, contain no more than the social labour required for its production, and from this point of view the market value of this entire commodity represents only necessary labour, but if this commodity has been produced in excess of the existing social needs, then so much of the social labour time is squandered and the mass of the commodity comes to represent a much smaller quantity of social labour in the market than is actually incorporated in it. (It is only where production is under the actual, predetermining control of society that the latter establishes a relation between the volume of social labour time applied in producing definite articles, and the volume of the social want to be satisfied by these articles.) For this reason, these commodities must be sold below their market value, and a portion of them may even be altogether unsaleable. The reverse applies if the quantity of social labour employed in the production of a certain kind of commodity is too small to meet the social demand for that commodity. But if the quantity of social labour expended in the production of a certain article corresponds to the social demand for that article, so that the produced quantity corresponds to the usual scale of reproduction and the demand remains unchanged, then the commodity is sold at its market value. The exchange, or sale, of commodities at their value is the rational state of affairs, i. e., the natural law of their equilibrium. It is this law that explains the deviations, and not vice versa, the deviations that explain the law.

Now let us look at the other side — the demand.

Commodities are bought either as means of production or means of subsistence to enter productive or individual consumption. It does not alter matters that some commodities may serve both purposes. There is, then, a demand for them on the part of producers (here capitalists, since we have assumed that means of production have been transformed into capital) and of consumers. Both appear at first sight to presuppose a given quantity of social want on the side of demand, corresponding on the other side to a definite quantity of social output in the various lines of production. If the cotton industry is to accomplish its annual reproduction on a given scale, it must have the usual supply of cotton, and, other circumstances remaining the same, an additional amount of cotton corresponding to the annual extension of reproduction caused by the accumulation of capital. This is equally true with regard to means of subsistence. The working class must find at least the same quantity of necessities on hand if it is to continue living in its accustomed average way, although they may be more or less differently distributed among the different kinds of commodities. Moreover, there must be an additional quantity to allow for the annual increase of population. The same, with more or less modification, applies to other classes.

It would seem, then, that there is on the side of demand a certain magnitude of definite social wants which require for their satisfaction a definite quantity of a commodity on the market. But quantitatively, the definite social needs are very elastic and changing. Their fixedness is only apparent. If the means of subsistence were cheaper, or money wages higher, the labourers would buy more of them, and a greater "social need" would arise for them, leaving aside the paupers, etc., whose "demand" is even below the narrowest limits of their physical wants. On the other hand, if cotton were cheaper, for example, the capitalists' demand for it would increase, more additional capital would be thrown into the cotton industry, etc. We must never forget that the demand for productive consumption is, under our assumption, a demand of the capitalist, whose essential purpose is the production of surplus value, so that he produces a particular commodity to this sole end. Still, this does not hinder the capitalist, so long as he appears in the market as a buyer of, say, cotton, from representing the need for this cotton, just as it is immaterial to the seller of cotton whether the buyer converts it into shirting or gun-cotton, or whether he intends to turn it into wads for his own, and the world's ears. But this does exert a considerable influence on the kind of buyer the capitalist is. His demand for cotton is substantially modified by the fact that it disguises his real need for making profit. The limits within which the need for commodities in the *market*, the demand, differs quantitatively from the *actual social* need, naturally vary consider-

ably for different commodities; what I mean is the difference between
the demanded quantity of commodities and the quantity which
would have been in demand at other money prices of commodities or
other money or living conditions of the buyers.

Nothing is easier than to realise the inconsistencies of demand and
supply, and the resulting deviation of market prices from market
values. The real difficulty consists in determining what is meant by
the equation of supply and demand.

Supply and demand coincide when their mutual proportions are
such that the mass of commodities of a definite line of production can
be sold at their market value, neither above nor below it. That is the
first thing we hear.

The second is this: If commodities are sold at their market values,
supply and demand coincide.

If supply equals demand, they cease to act, and for this very reason
commodities are sold at their market values. Whenever two forces
operate equally in opposite directions, they balance one another,
exert no outside influence, and any phenomena taking place in these
circumstances must be explained by causes other than the effect of
these two forces. If supply and demand balance one another, they
cease to explain anything, do not affect market values, and therefore
leave us so much more in the dark about the reasons why the market
value is expressed in just this sum of money and no other. It is evident
that the real inner laws of capitalist production cannot be explained
by the interaction of supply and demand (quite aside from a deeper
analysis of these two social motive forces, which would be out of place
here), because these laws cannot be observed in their pure state, until
supply and demand cease to act, i. e., are equated. In reality, supply
and demand never coincide, or, if they do, it is by mere accident,
hence scientifically = 0, and to be regarded as not having occurred. But
political economy assumes that supply and demand coincide with one
another.[a] Why? To be able to study phenomena in their fundamental
relations, in the form corresponding to their conception, that is, to
study them independent of the appearances caused by the movement
of supply and demand. The other reason is to find the actual tendencies of their movements and to some extent to record them. Since the
inconsistencies are of an antagonistic nature, and since they conti-

---

[a] Cf. present edition, Vol. 28, pp. 338-39.

nually succeed one another, they balance out one another through their opposing movements, and their mutual contradiction. Since, therefore, supply and demand never equal one another in any given case, their differences follow one another in such a way — and the result of a deviation in one direction is that it calls forth a deviation in the opposite direction — that supply and demand are always equated when the whole is viewed over a certain period, but only as an average of past movements, and only as the continuous movement of their contradiction. In this way, the market prices which have deviated from the market values adjust themselves, as viewed from the standpoint of their average number, to equal the market values, in that deviations from the latter cancel each other as plus and minus. And this average is not merely of theoretical, but also of practical importance to capital, whose investment is calculated on the fluctuations and compensations of a more or less fixed period.

On the one hand, the relation of demand and supply, therefore, only explains the deviations of market prices from market values. On the other, it explains the tendency to eliminate these deviations, i. e., to eliminate the effect of the relation of demand and supply. (Such exceptions as commodities which have a price without having a value are not considered here.) Supply and demand may eliminate the effect caused by their difference in many different ways. For instance, if the demand, and consequently the market price, fall, capital may be withdrawn, thus causing supply to shrink. It may also be that the market value itself shrinks and balances with the market price as a result of inventions which reduce the necessary labour time. Conversely, if the demand increases, and consequently the market price rises above the market value, this may lead to too much capital flowing into this line of production and production may swell to such an extent that the market price will even fall below the market value. Or, it may lead to a price increase, which cuts the demand. In some lines of production it may also bring about a rise in the market value itself for a shorter or longer period, with a portion of the desired products having to be produced under worse conditions during this period.

Supply and demand determine the market price, and so does the market price, and the market value in the further analysis, determine supply and demand. This is obvious in the case of demand, since it moves in a direction opposite to prices, swelling when prices fall, and vice versa. But this is also true of supply. Because the prices of means of production incorporated in the offered commodities determine the demand for these means of production, and thus the supply of commodities whose supply embraces the demand for these means of production. The prices of cotton are determinants in the supply of cotton goods.

To this confusion — determining prices through demand and supply, and, at the same time, determining supply and demand through prices — must be added that demand determines supply, just as supply determines demand, and production determines the market, as well as the market determines production.[31]

Even the ordinary economist (see footnote) agrees that the proportion between supply and demand may vary in consequence of a change in the market value of commodities, without a change being brought about in demand or supply by extraneous circumstances. Even he must admit that, whatever the market value, supply and demand must coincide in order for it to be established. In other words, the ratio of supply to demand does not explain the market value, but

---

[31] The following subtility is sheer nonsense: "Where the quantity of wages, capital, and land, required to produce an article, are become different from what they were, that which Adam Smith calls the natural price of it, is also different, and that price, which was previously its natural price, becomes, with reference to this alteration, its market price; because, though neither the supply, nor the quantity wanted, may have been changed" — both of them change here, just because the market value, or in the case of Adam Smith, the price of production, changes in consequence of a change of value — "that supply is not now exactly enough for those persons who are able and willing to pay what is now the cost of production, but is either greater or less than that; so that the proportion between the supply and what is with reference to the new cost of production the effectual demand, is different from what it was. An alteration in the rate of supply will then take place, if there is no obstacle in the way of it, and at last bring the commodity to its new natural price. It may then seem good to some persons to say that, as the commodity gets to its natural price by an alteration in its supply, the natural price is as much owing to one proportion between the demand and supply, as the market price is to another; and consequently, that the natural price, just as much as the market price, depends on the proportion that demand and supply bear to each other." ("The great principle of demand and supply is called into action to determine what A. Smith calls natural prices as well as market prices." — Malthus.[a]) (*Observations on Certain Verbal Disputes, etc.*, London, 1821, pp. 60-61.) The good man does not grasp the fact that it is precisely the change in the cost of production, and thus in the value, which caused a change in the demand, in the present case, and thus in the proportion between demand and supply, and that this change in the demand may bring about a change in the supply. This would prove just the reverse of what our good thinker wants to prove. It would prove that the change in the cost of production is by no means due to the proportion of demand and supply, but rather regulates this proportion.

---

[a] *Principles of Political Economy*, London, 1820, p. 75.

conversely, the latter rather explains the fluctuations of supply and demand. The author of the *Observations* continues after the passage quoted in the footnote:

*"This proportion" * (between demand and supply), * "however, if we still mean by 'demand' and 'natural price', what we meant just now, when referring to Adam Smith, must always be a proportion of equality; for it is only when the supply is equal to the effectual demand, that is, to that demand which will neither more nor less than pay the natural price, that the natural price is in fact paid; consequently, there may be two very different natural prices, at different times, for the same commodity, and yet the proportion, which the supply bears to the demand, be in both cases the same, namely, the proportion of equality." *

It is admitted, then, that with two different NATURAL PRICES of the same commodity, at different times, demand and supply are always able to, and must, balance one another if the commodity is to be sold at its NATURAL PRICE in both instances. Since there is no difference in the ratio of supply to demand in either case, but a difference in the magnitude of the NATURAL PRICE itself, it follows that this price is obviously determined independently of demand and supply, and thus that it can least of all be determined by them.

For a commodity to be sold at its market value, i. e., proportionally to the necessary social labour contained in it, the total quantity of social labour used in producing the total mass of this commodity must correspond to the quantity of the social want for it, i. e., the effective social want. Competition, the fluctuations of market prices which correspond to the fluctuations in the ratio of demand to supply, tend continually to reduce to this scale the total quantity of labour devoted to each kind of commodity.

The proportion of supply and demand recapitulates, first, the relation of use value to exchange value, of commodity to money, and of buyer to seller; and, second, that of producer to consumer, although both of them may be represented by third parties, the merchants. In considering buyer and seller, it suffices to counterpose them individually in order to present their relationship. Three individuals are enough for the complete metamorphosis of a commodity, and therefore for the process of sale and purchase taken as a whole. A converts his commodity into the money of B, to whom he sells his commodity, and reconverts his money again into commodities, when he uses it to make purchases from C; the whole process takes place among these three. Further, in the study of money it had been assumed that the commodities are sold at their values because there was absolutely no reason to consider prices divergent from values, it being merely a matter of changes of form which commodities undergo in their transformation into money and their reconversion from money into commodities.[a] As soon as a commodity has been sold and a new commodity bought with the receipts, we have before us the entire metamorphosis, and to this process as such it is immaterial whether the price of the commodity lies above or below its value. The value of the commodity remains important as a basis, because the concept of money cannot be developed on any other foundation, and price, in its general meaning, is but value in the form of money. At any rate, it is assumed in the study of money as a medium of circulation that there is not just *one* metamorphosis of a certain commodity. It is rather the social interrelation of these metamorphoses which is studied. Only thus do we arrive at the circulation of money and the development of its function as a medium of circulation. But however important this connection may be for the conversion of money into a circulating medium, and for its resulting change of form, it is of no moment to the transaction between individual buyers and sellers.

In the case of supply and demand, however, the supply is equal to the sum of sellers, or producers, of a certain kind of commodity, and the demand equals the sum of buyers, or consumers (both productive and individual) of the same kind of commodity. The sums react on one another as units, as aggregate forces. The individual counts here only as part of a social force, as an atom of the mass, and it is in this form that competition brings out the *social* character of production and consumption.

The side of competition which happens for the moment to be weaker is also the side in which the individual acts independently of, and often directly against, the mass of his competitors, and precisely in this manner is the dependence of one upon the other impressed upon them, while the stronger side acts always more or less as a united whole against its antagonist. If the demand for this particular kind of commodity is greater than the supply, one buyer outbids another — within certain limits — and so raises the price of the commodity for all of them above the market value,[b] while on the other hand the sellers unite in trying to sell at a high market price. If, conversely, the supply exceeds the demand, one begins to dispose of his

---

[a] See present edition, Vol. 35, pp. 113-14. - [b] In the 1894 German edition "market price".

goods at a cheaper rate and the others must follow, while the buyers unite in their efforts to depress the market price as much as possible below the market value. The common interest is appreciated by each only so long as he gains more by it than without it. And unity of action ceases the moment one or the other side becomes the weaker, when each tries to extricate himself on his own as advantageously as he possibly can. Again, if one produces more cheaply and can sell more goods, thus possessing himself of a greater place in the market by selling below the current market price, or market value, he will do so, and will thereby begin a movement which gradually compels the others to introduce the cheaper mode of production, and one which reduces the socially necessary labour to a new, and lower, level. If one side has the advantage, all belonging to it gain. It is as though they exerted their common monopoly. If one side is weaker, then one may try on his own hook to become the stronger (for instance, one who works with lower costs of production), or at least to get off as lightly as possible, and in such cases each for himself and the devil take the hindmost, although his actions affect not only himself, but also all his boon companions.[32]

Demand and supply imply the conversion of value into market value, and so far as they proceed on a capitalist basis, so far as the commodities are products of capital, they are based on capitalist production processes, i. e., on quite different relationships than the mere purchase and sale of goods. Here it is not a question of the formal conversion of the value of commodities into prices, i. e., not of a mere change of form. It is a question of definite deviations in quantity of the market prices from the market values, and, further, from the prices of production. In simple purchase and sale it suffices to have the producers of commodities as such counterposed to one another. In further analysis supply and demand presuppose the existence of different classes and sections of classes which divide the total revenue of a society and consume it among themselves as revenue, and, therefore, make up the demand created by revenue. While on the other hand it

---

[32] "If each man of a class could never have more than a given share, or aliquot part, of the gains and possessions of the whole, he would readily combine to raise the gain"; (he does it as soon as the proportion of demand to supply permits it) "this is monopoly. But where each man thinks that he may anyway increase the absolute amount of his own share, though by a process which lessens the whole amount, he will often do it; this is competition" (*An Inquiry into Those Principles Respecting the Nature of Demand, etc.*, London, 1821, p. 105).

requires an insight into the overall structure of the capitalist production process for an understanding of the supply and demand created among themselves by producers as such.

Under capitalist production it is not merely a matter of obtaining an equal mass of value in another form — be it that of money or some other commodity — for a mass of values thrown into circulation in the form of a commodity, but it is rather a matter of realising as much surplus value, or profit, on capital advanced for production, as any other capital of the same magnitude, or *pro rata* to its magnitude in whichever line it is applied. It is, therefore, a matter, at least as a minimum, of selling the commodities at prices which yield the average profit, i. e., at prices of production. In this form capital becomes conscious of itself as a *social power* in which every capitalist participates proportionally to his share in the total social capital.

First, capitalist production is in itself indifferent to the particular use value, and distinctive features of any commodity it produces. In every sphere of production it is only concerned with producing surplus value, and appropriating a certain quantity of unpaid labour incorporated in the product of labour. And it is likewise in the nature of the wage labour subordinated by capital that it is indifferent to the specific character of its labour and must submit to being transformed in accordance with the requirements of capital and to being transferred from one sphere of production to another.

Second, one sphere of production is, in fact, just as good or just as bad as another. Every one of them yields the same profit, and every one of them would be useless if the commodities it produced did not satisfy some social need.

Now, if the commodities are sold at their values, then, as we have shown, very different rates of profit arise in the various spheres of production, depending on the different organic composition of the masses of capital invested in them. But capital withdraws from a sphere with a low rate of profit and invades others, which yield a higher profit. Through this incessant outflow and influx, or, briefly, through its distribution among the various spheres, which depends on how the rate of profit falls here and rises there, it creates such a ratio of supply to demand that the average profit in the various spheres of production becomes the same, and values are, therefore, converted into prices of production. Capital succeeds in this equalisation, to a greater or lesser degree, depending on the extent of capitalist development in the given nation; i. e., on the extent the conditions in the country in question are adapted for the capitalist mode of production. With the progress of capitalist production, it also develops its own conditions and subordinates to its specific character and its immanent laws all the social prerequisites on which the production process is based.

The incessant equilibration of constant divergences is accomplished so much more quickly, 1) the more mobile the capital, i. e., the more easily it can be shifted from one sphere and from one place to another; 2) the more quickly labour power can be transferred from one sphere to another and from one production locality to another. The first condition implies complete freedom of trade within the society and the removal of all monopolies with the exception of the natural ones, those, that is, which naturally arise out of the capitalist mode of production. It implies, furthermore, the development of the credit system, which concentrates the inorganic mass of the disposable social capital vis-à-vis the individual capitalist. Finally, it implies the subordination of the various spheres of production to the control of capitalists. This last implication is included in our premises, since we assumed that it was a matter of converting values into prices of production in all capitalistically exploited spheres of production. But this equilibration itself runs into greater obstacles, whenever numerous and large spheres of production not operated on a capitalist basis (such as soil cultivation by small farmers), filter in between the capitalist enterprises and become linked with them. A great density of population is another requirement.— The second condition implies the abolition of all laws preventing the labourers from transferring from one sphere of production to another and from one local centre of production to another; indifference of the labourer to the nature of his labour; the greatest possible reduction of labour in all spheres of production to simple labour; the elimination of all vocational prejudices among labourers; and last but not least, a subjugation of the labourer to the capitalist mode of production. Further reference to this belongs to a special analysis of competition.

It follows from the foregoing that in each particular sphere of production the individual capitalist, as well as the capitalists as a whole, take direct part in the exploitation of the total working class by the totality of capital and in the degree of that exploitation, not only out of general class sympathy, but also for direct economic reasons. For, assuming all other conditions — among them the value of the total advanced constant capital — to be given, the average rate of profit depends on the intensity of exploitation of the sum total of labour by the sum total of capital.

The average profit coincides with the average surplus value produced for each 100 of capital, and so far as the surplus value is concerned the foregoing statements apply as a matter of course. In the case of the average profit the value of the advanced capital becomes an additional element determining the rate of profit. In fact, the direct interest taken by the capitalist, or the capital, of any individual sphere of production in the exploitation of the labourers who are directly employed is confined to making an extra gain, a profit exceeding the average, either through exceptional overwork, or reduction of the wage below the average, or through the exceptional productivity of the labour employed. Aside from this, a capitalist who would not in his line of production employ any variable capital, and therefore any labourer (in reality an exaggerated assumption), would nonetheless be as much interested in the exploitation of the working class by capital, and would derive his profit quite as much from unpaid surplus labour, as, say, a capitalist who would employ only variable capital (another exaggeration), and who would thus invest his entire capital in wages. But the degree of exploitation of labour depends on the average intensity of labour if the working day is given, and on the length of the working day if the intensity of exploitation is given. The degree of exploitation of labour determines the rate of surplus value, and therefore the mass of surplus value for a given total mass of variable capital, and consequently the magnitude of the profit. The individual capitalist, as distinct from his sphere as a whole, has the same special interest in exploiting the labourers he personally employs as the capital of a particular sphere, as distinct from the sum total of capital, has in exploiting the labourers directly employed in that sphere.

On the other hand, every particular sphere of capital, and every individual capitalist, have the same interest in the productivity of the social labour employed by the sum total of capital. For two things depend on this productivity: First, the mass of use values in which the average profit is expressed; and this is doubly important, since this average profit serves as a fund for the accumulation of new capital and as a fund for revenue to be spent for consumption. Second, the value of the total capital advanced (constant and variable), which, the amount of surplus value, or profit, for the whole capitalist class being given, determines the rate of profit, or the profit on a certain quantity of capital. The special productivity of labour in any particular sphere, or in any individual enterprise of this sphere, is of interest only to those capitalists who are directly engaged in it, since it enables that particular sphere, vis-à-vis the total capital, or that individual capitalist, vis-à-vis his sphere, to make an extra profit.

Here, then, we have a mathematically precise proof why capitalists form a veritable freemason society vis-à-vis the whole working class, while there is little love lost between them in competition among themselves.

The price of production includes the average profit. We call it price of production. It is really what Adam Smith calls NATURAL PRICE, Ricardo calls PRICE OF PRODUCTION, or COST OF PRODUCTION, and the Physiocrats call *prix nécessaire*, because in the long run it is a prerequisite of supply, of the reproduction of commodities in every individual sphere.[33] But none of them has revealed the difference between price of production and value. We can well understand why the same economists who oppose determining the value of commodities by labour time, i. e., by the quantity of labour contained in them, why they always speak of prices of production as centres around which market prices fluctuate. They can afford to do it because the price of production is an utterly external and *prima facie* meaningless form of the value of commodities, a form as it appears in competition, therefore in the mind of the vulgar capitalist, and consequently in that of the vulgar economist.

Our analysis has revealed how the market value (and everything said concerning it applies with appropriate modifications to the price of production) embraces a surplus profit for those who produce in any particular sphere of production under the most favourable conditions. With the exception of crises, and of overproduction in general, this applies to all market prices, no matter how much they may deviate from market values or market prices of production. For the market price signifies that the same price is paid for commodities of the same kind, although they may have been produced under very different individual conditions and hence may have considerably different cost prices. (We do not speak at this point of any surplus profits due

[33] Malthus.[a]

---

[a] *Principles of Political Economy*, London, 1836, p. 77 et seq.

to monopolies in the usual sense of the term, whether artificial or natural.)

A surplus profit may also arise if certain spheres of production are in a position to evade the conversion of the values of their commodities into prices of production, and thus the reduction of their profits to the average profit. We shall devote more attention to the further modifications of these two forms of surplus profit in the part dealing with ground rent.

Chapter XI

EFFECTS OF GENERAL WAGE FLUCTUATIONS
ON PRICES OF PRODUCTION

Let the average composition of social capital be $80_c + 20_v$, and the profit 20%. The rate of surplus value is then 100%. A general increase of wages, all else remaining the same, is tantamount to a reduction in the rate of surplus value. In the case of average capital, profit and surplus value are identical. Let wages rise 25%. Then the same quantity of labour, formerly set in motion with 20, will cost 25. We shall then have a turnover value of $80_c + 25_v + 15_p$ instead of $80_c + 20_v + 20_p$. As before, the labour set in motion by the variable capital produces a value of 40. If v rises from 20 to 25, the surplus s, or p, will amount to only 15. The profit of 15 on 105 is $14\frac{2}{7}\%$, and this would be the new average rate of profit. Since the price of production of commodities produced by the average capital coincides with their value, the price of production of these commodities would have remained inchanged. A wage increase would therefore have caused a drop in profit, but no change in the value and price of the commodities.

Formerly, as long as the average profit was 20%, the price of production of commodities produced in one period of turnover was equal to their cost price plus a profit of 20% on this cost price, therefore $= k + kp' = k + \frac{20k}{100}$. In this formula k is a variable magnitude, changing in accordance with the value of the means of production that go into the commodities, and with the amount of depreciation given up to the product by the fixed capital employed in its production. The price of production would then amount to $k + \frac{14\frac{2}{7}k}{100}$.

Let us now select a capital, whose composition is lower than the original composition of the average social capital of $80_c + 20_v$ (which has now changed into $76\frac{4}{21}{}_c + 23\frac{17}{21}{}_v$); say, $50_c + 50_v$. In this case, the price of production of the annual product before the wage increase would have been $50_c + 50_v + 20_p = 120$, assuming for the sake of simplicity that the entire fixed capital passes through depreciation into the annual product and that the period of turnover is the same as in the first case. For the same quantity of labour set in motion a wage increase of 25% means an increase of the variable capital from 50 to $62\frac{1}{2}$. If the annual product were sold at the former price of production of 120, this would give us $50_c + 62\frac{1}{2}{}_v + 7\frac{1}{2}{}_p$, or a rate of profit of $6\frac{2}{3}\%$. But the new average rate of profit is $14\frac{2}{7}\%$, and since we assume all other circumstances to remain the same, the capital of $50_c + 62\frac{1}{2}{}_v$ must also make this profit. Now, a capital of $112\frac{1}{2}$ makes a profit of $16\frac{1}{14}$ at a rate of profit of $14\frac{2}{7}\%$. Therefore, the price of production of the commodities produced by this capital is now $50_c + 62\frac{1}{2}{}_v + 16\frac{1}{14}{}_p = 128\frac{8}{14}$. Owing to a wage rise of 25%, the price of production of the same quantity of the same commodities, therefore, has here risen from 120 to $128\frac{8}{14}$, or more than 7%.

Conversely, suppose we take a sphere of production of a higher composition than the average capital; say, $92_c + 8_v$. The original average profit in this case would still be 20, and if we again assume that the entire fixed capital passes into the annual product and that the period of turnover is the same as in cases I and II, the price of production of the commodity is here also 120.

Owing to the rise in wages of 25% the variable capital for the same quantity of labour rises from 8 to 10, the cost price of the commodities from 100 to 102, while the average rate of profit falls from 20% to $14\frac{2}{7}\%$. But $100:14\frac{2}{7} = 102:14\frac{4}{7}$. The profit now falling to the share of 102 is therefore $14\frac{4}{7}$. For this reason, the total product sells at $k + kp' = 102 + 14\frac{4}{7} = 116\frac{4}{7}$. The price of production has therefore fallen from 120 to $116\frac{4}{7}$, or $3\frac{3}{7}$.

Consequently, if wages are raised 25%:

1) the price of production of the commodities of a capital of average social composition does not change;

2) the price of production of the commodities of a capital of lower composition rises, but not in proportion to the fall in profit;

3) the price of production of the commodities of a capital of higher composition falls, but also not in the same proportion as profit.

Since the price of production of the commodities of the average capital remained the same, equal to the value of the product, the sum of the prices of production of the products of all capitals remained the same as well, and equal to the sum total of the values produced by the aggregate capital. The increase on one side and the decrease on the other balance for the aggregate capital on the level of the average social capital.

If the price of production rises in case II and falls in case III, these opposite effects alone, which are brought about by a fall in the rate of surplus value or by a general wage increase, show that this cannot be a matter of compensation in the price for the rise in wages, since the fall in the price of production in case III cannot compensate the capitalist for the fall in profit, and since the rise of the price in case II does not prevent a fall in profit. Rather, in either case, whether the price rises or falls, the profit remains the same as that of the average capital, in which case the price remains unchanged. It is the same average profit which has fallen by $5\frac{5}{7}$, or somewhat over 25%, in the case of II as well as III. It follows from this that if the price did not rise in II and fall in III, II would have to sell below and III above the new reduced average profit. It is self-evident that, depending on whether 50, 25, or 10 per 100 units of capital are laid out for labour, the effect of a wage increase on a capitalist who has invested $\frac{1}{10}$ of his capital in wages must be quite different from that on one who has invested $\frac{1}{4}$ or $\frac{1}{2}$. An increase in the price of production on the one side, a fall on the other, depending on a capital being below or above the average social composition, occurs solely by virtue of the process of levelling the profit to the new reduced average profit.

How would a general reduction in wages, and a corresponding general rise of the rate of profit, and thus of the average profit, now affect the prices of production of commodities produced by capitals deviating in opposite directions from the average social composition? We have but to reverse the foregoing exposition to obtain the result (which Ricardo fails to analyse).

I. Average capital $= 80_c + 20_v = 100$; rate of surplus value $= 100\%$; price of production $=$ value of commodities $= 80_c + 20_v + 20_p = 120$; rate of profit $= 20\%$. Suppose wages fall by one-fourth. Then the same constant capital is set in motion by 15_v, instead of 20_v. Then the value of commodities $= 80_c + 15_v + 25_p = 120$. The quantity of labour performed by v remains unchanged, except that the value newly created by it is distributed differently between the capitalist and the labourer. The surplus value rises from 20 to 25 and the rate of surplus value from $\frac{20}{20}$ to $\frac{25}{15}$ or from 100% to $166\frac{2}{3}\%$. The profit on 95 now $= 25$, so that the rate of profit per $100 = 26\frac{6}{19}$. The new composition of the capital in per cent is now $84\frac{4}{19}\,_c + 15\frac{15}{19}\,_v = 100$.

II. Lower composition. Originally $50_c + 50_v$, as above. Due to the fall of wages by $\frac{1}{4}$ v is reduced to $37\frac{1}{2}$, and consequently the advanced total capital to $50_c + 37\frac{1}{2}\,_v = 87\frac{1}{2}$. If we apply the new rate of profit of $26\frac{6}{19}\%$ to this, we get $100 : 26\frac{6}{19} = 87\frac{1}{2} : 23\frac{1}{38}$. The same mass of commodities which formerly cost 120, now costs $87\frac{1}{2} + 23\frac{1}{38} = 110\frac{10}{19}$, this being a price reduction of almost 10.

III. Higher composition. Originally $92_c + 8_v = 100$. The reduction of wages by $\frac{1}{4}$ reduces 8_v to 6_v, and the total capital to 98. Consequently, $100 : 26\frac{6}{19} = 98 : 25\frac{15}{19}$. The price of production of the commodity, formerly $100 + 20 = 120$, is now, after the fall in wages, $98 + 25\frac{15}{19} = 123\frac{15}{19}$, this being a rise of almost 4.

It is evident, therefore, that we have but to follow the same development in the opposite direction with the appropriate modifications; that a general reduction of wages is attended by a general rise of surplus value, of the rate of surplus value and, other circumstances remaining the same, of the rate of profit, even if expressed in a different proportion; a fall in the prices of production for commodities produced by capitals of lower composition, and a rise in the prices of production for commodities produced by capitals of higher composition. The result is just the reverse of that observed for a general rise of wages.[34] In both cases — rise or fall of wages — it is assumed that the

---

[34] It is very peculiar that Ricardo[a] (who naturally proceeds differently from us, since he did not understand the levelling of values to prices of production) did not once consider this eventuality, but only the first case, that of a wage rise and its influence on the prices of production of commodities. And the *servum pecus imitatorum*[b] did not even attempt to make this extremely self-evident, actually tautological, practical application.

---

[a] D. Ricardo, *On the Principles of Political Economy...*, pp. 36-41. Cf. present edition, Vol. 31, pp. 421-22. - [b] Horace, *Epistles*, I, 19.

working day remains the same, and also the prices of all the necessary means of subsistence. In these circumstances a fall in wages is possible only if they stood higher than the normal price of labour, or if they are depressed below this price. The way in which the matter is modified if the rise or fall of wages is due to a change in value, and consequently the price of production of commodities usually consumed by the labourer, will be analysed at some length in the part dealing with ground rent. At this point, however, the following remarks are to be made once and for all:

Should the rise or fall in wages be due to a change in the value of the necessities of life, a modification of the foregoing findings can take place only to the extent that commodities, whose change of price raises or lowers the variable capital, also go into the constant capital as constituent elements and therefore affect more than just the wages alone. But if they affect only wages, the above analysis contains all that needs to be said.

In this entire chapter, the establishment of the general rate of profit and the average profit, and consequently, the transformation of values into prices of production, are assumed as given. The question merely was, how a general rise or fall in wages affected the assumed prices of production of commodities. This is but a very secondary question compared with the other important points analysed in this part. But it is the only relevant question treated by Ricardo, and, as we shall see,[32] he treated it one-sidedly and unsatisfactorily.

Chapter XII

SUPPLEMENTARY REMARKS

I. CAUSES IMPLYING A CHANGE IN THE PRICE OF PRODUCTION

There are just two causes that can change the price of production of a commodity:

First. A change in the general rate of profit. This can solely be due to a change in the average rate of surplus value, or, if the average rate of surplus value remains the same, to a change in the ratio of the sum of the appropriated surplus values to the sum of the advanced total social capital.

If the change in the rate of surplus value is not due to a depression of wages below normal, or their rise above normal — and movements of that kind are to be regarded merely as oscillations — it can only occur either through a rise, or fall, in the value of labour power, the one being just as impossible as the other unless there is a change in the productivity of the labour producing means of subsistence, i. e., in the value of commodities consumed by the labourer.

Or, through a change in the proportion of the sum of appropriated surplus values to the advanced total capital of society. Since the change in this case is not caused by the rate of surplus value, it must be caused by the total capital, or rather its constant part. The mass of this part, technically considered, increases or decreases in proportion to the quantity of labour power bought by the variable capital, and the mass of its value thus increases or decreases with the increase or decrease of its own mass. It also increases or decreases, therefore, proportionately to the mass of the value of the variable capital. If the same labour sets more constant capital in motion, it has become more productive. If the reverse, then less productive. Thus, there has been a change in the productivity of labour, and there must have occurred a change in the value of certain commodities.

The following law, then, applies to both cases: If the price of production of a commodity changes in consequence of a change in the general rate of profit, its own value may have remained unchanged. However, a change must have occurred in the value of other commodities.

Second. The general rate of profit remains unchanged. In this case the price of production of a commodity can change only if its own value has changed. This may be due to more, or less, labour being required to reproduce the commodity in question, either because of a change in the productivity of labour which produces this commodity in its final form, or of the labour which produces those commodities that go into its production. The price of production of cotton yarn may fall, either because raw cotton is produced cheaper than before, or because the labour of spinning has become more productive due to improved machinery.

The price of production, as we have seen, $= k + p$, equal to cost price plus profit. This, however, $= k + kp'$, in which k, the cost price, is a variable magnitude, which changes for different spheres of production and is everywhere equal to the value of the constant and variable capital consumed in the production of the commodity, and p' is the average rate of profit in percentage form. If $k = 200$,

and p′ = 20%, the price of production k + kp′ = 200 +
+ 200 · $\frac{20}{100}$ = 200 + 40 = 240. This price of production may clearly
remain the same, in spite of a change in the value of the commodities.

All changes in the price of production of commodities are reduced,
in the last analysis, to changes in value. But not all changes in the
value of commodities need express themselves in changes in the price
of production. The price of production is not determined by the value
of any one commodity alone, but by the aggregate value of all commodities. A change in commodity A may therefore be balanced by an
opposite change in commodity B, so that the general relation remains
the same.

II. PRICE OF PRODUCTION OF COMMODITIES OF AVERAGE COMPOSITION

We have seen how a deviation in prices of production from values
arises from:

1) adding the average profit instead of the surplus value contained
in a commodity to its cost price;

2) the price of production, which so deviates from the value of
a commodity, entering into the cost price of other commodities as one
of its elements, so that the cost price of a commodity may already
contain a deviation from the value of the means of production consumed by it, quite aside from a deviation of its own which may arise
through a difference between the average profit and the surplus
value.

It is therefore possible that even the cost price of commodities produced by capitals of average composition may differ from the sum of
the values of the elements which make up this component of their
price of production. Suppose, the average composition is $80_c + 20_v$.
Now, it is possible that in the actual capitals of this composition 80_c
may be greater or smaller than the value of c, i. e., the constant capital, because this c may be made up of commodities whose price of
production differs from their value. In the same way, 20_v might diverge from its value if the consumption of the wage includes commodities whose price of production diverges from their value; in which
case the labourer would work a longer, or shorter, time to buy them
back (to replace them) and would thus perform more, or less, necessary labour than would be required if the price of production of such
necessities of life coincided with their value.

However, this possibility does not detract in the least from the correctness of the theorems demonstrated which hold for commodities of average composition. The quantity of profit falling to these commodities is equal to the quantity of surplus value contained in them. For instance, in a capital of the given composition $80_c + 20_v$, the most important thing in determining surplus value is not whether these figures are expressions of actual values, but how they are related to one another, i. e., whether $v = \frac{1}{5}$ of the total capital, and $c = \frac{4}{5}$. Whenever this is the case, the surplus value produced by v is, as was assumed, equal to the average profit. On the other hand, since it equals the average profit, the price of production = cost price + profit = $k + p = k + s$; i. e., in practice it is equal to the value of the commodity. This implies that a rise or fall in wages would not change $k + p$ any more than it would change the value of the commodities, and would merely effect a corresponding opposite movement, a fall or a rise, in the rate of profit. For if a rise or fall of wages were here to bring about a change in the price of commodities, the rate of profit in these spheres of average composition would rise above, or fall below, the level prevailing in other spheres. The sphere of average composition maintains the same level of profit as the other spheres only so long as the price remains unchanged. The practical result is therefore the same as it would be if its products were sold at their real value. For if commodities are sold at their actual values, it is evident that, other conditions being equal, a rise, or fall, in wages will cause a corresponding fall or rise in profit, but no change in the value of commodities, and that under all circumstances a rise or fall in wages can never affect the value of commodities, but only the magnitude of the surplus value.

III. THE CAPITALIST'S GROUNDS FOR COMPENSATING

It has been said that competition levels the rates of profit of the different spheres of production into an average rate of profit and thereby turns the values of the products of these different spheres into prices of production. This occurs through the continual transfer of capital from one sphere to another, in which, for the moment, the profit happens to lie above average. The fluctuations of profit caused by the cycle of fat and lean years succeeding one another in any given branch of industry within given periods must, however, receive due consideration. This incessant outflow and inflow of capital between the different spheres of production creates trends of rise and fall in the rate of profit, which equalise one another more or less and thus have a tendency to reduce the rate of profit everywhere to the same common and general level.

This movement of capitals is primarily caused by the level of market prices, which lift profits above the general average in one place and depress them below it in another. Merchant's capital is left out of consideration as it is irrelevant at this point, for we know from the sudden paroxysms of speculation appearing in certain popular articles that it can withdraw masses of capital from one line of business with extraordinary rapidity and throw them with equal rapidity into another. Yet with respect to each sphere of actual production — industry, agriculture, mining, etc.— the transfer of capital from one sphere to another offers considerable difficulties, particularly on account of the existing fixed capital. Experience shows, moreover, that if a branch of industry, such as, say, the cotton industry, yields unusually high profits at one period, it makes very little profit, or even suffers losses, at another, so that in a certain cycle of years the average profit is much the same as in other branches. And capital soon learns to take this experience into account.

What competition does *not* show, however, is the determination of value, which dominates the movement of production; and the values that lie beneath the prices of production and that determine them in the last instance. Competition, on the other hand, shows: 1) the average profits, which are independent of the organic composition of capital in the different spheres of production, and therefore also of the mass of living labour appropriated by any given capital in any given sphere of exploitation; 2) the rise and fall of prices of production caused by changes in the level of wages, a phenomenon which at first glance completely contradicts the value relation of commodities; 3) the fluctuations of market prices, which reduce the average market price of commodities in a given period of time, not to the market *value*, but to a very different market price of production, which diverges considerably from this market value. All these phenomena *seem* to contradict the determination of value by labour time as much as the nature of surplus value consisting of unpaid surplus labour. *Thus everything appears reversed in competition.* The final pattern of economic relations as seen on the surface, in their real existence and consequently in the conceptions by which the bearers and agents of these relations seek to understand them, is very much different from, and indeed quite the reverse of, their inner but concealed essential pattern and the conception corresponding to it.[a]

Further. As soon as capitalist production reaches a certain level of development, the equalisation of the different rates of profit in individual spheres to general rate of profit no longer proceeds solely through the play of attraction and repulsion, by which market prices attract or repel capital. After average prices, and their corresponding market prices, become stable for a time it reaches the *consciousness* of the individual capitalists that this equalisation balances *definite differences*, so that they include these in their mutual calculations. The differences exist in the mind of the capitalist and are taken into account as grounds for compensating.

Average profit is the basic conception, the conception that capitals of equal magnitude must yield equal profits in equal time spans. This, again, is based on the conception that the capital in each sphere of production must share *pro rata* to its magnitude in the total surplus value squeezed out of the labourers by the total social capital; or, that every individual capital should be regarded merely as a part of the total capital, and every capitalist actually as a shareholder in the total enterprise, each sharing in the total profit *pro rata* to the magnitude of his share of capital.

This conception serves as a basis for the capitalist's calculations, for instance, that a capital whose turnover is slower than another's because its commodities take longer to be produced, or because they are sold in remoter markets, nevertheless charges the profit it loses in this way, and compensates itself by raising the price. Or else, that investments of capital in lines exposed to greater hazards, for instance in shipping, are compensated by higher prices. As soon as capitalist production, and with it the insurance business, are developed, the hazards are, in effect, made equal for all spheres of production (cf. Corbet[b]); but the more hazardous lines pay higher insurance rates, and recover them in the prices of their commodities. In practice all this means that every circumstance, which renders one line of production — and all of them are considered equally necessary within certain limits — less profitable, and another more profitable, is taken in-

---

[a] Cf. present edition, Vol. 33, p. 102. - [b] Th. Corbet, *An Inquiry into the Causes and Modes of the Wealth of Individuals...*, London, 1841, pp. 100-02. Cf. present edition, Vol. 33, pp. 243 and 281.

to account once and for all as valid ground for compensation, without always requiring the renewed action of competition to justify the motives or factors for calculating this compensation. The capitalist simply forgets — or rather fails to see, because competition does not point it out to him — that all these grounds for compensation mutually advanced by capitalists in calculating the prices of commodities of different lines of production merely come down to the fact that they all have an equal claim, *pro rata* to the magnitude of their respective capitals, to the common loot, the total surplus value. It rather *seems* to them that since the profit pocketed by them differs from the surplus value they squeezed out, these grounds for compensation do not level out their participation in the total surplus value, but *create the profit itself*, which seems to be derived from the additions made on one or another ground to the cost price of their commodities.

In other respects the statements made in Chapter VII, p. 116,[a] concerning the capitalists' assumptions as to source of surplus value, apply also to average profit. The present case appears different only in so far as a saving in cost price depends on individual business acumen, alertness, etc., assuming the market price of commodities and the exploitation of labour to be given.

---

[a] See this volume, p. 137.

Part III

THE LAW OF THE TENDENCY
OF THE RATE OF PROFIT TO FALL

Chapter XIII

THE LAW AS SUCH

Assuming a given wage and working day, a variable capital, for instance of 100, represents a certain number of employed labourers. It is the index of this number. Suppose £100 are the wages of 100 labourers for, say, one week. If these labourers perform equal amounts of necessary and surplus labour, if they work daily as many hours for themselves, i. e., for the reproduction of their wage, as they do for the capitalist, i. e., for the production of surplus value, then the value of their total product = £200, and the surplus value they produce would amount to £100. The rate of surplus value, $\frac{s}{v}$, would = 100%. But, as we have seen, this rate of surplus value would nonetheless express itself in very different rates of profit, depending on the different volumes of constant capital c and consequently of the total capital C, because the rate of profit = $\frac{s}{C}$. The rate of surplus value is 100%:

If c = 50, and v = 100, then p′ = $\frac{100}{150}$ = 66 $^2/_3$%;

" c = 100, and v = 100, then p′ = $\frac{100}{200}$ = 50%;

" c = 200, and v = 100, then p′ = $\frac{100}{300}$ = 33 $^1/_3$%;

" c = 300, and v = 100, then p′ = $\frac{100}{400}$ = 25%;

" c = 400, and v = 100, then p′ = $\frac{100}{500}$ = 20%.

This is how the same rate of surplus value would express itself under the same degree of labour exploitation in a falling rate of profit, because the material growth of the constant capital implies also

a growth — albeit not in the same proportion — in its value, and consequently in that of the total capital.[a]

If it is further assumed that this gradual change in the composition
of capital is not confined only to individual spheres of production, but
that it occurs more or less in all, or at least in the key spheres of production, so that it involves changes in the average organic composition of the total capital of a certain society, then the gradual growth
of constant capital in relation to variable capital must necessarily
lead to *a gradual fall of the general rate of profit*, so long as the rate of surplus value, or the intensity of exploitation of labour by capital, remain the same. Now we have seen that it is a law of capitalist production that its development is attended by a relative decrease of variable in relation to constant capital, and consequently to the total capital set in motion.[b] This is just another way of saying that owing to
the distinctive methods of production developing in the capitalist system the same number of labourers, i. e., the same quantity of labour
power set in motion by a variable capital of a given value, operate,
work up and productively consume in the same time span an ever-
increasing quantity of means of labour, machinery and fixed capital
of all sorts, raw and auxiliary materials — and consequently a constant capital of an ever-increasing value. This continual relative decrease of the variable capital vis-à-vis the constant, and consequently
the total capital, is identical with the progressively higher organic
composition of the social capital in its average. It is likewise just another expression for the progressive development of the social productive
power of labour, which is demonstrated precisely by the fact that
the same number of labourers, in the same time, i. e., with less
labour, convert an ever-increasing quantity of raw and auxiliary materials into products, thanks to the growing application of machinery
and fixed capital in general. To this growing quantity of value of the
constant capital — although indicating the growth of the real mass
of use values of which the constant capital materially consists only
approximately — corresponds a progressive cheapening of products.
Every individual product, considered by itself, contains a smaller
quantity of labour than it did on a lower level of production, where
the capital invested in labour occupies a far greater place compared
to the capital invested in means of production. The hypothetical se-

---

[a] Cf. present edition, Vol. 33, pp. 76-78. - [b] Ibid., Vol. 35, pp. 616-20.

ries drawn up at the beginning of this chapter expresses, therefore, the actual tendency of capitalist production. This mode of production produces a progressive relative decrease of the variable capital as compared to the constant capital, and consequently a continuously rising organic composition of the total capital. The immediate result of this is that the rate of surplus value, at the same, or even a rising, degree of labour exploitation, is represented by a continually falling general rate of profit. (We shall see later[a] why this fall does not manifest itself in an absolute form, but rather as a tendency toward a progressive fall.) The progressive tendency of the general rate of profit to fall is, therefore, just *an expression peculiar to the capitalist mode of production* of the progressive development of the social productive power of labour. This does not mean to say that the rate of profit may not fall temporarily for other reasons. But proceeding from the nature of the capitalist mode of production, it is thereby proved a logical necessity that in its development the general average rate of surplus value must express itself in a falling general rate of profit. Since the mass of the employed living labour is continually on the decline as compared to the mass of objectified labour set in motion by it, i. e., to the productively consumed means of production, it follows that the portion of living labour, unpaid and congealed in surplus value, must also be continually on the decrease compared to the amount of value represented by the invested total capital. Since the ratio of the mass of surplus value to the value of the invested total capital forms the rate of profit, this rate must constantly fall.

Simple as this law appears from the foregoing statements, all of political economy has so far had little success in discovering it, as we shall see in a later part.[1] The economists perceived the phenomenon and cudgelled their brains in tortuous attempts to interpret it. Since this law is of great importance to capitalist production, it may be said to be a mystery whose solution has been the goal of all political economy since Adam Smith, the difference between the various schools since Adam Smith having been in the divergent approaches to a solution. When we consider, on the other hand, that up to the present political economy has been running in circles round the distinction between constant and variable capital, but has never known how to define it accurately; that it has never separated surplus value from profit, and never even considered profit in its pure form as distinct

---

[a] See this volume, Ch. XIV.

from its different, self-established components, such as industrial profit, commercial profit, interest, and ground rent; that it has never thoroughly analysed the differences in the organic composition of capital, and, for this reason, has never thought of analysing the formation
of the general rate of profit—if we consider all this, the failure to
solve this riddle is no longer surprising.

We intentionally present this law before going on to the division of
profit into different self-established categories. The fact that this analysis is made independently of the division of profit into different
parts, which fall to the share of different categories of people, shows
from the outset that this law is, in its entirety, independent of this division, and just as independent of the mutual relations of the resultant
categories of profit. The profit to which we are here referring is but
another name for surplus value itself, which is presented only in its relation to total capital rather than to variable capital, from which it
arises. The drop in the rate of profit, therefore, expresses the falling
relation of surplus value to advanced total capital, and is for this reason independent of any division whatsoever of this surplus value
among the various categories.

We have seen that at a certain stage of capitalist development, where
the composition of capital c : v was 50 : 100, a rate of surplus value of 100% was expressed in a rate of profit of $66\frac{2}{3}$%, and that at a
higher stage, where c : v was 400 : 100, the same rate of surplus value
was expressed in a rate of profit of only 20%. What is true of different
successive stages of development in one country, is also true of different coexisting stages of development in different countries. In an undeveloped country, in which the former composition of capital is the
average, the general rate of profit would = $66\frac{2}{3}$%, while in a country with the latter composition and a much higher stage of development it would = 20%.

The difference between the two national rates of profit might
disappear, or even be reversed, if labour were less productive in
the less developed country, so that a larger quantity of labour were
to be represented in a smaller quantity of the same commodities,
and a larger exchange value were represented in less use value. The
labourer would then spend more of his time in reproducing his own
means of subsistence, or their value, and less time in producing surplus value; consequently, he would perform less surplus labour, with
the result that the rate of surplus value would be lower. Suppose, the
labourer of the less developed country were to work $\frac{2}{3}$ of the working

day for himself and $\frac{1}{3}$ for the capitalist; in accordance with the above illustration, the same labour power would then be paid with $133\frac{1}{3}$ and would furnish a surplus of only $66\frac{2}{3}$. A constant capital of 50 would correspond to a variable capital of $133\frac{1}{3}$. The rate of surplus value would amount to $66\frac{2}{3} : 133\frac{1}{3} = 50\%$, and the rate of profit to $66\frac{2}{3} : 183\frac{1}{3}$, or approximately $36\frac{1}{2}\%$.

Since we have not so far analysed the different component parts of profit, i. e., they do not for the present exist for us, we make the following remarks beforehand merely to avoid misunderstanding: In comparing countries in different stages of development it would be a big mistake to measure the level of the national rate of profit by, say, the level of the national rate of interest, namely when comparing countries with a developed capitalist production with countries in which labour has not yet been formally subjected to capital, although in reality the labourer is exploited by the capitalist (as, for instance, in India, where the ryot manages his farm as an independent producer whose production as such is not, therefore, as yet subordinated to capital, although the usurer may not only rob him of his entire surplus labour by means of interest, but may also, to use a capitalist term, hack off a part of his wage).[a] This interest comprises all the profit, and more than the profit, instead of merely expressing an aliquot part of the produced surplus value, or profit, as it does in countries with a developed capitalist production. On the other hand, the rate of interest is, in this case, mostly determined by relations (loans granted by usurers to owners of larger estates who draw ground rent) which have nothing to do with profit, and rather indicate to what extent usury appropriates ground rent.

As regards countries with capitalist production in different stages of development, and consequently capitals of different organic composition, a country where the normal working day is shorter than another's may have a higher rate of surplus value (one of the factors which determines the rate of profit). *First*, if the English ten-hour working day is, on account of its higher intensity, equal to an Austrian working day of 14 hours, then, dividing the working day equally in both instances, 5 hours of English surplus labour may represent a greater value on the world market than 7 hours of Austrian surplus labour.

---

[a] Cf. present edition, Vol. 34, pp. 118-19.

Second, a larger portion of the English working day than of the Austrian may represent surplus labour.

The law of the falling rate of profit, which expresses the same, or even a higher, rate of surplus value, states, in other words, that any quantity of the average social capital, say, a capital of 100, comprises an ever larger portion of means of labour, and an ever smaller portion of living labour. Therefore, since the aggregate mass of living labour added to the means of production decreases in relation to the value of these means of production, it follows that the unpaid labour and the portion of value in which it is expressed must decline as compared to the value of the advanced total capital. Or: An ever smaller aliquot part of invested total capital is converted into living labour, and this total capital, therefore, absorbs in proportion to its magnitude less and less surplus labour, although the unpaid part of the labour applied may at the same time grow in relation to the paid part. The relative decrease of the variable and increase of the constant capital, however much both parts may grow in absolute magnitude, is, as we have said, but another expression for greater productivity of labour.

Let a capital of 100 consist of $80_c + 20_v$, and the latter = 20 labourers. Let the rate of surplus value be 100%, i. e., the labourers work half the day for themselves and the other half for the capitalist. Now let the capital of 100 in a less developed country = $20_c + 80_v$, and let the latter = 80 labourers. But these labourers require $\frac{2}{3}$ of the day for themselves, and work only $\frac{1}{3}$ for the capitalist. Everything else being equal, the labourers in the first case produce a value of 40, and in the second of 120. The first capital produces $80_c + 20_v + 20_s = 120$; rate of profit = 20%. The second capital, $20_c + 80_v + 40_s = 140$; rate of profit = 40%. In the second case the rate of profit is, therefore, double the first, although the rate of surplus value in the first = 100%, which is double that of the second, where it is only 50%. But then, a capital of the same magnitude appropriates the surplus labour of only 20 labourers in the first case, and of 80 labourers in the second case.

The law of the progressive falling of the rate of profit, or the relative decline of appropriated surplus labour compared to the mass of objectified labour set in motion by living labour, does not rule out in any way that the absolute mass of exploited labour set in motion by the social capital, and consequently the absolute mass of the surplus labour it appropriates, may grow; nor, that the capitals controlled by individual capitalists may dispose of a growing mass of labour and, hence, of surplus labour, the latter even though the number of labourers they employ does not increase.

Take a certain working population of, say, two million. Assume, furthermore, that the length and intensity of the average working day, and the level of wages, and thereby the proportion between necessary and surplus labour, are given. In that case the aggregate labour of these two million, and their surplus labour expressed in surplus value, always produces the same magnitude of value. But with the growth of the mass of the constant (fixed and circulating) capital set in motion by this labour, this produced quantity of value declines in relation to the value of this capital, which value grows with its mass, even if not in quite the same proportion. This ratio, and consequently the rate of profit, shrinks in spite of the fact that the mass of commanded living labour is the same as before, and the same amount of surplus labour is absorbed by the capital. It changes because the mass of objectified labour set in motion by living labour increases, and not because the mass of living labour has shrunk. It is a relative decrease, not an absolute one, and has, in fact, nothing to do with the absolute magnitude of the labour and surplus labour set in motion. The drop in the rate of profit is not due to an absolute, but only to a relative decrease of the variable part of the total capital, i. e., to its decrease in relation to the constant part.

What applies to any given mass of labour and surplus labour, also applies to a growing number of labourers, and, thus, under the above assumption, to any growing mass of commanded labour in general, and to its unpaid part, the surplus labour, in particular. If the working population increases from two million to three, and if the variable capital paid out in wages also rises to three million from its former two million, while the constant capital rises from 4 million to 15 million, then, under the above assumption of a constant working day and a constant rate of surplus value, the mass of surplus labour, and of surplus value, rises by one-half, i. e., 50%, from 2 million to 3. Nevertheless, in spite of this growth of the absolute mass of surplus labour, and hence of surplus value, by 50%, the ratio of variable to constant capital would fall from 2 : 4 to 3 : 15, and the ratio of surplus value to total capital would be (in millions)

$$\text{I. } 4_c + 2_v + 2_s; \; C = 6, \; p' = 33\tfrac{1}{3}\%.$$
$$\text{II. } 15_c + 3_v + 3_s; \; C = 18, \; p' = 16\tfrac{2}{3}\%.$$

While the mass of surplus value has increased by one-half, the rate of profit has fallen by one-half. However, the profit is only the surplus value calculated in relation to the social capital, and the mass of profit, its absolute magnitude, is socially equal to the absolute magnitude of the surplus value. The absolute magnitude of the profit, its total amount, would, therefore, have grown by 50%, in spite of its enormous relative decrease compared to the advanced total capital, or in spite of the enormous decrease in the general rate of profit. The number of labourers employed by capital, hence the absolute mass of the labour set in motion by it, and therefore the absolute mass of surplus labour absorbed by it, the mass of the surplus value produced by it, and therefore the absolute mass of the profit produced by it, *can*, consequently, increase, and increase progressively, in spite of the progressive drop in the rate of profit. And this not only *can* be so. Aside from temporary fluctuations it *must* be so, on the basis of capitalist production.

Essentially, the capitalist production process is simultaneously a process of accumulation. We have shown that with the development of capitalist production the mass of values to be simply reproduced, or maintained, increases and grows as the productivity of labour grows, even if the labour power employed should remain constant.[a] But with the development of social productivity of labour the mass of produced use values, of which the means of production form a part, grows still more. And the additional labour, through whose appropriation this additional wealth can be reconverted into capital, does not depend on the value, but on the mass of these means of production (including means of subsistence), because in the production process the labourers have nothing to do with the value, but with the use value, of the means of production. Accumulation itself, however, and the concentration of capital that goes with it, is a material means of increasing productive power. Now, this growth of the means of production includes the growth of the working population, the creation of a working population, which corresponds to the surplus capital, or even exceeds its general requirements, thus leading to an overpopulation of workers. A momentary excess of surplus capital over the working population it has commandeered, would have a two-fold effect. It would, on the one hand, by raising wages, mitigate the adverse

---

[a] See present edition, Vol. 35, pp. 623-34.

conditions which decimate the offspring of the labourers and would make marriages easier among them, so as gradually to increase the population. On the other hand, by applying methods which yield relative surplus value (introduction and improvement of machinery) it would produce a far more rapid, artificial, relative overpopulation, which in its turn, would be a breeding ground for a really swift propagation of the population, since under capitalist production misery produces population.[a] It therefore follows of itself from the nature of the capitalist process of accumulation, which is but one facet of the capitalist production process, that the increased mass of means of production that is to be converted into capital always finds a correspondingly increased, even excessive, exploitable worker population. As the process of production and accumulation advances therefore, the mass of available and appropriated surplus labour, and hence the absolute mass of profit appropriated by the social capital, *must* grow. Along with the volume, however, the same laws of production and accumulation increase also the value of the constant capital in a mounting progression more rapidly than that of the variable part of capital, invested as it is in living labour. Hence, the same laws produce for the social capital a growing absolute mass of profit, and a falling rate of profit.

We shall entirely ignore here that with the advance of capitalist production and the attendant development of the productive power of social labour and multiplication of production branches, hence products, the same amount of value represents a progressively increasing mass of use values and enjoyments.

The development of capitalist production and accumulation lifts labour processes to an increasingly enlarged scale and thus imparts to them ever greater dimensions, and involves accordingly larger investments of capital for each individual establishment. A mounting concentration of capitals (accompanied, though on a smaller scale, by an increase in the number of capitalists) is, therefore, one of its material prerequisites as well as one of its results. Hand in hand with it, mutually interacting, there occurs a progressive expropriation of the more or less direct producers. It is, then, natural for the individual capitalists to command increasingly large armies of labourers (no matter how much the variable capital may decrease in relation to

---

[a] Ibid., Vol. 34, p. 165.

the constant), and natural, too, that the mass of surplus value, and hence profit, appropriated by them, should grow simultaneously with, and in spite of, the fall in the rate of profit. The causes which concentrate masses of labourers under the command of individual capitalists, are the very same that swell the mass of the employed fixed capital, and auxiliary and raw materials, in mounting proportion as compared to the mass of employed living labour.

It requires no more than a passing remark at this point to indicate that, given a certain labouring population, the mass of surplus value, hence the absolute mass of profit, must grow if the rate of surplus value increases, be it through a lengthening or intensification of the working day, or through a drop in the value of wages due to an increase in the productive power of labour, and that it must do so in spite of the relative decrease of variable capital in respect to constant.

The same development of the productive power of social labour, the same laws which express themselves in a relative decrease of variable as compared to total capital, and in the thereby facilitated accumulation, while this accumulation in its turn becomes a starting point for the further development of the productive power and for a further relative decrease of variable capital — this same development manifests itself, aside from temporary fluctuations, in a progressive increase of the total employed labour power and a progressive increase of the absolute mass of surplus value, and hence of profit.

Now, what must be the form of this double-edged law of a decrease in the *rate* of profit and a simultaneous increase in the absolute *mass* of profit arising from the same causes? A law based on the fact that under given conditions the appropriated mass of surplus labour, hence of surplus value, increases, and that, so far as the total capital is concerned, or the individual capital as an aliquot part of the total capital, profit and surplus value are identical magnitudes?

Let us take an aliquot part of capital upon which we calculate the rate of profit, e. g., 100. These 100 represent the average composition of the total capital, say, $80_c + 20_v$. We have seen in the second part of this book that the average rate of profit in the various branches of production is determined not by the particular composition of each individual capital, but by the average social composition. As the variable capital decreases relative to the constant, hence the total capital of 100, the rate of profit, or the relative magnitude of surplus value, i. e., its ratio to the advanced total capital of 100, falls even though the intensity of labour exploitation were to remain the same, or even to increase. But it is not this relative magnitude alone which falls. The magnitude of the surplus value or profit absorbed by the total capital of 100 also falls absolutely. At a rate of surplus value of 100%, a capital of $60_c + 40_v$ produces a mass of surplus value, and hence of profit, amounting to 40; a capital of $70_c + 30_v$ a mass of profit of 30; and for a capital of $80_c + 20_v$ the profit falls to 20. This falling applies to the mass of surplus value, and hence of profit, and is due to the fact that the total capital of 100 employs less living labour, and, the intensity of labour exploitation remaining the same, sets in motion less surplus labour, and therefore produces less surplus value. Taking any aliquot part of the social capital, i. e., a capital of average social composition, as a standard by which to measure surplus value — and this is done in all calculations of profit — a relative fall of surplus value is generally identical with its absolute fall. In the cases given above, the rate of profit sinks from 40% to 30% and to 20%, because, in fact, the mass of surplus value, and hence of profit, produced by the same capital falls absolutely from 40 to 30 and to 20. Since the magnitude of the value of the capital, by which the surplus value is measured, is given as 100, a fall in the proportion of surplus value to this given magnitude can be only another expression for the decrease of the absolute magnitude of surplus value and profit. This is, indeed, a tautology. But, as shown, the fact that this decrease occurs at all, arises from the nature of the development of the capitalist process of production.

On the other hand, however, the same causes which bring about an absolute decrease of surplus value, and hence profit, on a given capital, and consequently of the rate of profit calculated in per cent, produce an increase in the absolute mass of surplus value, and hence of profit, appropriated by the social capital (i. e., by all capitalists taken as a whole). How does this occur, what is the only way in which this can occur, or what are the conditions obtaining in this seeming contradiction?

If any aliquot part = 100 of the social capital, and hence any 100 of average social composition, is a given magnitude, for which therefore a fall in the rate of profit coincides with a fall in the absolute magnitude of the profit because the capital which here serves as a standard of measurement is a constant magnitude, then the magnitude of the total social capital like that of the capital in the hands of individual capitalists, is variable, and in keeping with our assumptions it must vary inversely with the decrease of its variable portion.

In our former illustration, when the percentage of composition was

$60_c + 40_v$, the corresponding surplus value, or profit, was 40, and hence the rate of profit 40%. Suppose, the total capital in this stage of composition was one million. Then the total surplus value, and hence the total profit, amounted to 400,000. Now, if the composition later $= 80_c + 20_v$, while the degree of labour exploitation remained the same, then the surplus value or profit for each $100 = 20$. But since the absolute mass of surplus value or profit increases, as demonstrated, in spite of the decreasing rate of profit or the decreasing production of surplus value by every 100 of capital—increases, say, from 400,000 to 440,000, then this occurs solely because the total capital which formed at the time of this new composition has risen to 2,200,000. The mass of the total capital set in motion has risen to 220%, while the rate of profit has fallen by 50%. Had the capital no more than doubled, it would have to produce as much surplus value and profit to obtain a rate of profit of 20% as the old capital of 1,000,000 produced at 40%. Had it grown to less than double, it would have produced less surplus value, or profit, than the old capital of 1,000,000, which, in its former composition, would have had to grow from 1,000,000 to no more than 1,100,000 to raise its surplus value from 400,000 to 440,000.

We again meet here the previously defined law [33] that the relative decrease of the variable capital, hence the development of the social productive power of labour, involves an increasingly large mass of total capital to set in motion the same quantity of labour power and absorb the same quantity of surplus labour. Consequently, the possibility of a relative surplus of labouring people develops proportionately to the advances made by capitalist production not because the productive power of social labour *decreases*, but because it *increases*. It does not therefore arise out of an absolute disproportion between labour and the means of subsistence, or the means for the production of these means of subsistence, but out of a disproportion occasioned by capitalist exploitation of labour, a disproportion between the progressive growth of capital and its relatively shrinking need for an increasing population.

Should the rate of profit fall by 50%, it would shrink one-half. If the mass of profit is to remain the same, the capital must be doubled. For the mass of profit made at a declining rate of profit to remain the same, the multiplier indicating the growth of the total capital must be equal to the divisor indicating the fall of the rate of profit. If the rate of profit falls from 40 to 20, the total capital must rise inversely at the rate of 20:40 to obtain the same result. If the rate of profit falls from 40 to 8, the capital would have to increase at the rate of 8:40, five-fold. A capital of 1,000,000 at 40% produces 400,000, and a capital of 5,000,000 at 8% likewise produces 400,000. This applies if we want the result to remain the same. But if the result is to be higher, then the capital must grow at a greater rate than the rate of profit falls. In other words, for the variable portion of the total capital not to remain the same in absolute terms, but to increase absolutely, in spite of its falling in percentage of the total capital, the total capital must grow at a faster rate than the percentage of the variable capital falls. It must grow so considerably that in its new composition it should require more than the old portion of variable capital to purchase labour power. If the variable portion of a capital = 100 should fall from 40 to 20, the total capital must rise higher than 200 to be able to employ a larger variable capital than 40.

Even if the exploited mass of the working population were to remain constant, and only the length and intensity of the working day were to increase, the mass of the employed capital would have to increase, since it would have to be greater in order to employ the same mass of labour under the old conditions of exploitation after the composition of capital changes.

Thus, the same development of the social productive power of labour expresses itself with the progress of capitalist production on the one hand in a tendency of the rate of profit to fall progressively and, on the other, in a constant growth of the absolute mass of the appropriated surplus value, or profit; so that on the whole a relative decrease of variable capital and profit is accompanied by an absolute increase of both. This two-fold effect, as we have seen, can express itself only in a growth of the total capital at a pace more rapid than that at which the rate of profit falls. For an absolutely increased variable capital to be employed in a capital of higher composition, or one in which the constant capital has increased relatively more, the total capital must not only grow proportionately to its higher composition, but still more rapidly. It follows, then, that as the capitalist mode of production develops, an ever larger quantity of capital is required to employ the same, let alone an increased, amount of labour power. Thus, on a capitalist foundation, the increasing productive power of labour necessarily and permanently creates a seeming overpopulation of labouring people. If the variable capital forms just $\frac{1}{6}$ of the total capital instead of the former $\frac{1}{2}$, the total capital must be trebled to employ the same amount of labour power. And if twice as much labour power is to be employed, the total capital must increase six-fold.

Political economy, which has until now been unable to explain the law of the tendency of the rate of profit to fall, pointed self-consolingly to the increasing mass of profit, i. e., to the growth of the absolute magnitude of profit, be it for the individual capitalist or for the social capital, but this was also based on mere platitude and speculation.

To say that the mass of profit is determined by two factors — first, the rate of profit, and, secondly, the mass of capital invested at this rate, is mere tautology. It is therefore but a corollary of this tautology to say that there is a possibility for the mass of profit to grow even though the rate of profit may fall at the same time. It does not help us one step farther, since it is just as possible for the capital to increase without the mass of profit growing, and for it to increase even while the mass of profit falls. For 100 at 25% yields 25, and 400 at 5% yields only 20.[35] But if the same causes which make the rate of profit fall, entail the accumulation, i. e., the formation, of additional capital, and if each additional capital employs additional labour and produces additional surplus value; if, on the other hand, the mere fall

[35] "We should also expect that, however the rate of the profits of stock might diminish in consequence of the accumulation of capital on the land and the rise of wages, yet the aggregate amount of profits would increase. Thus, supposing that, with repeated accumulations of £100,000, the rate of profit should fall from 20 to 19, to 18, to 17%, a constantly diminishing rate, we should expect that the whole amount of profits received by those successive owners of capital would be always progressive; that it would be greater when the capital was £200,000, than when £100,000; still greater when £300,000; and so on, increasing, though at a diminishing rate, with every increase of capital. This progression, however, is only true for a certain time; thus 19% on £200,000 is more than 20% on £100,000; again 18% on £300,000 is more than 19% on £200,000; but after capital has accumulated to a large amount, and profits have fallen, the further accumulation diminishes the aggregate of profits. Thus, suppose the accumulation should be £1,000,000, and the profits 7%, the whole amount of profits will be £70,000; now if an addition of £100,000 capital be made to the million, and profits should fall to 6%, £66,000 or a diminution of £4,000 will be received by the owners of the stock, although the whole amount of stock will be increased from 1,000,000 to 1,100,000." — Ricardo, *Political Economy*, Chap. VI (*Works*, ed. by MacCulloch, 1852, pp. 68-69).— The fact is, that the assumption has here been made that the capital increases from 1,000,000 to 1,100,000, that is, by 10%, while the rate of profit falls from 7 to 6, hence by $14\frac{2}{7}$%. *Hinc illae lacrimae!* [a]

[a] Hence those tears (Terence, *Andria*, I, 1, 99).

in the rate of profit implies that the constant capital, and with it the total old capital, have increased, then this process ceases to be mysterious. We shall see later [1] to what deliberate falsifications some people resort in their calculations to spirit away the possibility of an increase in the mass of profit simultaneous with a decrease in the rate of profit.[a]

We have shown how the same causes that bring about a tendency for the general rate of profit to fall necessitate an accelerated accumulation of capital and, consequently, an increase in the absolute magnitude, or total mass, of the surplus labour (surplus value, profit) appropriated by it. Just as everything appears reversed in competition, and thus in the consciousness of the agents of competition, so also this law, this inner and necessary connection between two seeming contradictions. It is evident that within the proportions indicated above a capitalist disposing of a large capital will receive a larger mass of profit than a small capitalist making seemingly high profits. Even a cursory examination of competition shows, furthermore, that under certain circumstances, when the greater capitalist wishes to make room for himself on the market, and to crowd out the smaller ones, as happens in times of crises, he makes practical use of this, i. e., he deliberately lowers his rate of profit in order to drive the smaller ones to the wall. Merchant's capital, which we shall describe in detail later, also notably exhibits phenomena which appear to attribute a fall in profit to an expansion of business, and thus of capital. The scientific expression for this false conception will be given later. Similar superficial observations result from a comparison of rates of profit in individual lines of business, distinguished either as subject to free competition, or to monopoly. The utterly shallow conception existing in the minds of the agents of competition is found in Roscher, namely, that a reduction in the rate of profit is "more prudent and humane".[b] The fall in the rate of profit appears in this case as an *effect* of an increase in capital and of the concomitant calculation of the capitalist that the mass of profits pocketed by him will be greater at a smaller rate of profit. This entire conception (with the exception of Adam Smith's, which we shall mention later [34]) rests on an utter misapprehension of what the general rate of profit is, and on the crude notion that prices are actually determined by adding a more or less arbitrary

---

[a] Cf. present edition, Vol. 32, pp. 170-74. - [b] W. Roscher, *Die Grundlage der National-ökonomie*, 3rd edition, Stuttgart and Augsburg, 1858, §108, p. 192.

quota of profit to the true value of commodities. Crude as these ideas are, they arise necessarily out of the inverted aspect which the immanent laws of capitalist production represent in competition.

―――――――

The law that a fall in the rate of profit due to the development of productiveness is accompanied by an increase in the mass of profit, also expresses itself in the fact that a fall in the price of commodities produced by a capital is accompanied by a relative increase of the masses of profit contained in them and realised by their sale.

Since the development of the productive power and the correspondingly higher composition of capital sets in motion an ever-increasing quantity of means of production through a constantly decreasing quantity of labour, every aliquot part of the total product, i. e., every single commodity, or each particular lot of commodities in the total mass of products, absorbs less living labour, and also contains less objectified labour, both in the depreciation of the fixed capital applied and in the raw and auxiliary materials consumed. Hence every single commodity contains a smaller sum of labour objectified in means of production and of labour newly added during production. This causes the price of the individual commodity to fall. But the mass of profits contained in the individual commodities may nevertheless increase if the rate of the absolute or relative surplus value grows. The commodity contains less newly added labour, but its unpaid portion grows in relation to its paid portion. However, this is the case only within certain limits. With the absolute amount of living labour newly incorporated in individual commodities decreasing enormously as production develops, the absolute mass of unpaid labour contained in them will likewise decrease, however much it may have grown as compared to the paid portion. The mass of profit on each individual commodity will shrink considerably with the development of the productive power of labour, in spite of a growth in the rate of surplus value. And this reduction, just as the fall in the rate of profit, is only delayed by the cheapening of the elements of constant capital and by the other circumstances set forth in the first part of this book, which increase the rate of profit at a given, or even falling, rate of surplus value.

That the price of individual commodities whose sum makes up the total product of capital falls, means simply that a certain quantity of labour is realised in a larger quantity of commodities, so that each individual commodity contains less labour than before. This is the case even if the price of one part of constant capital, such as raw material, etc., should rise. Outside of a few cases (for instance, if the productiveness of labour uniformly cheapens all elements of the constant, and the variable, capital), the rate of profit will fall, in spite of the higher rate of surplus value, 1) because even a larger unpaid portion of the smaller total amount of newly added labour is smaller than a smaller aliquot unpaid portion of the former larger amount, and 2) because the higher composition of capital is expressed in the individual commodity by the fact that the portion of its value in which newly added labour is represented decreases in relation to the portion of its value which represents raw and auxiliary material, and the wear and tear of fixed capital. This change in the proportion of the various component parts in the price of individual commodities, i. e., the decrease of that portion of the price in which newly added living labour is objectified and the increase of that portion of it in which formerly objectified labour is represented, is the form which expresses the decrease of the variable in relation to the constant capital through the price of the individual commodities. Just as this decrease is absolute for a certain amount of capital, say of 100, it is also absolute for every individual commodity as an aliquot part of the reproduced capital. However, the rate of profit, if calculated merely on the elements of the price of an individual commodity, would be different from what it actually is. And for the following reason:

//The rate of profit is calculated on the total capital invested, but for a definite time, actually a year. The rate of profit is the ratio of the surplus value, or profit, produced and realised in a year, to the total capital calculated in per cent. It is, therefore, not necessarily equal to a rate of profit calculated for the period of turnover of the invested capital rather than for a year. It is only if the capital is turned over exactly in one year that the two coincide.

On the other hand, the profit made in the course of a year is merely the sum of profits on commodities produced and sold during that same year. Now, if we calculate the profit on the cost price of commodities, we obtain a rate of profit $= \frac{p}{k}$ in which p stands for the profit realised during one year, and k for the sum of the cost prices of commodities produced and sold within the same period. It is evident that this rate of profit $\frac{p}{k}$ will not coincide with the actual rate of profit $\frac{p}{C}$, mass of profit divided by total capital, unless k = C, that is, unless the capital is turned over in exactly one year.

Let us take three different conditions of an industrial capital.

I. A capital of £8,000 produces and sells annually 5,000 pieces of a commodity at 30s. per piece, thus making an annual turnover of £7,500. It makes a profit of 10s. on each piece, or £2,500 per year. Every piece, then, contains 20s. advanced capital and 10s. profit, so that the rate of profit per piece is $\frac{10}{20}$ $=50\%$. The turned-over sum of £7,500 contains £5,000 advanced capital and £2,500 profit. Rate of profit per turnover, $\frac{p}{k}$, likewise $= 50\%$. But calculated on the total capital the rate of profit $\frac{p}{C} = \frac{2,500}{8,000} = 31^1/_4\%$.

II. The capital rises to £10,000. Owing to increased productivity of labour it is able to produce annually 10,000 pieces of the commodity at a cost price of 20s. per piece. Suppose, the commodity is sold at a profit of 4s., hence at 24s. per piece. In that case the price of the annual product = £12,000, of which £10,000 is advanced capital and £2,000 is profit. The rate of profit $\frac{p}{k} = \frac{4}{20}$ per piece, and $\frac{2,000}{10,000}$ for the annual turnover, or in both cases $= 20\%$. And since the total capital is equal to the sum of the cost prices, namely £10,000 it follows that $\frac{p}{C}$, the actual rate of profit, is in this case also 20%.

III. Let the capital rise to £15,000 owing to a constant growth of the productive power of labour, and let it annually produce 30,000 pieces of the commodity at a cost price of 13s. per piece, each piece being sold at a profit of 2s., or at 15s. The annual turnover therefore $= 30,000 \times 15s. = £22,500$, of which £19,500 is advanced capital and £3,000 profit. The rate of profit $\frac{p}{k}$ then $= \frac{2}{13} = \frac{3,000}{19,500} = 15^5/_{13}\%$. But $\frac{p}{C} = \frac{3,000}{15,000} = 20\%$.

We see, therefore, that only in case II, where the turned-over capital value is equal to the total capital, the rate of profit per piece, or per total amount of turnover, is the same as the rate of profit calculated on the total capital. In case I, in which the amount of the turnover is smaller than the total capital, the rate of profit calculated on the cost price of the commodity is higher; and in case III, in which the total capital is smaller than the amount of the turnover, it is lower than the actual rate of profit calculated on the total capital. This is a general rule.

In commercial practice, the turnover is generally calculated inaccurately. It is assumed that the capital has been turned over once as soon as the sum of the realised commodity prices equals the sum of the invested total capital. But the *capital* can complete one whole turn-over only when the sum of the *cost prices* of the realised commodi-ties equals the sum of the total capital.— *F. E.*//

This again shows how important it is in capitalist production to re-gard individual commodities, or the commodity product of a certain period, as products of advanced capital and in relation to the total cap-ital which produces them, rather than in isolation, by themselves, as mere commodities.[a]

The *rate* of profit must be calculated by measuring the mass of pro-duced and realised surplus value not only in relation to the consumed portion of capital reappearing in the commodities, but also to this part plus that portion of unconsumed but applied capital which con-tinues to operate in production. However, the *mass* of profit cannot be equal to anything but the mass of profit or surplus value, contained in the commodities themselves, and to be realised by their sale.

If the productivity of industry increases, the price of individual commodities falls. There is less labour in them, less paid and unpaid labour. Suppose, the same labour produces, say, triple its former prod-uct. Then $\frac{2}{3}$ less labour yields individual product. And since profit can make up but a portion of the amount of labour contained in an individual commodity, the mass of profit in the individual commod-ity must decrease, and this takes place within certain limits, even if the rate of surplus value should rise. In any case, the mass of profit on the total product does not fall below the original mass of profit so long as the capital employs the same number of labourers at the same de-gree of exploitation. (This may also occur if fewer labourers are em-ployed at a higher rate of exploitation.) For the mass of profit on the individual product decreases proportionately to the increase in the number of products. The mass of profit remains the same, but it is dis-tributed differently over the total amount of commodities. Nor does this alter the distribution between the labourers and capitalists of the amount of value created by newly added labour. The mass of profit cannot increase so long as the same amount of labour is employed, unless the unpaid surplus labour increases, or, should intensity of exploitation remain the same, unless the number of labourers grows. Or, both these causes may combine to produce this result. In all these cases — which, however, in accordance with our assumption, presup-

---

[a] Cf. present edition, Vol. 34, pp. 355-84.

pose an increase of constant capital as compared to variable, and an increase in the magnitude of total capital invested — the individual commodity contains a smaller mass of profit and the rate of profit falls even if calculated on the individual commodity. A given quantity of newly added labour materialises in a larger quantity of commodities. The price of the individual commodity falls. Considered abstractly the rate of profit may remain the same, even though the price of the individual commodity may fall as a result of greater productive power and a simultaneous increase in the number of this cheaper commodity if, for instance, the increase in productive power acts uniformly and simultaneously on all the elements of the commodity, so that its total price falls in the same proportion in which the productivity of labour increases, while, on the other hand, the mutual relation of the different elements of the price of the commodity remains the same. The rate of profit could even rise if a rise in the rate of surplus value were accompanied by a substantial reduction in the value of the elements of constant, and particularly of fixed, capital. But in reality, as we have seen, the rate of profit will fall in the long run. In no case does a fall in the price of any individual commodity by itself give a clue to the rate of profit. Everything depends on the magnitude of the total capital invested in its production. For instance, if the price of one yard of fabric falls from 3s. to $1\frac{2}{3}$ s., if we know that before this price reduction it contained $1\frac{2}{3}$ s. constant capital, yarn, etc., $\frac{2}{3}$ s. wages, and $\frac{2}{3}$ s. profit, while after the reduction it contains 1s. constant capital, $\frac{1}{3}$ s. wages, and $\frac{1}{3}$ s. profit, we cannot tell if the rate of profit has remained the same or not. This depends on whether, and by how much, the advanced total capital has increased, and how many yards more it produces in a given time.

The phenomenon, springing from the nature of the capitalist mode of production, that increasing productivity of labour implies a drop in the price of the individual commodity, or of a certain mass of commodities, an increase in the number of commodities, a reduction in the mass of profit on the individual commodity and in the rate of profit on the aggregate of commodities, and an increase in the mass of profit on the total quantity of commodities — this phenomenon appears on the surface only in a reduction of the mass of profit on the individual commodity, a fall in its price, an increase in the mass of profit on the augmented total number of commodities produced by the total social capital or an individual capitalist. It then appears as if the capitalist adds less profit to the price of the individual commodity of his own free will, and makes up for it through the greater number of commodities he produces. This conception rests upon the notion of PROFIT UPON ALIENATION,[a] [35] which, in its turn, is deduced from the conception of merchant capital.[b]

We have previously seen in Book I (4 and 7 Abschnitt[c]) that the mass of commodities growing along with the productive power of labour and the cheapening of the individual commodity as such (as long as these commodities do not enter the price of labour power as determinants) do not affect the proportion between paid and unpaid labour in the individual commodity, in spite of the falling price.

Since all things appear distorted, namely, reversed in competition, the individual capitalist may imagine: 1) that he is reducing his profit on the individual commodity by cutting its price, but still making a greater profit by selling a larger quantity of commodities; 2) that he fixes the price of the individual commodities and that he determines the price of the total product by multiplication, while the original process is really one of division (see Book I, Kap. X, S. 314/323[d]), and multiplication is only correct secondarily, since it is based on that division. The vulgar economist does practically no more than translate the singular concepts of the capitalists, who are in the thrall of competition, into a seemingly more theoretical and generalised language, and attempt to substantiate the justice of those conceptions.[e]

The fall in commodity prices and the rise in the mass of profit on the augmented mass of these cheapened commodities is, in fact, but another expression for the law of the falling rate of profit attended by a simultaneously increasing mass of profit.

The analysis of how far a falling rate of profit may coincide with rising prices no more belongs here than that of the point previously discussed in Book I (S. 314/323), concerning relative surplus value. A capitalist working with improved but not as yet generally adopted methods of production sells below the market price, but above his individual price of production; his rate of profit rises until competition levels it out. During this equalisation period the second requisite,

---

[a] In the 1894 German edition this English term is given in parentheses after its German equivalent. - [b] Cf. present edition, Vol. 34, pp. 368-70. - [c] English edition: Vol. I, parts IV and VII. - [d] English edition: Ch. XII (cf. present edition, Vol. 35, pp. 321-22). - [e] Ibid., Vol. 32, p. 395.

increase of the invested capital, makes its appearance. According to the degree of this expansion the capitalist will be able to employ a part of his former labourers, actually perhaps all of them, or even more, under the new conditions, and hence to produce the same, or a greater, mass of profit.[a]

Chapter XIV

COUNTERACTING INFLUENCES

If we consider the enormous development of the productive forces of social labour in the last 30 years alone as compared with all preceding periods; if we consider, in particular, the enormous mass of fixed capital, aside from the actual machinery, which goes into the process of social production as a whole, then the difficulty which has hitherto troubled the economists, namely to explain the falling rate of profit, gives place to its opposite, namely to explain why this fall is not greater and more rapid. There must be some counteracting influences at work, which cross and annul the effect of the general law, and which give it merely the characteristic of a tendency, for which reason we have referred to the fall of the general rate of profit as a tendency to fall. The following are the most general counterbalancing forces:

I. INCREASING INTENSITY OF EXPLOITATION

The degree of exploitation of labour, the appropriation of surplus labour and surplus value, is raised notably by lengthening the working day and intensifying labour. These two points have been comprehensively treated in Book I as incidental to the production of absolute and relative surplus value. There are many ways of intensifying labour which imply an increase of constant, as compared to variable, capital, and hence a fall in the rate of profit, such as compelling a labourer to operate a larger number of machines. In such cases — and in most procedures serving the production of relative surplus values — the same causes which increase the rate of surplus value, may also, from the standpoint of given quantities of invested total capital,

---

a Ibid., Vol. 33, pp. 35-36.

involve a fall in the mass of surplus value. But there are other aspects of intensification, such as the greater velocities of machinery, which consume more raw material in the same time, but, so far as the fixed capital is concerned, wear out the machinery so much faster, and yet do not in any way affect the relation of its value to the price of the labour which sets it in motion. But notably, it is prolongation of the working day, this invention of modern industry, which increases the mass of appropriated surplus labour without essentially altering the proportion of the employed labour power to the constant capital set in motion by it, and which rather tends to reduce this capital relatively. Moreover, it has already been demonstrated — and this constitutes the real secret of the tendency of the rate of profit to fall — that the manipulations to produce relative surplus value amount, on the whole, to transforming as much as possible of a certain quantity of labour into surplus value, on the one hand, and employing as little labour as possible in proportion to the advanced capital, on the other, so that the same reasons which permit raising the intensity of exploitation rule out exploiting the same quantity of labour as before by the same capital. These are the counteracting tendencies, which, while effecting a rise in the rate of surplus value, also tend to decrease the mass of surplus value, and hence the rate of profit produced by a certain capital. Mention should also be made here of the widespread introduction of female and child labour, in so far as the whole family must now perform more surplus labour for capital than before, even when the total amount of their wages increases, which is by no means always the case.[a] — Everything that promotes the production of relative surplus value by mere improvement in methods, as in agriculture, without altering the magnitude of the invested capital, has the same effect. The constant capital, it is true, does not, in such cases, increase in relation to the variable, inasmuch as we regard the variable capital as an index of the amount of labour power employed, but the mass of the product does increase in proportion to the labour power employed. The same occurs, if the productive power of labour (no matter, whether its product goes into the labourer's consumption or into the elements of constant capital) is freed from hindrances in communications, from arbitrary or other restrictions which have become obstacles in the course of time; from

---

[a] Cf. present edition, Vol. 30, pp. 332-35; Vol. 33, pp. 123-24; Vol. 34, pp. 24-25.

fetters of all kinds, without directly affecting the ratio of variable to constant capital.

It might be asked whether the factors that check the fall of the rate of profit, but that always hasten its fall in the last analysis, whether these include the temporary, but always recurring, elevations in surplus value above the general level, which keep occurring now in this and now in that line of production redounding to the benefit of those individual capitalists, who make use of inventions, etc., before these are introduced elsewhere. This question must be answered in the affirmative.

The mass of surplus value produced by a capital of a given magnitude is the product of two factors — the rate of surplus value multiplied by the number of labourers employed at this rate. At a given rate of surplus value it therefore depends on the number of labourers, and it depends on the rate of surplus value when the number of labourers is given. Generally, therefore, it depends on the composite ratio of the absolute magnitudes of the variable capital and the rate of surplus value. Now we have seen that, on the average, the same factors which raise the rate of relative surplus value lower the mass of the employed labour power. It is evident, however, that this will occur to a greater or lesser extent, depending on the definite proportion in which this conflicting movement obtains, and that the tendency towards a reduction in the rate of profit is notably weakened by a rise in the rate of absolute surplus value, which originates with the lengthening of the working day.

We saw in the case of the rate of profit that a drop in the rate was generally accompanied by an increase in the mass of profit, due to the increasing mass of total capital employed. From the standpoint of the total variable capital of society, the surplus value it has produced is equal to the profit it has produced. Both the absolute mass and the rate of surplus value have increased; the one because the quantity of labour power employed by society has grown, and the other, because the intensity of exploitation of this labour has increased. But in the case of a capital of a given magnitude, e. g., 100, the rate of surplus value may increase, while the average mass may decrease; for the rate is determined by the proportion, in which the variable capital produces value, while the mass is determined by the proportion of variable capital to the total capital.

The rise in the rate of surplus value is a factor which determines the mass of surplus value, and hence also the rate of profit, for it takes place especially under conditions, in which, as we have previously seen, the constant capital is either not increased at all, or not proportionately increased, in relation to the variable capital. This factor does not abolish the general law. But it causes that law to act rather as a tendency, i. e., as a law whose absolute action is checked, retarded, and weakened, by counteracting circumstances. But since the same influences which raise the rate of surplus value (even a lengthening of the working time is a result of large-scale industry) tend to decrease the labour power employed by a certain capital, it follows that they also tend to reduce the rate of profit and to retard this reduction.[a] If one labourer is compelled to perform as much labour as would rationally be performed by at least two, and if this is done under circumstances in which this one labourer can replace three, then this one labourer will perform as much surplus labour as was formerly performed by two, and the rate of surplus value will have risen accordingly. But he will not perform as much as three had performed, and the mass of surplus value will have decreased accordingly. But this reduction in mass will be compensated, or limited, by the rise in the rate of surplus value. If the entire population is employed at a higher rate of surplus value, the mass of surplus value will increase, in spite of the population remaining the same. It will increase still more if the population increases. And although this is tied up with a relative reduction of the number of employed labourers in proportion to the magnitude of the total capital, this reduction is moderated, or checked, by the rise in the rate of surplus value.

Before leaving this point, it is to be emphasised once more that with a capital of a given magnitude the *rate* of surplus value may rise, while its *mass* is decreasing, and vice versa. The mass of surplus value is equal to the rate multiplied by the number of labourers; however, the rate is never calculated on the total, but only on the variable capital, actually only for every working day. On the other hand, with a given magnitude of capital value, the *rate of profit* can neither rise nor fall without the *mass of surplus value* also rising or falling.

---

[a] Ibid., Vol. 35, p. 408.

II. DEPRESSION OF WAGES BELOW THE VALUE
OF LABOUR POWER

This is mentioned here only empirically, since, like many other things which might be enumerated, it has nothing to do with the general analysis of capital, but belongs in an analysis of competition, which is not presented in this work.[1] However, it is one of the most important factors checking the tendency of the rate of profit to fall.

III. CHEAPENING OF ELEMENTS OF CONSTANT CAPITAL

Everything said in Part I of this book about factors which raise the rate of profit while the rate of surplus value remains the same, or regardless of the rate of surplus value, belongs here. Hence also, with respect to the total capital, that the value of the constant capital does not increase in the same proportion as its material volume. For instance, the quantity of cotton worked up by a single European spinner in a modern factory has grown tremendously compared to the quantity formerly worked up by a European spinner with a spinning-wheel. Yet the value of the worked-up cotton has not grown in the same proportion as its mass. The same applies to machinery and other fixed capital. In short, the same development which increases the mass of the constant capital in relation to the variable reduces the value of its elements as a result of the increased productivity of labour, and therefore prevents the value of constant capital, although it continually increases, from increasing at the same rate as its material volume, i. e., the material volume of the means of production set in motion by the same amount of labour power. In isolated cases the mass of the elements of constant capital may even increase, while its value remains the same, or even falls.

The foregoing is bound up with the depreciation of existing capital (that is, of its material elements), which occurs with the development of industry. This is another continually operating factor which checks the fall of the rate of profit, although it may under certain circumstances encroach on the mass of profit by reducing the mass of the capital yielding a profit. This again shows that the same influences which tend to make the rate of profit fall, also moderate the effects of this tendency.

IV. RELATIVE OVERPOPULATION

Its propagation is inseparable from, and hastened by, the development of the productivity of labour as expressed by a fall in the rate of profit. The relative overpopulation becomes so much more apparent in a country, the more the capitalist mode of production is developed in it. This, again, is the reason why, on the one hand, the more or less imperfect subordination of labour to capital continues in many branches of production, and continues longer than seems at first glance compatible with the general stage of development. This is due to the cheapness and abundance of disposable or unemployed wage labourers, and to the greater resistance, which some branches of production, by their very nature, render to the transformation of manual work into machine production. On the other hand, new lines of production are opened up, especially for the production of luxuries, and it is these that take as their basis this relative overpopulation, often set free in other lines of production through the increase of their constant capital. These new lines start out predominantly with living labour, and by degrees pass through the same evolution as the other lines of production. In either case the variable capital makes up a considerable portion of the total capital and wages are below the average, so that both the rate and mass of surplus value in these lines of production are unusually high. Since the general rate of profit is formed by levelling the rates of profit in the individual branches of production, however, the same factor which brings about the tendency in the rate of profit to fall, again produces a counterbalance to this tendency and more or less paralyses its effects.

V. FOREIGN TRADE

Since foreign trade partly cheapens the elements of constant capital, and partly the necessities of life into which the variable capital is converted, it tends to raise the rate of profit by increasing the rate of surplus value and lowering the value of constant capital. It generally acts in this direction by permitting an expansion of the scale of production. It thereby hastens the process of accumulation, on the one hand, but causes the variable capital to shrink in relation to the constant capital, on the other, and thus hastens a fall in the rate of profit. In the same way, the expansion of foreign trade, although the basis of the capitalist mode of production in its infancy, has become its own product, however, with the further progress of the capitalist mode of production, through the innate necessity of this mode of production, its need for an ever-expanding market. Here we see once more the dual nature of this effect. (Ricardo has entirely overlooked this side of foreign trade.[a])

Another question — really beyond the scope of our analysis[1] because of its special nature — is this: Is the general rate of profit raised by the higher rate of profit produced by capital invested in foreign, and particularly colonial, trade?

Capitals invested in foreign trade can yield a higher rate of profit, because, in the first place, there is competition with commodities produced in other countries with inferior production facilities, so that the more advanced country sells its commodities above their value even though cheaper than the competing countries. In so far as the labour of the more advanced country is here realised as labour of a higher specific weight, the rate of profit rises, because labour which has not been paid as being of a higher quality is sold as such. The same may obtain in relation to the country, to which commodities are exported and to that from which commodities are imported; namely, the latter may offer more objectified labour *in natura* than it receives, and yet thereby receive commodities cheaper than it could produce them. Just as a manufacturer who employs a new invention before it becomes generally used, undersells his competitors and yet sells his commodity above its individual value, that is, realises the specifically higher productiveness of the labour he employs as surplus labour. He thus secures a surplus profit. As concerns capitals invested in colonies, etc., on the other hand, they may yield higher rates of profit for the simple reason that the rate of profit is higher there due to backward development, and likewise the exploitation of labour, because of the use of slaves, coolies, etc. It is hard to see why these higher rates of profit, realised by capitals invested in certain lines and sent home by them, should not, unless monopolies stand in the way, enter here into the equalisation of the general rate of profit and thus tend, *pro tanto*, to raise it.[36] It is

[36] Adam Smith[b] was right in this respect, contrary to Ricardo, who said: "They contend that the equality of profits will be brought about by the general rise of profits; and I am of the opinion that the profits of the favoured trade will speedily submit to the general level." (*Works*, ed. by MacCulloch, p. 73.)

[a] See D. Ricardo, *On the Principles of Political Economy, and Taxation*, 3rd edition, Ch. VII; cf. present edition, Vol. 32, pp. 73-74. - [b] *An Inquiry into the Nature and Causes of the Wealth of Nations*, Vol. I, London, 1776, Ch. 9.

hard to see this in particular if these spheres of investment of capital are subject to the laws of free competition. What Ricardo fancies, in contrast, is mainly this: with the higher prices realised abroad commodities are bought there and sent home. These commodities are thus sold on the home market, so that the result can at best be but a temporary extra advantage for these favoured spheres of production over others. This illusion falls away as soon as it is divested of its money form. The favoured country recovers more labour in exchange for less labour, although this difference, this excess is pocketed, as in any exchange between labour and capital, by a certain class. Since the rate of profit is higher, therefore, because it is generally higher in a colonial country, it may, provided natural conditions are favourable, go hand in hand with low commodity prices. A levelling takes place but not a levelling to the old level, as Ricardo feels.

This same foreign trade develops the capitalist mode of production in the home country, which implies the decrease of variable capital in relation to constant, and, on the other hand, causes overproduction in respect to foreign markets, so that in the long run it again has an opposite effect.

We have thus seen in a general way that the same influences which produce a tendency in the general rate of profit to fall, also call forth countereffects, which hamper, retard, and partly paralyse this fall. The latter do not do away with the law, but impair its effect. Otherwise, it would not be the fall of the general rate of profit, but rather its relative slowness, that would be incomprehensible. Thus, the law acts only as a tendency. And it is only under certain circumstances and only after long periods that its effects become strikingly pronounced.

Before we go on, in order to avoid misunderstandings, we should recall two, repeatedly treated, points.

First: The same process which brings about a cheapening of commodities in the course of the development of the capitalist mode of production, causes a change in the organic composition of the social capital invested in the production of commodities, and consequently lowers the rate of profit. We must be careful, therefore, not to identify the reduction in the relative cost of an individual commodity, including that portion of it which represents wear and tear of machinery, with the rise in the value of the constant in relation to variable capital, although, conversely, every reduction in the relative cost of the constant capital assuming the volume of its material elements remains the same, or increases, tends to raise the rate of profit, i. e., to reduce *pro tanto* the value of the constant capital in relation to the shrinking proportions of the employed variable capital.

Second: The fact that the newly added living labour contained in the individual commodities, which taken together make up the product of capital, decreases in relation to the materials they contain and the means of labour consumed by them; the fact, therefore, that an ever-decreasing quantity of newly added living labour is objectified in them, because their production requires less labour with the development of the social productiveness— this fact does not affect the ratio, in which the living labour contained in the commodities breaks up into paid and unpaid labour. Quite the contrary. Although the total quantity of newly added living labour contained in the commodities decreases, the unpaid portion increases in relation to the paid portion, either by an absolute or a relative shrinking of the paid portion; for the same mode of production which reduces the total quantity of newly added living labour in a commodity is accompanied by a rise in the absolute and relative surplus value. The tendency of the rate of profit to fall is bound up with a tendency of the rate of surplus value to rise, hence with a tendency for the rate of labour exploitation to rise. Nothing is more absurd, for this reason, than to explain the fall in the rate of profit by a rise in the rate of wages, although this may be the case by way of an exception.[a] Statistics is not able to make actual analyses of the rates of wages in different epochs and countries, until the conditions which shape the rate of profit are thoroughly understood. The rate of profit does not fall because labour becomes less productive, but because it becomes more productive. Both the rise in the rate of surplus value and the fall in the rate of profit are but specific forms through which growing productivity of labour is expressed under capitalism.

VI. THE INCREASE OF STOCK CAPITAL

The foregoing five points may still be supplemented by the following, which, however, cannot be more fully treated for the present. With the progress of capitalist production, which goes hand in hand

---

[a] See D. Ricardo, op. cit., pp. 120-21; cf. present edition, Vol. 32, p. 73.

with accelerated accumulation, a portion of capital is calculated and applied only as interest-bearing capital. Not in the sense in which every capitalist who lends out capital is satisfied with interest, while the industrial capitalist pockets the investor's profit. This has no bearing on the level of the general rate of profit, because for the latter profit = interest + profit of all kinds + ground rent, the division into these particular categories being immaterial to it. But in the sense that these capitals, although invested in large productive enterprises, yield only large or small amounts of interest, so-called dividends, after all costs have been deducted. In railways, for instance. These do not therefore go into levelling the general rate of profit, because they yield a lower than average rate of profit. If they did enter into it, the general rate of profit would fall much lower. Theoretically, they may be included in the calculation, and the result would then be a lower rate of profit than the seemingly existing rate, which is decisive for the capitalists; it would be lower, because the constant capital particularly in these enterprises is largest in its relation to the variable capital.

Chapter XV

EXPOSITION OF THE INTERNAL CONTRADICTIONS OF THE LAW

I. GENERAL

We have seen in the first part of this book that the rate of profit expresses the rate of surplus value always lower than it actually is. We have just seen that even a rising rate of surplus value has a tendency to express itself in a falling rate of profit. The rate of profit would equal the rate of surplus value only if $c = 0$, i. e., if the total capital were paid out in wages. A falling rate of profit does not express a falling rate of surplus value, unless the proportion of the value of the constant capital to the quantity of labour power which sets it in motion remains unchanged or the amount of labour power increases in relation to the value of the constant capital.

On the plea of analysing the rate of profit, Ricardo actually analyses the rate of surplus value alone, and this only on the assumption that the working day is intensively and extensively a constant magnitude.[a]

A fall in the rate of profit and accelerated accumulation are different expressions of the same process only in so far as both reflect the development of the productive power. Accumulation, in turn, hastens the fall of the rate of profit, inasmuch as it implies concentration of labour on a large scale, and thus a higher composition of capital. On the other hand, a fall in the rate of profit again hastens the concentration of capital and its centralisation through expropriation of minor capitalists, the few direct producers who still have anything left to be expropriated. This accelerates accumulation with regard to mass, although the rate of accumulation falls with the rate of profit.

On the other hand, the rate of self-expansion of the total capital, the rate of profit, being the goad of capitalist production (just as self-expansion of capital is its only purpose), its fall checks the formation of new independent capitals and thus appears as a threat to the development of the capitalist production process. It breeds overproduction, speculation, crises, and surplus capital alongside surplus population. Those economists, therefore, who, like Ricardo, regard the capitalist mode of production as absolute, feel at this point that it creates a barrier to itself, and for this reason attribute the barrier to Nature (in the theory of rent), not to production. But the main thing about their horror of the falling rate of profit is the feeling that the capitalist mode of production meets in the development of its productive forces a barrier which has nothing to do with the production of wealth as such; and this peculiar barrier testifies to the limitations and to the merely historical, transitory character of the capitalist mode of production; testifies that for the production of wealth, it is not an absolute mode, moreover, that at a certain stage it rather conflicts with its further development.[b]

True, Ricardo and his school considered only industrial profit, which includes interest. But the rate of ground rent likewise has a tendency to fall, although its absolute mass increases, and may also increase proportionately more than industrial profit. (See Ed. West,[c] who developed the law of ground rent *before* Ricardo). If we consider the total social capital C, and use p_1 for the industrial profit that

---

[a] Cf. present edition, Vol. 32, pp. 44, 51-52 and 60-67. - [b] Ibid., Vol. 33, p. 114. - [c] [E. West,] *Essay on the Application of Capital to Land...*, London, 1815; cf. present edition, Vol. 31, pp. 344-45.

remains after deducting interest and ground rent, i for interest, and r for ground rent, then $\frac{s}{C} = \frac{p}{C} = \frac{p_1 + i + r}{C} = \frac{p_1}{C} + \frac{i}{C} + \frac{r}{C}$. We have seen that while s, the total amount of surplus value, is continually increasing in the course of capitalist development, $\frac{s}{C}$ is just as steadily declining, because C grows still more rapidly than s. Therefore it is by no means a contradiction for p_1, i, and r to be steadily increasing, each individually, while $\frac{s}{C} = \frac{p}{C}$, as well as $\frac{p_1}{C}$, $\frac{i}{C}$, and $\frac{r}{C}$, should each by itself be steadily shrinking, or that p_1 should increase in relation to i, or r in relation to p_1, or to p_1 and i. With a rising total surplus value or profit s = p, and a simultaneously falling rate of profit $\frac{s}{C} = \frac{p}{C}$, the proportions of the parts p_1, i, and r, which make up s = p, may change at will within the limits set by the total amount of s without thereby affecting the magnitude of s or $\frac{s}{C}$.

The mutual variation of p_1, i, and r is merely a varying distribution of s among different classes. Consequently, $\frac{p_1}{C}$, $\frac{i}{C}$, or $\frac{r}{C}$, the rate of individual industrial profit, the rate of interest, and the ratio of ground rent to the total capital, may rise in relation to one another, while $\frac{s}{C}$, the general rate of profit, falls. The only condition is that the sum of all three $= \frac{s}{C}$. If the rate of profit falls from 50% to 25%, because the composition of a certain capital with, say, a rate of surplus value = 100% has changed from $50_c + 50_v$ to $75_c + 25_v$, then a capital of 1,000 will yield a profit of 500 in the first case, and in the second a capital of 4,000 will yield a profit of 1,000. We see that s or p have doubled, while p' has fallen by one-half. And if that 50% was formerly divided into 20 profit, 10 interest, and 20 rent, then $\frac{p_1}{C} = 20\%$, $\frac{i}{C} = 10\%$, and $\frac{r}{C} = 20\%$. If the proportions had remained the same after the change from 50% to 25%, then $\frac{p_1}{C} = 10\%$, $\frac{i}{C} = 5\%$, and $\frac{r}{C} = 10\%$. If, however, $\frac{p_1}{C}$ should fall to 8% and $\frac{i}{C}$ to 4%, then $\frac{r}{C}$ would rise to 13%. The relative magnitude of r would have risen as against p_1 and i, while p' would have remained the same. Under both assumptions, the sum of p_1, i, and r would have increased, because produced by a capital four times as large. Furthermore, Ricardo's assumption that originally industrial profit (plus interest) contains the entire surplus value is historically and logically false.[a] It

---

[a] Ibid., Vol. 31, p. 265.

is rather the progress of capitalist production which 1) gives the whole profit directly to the industrial and commercial capitalists for further distribution, and 2) reduces rent to the excess over the profit. On this capitalist basis, again, the rent grows, being a portion of profit (i. e., of the surplus value viewed as the product of the total capital), but not that specific portion of the product, which the capitalist pockets.

Given the necessary means of production, i. e., a sufficient accumulation of capital, the creation of surplus value is only limited by the labouring population if the rate of surplus value, i. e., the intensity of exploitation, is given; and no other limit but the intensity of exploitation if the labouring population is given. And the capitalist process of production consists essentially of the production of surplus value, represented in the surplus product or the aliquot portion of the produced commodities in which unpaid labour is objectified. It must never be forgotten that the production of this surplus value — and the reconversion of a portion of it into capital, or the accumulation, forms an integrate part of this production of surplus value — is the immediate purpose and compelling motive of capitalist production. It will never do, therefore, to represent capitalist production as something which it is not, namely as production whose immediate purpose is enjoyment or the manufacture of the means of enjoyment for the capitalist. This would be overlooking its specific character, which is revealed in all its inner essence.[a]

The creation of this surplus value makes up the direct process of production, which, as we have said, has no other limits but those mentioned above. As soon as all the surplus labour it was possible to squeeze out has been objectified in commodities, surplus value has been produced. But this production of surplus value completes but the first act of the capitalist process of production — the direct production process. Capital has absorbed so and so much unpaid labour. With the development of the process, which expresses itself in a drop in the rate of profit, the mass of surplus value thus produced swells to immense dimensions. Now comes the second act of the process. The entire mass of commodities, i. e., the total product, including the portion which replaces the constant and variable capital, and that representing surplus value, must be sold. If this is not done, or done only in part, or only at prices below the prices of production, the labourer

---

[a] Ibid., Vol. 28, pp. 339-40 and Vol. 32, p. 126.

has been indeed exploited, but his exploitation is not realised as such for the capitalist, and this can be bound up with a total or partial failure to realise the surplus value pressed out of him, indeed even with the partial or total loss of the capital. The conditions of direct exploitation, and those of realising it, are not identical. They diverge not only in place and time, but also logically. The first are only limited by the productive power of society, the latter by the proportional relation of the various branches of production and the consumer power of society. But this last-named is not determined either by the absolute productive power, or by the absolute consumer power, but by the consumer power based on antagonistic conditions of distribution, which reduce the consumption of the bulk of society to a minimum varying within more or less narrow limits. It is furthermore restricted by the tendency to accumulate, the drive to expand capital and produce surplus value on an extended scale. This is law for capitalist production, imposed by incessant revolutions in the methods of production themselves, by the depreciation of existing capital always bound up with them, by the general competitive struggle and the need to improve production and expand its scale merely as a means of self-preservation and under penalty of ruin. The market must, therefore, be continually extended, so that its interrelations and the conditions regulating them assume more and more the form of a natural law working independently of the producer, and become ever more uncontrollable. This internal contradiction seeks to resolve itself through expansion of the outlying field of production. But the more the productive power develops, the more it finds itself at variance with the narrow basis on which the conditions of consumption rest. It is no contradiction at all on this self-contradictory basis that there should be an excess of capital simultaneously with a growing surplus of population. For while a combination of these two would, indeed, increase the mass of produced surplus value, it would at the same time intensify the contradiction between the conditions under which this surplus value is produced and those under which it is realised.

If a certain rate of profit is given, the mass of profit will always depend on the magnitude of the advanced capital. The accumulation, however, is then determined by that portion of this mass which is reconverted into capital. As for this portion, being equal to the profit minus the revenue consumed by the capitalists, it will depend not merely on the value of this mass, but also on the cheapness of the commodities which the capitalist can buy with it, commodities which pass partly into his consumption, his revenue, and partly into his constant capital. (Wages are here assumed to be given.)

The mass of capital set in motion by the labourer, whose value he preserves by his labour and reproduces in his product, is quite different from the value which he adds to it. If the mass of the capital = 1,000 and the added labour = 100, the reproduced capital = 1,100. If the mass = 100 and the added labour = 20, the reproduced capital = 120. In the first case the rate of profit = 10%, in the second = 20%. And yet more can be accumulated out of 100 than out of 20. And thus the river of capital rolls on (aside from its depreciation through increase of the productive power), or its accumulation does, not in proportion to the rate of profit, but in proportion to the impetus it already possesses. So far as it is based on a high rate of surplus value, a high rate of profit is possible when the working day is very long, although labour is not productive. It is possible, because the wants of the labourers are very small, hence average wages very low, although the labour itself is unproductive. The low wages will correspond to the labourer's lack of energy. Capital then accumulates slowly, in spite of the high rate of profit. Population is stagnant and the working time which the product costs, is great, while the wages paid to the labourer are small.[a]

The rate of profit does not sink because the labourer is exploited any less, but because generally less labour is employed in proportion to the employed capital.

If, as shown, a falling rate of profit is bound up with an increase in the mass of profit, a larger portion of the annual product of labour is appropriated by the capitalist under the category of capital (as a replacement for consumed capital) and a relatively smaller portion under the category of profit. Hence the fantastic idea of priest Chalmers,[b] that the less of the annual product is expended by capitalists as capital, the greater the profits they pocket. In which case the state church comes to their assistance, to care for the consumption of the greater part of the surplus product, rather than having it used as capital. The preacher confounds cause with effect. Furthermore, the mass of profit increases in spite of its slower rate with the growth of the invested capital. However, this requires a simultaneous concentration

---

a Ibid., Vol. 32, pp. 434-35. - b Th. Chalmers, *On Political Economy in Connexion with the Moral State and Moral Prospects of Society*, Second edition, Glasgow, 1832, pp. 88-92; cf. present edition, Vol. 32, pp. 434-35.

of capital, since the conditions of production then demand employment of capital on a larger scale. It also requires its centralisation,
i. e., the swallowing up of the small capitalists by the big and their
deprivation of capital. It is again but an instance of separating — raised to the second power — the conditions of labour from the
producers to whose number these small capitalists still belong, since
their own labour continues to play a role in their case. The labour of
a capitalist stands altogether in inverse proportion to the size of his
capital, i. e., to the degree in which he is a capitalist. It is this same
severance of the conditions of labour, on the one hand, from the producers, on the other, that forms the conception of capital. It begins
with primitive accumulation (Buch I, Kap. XXIV[a]), appears as a
permanent process in the accumulation and concentration of capital,
and expresses itself finally as centralisation of existing capitals in a few
hands and a deprivation of many of their capital (to which expropriation is now changed). This process would soon bring about the
collapse of capitalist production if it were not for counteracting
tendencies, which have a continuous decentralising effect alongside
the centripetal one.

II. CONFLICT BETWEEN EXPANSION OF PRODUCTION
AND PRODUCTION OF SURPLUS VALUE

The development of the social productive power of labour is manifested in two ways: First, in the magnitude of the already produced
productive forces, the value and mass of the conditions of production
under which new production is carried on, and in the absolute magnitude of the already accumulated productive capital; secondly,
in the relative smallness of the portion of total capital laid out in
wages, i. e., in the relatively small quantity of living labour required
for the reproduction and self-expansion of a given capital, for mass
production. This also implies concentration of capital.

In relation to employed labour power the development of the
productive power again reveals itself in two ways: First, in the
increase of surplus labour, i. e., the reduction of the necessary labour
time required for the reproduction of labour power. Secondly, in the
decrease of the quantity of labour power (the number of labourers)
generally employed to set in motion a given capital.

---

[a] Ibid., Vol. 35, Ch. XXVI-XXVII.

The two movements not only go hand in hand, but mutually influence one another and are phenomena in which the same law expresses itself. Yet they affect the rate of profit in opposite ways. The total mass of profit is equal to the total mass of surplus value, the rate of profit $= \frac{s}{C} = \frac{\text{surplus value}}{\text{advanced total capital}}$. The surplus value, however, as a total, is determined first by its rate, and second by the mass of labour simultaneously employed at this rate, or, what amounts to the same, by the magnitude of the variable capital. One of these factors, the rate of surplus value, rises, and the other, the number of labourers, falls (relatively or absolutely). Inasmuch as the development of the productive power reduces the paid portion of employed labour, it raises the surplus value, because it raises its rate; but inasmuch as it reduces the total mass of labour employed by a given capital, it reduces the factor of the number by which the rate of surplus value is multiplied to obtain its mass. Two labourers, each working 12 hours daily, cannot produce the same mass of surplus value as 24 who work only 2 hours, even if they could live on air and hence did not have to work for themselves at all. In this respect, then, the compensation of the reduced number of labourers by intensifying the degree of exploitation has certain insurmountable limits. It may, for this reason, well check the fall in the rate of profit, but cannot prevent it altogether.[a]

With the development of the capitalist mode of production, therefore, the rate of profit falls, while its mass increases with the growing mass of the capital employed. Given the rate, the absolute increase in the mass of capital depends on its existing magnitude. But, on the other hand, if this magnitude is given, the proportion of its growth, i. e., the rate of its increment, depends on the rate of profit. The increase in the productive power (which, moreover, we repeat, always goes hand in hand with a depreciation of the available capital) can directly only increase the value of the existing capital if by raising the rate of profit it increases that portion of the value of the annual product which is reconverted into capital. As concerns the productive power of labour, this can only occur (since this productive power has nothing direct to do with the *value* of the existing capital) by raising the relative surplus value, or reducing the value of the constant capital, so that the commodities which enter either the reproduction of

---

labour power, or the elements of constant capital, are cheapened. Both imply a depreciation of the existing capital, and both go hand in hand with a reduction of the variable capital in relation to the constant. Both cause a fall in the rate of profit, and both slow it down. Furthermore, inasmuch as an increased rate of profit causes a greater demand of labour, it tends to increase the working population and thus the material, whose exploitation makes real capital out of capital.

Indirectly, however, the development of the productive power of labour contributes to the increase of the value of the existing capital by increasing the mass and variety of use values in which the same exchange value is represented and which form the material substance, i. e., the material elements of capital, the material objects making up the constant capital directly, and the variable capital at least indirectly. More products which may be converted into capital, whatever their exchange value, are created with the same capital and the same labour. These products may serve to absorb additional labour, hence also additional surplus labour, and therefore create additional capital. The amount of labour which a capital can command does not depend on its value, but on the mass of raw and auxiliary materials, machinery and elements of fixed capital and necessities of life, all of which it comprises, whatever their value may be. As the mass of the labour employed, and thus of surplus labour increases, there is also a growth in the value of the reproduced capital and in the surplus value newly added to it.

These two elements embraced by the process of accumulation, however, are not to be regarded merely as existing side by side in repose, as Ricardo does. They contain a contradiction which manifests itself in contradictory tendencies and phenomena.[a] These antagonistic agencies counteract each other simultaneously.

Alongside the stimulants of an actual increase of the labouring population, which spring from the increase of the portion of the total social product serving as capital, there are agencies which create a merely relative overpopulation.

Alongside the fall in the rate of profit mass of capitals grows, and hand in hand with this there occurs a depreciation of existing capitals which checks the fall and gives an accelerating motion to the accumulation of capital values.

Alongside the development of productivity there develops a higher

---

[a] Ibid., Vol. 32, pp. 167-74 and 158.

composition of capital, i. e., the relative decrease of the ratio of variable to constant capital.

These different influences may at one time operate predominantly side by side in space, and at another succeed each other in time. From time to time the conflict of antagonistic agencies finds vent in crises. The crises are always but momentary and forcible solutions of the existing contradictions. They are violent eruptions which for a time restore the disturbed equilibrium.

The contradiction, to put it in a very general way, consists in that the capitalist mode of production involves a tendency towards absolute development of the productive forces, regardless of the value and surplus value it contains, and regardless of the social conditions under which capitalist production takes place; while, on the other hand, its aim is to preserve the value of the existing capital and promote its self-expansion to the highest limit (i. e., to promote an ever more rapid growth of this value). The specific feature about it is that it uses the existing value of capital as a means of increasing this value to the utmost. The methods by which it accomplishes this include the fall of the rate of profit, depreciation of existing capital, and development of the productive forces of labour at the expense of already created productive forces.

The periodical depreciation of existing capital — one of the means immanent in capitalist production to check the fall of the rate of profit and hasten accumulation of capital value through formation of new capital — disturbs the given conditions, within which the process of circulation and reproduction of capital takes place, and is therefore accompanied by sudden stoppages and crises in the production process.

The decrease of variable in relation to constant capital, which goes hand in hand with the development of the productive forces, stimulates the growth of the labouring population, while continually creating an artificial overpopulation. The accumulation of capital in terms of value is slowed down by the falling rate of profit, to hasten still more the accumulation of use values, while this, in its turn, adds new momentum to accumulation in terms of value.

Capitalist production seeks continually to overcome these immanent barriers, but overcomes them only by means which again place these barriers in its way and on a more formidable scale.

The *real barrier* of capitalist production is *capital itself*. It is that capital and its self-expansion appear as the starting and the closing point, the motive and the purpose of production; that production is only production for *capital* and not vice versa, the means of production are not mere means for a constant expansion of the living process of the *society* of producers. The limits within which the preservation and self-expansion of the value of capital resting on the expropriation and pauperisation of the great mass of producers can alone move —these limits come continually into conflict with the methods of production employed by capital for its purposes, which drive towards unlimited extension of production, towards production as an end in itself, towards unconditional development of the social productivity of labour. The means — unconditional development of the productive forces of society — comes continually into conflict with the limited purpose, the self-expansion of the existing capital. The capitalist mode of production is, for this reason, a historical means of developing the material forces of production and creating an appropriate world market and is, at the same time, a continual conflict between this its historical task and its corresponding social relations of production.[a]

III. EXCESS CAPITAL AND EXCESS POPULATION

A drop in the rate of profit is attended by a rise in the minimum capital required by an individual capitalist for the productive employment of labour; required both for its exploitation generally, and for making the consumed labour time suffice as the labour time necessary for the production of the commodities, so that it does not exceed the average social labour time required for the production of the commodities. Concentration increases simultaneously, because beyond certain limits a large capital with a small rate of profit accumulates faster than a small capital with a large rate of profit. At a certain high point this increasing concentration in its turn causes a new fall in the rate of profit. The mass of small dispersed capitals is thereby driven along the adventurous road of speculation, credit frauds, stock swindles, and crises. The so-called plethora of capital always applies essentially to a plethora of the capital for which the fall in the rate of profit is not compensated through the mass of profit[b] — this is always

------

[a] Ibid., Vol. 28, p. 23 and Vol. 34, pp. 24-25. - [b] Ibid., Vol. 33, p. 112.

true of newly developing fresh offshoots of capital — or to a plethora which places capitals incapable of action on their own at the disposal of the managers of large enterprises in the form of credit. This plethora of capital arises from the same causes as those which call forth relative overpopulation, and is, therefore, a phenomenon supplementing the latter, although they stand at opposite poles — unemployed capital at one pole, and unemployed worker population at the other.

Overproduction of capital, not of individual commodities — although overproduction of capital always includes overproduction of commodities — is therefore simply overaccumulation of capital. To appreciate what this overaccumulation is (its closer analysis follows later), one need only assume it to be absolute. When would overproduction of capital be absolute? Overproduction which would affect not just one or another, or a few important spheres of production, but would be absolute in its full scope, hence would extend to all fields of production?

There would be absolute overproduction of capital as soon as additional capital for purposes of capitalist production = 0. The purpose of capitalist production, however, is self-expansion of capital, i. e., appropriation of surplus labour, production of surplus value, of profit. As soon as capital would, therefore, have grown in such a ratio to the labouring population that neither the absolute working time supplied by this population, nor the relative surplus working time, could be expanded any further (this last would not be feasible at any rate in the case when the demand for labour were so strong that there were a tendency for wages to rise); at a point, therefore, when the increased capital produced just as much, or even less, surplus value than it did before its increase, there would be absolute overproduction of capital; i. e., the increased capital $C + \Delta C$ would produce no more, or even less, profit than capital C before its expansion by ΔC. In both cases there would be a steep and sudden fall in the general rate of profit, but this time due to a change in the composition of capital not caused by the development of the productive power, but rather by a rise in the money value of the variable capital (because of increased wages) and the corresponding reduction in the proportion of surplus labour to necessary labour.

In reality, it would appear that a portion of the capital would lie completely or partially idle (because it would have to crowd out some of the active capital before it could expand its own value), and the other portion would produce values at a lower rate of profit, owing to the pressure of unemployed or but partly employed capital. It would be immaterial in this respect if a part of the additional capital were to take the place of the old capital, and the latter were to take its position in the additional capital. We should still always have the old sum of capital on one side, and the sum of additional capital on the other. The fall in the rate of profit would then be accompanied by an absolute decrease in the mass of profit, since the mass of employed labour power could not be increased and the rate of surplus value raised under the conditions we had assumed, so that the mass of surplus value could not be increased either. And the reduced mass of profit would have to be calculated on an increased total capital. But even if it is assumed that the employed capital continues to self-expand at the old rate of profit, and the mass of profit hence remains the same, this mass would still be calculated on an increased total capital, this likewise implying a fall in the rate of profit. If a total capital of 1,000 yielded a profit of 100, and after being increased to 1,500 still yielded 100, then, in the second case, 1,000 would yield only $66\frac{2}{3}$. Self-expansion of the old capital, in the absolute sense, would have been reduced. The capital = 1,000 would yield no more under the new circumstances than formerly a capital = $666\frac{2}{3}$.

It is evident, however, that this actual depreciation of the old capital could not occur without a struggle, and that the additional capital ΔC could not assume the functions of capital without a struggle. The rate of profit would not fall under the effect of competition due to overproduction of capital. It would rather be the reverse; it would be the competitive struggle which would begin because the fallen rate of profit and overproduction of capital originate from the same conditions. The part of ΔC in the hands of old functioning capitalists would be allowed to remain more or less idle to prevent a depreciation of their own original capital and not to narrow its place in the field of production. Or they would employ it, even at a momentary loss, to shift the need of keeping additional capital idle on newcomers and on their competitors in general.

That portion of ΔC which is in new hands would seek to assume a place for itself at the expense of the old capital, and would accomplish this in part by forcing a portion of the old capital to lie idle. It would compel the old capital to give up its old place and withdraw to join completely or partially unemployed additional capital.

A portion of the old capital has to lie unused under all circumstances;

it has to give up its characteristic quality as capital, so far as acting as such and producing value is concerned. The competitive struggle would decide what part of it would be particularly affected. So long as things go well, competition effects an operating fraternity of the capitalist class, as we have seen in the case of the equalisation of the general rate of profit, so that each shares in the common loot in proportion to the size of his respective investment. But as soon as it no longer is a question of sharing profits, but of sharing losses, everyone tries to reduce his own share to a minimum and to shove it off upon another. The class, as such, must inevitably lose. How much the individual capitalist must bear of the loss, i. e., to what extent he must share in it at all, is decided by strength and cunning, and competition then becomes a fight among hostile brothers. The antagonism between each individual capitalist's interests and those of the capitalist class as a whole, then comes to the surface, just as previously the identity of these interests operated in practice through competition.

How is this conflict settled and the conditions restored which correspond to the "sound" operation of capitalist production? The mode of settlement is already indicated in the very emergence of the conflict whose settlement is under discussion. It implies the withdrawal and even the partial destruction of capital amounting to the full value of additional capital ΔC, or at least a part of it. Although, as the description of this conflict shows, the loss is by no means equally distributed among individual capitals, its distribution being rather decided through a competitive struggle in which the loss is distributed in very different proportions and forms, depending on special advantages or previously captured positions, so that one capital is left unused, another is destroyed, and a third suffers but a relative loss, or is just temporarily depreciated, etc.

But the equilibrium would be restored under all circumstances through the withdrawal or even the destruction of more or less capital. This would extend partly to the material substance of capital, i. e., a part of the means of production, of fixed and circulating capital, would not operate, not act as capital; some of the operating establishments would then be brought to a standstill. Although, in this respect, time attacks and worsens all means of production (except land), the stoppage would in reality cause far greater damage to the means of production. However, the main effect in this case would be that these means of production would cease to function as such, that their function as means of production would be disturbed for a shorter or longer period.

The main damage, and that of the most acute nature, would occur in respect to capital, and in so far as the latter possesses the characteristic of value it would occur in respect to the *values* of capitals. That portion of the value of a capital which exists only in the form of claims on prospective shares of surplus value, i. e., profit, in fact in the form of promissory notes on production in various forms, is immediately depreciated by the reduction of the receipts on which it is calculated. A part of the gold and silver lies unused, i. e., does not function as capital. Part of the commodities on the market can complete their process of circulation and reproduction only through an immense contraction of their prices, hence through a depreciation of the capital which they represent. The elements of fixed capital are depreciated to a greater or lesser degree in just the same way. It must be added that definite, presupposed, price relations govern the process of reproduction, so that the latter is halted and thrown into confusion by a general drop in prices. This confusion and stagnation paralyses the function of money as a medium of payment, whose development is geared to the development of capital and is based on those presupposed price relations. The chain of payment obligations due at specific dates is broken in a hundred places. The confusion is augmented by the attendant collapse of the credit system, which develops simultaneously with capital, and leads to violent and acute crises, to sudden and forcible depreciations, to the actual stagnation and disruption of the process of reproduction, and thus to a real falling off in reproduction.[a]

But there would have been still other agencies at work at the same time. The stagnation of production would have laid off a part of the working class and would thereby have placed the employed part in a situation where it would have to submit to a reduction of wages even below the average. This has the very same effect on capital as an increase of the relative or absolute surplus value at average wages would have had. Prosperity would have led to more marriages among labourers and reduced the decimation of offspring. While implying a real increase in population, this does not signify an increase in the actual working population. But it affects the relations of the labourer

---

[a] Cf. present edition, Vol. 32, pp. 127-28.

to capital in the same way as an increase of the number of actually working labourers would have affected them. On the other hand, the fall in prices and the competitive struggle would have driven every capitalist to lower the individual value of his total product below its general value by means of new machines, new and improved working methods, new combinations, i. e., to increase the productive farmer of a given quantity of labour, to lower the proportion of variable to constant capital, and thereby to release some labourers; in short, to create an artificial overpopulation. Ultimately, the depreciation of the elements of constant capital would itself tend to raise the rate of profit. The mass of employed constant capital would have increased in relation to variable, but its value could have fallen. The ensuing stagnation of production would have prepared — within capitalistic limits — a subsequent expansion of production.

And thus the cycle would run its course anew. Part of the capital, depreciated by its functional stagnation, would recover its old value. For the rest, the same vicious circle would be described once more under expanded conditions of production, with an expanded market and increased productive forces.

However, even under the extreme conditions assumed by us this absolute overproduction of capital is not absolute overproduction, not absolute overproduction of means of production. It is overproduction of means of production only in so far as the latter *serve as capital*, and consequently include a self-expansion of value, must produce an additional value in proportion to the increased mass.

Yet it would still be overproduction, because capital would be unable to exploit labour to the degree required by a "sound", "normal" development of the process of capitalist production, to a degree which would at least increase the mass of profit along with the growing mass of the employed capital; to a degree which would, therefore, prevent the rate of profit from falling as much as the capital grows, or even more rapidly.

Overproduction of capital is never anything more than overproduction of means of production — of means of labour and necessities of life — which may serve as capital, i. e., may serve to exploit labour at a given degree of exploitation; a fall in the intensity of exploitation below a certain point, however, calls forth disturbances, and stoppages in the capitalist production process, crises, and destruction of capital. It is no contradiction that this overproduction of capital is accompanied by more or less considerable relative overpopulation. The circumstances which increased the productive power of labour, aug-mented the mass of produced commodities, expanded markets, accelerated accumulation of capital both in terms of its mass and its value, and lowered the rate of profit — these same circumstances have also created, and continuously create, a relative overpopulation, an overpopulation of labourers not employed by the surplus capital owing to the low degree of exploitation at which alone they could be employed, or at least owing to the low rate of profit which they would yield at the given degree of exploitation.

If capital is sent abroad, this is not done because it absolutely could not be applied at home, but because it can be employed at a higher rate of profit in a foreign country. But such capital is absolute excess capital for the employed labouring population and for the home country in general. It exists as such alongside the relative overpopula-tion, and this is an illustration of how both of them exist side by side, and mutually influence one another.

On the other hand, a fall in the rate of profit connected with accu-mulation necessarily calls forth a competitive struggle. Compensation of a fall in the rate of profit by a rise in the mass of profit applies only to the total social capital and to the big, firmly placed capitalists. The new additional capital operating independently does not enjoy any such compensating conditions. It must still win them, and so it is that a fall in the rate of profit calls forth a competitive struggle among cap-italists, not vice versa. To be sure, the competitive struggle is accom-panied by a temporary rise in wages and a resultant further tempo-rary fall of the rate of profit. The same occurs when there is an over-production of commodities, when markets are overstocked. Since the aim of capital is not to minister to certain wants, but to produce pro-fit, and since it accomplishes this purpose by methods which adapt the mass of production to the scale of production, not vice versa, a rift must continually ensue between the limited dimensions of consump-tion under capitalism and a production which forever tends to exceed this immanent barrier. Furthermore, capital consists of commodities, and therefore overproduction of capital implies overproduction of com-modities. Hence the peculiar phenomenon of economists who deny overproduction of commodities, admitting overproduction of capital.[a] To say that there is no general overproduction, but rather a dispropor-tion within the various branches of production, is no more than to say

---

[a] Ibid., Vol. 32, pp. 132-35 and Vol. 33, pp. 113-14.

that under capitalist production the proportionality of the individual branches of production springs as a continual process from disproportionality, because the cohesion of the aggregate production imposes itself as a blind law upon the agents of production, and not as a law which, being understood and hence controlled by their common mind, brings the production process under their joint control. It amounts furthermore to demanding that countries in which the capitalist mode of production is not developed, should consume and produce at a rate which suits the countries with the capitalist mode of production. If it is said that overproduction is only relative, this is quite correct; but the entire capitalist mode of production is only a relative one, whose barriers are not absolute. They are absolute only for this mode, i. e., on its basis. How could there otherwise be a shortage of demand for the very commodities which the mass of the people lack, and how would it be possible for this demand to be sought abroad, in foreign markets, to pay the labourers at home the average amount of necessities of life? This is possible only because in this specific capitalist interrelation the surplus product assumes a form in which its owner cannot offer it for consumption, unless it first reconverts itself into capital for him. If it is finally said that the capitalists have only to exchange and consume their commodities among themselves, then the entire nature of the capitalist mode of production is lost sight of; and also forgotten is the fact that it is a matter of expanding the value of the capital, not consuming it. In short, all these objections to the obvious phenomena of overproduction (phenomena which pay no heed to these objections) amount to the contention that the barriers of *capitalist* production are not barriers of *production generally*, and therefore not barriers of this specific, capitalist mode of production. The contradiction of the capitalist mode of production, however, lies precisely in its tendency towards an absolute development of the productive *forces*, which continually comes into conflict with the specific *conditions* of production in which capital moves, and alone can move.

There are not too many necessities of life produced, in proportion to the existing population. Quite the reverse. Too little is produced to decently and humanely satisfy the wants of the great mass.

There are not too many means of production produced to employ the able-bodied portion of the population. Quite the reverse. In the first place, too large a portion of the produced population is not really capable of working, and is through force of circumstances made dependent on exploiting the labour of others, or on labour which can pass under this name only under a miserable mode of production. In the second place, not enough means of production are produced to permit the employment of the entire able-bodied population under the most productive conditions, so that their absolute working period could be shortened by the mass and effectiveness of the constant capital employed during working hours.

On the other hand, too many means of labour and necessities of life are produced at times to permit of their serving as means for the exploitation of labourers at a certain rate of profit. Too many commodities are produced to permit of a realisation and conversion into new capital of the value and surplus value contained in them under the conditions of distribution and consumption peculiar to capitalist production, i. e., too many to permit of the continuation of this process without constantly recurring explosions.

Not too much wealth is produced. But at times too much wealth is produced in its capitalistic, self-contradictory forms.

The limitations of the capitalist mode of production come to the surface:

1) In that the development of the productive power of labour creates out of the falling rate of profit a law which at a certain point comes into antagonistic conflict with this development and must be overcome constantly through crises.

2) In that the expansion or contraction of production are determined by the appropriation of unpaid labour and the proportion of this unpaid labour to objectified labour in general, or, to speak the language of the capitalists, by profit and the proportion of this profit to the employed capital, thus by a definite rate of profit, rather than by the relation of production to social requirements, i. e., to the requirements of socially developed human beings. It is for this reason that the capitalist mode of production meets with barriers at a certain expanded stage of production which, if viewed from the other premiss, would reversely have been altogether inadequate. It comes to a standstill at a point fixed by the production and realisation of profit, and not by the satisfaction of requirements.

If the rate of profit falls, there follows, on the one hand, an exertion of capital in order that the individual capitalists, through improved methods, etc., may depress the value of their individual commodity below the social average value and thereby realise an extra profit at the prevailing market price. On the other hand, there appears swindling and a general promotion of swindling by recourse to frenzied ventures with new methods of production, new investments of capital, new adventures, all for the sake of securing a shred of extra profit which is independent of the general average and rises above it.

The rate of profit, i. e., the relative increment of capital, is above all important to all new offshoots of capital seeking to find an independent place for themselves. And as soon as formation of capital were to fall into the hands of a few established big capitals, for which the mass of profit compensates for the falling rate of profit, the vital flame of production would be altogether extinguished. It would die out. The rate of profit is the motive power of capitalist production. Things are produced only so long as they can be produced with a profit. Hence the concern of the English economists over the decline of the rate of profit.[a] The fact that the bare possibility of this happening should worry Ricardo, shows his profound understanding of the conditions of capitalist production. It is that which is held against him, it is his unconcern about "human beings", and his having an eye solely for the development of the productive forces, whatever the cost in human beings and capital *values*—it is precisely that which is the important thing about him.[b] Development of the productive forces of social labour is the historical task and justification of capital. This is just the way in which it unconsciously creates the material conditions of a higher mode of production. What worries Ricardo is the fact that the rate of profit, the stimulating principle of capitalist production, the fundamental premiss and driving force of accumulation, should be endangered by the development of production itself. And here the quantitative proportion means everything. There is, indeed, something deeper behind it, of which he is only vaguely aware. It comes to the surface here in a purely economic way—i. e., from the bourgeois point of view, within the limitations of capitalist understanding, from the standpoint of capitalist production itself—that it has its barrier, that it is relative, that it is not an absolute, but only a historical mode of production corresponding to a definite limited epoch in the development of the material conditions of production.

IV. SUPPLEMENTARY REMARKS

Since the development of the productive power of labour proceeds very disproportionately in the various lines of industry, and not only

---

[a] Ibid., Vol. 33, p. 112. - [b] Ibid., p. 114.

disproportionately in degree but frequently also in opposite directions, it follows that the mass of average profit (= surplus value) must be substantially below the level one would naturally expect after the development of the productive power in the most advanced branches of industry. The fact that the development of the productive power in different lines of industry proceeds at substantially different rates and frequently even in opposite directions, is not due merely to the anarchy of competition and the peculiarity of the bourgeois mode of production. Productivity of labour is also bound up with natural conditions, which frequently become less productive as productivity grows—inasmuch as the latter depends on social conditions. Hence the opposite movements in these different spheres—progress here, and retrogression there. Consider the mere influence of the seasons, for instance, on which the bulk of raw materials depends for its mass, the exhaustion of forest lands, coal and iron mines, etc.[a]

While the circulating part of constant capital, such as raw materials, etc., continually increases its mass in proportion to the productivity of labour, this is not the case with fixed capital, such as buildings, machinery, and lighting and heating facilities, etc. Although in absolute terms a machine becomes dearer with the growth of its bodily mass, it becomes relatively cheaper. If five labourers produce ten times as much of a commodity as before, this does not increase the outlay for fixed capital ten-fold; although the value of this part of constant capital increases with the development of the productive power it does not by any means increase in the same proportion.[b] We have frequently pointed out the difference in the ratio of constant to variable capital as expressed in the fall of the rate of profit, and the difference in the same ratio as expressed in relation to the individual commodity and its price with the development of the productivity of labour.

//The value of a commodity is determined by the total labour time of past and living labour incorporated in it.[c] The increase in labour productivity consists precisely in that the share of living labour is reduced while that of past labour is increased, but in such a way that the total quantity of labour incorporated in that commodity declines; in such a way, therefore, that living labour decreases more than past labour increases. The past labour contained in the value of a commodity—the constant part of capital—consists partly of the wear and tear of fixed, partly of circulating, constant capital entirely consumed

---

[a] Ibid., pp. 131 and 135. - [b] Ibid., pp. 131-32. - [c] Ibid., pp. 136-37.

by that commodity, such as raw and auxiliary materials. The portion of value deriving from raw and auxiliary materials must decrease with the increased productivity of labour, because with regard to these materials the productivity expresses itself precisely by reducing their value. On the other hand, it is most characteristic of the rising productive power of labour that the fixed part of constant capital is strongly augmented, and with it that portion of its value which is transferred by wear and tear to the commodities. For a new method of production to represent a real increase in productivity, it must transfer a smaller additional portion of the value of fixed capital to each unit of the commodity in wear and tear than the portion of value deducted from it through the saving in living labour; in short, it must reduce the value of the commodity. It must obviously do so even if, as it occurs in some cases, an additional value goes into the value of the commodity for more or dearer raw or auxiliary materials over and above the additional portion for wear and tear of the fixed capital. All additions to the value must be more than offset by the reduction in value resulting from the decrease in living labour.

This reduction of the total quantity of labour going into a commodity seems, accordingly, to be the essential criterion of increased productive power of labour, no matter under what social conditions production is carried on. Productivity of labour, indeed, would always be measured by this standard in a society, in which producers regulate their production according to a preconceived plan, or even under simple commodity production. But how does the matter stand under capitalist production?

Suppose, a certain branch of capitalist industry produces a normal unit of its commodity under the following conditions: The wear and tear of fixed capital amounts to $\frac{1}{2}$ shilling per piece; raw and auxiliary materials go into it to the amount of $17\frac{1}{2}$ shillings per piece; wages, 2 shillings; and surplus value, 2 shillings at a rate of surplus value of 100%. Total value = 22 shillings. We assume for the sake of simplicity that the capital in this branch of production has the average composition of social capital, so that the price of production of the commodity is identical with its value, and the profit of the capitalist with the created surplus value. Then the cost price of the commodity $=\frac{1}{2} + 17\frac{1}{2} + 2 = 20$s., the average rate of profit $\frac{2}{20} = 10\%$, and the price of production per piece of the commodity, like its value = 22s.

Suppose a machine is invented which reduces by half the living labour required per piece of the commodity, but trebles that portion of its value accounted for by the wear and tear of the fixed capital. In that case, the calculation is: Wear and tear = $1\frac{1}{2}$ s., raw and auxiliary materials, as before, $17\frac{1}{2}$ s., wages, 1s., surplus value 1s., total 21s. The commodity then falls 1s. in value; the new machine has certainly increased the productivity of labour. But the capitalist sees the matter as follows: his cost price is now $1\frac{1}{2}$ s. for wear, $17\frac{1}{2}$ s. for raw and auxiliary materials, 1s. for wages, total 20s., as before. Since the rate of profit is not immediately altered by the new machine, he will receive 10% over his cost price, that is, 2s. The price of production, then, remains unaltered = 22s., but is 1s. above the value. For a society producing under capitalist conditions the commodity has *not* cheapened. The new machine is *no* improvement for it. The capitalist is, therefore, not interested in introducing it. And since its introduction would make his present, not as yet worn-out, machinery simply worthless, would turn it into scrap-iron, hence would cause a positive loss, he takes good care not to commit this, what is for him a utopian, mistake.

The law of the increased productive power of labour is not, therefore, absolutely valid for capital. So far as capital is concerned, this productive power does not increase through a saving in living labour in general, but only through a saving in the *paid* portion of living labour, as compared to labour expended in the past, as we have already indicated in passing in Book I (Kap. XIII, 2, S. 409/398).[a] Here the capitalist mode of production is beset with another contradiction. Its historical mission is unconstrained development in geometrical progression of the productivity of human labour. It goes back on its mission whenever, as here, it checks the development of productivity. It thus demonstrates again that it is becoming senile and that it is more and more outlived.// [37]

———

Under competition, the increasing minimum of capital required with the increase in productivity for the successful operation of an in-

[37] The foregoing is placed in two oblique lines, because, though a rehash of the notes of the original manuscript, it goes in some points beyond the scope of the material found in the original.— *F. E.*

———

[a] English edition: Vol. I, Ch. XV, 2 (present edition, Vol. 35).

dependent industrial establishment, assumes the following aspect: As soon as the new, more expensive equipment has become universally established, smaller capitals are henceforth excluded from this industry. Smaller capitals can carry on independently in the various spheres of production only in the infancy of mechanical inventions. Very large undertakings, such as railways, on the other hand, which have an unusually high proportion of constant capital, do not yield the average rate of profit, but only a portion of it, only an interest. Otherwise the general rate of profit would have fallen still lower. But this offers direct employment to large concentrations of capital in the form of stocks.

Growth of capital, hence accumulation of capital, does not imply a fall in the rate of profit, unless it is accompanied by the aforementioned changes in the proportion of the organic constituents of capital. Now it so happens that in spite of the constant daily revolutions in the mode of production, now this and now that larger or smaller portion of the total capital continues to accumulate for certain periods on the basis of a given average proportion of those constituents, so that there is no organic change with its growth, and consequently no cause for a fall in the rate of profit. This constant expansion of capital, hence also an expansion of production, on the basis of the old method of production which goes quietly on while new methods are already being introduced at its side, is another reason, why the rate of profit does not decline as much as the total capital of society grows.

The increase in the absolute number of labourers does not occur in all branches of production, and not uniformly in all, in spite of the relative decrease of variable capital laid out in wages. In agriculture, the decrease of the element of living labour may be absolute.

At any rate, it is but a requirement of the capitalist mode of production that the number of wage workers should increase absolutely, in spite of its relative decrease. Labour power becomes redundant for it as soon as it is no longer necessary to employ it for 12 to 15 hours daily. A development of productive forces which would diminish the absolute number of labourers, i. e., enable the entire nation to accomplish its total production in a shorter time span, would cause a revolution, because it would put the bulk of the population out of the running. This is another manifestation of the specific barrier of capitalist production, showing also that capitalist production is by no means an absolute form for the development of the productive forces and for the creation of wealth, but rather that at a certain point it comes into

collision with this development. This collision appears partly in periodical crises, which arise from the circumstance that now this and
now that portion of the labouring population becomes redundant under its old mode of employment. The limit of capitalist production is
the excess time of the labourers. The absolute spare time gained by
society does not concern it. The development of the productive power
concerns it only in so far as it increases the surplus labour time of the
working class, not because it decreases the labour time for material
production in general. It moves thus in a contradiction.[a]

We have seen that the growing accumulation of capital implies its
growing concentration. Thus grows the power of capital, the alienation of the conditions of social production personified in the capitalist
from the real producers. Capital comes more and more to the fore as
a social power, whose agent is the capitalist. This social power no longer
stands in any possible relation to that which the labour of a single
individual can create. It becomes an estranged, independent, social
power, which stands opposed to society as an object, and as an object
that is the capitalist's source of power. The contradiction between the
general social power into which capital develops, on the one hand,
and the private power of the individual capitalists over these social
conditions of production, on the other, becomes ever more irreconcilable, and yet contains the solution of the problem, because it implies
at the same time the transformation of the conditions of production
into general, common, social, conditions. This transformation stems
from the development of the productive forces under capitalist production, and from the ways and means by which this development
takes place.

No capitalist ever voluntarily introduces a new method of production, no matter how much more productive it may be, and how much
it may increase the rate of surplus value, so long as it reduces the rate
of profit. Yet every such new method of production cheapens the
commodities. Hence, the capitalist sells them originally above their
prices of production, or, perhaps, above their value. He pockets the
difference between their costs of production and the market prices of
the same commodities produced at higher costs of production. He can
do this, because the average labour time required socially for the pro-

----

[a] Cf. present edition, Vol. 33, pp. 141-42.

duction of these latter commodities is higher than the labour time required for the new methods of production. His method of production stands above the social average. But competition makes it general and subject to the general law. There follows a fall in the rate of profit — perhaps first in this sphere of production, and eventually it achieves a balance with the rest — which is, therefore, wholly independent of the will of the capitalist.

It is still to be added to this point, that this same law also governs those spheres of production, whose product passes neither directly nor indirectly into the consumption of the labourers, or into the conditions under which their necessities are produced; it applies, therefore, also to those spheres of production, in which there is no cheapening of commodities to increase the relative surplus value or cheapen labour power. (At any rate, a cheapening of constant capital in all these branches may increase the rate of profit, with the exploitation of labour remaining the same.) As soon as the new production method begins to spread, and thereby to furnish tangible proof that these commodities can actually be produced more cheaply, the capitalists working with the old methods of production must sell their product below its full price of production, because the value of this commodity has fallen, and because the labour time required by them to produce it is greater than the social average. In one word — and this appears as an effect of competition — these capitalists must also introduce the new method of production, in which the proportion of variable to constant capital has been reduced.[a]

All the circumstances which lead to the use of machinery cheapening the price of a commodity produced by it, come down in the last analysis to a reduction of the quantity of labour absorbed by a single piece of the commodity; and secondly, to a reduction in the wear-and-tear portion of the machinery, whose value goes into a single piece of the commodity. The less rapid the wear of machinery, the more the commodities over which it is distributed, and the more living labour it replaces before its term of reproduction arrives. In both cases the quantity and value of the fixed constant capital increase in relation to the variable.

* "All other things being equal, the power of a nation to save from its profits varies with the rate of profits: is great when they are high, less, when low; but as the rate of

a Ibid., pp. 144-49.

profit declines, all other things do not remain equal.... A low rate of profit is ordinarily accompanied by a rapid rate of accumulation, relatively to the numbers of the people, as in England ... a high rate of profit by a slower rate of accumulation, relatively to the numbers of the people." * Examples: Poland, Russia, India, etc. (Richard Jones, *An Introductory Lecture on Political Economy*, London, 1833, p. 50 ff.)

Jones emphasises correctly that in spite of the falling rate of profit the INDUCEMENTS AND FACULTIES TO ACCUMULATE are augmented [a]; first, on account of the growing relative overpopulation; second, because the growing productivity of labour is accompanied by an increase in the mass of use values represented by the same exchange value, hence in the material elements of capital; third, because the branches of production become more varied; fourth, due to the development of the credit system, the stock companies, etc., and the resultant case of converting money into capital without becoming an industrial capitalist; fifth, because the wants and the greed for wealth increase; and, sixth, because the mass of investments in fixed capital grows, etc.

Three cardinal facts of capitalist production:

1) Concentration of means of production in few hands, whereby they cease to appear as the property of the immediate labourers and turn into social production capacities. Even if initially they are the private property of capitalists. These are the trustees of bourgeois society, but they pocket all the proceeds of this trusteeship.

2) Organisation of labour itself into social labour: through co-operation, division of labour, and the uniting of labour with the natural sciences.

In these two senses, the capitalist mode of production abolishes private property and private labour, even though in contradictory forms.[b]

3) Creation of the world market.

The stupendous productive power developing under the capitalist mode of production relative to population, and the increase, if not in the same proportion, of capital values (not just of their material substance), which grow much more rapidly than the population, contradict the basis, which constantly narrows in relation to the expanding wealth, and for which all this immense productive power works. They also contradict the conditions under which this swelling capital augments its value. Hence the crises.

---

a Ibid., p. 336. - b Ibid., pp. 342-43.

Part IV

CONVERSION OF COMMODITY CAPITAL AND MONEY CAPITAL INTO COMMERCIAL CAPITAL AND MONEY-DEALING CAPITAL (MERCHANT'S CAPITAL)

Chapter XVI

COMMERCIAL CAPITAL

Merchant's, or trading, capital breaks up into two forms or sub-divisions, namely, commercial capital and money-dealing capital, which we shall now define more closely, in so far as this is necessary for our analysis of capital in its basic structure. This is all the more necessary, because modern political economy, even in the persons of its best exponents, throws trading capital and industrial capital indiscriminately together and, in effect, wholly overlooks the characteristic peculiarities of the former.[a]

————

The movements of commodity capital have been analysed in Book II.[b] To take the total capital of society, one part of it — always made up of different elements and even changing in magnitude — always exists in the form of commodities on the market, to be converted into money. Another part exists on the market in the form of money, to be converted into commodities. It is always in the process of this transition, of this formal metamorphosis. Inasmuch as this function of capital in the process of circulation is at all set apart as a special function of a special capital, as a function established by virtue of the division of labour to a special group of capitalists, commodity capital becomes commercial capital.

We have explained (Book II, Chapter VI, "The Costs of Circulation," 2 and 3) to what extent the transport industry, storage and dis-

————

a Cf. present edition, Vol. 33, pp. 63-64. - b Ibid., Vol. 36, pp. 92-105.

tribution of commodities in a distributable form, may be regarded as production processes continuing within the process of circulation. These episodes incidental to the circulation of commodity capital are sometimes confused with the distinct functions of merchant's or commercial capital. Sometimes they are, indeed, practically bound up with these distinct, specific functions, although with the development of the social division of labour the function of merchant's capital evolves in a pure form, i. e., divorced from those real functions, and independent of them. Those functions are therefore irrelevant to our purpose, which is to define the specific difference of this special form of capital. In so far as capital solely employed in the circulation process, special commercial capital, partly combines those functions with its specific ones, it does not appear in its pure form. We obtain its pure form after stripping it of all these functions.

We have seen that the existence of capital as commodity capital and the metamorphosis it undergoes within the sphere of circulation, in the market, as commodity capital — a metamorphosis which resolves itself into buying and selling, converting commodity capital into money capital and money capital into commodity capital — that this forms a phase in the reproduction process of industrial capital, hence in its process of production as a whole. We have also seen, however, that it is distinguished in its function as a capital of circulation from its function as productive capital. These are two different and separate forms of existence of the same capital. One portion of the total social capital is continually on the market in the form of capital of circulation, passing through this process of transmutation, although for each individual capital its existence as commodity capital, and its metamorphosis as such, merely represent ever-vanishing and ever renewed points of transition — i. e., stages of transition in the continuity of its production process, and although the elements of commodity capital in the market vary continuously for this reason, being constantly withdrawn from the commodity market and equally periodically returned to it as new products of the process of production.

Commercial capital is nothing but a converted form of a part of this capital of circulation constantly to be found in the market, ever in the process of its metamorphosis, and always encompassed by the sphere of circulation. We say a part, because a part of the selling and buying of commodities always takes place directly between industrial capitalists. We leave this part entirely out of consideration in this analysis, because it contributes nothing to defining the conception, or to understanding the specific nature of merchant's capital, and because it has furthermore been exhaustively treated for our purpose in Book II.[a]

The dealer in commodities, as a capitalist generally, appears on the market primarily as the representative of a certain sum of money, which he advances as a capitalist, i. e., which he wants to turn from x (its original value) into x + Δx (the original sum plus profit). But it is evident to him — not being just a capitalist in general, but rather a special dealer in commodities — that his capital must first enter the market in the form of money capital, for he does not produce commodities. He merely trades in them, promotes their movement, and to operate with them he must first buy them, and, therefore, must be in possession of money capital.

Suppose that a dealer in commodities owns £3,000 which he invests as a trading capital. With these £3,000 he buys, say, 30,000 yards of linen from some linen manufacturer at 2s. per yard. He then sells the 30,000 yards. If the annual average rate of profit = 10% and he makes an annual profit of 10% after deducting all incidental expenses, then by the end of the year he has converted his £3,000 into £3,300. How he makes this profit is a question which we shall discuss later. At present, we intend to consider solely the form of the movement of his capital. With his £3,000 he keeps buying linen and selling it; he constantly repeats this operation of buying in order to sell, M — C — M′, the simple form of capital as it obtains entirely in the process of circulation, uninterrupted by the production process, which lies outside its own movement and function.

What is now the relation of this commercial capital to commodity capital as a mere form of existence of industrial capital? So far as the linen manufacturer is concerned, he has realised the value of his linen with the merchant's money and thereby completed the first phase in the metamorphosis of his commodity capital — its conversion into money. Other conditions being equal, he can now proceed to reconvert this money into yarn, coal, wages, etc., and into means of subsistence, etc., for the consumption of his revenue. Hence, leaving aside the revenue expenditure, he can go on with his process of reproduction.

---

[a] Ibid., Ch. III.

But while the sale of the linen, its metamorphosis into money, has taken place for him, as producer, it has not yet taken place for the linen itself. It is still on the market as commodity capital awaiting to undergo its first metamorphosis — to be sold. Nothing has happened to this linen besides a change in the person of its owner. As concerns its purpose, as concerns its place in the process, it is still commodity capital, a saleable commodity, with the only difference that it is now in the merchant's hands instead of the manufacturer's. The function of selling it, of effecting the first phase of its metamorphosis, has passed from the manufacturer to the merchant, has become the special business of the merchant, whereas previously it was a function which the producer had to perform himself after having completed the function of its production.

Let us assume that the merchant fails to sell the 30,000 yards of linen during the interval required by the linen manufacturer to bring another 30,000 yards to market at a value of £3,000. The merchant cannot buy them again, because he still has in stock the unsold 30,000 yards which have not as yet been reconverted into money capital. A stoppage ensues, i. e., an interruption of reproduction. The linen producer might, of course, have additional money capital at his disposal, which he could convert into productive capital, regardless of the sale of the 30,000 yards, in order to continue the production process. But this would not alter the situation. So far as the capital tied up in the 30,000 yards of linen is concerned, its process of reproduction is, and remains, interrupted. It is, indeed, easily seen here that the merchant's operations are really nothing but operations that must be performed at all events to convert the producer's commodity capital into money. They are operations which effect the functions of commodity capital in the circulation and reproduction processes. If it devolved upon the producer's clerk to attend exclusively to the sale, and also the purchase, instead of an independent merchant, this connection would not be obscured for a single moment.

Commercial capital is, therefore, nothing but the producer's commodity capital which has to undergo the process of conversion into money — to perform its function of commodity capital on the market — the only difference being that instead of representing an incidental function of the producer, it is now the exclusive operation of a special kind of capitalist, the dealer in commodities, and is set apart as the business of a special investment of capital.

This becomes evident, furthermore, in the specific form of circulation of commercial capital. The merchant buys a commodity and then sells it: M — C — M'. In the simple circulation of commodities, or even in the circulation of commodities as it appears in the circulation process of industrial capital, C' — M — C, circulation is effected by each piece of money changing hands twice. The linen manufacturer sells his commodity — linen, converting it into money; the buyer's money passes into his hands. With this same money he buys yarn, coal, labour, etc.— expends the money for reconverting the value of linen into the commodities which make up its production elements. The commodity he buys is not the same commodity, not the same kind of commodity which he sells. He has sold products and bought means of production. But it is different with respect to the movement of merchant's capital. With his £3,000 the linen merchant buys 30,000 yards of linen; he sells the same 30,000 yards of linen in order to retrieve his money capital (£3,000 and the profit) from circulation. It is not the same pieces of money, but rather the same commodity which here changes places twice; the commodity passes from the seller into the hands of the buyer, and from the hands of the buyer, who now becomes seller, into those of another buyer. It is sold twice, and may be sold repeatedly through the medium of a series of merchants. And it is precisely through this repeated sale, through this two-fold change of place of the same commodity, that the money advanced for its purchase by the first buyer is retrieved, its reflux to him effected. In one case, C' — M — C effects the two-fold change of place of the same money, the sale of a commodity in one form and the purchase of a commodity in another. In the other case, M — C — M' effects the two-fold change of place of the same commodity, the withdrawal of advanced money from circulation. It is evident that the commodity has not been finally sold when it passes from the producer into the hands of the merchant and that the latter merely carries on the operation of selling — or effects the function of commodity capital. But at the same time it is evident that what is C — M, a mere function of his capital in its transient form of commodity capital, for the productive capitalist, is M — C — M', a specific increase in the value of his advanced money capital, for the merchant. One phase of the metamorphosis of commodities appears here in respect to the merchant in the form of M — C — M', hence as evolution of a distinct kind of capital.

The merchant finally sells his commodity, that is, the linen, to the consumer, be it a productive consumer (for instance, a bleacher), or an individual who acquires the linen for his private use. The merchant thereby recovers his advanced capital (with a profit), and can repeat his operation anew. Had the money served merely as a means of payment in purchasing the linen, so that the merchant would have had to pay only after six weeks, and had he succeeded in selling before this term was out, he could have paid the linen manufacturer without advancing any money capital of his own. Had he not sold it, he would have had to advance his £3,000 on the date of expiration, instead of on delivery of the linen. And if a drop in the market prices had compelled him to sell below the purchase price, he would have had to make good the shortage out of his own capital.

What is it, then, that lends to commercial capital the character of an independently operating capital, whereas in the hands of the producer who does his own selling it is obviously merely a special form of his capital in a specific phase of the reproduction process during its sojourn in the sphere of circulation?

First: The fact that commodity capital is finally converted into money, that it performs its initial metamorphosis, i. e., its appropriate function on the market qua commodity capital while in the hands of an agent other than the producer, and that this function of commodity capital is effected by the merchant in his operations, his buying and selling, so that these operations assume the appearance of a separate undertaking distinct from the other functions of industrial capital — and hence of an independent undertaking. It is a distinct form of the social division of labour, so that part of the function ordinarily performed as a special phase of the reproduction process of capital, in this case — circulation, appears as the exclusive function of specific circulation agent distinct from the producer. But this alone would by no means give this particular business the aspect of a function of a specific capital distinct from, and independent of, industrial capital engaged in the process of reproduction; indeed, it does not so appear in cases where trade is carried on by travelling salesmen or other direct agents of the industrial capitalist. Therefore, there must be a second element involved.

Second: This arises from the fact that in his capacity as an independent circulation agent, the merchant advances money capital (his own or borrowed). The transaction which for industrial capital in the reproduction process amounts merely to C — M, i. e., converting commodity capital into money capital, or mere sale, assumes for the merchant the form of M — C — M', or purchase and sale of the same commodity, and thus of a reflux of money capital which leaves him in the purchase, and returns to him in the sale.

It is always C — M, the conversion of commodity capital into money capital, which for the merchant assumes the form of M — C — M, inasmuch as he advances capital to purchase commodities from their producers; it is always the first metamorphosis of commodity capital, although for a producer, or for industrial capital in process of reproduction, the same transaction may amount to M — C, to a reconversion of money into commodities (means of production), to the second phase of the metamorphosis. For the linen producer, the first metamorphosis was C — M, the conversion of his commodity capital into money capital. For the merchant the same act appears as M — C, as a conversion of his money capital into commodity capital. Now, if he sells this linen to a bleacher, it will mean M — C, i. e., the conversion of money capital into productive capital, this being the second metamorphosis of his commodity capital for the bleacher, while for the merchant it means C — M, the sale of the linen he had bought. But in fact it is only at this point that the commodity capital produced by the linen manufacturer has been finally sold. In other words, this M — C — M of the merchant represents no more than a middleman's function for C — M between two manufacturers. Or let us assume that the linen manufacturer buys yarn from a yarn dealer with a portion of the value of the sold linen. This is M — C for him. But for the merchant selling the yarn it is C — M, the resale of the yarn. As concerning the yarn in its capacity of commodity capital, it is no more than its final sale, whereby it passes from the sphere of circulation into that of consumption; it is C — M, the consummation of its first metamorphosis. Whether the merchant buys from, or sells to the industrial capitalist, his M — C — M, the circuit of merchant's capital, always expresses what is just C — M, or simply the completion of its first metamorphosis, with regard to the commodity capital, a transient form of industrial capital in process of reproduction. The M — C of merchant's capital is C — M only for the industrial capitalist, not for the commodity capital produced by him. It is but the transfer of commodity capital from the industrialist to the circulation agent. It is not until the merchant's capital closes C — M that functioning commodity capital performs its final C — M. M — C — M amounts solely to two C — M's of the same commodity capital, two successive sales of it, which merely effect its last and final sale.

Thus, commodity capital assumes in commercial capital the form of an independent type of capital because the merchant advances money capital, which is expanded and functions as capital only by serving exclusively to mediate the metamorphosis of commodity capital, its function as commodity capital, i. e., its conversion into money, and it accomplishes this by the continual purchase and sale of commodities. This is its exclusive operation. This activity of effecting the circulation process of industrial capital is the exclusive function of the money capital with which the merchant operates. By means of this function he converts his money into money capital, moulds his M into M — C — M′, and by the same process converts commodity capital into commercial capital.

So long and so far as commercial capital exists in the form of commodity capital, it is obviously nothing else — from the standpoint of the reproduction process of the total social capital — but a portion of industrial capital in the market in process of metamorphosis, which exists and functions as commodity capital. It is therefore only the *money* capital advanced by the merchant which is exclusively destined for purchase and sale and for this reason never assumes any other form but that of commodity capital and money capital, never that of productive capital, and is always confined to the sphere of circulation of capital — it is only this money capital which is now to be regarded with reference to the entire reproduction process of capital.

As soon as the producer, the linen manufacturer, has sold his 30,000 yards to the merchant for £3,000, he uses the money so obtained to buy the necessary means of production, so that his capital returns to the production process. His process of production continues without interruption.[a] So far as he is concerned, the conversion of his commodity into money is accomplished. But for the linen itself, as we have seen, its metamorphosis has not yet taken place. It has not yet been finally reconverted into money, has not yet passed as a use value into either productive or individual consumption. It is now the linen merchant who represents on the market the same commodity capital originally represented by the linen manufacturer. For the latter the process of transformation has been curtailed, only to be continued in the merchant's hands.

Had the linen producer been obliged to wait until his linen had really ceased being a commodity, until it has passed into the hands of its ultimate buyer, its productive or individual consumer, his process of

---

[a] Cf. present edition, Vol. 33, pp. 50-51.

reproduction would have been interrupted. Or, to avoid interrupting it, he would have had to curtail his operations, to convert a smaller portion of his linen into yarn, coal, labour, etc., in short, into the elements of productive capital, and to retain a larger portion of it as a money reserve, so that with one portion of his capital on the market in the shape of commodities, another would continue the process of production; one portion would be on the market in the form of commodities, while the other returned in the form of money. This division of his capital is not abolished by the merchant's intervention. But without it the portion of money reserve in the capital of circulation would always have to be greater in relation to the part employed in the form of productive capital, and the scale of reproduction would have to be restricted accordingly. Instead, however, the manufacturer is enabled to constantly employ a larger portion of his capital in the actual process of production, and a smaller portion as money reserve.

On the other hand, however, another portion of the social capital, in the form of merchant's capital, is kept continually within the sphere of circulation. It is employed all the time for the sole purpose of buying and selling. Hence there seems to have been no more than a replacement of persons holding this capital in their hands.

If, instead of buying £3,000 worth of linen with the purpose of selling it again, the merchant had applied these £3,000 productively, the productive capital of society would have increased. True, the linen manufacturer would then have been obliged to hold back a larger portion of his capital as money reserve, and likewise the merchant, now transformed into an industrial capitalist. On the other hand, if the merchant remains merchant, the manufacturer saves time in selling, which he can devote to supervising the production process, while the merchant must apply all his time to selling.

If merchant's capital does not overstep its necessary proportions, it is to be inferred:

1) that as a result of the division of labour the capital devoted exclusively to buying and selling (and this includes not only the money required to buy commodities, but also the money which must be invested in labour to maintain the merchant's establishment, and in his constant capital — the storehouses, transport, etc.) is smaller than it would be if the industrial capitalist were constrained to carry on the entire commercial part of his business on his own;

2) that because the merchant devotes all his time exclusively to

this business, the producer is able to convert his commodities more rapidly into money, and, moreover, the commodity capital itself passes more rapidly through its metamorphosis than it would in the hands of the producer;

3) that in viewing the aggregate merchant's capital in its relation to industrial capital, one turnover of merchant's capital may represent not only the turnovers of many capitals in one sphere of production, but the turnovers of a number of capitals in different spheres of production. The former is the case when, for instance, the linen merchant, after buying the product of some linen manufacturer with his £3,000, sells it before the same manufacturer brings another lot of the same quantity to market, and buys, and again sells, the product of another, or several other, linen manufacturers, thus effecting the turnovers of different capitals in the same sphere of production. The latter is the case if, for example, the merchant after selling his linen buys silk, thus effecting the turnover of a capital in a different sphere of production.[a]

In general, it may be noted that the turnover of industrial capital is limited not by the time of circulation alone, but also by the time of production. The turnover of merchant's capital dealing in one kind of commodity is not merely limited by the turnover of a single industrial capital, but by that of all industrial capitals in the same branch of production. After the merchant has bought and sold the linen of one producer he can buy and sell that of another, before the first brings another lot to the market. The same merchant's capital may, therefore, successively promote the different turnovers of capitals invested in a certain branch of production, with the effect that its turnover is not identical with the turnovers of a sole industrial capital, and does not therefore replace just the single money reserve which that one industrial capitalist would have had to hold *in petto*.[b] The turnover of merchant's capital in one sphere of production is naturally restricted by the total production of that sphere. But it is not restricted by the scale of production, or the period of turnover, of any one capital of the same sphere, so far as its period of turnover is qualified by its time of production. Suppose, A supplies a commodity requiring three months for its production. After the merchant has bought and sold it, say, in one month, he can buy and sell the same product of some other manufacturer. Or after he has sold, say, the corn of one farmer, he

---

[a] Ibid., pp. 51-53. - [b] within the breast, in reserve

can buy and sell that of another with the same money, etc. The turnover of his capital is restricted by the mass of corn he is able to buy and sell successively within a certain period, for instance, in one year, while the turnover of the farmer's capital is, regardless of the time of turnover, restricted by the time of production, which lasts one year.

However, the turnover of the same merchant's capital may equally well effect the turnovers of capitals in different branches of production.

In so far as the same merchant's capital serves in different turnovers to transform different commodity capitals successively into money, buying and selling them one after another, it performs the same function in its capacity of money capital with regard to commodity capital, which money in general performs by means of the number of its turnovers in a given period with regard to commodities.

The turnover of merchant's capital is not identical with the turnover, or a single reproduction, of an industrial capital of equal size; it is rather equal to the sum of the turnovers of a number of such capitals, whether in the same or in different spheres of production. The more quickly merchant's capital is turned over, the smaller the portion of total money capital serving as merchant's capital; and conversely, the more slowly it is turned over, the larger this portion. The less developed production, the larger the sum of merchant's capital in its relation to the sum of the commodities thrown into circulation; but the smaller in absolute terms, or in comparison with more developed conditions, and vice versa. In such undeveloped conditions, therefore, the greater part of the actual money capital is in the hands of merchants, whose fortune constitutes money wealth vis-à-vis the others.

The velocity of circulation of the money capital advanced by the merchant depends 1) on the speed with which the process of production is renewed and the different processes of production are linked together; and 2) on the velocity of consumption.[a]

To accomplish the turnover we have examined above, merchant's capital does not first have to buy commodities for its full amount of value, and then to sell them. Instead, the merchant performs both movements simultaneously. His capital then breaks up into two parts. One of them consists of commodity capital, and the other of money capital. He buys and converts his money into commodities at one place. Elsewhere, he sells and converts another part of his commodity

---

[a] Cf. present edition, Vol. 33, pp. 57-58.

capital into money. On one side, his capital returns to him in the form of money capital, while on the other he gets commodity capital. The larger the portion in one form, the smaller the portion in the other. This alternates and balances itself. If the use of money as a medium of circulation combines with its use as a means of payment and the attendant development of the credit system, then the money capital part of merchant's capital is reduced still more in relation to the volume of the transactions this merchant's capital effects. If I buy £3,000 worth of wine on 3 months' credit and sell all the wine for cash before this term expires, I do not need to advance a single penny for these transactions. In this case it is also quite obvious that the money capital, which here acts as merchant's capital, is nothing more than industrial capital in its money capital form, in its process of reflux in the form of money. (The fact that the manufacturer who sold £3,000 worth of wine on 3 months' credit may discount his promissory note at the banker's does not alter the matter at all and has nothing to do with the merchant's capital.) If market prices should fall in the meantime by, say, $\frac{1}{10}$, the merchant, far from making a profit, would recover only £2,700 instead of £3,000. He would have to put up £300 out of his own pocket. These £300 would serve merely as a reserve to balance the difference in price. But the same applies to the manufacturer. If he himself had sold at falling prices, he would likewise have lost £300, and would not be able to resume production on the same scale without reserve capital.

The linen dealer buys £3,000 worth of linen from the manufacturer. The latter pays, say, £2,000 of the £3,000 for yarn. He buys this yarn from a yarn dealer. The money which the manufacturer pays to the yarn dealer is not the linen dealer's money, for the latter has received commodities to this amount. It is the money form of the manufacturer's own capital. Now in the hands of the yarn dealer these £2,000 appear as returned money capital. But to what extent are they that as distinct from the £2,000 representing the discarded money form of the linen and the assumed money form of the yarn? If the yarn dealer bought on credit and sold for cash before the expiration of his term of payment, then these £2,000 do not contain one penny of merchant's capital as distinct from the money form which the industrial capital itself assumes in the course of its circuit. In so far as commercial capital is not, therefore, just a form of industrial capital in the merchant's hands as commodity capital or money capital, it is nothing but that portion of money capital which belongs to the merchant himself and circulates in the purchase and sale of commodities. On a reduced scale this portion represents that part of capital advanced for production which should always have to be in the hands of the industrialist as money reserve and means of purchase, and which should always have to circulate as his money capital. This portion, on a reduced scale, is now in the hands of merchant capitalists and always performs its functions as such in the process of circulation. It is that portion of the total capital which, aside from what is expended as revenue, must continually circulate on the market as a means of purchase in order to maintain the continuity of the process of reproduction. The more rapid the process of reproduction, and the more developed the function of money as a means of payment, i. e., the more developed the credit system,[38] the smaller that portion is in relation to the total capital.

Merchant's capital is simply capital functioning in the sphere of circulation. The process of circulation is a phase of the total process of

---

[38] To be able to classify merchant's capital as production capital, Ramsay confounds it with the transportation industry and calls commerce "the transport of commodities from one place to another" (*An Essay on the Distribution of Wealth*, p. 19). The same confusion by Verri (*Meditazioni sulla Economia Politica*, § 4[a] and by Say (*Traité d'économie politique*, I, pp. 14, 15). In his *Elements of Political Economy* (Andover and New York, 1835) S. P. Newman says: "In the existing economical arrangements of society, the very act, which is performed by the merchant, of standing between the producer and the consumer, advancing to the former capital and receiving products in return, and then handing over these products to the latter, receiving back capital in return, is a transaction which both facilitates the economical processes of the community, and adds value to the products in relation to which it is performed" (p. 174). Producer and consumer thus save time and money through the intervention of the merchant. This service requires an advance of capital and labour, and must be rewarded, "since it adds value to products, for the same products in the hands of consumers are worth more than in the hands of producers". And so commerce appears to him, as it does to M. Say, as "strictly an act of production" (p. 175). This Newman's view is fundamentally wrong. The *use value* of a commodity is greater in the hands of the consumer than in those of the producer, because it is first realised by the consumer. For the use value of a commodity does not serve its end, does not begin to function until the commodity enters the sphere of consumption. So long as it is in the hands of the producer, it exists only in potential form. But one does not pay twice for a commodity—first for its exchange value, and then for its use value. By paying for its exchange value, I appropriate its use value. And its exchange value is not in the least augmented by transferring the commodity from the producer or middleman to the consumer.[b]

---

[a] In *Scrittori Classici Italiani di Economia Politica*. Parte moderna, t. XV, p. 32.
- [b] Cf. present edition, Vol. 33, p. 239.

reproduction. But no value is produced in the process of circulation, and, therefore, no surplus value. Only changes of form of the same mass of value take place. In fact, nothing occurs there outside the metamorphosis of commodities, and this has nothing to do as such either with the creation or change of values. If a surplus value is realised in the sale of produced commodities, then this is only because it already existed in them. In the second act, the re-exchange of money capital against commodities (elements of production), the buyer therefore does not realise any surplus value either. He merely initiates the production of surplus value through exchanging his money for means of production and labour power. But so far as these metamorphoses require circulation time — time during which capital does not produce at all, least of all surplus value — it restricts the creation of values, and the surplus value expresses itself through the rate of profit in inverse ratio to the duration of the circulation period. Merchant's capital, therefore, does not create either value or surplus value, at least not directly. In so far as it contributes to shortening the time of circulation, it may help indirectly to increase the surplus value produced by the industrial capitalists. In so far as it helps to expand the market and effects the division of labour between capitals, hence enabling capital to operate on a larger scale, its function promotes the productivity of industrial capital, and its accumulation. In so far as it shortens circulation time, it raises the ratio of surplus value to advanced capital, hence the rate of profit. And to the extent that it confines a smaller portion of capital to the sphere of circulation in the form of money capital, it increases that portion of capital which is engaged directly in production.[a]

Chapter XVII

COMMERCIAL PROFIT

We have seen in Book II [b]that the pure functions of capital in the sphere of circulation — the operations which the industrial capitalist must perform, first, to realise the value of his commodities, and second, to reconvert this value into elements of production, operations effecting the metamorphosis of commodity capital, $C'-M-C$, hence

---

[a] Ibid., pp. 58-63.- [b] See present edition, Vol. 36, pp. 133-37.

the acts of selling and buying — produce neither value nor surplus value. It was rather seen that the time required for this purpose, objectively in regard to commodities and subjectively in regard to the capitalist, sets the limit to the production of value and surplus value. What is true of the metamorphosis of commodity capital in general, is, of course, not in the least altered by the fact that a part of it may assume the shape of commercial capital, or that the operations, effecting the metamorphosis of commodity capital, appear as the special concern of a special group of capitalists, or as the exclusive function of a portion of the money capital. If selling and buying commodities — and that is what the metamorphosis of commodity capital C′—M — C amounts to — by industrial capitalists themselves are not operations which create value or surplus value, they will certainly not create either of these when carried out by persons other than the industrial capitalists. Furthermore, if that portion of the total social capital, which must continually be on hand as money capital, in order that the process of reproduction is not interrupted by the process of circulation and proceeds continuously — if this money capital creates neither value nor surplus value, it cannot acquire the properties of creating them by being continually thrown into circulation by some section of capitalists other than the industrial capitalists, to perform the same function. We have already indicated to what extent merchant's capital may be indirectly productive, and we shall later discuss this point at greater length.

Commercial capital, therefore — stripped of all heterogeneous functions, such as storing, expressing, transporting, distributing, retailing, which may be connected with it, and confined to its true function of buying in order to sell — creates neither value nor surplus value, but acts as middleman in their realisation and thereby simultaneously in the actual exchange of commodities, i. e., in their transfer from hand to hand, in the social metabolism. Nevertheless, since the circulation phase of industrial capital is just as much a phase of the reproduction process as production is, the capital operating independently in the process of circulation must yield the average annual profit just as well as capital operating in the various branches of production. Should merchant's capital yield a higher percentage of average profit than industrial capital, then a portion of the latter would transform itself into merchant's capital. Should it yield a lower average profit, then the converse would result. A portion of the merchant's capital would then be transformed into industrial capital.

No species of capital changes its purpose, or function, with greater ease than merchant's capital.

Since merchant's capital does not itself produce surplus value, it is evident than the surplus value which it pockets in the form of average profit must be a portion of the surplus value produced by the total productive capital. But now the question arises: How does merchant's capital attract its share of the surplus value or profit produced by the productive capital? [a]

It is just an illusion that commercial profit is a mere addition to, or a nominal rise of, the prices of commodities above their value.

It is plain that the merchant can draw his profit only out of the price of the commodities he sells, and plainer still that the profit he makes in selling his commodities must be equal to the difference between his purchase price and his selling price, i. e., equal to the excess of the latter over the former.

It is possible that additional costs (costs of circulation) may enter into the commodities after their purchase and before their sale, and it is also possible that this may not happen. If such costs should occur, it is plain that the excess of the selling price over the purchase price would not be all profit. To simplify the analysis, we shall assume at this point that no such costs occur.

For the industrial capitalist the difference between the selling price and the purchase price of his commodities is equal to the difference between their price of production and their cost price, or, from the standpoint of the total social capital, equal to the difference between the value of the commodities and their cost price for the capitalists, which again comes down to the difference between the total quantity of labour objectified in them and the quantity of paid labour objectified in them. Before the commodities bought by the industrial capitalist are thrown back on the market as saleable commodities, they pass through the process of production, in which alone the portion of their price to be realised as profit is created. But it is different with the dealer in commodities. The commodities are in his hands only so long as they are in the process of circulation. He merely continues their sale, the realisation of their price which was begun by the productive capitalist, and therefore does not cause them to pass through any intermediate process in which they could again absorb surplus value. While the industrial capitalist merely realises the previously produced sur-

---

[a] Ibid., Vol. 33, pp. 64-68.

plus value, or profit, in the process of circulation, the merchant has not only to realise his profit during and through circulation, but must first make it. There appears to be no other way of doing this outside of selling the commodities bought by him from the industrial capitalist at their prices of production, or, from the standpoint of the total commodity capital, at their values in excess of their prices of production, making a nominal extra charge to their prices, hence, selling them, from the standpoint of the total commodity capital, above their value, and pocketing this excess of their nominal value over their real value; in short, selling them for more than they are worth.

This method of adding an extra charge is easy to grasp. For instance, one yard of linen costs 2s. If I want to make a 10% profit in reselling it, I must add $\frac{1}{10}$ to the price, hence sell the yard at 2s. $2\frac{2}{5}$ d. The difference between its actual price of production and its selling price is then $= 2\frac{2}{5}$ d., and this represents a profit of 10% on 2s. This amounts to my selling the yard to the buyer at a price which is in reality the price of $1\frac{1}{10}$ yard. Or, what amounts to the same, it is as though I sold to the buyer only $\frac{10}{11}$ of a yard for 2s. and kept $\frac{1}{11}$ of a yard for myself. In fact I can buy back $\frac{1}{11}$ of a yard for $2\frac{2}{5}$ d. at the price of 2s. $2\frac{2}{5}$ d. per yard. This would, therefore, be just a roundabout way of sharing in the surplus value and surplus product by a nominal rise in the price of commodities.

This is realisation of commercial profit by raising the price of commodities, as it appears at first glance. And, indeed, this whole notion that profit originates from a nominal rise in the price of commodities, or from their sale above their value, springs from the observations of commercial capital.

But it is quickly apparent on closer inspection that this is mere illusion. Assuming capitalist production to be predominant, commercial profit cannot be realised in this manner. (It is here always a question of averages, not of isolated cases.) Why do we assume that the dealer in commodities can realise a profit of no more than, say, 10% on his commodities by selling them 10% above their price of production? Because we assume that the producer of these commodities, the industrial capitalist (who appears as "*the producer*" before the outside world, being the personification of industrial capital), had sold them to the merchant at their prices of production. If the purchase price of commodities paid by the dealer is equal to their price of production, or, in the last instance, equal to their value, so that the price of production or, in the last instance, the value, represent the merchant's cost price, then, indeed, the excess of his selling price over his purchase price — and this difference alone is the source of his profit — must be an excess of their commercial price over their price of production, so that in the final analysis the merchant sells all commodities above their values. But why was it assumed that the industrial capitalist sells his commodities to the merchant at their prices of production? Or rather, what was taken for granted in that assumption? It was that merchant's capital (we are dealing with it as yet only in its capacity of commercial capital) did not go into forming the general rate of profit. We proceeded necessarily from this premiss in discussing the general rate of profit, first, because merchant's capital as such did not exist for us at the time, and, second, because average profit, and hence the general rate of profit, had first to be developed as a levelling of profits or surplus values actually produced by the industrial capitals in the different spheres of production. But in the case of merchant's capital we are dealing with a capital which shares in the profit without participating in its production. Hence, it is now necessary to supplement our earlier exposition.

Suppose, the total industrial capital advanced in the course of the year $= 720_c + 180_v = 900$ (say million $\pounds$), and that $s' = 100\%$. The product therefore $= 720_c + 180_v + 180_s$. Let us call this product or the produced commodity capital, C, whose value, or price of production (since both are identical for the totality of commodities) $= 1,080$, and the rate of profit for the total capital of $900 = 20\%$. These 20% are, according to our earlier analyses, the average rate of profit, since the surplus value is not calculated here on this or that capital of any particular composition, but on the total industrial capital of average composition. Thus, C $= 1,080$, and the rate of profit $= 20\%$. Let us now assume, however, that aside from these $\pounds900$ of industrial capital, there are still $\pounds100$ of merchant's capital, which shares in the profit *pro rata* to its magnitude just as the former. According to our assumption, it is $\frac{1}{10}$ of the total capital of 1,000. Therefore, it participates to the extent of $\frac{1}{10}$ in the total surplus value of 180, and thus secures a profit of 18%. Actually, then, the profit to be distributed among the other $\frac{9}{10}$ of the total capital is only $= 162$, or on the capital of 900 likewise $= 18\%$. Hence, the price at which C is sold by the owners of the industrial capital of 900 to the dealers in commodities $= 720_c + 180_v + 162_s = 1,062$. If the merchant then adds the average profit of 18% to his capital of 100, he sells the commodities at

1,062 + 18 = 1,080, i. e., at their price of production, or, from the standpoint of the total commodity capital, at their value, although he makes his profit only during and through the circulation process, and only from an excess of his selling price over his purchase price. Yet he does not sell the commodities above their value, or above their price of production, precisely because he has bought them from the industrial capitalist below their value, or below their price of production.

Thus, merchant's capital enters the formation of the general rate of profit as a determinant *pro rata* to its part in the total capital. Hence, if we say in the given case that the average rate of profit = 18%, it would = 20%, if it were not that $\frac{1}{10}$ of the total capital was merchant's capital and the general rate of profit thereby lowered by $\frac{1}{10}$. This leads to a closer and more comprehensive definition of the price of production. By price of production we mean, just as before, the price of a commodity = its costs (the value of the constant + variable capital contained in it) + the average profit. But this average profit is now determined differently. It is determined by the total profit produced by the total productive capital; but not as calculated on the total productive capital alone, so that if this = 900, as assumed above, and the profit = 180, then the average rate of profit = $\frac{180}{900}$ = 20%. But, rather, as calculated on the total productive + merchant's capital, so that with 900 productive and 100 merchant's capital, the average rate of profit = $\frac{180}{1,000}$ = 18%. The price of production is, therefore = k (the costs) + 18, instead of k + 20. The share of the total profit falling to merchant's capital is thus included in the average rate of profit. The actual value, or price of production, of the total commodity capital is therefore = k + p + m (where m is commercial profit). The price of production, or the price at which the industrial capitalist as such sells his commodities, is thus smaller than the actual price of production of the commodity; or in terms of all commodities taken together, the prices at which the class of industrial capitalists sell their commodities are lower than their value. Hence, in the above case, 900 (costs) + 18% on 900, or 900 + 162 = 1,062. It follows, then, that in selling a commodity at 118 for which he paid 100 the merchant does, indeed, add 18% to the price. But since this commodity, for which he paid 100, is really worth 118, he does not sell it above its value. We shall henceforth use the term price of production in this, its more precise, sense. It is evident, therefore, that the profit of the industrial capitalist equals the excess of the price of production of the commodity over its cost price, and that commercial profit, as distinct from this industrial profit, equals the excess of the selling price over the price of production of the commodity which, for the merchant, is its purchase price; but that the actual price of the commodity = its price of production + the commercial profit. Just as industrial capital realises only such profits as already exist in the value of commodities as surplus value, so merchant's capital realises profits only because the entire surplus value, or profit, has not as yet been fully realised in the price charged for the commodities by the industrial capitalist.[39] The merchant's selling price thus exceeds the purchase price not because the former exceeds the total value, but because the latter is below this value.

Merchant's capital, therefore, participates in levelling surplus value to average profit, although it does not take part in the production of this surplus value. Thus, the general rate of profit contains a deduction from surplus value due to merchant's capital, hence a deduction from the profit of industrial capital.[b]

It follows from the foregoing:

1) The larger the merchant's capital in proportion to the industrial capital, the smaller the rate of industrial profit, and vice versa.

2) It was demonstrated in the first part that the rate of profit is always lower than the rate of the actual surplus value, i.e., it always understates the intensity of exploitation, as in the above case, $720_c + 180_v + 180_s$, the rate of surplus value of 100% and a rate of profit of only 20%. And the difference becomes still greater, inasmuch as the average rate of profit appears smaller again, dropping from 20% to 18%, if the share falling to merchant's capital is also taken into account. The average rate of profit of the direct capitalist exploiter, therefore, expresses a rate of profit smaller than it actually is.

Assuming all other circumstances remaining the same, the relative volume of merchant's capital (with the exception of the small dealer who represents a hybrid form) is in inverse proportion to the velocity of its turnover, hence in inverse proportion to the energy of the process of reproduction in general. In the course of scientific analysis, the formation of a general rate of profit appears to result from industrial

[39] John Bellers.[a]

---

[a] *Essays About the Poor, Manufactures, Trade, Plantations, and Immorality...*, London, 1699, p. 10. - [b] Cf. present edition, Vol. 33, p. 154.

capitals and their competition, and is only later corrected, supplemented, and modified by the intervention of merchant's capital. In the course of its historical development, however, the process is really reversed. It is the commercial capital which first determines the prices of commodities more or less in accordance with their values, and it is the sphere of circulation, the sphere that promotes the process of reproduction, in which a general rate of profit initially takes shape. It is originally the commercial profit which determines the industrial profit. Not until the capitalist mode of production has asserted itself and the producer himself has become merchant, is commercial profit reduced to that aliquot part of the total surplus value falling to the share of merchant's capital as an aliquot part of the total capital engaged in the social process of reproduction.[a]

It was seen in the supplementary equalisation of profit through the intervention of merchant's capital that no additional element entered the value of commodities with the merchant's advanced money capital, and that the extra charge to the price, whereby the merchant makes his profit, was merely equal to that portion of the value of the commodities, which productive capital had not calculated in the price of production, i. e., had left out. The case of this money capital is similar to that of the industrial capitalist's fixed capital, since it is not consumed and its value, therefore, does not make up an element of the value of commodity. It is in the purchase price of commodity capital that the merchant replaces its price of production = M, in money. His own selling price, as previously shown, is = $M + \Delta M$, where ΔM stands for the addition to the price of commodities determined by the general rate of profit. Once he sells the commodities, his original money capital, which he advanced for their purchase, returns to him together with this ΔM. We see once more that his money capital is nothing but the industrial capitalist's commodity capital transformed into money capital, which affects the magnitude of the value of this commodity capital no more than would a direct sale of the latter to the ultimate consumer, instead of to the merchant. In fact, it merely anticipates the payment of the consumer. However, this is correct only on the condition hitherto assumed, that the merchant has no overhead expenses, or that aside from the money capital which he must advance to buy commodities from the producer he need not advance any other capital, circulating or fixed, in the process of commodity meta-

---

a Ibid., p. 155.

morphosis, the process of buying and selling. But this is not so in reality, as we have seen in the analysis of the costs of circulation (Book II, Chap. VI).[a] These costs of circulation are partly expenses which the merchant has to reclaim from other agents of circulation, and partly expenses arising directly from his specific business.

No matter what the nature of these costs of circulation — whether they arise from the purely commercial nature of the merchant's establishment as such and hence belong to the merchant's specific costs of circulation, or represent items which are charges for subsequent processes of production added in the process of circulation, such as expressage, transport, storage, etc.— they always require of the merchant, aside from his money capital, advanced to the purchase of commodities, some additional capital for the purchase and payment of such means of circulation. As much of this element of cost as consists of circulating capital passes wholly as an additional element into the selling price of the commodities; and as much of it as consists of fixed capital only to the extent of its wear and tear. But only as an element which forms a nominal value, even if as the purely commercial costs of circulation, it does not add any real value to the commodities. But whether fixed or circulating, this entire additional capital participates in forming the general rate of profit.

The purely commercial costs of circulation (hence, excluding costs of expressage, shipping, storage, etc.) resolve themselves into costs required to realise the value of commodities, to transform it from commodities into money, or from money into commodities, to effect their exchange. We leave entirely out of consideration all possible processes of production which may continue in the process of circulation, and from which the merchant's business can be altogether separated; as, in fact, the actual transport industry and expressage may be, and are, industrial branches entirely distinct from commercial; and purchaseable and saleable commodities may be stored in DOCKS or in other public premises, with the resultant cost of storage being charged to the merchant by third persons inasmuch as he has to advance it. All this takes place in actual wholesale commerce, where merchant's capital appears in its purest form, unmixed with other functions. The express company owner, the railway director, and the shipowner, are not "merchants". The costs which we consider here are those of buying and selling. We have already remarked earlier that these resolve

---

[a] See present edition, Vol. 36.

themselves into accounting, book-keeping, marketing, correspondence, etc. The constant capital required for this purpose consists of offices, paper, postage, etc. The other costs break up into variable capital advanced for the employment of mercantile wage workers. (Expressage, transport costs, advances for customs duties, etc., may partly be considered as being advanced by the merchant in purchasing commodities and thus enter the purchase price as far as he is concerned.)

All these costs are not incurred in producing the use value of commodities, but in realising their value. They are pure costs of circulation. They do not enter into the immediate process of production, but since they are part of the process of circulation they are also part of the total process of reproduction.

The only portion of these costs of interest to us at this point is that advanced as variable capital. (The following questions should also be analysed: First, how does the law that only necessary labour enters the value of commodities operate in the process of circulation? Second, how does accumulation obtain in merchant's capital? Third, how does merchant's capital function in the actual aggregate reproduction process of society?)

These costs arise due to the product having the economic form of a commodity.[a]

If the labour time which the industrial capitalists themselves lose while directly selling commodities to one another — hence, speaking objectively, the circulation time of the commodities — does not add value to these commodities, it is evident that this labour time does not change its nature in the least by falling to the merchant instead of the industrial capitalist. The conversion of commodities (products) into money, and of money into commodities (means of production) is a necessary function of industrial capital and, therefore, a necessary operation of the capitalist — who is actually but personified capital endowed with a consciousness of its own and a will. But these functions neither increase value, nor produce surplus value. By performing these operations and carrying on the functions of capital in the sphere of circulation after the productive capitalist has ceased to be involved the merchant merely takes the place of the industrial capitalist. The labour time required in these operations is devoted to certain necessary operations of the reproduction process of capital, but

---

[a] Ibid., Vol. 33, pp. 157-58.

yields no additional value. If the merchant did not perform these operations (hence, did not expend the labour time entailed), he would not be applying his capital as a circulation agent of industrial capital; he would not then be continuing the interrupted function of the industrial capitalist, and consequently could not participate as a capitalist, *pro rata* to his advanced capital, in the mass of profit produced by the class of industrial capitalists. In order to share in the mass of surplus value, to expand the value of his advance as capital, the commercial capitalist need not employ wage workers. If his business and capital are small, he may be the only worker in it. He is paid with that portion of the profit which falls to him through the difference between the purchase price paid by him for commodities and their actual price of production.

But, on the other hand, the profit realised by the merchant on a small amount of advanced capital may be no larger, or may even be smaller, than the wages of one of the better-paid skilled wage workers. In fact, he brushes shoulders with many direct commercial agents of the productive capitalist, such as buyers, sellers, travellers, who enjoy the same or a higher income either in the form of wages, or in the form of a share in the profit (percentages, bonuses) made from each sale. In the first case, the merchant pockets the mercantile profit as an independent capitalist; in the other, the salesman, the industrial capitalist's wage labourer, receives a portion of the profit either in the form of wages, or as a proportional share in the profit of the industrial capitalist, whose direct agent he is, while his employer pockets both the industrial and the commercial profit. But in all these cases, although his income may appear to the circulation agent as an ordinary wage, as payment for work performed, and although, where it does not so appear, the profit may be no larger than the wage of a better-paid labourer, his income is derived solely from the mercantile profit. This follows from his labour not being labour which produces value.

The lengthening of the act of circulation represents for the industrial capitalist 1) a personal loss of time, since it prevents him from performing in person his function as manager of the productive process; 2) a longer stay of his product in money or commodity form, in the circulation process, hence in a process where it does not expand value and where the direct production process is interrupted. If this process is not to be interrupted, production must either be curtailed, or more money capital must be advanced to maintain the process of production on the same scale. This means that each time either a smaller profit is made on the capital hitherto invested, or that additional money capital must be advanced to make the previous profit. All this remains unchanged when the merchant takes the place of the industrial capitalist. Instead of the industrial capitalist devoting more time to the process of circulation, it is the merchant who is so engaged; instead of the industrial capitalist it is the merchant who advances additional capital for circulation; or, what amounts to the same thing, instead of a large portion of the industrial capital being continually diverted into the process of circulation, it is the merchant's capital which is wholly tied up in it; and instead of making a smaller profit, the industrial capitalist must yield a portion of his profit wholly to the merchant. So long as merchant's capital remains within the bounds in which it is necessary, the only difference is that this division of the functions of capital reduces the time exclusively used up in the process of circulation, that less additional capital is advanced for this purpose, and that the loss in total profit, represented by mercantile profit, is smaller than it would otherwise have been. If in the above example, $720_c + 180_v + 180_s$, assisted by a merchant's capital of 100, produces a profit of 162, or 18%, for the industrial capitalist, hence implying a deduction of 18, then, but for this independent merchant's capital, the additional capital required would probably be 200, and we should have a total advance by the industrial capitalist of 1,100 instead of 900, which, based upon a surplus value of 180, would yield a rate of profit of only $16\frac{4}{11}\%$.

If the industrial capitalist who acts as his own merchant advances not only the additional capital to buy new commodities before his product in the process of circulation has been reconverted into money, but also capital (office expenses and wages for commercial employees) to realise the value of his commodity capital, or, in other words, for the process of circulation, then these supplements form additional capital, but do not create surplus value. They must be made good out of the value of the commodities, because a portion of the value of these commodities must be reconverted into these circulation costs. But no additional surplus value is created thereby. So far as this concerns the total capital of society, it means in fact that a portion of it must be set aside for secondary operations which are no part of the self-expansion process, and that this portion of the social capital must be continually reproduced for this purpose. This reduces the rate of profit for the individual capitalist and for the entire class of industrial capitalists, an effect arising from every new investment of additional capital whenever such capital is required to set in motion the same mass of variable capital.

In so far as these additional costs connected with the business of circulation are transferred from the industrial to the commercial capitalist, there takes place a similar reduction in the rate of profit, but to a lesser degree and in a different way. It now develops that the merchant advances more capital than would be necessary if these costs did not exist, and that the profit on this additional capital increases the amount of the commercial profit, so that more of the merchant's capital joins industrial capital in levelling the average rate of profit and thereby the average profit falls. If in our above example an additional capital of 50 is advanced besides the merchant's capital of 100 to cover the costs in question, then the total surplus value of 180 is distributed with respect to a productive capital of 900 plus a merchant's capital of 150, together = 1,050. The average rate of profit, therefore, sinks to $17\frac{1}{7}\%$. The industrial capitalist sells his commodities to the merchant at $900 + 154\frac{2}{7} = 1,054\frac{2}{7}$, and the merchant sells them at 1,130 (1,080 + 50 for costs which he must recover). Moreover, it must be admitted that the division between merchant's and industrial capital is accompanied by a centralisation of the commercial expenses and, consequently, by their reduction.

The question now arises: What about the commercial wage workers employed by the commercial capitalist, here the dealer in commodities?

In one respect, such a commercial employee is a wage worker like any other. In the first place, his labour is bought with the variable capital of the merchant, not with money expended as revenue, and consequently it is not bought for private service, but for the purpose of expanding the value of the capital advanced for it. In the second place, the value of his labour power, and thus his wages, are determined as those of other wage workers, i. e., by the cost of production and reproduction of his specific labour power, not by the product of his labour.[a]

However, we must make the same distinction between him and the workers directly employed by industrial capital which exists between industrial capital and merchant's capital, and thus between the industrial capitalist and the merchant. Since the merchant, as a mere

---

[a] Ibid., Vol. 33, p. 156.

agent of circulation, produces neither value nor surplus value (for the additional value which he adds to the commodities through his expenses resolves itself into an addition of previously existing values, although the question here poses itself, how he preserves this value of his constant capital?) it follows that the mercantile workers employed by him in these same functions cannot directly create surplus value for him. Here, as in the case of productive labourers, we assume that wages are determined by the value of the labour power, and that, hence, the merchant does not enrich himself by depressing wages, so that he does not enter into his cost account an advance for labour which he has paid only in part; in other words, that he does not enrich himself through cheating his clerks, etc.

The difficulty as concerns mercantile wage workers is by no means to explain how they produce direct profits for their employer without creating any direct surplus value (of which profit is but a converted form). This question has, indeed, already been solved in the general analysis of commercial profits. Just as industrial capital makes profit by selling labour embodied and realised in commodities, for which it has not paid any equivalent, so merchant's capital derives profit from not paying in full to productive capital for all the unpaid labour contained in the commodities (in commodities, in so far as capital invested in their production functions as an aliquot part of the total industrial capital), and by demanding payment for this unpaid portion still contained in the commodities when making a sale. The relation of merchant's capital to surplus value is different from that of industrial capital. The latter produces surplus value by directly appropriating the unpaid labour of others. The former appropriates a portion of this surplus value by having this portion transferred from industrial capital to itself.

It is only through its function of realising values that merchant's capital acts as capital in the process of reproduction, and hence as functioning capital draws on the surplus value produced by the total capital. The mass of the individual merchant's profits depends on the mass of capital that he can apply in this process, and he can apply so much more of it in buying and selling, the more the unpaid labour of his clerks. The very function, by virtue of which the merchant's money becomes capital, is largely done through his employees. The unpaid labour of these clerks, while it does not create surplus value, enables him to appropriate surplus value, which, in effect, amounts to the same thing with respect to this capital. It is, therefore, a source of profit for him. Otherwise commercial business could never be conducted on a large scale, capitalistically.[a]

Just as the labourer's unpaid labour directly creates surplus value for productive capital, so the unpaid labour of the commercial wage worker secures a share of this surplus value for merchant's capital.

The difficulty lies here: Since the merchant's labour time and labour do not create value, although they secure for him a share of already produced surplus value, how does the matter stand with the variable capital which he lays out in purchasing commercial labour power? Is this variable capital to be included in the cost outlays of the advanced merchant's capital? If not, this appears to conflict with the law of equalisation of the rate of profit; what capitalist would advance 150 if he could charge only 100 to advanced capital? If so, it seems to conflict with the nature of merchant's capital, since this kind of capital does not act as capital by setting in motion the labour of others, as industrial capital does, but rather by doing its own work, i. e., performing the functions of buying and selling, this being precisely the means and the reason why it transfers to itself a portion of the surplus value produced by the industrial capital.

(We must therefore analyse the following points: the merchant's variable capital; the law of necessary labour in the sphere of circulation; how the merchant's labour maintains the value of his constant capital; the part played by merchant's capital in the process of reproduction as a whole; and, finally, the duplication in commodity capital and money capital, on the one hand, and in commercial capital and money-dealing capital on the other.)

If every merchant had only as much capital as he himself were able to turn over by his own labour, there would be infinite fragmentation of merchant's capital. This fragmentation would increase in the same proportion as productive capital raised production and operated with greater masses in the forward march of the capitalist mode of production. Hence, an increasing disproportion of the two. Capital in the sphere of circulation would become decentralised in the same proportion as it became centralised in the sphere of production. The purely commercial business of the industrial capitalist, and thus his purely commercial expenses, would expand infinitely thereby, for he would have to deal with, say, 1,000 merchants, instead of 100. Thus, the advantages of independently operating merchant's capital would large-

---

[a] Ibid., pp. 156 and 165-66.

ly be lost. And not the purely commercial expenses alone, but also the other costs of circulation, such as sorting, expressage, etc., would grow. This, as far as the industrial capital is concerned. Now let us consider merchant's capital. Firstly, the purely commercial operations. It does not take more time to deal with large figures than with small ones. It takes ten times as much time to make 10 purchases at £100 each as it does to make *one* purchase at £1,000. It takes ten times as much correspondence, paper, and postage, to correspond with 10 small merchants as it does with *one* large merchant. The clearly defined division of labour in a commercial office, in which one keeps the books, another looks after money matters, a third has charge of correspondence, one buys, another sells, a third travels, etc., saves immense quantities of labour time, so that the number of workers employed in wholesale commerce are in no way related to the comparative size of the establishment. This is so, because in commerce much more than in industry the same function requires the same labour time, whether performed on a large or a small scale. This is the reason why concentration appears earlier historically in the merchant's business than in the industrial workshop. Further, regarding outlays in constant capital. One hundred small offices cost incomparably more than one large office, 100 small warehouses more than a large one, etc. The costs of transport, which enter the accounts of a commercial establishment at least as costs to be advanced, grow with the fragmentation.

The industrial capitalist would have to lay out more in labour and in circulation costs in the commercial part of his business. The same merchant's capital, when divided among many small merchants, would, owing to this fragmentation, require more labourers to perform its functions, and more merchant's capital would, furthermore, be needed to turn over the same commodity capital.

Suppose B is the entire merchant's capital directly applied in buying and selling commodities, and b the corresponding variable capital paid out in wages to the commercial employees. Then B + b is smaller than the total merchant's capital, B, would be if every merchant had to get along without assistants, hence would invest nothing in b. However, we have not yet overcome the difficulty.

The selling price of the commodities must suffice 1) to pay the average profit on B + b. This is explained if only by the fact that B + b is generally a reduction of the original B, representing a smaller merchant's capital than would be required without b. But this selling price must suffice 2) to cover not only the additional profit on b, but to replace also the paid wages, the merchant's variable capital = b. This last consideration gives rise to the difficulty. Does b represent a new constituent of the price, or is it merely a part of the profit made by means of B + b, which appears as wages only so far as the mercantile worker is concerned, and as concerns the merchant simply replaces variable capital? In the latter case, the merchant's profit on his advanced capital B + b would just equal the profit due to B by virtue of the general rate, plus b, which he pays out in the form of wages, but which does not itself yield a profit.

The crux of the matter is, indeed, to find the limits (mathematically speaking) of b. Let us first accurately define the problem. Let B stand for capital invested directly in buying and selling commodities, K for the constant capital (actual handling costs) consumed in this function, and b for the variable capital invested by the merchant.

Recovering B offers no difficulties at all. For the merchant it is simply the realised purchase price, and the price of production for the manufacturer. It is the price paid by the merchant, and in reselling he recovers B as part of his selling price; in addition to this B, he makes a profit on B, as previously explained. For example, let the commodity cost £100. Suppose the profit is 10%. In that case, the commodity is sold at 110. The commodity previously cost 100, and the merchant's capital of 100 merely adds 10 to it.

Now if we look at K, it is at most as large as, but in fact smaller than, the portion of constant capital which the producer would use up in buying and selling, but then it would form an addition to the constant capital he requires directly in production. This portion, nonetheless, must be continually recovered in the price of the commodity, or, what amounts to the same, a corresponding portion of the commodity must be continually expended in this form, or, from the standpoint of the total capital of society, must be continually reproduced in this form. This portion of the advanced constant capital would have a limiting effect on the rate of profit, just as the entire mass of it directly invested in production. In so far as the industrial capitalist leaves the commercial part of his business to the merchant, he need not advance this part of the capital. The merchant advances it in his stead. In a way, he does this but nominally, since a merchant neither produces, nor reproduces, the constant capital consumed by him (the actual handling costs). Its production appears a separate business, or at least a part of the business, of some industrial capitalists who thus play a role similar to those who supply constant capital to producers of necessities of life. First, therefore, the merchant has this constant capital recovered for him and, secondly, receives his profit on it. Through both of these, therefore, the industrial capitalist's profit is reduced. But owing to economising and concentration which are bound up with division of labour, it shrinks less than it would if he himself had to advance this capital. The reduction in the rate of profit is less, because the capital thus advanced is less.

So far, then, the selling price is made up of $B + K +$ the profit on $B + K$. This portion of it offers no further difficulties. But now b, the variable capital advanced by the merchant, enters into it.

The resultant selling price is $B + K + b +$ the profit on $B + K$, $+$ the profit on b.

B merely recovers the purchase price and adds nothing to it but the profit on B. K adds the profit on K, and K itself; but $K +$ the profit on K, the part of the circulation costs advanced in the form of constant capital $+$ the corresponding average profit, would be larger in the hands of the industrial capitalist than in the merchant's. The shrinking of the average profit appears in the form of the full average profit calculated after deducting $B + K$ from the advanced industrial capital, with the deduction from the average profit on $B + K$ paid to the merchant, so that this deduction appears as the profit of a specific capital, merchant's capital.

But the situation is different with respect to b $+$ the profit on b, or, in the present case, where the rate of profit is assumed $= 10\%$ with $b + \frac{1}{10}b$. And the real difficulty lies here.

What the merchant buys with b is, according to our assumption, nothing but commercial labour, hence labour required to perform the functions of circulating capital, $C - M$ and $M - C$. But commercial labour is the labour generally necessary for a capital to operate as merchant's capital, to help convert commodities into money and money into commodities. It is labour which realises, but does not create, values. And only in so far as a capital performs these functions — hence a capitalist performs these operations, or this work with his capital — does it serve as merchant's capital and participate in regulating the general rate of profit, i. e., draw its dividends out of the total profit. But (b $+$ the profit on b) appears to include, first, payment for labour (for it makes no difference whether the industrial capitalist pays the merchant for his own labour, or the labour of the clerks paid by the merchant), and, secondly, the profit on the payment for this labour, which the merchant would have to perform in person. First, merchant's capital gets its b refunded, and, secondly, he makes the profit on it. This arises from the fact, therefore, that, first, it requires payment for the work whereby it operates as *merchant's* capital, and that, secondly, it demands the profit, because it operates as *capital*, i. e., because it performs work for which profit is paid to it as functioning capital. This is, therefore, the question to be solved.

Let us assume that $B = 100$, $b = 10$, and the rate of profit $= 10\%$. We take it that $K = 0$, in order to leave out of consideration this element of the purchase price, which does not belong here and has already been accounted for. Hence, the selling price would $= B + p + b + p$ ($= B + Bp' + b + bp'$; where p' stands for the rate of profit) $= 100 + 10 + 10 + 1 = 121$.

But if b were not invested by the merchant in wages—since b is paid only for commercial labour, hence labour required to realise the value of the commodity capital thrown on the market by industrial capital—the matter would stand as follows: to buy or sell for $B = 100$, the merchant would devote his time, and we wish to assume that this is the only time at his disposal. The commercial labour represented by b, or 10, if paid for by profit instead of wages, would presuppose another merchant's capital $= 100$, since at 10% this makes $b = 10$. This second $B = 100$ would not additionally go into the price of commodities, but the 10% would. There would, hence, be two operations at $100 = 200$, that would buy commodities at $200 + 20 = 220$.

Since merchant's capital is absolutely nothing but self-established form of a portion of industrial capital engaged in the process of circulation, all questions referring to it must be solved by representing the problem primarily in a form, in which the phenomena peculiar to merchant's capital do not yet appear independently, but still in direct connection with industrial capital, as a branch of it. As an office, distinct from a workshop, mercantile capital operates continually in the circulation process. It is here — in the office of the industrial capitalist himself— that we must first analyse the b now under consideration.[a]

The office is from the outset always infinitesimally small compared to the industrial workshop. As for the rest, it is clear that as the scale of production is extended, commercial operations required constantly for the circulation of industrial capital, in order to sell the product

a Ibid., p. 159.

existing as commodity capital, to reconvert the money so received into means of production, and to keep account of the whole process, multiply accordingly. Calculation of prices, book-keeping, managing funds, correspondence — all belong under this head. The more developed the scale of production, the greater, even if not proportionately greater, the commercial operations of the industrial capital, and consequently the labour and other costs of circulation involved in realising value and surplus value. This necessitates the employment of commercial wage workers who make up the actual office staff. The outlay for these, although made in the form of wages, differs from the variable capital laid out in purchasing productive labour. It increases the outlay of the industrial capitalist, the mass of the capital to be advanced, without directly increasing surplus value. Because it is an outlay for labour employed solely in realising value already created. Like every other outlay of this kind, it reduces the rate of profit because the advanced capital increases, but not the surplus value. If surplus value s remains constant while advanced capital C increases to $C + \Delta C$, then the rate of profit $\frac{s}{C}$ is replaced by the smaller rate of profit $\frac{s}{C + \Delta C}$. The industrial capitalist endeavours, therefore, to cut these expenses of circulation down to a minimum, just as his expenses for constant capital. Hence, industrial capital does not maintain the same attitude to its commercial wage labourers as it does to its productive wage labourers. The more productive wage labourers it employs under otherwise equal circumstances, the greater the output, and the greater the surplus value, or profit. Conversely, however, the larger the scale of production, the greater the quantity of value and surplus value to be realised, the greater the produced commodity capital, the greater are the absolute, if not relative, office costs, giving rise to a kind of division of labour. To what extent profit is the precondition for these outlays, is seen, among other things, from the fact that with the increase of commercial salaries, a part of them is frequently paid by a share in the profit. It is in the nature of things that labour consisting merely of intermediate operations connected partly with calculating values, partly with realising them, and partly with reconverting the realised money into means of production, is a labour whose magnitude therefore depends on the quantity of the produced ·values that have to be realised, and does not act as the cause, like directly productive labour, but rather as an effect, of the respective magnitudes and masses of these values. The same applies to the other costs of circulation. To do much measuring, weighing, packing, and transporting, much must be on hand. The amount of packing, transporting, etc., depends on the quantity of commodities which are the objects of this activity, not vice versa.

The commercial worker produces no surplus value directly. But the price of his labour is determined by the value of his labour power, hence by its costs of production, while the application of this labour power, its exertion, expenditure of energy, and wear and tear, is as in the case of every other wage labourer by no means limited by its value. His wage, therefore, is not necessarily proportionate to the mass of profit which he helps the capitalist to realise. What he costs the capitalist and what he brings in for him, are two different things. He creates no direct surplus value, but adds to the capitalist's income by helping him to reduce the cost of realising surplus value, inasmuch as he performs partly unpaid labour. The commercial worker, in the strict sense of the term, belongs to the better-paid class of wage workers — to those whose labour is classed as skilled and stands above average labour. Yet the wage tends to fall, even in relation to average labour, with the advance of the capitalist mode of production. This is due partly to the division of labour in the office, implying a one-sided development of the labour capacity, the cost of which does not fall entirely on the capitalist, since the labourer's skill develops by itself through the exercise of his function, and all the more rapidly as division of labour makes it more one-sided. Secondly, because the necessary training, knowledge of commercial practices, languages, etc., is more and more rapidly, easily, universally and cheaply reproduced with the progress of science and public education the more the capitalist mode of production directs teaching methods, etc., towards practical purposes. The universality of public education makes it possible to recruit such labourers from classes that formerly had no access to such trades and were accustomed to a lower standard of living. Moreover, this increases supply, and hence competition. With few exceptions, the labour power of these people is therefore devaluated with the progress of capitalist production. Their wage falls, while their labour capacity increases.[a] The capitalist increases the number of these labourers whenever he has more value and profits to realise. The increase of this labour is always a result, never a cause of more surplus value.[39a]

[39a] How well this forecast of the fate of the commercial proletariat, written in 1865, has stood the test of time can be corroborated by hundreds of German clerks,

There is duplication, therefore. On the one hand, the functions as commodity capital and money capital (hence further designated as merchant's capital) are general definite forms assumed by industrial capital. On the other hand, specific capitals, and therefore specific groups of capitalists, are exclusively devoted to these functions; and these functions thus develop into specific spheres of self-expansion of capital.[b]

In the case of mercantile capital, the commercial functions and circulation costs are found only in a self-established form. That side of industrial capital which is devoted to circulation, continuously exists not only in the shape of commodity capital and money capital, but also in the office alongside the workshop. But it becomes independent in the case of mercantile capital. In the latter's case, the office is its only workshop. The portion of capital employed in the form of circulation costs appears much larger in the case of the big merchant than in that of the industrialist, because besides their own offices connected with every industrial workshop, that part of capital which would have to be so applied by the entire class of industrial capitalists is concentrated in the hands of a few merchants, who in carrying out the functions of circulation also provide for the growing expenses incidental to their continuation.

To industrial capital the costs of circulation appear as unproductive expenses, and so they are. To the merchant they appear as a source of his profit, proportional, given the general rate of profit, to their size. The outlay to be made for these circulation costs is, therefore, a productive investment of mercantile capital. And for this reason, the commercial labour which it buys is likewise immediately productive for it.[c]

who are trained in all commercial operations and acquainted with three or four languages, and offer their services in vain in London City at 25 shillings per week, which is far below the wages of a skilled fitter. A blank of two pages in the manuscript indicates that this point was to have been treated at greater length. For the rest, we refer the reader to Book II (Kap. VI, S. 105-13)[a] ("The Costs of Circulation"), where various matters belonging under this head have already been discussed.— *F. E.*

[a] Ibid., Vol. 36, pp. 133-39. - [b] Ibid., Vol. 33, p. 48. - [c] Ibid., pp. 163-66.

Chapter XVIII

THE TURNOVER OF MERCHANT'S CAPITAL.
PRICES

The turnover of industrial capital is a combination of its period of production and time of circulation, and therefore embraces the entire process of production. The turnover of merchant's capital, on the other hand, being in reality nothing but an independent movement of commodity capital, represents only the first phase in the metamorphosis of a commodity, $C-M$, as the refluent movement of a specific capital; $M-C$, $C-M$, is, from the mercantile point of view, the turnover of merchant's capital. The merchant buys, converting his money into commodities, then sells, converting the latter back into money, and so forth in constant repetition. Within circulation, the metamorphosis of industrial capital always presents itself in the form of C_1-M-C_2; the money realised by the sale of the produced commodity C_1 is used to purchase new means of production, C_2. This amounts to a practical exchange of C_1 for C_2, and the same money thus changes hands twice. Its movement mediates the exchange of two different kinds of commodities, C_1 and C_2, But in the case of the merchant, it is, conversely, the same commodity which changes hands twice in $M-C-M'$. It merely promotes the reflux of his money.

If, for example, a certain merchant's capital is £100, and for these £100 the merchant buys commodities and sells them for £110, then his capital of £100 has completed one turnover, and the number of such turnovers per year depends on the number of times this movement $M-C-M'$ is repeated.

We here leave entirely out of consideration the costs which may be concealed in the difference between the purchase price and the selling price, since these do not alter in any way the form, which we are now analysing.

The number of turnovers of a given merchant's capital, therefore, is analogous in this case to the repeated cycles of money as a mere medium of circulation. Just as the same thaler buys ten times its value in commodities in making ten cycles, so the same money capital of the merchant, when turned over ten times, buys ten times its value in commodities, or realises, a total commodity capital of ten times its value; a merchant's capital of 100, for instance, a ten-fold value

= 1,000. But there is this difference: In the cycle of money as a medium of circulation it is the same piece of money that passes through
different hands, thus repeatedly performing the same function and
hence making up for the mass of the circulating pieces of money by its
velocity. But in the merchant's case it is the same money capital, the
same money value, regardless of what pieces of money it may be composed, which repeatedly buys and sells commodity capital to the
amount of its value and which therefore returns to the same hands,
the same point of departure as $M + \Delta M$, i. e., value plus surplus value.[a] This characterises its turnover as a capital turnover. It always
withdraws more money from circulation than it throws in. It is self-
evident, at any rate, that an accelerated turnover of merchant's capital (given a developed credit system, the function of money as a
means of payment predominates) implies a more rapid circulation of
the same quantity of money.

A repeated turnover of commercial capital, however, never connotes more than repeated buying and selling; while a repeated turnover
of industrial capital connotes the periodicity and renovation of the
entire reproduction process (which includes the process of consumption). For merchant's capital, on the other hand, this appears merely
as an external condition. Industrial capital must continually bring
commodities to the market and withdraw them from it, in order that
rapid turnover of merchant's capital may remain possible. If the process of reproduction is slow, then so is the turnover of merchant's capital. True, merchant's capital promotes the turnover of productive
capital, but only in so far as it shortens its time of circulation. It has
no direct influence on the time of production, which is also a barrier
to the period of turnover of industrial capital. This is the first barrier
for the turnover of merchant's capital. Secondly, aside from the barrier formed by reproductive consumption, the turnover of merchant's
capital is ultimately limited by the velocity and volume of the total
individual consumption, since the entire part of the commodity capital which enters the consumption fund depends on it.

However (aside from the turnovers in the world of commerce, in
which one merchant always sells the same commodity to another,
and this sort of circulation may appear highly prosperous in times of
speculation), the merchant's capital, in the first place, curtails phase
C—M for productive capital. Secondly, under the modern credit sys-

---

[a] Cf. present edition, Vol. 33, pp. 48-49.

tem it disposes of a large portion of the total social money capital, so that it can repeat its purchases even before it has definitely sold what has previously been purchased. And it is immaterial in this case, whether our merchant sells directly to the ultimate consumer, or there are a dozen other intermediate merchants between them. Owing to the immense elasticity of the reproduction process, which may always be pushed beyond any given bounds, it does not encounter any obstacle in production itself, or at best a very elastic one. Aside from the separation of C — M and M — C, which follows from the nature of the commodities, a fictitious demand is then created. In spite of its independent status, the movement of merchant's capital is never more than the movement of industrial capital within the sphere of circulation. But by virtue of its independent status it moves, within certain limits, independently of the bounds of the reproduction process and thereby even drives the latter beyond its bounds. This internal dependence and external independence push merchant's capital to a point where the internal connection is violently restored through a crisis.

Hence the phenomenon that crises do not come to the surface, do not break out, in the retail business first, which deals with direct consumption, but in the spheres of wholesale trade, and of banking, which places the money capital of society at the disposal of the former.

The manufacturer may actually sell to the exporter, and the exporter, in his turn, to his foreign customer; the importer may sell his raw materials to the manufacturer, and the latter may sell his products to the wholesale merchant, etc. But at some particular imperceptible point the goods lie unsold, or else, again, all producers and middlemen may gradually become overstocked. Consumption is then generally at its highest, either because one industrial capitalist sets a succession of others in motion; or because the labourers employed by them are fully employed and have more to spend than usual. The capitalists' expenditures increase together with their growing income. Besides, as we have seen (Book II, Part III[a]), continuous circulation takes place between constant capital and constant capital (even regardless of accelerated accumulation). It is at first independent of individual consumption because it never enters the latter. But this consumption definitely limits it nevertheless, since constant capital is never produced for its own sake but solely because more of it is needed

---

[a] Ibid., Vol. 36, pp. 427-32.

in spheres of production whose products go into individual consumption. However, this may go on undisturbed for some time, stimulated by prospective demand, and in such branches, therefore, the business of merchants and industrialists goes briskly forth. The crisis occurs when the returns of merchants who sell in distant markets (or whose supplies have also accumulated on the home market) become so slow and meagre that the banks press for payment, or promissory notes for purchased commodities become due before the latter have been resold. Then forced sales take place, sales in order to meet payments. Then comes the crash, which brings the illusory prosperity to an abrupt end.

But the superficiality and meaninglessness of the turnover of merchant's capital are still greater, because the turnover of one and the same merchant's capital may simultaneously or successively promote the turnovers of several productive capitals.

The turnover of merchant's capital does not just promote the turnovers of several industrial capitals, it can also mediate the opposite phases of the metamorphosis of commodity capital. For instance, the merchant buys linen from the manufacturer and sells it to the bleacher. In this case therefore the turnover of the same merchant's capital — in fact, the same $C - M$, a realisation of the linen — represents two opposite phases for two different industrial capitals. Inasmuch as the merchant sells for productive consumption, his $C - M$ is always $M - C$ for one industrial capitalist, and his $M - C$ always $C - M$ for another industrial capitalist.

If we leave out K, the circulation costs, as we do in this chapter, if, in other words, we leave aside that portion of capital which the merchant advances along with the money required to purchase commodities, it follows that we also omit ΔK, the additional profit made on this additional capital. This is thus the strictly logical and mathematically correct mode of analysis if we want to see how profit and turnover of merchant's capital affect prices.

If the price of production of 1 lb. of sugar were £1, the merchant could buy 100 lbs of sugar with £100. If he buys and sells this quantity in the course of the year, and if the average annual rate of profit is 15%, he would add £15 to the £100, and 3s. to £1, the price of production of 1 lb. of sugar. That is, he would sell 1 lb. of sugar at £1 3s. But if the price of production of 1 lb. of sugar should fall to 1s., the merchant could buy 2,000 lbs of sugar with £100, and sell the sugar at 1s. $1\frac{4}{5}$ d. per lb. The annual profit on capital invested in the sugar business would still be £15 on each £100. But the merchant has to sell 100 lbs in the first case, and 2,000 lbs in the second. The high or low level of the price of production has nothing to do with the rate of profit. But it would greatly and decisively affect that aliquot part of the selling price of each lb. of sugar, which resolves itself in mercantile profit, i. e., the addition to the price which the merchant makes on a certain quantity of commodities or products. If the price of production of a commodity is small, so, too, the amount the merchant advances in its purchase price, i. e., for a certain quantity of it. Hence, with a given rate of profit, the amount of profit he makes on this quantity of cheap commodities is small as well. Or, what amounts to the same, he can then buy with a certain amount of capital, say, 100, a larger quantity of these cheap commodities, and the total profit of 15, which he makes per 100, breaks up into small fractions over each individual piece or portion of this mass of commodities. If the opposite takes place, then the reverse is true. This depends entirely on the greater or smaller productivity of the industrial capital in whose products he trades. If we except the cases in which the merchant is a monopolist and simultaneously monopolises production, as did the Dutch East India Company [36] in its day, nothing can be more ridiculous than the current idea that it depends on the merchant whether he sells many commodities at a small profit or few commodities at a large profit on each individual piece of the commodities. The two limits of his selling price are: on the one hand, the price of production of the commodities, over which he has no control; on the other hand, the average rate of profit, over which he has just as little control. The only thing up to him to decide is whether he wants to deal in dear or in cheap commodities, and even here the size of his available capital and other circumstances also have their effect. Therefore, it depends wholly on the degree of development of the capitalist mode of production, not on the merchant's goodwill, what course he shall follow. A purely commercial company like the old Dutch East India Company, which had a monopoly of production, believed that it could continue a method adapted at best to the beginnings of capitalist production, under entirely changed conditions.[40]

The following circumstances, among others, help to maintain that

[40] "Profit, on the general principle, is always the same, whatever be price; keeping its place like an incumbent body on the swelling or sinking tide. As, therefore, prices rise, a tradesman raises price; as prices fall, a tradesman lowers price" (Corbet, *An In-*

popular prejudice, which, like all false conceptions of profit, etc., arises from the observation of pure commerce and merchants' prejudice:

First: phenomena of competition, which, however, apply merely to the distribution of mercantile profit among individual merchants, the shareholders of the total merchant's capital; if one, for example, sells cheaper, in order to drive his competitors off the field.

Secondly: an economist of the calibre of Professor Roscher may still imagine in Leipzig that it was "common sense and humanitarian"[b] grounds, which produced the change in selling prices, and that it was not a result of a revolutionised mode of production.

Thirdly: if production prices fall due to greater productive power of labour, and selling prices fall for the same reason, the demand, and with it the market prices, often rise even faster than the supply, so that selling prices yield more than the average profit.

Fourthly: a merchant may reduce his selling price (which is never more than a reduction of the usual profit that he adds to the price) so as to turn over a larger capital more rapidly. All these are matters that only concern competition between the merchants themselves.

We have already shown in Book I that high or low commodity prices do not determine either the mass of surplus value produced by a given capital, or the rate of surplus value; although the unit price of a commodity, and with it the share of surplus value in this price, are greater or smaller, depending on the relative quantity of commodities produced by a given quantity of labour.[c] The prices of every specified quantity of a commodity are, so far as they correspond to the values, determined by the total quantity of labour objectified in this commodity. If little labour is objectified in much commodity, the unit price of the commodity is low and the surplus value in it is small. How this labour incorporated in a commodity breaks up into paid and unpaid labour and what portion of its price, therefore, represents surplus value, has nothing to do with this total quantity of labour, nor, conse-

---

quiry into the Causes and Modes of the Wealth of Individuals..., London, 1841, p. 20.[a]) — Here, as in the text generally, it is only a matter of ordinary commerce, not of speculation. The analysis of speculation, as well as everything else pertaining to the division of mercantile capital, falls outside the field of our inquiry. "The profit of trade is a value added to capital which is independent of price, the second" (speculation profit) "is founded on the variation in the value of capital or in price itself" (l. c., p. 128).

---

[a] Ibid., Vol. 33, p. 242. - [b] W. Roscher, *Die Grundlagen der Nationalökonomie...*, p. 192. - [c] See present edition, Vol. 34, pp. 369-70.

quently, with the price of the commodity. But the rate of surplus value does not depend on the absolute magnitude of the surplus value contained in the unit price of the commodity. It depends on its relative magnitude, its proportion to the wages contained in the same commodity. The rate of surplus value may therefore be large, while the absolute magnitude of surplus value in each unit of the commodity is small. This absolute magnitude of surplus value in each piece of the commodity depends primarily on the productivity of labour, and only secondarily on its division into paid and unpaid labour.

Now, in the case of the commercial selling price, the price of production is a given external precondition.

The high commercial commodity prices in former times were due 1) to the high prices of production, i. e., the unproductiveness of labour; 2) to the absence of a general rate of profit, with merchant's capital absorbing a much larger quota of surplus value than would have fallen to its share if capitals enjoyed greater general mobility. The ending of this situation, in both its aspects, is therefore the result of the development of the capitalist mode of production.

The turnovers of merchant's capital vary in duration, their annual number consequently being greater or smaller, in different branches of commerce. Within the same branch the turnover is more or less rapid in the different phases of the economic cycle. Yet there is an average number of turnovers, determined by experience.

We have already seen that the turnover of merchant's capital differs from that of industrial capital. This is in the nature of things. One single phase in the turnover of industrial capital appears as a complete turnover of an independently constituted merchant's capital, or yet of its part. It also stands in a different relation to the determination of profit and price.

In the case of industrial capital, its turnover expresses, on the one hand, the periodicity of reproduction, and, therefore, the mass of commodities thrown on the market in a certain period depends on it. On the other hand, its time of circulation creates a barrier, an extensible one, and exerts more or less of a restraint on the creation of value and surplus value, because it affects the volume of the production process. The turnover, therefore, acts as a determining element on the mass of annually produced surplus value, and hence on the formation of the general rate of profit, but it acts as a limiting, rather than positive, element. For merchant's capital, on the contrary, the average rate of profit is a given magnitude. The merchant's capital does not directly participate in creating profit or surplus value, and joins in shaping the general rate of profit only in so far as it draws a dividend proportionate to its share in the total capital, out of the mass of profit produced by industrial capital.

The greater the number of turnovers of an industrial capital under conditions described in Book II, Part II, the greater the mass of profit it creates. True, through the formation of a general rate of profit, the total profit is distributed among the different capitals not in proportion to their actual part in its production, but in proportion to the aliquot part they make up of the total capital, i. e., in proportion to their magnitude. But this does not alter the essence of the matter. The greater the number of turnovers of the total industrial capital, the greater the mass of profit, the mass of annually produced surplus value, and, therefore, other circumstances remaining unchanged, the rate of profit. It is different with merchant's capital. The rate of profit is a given magnitude with respect to it, determined on the one hand by the mass of profit produced by industrial capital, and on the other by the relative magnitude of the total merchant's capital, by its quantitative relation to the sum of capital advanced in the processes of production and circulation. The number of its turnovers does, indeed, decisively affect its relation to the total capital, or the relative magnitude of merchant's capital required for the circulation, for it is evident that the absolute magnitude of the required merchant's capital and the velocity of its turnovers stand in inverse proportion. But, all other conditions remaining equal, the relative magnitude of merchant's capital, or the part it makes up of the total capital, is determined by its absolute magnitude. If the total capital is 10,000, and the merchant's capital $\frac{1}{10}$ of that sum, it is = 1,000; if the total capital is 1,000 then $\frac{1}{10}$ of it = 100. The absolute magnitude of merchant's capital varies, depending on the magnitude of the total capital, although its relative magnitude remains the same. But here we assume that its relative magnitude, say, $\frac{1}{10}$ of the total capital, is given. This relative magnitude, however, is again determined by the turnover. If it is turned over rapidly, its absolute magnitude, for example, will = = £1,000 in the first case, = 100 in the second, and hence its relative magnitude = $\frac{1}{10}$. With a slower turnover its absolute magnitude is, say, = 2,000 in the first case, and = 200 in the second. Its relative magnitude will then have increased from $\frac{1}{10}$ to $\frac{1}{5}$ of the total capital. Circumstances which reduce the average turnover of merchant's capital, like the development of means of transportation, for instance, reduce *pro tanto* the absolute magnitude of merchant's capital, and thereby increase the general rate of profit. If the opposite takes place, then the reverse is true. A developed capitalist mode of production, compared with earlier conditions, exerts a two-fold influence on merchant's capital. On the one hand, the same quantity of commodities is turned over with a smaller mass of actually functioning merchant's capital; owing to the more rapid turnover of merchant's capital, and the more rapid reproduction process, on which this depends, the relation of merchant's capital to industrial capital diminishes. On the other hand, with the development of the capitalist mode of production all production becomes the production of commodities, which places all products into the hands of agents of circulation. It is to be added that under the previous mode of production, which produced on a small scale, a very large portion of the producers sold their goods directly to the consumers, or worked on their personal orders, save for the mass of products consumed directly, *in natura,* by the producer himself, and the mass of services performed *in natura.* While, therefore, under former modes of production commercial capital was greater in relation to the commodity capital which it turned over, it was:

1) absolutely smaller, because a disproportionately smaller part of the total product was produced as commodities, and passed as commodity capital into circulation, falling into the hands of merchants. It was smaller, because the commodity capital was smaller. But at the same time it was proportionately larger, not only because its turnover was slower and not only in relation to the mass of commodities turned over by it. It was larger also because the price of this mass of commodities, and hence the merchant's capital to be advanced for it, were greater than under capitalist production on account of a lower productivity of labour, so that the same value was incorporated in a smaller mass of commodities.

2) It is not only that a larger mass of commodities is produced on the basis of the capitalist mode of production (taking into account also the reduced value of this mass of commodities), but the same mass of products, for instance, of corn, also forms a greater commodity mass, i. e., more and more of it becomes an object of commerce. As a consequence, there is an increase not only of the mass of merchant's capital, but of all capital applied in circulation, such as in marine shipping, railways, telegraph, etc.

3) However, and this is an aspect which belongs to the discussion of "competition among capitals" [1]: idle or only half-functioning merchant's capital grows with the progress of the capitalist mode of production, with the ease of entering retail trade, with speculation, and the redundance of released capital.

But, assuming the relative magnitude of merchant's capital to total capital to be given, the difference of turnovers in the various branches of commerce does not affect either the magnitude of the total profit falling to the share of merchant's capital, or the general rate of profit. The merchant's profit is not determined by the mass of commodity capital turned over by him, but by the dimensions of the money capital advanced by him to promote this turnover. If the general annual rate of profit is 15%, and the merchant advances £100, which he turns over once a year, he will sell his commodities at 115. If his capital turns over five times a year, he will sell a commodity capital he bought at 100 at 103 five times a year, hence in a year a commodity capital of 500 at 515. This gives the same annual profit of 15 on his advanced capital of 100. If this were not so, merchant's capital would yield a much higher profit, proportionate to the number of its turnovers, than industrial capital, which would be in conflict with the law of the general rate of profit.

Hence, the number of turnovers of merchant's capital in the various branches of commerce has a direct influence on the mercantile prices of commodities. The amount added to the mercantile price, the aliquot part of mercantile profit of a given capital, which falls upon the price of production of an individual commodity, is in inverse proportion to the number of turnovers, or the velocity of turnover, of merchants' capitals in the various branches of commerce. If a certain merchant's capital is turned over five times a year, it will add to a commodity capital of equal value but $\frac{1}{5}$ of what another merchant's capital, which turns over just once a year, adds to a commodity capital of equal value.

The modification of selling prices by the average period of turnover of capitals in different branches of commerce amounts to this: The same mass of profits, determined for any given magnitude of merchant's capital by the general annual rate of profit, hence determined independently of the specific character of the commercial operations of this capital, is differently distributed — proportionately to the velocity of turnover — over masses of commodities of equal value, so that, for instance, if a merchant's capital is turned over five times a year, $\frac{15}{5} = 3\%$, and if once a year, 15%, is added to the price of the commodities.

The same percentage of commercial profit in different branches of commerce, therefore, increases the selling prices of commodities by quite different percentages of their values, all depending on their periods of turnover.

On the other hand, in the case of industrial capital, the period of turnover does not in any way affect the magnitude of the value of individual commodities produced, although it does affect the mass of values and surplus values produced in a given time by a given capital, because it affects the mass of exploited labour. This is concealed, to be sure, and seems to be otherwise as soon as one turns to prices of production. But this is due solely to the fact that, according to previously analysed laws, the prices of production of various commodities deviate from their values. If we look upon the process of production as a whole, and upon the mass of commodities produced by the total industrial capital, we shall at once find the general law vindicated.

While, therefore, a closer inspection of the influence of the period of turnover on the formation of values by industrial capital leads us back to the general law and to the basis of political economy, that the values of commodities are determined by the labour time contained in them, the influence of the turnovers of merchant's capital on mercantile prices reveals phenomena which, without benefit of a very far-reaching analysis of the connecting links, seem to point to a purely arbitrary determination of prices; namely, that they are fixed by a capital simply bent upon pocketing a certain quantity of profit in a year. Due particularly to this influence of turnovers, it appears that within certain limits the process of circulation as such determines commodity prices independently of the process of production. All superficial and false conceptions of the process of reproduction as a whole are derived from examinations of merchant's capital and from the conceptions which its peculiar movements call forth in the minds of circulation agents.

If, as the reader will have realised to his great dismay, the analysis of the actual intrinsic relations of the capitalist process of production is a very complicated matter and a very extensive work; if it is a work of science to resolve the visible, merely external movement into the true intrinsic movement, it is self-evident that conceptions which arise about the laws of production in the minds of agents of capitalist production and circulation will diverge drastically from these real laws

and will merely be the conscious expression of the apparent movement. The conceptions of the merchant, stockbroker, and banker, are
necessarily quite distorted. Those of the manufacturers are vitiated
by the acts of circulation to which their capital is subject, and by the
levelling of the general rate of profit.[41] Competition likewise assumes
a completely distorted role in their minds. If the limits of value and
surplus value are given, it is easy to grasp how competition of capitals
transforms values into prices of production and further into mercantile prices, and surplus value into average profit. But without these
limits, it is absolutely unintelligible why competition should reduce
the general rate of profit to one level instead of another, e. g., make it
15% instead of 1,500%. Competition can at best only reduce the general rate of profit to *one* level. But it contains no element by which it
could determine this level itself.

From the standpoint of merchant's capital, therefore, it is the turnover which appears to determine prices. On the other hand, while
the velocity of turnover of industrial capital, in so far as it enables a
certain capital to exploit more or less labour, exerts a determining
and limiting influence on the mass of profit, and thus on the general
rate of profit, this rate of profit obtains for merchant's capital as an
external fact, its internal connection with the production of surplus
value being entirely obliterated. If, under otherwise equal circumstances and particularly the same organic composition, the same industrial capital is turned over four times a year instead of twice, it
produces twice as much surplus value and, consequently, profit. And
this is apparent as soon, and as long, as this capital has a monopoly
on an improved method of production, which makes this accelerated
turnover possible. Conversely, differences in the periods of turnover
in different branches of commerce manifest themselves in the fact that
profit made on the turnover of a given commodity capital is in inverse
proportion to the number of times the money capital turns over this
commodity capital. SMALL PROFITS AND QUICK RETURNS appear to the SHOP-
KEEPER to be the principle which he follows out of sheer principle.

For the rest, it is self-evident that regardless of alternating, mutually
compensating, speedier and slower turnovers, this law of turnover of

---

[41] This is a very naive, but also a very correct remark: "Surely the fact that one
and the same commodity may be had from different sellers at considerably different
prices is frequently due to mistakes of calculation" (Feller and Odermann, *Das Ganze
der kaufmännischen Arithmetik*, 7th ed., 1859, [p. 451]). This shows how purely theoretical,
that is, abstract, becomes the determination of prices.

merchant's capital holds good in each branch of commerce only for the average turnovers made by the entire merchant's capital invested in each particular branch. The capital of A, who deals in the same branch as B, may make more or less than the average number of turnovers. In this case the others make less or more. This does not alter the turnover of the total mass of merchant's capital invested in this branch. But it is of decisive moment for the individual merchant or shopkeeper. In this case he makes an extra profit, just as industrial capitalists make extra profits if they produce under better than average conditions. If competition compels him, he can sell cheaper than his companions without lowering his profit below the average. If the conditions which would enable him to turn over his capital more rapidly, are themselves for sale, such as a favourable shop location, he can pay extra rent for it, i. e., convert a portion of his surplus profit into ground rent.

Chapter XIX

MONEY-DEALING CAPITAL

The purely technical movements performed by money in the circulation process of industrial, and, as we may now add, of commercial capital (since it takes over a part of the circulation movement of industrial capital as its own, peculiar movement), if individualised as a function of some particular capital performing just these, and only these, operations as its specific operations, convert this capital into money-dealing capital. A portion of industrial capital, and, more precisely, also of commercial capital, not only obtains all the time in the form of money, as money capital in general, but as money capital, engaged precisely in these technical functions. A definite part of the total capital dissociates itself from the rest and stands apart in the form of money capital, whose capitalist function consists exclusively in performing these operations for the entire class of industrial and commercial capitalists. As in the case of commercial capital, a portion of industrial capital engaged in the circulation process in the form of money capital separates from the rest and performs these operations of the reproduction process for all the other capital. The movements of this money capital are, therefore, once more merely movements of an individualised part of industrial capital engaged in the reproduction process.

It is only when, and in so far as, capital is newly invested — which also applies to accumulation — that capital in money form appears as the starting-point and the end result of the movement. But for all capitals already engaged in the process, these first and last points appear merely as points of transit. Since, as already seen in the case of simple commodity circulation, from the moment of leaving the sphere of production to the moment of its re-entry industrial capital undergoes the metamorphosis C' — M — C, M in fact represents the end result of one phase of the metamorphosis, just to become the starting-point of the reverse phase, which supplements it. And although the C — M of industrial capital is always M — C — M for merchant's capital, the actual process for the latter is continually also C — M — C once it has begun to function. But merchant's capital performs the acts C — M and M — C simultaneously. This is to say that there is not just *one* capital in the stage C — M while another is in the stage M — C, but that the same capital buys continually and sells continually at one and the same time because of the continuity of the production process. It is to be found always in both stages at one and the same time. While one of its parts turns into money, later to be reconverted into commodities, another turns simultaneously into commodities, to be reconverted into money.

It all depends on the form of the commodity exchange whether the money serves here as a means of circulation or of payment. In both cases the capitalist has to pay out money constantly to many persons, and to receive money continually from many persons. This purely technical operation of disbursing and receiving money is in itself labour which, as long as the money serves as a means of payment, necessitates drawing up payment balances and acts of balancing accounts. This labour is a cost of circulation, i. e., not labour creating value. It is shortened in being carried out by a special section of agents, or capitalists, for the rest of the capitalist class.

A definite portion of the capital must be on hand constantly as a hoard, as potential money capital — a reserve of means of purchase, a reserve of means of payment, and idle capital in the form of money waiting to be put to work. Another portion streams back continually in this form. Aside from collecting, paying, and book-keeping, this entails safekeeping the hoard, which is an operation all in itself. It is, indeed, a continuous conversion of the hoard into means of circulation and means of payment, and its restoration by means of money secured through sales and from payments due. This constant movement of the part of capital existing as money, dissociated from the function of capital itself, this purely technical function, causes its own labour and expense, classified as costs of circulation.

The division of labour brings it about that these technical operations, dependent upon the functions of capital, should be performed for the entire capitalist class as much as possible by a special section of agents or capitalists as their exclusive function—or that these operations should be concentrated in their hands. We have here, as in merchant's capital, division of labour in a twofold sense. It becomes a specialised business, and because performed as a specialised business for the money mechanism of the whole class, it is concentrated and conducted on a large scale. A further division of labour takes place within it, both through division into various independent branches, and through segmentation of work within these branches (large offices, numerous book-keepers and cashiers, and far-reaching division of labour). Paying and receiving money, settling accounts, keeping current accounts, storing money, etc.—all this, dissociated from the acts necessitating these technical operations, makes money-dealing capital of the capital advanced for these functions.[a]

The various operations, whose individualisation into specific businesses gives rise to the money trade, spring from the different purposes of money itself and from its functions, which capital in its money form must therefore likewise carry out.

I have pointed out earlier that finance developed originally from the exchange of products between different communities.[42]

Trading in money, commerce in the money commodity, first developed therefore out of international commerce. Even since different national coins have existed merchants buying in foreign countries have had to exchange their national coins for local coins, and vice versa, or to exchange different coins for uncoined pure silver or gold—the world money. Hence the exchange business which is to be regarded as one of the natural foundations of modern finance.[43] Out of it devel-

---

[42] *Zur Kritik der politischen Oekonomie*, S. 27.[b]

[43] "The great differences among coins as concerns their grain and coinage by many princes and towns that were privileged to coin money, necessitated the creation of business establishments to enable merchants to use local money wherever compensation for the different coins was required. To be able to make cash payments, merchants who travelled to a foreign market provided themselves with uncoined pure silver, or

---

[a] Cf. present edition, Vol. 33, pp. 166-68. - [b] Ibid., Vol. 29, pp. 282-83.

oped banks of exchange, in which silver (or gold) serves as world money—now called bank money or commercial money—as distinct from currency. Exchange transactions, in the sense of mere notes of payment to travellers from a money changer in one country to a changer in another country, developed back in Rome and Greece out of the actual money-changing.

Trading in gold and silver as commodities (raw materials for the making of luxury articles) is the natural basis of the BULLION TRADE,[a] or the trade which acts as a medium for the functions of money as world money. These functions, as previously explained (Buch I, Kap. III, 3, c[b]), are two-fold: currency movement back and forth between the various national spheres of circulation in order to balance international payments and in connection with the migrations of capital in quest of interest; simultaneously, flow of precious metals from their sources of production via the world market and their distribution among the various national spheres of circulation. Goldsmiths acted as bankers still during the greater part of the 17th century in England. We shall completely disregard the way in which the balancing of international accounts developed further in the bill jobbing, etc., and everything referring to transactions in valuable papers; in short, we shall leave

gold. In the same way they exchanged money received in local markets for uncoined silver or gold when returning home. The business of exchanging money, the exchange of uncoined precious metals for local coins, and vice versa, thus became a widespread and paying business" (Hüllmann, *Städtewesen des Mittelalters*, Bonn, 1826-29, I, S. 437-38). "Banks of exchange do not owe their name to the fact that they issue bills of exchange ... but to the fact that they used to exchange coins. Long before the establishment of the Amsterdam Bank of Exchange in 1609, there existed in the Dutch merchant towns money changers and exchange houses, even exchange banks.... The business of these money changers consisted in exchanging the numerous varieties of coin brought into the country by foreign traders for the currency of the realm. Gradually their circle of activity extended.... They became the bankers and cashiers of their times. But the government of Amsterdam viewed as dangerous the combination of cashier and exchange businesses, and to meet this danger it was resolved to establish a large chartered institution able to perform both the cashier and exchange operations. This institution was the famous Amsterdam Bank of Exchange of 1609. In like manner, the exchange banks of Venice, Genoa, Stockholm, Hamburg, owe their origin to the continual necessity of changing money. Of all these, the Hamburg Exchange is the only one today still doing business, because the need for such an institution is still felt in that merchants' town, which has no Mint of its own, etc." (S. Vissering, *Handboek van Praktische Staathuishoudkunde*, Amsterdam, 1860-61, I, 247-48).

---

[a] In the 1894 German edition this English term is given in parentheses after its German equivalent. - [b] See present edition, Vol. 35.

out of consideration all special forms of the credit system, which do not as yet concern us here.[a]

National money discards its local character in the capacity of world money; one national currency is expressed in another, and thus all of them are reduced to their content of gold or silver, while the latter, being the two commodities circulating as world money, are simultaneously reduced to their reciprocal value ratio, which changes continually. It is this intermediate operation which the money trader makes his special occupation. Money-changing and the bullion trade are thus the original forms of the money trade, and spring from the two-fold functions of money — as national money and world money.[b]

The capitalist process of production, just as commerce in general, even under precapitalist methods, imply:

First, the accumulation of money as a hoard, i. e., here as that part of capital which must always be on hand in the form of money as a reserve fund of means of payment and purchase. This is the first form of a hoard, as it reappears under the capitalist mode of production, and as it appears generally with the development of merchant's capital, at least for the purposes of this capital. Both remarks apply to national, as well as international, circulation. The hoard is in continuous flux, pours ceaselessly into circulation, and returns ceaselessly from it. The second form of a hoard is that of idle, temporarily unemployed capital in the shape of money, including newly accumulated and not yet invested money capital. The functions entailed by this formation of a hoard are primarily those of safekeeping, bookkeeping, etc.[c]

Secondly, however, this involves outlays of money for purchases, collecting money from sales, making and receiving payments, balancing payments, etc. The money dealer performs all these services at first as a simple *cashier* of the merchants and industrial capitalists.[44]

---

[44] "The institution of cashier has probably nowhere preserved its original independent character so pure as in the Dutch merchant towns (cf. on the origin of the cashier business in Amsterdam, E. Luzac, *Holland's Rijkdom*, Part III). Its functions coincide in part with those of the old Amsterdam Bank of Exchange. The cashier receives from the merchants, who employ his services, a certain amount of money, for which he opens a 'credit' for them in his books. Later, they send him their claims, which he collects for them and credits to their account. At the same time, he makes payments on their drafts (*kassiers briefjes*) and charges the amounts to their account. He makes a small charge for these receipts and payments, which yields him a remuneration for his labours only corresponding to the size of the turnover accomplished between the two

---

[a] Ibid., Vol. 33, pp. 169-70. - [b] Ibid., p. 46. - [c] Ibid., p. 43.

The money trade becomes fully developed, even in its first stages, as soon as its ordinary functions are supplemented by lending and borrowing and by credit. Of this more in the next part, which deals with interest-bearing capital.

The bullion trade itself, the transfer of gold or silver from one country to another, is merely the result of trading in commodities. It is determined by the rate of exchange which expresses the standing of international payments and the interest rates in the different markets. The bullion trader as such acts merely as an intermediary of the results.

In discussing money and the way its movements and forms develop out of simple commodity circulation, we saw (Buch I, Kap. III) that the movements of the mass of money circulating as means of purchase and payment depend on the metamorphosis of commodities, on the volume and velocity of this metamorphosis, which we now know to be but a phase in the entire process of reproduction. As for securing the money materials — gold and silver — from their sources of production, this resolves itself into a direct exchange of commodities, an exchange of gold and silver as commodities for other commodities. Hence, it is itself as much a phase of the exchange of commodities as the securing of iron or other metals. However, so far as the movement of precious metals on the world market is concerned (we here leave aside movements expressing the transfer of capital by loans — a type of transfer which also obtains in the shape of commodity capital), it is quite as much determined by the international exchange of commodities as the movement of money as a national means of purchase and

parties. If payments are to be balanced between two merchants, who both deal with the same cashier, such payments are settled very simply by mutual entries in the books, for the cashiers balance their mutual claims from day to day. The cashier's actual business thus consists basically of this mediation in payments. Therefore, it excludes industrial enterprises, speculation, and opening of unlimited credits; for it must be the rule in this business that the cashier makes no payment over and above the credit of any one keeping an account with him" (Vissering, l. c., p. 243-244). Re the banking associations of Venice: "The requirements and locality of Venice, where carrying bullion was less convenient than in other places, induced the large merchants of that city to found banking associations under due safeguards, supervision and management. Members of such associations deposited certain sums, on which they drew drafts for their creditors, whereupon the paid sum was deducted from the debtor's account on the page of the book reserved for that purpose and added to the sum credited in the same book to the creditor. This is the earliest beginning of the so-called giro banks. These associations are indeed old. But if attributed to the 12th century, they are being confounded with the State Loan Institute established in 1171" (Hüllmann, l. c., pp. 453-54).

payment is determined by the exchange of commodities in the home market. The inflow and outflow of precious metals from one national sphere of circulation to another, inasmuch as this is caused merely by a depreciation of the national currency, or by a double standard,[10] are alien to money circulation as such and merely represent corrections of deviations brought about arbitrarily by state decrees. Finally, as concerns the formation of hoards which constitute reserve funds for means of purchase and payment, be it for home or foreign trade, and which also merely represent a form of temporarily idle capital, they are in both cases necessary precipitates of the circulation process.

If the entire circulation of money is in volume, form and movement purely a result of commodity circulation, which, in its turn, from the capitalist point of view, is only the circulation process of capital (also embracing the exchange of capital for revenue, and of revenue for revenue, so far as outlay of revenue is effected through retail trade), it is self-evident that dealing in money does not merely promote the circulation of money, a mere result and phenomenon of commodity circulation. This circulation of money itself, a phase in commodity circulation, is taken for granted in money-dealing. What the latter promotes is merely the technical operations of money circulation which it concentrates, shortens, and simplifies. Dealing in money does not form the hoards. It provides the technical means by which the formation of hoards may, so far as it is voluntary (hence, not an expression of unemployed capital or of disturbances in the reproduction process), be reduced to its economic minimum because, if managed for the capitalist class as a whole, the reserve funds of means of purchase and payment need not be as large as they would have to be if each capitalist were to manage his own. The money dealers do not buy the precious metals. They merely handle their distribution as soon as the commodity trade has bought them. They facilitate the settling of balances, inasmuch as money serves as the means of payment, and reduce through the artificial mechanism of these settlements the amount of money required for this purpose. But they do not determine either the connections, or the volume, of the mutual payments. The bills of exchange and the cheques, for instance, which are exchanged for one another in banks and CLEARING HOUSES, represent quite independent transactions and are the results of given operations, and it is merely a question of a better technical settlement of these results. So far as money circulates as a means of purchase, the volume and number of purchases and sales have no connection whatever with money-dealing. The latter can do no more than shorten the technical operations that go with buying and selling, and thus reduce the amount of cash money required to turn over the commodities.

Money-dealing in its pure form, which we consider here, i. e., set apart from the credit system, is thus concerned only with the technique of a certain phase of commodity circulation, namely, that of money circulation and the different functions of money arising in its circulation.

This substantially distinguishes dealing in money from the dealing in commodities, which promotes the metamorphosis of commodities and their exchange, or even gives this process of the commodity capital the appearance of a process of a capital set apart from industrial capital. While, therefore, commercial capital has its own form of circulation, $M — C — M$, in which the commodity changes hands twice and thus provides a reflux of money, as distinct from $C — M — C$, in which money changes hands twice and thus promotes commodity exchange, there is no such special form in the case of money-dealing capital.

In so far as money capital is advanced by a separate class of capitalists in this technical promotion of money circulation — a capital which on a reduced scale represents the additional capital the merchants and industrial capitalists would otherwise have to advance themselves for these purposes — the general form of capital, $M — M'$, occurs here as well. By advancing M, the advancing capitalist secures $M + \Delta M$. But promotion of $M — M'$ does not here concern the material, but only the technical, processes of the metamorphosis.

It is evident that the mass of money capital with which the money dealers operate is the money capital of merchants and industrialists in the process of circulation, and that the money dealers' operations are actually operations of merchants and industrialists, in which they act as mediators.

It is equally evident that the money dealers' profit is nothing but a deduction from the surplus value, since they operate with already realised values (even when realised in the form of creditors' claims).

Just as in the commodity trade, there is a duplication of functions, because a part of the technical operations connected with money circulation must be carried out by the dealers and producers of commodities themselves.

Chapter XX

HISTORICAL FACTS ABOUT MERCHANT'S CAPITAL

The particular form in which commercial and money-dealing capitals accumulate money will be discussed in the next part.

It is self-evident from what has gone before that nothing could be more absurd than to regard merchant's capital, whether in the shape of commercial or of money-dealing capital, as a particular variety of industrial capital, such as, say, mining, agriculture, cattle-raising, manufacturing, transport, etc., which are side lines of industrial capital occasioned by the division of social labour, and hence different spheres of investment. The simple observation that in the circulation phase of its reproduction process every industrial capital performs as commodity capital and as money capital the very functions which appear as the exclusive functions of the two forms of merchant's capital, should rule out such a crude notion. On the other hand, in commercial and money-dealing capital the differences between industrial capital as productive capital and the same capital in the sphere of circulation are individualised through the fact that the definite forms and functions which capital assumes for the moment appear as independent forms and functions of a separate portion of the capital and are exclusively bound up with it. The converted form of industrial capital and the material differences between productive capitals applied in different branches of industry, which arise from the nature of these various branches, are worlds apart.[a]

Aside from the crudity with which the economist generally considers distinctions of form, which really concern him only from their material side, this misconception by the vulgar economist is explained on two additional counts. First, his inability to explain the peculiar nature of mercantile profit; and, secondly, his apologetic endeavours to deduce commodity capital and money capital, and later commercial capital and money-dealing capital as forms arising necessarily from the process of production as such, whereas they are due to the specific form of the capitalist mode of production, which above all presupposes the circulation of commodities, and hence of money, as its basis.

If commercial capital and money-dealing capital do not differ from

---

[a] Cf. present edition, Vol. 33, pp. 47-48.

grain production any more than this differs from cattle-raising and manufacturing, it is plain as day that production and capitalist production are altogether identical, and that, among other things, the distribution of the social products among the members of a society, be it for productive or individual consumption, must just as consistently be handled by merchants and bankers as the consumption of meat by cattle-raising and that of clothing by their manufacture.[45]

The great economists, such as Smith, Ricardo, etc., are perplexed over mercantile capital being a special variety, since they consider the basic form of capital, capital as industrial capital, and circulation capital (money capital and commodity capital) solely because it is a phase in the reproduction process of every capital. The rules concerning the formation of value, profit, etc., immediately deduced by them from their study of industrial capital, do not extend directly to merchant's capital. For this reason, they leave merchant's capital entirely aside and mention it only as a kind of industrial capital. Wherever they make a special analysis of it, as Ricardo[b] does in dealing with foreign trade, they seek to demonstrate that it creates no value (and consequently no surplus value). But whatever is true of foreign trade, is also true of home trade.[c]

Hitherto we have considered merchant's capital merely from the

---

[45] The sage Mr. Roscher has figured out[a] that, since certain people designate trade as "mediation" between producers and consumers, "one" might just as well designate production itself as "mediation" of consumption (between whom?), and this implies, of course, that merchant's capital is as much a part of productive capital as agricultural and industrial capital. In other words, because I can say, that man can mediate his consumption only by means of production (and he has to do this even without getting his education at Leipzig), or that labour is required for the appropriation of the products of Nature (which might be called "mediation"), it follows, of course, that social "mediation" arising from a specific social form of production — *because* mediation — has the same absolute character of necessity, and the same rank. The word "mediation" settles everything. By the way, the merchants are not mediators between producers and consumers (consumers as distinct from producers, consumers, that is, who do not produce, are left aside for the moment), but mediators in the exchange of the products of these producers among themselves. They are but middlemen in an exchange, which in thousands of cases proceeds without them.

---

[a] *Die Grundlagen der Nationalökonomie*, § 60, S. 103. - [b] See D. Ricardo, *On the Principles of Political Economy...*, 3rd ed., p. 413; cf. also present edition, Vol. 32, pp. 70-72. - [c] Ibid., Vol. 33, p. 64.

standpoint, and within the limits, of the capitalist mode of production. However, not commerce alone, but also merchant's capital, is older than the capitalist mode of production, is, in fact, historically the oldest free mode of existence of capital.

Since we have already seen that money-dealing and the capital advanced for it require nothing more for their development than the existence of wholesale commerce, and further of commercial capital, it is only the latter which we must occupy ourselves with here.

Since merchant's capital is penned in the sphere of circulation, and since its function consists exclusively in promoting the exchange of commodities, it requires no other conditions for its existence — aside from the undeveloped forms arising from direct barter — outside those necessary for the simple circulation of commodities and money. Or rather, the latter is the condition of *its* existence. No matter what the basis on which products are produced, which are thrown into circulation as commodities — whether the basis of the primitive community, of slave production, of small peasant and petty bourgeois, or the capitalist basis, the character of products as commodities is not altered, and as commodities they must pass through the process of exchange and its attendant changes of form. The extremes between which merchant's capital acts as mediator exist for it as given, just as they are given for money and for its movements. The only necessary thing is that these extremes should be on hand as commodities, regardless of whether production is wholly a production of commodities, or whether only the surplus of the independent producers' immediate needs, satisfied by their own production, is thrown on the market. Merchant's capital promotes only the movements of these extremes, of these commodities, which are preconditions of its own existence.

The extent to which products enter trade and go through the merchants' hands depends on the mode of production, and reaches its maximum under the full development of capitalist production, where the product is produced solely as a commodity, and not as a direct means of subsistence. On the other hand, on the basis of every mode of production, trade facilitates the production of surplus products destined for exchange, in order to increase the enjoyments, or the wealth, of the producers (here meant are the owners of the products). Hence, commerce imparts to production a character directed more and more towards exchange value.[a]

---

a Ibid., Vol. 29, pp. 233-34 and 480-81.

The metamorphosis of commodities, their movement, consists 1) materially, of the exchange of different commodities for one another, and 2) formally, of the conversion of commodities into money by sale, and of money into commodities by purchase. And the function of merchant's capital resolves itself into these very acts of buying and selling commodities. It therefore merely promotes the exchange of commodities; yet this exchange is not to be conceived at the outset as a bare exchange of commodities between direct producers. Under slavery, feudalism and vassalage (so far as primitive communities are concerned) it is the slave-owner, the feudal lord, the tribute-collecting state, who are the owners, hence sellers, of the products. The merchant buys and sells for many. Purchases and sales are concentrated in his hands and consequently are no longer bound to the direct requirements of the buyer (as merchant).

But whatever the social organisation of the spheres of production whose commodity exchange the merchant promotes, his wealth exists always in the form of money, and his money always serves as capital. Its form is always $M — C — M'$. Money, the independent form of exchange value, is the point of departure, and increasing the exchange value an end in itself. Commodity exchange as such and the operations effecting it — separated from production and performed by non-producers — are just a means of increasing wealth not as mere wealth, but as wealth in its most universal social form, as exchange value. The compelling motive and determining purpose are the conversion of M into $M + \Delta M$. The transactions $M — C$ and $C — M'$, which promote $M—M'$, appear merely as stages of transition in this conversion of M into $M + \Delta M$. This $M — C — M'$, the characteristic movement of merchant's capital, distinguishes it from $C — M — C$, trade in commodities directly between producers, which has for its ultimate end the exchange of use values.

The less developed the production, the more wealth in money is concentrated in the hands of merchants or appears in the specific form of merchants' wealth.

Within the capitalist mode of production — i. e., as soon as capital has established its sway over production and imparted to it a wholly changed and specific form — merchant's capital appears merely as a capital with a *specific* function. In all previous modes of production, and all the more, wherever production ministers to the immediate wants of the producer, merchant's capital appears to perform the function *par excellence* of capital.

There is, therefore, not the least difficulty in understanding why merchant's capital appears as the historical form of capital long before capital established its own domination over production. Its existence and development to a certain level are in themselves historical premises for the development of capitalist production 1) as a precondition for the concentration of money wealth, and 2) because the capitalist mode of production presupposes production for trade, selling on a large scale, and not to the individual customer, hence also a merchant who does not buy to satisfy his personal wants but concentrates the purchases of many buyers in his one purchase. On the other hand, all development of merchant's capital tends to give production more and more the character of production for exchange value and to turn products more and more into commodities. Yet its development, as we shall presently see, is incapable by itself of promoting and explaining the transition from one mode of production to another.

Within capitalist production merchant's capital is reduced from its former independent existence to a special phase in the investment of capital in general, and the levelling of profits reduces its rate of profit to the general average. It functions only as an agent of productive capital. The special social conditions that take shape with the development of merchant's capital, are here no longer paramount. On the contrary, wherever merchant's capital still predominates we find obsolete conditions. This is true even within one and the same country, in which, for instance, the specifically merchant towns present far more striking analogies with past conditions than manufacturing towns.[46]

The independent and predominant development of capital as mer-

---

[46] Herr W. Kiesselbach (in his *Der Gang des Welthandels im Mittelalter*, 1860) is indeed still enwrapped in the ideas of a world, in which merchant's capital is the general form of capital. He has not the least idea of the modern meaning of capital, any more than Herr Mommsen when he speaks in his *Römische Geschichte* of "capital"and the rule of capital. In modern English history, the commercial estate proper and the merchant towns are also politically reactionary and in league with the landed and financial aristocracy against industrial capital. Compare, for instance, the political role of Liverpool with that of Manchester and Birmingham. The complete rule of industrial capital was not acknowledged by English merchant's capital and MONEYED INTEREST[a] until after the abolition of the corn duties,[22] etc.

---

[a] In the 1894 German edition this English term is given in parentheses after its German equivalent.

chant's capital is tantamount to the non-subjection of production to capital, and hence to capital developing on the basis of an alien social mode of production which is also independent of it. The independent development of merchant's capital, therefore, stands in inverse proportion to the general economic development of society.

Independent mercantile wealth as a predominant form of capital represents the separation of the circulation process from its extremes, and these extremes are the exchanging producers themselves. These extremes remain independent of the circulation process, just as the latter remains independent of them. The product becomes a commodity by way of commerce. It is commerce which here turns products into commodities, not the produced commodity which by its movements gives rise to commerce. Thus, capital appears here first as capital in the process of circulation. It is in the circulation process that money develops into capital. It is in circulation that products first develop as exchange values, as commodities and as money. Capital can, and must, form in the process of circulation, before it learns to control its extremes — the various spheres of production between which circulation mediates. Money and commodity circulation can mediate between spheres of production of widely different organisation, whose internal structure is still chiefly adjusted to the output of use values. This individualisation of the circulation process, in which spheres of production are interconnected by means of a third, has a two-fold significance. On the one hand, that circulation has not as yet established a hold on production, but is related to it as to a given premiss. On the other hand, that the production process has not as yet absorbed circulation as a mere phase of production. Both, however, are the case in capitalist production. The production process rests wholly upon circulation, and circulation is a mere transitional phase of production, in which the product created as a commodity is realised and its elements of production, likewise created as commodities, are replaced. That form of capital — merchant's capital — which developed directly out of circulation appears here merely as one of the forms of capital occurring in its reproduction process.[a]

The law that the independent development of merchant's capital is inversely proportional to the degree of development of capitalist production is particularly evident in the history of the CARRYING TRADE,[b] as

---

[a] Cf. present edition, Vol. 33, pp. 14-15. - [b] In the 1894 German edition this English term is given in parentheses after its German equivalent.

among the Venetians, Genoese, Dutch, etc., where the principal gains were not thus made by exporting domestic products, but by promoting the exchange of products of commercially and otherwise economically undeveloped societies, and by exploiting both producing countries.[47] Here, merchant's capital is in its pure form, separated from the extremes — the spheres of production between which it mediates. This is the main source of its formation. But this monopoly of the carrying trade disintegrates, and with it this trade itself, proportionately to the economic development of the peoples, whom it exploits at both ends of its course, and whose lack of development was the basis of its existence. In the case of the carrying trade this appears not only as the decline of a special branch of commerce, but also that of the predominance of the purely trading nations, and of their commercial wealth in general, which rested upon the carrying trade. This is but a special form, in which is expressed the subordination of commercial to industrial capital with the advance of capitalist production. The behaviour of merchant's capital wherever it directly rules over production is strikingly illustrated not only by the colonial economy (the so-called colonial system) in general, but quite specifically by the methods of the old Dutch East India Company.[36]

Since the movement of merchant's capital is $M - C - M'$, the merchant's profit is made, first, in acts which occur only within the circulation process, hence in the two acts of buying and selling; and, secondly, it is realised in the last act, the sale. It is therefore PROFIT UPON ALIENATION.[b][35] *Prima facie*, a pure and independent commercial profit seems impossible so long as products are sold at their value. To buy cheap in order to sell dear is the rule of trade. Hence, not the exchange of equivalents. The conception of value is included in it in so

---

[47] "The inhabitants of trading cities, by importing the improved manufactures and expensive luxuries of richer countries afforded some food to the vanity of the great proprietors, who eagerly purchased them with great quantities of the rude produce of their own lands. The commerce of a great part of Europe in those times, accordingly consisted chiefly, in the exchange of their own rude produce for the manufactured produce of more civilised nations.... When this taste became so general as to occasion a considerable demand, the merchants, in order to save the expense of carriage, naturally endeavoured to establish some manufactures of the same kind in their own country" (Adam Smith, Book III, Ch. III).[a]

---

[a] *An Inquiry into the Nature and Causes of the Wealth of Nations*, Vol. I, London, 1776, pp. 489 and 490; cf. also present edition, Vol. 33, p. 19. - [b] In the 1894 German edition this English term is given in parentheses after its German equivalent.

far as the various commodities are all values, and therefore money. In respect to quality they are all expressions of social labour. But they are not values of equal magnitude. The quantitative ratio in which products are exchanged is at first quite arbitrary. They assume the form of commodities inasmuch as they are exchangeables, i. e., expressions of one and the same third. Continued exchange and more regular reproduction for exchange reduces this arbitrariness more and more. But at first not for the producer and consumer, but for their go-between, the merchant, who compares money prices and pockets the difference. It is through his own movements that he establishes equivalence.

Merchant's capital is originally merely the intervening movement between extremes which it does not control, and between premises which it does not create.

Just as money originates from the bare form of commodity circulation, $C — M — C$, not only as a measure of value and a medium of circulation, but also as the absolute form of commodity, and hence of wealth, as hoard, so that its conservation and accumulation as money becomes an end in itself, so, too, does money, the hoard, as something that preserves and increases itself through mere alienation, originate from the bare form of the circulation of merchant's capital, $M — C — M'$.[a]

The trading nations of ancient times existed like the gods of Epicurus in the intermediate worlds of the universe,[37] or rather like the Jews in the pores of Polish society. The trade of the first independent flourishing merchant towns and trading nations rested as a pure carrying trade upon the barbarism of the producing nations, between whom they acted the middleman.

In the precapitalist stages of society commerce ruled industry. In modern society the reverse is true. Of course, commerce will have more or less of a countereffect on the communities between which it is carried on. It will subordinate production more and more to exchange value by making luxuries and subsistence more dependent on sale than on the immediate use of the products. Thereby it dissolves the old relationships. It multiplies money circulation. It encompasses no longer merely the surplus of production, but bites deeper and deeper into the latter, and makes entire branches of production dependent upon it. Nevertheless this disintegrating effect depends very much on the nature of the producing community.[b]

---

[a] Cf. present edition, Vol. 33, pp. 9-10. - [b] Ibid., p. 20.

So long as merchant's capital promotes the exchange of products between undeveloped societies, commercial profit not only appears as outbargaining and cheating, but also largely originates from them. Aside from the fact that it exploits the difference between the prices of production of various countries (and in this respect it tends to level and fix the values of commodities), those modes of production bring it about that merchant's capital appropriates an overwhelming portion of the surplus product partly as a mediator between communities which still substantially produce for use value, and for whose economic organisation the sale of the portion of their product entering circulation, or for that matter any sale of products at their value, is of secondary importance; and partly, because under those earlier modes of production the principal owners of the surplus product with whom the merchant dealt, namely, the slave-owner, the feudal lord, and the state (for instance, the oriental despot) represent the consuming wealth and luxury which the merchant seeks to trap, as Adam Smith correctly scented in the passage on feudal times quoted earlier. Merchant's capital, when it holds a position of dominance, stands everywhere for a system of robbery,[48] so that its development among the

[48] "Now there is among merchants much complaint about the nobles, or robbers, because they must trade under great danger and run the risk of being kidnapped, beaten, blackmailed, and robbed. If they would suffer these things for the sake of justice, the merchants would be saintly people.... But since such great wrong and unchristian thievery and robbery are committed all over the world by merchants, and even among themselves, is it any wonder that God should procure that such great wealth, gained by wrong, should again be lost or stolen, and they themselves be hit over the head or made prisoner?... And the princes should punish such unjust bargains with due rigour and take care that their subjects shall not be so outrageously abused by merchants. Because they fail to do so, God employs knights and robbers, and punishes the merchants through them for the wrongs they committed, and uses them as his devils, just as he plagues Egypt and all the world with devils, or destroys through enemies. He thus pits one against the other, without thereby insinuating that knights are any the less robbers than merchants, although the merchants daily rob the whole world, while a knight may rob one or two once or twice a year." "Go by the word of Isaiah [a]: Thy princes have become the companions of robbers. For they hang the thieves, who have stolen a gulden or a half gulden, but they associate with those, who rob all the world and steal with greater assurance than all others, so that the proverb remains true: Big thieves hang little thieves; and as the Roman senator Cato said: Mean thieves lie in prisons and stocks, but public thieves are clothed in gold and silks. But what will God say finally? He will do as he said to Ezekiel [b]; he will amalgamate princes and merchants, one thief with another, like lead and iron, as when a city burns down, leaving neither princes nor merchants" (Martin Luther, *Von Kauffshandlung und Wucher*, 1524, S. 296-97).[c]

[a] Isaiah 1 : 23. - [b] Ezekiel 22 : 18-22. - [c] Cf. present edition, Vol. 32, pp. 531-32.

trading nations of old and modern times is always directly connected with plundering, piracy, kidnapping slaves, and colonial conquest; as in Carthage, Rome, and later among the Venetians, Portuguese, Dutch, etc.

The development of commerce and merchant's capital gives rise everywhere to the tendency towards production of exchange values, increases its volume, multiplies it, makes it cosmopolitan, and develops money into world money. Commerce, therefore, has a more or less dissolving influence everywhere on the producing organisation, which it finds at hand and whose different forms are mainly carried on with a view to use value. To what extent it brings about a dissolution of the old mode of production depends on its solidity and internal structure. And whither this process of dissolution will lead, in other words, what new mode of production will replace the old, does not depend on commerce, but on the character of the old mode of production itself. In the ancient world the effect of commerce and the development of merchant's capital always resulted in a slave economy; depending on the point of departure, only in the transformation of a patriarchal slave system devoted to the production of immediate means of subsistence into one devoted to the production of surplus value. However, in the modern world, it results in the capitalist mode of production. It follows therefrom that these results spring in themselves from circumstances other than the development of merchant's capital.

It is in the nature of things that as soon as urban industry as such separates from agricultural industry, its products are from the outset commodities and thus require the mediation of commerce for their sale. The leaning of commerce towards the development of towns, and, on the other hand, the dependence of towns upon commerce, are so far natural. However, it depends on altogether different circumstances to what measure industrial development will go hand in hand with this development. Ancient Rome, in its later republican days, developed merchant's capital to a higher degree than ever before in the ancient world, without showing any progress in the development of crafts, while in Corinth and other Grecian towns in Europe and Asia Minor the development of commerce was accompanied by highly developed crafts. On the other hand, quite contrary to the growth of towns and attendant conditions, the trading spirit and the development of merchant's capital occur frequently among unsettled nomadic peoples.

There is no doubt — and it is precisely this fact which has led to wholly erroneous conceptions — that in the 16th and 17th centuries the great revolutions, which took place in commerce with the geographical discoveries [38] and speeded the development of merchant's capital, constitute one of the principal elements in furthering the transition from feudal to capitalist mode of production. The sudden expansion of the world market, the multiplication of circulating commodities, the competitive zeal of the European nations to possess themselves of the products of Asia and the treasures of America, and the colonial system — all contributed materially toward destroying the feudal fetters on production. However, in its first period — the manufacturing period — the modern mode of production developed only where the conditions for it had taken shape within the Middle Ages. Compare, for instance, Holland with Portugal.[49] And when in the 16th, and partially still in the 17th, century the sudden expansion of commerce and emergence of a new world market overwhelmingly contributed to the fall of the old mode of production and the rise of capitalist production, this was accomplished conversely on the basis of the already existing capitalist mode of production. The world market itself forms the basis for this mode of production. On the other hand, the immanent necessity of this mode of production to produce on an ever-enlarged scale tends to extend the world market continually, so that it is not commerce in this case which revolutionises industry, but industry which constantly revolutionises commerce. Commercial supremacy itself is now linked with the prevalence to a greater or lesser degree of conditions for a large industry. Compare, for instance, England and Holland. The history of the decline of Holland as the ruling trading nation is the history of the subordination of

---

[49] How predominant fishery, manufacture and agriculture, aside from other circumstances, were as the basis for Holland's development, has already been explained by 18th-century writers, such as Massie.[a] In contradistinction to the former view, which underrated the volume and importance of commerce in Asia, in Antiquity, and in the Middle Ages, it has now come to be the custom to extremely overrate it. The best antidote against this conception is to study the imports and exports of England in the early 18th century and to compare them with modern imports and exports. And yet they were incomparably greater than those of any former trading nation. (See Anderson, *History of Commerce.*) [b]

---

[a][J. Massie,] *An Essay on the Governing Causes of the Natural Rate of Interest...*, London, 1750, p. 60; cf. also present edition, Vol. 34, pp. 91-93. - [b] [A. Anderson,] *An Historical and Chronological Deduction of the Origin of Commerce...*, Vol. 1, London, 1764, p. 261.

merchant's capital to industrial capital. The obstacles presented by the internal solidity and organisation of precapitalistic, national modes of production to the corrosive influence of commerce are strikingly illustrated in the intercourse of the English with India and China. The broad basis of the mode of production here is formed by the unity of small-scale agriculture and home industry, to which in India we should add the form of village communities resting upon the common ownership of land, which, incidentally, was the original form in China as well. In India the English lost no time in exercising their direct political and economic power, as rulers and landlords, to disrupt these small economic communities.[50] English commerce exerted here a revolutionising influence on the mode of production only in so far as the low prices of its goods served to destroy the spinning and weaving industries, which were an ancient integrating element of this unity of industrial and agricultural production, and thus tore the community apart. And even so this work of dissolution proceeds very gradually. And still more slowly in China, where it is not reinforced by direct political power. The substantial economy and saving in time afforded by the association of agriculture with manufacture put up a stubborn resistance to the products of the big industries, whose prices include the *faux frais* [a] of the circulation process which pervades them. Unlike the English, Russian commerce, on the other hand, leaves the economic groundwork of Asiatic production untouched.[51]

The transition from the feudal mode of production is two-fold. The producer becomes merchant and capitalist, in contrast to the natural agricultural economy and the guild-bound handicrafts of the medieval urban industries. This is the really revolutionising path. Or else, the merchant establishes direct sway over production. However much this serves historically as a stepping-stone — witness the English 17th-century CLOTHIER, who brings the weavers, independent as they

[50] If any nation's history is a string of futile and really absurd (in practice infamous) economic experiments, then it is the history of the English management in India. In Bengal they created a caricature of large-scale English landed estates; in southeastern India a caricature of small parcelled property; in the north-west they did all they could to transform the Indian economic community with common ownership of the soil into a caricature of itself.

[51] Since Russia has been making frantic exertions to develop its own capitalist production, which is exclusively dependent upon its domestic and the neighbouring Asiatic market, this is also beginning to change.— *F. E.*

---

[a] overhead costs

are, under his control by selling their wool to them and buying their cloth — it cannot by itself contribute to the overthrow of the old mode of production, but tends rather to preserve and retain it as its precondition. The manufacturer in the French silk industry and in the English hosiery and lace industries, for example, was thus mostly but nominally a manufacturer until the middle of the 19th century. In point of fact, he was merely a merchant, who let the weavers carry on in their old unorganised way and exerted only a merchant's control, for that was for whom they really worked.[52] This system presents everywhere an obstacle to the real capitalist mode of production and goes under with its development. Without revolutionising the mode of production, it only worsens the condition of the direct producers, turns them into mere wage workers and proletarians under conditions worse than those under the immediate control of capital, and appropriates their surplus labour on the basis of the old mode of production. The same conditions exist in somewhat modified form in part of the London handicraft furniture industry. It is practised notably in the Tower Hamlets on a very large scale. The whole production is divided into very numerous separate branches of business independent of one another. One establishment makes only chairs, another only tables, a third only bureaus, etc. But these establishments themselves are run more or less like handicrafts by a single minor master and a few journeymen. Nevertheless, production is too large to work directly for private persons. The buyers are the owners of furniture stores. On Saturdays the master visits them and sells his product, the transaction being closed with as much haggling as in a pawnshop over a loan. The masters depend on this weekly sale, if for no other reason than to be able to buy raw materials for the following week and to pay out wages. Under these circumstances, they are really only middlemen between the merchant and their own labourers. The merchant is the actual capitalist who pockets the lion's share of the surplus value.[53] Almost the same applies in the transition to manufacture of branches formerly carried on as handicrafts or side lines to

[52] The same is true of the ribbon and basting makers and the silk weavers of the Rhine. Even a railway has been built near Krefeld for the intercourse of these rural hand-weavers with the town "manufacturers". But this was later put out of business, together with the hand-weavers, by the mechanical weaving industry.— *F. E.*

[53] This system has been developed since 1865 on a still larger scale. For details see the First Report of the Select Committee of the House of Lords on the Sweating System, London, 1888.— *F. E.*

rural industries. The transition to large-scale industry depends on the technical development of these small owner-operated establishments — wherever they employ machinery that admits of a handicraft-like operation. The machine is driven by steam, instead of by hand. This is of late the case, for instance, in the English hosiery industry.[a]

There is, consequently, a three-fold transition. *First*, the merchant becomes directly an industrialist. This is true in crafts based on trade, especially crafts producing luxuries, which are imported by merchants together with the raw materials and labourers from foreign lands, as in Italy from Constantinople in the 15th century. *Second*, the merchant turns the small masters into his MIDDLEMEN,[b] or buys directly from the independent producer, leaving him nominally independent and his mode of production unchanged. *Third*, the industrialist becomes merchant and produces directly for the wholesale market.

In the Middle Ages, the merchant was merely one who, as Poppe rightly says, "transferred" the goods produced by guilds or peasants.[c] The merchant becomes industrialist, or rather, makes craftsmen, particularly the small rural producers, work for him. Conversely, the producer becomes merchant. The master weaver, for instance, buys his wool or yarn himself and sells his cloth to the merchant, instead of receiving his wool from the merchant piecemeal and working for him together with his journeymen. The elements of production pass into the production process as commodities bought by himself. And instead of producing for some individual merchant, or for specified customers, he produces for the world of trade. The producer is himself a merchant. Merchant's capital does no more than carry on the process of circulation. Originally, commerce was the precondition for the transformation of the crafts, the rural domestic industries, and feudal agriculture, into capitalist enterprises. It develops the product into a commodity, partly by creating a market for it, and partly by introducing new commodity equivalents and supplying production with new raw and auxiliary materials, thereby opening new branches of production based from the first upon commerce, both as concerns production for the home and world-market, and as concerns conditions of production originating in the world market. As soon as manufacture gains sufficient strength, and particularly large-scale industry,

---

[a] Cf. present edition, Vol. 33, p. 369. - [b] In the 1894 German edition this English term is given in parentheses after its German equivalent. - [c] J. H. M. Poppe, *Geschichte der Technologie...*, Band I, Göttingen, 1807, S. 70.

it creates in its turn a market for itself, by capturing it through its commodities. At this point commerce becomes the servant of industrial production, for which continued expansion of the market becomes a vital necessity. Ever more extended mass production floods the existing market and thereby works continually for a still greater expansion of this market, for breaking out of its limits. What restricts this mass production is not commerce (in so far as it expresses the existing demand), but the magnitude of employed capital and the level of development of the productive power of labour. The industrial capitalist always has the world market before him, compares, and must constantly compare, his own cost prices with the market prices at home, and throughout the world. In the earlier period such comparison fell almost entirely to the merchants, and thus secured the predominance of merchant's capital over industrial capital.[a]

The first theoretical treatment of the modern mode of production — the mercantile system — proceeded necessarily from the superficial phenomena of the circulation process as individualised in the movement of merchant's capital, and therefore grasped only the appearance of matters. Partly because merchant's capital is the first free state of existence of capital in general. And partly because of the overwhelming influence which it exerted during the first revolutionising period of feudal production — the genesis of modern production. The real science of modern economy only begins when the theoretical analysis passes from the process of circulation to the process of production. Interest-bearing capital is, indeed, likewise a very old form of capital. But we shall see later why mercantilism does not take it as its point of departure, but rather carries on a polemic against it.

---

[a] Cf. present edition, Vol. 32, pp. 465-66.

Part V

DIVISION OF PROFIT
INTO INTEREST AND PROFIT
OF ENTERPRISE.
INTEREST-BEARING CAPITAL

Chapter XXI

INTEREST-BEARING CAPITAL

In our first discussion of the general, or average, rate of profit (Part II of this book) we did not have this rate before us in its complete form, the equalisation of profit appearing only as equalisation between industrial capitals invested in different spheres. This was supplemented in the preceding part, which dealt with the participation of merchant's capital in this equalisation, and also commercial profit. The general rate of profit and the average profit now appeared in narrower limits than before. It should be remembered in the course of our analysis that in any future reference to the general rate of profit or to average profit we mean this latter connotation, hence only the final form of average rate. And since this rate is the same for mercantile, as well as industrial, capital, it is no longer necessary, so far as this average profit is concerned, to make a distinction between industrial and commercial profit. Whether industrially invested in the sphere of production, or commercially in the sphere of circulation, capital yields the same average annual profit *pro rata*[a] to its magnitude.

Money — here taken as the independent expression of a certain amount of value existing either actually as money or as commodities — may be converted into capital on the basis of capitalist production, and may thereby be transformed from a given value to a self-expanding, or increasing, value. It produces profit, i. e., it enables the capitalist to extract a certain quantity of unpaid labour, surplus product and surplus value, from the labourers, and to appropriate it. In this way, aside from its use value as money, it acquires an additional

---

[a] in proportion to

use value, namely that of serving as capital. Its use value then consists precisely in the profit it produces when converted into capital. In this capacity of potential capital, of a means of producing profit, it becomes a commodity, but a commodity *sui generis*. Or, what amounts to the same, capital as capital becomes a commodity.[54]

Suppose the annual average rate of profit is 20%. In that case a machine valued at £100, employed as capital under average conditions and an average amount of intelligence and purposive effort, would yield a profit of £20. A man in possession of £100, therefore, possesses the power to make £120 out of £100, or to produce a profit of £20. He possesses a potential capital of £100. If he gives these £100 to another for one year, so the latter may use them as real capital, he gives him the power to produce a profit of £20 — a surplus value which costs this other nothing, and for which he pays no equivalent. If this other should pay, say, £5 at the close of the year to the owner of the £100 out of the profit produced, he would thereby pay the use value of the £100 — the use value of its function as capital, the function of producing a profit of £20. The part of the profit paid to the owner is called interest, which is just another name, or special term, for a part of the profit given up by capital in the process of functioning to the owner of the capital, instead of putting it into its own pocket.

It is plain that the possession of £100 gives their owner the power to pocket the interest — that certain portion of profit produced by means of his capital. If he had not given the £100 to the other person, the latter could not have produced any profit, and could not at all have acted as a capitalist with reference to these £100.[55]

To speak here of natural justice, as Gilbart does (see note), is nonsense. The justice of the transactions between agents of production rests on the fact that these arise as natural consequences out of the production relationships. The juristic forms in which these economic transactions appear as wilful acts of the parties concerned, as expressions of their common will and as contracts that may be enforced by

[54] At this point certain passages may be quoted, in which the economists so conceive the matter.— "You" (the Bank of England): "are very large dealers in the *commodity of capital?*" is the question posed to a director of this bank when he was interrogated for the Report on Bank Acts on the witness stand. (H. of C. 1857, [p. 104].)

[55] "That a man who borrows money with a view of making a profit by it, should give some portion of his profit to the lender, is a self-evident principle of natural justice" (Gilbart, *The History and Principles of Banking*, London, 1834, p. 163).

law against some individual party, cannot, being mere forms, determine this content. They merely express it. This content is just whenever it corresponds, is appropriate, to the mode of production. It is unjust whenever it contradicts that mode. Slavery on the basis of capitalist production is unjust; likewise fraud in the quality of commodities.

The £100 produce the profit of £20 because they function as capital, be it industrial or mercantile. But the *sine qua non*[a] of this function as capital is that they are expended as capital, i. e., are expended in purchasing means of production (in the case of industrial capital) or commodities (in the case of mercantile capital). But to be expended, they must be available. If A, the owner of the £100, were either to spend them for personal consumption, or to keep them as a hoard, they could not have been invested as capital by B in his capacity of functioning capitalist. B does not expend his own capital, but A's; however, he cannot expend A's capital without A's consent. Therefore, it is really A who originally expends the £100 as capital, albeit his function as capitalist is limited to this outlay of £100 as capital. In respect to these £100, B acts as capitalist only because A lends him the £100, thus expending them as capital.

Let us first consider the singular circulation of interest-bearing capital. We shall then secondly have to analyse the peculiar manner in which it is sold as a commodity, namely loaned instead of relinquished once and for all.

The point of departure is the money which A advances to B. This may be done with or without security. The first-named form, however, is the more ancient, save advances on commodities or paper, such as bills of exchange, shares, etc. These special forms do not concern us at this point. We are dealing here with interest-bearing capital in its usual form.

In B's possession the money is actually converted into capital, passes through M—C—M' and returns to A as M', as M + ΔM, where ΔM represents the interest. For the sake of simplicity we shall not consider here the case, in which capital remains in B's possession for a longer term and interest is paid at regular intervals.

The movement, therefore, is

$$M - M - C - M' - M'.$$

---

[a] the indispensable condition

What appears duplicated here, is 1) the outlay of money as capital, and 2) its reflux as realised capital, as M′ or M + ΔM.

In the movement of merchant's capital, M—C—M′, the same commodity changes hands twice, or more than twice, if merchant sells to merchant. But every such change of place of the same commodity indicates a metamorphosis, a purchase or sale of the commodity, no matter how often the process may be repeated, until it finally enters consumption.

On the other hand, the same money changes hands twice in C—M—C, but this indicates the complete metamorphosis of the commodity, which is first converted into money and then from money back into another commodity.

But in interest-bearing capital the first time M changes hands is by no means a phase either of the commodity metamorphosis, or of reproduction of capital. It first becomes one when it is expended a second time, in the hands of the functioning capitalist who carries on trade with it, or transforms it into productive capital. M's first change of hands does not express anything here, beyond its transfer from A to B—a transfer which usually takes place under certain legal forms and stipulations.

This double outlay of money as capital, of which the first is merely a transfer from A to B, is matched by its double reflux. As M′, or M + ΔM, it flows back out of the process to B, the person acting as capitalist. The latter then transfers it back to A, but together with a part of the profit, as realised capital, as M + ΔM, in which ΔM is not the entire profit, but only a portion of the profit—the interest. It flows back to B only as what he had expended, as functioning capital, but as the property of A. To make its reflux complete, B must consequently return it to A. But in addition to the capital, B must also turn over to A a portion of the profit, a part which goes under the name of interest, which he had made with this capital since A had given him the money only as a capital, i. e., as value which is not only preserved in its movement, but also creates surplus value for its owner. It remains in B's hands only so long as it is functioning capital. And with its reflux—on the stipulated date—it ceases to function as capital. When no longer acting as capital, however, it must again be returned to A, who had never ceased being its legal owner.

The form of lending, which is peculiar to this commodity, to capital as commodity, and which also occurs in other transactions, instead of that of sale, follows from the simple definition that capital obtains here as a commodity, or that money as capital becomes a commodity.

A distinction should be made here.

We have seen (Book II, Chap. I),[a] and recall briefly at this point, that in the process of circulation capital serves as commodity capital and money capital. But in neither form does capital become a commodity as capital.

As soon as productive capital turns into commodity capital it must be placed on the market to be sold as a commodity. There it acts simply as a commodity. The capitalist then appears only as the seller of commodities, just as the buyer is only the buyer of commodities. As a commodity the product must realise its value, must assume its converted form, the form of money, in the process of circulation by its sale. It is also quite immaterial for this reason whether this commodity is bought by a consumer as a necessity of life, or by a capitalist as means of production, i. e., as a component part of his capital. In the act of circulation commodity capital acts only as a commodity, not as a capital. It is commodity *capital*, as distinct from an ordinary commodity, 1) because it is weighted with surplus value, the realisation of its value, therefore, being simultaneously the realisation of surplus value, but this alters nothing about its simple existence as a commodity, as a product with a certain price; 2) because its function as a commodity is a phase in its process of reproduction as capital, and therefore its movement as a commodity being only a partial movement of its process, is simultaneously its movement as capital. Yet it does not become that through the sale as such, but only through the connection of the sale with the whole movement of this specific quantity of value in the capacity of capital.

In the same way as money capital it really acts simply as money, i. e., as a means of buying commodities (the elements of production). The fact that this money is simultaneously money capital, a form of capital, does not emerge from the act of buying, the actual function which it here performs as money, but from the connection of this act with the total movement of capital, since this act, performed by capital as money, initiates the capitalist production process.

But in so far as they actually function, actually play a role in the process, commodity capital acts here only as a commodity and money capital only as money. At no time during the metamorphosis, viewed

---

[a] See present edition, Vol. 36.

by itself, does the capitalist sell his commodities as *capital* to the buyer, although to him they represent capital; nor does he give up money as capital to the seller. In both cases he gives up his commodities simply as commodities, and money simply as money, as a means of purchasing commodities.

It is only in connection with the entire process, at the moment where the point of departure appears simultaneously as the point of return, in $M — M'$ or $C — C'$, that capital in the process of circulation appears as capital (whereas in the process of production it appears as capital through the subordination of the labourer to the capitalist and the production of surplus value). In this moment of return, however, the connection disappears. What we have then is M', or $M + \Delta M$, a sum of money equal to the sum originally advanced plus an increment — the realised surplus value (regardless of whether the amount of value increased by ΔM exists in the form of money, or commodities, or elements of production). And it is precisely at this point of return where capital exists as realised capital, as an expanded value, that it never enters the circulation in this form — in so far as this point is fixed as a point of rest, whether real or imaginary — but rather appears to have been withdrawn from circulation as a result of the whole process. Whenever it is again expended, it is never given up to another *as capital*, but is sold to him as an ordinary commodity, or given to him as ordinary money in exchange for commodities. It never appears as capital in its process of circulation, only as commodity or money, and at this point this is the only form of its existence *for others*. Commodities and money are here capital not because commodities change into money, or money into commodities, not in their actual relations to sellers or buyers, but only in their ideal relations to the capitalist himself (subjectively speaking), or as phases in the process of reproduction (objectively speaking). Capital exists as capital in actual movement, not in the process of circulation, but only in the process of production, in the process by which labour power is exploited.

The matter is different with interest-bearing capital, however, and it is precisely this difference which lends it its specific character. The owner of money who desires to enhance his money as interest-bearing capital, turns it over to a third person, throws it into circulation, turns it into a commodity as *capital*; not just capital for himself, but also for others. It is not capital merely for the man who gives it up, but is from the very first given to the third person as capital, as a value endowed with the use value of creating surplus value, of creating profit; as a value which preserves itself in its movement and returns to its original owner, in this case the owner of money, after performing its function. Hence it leaves him only for a specified time, passes but temporarily out of the possession of its owner into the possession of a functioning capitalist; it is therefore neither given up in payment nor sold, but merely loaned, merely relinquished with the understanding that, first, it shall return to its point of departure after a definite time interval, and, second, that it shall return as realised capital — a capital having realised its use value, its power of creating surplus value.

Commodities loaned out as capital are loaned either as fixed or as circulating capital, depending on their properties. Money may be loaned out in either form. It may be loaned as fixed capital, for instance, if it is paid back in the form of an annuity, whereby a portion of the capital always flows back together with the interest. Certain commodities, such as houses, ships, machines, etc., can be loaned out only as fixed capital by the nature of their use values. Yet all loaned capital, whatever its form, and no matter how the nature of its use value may modify its return, is always only a specific form of money capital. Because what is loaned out here is always a definite sum of money, and it is this sum on which interest is calculated. Should whatever is loaned out be neither money nor circulating capital, it is also paid back in the way fixed capital returns. The lender periodically receives interest and a portion of the consumed value of the fixed capital itself, this being an equivalent for the periodic wear and tear. And at the end of the stipulated term the unconsumed portion of the loaned fixed capital is returned in kind. If the loaned capital is circulating capital, it is likewise returned to the lender in the manner peculiar to circulating capital.[a]

The *manner* of reflux is, therefore, always determined by the actual circuit described by capital in the act of reproduction and by its specific varieties. But as for loaned capital, its reflux assumes the *form* of return payments, because its advance, by which it is alienated, possesses the form of a loan.

In this chapter we treat only of actual money capital, from which the other forms of loaned capital are derived.

The loaned capital flows back in two ways. In the process of repro-

---

[a] Cf. present edition, Vol. 32, p. 522.

duction it returns to the functioning capitalist, and then its return repeats itself once more as transfer to the lender, the money capitalist, as return payment to the real owner, its legal point of departure.

In the actual process of circulation, capital appears always as a commodity or as money, and its movement is broken up into a series of purchases and sales. In short, the process of circulation resolves itself into the metamorphosis of commodities. It is different, when we consider the process of reproduction as a whole. If we start out with money (and the same is true if we start out with commodities, since in this case we begin with their value, hence view them *sub specie* as money), we shall see that a certain sum of money is expended and returns after a certain period with an increment. The advanced sum of money returns together with a surplus value. It has preserved and expanded itself in making a certain cycle. But now, being loaned out as capital, money is loaned as just a sum of money which preserves and expands itself, which returns after a certain period with an increment, and is always ready to perform the same process over again. It is expended neither as money nor as a commodity, thus, neither exchanged against a commodity when advanced in the form of money, nor sold in exchange for money when advanced as a commodity; rather, it is expended as capital. This relation to itself, in which capital presents itself when the capitalist production process is viewed as a whole and a totality, and in which capital appears as money that begets money, is here embodied in it as its character, its designation, without any intermediary movement. And it is alienated in this designation when loaned out as money capital.

A queer conception of the role of money capital is held by Proudhon (*Gratuité du Crédit. Discussion entre M. Fr. Bastiat et M. Proudhon*, Paris, 1850).[a] Loaning seems an evil to Proudhon because it is not selling.

Loaning for an interest

"is the ability of selling the same object over and over again, and receiving the price of it, over and over again, without ever giving up the ownership of what is sold" (p. 9).[b]

The object — money, a house, etc.— does not change owners as in selling and buying. But Proudhon does not see that no equivalent is

---

[a] Ibid., Vol. 32, pp. 529-30 and Vol. 29, pp. 219-21. - [b] *Gratuité du crédit*, First Letter of Chevé, one of the editors of *La Voix du peuple*. Marx is quoting in French. Below, when analysing Proudhon's views, he uses quite a few French expressions.

received in return for money given away in the form of interest-bearing capital. True, the object is given away in every act of buying and selling, so far as there are processes of exchange at all. Ownership of the sold article is always relinquished. But its value is not given up. In a sale the commodity is given away, but not its value, which is returned in the form of money, or in what is here just another form of it—promissory notes, or titles of payment. When purchasing, the money is given away, but not its value, which is replaced in the form of commodities. The industrial capitalist retains the same value in his hands throughout the process of reproduction (excluding surplus value), but in different forms.

Inasmuch as there is an exchange, i. e., an exchange of articles, there is no change in the value. The same capitalist always retains the same value. But so long as surplus value is produced by the capitalist, there is no exchange. As soon as an exchange occurs, the surplus value is already incorporated in the commodities. If we view the entire circuit made by capital, M—C—M′, rather than individual acts of exchange, we shall see that a definite amount of value is continually advanced, and that this same amount plus surplus value, or profit, is withdrawn from circulation. The simple acts of exchange do not, at any rate, reveal how this process is promoted. And it is precisely this process of M as capital, on which the interest of the money-lending capitalist rests, and from which it is derived.

"Actually," says Proudhon, "the hatter who sells hats... obtains the value of them, neither more nor less. But the capitalist who loans out his capital ... not merely gets his capital back in full; he gets back more than his capital, more than he brought to the exchange; over and above his capital, he gets an interest" (p. 69).

Here the hatter represents the productive capitalist as distinct from the loan capitalist. Proudhon has obviously failed to grasp the secret of how the productive capitalist can sell commodities at their value (equalisation through prices of production is here immaterial to his conception) and precisely by doing so receive a profit over and above the capital he flings into exchange. Suppose the price of production of 100 hats = £115, and that this price of production happens to coincide with the value of the hats, which means that the capital producing the hats is of the same composition as the average social capital. Should the profit = 15%, the hatter makes a profit of £15 by selling his commodities at their value of £115. They cost him only £100. If he produced them with his own capital, he pockets the entire surplus of £15 but if with borrowed capital, he may have to give up £5 as interest. This alters nothing in the value of the hats, only in the distribution among different persons of the surplus value already contained in this value. Since, therefore, the value of the hats is not affected by the payment of interest, it is nonsense on Proudhon's part to say:

"It is impossible, with interest on capital being added in commerce to the workers' wages to make up the price of the commodity, for the worker to be able to buy back what he himself has produced. *Vivre en travaillant*[a] is a principle which, under the rule of interest, is implicitly self-contradictory" (p. 105).[56]

How little Proudhon understood the nature of capital is shown in the following statement, in which he describes the movement of capital in general as a movement peculiar to interest-bearing capital:

"As, by the accumulation of interest, capital-money, from exchange to exchange, always returns to its source, it follows that the re-lending, always done by the same hand, always profits the same person" [p. 154].[c]

What is it that still puzzles him in the peculiar movement of interest-bearing capital? The categories: buying, price, giving up articles, and the immediate form in which surplus value appears here; in short, the phenomenon that capital as such has become a commodity, that selling, consequently, has turned into lending and price into a share of the profit.

The return of capital to its point of departure is generally the characteristic movement of capital in its total circuit. This is by no means a feature of interest-bearing capital alone. What singles it out is rather the external form of its return without the intervention of any circuit. The loaning capitalist gives away his capital, transfers it to the industrial capitalist, without receiving any equivalent. His transfer is not an act belonging to the real circulation process of capital at all. It serves merely to introduce this circuit, which is effected by the

---

[56] "A house", "money", etc., are not to be loaned as "capital" if Proudhon is to have his way, but are to be sold as "commodities ... at cost price" (pp. 43, 44). Luther stood somewhat above Proudhon. He knew that profit-making does not depend on the manner of lending or buying: "They also make a usury out of buying and selling. But this is too much to deal with in one single bite. We must deal with one thing now, with usury as regards loans; when we have put a stop to this (as on the Day of Judgement), then we will surely read the lesson with regard to *usurious trade*" (Martin Luther, *An die Pfarrherrn wider den Wucher zu predigen*, Wittenberg, 1540).[b]

---

[a] To live by working - [b] See present edition, Vol. 32, p. 536. - [c] Marx is quoting Proudhon in French.

industrial capitalist. This first change of position of money does not express any act of the metamorphosis—neither buying nor selling. Ownership is not relinquished, because there is no exchange and no equivalent is received. The return of the money from the hands of the industrial capitalist to those of the loaning capitalist merely supplements the first act of giving away the capital. Advanced in the form of money, the capital again returns to the industrial capitalist through the circular process in the form of money. But since it did not belong to him when he invested it, it cannot belong to him on its return. Passing through the process of reproduction cannot by any means turn the capital into his property. He must therefore restore it to the lender. The first expenditure, which transfers the capital from the lender to the borrower, is a legal transaction which has nothing to do with the actual process of reproduction of capital. It is merely a prelude to this process. The return payment, which again transfers the capital that has flowed back from the borrower to the lender, is another legal transaction, a supplement of the first. One introduces the actual process, the other is an act supplementary to this process. Point of departure and point of return, the giving away and the recovery of the loaned capital, thus appear as arbitrary movements promoted by legal transactions, which take place before and after the actual movement of capital and have nothing to do with it as such. It would have been all the same as concerns this actual movement if the capital had from the first belonged to the industrial capitalist and had returned to him, therefore, as his own.[a]

In the first introductory act the lender gives his capital to the borrower. In the supplemental and closing act the borrower returns the capital to the lender. As concerns the transaction between these two—and aside from the interest for the present—as concerns the movement of the loaned capital between lender and borrower, therefore, the two acts (separated by a longer or shorter time interval, during which the actual reproduction process of the capital takes place) embrace the entire movement. And this movement, disposing on condition of returning, constitutes *per se* the movement of lending and borrowing, that specific form of conditionally alienating money or commodities.

The characteristic movement of capital in general, the return of the money to the capitalist, i. e., the return of capital to its point of

---

[a] Cf. present edition, Vol. 32, pp. 453-54.

departure, assumes in the case of interest-bearing capital a wholly external appearance, separated from the actual movement, of which it is a form. A gives away his money not as money, but as capital. No transformation occurs in the capital. It merely changes hands. Its real transformation into capital does not take place until it is in the hands of B. But for A it becomes capital as soon as he gives it to B. The actual reflux of capital from the processes of production and circulation takes place only for B. But for A the reflux assumes the same form as the alienation. The capital returns from B to A. Giving away, i. e., loaning money for a certain time and receiving it back with interest (surplus value) is the complete form of the movement peculiar to interest-bearing capital as such. The actual movement of loaned money as capital is an operation lying outside the transactions between lender and borrower. In these transactions the intermediate act is obliterated, invisible, not directly included. A special sort of commodity, capital has its own peculiar mode of alienation. Neither does its return, therefore, express itself as the consequence and result of some definite series of economic processes, but as the effect of a specific legal agreement between buyer and seller. The time of return depends on the progress of the process of reproduction; in the case of interest-bearing capital, its return as capital *seems* to depend on the mere agreement between lender and borrower. So that in regard to this transaction the return of capital no longer appears as a result arising out of the process of production; it appears as if the loaned capital never lost the form of money. To be sure, these transactions are really determined by the actual reproductive returns. But this is not evident in the transaction itself.[a] Nor is it by any means always the case in practice. If the actual return does not take place in due time, the borrower must look for other resources to meet his obligations vis-à-vis the lender. The bare *form* of capital — money expended as a certain sum, A, which returns as sum $A + \frac{1}{x} A$ after a given lapse of time without any other intermediate act save this lapse of time — is only a meaningless form of the actual movement of capital.

In the actual movement of capital its return is a phase in the process of circulation. The money is first converted into means of production; the production process converts it into commodities; through the sale of the commodities it is reconverted into money and returns

---

a   Ibid., pp. 453-54.

in this form into the hands of the capitalist who had originally advanced the capital in the form of money. But in the case of interest-bearing capital, the return, like alienation, is merely the result of a legal transaction between the owner of the capital and a second party. We see only the alienation and the return payment. Whatever passes in the interim is obliterated.

But since money advanced as capital has the property of returning to the person who advanced it, to the one who expended it as capital, and since $M - C - M'$ is the immanent form of the movement of capital, the owner of the money can, for this very reason, loan it out as capital, as something that has the property of returning to its point of departure, of preserving, and increasing, its value in the course of its movement. He gives it away as capital, because it returns to its point of departure after having been employed as capital, hence can be restored by the borrower after a certain period precisely because it has come back to him.

Loaning money as capital—its alienation on the condition of it being returned after a certain time—presupposes, therefore, that it will be actually employed as capital, and that it actually flows back to its starting-point. The real cycle made by money as capital is, therefore, the premise for the legal transaction by which the borrower must return the money to the lender. If the borrower does not use the money as capital, that is his own business. The lender loans it as capital, and as such it is supposed to perform the functions of capital, which include the circuit of money capital until it returns to its starting-point in the form of money.

The acts of circulation, $M - C$ and $C - M'$, in which a certain amount of value functions as money or as commodities, are but intermediate processes, mere phases of the total movement. As capital, it performs the entire movement $M - M'$. It is advanced as money or a sum of values in one form or another, and returns as a sum of values. The lender of money does not expend it in purchasing commodities, or, if this sum of values is in commodity form, does not sell it for money. He advances it as capital, as $M - M'$, as a value, which returns to its point of departure after a certain term. He lends instead of buying or selling. This lending, therefore, is the appropriate form of alienating value as *capital*, instead of alienating it as money or commodities. It does not follow, however, that lending cannot also take the form of transactions which have nothing to do with the capitalist process of reproduction.

We have so far only considered the movements of loaned *capital* between its owner and the industrial capitalist. Now we must inquire into *interest*.

The lender expends his money as capital; the amount of value, which he relinquishes to another, is capital, and consequently returns to him. But the mere return of it would not be the reflux of the loaned sum of value *as capital*, but merely the return of a loaned sum of value. To return as capital, the advanced sum of value must not only be preserved in the movement but must also expand, must increase in value, i. e., must return with a surplus value, as $M + \Delta M$, the latter being interest or a portion of the average profit, which does not remain in the hands of the functioning capitalist, but falls to the share of the money capitalist.

The fact that the latter has relinquished it as capital implies that it must be restored to him as $M + \Delta M$. Later, we shall also have to turn our attention to the form in which interest is paid in the meantime at fixed intervals, but without the capital, whose return follows at the end of a lengthy period.

What does the money capitalist give to the borrower, the industrial capitalist? What does he really turn over to him? It is only this act of alienating money which changes lending money into alienation of money as capital, i. e., alienation of capital as a commodity.

It is only by this act of alienating that capital is loaned by the money lender as a commodity, or that the commodity at his disposal is given to another as capital.

What is alienated in an ordinary sale? Not the value of the sold commodity, for this merely changes its form. The value exists ideally in a commodity as its price before it actually passes as money into the hands of the seller. The same value and the same amount of value merely change their form here. In the one instance they exist in commodity form, in the other in the form of money. What is really alienated by the seller, and, therefore, passes into the individual or productive consumption of the buyer, is the use value of the commodity — the commodity as a use value.

What, now, is the use value which the money capitalist gives up for the period of the loan and relinquishes to the productive capitalist — the borrower? It is the use value which the money acquires by being capable of becoming capital, of performing the functions of capital, and creating a definite surplus value, the average profit (whatever is above or below it appears here as a mere accident) during its process, besides preserving its original magnitude of value. In the case of the other commodities the use value is ultimately consumed. Their substance disappears, and with it their value. In contrast, the commodity capital is peculiar in that its value and use value not only remain intact but also increase, through consumption of its use value.

It is this use value of money as capital—this faculty of producing an average profit—which the money capitalist relinquishes to the industrial capitalist for the period, during which he places the loaned capital at the latter's disposal.

Money thus loaned has in this respect a certain similarity with labour power in its relation to the industrial capitalist. With the difference that the latter pays for the value of labour power, whereas he simply pays back the value of the loaned capital. The use value of labour power for the industrial capitalist is that labour power creates more value (profit) in its consumption than it possesses itself, and than it costs. This additional value is use value for the industrial capitalist. And in like manner the use value of loaned capital appears as its faculty of begetting and increasing value.

The money capitalist, in fact, alienates a use value, and thus whatever he gives away is given as a commodity. It is to this extent that the analogy with a commodity *per se* is complete. In the first place, it is a value which passes from one hand to another. In the case of an ordinary commodity, a commodity as such, the same value remains in the hands of the buyer and seller, only in different forms; both have the same value which they had before and after the transaction, and which they had alienated—the one in the form of a commodity, the other in the form of money. The difference is that in a loan the money capitalist is the only one in the transaction who gives away value; but he preserves it through the prospective return. In the loan transaction just one party receives value, since only one party relinquishes value.— In the second place, a real use value is alienated on the one side, and received and consumed on the other. But in contrast to ordinary commodities this use value is value in itself, namely the excess over the original value realised through the use of money as capital. The profit is this use value.

The use value of the loaned money lies in its being able to serve as capital and, as such, to produce the average profit under average conditions.[57]

___

[57] "The equitableness of taking interest depends not upon a man's making or not

What, now, does the industrial capitalist pay, and what is, therefore, the price of the loaned capital?

"That which men pay as interest for the use of what they borrow" is, according to Massie, *"a part of the profit it is capable of producing."* 58)

What the buyer of an ordinary commodity buys is its use value; what he pays for is its value. What the borrower of money buys is likewise its use value as capital; but what does he pay for? Surely not its price, or value, as in the case of other commodities. No change of form occurs in the value passing between borrower and lender, as occurs between buyer and seller when it exists in one instance in the form of money, and in another in the form of a commodity. The sameness of the given away and returned value is revealed here in an entirely different way. The sum of value, i. e., the money, is given away without an equivalent, and is returned after a certain period. The lender always remains the owner of the same value, even after it passes from his hands into those of the borrower. In an ordinary exchange of commodities money always comes from the buyer's side; but in a loan it comes from the side of the seller. He is the one who gives away money for a certain period, and the buyer of capital is the one who receives it as a commodity. But this is only possible as long as the money acts as capital and is therefore advanced. The borrower borrows money as capital, as a value producing more value. But at the moment when it is advanced it is still only potential capital, like any other capital at its starting-point, the moment it is advanced. It is only through its employment that it expands its value and realises itself as capital. However, it has to be returned by the borrower as *realised* capital, hence as value plus surplus value (interest). And the latter can only be a portion of the realised profit. Only a portion, not all of it. For the use value of the loaned capital to the borrower consists in producing profit for him. Otherwise there would not have been any alienation of use value on the lender's part. On the other hand, not all the profit can fall to the borrower's share. Otherwise he

making profit, but upon its" (the borrowed) "being capable of producing profit if rightly employed" (*An Essay on the Governing Causes of the Natural Rate of Interest, wherein the sentiments of Sir W. Petty and Mr. Locke, on that head, are considered*, London, 1750, p. 49. The author of this anonymous work is J. Massie).

58) [Ibid., p. 49.] "Rich people, instead of employing their money themselves ... let it out to other people for them to make profit of, reserving for the owners a proportion of the profits so made" (l. c., pp. 23, 24).

would pay nothing for the alienated use value, and would return the advanced money to the lender as ordinary money, not as capital, as realised capital, for it is realised capital only as $M + \Delta M$.

Both of them, lender and borrower, expend the same sum of money as capital. But it is only in the hands of the latter that it serves as capital. The profit is not doubled by the double existence of the same sum of money as capital for two persons. It can serve as capital for both of them only by dividing the profit. The portion which falls to the lender is called interest.

The entire transaction, as assumed, takes place between two kinds of capitalists — the money capitalist and the industrial or merchant capitalist.

It must always be borne in mind that here capital as capital is a commodity, or that the commodity here discussed is capital. All the relations in evidence here would therefore be irrational from the standpoint of an ordinary commodity, or from that of capital in so far as it acts as a commodity capital in the process of reproduction. Lending and borrowing, instead of selling and buying, is a distinction which here springs from the specific nature of the commodity — capital. Similarly, the fact that it is interest, not the price of the commodity, which is paid here. If we want to call interest the price of money capital, then it is an irrational form of price quite at variance with the conception of the price of commodities.[59] The price is here reduced to its purely abstract and meaningless form, signifying that it is a certain sum of money paid for something serving in one way or another as a use value; whereas the conception of price really signifies the value of some use value expressed in money.

Interest, signifying the price of capital, is from the outset quite an irrational expression. The commodity in question has a double value, first a value, and then a price different from this value, while price represents the expression of value in money. Money capital is nothing

---

[59] "The term 'VALUE',[a] when applied to CURRENCY, has three meanings ... 2) CURRENCY ACTUALLY IN HAND... compared with the same amount of CURRENCY to be received upon a future day. In this case the value of currency is measured by the rate of interest, and the rate of interest being determined BY THE RATIO BETWEEN THE AMOUNT OF LOANABLE CAPITAL AND THE DEMAND FOR IT" (Colonel R. Torrens, *On the Operation of the Bank Charter Act of 1844, etc.*, 2nd ed., 1847, [pp. 5, 6]).

---

[a] In the 1894 German edition this English word is given in parentheses after its German equivalent.

but a sum of money, or the value of a certain quantity of commodities fixed in a sum of money. If a commodity is loaned out as capital, it is only a disguised form of a sum of money. Because what is loaned out as capital is not so and so many pounds of cotton, but so much and so much money existing in the form of cotton as its value. The price of capital, therefore, refers to it as to a sum of money, even if not currency, as Mr. Torrens thinks (see Footnote [59]). How, then, can a sum of value have a price besides its own price, besides the price expressed in its own money form? Price, after all, is the value of a commodity (this is also true of the market price, whose difference from value is not one of quality, but only one of quantity, referring only to the magnitude of value) as distinct from its use value. A price which differs from value in quality is an absurd contradiction.[60]

Capital manifests itself as capital through self-expansion. The degree of its self-expansion expresses the quantitative degree in which it realises itself as capital. The surplus value or profit produced by it — its rate or magnitude — is measurable only by comparison with the value of the advanced capital. The greater or lesser self-expansion of interest-bearing capital is, therefore, likewise only measurable by comparing the amount of interest, its share in the total profits, with the value of the advanced capital. If, therefore, price expresses the value of the commodity, then interest expresses the self-expansion of money capital and thus appears as the price paid for it to the lender. This shows how absurd it is from the very first to apply hereto the simple relations of exchange through the medium of money in buying and selling, as Proudhon does. The basic premise is precisely that money functions as capital and may thus be transferred as such, i. e., as potential capital, to a third person.

Capital, however, appears here as a commodity, inasmuch as it is offered on the market, and the use value of money is actually alienated as capital. Its use value, however, lies in producing profit. The value of money or of commodities employed as capital does not depend on their value as money or as commodities, but on the quantity of surplus value they produce for their owner. The product of capital is profit. On the basis of capitalist production it is merely a dif-

[60] "The ambiguity of the term 'value of money' or 'of the currency', when employed indiscriminately as it is, to signify both value in exchange for commodities and value in use of capital, is a constant source of confusion" (Tooke, *Inquiry into the Currency Principle*, p. 77). The main confusion (implied in the matter itself) that value as such (interest) becomes the use value of capital, has escaped Tooke.

ferent use of money — whether it is expended as money, or advanced as capital. Money, or commodities, is in itself potentially capital, just as labour power is potential capital. Because, 1) money may be converted into elements of production and is, as is, merely an abstract expression of them — their existence as value; 2) the material elements of wealth have the property of potentially becoming capital, because their supplementary opposite, which makes them into capital, namely wage labour, is available on the basis of capitalist production.

The antithetical social features of material wealth — its antagonism to labour as wage labour — are already expressed in capitalist property as such, independently of the production process. This particular moment — separated from the capitalist production process itself of which it is the constant result, and as its constant result it is also its constant prerequisite — manifests itself in the fact that money, commodities are as such, latently, potentially capital, that they can be sold as capital, and that in this form they command the labour of others, claim to appropriate the labour of others, and therefore represent self-expanding values. It also becomes clearly apparent that this relationship, and not the labour offered as an equivalent on the part of the capitalist, supplies the title and the means to appropriate the labour of others.[a]

Furthermore, capital appears as a commodity, inasmuch as the division of profit into interest and profit proper is regulated by supply and demand, that is, by competition, just as the market prices of commodities. But the difference here is just as apparent as the analogy. If supply and demand coincide, the market price of commodities corresponds to their price of production, i. e., their price then appears to be regulated by the immanent laws of capitalist production, independently of competition, since the fluctuations of supply and demand explain nothing but deviations of market prices from prices of production. These deviations mutually balance one another, so that in the course of certain longer periods the average market prices equal the prices of production. As soon as supply and demand coincide, these forces cease to operate, i. e., compensate one another, and the general law determining prices then also comes to apply to individual cases. The market price then corresponds even in its immediate form, and not only as the average of market price movements, to the price of production, which is regulated by the immanent laws of the mode of

---

[a] Cf. present edition, Vol. 32, p. 474.

production itself. The same applies to wages. If supply and demand coincide, they neutralise each other's effect, and wages equal the value of labour power. But it is different with the interest on money capital. Competition does not, in this case, determine the deviations from the rule. There is rather no law of division except that enforced by competition, because, as we shall later see, no such thing as a "natural" rate of interest exists. By the natural rate of interest people merely mean the rate fixed by free competition. There are no "natural" limits for the rate of interest. Whenever competition does not merely determine the deviations and fluctuations, whenever, therefore, the neutralisation of opposing forces puts a stop to any and all determination, the thing to be determined becomes something arbitrary and lawless. More on this in the next chapter.

In the case of interest-bearing capital everything appears superficial: the advance of capital as mere transfer from lender to borrower; the reflux of realised capital as mere transfer back, as a return payment with interest, by borrower to lender. The same is true of the fact, immanent in the capitalist mode of production, that the rate of profit is not only determined by the relation of profit made in one single turnover to advanced capital value, but also by the length of this period of turnover, hence determined as profit yielded by industrial capital within definite spans of time. In the case of interest-bearing capital this likewise appears on the surface to mean that a definite interest is paid to the lender for a definite time span.

With his usual insight into the internal connection of things, the romantic Adam Müller says (*Elemente der Staatskunst*, Berlin, 1809, [Dritter Theil,] S. 138):

"In determining the prices of things, time is not considered; while in determining interest, time is the principal factor."

He does not see how the time of production and the time of circulation enter into the determination of commodity prices, and how this is just what determines the rate of profit for a given period of turnover of capital, whereas interest is determined by precisely this determination of profit for a given period. His sagacity here, as elsewhere, consists in observing the clouds of dust on the surface and presumptuously declaring this dust to be something mysterious and important.[a]

---

[a] See present edition, Vol. 33, pp. 225-26.

Chapter XXII

DIVISION OF PROFIT. RATE OF INTEREST.
"NATURAL" RATE OF INTEREST

The subject of this chapter, like all the other phenomena of credit we shall come across later on, cannot be analysed here in detail. The competition between lenders and borrowers and the resultant minor fluctuations of the money market fall outside the scope of our inquiry. The circuit described by the rate of interest during the industrial cycle requires for its presentation the analysis of this cycle itself, but this likewise cannot be given here. The same applies to the greater or lesser approximate equalisation of the rate of interest in the world market. We are here concerned with the independent form of interest-bearing capital and the individualisation of interest, as distinct from profit.

Since interest is merely a part of profit paid, according to our earlier assumption, by the industrial capitalist to the money capitalist, the maximum limit of interest is the profit itself, in which case the portion pocketed by the functioning capitalist would $= 0$. Aside from exceptional cases, in which interest might actually be larger than profit, but then could not be paid out of the profit, one might consider as the maximum limit of interest the total profit minus the portion (to be subsequently analysed) which resolves itself into WAGES OF SUPERINTENDENCE.[a] The minimum limit of interest is altogether indeterminable. It may fall to any level. Yet in that case there will always be counteracting influences to raise it again above this relative minimum.

"The relation between the sum paid for the use of capital and the capital itself expresses the rate of interest as measured in money."—"The rate of interest depends 1) on the rate of profit; 2) on the proportion in which the entire profit is divided between the lender and borrower" (*Economist*, January 22, 1853, [p. 89]). "If that which men pay as interest for the use of what they borrow, be a part of the profits it is capable of producing, this interest must always be governed by those profits" (Massie, l. c., p. 49).

Let us first assume that there is a fixed relation between the total profit and that part of it which has to be paid as interest to the money capitalist. It is then clear that the interest will rise or fall with the total profit, and the latter is determined by the general rate of profit

---

[a] In the 1894 German edition this English term is given in parentheses after its German equivalent.

and its fluctuations. For instance, if the average rate of profit were $= 20\%$ and the interest $= \frac{1}{4}$ of the profit, the rate of interest would $= 5\%$; if the average rate of profit were $= 16\%$, the rate of interest would $= 4\%$. With the rate of profit at 20%, the rate of interest might rise to 8%, and the industrial capitalist would still make the same profit as he would at a rate of profit $= 16\%$ and a rate of interest $= 4\%$, namely 12%. Should the interest rise only to 6% or 7%, he would still keep a larger share of the profit. If the interest amounted to a constant quota of the average profit, it would follow that the higher the general rate of profit, the greater the absolute difference between the total profit and the interest, and the greater the portion of the total profit pocketed by the functioning capitalist, and vice versa. Take it that the interest $= \frac{1}{5}$ of the average profit. One-fifth of 10 is 2; the difference between the total profit and the interest $= 8$. One-fifth of $20 = 4$; difference $= 20 - 4 = 16$; $\frac{1}{5}$ of $25 = 5$; difference $= 25 - 5 = 20$; $\frac{1}{5}$ of $30 = 6$; difference $= 30 - 6 = 24$; $\frac{1}{5}$ of $35 = 7$; difference $= 35 - 7 = 28$. The different rates of interest of 4, 5, 6, 7% would here always represent no more than $\frac{1}{5}$, or 20% of the total profit. If the rates of profit are different, therefore, different rates of interest may represent the same aliquot parts of the total profit, or the same percentage of the total profit. With such constant proportions of interest, the industrial profit (the difference between the total profit and the interest) would rise proportionately to the general rate of profit, and conversely.

All other conditions taken as equal, i. e., assuming the proportion between the interest and the total profit to be more or less constant, the functioning capitalist is able and willing to pay a higher or lower interest directly proportional to the level of the rate of profit.[61] Since we have seen that the rate of profit is inversely proportional to the development of capitalist production, it follows that the higher or lower rate of interest in a country is in the same inverse proportion to the degree of industrial development, at least in so far as the difference in the rate of interest actually expresses the difference in the rates of profit. It shall later develop that this need not always be the case. In this sense it may be said that interest is regulated through profit, or, more precisely, the general rate of profit. And this mode of regulating interest applies even to its average.

---

[61] "The natural rate of interest is governed by the profits of trade to particulars" (Massie, l. c., p. 51).

In any event the average rate of profit is to be regarded as the ultimate determinant of the maximum limit of interest.

The fact that interest is to be related to average profit will be considered presently at greater length. Whenever a specified entity, such as profit, is to be divided between two parties, the matter naturally hinges above all on the magnitude of the entity which is to be divided, and this, the magnitude of profit, is determined by its average rate. Suppose the general rate of profit, hence the magnitude of profit, for a capital of given size, say, = 100, is assumed as given. Then the variations of interest will obviously be inversely proportional to those of the part of profit remaining in the hands of the producing capitalist, working with a borrowed capital. And the circumstances determining the amount of profit to be distributed, of the value produced by unpaid labour, differ widely from those which determine its distribution between these two kinds of capitalists, and frequently produce entirely opposite effects.[62]

If we observe the cycles in which modern industry moves—state of inactivity, mounting revival, prosperity, overproduction, crisis, stagnation, state of inactivity, etc., cycles which fall beyond the scope of our analysis—we shall find that a low rate of interest generally corresponds to periods of prosperity or extra profit, a rise in interest separates prosperity and its reverse, and a maximum of interest up to a point of extreme usury corresponds to the period of crisis.[63] The summer of 1843 ushered in a period of remarkable prosperity; the rate of interest, still $4\frac{1}{2}\%$ in the spring of 1842, fell to 2% in the spring and summer of 1843[64]; in September it fell as low as $1\frac{1}{2}\%$ (Gilbart, l. c., I, p. 166); whereupon it rose to 8% and higher during the crisis of 1847.

[62] At this point the manuscript contains the following remark: "The course of this chapter shows that it is preferable, before analysing the laws of the distribution of profits, to ascertain first the way in which the division of quantity becomes one of quality. To make a transition from the previous chapter, we need but assume that interest is a certain indefinite portion of profit." [F. E.]

[63] "In the first period, immediately after pressure, money is abundant without speculation; in the second period, money is abundant and speculations abound; in the third period, speculation begins to decline and money is in demand; in the fourth period, money is scarce and a pressure arrives" (Gilbart, A Practical Treatise on Banking, 5th ed., Vol. I, London, 1849, p. 149).

[64] Tooke explains this "by the accumulation of surplus capital necessarily accompanying the scarcity of profitable employment for it in previous years, by the release of hoards, and by the revival of confidence in commercial prospects" (History of Prices from 1839 to 1847, London, 1848, p. 54).

It is possible, however, for low interest to go along with stagnation, and for moderately rising interest to go along with revived activity. The rate of interest reaches its peak during crises, when money is borrowed to meet payments at any cost. Since a rise in interest implies a fall in the price of securities, this simultaneously offers a fine opportunity to people with available money capital, to acquire at ridiculously low prices such interest-bearing securities as must, in the regular course of things, at least regain their average price as soon as the rate of interest falls again.[65]

However, the rate of interest also has a tendency to fall quite independently of the fluctuations in the rate of profit. And, indeed, due to two main causes:

I. "Were we even to suppose that capital was never borrowed with any view but to productive employment, I think it very possible that interest might vary without any change in the rate of gross profits. For, as a nation advances in the career of wealth, a class of men springs up and increases more and more, who by the labours of their ancestors find themselves in the possession of funds sufficiently ample to afford a handsome maintenance from the interest alone. Very many also who during youth and middle age were actively engaged in business, retire in their latter days to live quietly on the interest of the sums they have themselves accumulated. This class, as well as the former, has a tendency to increase with the increasing riches of the country, for those who begin with a tolerable stock are likely to make an independence sooner than they who commence with little. Thus it comes to pass, that in old and rich countries, the amount of national capital belonging to those who are unwilling to take the trouble of employing it themselves, bears a larger proportion to the whole productive stock of the society, than in newly settled and poorer districts. How much more numerous in proportion to the population is the class of *rentiers* ... in England! As the class of *rentiers* increases, so also does that of lenders of capital, for they are one and the same" (Ramsay, *An Essay on the Distribution of Wealth*, pp. 201, 202).

II. The development of the credit system and the attendant ever-growing control of industrialists and merchants over the money savings of all classes of society that is effected through the bankers, and the progressive concentration of these savings in amounts which can serve as money capital, must also depress the rate of interest. More about this later.

With reference to the determination of the rate of interest, Ramsay says that it

[65] "An old customer of a banker was refused a loan upon a £200,000 bond; when about to leave to make known his suspension of payment, he was told there was no necessity for the step, under the circumstances the banker would buy the bond at £150,000" ([H. Roy], *The Theory of the Exchanges. The Bank Charter Act of 1844, etc.*, London, 1864, p. 80).

"depends partly upon the rate of gross profits, partly on the proportion in which these are separated into PROFITS of capital and those OF ENTERPRISE.[a] This proportion again depends upon the competition between the lenders of capital and the borrowers; which competition is influenced, though by no means entirely regulated, by the rate of gross profits expected to be realised.[66] And the reason why competition is not exclusively regulated by this cause, is, because, on the one hand, many borrow without any view to productive employment; and, on the other, because the proportion of the whole capital to be lent, varies with the riches of the country independently of any change in gross profits" (Ramsay, l. c., pp. 206-07).

To determine the average rate of interest we must 1) calculate the average rate of interest during its variations in the major industrial cycles; and 2) find the rate of interest for investments which require long-term loans of capital.

The average rate of interest prevailing in a certain country—as distinct from the continually fluctuating market rates—cannot be determined by any law. In this sphere there is no such thing as a natural rate of interest in the sense in which economists speak of a natural rate of profit and a natural rate of wages. Massie has rightly said in this respect:

"The only thing which any man can be in doubt about on this occasion, is, what proportion of these profits do of right belong to the borrower, and what to the lender; and this there is no other method of determining than by the opinions of borrowers and lenders in general; for right and wrong, in this respect, are only what common consent makes so" (Massie, l. c., p. 49).

Equating supply and demand—assuming the average rate of profit as given—is of no consequence at all here. Wherever else this formula is resorted to (and this is then practically correct), it serves as a formula to find the fundamental rule (the regulating limits or limiting magnitudes) which is independent of, and rather determines, competition; notably as a formula for those who are held captive by the practice of competition, and by its phenomena and the conceptions arising out of them, to arrive at what is again but a superficial idea of the inner connection of economic relations obtaining within competi-

---

[66] Since the rate of interest is on the whole determined by the average rate of profit, inordinate swindling is often bound up with a low rate of interest. For instance, the railway swindle in the summer of 1844. The rate of interest of the Bank of England was not raised to 3% until 16th October, 1844.

---

[a] In the 1894 German edition the term "profits of enterprise" is given in parentheses after its German equivalent.

tion. It is a method to pass from the variations that go with competition to the limits of these variations. This is not the case with the average rate of interest. There is no good reason why average conditions of competition, the balance between lender and borrower, should give the lender an interest rate of 3, 4, 5%, etc., or else a certain percentage of the gross profits, say 20% or 50%, on his capital. Where competition as such is the determining factor, the particular rate fixed is accidental, purely empirical, and only pedantry or fantasy would seek to represent this accident as a necessity.[67] Nothing is more amusing in the reports of Parliament for 1857 and 1858 concerning bank legislation and commercial crises than to hear of "THE REAL RATE PRODUCED" as the directors of the Bank of England, London bankers, country bankers, and professional theorists chatter back and forth, never getting beyond such commonplaces as that "the price paid for the use of loanable capital should vary with the supply of such capital", that "a high rate and a low profit cannot permanently exist", and similar platitudes.[68] Customs, juristic tradition, etc., have as much to do with determining the average rate of interest as competition itself, in so far as it exists not merely as an average, but rather as actual magnitude. In many law disputes, where interest has to be calculated, an average rate of interest has to be assumed as the legal rate. If we

---

[67] J. G. Opdyke, for instance, in his *Treatise on Political Economy*, New York, 1851, [pp. 86-87], makes a very unsuccessful attempt to explain the universality of a 5% rate of interest by eternal laws. Mr. Karl Arnd is still more naive in *Die naturgemässe Volkswirtschaft, gegenüber dem Monopoliengeist und dem Kommunismus, etc.*, Hanau, 1845. It is stated there: "In the natural course of goods production there is just *one* phenomenon, which, in the fully settled countries, seems in some measure to regulate the rate of interest; this is the proportion in which the timber in European forests is augmented through their annual growth. This new growth occurs quite independently of their exchange value, at the rate of 3 or 4 to 100." (How queer that trees should see to their new growth independently of their exchange value!) "According to this a drop in the rate of interest below its present level in the richest countries cannot be expected" (pp. 124-25). (He means, because the new growth of the trees is independent of their exchange value, however much their exchange value may depend on their new growth.) This deserves to be called "the primordial forest rate of interest". Its discoverer makes a further laudable contribution in this work to "our science" as the "philosopher of the dog tax".[39]

[68] The Bank of England raises and lowers the rate of its discount, always, of course, with due consideration to the rate prevailing in the open market, in accordance with imports and exports of gold. "By which gambling in discounts, by anticipation of the alterations in the bank rate, has now become half the trade of the great heads of the money centre" — i. e., of the London money market. ([H. Roy], *The Theory of the Exchanges, etc.*, p. 113.)

inquire further as to why the limits of an average rate of interest cannot be deduced from general laws, we find the answer lies simply in the nature of interest. It is merely a part of the average profit. The same capital appears in two roles — as loanable capital in the lender's hands and as industrial, or commercial, capital in the hands of the functioning capitalist. But it functions just once, and produces profit just once. In the production process itself the nature of capital as loanable capital plays no role. How the two parties who have claim to it divide the profit is in itself just as purely empirical a matter belonging to the realm of accident as the distribution of percentage shares of a common profit in a business partnership. Two entirely different elements — labour power and capital — act as determinants in the division between surplus value and wages, which division essentially determines the rate of profit; these are functions of two independent variables, which limit one another; and it is their *qualitative difference* that is the source of the *quantitative division* of the produced value. We shall see later that the same occurs in the division of surplus value into rent and profit. Nothing of the kind occurs in the case of interest. Here the *qualitative differentiation*, as we shall presently see, proceeds rather from the *purely quantitative division* of the same sum of surplus value.

It follows from the aforesaid that there is no such thing as a "natural" rate of interest. But if, on the one hand, unlike in the case of the general rate of profit, there is no general law to determine the limits of the average interest, or average rate of interest, as distinct from the continually fluctuating market rates of interest, because it is merely a question of dividing the gross profit between two owners of capital under different titles, the rate of interest, be it the average or the market rate prevalent in each particular case, on the other hand, appears as a uniform, definite and tangible magnitude in a quite different way from the general rate of profit.[69]

The rate of interest is similarly related to the rate of profit as the market price of a commodity is to its value. In so far as the rate of interest is determined by the rate of profit, this is always the general rate

---

[69] "'The price of commodities fluctuates' continually; they are all made for different uses; the money serves for all purposes. The commodities, even those of the same kind, differ according to quality; cash money is always of the same value, or at least is assumed to be so. Thus it is that the price of money, which we designate by the term interest, has a greater stability and uniformity than that of any other thing" (J. Steuart, *Principles of Political Economy*, French translation, 1789, IV, p. 27).

of profit and not any specific rate of profit prevailing in some particular branch of industry, and still less any extra profit which an individual capitalist may make in a particular sphere of business.[70] It is a fact, therefore, that the general rate of profit appears as an empirical, given reality in the average rate of interest, although the latter is not a pure or reliable expression of the former.

It is indeed true that the rate of interest itself varies continually in accordance with the different classes of securities offered by borrowers, and in accordance with the length of time for which the money is borrowed; but it is uniform in each of these classes at a given moment. This distinction, then, does not militate against a fixed and uniform appearance of the rate of interest.[71]

The average rate of interest appears in every country over fairly long periods as a constant magnitude, because the general rate of profit varies only at longer intervals—in spite of constant variations in specific rates of profit, in which a change in one sphere is offset by an opposite change in another. And its relative constancy is revealed

---

[70] "This rule of dividing profits is not, however, to be applied particularly to every lender and borrower, but to lenders and borrowers in general ... remarkably great and small gains are the reward of skill and the want of understanding, which lenders have nothing at all to do with; for as they will not suffer by the one, they ought not to benefit by the other. What has been said of particular men in the same business is applicable to particular sorts of business; if the merchants and tradesmen employed in any one branch of trade get more by what they borrow than the common profits made by other merchants and tradesmen of the same country, the extraordinary gain is theirs, though it required only common skill and understanding to get it; and not the lenders', who supplied them with money ... for the lenders would not have lent their money to carry on any branch of trade upon lower terms than would admit of paying so much as the common rate of interest; and therefore they ought not to receive more than that, whatever advantages may be made by their money" (Massie, l. c., pp. 50, 51).

[71] * Bank rate 5%
Market rate of discount, 60 days' drafts .... $3^5/_8\%$
Ditto, 3 months' .... $3^1/_2\%$
Ditto, 6 months' .... $3^5/_{16}\%$
Loans to bill-brokers, day to day .... 1 to 2%
Ditto, for one week 3%
Last rate for fortnight, loans to stockbrokers .... $4^3/_4$ to 5%
Deposit allowance (banks) .... $3^1/_2\%$
Ditto (discount houses) .... 3 to $3^1/_4\%$ *

How large this difference may be for one and the same day is shown in the preceding figures of the rate of interest of the London money market on December 9, 1889, taken from the City article of the *Daily News* of December 10. The minimum is 1%, the maximum 5%. [*F. E.*]

precisely in this more or less constant nature of the AVERAGE, OR COMMON, RATE OF INTEREST.[a]

As concerns the perpetually fluctuating market rate of interest, however, it exists at any moment as a fixed magnitude, just as the market price of commodities, because in the money market all loanable capital continually faces functioning capital as an aggregate mass, so that the relation between the supply of loanable capital on one side, and the demand for it on the other, decides the market level of interest at any given time. This is all the more so, the more the development, and the attendant concentration, of the credit system gives to loanable capital a general social character and throws it all at once on the money market. On the other hand, the general rate of profit is never anything more than a tendency, a movement to equalise specific rates of profit. The competition between capitalists — which is itself this movement toward equilibrium — consists here of their gradually withdrawing capital from spheres in which profit is for an appreciable length of time below average, and gradually investing capital into spheres in which profit is above average. Or it may also consist in additional capital distributing itself gradually and in varying proportions among these spheres. It is continual variation in supply and withdrawal of capital in regard to these different spheres, and never a simultaneous mass effect, as in the determination of the rate of interest.

We have seen that interest-bearing capital, although a category which differs absolutely from a commodity, becomes a commodity *sui generis*,[b] so that interest becomes its price, fixed at all times by supply and demand like the market price of an ordinary commodity. The market rate of interest, while fluctuating continually, appears therefore at any given moment just as constantly fixed and uniform as the market price of a commodity prevailing in each individual case. Money capitalists supply this commodity, and functioning capitalists buy it, creating the demand for it. This does not occur when equalisation creates a general rate of profit. If prices of commodities in one sphere are below or above the price of production (wherein we leave aside the fluctuations attendant upon the various phases of the industrial cycle in each and every enterprise) equalisation occurs through the expansion or curtailment of production, i. e., the expansion or

---

[a] In the 1894 German edition this English term is given in parentheses after its German equivalent. - [b] peculiar

curtailment of the masses of commodities thrown on the market by industrial capitals — caused by inflow or outflow of capital to and from individual spheres of production. It is by this equalisation of the average market prices of commodities to prices of production that deviations of specific rates of profit from the general, or average, rate of profit are corrected. It cannot be that in this process industrial or mercantile capital *as such* should ever assume the appearance of commodities vis-à-vis the buyer, as in the case of interest-bearing capital. If perceptible at all, this process is so only in the fluctuations and equalisations of market prices of commodities to prices of production, not as a direct fixation of the average profit. The general rate of profit is, indeed, determined 1) by the surplus value produced by the total capital, 2) by the proportion of this surplus value to the value of the total capital, and 3) by competition, but only in so far as this is a movement whereby capitals invested in particular production spheres seek to draw equal dividends out of this surplus value in proportion to their relative magnitudes. The general rate of profit, therefore, derives actually from causes far different and far more complicated than the market rate of interest, which is directly and immediately determined by the proportion between supply and demand, and hence is not as tangible and obvious a fact as the rate of interest. The specific rates of profit in various spheres of production are themselves more or less uncertain; but in so far as they appear, it is not their uniformity but their differences which are perceptible. The general rate of profit, however, appears only as the lowest limit of profit, not as an empirical, directly visible form of the actual rate of profit.

In emphasising this difference between the rate of interest and the rate of profit, we still omit the following two points, which favour consolidation of the rate of interest: 1) the historical preexistence of interest-bearing capital and the existence of a traditional general rate of interest; 2) the far greater direct influence exerted by the world market on establishing the rate of interest, irrespective of the economic conditions of a country, as compared with its influence on the rate of profit.

The average profit does not appear as a directly established fact, but rather is to be determined as an end result of the equalisation of opposite fluctuations. Not so with the rate of interest. It is a thing fixed daily in its general, at least local, validity — a thing which serves industrial and mercantile capitals even as a prerequisite and a factor in the calculation of their operations. It becomes the general endowment of every sum of money of £100 to yield 2, 3, 4, 5%. Meteorological reports never denote the readings of the barometer and thermometer with greater accuracy than stock exchange reports denote the rate of interest, not for one or another capital, but for capital in the money market, i. e., for loanable capital generally.[a]

In the money market only lenders and borrowers face one another. The commodity has the same form — money. All specific forms of capital in accordance with its investment in particular spheres of production or circulation are here obliterated. It exists in the undifferentiated homogeneous form of independent value — money. The competition of individual spheres does not affect it. They are all thrown together as borrowers of money, and capital confronts them all in a form in which it is as yet indifferent to the particular manner of its employment. Here, in the supply and demand of capital, it appears most emphatically as *essentially the common capital of a class* — something industrial capital does only in the movement and competition between the individual spheres. On the other hand, money capital in the money market actually possesses the form, in which, indifferent to its specific employment, it is divided as a common element among the various spheres, among the capitalist class, as the requirements of production in each individual sphere may dictate. Moreover, with the development of large-scale industry money capital, so far as it appears on the market, is not represented by some individual capitalist, not the owner of one or another fraction of the capital in the market, but assumes the nature of a concentrated, organised mass, which, quite different from actual production, is subject to the control of bankers, i. e., the representatives of social capital. So that, as concerns the form of demand, loanable capital is confronted by the class as a whole, whereas in the province of supply it is loanable capital which obtains *en masse*.

These are some of the reasons why the general rate of profit appears blurred and hazy alongside the definite interest rate, which may fluctuate in magnitude, but always confronts borrowers as given and fixed because it varies uniformly for all of them. Just as variations in the value of money do not prevent it from having the same value vis-à-vis all commodities. Just as the daily fluctuations in market prices of commodities do not prevent them from being daily reported in

---

[a] Cf. present edition, Vol. 32, pp. 459-60.

the papers. So the rate of interest is regularly reported as "the price of money". It is so, because capital itself is being offered here in the form of money as a commodity. The fixation of its price is thus a fixation of its market price, as with all other commodities. The rate of interest, therefore, always appears as the general rate of interest, as so much money for so much money, as a definite quantity. The rate of profit, on the other hand, may vary even within the same sphere for commodities with the same market prices, depending on different conditions under which individual capitals produce the same commodity, because the rate of profit of an individual capital is not determined by the market price of a commodity, but rather by the difference between market price and cost price. And these different rates of profit can strike a balance — first within the same sphere and then between different spheres — only through continual fluctuations.[a]

(Note for later elaboration.) A specific form of credit: It is known that when money serves as a means of payment instead of a means of purchase, the commodity is alienated, but its value is realised only later. If payment is not made until after the commodity has again been sold, this sale does not appear as the result of the purchase; rather it is through this sale that the purchase is realised. In other words, the sale becomes a means of purchase. Secondly: titles to debts, bills of exchange, etc., become means of payment for the creditor. Thirdly: the compensation of titles to debts replaces money.

Chapter XXIII

INTEREST AND PROFIT OF ENTERPRISE

Interest, as we have seen in the two preceding chapters, appears originally, is originally, and remains in fact merely a portion of the profit, i.e., of the surplus value, which the functioning capitalist, industrialist or merchant has to pay to the owner and lender of money capital whenever he uses loaned capital instead of his own. If he employs only his own capital, no such division of profit takes place; the latter is then entirely his. Indeed, as long as the owners of the capital employ it on their own in the reproduction process, they do not compete in determining the rate of interest. This alone shows that the

---

[a] Ibid., pp. 461-62.

category of interest—impossible without determining the rate of interest—is alien to the movements of industrial capital as such.

* The rate of interest may be defined to be that proportional sum which the lender is content to receive, and the borrower to pay, for a year or for any longer or shorter period, for the use of a certain amount of moneyed capital.... When the owner of a capital employs it actively in reproduction, he does not come under the head of those capitalists, the proportion of whom, to the number of borrowers, determines the rate of interest" * (Th. Tooke, *A History of Prices*, London, 1838, II, pp. 355-56.)

It is indeed only the division of capitalists into money capitalists and industrial capitalists that transforms a portion of the profit into interest, that generally creates the category of interest; and it is only the competition between these two kinds of capitalists which creates the rate of interest.

As long as capital functions in the process of reproduction—even assuming that it belongs to the industrial capitalist and he has no need of paying it back to a lender—the capitalist, as a private individual, does not have at his disposal this capital itself, but only the profit, which he may spend as revenue. As long as his capital functions as capital, it belongs to the process of reproduction, is tied up in it. He is, indeed, its owner, but this ownership does not enable him to dispose of it in any other way, so long as he uses it as capital for the exploitation of labour. The same is true of the money capitalist. So long as his capital is loaned out and thereby serves as money capital, it brings him interest, a portion of the profit, but he cannot dispose of the principal. This is evident whenever he loans out his capital for, say, a year, or more, and receives interest at certain stipulated times without the return of his principal. But even the return of the principal makes no difference here. If he gets it back, he must always loan it out again, so long as it is to function for him as capital—here as money capital. As long as he keeps it in his own hands, it does not collect interest and does not act as capital; and as long as it does gather interest and does serve as capital, it is out of his hands. Hence the possibility of loaning out capital for all time. The following remarks by Tooke directed against Bosanquet are, therefore, entirely wrong. He quotes Bosanquet (*Metallic, Paper, and Credit Currency*, p. 73):

"Were the rate of interest reduced as low as 1%, capital borrowed would be placed nearly ON A PAR [a] with capital possessed."

---

[a] In the 1894 German edition this English expression is given in parentheses after its German equivalent.

To this Tooke adds the following marginal note:

"That a capital borrowed at that, or even a lower rate, should be considered nearly on a par with capital possessed, is a proposition so strange as hardly to warrant serious notice were it not advanced by a writer so intelligent, and, on some points of the subject, so well informed. Has he overlooked the circumstance, or does he consider it of little consequence, that there must, by the supposition, be a condition of repayment?" (Th. Tooke, *An Inquiry into the Currency Principle*, 2nd ed., London, 1844, p. 80.)

If interest were = 0, the industrial capitalist operating on borrowed capital would stand on a par with a capitalist using his own capital. Both would pocket the same average profit, and capital, whether borrowed or owned, serves as capital only as long as it produces profit. The condition of return payment would alter nothing. The nearer the rate of interest approaches zero, falling, for instance, to 1%, the nearer borrowed capital is to being on a par with owner's capital. So long as money capital is to exist as money capital, it must always be loaned out, and indeed at the prevailing rate of interest, say of 1%, and always to the same class of industrial and commercial capitalists. So long as these function as capitalists, the sole difference between the one working with borrowed capital and the other with his own is that the former must pay interest and the latter must not; the one pockets the entire profit p, and the other p — i, the profit minus the interest. The nearer interest approaches zero, the nearer p — i approaches p, and hence the nearer the two capitals are to being on a par. The one must pay back the capital and borrow anew; yet the other must likewise advance it again and again to the production process, so long as his capital is to function, and cannot dispose of it freely, independent of this process. The sole remaining difference between the two is the obvious difference that one is the owner of his capital, and the other is not.

The question which now arises is this. How does this purely quantitative division of profit into net profit and interest turn into a qualitative one? In other words, how is it that a capitalist who employs solely his own, not borrowed capital, classifies a portion of his gross profit under the specific category of interest and as such calculates it separately? And, furthermore, how is it that all capital, whether borrowed or not, is differentiated as interest-bearing capital from itself as capital producing a net profit?

It is understood that not every accidental quantitative division of profit turns in this manner into a qualitative one. For instance, some industrial capitalists join hands to operate a business and then divide the profit among themselves in accordance with some legal agreement. Others do their business, each on his own, without any partners. These last do not calculate their profit under two heads — one part as individual profit, and the other as company profit for their non-existent partners. In this case the quantitative division therefore does not become a qualitative one. This occurs whenever ownership happens to be vested in several juridical persons. It does not occur whenever this is not the case.

In order to answer this question, we must dwell somewhat longer on the actual point of departure in the formation of interest; that is, we must proceed from the assumption that the money capitalist and the productive capitalist really confront one another not just as legally different persons, but as persons playing entirely different roles in the reproduction process, or as persons in whose hands the same capital really performs a two-fold and wholly different movement. The one merely loans it, the other employs it productively.

For the productive capitalist who works on borrowed capital, the gross profit falls into two parts — the interest, which he is to pay the lender, and the surplus over and above the interest, which makes up his own share of the profit. If the general rate of profit is given, this latter portion is determined by the rate of interest; and if the rate of interest is given, then by the general rate of profit. And furthermore: no matter how the gross profit, the actual value of the total profit, may diverge in each individual case from the average profit, the portion which belongs to the functioning capitalist is determined by the interest, since this is fixed by the general rate of interest (leaving aside any special legal stipulations) and assumed to be given beforehand, before the process of production begins, hence before its result, the gross profit, is achieved. We have seen that the actual specific product of capital is surplus value, or, more precisely, profit. But for the capitalist working on borrowed capital it is not profit, but profit minus interest, that portion of profit which remains to him after paying interest. This portion of the profit, therefore, necessarily appears to him to be the product of a capital as long as it is operative; and this it is, as far as he is concerned, because he represents capital only as functioning capital. He is its personification as long as it functions, and it functions as long as it is profitably invested in industry or commerce and such operations are undertaken with it through its employer as are prescribed by the branch of industry concerned. As distinct from interest, which he has to pay to the lender out of the gross profit, the portion of profit which falls to his share necessarily assumes the form of industrial or commercial profit, or, to use a German term embracing both, the form of *Unternehmergewinn* (profit of enterprise). If the gross profit equals the average profit, the size of the profit of enterprise is determined exclusively by the rate of interest. If the gross profit deviates from the average profit, its difference from the average profit (after interest is deducted from both) is determined by all the circumstances which cause a temporary deviation, be it of the rate of profit in any particular sphere of production from the general rate of profit, or the profit of some individual capitalist in a certain sphere from the average profit of this particular sphere. We have seen however that the rate of profit within the production process itself does not depend on surplus value alone, but also on many other circumstances, such as purchase prices of the means of production, methods more productive than the average, savings of constant capital, etc. And aside from the price of production, it depends on special circumstances, and in every single business transaction on the greater or lesser shrewdness and industry of the capitalist, whether, and to what extent, he buys or sells above or below the price of production and thus appropriates a greater or smaller portion of the total surplus value in the process of circulation. In any case, the quantitative division of the gross profit turns here into a qualitative one, and all the more so because the quantitative division itself depends on *what* is to be divided, the *manner* in which the active capitalist manages his capital, and what gross profit it yields to him as a functioning capital, i. e., in consequence of his functions as an active capitalist. The functioning capitalist is here assumed as a non-owner of capital. Ownership of the capital is represented in relation to him by the money capitalist, the lender. The interest he pays to the latter thus appears as that portion of gross profit which is due to the ownership of capital as such. As distinct from this, that portion of profit which falls to the active capitalist appears now as profit of enterprise, deriving solely from the operations, or functions, which he performs with the capital in the process of reproduction, hence particularly those functions which he performs as entrepreneur in industry or commerce. In relation to him interest appears therefore as the mere fruit of owning capital, of capital as such abstracted from the reproduction process of capital, inasmuch as it does not "work", does not function; while profit of enterprise appears to him as the exclusive fruit of the functions which he performs with the capital, as the fruit of the movement and performance of capital, of a performance which appears to him as his own activity, as opposed to the inactivity, the non-participation of the money capitalist in the production process. This qualitative distinction between the two portions of gross profit that interest is the fruit of capital as such, of the ownership of capital irrespective of the production process, and that profit of enterprise is the fruit of performing capital, of capital functioning in the production process, and hence of the active role played by the employer of the capital in the reproduction process — this qualitative distinction is by no means merely a subjective notion of the money capitalist, on the one hand, and the industrial capitalist, on the other. It rests upon an objective fact, for interest flows to the money capitalist, to the lender, who is the mere owner of capital, hence represents only ownership of capital before the production process and outside of it; while the profit of enterprise flows to the functioning capitalist alone, who is non-owner of the capital.

The merely quantitative division of the gross profit between two different persons who both have different legal claims to the same capital, and hence to the profit produced by it, thus turns into a qualitative division for both the industrial capitalist in so far as he is operating on borrowed capital, and for the money capitalist, in so far as he does not himself apply his capital. One portion of the profit appears now as fruit due as such to capital in *one* form, as interest; the other portion appears as a specific fruit of capital in an opposite form, and thus as profit of enterprise. One appears exclusively as the fruit of owning the capital, the other as the fruit of operating with the capital, the fruit of performing capital, or of the functions performed by the active capitalist. And this ossification and individualisation of the two parts of the gross profit in respect to one another, as though they originated from two essentially different sources, must now take firm shape for the entire capitalist class and the total capital. And, indeed, regardless of whether the capital employed by the active capitalist is borrowed or not, and whether the capital belonging to the money capitalist is employed by himself or not. The profit of every capital, and consequently also the average profit established by the equalisation of capitals, splits, or is separated, into two qualitatively different, mutually independent and self-established parts, to wit — interest and profit of enterprise — both of which are determined by particular laws. The capitalist operating with his own capital, like the one operating with borrowed capital, divides the gross profit into interest due to himself as owner, as his own lender, and into profit of enterprise due to him as to an active capitalist performing his function. As concerns this division, therefore, as a qualitative one, it is immaterial whether the capitalist really has to share with another, or not. The employer of capital, even when working with his own capital, splits into two personalities — the owner of capital and the employer of capital; with reference to the categories of profit which it yields, his capital also splits into capital-*property*, capital *outside* the production process, yielding interest of itself, and capital *in* the production process which yields a profit of enterprise through its function.

Interest, therefore, becomes firmly established in a way that it no longer appears as a division of gross profit of indifference to production, which occurs occasionally when the industrial capitalist operates with someone else's capital. His profit splits into interest and profit of enterprise even when he operates with his own capital. A merely quantitative division thus turns into a qualitative one. It occurs regardless of the fortuitous circumstance whether the industrial capitalist is, or is not, the owner of his capital. It is not only a matter of different quotas of profit assigned to different persons, but two different categories of profit which are differently related to the capital, hence related to different aspects of the capital.

Now that this division of gross profit into interest and profit of enterprise has become a qualitative one, it is very easy to discover the reasons why it acquires this character of a qualitative division for the total capital and the entire class of capitalists.[a]

Firstly, this follows from the simple empirical circumstance that the majority of industrial capitalists, even if in different numerical proportions, work with their own and with borrowed capital, and that at different times the proportion between one's own and borrowed capital changes.

Secondly, the transformation of a portion of the gross profit into the form of interest converts its other portion into profit of enterprise. The latter is, indeed, but the opposite form assumed by the excess of gross profit over interest as soon as this exists as a special category. The entire analysis of the problem how gross profit is differentiated into interest and profit of enterprise, resolves itself into the inquiry of

---

[a] Cf. present edition, Vol. 32, p. 493.

how a portion of the gross profit becomes universally ossified and individualised as interest. Yet historically interest-bearing capital existed as a completed traditional form, and hence interest as a completed subdivision of surplus value produced by capital, long before the
capitalist mode of production and its attendant conceptions of capital
and profit. Thus it is that to the popular mind money capital, or interest-bearing capital, is still capital as such, as capital *par excellence*.
Thus it is, on the other hand, that up to the time of Massie the notion
prevailed that it is money as such which is paid in interest. The fact
that loaned capital yields interest whether actually employed as capital or not — even when borrowed only for consumption — lends
strength to the idea that this form of capital exists independently. The
best proof of the independence which interest possessed during the
early periods of the capitalist mode of production in reference to profit, and which interest-bearing capital possessed in reference to industrial capital, is that it was discovered (by Massie and after him by
Hume [a]) as late as the middle of the 18th century, that interest is but a
portion of the gross profit, and that such a discovery was at all necessary.

Thirdly, whether the industrial capitalist operates with his own or
with borrowed capital does not alter the fact that the class of money
capitalists confronts him as a special kind of capitalists, money capital
as an independent kind of capital, and interest as an independent
form of surplus value peculiar to this specific capital.

Qualitatively speaking, interest is surplus value yielded by the
mere ownership of capital; it is yielded by capital as such, even
though its owner remains outside the reproduction process. Hence it
is surplus value yielded by capital outside of its process.

Quantitatively speaking, that portion of profit which forms interest
does not seem to be related to industrial or commercial capital as
such, but to money capital, and the rate of this portion of surplus value, the rate of interest, reinforces this relation. Because, in the first
place, the rate of interest is independently determined despite its dependence upon the general rate of profit, and, in the second place,
like the market price of commodities, it appears in contrast to the in-
tangible rate of profit as a fixed, uniform, tangible and always given

---

[a] [J. Massie,] *An Essay on the Governing Causes of the Natural Rate of Interest....* D. Hume,
"Of Interest" in: D. Hume, *Essays and Treatises on Several Subjects*, Vol. I, London, 1764.
See also present edition, Vol. 34, pp. 89-92.

relation for all its variations. If all capital were in the hands of the industrial capitalists there would be no such thing as interest and rate of interest. The independent form assumed by the quantitative division of gross profit creates the qualitative one. If the industrial capitalist were to compare himself with the money capitalist, it would be his profit of enterprise alone, the excess of his gross profit over the average interest—the latter appearing to be empirically given by virtue of the rate of interest—that would distinguish him from the other person. If, on the other hand, he compares himself with the industrial capitalist working with his own, instead of borrowed, capital, the latter differs from him only as a money capitalist in pocketing the interest instead of paying it to someone else. The portion of gross profit distinguished from interest appears to him in either case as profit of enterprise, and interest itself as a surplus value yielded by capital as such, which it would yield even if not applied productively.

This is correct in the practical sense for the individual capitalist. He has the choice of making use of his capital by lending it out as interest-bearing capital, or of expanding its value on his own by using it as productive capital, regardless of whether it exists as money capital from the very first, or whether it still has to be converted into money capital. But to apply it to the total capital of society, as some vulgar economists do, and to go so far as to define it as the cause of profit, is, of course, preposterous.[a] The idea of converting all the capital into money capital, without there being people who buy and put to use means of production, which make up the total capital outside of a relatively small portion of it existing in money, is, of course, sheer absurdity. It would be still more absurd to presume that capital would yield interest on the basis of the capitalist mode of production without performing any productive function, i. e., without creating surplus value, of which interest is just a part; that the capitalist mode of production would run its course without capitalist production. If an untowardly large section of capitalists were to convert their capital into money capital, the result would be a frightful depreciation of money capital and a frightful fall in the rate of interest; many would at once face the impossibility of living on their interest, and would hence be compelled to reconvert into industrial capitalists. But we repeat that it is a fact for the individual capitalist. For this reason, even when operating with his own capital, he necessarily considers the part

---

[a] Ibid., p. 475.

of his average profit which equals the average interest as fruit of his capital as such, set apart from the process of production; and as distinct from this portion singled out as interest, he considers the excess of the gross profit as mere profit of enterprise.

Fourthly: [A blank in the manuscript.]

We have seen, therefore, that the portion of profit which the functioning capitalist has to pay to the owner of borrowed capital is transformed into an independent form for a portion of the profit, which all capital as such, whether borrowed or not, yields under the name of interest. How large this portion is depends on the average rate of interest. Its origin is only revealed in the fact that the functioning capitalist, when owner of his capital, does not compete — at least not actively — in determining the interest rate. The purely quantitative division of the profit between two persons who have different legal titles to it has turned into a qualitative division, which seems to spring from the very nature of capital and profit. Because, as we have seen, as soon as a portion of profit universally assumes the form of interest, the difference between average profit and interest, or the portion of profit over and above the interest, assumes a form opposite to interest — the form of profit of enterprise. These two forms, interest and profit of enterprise, exist only as opposites. Hence, they are not related to surplus value, of which they are but parts placed under different categories, heads or names, but rather to one another. It is because one portion of profit turns into interest, that the other appears as profit of enterprise.

By profit we here always mean average profit, since variations do not concern us in this analysis, be they of individual profits or of profits in different spheres of production — hence variations caused by the competitive struggle and other circumstances affecting the distribution of the average profit, or surplus value. This applies generally to this entire inquiry.

Interest is then net profit, as Ramsay calls it,[a] which the ownership of capital yields as such, either simply to the lender, who remains outside the reproduction process, or to the owner who employs his capital productively. But in the latter's case, too, capital yields this net profit to him not in his capacity of functioning capitalist, but of money capitalist, of lender of his own capital as interest-bearing capital to himself as to a functioning capitalist. Just as the conversion of mon-

---

a See this volume, pp. 360 and 377.

ey, and of value in general, into capital is the constant result of capitalist production, so is its existence as capital its constant precondition. By its ability to be transformed into means of production it continually commands unpaid labour and thereby transforms the processes of production and circulation of commodities into the production of surplus value for its owner. Interest is, therefore, the expression of the fact that value in general — objectified labour in its general social form — value which assumes the form of means of production in the actual process of production, confronts living labour power as an independent power, and is a means of appropriating unpaid labour; and that it is such a power because it confronts the labourer as the property of another. But on the other hand, this antithesis to wage labour is obliterated in the form of interest, because interest-bearing capital as such has not wage labour, but productive capital for its opposite. The lending capitalist as such faces the capitalist performing his actual function in the process of reproduction, not the wage worker, who, precisely under capitalist production, is expropriated of the means of production. Interest-bearing capital is capital as *property* as distinct from capital as a *function*. But so long as capital does not perform its function, it does not exploit labourers and does not come into opposition to labour.

On the other hand, profit of enterprise is not related as an opposite to wage labour, but only to interest.

Firstly, assuming the average profit to be given, the rate of the profit of enterprise is not determined by wages, but by the rate of interest. It is high or low in inverse proportion to it.[72]

Secondly, the functioning capitalist derives his claim to profits of enterprise, hence the profit of enterprise itself, not from his ownership of capital, but from the function of capital, as distinct from the definite form in which it is only inert property. This stands out as an immediately apparent contrast whenever he operates with borrowed capital, and interest and profit of enterprise therefore go to two different persons. The profit of enterprise springs from the function of capital in the reproduction process, hence as a result of the operations, the acts by which the functioning capitalist promotes these functions of industrial and commercial capital. But to represent functioning capi-

---

[72] * "The profits of enterprise depend upon the net profits of capital, not the latter upon the former." * (Ramsay, *Essay on the Distribution of Wealth*, p. 214. For Ramsay net profits always mean interest.)

tal is not a sinecure, like representing interest-bearing capital. On the basis of capitalist production, the capitalist directs the processes of production and circulation. Exploiting productive labour entails exertion, whether he exploits it himself or has it exploited by someone else on his behalf. Therefore, as distinct from interest, his profit of enterprise appears to him as independent of the ownership of capital, but rather as the result of his functions as a non-proprietor — a *labourer*.

He necessarily conceives the idea for this reason that his profit of enterprise, far from being counterposed to wage labour and far from being the unpaid labour of others, is itself rather a *wage* or WAGES OF SUPERINTENDENCE OF LABOUR,[a] higher than a common labourer's, 1) because the work is far more complicated, and 2) because he pays them to himself. The fact that his function as a capitalist consists in creating surplus value, i. e., unpaid labour, and creating it under the most economical conditions, is entirely lost sight of in the contrast that interest falls to the share of the capitalist even when he does not perform the function of a capitalist and is merely the owner of capital; and that, on the other hand, profit of enterprise does fall to the share of the functioning capitalist even when he is not the owner of the capital with which he operates. He forgets, due to the antithetical form of the two parts into which profit, hence surplus value, is divided, that both are merely parts of the surplus value, and that this division alters nothing in the nature, origin, and way of existence of surplus value.

In the process of reproduction the functioning capitalist represents capital as the property of another vis-à-vis the wage labourers, and the money capitalist, represented by the functioning capitalist, takes a hand in exploiting labour. The fact that the investing capitalist can perform his function of making the labourers work for him, or of employing means of production as capital, only as the personification of the means of production vis-à-vis the labourers, is forgotten over the contradiction between the function of capital in the reproduction process and the mere ownership of capital outside of the reproduction process.

In fact, the form of interest and profit of enterprise assumed by the two parts of profit, i. e., of surplus value, expresses no relation to labour, because this relation exists only between labour and profit, or

---

[a] In the 1894 German edition this English term is given in parentheses after its German equivalent.

rather the surplus value as a sum, a whole, the unity of these two parts. The proportion in which the profit is divided, and the different legal titles by which this division is sanctioned, are based on the assumption that profit is already in existence. If, therefore, the capitalist is the owner of the capital with which he operates, he pockets the whole profit, or surplus value. It is absolutely immaterial to the labourer whether the capitalist does this, or whether he has to pay a part of it to a third person as its legal proprietor. The reasons for dividing the profit among two kinds of capitalists thus turn imperceptibly into the reasons for the existence of the profit, the surplus value, that is to be divided, and which capital as such derives from the reproduction process regardless of any subsequent division. Since interest is opposed to profit of enterprise, and profit of enterprise to interest, and since they are both counterposed to one another, but not to labour, it follows that profit of enterprise plus interest, i. e., profit, and further surplus value, are derived — from what? From the antithetical form of its two parts! But profit is produced before its division is undertaken, and before there can be any thought of it.

Interest-bearing capital remains as such only so long as the loaned money is actually converted into capital and a surplus is produced with it, of which interest is a part. But this does not rule out that drawing interest, regardless of the process of production, is its organic property. So does labour power preserve its property of producing value only so long as it is employed and realised in the labour process; yet this does not argue against the fact that it is potentially, as a power, an activity which creates value, and that as such it does not spring from the process of production, but rather antecedes it. It is bought as such a capacity for creating value. One might also buy it without setting it to work productively; for purely personal ends, for instance, for personal services, etc. The same applies to capital. It is the borrower's affair whether he employs it as capital, hence actually sets in motion its inherent property of producing surplus value. What he pays for, is in either case the potential surplus value inherently contained in capital as a commodity.[a]

————

Let us now consider profit of enterprise in greater detail.

Since the specific social attribute of capital under the capitalist mode

————

[a] Cf. present edition, Vol. 32, pp. 487-89.

of production — that of being property commanding the labour power of another — becomes fixed, so that interest appears as a part of surplus value produced by capital in this interrelation, the other part of surplus value — profit of enterprise — must necessarily appear as coming not from capital as such, but from the process of production, separated from its specific social attribute, whose distinct mode of existence is already expressed by the term interest on capital. But the process of production, separated from capital, is simply a labour process. Therefore, the industrial capitalist, as distinct from the owner of capital, does not appear as operating capital, but rather as a functionary irrespective of capital, or, as a simple agent of the labour process in general, as a labourer, and indeed as a wage labourer.[a]

Interest as such expresses precisely the existence of the conditions of labour as capital, in their social antithesis to labour, and in their transformation into personal power vis-à-vis and over labour. It represents the ownership of capital as a means of appropriating the products of the labour of others. But it represents this characteristic of capital as something which belongs to it outside the production process and by no means is the result of the specifically capitalist attribute of this production process itself. Interest represents this characteristic not as directly counterposed to labour, but rather as unrelated to labour, and simply as a relationship of one capitalist to another. Hence, as an attribute outside of and irrelevant to the relation of capital to labour. In interest, therefore, in that specific form of profit in which the antithetical character of capital assumes a self-established form, this is done in such a way that the antithesis is completely obliterated and abstracted. Interest is a relationship between two capitalists, not between capitalist and labourer.

On the other hand, this form of interest lends the other portion of profit the qualitative form of profit of enterprise, and further of wages of superintendence. The specific functions which the capitalist as such has to perform, and which fall to him as distinct from and opposed to the labourer, are presented as mere functions of labour. He creates surplus value not because he works *as a capitalist*, but because he *also* works, regardless of his capacity of capitalist. This portion of surplus value is thus no longer surplus value, but its opposite, an equiv-

---

[a] Ibid., pp. 492-93.

alent for labour performed. Due to the estranged character of capital, its antithesis to labour, being relegated to a place outside the actual process of exploitation, namely to the interest-bearing capital, this process of exploitation itself appears as a simple labour process in which the functioning capitalist merely performs a different kind of labour than the labourer. So that the labour of exploiting and the exploited labour both appear identical as labour. The labour of exploiting is just as much labour as exploited labour.[a] The social form of capital falls to interest, but expressed in a neutral and indifferent form. The economic function of capital falls to profit of enterprise, but abstracted from the specific capitalist character of this function.

The same thing passes through the mind of the capitalist in this case as in the case of the reasons indicated in Part II of this book for compensation in the equalisation to average profit. These reasons for compensation which enter the distribution of surplus value as determinants are distorted in a capitalist's mind to appear as bases of origin and the (subjective) justifications of profit itself.

The conception of profit of enterprise as the wages of superintendence, arising from the antithesis of profit of enterprise to interest, is further strengthened by the fact that a portion of profit may, indeed, be separated, and is separated in reality, as wages, or rather the reverse, that a portion of wages appears under the capitalist mode of production as integral part of profit. This portion, as Adam Smith correctly deduced,[b] presents itself in pure form, independently and wholly separated from profit (as the sum of interest and profit of enterprise), on the one hand, and on the other, from that portion of profit which remains, after interest is deducted, as profit of enterprise in the salary of management of those branches of business whose size, etc., permits of a sufficient division of labour to justify a special salary for a manager.[c]

The labour of superintendence and management is naturally required wherever the direct process of production assumes the form of a combined social process, and not of the isolated labour of independent producers.[73] However, it has a double nature.

---

[73] "Superintendence is here" (in the case of the farm owner) "completely dispensed with" (J. E. Cairnes, *The Slave Power*, London, 1862, pp. 48, 49).

---

[a] Cf. present edition, Vol. 32, p. 495. - [b] A. Smith, *An Inquiry into the Nature and Causes of the Wealth of Nations*, Book I, Ch. VI. - [c] Cf. present edition, Vol. 32, pp. 495-96.

On the one hand, all labour in which many individuals cooperate necessarily requires a commanding will to coordinate and unify the process, and functions which apply not to partial operations but to the total activity of the workshop, much as that of an orchestra conductor. This is a productive job, which must be performed in every combined mode of production.

On the other hand — quite apart from any commercial department — this supervision work necessarily arises in all modes of production based on the antithesis between the labourer, as the direct producer, and the owner of the means of production. The greater this antithesis, the greater the role played by supervision. Hence it reaches its peak in the slave system.[74] But it is indispensable also in the capitalist mode of production, since the production process in it is simultaneously a process by which the capitalist consumes labour power. Just as in despotic states, supervision and all-round interference by the government involves both the performance of common activities arising from the nature of all communities, and the specific functions arising from the antithesis between the government and the mass of the people.

In the works of ancient writers, who had the slave system before them, both sides of the work of supervision are as inseparably combined in theory as they were in practice. Likewise in the works of modern economists, who regard the capitalist mode of production as absolute. On the other hand, as I shall presently illustrate with an example, the apologists of the modern slave system utilise the work of supervision quite as much as a justification of slavery, as the other economists do to justify the wage system.

The *villicus* in Cato's time:

"At the head of the estate with slave economy (*familia rustica*) stands the manager (*villicus*, derived from *villa*), who receives and expends, buys and sells, takes instructions from the master, in whose absence he gives orders and metes out punishment.... The manager naturally had more freedom of action than the other slaves; the Magonian books advise that he be permitted to marry, raise children, and have his own funds, and Cato recommends that he be married to the female manager; he alone probably had the prospect of winning his freedom from the master in the event of good behaviour. As for the rest, all formed a common household.... Every slave, including the

[74] * "If the nature of the work requires that the workmen" (viz., the slaves) "should be dispersed over an extended area, the number of overseers, and, therefore, the cost of the labour which requires this supervision, will be proportionately increased" * (Cairnes, l. c., p. 44).

manager himself, was supplied his necessities at his master's expense at definite intervals and fixed rates, and had to get along on them...The quantity varied in accordance with labour, which is why the manager, for example, whose work was lighter than the other slaves', received a smaller ration than they" (Mommsen, *Römische Geschichte*, 2nd ed., 1856, I, pp. 809-10).

Aristotle:

" Ὁ γὰρ δεσπότης οὐκ ἐν τῷ κτᾶσθαι τοὺς δούλους, ἀλλ'ἐν τῷ χρῆσθαι δούλους." ("For the master" — the capitalist — "proves himself such not by obtaining slaves" — ownership of capital which gives him power to buy labour power — "but in employing slaves" — using labourers, nowadays wage labourers, in the production process.) " Ἐστὶ δε αὐτὴ ἡ ἐπιστήμη οὐδὲν μέγα ἔχουσα οὐδὲ σεμνόν" ("But there is nothing great or sublime about this science") "ἃ γὰρ τὸν δοῦλον ἐπίστασθαι δεῖ ποιεῖν, ἐκεῖνον δεῖ ταῦτα ἐπίστασθαι ἐπιτάττειν." ("But whatever the slave must be able to perform, the master must be able to order." "Διὸ ὅσοις ἐξουσία μὴ αὐτοὺς κακοπαθεῖν, ἐπίτροπος λαμβάνει ταύτην τὴν τιμήν, αὐτοὶ δὲ πολιτεύονται ἢ φιλοσοφοῦσιν." ("Whenever the masters are not compelled to plague themselves with supervision, the manager assumes *this honour*, while the masters attend to affairs of state or study philosophy." (Aristotle, *De republica*, Bekker edition, Book I, 7.).

Aristotle says in just so many words that supremacy in the political and economic fields imposes the functions of government upon the ruling powers, and hence that they must, in the economic field, know the art of consuming labour power. And he adds that this supervisory work is not a matter of great moment and that for this reason the master leaves the "honour" of this drudgery to an overseer as soon as he can afford it.

The labour of management and superintendence — so far as it is not a special function determined by the nature of all combined social labour, but rather by the antithesis between the owner of means of production and the owner of mere labour power, regardless of whether this labour power is purchased by buying the labourer himself, as it is under the slave system, or whether the labourer himself sells his labour power, so that the production process also appears as a process by which capital consumes his labour — this function arising out of the servitude of the direct producers has all too often been quoted to justify this relationship. And exploitation, the appropriation of the unpaid labour of others, has quite as often been represented as the reward justly due to the owner of capital for his work; but never better than by a champion of slavery in the United States, a lawyer named O'Connor, at a meeting held in New York on December 19, 1859, under the slogan of "Justice for the South".

"NOW, GENTLEMEN," he said amid thunderous applause, "to that condition of bondage the Negro is assigned by Nature... He has strength, and has the power to labour; but the Nature which created the power denied to him either the intellect to govern, or willingness to work." (Applause.) "Both were denied to him. And that Nature, which deprived him of the will to labour, gave him a master to coerce that will, and to make him a useful... servant in the clime in which he was capable of living useful for himself and for the master who governs him... I maintain that it is not injustice to leave the Negro in the condition in which Nature placed him, to give him a master to govern him ... nor is it depriving him of any of his rights to compel him to labour in return, and afford to that master just compensation for the labour and talent employed in governing him and rendering him useful to himself and to the society."[a]

Now, the wage labourer, like the slave, must have a master who puts him to work and rules over him. And assuming the existence of this relationship of lordship and servitude, it is quite proper to compel the wage labourer to produce his own wages and also the wages of supervision, as compensation for the labour of ruling and supervising him, or

"just compensation for the labour and talent employed in governing him and rendering him useful to himself and to the society".

The labour of superintendence and management, arising as it does out of an antithesis, out of the supremacy of capital over labour, and being therefore common to all modes of production based on class contradictions like the capitalist mode, is directly and inseparably connected, also under the capitalist system, with productive functions which all combined social labour assigns to individuals as their special tasks. The wages of an *epitropos*, or *régisseur*, as he was called in feudal France, are entirely divorced from profit and assume the form of wages for skilled labour whenever the business is operated on a sufficiently large scale to warrant paying for such a MANAGER,[b] although, for all that, our industrial capitalists are far from "attending to affairs of state or studying philosophy".

It has already been remarked by Mr. Ure[75] that it is not the industrial capitalists, but the industrial MANAGERS who are "the soul of our industrial system". Whatever concerns the commercial part of an

---

[75] A. Ure, *Philosophy of Manufactures*, French translation, 1836, I, p. 67, where this Pindar of the manufacturers at the same time testifies that most manufacturers have not the slightest understanding of the mechanism which they set in motion.[c]

---

[a] *New-York Daily Tribune*, No. 5852, December 20, 1859, pp. 7-8. - [b] In the 1894 German edition this English word is given in parentheses after its German equivalent. - [c] Cf. present edition, Vol. 33, pp. 495 and 501.

establishment we have already said all that is necessary in the preceding part.[a]

The capitalist mode of production itself has brought matters to a point where the labour of superintendence, entirely divorced from the ownership of capital, is always readily obtainable. It has, therefore, come to be useless for the capitalist to perform it himself. An orchestra conductor need not own the instruments of his orchestra, nor is it within the scope of his duties as conductor to have anything to do with the "wages" of the other musicians. Cooperative factories furnish proof that the capitalist has become no less redundant as a functionary in production as he himself, looking down from his high perch, finds the big landowner redundant. Inasmuch as the capitalist's labour does not originate in the purely capitalistic process of production, and hence does not cease on its own when capital ceases; inasmuch as it does not confine itself solely to the function of exploiting the labour of others; inasmuch as it therefore originates from the social form of the labour process, from combination and cooperation of many in pursuance of a common result, it is just as independent of capital as that form itself as soon as it has burst its capitalistic shell. To say that this labour is necessary as capitalistic labour, or as a function of the capitalist, only means that the *vulgus* is unable to conceive the forms developed in the lap of the capitalist mode of production, separate and free from their antithetical capitalist character.[b] The industrial capitalist is a worker, compared to the money capitalist, but a worker in the sense of capitalist, i. e., an exploiter of the labour of others. The wage which he claims and pockets for this labour is exactly equal to the appropriated quantity of another's labour and depends directly upon the rate of exploitation of this labour, in so far as he undertakes the effort required for exploitation; it does not, however, depend on the degree of exertion that such exploitation demands, and which he can shift to a manager for moderate pay. After every crisis there are enough ex-manufacturers in the English factory districts who will supervise, for low wages, what were formerly their own factories in the capacity of managers of the new owners, who are frequently their creditors.[76]

[76] In a case known to me, following the crisis of 1868, a bankrupt manufacturer became the paid wage labourer of his own former labourers. The factory was operated after the bankruptcy of its owner by a labourers' cooperative, and its former owner was employed as manager.— *F. E.*

---

[a] See this volume, pp. 287-89. - [b] Cf. present edition, Vol. 32, pp. 497-98 and 504.

The wages of management both for the commercial and industrial manager are completely isolated from the profits of enterprise in the cooperative factories of labourers, as well as in capitalist stock companies. The separation of wages of management from profits of enterprise, purely accidental at other times, is here constant. In a cooperative factory the antagonistic nature of the labour of supervision disappears, because the manager is paid by the labourers instead of representing capital counterposed to them. Stock companies in general — developed with the credit system — have an increasing tendency to separate this work of management as a function from the ownership of capital, be it self-owned or borrowed. Just as the development of bourgeois society witnessed a separation of the functions of judges and administrators from landownership, whose attributes they were in feudal times. But since, on the one hand, the mere owner of capital, the money capitalist, has to face the functioning capitalist, while money capital itself assumes a social character with the advance of credit, being concentrated in banks and loaned out by them instead of by its direct owners, and since, on the other hand, the mere manager who has no title whatever to the capital, whether through borrowing it or otherwise, performs all the real functions pertaining to the functioning capitalist as such, only the functionary remains and the capitalist disappears as superfluous from the production process.

It is manifest from the public accounts of the cooperative factories in England [77] that — after deducting the manager's wages, which form a part of the invested variable capital much the same as wages of other labourers — the profit was higher than the average profit, although at times they paid a much higher interest than did private manufacturers. The source of greater profits in all these cases was greater economy in the application of constant capital. What interests us in this, however, is the fact that here the average profit (= interest + profit of enterprise) presents itself actually and palpably as a magnitude wholly independent of the wages of management. Since the profit was higher here than average profit, the profit of enterprise was also higher than usual.

The same situation is observed in relation to some capitalist stock

---

[77] The accounts quoted here go no further than 1864, since the above was written in 1865.— *F. E.*

companies, such as JOINT-STOCK BANKS[a]. The London and Westminster Bank paid. an annual dividend of 30% in 1863, while the Union Bank of London and others paid 15%. Aside from the directors' salary the interest paid for deposits is here deducted from gross profit. The high profit is to be explained here by the moderate proportion of paid-in capital to deposits. For instance, in the case of the London and Westminster Bank, in 1863: paid-in capital, £1,000,000; deposits, £14,540,275. As for the Union Bank of London, in 1863: paid-in capital, £600,000; deposits, £12,384,173.

Profit of enterprise and wages of supervision, or management, were confused originally due to the antagonistic form assumed in respect to interest by the excess of profit. This was further promoted by the apologetic aim of representing profit not as a surplus value derived from unpaid labour, but as the capitalist's wages for work performed by him. This was met on the part of socialists by a demand to reduce profit actually to what it pretended to be theoretically, namely, mere wages of superintendence.[b] And this demand was all the more obnoxious to theoretical embellishment, the more these wages of superintendence, like any other wage, found their definite level and definite market price, on the one hand, with the development of a numerous class of industrial and commercial managers,[78] and the more they fell, on the other, like all wages for skilled labour, with the general development which reduces the cost of production of specially trained labour power.[79] With the development of cooperation on the part of the labourers, and of stock enterprises on the part of the bourgeoisie, even the last pretext for the confusion of profit of enterprise and wages of management was removed, and profit appeared also in practice

---

[78] "Masters are labourers as well as their journeymen. In this character their interest is precisely the same as that of their men. But they are also either capitalists, or the agents of the capitalists, and in this respect their interest is decidedly opposed to the interests of the workmen" (p. 27). "The wide spread of education among the journeymen mechanics of this country diminishes daily the value of the labour and skill of almost all masters and employers by increasing the number of persons who possess their peculiar knowledge" (p. 30, Hodgskin, *Labour Defended Against the Claims of Capital, etc.*, London, 1825).

[79] "The general relaxation of conventional barriers, the increased facilities of education tend to bring down the wages of skilled labour instead of raising those of the unskilled" (J. St. Mill, *Principles of Political Economy*, 2nd ed., London, 1849, I, p. 479).

---

[a] In the 1894 German edition this English term is given in parentheses after its German equivalent. - [b] Cf. present edition, Vol. 32, p. 497.

as it undeniably appeared in theory, as mere surplus value, a value for which no equivalent was paid, as realised unpaid labour. It was then seen that the functioning capitalist really exploits labour, and that the fruit of his exploitation, when working with borrowed capital, was divided into interest and profit of enterprise, an excess of profit over interest.

On the basis of capitalist production a new swindle develops in stock enterprises with respect to wages of management, in that boards of numerous managers or directors are placed next and above the actual director, for whom supervision and management serve only as a pretext to plunder the stockholders and amass wealth. Very curious details concerning this are to be found in *The City or the Physiology of London Business; with Sketches on 'Change, and the Coffee Houses*, London, 1845.

What bankers and merchants gain by the direction of eight or nine different companies, may be seen from the following illustration: The private balance sheet of Mr. Timothy Abraham Curtis, presented to the Court of Bankruptcy when that gentleman failed, exhibited a sample of the income netted from directorship ... between £800 and £900 a year. Mr. Curtis having been associated with the Courts of the Bank of England, and the East India House, it was considered quite a plum for a public company to acquire his services in the boardroom" (pp. [81,] 82).

The remuneration of the directors of such companies for each weekly meeting is at least one guinea. The proceedings of the Court of Bankruptcy show that these wages of supervision were, as a rule, inversely proportional to the actual supervision performed by these nominal directors.

Chapter XXIV

EXTERNALISATION OF THE RELATIONS OF CAPITAL
IN THE FORM OF INTEREST-BEARING CAPITAL

The relations of capital assume their most external and most fetish-like form in interest-bearing capital. We have here $M — M'$, money creating more money, self-expanding value, without the process that mediates these two extremes. In merchant's capital, $M — C — M'$, there is at least the general form of the capitalistic movement, although it confines itself solely to the sphere of circulation, so that profit appears merely as profit derived from alienation; but it is at least seen to be the product of a social *relation*, not the product of a mere *thing.* The form of merchant's capital at least presents a process, a unity of opposing phases, a movement that breaks up into two opposite actions — the purchase and the sale of commodities. This is obliterated in M — M', the form of interest-bearing capital. For instance, if £1,000 are loaned out by a capitalist at a rate of interest of 5%, the value of £1,000 as a capital for one year $= C + Ci'$; where C is the capital and i' the rate of interest. Hence, $5\% = \frac{5}{100} = \frac{1}{20}$, and $1,000 + 1,000 \times \frac{1}{20} = £1,050$. The value of £1,000 as capital $= £1,050$, i. e., capital is not a simple magnitude. It is a *relationship* of magnitudes, a relationship of the principal sum, as a given value, to itself as a self-expanding value, as a principal sum which has produced a surplus value.[a] And capital as such, as we have seen, assumes this form of a directly self-expanding value for all active capitalists, whether they operate with their own or borrowed capital.

M — M'. We have here the original starting-point of capital, money in the formula M — C — M' reduced to its two extremes M — M', in which $M' = M + \Delta M$, money creating more money. It is the primary and general formula of capital reduced to a meaningless condensation. It is ready capital, a unity of the process of production and the process of circulation, and hence capital yielding a definite surplus value in a particular period of time. In the form of interest-bearing capital this appears directly, unassisted by the processes of production and circulation. Capital appears as a mysterious and self-creating source of interest — the source of its own increase. The *thing* (money, commodity, value) is now capital even as a mere thing, and capital appears as a mere thing. The result of the entire process of reproduction appears as a property inherent in the thing itself. It depends on the owner of the money, i. e., of the commodity in its continually exchangeable form, whether he wants to spend it as money or loan it out as capital. In interest-bearing capital, therefore, this automatic fetish, self-expanding value, money generating money, is brought out in its pure state and in this form it no longer bears the birthmarks of its origin. The social relation is consummated in the relation of a thing, of money, to itself.[b] Instead of the actual transformation of money into capital, we see here only form without content. As in the case of labour power, the use value of money here is its capacity of creating value — a value greater than it contains. Money as

---

a See present edition, Vol. 32, pp. 476-77. - b Ibid., p. 451.

money is potentially self-expanding value and is loaned out as such — which is the form of sale for this singular commodity. It becomes a property of money to generate value and yield interest, much as it is an attribute of pear-trees to bear pears. And the money lender sells his money as just such an interest-bearing thing. But that is not all. The actually functioning capital, as we have seen, presents itself in such a light, that it seems to yield interest not as a functioning capital, but as capital in itself, as money capital.[a]

This, too, becomes distorted. While interest is only a portion of the profit, i. e., of the surplus value, which the functioning capitalist squeezes out of the labourer, it appears now, on the contrary, as though interest were the typical product of capital, the primary matter, and profit, in the shape of profit of enterprise, were a mere accessory and by-product of the process of reproduction. Thus we get the fetish form of capital and the conception of fetish capital. In M — M′ we have the meaningless form of capital, the perversion and materialisation of production relations in their highest degree, the interest-bearing form, the simple form of capital, in which it antecedes its own process of reproduction. It is the capacity of money, or of a commodity, to expand its own value independently of reproduction — which is a mystification of capital in its most flagrant form.

For vulgar political economy, which seeks to represent capital as an independent source of value, of value creation, this form is naturally a veritable find, a form in which the source of profit is no longer discernible, and in which the result of the capitalist process of production — divorced from the process — acquires an independent existence.[b]

It is not until capital is money capital that it becomes a commodity, whose capacity for self-expansion has a definite price quoted in every prevailing rate of interest.

As interest-bearing capital, and particularly in its direct form of interest-bearing money capital (the other forms of interest-bearing capital, which do not concern us here, are derivatives of this form and presuppose its existence), capital assumes its pure fetish form, M — M′ being the subject, the saleable thing. *Firstly*, through its continual existence as money, a form, in which all its specific attributes are obliterated and its real elements invisible. For money is precisely that form in which the distinctive features of commodities as use

---

[a] Ibid., p. 457. - [b] Ibid., p. 458.

values are obscured, and hence also the distinctive features of the industrial capitals which consist of these commodities and conditions of their production. It is that form, in which value — in this case capital — exists as an independent exchange value. In the reproduction process of capital, the money form is but transient — a mere point of transit. But in the money market capital always exists in this form. *Secondly*, the surplus value produced by it, here again in the form of money, appears as an inherent part of it. As the growing process is to trees, so generating money (τόχος)[a] appears innate in capital in its form of money capital.[b]

In interest-bearing capital the movement of capital is contracted. The intervening process is omitted. In this way, a capital = 1,000 is fixed as a thing, which in itself = 1,100, and which is transformed after a certain period into 1,100 just as wine stored in a cellar improves its use value after a certain period. Capital is now a thing, but as a thing it is capital. Money now has love in its body.[c] As soon as it is loaned out, or invested in the reproduction process (inasmuch as it yields interest to the functioning capitalist as its owner, separate from profit of enterprise), interest on it grows, no matter whether it is awake or asleep, is at home or abroad, by day or by night. Thus interest-bearing money capital (and all capital is money capital in terms of its value, or is considered as the expression of money capital) fulfils the most fervent wish of the hoarder.

It is this ingrown existence of interest in money capital as in a thing (this is how the production of surplus value through capital appears here), which occupies Luther's attention so thoroughly in his naïve onslaught against usury.[d] After demonstrating that interest may be demanded if the failure to repay a loan on a definite date caused a loss to a lender, who himself required it to make some payment, or resulted in his missing an opportunity to make a profit on a bargain, for instance, in buying a garden, Luther continues:

"But since I lent you the hundred guilders, you have caused me to suffer two-fold damage because I cannot pay on the one hand and cannot buy on the other and thus must suffer loss on both sides. This is called *duplex interesse, damni emergentis et lucri cessantis*...[e] Having heard that Hans has suffered loss on the hundred guilders which he

---

[a] *Tokos* — to bear, produce, product; figuratively: interest on money lent. - [b] Cf. present edition, Vol. 32, pp. 462-63. - [c] Allusion to a passage in Goethe's *Faust*, Part I, Scene 5, "Auerbach's Cellar in Leipzig"; cf. present edition, Vol. 30, p.112 and Vol. 32, p. 526. - [d] Ibid., pp. 535-38. - [e] Twofold compensation, for the loss incurred and for the gain missed.

lent and demands just recompense for this loss, they rush in and charge such double compensation on every 100 guilders, namely, for expenses incurred and for the inability to buy the garden, just *as though every hundred guilders could grow double interest naturally,* so that whenever they have a hundred guilders, they loan them out and charge for two such losses which however they have not incurred at all... Therefore thou art a usurer, who makes good thine own imagined losses with your neighbour's money, losses which no one has caused thee and which thou canst neither prove nor calculate.The lawyers call such losses *non verum, sed phantasticum interesse*.[a] A loss which each man dreams up for himself... It will not do to say I might incur a loss because I might not have been able to pay or buy. That would mean *ex contingente necessarium*,[b] making something that must be out of something which is not, to turn a thing which is uncertain into a thing which is absolutely sure. Would such usury not eat up the world in a few years?... If the lender accidentally incurs a loss through no fault of his own, he must be recompensed, but it is different in such deals and just the reverse. There he seeks and invents losses to the detriment of his needy neighbours; thus he wants to maintain himself and get rich, to be lazy and idle and to live in luxury and splendour on other people's labour and worry, danger and loss. So that I sit behind the stove and let my hundred guilders gather wealth for me throughout the land, and, because they are only loaned, I keep them safely in my purse without any risk or worry; my friend, who would not like that?" (Martin Luther, *An die Pfarrherrn wider den Wucher zu predigen, etc.*, Wittenberg, 1540).

The conception of capital as a self-reproducing and self-expanding value, lasting and growing eternally by virtue of its innate properties — hence by virtue of the hidden quality of scholasticists — has led to the fabulous fancies of Dr. Price, which outdo by far the fantasies of the alchemists; fancies, in which Pitt[c] believed in all earnest, and which he used as pillars of his financial administration in his laws concerning the sinking fund.[40]

"Money bearing compound interest increases at first slowly. But, the rate of increase being continually accelerated, it becomes in some time so rapid, as to mock all the powers of the imagination. One penny, put out at our Saviour's birth to 5 per cent compound interest, would, before this time, have increased to a greater sum, than would be contained in a hundred and fifty millions of earths, all solid gold. But if put out to simple interest, it would, in the same time, have amounted to no more than seven shillings and four pence half-penny. Our government has hitherto chosen to improve money in the last, rather than the first of these ways."[80]

[80] Richard Price, *An Appeal to the Public on the Subject of the National Debt*, London, 1772, [pp. 18-19]. He cracks the naïve joke: "It is borrowing money at simple interest, in order to improve it at compound interest" (R. Hamilton, *An Inquiry Concerning the Rise and Progress of the National Debt of Great Britain*, 2nd ed., Edinburgh, 1814, [p. 133]). According to this, borrowing would be the safest means also for private people to gather wealth. But if I borrow £100 at 5% annual interest, I have to pay £5 at

---

[a] not real but imagined losses. - [b] making a necessity out of accident. - [c] See present edition, Vol. 33, pp. 222-24.

His fancy flies still higher in his *Observations on Reversionary Payments, etc.,* London, 1772.

"A shilling put out to 6% compound interest at our Saviour's birth" (presumably in the Temple of Jerusalem) "would ... have increased to a greater sum than the whole solar system could hold, supposing it a sphere equal in diameter to the diameter of Saturn's orbit." "A state need never therefore be under any difficulties; for with the smallest savings it may in as little time as its interest can require pay off the largest debts" [pp. XIII, XIV].

What a pretty theoretical introduction to the national debt of England!

Price was simply dazzled by the gargantuan dimensions obtained in a geometrical progression. Since he took no note of the conditions of reproduction and labour, and regarded capital as a self-regulating automaton, as a mere number that increases itself (just as Malthus did with respect to population in his geometrical progression),[a] he was struck by the thought that he had found the law of its growth in the formula $s = c(1 + i)^n$, in which s = the sum of capital + compound interest, c = advanced capital, i = rate of interest (expressed in aliquot parts of 100) and n stands for the number of years in which this process takes place.

Pitt takes Dr. Price's mystification quite seriously. In 1786 the House of Commons had resolved to raise £1 million for the public weal. According to Price, in whom Pitt believed, there was, of course, no better way than to tax the people, so as to "accumulate" this sum after raising it, and thus to spirit away the national debt through the mystery of compound interest. The above resolution of the House of

the end of the year, and even if the loan lasts for 100 million years, I have meanwhile only £100 to loan every year and £5 to pay every year. I can never manage by this process to loan £105 when borrowing £100. And how am I going to pay 5%? By new loans, or, if it is the state, by new taxes. Now, if the industrial capitalist borrows money, and his profit amounts to, say, 15%, he may pay 5% interest, spend 5% for his private expenses (although his appetite grows with his income), and capitalise 5%. In this case, 15% is the precondition for paying continually 5% interest. If this process continues, the rate of profit, for the reasons indicated in former chapters, will fall from 15% to, say, 10%. But Price entirely forgets that the interest of 5% presupposes a rate of profit of 15%, and assumes it to continue with the accumulation of capital. He has nothing whatsoever to do with the actual process of accumulation, but rather only with lending money and getting it back with compound interest. How that is accomplished is immaterial to him, since it is the innate property of interest-bearing capital.

---

[a] [Th. R. Malthus], *An Essay on the Principle of Population...,* London, 1798, pp. 25-26.

Commons was soon followed up by Pitt with a law which ordered the accumulation of £250,000

"until, with the expired annuities, the fund should have grown to £4,000,000 annually" (Act 26, George III, Chap. 31).[a]

In his speech of 1792, in which Pitt proposed that the amount devoted to the sinking fund be increased, he mentioned machines, credit, etc., among the causes of England's commercial supremacy, but as

"the most wide-spread and enduring cause, that of accumulation. This principle, he said, was completely developed in the work of Smith, that genius ... and this accumulation, he continued, was accomplished by laying aside at least a portion of the annual profit for the purpose of increasing the principal, which was to be employed in the same manner the following year, and which thus yielded a continual profit" [pp. 178-79].

With Dr. Price's aid Pitt thus converts Smith's theory of accumulation into enrichment of a nation by means of accumulating debts, and thus arrives at the pleasant progression of an infinity of loans — loans to pay loans.[b]

It had already been noted by Josiah Child, the father of modern banking, that " £100 at 10% would produce in 70 years by compound interest £102,400". (*Traités sur le commerce, etc.*, par J. Child, traduit, etc., Amsterdam et Berlin, 1754, p. 115. Written in 1669.) [41]

How thoughtlessly Dr. Price's conception is applied by modern economists, is shown in the following passage from the *Economist:*

*Capital, with compound interest on every portion of capital saved, is so all-engrossing that all the wealth in the world from which income is derived, has long ago become the interest of capital... All rent is now the payment of interest on capital previously invested in the land." * (*Economist*, July 19, 1851.)

In its capacity of interest-bearing capital, capital claims the ownership of all wealth which can ever be produced, and everything it has received so far is but an instalment for its all-engrossing appetite. By its innate laws, all surplus labour which the human race can ever perform belongs to it. Moloch.

In conclusion, the following hodge-podge by the romantic Müller:

"Dr. Price's enormous increase of compound interest, or of the self-accelerating

---

[a] "An Act for vesting certain sums in commissioners, at the end of every quarter of a year, to be by them applied to the reduction of the national debt" (Anno 26 Georgii III, Regis, cap. 31). - [b] Cf. present edition, Vol. 33, pp. 223-24.

forces of man, presupposes, if it is to produce such enormous effects, an undivided, or uninterrupted, uniform order for several centuries. As soon as capital is divided, cut up into several independently growing shoots, the total process of accumulating forces begins anew. Nature has distributed over a span of about 20 to 25 years the progression of energy which falls on an average to the share of every labourer (!). After the lapse of this time the labourer leaves his career and must transfer the capital accumulated by the compound interest of labour to a new labourer, mostly distributing it among several labourers or children. These must first learn to activate and apply their share of capital, before they can draw any actual compound interest on it. Furthermore, an enormous quantity of capital gained by civil society even in the most restless communities, is gradually accumulated over many years and not employed for any immediate expansion of labour. Instead, as soon as an appreciable sum is gathered together, it is transferred to another individual, a labourer, bank or state, under the head of a loan. And the receiver then sets the capital into actual motion and draws compound interest on it, so that he can easily pledge to pay simple interest to the lender. Finally, the law of consumption, greed, and waste opposes those huge progressions, in which man's powers and their products would multiply if the law of production, or thrift, were alone effective" (A. Müller, *Elemente der Staatskunst,* 1809, Part III, pp. 147-49).

It is impossible to concoct a more hair-raising absurdity in so few lines. Leaving aside the droll confusion of labourer and capitalist, value of labour power and interest on capital, etc., the charging of compound interest is supposed to be explained by the fact that capital is "loaned out" to bring in "compound interest". The method employed by our Müller is characteristic of the romanticism in all walks of life. It is made up of current prejudices, skimmed from the most superficial semblance of things. This incorrect and trite content should then be "exalted" and rendered sublime through a mystifying mode of expression.[a]

The process of accumulation of capital may be conceived as an accumulation of compound interest in the sense that the portion of profit (surplus value) which is reconverted into capital, i. e., serves to absorb more surplus labour, may be called interest. But:

1) Aside from all incidental interference, a large part of available capital is constantly more or less depreciated in the course of the reproduction process, because the value of commodities is not determined by the labour time originally expended in their production, but by the labour time expended in their reproduction, and this decreases continually owing to the development of the social productivity of labour. On a higher level of social productivity, all available capital appears, for this reason, to be the result of a relatively short period

---

[a] Ibid., pp. 225-26.

of reproduction, instead of a long process of accumulation of capital.[81]

2) As demonstrated in Part III of this book, the rate of profit decreases in proportion to the mounting accumulation of capital and the correspondingly increasing productivity of social labour, which is expressed precisely in the relative and progressive decrease of the variable as compared to the constant portion of capital. To produce the same rate of profit after the constant capital set in motion by one labourer increases ten-fold, the surplus labour time would have to increase ten-fold, and soon the total labour time, and finally the entire 24 hours of a day, would not suffice, even if wholly appropriated by capital. The idea that the rate of profit does not shrink is, however, the basis of Price's progression and in general the basis of "ALL-ENGROSSING CAPITAL, WITH COMPOUND INTEREST".[82]

The identity of surplus value and surplus labour imposes a qualitative limit upon the accumulation of capital. This consists of the *total working day*, and the prevailing development of the productive forces and of the population, which limits the number of simultaneously exploitable working days. But if one conceives of surplus value in the meaningless form of interest, the limit is merely quantitative and defies all fantasy.

Now, the conception of capital as a fetish reaches its height in interest-bearing capital, being a conception which attributes to the accumulated product of labour, and at that in the fixed form of money, the inherent secret power, as an automaton, of creating surplus value in geometrical progression, so that the accumulated product of labour, as the *Economist* thinks, has long discounted all the wealth of the world for all time as belonging to it and rightfully coming to it. The

---

[81] See Mill and Carey, and Roscher's mistaken commentary on this score.[a]

[82] "It is clear that no labour, no productive power, no ingenuity, and no art, can answer the overwhelming demands of compound interest. But all saving is made from the revenue of the capitalist, so that actually these demands are constantly made and as constantly the productive power of labour refuses to satisfy them. A sort of balance is, therefore, constantly struck" (*Labour Defended Against the Claims of Capital*, p. 23. By Hodgskin).[b]

---

[a] Marx, presumably, refers to the following works: J. St. Mill, *Principles of Political Economy*, Vol. I, London, 1849, pp. 91-92; H. Ch. Carey, *Principles of Social Science*, Vol. III, Philadelphia, London, Paris, 1859, pp. 71-73; W. Roscher, *Die Grundlagen der Nationalö konomie*, Stuttgart und Augsburg, 1858, pp. 77-79. - [b] Cf. present edition, Vol. 32, p. 431.

product of past labour, the past labour itself, is here pregnant in itself with a portion of present or future living surplus labour. We know, however, that in reality the preservation, and to that extent also the reproduction of the value of products of past labour is *only* the result of their contact with living labour; and secondly, that the domination of the products of past labour over living surplus labour lasts only as long as the relations of capital, which rest on those particular social relations in which past labour independently and overwhelmingly dominates over living labour.

Chapter XXV

CREDIT AND FICTITIOUS CAPITAL

An exhaustive analysis of the credit system and of the instruments which it creates for its own use (credit money, etc.) lies beyond our plan.[1] We merely wish to dwell here upon a few particular points, which are required to characterise the capitalist mode of production in general. We shall deal only with commercial and bank credit. The connection between the development of this form of credit and that of public credit will not be considered here.

I have shown earlier (Buch I, Kap. III, 3, b[a]) how the function of money as a means of payment, and therewith a relation of creditor and debtor between the producer and trader of commodities, develop from the simple circulation of commodities. With the development of commerce and of the capitalist mode of production, which produces solely with an eye to circulation, this natural basis of the credit system is extended, generalised, and worked out. Money serves here, by and large, merely as a means of payment, i. e., commodities are not sold for money, but for a written promise to pay for them at a certain date. For brevity's sake, we may put all these promissory notes under the general head of bills of exchange. Such bills of exchange, in their turn, circulate as means of payment until the day on which they fall due; and they form the actual commercial money. Inasmuch as they ultimately neutralise one another through the balancing of claims and debts, they act absolutely as money, although there is no eventual transformation into actual money. Just as these mutual advances of producers and merchants make up the real foundation of credit, so

---

[a] See present edition, Vol. 35.

does the instrument of their circulation, the bill of exchange, form the basis of credit money proper, of banknotes, etc. These do not rest upon the circulation of money, be it metallic or government-issued paper money, but rather upon the circulation of bills of exchange.

W. Leatham (banker of Yorkshire) writes in his *Letters on the Currency*, 2nd ed., London, 1840:

"I find, then, the amount for the whole of the year of 1839 ... to be £528,493,842" (he assumed that the foreign bills of exchange made up about one-fifth of the total) "and the amount of bills out at one time in the above year, to be £132,123,460" (pp. 55, 56). The bills of exchange make up "one component part greater in amount than all the rest put together" (pp. 3, 4). "This enormous superstructure of bills of exchange rests (!) upon the base formed by the amount of banknotes and gold, and when, by events, this base becomes too much narrowed, its solidity and very existence is endangered" (p. 8). "If I estimate the whole currency"

//he means the banknotes//

"and the amount of the liabilities of the Bank and country bankers, payable on demand, I find a sum of 153 million, which, by law, can be converted into gold ... and the amount of gold to meet this demand only 14 million" (p. 11). "The bills of exchange are not ... placed under any control, except by preventing the abundance of money, and low rates of interest or discount, which create a part of them, and encourage their great and dangerous expansion. It is impossible to decide what part arises out of real *bonâ fide* transactions, such as actual bargain and sale, or what part is FICTITIOUS[a] and mere accommodation paper, that is, where one bill of exchange is drawn to take up another running, in order to raise a fictitious capital, by creating so much currency. In times of abundance and cheap money this I know reaches an enormous amount" (pp. 43-44).

J. W. Bosanquet, *Metallic, Paper, and Credit Currency*, London, 1842:

"An average amount of payments to the extent of upwards of £3,000,000 is settled through the CLEARING HOUSE

//where the London bankers exchange due bills and filed cheques//

every day of business in the year, and the daily amount of money required for the purpose is little more than £200,000" (p. 86).

//In 1889, the total turnover of the CLEARING HOUSE amounted to £7,618$\frac{3}{4}$ million, which, in roughly 300 business days, averages £25$\frac{1}{2}$ million daily. —F. E.//

"Bills of exchange act undoubtedly as CURRENCY,[a] independent of money, inasmuch as they transfer property from hand to hand by endorsement" (pp. 92-93). "It

---

[a] In the 1894 German edition this English word is given in parentheses after its German equivalent.

may be assumed that upon an average there are two endorsements upon every bill in circulation, and ... each bill performs two payments before it becomes due. Upon this assumption it would appear, that by endorsement alone property changed hands, by means of bills of exchange, to the value of twice five hundred and twenty-eight million, or £1,056,000,000, being at the rate of more than £3,000,000 per day, in the course of the year 1839. We may safely therefore conclude, that deposits and bills of exchange together, perform the functions of money, by transferring property from hand to hand without the aid of money, to an extent daily of not less than £18,000,000" (p. 93).

Tooke says the following about credit in general:

"Credit, in its most simple expression, is the confidence which, well, or ill-founded, leads a person to entrust another with a certain amount of capital, in money, or in goods computed at a value in money agreed upon, and in each case payable at the expiration of a fixed term. In the case where the capital is lent in money, that is whether in banknotes, or in a cash credit, or in an order upon a correspondent, an addition for the use of the capital of so much upon every £100 is made to the amount to be repaid. In the case of goods the value of which is agreed in terms of money, constituting a sale, the sum stipulated to be repaid includes a consideration for the use of the capital and for the risk, till the expiration of the period fixed for payment. Written obligations of payment at fixed dates mostly accompany these credits, and the obligations or promissory notes after date being transferable, form the means by which the lenders, if they have occasion for the use of their capital, in the shape whether of money or goods, before the expiration of the term of the bills they hold, are mostly enabled to borrow or to buy on lower terms, by having their own credit strengthened by the names on the bills in addition to their own" (*Inquiry into the Currency Principle*, p. 87).

Ch. Coquelin, *Du Crédit et des Banques dans l'Industrie*, Revue des deux Mondes, 1842, tome 31 [p. 797]:

"In every country the majority of credit transactions takes place within the circle of industrial relations... The producer of the raw material advances it to the processing manufacturer, and receives from the latter a promise to pay on a certain day. The manufacturer, having completed his share of the work, in his turn advances his product on similar terms to another manufacturer, who has to process it further, and in this way credit stretches on and on, from one to the other, right up to the consumer. The wholesale dealer gives the retailer commodities on credit, while receiving credit from a manufacturer or commission agent. All borrow with one hand and lend with the other, sometimes money, but more frequently products. In this manner an incessant exchange of advances, which combine and intersect in all directions, takes place in industrial relations. The development of credit consists precisely in this multiplication and growth of mutual advances, and therein is the real seat of its power."

The other side of the credit system is connected with the development of money-dealing, which, of course, keeps step under capitalist production with the development of dealing in commodity. We have seen in the preceding part (Chap. XIX) how the care of the reserve funds of businessmen, the technical operations of receiving and disbursing money, of international payments, and thus of the bullion trade, are concentrated in the hands of the money dealers. The other side of the credit system — the management of interest-bearing capital, or money capital, develops alongside this money-dealing as a special function of the money dealers. Borrowing and lending money becomes their particular business. They act as middlemen between the actual lender and the borrower of money capital. Generally speaking, this aspect of the banking business consists of concentrating large amounts of the loanable money capital in the bankers' hands, so that, in place of the individual money lender, the bankers confront the industrial and commercial capitalists as representatives of all money lenders. They become the general managers of money capital. On the other hand by borrowing for the entire world of commerce, they concentrate all the borrowers vis-à vis all the lenders. A bank represents a centralisation of money capital, of the lenders, on the one hand, and on the other a centralisation of the borrowers. Its profit is generally made by borrowing at a lower rate of interest than it receives in loaning.

The loanable capital which the banks have at their disposal streams to them in various ways. In the first place, being the cashiers of the industrial capitalists, all the money capital which every producer and merchant keeps as a reserve fund, or receives in payment, is concentrated in their hands. These funds are thus converted into loanable money capital. In this way, the reserve fund of the commercial world, because it is concentrated in a common treasury, is reduced to its necessary minimum, and a portion of the money capital which would otherwise have to lie slumbering as a reserve fund, is loaned out and serves as interest-bearing capital. In the second place, the loanable capital of the banks is formed by the deposits of money capitalists who entrust them with the business of loaning them out. Furthermore, with the development of the banking system, and particularly as soon as banks come to pay interest on deposits, money savings and the temporarily idle money of all classes are deposited with them. Small amounts, each in itself incapable of acting in the capacity of money capital, merge together into large masses and thus form a money power. This aggregation of small amounts must be distinguished as a specific function of the banking system from its mediatory activities between the money capitalists proper and the borrowers. In the final analysis, the revenues, which are but gradually consumed, are also deposited with the banks.

The loan is made (we refer here strictly to commercial credit) by discounting bills of exchange — by converting bills of exchange into money before they come due — and by advances of various kinds: direct advances on personal credit, loans against securities, such as interest-bearing paper, government paper, stocks of all sorts, and, notably, overdrafts against bills of lading, DOCK WARRANTS, and other certified titles of ownership of commodities and overdrawing deposits, etc.

The credit given by a banker may assume various forms, such as bills of exchange on other banks, cheques on them, credit accounts of the same kind, and finally, if the bank is entitled to issue notes — banknotes of the bank itself. A banknote is nothing but a draft upon a banker, payable at any time to the bearer, and given by the banker in place of private drafts. This last form of credit appears particularly important and striking to the layman, first, because this form of credit money breaks out of the confines of mere commercial circulation into general circulation, and serves there as money; and because in most countries the principal banks issuing notes, being a peculiar mixture of national and private banks, actually have the national credit to back them, and their notes are more or less legal tender; because it is apparent here that the banker deals in credit itself, a banknote being merely a circulating token of credit. But the banker also deals in credit in all its other forms, even when he advances the cash money deposited with him. In fact, a banknote simply represents the coin of wholesale trade, and it is always the deposit which carries the most weight with banks. The best proof of this is furnished by the Scottish banks.

Special credit institutions, like special forms of banks, need no further consideration for our purpose.

"The business of bankers ... may be divided into two branches... One branch of the banker's business is to collect capital from those who have not immediate employment for it, and to distribute or transfer it to those who have. The other branch is to receive deposits of the incomes of their customers, and to pay out the amount, as it is wanted for expenditure by the latter in the objects of their consumption... The former being a circulation of *capital*, the latter of CURRENCY.[a]"—"One relates to the concentration of capital on the one hand and the distribution of it on the other, the other is employed in administering the circulation for local purposes of the district." Tooke, *An Inquiry into the Currency Principle*, pp. 36, 37.

---

[a] In the 1894 German edition this English term is given in parentheses after its German equivalent.

//We shall revert to this passage later, in Chapter XXVIII.ᵃ//

Reports of Committees, Vol. VIII. Commercial Distress, Vol. II, Part I, 1847-48, Minutes of Evidence. (Further quoted as Commercial Distress, 1847-48.) In the forties, when discounting bills of exchange in London, 21-day drafts of one bank on another were often accepted in lieu of banknotes. (Testimony of J. Pease, country banker, Nos. 4636 and 4645.) According to the same report, bankers were in the habit of giving such bills of exchange regularly in payment to their customers whenever money was tight. If the receiver wanted banknotes, he had to rediscount this bill. For the banks this amounted to a privilege of coining money. Messrs. Jones, Loyd and Co. made payments in this way "from time immemorial", as soon as money was scarce and the rate of interest rose above 5%. The customer was glad to get such banker's bills because bills from Jones, Loyd and Co. were easier discounted than his own; besides, they often passed through twenty to thirty hands (Ibid., Nos. 901 to 905, 992).

All these forms serve to make the payments claim transferable.

"There is scarcely any shape into which credit can be cast, in which it will not at times be called to perform the functions of money; and whether that shape be a banknote, or a bill of exchange, or a banker's cheque, the process is in every essential particular the same, and the result is the same." Fullarton, *On the Regulation of Currencies*, 2nd ed., London, 1845, p. 38.—"Banknotes are the small change of credit" (p. 51).

The following from J. W. Gilbart's *The History and Principles of Banking*, London, 1834:

"The trading capital of a bank may be divided into two parts: the invested capital, and the borrowed BANKING CAPITALᵇ" (p. 117). "There are three ways of raising a banking or borrowed capital. First, by receiving deposits; secondly, by the issuing of notes; thirdly, by the drawing of bills. If a person will lend me £100 for nothing, and I lend that £100 to another person at four per cent interest, then, in the course of a year, I shall gain £4 by the transaction. Again, if a person will take my 'promise to pay'" ("I PROMISE TO PAY" is the usual formula for English banknotes) "and bring it back to me at the end of the year, and pay me four per cent for it, just the same as though I had lent him 100 sovereigns, then I shall gain £4 by that transaction; and again, if a person in a country town brings me £100 on condition that, twenty-one days afterwards, I shall pay the same amount to a person in London, then whatever interest I can make of the money during the twenty-one days, will be my profit. This is a fair representation of the operations of banking, and of the way in which a banking capital is created by means of deposits, notes, and bills" (p. 117)."The profits of a banker are generally in proportion to the amount of his banking or borrowed capital... To ascertain the real

ᵃ See this volume, p. 439. - ᵇ In the 1894 German edition this English term is given in parentheses after its German equivalent.

profit of a bank, the interest upon the invested capital should be deducted from the gross profit, and what remains is the banking profit" (p. 118)."*The advances of bankers to their customers are made with other people's money*" (p. 146). "Precisely those bankers who do not issue notes, create a banking capital by the discounting of bills. They render their discounts subservient to the increase of their deposits. The London bankers will not discount except for those houses who have deposit accounts with them" (p. 119)."A party who has had bills discounted, and has paid interest on the whole amount, must leave some portion of that amount in the hands of the banker without interest. By this means the banker obtains more than the current rate of interest on the money actually advanced, and raises a banking capital to the amount of the balance left in his hands" (p. 120).

Economising on reserve funds, deposits, cheques:

"Banks of deposit serve to economise the use of the circulating medium. This is done upon the principle of transfer of titles.... Thus it is that banks of deposit ... are enabled to settle a large amount of transactions with a small amount of money. The money thus liberated, is employed by the banker in making advances, by discount or otherwise, to his customers. Hence the principle of transfer gives additional efficiency to the deposit system..." (p. 123). "It matters not whether the two parties, who have dealings with each other, keep their accounts with the same banker or with different bankers; for, as the bankers exchange their cheques with each other at the clearing house.... The deposit system might thus, by means of transfers, be carried to such an extent as wholly to supersede the use of a metallic currency. Were every man to keep a deposit account at a bank, and make all his payments by cheques... cheques become the sole circulating medium. In this case, however, it must be supposed that the banker has the money in his hands, or the cheques would have no value" (p. 124).

Centralisation of local transactions in the hands of the banks is effected 1) through branch banks. Country banks have branch establishments in the smaller towns of their district, and London banks in different districts of the city. 2) Through agencies.

"Each country banker employs a London agent to pay his notes or bills ... and to receive sums that may be lodged by parties residing in London for the use of parties residing in the country" (p. 127). "Each banker accepts the notes of others, but does not reissue them. In all larger cities they come together once or twice a week and exchange their notes. The balance is paid by a draft on London" (p. 134). "It is the object of banking to give facilities to trade, and whatever gives facilities to trade gives facilities to speculation. Trade and speculation are in some cases so nearly allied, that it is impossible to say at what precise point trade ends and speculation begins.... Wherever there are banks, capital is more readily obtained, and at a cheaper rate. The cheapness of capital gives facilities to speculation, just in the same way as the cheapness of beef and of beer gives facilities to gluttony and drunkenness" (pp. 137, 138). "As banks of circulation always issue their own notes, it would seem that their discounting business was carried on exclusively with this last description of capital, but it is not so. It is very possible for a banker to issue his own notes for all the bills he discounts, and yet nine-tenths of the bills in his possession shall represent real capital. For, although in the first instance, the banker's notes are given for the bill, yet these notes may not stay in circulation until the bill becomes due — the bill may have three months to run, the notes may return in three days" (p. 172). "The overdrawing of a cash credit account is a regular matter of business; it is, in fact, the purpose for which the cash credit has been granted.... Cash credits are granted not only upon personal security, but also upon the security of the Public Funds" (pp. 174, 175). "Capital advanced, by way of loan, on the securities of merchandise, would produce the same effects as if advanced in the discounting of bills. If a party borrows £100 on the security of his merchandise, it is the same as though he had sold his merchandise for a £100 bill, and got it discounted with the banker. By obtaining this advance he is enabled to hold over this merchandise for a better market, and avoids a sacrifice which, otherwise, he might be induced to make, in order to raise the money for urgent purposes" (pp. 180-81).

The Currency Theory Reviewed, etc., pp. 62-63:

"It is unquestionably true that the £1,000 which you deposit at A today may be re-issued tomorrow, and form a deposit at B. The day after that, reissued from B, it may form a deposit at C ... and so on to infinitude; and that the same £1,000 in money may thus, by a succession of transfers, multiply itself into a sum of deposits absolutely indefinite. It is possible, therefore, that *nine-tenths of all the deposits in the United Kingdom may have no existence beyond their record in the books of the bankers* .... Thus in Scotland, for instance, currency //mostly paper money at that!// has never exceeded £3 million, the deposits in the banks are estimated at £27 million.... Unless A RUN ON THE BANKS[a] be made, the same £1,000 would, if sent back upon its travels, cancel with the same facility a sum equally indefinite. As the same £1,000 with which you cancel your debt to a tradesman today, may cancel his debt to the merchant tomorrow, the merchant's debt to the bank the day following, and so on without end; so the same £1,000 may pass from hand to hand, and bank to bank, and cancel any conceivable sum of deposits."

//We have seen that Gilbart knew even in 1834 that

"whatever gives facilities to trade gives facilities to speculation. Trade and speculation are in some cases so nearly allied, that it is impossible to say at what precise point trade ends and speculation begins".

The easier it is to obtain advances on unsold commodities, the more such advances are taken, and the greater the temptation to manufacture commodities, or dump already manufactured commodities in distant markets, just to obtain advances of money on them. To what extent the entire business world of a country may be seized by such swindling, and what it finally comes to, is amply illustrated by the history of English trade during 1845-47. It shows us what credit can accomplish. Before passing on to the following examples, a few preliminary remarks.

At the close of 1842 the pressure which English industry suffered almost uninterruptedly since 1837, began to abate. During the follow-

---

[a] In the 1894 German edition this English expression is given in parentheses after its German equivalent.

ing two years foreign demand for English manufactured goods increased still more; 1845 and 1846 marked a period of greatest prosperity.. In 1843 the Opium War had opened China to English commerce.[42] The new market gave a new impetus to the further expansion of industry, particularly the cotton industry. "How can we ever produce too much? We have to clothe 300 million people," a Manchester manufacturer said to this writer at the time. But all the newly erected factory buildings, steam-engines, and spinning and weaving machines did not suffice to absorb the surplus value pouring in from Lancashire. With the same zeal as was shown in expanding production, people engaged in building railways. The thirst for speculation of manufacturers and merchants at first found gratification in this field, and as early as in the summer of 1844. Stock was fully underwritten, i. e., so far as there was money to cover the initial payments. As for the rest, time would show! But when further payments were due— Question 1059, C. D. 1848/57, indicates that the capital invested in railways in 1846-47 amounted to £75 million— recourse had to be taken to credit, and in most cases the basic enterprises of the firm had also to bleed.

And in most cases these basic enterprises were already overburdened. The enticingly high profits had led to far more extensive operations than justified by the available liquid resources. Yet there was credit — easy to obtain and cheap. The bank discount rate stood low: $1\frac{3}{4}$ to $2\frac{3}{4}$ % in 1844, less than 3% until October 1845, rising to 5% for a while (February 1846), then dropping again to $3\frac{1}{4}$ % in December 1846. The Bank of England had an unheard-of supply of gold in its vaults. All inland quotations were higher than ever before. Why then allow this splendid opportunity to escape? Why not go in for all one was worth? Why not send all one could manufacture to foreign markets which pined for English goods? And why should not the manufacturer himself pocket the double gain arising from selling yarn and fabrics in the Far East, and the return cargo in England?

Thus arose the system of mass consignments to India and China against advance payments, and this very soon developed into a system of consignments purely for the sake of getting advances, as described in greater detail in the following notes, which led inevitably to overflooding the markets and a crash.

The crash was precipitated by the crop failure of 1846. England, and particularly Ireland, required enormous imports of foodstuffs, notably corn and potatoes. But the countries which supplied them could be paid with the products of English industry only to a very limited extent. Precious metals had to be given out. Gold worth at least nine million was sent abroad. Of this amount no less than seven and a half million came from the treasury of the Bank of England, whose freedom of action on the money market was thereby considerably impaired. Other banks, whose reserves were deposited with the Bank of England and were practically identical with those of that Bank, were thus also compelled to curtail accommodation of money. The rapid and easy flow of payments was obstructed, first here and there, then generally. The banking discount rate, still 3 to $3\frac{1}{2}$% in January 1847, rose to 7% in April, when the first panic broke out. The situation eased somewhat in the summer ($6\frac{1}{2}$%, 6%), but when the new crop failed as well panic broke out afresh and even more violently. The official minimum bank discount rose in October to 7 and in November to 10%; i. e., the overwhelming mass of bills of exchange was discountable only at outrageous rates of interest, or no longer discountable at all. The general cessation of payments caused the failure of several leading and very many medium-sized and small firms. The Bank itself was in danger due to the limitations imposed by the artful Bank Act of 1844.[a] The government yielded to the general clamour and suspended the Bank Act on October 25, thereby eliminating the absurd legal fetters imposed on the Bank. Now it could throw its supply of banknotes into circulation without hindrance. The credit of these banknotes being in practice guaranteed by the credit of the nation, and thus unimpaired, the money stringency was thus instantly and decisively relieved. Naturally, quite a number of hopelessly enmeshed large and small firms failed nevertheless, but the peak of the crisis was overcome, the banking discount dropped to 5% in December, and in the course of 1848 a new wave of business activity began which took the edge off the revolutionary movements on the continent in 1849, and which inaugurated in the fifties an unprecedented industrial prosperity, but then ended again—in the crash of 1857.—*F. E.*//

I. A document issued by the House of Lords in 1848 deals with the colossal depreciation of government paper and bonds during the 1847 crisis. According to it the depreciation of October 23, 1847, compared with the level in February of the same year, amounted to:

---

[a] See this volume, Chapter XXXIV.

On English government bonds £93,824,217
On dock and canal stock £1,358,288
On railway stock £19,579,820

Total £114,762,325

II. With reference to the swindle in East Indian trade, in which drafts were no longer drawn because commodities were being bought, but rather commodities were bought to be able to make out discountable drafts convertible into money, the *Manchester Guardian* of November 24, 1847, remarks:

Mr. A in London instructs a Mr. B. to buy from the manufacturer C in Manchester commodities for shipment to a Mr. D in East India. B pays C in six months' drafts to be made out by C on B. B secures himself by six months' drafts on A. As soon as the goods are shipped A makes out six months' drafts on D against the mailed bill of lading.

"The shipper and the co-signee were thus both put in possession of funds — months before they actually paid for the goods; and, very commonly, these bills were renewed at maturity, on pretence of affording time for the returns in a 'long trade'. Unfortunately, losses by such a trade, instead of leading to its contraction, led directly to its increase. The poorer men became, the greater need they had to purchase, in order to make up, by new advances, the capital they had lost on the past adventures. Purchases thus became, not a question of supply and demand, but the most important part of the finance operations of a firm labouring under difficulties. But this is only one side of the picture. What took place in reference to the export of goods at home, was taking place in the purchase and shipment of produce abroad. Houses in India, who had credit to pass their bills, were purchasers of sugar, indigo, silk, or cotton — not because the prices advised from London by the last overland mail promised a profit on the prices current in India, but because former drafts upon the London house would soon fall due, and must be provided for. What was so simple as to purchase a cargo of sugar, pay for it in bills upon the London house at ten months' date, transmit the shipping documents by the overland mail; and, in less than two months the goods on the high seas...were pawned in Lombard Street — putting the London house in funds eight months before the drafts against those goods fell due. And all this went on without interruption or difficulty, as long as bill-brokers had abundance of money 'at call,' to advance on bills of lading and dock warrants, and to discount, without limit, the bills of India houses drawn upon the eminent firms in Mincing Lane."

//This fraudulent procedure remained in vogue so long as goods to and from India had to round the Cape in sailing vessels. But ever since they are being shipped in steamboats via the Suez Canal this method of fabricating fictitious capital has been deprived of its basis — the long freight voyage. And ever since the telegraph informs the English businessman about the Indian market and the Indian merchant about the English market, on the same day this method has become totally impracticable.— *F. E.*//

III. The following is taken from the quoted Report on Commercial Distress, 1847-48:

"In the last week of April 1847, the Bank of England advised the Royal Bank of Liverpool that it would thereafter reduce its discount business with the latter bank by one-half. The announcement operated with peculiar hardship on this account, that the payments into Liverpool had latterly been much more in bills than in cash; and the merchants who generally brought to the Bank a large proportion of cash with which to pay their acceptances, had latterly been able to bring only bills which they had received for their cotton and other produce, and that increased very rapidly as the difficulties increased.... The acceptances ... which the Bank had to pay for the merchants, were acceptances drawn chiefly upon them from abroad, and they have been accustomed to meet those acceptances by whatever payment they received for their produce.... The bills that the merchants brought ... in lieu of cash... were of various dates, and of various descriptions; a considerable number of them were bankers' bills, of three months' date, the large bulk being cotton bills. These bills of exchange, when bankers' bills, were accepted by London bankers, and by merchants in every trade that we could mention — the Brazilian, the American, the Canadian, the West Indian.... The merchants did not draw upon each other; but the parties in the interior, who had purchased produce from the merchants, remitted to the merchants bills on London bankers, or bills on various parties in London, or bills upon anybody. The announcement of the Bank of England caused a reduction of the maturity terms of bills drawn against sales of foreign products, frequently extending to over three months" (pp. 26, 27).

The period of prosperity in England from 1844 to 1847, was, as described above, connected with the first great railway swindle. The above-named report makes the following reference to the effect of this swindle on business in general:

In April 1847 "almost all mercantile houses had begun TO STARVE THEIR BUSINESS[a] more or less ... by taking part of their commercial capital for railways" (p. 42). "Loans were made on railway shares at a high rate of interest, say, 8%, by private individuals, by bankers and by fire-offices" (p. 66). "Loans to so great an extent by commercial houses to railways induced them to lean too much upon banks by the discount of paper, whereby to carry on their commercial operations" (p. 67). (Question:) "Should you say that the railway calls had had a great effect in producing the pressure which there was" //on the money market// "in April and October" //1847//? — (Answer:) "I should say that they had had hardly any effect at all in producing the pressure in April; I should imagine that up to April, and up, perhaps, to the summer, they had increased the power of bankers in some respects rather than diminished it; for the expenditure had not been nearly so rapid as the calls; the consequence was, that most of the banks had rather a large amount of railway money in their hands in the beginning of the year."

//This is corroborated in numerous statements made by bankers in C. D. 1848-57.//

---

[a] In the 1894 German edition this English expression is given in parentheses after its German equivalent.

"In the summer that melted gradually away, and on the 31st of December it was materially less. One cause ... of the pressure in October was the gradual diminution of the railway money in the bankers' hands; between the 22nd of April and the 31st of December the railway balances in our hands were reduced one-third; and the railway calls have also had this effect ... throughout the Kingdom; they have been gradually draining the deposits of bankers" (pp. 43, 44).

Samuel Gurney //head of the ill-famed firm of Overend, Gurney and Co.// similarly says:

"During the year 1846 ... there had been a considerable demand for capital, for the establishment of railways ... but it did not increase the value of money.... There was a condensation of small sums into large masses, and those large masses were used in our market; so that, upon the whole, the effect was to throw more money into the money market of the City than to take it out" [p. 159].

A. Hodgson, Director of the Liverpool Joint-Stock Bank, shows how much bills of exchange may constitute a reserve for bankers:

"It has been our habit to keep at least nine-tenths of all our deposits, and all money we have of other persons, in our bill case, in bills that are falling due from day to day... so much so, that during the time of the run, the bills falling due were almost equal to the amount of the run upon us day by day" (p. 53).

Speculative bills.

"5092. Who were those bills" (against sold cotton) generally accepted by?" — //R.Gardner, the cotton manufacturer repeatedly mentioned in this work:// "Produce brokers: a person buys cotton, and places it in the hands of a broker, and draws upon that broker, and gets the bills discounted." — "5094. And they are taken to the banks at Liverpool, and discounted? — Yes, and in other parts besides.... I believe if it had not been for the accommodation thus granted, and principally by the Liverpool banks, cotton would never have been so high last year as it was by $1\frac{1}{2}$ d. or 2d. a pound." — "600. You have stated that a vast amount of bills were put in circulation, drawn by speculators upon cotton brokers in Liverpool; does that system extend to your advance on acceptances upon colonial and foreign produce as well as on cotton?" //A. Hodgson, a Liverpool banker:// "It refers to all kinds of colonial produce, but to cotton most especially." — "601. Do you, as a banker, discourage as far as you can that description of paper? — We do not; we consider it a very legitimate description of paper, when kept in moderation. This description of paper is frequently renewed."

Swindling in the East Indian and Chinese Market, 1847.— Charles Turner (head of one of the leading East Indian houses in Liverpool):

"We are all aware of the events which have taken place as regards the Mauritius trade, and other trades of that kind. The brokers have been in the habit ... not only of advancing upon goods after their arrival to meet the bills drawn against those goods, which is perfectly legitimate, and upon the bills of lading ... but ... they have advanced upon the produce before it was shipped, and in some cases before it was manufactured. Now, to speak of my own individual instance: I have bought bills in Calcutta to the extent of six or seven thousand pounds in one particular instance; the proceeds of the bills went down to the Mauritius, to help in the growth of sugar; those bills came to England, and above half of them were protested; for when the shipments of sugar came forward, instead of being held to pay those bills, it had been mortgaged to third parties... before it was shipped, in fact almost before it was boiled" (p. 78). "Now manufacturers are insisting upon cash but it does not amount to much, because if a buyer has any credit in London, he can draw upon the house, and get the bill discounted; he goes to London, where discounts now are cheap; he gets the bill discounted, and pays cash to the manufacturer.... It takes twelve months, at least, for the shipper of goods to get his return from India ... a man with ten or fifteen thousand pounds would go into the Indian trade; he would open a credit with a house in London, to a considerable extent, giving that house one per cent; he, drawing upon the house in London, on the understanding that the proceeds of the goods that go out are to be returned to the house in London, but it being perfectly understood by both parties that the man in London is to be kept out of a cash advance; that is to say, in other words, the bills are to be renewed till the proceeds come home. The bills were discounted at Liverpool, Manchester ... or in London ... many of them lie in the Scotch banks" (p. 79).— "786. There is one house which failed in London the other day, and in examining their affairs, a transaction of this sort was proved to have taken place; there is a house of business at Manchester, and another at Calcutta; they opened a credit account with a house in London to the extent of £200,000; that is to say, the friends of this house in Manchester, who consigned goods to the East India House from Glasgow and from Manchester, had the power of drawing upon the house in London to the extent of £200,000; at the same time, there was an understanding that the corresponding house in Calcutta were to draw upon the London house to the extent of £200,000; with the proceeds of those bills sold in Calcutta, they were to buy other bills, and remit them to the house in London, to take up the first bills drawn from Glasgow or Manchester... There would have been £600,000 of bills created upon that transaction." — "971. At present, if a house in Calcutta purchase a cargo" //for England//, "and give their own bills upon their correspondent in London in payment, and they send the bills of lading home to this country, those bills of lading ... immediately become available to them in Lombard Street for advances, and they have eight months' use of the money before their correspondents are called upon to pay."

IV. In 1848 a secret committee of the House of Lords investigated the causes of the 1847 crisis. The evidence given to the committee was not published, however, until 1857 (Minutes of Evidence, taken before the Secret Committee of the H. of L. appointed to inquire into the Causes of Distress, etc., 1857; quoted as C. D. 1848/57). Here Mr. Lister, Director of the Union Bank of Liverpool, testified, among other things, to the following:

"2444. In the spring of 1847 there was an undue extension of credit... because a man transferred property from business into railways and was still anxious to carry on the same extent of business. He probably first thought that he could sell the railway shares at a profit and replace the money in his business. Perhaps he found that could not be done, and he then got credit in his business where formerly he paid in cash. There was an extension of credit from that circumstance."

"2500. Were those bills ... upon which the banks had sustained a loss by holding them, principally bills upon corn or bills upon cotton?" — "They were bills upon all kinds of produce, corn and cotton and sugar, all foreign produce of all descriptions. There was scarcely any thing perhaps with the exception of oil, that did not go down." — "2506. A broker who accepts a bill will not accept it without a good margin as to the value."

"2512. There are two kinds of bills drawn against produce; the first is the original bill drawn abroad upon the merchant, who imports it.... The bills which are drawn against produce frequently fall due before the produce arrives. The merchant, therefore, when it arrives, if he has not sufficient capital, has to pledge that produce with the broker till he has time to sell that produce. Then a new species of bill is immediately drawn by the merchant in Liverpool upon the broker, on the security of that produce.... Then it is the business of the banker to ascertain from the broker whether he has the produce, and to what extent he has advanced upon it. It is his business to see that the broker has property to protect himself if he makes a loss."

"2516. We also receive bills from abroad.... A man buys a bill abroad on England, and sends it to a house in England; we cannot tell whether that bill is drawn prudently or imprudently, whether it is drawn for produce or for wind."

"2533. You said that almost every kind of foreign produce was sold at a great loss. Do you think that that was in consequence of undue speculation in that produce? — It arose from a very large import, and there not being an equal consumption to take it off. It appears that consumption fell off a great deal." — "2534. In October produce was almost unsaleable."

How a general *sauve qui peut*[a] develops at the height of a crisis is revealed in the same report by a first-rate expert, the esteemed crafty Quaker, Samuel Gurney, of Overend, Gurney and Co.:

"1262. ... When a panic exists a man does not ask himself what he can get for his banknotes, or whether he shall lose one or two per cent by selling his exchequer bills, or three per cent. If he is under the influence of alarm he does not care for the profit or loss, but makes himself safe and allows the rest of the world to do as they please."

V. Concerning the mutual satiation of the two markets Mr. Alexander, a merchant in the East India trade, testifies before the Committee of the Lower House on the Bank Act of 1857 (quoted as B. C. 1857):

"4330. At the present moment, if I lay out 6s. in Manchester, I get 5s. back in India; if I lay out 6s. in India, I get 5s. back in London."

So that the Indian market is, therefore, drugged by England, and the English by India. This was, indeed, the case in the summer of 1857, barely ten years after the bitter experience of 1847!

---

[a] save yourself if you can

Chapter XXVI

ACCUMULATION OF MONEY CAPITAL.
ITS INFLUENCE ON THE INTEREST RATE

"In England there takes place a steady accumulation of additional wealth, which has a tendency ultimately to assume the form of money. Now next in urgency, perhaps, to the desire to acquire money, is the wish to part with it again for some species of investment that shall yield either interest or profit; for money itself, as money, yields neither. Unless, therefore, concurrently with this ceaseless influx of surplus capital, there is a gradual and sufficient extension of the field for its employment, we must be subject to periodical accumulations of money seeking investment, of more or less volume, according to the movement of events. For a long series of years, the grand absorbent of the surplus wealth of England was our public debt.... As soon as in 1816 the debt reached its maximum, and operated no longer as an absorbent, a sum of at least seven-and-twenty million per annum was necessarily driven to seek other channels of investment. What was more, various return payments of capital were made.... Enterprises which entail a large capital and create an opening from time to time for the excess of unemployed capital ... are absolutely necessary, at least in our country, so as to take care of the periodical accumulations of the superfluous wealth of society, which is unable to find room in the usual fields of application" (*The Currency Theory Reviewed*, Edinburgh, 1845, pp. 32-34).

Of 1845 the same work says:

"Within a very recent period prices have sprung upwards from the lowest point of depression.... Consols touch par.... The bullion in the vaults of the Bank of England has ... exceeded in amount the treasure held by that establishment since its institution. Shares of every description range at prices on the average wholly unprecedented, and interest has declined to rates which are all but nominal. If these be not evidences that another heavy accumulation of unemployed wealth exists at this hour in England, that another period of speculative excitement is at hand" (ibid., p. 36).

"Although ... the import of bullion is no sure sign of gain upon the foreign trade, yet, in the absence of any explanatory cause, it does *prima facie* represent a portion of it" (J. G. Hubbard, *The Currency and the Country*, London, 1843, p. 41). "Suppose ... that at a period of steady trade, fair prices ... and full, but not redundant circulation, a deficient harvest should give occasion for an import of corn, and an export of gold to the value of five million. The circulation"

//meaning, as we shall presently see, idle money capital rather than means of circulation—*F. E.*//

"would of course be reduced by the same amount. An equal quantity of the circulation might still be held by individuals, but the deposits of merchants at their bankers, the balances of bankers with their money brokers, and the reserve in their till, will all be diminished, and the immediate result of this reduction in the amount of unemployed capital will be a rise in the rate of interest. I will assume from 4 per cent to 6. Trade being in a sound state, confidence will not be shaken, but credit will be more highly valued" (ibid., p. 42). "But imagine ... that all prices fall.... The superfluous currency returns to the bankers in increased deposits—the abundance of unemployed capital lowers the rate of interest to a minimum, and this state of things lasts until either a return of higher prices or a more active trade call the dormant currency into service, or until it is absorbed by investments in foreign stocks or foreign goods" (p. 68).

The following extracts are also taken from the Parliamentary Report on Commercial Distress, 1847-48.—Owing to the crop failure and famine of 1846-47 large-scale imports of foodstuffs became necessary.

"These circumstances caused the imports of the country to be very largely in excess over ... exports ... a considerable drain upon the banks, and an increased application to the discount brokers ... for the discount of bills.... They began to scrutinise the bills. ...The facilities of houses then began to be very seriously curtailed, and the weak houses began to fail. Those houses which ... relied upon their credit... went down. This increased the alarm that had been previously felt; and the bankers and others finding that they would not rely with the same degree of confidence that they had previously done upon turning their bills and other money securities into banknotes, for the purpose of meeting their engagements, still further curtailed their facilities, and in many cases refused them altogether; they locked up their banknotes, in many instances to meet their own engagements; they were afraid of parting with them.... The alarm and confusion were increased daily; and unless Lord John Russell .... had issued the letter to the Bank ... universal bankruptcy would have been the issue" (pp. 74-75).

Russell's letter suspended the Bank Act.—The previously mentioned Charles Turner testifies:

"Some houses had large means, but not available. The whole of their capital was locked up in estates in the Mauritius, or indigo factories, or sugar factories. Having incurred liabilities to the extent of £500,000 or £600,000 they had no available assets to pay their bills, and eventually it proved that to pay their bills they were entirely dependent upon their credit" (p. 81).

The aforementioned S. Gurney said:

[1664]: "At present" (1848) "there is a limitation of transaction and a great superabundance of money." — "1763. I do not think it was owing to the want of capital; it was owing to THE ALARM [a] that existed that the rate of interest got so high."

In 1847 England paid at least £9 million gold to foreign countries of imported foodstuffs. Of this amount £7$\frac{1}{2}$ million came from the Bank of England and 1$\frac{1}{2}$ million from other sources (p. 245). —Morris, Governor of the Bank of England:

"The public stocks in the country and canal and railway shares had already by the 23rd of October 1847 been depreciated in the aggregate to the amount of £114,752,225" (p. 312).

[a] In the 1894 German edition this English term is given in parentheses after its German equivalent.

Again Morris, when questioned by Lord G. Bentinck:

"Are you not aware that all property invested in stocks and produce of every description was depreciated in the same way; that raw cotton, raw silk and unmanufactured wool were sent to the continent at the same depreciated price... and that sugar, coffee and tea were sacrificed as at forced sales? — It was ... inevitable that the country should make a considerable sacrifice for the purpose of meeting the efflux of bullion which had taken place in consequence of the large importation of food." — [3848] "Do not you think it would have been better to trench upon the £8,000,000 lying in the coffers of the Bank than to have endeavoured to get the gold back again at such a sacrifice? — *No, I do not.*" —

Now to the commentaries on such heroism. Disraeli questions Mr. W. Cotton, a Director and former Governor of the Bank of England:

"What was the rate of dividend paid to the Bank proprietors in 1844? — It was 7 per cent for the year." — "What is the dividend ... for 1847? — Nine per cent." — "Does the Bank pay the income tax for its proprietors in this year? — It does." — "Did it do so in 1844? — It did not." [83]— "Then this Bank Act" (of 1844) "has worked very well for the proprietors?... The result is, that since the passing of the Act, the dividend to the proprietors has been raised from 7 per cent to 9 per cent, and the income tax, that previously to the Act was paid by the proprietors, is now paid by the Bank? — *It is so.*" (Nos. 4356-61).

Mr. Pease, a country banker, had the following to say concerning hoarding in banks during the crisis of 1847:

"4605. As the Bank was obliged still to raise its rate of interest, every one seemed apprehensive; country bankers increased the amount of bullion in their hands, and increased their reserve of notes, and many of us who were in the habit of keeping, perhaps, a few hundred pounds of gold and banknotes, immediately laid up thousands in our desks and drawers, as there was an uncertainty about discounts, and about our bills being current in the market, a general hoarding ensued."

A member of the Committee remarks:

"4691. Then, whatever may have been the cause during the last 12 years, the result has been rather in favour of the Jew and money dealer, than the productive classes generally."

How much a money dealer takes advantage of times of crisis is revealed by Tooke:

[83] In other words, formerly they first fixed the dividend, and then deducted the income tax as the dividend was paid to the individual stockholder; after 1844, however, the Bank first paid the income tax on its total profit, and then paid the dividend "FREE OF INCOME TAX". The same nominal percentages are, therefore, higher in the latter case by the amount of the tax.— *F. E.*

"In the hardware districts of Warwickshire and Staffordshire, a great many orders for goods were declined to be accepted in 1847, because the rate of interest which the manufacturer had to pay for discounting his bills more than absorbed all his profit" (No. 5451).

Let us now take another parliamentary report cited earlier: Report from the Select Committee on Bank Acts, communicated from the Commons to the Lords, 1857 (quoted further as B. C. 1857). In it Mr. Norman, Director of the Bank of England and a leading figure among the champions of the CURRENCY PRINCIPLE,[43] is interrogated as follows:

"3635. You stated, that you consider that the rate of interest depends, not upon the amount of notes, but upon the supply and demand of capital. Will you state what you include in 'capital', besides notes and coin? — I believe that the ordinary definition of 'capital' is commodities or services used in production." — "3636. Do you mean to include all commodities in the word 'capital' when you speak of the rate of interest? — All commodities used in production." — "3637.You include all that in the word 'capital', when you speak of what regulates the rate of interest? — Yes. Supposing a cotton manufacturer to want cotton for his factory, the way in which he goes to work to obtain it is, probably, by getting an advance from his banker, and with the notes so obtained he goes to Liverpool, and makes a purchase.What he really wants is the cotton; he does not want the notes or the gold, except as a means of getting the cotton. Or he may want the means of paying his workmen; then again, he borrows the notes, and he pays the wages of the workmen with the notes; and the workmen, again, require food and lodging, and the money is the means of paying for those." — "3638. But interest is paid for the money? — It is, in the first instance; but take another case. Supposing he buys the cotton on credit, without going to the bank for an advance, then the difference between the ready-money price and the credit price at the time at which he is to pay for it is the measure of the interest. Interest would exist if there was no money at all."

This self-complacent rubbish is quite fitting for this pillar of the CURRENCY PRINCIPLE. First, the brilliant discovery that banknotes or gold are means of buying something, and that they are not borrowed for their own sake. And this is advanced to explain that the rate of interest is regulated — but by what? By the demand and supply of commodities, which heretofore were known to regulate only the market prices of commodities. However, very different rates of interest are compatible with the same market prices of commodities.— But now this cunning. He is confronted with the correct remark: "But interest is paid for the money," which, of course, contains the implication: "What has interest received by the banker, who does not deal in commodities at all, to do with these commodities? And do not manufacturers receive money at the same rate of interest, although they invest it in widely different markets, hence in markets with widely different conditions of demand and supply for the commodities used in production?" All that this celebrated genius has to say in reply to these questions is that if the manufacturer buys cotton on credit "the difference between the price and the credit price at the time at which he is to pay for it is the measure of the interest". Quite the contrary. The prevailing rate of interest whose regulation the great intellect Norman was asked to explain is the measure of the difference between the cash price and the credit price until payment is due. First the cotton is to be sold at its cash price, and this is determined by the market price, itself regulated by the state of supply and demand. Say the price = £1,000. This concludes the transaction between the manufacturer and the cotton broker so far as buying and selling is concerned. Now comes a second transaction. This is one between lender and borrower. The value of £1,000 is advanced to the manufacturer in cotton, and he has to repay it in money, say, in three months. And three months' interest for £1,000, determined by the market rate of interest, makes up the extra charge over and above the cash price. The price of cotton is determined by supply and demand. But the price of the advanced value of cotton, of £1,000 advanced for three months, is determined by the rate of interest. And this fact, that cotton is thus transformed into money capital, proves to Mr. Norman that interest would exist even if there had been no money. If there were no money at all, there would certainly be no general rate of interest.

There is, to begin with, a vulgar conception of capital as "commodities used in production". In so far as these commodities serve as capital, their value as *capital*, as distinct from their value as *commodities*, is expressed in the profit which is derived from their productive or mercantile employment. And the rate of profit under all circumstances has something to do with the market price of the purchased commodities and with their supply and demand, but is determined by entirely different circumstances. And there is no doubt that the interest rate is generally limited by the rate of profit. But Mr. Norman should tell us just how this limit is determined. And it is determined by the supply and demand of money capital *as distinguished* from the other forms of capital. It could be further asked: How are demand and supply of money capital determined? It is doubtlessly true that a tacit connection exists between the supply of material capital and the supply of money capital, and, likewise, that the demand of industrial capitalists for money capital is determined by conditions of actual production. Instead of enlightening us on this point, Norman offers us the sage opinion that the demand for money capital is not identical with the demand for money as such; and this sagacity alone, because he, Overstone, and the other Currency prophets, constantly have pricks of conscience since they are striving to make capital out of means of circulation as such through the artificial intervention of legislation, and to raise the interest rate.

Now to Lord Overstone, alias Samuel Jones Loyd, as he is asked to explain why he takes 10% for his "money" because "capital" is so scarce in his country.

"3653. The fluctuations in the rate of interest arise from one of two causes: an alteration in the value of capital"

(excellent! Value of capital, generally speaking, signifies precisely the rate of interest! A change in the rate of interest is thus made to spring from a change in the rate of interest. "Value of capital", as we have shown elsewhere, is never conceived otherwise in theory. Or else, if Lord Overstone means the rate of profit by the phrase value of capital, then the profound thinker returns to the notion that the interest rate is regulated by the rate of profit!)

"or an alteration in the amount of money in the country. All great fluctuations of interest, great either in their duration or in the extent of the fluctuation, may be distinctly traced to alterations in the value of capital. Two more striking practical illustrations of that fact cannot be furnished than the rise in the rate of interest in 1847 and during the last two years (1855-56); the minor fluctuations in the rate of interest, which arise from an alteration in the quantity of money, are small both in extent and in duration. They are frequent, and the more rapid and frequent they are, the more effectual they are for accomplishing their destined purpose",

which is to enrich bankers like Overstone. Friend Samuel Gurney expresses it very naïvely before the Committee of Lords, C. D. 1848 [1857]:

"1324. Do you think that the great fluctuations in the rate of interest which have taken place in the last year are advantageous or not to bankers or dealers in money? — I think they are advantageous to dealers in money. All fluctuations in trade are advantageous TO THE KNOWING MAN." [a]

"1325. May not the banker suffer eventually from the high rates of interest, by impoverishing his best customers? — No; I do not think it has that effect perceptibly."

Voilà ce que parler veut dire.[b]

---

[a] In the 1894 German edition these English words are given in parentheses after their German equivalents. - [b] This is what had to be said.

We shall eventually return to the influence of the quantity of available money on the rate of interest. But it is to be noted right here that Overstone again makes a *quid pro quo*.[a] The demand for money capital in 1847 (before October there was no anxiety over money stringency, or the "quantity of money", as he called it) increased for various reasons, such as rising prices for corn and cotton, lack of buyers of sugar due to overproduction, railway speculation and the crash, overcrowding of foreign markets with cotton goods, and the forced export to, and import from, India for the purpose of speculation in bills of exchange, which was described above.[b] All these things, overproduction in industry and underproduction in agriculture — in other words, greatly differing causes — gave rise to an increased demand for money capital, i. e., for credit and money. The increased demand for money capital had its origin in the course of the production process itself. But whatever may have been the cause, it was the demand for *money* capital which made the interest rate, the value of money capital, climb. If Overstone means to say that the value of money capital rose *because* it rose, then it is tautology. But if, by "value of capital", he means a rise in the rate of profit as the cause of the rise in the rate of interest, we shall immediately see that this is wrong. The demand for money capital, and consequently the "value of capital", may rise even though the profit may decrease; as soon as the relative supply of money capital shrinks, its "value" increases. What Overstone wished to prove is that the crisis of 1847, and the attendant high interest rate, had nothing to do with the "quantity of money", i. e., with the regulations of the Bank Act of 1844 which he had inspired; although it was, indeed, connected with them, inasmuch as the fear of exhausting the bank reserve — a creation of Overstone — contributed a money panic to the crisis of 1847-48. But this is not the issue here. There was a dearth of money capital, caused by the excessive volume of operations compared to the available means and precipitated by the disturbance in the reproduction process due to a crop failure, overinvestment in railways, overproduction, particularly of cotton goods, swindling operations in trade with India and China, speculation, superfluous sugar imports, etc. What the people, who had bought corn at 120 shillings per quarter, lacked when it fell to 60 shillings, were the 60 shillings which they had overpaid and the corresponding credit for that amount in Lombard Street advances on the

---

[a] takes one thing for another - [b] See this volume, pp. 409-10.

corn. It was by no means a lack of banknotes that prevented them from converting their corn into money at its old price of 120 shillings. The same applied to those who had imported an excess of sugar, which became almost unsaleable. It applied likewise to the gentlemen who had tied up their FLOATING CAPITAL [a] in railways and relied on credit to replace it in their "legitimate" business. To Overstone all this signifies "A MORAL SENSE OF THE ENHANCED VALUE OF HIS MONEY".[a] But this enhanced value of money capital corresponded directly on the other hand to the depreciated money value of real capital (commodity capital and productive capital). The value of capital in the one form rose because the value of capital in the other fell. Overstone, however, seeks to identify these two values of different sorts of capital in a single value of capital in general, and he tries to do so by opposing both of them to a scarcity of the medium of circulation, of available money. But the same amount of money capital may be loaned with very different quantities of the circulation medium.

Take his example of 1847. The official bank rate of interest stood at 3 to $3\frac{1}{2}$ % in January; 4 to $4\frac{1}{2}$ % in February. In March it was generally 4%. April (panic) 4 to $7\frac{1}{2}$%. May 5 to $5\frac{1}{2}$%, June, on the whole, 5%. July 5%. August 5 to $5\frac{1}{2}$%. September 5% with trifling variations of $5\frac{1}{4}$, $5\frac{1}{2}$, 6%. October 5, $5\frac{1}{2}$, 7%. November 7-10%. December 7 to 5%.— In this case the interest rose because profits decreased and the money values of commodities fell enormously. If, therefore, Overstone says here that the rate of interest rose in 1847 because the value of capital rose, he cannot mean anything by value of capital but the value of money capital, and the value of money capital is the rate of interest, and nothing else. But later he showed the cloven hoof and identified the value of capital with the rate of profit.

As for the high rate of interest paid in 1856, Overstone was indeed ignorant of the fact that this was partially a symptom that the credit jobbers were coming to the fore, who paid interest not from their profit, but with the capital of others; he maintained just a few months before the crisis of 1857 that "business is quite sound".

He testified furthermore:

"3722. That idea of the profits of trade being destroyed by a rise in the rate of interest is most erroneous. In the first place, a rise in the rate of interest is seldom of any long

---

[a] In the 1894 German edition these English phrases are given in parentheses after their German equivalents.

duration; in the second place, if it is of long duration, and of great extent, it is really a rise in the value of capital, and why does value of capital rise? Because the rate of profit is increased."

Here, then, we learn, at last, what the meaning of "value of capital" is. Furthermore, the rate of profit may be high for a lengthy period, and yet the profit of enterprise may fall and the rate of interest rise to a point where it swallows the greater portion of the profit.

"3724. The rise in the rate of interest has been in consequence of the great increase in the trade of the country, and the great rise in the rate of profits; and to complain of the rise in the rate of interest as being destructive of the two things, which have been its own cause, is a sort of logical absurdity, which one does not know how to deal with."

This is just as logical as if he were to say: The rise in the rate of profit has been in consequence of the rise in commodity prices by speculation, and to complain that the rise in prices destroys its own cause, namely, speculation, is a logical absurdity, etc. That anything can ultimately destroy its own cause is a logical absurdity only for the usurer enamoured of the high interest rate. The greatness of the Romans was the cause of their conquests, and their conquests destroyed their greatness. Wealth is the cause of luxury and luxury has a destructive effect on wealth. The wiseacre! The idiocy of the present-day bourgeois world cannot be better described than by the respect, which the "logic" of the millionaire— the DUNGHILL ARISTOCRAT— inspired in all England. Furthermore, if a high rate of profit and an expansion of business may be causes of a high interest rate, a high rate of interest is, therefore, by no means a cause of high profit. The question is precisely whether such a high interest (as was actually discovered during the crisis) continued or, what is more, reached its climax after the high rate of profit had long gone the way of all flesh.

"3718. With regard to a great rise in the rate of discount, that is a circumstance entirely arising from the increased value of capital, and the cause of that increased value of capital I think any person may discover with perfect clearness. I have already alluded to the fact that during the 13 years this Act has been in operation, the trade of this country has increased from £45,000,000 to £120,000,000. Let any person reflect upon all the events which are involved in that short statement; let him consider the enormous demand upon capital for the purpose of carrying on such a gigantic increase of trade, and let him consider at the same time that the natural source from which that great demand should be supplied, namely, the annual savings of this country, has for the last three or four years been consumed in the unprofitable expenditure of war. I confess that my surprise is, that the rate of interest is not much higher than it is; or, in other words, my surprise is, that the pressure for capital to carry on these gigantic operations, is not far more stringent than you have found it to be."

What an amazing jumble of words by our logician of usury! Here he comes again with his increased value of capital! He seems to think that this enormous expansion of the reproduction process, hence accumulation of real capital, took place on one side, and that on the other there existed a "capital", for which there arose an "enormous demand", in order to accomplish this gigantic increase of commerce! Was not this enormous increase of production an increase of capital itself, and if it created a demand, did it not also create the supply, and, simultaneously, an increased supply of money capital? If the interest rate rose very high, then merely because the demand for money capital increased still more rapidly than its supply, which implies, in other words, that with the expansion of industrial production its operation on a credit basis expanded as well. That is to say, the actual industrial expansion caused an increased demand for "accommodation", and the latter demand is evidently what our banker means by the "enormous demand for capital". It was surely not the expansion of this *demand* for capital alone, which raised the export business from £45 to £120 million. And furthermore, what does Overstone mean when he says that the country's annual savings swallowed by the Crimean War form the natural source of supply for this big demand? In the first place, how did England achieve accumulation in 1792-1815, which was a far different war from the little Crimean one [44]? In the second place, if the natural source was dry, from what source did capital flow at all? It is well known that England did not request loans from foreign countries. Yet if there is an artificial source besides the natural one, it would have been best for a nation to utilise the natural source in war and the artificial one in business. But if only the old money capital was available, could it double its effectiveness through a high rate of interest? Mr. Overstone evidently thinks that the country's annual savings (which, however, were supposed to have been consumed in this case) are converted only into money capital. But if no real accumulation, i. e., expansion of production and augmentation of the means of production, had taken place, what good would there be from the accumulation of debtor's money claims on this production?

The increase in the "value of capital" springing from a high rate of profit is identified by Overstone with an increase caused by a greater demand for money capital. This demand may climb for reasons quite independent of the rate of profit. He himself cites the example of its rise in 1847 as a result of the depreciation of real capital. Depending on what suits his purpose, he ascribes the value of capital to real capital or money capital.

The dishonesty of our banking lord, and his narrow-minded banker's point of view with its didactic flavouring are further revealed in the following:

3728. (Question:) "You have stated that the rate of discount is of no material moment you think to the merchant; will you be kind enough to state what you consider the ordinary rate of profit?"

Mr. Overstone declares that it is "impossible" to answer this question.

"3729. Supposing the average rate of profit to be, say, from 7 to 10%, a variation of from 2 to 7 or 8% in the rate of discount must materially affect the rate of profit, must it not?"

(This question itself lumps together the rate of profit of enterprise with the rate of profit, and passes over the fact that the rate of profit is the common source of interest and profit of enterprise. The interest rate may leave the rate of profit untouched, but not the profit of enterprise. Overstone replied:)

"In the first place parties will not pay a rate of discount which seriously interrupts their profits; they will discontinue their business rather than do that."

(Yes, if they can do so without ruining themselves. So long as their profit is high, they pay the discount because they wish to, and when it is low, because they have to.)

"What is the meaning of discount? Why does a person discount a bill?... Because he wants to obtain the command of a greater quantity of capital."

(*Halte-là!* [a] Because he wants to anticipate the return in money of his tied-up capital and to prevent his business from stopping; because he must meet payments due. He demands more capital only when business is good, or when he speculates on another's capital, though business may be bad. The discount is by no means simply a device to expand business.)

"And why does he want to obtain the command of a greater quantity of capital? Because he wants to employ that capital; and why does he want to employ that capital? Because it is profitable to him to do so; it would not be profitable to him to do so if the discount destroyed his profit."

---

[a] Hold on!

This smug logician assumes that bills of exchange are discounted only for the purpose of expanding business, and that business is expanded because it is profitable. The first assumption is wrong. The ordinary businessman discounts, in order to anticipate the money form of his capital and thereby to keep his process of reproduction in flow; not in order to expand his business or secure additional capital, but in order to balance the credit he gives by the credit he receives. And if he wants to expand his business on credit, discounting bills will do him little good because it is merely conversion of the money capital which he already has in his hands from one form into another; he will rather take a direct loan for a longer period. The credit swindler will get his accommodation bills discounted to expand his business activity, to cover one squalid business deal by another; not to make profits but to obtain possession of another's capital.

After Mr. Overstone has thus identified discounting with borrowing additional capital (instead of with converting bills representing capital into hard cash), he beats an instant retreat as soon as the screws are applied to him.

3730. (Question:) "Merchants being engaged in business, must they not for a certain period carry on their operations in spite of any temporary increase in the rate of discount?" — (Overstone:) "There is no doubt that in any particular transaction, if a person can get his command of capital at a low rate of interest rather than at a high rate of interest, taken in that limited view of the matter, that is convenient to him."

But it is a very unlimited point of view, on the other hand, which enables Mr. Overstone quite suddenly to understand only his, banker's capital, as "capital", and to assume that the man who discounts a bill of exchange with him is a man without capital, just because his capital exists in the form of commodities, or because the money form of his capital is a bill of exchange, which Mr. Overstone converts into another money form.

"3732. With reference to the Act of 1844, can you state what has been about the average rate of interest in proportion to the amount of bullion in the Bank; would it be a fact that when the amount of bullion has been about £9,000,000 or £10,000,000 the rate of interest has been 6 or 7 per cent, and that when it has been £16,000,000, the rate of interest has been, say, from 3 to 4 per cent?"

(The examiner wishes to press him to explain the rate of interest, so far as it is influenced by the amount of bullion in the Bank, on the basis of the rate of interest, so far as it is influenced by the value of capital.)

"I do not apprehend that that is so... but if it is, then I think we must take still more stringent measures than those adopted by the Act of 1844, because if it be true that the greater the store of bullion, the lower the rate of interest, we ought to set to work, according to that view of the matter, to increase the store of bullion to an indefinite amount, and then we should get the interest down to nothing."

The examiner, Cayley, unmoved by this poor joke, continues:

"3733. If that be so, supposing that £5,000,000 of bullion was to be restored to the Bank, in the course of the next six months the bullion then would amount, say, to £16,000,000, and supposing that the rate of interest was thus to fall to 3 or 4 per cent, how could it be stated that that fall in the rate of interest arose from a great decrease of the trade of the country? — I said that the recent rise in the rate of interest, not that the fall in the rate of interest, was closely connected with the great increase in the trade of the country."

But what Cayley says is this: If a rise of interest rate together with a contraction of the gold reserve, is an indication of an expansion in business, then a fall of the interest rate together with an expansion of the gold reserve, must be an indication of a contraction of business. Overstone has no answer to this.

3736. (Question:) "I observed you" (in the text always "YOUR LORDSHIP") "to say that money was the instrument for obtaining capital."

(Precisely this is the mistake, to conceive money as an instrument; it is a form of capital.)

"Under a drain of bullion//of the Bank of England//is not the great strain, on the contrary, for *capitalists* to obtain money?" —//Overstone://"No, it is not the capitalists, it is those who are not capitalists, who want to obtain money and why do they want to obtain money?... Because through the money they obtain the command of the capital of the capitalist to carry on the business of the persons who are not capitalists."

Here he declares point-blank that manufacturers and merchants are not capitalists, and that the capitalist's capital is only money capital.

"3737. Are not the parties who draw bills of exchange capitalists? — The parties who draw bills of exchange may be, and may not be, capitalists."

Here he is stuck.

He is then asked whether merchants' bills of exchange represent commodities which have been sold or shipped. He denies that these bills represent the value of commodities in the same way that a banknote represents gold (3740, 3741). This is somewhat insolent.

"3742. Is it not the merchant's object to get money? — No; getting money is not the object in drawing the bill; getting money is the object in discounting the bill."

Drawing bills of exchange is converting commodities into a form of credit money, just as discounting bills of exchange is converting this credit money into another, namely banknotes. At any rate, Mr. Overstone admits here that the purpose of discounting is to obtain money. A while ago he said that discounting was a way not of converting capital from one form into another, but of obtaining additional capital.

"3743. What is the great desire of the mercantile community under pressure of panic, such as you state to have occurred in 1825, 1837 and 1839; is their object to get possession of capital or the legal tender? — Their object is to get the command of capital to support their business."

Their purpose is to obtain means of payment for due bills of exchange on themselves, on account of the prevailing lack of credit, so that they will not have to let their commodities go below price. If they have no capital at all themselves, they receive it, naturally, along with the means of payment, because they receive value without an equivalent. The urge to obtain money as such consists always in the wish to convert value from the form of commodities or creditor's claims into the form of money. Hence, even aside from the crises, the great difference between borrowing capital and discount, the latter being a mere conversion of money claims from one form into another, or into real money.

//I take the liberty at this point in my capacity of editor to interpolate a few remarks.

With respect to Norman, as well as Loyd-Overstone, the banker is always the one who "advances capital" to others, and his customers are those who demand "capital" from him. Thus, Overstone says that people have bills of exchange discounted through him, "because they wish to obtain the command of *capital*" (3729), and that it is pleasant for such people if they can "get *command of capital* at a low rate of interest" (3730). "Money is the instrument for obtaining *capital*" (3736), and during a panic the great desire of the mercantile community is to "get the command of *capital*" (3743). For all of Loyd-Overstone's confusion over what capital is, it is at least clear that he designates what the banker gives to his client as capital, as a capital which the client did not formerly possess, but which was advanced to him to supplement what he already possessed.

The banker has become so accustomed to act as distributor (through loans) of the social capital available in money form that he considers every function whereby he hands out money, as loaning. All the money he pays out appears to him as a loan. If the money is directly loaned, this is literally true. If it is invested in the bill-discounting business, it is in fact advanced by himself until the bill becomes due. The notion thus grows on him that all the payments he makes are advances; furthermore, that they are advances not merely in the sense that every investment of money with the object of deriving interest or profit, is economically considered an advance of money which the owner of money concerned, in his capacity of private individual, makes to himself in his capacity as entrepreneur, but advances in the definite sense that the banker lends his client a sum of money which augments the capital already at the latter's disposal.

It is this conception, which, transferred from the banker's office to political economy, has created the confusing controversy, whether that which the banker places at his client's disposal in hard cash is capital or mere money, a medium of circulation, or CURRENCY. To decide this—fundamentally simple—controversy, we must put ourselves in the place of a bank client. It all depends on what this customer requests and receives.

If the bank allows its client a loan simply on his personal credit, without any security on his part, then the matter is clear. He then certainly receives an advance of definite value as a supplement to the capital he has already invested. He receives it in the form of money; hence, not merely money, but also money *capital*.

If, on the other hand, he receives the advance against securities, etc., then it is an advance in the sense of money paid to him on condition that he pay it back. But it is not an advance of capital. For the securities also represent capital, and a larger amount at that than the advance. The recipient therefore receives less capital value than he deposits as security; this represents for him no acquisition of additional capital. He does not enter into the transaction because he needs capital—he has that in his securities—but because he needs money. Here we, therefore, have an advance of *money*, not of capital.

If the loan is granted by discounting bills, then even the *form* of an advance disappears. Then it is purely a matter of buying and selling. The bill passes by endorsement into the possession of the bank, while the money passes into the possession of the client; there is no question of any return payment on his part. If the client buys hard cash with a bill of exchange or some similar instrument of credit, it is no more and no less an advance than were he to buy cash money with his other commodities, such as cotton, iron, or corn. Still less can this be called an advance of *capital*. Every purchase and sale between one merchant and another is a transfer of capital. But an advance occurs only when the transfer of capital is not reciprocal, but unilateral and for a period of time. An advance of capital through discount can, therefore, only occur when a bill is a speculative one, which does not represent any sold commodities, and no banker will take such a bill if he is aware of its nature. In the regular discounting business the bank client does not, therefore, receive an advance, either of capital or of money.What he receives is money for sold commodities.

The cases in which the customer demands and receives capital from a bank are thus clearly distinguished from those, in which he merely receives an advance of money, or buys money from the bank. And since least of all Mr. Loyd-Overstone ever advanced his funds without collateral except on the rarest occasions (he was the banker of my firm [a] in Manchester), it is likewise evident that his lyric descriptions of the great quantities of capital loaned by generous bankers to manufacturers in need of capital are gross inventions.

By the way, in Chapter XXXII Marx says essentially the same thing: "The demand for means of payment is a mere demand for *convertibility into money*, so far as merchants and producers have good securities to offer; it is a demand for *money capital* whenever there is no collateral, so that an advance of means of payment gives them not only the *form of money*, but also the *equivalent* they lack, whatever its form, with which to make payment." [b]— And again in Chapter XXXIII: "Under a developed system of credit, with the money concentrated in the hands of bankers, it is they, *at least nominally*, who advance it. This advance refers only to money in circulation. It is an advance of *circulation*, not an advance of capitals which it circulates." [c] Mr. Chapman, who should know, likewise corroborates this conception of the discounting business, B. C. 1857:

"The banker has the bill, the banker has *bought the bill*." Evid. Question 5139.

We shall, however, return to this subject in Chapter XXVIII.[d]— F. E.//

---

[a] A reference to Ermen and Engels firm. - [b] See this volume, p. 513. - [c] Ibid., p. 528. - [d] Ibid., pp. 452-54.

"3744. Will you be good enough to describe what you actually mean by the term 'capital'?" — //Overstone://"CAPITAL CONSISTS OF VARIOUS COMMODITIES; BY THE MEANS OF WHICH TRADE IS CARRIED ON [a]; there is fixed capital and there is circulating capital. Your ships, your docks, your wharves ... are fixed capital; your provisions, your clothes, etc., are circulating capital."

"3745. Is the country oppressed under a drain of bullion? — Not in the rational sense of the word."

(Then comes the old Ricardian theory of money.[b])

"In the natural state of things the money of the world is distributed amongst the different countries of the world in certain proportions, those proportions being such that under that distribution//of money//the intercourse between any one country and all the other countries of the world jointly will be an intercourse of barter; but disturbing circumstances will arise from time to time to affect that distribution, and when those arise, a certain portion of the money of any given country passes to other countries." — "3746. Your Lordship now uses the term 'money'. I understood you before to say that it was a loss of capital.— That what was a loss of capital?" — "3747. The export of bullion? — No, I did not say so. If you treat bullion as capital, no doubt it is a loss of capital; it is parting with a certain proportion of those precious metals which constitute the money of the world." — "3748. I understood Your Lordship to say that an alteration in the rate of discount was a mere sign of an alteration in the value of capital? — I did." — "3749. And that the rate of discount generally alters with the state of the store of bullion in the Bank of England? — Yes, but I have already stated that the fluctuations in the rate of interest, which arise from an alteration in the quantity of money" (what he therefore means here is the quantity of actually existing gold) "in a country, are very small..."

"3750. Then, does Your Lordship mean that there is less capital than there was, when there is a more continuous yet temporary increase in the rate of discount than usual? — Less, in one sense of the word. The proportion between capital and the demand for it is altered; it may be by an increased demand, not by a diminution of the quantity of capital."

(But a moment ago it was capital = money or gold, and a little before that he had explained the rise in interest rate by a high rate of profit, due to an expansion rather than a contraction of business or capital.)

"3751. What is the capital which you particularly allude to? — That depends entirely upon what the capital is which each person wants. It is the capital which the country has at its command for conducting its business, and when that business is doubled, there must be a great increase in the demand for the capital with which it is to be carried on."

(This shrewd banker doubles first the business activity and then the

---

[a] In the 1894 German edition this English phrase is given in parentheses after its German equivalent. - [b] See present edition, Vol. 29, pp. 400-09.

demand for capital with which it is to be doubled. All he sees is his client, who asks Mr. Loyd for more capital by which to double the volume of his business.)

"Capital is like any other commodity" (but according to Mr. Loyd capital is nothing but the totality of commodities), "it will vary in its price" (hence, commodities change their price twice, one time as commodities and the second as capital), "according to the supply and demand."

"3752. The changes in the rate of discount are generally connected with the changes in the amount of gold which there is in the coffers of the Bank. Is it that capital to which Your Lordship refers? — No." — "3753. Can Your Lordship point to any instance in which there has been a large store of capital in the Bank of England connected with a high rate of discount? — The Bank of England is not a place for the deposit of capital, it is a place for the deposit of money." — "3754. Your Lordship has stated that the rate of interest depends upon the amount of capital; will you be kind enough to state what capital you mean, and whether you can point to any instance in which there has been a large store of bullion in the Bank and at the same time a high rate of interest? — It is very probable" (aha!) "that the accumulation of bullion in the Bank may be coincident with a low rate of interest, because a period in which there is a diminished demand for capital"

(namely, money capital; the period to which reference is made here, 1844 and 1845, was a period of prosperity)

"is a period, during which, of course, the means or instrument through which you command capital may accumulate." — "3755. Then you think that there is no connection between the rate of discount and the amount of bullion in the coffers of the Bank? — There may be a connection, but it is not a connection of principle" (his Bank Act of 1844, however, made it a principle of the Bank of England to regulate the interest rate by the quantity of bullion in its possession), "THERE MAY BE A COINCIDENCE OF TIME." [a]— "3758. Do I rightly understand you to say, that the difficulty of merchants in this country, under a state of pressure, in consequence of a high rate of discount, is in getting capital, and not in getting money? — You are putting two things together which I do not join in that form; their difficulty is in getting capital, and their difficulty also is in getting money.... The difficulty of getting money and the difficulty of getting capital is the same difficulty taken in two successive stages of its progress."

Here the fish is caught in the net again. The first difficulty is to discount a bill of exchange, or to obtain a loan against the security of commodities. It is the difficulty of converting capital, or a commercial token of capital, into money. And this difficulty is manifested, among other things, in a high rate of interest. But as soon as the money is obtained, what is the second difficulty? Does anyone ever find any difficulty in getting rid of his money when it is merely a matter of

---

[a] In the 1894 German edition this English phrase is given in parentheses after its German equivalent.

paying? And if it is a matter of buying, has anyone ever had any difficulty in purchasing during times of crisis? And, for the sake of argument, should this refer to a specific dearth in corn, cotton, etc., this
difficulty could only appear in the price of these commodities, not in
the value of money capital, i. e., not in the rate of interest; and this
difficulty is overcome, in the final analysis, by the fact that our man
now has the money to buy them."

"3760. But a higher rate of discount is an increased difficulty of getting money? —
It is an increased difficulty of getting money, but it is not because you want to have the
money; it is only the form" (and this form brings profit into the banker's pocket) "in
which the increased difficulty of getting capital presents itself according to the complicated relations of a civilised state."

"3763.//Overstone's reply://The banker is the go-between who receives deposits
on the one side, and on the other applies those deposits, entrusting them, *in the form of
capital*, to the hands of persons, who, etc."

At last we have what he means by capital. He converts money into
capital by "entrusting" it, less euphemistically, by loaning it at interest.

After Mr. Overstone has stated that a change in the rate of discount is not essentially connected with a change in quantity of the
gold reserve in a bank, or in the quantity of available money, but that
there is at best only a coincidence in time, he repeats:

"3805. When the money in the country is diminished by a drain, its value increases,
and the Bank of England must conform to that alteration in the value of money"

(hence, the value of money *as capital*; in other words, the rate of
interest, for the value of money *as money*, compared with commodities,
remains the same),

"which is meant by the technical term of raising the rate of interest."
"3819. I never confound those two."

Meaning money and capital, and for the simple reason that he
never differentiates between them.

"3834. The very large sum, which had to be paid" (for corn in 1847), "which was
in point of fact capital, for the supply of the necessary provisions of the country."

"3841. The variations in the rate of discount have no doubt a very close relation to
the state of the reserve"//of the Bank of England//"because the state of the reserve is
the indicator of the increase or the decrease of the quantity of money in the country;
and in proportion as the money in the country increases or decreases, the value of that
money will increase or decrease, and the bankrate of discount will conform to that
change."

Thus, Overstone admits here what he emphatically denied in No. 3755.

"3842. There is an intimate connection between them."

Meaning the quantity of bullion in the ISSUE DEPARTMENT, on the one hand, and the reserve of notes in the BANKING DEPARTMENT, on the other. Here he explains the change in the rate of interest by the change in the quantity of money. But this statement is wrong. The reserve may shrink because the circulating money in the country increases. This is the case when the public takes more notes and the hoard of metal does not decrease. But in such case the interest rate rises, because then the banking capital of the Bank of England is limited by the Act of 1844. But he dare not mention this, because due to this law the two departments have nothing to do with one another.

"3859. A high rate of profit will always create a great demand for capital; a great demand for capital will raise the value of it."

Here, at last, we have the connection between a high rate of profit and a demand for capital as Overstone conceives it. Now, a high rate of profit prevailed in, for example, 1844-45 in the cotton industry, because raw cotton was cheap, and remained so, whereas the demand for cotton goods was strong. The value of capital (and in an earlier statement Overstone calls capital that which everyone needs in his business), in this case therefore the value of raw cotton, was not increased for the manufacturer. The high rate of profit may have induced some cotton manufacturer to obtain money on credit for the purpose of expanding his business. Thereby his demand rose for *money* capital, but for nothing else.

"3889. Bullion may or may not be money, just as paper may or may not be a banknote."

"3896. Do I correctly understand Your Lordship that you give up the argument, which you used in 1840, that the fluctuations in the notes out of the Bank of England ought to conform to the fluctuations in the amount of bullion? — I give it up so far as this... that now with the means of information which we possess, the notes out of the Bank of England must have added to them the notes which are in the banking reserve of the Bank of England."

This is superlative. The arbitrary provision that the Bank may make out as many paper notes as it has gold in the treasury and 14 million more, implies, of course, that its issue of notes fluctuates with the fluctuations of the gold reserve. But since the present "means of information which we possess" clearly showed that the mass of notes, which the Bank can thus manufacture (and which the ISSUE DEPARTMENT transfers to the BANKING DEPARTMENT) — that this circulation between the two departments of the Bank of England, fluctuating with the fluctuations of the gold reserve, does not determine the fluctuations in the circulation of banknotes outside the Bank of England, then the latter — the real circulation — becomes a matter of indifference to the bank administration, and the circulation between the two departments of the Bank, whose difference from the real circulation is mirrored in the reserve, alone becomes decisive. To the outside world this circulation is significant only because the reserve indicates how close the Bank is approaching the legal maximum of its note issue, and how much its clients can still receive from the BANKING DEPARTMENT.

The following is a brilliant example of Overstone's *mala fides*[a]:

"4243. Does the quantity of capital, do you think, oscillate from month to month to such a degree as to alter its value in the way exhibited of late years in the oscillations in the rate of discount? — The relation between the demand and the supply of capital may undoubtedly fluctuate, even within short periods.... If France tomorrow put out a notice that she wishes to borrow a very large loan, there is no doubt that it would immediately cause a great alteration *in the value of money*, that is to say, *in the value of capital*, in this country."

"4245. If France announces, that she wants suddenly, for any purpose, 30 million's worth of commodities there will be a great demand for *capital*, to use the more scientific and the simpler term."

"4246. The *capital*, which France would wish to buy with her loan, is *one* thing, and the *money* with which she buys it is *another*, is it the *money*, which alters in value, or not? — We seem to be reviving the old question, which I think is more fit for the chamber of a student than for this committee room."

And with this he retires, but not into the chamber of a student.[84]

Chapter XXVII

THE ROLE OF CREDIT IN CAPITALIST PRODUCTION

The general remarks, which the credit system so far elicited from us, were the following:

I. Its necessary development to effect the equalisation of the rate of

---

[84] More on Overstone's confusion of terms in matters concerning capital at the close of Chapter XXXII.[b]

---

[a] dishonesty - [b] See this volume, p. 517.

profit, or the movements of this equalisation, upon which the entire capitalist production rests.

II. Reduction of the costs of circulation.

1) One of the principal costs of circulation is money itself, being value in itself. It is economised through credit in three ways.

A. By dropping it away entirely in a great many transactions.

B. By the accelerated circulation of the circulating medium.[85] This corresponds in part with what is to be said under 2). On the one hand, the acceleration is technical; i. e., with the same magnitude and number of actual turnovers of commodities for consumption, a smaller quantity of money or money tokens performs the same service. This is bound up with the technique of banking. On the other hand, credit accelerates the velocity of the metamorphosis of commodities and thereby the velocity of money circulation.

C. Substitution of paper for gold money.

2) Acceleration, by means of credit, of the individual phases of circulation or of the metamorphosis of commodities, later the metamorphosis of capital, and with it an acceleration of the process of reproduction in general. (On the other hand, credit helps to keep the acts of buying and selling longer apart and serves thereby as a basis for speculation.) Contraction of reserve funds, which may be viewed in two ways: as a reduction of the circulating medium, on the one hand, and, on the other, as a reduction of that part of capital which must always exist in the form of money.[86]

[85] "The average of notes in circulation during the year was, in 1812, 106,538,000 francs; in 1818, 101,205,000 francs; whereas the movement of the currency, or the annual aggregate of disbursements and receipts upon all accounts, was, in 1812, 2,837,712,000 francs; in 1818, 9,665,030,000 francs. The activity of the currency in France, therefore, during the year 1818, as compared with its activity in 1812, was in the proportion of three to one. The great regulator of the velocity of circulation is credit.... This explains, why a severe pressure upon the money market is generally coincident with a full circulation" (*The Currency Theory Reviewed, etc.*, p. 65).— "Between September 1833 and September 1843 nearly 300 banks were added to the various issuers of notes throughout the United Kingdom; the result was a reduction in the circulation to the extent of two million and a half; it was £36,035,244 at the close of September 1833, and £33,518,554 at the close of September 1843" (l. c., p. 53).— "The prodigious activity of Scottish circulation enables it, with £100, to effect the same quantity of monetary transactions, which in England it requires £420 to accomplish" (l. c., p. 55. This last refers only to the technical side of the operation).

[86] "Before the establishment of the banks ... the amount of capital withdrawn for the purposes of currency was greater, at all times, than the actual circulation of commodities required" (*Economist*, [March 15,] 1845, p. 238).

III. Formation of stock companies. Thereby:

1) An enormous expansion of the scale of production and of enterprises, that was impossible for individual capitals. At the same time, enterprises that were formerly government enterprises, become public.

2) The capital, which in itself rests on a social mode of production and presupposes a social concentration of means of production and labour power, is here directly endowed with the form of social capital (capital of directly associated individuals) as distinct from private capital, and its undertakings assume the form of social undertakings as distinct from private undertakings. It is the abolition of capital as private property within the framework of the capitalist mode of production itself.

3) Transformation of the actually functioning capitalist into a mere manager, administrator of other people's capital, and of the owner of capital into a mere owner, a mere money capitalist. Even if the dividends which they receive include the interest and the profit of enterprise, i. e., the total profit (for the salary of the manager is, or should be, simply the wage of a specific type of skilled labour, whose price is regulated in the labour market like that of any other labour), this total profit is henceforth received only in the form of interest, i. e., as mere compensation for owning capital that now is entirely divorced from the function in the actual process of reproduction, just as this function in the person of the manager is divorced from ownership of capital. Profit thus appears (no longer only that portion of it, the interest, which derives its justification from the profit of the borrower) as a mere appropriation of the surplus labour of others, arising from the conversion of means of production into capital, i. e., from their estrangement vis-à-vis the actual producer, from their antithesis as another's property to every individual actually at work in production, from manager down to the last day labourer. In stock companies the function is divorced from capital ownership, hence also labour is entirely divorced from ownership of means of production and surplus labour. This result of the ultimate development of capitalist production is a necessary transitional phase towards the reconversion of capital into the property of producers, although no longer as the private property of the individual producers, but rather as the property of associated producers, as direct social property. On the other hand, the stock company is a transition toward the conversion of all functions in the reproduction process which still remain linked with

capitalist property, into mere functions of associated producers, into social functions.

Before we go any further, there is still the following economically important fact to be noted: Since profit here assumes the pure form of interest, undertakings of this sort are still possible if they yield bare interest, and this is one of the causes, stemming the fall of the general rate of profit, since such undertakings, in which the ratio of constant capital to the variable is so enormous, do not necessarily enter into the equalisation of the general rate of profit.

//Since Marx wrote the above, new forms of industrial enterprises have developed, as we know, representing the second and third degree of stock companies. The daily growing speed with which production may be enlarged in all fields of large-scale industry today, is offset by the ever-greater slowness with which the market for these increased products expands. What the former turns out in months, can scarcely be absorbed by the latter in years. Add to this the protective tariff policy, by which every industrial country shuts itself off from all others, particularly from England, and also artificially increases domestic production capacity. The results are a general chronic overproduction, depressed prices, falling and even wholly disappearing profits; in short, the old boasted freedom of competition has reached the end of its tether and must itself announce its obvious, scandalous bankruptcy. And in every country this is taking place through the big industrialists of a certain branch joining in a cartel for the regulation of production. A committee fixes the quantity to be produced by each establishment and is the final authority for distributing the incoming orders. Occasionally even international cartels were established, as between the English and German iron industries. But even this form of association in production did not suffice. The antagonism of interests between the individual firms broke through it only too often, restoring competition. This led in some branches, where the scale of production permitted, to the concentration of the entire production of that branch of industry in *one* big joint-stock company under single management. This has been repeatedly effected in America; in Europe the biggest example so far is the United Alkali Trust, which has brought all British alkali production into the hands of a single business firm. The former owners of the more than thirty individual plants have received shares for the appraised value of their entire establishments, totalling about £5 million, which represent the fixed capital of the trust. The technical management remains in the same hands as before, but business control is concentrated in the hands of the general management. The FLOATING CAPITAL,[a] totalling about £1 million, was offered to the public for subscription. The total capital is, therefore, £6 million. Thus, in this branch, which forms the basis of the whole chemical industry, competition has been replaced by monopoly in England, and the road has been paved, most gratifyingly, for future expropriation by the whole of society, the nation.—*F. E.*||

This is the abolition of the capitalist mode of production within the capitalist mode of production itself, and hence a self-dissolving contradiction, which *prima facie* represents a mere phase of transition to a new form of production. It manifests itself as such a contradiction in its effects. It establishes a monopoly in certain spheres and thereby requires state interference. It reproduces a new financial aristocracy, a new variety of parasites in the shape of promoters, speculators and simply nominal directors; a whole system of swindling and cheating by means of corporation promotion, stock issuance, and stock speculation. It is private production without the control of private property.

IV. Aside from the stock-company business, which represents the abolition of capitalist private industry on the basis of the capitalist system itself and destroys private industry as it expands and invades new spheres of production, credit offers to the individual capitalist, or to one who is regarded a capitalist, absolute control within certain limits over the capital and property of others, and thereby over the labour of others.[87] The control over social capital, not the individual

---

[87] See, for instance, in the *Times* the list of business bankruptcies in a crisis year such as 1857 and compare the private property of those bankrupt with the amount of their debts. "The truth is that the power of purchase by persons having capital and credit is much beyond anything that those who are unacquainted practically with speculative markets have any idea of" (Tooke, *An Inquiry into the Currency Principle*, p. 79). "A person having the reputation of capital enough for his regular business, and enjoying good credit in his trade, if he takes a sanguine view of the prospect of a rise of price of the article in which he deals, and is favoured by circumstances in the outset and progress of his speculation, may effect purchases to an extent perfectly enormous compared with his capital" (ibid, p. 136). "Merchants, manufacturers, etc., carry on operations much beyond these which the use of their own capital alone would enable them to do.... Capital is rather the foundation upon which a good credit is built than the limit of the transactions of any commercial establishment" (*Economist*, [November 20,] 1847, p. 1333).

---

[a] In the 1894 German edition this English term is given in parentheses after its German equivalent.

capital of his own, gives him control over social labour. The capital itself, which a man really owns or is supposed to own in the opinion of the public, becomes purely a basis for the superstructure of credit. This is particularly true of wholesale commerce, through which the greatest portion of the social product passes. All standards of measurement, all excuses more or less still justified under capitalist production, disappear here. What the speculating wholesale merchant risks is social property, not *his own*. Equally sordid becomes the phrase relating the origin of capital to savings, for what he demands is that *others* should save for him. //Just as all France recently saved up one and a half billion francs for the Panama Canal swindlers.[45] In fact, a description of the entire Panama swindle is here correctly anticipated, fully twenty years before it occurred.— *F. E.*// The other phrase concerning abstention is squarely refuted by his luxury, which is now itself a means of credit. Conceptions which have some meaning on a less developed stage of capitalist production, become quite meaningless here. Success and failure both lead here to a centralisation of capital, and thus to expropriation on the most enormous scale. Expropriation extends here from the direct producers to the smaller and the medium-sized capitalists themselves. It is the point of departure for the capitalist mode of production; its accomplishment is the goal of this production. In the last instance, it aims at the expropriation of the means of production from all individuals. With the development of social production the means of production cease to be means of private production and products of private production, and can thereafter be only means of production in the hands of associated producers, i. e., the latter's social property, much as they are their social products. However, this expropriation appears within the capitalist system in a contradictory form, as appropriation of social property by a few; and credit lends the latter more and more the aspect of pure adventurers. Since property here exists in the form of stock, its movement and transfer become purely a result of gambling on the stock exchange, where the little fish are swallowed by the sharks and the lambs by the stock-exchange wolves. There is antagonism against the old form in the stock companies, in which social means of production appear as individual property; but the conversion to the form of stock still remains ensnared in the trammels of capitalism; hence, instead of overcoming the antithesis between the character of wealth as social and as private wealth, the stock companies merely develop it in a new form.

The cooperative factories of the labourers themselves represent within the old form the first sprouts of the new, although they naturally reproduce, and must reproduce, everywhere in their actual organisation all the shortcomings of the prevailing system. But the antithesis between capital and labour is overcome within them, if at first only by way of making the associated labourers into their own capitalist, i. e., by enabling them to use the means of production for the employment of their own labour. They show how a new mode of production naturally grows out of an old one, when the development of the material forces of production and of the corresponding forms of social production have reached a particular stage. Without the factory system arising out of the capitalist mode of production there could have been no cooperative factories. Nor could these have developed without the credit system arising out of the same mode of production. The credit system is not only the principal basis for the gradual transformation of capitalist private enterprises into capitalist stock companies, but equally offers the means for the gradual extension of cooperative enterprises on a more or less national scale. The capitalist stock companies, as much as the cooperative factories, should be considered as transitional forms from the capitalist mode of production to the associated one, with the only distinction that the antagonism is resolved negatively in the one and positively in the other.

So far we have considered the development of the credit system— and the implicit latent abolition of capitalist property—mainly with reference to industrial capital. In the following chapters we shall consider credit with reference to interest-bearing capital as such, and to its effect on this capital, and the form it thereby assumes; and there are generally a few more specifically economic remarks still to be made.

But first this:

The credit system appears as the main lever of overproduction and overspeculation in commerce solely because the reproduction process, which is elastic by nature, is here forced to its extreme limits, and is so forced because a large part of the social capital is employed by people who do not own it and who consequently tackle things quite differently than the owner, who anxiously weighs the limitations of his private capital in so far as he handles it himself. This simply demonstrates the fact that the self-expansion of capital based on the contradictory nature of capitalist production permits an actual free development only up to a certain point, so that in fact it constitutes an immanent fetter and barrier to production, which are continually broken through by the credit system.[88] Hence, the credit system accelerates the material development of the productive forces and the establishment of the world market. It is the historical mission of the capitalist mode of production to raise these material foundations of the new form of production to a certain degree of perfection. At the same time credit accelerates the violent eruptions of this contradiction — crises — and thereby the elements of disintegration of the old mode of production.

The two characteristics immanent in the credit system are, on the one hand, to develop the incentive of capitalist production, enrichment through exploitation of the labour of others, to the purest and most colossal form of gambling and swindling, and to reduce more and more the number of the few who exploit the social wealth; on the other hand, to constitute the form of transition to a new mode of production. It is this ambiguous nature, which endows the principal spokesmen of credit from Law to Isaac Péreire with the pleasant character mixture of swindler and prophet.

Chapter XXVIII

MEDIUM OF CIRCULATION AND CAPITAL;
VIEWS OF TOOKE AND FULLARTON

The distinction between currency and capital, as Tooke,[89] Wilson, and others draw it, whereby the differences between medium of circu-

---

[88] Th. Chalmers. [a]

[89] We here give the related passage from Tooke in the original, which was cited in German on p. 390 [b]: * "The business of bankers, setting aside the issue of promissory notes payable on demand, may be divided into two branches, corresponding with the distinction pointed out by Dr. (Adam) Smith of the transactions between dealers and dealers, and between dealers and consumers. One branch of the bankers' business is to collect *capital* from those who have not immediate employment for it, and to distribute or transfer it to those who have. The other branch is to receive deposits of the *incomes* of their customers, and to pay out the amount, as it is wanted for expenditure by the latter in the objects of their consumption ... the former being a circulation of *capital*, the latter of *currency*" * (Tooke, *Inquiry into the Currency Principle*, p. 36). The first is

---

[a] *On Political Economy etc.*, Glasgow, 1832, Ch. V. "On the Possibility of Overproduction or of a General Glut." - [b] See this volume, p. 401.

lation as money, as money capital generally, and as interest-bearing capital (MONEYED CAPITAL in the English sense) are thrown together pell-mell, comes down to two things.

Currency circulates on the one hand as *coin* (money), so far as it promotes the *expenditure of revenue*, hence the traffic between the individual consumers and the retail merchants, to which category belong all merchants who sell to the consumers — to the individual consumers as distinct from productive consumers or producers. Here money circulates in the function of coin, although it continually *replaces capital*. A certain portion of money in a particular country is continually devoted to this function, although this portion consists of perpetually changing individual coins. In so far as money promotes the *transfer of capital*, however, either as a means of purchase (medium of circulation) or as a means of payment, it is *capital*. It is, therefore, neither its function as a means of purchase, nor that as a means of payment, which distinguishes it from coin, for it may also act as a means of purchase between one dealer and another so far as they buy from one another in hard cash, and also as a means of payment between dealer and consumer so far as credit is given and the revenue consumed before it is paid. The difference is, therefore, that in the second case this money not only replaces the capital for one side, the seller, but is expended, advanced, by the other side, the buyer, as capital. The difference, then, is in fact that between *the money form of revenue*

* "the concentration of capital on the one hand and the distribution of it on the other"; * the latter is * "administering the circulation for local purposes of the district" * (ibid., p. 37). A far more correct conception is outlined in the following passage by Kinnear: "Money ... is employed to perform two operations essentially distinct.... As a medium of exchange between dealers and dealers, it is the instrument by which transfers of capital are effected; that is, the exchange of a certain amount of capital in money for an equal amount of capital in commodities. But money employed in the payment of wages and in purchase and sale between dealers and consumers is not capital, but income; that portion of the incomes of the community, which is devoted to daily expenditure. It circulates in constant daily use, and is that alone which can, with strict propriety, be termed CURRENCY.[a] Advances of capital depend entirely on the will of the Bank and other possessors of capital, for borrowers are always to be found; but the amount of the currency depends on the wants of the community, among whom the money circulates, for the purposes of daily expenditure" (J. G. Kinnear, *The Crisis and the Currency*, London, 1847, [pp. 3-4]).

---

[a] In the 1894 German edition this English word is given in parentheses after its German equivalent.

and *the money form of capital*, but not that between currency and capital, for a certain quantity of money *circulates* in the transactions between dealers as well as in the transactions between consumers and dealers. It is, therefore, equally *currency* in *both* functions. Tooke's conception introduces confusion into this question in various ways:

1) by confusing the functional distinctions;

2) by introducing the question of the quantity of money circulating together in both functions;

3) by introducing the question of the relative proportions of the quantities of currency circulating in both functions and thus in both spheres of the reproduction process.

Ad 1) Confusing the functional distinctions that money in one form is CURRENCY,[a] and capital in the other. In so far as money serves in one or another function, be it to realise revenue or transfer capital, it functions in buying and selling, or in paying, as a means of purchase or a means of payment, and, in the wider sense of the word, as currency. The further purpose which it has in the calculations of its spender or recipient, of being capital or revenue for him, alters absolutely nothing, and this is doubly demonstrated. Although the kinds of money circulating in the two spheres are different, the same piece of money, for instance a five-pound note, passes from one sphere into the other and alternately performs both functions; which is inevitable, if only because the retail merchant can give his capital the form of money only in the shape of the coin which he receives from his customers. It may be assumed that the actual small change has its circulation centre of gravity in the domain of retail trade; the retail dealer needs it continually to make change and receives it back continually in payment from his customers. But he also receives money, i. e., coin, in that metal which serves as a standard of value, hence in England one-pound coins, or even banknotes, particularly notes of small denominations, such as five- and ten-pound notes. These gold coins and notes, with whatever small change he has to spare, are deposited by the retail dealer every day, or every week, in his bank, and he pays for his purchases by drawing cheques on his bank deposit. But the same gold coins and banknotes are just as continually withdrawn from the bank, directly or indirectly (for instance, small change by manufac-

---

[a] In the 1894 German edition this English word is given in parentheses after its German equivalent.

turers for the payment of wages), as the money form of its revenue by the entire public in its capacity of consumer, and flow continually back to the retail dealers, for whom they thus again realise a portion of their capital, but at the same time also a portion of their revenue. This last circumstance is important, and is wholly overlooked by Tooke. Only where money is expended as money capital, early in the reproduction process (Book II, Part I [a]), does capital value exist purely as such. For the produced commodities contain not merely capital, but also surplus value; they are not only capital in themselves, but already capital realised as capital, capital with the source of revenue incorporated in it. What the retail dealer gives away for the money returning to him, his commodities, therefore, is for him capital plus profit, capital plus revenue.

Furthermore, in returning to the retailer, circulating money restores the money form of his capital.

To reduce the difference between circulation as circulation of revenue and circulation of capital into a difference between currency and capital is, therefore, altogether wrong. This mode of expression is in Tooke's case due to his simply assuming the standpoint of a banker issuing his own banknotes. Those of his notes which are continually in the public's hands (even if consisting of ever different notes) and serving as currency cost him nothing, save the cost of the paper and the printing. They are circulating certificates of indebtedness (bills of exchange) made out in his own name, but they bring him money and thus serve as a means of expanding his capital. They differ from his capital, however, whether it be his own or borrowed. That is why there is a special distinction for him between currency and capital, which, however, has nothing to do with the definition of these terms as such, least of all with that made by Tooke.

The distinct attribute— whether it serves as the money form of revenue or of capital — changes nothing in the character of money as a medium of circulation; it retains this character no matter which of the two functions it performs. True, money serves more as an actual medium of circulation (coin, means of purchase) when acting as the money form of revenue, due to the dispersion of purchases and sales, and because the majority of disbursers of revenue, the labourers, can buy relatively little on credit; whereas in the traffic of the business world, where the medium of circulation is the money form of capital, money

[a] See present edition, Vol. 36, pp. 31-40.

serves mainly as a means of payment, partly on account of the concentration, and partly on account of the prevailing credit system. But the distinction between money as a means of payment and money as a means of purchase (medium of circulation) is a distinction that refers to the money itself. It is not a distinction between money and capital. More copper and silver circulate in the retail business, and more gold in the wholesale business. Yet the distinction between silver and copper on the one hand, and gold on the other, is not the distinction between currency and capital.

Ad 2) Introducing the question of the quantity of money circulating together in both functions: So far as money circulates, be it as a means of purchase or as a means of payment — no matter in which of the two spheres and independently of its function of realising revenue or capital — the quantity of its circulating mass comes under the laws developed previously in discussing the simple circulation of commodities (Book I, Chap. III, 2, b[a]). The velocity of circulation, hence the number of repetitions of the same function as means of purchase and means of payment by the same pieces of money in a given term, the mass of simultaneous purchases and sales, or payments, the sum of the prices of the circulating commodities, and finally the balances of payments to be settled in the same period, determine in either case the mass of circulating money, of CURRENCY. Whether money so employed represents capital or revenue for the payer or receiver, is immaterial, and in no way alters the matter. Its mass is simply determined by its function as a means of purchase and payment.

Ad 3) On the question of the relative proportions of the quantities of currency circulating in both functions and thus in both spheres of the reproduction process. Both spheres of circulation are connected internally, for, on the one hand, the mass of revenues to be spent expresses the volume of consumption, and, on the other, the magnitude of the masses of capital circulating in production and commerce expresses the volume and velocity of the reproduction process. Nevertheless, the same circumstances have a different effect, working even in opposite directions, upon the quantities of money circulating in both functions or spheres, or on the amount of currency, as the English put it in banking parlance. And this gives new cause for Tooke's vulgar distinction between capital and currency. The fact that the

---

[a] Ibid., Vol. 35.

gentlemen of the CURRENCY Theory [43] confuse two different things is no reason to present them as two different concepts.

In times of prosperity, intense expansion, acceleration and vigour of the reproduction process, labourers are fully employed. Generally, there is also a rise in wages which makes up in some measure for their fall below average during other periods of the commercial cycle. At the same time, the revenues of the capitalists grow considerably. Consumption increases generally. Commodity prices also rise regularly, at least in the various vital branches of business. Consequently, the quantity of circulating money grows at least within definite limits, since the greater velocity of circulation, in turn, sets up certain barriers to the growth of the amount of currency. Since that portion of the social revenue which consists of wages is originally advanced by the industrial capitalist in the form of variable capital, and always in money-form, it requires more money for its circulation in times of prosperity. But we must not count this twice—first as money required for the circulation of variable capital, and then as money required for the circulation of the labourers' revenue. The money paid to the labourers as wages is spent in retail trade and returns about once a week to the banks as the retailers' deposits, after negotiating miscellaneous intermediary transactions in smaller cycles. In times of prosperity the reflux of money proceeds smoothly for the industrial capitalists, and thus the need for money accommodation does not increase because more wages have to be paid and more money is required for the circulation of their variable capital.

The total result is that the mass of circulating medium serving the expenditure of revenue grows decidedly in periods of prosperity.

As concerns the circulation required for the transfer of capital, hence required exclusively between capitalists, a period of brisk business is simultaneously a period of the most elastic and easy credit. The velocity of circulation between capitalist and capitalist is regulated directly by credit, and the mass of circulating medium required to settle payments, and even in cash purchases, decreases accordingly. It may increase in absolute terms, but decreases relatively under all circumstances compared to the expansion of the reproduction process. On the one hand, greater mass payments are settled without the mediation of money; on the other, owing to the vigour of the process, there is a quicker movement of the same amounts of money, both as means of purchase and of payment. The same quantity of money promotes the reflux of a greater number of individual capitals.

On the whole, the circulation of money in such periods appears FULL,[a] although its Department II (transfer of capital) is, at least relatively, contracted, while its Department I (expenditure of revenue) expands in absolute terms.

The refluxes express the reconversion of commodity capital into money, $M — C — M'$, as we have seen in the discussion of the reproduction process, Book II, Part I. Credit renders the reflux in money form independent of the time of actual reflux both for the industrial capitalist and the merchant. Both of them sell on credit; their commodities are thus alienated before they are reconverted into money for them, hence before they flow back to them in money form. On the other hand, they buy on credit, and in this way the value of their commodities is reconverted, be it into productive capital or commodity capital, even before this value has really been transformed into money, i. e., before the commodity price is due and paid for. In such times of prosperity the reflux passes off smoothly and easily. The retailer securely pays the wholesaler, the wholesaler pays the manufacturer, the manufacturer pays the importer of raw materials, etc. The appearance of rapid and reliable refluxes always keeps up for a longer period after they are over in reality by virtue of the credit that is under way, since credit refluxes take the place of the real ones. The banks scent danger as soon as their clients deposit more bills of exchange than money. See the above-mentioned testimony of the Liverpool bank director, p. 398.[b]

To insert what I have noted earlier: "In periods of expanding credit the velocity of currency increases faster than the prices of commodities, whereas in periods of contracting credit the velocity of currency declines faster than the prices of commodities." (*Zur Kritik der politischen Oekonomie*, 1859, S. 83, 84.)[c]

The reverse is true in a period of crisis. Circulation No. I contracts, prices fall, similarly wages; the number of employed labourers is reduced, the mass of transactions decreases. On the contrary, the need for money accommodation increases in circulation No. II with the contraction of credit. We shall examine this point in greater detail immediately.

There is no doubt that with the decrease of credit which goes hand

---

in hand with stagnation in the reproduction process, the circulation mass required for No. I, the expenditure of revenue, contracts, while that required for No. II, the transfer of capital, expands. But to what extent this statement coincides with what is maintained by Fullarton and others still remains to be analysed:

* "A demand for capital on loan and a demand for additional circulation are quite distinct things, and not often found associated." * (Fullarton, l. c., p. 82, title of Chapter 5.) [90]

[90] "It is a great error, indeed, to imagine that the demand for pecuniary accommodation" (that is, for the loan of capital) "is identical with a demand for additional means of circulation, or even that the two are frequently associated. Each demand originates in circumstances peculiarly affecting itself, and very distinct from each other. It is when everything looks prosperous, when wages are high, prices on the rise, and factories busy, that an additional supply of *currency* is usually required to perform the additional functions inseparable from the necessity of making larger and more numerous payments; whereas it is chiefly in a more advanced stage of the commercial cycle, when difficulties begin to present themselves, when markets are overstocked, and returns delayed, that interest rises, and a pressure comes upon the Bank for advances of *capital*. It is true that there is no medium through which the Bank is accustomed to advance capital except that of its promissory notes; and that to refuse the notes, therefore, is to refuse the accommodation. But the accommodation once granted, everything adjusts itself in conformity with the necessities of the market; the loan remains, and the currency, if not wanted, finds its way back to the issuer. Accordingly, a very slight examination of the Parliamentary Returns may convince any one, that the securities in the hands of the Bank of England fluctuate more frequently in an opposite direction to its circulation than in concert with it, and that the example, therefore, of that great establishment furnishes no exception to the doctrine so strongly pressed by the country bankers, to the effect that no bank can enlarge its circulation, if that circulation be already adequate to the purposes to which a banknote currency is commonly applied; but that every addition to its advances, after that limit is passed, must be made from its capital, and supplied by the sale of some of its securities in reserve, or by abstinence from further investment in such securities. The table compiled from the Parliamentary Returns for the interval between 1833 and 1840, to which I have referred in a preceding page, furnishes continued examples of this truth; but two of these are so remarkable that it will be quite unnecessary for me to go beyond them. On the 3rd of January, 1837, when the resources of the Bank were strained to the uttermost to sustain credit and meet the difficulties of the money market, we find its advances on loan and discount carried to the enormous sum of £17,022,000, an amount scarcely known since the war, and almost equal to the entire aggregate issues which, in the meanwhile, remain unmoved at so low a point as £17, 076, 000. On the other hand, we have on the 4th of June, 1833, a circulation of £18,892,000, with a return of private securities in hand, nearly, if not the very lowest on record for the last half-century, amounting to no more than £972,000" (Fullarton, l. c., pp. 97, 98). That a DEMAND FOR PECUNIARY ACCOMMODATION need not be identical by any means with a DEMAND FOR GOLD (what Wilson, Tooke and others call capital) is seen from the following testimony of Mr. We-

In the first place it is evident that in the first of the two cases mentioned above, during times of prosperity, when the mass of the circulating medium must increase, the demand for it increases. But it is likewise evident that, when a manufacturer draws more or less of his deposit out of a bank in gold or banknotes because he has to expend more capital in the form of money, his demand for capital does not thereby increase. What increases is merely his demand for this particular form in which he expends his capital. The demand refers only to the technical form, in which he throws his capital into circulation. Just as in the case of a different development of the credit system, the same variable capital, for example, or the same quantity of wages, requires a greater mass of means of circulation in one country than in another; in England more than in Scotland, for instance, and in Germany more than in England. Likewise in agriculture, the same capital active in the reproduction process requires different quantities of money in different seasons for the performance of its function.

But the contrast drawn by Fullarton is not correct. It is by no means the strong demand for loans, as he says, which distinguishes the period of depression from that of prosperity, but the ease with which this demand is satisfied in periods of prosperity, and the difficulties which it meets in periods of depression. It is precisely the enormous development of the credit system during a prosperity period, hence also the enormous increase in the demand for loan capital and the readiness with which the supply meets it in such periods, which brings about a shortage of credit during a period of depression. It is not, therefore, the difference in volume of demand for loans which characterises both periods.

guelin, Governor of the Bank of England: "The discounting of bills to that extent" (one million daily for three successive days) "would not reduce the reserve" (of banknotes), "unless the public demanded a greater amount of active circulation. The notes issued on the discount of bills would be returned through the medium of the bankers and through deposits. Unless these transactions were for the purpose of exporting bullion, and unless there were an amount of internal panic which induced people to lock up their notes, and not to pay them into the hands of the bankers ... the reserve would not be affected by the magnitude of the transactions."—"The Bank may discount a million and a half a day, and that is done constantly, without its reserve being in the slightest degree affected, the notes coming back again as deposits, and no other alteration taking place than the mere transfer from one account to another" (Report on Bank Acts, 1857, Evidence Nos. 241, 500). The notes therefore serve here merely as means of transferring credits.

As we have previously remarked, both periods are primarily distinguished by the fact that the demand for currency between consumers and dealers predominates in periods of prosperity, and the demand for currency between capitalists predominates in periods of depression. During a depression the former decreases, and the latter increases.

What strikes Fullarton and others as decisively important is the phenomenon that in such periods when SECURITIES in possession of the Bank of England are on the increase, its circulation of notes decreases, and vice versa. The level of the SECURITIES, however, expresses the volume of the pecuniary accommodation, the volume of discounted bills of exchange and of advances made against marketable collateral. Thus Fullarton says in the above passage (Footnote 90, p. 435[a]) that the SECURITIES[b] in the hands of the Bank of England fluctuate more frequently in an opposite direction to its circulation, and this corroborates the view long held by private banks that no bank can increase its issue of banknotes beyond a certain point determined by the needs of its public; but if a bank wants to make advances beyond this limit, it must make them out of its capital, hence it must either realise on securities or utilise money deposits which it would otherwise have invested in securities.

This, however, reveals also what Fullarton means by capital. What does capital signify here? That the Bank can no longer make advances with its own banknotes, or promissory notes, which, of course, cost it nothing. But what does it make advances with in that case? With the sums realised from the sale of SECURITIES IN RESERVE, i. e., government bonds, stocks, and other interest-bearing paper. And what does it get in payment for the sale of such paper? Money — gold or banknotes, so far as the latter are legal tender, such as those of the Bank of England. What the bank advances, therefore, is under all circumstances money. This money, however, now constitutes a part of its capital. If it advances gold, this is understandable. If it advances notes, then these notes represent capital, because it has given up some actual value for them, such as interest-bearing paper. In the case of private banks the notes secured by them through the sale of securities cannot be anything else, in the main, but Bank of England notes or their own notes, since others would hardly be taken in payment for securities. If it is

---

[a] See this volume, pp. 446-47. - [b] In the 1894 German edition this English term is given in parentheses after its German equivalent.

the Bank of England itself, then its own notes, which it receives in return, cost it capital, that is, interest-bearing paper. Besides, it thereby withdraws its own notes from circulation. Should it reissue these notes, or issue new notes in their stead to the same amount, they now represent capital. And they do so equally well, when used for advances to capitalists, or when used later, when the demand for such pecuniary accommodation decreases, for reinvestment in securities. In all these cases the term capital is employed only from the banker's point of view, and means that the banker is compelled to loan more than his mere credit.

As is known, the Bank of England makes all its advances in its own notes. Now, if despite this, as a rule, the banknote circulation of the Bank decreases in proportion as the discounted bills of exchange and collateral in its hands, and thus its advances increase — what becomes of the notes thrown into circulation? How do they return to the Bank?

To begin with, if the demand for money accommodation arises from an unfavourable national balance of payments and thereby implies a drain of gold, the matter is very simple. The bills of exchange are discounted in banknotes. The banknotes are exchanged for gold by the Bank itself, in its ISSUE DEPARTMENT, and this gold is exported. It is as though the Bank paid out gold directly, without the mediation of notes, on discounting bills. Such an increased demand, which may in certain cases be £7 to £10 million, naturally does not add a single five-pound note to the country's domestic circulation. If it is now said that the Bank advances capital, and not currency, this means two things. First, that it does not advance credit, but actual values, a part of its own capital or of capital deposited with it. Secondly, that it does not advance money for inland, but for international circulation, that it advances world money; and for this purpose money must always exist in its form of a hoard, in its metallic state; in the form in which it is not merely a form of value, but value itself, whose money form it is. Although this gold now represents capital, both for the Bank and for the exporting gold dealer, i. e., banking or merchant's capital, the demand for it arises not as demand for capital, but for the absolute form of money capital. This demand arises precisely at the moment when foreign markets are overcrowded with unsaleable English commodity capital. What is wanted, therefore, is capital, not as *capital*, but capital as *money*, in the form in which money serves as a universal world-market commodity; and this is its original form of precious metal.

The drain of gold is not, therefore, as Fullarton, Tooke, etc., claim, "A MERE QUESTION OF CAPITAL". Rather, it is "A QUESTION OF MONEY", even if in a specific function. The fact that it is not a question of *inland* circulation, as the advocates of the CURRENCY Theory maintain, does not prove at all, as Fullarton and others think, that it is merely A QUESTION OF CAPITAL. It is A QUESTION OF MONEY in the form in which money is an international means of payment.

* "Whether that capital" * (the purchase price for the million of quarters of foreign wheat after a crop failure in the home country) * "is transmitted in merchandise or in specie, is a point which in no way affects the nature of the transaction" * (Fullarton, l c., p. 131).

But it significantly affects the question, whether there is a drain of gold, or not. Capital is transferred in the form of precious metal, because it either cannot be transferred at all, or only at a great loss in the shape of commodities. The fear which the modern banking system has of gold drain exceeds anything ever imagined by the monetary system, which considered precious metals as the only true wealth.[a] Take, for instance, the following evidence of the Governor of the Bank of England, Morris, before the Parliamentary Committee on the crisis of 1847-48:

3846. //Question.// When I spoke of the depreciation of STOCKS[b] and fixed capital, are you not aware that all property invested in stocks and produce of every description was depreciated in the same way; that raw cotton, raw silk, and unmanufactured wool were sent to the continent at the same depreciated price, and that sugar, coffee and tea were sacrificed as at forced sales? — It was inevitable that the country should make *a considerable sacrifice* for the purpose of meeting the *efflux of bullion* which had taken place in consequence of the large importation of food."—"3848. Do not you think it would have been better to trench upon the £8 million lying in the coffers of the Bank, than to have endeavoured to get the gold back again at such a sacrifice? — *No, I do not.*"

It is gold which here stands for the only true wealth. Fullarton quotes the discovery by Tooke that

* "with only one or two exceptions, and those admitting of satisfactory explanation, every remarkable fall of the exchange, followed by a drain of gold, that has occurred during the last half-century, has been coincident throughout with a comparatively low state of the circulating medium, and vice versa" * (Fullarton, p. 121).

---

[a] Cf. present edition, Vol. 28, pp. 164-65. - [b] In the 1894 German edition this English word is given in parentheses after its German equivalent.

This discovery proves that such drains of gold occur generally after a period of animation and speculation, as

* "a signal of a collapse already commenced ... an indication of overstocked markets, of a cessation of the foreign demand for our productions, of delayed returns, and, as the necessary sequel of all these, of commercial discredit, manufactories shut up, artisans starving, and a general stagnation of industry and enterprise" * (p. 129).

This, naturally, is at once the best refutation of the claim of the advocates of the CURRENCY Theory, that

* "a full circulation drives out bullion and a low circulation attracts it" *.

On the contrary, while the Bank of England generally carries a strong gold reserve during a period of prosperity, this hoard is generally formed during the slack period, which follows after a storm.

All this sagacity concerning the drain of gold, then, amounts to saying that the demand for *international* media of circulation and payment differs from the demand for *internal* media of circulation and payment (and it goes without saying, therefore, that "THE EXISTENCE OF A DRAIN DOES NOT NECESSARILY IMPLY ANY DIMINUTION OF THE INTERNAL DEMAND FOR CIRCULATION", as Fullarton has it on page 112 of his work) and that the export of precious metal and its being thrown into international circulation is not the same as throwing notes or specie into internal circulation. As for the rest, I have shown on a previous occasion[a] that the movements of a hoard concentrated as a reserve fund for international payments have as such nothing to do with the movements of money as a medium of circulation. At any rate, the question is complicated by the fact that the different functions of a hoard, which I have developed from the nature of money — such as its function as a reserve fund of means of payment to cover due bills in domestic business; the function of a reserve fund of currency; and finally, the function of a reserve fund of world money — are here attributed to one sole reserve fund. It also follows from this that under certain circumstances a drain of gold from the Bank to the home market may combine with a drain abroad. The question is further complicated, however, by the fact that this hoard is arbitrarily burdened with the additional function of serving as a fund guaranteeing the convertibility of banknotes in countries, in which the credit system and credit money are developed. And in addition to all this comes 1) the concentration of the national reserve fund in one single central bank,

---

[a] See present edition, Vol. 29, pp. 382-84.

and 2) its reduction to the smallest possible minimum. Hence, also, Fullarton's complaint (p. 143):

* "One cannot contemplate the perfect silence and facility with which variations of the exchange usually pass off in continental countries, compared with the state of feverish disquiet and alarm always produced in England whenever the treasure in the Bank seems to be at all approaching to exhaustion, without being struck with the great advantage in this respect which a metallic currency possesses." *

However, if we now leave aside the drain of gold, how can a bank that issues notes, like the Bank of England, increase the amount of money accommodation granted by it without increasing its issue of banknotes?

So far as the bank itself is concerned, all the notes outside its walls, whether circulating or in private hoards, are in circulation, i. e., are out of its hands. Hence, if the bank extends its discounting and money-lending business, its advances on SECURITIES, all the banknotes issued by it for that purpose must return, for otherwise they would increase the volume of circulation, something which is not supposed to happen. This return may take place in two ways.

First: The bank pays A notes against securities; A uses them to pay for bills of exchange due to B, and B deposits notes once more in the bank. This brings to a close the circulation of these notes, but the loan remains.

* "The loan remains, and the currency, if not wanted, finds its way back to the issuer" * (Fullarton, p. 97).

The notes, which the bank advanced to A, have now returned to it; but it is the creditor of A, or whoever may have been the drawer of the bill discounted by A, and the debtor of B for the amount of value expressed in these notes, and B thus disposes of a corresponding portion of the capital of the bank.

Secondly: A pays to B, and B himself, or C, to whom he pays the notes, uses these notes to pay bills due to the bank, directly or indirectly. In that case the bank is paid in its own notes. This concludes the transaction (pending A's return payment to the bank).

To what extent, now, shall the bank's advance to A be regarded as an advance of capital, or as a mere advance of means of payment? [91]

[91] The passage that follows in the original is unintelligible in this context and has been rewritten by the editor to the end of the oblique lines. In another context this point has already been touched upon in Chapter XXVI.[a]

---

[a] See this volume, pp. 425-27.

//This depends on the nature of the loan itself. Three cases must be distinguished.

First case.— A receives from the bank amounts loaned on his own personal credit, without giving any security for them. In this case he does not merely receive means of payment, but also unquestionably a new capital, which he may employ in his business and realise as an additional capital until the maturity date.

Second case.— A has given to the bank securities, national bonds, or stocks as collateral, and received for them, say, up to two-thirds of their momentary value as a cash loan. In this case he has received the means of payment he needed, but no additional capital, for he entrusted to the bank a larger capital value than he received from it. But this larger capital value was, on the one hand, unavailable for his momentary needs (means of payment), because invested in a particular interest-bearing form; on the other hand, A had his own reasons for not wanting to convert this capital value directly into means of payment by selling it. His securities served, among other things, as a reserve capital, and he set them in motion as such. The transaction between A and the bank, therefore, consists in a temporary mutual transfer of capital, so that A does not receive any additional capital (quite the contrary!) although he receives the desired means of payment. For the bank, on the other hand, this transaction constitutes a temporary lodgement of money capital in the form of a loan, a conversion of money capital from one form into another, and this conversion is precisely the essential function of the banking business.

Third case.— A had the bank discount a bill of exchange and received its value in cash after the deduction of discount. In this case he sold a non-convertible money capital to the bank for the amount of value in convertible form. He sold his still running bill for cash money. The bill is now the property of the bank. It does not alter the matter that A as the last endorser of the bill is responsible for it to the bank in default of payment. He shares this responsibility with the other endorsers and with the drawer of the bill, all of whom are duly responsible to him. In this case, therefore, we do not have a loan, but only an ordinary purchase and sale. For this reason, A has nothing to pay back to the bank. It reimburses itself by cashing the bill when it becomes due. Here, too, a transfer of capital has taken place between A and the bank, and in exactly the same manner as in the sale and purchase of any other commodity, and for this very reason A did not receive any additional capital. What he needed and received were means of payment, and he received them by having the bank convert one form of his money capital — his bill — into another — money.

It is therefore only in the first case that there is any question of a real advance of capital; in the second and third cases, the matter can be so regarded only in the sense that every investment of capital implies an "advance of capital". In this sense the bank advances money capital to A; but for A it is *money capital* at best in the sense that it is a portion of his capital in general. And he requires it and uses it not specifically as capital, but rather as specifically a means of payment. Otherwise, every ordinary sale of commodities by which means of payment are secured might be considered as receiving an advance of capital.— *F. E.*//

In the case of the private bank which issues its own notes we have this difference, that if its notes remain neither in local circulation, nor return to it in the form of deposits, or in payment for due bills of exchange, they fall into the hands of persons who compel the private bank to cash these notes in gold or in notes of the Bank of England. In this event, therefore, its loan in fact represents an advance of notes of the Bank of England, or, what amounts to the same thing for the private bank, of gold, hence a portion of its banking capital. The same holds good in case the Bank of England itself, or some other bank, which has a fixed legal maximum for its issue of notes, must sell securities to withdraw its own notes from circulation and then issue them once more in the shape of advances; in that case, the bank's own notes represent a portion of its mobilised banking capital.

Even if the circulation were purely metallic, it would be possible 1) for a drain of gold //Marx evidently refers here to a drain of gold that would, at least partially, go abroad — *F. E.*// to empty the treasury, and 2) since gold would be chiefly wanted by the bank to make payments (in settlement of erstwhile transactions), the advance against collateral could grow considerably, but would flow back to it in the form of deposits or in payment of due bills of exchange; so that, on one side, the total treasure of the bank would decrease with an increase of the securities in its hands, while on the other, it would now be holding the same amount, which it possessed formerly as owner, as debtor of its depositors, and finally the total mass of currency would decrease.

Our assumption so far has been that the loans are made in notes, so that they carry with them at least a fleeting, even if instantly disappearing, increase in the issue of notes. But this is not necessary. Instead of a paper note, the bank may open a credit account for A, in which case this A, the bank's debtor, becomes its imaginary depositor. He pays his creditors with cheques on the bank, and the recipient of these cheques passes them on to his own banker, who exchanges them for the cheques outstanding against him in the CLEARING HOUSE. In this case no mediation of notes takes place at all, and the entire transaction is confined to the fact that the bank settles its own debt with a cheque drawn on itself, and its actual recompense consists in its claim on A. In this case the bank has loaned a portion of its banking capital, because its own debt claims, to A.

In so far as this demand for pecuniary accommodation is a demand for capital, it is so only for money capital; capital from the standpoint of the banker, namely for gold (in the case of gold exports abroad) or notes of the National Bank, which a private bank can obtain only by purchase against an equivalent, and which, therefore, represent capital for it. Or, again, it is a case of interest-bearing papers, government bonds, stocks, etc., which must be sold in order to obtain gold or banknotes. Such papers, however, if in government bonds, are capital only for the buyer, for whom they represent the purchase price, the capital he invested in them. In themselves they are not capital, but merely debt claims. If mortgages, they are mere titles on future ground rent. And if they are shares of stock, they are mere titles of ownership, which entitle the holder to a share in future surplus value. All of these are not real capital. They do not form constituent parts of capital, nor are they values in themselves. By way of similar transactions money belonging to the bank may be transformed into deposits, so that the bank becomes the debtor instead of owner of this money, and holds it under a different title of ownership. However important this may be to the bank itself, it alters nothing in the mass of reserve capital, or even of money capital available in a particular country. Capital, therefore, represents here only money capital, and, if not available in the actual form of money, it represents a mere title on capital. This is very important, since a scarcity of, and pressing demand for, *banking* capital is confounded with a decrease of *actual* capital, which, conversely, is in such cases rather abundant in the form of means of production and products, and swamps the markets.

It is, therefore, easy to explain how the mass of securities held by a bank as collateral increases, hence how the growing demand for pecuniary accommodation can be satisfied by the bank, while the total mass of currency remains the same or decreases. This total mass is held in check during such periods of money stringency in two ways: 1) by a drain of gold; 2) by a demand for money in its capacity as a mere means of payment, when the issued banknotes return immediately; or when the transactions take place without the mediation of notes by means of book credit; when, therefore, payments are made simply through a credit transaction, the settlement of these payments being the sole purpose of the operation. It is a peculiarity of money, when it serves merely to settle accounts (and in times of crises loans are taken up to pay, rather than to buy; to wind up previous transactions, not to initiate new ones), that its circulation is no more than fleeting, even where balances are not settled by mere credit operations, without any intervention of money, so that, when there is a strong demand for pecuniary accommodation, an enormous quantity of such transactions can take place without expanding the circulation. But the mere fact that the circulation of the Bank of England remains stable or even decreases simultaneously with an extensive accommodation of money on its part, does not *prima facie* prove, as Fullarton, Tooke and others assume (owing to their erroneous notion that pecuniary accommodation is identical with receiving CAPITAL ON LOAN as additional capital), that the circulation of money (of banknotes) in its function as a means of payment is not increased and extended. Since the circulation of notes as means of purchase decreases during a business depression, when such extensive accommodation is necessary, their circulation as means of payment may increase, and the aggregate amount of the circulation, the sum of notes functioning as means of purchase and payment, may remain stable or may even decrease. The circulation as a means of payment of banknotes immediately returning to the bank that issues them is simply not circulation in the eyes of those economists.

Should circulation as a means of payment increase at a higher rate than it decreases as a means of purchase, the aggregate circulation would increase, although the money serving as a means of purchase would decrease considerably in quantity. And this actually occurs in certain periods of crisis, namely, when credit collapses completely and when not only commodities and securities are unsaleable but bills of exchange are undiscountable and nothing counts any more but money payment, or, as the merchant puts it, cash. Since Fullarton *et al.* do not understand that the circulation of notes as a means of payment is the characteristic feature of such periods of money shortage, they treat this phenomenon as accidental.

* "With respect again to those examples of eager competition for the possession of banknotes, which characterise seasons of panic and which may sometimes, as at the close of 1825, lead to a sudden, though only temporary, enlargement of the issues, even while the efflux of bullion is still going on, these, I apprehend, are not to be regarded as among the natural or necessary concomitants of a low exchange; the demand in such cases is not for circulation" * (read circulation as a means of purchase), * "but for hoarding, a demand on the part of alarmed bankers and capitalists which arises generally in the last act of the crisis" * (hence, for a reserve of means of payment), * "after a long continuation of the drain, and is the precursor of its termination" * (Fullarton, p. 130).

In the discussion of money as a means of payment (Book I, Chap. III, 3, b[a]) we have already explained, in what manner, when the chain of payments is suddenly interrupted, money turns from its ideal form into a material and, at the same time, absolute form of value vis-à-vis the commodities. This was illustrated by some examples (footnotes 100 and 101 [b]). This interruption itself is partly an effect, partly a cause of the instability of credit and of the circumstances accompanying it, such as overstocking of markets, depreciation of commodities, interruption of production, etc.

It is evident, however, that Fullarton transforms the distinction between money as a means of purchase and money as a means of payment into a false distinction between CURRENCY and capital. This is again due to the narrow-minded banker's conception of circulation.

It might yet be asked: which is it, capital or money in its specific function as a means of payment, that is in short supply in such periods of stringency? And this is a well-known controversy.

In the first place, so far as the stringency is marked by a drain of gold, it is evidently international means of payment that are demanded. But money in its specific capacity of international means of payment is gold in its metallic actuality, as a valuable substance in itself, as a quantity of value. It is at the same time capital, not capital as commodity capital, but as money capital, capital not in the form of commodities but in the form of money (and, at that, of money in the eminent sense of the word, in which it exists as universal world-market commodity). It is not a contradiction here between a demand for money as a means of payment and a demand for capital. The contradiction is rather between capital in its money form and capital in its commodity form; and the form in which it is here demanded and in which alone it can function, is its money form.

---

[a] See present edition, Vol. 35. - [b] Ibid., p. 149, notes 1, 2.

Aside from this demand for gold (or silver) it cannot be said that there is any dearth whatever of capital in such periods of crisis. Under extraordinary circumstances, such as rise in the price of corn, or a cotton famine, etc., this may be the case; but these phenomena are not necessary or regular accompaniments of such periods; and the existence of such a lack of capital cannot be assumed beforehand without further ado from the mere fact that there is a heavy demand for pecuniary accommodation. On the contrary. The markets are overstocked, swamped with commodity capital. Hence, it is not, in any case, a lack of *commodity* capital which causes the stringency. We shall return to this question later.

BOOK III

THE PROCESS
OF CAPITALIST PRODUCTION
AS A WHOLE

II

Part V

DIVISION OF PROFIT INTO INTEREST AND PROFIT OF ENTERPRISE. INTEREST-BEARING CAPITAL (*CONTINUED*)

Chapter XXIX

COMPONENT PARTS OF BANK CAPITAL

It is now necessary to examine the component parts of bank capital in greater detail.

We have just seen that Fullarton and others transform the distinction between money as a medium of circulation and money as a means of payment — also world money in so far as it concerns a drain of gold — into a distinction between CURRENCY[a] and capital.

The peculiar role played by capital in this instance is the reason why bankers' economics teaches that money is indeed capital *par excellence* as insistently as enlightened economics taught that money is not capital.[46]

In subsequent analyses, we shall demonstrate that money capital is being confused here with MONEYED CAPITAL in the sense of interest-bearing capital, while in the former sense, money capital is always merely a transient form of capital — in contradistinction to the other forms of capital, namely, commodity capital and productive capital.

Bank capital consists of 1) cash money, gold or notes; 2) securities. The latter can be subdivided into two parts: commercial paper or bills of exchange, which run for a period, become due from time to time, and whose discounting constitutes the essential business of the banker; and public securities, such as government bonds, treasury notes, stocks of all kinds, in short, interest-bearing paper which is however significantly different from bills of exchange. Mortgages may

---

[a] In the 1894 German edition this English term is given in parentheses after its German equivalent.

also be included here. The capital composed of these tangible compo-nent parts can again be divided into the banker's invested capital and into deposits, which constitute his BANKING CAPITAL, or borrowed capi-tal. In the case of banks which issue notes, these must also be includ-ed. We shall leave the deposits and notes out of consideration for the present. It is evident at any rate that the actual component parts of the banker's capital (money, bills of exchange, deposit currency) remain unaffected whether the various elements represent the ban-ker's own capital or deposits, i. e., the capital of other people. The same division would remain, whether he were to carry on his business with only his own capital or only with deposited capital.

The form of interest-bearing capital is responsible for the fact that every definite and regular money REVENUE appears as interest on some capital, whether it arises from some capital or not. The money in-come is first converted into interest, and from the interest one can determine the capital from which it arises. In like manner, in the case of interest-bearing capital, every sum of value appears as capital as long as it is not expended as REVENUE; that is, it appears as PRINCIPAL[a] in contrast to possible or actual interest which it may yield.

The matter is simple. Let the average rate of interest be 5% an-nually. A sum of £500 would then yield £25 annually if converted in-to interest-bearing capital. Every fixed annual income of £25 may then be considered as interest on a capital of £500. This, however, is and remains a purely illusory conception, except in the case where the source of the £25, whether it be a mere title of ownership or claim, or an actual element of production such as real estate, is di-rectly transferable or assumes a form in which it becomes transfer-able. Let us take the national debt and wages as illustrations.

The state has to annually pay its creditors a certain amount of inter-est for the capital borrowed from them. In this case, the creditor can-not recall his investment from his debtor, but can only sell his claim, or his title of ownership. The capital itself has been consumed, i. e., expended by the state. It no longer exists. What the creditor of the state possesses is 1) the state's promissory note, amounting to, say, £100; 2) this promissory note gives the creditor a claim upon the an-nual revenue of the state, that is, the annual tax proceeds, for a cer-tain amount, e. g., £5 or 5%; 3) the creditor can sell this promissory

---

[a] In the 1894 German edition this English term is given in parentheses after its Ger-man equivalent.

note of £100 at his discretion to some other person. If the rate of interest is 5%, and the security given by the state is good, the owner A can sell this promissory note, as a rule, to B for £100; for it is the same to B whether he lends £100 at 5% annually, or whether he secures for himself by the payment of £100 an annual tribute from the state amounting to £5. But in all these cases, the capital, as whose offshoot (interest) state payments are considered, is illusory, fictitious capital. Not only that the amount loaned to the state no longer exists, but it was never intended that it be expended as capital, and only by investment as capital could it have been transformed into a self-preserving value. To the original creditor A, the share of annual taxes accruing to him represents interest on his capital, just as the share of the spendthrift's fortune accruing to the usurer appears to the latter, although in both cases the loaned amount was not invested as capital. The possibility of selling the state's promissory note represents for A the potential means of regaining his principal. As for B, his capital is invested, from his individual point of view, as interest-bearing capital. So far as the transaction is concerned, B has simply taken the place of A by buying the latter's claim on the state's revenue. No matter how often this transaction is repeated, the capital of the state debt remains purely fictitious, and, as soon as the promissory notes become unsaleable, the illusion of this capital disappears. Nevertheless, this fictitious capital has its own laws of motion, as we shall presently see.

We shall now consider labour power in contrast to the capital of the national debt, where a negative quantity appears as capital — just as interest-bearing capital, in general, is the fountain-head of all manner of insane forms, so that debts, for instance, can appear to the banker as commodities. Wages are conceived here as interest, and therefore labour power as the capital yielding this interest. For example, if the wage for one year amounts to £50 and the rate of interest is 5%, the annual labour power is equal to a capital of £1,000. The insanity of the capitalist mode of conception reaches its climax here, for instead of explaining the expansion of capital on the basis of the exploitation of labour power, the matter is reversed and the productivity of labour power is explained by attributing this mystical quality of interest-bearing capital to labour power itself. In the second half of the 17th century, this used to be a favourite conception (for example, of Petty),[47] but it is used even nowadays in all seriousness by some vulgar economists and more particularly by some German statisticians.[1] Unfortunately two disagreeably frustrating facts mar this thoughtless conception. In the first place, the labourer must work in order to obtain this interest. In the second place, he cannot transform the capital value of his labour power into cash by transferring it. Rather, the annual value of his labour power is equal to his average annual wage, and what he has to give the buyer in return through his labour is this same value plus a surplus value, i. e., the increment added by his labour. Under a slave system, the labourer has a capital value, namely, his purchase price. And when he is hired out, the hirer must pay, in the first place, the interest on this purchase price, and, in addition, replace the annual wear and tear of the capital.

The formation of a fictitious capital is called capitalisation. Every regularly repeated income is capitalised by calculating it on the basis of the average rate of interest, as an income which would be yielded by a capital loaned at this rate of interest. For example, if the annual income = £100 and the rate of interest = 5%, then the £100 would represent the annual interest on £2,000, and the £2,000 is regarded as the capital value of the legal title of ownership on the £100 annually. For the person who buys this title of ownership, the annual income of £100 represents indeed the interest on his capital invested at 5%. All connection with the actual expansion process of capital is thus completely lost, and the conception of capital as something with automatic self-expansion properties is thereby strengthened.

Even when the promissory note — the security — does not represent a purely fictitious capital, as it does in the case of state debts, the capital value of such paper is nevertheless wholly illusory. We have previously seen[a] in what manner the credit system creates associated capital. The paper serves as title of ownership which represents this capital. The stocks of railways, mines, navigation companies, and the like, represent actual capital, namely, the capital invested and functioning in such enterprises, or the amount of money advanced by the stockholders for the purpose of being used as capital in such enterprises. This does not preclude the possibility that these may re-

---

[1] "The labourer possesses [...] capital value, which is arrived at by considering the money value of his annual wage as income from interest.... Capitalising ... the average daily wage at 4%, we obtain the average value of a male agricultural labourer to be: German Austria, 1,500 taler; Prussia, 1,500; England, 3,750; France, 2,000; inner Russia, 750 taler" (Von Reden, *Vergleichende Kultur-Statistik*, Berlin, 1848, p. 434).

---

[a] See this volume, pp. 433-34.

Das Kapital.

Kritik der politischen Oekonomie.

Von

Karl Marx.

Drittes Buch

Buch III:
Der Gesammtprocess der kapitalistischen Produktion.
Zweiter Theil.

Herausgegeben von Friedrich Engels.

Hamburg
Verlag von Otto Meissner.
1894.

Title page of the first German edition
of Vol. III, II, of *Capital*

present pure swindle. But this capital does not exist twice, once as the capital value of titles of ownership (stocks) and the other time as the actual capital invested, or to be invested, in those enterprises. It exists only in the latter form, and a share of stock is merely a title of ownership to a certain portion of the surplus value to be realised by it. A may sell this title to B, and B may sell it to C. These transactions do not alter anything in the nature of the problem. A or B then has his title in the form of capital, but C has transformed his capital into a mere title of ownership to the anticipated surplus value from the stock capital.

The independent movement of the value of these titles of ownership, not only of government bonds but also of stocks, adds weight to the illusion that they constitute real capital alongside of the capital or claim to which they may have title. For they become commodities, whose price has its own characteristic movement and is established in its own way. Their market value is determined differently from their nominal value, without any change in the value (even though the expansion may change) of the actual capital. On the one hand, their market value fluctuates with the amount and reliability of the proceeds to which they afford legal title. If the nominal value of a share of stock, that is, the invested sum originally represented by this share, is £100, and the enterprise pays 10% instead of 5%, then its market value, everything else remaining equal, rises to £200, as long as the rate of interest is 5%, for when capitalised at 5%, it now represents a fictitious capital of £200. Whoever buys it for £200 receives a revenue of 5% on this investment of capital. The converse is true when the proceeds from the enterprise diminish. The market value of this paper is in part speculative, since it is determined not only by the actual income, but also by the anticipated income, which is calculated in advance. But assuming the expansion of the actual capital as constant, or where no capital exists, as in the case of state debts, the annual income to be fixed by law and otherwise sufficiently secured, the price of these securities rises and falls inversely as the rate of interest. If the rate of interest rises from 5% to 10%, then securities guaranteeing an income of £5 will now represent a capital of only £50. Conversely, if the rate of interest falls to $2\frac{1}{2}$%; the same securities will represent a capital of £200. Their value is always merely capitalised income, that is, the income calculated on the basis of a fictitious capital at the prevailing rate of interest. Therefore, when the money market is tight these securities will fall in price for two reasons: first, because the rate of interest rises, and secondly, because they are thrown on the market in large quantities in order to convert them into cash. This drop in price takes place regardless of whether the income that this paper guarantees its owner is constant, as is the case with government bonds, or whether the expansion of the actual capital, which it represents, as in industrial enterprises, is possibly affected by disturbances in the reproduction process. In the latter event, there is only still another depreciation added to that mentioned above. As soon as the storm is over, this paper again rises to its former level, in so far as it does not represent a business failure or swindle. Its depreciation in times of crisis serves as a potent means of centralising fortunes.[2]

To the extent that the depreciation or increase in value of this paper is independent of the movement of value of the actual capital that it represents, the wealth of the nation is just as great before as after its depreciation or increase in value.

"The public stocks and canal and railway shares had already by the 23rd of October, 1847, been depreciated in the aggregate to the amount of £114,752,225" (Morris, Governor of the Bank of England, testimony in the Report on Commercial Distress, 1847-48).[b]

Unless this depreciation reflected an actual stoppage of production and of traffic on canals and railways, or a suspension of already initiated enterprises, or squandering capital in positively worthless ventures, the nation did not grow one cent poorer by the bursting of this soap bubble of nominal money capital.

All this paper is actually nothing more than accumulated claims, or legal titles, to future production whose money or capital value represents either no capital at all, as in the case of state debts, or is regulated independently of the value of real capital which it represents.

[2] //Immediately after the February Revolution, when commodities and securities were extremely depreciated and utterly unsaleable in Paris, a Swiss merchant in Liverpool, Mr. R. Zwilchenbart—who told this to my father—cashed all his belongings, travelled with cash in hand to Paris and sought out Rothschild, offering to participate in a joint enterprise with him. Rothschild looked at him fixedly, rushed towards him, grabbed him by his shoulders and asked: "*Avez-vous de l'argent sur vous?*" — "*Oui, M. le baron.*" — "*Alors vous êtes mon homme!*"[a]—And they did a thriving business together.—F. E.//

---

[a] "Have you money in your possession?" — "Yes, Baron." — "Then you are my man!" - [b] First Report from the Secret Committee on Commercial Distress with the Minutes of Evidence, p. 288, No. 3800.

In all countries based on capitalist production, there exists in this form an enormous quantity of so-called interest-bearing capital, or MONEYED CAPITAL. And by accumulation of money capital nothing more, in the main, is connoted than an accumulation of these claims on production, an accumulation of the market price, the illusory capital value of these claims.

A part of the banker's capital is now invested in this so-called interest-bearing paper. This is itself a portion of the reserve capital, which does not perform any function in the actual business of banking. The most important portion of this paper consists of bills of exchange, that is, promises to pay made by industrial capitalists or merchants. For the money lender these bills of exchange are interest-bearing papers, in other words, when he buys them, he deducts interest for the time which they still have to run. This is called discounting. It depends on the prevailing rate of interest, how much of a deduction is made from the sum represented by the bill of exchange.

Finally, the last part of the capital of a banker consists of his money reserve in gold and notes. The deposits, unless tied up by agreement for a certain time, are always at the disposal of the depositors. They are in a state of continual fluctuation. But while one depositor draws on his account, another deposits, so that the general average sum total of deposits fluctuates little during periods of normal business.

The reserve funds of the banks, in countries with developed capitalist production, always express on the average the quantity of money existing in the form of a hoard, and a portion of this hoard in turn consists of paper, mere drafts upon gold, which have no value in themselves. The greater portion of banker's capital is, therefore, purely fictitious and consists of claims (bills of exchange), government securities (which represent spent capital), and stocks (drafts on future revenue). And it should not be forgotten that the money value of the capital represented by this paper in the safes of the banker is itself fictitious, in so far as the paper consists of drafts on guaranteed revenue (e. g., government securities), or titles of ownership to real capital (e. g., stocks), and that this value is regulated differently from that of the real capital, which the paper represents at least in part; or, when it represents mere claims on revenue and no capital, the claim on the same revenue is expressed in continually changing fictitious money capital. In addition to this, it must be noted that this fictitious banker's capital represents largely, not his own capital, but that of the public, which makes deposits with him, either interest-bearing or not.

Deposits are always made in money, in gold or notes, or in drafts upon these. With the exception of the reserve fund, which contracts or expands in accordance with the requirements of actual circulation, these deposits are in fact always in the hands of the industrial capitalists and merchants, on the one hand, whose bills of exchange are thereby discounted and who thus receive advances; on the other hand, they are in the hands of dealers in securities (exchange brokers), or in the hands of private parties who have sold their securities, or in the hands of the government (in the case of treasury notes and new loans). The deposits themselves play a double role. On the one hand, as we have just mentioned, they are loaned out as interest-bearing capital and are, therefore, not in the safes of the banks, but figure merely on their books as credits of the depositors. On the other hand, they function merely as such book entries, in so far as the mutual claims of the depositors are balanced by cheques on their deposits and can be written off against each other. In this connection, it is immaterial whether these deposits are entrusted to the same banker, who can thus balance the various accounts against each other, or whether this is done in different banks, which mutually exchange cheques and pay only the balances to one another.

With the development of interest-bearing capital and the credit system, all capital seems to double itself, and sometimes treble itself, by the various modes in which the same capital, or perhaps even the same claim on a debt, appears in different forms in different hands.[3] The greater portion of this "money capital" is purely fictitious. All the deposits, with the exception of the reserve fund, are merely claims

---

[3] //This doubling and trebling of capital has developed considerably further in recent years, for instance, through FINANCIAL TRUSTS, which already occupy a heading of their own in the report of the London Stock Exchange. A company is organised for the purchase of a certain class of interest-bearing paper, e. g., of foreign government securities, English municipal or American public bonds, railway stocks, etc. The capital, for example, £2 million, is raised by stock subscriptions. The Board of Directors buys up the values in question or speculates more or less actively therein, and after deducting the expenses distributes among the stockholders the annual interest as dividends. Furthermore, some stock companies have adopted the custom of dividing the common stock into two classes, PREFERRED and DEFERRED. The PREFERRED receive a fixed rate of interest, say, 5%, provided that the total profit permits it; if there is anything left after that, the DEFERRED receive it. In this manner, the "solid" investment of capital in PREFERRED shares is more or less separated from actual speculation — with DEFERRED shares. Since a few large enterprises have been unwilling to adopt this new custom, the expedient has been resorted to of organising new companies which invest a million or several million pounds sterling in shares of the former companies and then issue new

on the banker, which, however, never exist as deposits. To the extent that they serve in clearing-house transactions, they perform the function of capital for the bankers — after the latter have loaned them out. They pay one another their mutual drafts upon the non-existing deposits by balancing their mutual accounts.

Adam Smith says with regard to the role played by capital in the loaning of money:

"Even in the moneyed interest, however, the money is, as it were, but the deed of assignment which conveys from one hand to another those capitals which the owners do not care to employ themselves. Those capitals may be greater in almost any proportion than the amount of the money which serves as the instrument of their conveyance, the same pieces of money successively serving for many different loans, as well as for many different purchases. A, for example, lends to W £1,000, with which W immediately purchases of B £1,000 worth of goods. B, having no occasion for the money himself, lends the identical pieces to X, with which X immediately purchases of C another £1,000 worth of goods. C, in the same manner, and for the same reason, lends them to Y, who again purchases goods with them of D. In this manner the same pieces, either of coin or of paper, may, in the course of a few days, serve as the instrument of three different loans, and of three different purchases, each of which is, in value, equal to the whole amount of those pieces. What the three moneyed men, A, B and C, assign to the three borrowers, W, X and Y, is the power of making those purchases. In this power consist both the value and the use of the loans. The stock lent by the three moneyed men is equal to the value of the goods which can be purchased with it, and is three times greater than that of the money with which the purchases are made. Those loans, however, may be all perfectly well secured, the goods purchased by the different debtors being so employed, as, in due time, to bring back, with a profit, an equal value either of coin or of paper. And as the same pieces of money can thus serve as the instrument of different loans to three, or for the same reason, to thirty times their value, so they may likewise successively serve as the instrument of repayment" (BOOK II, CHAP. IV).[a]

Since the same piece of money can be used for various purchases, corresponding to its velocity of circulation, it can similarly be used for various loans, since the purchases take it from one person to another, and a loan is but a transfer from one person to another without the mediation of a purchase. To every seller, money represents the converted form of his commodities. Nowadays, when every value is expressed as capital value, it represents in the various loans various ca-

shares amounting to the nominal value of the purchased shares, but half of them are issued as PREFERRED and the other half as DEFERRED. In such cases the original shares are doubled, since they serve as a basis for a new issue of shares.—*F. E.*||

---

[a] A. Smith, *An Inquiry into the Nature and Causes of the Wealth of Nations*, Vol. I, pp. 428-29.

pitals in succession. This is simply another way of expressing the earlier statement that it can successively realise various commodity values. At the same time it serves as a medium of circulation, in order to transfer the material capitals from person to person. In the case of loans, it does not pass from person to person as a medium of circulation. As long as it remains in the hands of the lender, it is in his hands not a medium of circulation, but the value existence of his capital. And in this form he transfers it when lending it to a third party. If A had lent the money to B, and B to C, without the mediation of purchases, the same money would not represent three capitals, but only one — a *single* capital value. The number of capitals which it actually represents depends on the number of times that it functions as the value form of various commodity capitals.

The same thing that Adam Smith says about loans in general also applies to deposits, which are merely another name for the loans which the public makes to the bankers. The same pieces of money serve as the instruments for any number of deposits.

"It is unquestionably true that the £1,000 which you deposit at A today may be reissued tomorrow, and form a deposit at B. The day after that, reissued from B, it may form a deposit at C... and so on to infinitude; and that the same £1,000 in money may, thus, by a succession of transfers, multiply itself into a sum of deposits absolutely indefinite. It is possible, therefore, that nine-tenths of all the deposits in the United Kingdom may have no existence beyond their record in the books of the bankers.... Thus in Scotland, for instance, currency has never exceeded £3 million, the deposits in the banks are estimated at £27 million. Unless a run on the banks be made, the same £1,000 would, if sent back upon its travels, cancel with the same facility a sum equally indefinite. As the same £1,000, with which you cancel your debt to a tradesman today, may cancel his debt to the merchant tomorrow, the merchant's debt to the bank the day following, and so on without end; so the same £1,000 may pass from hand to hand, and bank to bank, and cancel any conceivable sum of deposits" (*The Currency Theory Reviewed*, pp. 62-63).

Just as everything in this credit system is doubled and trebled and transformed into a mere phantom of the imagination, so it is with the "reserve fund", where one would at last hope to grasp on to something solid.

Let us listen once more to Mr. Morris, Governor of the Bank of England:

"The reserves of the private bankers are in the hands of the Bank of England in the shape of deposits.... An export of gold acts exclusively, in the first instance, upon the reserve of the Bank of England; but it would also be acting upon the reserves of the bankers, inasmuch as it is a withdrawal of a portion of the reserves which they have in the

Bank of England. It would be acting upon the reserves of all the bankers throughout the country" (Commercial Distress, 1847-48).[a]

Ultimately, then, the reserve funds actually merge with the reserve fund of the Bank of England.[4] However, this reserve fund also has a double existence. The reserve fund of the BANKING DEPARTMENT is equal to the surplus of notes which the Bank is authorised to issue over and above the notes in circulation. The legal maximum of the note issue = £14 million (for which no bullion reserve is required; it is the approximate amount owed by the state to the Bank) plus the amount of the Bank's supply of precious metal. If the supply of precious metal in the Bank = £14 million, the Bank can thus issue £28 million in notes, and if £20 million of these are in circulation, the reserve fund of the BANKING DEPARTMENT = £8 million. These £8 million's worth of notes

[4] //To what extent this has intensified since then is shown by the following official tabulation of the bank reserves of the fifteen largest London banks in November 1892, taken from the *Daily News* of December 15, 1892:

Name of Bank	Liabilities	Cash Reserves	Percentages
City	£9,317,629	£746,551	8.01
Capital and Counties	11,392,744	1,307,483	11.47
Imperial	3,987,400	447,157	11.22
Lloyds	23,800,937	2,966,806	12.46
London & Westminster	24,671,559	3,818,885	15.50
London & S. Western	5,570,268	812,353	14.58
London Joint Stock	12,127,993	1,288,977	10.62
London and Midland	8,814,499	1,127,280	12.79
London and County	37,111,035	3,600,374	9.70
National	11,163,829	1,426,225	12.77
National Provincial	41,907,384	4,614,780	11.01
Parrs and the Alliance	12,794,489	1,532,707	11.98
Prescott & Co	4,041,058	538,517	13.07
Union of London	15,502,618	2,300,084	14.84
Williams, Deacon & Manchester & Co	10,452,381	1,317,628	12.60
Total	£232,655,823	£27,845,807	11.97

Of this total reserve of almost 28 million, at least 25 million are deposited in the Bank of England, and at most 3 million are in cash in the safes of the 15 banks themselves. But the cash reserve of the banking department of the Bank of England amounted to less than 16 million during that same month of November 1892!—*F. E.*//

[a] First Report from the Secret Committee on Commercial Distress..., p. 277, Nos 3641 and 3642, testimony of J. Morris and H. Prescott (paraphrased).

are then legally the banker's capital at the disposal of the Bank, and at the same time the reserve fund for its deposits. Now, if a drain of gold takes place, whereby the supply of precious metal in the Bank is reduced by £6 million — requiring the destruction of an equivalent number of notes — the reserve of the BANKING DEPARTMENT would fall from £8 million to £2 million. On the one hand, the Bank would raise its rate of interest considerably; on the other hand, the banks having deposits with it, and the other depositors, would observe a large decrease in the reserve fund covering their own credits in the Bank. In 1857, the four largest stock banks of London threatened to call in their deposits, and thereby bankrupt the BANKING DEPARTMENT, unless the Bank of England would secure a "government letter" suspending the Bank Act of 1844.[5] In this way the BANKING DEPARTMENT could fail, as in 1847, while any number of millions (e. g., 8 million in 1847) are held in its ISSUE DEPARTMENT to guarantee the convertibility of the circulating notes. But this is again illusory.

"That large portion (of deposits) for which the bankers themselves have no immediate demand passes into the hands of the BILL-BROKERS, who give to the banker in return commercial bills already discounted by them for persons in London and in different parts of the country as a security for the sum advanced by the banker. The BILL-BROKER is responsible to the banker for payment of this MONEY AT CALL[a]; and such is the magnitude of these transactions, that Mr. Neave, the present Governor of the Bank //of England//, stated in evidence, 'We know that one BROKER had 5 million, and we were led to believe that another had between 8 and 10 million; there was one with 4, another with $3\frac{1}{2}$, and a third with above 8. I speak of deposits with the brokers' " (Report of Committee on Bank Acts, 1857-58, p. V, Section 8).

"The London BILL-BROKERS carried on their enormous transactions without any cash reserve, relying on the run off of their bills falling due, or in extremity, on the power of obtaining advances from the Bank of England on the security of bills under discount" [Ibid., p. VIII, Section 17]. "Two BILL-BROKING houses in London suspended payment in 1847; both afterwards resumed business. In 1857, both suspended again. The liabilities of one house in 1847 were, in round numbers, £2,683,000, with a capital of £180,000; the liabilities of the same house, in 1857, were £5,300,000, the capital probably not more than one-fourth of what it was in 1847. The liabilities of the other firm were between £3,000,000 and £4,000,000 at each period of stoppage, with a capital not exceeding £45,000" (Ibid., p. XXI, Section 52).

[5] //The suspension of the Bank Act of 1844 [48] permits the Bank to issue any quantity of banknotes regardless of the gold reserve backing in its possession; thus, to create an arbitrary quantity of fictitious paper money capital, and to use it for the purpose of making loans to banks, exchange brokers, and through them to commerce.—F. E.//

---

[a] In 1894 German edition this English term is explained in German in parentheses.

Chapter XXX

MONEY CAPITAL AND REAL CAPITAL. I

The only difficult questions, which we are now approaching in connection with the credit system, are the following:

First: The accumulation of the actual money capital. To what extent is it, and to what extent is it not, an indication of an actual accumulation of capital, i. e., of reproduction on an extended scale? Is the so-called PLETHORA of capital — an expression used only with reference to the interest-bearing capital, i. e., money capital — only a special way of expressing industrial overproduction, or does it constitute a separate phenomenon alongside of it? Does this PLETHORA, or excessive supply of money capital, coincide with the existence of stagnating masses of money (bullion, gold coin and banknotes), so that this superabundance of actual money is the expression and external form of that PLETHORA of loan capital?

Secondly: To what extent does a scarcity of money, i. e., a shortage of loan capital, express a shortage of real capital (commodity capital and productive capital)? To what extent does it coincide, on the other hand, with a shortage of money as such, a shortage of the medium of circulation?

In so far as we have hitherto considered the peculiar form of accumulation of money capital and of money wealth in general, it has resolved itself into an accumulation of claims of ownership upon labour. The accumulation of the capital of the national debt has been revealed to mean merely an increase in a class of state creditors, who have the privilege of a firm claim upon a certain portion of the tax revenue.[6] By means of these facts, whereby even an accumulation of

---

[6] "The public fund is nothing but imaginary capital, which represents that portion of the annual revenue, which is set aside to pay the debt. An equivalent amount of capital has been spent; it is this which serves as a denominator for the loan, but it is not this which is represented by the public fund; for the capital no longer exists. New wealth must be created by the work of industry; a portion of this wealth is annually set aside in advance for those who have loaned that wealth which has been spent; this portion is taken by means of taxes from those who produce it, and is given to the creditors of the state, and, according to the customary proportion between capital and interest in the country, an imaginary capital is assumed equivalent to that which could give rise to the annual income which these creditors are to receive" (Sismondi, *Nouveaux principes*, II, p. 230).[a]

---

[a] The footnote is written in French.

debts may appear as an accumulation of capital, the height of distortion taking place in the credit system becomes apparent. These promissory notes, which are issued for the originally loaned capital long since spent, these paper duplicates of consumed capital, serve for their owners as capital to the extent that they are saleable commodities and may, therefore, be reconverted into capital.

Titles of ownership to public works, railways, mines, etc., are indeed, as we have also seen, titles to real capital. But they do not place this capital at one's disposal. It is not subject to withdrawal. They merely convey legal claims to a portion of the surplus value to be obtained by it. But these titles likewise become paper duplicates of the real capital; it is as though a bill of lading were to acquire a value separate from the cargo, both concomitantly and simultaneously with it. They come to nominally represent non-existent capital. For the real capital exists side by side with them and does not change hands as a result of the transfer of these duplicates from one person to another. They assume the form of interest-bearing capital, not only because they guarantee a certain income, but also because, through their sale, their repayment as capital values can be obtained. To the extent that the accumulation of this paper expresses the accumulation of railways, mines, steamships, etc., to that extent does it express the extension of the actual reproduction process — just as the extension of, for example, a tax list on movable property indicates the expansion of this property. But as duplicates which are themselves objects of transactions as commodities, and thus able to circulate as capital values, they are illusory, and their value may fall or rise quite independently of the movement of value of the real capital for which they are titles. Their value, that is, their quotation on the Stock Exchange, necessarily has a tendency to rise with a fall in the rate of interest — in so far as this fall, independent of the characteristic movements of money capital, is due merely to the tendency for the rate of profit to fall; therefore, this imaginary wealth expands, if for this reason alone, in the course of capitalist production in accordance with the expressed value for each of its aliquot parts of specific original nominal value.[7]

Gain and loss through fluctuations in the price of these titles of

---

[7] A portion of the accumulated loanable money capital is indeed merely an expression of industrial capital. For instance, when England, in 1857, had invested £80 million in American railways and other enterprises, this investment was transacted almost completely by the export of English commodities for which the Americans did not have to make payment in return. The English exporter drew bills of exchange for these

ownership, and their centralisation in the hands of railway kings, etc., become, by their very nature, more and more a matter of gamble, which appears to take the place of labour as the original method of acquiring capital wealth and also replaces naked force. This type of imaginary money wealth not only constitutes a very considerable part of the money wealth of private people, but also of banker's capital, as we have already indicated.

In order to quickly settle this question, let us point out that one could also mean by the accumulation of money capital the accumulation of wealth in the hands of bankers (money lenders by profession), acting as middlemen between private money capitalists on the one hand, and the state, communities, and reproducing borrowers on the other. For the entire vast extension of the credit system, and all credit in general, is exploited by them as their private capital. These fellows always possess capital and incomes in money form or in direct claims on money. The accumulation of the wealth of this class may take place completely differently than actual accumulation, but it proves at any rate that this class pockets a good deal of the real accumulation.

Let us reduce the scope of the problem before us. Government securities, like stocks and other securities of all kinds, are spheres of investment for loanable capital — capital intended for bearing interest. They are forms of loaning such capital. But they themselves are not the loan capital, which is invested in them. On the other hand, in so far as credit plays a direct role in the reproduction process, what the industrialist or merchant needs when he wishes to have a bill discounted or a loan granted is neither stocks nor government securities. What he needs is money. He, therefore, pledges or sells those securities if he cannot secure money in any other way. It is the accumulation of *this* loan capital with which we have to deal here, and more particularly accumulation of loanable money capital. We are not concerned here with loans of houses, machines, or other fixed capital. Nor are we concerned with the advances industrialists and merchants make to one another in commodities and within the compass of the reproduction process; although we must also investigate this point beforehand in more detail. We are concerned exclusively with money loans, which are made by bankers, as middlemen, to industrialists and merchants.

commodities on America, which the English stock subscribers bought up and which were sent to America for purchasing the stock subscriptions.

Let us then, to begin with, analyse commercial credit, that is, the credit which the capitalists engaged in reproduction give to one another. It forms the basis of the credit system. It is represented by the bill of exchange, a promissory note with a definite term of payment, i. e., a DOCUMENT OF DEFERRED PAYMENT. Everyone gives credit with one hand and receives credit with the other. Let us completely disregard, for the present, banker's credit, which constitutes an entirely different sphere. To the extent that these bills of exchange circulate among the merchants themselves as means of payment again, by endorsement from one to another — without, however, the mediation of discounting — it is merely a transfer of the claim from A to B and does not change the picture in the least. It merely replaces one person by another. And even in this case, the liquidation can take place without the intervention of money. Spinner A, for example, has to pay a bill to cotton broker B, and the latter to importer C. Now, if C also exports yarn, which happens often enough, he may buy yarn from A on a bill of exchange and the spinner A may pay the broker B with the broker's own bill which was received in payment from C. At most, a balance will have to be paid in money. The entire transaction then consists merely in the exchange of cotton and yarn. The exporter represents only the spinner, and the cotton broker, the cotton planter.

Two things are now to be noted in the circuit of this purely commercial credit.

First: The settlement of these mutual claims depends upon the return flow of capital, that is, on C — M, which is merely deferred. If the spinner has received a bill of exchange from a cotton goods manufacturer, the manufacturer can pay if the cotton goods which he has on the market have been sold in the interim. If the corn speculator has a bill of exchange drawn upon his agent, the agent can pay the money if the corn has been sold in the interim at the expected price. These payments, therefore, depend on the fluidity of reproduction, that is, the production and consumption processes. But since the credits are mutual, the solvency of one depends upon the solvency of another; for in drawing his bill of exchange, one may have counted either on the return flow of the capital in his own business or on the return flow of the capital in a third party's business whose bill of exchange is due in the meantime. Aside from the prospect of the return flow of capital, payment can only be possible by means of reserve capital at the disposal of the person drawing the bill of exchange, in order to meet his obligations in case the return flow of capital should be delayed.

Secondly: This credit system does not do away with the necessity for cash payments. For one thing, a large portion of expenses must always be paid in cash, e. g., wages, taxes, etc. Furthermore, capitalist B, who has received from C a bill of exchange in place of cash payment, may have to pay a bill of his own which has fallen due to D before C's bill becomes due, and so he must have ready cash. A complete circuit of reproduction as that assumed above, i. e., from cotton planter to cotton spinner and back again, can only constitute an exception; it will be constantly interrupted at many points. We have seen in the discussion of the reproduction process (Book II, Part III ^a) that the producers of constant capital exchange, in part, constant capital among themselves. As a result, the bills of exchange can, more or less, balance each other out. Similarly, in the ascending line of production, where the cotton broker draws on the cotton spinner, the spinner on the manufacturer of cotton goods, the manufacturer on the exporter, the exporter on the importer (perhaps of cotton again). But the circuit of transactions, and, therefore, the turn about of the series of claims, does not take place at the same time. For example, the claim of the spinner on the weaver is not settled by the claim of the coal-dealer on the machine-builder. The spinner never has any counter-claims on the machine-builder, in his business, because his product, yarn, never enters as an element in the machine-builder's reproduction process. Such claims must, therefore, be settled by money.

The limits of this commercial credit, considered by themselves, are 1) the wealth of the industrialists and merchants, that is, their command of reserve capital in case of delayed returns; 2) these returns themselves. These returns may be delayed, or the prices of commodities may fall in the meantime or the commodities may become momentarily unsaleable due to a stagnant market. The longer the bills of exchange run, the larger must be the reserve capital, and the greater the possibility of a diminution or delay of the returns through a fall in prices or a glut on the market. And, furthermore, the returns are so much less secure, the more the original transaction was conditioned upon speculation on the rise or fall of commodity prices. But it is evident that with the development of the productive power of labour, and thus of production on a large scale: 1) the markets expand and

---

^a See present edition, Vol. 36.

become more distant from the place of production; 2) credits must, therefore, be prolonged; 3) the speculative element must thus more and more dominate the transactions. Production on a large scale and for distant markets throws the total product into the hands of commerce; but it is impossible that the capital of a nation should double itself in such a manner that commerce should itself be able to buy up the entire national product with its own capital and to sell it again. Credit is, therefore, indispensable here; credit, whose volume grows with the growing volume of value of production and whose time duration grows with the increasing distance of the markets. A mutual interaction takes place here. The development of the production process extends the credit, and credit leads to an extension of industrial and commercial operations.

When we examine this credit detached from banker's credit, it is evident that it grows with an increasing volume of industrial capital itself. Loan capital and industrial capital are identical here. The loaned capital is commodity capital which is intended either for ultimate individual consumption or for the replacement of the constant elements of productive capital. What appears here as loan capital is always capital existing in some definite phase of the reproduction process, but which by means of purchase and sale passes from one person to another, while its equivalent is not paid by the buyer until some later stipulated time. For example, cotton is transferred to the spinner for a bill of exchange, yarn to the manufacturer of cotton goods for a bill of exchange, cotton goods to the merchant for a bill, from whose hands they go to the exporter for a bill, and then, for a bill to some merchant in India, who sells the goods and buys indigo instead, etc. During this transfer from hand to hand the transformation of cotton into cotton goods is effected, and the cotton goods are finally transported to India and exchanged for indigo, which is shipped to Europe and there enters into the reproduction process again. The various phases of the reproduction process are promoted here by credit, without any payment on the part of the spinner for the cotton, the manufacturer of cotton goods for the yarn, the merchant for the cotton goods, etc. In the first stages of the process, the commodity, cotton, goes through its various production phases, and this transition is promoted by credit. But as soon as the cotton has received in production its ultimate form as a commodity, the same commodity capital passes only through the hands of various merchants who promote its transportation to distant markets, and the last of whom finally sells these commodities to the consumer and buys other commodities in their stead, which either become consumed or go into the reproduction process. It is necessary, then, to differentiate between two stages here: in the first stage, credit promotes the actual successive phases in the production of the same article; in the second, credit merely promotes the transfer of the article, including its transportation, from one merchant to another, in other words, the process $C — M$. But here also the commodity is at least in the act of circulation, that is, in a phase of the reproduction process.

It follows, then, that it is never idle capital which is loaned here, but capital which must change its form in the hands of its owner; it exists in a form that for him is merely commodity capital, i. e., capital which must be retransformed, and, to begin with, at least converted into money. It is, therefore, the metamorphosis of commodities that is here promoted by credit; not merely $C — M$, but also $M — C$ and the actual production process. A large quantity of credit within the reproductive circuit (banker's credit excepted) does not signify a large quantity of idle capital, which is being offered for loan and is seeking profitable investment. It means rather a large employment of capital in the reproduction process. Credit, then, promotes here 1) as far as the industrial capitalists are concerned, the transition of industrial capital from one phase into another, the connection of related and dovetailing spheres of production; 2) as far as the merchants are concerned, the transportation and transition of commodities from one person to another until their definite sale for money or their exchange for other commodities.

The maximum of credit is here identical with the fullest employment of industrial capital, that is, the utmost exertion of its reproductive power without regard to the limits of consumption. These limits of consumption are extended by the exertions of the reproduction process itself. On the one hand, this increases the consumption of revenue on the part of labourers and capitalists, on the other hand, it is identical with an exertion of productive consumption.

As long as the reproduction process is continuous and, therefore, the return flow assured, this credit exists and expands, and its expansion is based upon the expansion of the reproduction process itself. As soon as a stoppage takes place, as a result of delayed returns, glutted markets, or fallen prices, a superabundance of industrial capital becomes available, but in a form in which it cannot perform its functions. Huge quantities of commodity capital, but unsaleable. Huge quantities of fixed capital, but largely idle due to stagnant reproduction. Credit is contracted 1) because this capital is idle, i. e., blocked in one of its phases of reproduction because it cannot complete its metamorphosis; 2) because confidence in the continuity of the reproduction process has been shaken; 3) because the demand for this commercial credit diminishes. The spinner, who curtails his production and has a large quantity of unsold yarn in stock, does not need to buy any cotton on credit; the merchant does not need to buy any commodities on credit because he has more than enough of them.

Hence, if there is a disturbance in this expansion or even in the normal flow of the reproduction process, credit also becomes scarce; it is more difficult to obtain commodities on credit. However, the demand for cash payment and the caution observed toward sales on credit are particularly characteristic of the phase of the industrial cycle following a crash. During the crisis itself, since everyone has products to sell, cannot sell them, and yet must sell them in order to meet payments, it is not the mass of idle and investment-seeking capital, but rather the mass of capital impeded in its reproduction process, that is greatest just when the shortage of credit is most acute (and therefore the rate of discount highest for banker's credit). The capital already invested is then, indeed, idle in large quantities because the reproduction process is stagnant. Factories are closed, raw materials accumulate, finished products flood the market as commodities. Nothing is more erroneous, therefore, than to blame a scarcity of productive capital for such a condition. It is precisely at such times that there is a superabundance of productive capital, partly in relation to the normal, but temporarily reduced scale of reproduction, and partly in relation to the paralysed consumption.

Let us suppose that the whole of society is composed only of industrial capitalists and wage workers. Let us furthermore disregard price fluctuations, which prevent large portions of the total capital from replacing themselves in their average proportions and which, owing to the general interrelations of the entire reproduction process as developed in particular by credit, must always call forth general stoppages of a transient nature. Let us also disregard the sham transactions and speculations, which the credit system favours. Then, a crisis could only be explained as the result of a disproportion of production in various branches of the economy, and as a result of a disproportion between the consumption of the capitalists and their accumulation. But as matters stand, the replacement of the capital invested in production depends largely upon the consuming power of the non-producing classes; while the consuming power of the workers is limited partly by the laws of wages, partly by the fact that they are used only as long as they can be profitably employed by the capitalist class. The ultimate reason for all real crises always remains the poverty and restricted consumption of the masses as opposed to the drive of capitalist production to develop the productive forces as though only the absolute consuming power of society constituted their limit.

A real lack of productive capital, at least among capitalistically developed nations, can be said to exist only in times of general crop failures, either in the principal foodstuffs or in the principal industrial raw materials.

However, in addition to this commercial credit we have actual money credit. The advances of the industrialists and merchants among one another are amalgamated with the money advances made to them by the bankers and money lenders. In discounting bills of exchange the advance is only nominal. A manufacturer sells his product for a bill of exchange and gets this bill discounted by some BILL-BROKER. In reality, the latter advances only the credit of his banker, who in turn advances to the broker the money capital of his depositors. The depositors consist of the industrialists and merchants themselves and also of workers (through savings banks) — as well as ground rent recipients and other unproductive classes. In this way every individual industrial manufacturer and merchant gets around the necessity of keeping a large reserve capital and being dependent upon his actual returns. On the other hand, the whole process becomes so complicated, partly by simply manipulating bills of exchange, partly by commodity transactions for the sole purpose of manufacturing bills of exchange, that the semblance of a very solvent business with a smooth flow of returns can easily persist even long after returns actually come in only at the expense partly of swindled money lenders and partly of swindled producers. Thus business always appears almost excessively sound right on the eve of a crash. The best proof of this is furnished, for instance, by the Reports on Bank Acts of 1857 and 1858, in which all bank directors, merchants, in short all the invited experts with Lord Overstone at their head, congratulated one another on the prosperity and soundness of business — just one month before the outbreak of the crisis in August 1857.[a] And, strange-

---

[a] See Report from the Select Committee on Bank Acts, Part I, 1857, pp. 327-419.

ly enough, Tooke in his *History of Prices* succumbs to this illusion once again as historian for each crisis.[a] Business is always thoroughly sound and the campaign in full swing, until suddenly the debacle takes place.

––––––––––

We revert now to the accumulation of money capital.

Not every augmentation of loanable money capital indicates a real accumulation of capital or expansion of the reproduction process. This becomes most evident in the phase of the industrial cycle immediately following a crisis, when loan capital lies idle in great quantities. And such times, when the production process is curtailed (production in the English industrial districts was reduced by one-third after the crisis of 1847), when the prices of commodities are at their lowest level, when the spirit of enterprise is paralysed, the rate of interest is low, which in this case indicates nothing more than an increase in loanable capital precisely as a result of contraction and paralysation of industrial capital. It is quite obvious that a smaller quantity of a circulation medium is required when the prices of commodities have fallen, the number of transactions decreased, and the capital laid out for wages reduced; that, on the other hand, no additional money is required to function as world money after foreign debts have been liquidated either by the export of gold or as a result of bankruptcies; that, finally, the volume of business connected with discounting bills of exchange diminishes in proportion with the reduced number and magnitudes of the bills of exchange themselves. Hence the demand for loanable money capital, either to act as a medium of circulation or as a means of payment (the investment of new capital is still out of the question), decreases and this capital, therefore, becomes relatively abundant. Under such circumstances, however, the supply of loanable money capital also increases, as we shall later see.

Thus, the situation after the crisis of 1847 was characterised by "a limitation of transaction and a great superabundance of money" (Commercial Distress, 1847-48, Evidence No. 1664). The rate of interest was very low because of the "almost perfect destruction of commerce and the almost total want of means of employing money" (l. c., p. 45, tes-

––––––––––

[a] Th. Tooke, *A History of Prices, and of the State of the Circulation, from 1839 to 1847 Inclusive*, pp. 329-48 and *A History of Prices, and of the State of the Circulation, During the Nine Years 1848-1856*, Vol. VI, pp. 218-29.

timony of Hodgson, Director of the Royal Bank of Liverpool).[a] What nonsense these gentlemen concocted (and Hodgson is, moreover, one of the best of them) in order to explain these facts, can be seen from the following remark:

"The pressure" (1847) "arose from the real diminution of the moneyed capital of the country, caused partly by the necessity of paying in gold for imports from all parts of the world, and partly by the absorption of FLOATING into fixed CAPITAL."[b]

How the conversion of floating capital into fixed capital reduces the money capital of a country is unintelligible. For, in the case of railways, e. g., in which capital was mainly invested at that time, neither gold nor paper is used for viaducts and rails, and the money for the railway stocks, to the extent that it had been deposited solely in payment, performed exactly the same functions as any other money deposited in banks and even increased the loanable money capital temporarily, as already shown above[c]; but to the extent that it had actually been spent for construction, it circulated in the country as a medium of purchase and of payment. Only in so far as fixed capital cannot be exported, so that with the impossibility of its export the available capital secured from returns for exported articles also drops out of the picture — including the returns in cash or bullion — only to that extent could the money capital be affected. But at that time English export articles were also piled up in huge quantities on the foreign markets without being able to be sold. It is true, the FLOATING CAPITAL of the merchants and manufacturers of Manchester, etc., who had a portion of their normal business capital tied up in railway stocks and were therefore dependent upon borrowed capital for running their business, had become fixed, and they, therefore, had to suffer the consequences. But it would have been the same, if the capital belonging to their business, but withdrawn from it, had been invested, say, in mines instead of railways — mining products like iron, coal, copper being themselves in turn FLOATING CAPITAL. The actual reduction of available money capital through crop failures, corn imports, and gold exports constituted, naturally, an event that had nothing to do with the railway swindle.

"Almost all mercantile houses had begun to starve their business more or less ... by taking part of their commercial capital for railways" [l.c., p. 42].—"Loans to so great

---

[a] Op. cit., p. 21, No. 231. The page given in the text is wrong. - [b] See First Report from the Select Committee..., p. 39, No. 466, paraphrased. - [c] See this volume, pp. 464-67.

an extent by commercial houses to railways induced them to lean too much upon ... banks by the discount of paper, whereby to carry on their commercial operations" (the same Hodgson, l. c., p. 67). "In Manchester there have been immense losses in consequence of the speculation in railways" (R. Gardner, previously cited in Buch I, Kap. XIII, 3, c.[a] and in several other places; Evidence No. 4884, l. c.).

One of the principal causes of the crisis of 1847 was the colossal flooding of the market and the fabulous swindle in the East Indian trade with commodities. But there were also other circumstances which bankrupted very rich firms in this line:

"They had large means, but not available. The whole of their capital was locked up in estates in the Mauritius, or indigo factories, or sugar factories. Having incurred liabilities to the extent of £500,000-600,000, they had no available assets to pay their bills, and eventually it proved that to pay their bills they were entirely dependent upon their credit" (Ch. Turner, big East Indian merchant in Liverpool, No. 730, l. c.).

See also Gardner (No. 4872, l. c.):

"Immediately after the China treaty, so great a prospect was held out to the country of a great extension of our commerce with China, that there were many large mills built with a view to that trade exclusively, in order to manufacture that class of cloth which is principally taken for the China market, and our previous manufactures had the addition of all those."—"4874. How has that trade turned out? — Most ruinous, almost beyond description; I do not believe that of the whole of the shipments that were made in 1844 and 1845 to China, above two-thirds of the amount have ever been returned; in consequence of tea being the principal article of repayment and of the expectation that was held out, we, as manufacturers, fully calculated upon a great reduction in the duty on tea."

And now, naïvely expressed, comes the characteristic credo of the English manufacturer:

"Our commerce with no foreign market is limited by their power to purchase the commodity, but it is limited in this country by our capability of consuming that which we receive in return for our manufactures."

(The relatively poor countries, with whom England trades, are, of course, able to pay for and consume any amount of English products, but unfortunately wealthy England cannot assimilate the products sent in return.)

"4876. I sent out some goods in the first instance, and the goods sold at about 15 per cent loss, from the full conviction that the price at which my agents could purchase tea would leave so great a profit in this country as to make up the deficiency... but instead of profit I lost in some instances 25 and up to 50 per cent."—"4877. Did the manufacturers generally export on their own account? — Principally; the merchants, I think, very soon saw that the thing would not answer, and they rather encouraged the manufacturers to consign than take a direct interest themselves."

---

[a] English edition: Ch. XV, 3, c (present edition, Vol. 35).

In 1857, on the other hand, the losses and failures fell mainly upon the merchants, since the manufacturers left them the task of flooding the foreign markets "on their own account".

––––––

An expansion of money capital, which arises out of the fact that, in view of the expansion of banking (see, below, the example of Ipswich, where in the course of a few years immediately preceding 1857 the deposits of the farmers quadrupled[a]), what was formerly a private hoard or coin reserve is always converted into loanable capital for a definite time, does not indicate a growth in productive capital any more than the increasing deposits with the London stock banks when the latter began to pay interest on deposits. As long as the scale of production remains the same, this expansion leads only to an abundance of loanable money capital as compared with the productive. Hence the low rate of interest.

After the reproduction process has again reached that state of prosperity which precedes that of overexertion, commercial credit becomes very much extended; this forms, indeed, the "sound" basis again for a ready flow of returns and extended production. In this state the rate of interest is still low, although it rises above its minimum. This is, in fact, the *only* time that it can be said a low rate of interest, and consequently a relative abundance of loanable capital, coincides with a real expansion of industrial capital. The ready flow and regularity of the returns, linked with extensive commercial credit, ensures the supply of loan capital in spite of the increased demand for it, and prevents the level of the rate of interest from rising. On the other hand, those cavaliers who work without any reserve capital or without any capital at all and who thus operate completely on a money credit basis begin to appear for the first time in considerable numbers. To this is now added the great expansion of fixed capital in all forms, and the opening of new enterprises on a vast and far-reaching scale. The interest now rises to its average level. It reaches its maximum again as soon as the new crisis sets in. Credit suddenly stops then, payments are suspended, the reproduction process is paralysed, and with the previously mentioned exceptions, a superabundance of idle industrial capital appears side by side with an almost absolute absence of loan capital.

––––––

[a] See this volume, p. 495.

On the whole, then, the movement of loan capital, as expressed in the rate of interest, is in the opposite direction to that of industrial capital. The phase wherein a low rate of interest, but above the minimum, coincides with the "improvement" and growing confidence after a crisis, and particularly the phase wherein the rate of interest reaches its average level, exactly midway between its minimum and maximum, are the only two periods during which an abundance of loan capital is available simultaneously with a great expansion of industrial capital. But at the beginning of the industrial cycle, a low rate of interest coincides with a contraction, and at the end of the industrial cycle, a high rate of interest coincides with a superabundance of industrial capital. The low rate of interest that accompanies the "improvement" shows that the commercial credit requires bank credit only to a slight extent because it is still self-supporting.

The industrial cycle is of such a nature that the same circuit must periodically reproduce itself, once the first impulse has been given.[8] During a period of slack, production sinks below the level, which it

---

[8] //As I have already stated elsewhere, a change has taken place here since the last major general crisis. The acute form of the periodic process, with its former ten-year cycle, appears to have given way to a more chronic, long drawn out, alternation between a relatively short and slight business improvement and a relatively long, indecisive depression — taking place in the various industrial countries at different times. But perhaps it is only a matter of a prolongation of the duration of the cycle. In the early years of world commerce, 1815-47, it can be shown that these cycles lasted about five years; from 1847 to 1867 the cycle is clearly ten years; is it possible that we are now in the preparatory stage of a new world crash of unparalleled vehemence? Many things seem to point in this direction. Since the last general crisis of 1867 profound changes have taken place. The colossal expansion of the means of transportation and communication — ocean liners, railways, electrical telegraphs, the Suez Canal — has made a real world market a fact. The former monopoly of England in industry has been challenged by a number of competing industrial countries; infinitely greater and varied fields have been opened in all parts of the world for the investment of surplus European capital, so that it is far more widely distributed and local overspeculation may be more easily overcome. By means of all this, most of the old breeding-grounds of crises and opportunities for their development have been eliminated or strongly reduced. At the same time, competition in the domestic market recedes before the cartels and trusts, while in the foreign market it is restricted by protective tariffs, with which all major industrial countries, England excepted, surround themselves. But these protective tariffs are nothing but preparations for the ultimate general industrial war, which shall decide who has supremacy on the world market. Thus every factor, which works against a repetition of the old crises, carries within itself the germ of a far more powerful future crisis.— F. E.//

had attained in the preceding cycle and for which the technical basis has now been laid. During prosperity — the middle period — it continues to develop on this basis. In the period of overproduction and swindle, it strains the productive forces to the utmost, even beyond the capitalistic limits of the production process.

It is self-evident that there is a shortage of means of payment during a period of crisis. The convertibility of bills of exchange replaces the metamorphosis of commodities themselves, and so much more so exactly at such times the more a portion of the firms operates on pure credit. Ignorant and mistaken bank legislation, such as that of 1844-45,[a] can intensify this money crisis. But no kind of bank legislation can eliminate a crisis.

In a system of production, where the entire continuity of the reproduction process rests upon credit, a crisis must obviously occur — a tremendous rush for means of payment — when credit suddenly ceases and only cash payments have validity. At first glance, therefore, the whole crisis seems to be merely a credit and money crisis. And in fact it is only a question of the convertibility of bills of exchange into money. But the majority of these bills represent actual sales and purchases, whose extension far beyond the needs of society is, after all, the basis of the whole crisis. At the same time, an enormous quantity of these bills of exchange represents plain swindle, which now reaches the light of day and collapses; furthermore, unsuccessful speculation with the capital of other people; finally, commodity capital which has depreciated or is completely unsaleable, or returns that can never more be realised again. The entire artificial system of forced expansion of the reproduction process cannot, of course, be remedied by having some bank, like the Bank of England, give to all the swindlers the deficient capital by means of its paper and having it buy up all the depreciated commodities at their old nominal values. Incidentally, everything here appears distorted, since in this paper world, the real price and its real basis appear nowhere, but only bullion, metal coin, notes, bills of exchange, securities. Particularly in centres where the entire money business of the country is concentrated, like London, does this distortion become apparent; the entire process becomes incomprehensible; it is less so in centres of production.

Incidentally in connection with the superabundance of industrial

---

[a] See this volume, pp. 542-59.

capital which appears during crises the following should be noted: commodity capital is in itself simultaneously money capital, that is, a definite amount of value expressed in the price of the commodities. As use value it is a definite quantum of objects of utility, and there is a surplus of these available in times of crises. But as money capital in itself, as potential money capital, it is subject to continual expansion and contraction. On the eve of a crisis, and during it, commodity capital in its capacity as potential money capital is contracted. It represents less money capital for its owner and his creditors (as well as security for bills of exchange and loans) than it did at the time when it was bought and when the discounts and mortgages based on it were transacted. If this is the meaning of the contention that the money capital of a country is reduced in times of stringency, this is identical with saying that the prices of commodities have fallen. Such a collapse in prices merely balances out their earlier inflation.

The incomes of the unproductive classes and of those who live on fixed incomes remain in the main stationary during the inflation of prices which goes hand in hand with overproduction and overspeculation. Hence their consuming capacity diminishes relatively, and with it their ability to replace that portion of the total reproduction which would normally enter into their consumption. Even when their demand remains nominally the same, it decreases in reality.

It should be noted in regard to imports and exports, that, one after another, all countries become involved in a crisis and that it then becomes evident that all of them, with few exceptions, have exported and imported too much, so that *they all have an unfavourable balance of payments*. The trouble, therefore, does not actually lie with the balance of payments. For example, England suffers from a drain of gold. It has imported too much. But at the same time all other countries are oversupplied with English goods. They have thus also imported too much, or have been made to import too much. (There is, indeed, a difference between a country which exports on credit and those which export little or nothing on credit. But the latter then import on credit; and this is only then not the case when commodities are sent to them on consignment.) The crisis may first break out in England, the country which advances most of the credit and takes the least, because the balance of payments, the balance of payments due, which must be settled immediately, is *unfavourable*, even though the general balance of trade is *favourable*. This is explained partly as a result of the credit which it has granted, and partly as a result of the huge

quantity of capital loaned to foreign countries, so that a large quantity of returns flow back to it in commodities, in addition to the actual
trade returns. (However, the crisis has at times first broken out in
America, which takes most of the commercial and capital credit from
England.) The crash in England, initiated and accompanied by a
gold drain, settles England's balance of payments, partly by a bankruptcy of its importers (about which more below), partly by disposing
of a portion of its commodity capital at low prices abroad, and partly
by the sale of foreign securities, the purchase of English securities, etc.
Now comes the turn of some other country. The balance of payments
was momentarily in its favour; but now the time lapse normally existing between the balance of payments and balance of trade has been
eliminated or at least reduced by the crisis: all payments are supposed
to be made at once. The same thing is now repeated here. England
now has a return flow of gold, the other country a gold drain. What
appears in one country as excessive imports, appears in the other as
excessive exports, and vice versa. But overimports and overexports
have taken place in all countries (we are not speaking here about crop
failures, etc., but about a general crisis); that is overproduction promoted by credit and the general inflation of prices that goes with it.

In 1857, the crisis broke out in the United States. A flow of gold
from England to America followed. But as soon as the bubble in
America burst, the crisis broke out in England and the gold flowed
from America to England. The same took place between England
and the continent. The balance of payments is in times of general crisis unfavourable to every nation, at least to every commercially developed nation, but always to each country in succession, as in volley
firing, i. e., as soon as each one's turn comes for making payments;
and once the crisis has broken out, e. g., in England, it compresses the
series of these terms into a very short period. It then becomes evident
that all these nations have simultaneously overexported (thus over-
produced) and overimported (thus overtraded), that prices were inflated in all of them, and credit stretched too far. And the same break-
down takes place in all of them. The phenomenon of a gold drain
then takes place successively in all of them and proves precisely by its
general character 1) that gold drain is just a phenomenon of a crisis,
not its cause; 2) that the sequence in which it hits the various countries indicates only when their judgment-day has come, i. e., when the
crisis started and its latent elements come to the fore there.

It is characteristic of the English economic writers — and the economic literature worth mentioning since 1830 resolves itself mainly into a literature on CURRENCY, credit, and crises — that they look upon the export of precious metals in times of crisis, in spite of the alteration in the rates of exchange, only from the standpoint of England, as a purely national phenomenon, and resolutely close their eyes to the fact that all other European banks raise their rate of interest when their bank raises its own in times of crisis, and that, when the cry of distress over the drain of gold is raised in their country today, it is taken up in America tomorrow and in Germany and France the day after.

In 1847 "the engagements running upon this country had to be met" //mostly for corn//. "Unfortunately, they were met to a great extent by failures" //wealthy England secured relief by bankruptcies in its obligations toward the continent and America//, "but to the extent to which they were not met by failures, they were met by the exportation of bullion" (Report of Committee on Bank Acts, 1857).

In other words, in so far as a crisis in England is intensified by bank legislation, this legislation is a means of cheating the corn-exporting countries in periods of famine, first on their corn and then on the money for the corn. A prohibition on the export of corn during such periods for countries which are themselves labouring more or less under scarcities, is, therefore, a very rational measure to thwart this plan of the Bank of England to "meet obligations" for corn imports "by bankruptcies". It is after all much better that the corn producers and speculators lose a portion of their profit for the good of their own country than their capital for the good of England.

It follows from the above that commodity capital, during crises and during periods of business depression in general, loses to a large extent its capacity to represent potential money capital. The same is true of fictitious capital, interest-bearing paper, in so far as it circulates on the stock exchange as money capital. Its price falls with rising interest. It falls, furthermore, as a result of the general shortage of credit, which compels its owners to dump it in large quantities on the market in order to secure money. It falls, finally, in the case of stocks, partly as a result of the decrease in revenues for which it constitutes drafts and partly as a result of the spurious character of the enterprises which it often enough represents. This fictitious money capital is enormously reduced in times of crisis, and with it the ability of its owners to borrow money on it on the market. However, the reduction of the money equivalents of these securities on the stock exchange list has nothing to do with the actual capital which they represent, but very much indeed with the solvency of their owners.

Chapter XXXI

MONEY CAPITAL AND REAL CAPITAL. II
(*CONTINUED*)

We are still not finished with this question: to what extent does the accumulation of capital in the form of loanable money capital coincide with actual accumulation, i. e., the expansion of the reproduction process.

The transformation of money into loanable money capital is a much simpler matter than the transformation of money into productive capital. But two things should be distinguished here:

1) the mere transformation of money into loan capital;

2) the transformation of capital or revenue into money, which is transformed into loan capital.

It is only the latter point which can involve a positive accumulation of loan capital connected with an actual accumulation of industrial capital.

1. TRANSFORMATION OF MONEY INTO LOAN CAPITAL

We have already seen that a large build-up or superabundance of loan capital can occur, which is connected with productive accumulation only to the extent that it is inversely proportional to it. This is the case in two phases of the industrial cycle, namely, first, when industrial capital in both its forms of productive and commodity capital is contracted, i. e., at the beginning of the cycle after the crisis; and, secondly, when the improvement begins, but when commercial credit still does not use banking credit to a great extent. In the first case, money capital, which was formerly employed in production and commerce, appears as idle loan capital; in the second case, it appears used to an increasing extent, but at a very low rate of interest, because the industrial and commercial capitalists now prescribe terms to the money capitalist. The excess of loan capital expresses, in the first case, a stagnation of industrial capital, and in the second, a relative independence of commercial credit from banking credit — based on the fluidity of the returns, short-term credit, and a preponderance of operations with one's own capital. The speculators, who count on the credit capital of other people, have not yet appeared on the field; the people who work with their own capital are still far removed from approximately pure credit operations. In the former phase, the surplus of loan capital is directly opposite to expressing actual accumulation. In the second phase, it coincides with a renewed expansion of the reproduction process — it accompanies it, but is not its cause. The surplus of loan capital is already decreasing, i. e., it is still only relative compared to the demand. In both cases, the expansion of the actual process of accumulation is promoted by the fact that the low interest — which coincides in the first case with low prices and in the second, with slowly rising prices — increases that portion of the profit which is transformed into profit of enterprise. This takes place to an even greater extent when interest rises to its average level during the height of the period of prosperity, when it has indeed grown, but not relative to profit.

We have seen, on the other hand, that an accumulation of loan capital can take place without any actual accumulation, i. e., by mere technical means such as an expansion and concentration of the banking system; and a saving in the circulation reserve, or in the reserve fund of private means of payment, which are then always transformed into loan capital for a short time. Although this loan capital, which, for this reason, is also called FLOATING CAPITAL,[a] always retains the form of loan capital only for short periods of time (and should indeed also be used for discounting only for short periods of time), there is a continual ebb and flow of it. If one draws some away, another adds to it. The mass of loanable money capital thus grows quite independently of the actual accumulation (we are not speaking here at all about loans for a number of years but only of short-term ones on bills of exchange and deposits).

Bank Committee, 1857. Question 501. "What do you mean by 'FLOATING CAPITAL'?"— //Answer of Mr. Weguelin, Governor of the Bank of England:// "It is capital applicable to loans of money for short periods.... (502) The Bank of England notes ... the country banks circulation, and the amount of coin which is in the country." — //Question:// "It does not appear from the returns before the Committee, if by FLOATING CAPITAL you mean the active circulation" //of the notes of the Bank of England//, "that there is any very great variation in the active circulation?" //But there is a very great difference whether this active circulation is advanced by the money lender or by the reproductive capitalist himself. Weguelin's answer:// "I include in FLOATING CAPITAL the reserves of the bankers, in which there is a considerable fluctuation."

That is to say, there is considerable fluctuation in that portion of

---

[a] In the 1894 German edition this English term is given in parentheses after its German equivalent.

the deposits which the bankers have not loaned out again, but which figures as their reserve and for the greater part also as the reserve of the Bank of England, where they are deposited. Finally, the same gentleman says: FLOATING CAPITAL may be BULLION, that is, bar and coin (503). It is truly wonderful how in this credit gibberish of the money market all categories of political economy receive a different meaning and a different form. FLOATING CAPITAL is the expression there for CIRCULATING CAPITAL, which is, of course, something quite different, and MONEY is CAPITAL, and BULLION is CAPITAL, and banknotes are CIRCULATION, and capital is a COMMODITY, and debts are COMMODITIES, and FIXED CAPITAL is money invested in hard-to-sell paper!

"The joint-stock banks of London ... have increased their deposits from £8,850,774 in 1847 to £43,100,724 in 1857.... The evidence given to your Committee leads to the inference that of this vast amount, a large part has been derived from sources not heretofore made available for this purpose; and that the practice of opening accounts and depositing money with bankers has extended to numerous classes who did not formerly employ their capital(!) in that way. It is stated by Mr. Rodwell, the Chairman of the Association of the Private Country Bankers" //distinguished from joint-stock banks//, "and delegated by them to give evidence to your Committee, that in the neighbourhood of Ipswich this practice has lately increased four-fold among the farmers and shopkeepers of that district; that almost every farmer, even those paying only £50 per annum rent, now keeps deposits with bankers. The aggregate of these deposits of course finds its way to the employments of trade, and especially gravitates to London, the centre of commercial activity, where it is employed first in the discount of bills, or in other advances to the customers of the London bankers. That large portion, however, for which the bankers themselves have no immediate demand passes into the hands of the BILL-BROKERS, who give to the banker in return commercial bills already discounted by them for persons in London and in different parts of the country, as a security for the sum advanced by the banker" (Bank Committee, 1858, p. 8[a]).

By making advances to the BILL-BROKER on bills of exchange which this BILL-BROKER has already discounted once, the banker does, in fact, rediscount them; but in reality, very many of these bills have already been rediscounted by the BILL-BROKER, and with the same money that the banker uses to rediscount the bills of the BILL-BROKER, the latter rediscounts new bills. What this leads to is shown by the following:

"Extensive fictitious credits have been created by means of accommodation bills, and open credits, great facilities for which have been afforded by the practice of joint-stock country banks discounting such bills, and rediscounting them with the BILL-BROKERS in the London market, upon the credit of the bank alone, without reference to the quality of the bills otherwise"(l. c.).[b]

---

[a] Should be: p. V, No. 8. - [b] Should be: p. XXI, No. 54.

Concerning this rediscounting and the assistance which this purely
technical increase of loanable money capital gives to credit swindles,
the following extract from the *Economist* is of interest:

"For some years past capital" //namely, loanable money capital// "has accumulated in some districts of the country more rapidly than it could be used, while, in others,
the means of employing capital have increased more rapidly than the capital itself.
While the bankers in the purely agricultural districts throughout the kingdom found
no sufficient means of profitably and safely employing their deposits in their own districts,
those in the large mercantile towns, and in the manufacturing and mining districts,
have found a larger demand for capital than their own means could supply. The effect
of this relative state of different districts has led, of late years, to the establishment and
rapid extension of a new class of houses in the distribution of capital, who, though
usually called BILL-BROKERS, are in reality bankers upon an immense scale. The business of these houses has been to receive, for such periods, and at such rates of interest as
were agreed upon, the surplus capital of bankers in those districts where it could not be
employed, as well as the temporary unemployed moneys of public companies and extensive mercantile establishments, and advance them at higher rates of interest to bankers in those districts where capital was more in demand, generally by rediscounting
the bills taken from their customers ... and in this way Lombard Street has become the
great centre in which the transfer of spare capital has been made from one part of the
country, where it could not be profitably employed, to another, where a demand existed for it, as well as between individuals similarly circumstanced. At first these transactions were confined almost exclusively to borrowing and lending of banking securities.
But as the capital of the country rapidly accumulated, and became more economised
by the establishment of banks, the funds at the disposal of these discount houses became
so large that they were induced to make advances first on DOCK WARRANTS of merchandise (storage bills on commodities in docks), and next on bills of lading, representing produce not even arrived in this country, though sometimes, if not generally, secured by bills drawn by the merchant upon his broker. This practice rapidly changed the
whole character of English commerce. The facilities thus afforded in Lombard Street
gave extensive powers to the brokers in Mincing Lane, who on their part ... offered the
full advantage of them to the importing merchant; who so far took advantage of them,
that, whereas 25 years ago, the fact that a merchant received advances on his bills of
lading, or even his DOCK WARRANTS, would have been fatal to his credit, the practice
has become so common of late years that it may be said to be now the general rule, and
not the rare exception, as it was 25 years ago. Nay, so much further has this system been
carried, that large sums have been raised in Lombard Street on bills drawn against the
forthcoming crops of distant colonies. The consequence of such facilities being thus granted to the importing merchants led them to extend their transactions abroad, and to invest their FLOATING[a] capital with which their business has hitherto been conducted, in
the most objectionable of all fixed securities—foreign plantations—over which they
could exercise little or no control. And thus we see the direct chain of credits through
which the capital of the country, collected in our rural districts, and in small amounts
in the shape of deposits in country banks, and centred in Lombard Street for employ-

---

[a] In the 1894 German edition this English term is given in parentheses after its German equivalent.

ment, has been, first, made available for the extending operations in our mining and manufacturing districts, by the rediscount of bills to banks in those localities; next, for granting greater facilities for the importation of foreign produce by advances upon DOCK WARRANTS and bills of lading, and thus liberating the 'legitimate' mercantile capital of houses engaged in foreign and colonial trade, and inducing to its most objectionable advances on foreign plantations" (*Economist*, 1847, p. 1334).[a]

This is how credits are "nicely" chained. The rural depositor fancies that he deposits only with his banker, and fancies furthermore that when his banker lends to others, it is done to private persons whom he knows. He has not the slightest suspicion that this banker places his deposit at the disposal of some London BILL-BROKER, over whose operations neither of them has the slightest control.

We have already seen how large public enterprises, such as railways, may momentarily increase loan capital, owing to the circumstance that the deposited amounts always remain at the disposal of the bankers for a certain length of time until they are really used.

––––––––––

Incidentally, the mass of loan capital is quite different from the quantity of circulation. By the quantity of circulation we mean here the sum of all the banknotes and coin, including bars of precious metals, existing and circulating in a country. A portion of this quantity constitutes the reserve of the banks which continuously vary in magnitude.

"On November 12, 1857" //the date of the suspension of the Bank Act of 1844//, "the entire reserve of the Bank of England was only £580,751 (including London and all its branches); their deposits at the same time amounting to £22,500,000; of which near six and a half million belonged to London bankers" (Bank Acts, 1858, p. LVII[b]).

The variations in the interest rate (aside from those occurring over longer periods or the variation in the interest rate among various countries; the former are dependent upon variations in the general rate of profit, the latter on differences in the rates of profit and in the development of credit) depend upon the supply of loan capital (all other circumstances, state of confidence, etc., being equal), that is, of capital loaned in the form of money, coin and notes; in contradistinction to industrial capital, which, as such — in commodity form — is loaned by means of commercial credit among the agents of reproduction themselves.

––––––––––

[a] "The Changed Distribution of Capital", *The Economist*, No. 221, November 20, 1847.
- [b] Should be: p. VIII.

However, the mass of this loanable money capital is different from, and independent of, the mass of circulating money.

For example, if £20 were loaned five times per day, a money capital of £100 would be loaned, and this would imply at the same time that this £20 would have served, moreover, at least four times as a means of purchase or payment; for, if no purchase and payment intervened — so that it would not have represented at least four times the converted form of capital (commodities, including labour power) — it would not constitute a capital of £100, but only five claims of £20 each.

In countries with a developed credit, we can assume that all money capital available for lending exists in the form of deposits with banks and money lenders. This is at least true for business as a whole. Moreover, in times of flourishing business, before the real speculation gets underway — when credit is easy and confidence is growing — most of the functions of circulation are settled by a simple transfer of credit, without the help of coin or paper money.

The mere possibility of large sums of deposits existing when a relatively small quantum of a medium of circulation is available, depends solely on:

1) the number of purchases and payments which the same coin performs;

2) the number of return excursions, whereby it goes back to the banks as deposits, so that its repeated function as a means of purchase and payment is promoted through its renewed transformation into deposits. For example, a small dealer deposits weekly with his banker £100 in money; the banker pays out a portion of the deposit of a manufacturer with this; the latter pays it to his workers; and the workers use it to pay the small dealer, who deposits it in the bank again. The £100 deposited by this small dealer have served, therefore, first, to pay the manufacturer a deposit of his; secondly, to pay the workers; thirdly, to pay the dealer himself; fourthly, to deposit another portion of the money capital of the same small dealer; thus at the end of 20 weeks, if he himself did not have to draw against this money, he would have deposited £2,000 in the bank by means of the same £100.

To what extent this money capital is idle, is shown only by the ebb and flow in the reserve fund of the banks. Therefore, Mr. Weguelin, Governor of the Bank of England in 1857, concludes that the gold of the Bank of England is the "only" reserve capital:

"1258. Practically, I think, the rate of discount is governed by the amount of unemployed capital which there is in the country. The amount of unemployed capital is represented by the reserve of the Bank of England, which is practically a reserve of bullion. When, therefore, the bullion is drawn upon, it diminishes the amount of unemployed capital in the country, and consequently raises the value of that which remains."— "1364. The reserve of bullion in the Bank of England is, in truth, the central reserve or hoard of treasure upon which the whole trade of the country is carried on... And it is upon that hoard or reservoir that the action of the foreign exchanges always falls"[a] (Report on Bank Acts, 1857).

————

The statistics of exports and imports furnish a measure of the accumulation of real, i. e., productive and commodity capital. These always show that, during the ten-year cyclical periods of development of British industry (1815 to 1870), the maximum of the last prosperity *before* the crisis always reappears as the minimum of the following prosperity, whereupon it rises to a new and far higher peak.

The actual or declared value of the exported products from Great Britain and Ireland in the prosperity year of 1824 was £40,396,300. With the crisis of 1825, the amount of exports then falls below this sum and fluctuates between 35 and 39 million annually. With the return of prosperity in 1834, it rises above the former maximum to £41,649,191, and reaches in 1836 the new maximum of £53,368,571. Beginning with 1837, it falls again to 42 million, so that the new minimum is already higher than the old maximum, and then fluctuates between 50 and 53 million. The return of prosperity lifts the amount of exports in 1844 to £58,500,000, whereby the peak of 1836 is again already far exceeded. In 1845, it reaches £60,111,082; it then falls to something over 57 million in 1846, reaches in 1847 almost 59 million, in 1848 almost 53 million, rises in 1849 to 63,500,000, in 1853 to nearly 99 million, in 1854 to 97 million, in 1855 to 94,500,000, in 1856 almost 116 million and reaches a peak of 122 million in 1857. It falls in 1858 to 116 million, rises already in 1859 to 130 million, in 1860 to nearly 136 million, in 1861 only 125 million (the new minimum is here again higher than the former maximum), in 1863 to 146,500,000.

Of course, the same thing could be demonstrated in the case of imports, which show the expansion of the market; here it is only a mat-

————

[a] The last testimony is by W. Newmarch.

ter of the scale of production. //Of course, this holds true of England only for the time of its actual industrial monopoly; but it applies in general to the whole complex of countries with modern large-scale industries, as long as the world market is still expanding.— *F. E.//*

2. TRANSFORMATION OF CAPITAL OR REVENUE
INTO MONEY THAT IS TRANSFORMED INTO LOAN CAPITAL

We will consider here the accumulation of money capital, in so far as it is not an expression either of a stoppage in the flow of commercial credit or of an economy — whether it be an economy in the actual circulating medium or in the reserve capital of the agents engaged in reproduction.

Aside from these two cases, an accumulation of money capital can arise through an unusual inflow of gold, as in 1852 and 1853 as a result of the new Australian and Californian gold mines. This gold was deposited in the Bank of England. The depositors received notes for it, which they did not directly redeposit with bankers. By this means the circulating medium was unusually increased. (Testimony of Weguelin, Bank Committee, 1857, No. 1329.) The Bank strove to utilise these deposits by lowering its discount to 2%. The mass of gold accumulated in the Bank rose during six months of 1853 to 22-23 million.

The accumulation of all money-lending capitalists naturally always takes place directly in money form, whereas we have seen that the actual accumulation of industrial capitalists is accomplished, as a rule, by an increase in the elements of reproductive capital itself. Hence, the development of the credit system and the enormous concentration of the money-lending business in the hands of large banks must, by themselves alone, accelerate the accumulation of loanable capital, as a form distinct from actual accumulation. This rapid development of loan capital is, therefore, a result of actual accumulation, for it is a consequence of the development of the reproduction process, and the profit which forms the source of accumulation for these money capitalists is only a deduction from the surplus value which the reproductive ones filch (and it is at the same time the appropriation of a portion of the interest from the savings *of others*). Loan capital accumulates at the expense of both the industrial and commercial capitalists. We have seen that in the unfavourable phases of the industrial cycle the rate of interest may rise so high that it temporarily consumes the whole profit of some lines of business which are particularly handicapped. At the same time, prices of government and other securities fall. It is at such times that the money capitalists buy this depreciated paper in huge quantities which in the later phases soon regains its former level and rises above it. It is then sold again and a portion of the money capital of the public is thus appropriated. That portion which is not sold yields a higher interest because it was bought below par. But the money capitalists convert all profits made, and reconverted by them into capital, first into loanable money capital. The accumulation of the latter — as distinct from the actual accumulation, although its offshoot — thus takes place, even when we consider only the money capitalists, bankers, etc., by themselves, as an accumulation of this particular class of capitalists. And it must grow with every expansion of the credit system which accompanies the actual expansion of the reproduction process.

If the interest rate is low, this depreciation of the money capital falls principally upon the depositors, not upon the banks. Before the development of stock banks, $\frac{3}{4}$ of all the deposits in England lay in the banks without yielding interest. While interest is now paid on them, it amounts to at least 1% less than the current rate of interest.

As for the money accumulation of the other classes of capitalists, we desregard that portion of it which is invested in interest-bearing paper and accumulates in this form. We consider only that portion which is thrown upon the market as loanable money capital.

In the first place, we have here that portion of the profit which is not spent as revenue, but is set aside for accumulation — for which, however, the industrial capitalists have no use in their own business at the moment. This profit exists directly in commodity capital, a part of whose value it constitutes, and along with which it is realised in money. Now, if it is not reconverted into the production elements of commodity capital (we leave out of consideration for the present the merchant, whom we shall discuss separately), it must remain for a length of time in the form of money. This amount increases with the amount of capital itself, even when the rate of profit declines. That portion which is to be spent as revenue is gradually consumed, but, in the meantime, as deposits, it constitutes loan capital with the banker. Thus, even the growth of that portion of profit which is spent as revenue expresses itself as a gradual and continually repeated accumulation of loan capital. The same is true of the other portion, which is intended for accumulation. Therefore, with the development of the credit system and its organisation, even an increase in revenue, i. e., the consumption of the industrial and commercial capitalists, expresses itself as an accumulation of loan capital. And this holds true for all revenues so far as they are consumed gradually, in other words, for ground rent, wages in their higher form, incomes of unproductive classes, etc. All of them assume for a certain time the form of money revenue and are, therefore, convertible into deposits and thus into loan capital. All revenue — whether it be intended for consumption or accumulation — as long as it exists in some form of money, is a part of the value of commodity capital transformed into money, and is, for this reason, an expression and result of actual accumulation, but is not productive capital itself. When a spinner has exchanged his yarn for cotton — but that portion which constitutes revenue for money — the real existence of his industrial capital is the yarn, which has passed into the hands of the weaver or, perhaps, of some private consumer, and the yarn is, in fact, the existence — whether it is for reproduction or consumption — of the capital value as well as the surplus value contained in it. The magnitude of the surplus value transformed into money depends upon the magnitude of the surplus value contained in the yarn. But as soon as it has been transformed into money, this money is only the value existence of this surplus value. And as such it becomes a moment of loan capital. For this purpose, nothing more is required than that it be transformed into a deposit, if it has not already been loaned out by its owner. But in order to be reconverted into productive capital, it must, on the other hand, already have reached a certain minimum limit.

Chapter XXXII

MONEY CAPITAL AND REAL CAPITAL. III
(CONCLUDED)

The mass of money reconverted into capital in this manner is a result of the enormous reproduction process, but considered by itself, as loanable money capital, it is not itself a mass of reproductive capital.

The most important point of our presentation so far is that the expansion of the part of the revenue intended for consumption (leaving out of consideration the worker, because his revenue is = to the variable capital) shows itself at first as an accumulation of money capital.

A factor, therefore, enters into the accumulation of money capital that is essentially different from the actual accumulation of industrial capital; for the portion of the annual product which is intended for consumption does not by any means become capital. A portion of it *replaces* capital, i. e., the constant capital of the producers of means of consumption, but to the extent that it is actually transformed into capital, it exists in the natural form of the revenue of the producers of this constant capital. The same money, which represents the revenue and serves merely for the promotion of consumption, is regularly transformed into loanable money capital for a period of time. In so far as this money represents wages, it is at the same time the money form of the variable capital; and in so far as it replaces the constant capital of the producers of means of consumption, it is the money form temporarily assumed by their constant capital and serves to purchase the components of their constant capital to be replaced in kind. Neither in the one nor in the other form does it express in itself accumulation, although its quantity increases with the growth of the reproduction process. But it performs temporarily the function of loanable money, i. e., of money capital. In this respect, therefore, the accumulation of money capital must always reflect a greater accumulation of capital than actually exists, owing to the fact that the extension of individual consumption, because it is promoted by means of money, appears as an accumulation of money capital, since it furnishes the money form for actual accumulation, i. e., for money which permits new investments of capital.

Thus, the accumulation of loanable money capital expresses in part only the fact that all money into which industrial capital is transformed in the course of its circuit assumes the form not of money *advanced* by the reproductive capitalists, but of money *borrowed* by them; so that indeed the advance of money that must take place in the reproduction process appears as an advance of borrowed money. In fact, on the basis of commercial credit, one person lends to another the money required for the reproduction process. But this now assumes the following form: the banker, who receives the money as a loan from one group of the reproductive capitalists, lends it to another group of reproductive capitalists, so that the banker appears in the role of a supreme benefactor; and at the same time, the control over this capital falls completely into the hands of the banker in his capacity as middleman.

A few special forms of accumulation of money capital still remain to be mentioned. For example, capital is released by a fall in the price of the elements of production, raw materials, etc. If the industrial capitalist cannot expand his reproduction process immediately, a portion of his money capital is expelled from the circuit as superfluous and is transformed into loanable money capital. Secondly, however, capital in the form of money is released especially by the merchant, whenever interruptions in his business take place. If the merchant has completed a series of transactions and cannot begin a new series because of such interruptions until later, the money realised represents for him only a hoard, surplus capital. But at the same time, it represents a direct accumulation of loanable money capital. In the first case, the accumulation of money capital expresses a repetition of the reproduction process under more favourable conditions, an actual release of a portion of formerly tied-up capital; in other words, an opportunity for expanding the reproduction process with the same amount of money. But in the other case, it expresses merely an interruption in the flow of transactions. However, in both cases it is converted into loanable money capital, represents its accumulation, influences equally the money market and the rate of interest— although it expresses a promotion of the actual accumulation process in one case and its obstruction in the other. Finally, accumulation of money capital is influenced by the number of people who have feathered their nests and have withdrawn from reproduction. Their number increases as more profits are made in the course of the industrial cycle. In this case, the accumulation of loanable money capital expresses, on the one hand, an actual accumulation (in accordance with its relative extent), and, on the other hand, only the extent of the transformation of the industrial capitalists into mere money capitalists.

As for the other portion of profit, which is not intended to be consumed as revenue, it is converted into money capital only when it is not immediately able to find a place for investment in the expansion of business in the productive sphere in which it has been made. This may be due to two causes. Either because this sphere of production is saturated with capital, or because accumulation must first reach a certain volume before it can serve as capital, depending on the investment magnitudes of new capital required in this particular sphere. Hence it is converted for a while into loanable money capital and serves in the expansion of production in other spheres. Assuming all other conditions being equal, the quantity of profits intended for transformation back into capital will depend on the quantity of profits made and thus on the extension of the reproduction process itself. But if this new accumulation meets with difficulties in its employment, through a lack of spheres for investment, i. e., due to a surplus in the branches of production and an oversupply of loan capital, this PLETHORA of loanable money capital merely shows the limitations of *capitalist* production. The subsequent credit swindle proves that no real obstacle stands in the way of the employment of this surplus capital. However, an obstacle is indeed immanent in its laws of expansion, i. e., in the limits in which capital can realise itself as capital. A PLETHORA of money capital as such does not necessarily indicate overproduction, not even a shortage of spheres of investment for capital.

The accumulation of loan capital consists simply in the fact that money is precipitated as loanable money. This process is very different from an actual transformation into capital; it is merely the accumulation of money in a form in which it can be transformed into capital. But this accumulation can reflect, as we have shown, events which are greatly different from actual accumulation. As long as actual accumulation is continually expanding, this extended accumulation of money capital may be partly its result, partly the result of circumstances which accompany it but are quite different from it, and, finally, even partly the result of impediments to actual accumulation. If for no other reason than that accumulation of loan capital is inflated by such circumstances, which are independent of actual accumulation but nevertheless accompany it, there must be a continuous PLETHORA of money capital in definite phases of the cycle and this PLETHORA must develop with the expansion of credit. And simultaneously with it, the necessity of driving the production process beyond its capitalistic limits must also develop: overtrade, overproduction, and excessive credit. At the same time, this must always take place in forms that call forth a reaction.

As far as accumulation of money capital from ground rent, wages, etc., is concerned, it is not necessary to discuss that matter here. Only one aspect should be emphasised and that is that the business of actual saving and abstinence (by hoarders), to the extent that it furnishes elements of accumulation, is left by the division of labour, which comes with the progress of capitalist production, to those who receive the minimum of such elements, and who frequently enough lose even their savings, as do the labourers when banks fail. On the one hand, the capital of the industrial capitalist is not "saved" by himself, but he has command of the savings of others in proportion to the magnitude of his capital; on the other hand, the money capitalist makes of the savings of others his own capital, and of the credit, which the reproductive capitalists give to one another and which the public gives to them, a private source for enriching himself. The last illusion of the capitalist system, that capital is the fruit of one's own labour and savings, is thereby destroyed. Not only does profit consist in the appropriation of other people's labour, but the capital, with which this labour of others is set in motion and exploited, consists of other people's property, which the money capitalist places at the disposal of the industrial capitalist, and for which he in turn exploits the latter.

A few remarks remain to be made about credit capital.

How often the same piece of money can figure as loan capital wholly depends, as we have already previously shown, on:

1) how often it realises commodity values in sale or payment, thus transfers capital, and furthermore how often it realises revenue. How often it gets into other hands as realised value, either of capital or of revenue, obviously depends, therefore, on the extent and magnitude of the actual transactions;

2) this depends on the economy of payments and the development and organisation of the credit system;

3) finally, on the concatenation and velocity of action of credits, so that when a deposit is made at one point it immediately starts off as a loan at another.

Even assuming that the form in which loan capital exists is exclusively that of real money, gold or silver — the commodity whose substance serves as a measure of value — a large portion of this money capital is always necessarily purely fictitious, that is, a title to value — just as tokens of value. In so far as money functions in the circuit of capital, it constitutes indeed, for a moment, money capital; but it does not transform itself into loanable money capital; it is rather exchanged for the elements of productive capital, or paid out as a medium of circulation in the realisation of revenue, and cannot, therefore, transform itself into loan capital for its owner. But in so far as it is transformed into loan capital, and the same money repeatedly represents loan capital, it is evident that it exists only at *one* point in the form of metallic money; at all other points it exists only in the form of claims to capital. With the assumption made, the accumulation of these claims arises from actual accumulation, that is, from the transformation of the value of commodity capital, etc., into money;

but nevertheless the accumulation of these claims or titles as such differs from the actual accumulation from which it arises, as well as from the future accumulation (the new production process), which is promoted by the lending of this money.

Prima facie loan capital always exists in the form of money,[9] later as a claim to money, since the money in which it originally exists is now in the hands of the borrower in actual money form. For the lender it has been transformed into a claim to money, into a title of ownership. The same mass of actual money can, therefore, represent very different masses of money capital. Mere money, whether it represents realised capital or realised revenue, becomes loan capital through the simple act of lending, through its transformation into a deposit, if we consider the general form in a developed credit system. The deposit is money capital for the depositor. But in the hands of the banker it may be only potential money capital, which lies idle in his safe instead of in its owner's.[10]

[9] B. A. 1857. Testimony of Twells, banker: "4516. As a banker, do you deal in capital or in money? — We deal in money." — "4517. How are the deposits paid into your bank? — In money." — "4518. How are they paid out? — In money." — "Then can they be called anything else but money? — No."[a]

Overstone (see Chapter XXVI) confuses continually "CAPITAL" and "MONEY". "VALUE OF MONEY" also means interest to him, but in so far as it is determined by the mass of money, "VALUE OF CAPITAL" is supposed to be interest, in so far as it is determined by the demand for productive capital and the profit made by it. He says: "4140. The use of the word 'capital' is very dangerous." — "4148. The export of bullion from this country is a diminution of the quantity of money in this country, and a diminution of the quantity of money in this country must of course create a pressure upon the money market generally" //but not in the capital market, according to this//. — "4112. As the money goes out of the country, the quantity in the country is diminished. That diminution of the quantity remaining in the country produces an increased value of that money" //this originally means in his theory an increase in the value of money as such through a contraction of circulation, as compared to the values of commodities; in other words, an increase in the value of money is the same as a fall in the value of commodities. But since in the meantime even he has been convinced beyond peradventure that the mass of circulating money *does not* determine prices, it is now the diminution in money as a medium of circulation which is supposed to raise its value as interest-bearing capital, and thus the rate of interest//. "And that increased value of what remains stops the exit of money, and is kept up until it has brought back that quantity of money which is necessary to restore the equilibrium." — More of Overstone 's contradictions later on.

[10] At this point the confusion starts: both of these things are supposed to be "money", namely, the deposit as a claim to payment from the banker, and the deposit-

[a] No. 4519.

With the growth of material wealth the class of money capitalists grows; on the one hand, the number and the wealth of retiring capitalists, rentiers, increases; and on the other hand, the development of the credit system is promoted, thereby increasing the number of bankers, money lenders, financiers, etc. With the development of the available money capital, the quantity of interest-bearing paper, government securities, stocks, etc., also grows as we have previously shown. However, at the same time the demand for available money capital also grows, the jobbers, who speculate with this paper, playing a prominent role on the money market. If all the purchases and sales of this paper were only an expression of actual investments of capital, it would be correct to say that they could have no influence on the demand for loan capital, since when A sells his paper, he draws exactly as much money as B puts into the paper. But even if the paper itself exists, though not the capital (at least not as money capital) originally represented by it, it always creates *pro tanto* a new demand for such money capital. But at any rate it is then money capital, which was previously at the disposal of B but is now at the disposal of A.

B. A. 1857. No. 4886. "Do you consider that it is a correct description of the causes which determined the rate of discount, to say that it is fixed by the quantity of capital

ed money in the hands of the banker. Banker Twells, before the Banking Committee of 1857, offers the following example: "If I begin business with £10,000, I buy with £5,000 commodities and put them into a warehouse. I deposit the other £5,000 with a banker, to draw upon it and use it as I require it. I consider it still £10,000 capital to me, though £5,000 is in the shape of deposits or money" (4528).— This now gives rise to the following peculiar debate.— "4531. You have parted with your £5,000 of notes to somebody else? — Yes." — "4532. Then he has £5,000 of deposits? — Yes." — "4533. And you have £5,000 of deposits left? — Exactly." — "4534. He has £5,000 in money, and you have £5,000 in money? — Yes." — "4535. But it is nothing but money at last? — No." This confusion is due partly to the circumstance that A, who has deposited £5,000, can draw on it and dispose of it as though he still had it. To that extent it serves him as potential money. However, in all cases in which he draws on it he destroys his deposit *pro tanto*. If he draws out real money, and his own money has already been lent to someone else, he is not paid with his own money, but with that of some other depositor. If he pays a debt to B with a cheque on his banker, and B deposits this cheque with his banker, and the banker of A also has a cheque on the banker of B, so that the two bankers merely exchange cheques, the money deposited by A has performed the function of money twice; first, in the hands of the one who has received the money deposited by A; secondly, in the hands of A himself. In the second function, it is a balancing of claims (the claim of A on his banker, and the claim of the latter on the banker of B) without using money. Here the deposit acts twice as money, namely, as real money and then as a claim on money. Mere claims on money can take the place of money only by a balancing of claims.

in the market which is applicable to the discount of mercantile bills, as distinguished from other classes of securities?"—//Chapman:// "No; I think that the question of interest is affected by ALL CONVERTIBLE SECURITIES OF A CURRENT CHARACTER [a]; it would be wrong to limit it simply to the discount of bills, because it would be absurd to say that when there is a great demand for money upon" //the deposit of// "consols, or even upon Exchequer bills, as has ruled very much of late, at a rate much higher than the commercial rate, our commercial world is not affected by it; it is very materially affected by it."—"4890. When sound and current securities, such as bankers acknowledge to be so, are in the market, and people want to borrow money upon them, it certainly has its effect upon commercial bills; for instance, I can hardly expect a man to let me have money at 5% upon commercial bills, if he can lend his money at the same moment at 6% upon consols, or whatever it may be; it affects us in the same manner; a man can hardly expect me to discount bills at 5 $\frac{1}{2}$%, if I can lend my money at 6%."—"4892. We do not talk of investors who buy their £2,000, or £5,000, or £10,000 as affecting the money market materially. If you ask me as to the rate of interest upon" //a deposit of// "consols, I allude to people, who deal in hundreds of thousands of pounds, who are what are called jobbers, who take large portions of loans, or make purchases in the market, and have to hold that stock till the public take it off their hands at a profit; these men, therefore, want money."

With the development of the credit system, great concentrated money markets are created, such as London, which are at the same time the main seats of trade in this paper. The bankers place huge quantities of the public's money capital at the disposal of this unsavoury crowd of dealers, and thus this brood of gamblers multiplies.

"Money upon the Stock Exchange is, generally speaking, cheaper than it is elsewhere," says the incumbent of the Governor's chair of the Bank of England [b] in 1848 before the Secret Committee of Lords (C. D. 1848, PRINTED 1857, No. 219).

In the discussion on interest-bearing capital, we have already shown that the average interest over a long period of years, other conditions remaining equal, is determined by the average rate of profit; not profit of enterprise, which is nothing more than profit minus interest.[c]

It has also been mentioned, and will be further analysed in another place, that also for the variations in commercial interest, that is, interest calculated by the money lenders for discounts and loans within the commercial world, a phase is reached, in the course of the industrial cycle, in which the rate of interest exceeds its minimum and reaches its mean level (which it exceeds later) and that this movement is a result of a rise in profits.

In the meantime, two things are to be noted here.

---

[a] In the 1894 German edition this English phrase is given in parentheses after its German equivalent. - [b] James Morris. - [c] See this volume, pp. 363-64.

First: When the rate of interest stays up for a long time (we are speaking here of the rate of interest in a given country like England, where the average rate of interest is given over a lengthy period of time, and also shows itself in the interest paid on long-term loans—what could be called private interest), it is *prima facie* proof that the rate of profit is high during this period, but it does not prove necessarily that the rate of profit of enterprise is high. This latter distinction is more or less removed for capitalists, who operate mainly with their own capital; they realise the high rate of profit, since they pay the interest to themselves. The possibility of a high rate of interest of long duration is present when the rate of profit is high; this does not refer, however, to the phase of actual squeeze. But it is possible that this high rate of profit may leave only a low rate of profit of enterprise, after the high rate of interest has been deducted. The rate of profit of enterprise may shrink, while the high rate of profit continues. This is possible because the enterprises must be continued, once they have been started. During this phase, operations are carried on to a large extent with pure credit capital (capital of other people); and the high rate of profit may be partly speculative and prospective. A high rate of interest can be paid with a high rate of profit but decreasing profit of enterprise. It can be paid (and this is done in part during times of speculation), not out of the profit, but out of the borrowed capital itself, and this can continue for a while.

Secondly: The statement that the demand for money capital, and therefore the rate of interest, grows, because the rate of profit is high, is not identical with the statement that the demand for industrial capital grows and therefore the rate of interest is high.

In times of crisis, the demand for loan capital, and therefore the rate of interest, reaches its maximum; the rate of profit, and with it the demand for industrial capital, has to all intents and purposes disappeared. During such times, everyone borrows only for the purpose of paying, in order to settle previously contracted obligations. On the other hand, in times of renewed activity after a crisis, loan capital is demanded for the purpose of buying and for the purpose of transforming money capital into productive or commercial capital. And then it is demanded either by the industrial capitalist or the merchant. The industrial capitalist invests it in means of production and in labour power.

The rising demand for labour power can never by itself be a cause for a rising rate of interest, in so far as the latter is determined by the rate of profit. Higher wages are never a cause for higher profits, although they may be one of the consequences of higher profits during some particular phases of the industrial cycle.

The demand for labour power can increase because the exploitation of labour takes place under especially favourable circumstances, but the rising demand for labour power, and thus for variable capital, does not in itself increase the profit; it, on the contrary, lowers it *pro tanto*. But the demand for variable capital can nevertheless increase at the same time, thus also the demand for money capital — which can raise the rate of interest. The market price of labour power then rises above its average, more than the average number of labourers are employed, and the rate of interest rises at the same time because under such circumstances the demand for money capital rises. The rising demand for labour power raises the price of this commodity, as every other, increases its price; but not the profit, which depends mainly upon the relative cheapness of this commodity in particular. But it raises at the same time — under the assumed conditions — the rate of interest, because it increases the demand for money capital. If the money capitalist, instead of lending the money, should transform himself into an industrialist, the fact that he has to pay more for labour would not increase his profit but would rather decrease it *pro tanto*. The state of business may be such that his profit may nevertheless rise, but it would never be so because he pays more for labour. The latter circumstance, in so far as it increases the demand for money capital, is, however, sufficient to raise the rate of interest. If wages should rise for some reason during an otherwise unfavourable state of business, the rise in wages would lower the rate of profit, but raise the rate of interest to the extent that it increased the demand for money capital.

Leaving labour aside, the thing called "demand for capital" by Overstone consists only in a demand for commodities. The demand for commodities raises their price, either because it rises above average, or because the supply of commodities falls below average. If the industrial capitalist or merchant must now pay, e. g., £150 for the same amount of commodities for which he used to pay £100, he would now have to borrow £150 instead of the former £100, and if the rate of interest were 5%, he would now have to pay an interest of £7$\frac{1}{2}$ as compared with £5 formerly. The amount of interest to be paid by him would rise because he now has to borrow more capital.

The whole endeavour of Mr. Overstone consists in representing the interests of loan capital and industrial capital as being identical, whereas his Bank Act is precisely calculated to exploit this very difference of interests to the advantage of money capital.

It is possible that the demand for commodities, in case their supply has fallen below average, does not absorb any more money capital than formerly. The same sum, or perhaps a smaller one, has to be paid for their total value, but a smaller quantity of use values is received for the same sum. In this case, the demand for loanable capital will be unchanged and therefore the rate of interest will not rise, although the demand for commodities would have risen as compared to their supply and consequently the price of commodities would have become higher. The rate of interest cannot be affected, unless the total demand for loan capital increases, and this is not the case under the above assumptions.

The supply of an article can also fall below average, as it does when crop failures in corn, etc., occur; and the demand for loan capital can increase because speculation in these commodities counts on further rise in prices and the easiest way to make them rise is to temporarily withdraw a portion of the supply from the market. But in order to pay for the purchased commodities without selling them, money is secured by means of the commercial "bill of exchange operations". In this case, the demand for loan capital increases, and the rate of interest can rise as a result of this attempt to artificially prevent the supply of this commodity from reaching the market. The higher rate of interest then reflects an artificial reduction in the supply of commodity capital.

On the other hand, the demand for an article can grow because its supply has increased and the article sells below its average price.

In this case, the demand for loan capital can remain the same, or even fall, because more commodities can be had for the same sum of money. Speculative stock-piling could also occur, either for the purpose of taking advantage of the most favourable moment for production purposes, or in expectation of a future rise in prices. In this case, the demand for loan capital could grow, and the rise in the rate of interest would then be a reflection of capital investment in surplus stock-piling of elements of productive capital. We are only considering here the demand for loan capital as it is influenced by the demand for, and supply of, commodity capital. We have already discussed how the varying state of the reproduction process in the phases of the industrial cycle influences the supply of loan capital. The trivial proposition that the market rate of interest is determined by the supply and demand of (loan) capital is shrewdly jumbled up by Overstone with his own postulate, namely, that loan capital is identical with capital in general; and in this way he tries to transform the usurer into the only capitalist and his capital into the only capital.

In times of stringency, the demand for loan capital is a demand for means of payment and nothing else; it is by no means a demand for money as a means of purchase. At the same time, the rate of interest may rise very high, regardless whether real capital, i. e., productive and commodity capital, exists in abundance or is scarce. The demand for means of payment is a mere demand for convertibility into *money*, so far as merchants and producers have good securities to offer; it is a demand for *money capital* whenever there is no collateral, so that an advance of means of payment gives them not only the *form of money* but also the *equivalent* they lack, whatever its form, with which to make payment. This is the point where both sides of the controversy on the prevalent theory of crises are at the same time right and wrong. Those who say that there is merely a lack of means of payment, either have only the owners of *bona fide* securities in mind, or they are fools who believe that it is the duty and power of banks to transform all bankrupt swindlers into solvent and respectable capitalists by means of pieces of paper. Those who say that there is merely a lack of capital, are either just quibbling about words, since precisely at such times there is a mass of *inconvertible* capital as a result of over-imports and overproduction, or they are referring only to such cavaliers of credit who are now, indeed, placed in the position where they can no longer obtain other people's capital for their operations and now demand that the bank should not only help them to pay for the lost capital, but also enable them to continue with their swindles.

It is a basic principle of capitalist production that money, as an independent form of value, stands in opposition to commodities, or that exchange value must assume a self-established form in money; and this is only possible when a definite commodity becomes the material whose value becomes a measure of all other commodities, so that it thus becomes the general commodity, the commodity *par excellence*— as distinguished from all other commodities. This must manifest itself in two respects, particularly among capitalistically developed nations, which to a large extent replace money, on the one hand, by credit operations, and on the other, by credit money. In times of a squeeze, when credit contracts or ceases entirely, money suddenly stands as the only means of payment and true existence of value in absolute opposition to all other commodities. Hence the universal depreciation of commodities, the difficulty or even impossibility of transforming them into money, i. e., into their own purely fantastic form. Secondly, however, credit money itself is only money to the extent that it absolutely takes the place of actual money to the amount of its nominal value. With a drain of gold its convertibility, i. e., its identity with actual gold, becomes problematic. Hence coercive measures, raising the rate of interest, etc., for the purpose of safeguarding the conditions of this convertibility. This can be carried more or less to extremes by mistaken legislation, based on false theories of money and enforced upon the nation by the interests of the money dealers, the Overstones and their ilk. The basis, however, is given with the basis of the mode of production itself. A depreciation of credit money (not to mention, incidentally, a purely imaginary depreciation) would unsettle all existing relations. Therefore, the value of commodities is sacrificed for the purpose of safeguarding the fantastic and independent existence of this value in money. As money value, it is secure only as long as money is secure. For a few millions in money, many millions in commodities must therefore be sacrificed. This is inevitable under capitalist production and constitutes one of its beauties. In former modes of production, this does not occur because, on the narrow basis upon which they move, neither credit nor credit money can develop greatly. As long as the *social* character of labour appears as the *money existence* of commodities, and thus as a *thing* external to actual production, money crises—independent of or as an intensification of actual crises—are inevitable. On the other hand, it is clear that as long as the credit of a bank is not shaken, it will alleviate the panic in such cases by increasing credit money and intensify it by contracting the latter. The entire history of modern industry shows that metal would indeed be required only for the balancing of international commerce, whenever its equilibrium is momentarily disturbed, if only domestic production were organised. That the domestic market does not need any metal money even now is shown by the suspension of the cash payments of the so-called national banks, which resort to this expedient in all extreme cases as the sole relief.

In the case of two individuals, it would be ridiculous to say that in their transactions with one another both have an unfavourable balance of payments. If they are reciprocally creditor and debtor of one another, it is evident that when their claims do not balance, one must

be the creditor and the other the debtor for the balance. With nations
this is by no means the case. And that this is not the case is acknowledged by all economists when they admit that the balance of payments can be favourable or unfavourable for a nation, though its
trade balance must ultimately be settled. The balance of payments
differs from the balance of trade in that it is a balance of trade which
must be settled at a definite time. What the crises now accomplish is
to narrow the difference between the balance of payments and the
balance of trade to a short interval; and the specific conditions which
develop in the nation suffering from a crisis and, therefore, having its
payments become due — these conditions already lead to such a contraction of the time of settlement. First, shipping away precious metals; then selling consigned commodities at low prices; exporting commodities to dispose of them or to obtain money advances on them at
home; increasing the rate of interest, recalling credit, depreciating securities, disposing of foreign securities, attracting foreign capital for
investment in these depreciated securities, and finally bankruptcy,
which settles a mass of claims. At the same time, metal is still often
sent to the country where a crisis has broken out, because the drafts
drawn on it are insecure and payment in specie is most trustworthy.
Furthermore, in regard to Asia, all capitalist nations are usually simultaneously — directly or indirectly — its debtors. As soon as these
various circumstances exert their full effect upon the other involved
nation, it likewise begins to export gold and silver, in short, its payments become due and the same phenomena are repeated.

In commercial credit, the interest — as the difference between credit price and cash price — enters into the price of commodities only in
so far as the bills of exchange have a longer than ordinary running
time. Otherwise it does not. And this is explained by the fact that everyone takes credit with one hand and gives it with the other.//This
does not agree with my experience.— *F. E.*// But in so far as discount
in this form enters here, it is not regulated by this commercial credit,
but by the money market.

If supply and demand of money capital, which determine the rate
of interest, were identical with supply and demand of actual capital,
as Overstone maintains, the interest would be simultaneously low
and high, depending on whether various commodities or various
phases (raw material, semi-finished product, finished product) of the
same commodity were being considered. In 1844, the rate of interest
of the Bank of England fluctuated between 4% (from January to Sep-

tember) and $2\frac{1}{2}$ and 3% (from November to the end of the year). In 1845, it was $2\frac{1}{2}$, $2\frac{3}{4}$, and 3% from January to October, and between 3 and 5% during the remaining months. The average price of FAIR ORLEANS cotton was $6\frac{1}{4}$ d. in 1844 and $4\frac{7}{8}$ d. in 1845. On March 3, 1844, the cotton supply in Liverpool was 627,042 bales, and on March 3, 1845, it was 773,800 bales. To judge by the low price of cotton, the rate of interest should have been low in 1845, and it was indeed for the greater part of this time. But to judge by the yarn, the rate of interest should have been high, for the prices were relatively high and the profits absolutely high. From cotton at 4d. per pound, yarn could be spun in 1845 with a spinning cost of 4d. (good SECUNDA MULE TWIST No. 40), or a total cost of 8d. to the spinner, which he could sell in September and October 1845 at $10\frac{1}{2}$ or $11\frac{1}{2}$ d. per pound. (See the testimony of Wylie below.)

The entire matter can be resolved as follows:

Supply and demand of loan capital would be identical with supply and demand of capital generally (although this last statement is absurd; for the industrialist or merchant a commodity is a form of his capital, yet he never asks for capital as such, but only for the particular commodity as such, he buys and pays for it as a commodity, e. g., corn or cotton, regardless of the role that it has to play in the circuit of his capital), if there were no money lenders, and if in their stead the lending capitalists were in possession of machinery, raw materials, etc., which they would lend or hire out, as houses are rented out now, to the industrial capitalists, who are themselves owners of some of these objects. Under such circumstances, the supply of loan capital would be identical with the supply of elements of production for the industrial capitalist and commodities for the merchant. But it is clear that the division of profit between the lender and borrower would then, to begin with, completely depend on the relation of the capital which is lent to that which is the property of the one who employs it.

According to Mr. Weguelin (B. A. 1857), the rate of interest is determined by "the amount of unemployed capital" (252); it is "but an indication of a large amount of capital which is seeking employment" (271); later this unemployed capital becomes "FLOATING CAPITAL" (485) and by this he means "the Bank of England notes and other kinds of circulation in the country, for instance, the country banks circulation and the amount of coin which is in the country ... I include in FLOATING CAPITAL the reserves of the bankers" (502, 503), and later also gold bullion (503). Thus the same Mr. Weguelin says that the Bank of England exerts great influence upon the rate of interest in times, when "we" //the Bank of England// "are holders of the greater portion of the unemployed capital" (1198), while, according to the above testimony of Mr. Overstone, the Bank of England "is no place for capital." Mr. Weguelin further says:

"I think the rate of discount is governed by the amount of unemployed capital which there is in the country. The amount of unemployed capital is represented by the reserve of the Bank of England, which is practically a reserve of bullion. When, therefore, the bullion is drawn upon, it diminishes the amount of unemployed capital in the country and consequently raises the value of that which remains" (1258).

J. Stuart Mill says (2102):

"The Bank is obliged to depend for the solvency of its BANKING DEPARTMENT upon what it can do to replenish the reserve in that department; and therefore as soon as it finds that there is any drain in progress, it is obliged to look to the safety of its reserve, and to commence contracting its discounts or selling securities."

The reserve, in so far as only the BANKING DEPARTMENT is considered, is a reserve for the deposits only. According to the Overstones, the BANKING DEPARTMENT is supposed to act only as a banker, without regard to the "automatic" issue of notes. But in times of actual stringency the Bank, independently of the reserve of the BANKING DEPARTMENT, which consists only of notes, keeps a sharp eye on the bullion reserve, and must do so if it does not wish to fail. For, to the extent that the bullion reserve dwindles, so the reserve of banknotes also dwindles, and no one should be better informed of this than Mr. Overstone, who precisely by his Bank Act of 1844 has so sagaciously arranged this.

Chapter XXXIII

THE MEDIUM OF CIRCULATION
IN THE CREDIT SYSTEM

"The great regulator of the velocity of the currency is credit. This explains why a severe pressure upon the money market is generally coincident with a full circulation" (*The Currency Theory Reviewed*, p. 65).

This is to be taken in a double sense. On the one hand, all methods which save on medium of circulation are based upon credit. On the other hand, however, take, for example, a 500-pound note. A gives it to B on a certain day in payment for a bill of exchange; B deposits it on the same day with his banker; the latter discounts a bill of exchange with it on the very same day for C; C pays it to his bank, the bank gives it to the BILL-BROKER as an advance, etc. The velocity with which the note circulates here, to serve for purchases and payments, is effected by the velocity with which it repeatedly returns to someone in the form of a deposit and passes over to someone else again in the form of a loan. The pure economy in medium of circulation appears most highly developed in the CLEARING HOUSE — in the simple exchange of bills of exchange that are due — and in the preponderant function of money as a means of payment for merely settling balances. But the very existence of these bills of exchange depends in turn on credit, which the industrialists and merchants mutually give one another. If this credit declines, so does the number of bills, particularly long-term ones, and consequently also the effectiveness of this method of balancing accounts. And this economy, which consists in eliminating money from transactions and rests entirely upon the function of money as a means of payment, which in turn is based upon credit, can only be of two kinds (aside from the more or less developed technique in the concentration of these payments): mutual claims, represented by bills of exchange or cheques, are balanced out either by the same banker, who merely transcribes the claim from the account of one to that of another, or by the various bankers among themselves.[11] The concentration of 8 to 10 million bills of exchange in the hands of one BILL-BROKER, such as the firm of Overend, Gurney & Co., was one of the principal means of expanding the scale of such balancing locally. The effectiveness of the medium of circulation is increased through this economy in so far as a smaller quantity of it is required simply to balance accounts. On the other hand the velocity of the money flowing as medium of circulation (by which it is also economised) depends entirely upon the flow of purchases and sales, and on the chain of payments, in so far as they occur successively in money. But credit pro-

[11] Average number of days during which a banknote remained in circulation:

Year	£5 Note	£10 Note	£20-100	£200-500	£1,000
1792	—	236	209	31	22
1818	148	137	121	18	13
1846	79	71	34	12	8
1856	70	58	27	9	7

(Compilation by Marshall, Cashier of the Bank of England, in Report on Bank Acts, 1857. II. Appendix, pp. 300-01.)

motes and thereby increases the velocity of circulation. A single piece of money, for instance, can effect only five moves, and remains longer in the hands of each individual as mere medium of circulation without credit mediating — when A, its original owner, buys from B, B from C, C from D, D from E, and E from F, that is, when its transition from one hand to another is due only to actual purchases and sales. But when B deposits the money received in payment from A with his banker and the latter uses it in discounting bills of exchange for C, C in turn buys from D, D deposits it with his banker and the latter lends it to E, who buys from F, then even its velocity as mere medium of circulation (means of purchase) is promoted by several credit operations: B's depositing with his banker and the latter's discounting for C, D's depositing with his banker, and the latter's discounting for E; in other words through four credit operations. Without these credit operations, the same piece of money would not have performed five purchases successively in the given period of time. The fact that it changed hands without mediation of actual sales and purchases, through depositing and discounting, has here accelerated its change of hands in the series of actual transactions.

We have seen previously that one and the same banknote can constitute deposits in several banks. Similarly, it can also constitute various deposits in the same bank. The banker discounts, with the note which A has deposited, B's bill of exchange, B pays C, and C deposits the same note in the same bank that issued it.

We have already demonstrated in the discussion of simple money circulation (Buch I, Kap. III, 2 [a]) that the mass of actual circulating money, assuming the velocity of circulation and economy of payments as given, is determined by the prices of commodities and the quantity of transactions. The same law governs the circulation of notes.

In the following table, the annual average number of notes of the Bank of England, in so far as they were in the hands of the public, are recorded, namely, the 5- and 10-pound notes, the 20- to 100-pound notes, and the larger denominations between 200 and 1,000 pounds sterling; also the percentages of the total circulation that each one of these groupings constitutes. The amounts are in thousands, i. e., the last three figures are omitted.

----

[a] See present edition, Vol. 35.

Year	£5-10 Notes	%	£20-100 Notes	%	£200-1,000 Notes	%	Totals in £
1844	9,263	45.7	5,735	28.3	5,253	26.0	20,241
1845	9,698	46.9	6,082	29.3	4,942	23.8	20,722
1846	9,918	48.9	5,778	28.5	4,590	22.6	20,286
1847	9,591	50.1	5,498	28.7	4,066	21.2	19,155
1848	8,732	48.3	5,046	27.9	4,307	23.8	18,085
1849	8,692	47.2	5,234	28.5	4,477	24.3	18,403
1850	9,164	47.2	5,587	28.8	4,646	24.0	19,398
1851	9,362	48.1	5,554	28.5	4,557	23.4	19,473
1852	9,839	45.0	6,161	28.2	5,856	26.8	21,856
1853	10,699	47.3	6,393	28.2	5,541	24.5	22,653
1854	10,565	51.0	5,910	28.5	4,234	20.5	20,709
1855	10,628	53.6	5,706	28.9	3,459	17.5	19,793
1856	10,680	54.4	5,645	28.7	3,323	16.9	19,648
1857	10,659	54.7	5,567	28.6	3,241	16.7	19,467

(B. A. 1858, p. XXVI.)

The total sum of circulating banknotes, therefore, positively decreased from 1844 to 1857, although commercial business, as indicated by exports and imports, had more than doubled. The smaller banknotes of £5 and £10 increased, as the table shows, from £9,263,000 in 1844 to £10,659,000 in 1857. And this took place simultaneously with the particularly heavy increase in gold circulation at that time. On the other hand, there was a decrease in the notes of higher denominations (£200 to £1,000) from £5,856,000 in 1852 to £3,241,000 in 1857, i. e., a decrease of more than $2\frac{1}{2}$ million. This is explained as follows:

"On the 8th June 1854, the private bankers of London admitted the joint-stock banks to the arrangements of the CLEARING HOUSE, and shortly afterwards the final CLEARING was adjusted in the Bank of England. The daily clearances are now effected by transfers in the accounts which the several banks keep in that establishment. In consequence of the adoption of this system, the large notes which the bankers formerly employed for the purpose of adjusting their accounts are no longer necessary" (B. A. 1858, p. V).

To what small minimum the use of money in wholesale trade has been reduced, can be deduced from the table reprinted in Book I (Ch. III, Note 103),[a] which was presented to the Bank Committee by Morrison, Dillon & Co., one of the largest of those London firms from which a small dealer can buy his entire assortment of commodities.

---

[a] Ibid.

According to the testimony of W. Newmarch before the Bank Committee 1857, No. 1741, other circumstances also contributed to economy in the circulating medium: penny postage, railways, telegraphy, in short, the improved means of communication; thus England can now carry on five to six times more business with about the same circulation of banknotes. This is also essentially due to the withdrawal from circulation of notes of higher denomination than £10. Here Newmarch sees a natural explanation for the phenomenon that in Scotland and Ireland, where one-pound notes also circulate, note circulation has risen by about 31% (1747). The total circulation of banknotes in the United Kingdom, including one-pound notes, is said to be £39 million (1749). The gold circulation = £70 million (1750). In Scotland, the circulation of notes was £3,120,000 in 1834; £3,020,000 in 1844; and £4,050,000 in 1854 (1752).

From these figures alone, it is evident that banks issuing notes can by no means increase the number of circulating notes at will, as long as these notes are at all times exchangeable for money. //Inconvertible paper money is not considered here at all; inconvertible banknotes can become a universal medium of circulation only where they are actually backed by state credit, as is the case in Russia at present.[49] They then fall under the laws of inconvertible paper money issued by the state, which have already been developed (Buch I, Kap. III, 2, c: "Coin and Symbols of Value").— F. E.//

The quantity of circulating notes is regulated by the turnover requirements, and every superfluous note wends its way back immediately to the issuer. Since in England only the notes of the Bank of England circulate universally as legal means of payment, we can disregard at this point the insignificant, and merely local, note circulation of the country banks.

Before the Bank Committee 1858, Mr. Neave, Governor of the Bank of England, testifies:

No. 947. (Question:) "Whatever measures you resort to, the amount of notes with the public, you say, remains the same; that is somewhere about £20,000,000? — In ordinary times, the uses of the public seem to want about £20,000,000. There are special periodical moments when, through the year, they rise to another £1,000,000 or £1,500,000. I stated that, if the public wanted more, they could always take it from the Bank of England." — "948. You stated that during the panic the public would not allow you to diminish the amount of notes; I want you to account for that.— In moments of panic, the public have, as I believe, the full power of helping themselves as to notes; and of course, as long as the Bank has a liability, they may use that liability to take the notes from the Bank." — "949. Then there seems to be required, at all times, somewhere about £20,000,000 of legal tender? — £20,000,000 of notes with the public; it varies. It is £18,500,000, £19,000,000, £20,000,000, and so on; but taking the average, you may call it from £19,000,000 to £20,000,000."

Testimony of Thomas Tooke before the Committee of Lords on Commercial Distress (C. D. 1848/57):

> No. 3094. "The Bank has no power of its own volition to extend the amount of its circulation in the hands of the public; but it has the power of reducing the amount of the notes in the hands of the public, not however without a very violent operation."

J. C. Wright, a banker for 30 years in Nottingham, having explained at length the impossibility for a country bank to be able to keep more notes in circulation than the public needs and wants, says about notes of the Bank of England (C. D. 1848/57):

> No. 2844. "I am not aware that there is any check" (for note issue) "upon the Bank of England, but any excess of circulation will go into the deposits and thus assume a different name."

The same holds true for Scotland, where almost nothing but paper circulates, because there as well as in Ireland one-pound notes are also in use and "THE SCOTCH HATE GOLD". Kennedy, Director of a Scottish bank, declares that banks could not even contract their circulation of notes and

> "conceives that so long as there are internal transactions requiring notes or gold to perform them, bankers must, either through the demands of their depositors or in one shape or another, furnish as much currency as those transactions require.... The Scottish banks can restrict their transactions, but they cannot control their currency" (ibid., Nos. 3446, 3448).

Similarly, Anderson, Director of the UNION BANK OF SCOTLAND, states (ibid., No. 3578):

> "The system of exchanges between yourselves" //among the Scottish banks// "prevents any over-issue on the part of any one bank? — Yes; there is a more powerful preventive than the system of exchanges"

//which has really nothing to do with this, but does indeed guarantee the ability of the notes of each bank to circulate throughout Scotland//,

> "the universal practice in Scotland of keeping a bank account; everybody who has any money at all has a bank account and puts in every day the money which he does not immediately want, so that at the close of the business of the day there is no money scarcely out of the banks except what people have in their pockets."

The same applies to Ireland, as indicated in the testimony of the Governor of the Bank of Ireland, MacDonnell, and the Director of the PROVINCIAL BANK OF IRELAND, Murray, before the same Committee. Note circulation is just as independent of the state of the gold reserve in the vaults of the bank which guarantees the convertibility of these notes, as it is of the will of the Bank of England.

"On September 18, 1846, the circulation of the Bank of England was £20,900,000 and the bullion in the Bank £16,273,000; and on April 5, 1847, the notes in circulation were £20,815,000 and the bullion £10,246,000.... It is evident that six million of gold were exported, without any contraction of the currency of the country" (J. G. Kinnear, *The Crisis and the Currency*, London, 1847, p. 5).

Of course, this applies only under present conditions prevailing in England, and even here only in so far as legislation does not decree a different relationship between the note issue and metal reserve.

Hence only the requirements of business itself exert an influence on the quantity of circulating money — notes and gold. To be noted here, in the first instance, are the periodic fluctuations, which repeat themselves annually regardless of the general condition of business, so that for the past 20 years

"the circulation is high in one month, and it is low in another month, and in a certain other month occurs a medium point" (Newmarch, B. A. 1857, No. 1650).

Thus, in August of every year a few millions, generally in gold, pass from the Bank of England into domestic circulation to pay the harvest expenses; since wages are the principal payments to be made here, banknotes are less serviceable in England for this purpose. By the close of the year this money has streamed back to the Bank. In Scotland, there are almost nothing but one-pound notes instead of sovereigns; here, then, the note circulation is expanded in the corresponding situation, namely, twice a year — in May and November — from 3 million to 4 million; after a fortnight the return flow begins, and is almost completed in one month (Anderson, l. c., Nos. 3595-3600).[a]

The note circulation of the Bank of England also experiences a momentary fluctuation every three months because of the quarterly payment of "dividends", that is, interest on the national debt, whereby banknotes are first withdrawn from circulation and then again released to the public; but they flow back very soon again. Weguelin (B. A. 1857, No. 38) states that this fluctuation in the note circulation amounts to $2\frac{1}{2}$ million. Mr. Chapman of the notorious firm of

---

[a] See Report from the Secret Committee of the House of Lords, Appointed to Inquire into the Causes of the Distress...

Overend, Gurney & Co., however, estimates the amount of disturbance thus created in the money market as being much higher.

"When you abstract from the circulation £6,000,000 or £7,000,000 of revenue in anticipation of dividends, somebody must be the medium of supplying that in the intermediate times" (B. A. 1857, No. 5196).

Far more significant and enduring are the fluctuations in quantity of circulating medium corresponding to the various phases of the industrial cycle. Let us listen to another *associé* of that firm on this question, the esteemed Quaker Samuel Gurney (C. D. 1848/57, No. 2645):

"At the end of October (1847) the amount of banknotes in the hands of the public was £20,800,000. At that period there was great difficulty in getting possession of banknotes in the money market. This arose from the alarm of not being able to get them in consequence of the restriction of the Act of 1844. At present //March 1848// the amount of banknotes in the hands of the public is ... £17,700,000, but there being now no commercial alarm whatsoever, it is much beyond what is required. There is no banking house or money dealer in London, but what has a larger amount of banknotes than they can use." — "2650. The amount of banknotes ... out of the custody of the Bank of England affords a totally insufficient exponent of the active state of the circulation, without taking into consideration likewise ... the state of the commercial world and the state of credit." — "2651. The feeling of surplus that we have under the present amount of circulation in the hands of the public arises in a large degree from our present state of great stagnation. In a state of high prices and excitement of transaction £17,700,000 would give us a feeling of restriction."

//As long as the state of business is such that returns of loans made come in regularly and credit thus remains unshaken, the expansion and contraction of circulation depend simply upon the requirements of industrialists and merchants. Since gold, at least in England, does not come into question in the wholesale trade and the circulation of gold, aside from seasonal fluctuations, may be regarded as rather constant over a long period of time, the note circulation of the Bank of England constitutes a sufficiently accurate measure of these changes. In the period of stagnation following a crisis, circulation is smallest; with the renewed demand, a greater need for circulating medium develops, which increases with rising prosperity; the quantity of circulating medium reaches its apex in the period of overtension and over-speculation — the crisis precipitously breaks out and overnight banknotes which yesterday were still so plentiful disappear from the market and with them the discounters of bills, lenders of money on securities, and buyers of commodities. The Bank of England is called upon for help — but even its powers are soon exhausted, for the Bank Act of 1844 compels it to contract its note circulation at the very moment when the whole world cries out for notes; when owners of commodities cannot sell, yet are called upon to pay and are prepared for any sacrifice, if only they can secure banknotes.

"During an alarm," says the earlier mentioned banker Wright (l. c., No. 2930), "the country requires twice as much circulation as in ordinary times, because the circulation is hoarded by bankers and others."

Once the crisis has broken out, it becomes from then on only a question of means of payment. But since every one is dependent upon someone else for the receipt of these means of payment, and no one knows whether the next one will be able to meet his payments when due, a regular stampede ensues for those means of payment available on the market, that is, for banknotes. Everyone hoards as many of them as he can lay hand on, and thus the notes disappear from circulation on the very day when they are most needed. Samuel Gurney (C. D. 1848/57, No. 1116) estimates the amount of banknotes brought under lock and key in October 1847, at a time of such alarm, to have reached £4 to £5 million.— F. E.//

In this connection, the cross-examination of Chapman, Gurney's *associé* who has been previously mentioned, before the Bank Committee of 1857 is especially interesting. I present here its principal contents in context, although certain points are touched upon which we shall not examine until later.

Mr. Chapman has the following to say:

"4963. I have also no hesitation in saying that I do not think it is a proper condition of things that the money market should be under the power of any individual capitalist (such as does exist in London), to create a tremendous scarcity and pressure, when we have a very low state of circulation out.... That is possible ... there is more than one capitalist, who can withdraw from the circulating medium £1,000,000 or £2,000,000 of notes, if they have an object to attain by it."

4965. A big speculator can sell £1,000,000 or £2,000,000 of consols and thus take the money out of the market. Something similar to this has happened quite recently, "it creates a most violent pressure".

4967. The notes are then indeed unproductive.

"But that is nothing, if it effects his great object; his great object is to knock down the funds, to create a scarcity, and he has it perfectly in his power to do so."

An illustration: One morning there was a great demand for money in the Stock Exchange; nobody knew its cause; somebody asked Chapman to lend him £50,000 at 7%. Chapman was astonished, for his rate of interest was much lower; he accepted. Soon after that the man returned, borrowed another £50,000 at $7\frac{1}{2}$ %, then £100,000 at 8%, and wanted still more at $8\frac{1}{2}$ %. Then even Chapman became uneasy. Later it turned out that a considerable sum of money had been suddenly withdrawn from the market. But, says Chapman,

"I did lend a large sum at 8%; I was afraid to go beyond; I did not know what was coming."

It must never be forgotten that, although £19 to £20 million in notes are almost constantly supposed to be in the hands of the public, nevertheless, the portion of these notes which actually circulates, and, on the other hand, the portion which is held idle by the banks as a reserve, continually and significantly vary with respect to each other. If this reserve is large, and therefore the actual circulation small, it means, from the point of view of the money market, that THE CIRCULATION IS FULL, MONEY IS PLENTIFUL[a]; if the reserve is small, and therefore the actual circulation full, in the language of the money market THE CIRCULATION IS LOW, MONEY IS SCARCE[a]— in other words, the portion representing idle loan capital is small. A real expansion or contraction of the circulation, that is independent of the phases of the industrial cycle — with the amount needed by the public, however, remaining the same — occurs only for technical reasons, for instance, on the dates when taxes or the interest on the national debt are due. When taxes are paid, more notes and gold than usual flow into the Bank of England and, in effect, contract the circulation without regard to its needs. The reverse takes place when the dividends on the national debt are paid out. In the former case, loans are made from the Bank in order to obtain circulating medium. In the latter case, the rate of interest falls in private banks because of the momentary growth of their reserves. This has nothing to do with the absolute quantity of circulating medium; it does, however, concern the banking firm which sets this circulating medium in motion and for which this process consists in the alienation of loan capital and for which it pockets the profits thereby.

In the one case, there is merely a temporary displacement of circulating medium, which the Bank of England balances by short-term loans at low interest shortly before the quarterly taxes and also before the quarterly dividends on the national debt become due; the issue of these supernumerary notes first fills up the gap caused by the pay-

a In the 1894 German edition this English phrase is given in parentheses after its German equivalent.

ment of taxes, while their return payment to the Bank soon thereafter brings back the excess of notes obtained by the public through the payment of dividends.

In the other case, low or full circulation is always simply a matter of different distribution of the same quantity of circulating medium into active circulation and deposits, i. e., an instrument of loans.

On the other hand, if, for example, the number of notes issued is increased on the basis of a flow of gold into the Bank of England, these notes assist in discounting bills outside of the Bank and return to it through the repayment of loans, so that the absolute quantity of circulating notes is only momentarily increased.

If the circulation is full because of business expansion (which may take place even though prices are relatively low), then the rate of interest can be relatively high because of the demand for loan capital as a result of rising profits and increased new investments. If it is low, because of business contraction, or perhaps because credit is very plentiful, the rate of interest can be low even though prices are high. (See Hubbard.[a])

The absolute amount of circulation has a determining influence on the rate of interest only in times of stringency. The demand for full circulation can either reflect merely a demand for a hoarding medium (disregarding the reduced velocity of the money circulation and the continuous conversion of the same identical pieces of money into loan capital) owing to lack of credit, as was the case in 1847 when the suspension of the Bank Act did not cause any expansion of the circulation, but sufficed to draw forth the hoarded notes and to channel them into circulation; or it may be that more means of circulation are actually required under the circumstances, as was the case in 1857 when the circulation actually expanded for some time after the suspension of the Bank Act.

Otherwise, the absolute quantity of circulation has no influence whatever upon the rate of interest, since — assuming the economy and velocity of currency to be constant — it is determined in the first place by commodity prices and the quantity of transactions (whereby one of these generally neutralises the effect of the other), and finally by the state of credit, whereas it by no means exerts the reverse effect upon the latter; and, secondly, since commodity prices and interest do not necessarily stand in any direct correlation to each other.

---

[a] See this volume, pp. 546 - 47.

During the life of the BANK RESTRICTION ACT (1797-1819)[50] a surplus of CURRENCY existed and the rate of interest was always much higher than after the resumption of cash payments. Later, it fell rapidly with the restriction of the note issue and rising bill quotations. In 1822, 1823, and 1832, the general circulation was low, and so was the rate of interest. In 1824, 1825, and 1836, the circulation was full and the rate of interest rose. In the summer of 1830 the circulation was full and the rate of interest low. Since the gold discoveries, money circulation throughout Europe has expanded, and the rate of interest risen. Therefore, the rate of interest does not depend upon the quantity of circulating money.

The difference between the issue of circulating medium and the lending of capital is best demonstrated in the actual reproduction process. We have seen (Book II, Part III) in what manner the different component parts of production are exchanged for one another. For example, variable capital consists materially of the means of subsistence of the labourers, a portion of their own product. But this is paid out to them piecemeal in money. The capitalist has to advance this, and it is very greatly dependent on the credit system organisation whether he can pay out the new variable capital the following week with the old money which he paid out in the previous week. The same holds for exchange among various component parts of the total social capital, for instance, between means of consumption and means of production of means of consumption. The money for their circulation, as we have seen, must be advanced by one or both of the exchanging parties. It remains thereupon in circulation, but returns after the exchange has been completed to the one who advanced it, since it had been advanced by him over and above his actually employed industrial capital (Book II, Chap. XX[a]). Under a developed system of credit, with the money concentrated in the hands of bankers, it is they, at least nominally, who advance it. This advance refers only to money in circulation. It is an advance of circulation, not an advance of capitals which it circulates.

Chapman: "5062. There may be times when the notes in the hands of the public, though they may be large, are not to be had."

Money also exists during a panic; but everyone takes good care not to convert it into loanable capital, i. e., loanable money; everyone holds on to it for the purpose of meeting real payment needs.

---

[a] See present edition, Vol. 36, pp. 410-20.

"5099. The country bankers in rural districts send up their unemployed balances to yourselves and other houses? — Yes."—"5100. On the other hand, the Lancashire and Yorkshire districts require discounts from you for the use of their trades? — Yes."—"5101. Then by that means the surplus money of one part of the country is made available for the demands of another part of the country? — Precisely so."

Chapman states that the custom of banks to invest their surplus money capital for short periods in consols and treasury notes has decreased considerably of late, ever since it has become customary to lend this money AT CALL, i. e., payable on demand. He personally considers the purchase of such paper for his business very impractical. He, therefore, invests his money in reliable bills of exchange, some of which become due every day, so that he always knows how much ready money he can count on from day to day //5101 to 5105//.

Even the growth of exports expresses itself more or less for every country, but particularly for the country granting credit, as an increasing demand on the domestic money market, which is not felt, however, until a period of stringency. When exports increase, British manufacturers usually draw long-term bills of exchange on the export merchants against consignments of British goods (5126).

"5127. Is it not frequently the case that an understanding exists that those bills are to be redrawn from time to time?" — //Chapman:// "That is a thing which they keep from us; we should not admit any bill of that sort. ...I dare say it is done, but I cannot speak to a thing of the kind." //The innocent Chapman// "5129. If there is a large increase of the exports of the country, as there was last year, of £20 million, will not that naturally lead to a great demand for capital for the discount of bills representing those exports? — No doubt."—"5130. Inasmuch as this country gives credit, as a general rule, to foreign countries for all exports, it would be an absorption of a corresponding increase of capital for the time being? — This country gives an immense credit; but then it takes credit for its raw material. We are drawn upon from America always at 60 days, and from other parts at 90 days. On the other hand we give credit; if we send goods to Germany, we give two or three months."

Wilson inquires of Chapman (5131), whether bills of exchange on England are not drawn simultaneously with the loading of these imported raw materials and colonial goods and whether these bills of exchange do not arrive simultaneously with the bills of lading. Chapman believes so, but does not profess to know anything about such "commercial" transactions and suggests that experts in this field be questioned.— In exporting to America, remarks Chapman, "the goods are symbolised *in transitu*"; this gibberish is supposed to mean that the English export merchant draws against his commodities bills of exchange with a four-month term on one of the big American banking houses in London and this firm receives collateral from America.[a]

"5136. As a general rule, are not the more remote transactions conducted by the merchant, who waits for his capital until the goods are sold? — There may be houses of great private wealth, who can afford to lay out their own capital and not take any advance upon the goods; but the most part are converted into advances by the acceptances of some well-known established houses."—"5137. Those houses are resident in ... London, or Liverpool, or elsewhere."—"5138. There, it makes no difference, whether the manufacturer lays out his money, or whether he gets a merchant in London or Liverpool to advance it; it is still an advance in this country? — Precisely. The manufacturer in few cases has anything to do with it" //but in 1847 in almost every case//. "A man dealing in manufactured goods, for instance, at Manchester, will buy his goods and ship them through a house of respectability in London; when the London house is satisfied that they are all packed according to the understanding, he draws upon this London house for six months against these goods to India or China, or wherever they are going; then the banking world comes in and discounts that bill for him; so that, by the time he has to pay for those goods, he has the money all ready by the discount of that bill."—"5139. Although he has the money, the banker is laying out of his money? — *The banker has the bill; the banker has bought the bill*[b]; he uses his banking capital in that form, namely, in discounting commercial bills."

//Hence even Chapman does not regard the discounting of bills as an advance of money, but as a purchase of commodities.— *F. E.*//

"5140. Still that forms part of the demand upon the money market in London? — No doubt; it is the substantial occupation of the money market and of the Bank of England. The Bank of England are as glad to get these bills as we are, because they know them to be good property."—"5141. In that way, as the export trade increases, the demand upon the money market increases also? — As the prosperity of the country increases, we" //the Chapmans// "partake of it."—"5142. Then when these various fields for the employment of capital increase suddenly, of course, the natural consequence is that the rate of interest is higher? — No doubt about it."

In 5143 Chapman cannot "quite understand, that under our large exports we have had such occasion for bullion".

In 5144 the esteemed Wilson asks:

"May it not be that we give larger credits upon our exports than we take credits upon our imports? — I rather doubt that point myself. If a man accepts against his Manchester goods sent to India, you cannot accept for less than 10 months. We have had to pay America for her cotton (that is perfectly true) some time before India pays us; but still it is rather refined in its operation."—"5145. If we have had an increase, as we had last year, of £20 million in our exports of manufactures, we must have had a very large increase of imports of raw material previously to that" //and in this way overexports are already identified with overimports, and overproduction with overtrading//, "in order to make up that increased quantity of goods? — No

---

[a] See Report from the Select Committee on Bank Acts..., 1857, No. 5133. - [b] Italicised by Marx.

doubt."—"We should have to pay a very considerable balance, that is to say, the balance, no doubt, would run against us during that time, but in the long run, with America ... the exchanges are in our favour, and we have been receiving for some time past large supplies of bullion from America."[a]

5148. Wilson asks the arch-usurer Chapman, whether he does not regard his high rate of interest as a sign of great prosperity and high profits. Chapman, evidently surprised at the naïveté of this sycophant, affirms this, of course, but has enough integrity to add the following:

"There are some, who cannot help themselves; they have engagements to meet, and they must fulfil them, whether it is profitable or not; but, for a continuance" //of the high rate of interest//, "it would indicate prosperity."

Both forget that a high rate of interest can also indicate, as it did in 1857, that the country is undermined by the roving cavaliers of credit who can afford to pay a high interest because they pay it out of other people's pockets (whereby, however, they help to determine the rate of interest for all), and meanwhile they live in grand style on anticipated profits. Simultaneously, precisely this can incidentally provide a very profitable business for manufacturers and others. Returns become wholly deceptive as a result of the loan system. This also explains the following, which should require no explanation so far as the Bank of England is concerned, since it discounts at a lower rate than others when the interest rate is high.

"5156. I should say," says Chapman, "that our discounts, taking the present moment, when we have had for so long a high rate of interest, are at their maximum."

//Chapman made this statement on July 21, 1857, a couple of months before the crash.//

"5157. In 1852" //when the interest rate was low// "they were not nearly so large."

For business was indeed a great deal sounder then.

"5159. If there was a great flood of money in the market ... and the bank rate low, we should get a decrease of bills. ... In 1852 there was a totally different phase of things. The exports and imports of the country were as nothing then compared to the present."—"5161. Under this high rate of discount our discounts are as large as they were in 1854." //When the rate of interest was between 5 and $5\frac{1}{2}\%$.//

A very amusing part of Chapman's testimony reveals how these people really regard public money as their own and assume for

---

[a] Op. cit., No. 5146.

themselves the right to constant convertibility of the bills of exchange discounted by them. The questions and replies show great naïveté. It becomes the obligation of legislation to make those bills which are accepted by large firms convertible at all time; to ensure that the Bank of England should under all circumstances continue to rediscount them for BILL-BROKERS. And yet three of such BILL-BROKERS went bankrupt in 1857, owing about 8 million and their own infinitesimally small capital compared with these debts.

"5177. Do you mean by that that you think that they" //that is bills accepted by Barings or Loyds// "ought to be discountable on compulsion, in the same way that a Bank of England note is now exchangeable against gold by compulsion? — I think it would be a very lamentable thing that they should not be discountable; a most extraordinary position, that a man should stop payment who had the acceptances of Smith, Payne & Co., or Jones, Loyd & Co. in his hands, because he could not get them discounted."—"5178. Is not the engagement of Messrs. Baring an engagement to pay a certain sum of money when the bill is due? — That is perfectly true; but Messrs. Baring, when they contract that engagement, and every other merchant who contracts an engagement, never dream that they are going to pay it in sovereigns; they expect that they are going to pay it at the CLEARING HOUSE."—"5180. Do you think that there should be any machinery contrived by which the public would have a right to claim money before that bill was due by calling upon somebody to discount it? — No, not from the acceptor; but if you mean by that that we are not to have the possibility of getting commercial bills discounted, we must alter the whole constitution of things." —"5182. Then you think that it" //commercial bill// "ought to be convertible into money, exactly in the same way that a Bank of England note ought to be convertible into gold? — Most decidedly so, under certain circumstances."—"5184. Then you think that the provisions of the CURRENCY should be so shaped that a bill of exchange of undoubted character ought at all times to be as readily exchangeable against money as a banknote?— I do."—"5185. You do not mean to say that either the Bank of England or any individual should, by law, be compelled to exchange it? — I mean to say this, that in framing a bill for the CURRENCY, we should make provision to prevent the possibility of an inconvertibility of the bills of exchange of the country arising, assuming them to be undoubtedly solid and legitimate."

This is the convertibility of the commercial bill as compared with the convertibility of banknotes.

"5190. The money dealers of the country only, in point of fact, represent the public."

As did Mr. Chapman later before the court of assizes in the Davidson case. See the *Great City Frauds*.[51]

"5196. During the quarters" //when the dividends are paid// "it is ... absolutely necessary that we should go to the Bank of England. When you abstract from the circulation £6,000,000 or £7,000,000 of revenue in anticipation of the dividends, somebody must be the medium of supplying that in the intermediate time."

//In this case it is then a question of a supply of money, not of capital or loan capital.//

"5169. Everybody acquainted with our commercial circle must know that when we are in such a state that we find it impossible to sell Exchequer bills, when India bonds are perfectly useless, when you cannot discount the first commercial bills, there must be great anxiety on the part of those whose business renders them liable to pay the circulating medium of the realm on demand, which is the case with all bankers. Then the effect of that is to make every man double his reserve. Just see what the result of that is throughout the country, that every country banker, of whom there are about 500, has to send up to his London correspondent to remit him £5,000 in banknotes. Taking such a limited sum as that as the average, which is quite absurd, you come to £2,500,000 taken out of the circulation. How is that to be supplied?"

On the other hand, the private capitalists, etc., who have money do not let go of it at any interest, for they say after the manner of Chapman,

"5195. We would rather have no interest at all, than have a doubt about our getting the money in case we require it."

"5173. Our system is this: That we have £300,000,000 of liabilities which may be called for at a single moment to be paid in the coin of the realm, and that coin of the realm, if the whole of it is substituted, amounts to £23,000,000, or whatever it may be; is not that a state which may throw us into convulsions at any moment?"

Hence the sudden change of the credit system into a monetary system during crises.

Aside from the domestic panic during crises, one can speak of the quantity of money only in so far as it concerns bullion, universal money. And this is precisely what Chapman excludes, he speaks only of 23 million in *banknotes*.

The same Chapman:

"5218. The primary cause of the derangement of the money market" //in April and later in October 1847// "no doubt was in the quantity of money which was required to regulate our exchanges, in consequence of the extraordinary importations of the year."

In the first place, this reserve of world-market money had then been reduced to its minimum. Secondly, it served at the same time as security for the convertibility of credit money, banknotes. It combined in this manner two quite different functions, both of which, however, stem from the nature of money, since real money is always world-market money, and credit money always rests upon world-market money.

In 1847, without the suspension of the Bank Act of 1844,

"the CLEARING HOUSES could not have been settled" (5221).

That Chapman had an inkling of the imminent crisis, after all:

"5236. There are certain conditions of the money market (and the present is not very far from it) where money is exceedingly difficult, and recourse must be had to the Bank."

"5239. With reference to the sums which we took from the Bank on the Friday, Saturday and Monday, the 19th, 20th, and 22nd of October, 1847, ... we should only have been too thankful to have got the bills back on the Wednesday following; the money reflowed to us directly the panic was over."

On Tuesday, October 23, the Bank Act was suspended and the crisis was thus broken.

Chapman believes (5274) that the bills of exchange running simultaneously on London amount to £100 or £120 million. This does not include local bills made on provincial firms.

"5287. Whereas in October 1856, the amount of the notes in the hands of the public ran up to £21,155,000, there was an extraordinary difficulty in obtaining money; notwithstanding that the public held so much, we could not touch it."

This was due to the fear caused by the squeeze in which the EASTERN BANK found itself for a period of time (March 1856).

5290. As soon as the panic is over,

"all bankers deriving their profit from interest begin to employ the money immediately".

5302. Chapman does not explain the uneasiness that exists when the bank reserve decreases as being due to apprehension concerning deposits, but rather that all those who suddenly may be compelled to pay large sums of money are well aware they may be driven to seek their last refuge in the bank when there is a stringency in the money market; and

"if the banks have a very small reserve, they are not glad to receive us; but on the contrary".

It is pretty, incidentally, to observe how the reserve as a real magnitude dwindles away. Bankers hold a minimum for current business needs either in their own hands or the Bank of England. BILL-BROKERS hold the "loose bank money of the country" without any reserve. And the Bank of England has nothing to offset its liabilities for deposits but the reserves of bankers and others, together with some PUBLIC DEPOSITS, etc., which it permits to drop to a very low level, for instance, to £2 million. Aside from these £2 million in paper, then, this whole swindle has absolutely no other reserve but the bullion reserve in times of stringency (and this reduces the reserve, because the notes which come in to replace outgoing bullion must be cancelled), and thus every reduction of this reserve by drain of gold increases the crisis.

"5306. If there should not be currency to settle the transactions at the CLEARING HOUSE, the only next alternative which I can see is to meet together, and to make our payments in first-class bills, bills upon the Treasury, and Messrs. Smith, Payne, and so forth." — "5307. Then, if the government failed to supply you with a circulating medium, you would create one for yourselves? — What can we do? The public come in, and take the circulating medium out of our hands; it does not exist." — "5308. You would only then do in London what they do in Manchester every day of the week? — Yes."

Particularly clever is Chapman's reply to a question posed by Cayley (a Birmingham man of the Attwood school [52]) regarding Overstone's conception of capital:

"5315. It has been stated before this Committee, that in a pressure like that of 1847, men are not looking for money, but are looking for capital; what is your opinion in that respect? — I do not understand it; we only deal in money; I do not understand what you mean by it." — "5316. If you mean thereby" (commercial capital) "the quantity of money which a man has of his own in his business, if you call that capital, it forms, in most cases, a very small proportion of the money which he wields in his affairs through the credit which is given him by the public" — through the mediation of the Chapmans.
"5339. Is it the want of property that makes us give up our specie payments? — Not at all.... It is not that we want property, but it is that we are moving under a highly artificial system; and if we have an immense SUPERINCUMBENT[a] demand upon our currency, circumstances may arise to prevent our obtaining that currency. Is the whole commercial industry of the country to be paralysed? Shall we shut up all the avenues of employment?" — "5338. If the question should arise whether we should maintain specie payments, or whether we should maintain the industry of the country, I have no hesitation in saying which I should drop."

Concerning the hoarding of banknotes "with a view to aggravate the pressure and to take advantage of the consequences" //5358//, he says that this can very easily occur. Three large banks would be sufficient.

"5383. Must it not be within your knowledge, as a man conversant with the great transactions of this metropolis, that capitalists do avail themselves of these crises to make enormous profit out of the ruin of the people who fall victims to them? — There can be no doubt about it."

And we may well believe Mr. Chapman on this score, although he finally broke his own neck, commercially speaking, in an attempt at

---

[a] In the 1894 German edition this English word is given in parentheses after its German equivalent.

making "enormous profit out of the ruin of victims". For while his *associé* Gurney says: Every change in business is advantageous for one who is well informed, Chapman says:

"The one section of the community knows nothing of the other; one is the manufacturer, for instance, who exports to the continent, or imports his raw commodity; he knows nothing of the man who deals in bullion" (5046).

And thus it happened that one fine day Gurney and Chapman themselves "were not well informed" and went into ill-famed bankruptcy.

We have previously seen that note issue does not in all cases signify an advance of capital. The following testimony by Tooke before the C. D. Committee of Lords, 1848, indicates merely that an advance of capital, even if accomplished by the bank through an issue of new notes, does not unqualifiedly signify an increase in the number of circulating notes:

"3099. Do you think that the Bank of England for instance might enlarge its advances greatly, and yet lead to no additional issue of notes? — There are facts in abundance to prove it; one of the most striking instances was in 1835, when the Bank made use of the West India deposits and of the loan from the East India Company [53] in extended advances to the public. At that time the amount of notes in the hands of the public was actually rather diminished.... And something like the same discrepancy is observable in 1846 at the time of the payment of the railway deposits into the Bank; the securities" //in discount and deposits// "were increased to about thirty million, while there was no perceptible effect upon the amount of notes in the hands of the public."

Aside from banknotes, wholesale trade has another medium of circulation, which is far more important to it, namely, bills of exchange. Mr. Chapman showed us how essential it is for the regular flow of business that good bills of exchange be accepted in payment everywhere and under all conditions.

"Gilt nicht mehr der Tausves Jontof, was soll gelten, Zeter, Zeter!"[a]

How are these two media of circulation related to one another? Gilbart writes on this score:

"The reduction of the amount of the note circulation uniformly increases the amount of the bill circulation. These bills are of two classes — commercial bills and bankers' bills ... when money becomes scarce, the money lenders say, 'draw upon us and we will accept'. And when a country banker discounts a bill for his customer, instead of giving him the cash, he will give him his own draft at twenty-one days upon

---

[a] "If the Tausves-Jontof's nothing, What is left? O vile detractor!" (Heine, *Disputation*).

his London agent. These bills serve the purpose of a currency" (J. W. Gilbart, *An Inquiry into the Causes of the Pressure, etc.*, p. 31).

This is corroborated in somewhat modified form by Newmarch, B. A. 1857, No.1426:

"There is no connection between the variations in the amount of bill circulation and the variations in the banknote circulation ... the only pretty uniform result is ...that whenever there is any pressure upon the money market, as indicated by a rise in the rate of discount, then the volume of the bill circulation is very much increased, and vice versa."

However, the bills of exchange drawn at such times are by no means only the short-term bank bills mentioned by Gilbart. On the contrary, they are largely bills of accommodation, which represent no real transaction at all, or simply transactions made for the sole purpose of drawing bills of exchange on them; we have presented sufficient illustrations of both. Hence the *Economist* (Wilson) says in comparing the security of such bills with that of banknotes:

"Notes payable on demand can never be kept out in excess, because the excess would always return to the bank for payment, while bills at two months may be issued in great excess, there being no means of checking the issue till they have arrived at maturity, when they may have been replaced by others. For a people to admit the safety of the circulation of bills payable only on a distant day, and to object to the safety of a circulation of paper payable on demand, is, to us, perfectly unaccountable" (*Economist*, 1847, p. 575).

The quantity of circulating bills of exchange, therefore, like that of banknotes, is determined solely by the requirements of commerce; in ordinary times, there circulated in the fifties in the United Kingdom, in addition to 39 million in banknotes, about 300 million in bills of exchange — of which 100-120 million were made out on London alone. The volume of circulating bills of exchange has no influence on note circulation and is influenced by the latter only in times of money tightness, when the quantity of bills increases and their quality deteriorates. Finally, in a period of crisis, the circulation of bills collapses completely; nobody can make use of a promise to pay since everyone will accept only cash payment; only the banknote retains, at least thus far in England, its ability to circulate, because the nation with its total wealth backs up the Bank of England.

We have seen that even Mr. Chapman, who after all was himself a magnate on the money market in 1857, complains bitterly that there were several large money capitalists in London strong enough

to disrupt the whole money market at any given moment and thereby
bleed white the smaller money dealers. There were several such money sharks, he said, who could considerably intensify a stringency by
selling one or two million's worth of consols and thereby withdrawing
an equal amount of banknotes (and simultaneously available loan
capital) from the market. The joint action of three large banks would
suffice to transform a stringency into a panic by a similar manoeuvre.

The largest capital power in London is, of course, the Bank of England, which, however, is prevented by its status as a semi-government
institution from showing its domination in such a brutal manner.
Nevertheless it also knows enough about ways and means of feather-
ing its nest, particularly since the Bank Act of 1844.[48]

The Bank of England has a capital of £14,553,000, and in addition
has at its disposal about £3 million "balance", that is, undistributed
profits, as well as all money collected by the government for taxes,
etc., which must be deposited with the Bank until it is needed. If we
add to this the sum of other deposits (about £30 million in ordinary
times), and the banknotes issued without reserve backing, we shall
find that Newmarch made a rather conservative estimate in stating
(B. A. 1857, No. 1889):

"I satisfied myself that the amount of funds constantly employed in the //London//
money market may be described as something like £120,000,000; and of that
£120,000,000 a very considerable proportion, something like 15 or 20 per cent, is
wielded by the Bank of England."

In so far as the Bank issues notes which are not covered by the bullion reserve in its vaults, it creates symbols of value that constitute for
it not only circulating medium, but also additional — even if fictitious — capital to the nominal amount of these unbacked notes. And
this additional capital yields additional profit.— In B. A. 1857, Wilson questions Newmarch:

"1563. The circulation of a banker, so far as it is kept out upon the average, is an
addition to the effective capital of that banker, is it not? — Certainly."—"1564. Then
whatever profit he derives from that circulation is a profit derived from credit, and not
from a capital which he actually possesses? — Certainly."

The same is true, of course, for private banks issuing notes. In his
replies Nos. 1866 to 1868, Newmarch considers two-thirds of all banknotes issued by them (the last third has to be covered by bullion
reserve in these banks) as "the creation of so much capital", because
this amount of coin is saved. The profit of the banker as a result of

this may not be larger than that of other capitalists. The fact remains that he draws the profit out of this national saving of coin. The fact that a national saving becomes a private profit does not shock the bourgeois economist in the least, since profit is generally the appropriation of national labour. Is there anything more absurd, for instance, than the Bank of England (1797 to 1817) — whose notes have credit only thanks to the state — taking payment from the state, i. e., from the public, in the form of interest on government loans, for the power granted it by the state to transform these same notes from paper into money and then to lend it back to the state?

The banks, incidentally, have still other means of creating capital. Again according to Newmarch, the country banks, as mentioned above, are accustomed to send their superfluous funds (that is, Bank of England notes) to London BILL-BROKERS, in return for discounted bills of exchange. With these bills of exchange, the bank serves its customers, since it follows a rule not to reissue bills of exchange received from its local customers, in order to prevent their business transactions from becoming known in their own neighbourhood. These bills, received from London, not only serve the purpose of being issued to customers who have to make direct payments in London, in the event they do not prefer to get the bank's own draft on London; they also serve to settle payments locally, since the banker's endorsement secures local credit for them. Thus, in Lancashire, for instance, all the local banks' own notes and a large portion of the Bank of England notes have been pushed out of circulation by such bills (ibid., 1568 to 1574).

Thus we see here how banks create credit and capital by 1) issuing their own notes, 2) writing out drafts on London running up to 21 days, but paid in cash to them immediately on issue and 3) paying out discounted bills of exchange, which are endowed with credit primarily and essentially by endorsement through the bank — at least as far as concerns the local district.

The power of the Bank of England is revealed by its regulation of the market rate of interest. In times of normal activity, it may happen that the Bank cannot prevent a moderate drain of gold from its bullion reserve by raising the discount rate [12] because the demand for

---

[12] At the general meeting of stockholders of the UNION BANK OF LONDON on January 17, 1894, President Ritchie relates that the Bank of England raised the discount in 1893 from $2\frac{1}{2}$ % in July to 3 and 4% in August, and since it lost within four weeks fully £$4\frac{1}{2}$ million in gold despite this, it raised the bank rate to 5%, whereupon gold flowed

540 Part V.— Division of Profit into Interest and Profit of Enterprise

means of payment is satisfied by private banks, stock banks and
BILL-BROKERS, who have gained considerably in capital power during
the last thirty years. In such cases, the Bank of England must have
recourse to other means. But the statement made by banker Glyn
(of Glyn, Mills, Currie & Co.) before the C. D. 1848/57 still holds
good for critical periods:

"1709. Under circumstances of great pressure upon the country the Bank of England commands the rate of interest."—"1710. In times of extraordinary pressure ...
whenever the discounts of the private bankers or brokers become comparatively limited, they fall upon the Bank of England, and then it is that the Bank of England has
the power of commanding the market rate."

Nevertheless, the Bank of England, being a public institution
under government protection and enjoying corresponding privileges,
cannot exploit its power as ruthlessly as does private business. For this
reason Hubbard remarks before the Banking Committee B. A. 1857:

"2844. //Question:// Is not it the case that when the rate of discount is highest, the
Bank is the cheapest place to go, and that when it is the lowest, the bill-brokers are the
cheapest parties?"— //Hubbard:// "That will always be the case, because the Bank of
England never goes quite so low as its competitors, and when the rate is highest, it is
never quite as high."

But it is a serious event in business life nevertheless when, in time of
stringency, the Bank of England puts on the screw, as the saying goes,
that is, when it raises still higher the interest rate which is already
above average.

"As soon as the Bank puts on the screw, all purchases for foreign exportation immediately cease ... the exporters wait until prices have reached the lowest point of depression, and then, and not till then, they make their purchases. But when this point has
arrived, the exchanges have been rectified — gold ceases to be exported before the
lowest point of depression has arrived. Purchases of goods for exportation may have the
effect of bringing back some of the gold which has been sent abroad, but they come too
late to prevent the drain" (J. M. Gilbart, *An Inquiry into the Causes of the Pressure on
the Money Market*, p. 35). "Another effect of regulating the currency by the foreign
exchanges is that it leads in seasons of pressure to an enormous rate of interest" (l. c.,
p. 40). "The cost of rectifying the exchanges falls upon the productive industry of the
country, while during the process the profits of the Bank of England are actually aug-

back to it and the bank rate was reduced to 4% in September and then to 3% in October. But this bank rate was not recognised in the market. "When the bank rate was
5%, the market rate was $3\frac{1}{2}$%, and the rate for money $2\frac{1}{2}$%; when the bank rate fell
to 4%, the discount rate was $2\frac{3}{8}$% and the money rate $1\frac{3}{4}$%, when the bank rate was
3%, the discount rate fell to $1\frac{1}{2}$% and the money rate to something below that" (*Daily
News*, January 18, 1894).— *F. E.*

mented in consequence of carrying on her business with a less amount of treasure" (l. c., p. 52).

But, says friend Samuel Gurney,

"The great fluctuations in the rate of interest are advantageous to bankers and dealers in money—all fluctuations in trade are advantageous to the knowing man."

And even though the Gurneys skim off the cream by ruthlessly exploiting the precarious state of business, whereas the Bank of England cannot do so with the same liberty, nevertheless it also makes a very pretty profit—not to mention the personal profits falling into the laps of its directors, as a result of their exceptional opportunity for ascertaining the general state of business. According to data submitted to the LORDS' COMMITTEE of 1817 when cash payments were resumed, these profits accruing to the Bank of England for the entire period from 1797 to 1817 were as follows:

Bonuses and increased dividends	7,451,136
New stock divided among proprietors	7,276,500
Increased value of capital	14,553,000
Total	29,280,636

This, on a capital of £11,642,400 over a period of 19 years (D. Hardcastle, *Banks and Bankers*, 2nd ed., London, 1843, p. 120).

If we estimate the total gain of the Bank of Ireland, which also suspended cash payments in 1797, by the same method, we obtain the following result:

Dividends as by returns due 1821	4,736,085
Declared bonus	1,225,000
Increased assets	1,214,800
Increased value of capital	4,185,000
Total	11,360,885

This, on a capital of £3 million (ibid., pp. 363-64).

Talk about centralisation! The credit system, which has its focus in the so-called national banks and the big money lenders and usurers surrounding them, constitutes enormous centralisation, and gives to this class of parasites the fabulous power, not only to periodically despoil industrial capitalists, but also to interfere in actual production in a most dangerous manner—and this gang knows nothing about production and has nothing to do with it. The Acts of 1844 and 1845 are proof of the growing power of these bandits, who are joined by financiers and STOCK-JOBBERS.

Should anyone still doubt that these esteemed bandits exploit the national and world production solely in the interests of production and the exploited themselves, he will surely learn better from the following homily on the high moral worth of bankers:

"Banking establishments are ... moral and religious institutions.... How often has the fear of being seen by the watchful and reproving eye of his banker deterred the young tradesman from joining the company of riotous and extravagant friends?... What has been his anxiety to stand well in the estimation of his banker?... Has not the frown of his banker been of more influence with him than the jeers and discouragements of his friends? Has he not trembled to be supposed guilty of deceit or the slightest misstatement, lest it should give rise to suspicion, and his accommodation be in consequence restricted or discontinued? ... And has not that friendly advice been of more value to him than that of priest?" (G. M. Bell, a Scottish bank director, in *The Philosophy of Joint Stock Banking*, London, 1840, pp. 46, 47).

Chapter XXXIV

THE CURRENCY PRINCIPLE
AND THE ENGLISH BANK LEGISLATION OF 1844

//In a former work,[13] Ricardo's theory on the value of money as related to commodity prices has been analysed; we can, therefore, confine ourselves here to the indispensable. According to Ricardo, the value of metallic money is determined by the labour time objectified in it, but only as long as the quantity of money stands in correct relationship to amount and price of commodities to be exchanged. If the quantity of money rises above this ratio, its value falls and commodity prices rise; if it falls below the correct ratio, its value rises and commodity prices fall — assuming all other conditions equal. In the first case, the country in which this excess gold exists will export the gold whose value has depreciated and import commodities; in the second case, gold will flow to those countries in which it is assessed above its value, while the under-assessed commodities flow from these countries to other markets, where they command normal prices. Since under these circumstances "even gold in the form of coin or bullion

---

[13] K. Marx, *Zur Kritik der politischen Oekonomie*, Berlin, 1859, s. 150 ff.[a]

---

[a] K. Marx, *A Contribution to the Critique of Political Economy* (present edition, Vol. 29, pp. 404-15).

can become a value token representing a larger or smaller metallic value than its own, it is obvious that any convertible banknotes that are in circulation must share the same fate. Although banknotes are convertible, and their real value accordingly corresponds to their nominal value, THE AGGREGATE CURRENCY CONSISTING OF METAL AND OF CONVERTIBLE NOTES[a] may appreciate or depreciate if, for reasons described earlier, the total quantity either rises above or falls below the level which is determined by the exchange value of the commodities in circulation and the metallic value of gold.... This depreciation, not of notes in relation to gold, but of gold and notes taken together, i. e., of the aggregate means of circulation of a country, is one of Ricardo's main discoveries, which Lord Overstone and Co. pressed into their service and turned into a fundamental principle of Sir Robert Peel's bank legislation of 1844 and 1845" (l. c., p. 155).[b]

We need not here repeat a demonstration of the incorrectness of this Ricardian theory which is given in the cited work. We are merely interested in the way Ricardo's theses were elaborated by that school of bank theorists who dictated Peel's above-mentioned Bank Acts.

"The commercial crises of the nineteenth century, and in particular the great crises of 1825 and 1836, did not lead to any further development of Ricardo's currency theory, but rather to new practical applications of it. It was no longer a matter of single economic phenomena — such as the depreciation of precious metals in the sixteenth and seventeenth centuries confronting Hume, or the depreciation of paper currency during the eighteenth century and the beginning of the nineteenth confronting Ricardo — but of big storms on the world market, in which the antagonism of all elements in the bourgeois process of production explodes; the origin of these storms and the means of defence against them were sought within the sphere of currency, the most superficial and abstract sphere of this process. The theoretical assumption which actually serves the school of economic weather experts as their point of departure is the dogma that Ricardo had discovered the laws governing purely metallic currency. It was thus left to them to subsume the circulation of credit money or banknotes under these laws.

"The most common and conspicuous phenomenon accompanying commercial crises is a sudden fall in the general level of commodity

---

[a] In the 1894 German edition this English phrase is given in parentheses after its German equivalent. - [b] See present edition, Vol. 29, p. 404.

prices occurring after a prolonged general rise of prices. A general fall of commodity prices may be expressed as a rise in the value of money relative to all other commodities, and, on the other hand, a general rise of prices may be defined as a fall in the relative value of money. Either of these statements describes the phenomenon but does not explain it.... The different terminology has just as little effect on the task itself as a translation of the terms from German into English would have. Ricardo's monetary theory proved to be singularly apposite since it gave to a tautology the semblance of a causal relation. What is the cause of the general fall in commodity prices which occurs periodically? It is the periodically occurring rise in the relative value of money. What on the other hand is the cause of the recurrent general rise in commodity prices? It is the recurrent fall in the relative value of money. It would be just as correct to say that the recurrent rise and fall of prices is brought about by their recurrent rise and fall. ...Once the transformation of the tautology into a causal relationship is taken for granted, everything else follows easily. The rise in commodity prices is due to a fall in the value of money, the fall in the value of money, however, as we know from Ricardo, is due to excessive currency, that is to say, to the fact that the amount of money in circulation rises above the level determined by its own intrinsic value and the intrinsic value of commodities. Similarly in the opposite case, the general fall of commodity prices is due to the value of money rising above its intrinsic value as a result of an insufficient amount of currency. Prices therefore rise and fall periodically, because periodically there is too much or too little money in circulation. If it is proved, for instance, that the rise of prices coincided with a decreased amount of money in circulation, and the fall of prices with an increased amount, then it is nevertheless possible to assert that, in consequence of some reduction or increase — which can in no way be ascertained statistically — of commodities in circulation, the amount of money in circulation has relatively, though not absolutely, increased or decreased. We have seen that, according to Ricardo, even when a purely metallic currency is employed, these variations in the level of prices must take place, but, because they occur alternately, they neutralise one another. For example, an insufficient amount of currency brings about a fall in commodity prices, the fall of commodity prices stimulates an export of commodities to other countries, but this export leads to an influx of money into the country, the influx of money causes again a rise in commodity prices. When there is an excessive amount of currency the reverse occurs: commodities are imported and money exported. Since notwithstanding these general price movements, which arise from the very nature of Ricardo's metallic currency, their severe and vehement form, the form of crisis, belongs to periods with developed credit systems, it is clear that the issue of banknotes is not exactly governed by the laws of metallic currency. The remedy applicable to metallic currency is the import and export of precious metals, which are immediately thrown into circulation as coin, their inflow or outflow thus causing commodity prices to fall or to rise. The banks must now artificially exert the same influence on commodity prices by imitating the laws of metallic currency. If gold is flowing in from abroad, it is a proof that there is an insufficient amount of currency, that the value of money is too high and commodity prices too low, and banknotes must therefore be thrown into circulation in accordance with the newly imported gold. On the other hand, banknotes must be taken out of circulation in accordance with an outflow of gold from the country. In other words the issue of banknotes must be regulated according to the import and export of the precious metals or according to the rate of exchange. Ricardo's wrong assumption that gold is simply specie and that consequently the whole of the imported gold is used to augment the money in circulation thus causing prices to rise, and that the whole of the gold exported represents a decrease in the amount of specie and thus causes prices to fall — this theoretical assumption is now turned *into a practical experiment by making the amount of specie in circulation correspond always to the quantity of gold in the country.* Lord Overstone (Jones Loyd, the banker), Colonel Torrens, Norman, Clay, Arbuthnot and numerous other writers known in England as the "CURRENCY PRINCIPLE"[43] school have not only preached this doctrine, but have made it the basis of the present English and Scottish banking legislation by means of Sir Robert Peel's Bank Acts of 1844 and 1845.[48] The analysis of the ignominious fiasco they suffered both in theory and practice, after experiments on the largest national scale, can only be made in the section dealing with the theory of credit"[54] (l. c., pp. 165-68).[a]

The critique of this school was furnished by Thomas Tooke, James Wilson (in the *Economist* of 1844 to 1847) and John Fullarton. But we have seen on several occasions, particularly in Chapter XXVIII of this book, how incompletely they, too, saw through the nature of

---

[a] Ibid., pp. 412-14.

gold, and how unclear they were about the relationship of money and capital. We quote here merely a few instances in connection with the transactions of the Committee of the Lower House of 1857 concerning Peel's Bank Acts (B. C. 1857).— *F. E.*//

J. G. Hubbard, former Governor of the Bank of England, testifies:

"2400. The effect of the export of bullion ... has no reference whatever to the prices of commodities. It has an effect, and a very important one, upon the price of interest-bearing securities, because, as the rate of interest varies, the value of commodities which embodied that interest is necessarily powerfully affected."

He presents two tables covering the years 1834 to 1843, and 1844 to 1853,[a] which show that the price variations of fifteen major commercial articles were quite independent of the export and import of gold and the interest rate. On the other hand, they show a close connection between the export and import of gold, which is, indeed, the "representative of our uninvested capital", and the interest rate.

"In 1847, a very large amount of American securities were retransferred to America, and Russian securities to Russia, and other continental securities were transferred to those places from which we drew our supplies of grain."[b]

The fifteen major articles on which the following tables of Hubbard are based include cotton, cotton yarn, cotton fabrics, wool, woolen cloth, flax, linen, indigo, pig-iron, tin, copper, tallow, sugar, coffee, and silk.

I. 1834-1843

Date	Bullion Reserve of Bank	Market Rate of Discount	Of Fifteen Major Articles		
			Price Increase	Price Decrease	Unchanged
1834, March 1	£9,104,000	$2^3/_4\%$	—	—	—
1835, March 1	6,274,000	$3^3/_4\%$	7	7	1
1836, March 1	7,918,000	$3^1/_4\%$	11	3	1
1837, March 1	4,077,000	5%	5	9	1
1838, March 1	10,471,000	$2^3/_4\%$	4	11	—
1839, Sept. 1	2,684,000	6%	8	5	2
1840, June 1	4,571,000	$4^3/_4\%$	5	9	1
1840, Dec. 1	3,642,000	$5^3/_4\%$	7	6	2
1841, Dec. 1	4,873,000	5%	3	12	—
1842, Dec. 1	10,603,000	$2^1/_2\%$	2	13	—
1843, June 1	11,566,000	$2^1/_4\%$	1	14	—

---

[a] In the 1894 German edition: "1845-56". - [b] Report from the Select Committee on Bank Acts. Part I, No. 2402.

II. 1844-1853

Date	Bullion Reserve of Bank	Market Rate of Discount	Of Fifteen Major Articles		
			Price Increase	Price Decrease	Unchanged
1844, March 1	£16,162,000	2¼%	—	—	—
1845, Dec. 1	13,237,000	4½%	11	4	—
1846, Sept. 1	16,366,000	3%	7	8	—
1847, Sept. 1	9,140,000	6%	6	6	3
1850, March 1	17,126,000	2½%	5	9	1
1851, June 1	13,705,000	3%	2	11	2
1852, Sept. 1	21,853,000	1¾%	9	5	1
1853, Dec. 1	15,093,000	5%	14	—	1

Hubbard comments in this regard:

"As in the 10 years 1834-43, so in 1844-53, movements in the bullion of the Bank were invariably accompanied by a decrease or increase in the loanable value of money advanced on discount; and the variations in the prices of commodities in this country exhibit an entire independence of the amount of circulation as shown in the fluctuations in bullion at the Bank of England" (Bank Acts Report, 1857, II, pp. 290, 291).

Since the demand and supply of commodities regulate their market prices, it becomes evident here how wrong Overstone is in identifying the demand for loanable money capital (or rather the deviations of supply therefrom), as expressed by the discount rate, with the demand for actual "capital". The contention that commodity prices are regulated by fluctuations in the quantity of currency is now concealed by the phrase that discount rate fluctuations express fluctuations in the demand for actual material capital, as distinct from money capital. We have seen that before the same Committee both Norman and Overstone actually contended this, and that the latter especially was compelled to resort to very lame subterfuges, until he was finally cornered (Chap. XXVI). It is indeed an old humbug that changes in the existing quantity of gold in a particular country must raise or lower commodity prices within this country by increasing or decreasing the quantity of the medium of circulation. If gold is exported, then, according to this CURRENCY Theory, commodity prices must rise in the country importing this gold, and thereby the value of exports from the gold-exporting country on the gold-importing country's market; on the other hand, the value of the gold-importing country's exports would fall on the gold-exporting country's market while it would rise on the domestic market, i. e., the country receiving the gold. But, in fact, a decrease in the quantity of gold raises only the interest rate, whereas an increase in the quantity of gold lowers the interest rate; and if not for the fact that the fluctuations in the interest rate enter into the determination of cost prices, or in the determination of demand and supply, commodity prices would be wholly unaffected by them.

In the same report, N. Alexander, head of a large firm doing business with India, expresses the following views on the heavy drain of silver to India and China in the mid-fifties. This was partly due to the Chinese Civil War,[55] which checked the sale of English fabrics in China, and partly due to the disease among silkworms in Europe, which sharply reduced silkworm breeding in Italy and France:

"4337. Is the drain for China or for India? — You send the silver to India, and you buy opium with a great deal of it, all of which goes on to China to lay down funds for the purchase of the silk; and the state of the markets in India" (in spite of the accumulation of silver there) "makes it a more profitable investment for the merchant to lay down silver than to send piece-goods or English manufactures."—"4338. In order to obtain the silver, has there not been a great drain from France? — Yes, very large."—"4344. Instead of bringing in silk from France and Italy, we are sending it there in large quantities, both from Bengal and from China."

In other words, silver, the money metal of that continent, was sent to Asia instead of commodities, not because commodity prices had risen in the country which produced them (England), but because prices had fallen as a result of overimports in the country which imported them; and this despite the fact that the silver was received by England from France and had to be paid for partly in gold. According to the Currency Theory, prices should have fallen in England and risen in India and China as a result of such imports.

Another illustration. Before the Lords' Committee (C. D. 1848/57), Wylie, one of the first Liverpool merchants, testifies as follows:

"1994. At the close of 1845 there was no trade that was more remunerating, and in which there were such large profits //than cotton spinning//. The stock of cotton was large and good, useful cotton could be bought at 4d. per pound, and from such cotton good SECUNDA MULE TWIST No. 40 was made at an expense not exceeding a like amount, say at a cost of 8d. per pound in all to the spinner. This yarn was largely sold and contracted for in September and October 1845 at $10\frac{1}{2}$ and $11\frac{1}{2}$ d. per pound, and in some instances the spinners realised a profit equal to the first cost of the cotton."—"1996. The trade continued to be remunerative until the beginning of 1846."—"2000. On March 3, 1844, the stock of cotton //627,042 bales// was more than double what it is this day //on March 7, 1848, when it was 301,070 bales// and yet the price then was $1\frac{1}{4}$ d. per pound dearer." //$6\frac{1}{4}$ d. as against 5d.//—At the same time yarn, good SECUNDA MULE TWIST No. 40, had fallen from $11\frac{1}{2}$ -12d. to $9\frac{1}{2}$d. per 1b. in October, and to $7\frac{3}{4}$ d. at the end of December 1847; yarn was sold at the purchase price of the cotton from which it had been spun (ibid., Nos. 2021 and 2023).

This shows the self-interest of Overstone's sagacity according to which money should be "dear" because capital is "scarce". On March 3, 1844, the bank interest rate stood at 3%; in October and November of 1847 it rose to 8 and 9%, and was still 4% on March 7, 1848. The prices of cotton were depressed far below the price which corresponded to the state of supply by the complete stoppage of sales and the panic with its ensuing high rate of interest. As a result, there was an enormous decrease in imports in 1848, on the one hand, and, on the other, a decrease in production in America; hence a new rise in cotton prices in 1849. According to Overstone, the commodities were too dear because there was too much money in the country.

"2002. The late decline in the condition of the cotton manufactories is not to be ascribed to the want of the raw material, as the price seems to have been lower, though the stock of the raw material is very much diminished."

How nicely Overstone confuses prices, or the value of commodities, with the value of money, that is, the interest rate. In his reply to Question 2026, Wylie sums up his general judgement of the CURRENCY Theory, based on which Cardwell and Sir Charles Wood, in May 1847,

"asserted the necessity of carrying out the Bank Act of 1844 in its full and entire integrity". "These principles seemed to me to be of a nature that would give an artificial high value to money and an artificial and ruinously low value to all commodities and produce."

He says, furthermore, concerning the effects of this Bank Act on business in general:

"As bills at four months, which is the regular course of drafts, from manufacturing towns on merchants and bankers for the purchase of goods going to the United States, could not be discounted except at great sacrifices, the execution of orders was checked to a great extent, until after the Government Letter of October 25" (suspension of the Bank Act), "when those four months' bills became discountable" (2097).

We see, then, that the suspension of this Bank Act was received with relief in the provinces as well.

"2102. Last October //1847// there was scarcely an American buyer purchasing goods here who did not at once curtail his orders as much as he possibly could; and when our advices of the dearness of money reached America, all fresh orders ceased."—"2134. Corn and sugar were special. The corn market was affected by the prospects of the harvest, and sugar was affected by the immense stocks and imports. "—" 2163. Of our indebtedness to America ... much was liquidated by forced sales of consigned goods, and I fear that much was cancelled by the failures here."—"2196. If I recollect rightly, *70 per cent was paid* on our Stock Exchange *in October 1847.*"[a]

//The crisis of 1837 with its protracted aftermath, followed in 1842 by a regular post-crisis, and the self-interested blindness of industrialists and merchants, who absolutely refused to see any overproduction—for such a thing was absurd and impossible according to vulgar economy—had ultimately achieved that confusion of thought which enabled the CURRENCY School to put its dogma into practice on a national scale. The bank legislation of 1844 and 1845 was passed.

The Bank Act of 1844 divides the Bank of England into an issue department and a banking department. The former receives securities — principally government obligations — amounting to 14 million, and the entire metal hoard, of which not more than one-quarter is to consist of silver, and issues notes to the full amount of the total. In so far as these notes are not in the hands of the public, they are held in the banking department and, together with the small amount of coin required for daily use (about one million), constitute its ever ready reserve. The issue department gives the public gold for notes and notes for gold; the remaining transactions with the public are carried on by the banking department. Private banks in England and Wales authorised in 1844 to issue their own notes retained this privilege, but their note issue was fixed; if one of these banks ceases to issue its own notes, the Bank of England can increase its unbacked notes by two-thirds of the quota thus made available; in this way its issue was increased by 1892 from £14 to £16$\frac{1}{2}$ million (to be exact, £16,450,000).

Thus, for every five pounds in gold which leave the bank treasury, a five-pound note returns to the issue department and is destroyed; for every five sovereigns going into the treasury a new five-pound note comes into circulation. In this manner, Overstone's ideal paper circulation, which strictly follows the laws of metallic circulation, is carried out in practice, and by this means, according to the advocates of the CURRENCY Theory, crises are made impossible for all time.

But in reality the separation of the Bank into two independent departments deprived its management of the possibility of freely utilising its entire available means at critical times, so that situations could arise in which the banking department might be on the verge of

---

[a] Italicised by Marx.

bankruptcy while the issue department still had intact several millions in gold and, in addition, its entire 14 million in securities. And this could take place so much more easily since there is a period in almost every crisis when heavy exports of gold take place which must be covered in the main by the metal reserve of the bank. But for every five pounds in gold which then go abroad, the domestic circulation is deprived of a five-pound note, so that the quantity of circulating medium is reduced precisely at a time when the largest quantity is most needed. The Bank Act of 1844 thus directly induces the entire commercial world forthwith to hoard a reserve fund of banknotes at the outbreak of a crisis; in other words, to accelerate and intensify the crisis. By such artificial intensification of demand for money accommodation, that is, for means of payment at the decisive moment, and the simultaneous restriction of the supply the Bank Act drives the rate of interest to a hitherto unknown height during a crisis. Hence, instead of eliminating crises, the Act, on the contrary, intensifies them to a point where either the entire industrial world must go to pieces, or else the Bank Act. Both on October 25, 1847, and on November 12,[a] the crisis reached such a point; the government then lifted the restriction for the Bank in issuing notes by suspending the Act of 1844, and this sufficed in both cases to overcome the crisis. In 1847, the assurance that banknotes would again be issued for first-class securities sufficed to bring to light the £4 to £5 million of hoarded notes and put them back into circulation; in 1857, the issue of notes exceeding the legal amount reached almost one million, but this lasted only for a very short time.

It should also be mentioned that the 1844 legislation still shows traces recalling the first twenty years of the 19th century, the period when specie payments were suspended and notes devaluated. The fear that notes may lose their credit is still plainly in evidence. But this fear is quite groundless, since even in 1825 the issue of a discovered old supply of one-pound notes, which had been taken out of circulation, broke the crisis and proved thereby that the credit of the notes remained unshaken even in times of the most general and deepest mistrust. And this is quite understandable; for, after all, the entire nation backs up these symbols of value with its credit.— *F. E.*//

Let us now turn to a few comments on the effect of the Bank Act. John Stuart Mill believes that the Bank Act of 1844 kept down overspeculation. Happily this sage spoke on June 12, 1857. Four months

---

[a] 1857

later the crisis broke out. He literally congratulated the "bank directors and the commercial public generally" on the fact that they

"understand much better than they did the nature of a commercial crisis, and the
extreme mischief which they do both to themselves and to the public by upholding
overspeculation" (B. C. 1857, No. 2031).

The sagacious Mr. Mill thinks that if one-pound notes are issued

"as advances to manufacturers and others, who pay wages ... the notes may get
into the hands of others who expend them for consumption, and in that case the notes
do constitute in themselves a demand for commodities and may for some time tend
to promote a rise of prices".[a]

Does Mr. Mill assume, then, that manufacturers will pay higher
wages because they pay them in paper instead of gold? Or does he believe that if a manufacturer receives his loan in £100 notes and exchanges them for gold, these wages would constitute less demand
than if paid immediately in one-pound notes? And does he not know
that, for instance, in certain mining districts wages were paid in the
notes of local banks, so that several labourers together received one
five-pound note? Does this increase their demand? Or will bankers
advance money to manufacturers more easily and in larger quantities
in small notes than in large ones?

//This singular fear which Mill has for one-pound notes would be
inexplicable if his whole work on political economy did not reveal an
eclecticism which shows no hesitation in the face of any contradiction.
On the one hand, he agrees on many points with Tooke as opposed to
Overstone; on the other, he believes that commodity prices are determined by the quantity of available money. He is thus by no means
convinced that, all other conditions being equal, a sovereign will find
its way into the coffers of the Bank for every one-pound note issued.
He fears that the quantity of circulating medium could be increased
and thereby devaluated, that is, commodity prices might rise. This
and nothing more is concealed behind the above-mentioned apprehension.— F. E.//

Tooke expresses the following views before the C. D. 1848/57 concerning the division of the Bank into two departments and the excessive precautions taken to safeguard the cashing of notes:

The greater fluctuations of the interest rate in 1847, as compared with 1837 and
1839, are due solely to the separation of the Bank into two departments (3010).— The

---

[a] Ibid., No. 2066.

safety of banknotes was affected neither in 1825 nor in 1837 and 1839 (3015).— The demand for gold in 1825 was aimed only at filling the vacuum created by the complete discredit of the one-pound notes of country banks; this vacuum could be filled only by gold, until such time as the Bank of England also issued one-pound notes (3022).— In November and December 1825 not the slightest demand existed for gold for export purposes (3023).

"In point of discredit at home as well as abroad, a failure in paying the dividends and the deposits would be of far greater consequence than the suspending of the payment of the banknotes (3028)."

"3035. Would you not say that any circumstance, which had the effect of ultimately endangering the convertibility of the note, would be one likely to add serious difficulty in a moment of commercial pressure? — Not at all."

"In the course of 1847 ... an increased issue from the circulating department might have contributed to replenish the coffers of the Bank, as it did in 1825" (3058).

Before the Committee on B. A. 1857, Newmarch testifies:

"1357. The first mischievous effect ... of that separation of departments" (of the Bank) "and ... a necessary consequence from the cutting in two of the reserve of bullion has been that the banking business of the Bank of England, that is to say, the whole of that part of the operation of the Bank of England which brings it more immediately into contact with the commerce of the country, has been carried on upon a moiety only of its former amounts of reserve. Out of that division of the reserve has arisen, therefore, this state of things, that whenever the reserve of the banking department has been diminished, even to a small extent, it has rendered necessary an action by the Bank upon its rate of discount. That diminished reserve, therefore, has produced a frequent succession of changes and jerks in the rate of discount."—"1358. The alterations since 1844" (until June 1857) "have been some 60 in number, whereas the alterations prior to 1844 in the same space of time certainly did not amount to a dozen."

Of special interest is the testimony of Palmer, a Director of the Bank of England since 1811 and for a while its Governor, before the Lords' Committee on C. D. 1848/57:

"828. In December 1825, there was about £1,100,000 of bullion remaining in the Bank. At that period it must undoubtedly have failed *in toto*, if this Act had been in existence" (meaning the Act of 1844). "The issue in December, I think, was 5 or 6 millions of notes in a week, which relieved the panic that existed at that period."

"825. The first period" (since July 1, 1825) "when the present Act would have failed, if the Bank had attempted to carry out the transactions then undertaken, was on the 28th of February 1837; at that period there were £3,900,000 to £4,000,000 of bullion in the possession of the Bank, and then the Bank would have been left with £650,000 only in the reserve. Another period is in the year 1839, which continued from the 9th of July to the 5th of December."—"826. What was the amount of the reserve in that case? — THE RESERVE WAS MINUS ALTOGETHER £200,000[a] upon the 5th of September. On the 5th of November it rose to about a million or a million and a half."— "830. The Act of 1844 would have prevented the Bank giving assistance to the

[a] In the 1894 German edition this English phrase is given in parentheses after its German equivalent.

American trade in 1837."—"831. There were three of the principal American houses that failed. ... Almost every house connected with America was in a state of discredit, and unless the Bank had come forward at that period, I do not believe that there would have been more than one or two houses that could have sustained themselves."— "836.The pressure in 1837 is not to be compared with that of 1847. The pressure in the former year was chiefly confined to the American trade."—838. (Early in June 1837 the management of the Bank discussed the question of overcoming the pressure.) "Some gentlemen alvocated the opinion ... that the correct principle was to raise the rate of interest, by which the price of commodities would be lowered; in short, to make money dear and commodities cheap, BY WHICH THE FOREIGN PAYMENT WOULD BE AC-COMPLISHED." [a]—"906. The establishment of an artificial limitation of the powers of the Bank under the Act of 1844, instead of the ancient and natural limitation of the Bank's powers, namely, the actual amount of its specie, tends to create artificial diffi-culty, and therefore an operation upon the prices of merchandise that would have been unnecessary but for the provisions of the Act."—"968. You cannot, by the working of the Act of 1844, materially reduce the bullion, under ordinary circumstances, below nine million and a half. It would then cause a pressure upon prices and credit which would occasion such an advance in the exchange with foreign countries as to increase the import of bullion, and to that extent add to the amount in the issue department."— "996. Under the limitation that you" (the Bank) "are now subject to, you have not the command of silver to an extent that you require at a time when silver would be required for an action upon the foreign exchanges."—"999. What was the object of the regulation restricting the Bank as to the amount of silver to one-fifth? — I cannot answer that question."

The purpose was to make money dear; aside from the CURRENCY Theory, the separation of the two bank departments and the require-ment for Scottish and Irish banks to hold gold in reserve for backing notes issued beyond a certain amount had the same purpose. This brought about a decentralisation of the national metal reserve, which decreased its capability of correcting unfavourable exchange rates. All the following stipulations aim to raise the interest rate: that the Bank of England shall not issue notes exceeding 14 million except against gold reserve; that the banking department shall be adminis-tered as an ordinary bank, forcing the interest rate down when money is plentiful and driving it up when money is scarce; limiting the silver reserve, the principal means of rectifying the rates of exchange with the continent and Asia; the regulations concerning the Scottish and Irish banks, which never require gold [b] for export but must now keep it under the pretence of ensuring an actually illusory con-vertibility of their notes. The fact is that the Act of 1844 caused a run on the Scottish banks for gold in 1857 for the first time. Nor does

---

[a] In the 1894 German edition this English phrase is given in parentheses after its Ger-man equivalent. - [b] In the original: "money"; corrected after Marx's manuscript.

the new bank legislation make any distinction between a drain of gold abroad or for domestic purposes, although it goes without saying that their effects are quite different. Hence the continual large fluctuations in the market rate of interest. With reference to silver, Palmer says on two separate occasions, 992 and 994, that the Bank can buy silver for notes only when the rate of exchange is favourable for England, i. e., silver is superfluous; for:

"1003. The only object in holding a considerable amount of bullion in silver is to facilitate making the foreign payment so long as the exchanges are against the country."—"1004. Silver is ... a commodity which, being money in every other part of the world, is therefore the most direct commodity ... for the purpose" (payments abroad). "The United States latterly have taken gold alone."

In his opinion, the Bank did not have to raise the interest rate above its old level of 5% in times of stringency, so long as unfavourable exchange rates do not drain gold to foreign countries. Were it not for the Act of 1844, the Bank would be able to discount all FIRST-CLASS BILLS[a] presented to it without difficulty. (1018-20). But under the Act of 1844 and in the state in which the Bank found itself in October 1847,

"there was no rate of interest which the Bank could have charged to houses of credit, which they would not have been willing to pay to carry on their payments".[b]

And this high interest rate was precisely the purpose of the Act.

"1029. ... Great distinction which I wish to draw between the action of the rate of interest upon a foreign demand" (for precious metal) "and an advance in the rate for the object of checking a demand upon the Bank during a period of internal discredit."—"1023. Previously to the Act of 1844 ... when the exchanges were in favour of the country, and positive panic and alarm existed through the country, there was no limit put upon the issue, by which alone that state of distress could be relieved."

So speaks a man who has occupied a post for 39 years in the administration of the Bank of England. Let us now listen to a private banker, Twells, an associate of Spooner, Attwood & Co. since 1801. He is alone among the witnesses before the B. C. 1857 who provides us with an insight into the country's actual state of affairs and who sees the crisis approaching. In other respects, however, he is a sort of LITTLE-SHILLING MAN from Birmingham,[52] like his associates, the Attwood brothers, who are the founders of this school. (See *Zur Kritik der pol. Oek.*, S. 59.)[c] He testifies:

---

[a] In the 1894 German edition these English words are given in parentheses after their German equivalent. - [b] Ibid., No. 1022. - [c] See present edition, Vol. 29, p. 319.

"4488. How do you think that the Act of 1844 has operated? — If I were to answer you as a banker, I should say that it has operated exceedingly well, for it has afforded a rich harvest to bankers and" (money) "capitalists of all kinds. But it has operated very badly to the honest industrious tradesman who requires steadiness in the rate of discount, that he may be enabled to make his arrangements with confidence.... It has made money lending a most profitable pursuit."—"4489. It" (the Bank Act) "enables the London joint-stock banks to return from 20 to 22% to their proprietors? — The other day one of them was paying 18% and I think another 20%; they ought to support the Act of 1844 very strongly."—"4490. The little tradesmen and respectable merchants, who have not a large capital ... it pinches them very much indeed.... The only means that I have of knowing is that I observe such an amazing quantity of their acceptances unpaid. They are always small, perhaps ranging from £20 to £100, a great many of them are unpaid and go back unpaid to all parts of the country, which is always an indication of suffering amongst ... little shopkeepers."

4494. He declares that business is not profitable now. The following remarks of his are important because they show that he saw the latent existence of the crisis when none of the others had even an inkling of it.

"4494. Things keep their prices in Mincing Lane, but we sell nothing, we cannot sell upon any terms; we keep the nominal price."

4495. He relates the following case: A Frenchman sends a broker in Mincing Lane commodities for £3,000 to be sold at a certain price. The broker cannot obtain the requested price, and the Frenchman cannot sell below this price. The commodities remain unsold, but the Frenchman needs money. The broker therefore makes him an advance of £1,000 and has the Frenchman draw a bill of exchange of £1,000 for three months on the broker against his commodities as security. At the end of the three months the bill becomes due, but the commodities still remain unsold. The broker must then pay the bill, and although he possesses security for £3,000, he cannot convert it into cash and as a result faces difficulties. In this manner, one person drags another down with him.

"4496. With regard to the large exports ... where there is a depressed state of trade at home, it necessarily forces large exportation."—"4497. Do you think that the home consumption has been diminished? — *Very much indeed ... immensely ...* the shopkeepers are the best authorities."—"4498. Still the importations are very large; does not that indicate a large consumption? — It does, *if you can sell*; but many of the warehouses are full of these things; in this very instance which I have been relating, there is £3,000 worth imported, which cannot be sold."

"4514. When money is dear, would you say that capital would be cheap? — Yes."

This man, then, is by no means of Overstone's opinion that a high rate of interest is the same as dear capital.

The following shows how business is now conducted:

"4616. Others are going to a very great extent, carrying on a prodigious trade in exports and imports, to an extent far beyond what their capital justifies them in doing; there can be no doubt of all of that. These men may succeed; they may by some lucky venture get large fortunes, and put themselves right. That is very much the system in which a great deal of trade is now carried on. Persons will consent to lose 20, 30, and 40 per cent upon a shipment; the next venture may bring it back to them. If they fail in one after another, then they are broken up; and that is just the case which we have often seen recently; mercantile houses have broken up, without one shilling of property being left."

"4791. The low rate of interest" (during the last ten years) "operates against bankers, it is true, but I should have very great difficulty in explaining to you, unless I could show you the books, how much higher the profits" (his own) "are now than they used to be formerly. When interest is low, from excessive issues, we have large deposits; when interest is high, we get the advantage in that way."—"4794. When money is at a moderate rate, we have more demand for it; we lend more; it operates in that way" (for us, the bankers). "When it gets higher, we get more than a fair proportion for it; we get more than we ought to do."

We have seen that the credit of the Bank of England notes is considered beyond question by all experts. Nevertheless, the Bank Act completely ties up nine to ten million in gold for the convertibility of these notes. The sacredness and inviolability of this reserve is thereby carried much farther than among hoarders of olden times. Mr. Brown (Liverpool) testifies, C. D. 1847/57:

"2311: This money" (the metal reserve in the issue department) "might as well have been thrown into the sea from any use that it was of at that time, there being no power to employ any of it without violating the Act of Parliament."

The building contractor E. Capps, already cited earlier, whose testimony is also used to illustrate the modern building system in London (Book II, Chap. XII [a]), sums up his opinion of the Bank Act of 1844 as follows (B. A. 1857):

"5508. Then upon the whole ... you think that the present system" (of bank legislation) "is a somewhat adroit scheme for bringing the profits of industry periodically into the usurer's bag? — I think so. I know that it has operated so in the building trade."

As mentioned before, the Scottish banks were forced by the Bank Act of 1845 into a system resembling that of the English. They were obliged to hold gold in reserve for their note issue beyond the limit fixed for each bank. The effect of this may be seen from the following testimony before the C. D. 1848/57.

---

[a] Ibid., Vol. 36, pp. 235-36.

Kennedy, Director of a Scottish bank:

"3375. Was there anything that you can call a circulation of gold in Scotland previously to the passing of the Act of 1845? — None whatever."—"3376. Has there been any additional circulation of gold since? — None whatever; THE PEOPLE DISLIKE GOLD." [a]

3450. The sum of about £900,000 in gold, which the Scottish banks are compelled to keep since 1845, can only be injurious in his opinion and

"absorbs unprofitably so much of the capital of Scotland".

Furthermore, Anderson, Director of the Union Bank of Scotland:

"3588. The only pressure upon the Bank of England by the banks in Scotland for gold was for foreign exchanges? — It was; and that is not to be relieved by holding gold in Edinburgh."—"3590. Having the same amount of securities in the Bank of England" (or in the private banks of England) "we have the same power that we had before of making a drain upon the Bank of England."

Finally, we quote an article from the *Economist* (Wilson):

"The Scotch banks keep unemployed amounts of cash with their London agents; these keep them in the Bank of England. This gives to the Scotch banks, within the limits of these amounts, command over the metal reserve of the Bank, and here it is always in the place where it is needed, when foreign payments are to be made."

This system was disturbed by the Act of 1845:

"In consequence of the Act of 1845 for Scotland of late a large drain of the coin of the Bank has taken place, to supply a mere contingent demand in Scotland, which may never occur... Since that period there has been a large sum uniformly locked up in Scotland, and another considerable sum constantly travelling back and forward between London and Scotland. If a period arrives when a Scotch bank expects an increased demand for its notes, a box of gold is brought down from London; when this period is past, the same box, generally unopened, is sent back to London" (*Economist*, October 23, 1847).[b]

//And what does the father of the Bank Act, banker Samuel Jones Loyd, alias Lord Overstone, say to all this?

Already in 1848 he repeated before the Lords' Committee (C. D. 1848/57) that

"pressure, and a high rate of interest caused by the want of sufficient capital, cannot be relieved by an extra issue of banknotes" (1514),

---

[a] In the 1894 German edition this English phrase is given in parentheses after its German equivalent. - [b] "The Scotch Bank Bill — 1845", *The Economist*, No. 217, October 23, 1847.

in spite of the fact that the mere *authority* to increase the note issue, given by the Government's Letter of October 25, 1847, had sufficed to take the edge off the crisis.

He holds to the view that

"the high rate of interest and the depression of the manufacturing interests was the necessary result of the diminution of the *material* capital applicable to manufacturing and trading purposes" (1604).

And yet the depressed condition of the manufacturing industry had for months consisted in material commodity capital filling the warehouses to overflowing and being actually unsaleable; so that for precisely this reason, material productive capital lay wholly or partly idle, in order not to produce still more unsaleable commodity capital.

And before the Bank Committee of 1857 he says:

"By strict and prompt adherence to the principles of the Act of 1844, everything has passed off with regularity and ease, the monetary system is safe and unshaken, the prosperity of the country is undisputed, the public confidence in the wisdom of the Act of 1844 is daily gaining strength, and if the Committee wish for further practical illustration of the soundness of the principles on which it rests, or of the beneficial results which it has ensured, the true and sufficient answer to the Committee is, look around you, look at the present state of the trade of this country, ... look at the contentment of the people, look at the wealth and prosperity which pervades every class of the community, and then having done so, the Committee may be fairly called upon to decide whether they will interfere with the continuance of an Act under which those results have been developed." (B. C. 1857, No. 4189.)

To this song of praise by Overstone before the Committee on July 14, the antistrophe was given on November 12 of the same year in the shape of a letter to the Bank's management, in which the government suspended the miracle-working law of 1844 to save what could still be saved.—*F. E.*//

Chapter XXXV

PRECIOUS METAL AND RATE OF EXCHANGE

I. MOVEMENT OF THE GOLD RESERVE

It should be noted in regard to the accumulation of notes in times of stringency, that it is a repetition of the hoarding of precious metal as used to take place in troubled times in the most primitive conditions of society. The Act of 1844 is interesting in its operation because it seeks to transform all precious metal existing in the country into a circulating medium; it seeks to equate a drain of gold with a contraction of the circulating medium and a return flow of gold with an expansion of the circulating medium. As a result, the experiment proved the contrary to be the case. With a single exception, which we shall mention shortly, the quantity of circulating notes of the Bank of England has never, since 1844, reached the maximum which it was authorised to issue. The crisis of 1857 proved on the other hand that this maximum does not suffice under certain circumstances. From November 13 to 30, 1857, a daily average of £488,830 above this maximum was circulating (B. A. 1858, p. XI). The legal maximum was at that time £14,475,000, plus the amount of metal reserve in the vaults of the Bank.

Concerning the outflow and inflow of precious metal, the following is to be noted:

First, a distinction should be made between the back and forth movement of metal within a region which does not produce any gold and silver, on the one hand, and, on the other, the flow of gold and silver from their sources of production to various other countries and the distribution of this additional metal among them.

Before the gold mines of Russia,[56] California and Australia made their influence felt, the supply since the beginning of the 19th century sufficed only for the replacement of worn-out coins, for general use in articles of luxury, and for the export of silver to Asia.

However, in the first place, silver exports to Asia have since increased extraordinarily, owing to the Asiatic trade of America and Europe. The silver exported from Europe was largely replaced by the additional supply of gold. Secondly, a portion of the newly imported gold was absorbed by internal money circulation. It is estimated that up to 1857 about 30 million in gold were added to England's internal circulation.[14] Furthermore, the average level of metal reserves in all

---

[14] The effect this had on the money market is indicated by the following testimony of Newmarch [a]: "1509. At the close of 1853, there was a considerable apprehension in the public mind, and in September of that year the Bank of England raised its discount on three occasions... In the early part of October there was a considerable degree of apprehension and alarm in the public mind. That apprehension and alarm was relieved to a very great extent before the end of November, and was almost wholly removed, in consequence of the arrival of nearly £5,000,000 of treasure from Australia... The same thing happened in the autumn of 1854, by the arrival in the months of October and November of nearly £6,000,000 of treasure. The same thing happened again in the

[a] Report from the Select Committee on Bank Acts... 1857.

the central banks of Europe and North America increased since 1844. The expansion of domestic money circulation resulted at the same time in bank reserves growing more rapidly in the period of stagnation following upon the panic, because of the larger quantity of gold coins thrust out of domestic circulation and immobilised. Finally, the consumption of precious metal for luxury articles increased since the discovery of new gold deposits as a consequence of the increased wealth.

Secondly, precious metal flows back and forth between countries which do not produce any gold or silver, the same country continually importing, and also exporting. It is only the preponderance of this movement in one or another direction which, in the final analysis, determines whether a drain or an augmentation has taken place, since the mere oscillations and frequently parallel movements largely neutralise one another. But for this reason, in so far as the result is concerned, the continuity and, in the main, the parallel course of both movements is overlooked. A greater import or a greater export of precious metal is always interpreted to be solely the effect and expression of the relation between the imports and exports of commodities, whereas it is simultaneously indicative of the relation between exports and imports of precious metal itself, quite independent of commodity trade.

Thirdly, the preponderance of imports over exports, and vice versa, is measured on the whole by the increase or decrease in metal reserves of the central banks. The greater or lesser precision of this criterion naturally depends primarily on the degree of centralisation of the banking business in general. For on this depends the extent that precious metal in general accumulated in the so-called national banks represents the national metal reserve. But assuming this to be the case, the criterion is not accurate because an additional import may be absorbed under certain circumstances by domestic circulation and the growing consumption of gold and silver in producing luxury articles; furthermore, because without additional import, a withdrawal of gold coin for domestic circulation could take place,

autumn of 1855, which we know was a period of excitement and alarm, by the arrivals, in the three months of September, October and November, of nearly £8,000,000 of treasure; and then at the close of last year, 1856, we find exactly the same occurrence. In truth, I might appeal to the observation almost of any member of the Committee, whether the natural and complete solvent to which we have got into the habit of looking for any financial pressure, is not the arrival of a gold ship".

and thus the metal reserve could decrease even without a simultaneous increase in exports.

Fourthly, an export of metal assumes the aspect of a DRAIN[a] when the movement of decrease continues for a long time, so that the decrease represents a tendency of movement and depresses the metal reserve of the bank considerably below its average level, down to approximately its average minimum. This minimum is more or less arbitrarily fixed, in so far as it is differently determined in every individual case by legislation concerning backing for the cashing of notes, etc. Concerning the quantitative limits which such a drain can reach in England, Newmarch testified before the Committee on B. A. 1857, Evidence No. 1494:

"Judging from experience, it is very unlikely that the efflux of treasure arising from any oscillation in the foreign trade will proceed beyond £3,000,000 or £4,000,000."

In 1847, the lowest gold reserve level of the Bank of England, occurring on October 23, showed a decrease of £5,198,156 as compared with that of December 26, 1846, and a decrease of £6,453,748 as compared with the highest level of 1846 (August 29).

Fifthly, the determination of the metal reserve of the so-called national bank, a determination, however, which does not by itself regulate the magnitude of this metal hoard, for it can grow solely by the paralysis of domestic and foreign trade, is threefold: 1) reserve fund for international payments, in other words, reserve fund of world money; 2) reserve fund for alternately expanding and contracting domestic metal circulation; 3) reserve fund for the payment of deposits and for the convertibility of notes (this is connected with the function of the bank and has nothing to do with the functions of money as such). The reserve fund can, therefore, also be influenced by conditions which affect every one of these three functions. Thus, as an international fund it can be influenced by the balance of payments, no matter by what factors the latter may be determined and whatever its relation to the balance of trade may be. As a reserve fund for domestic metal circulation it can be influenced by the latter's expansion or contraction. The third function — that of a security fund — does not, admittedly, determine the independent movement of the metal reserve, but has a two-fold effect. If notes are issued which

---

[a] In the 1894 German edition this English term is given in parentheses after its German equivalent.

replace metallic money (also including silver coins in countries where silver is a measure of value) in domestic circulation, the function of the reserve fund under 2) drops away. And a portion of the precious metal, which served to perform this function, will for a long time find its way abroad. In this case metallic coins are not withdrawn for domestic circulation, and thus the temporary augmentation of the metal reserve by immobilising a part of the circulating coined metal simultaneously falls away. Furthermore, if a minimum metal reserve must be maintained under all circumstances for the payment of deposits and for the convertibility of notes, this affects in its own way the results of a drain or return flow of gold; it affects that part of the reserve which the bank is obliged to maintain under all circumstances, or that part which it seeks to get rid of as useless at certain times. If the circulation were purely metallic and the banking system concentrated, the bank would likewise have to consider its metal reserve as security for the payment of its deposits, and a drain of metal could cause a panic such as was witnessed in Hamburg in 1857.

Sixthly, with the exception of perhaps 1837, the real crisis always broke out only after a change in the rates of exchange, that is, as soon as the import of precious metal had again gained preponderance over its export.

In 1825, the real crash came after the drain of gold had ceased. In 1839, there was a drain of gold, but it did not bring about a crash. In 1847, the drain of gold ceased in April and the crash came in October. In 1857, the drain of gold to foreign countries had ceased in early November, and the crash did not come until later that same month.

This is particularly evident in the crisis of 1847, when the drain of gold ceased in April after causing a slight preliminary crisis, and the real business crisis did not come until October.

The following testimony was presented at the Secret Committee of the House of Lords on Commercial Distress, 1848, This evidence[a] was not printed until 1857 (also cited as C. D. 1848/57).

Evidence of Tooke:

In April 1847, a stringency arose, which, strictly speaking, equalled a panic, but was of relatively short duration and not accompanied by any commercial failures of importance. In October the stringency was far more intensive than at any time during

---

[a] In the 1894 German edition this English word is given in parentheses after its German equivalent.

April, an almost unheard-of number of commercial failures taking place (2996).— In April the rates of exchange, particularly with America, compelled us to export a considerable amount of gold in payment for unusually large imports; only by an extreme effort did the Bank stop the drain and drive the rates higher (2997).— In October the rates of exchange favoured England (2998).— The change in the rates of exchange had begun in the third week of April (3000).— They fluctuated in July and August; since the beginning of August they always favoured England (3001).— The drain on gold in August arose from a demand for internal circulation.[a]

J. Morris, Governor of the Bank of England:

Although the rate of exchange favoured England since August 1847, and an import of gold had taken place in consequence, the bullion reserve of the Bank decreased.

"£2,200,000 went out into the country in consequence of the internal demand" (137).— This is explained on the one hand by an increased employment of labourers in railway construction, and on the other by the "circumstance of the bankers wishing to provide themselves with gold in times of distress" (147).

Palmer, ex-Governor and a Director of the Bank of England since 1811:

"684. During the whole period from the middle of April 1847 to the day of withdrawing the restrictive clause in the Act of 1844 the foreign exchanges were in favour of this country."

The drain of bullion, which created an independent money panic in April 1847, was here therefore, as always, but a precursor of the crisis, and a turn had already taken place before it broke out. In 1839, a heavy drain of bullion took place for grain, etc., while business was strongly depressed, but there was no crisis or money panic.

Seventhly, as soon as general crises have spent themselves, gold and silver— leaving aside the inflow of new precious metal from the producing countries— distribute themselves once more in the proportions in which they existed in a state of equilibrium as individual hoards of the various countries. Other conditions being equal, the relative magnitude of a hoard in each country will be determined by the role of that country in the world market. They flow from the country which had more than its normal share to other countries. These movements of outgoing and incoming metal merely restore the original distribution among the various national reserves. This redistribution, however, is brought about by the effects of various circumstances, which will be taken up in our treatment of rates of exchange. As soon as the normal distribution is once more re-

---

[a] Ibid., No. 3003.

stored — beginning with this moment — a stage of growth sets in and then again a drain.//This last statement applies, of course, only to England, as the centre of the world money market.— *F. E.*//

Eighthly, a drain of metal is generally the symptom of a change in the state of foreign trade, and this change in turn is a premonition that conditions are again approaching a crisis.[15]

Ninthly, the balance of payments can favour Asia against Europe and America.[16]

An import of precious metal takes place mainly during two periods. On the one hand, it takes place in the first phase of a low interest rate, which follows upon a crisis and reflects a restriction of production; and then in the second phase, when the interest rate rises, but before it attains its average level. This is the phase during which returns come quickly, commercial credit is abundant, and therefore the demand for loan capital does not grow in proportion to the expansion of production. In both phases, with loan capital relatively abundant, the superfluous addition of capital existing in the form of gold and silver, i. e., a form in which it can primarily serve only as loan capital, must seriously affect the rate of interest and concomitantly the atmosphere of business in general.

On the other hand, a drain, a continued and heavy export of precious metal, takes place as soon as returns no longer flow, markets are overstocked, and an illusory prosperity is maintained only by means of credit; in other words, as soon as a greatly increased demand for loan capital exists and the interest rate, therefore, has reached at least its average level. Under such circumstances, which are reflected pre-

---

[15] According to Newmarch,[a] a drain of gold to foreign countries can arise from three causes: 1) from purely commercial conditions, that is, if imports have exceeded exports, as was the case in 1836 to 1844, and again in 1847 — principally a heavy import of grain; 2) in order to secure the means for investing English capital in foreign countries, as in 1857 for railways in India, and 3) for definite expenditures abroad, as in 1853 and 1854 for war purposes in the Orient.

[16] 1918. Newmarch. "When you combine India and China, when you bring into account the transactions between India and Australia, and the still more important transactions between China and the United States, the trade being a triangular one, and the adjustment taking place through us ... then it is true that the balance of trade was not merely against this country, but against France, and against the United States." — (B. A. 1857.)

---

[a] Ibid., Nos. 1498-1509.

cisely in a drain of precious metal, the effect of continued withdrawal of capital, in a form in which it exists directly as loanable money capital, is considerably intensified. This must have a direct influence on the interest rate. But instead of restricting credit transactions, the rise in interest rate extends them and leads to an overstraining of all their auxiliary resources. This period, therefore, precedes the crash.

Newmarch is asked (B. A. 1857):

"1520. But then the volume of bills in circulation increases with the rate of discount?— It seems to do so."—"1522. In quiet ordinary times the ledger is the real instrument of exchange; but when any difficulty arises; when, for example, under such circumstances as I have suggested, there is a rise in the bank rate of discount ... then the transactions naturally resolve themselves into drawing bills of exchange, those bills of exchange being not only more convenient as regards legal proof of the transaction which has taken place, but also being more convenient in order to effect purchases elsewhere, and being pre-eminently convenient as a means of credit by which capital can be raised."

Furthermore, as soon as somewhat threatening conditions induce the bank to raise its discount rate — whereby the probability exists at the same time that the bank will cut down the running time of the bills to be discounted by it — the general apprehension spreads that this will rise in crescendo. Everyone, and above all the credit swindler, will therefore strive to discount the future and have as many means of credit as possible at his command at the given time. These reasons, then, amount to this: it is not that the mere quantity of imported or exported precious metal as such which makes its influence felt, but that it exerts its effect, firstly, by virtue of the specific character of precious metal as capital in money form, and secondly, by acting like a feather which, when added to the weight on the scales, suffices to tip the oscillating balance definitely to one side; it acts because it arises under conditions when any addition decides in favour of one or the other side. Without these grounds, it would be quite inexplicable why a drain of gold amounting to, say, £5,000,000 to £8,000,000 — and this is the limit of experience to date — should have any appreciable effect. This small decrease or increase of capital, which seems insignificant even compared to the £70 million in gold which circulate on an average in England, is really a negligibly small magnitude when compared to production of such volume as that of the English.[17] But it is precisely the development of the credit and

[17] See, for instance, the ridiculous reply of Weguelin, where he states that a drain of five million in gold is so much capital less, and thus attempts to explain certain phe-

banking system, which tends, on the one hand, to press all money capital into the service of production (or what amounts to the same thing, to transform all money income into capital), and which, on the other hand, reduces the metal reserve to a minimum in a certain phase of the cycle, so that it can no longer perform the functions for which it is intended—it is this developed credit and banking system which creates this over-sensitiveness of the whole organism. At less developed stages of production, the decrease or increase of the hoard below or above its average level is a relatively insignificant matter. Similarly, on the other hand, even a very considerable drain of gold is relatively ineffective if it does not occur in the critical period of the industrial cycle.

In the given explanation we have not considered cases in which a drain of gold takes place as a result of crop failures, etc. In such cases the large and sudden disturbance of the equilibrium of production, which is expressed by this drain, requires no further explanation as to its effect. This effect is that much greater the more such a disturbance occurs in a period when production is in full swing.

We have also omitted from consideration the function of the metal reserve as a security for banknote convertibility and as the pivot of the entire credit system. The central bank is the pivot of the credit system. And the metal reserve, in turn, is the pivot of the bank.[18] The changeover from the credit system to the monetary system is necessary, as I have already shown in Book I, Ch. III in discussing means of payment.[a] That the greatest sacrifices of real wealth are necessary to maintain the metallic basis in a critical moment has been admitted by both Tooke and Loyd-Overstone. The controversy revolves merely round a plus or a minus and round the more or less

nomena which do *not* take place when there is an infinitely greater increase in prices or depreciation, expansion or contraction of real industrial capital. On the other hand, it is just as ridiculous to attempt to explain these phenomena directly as symptoms of an expansion or contraction of the mass of real capital (considered from the viewpoint of its material elements).

[18] Newmarch (B. A. 1857): "1364. The reserve of bullion in the Bank of England is, in truth ... the central reserve or hoard of treasure upon which the whole trade of the country is made to turn; all the other banks in the country look to the Bank of England as the central hoard or reservoir from which they are to draw their reserve of coin; and it is upon that hoard or reservoir that the action of the foreign exchanges always falls."

[a] See present edition, Vol. 35.

rational treatment of the inevitable.[19] A certain quantity of metal, insignificant compared with the total production, is admitted to be the pivotal point of the system. Hence the superb theoretical dualism, aside from the appalling manifestation of this characteristic that it possesses as the pivotal point during crises. So long as enlightened economy treats "of capital" *ex professo*, it looks down upon gold and silver with the greatest disdain, considering them as the most indifferent and useless form of capital. But as soon as it treats of the banking system, everything is reversed, and gold and silver become capital *par excellence*, for whose preservation every other form of capital and labour is to be sacrificed. But how are gold and silver distinguished from other forms of wealth? Not by the magnitude of their value, for this is determined by the quantity of labour incorporated in them; but by the fact that they represent independent incarnations, expressions of the *social* character of wealth. //The wealth of society exists only as the wealth of private individuals, who are its private owners. It preserves its social character only in that these individuals mutually exchange qualitatively different use values for the satisfaction of their wants. Under capitalist production they can do so only by means of money. Thus the wealth of the individual is realised as social wealth only through the medium of money. It is in money, in this thing, that the social nature of this wealth is incarnated.— *F. E.//* This social existence of wealth therefore assumes the aspect of a world beyond, of a thing, matter, commodity, alongside of and external to the real elements of social wealth. So long as production is in a state of flux this is forgotten. Credit, likewise a social form of wealth, crowds out money and usurps its place. It is faith in the social character of production which allows the money form of products to assume the aspect of something that is only evanescent and ideal, something merely imaginative. But as soon as credit is shaken — and this phase of necessity always appears in the modern industrial cycle — all the real wealth is to be actually and suddenly transformed into money, into

---

[19] "Practically, then, both Mr. Tooke and Mr. Loyd would meet an additional demand for gold ... by an early ... contraction of credit by raising the rate of interest, and restricting advances of capital.... But the principles of Mr. Loyd lead to certain" (legal) "restrictions and regulations which ... produce the most serious inconvenience" (*Economist*, 1847, p. 1418).[a]

---

[a] "Conformity of Convertible Notes with a Metallic Currency", *The Economist*, No. 224, December 11, 1847.

gold and silver — a mad demand, which, however, grows necessarily out of the system itself. And all the gold and silver which is supposed to satisfy these enormous demands amounts to but a few millions in the vaults of the Bank.[20] Among the effects of the gold drain, then, the fact that production as social production is not really subject to social control, is strikingly emphasised by the existence of the social form of wealth as a *thing* external to it. The capitalist system of production, in fact, has this feature in common with former systems of production, in so far as they are based on trade in commodities and private exchange. But only in the capitalist system of production does this become apparent in the most striking and grotesque form of absurd contradiction and paradox, because, in the first place, production for direct use value, for consumption by the producers themselves, is most completely eliminated under the capitalist system, so that wealth exists only as a social process expressed as the intertwining of production and circulation; and, secondly, because with the development of the credit system, capitalist production continually strives to overcome the metal barrier, which is simultaneously a material and imaginative barrier of wealth and its movement, but again and again it breaks its back on this barrier.

In the crisis, the demand is made that all bills of exchange, securities and commodities shall be simultaneously convertible into bank money, and all this bank money, in turn, into gold.

II. THE RATE OF EXCHANGE

//The rate of exchange is known to be the barometer for the international movement of money metals. If England has more payments to make to Germany than Germany to England, the price of marks, expressed in sterling, rises in London, and the price of sterling, expressed in marks, falls in Hamburg and Berlin. If this preponderance of England's payment obligations towards Germany is not balanced again, for instance, by a preponderance of purchases by Germany in

---

[20] "You quite agree that there is no mode by which you can modify the demand for bullion except by raising the rate of interest?" — Chapman (associate member of the great bill-brokers' firm of Overend, Gurney & Co.): "I should say so.... When our bullion falls to a certain point, we had better sound the tocsin at once and say we are drooping, and every man sending money abroad must do it at his own peril." B. A. 1857, Evid. No. 5057.

England, the sterling price of bills of exchange in marks on Germany must rise to the point where it will pay to send metal (gold coin or bullion) from England to Germany in payment of obligations, instead of sending bills of exchange. This is the typical course of events.

If this export of precious metal assumes a larger scope and lasts for a longer period, then the English bank reserve is affected, and the English money market, particularly the Bank of England, must take protective measures. These consist mainly, as we have already seen, in raising the interest rate. When the drain of gold is considerable, the money market as a rule becomes tight, that is, the demand for loan capital in the form of money significantly exceeds the supply and the higher interest rate follows quite naturally from this; the discount rate fixed by the Bank of England corresponds to this situation and asserts itself on the market. However there are cases when the drain of bullion is due to other than ordinary combinations of business transactions (for instance, loans to foreign states, investment of capital in foreign countries, etc.), and the London money market as such does not justify an effective rise in the interest rate; the Bank of England must then first "make money scarce", as the phrase goes, through heavy loans in the "open market" and thus artificially create a situation which justifies, or renders necessary, a rise in the interest rate; such a manoeuvre becomes more difficult from year to year.— *F. E.*||

How this raising of the interest rate affects the rates of exchange is shown by the following testimony before the Committee of the Lower House concerning bank legislation in 1857 (quoted as B. A. or B. C. 1857).

John Stuart Mill:

"2176. When there is a state of commercial difficulty there is always ... a considerable fall in the price of securities ... foreigners send over to buy railway shares in this country, or English holders of foreign railway shares sell their foreign railway shares abroad ... there is so much transfer of bullion prevented."—"2182. A large and rich class of bankers and dealers in securities, through whom the equalisation of the rate of interest and the equalisation of commercial PRESSURE[a] between different countries usually takes place ... are always on the look out to buy securities which are likely to rise.... The place for them to buy securities will be the country which is sending bullion away."—"2184. These investments of capital took place to a very considerable extent in 1847, to a sufficient extent to have relieved the drain considerably."

***

[a] In the 1894 German edition this English word is given in parentheses after its German equivalent.

J. G. Hubbard, ex-Governor, and a Director of the Bank of England since 1838:

"2545. There are great quantities of European securities ... which have a European currency in all the different money markets, and those bonds, as soon as their value is ... reduced by 1 or 2 per cent in one market, are immediately purchased for transmission to those markets where their value is still unimpaired."—"2565. Are not foreign countries considerably in debt to the merchants of this country? — Very largely. "— "2566. Therefore, the cashment of those debts might be sufficient to account for a very large accumulation of capital in this country? — In 1847, the ultimate restoration of our position was effected by our striking off so many millions previously due by America, and so many millions due by Russia to this country."

//At the same time, England owed these same countries "so and so many millions" for grain and also did not fail to "draw a line" through the greater portion of these millions via the bankruptcy of the English debtors. See the report on Bank Acts, 1857, Chapter XXX, p. 31 [a] above.

"2572. In 1847, the exchange between this country and St. Petersburg was very high. When the Government Letter came out authorising the Bank to issue irrespectively of the limitation of £14,000,000" (above and beyond the gold reserve), "the stipulation was that the rate of discount should be 8%. At that moment, with the then rate of discount, it was a profitable operation to order gold to be shipped from St. Petersburg to London and on its arrival to lend it at 8% up to the maturity of the three months' bills drawn against the purchase of gold."—"2573. In all bullion operations there are many points to be taken into consideration; there is the rate of exchange and the rate of interest, which is available for the investment during the period of the maturity of the bill" (drawn against it).

RATE OF EXCHANGE WITH ASIA

The following points are important because, on the one hand, they show how England recoups its losses, when its rate of exchange with Asia is unfavourable, at the expense of other countries, whose imports from Asia are paid through English middlemen. On the other hand, they are important because Mr. Wilson once again makes the foolish attempt here to identify the effect of the export of precious metal on the rates of exchange with the effect of the export of capital in general upon these rates; the export being in both cases not as a means of paying or buying, but for capital investment. In the first place, it goes without saying that whether so many millions of pounds sterling are

---

[a] See this volume, pp. 491-92.

sent to India in precious metal or iron rails, to be invested in railways there, these are merely two different forms of transferring the same amount of capital to another country; namely, a transfer which does not enter the calculation of ordinary mercantile business, and for which the exporting country expects no other return than the future annual revenue from the income of these railways. If this export is made in the form of precious metal, it will exert a direct influence upon the money market and with it upon the interest rate of the country exporting this precious metal; if not necessarily under all circumstances, then under the previously outlined conditions, since it is precious metal and as such is directly loanable money capital and the basis of the entire money system. Similarly, this export also directly affects the rate of exchange. Precious metal is exported only for the reason, and to the extent, that bills of exchange, say on India, which are offered in the London money market, do not suffice to make these extra remittances. In other words, there is a demand for Indian bills of exchange which exceeds their supply, and so the rates turn for a time against England, not because it is in debt to India, but because it has to send extraordinary sums to India. In the long run, such a shipment of precious metal to India must have the effect of increasing the Indian demand for English commodities, because it indirectly increases the consuming power of India for European goods. But if the capital is shipped in the form of rails, etc., it cannot have any influence on the rates of exchange, since India has no return payment to make for it. Precisely for this reason, it need not have any influence on the money market. Wilson seeks to establish the existence of such an influence by declaring that such an extra expenditure would bring about an additional demand for money accommodation and would thus influence the interest rate. This may be the case; but to maintain that it must take place under all circumstances is totally wrong. No matter where the rails are shipped and whether laid on English or Indian soil, they represent nothing but a definite expansion of English production in a particular sphere. To contend that an expansion of production, even within very broad limits, cannot take place without driving up the interest rate, is absurd. Money accommodation, i. e., the amount of business transacted which includes credit operations, may grow; but these credit operations can increase while the interest rate remains unchanged. This was actually the case during the railway mania in England in the forties. The interest rate did not rise. And it is evident that, so far as actual capital is concerned, in this case commodities, the effect on the money market will be just the same, whether these commodities are destined for foreign countries or for domestic consumption. It could only make a difference when capital investments by England in foreign countries exerted a restraining influence upon its commercial exports, i. e., exports for which payment must be made, thus giving rise to a return flow, or to the extent that these capital investments are already general symptoms indicating the overexertion of credit and the initiation of swindling operations.

In the following, Wilson puts the questions and Newmarch replies.

"1786. On a former day you stated, with reference to the demand for silver for the East, that you believed that the exchanges with India were in favour of this country, notwithstanding the large amount of bullion that is continually transmitted to the East; have you any ground for supposing the exchanges to be in favour of this country? — Yes, I have.... I find that the real value of the exports from the United Kingdom to India in 1851 was £7,420,000; to that is to be added the amount of India House drafts, that is, the funds drawn from India by the East India Company for the purpose of their own expenditure. Those drafts in that year amounted to £3,200,000, making, therefore, the total export from the United Kingdom to India £10,620,000. In 1855 ... the actual value of the export of goods from the United Kingdom had risen to £10,350,000 and the India House drafts were £3,700,000, making, therefore, the total export from this country £14,050,000. Now as regards 1851, I believe there are no means of stating what was the real value of the import of goods from India to this country, but in 1854 and 1855 we have a statement of the real value; in 1855, the total real value of the imports of goods from India to this country was £12,670,000 and that sum, compared with the £14,050,000 I have mentioned, left a balance in favour of the United Kingdom, as regards the direct trade between the two countries, of £1,380,000." [a]

Thereupon Wilson remarks that the rates of exchange are also affected by indirect commerce. For instance, exports from India to Australia and North America are covered by drafts on London, and therefore affect the rate of exchange just as though the commodities had gone directly from India to England. Furthermore, when India and China are considered together, the balance is against England, since China has constantly to make heavy payments to India for opium, and England has to make payments to China, so that the sums go by this circuitous route to India (1787, 1788).

1791. Wilson now asks if the effect on the rates of exchange will not be the same whether capital

"went in the form of iron rails and locomotives, or whether it went in the form of coin".

---

[a] See Report from the Select Committee on Bank Acts.... 1857.

Newmarch correctly answers:

The £12 million which have been sent during the last few years to India for railway construction served to purchase an annuity which India has to pay at regular intervals to England.

"But as far as regards the immediate operation on the bullion market, the investments of the £12 million would only be operative as far as bullion was required to be sent out for actual money disbursements." [1792]

1797. //Weguelin asks:// "If no return is made for this iron" (rails), "how can it be said to affect the exchanges? — I do not think that that part of the expenditure which is sent out in the form of commodities affects the computation of the exchange.... The computation of the exchange between two countries is affected, one might say, solely by the quantity of obligations or bills offering in one country, as compared with the quantity offering in the other country against it; that is the rationale of the exchange. Now, as regards the transmission of those £12,000,000, the money in the first place is subscribed in this country ... now, if the nature of the transaction was such that the whole of that £12,000,000 was required to be laid down in Calcutta, Bombay, and Madras in treasure ... a sudden demand would very violently operate upon the price of silver, and upon the exchange, just the same as if the India Company were to give notice tomorrow that their drafts were to be raised from £3,000,000 to £12,000,000. But half of those £12,000,000 is spent ... in buying commodities in this country ... iron rails and timber, and other materials ... it is an expenditure in this country of the capital of this country for a particular kind of commodity to be sent out to India, and there is an end of it."—"1798. //Weguelin:// But the production of those articles of iron and timber necessary for the railways produces a large consumption of foreign articles, which might affect the exchange? — Certainly."

Wilson now thinks that iron represents labour to a large extent, and that the wage paid for this labour largely represents imported goods (1799), and then questions further:

"1801. But speaking quite generally, it would have the effect of turning the exchanges against this country if you sent abroad the articles which were produced by the consumption of the imported articles without receiving any remittance for them either in the shape of produce or otherwise? — That principle is exactly what took place in this country during the time of the great railway expenditure" (1845). "For three or four or five years, you spent upon railways £30,000,000, nearly the whole of which went in the payment of wages. You sustained in three years a larger population employed in constructing railways, and locomotives, and carriages, and stations than you employed in the whole of the factory districts. The people ... spent those wages in buying tea and sugar and spirits and other foreign commodities; those commodities were imported; but it was a fact, that during the time this great expenditure was going on the foreign exchanges between this country and other countries were not materially deranged. There was no efflux of bullion, on the contrary, there was rather an influx."

1802. Wilson insists that with an equalised trade balance and par rates between England and India the extra shipment of iron and locomotives "would affect the exchanges with India". Newmarch cannot see it that way so long as the rails are sent out as capital investment and India has no payment to make for them in one form or another; he adds:

> "I agree with the principle that no one country can have permanently against itself an adverse state of exchange with all the other countries, with which it deals; an adverse exchange with one country necessarily produces a favourable exchange with another."

Wilson retorts with this triviality:

> "1803. But would not a transfer of capital be the same whether it was sent in one form or another? — As regards the obligation it would."—"1804. The effect therefore of making railways in India, whether you send bullion or whether you send materials, would be the same upon the capital market here in increasing the value of capital as if the whole was sent out in bullion?"

If iron prices did not rise, it was in any case proof that the "value" of "capital" contained in the rails had not been increased. What we are here concerned with is the value of money capital, i. e., the interest rate. Wilson would like to identify money capital with capital in general. The simple fact is essentially that 12 million were subscribed in England for Indian railways. This is a matter which has nothing directly to do with the rates of exchange, and the designation of the £12 million is also the same to the money market. If the money market is in good shape, it need not produce any effect at all on it, just as the English railway subscriptions in 1844 and 1845 left the money market unaffected. If the money market is already in somewhat difficult straits, the interest rate might indeed be affected by it, but certainly only in an upward direction, and this, according to Wilson's theory, would favourably affect the rates of exchange for England, that is, it would work against the tendency to export precious metal; if not to India, then to some other country. Mr. Wilson jumps from one thing to another. In Question 1802 it is the rates of exchange that are supposed to be affected, and in Question 1804 the "value of capital"— which are two very different things. The interest rate may affect the rates of exchange, and the rates of exchange may affect the interest rate, but the latter can be stable while the rates of exchange fluctuate, and the rates of exchange can be stable while the interest rate fluctuates. Wilson cannot get it through his head that the mere form in which capital is shipped abroad makes such a difference in the effect, i. e., that the difference in the form of capital is of such importance, and particularly its money form, which runs very much counter to the explanations of economists. Newmarch replies to Wilson one-sidedly in that he does not indicate that he has jumped so suddenly and without reason from rate of exchange to interest rate. Newmarch answers Question 1804 with uncertainty and equivocation:

"No doubt, if there is a demand for £12,000,000 to be raised, it is immaterial, as regards the general rate of interest, whether that £12 million is required to be sent in bullion or in materials. I think, however"

//a fine transition, this "however", when he intends to say the exact opposite//

"it is not quite immaterial"

//it is immaterial, but, nevertheless, it is not immaterial//

"because in the one case the £6 million would be returned immediately; in the other case it would not be returned so rapidly. Therefore it would make some"

//what definiteness!//

"difference, whether the £6 million was expended in this country or sent wholly out of it."

What does he mean when he says six million would return immediately? In so far as the £6 million have been expended in England, they exist in rails, locomotives, etc., which are to be shipped to India, whence they do not return; their value returns very slowly through amortisation, whereas the six million in precious metal may perhaps return very quickly in kind. In so far as the six million have been expended in wages, they have been consumed; but the money used for payment circulates in the country the same as ever, or forms a reserve. The same holds true for the profits of rail producers and that portion of the six million which replaces their constant capital. Thus, this ambiguous statement about returns is used by Newmarch only to avoid saying directly: The money has remained in the country, and in so far as it serves as loanable money capital the difference for the money market (aside from the possibility that circulation could have absorbed more coin) is only that it is charged to the account of A instead of B. An investment of this kind, where capital is transferred to other countries in commodities, not in precious metal, can affect the rate of exchange (but not the rate of exchange with the country in which the exported capital is invested) only in so far as the production of these exported commodities requires an additional import of other foreign commodities. This production then cannot balance out the additional import. However, the same thing happens with every export on credit, no matter whether intended for capital investment or ordinary commercial purposes. Moreover, this additional import can also call forth by way of reaction an additional demand for English goods, for instance, on the part of the colonies or the United States.

––––––––

Previously,[a] Newmarch stated that, owing to drafts of the East India Company, exports from England to India were larger than imports. Sir Charles Wood cross-examines him on this score. This preponderance of English exports to India over imports from India is actually brought about by imports from India for which England does not pay any equivalent. The drafts of the East India Company (now the East India government) resolve themselves into a tribute levied on India. For instance, in 1855, imports from India to England amounted to £12,670,000; English exports to India amounted to £10,350,000; balance in India's favour £2,250,000.

"If that was the whole state of the case, that £2,250,000 would have to be remitted in some form to India. But then come in the advertisements from the India House. The India House advertise to this effect that they are prepared to grant drafts on the various presidencies in India to the extent of £3,250,000."

//This amount was levied for the London expenses of the East India Company and for the dividends to be paid to stockholders.//

"And that not merely liquidates the £2,250,000 which arose out of the course of trade, but it presents £1,000,000 of surplus" (1917).

"1922. //Wood:// Then the effect of those India House drafts is not to increase the exports to India, but *pro tanto* to diminish them?"

//This should read: to reduce the necessity of covering the imports from India by exports to that country to the same amount.// Mr. Newmarch explains this by saying that the British import "good government" into India for these £3,700,000 (1925). Wood, as Minister for India, knows full well the kind of "good government" which the British import to India, and correctly replies with irony:

"1926. Then the export, which, you state, is caused by the East India drafts, is an export of good government, and not of produce."

Since England exports a good deal "in this way" for "good government" and as capital investment in foreign countries — thus obtaining imports which are completely independent of the ordinary run of

––––––––

[a] See Report from the Select Committee on Bank Acts... 1857. No. 1786.

business, tribute partly for exported "good government" and partly in the form of revenues from capital invested in the colonies or elsewhere, i. e., tribute for which it does not have to pay any equivalent—it is evident that the rates of exchange are not affected when England simply consumes this tribute without exporting anything in return. Hence, it is also evident that the rates of exchange are not affected when it reinvests this tribute, not in England, but productively or unproductively in foreign countries; for instance, when it sends munitions for it to the Crimea.[a] Moreover, to the extent that imports from abroad enter into the revenue of England—of course, they must be paid for in the form of tribute, for which no equivalent return is necessary, or by exchange for this unpaid tribute or in the ordinary course of commerce—England can either consume them or reinvest them as capital. In neither case are the rates of exchange affected, and this is overlooked by the sage Wilson. Whether a domestic or a foreign product constitutes a part of the revenue—whereby the latter case merely requires an exchange of domestic for foreign products—the consumption of this revenue, be it productive or unproductive, alters nothing in the rates of exchange, even though it may alter the scale of production. The following should be read with the foregoing in mind:

1934. Wood asks Newmarch how the shipment of war supplies to the Crimea would affect the rate of exchange with Turkey. Newmarch replies:

"I do not see that the mere transmission of warlike stores would necessarily affect the exchange, but certainly the transmission of treasure would affect the exchange."

In this case he thus distinguishes capital in the form of money from capital in other forms. But now Wilson asks:

"1935. If you make an export of any article to a great extent, for which there is to be no corresponding import"

//Mr. Wilson forgets that there are very considerable imports into England for which corresponding exports have never taken place, except in the form of "good government" or of previously exported investment capital; in any case imports which do not enter into normal commercial movement. But these imports are again exchanged, for instance, for American products, and the circumstance that Amer-

---

[a] Shipment of munitions during the Crimean War of 1853-56.

ican goods are exported without corresponding imports does not alter the fact that the value of these imports can be consumed without an equivalent flow abroad; they have been received without reciprocal exports and can therefore be consumed without entering into the balance of trade//,

"you do not discharge the foreign debt you have created by your imports"

//but, if you have previously paid for these imports, for instance, by credit given abroad, then no debt is contracted thereby, and the question has nothing to do with the international balance; it resolves itself into productive and unproductive expenditures, no matter whether the products so consumed are domestic or foreign//,

"and therefore you must by that transaction affect the exchanges by not discharging the foreign debt, by reason of your export having no corresponding imports? — That is true as regards countries generally."

This lecture by Wilson amounts to saying that every export with no corresponding import is simultaneously an import with no corresponding export, because foreign, i. e., imported, commodities enter into the production of the exported article. The assumption is that every export of this kind is based on, or creates, an unpaid import and thus presupposes a debt abroad. This is wrong, even when the following two circumstances are disregarded: 1) England receives certain imports free of charge for which it pays no equivalent, e. g., a portion of its Indian imports. It can exchange these for American imports and export the latter without importing in return; in any case, so far as the value is concerned, it has only exported something that has cost it nothing. 2) England may have paid for imports, for instance, American imports, which constitute additional capital; if it consumes these unproductively, for instance, as war materials, this does not constitute any debt towards America and does not affect the rate of exchange with America. Newmarch contradicts himself in Nos. 1934 and 1935, and Wood calls this to his attention in No. 1938:

"If no portion of the goods which are employed in the manufacture of the articles exported without return" (war materials) "came from the country to which those articles are sent, how is the exchange with that country affected; supposing the trade with Turkey to be in an ordinary state of equilibrium, how is the exchange between this country and Turkey affected by the export of warlike stores to the Crimea?"

Here Newmarch loses his equanimity; he forgets that he has answered the same simple question correctly in No. 1934, and says:

"We seem, I think, to have exhausted the practical question, and to have now attained a very elevated region of metaphysical discussion."

––––––––

//Wilson has still another version of his claim that the rate of exchange is affected by every transfer of capital from one country to another, no matter whether in the form of precious metal or commodities. Wilson knows, of course, that the rate of exchange is affected by the interest rate, particularly by the relation of the rates of interest prevailing in the two countries whose mutual rates of exchange are under discussion. If he can now demonstrate that surpluses of capital in general, i. e., in the first place, of commodities of all kinds including precious metal, have a hand in influencing the interest rate, then he is a step closer to his goal; a transfer of any considerable portion of this capital to some other country must then change the interest rate in both countries, with the change taking place in opposite directions. Thereby, in a secondary way, the rate of exchange between both countries is also altered.— *F. E.*//

He then says in the *Economist*, 1847, page 574, which he edited at the time [a]:

"No doubt, however, such abundance of capital as is indicated by large stocks of commodities of all kinds, including bullion, would necessarily lead, not only to low prices of commodities in general, but also to a lower rate of interest for the use of capital (1). If we have a stock of commodities on hand, which is sufficient to serve the country for two years to come, a command over those commodities would be obtained for a given period at a much lower rate than if the stocks were barely sufficient to last us two months (2). All loans of money, in whatever shape they are made, are simply a transfer of a command over commodities from one to another. Whenever, therefore, commodities are abundant, the interest of money must be low, and when they are scarce, the interest of money must be high (3). As commodities become abundant, the number of sellers, in proportion to the number of buyers, increases, and, in proportion as the quantity is more than is required for immediate consumption, so must a larger portion be kept for future use. Under these circumstances, the terms on which a holder becomes willing to sell for a future payment, or on credit, become lower than if he were certain that his whole stock would be required within a few weeks" (4).

In regard to statement (1), it is to be noted that a large *influx* in precious metal can take place simultaneously with a *contraction* in production, as is always the case in the period following a crisis. In the

––––––––

[a] "A Reply to Further Remarks on the Proposed Substitution of One-Pound Notes for Gold", *The Economist*, No. 195, May 22, 1847.

subsequent phase, precious metal may come in from countries which mainly produce precious metal; imports of other commodities are generally balanced by exports during this period. In these two phases, the interest rate is low and rises but slowly; we have already discussed the reason for this. This low interest rate could always be explained without recourse to the influence of any "large stocks of commodities of all kinds". And how is this influence to take place? The low price of cotton, for instance, renders possible the high profits of the spinners, etc. Now why is the interest rate low? Surely not because the profit, which may be made on borrowed capital, is high. But simply and solely because, under existing conditions, the demand for loan capital does not grow in proportion to this profit; in other words, because loan capital has a movement different from industrial capital. What the *Economist* wants to prove is exactly the reverse, namely, that the movements of loan capital are identical with those of industrial capital.

In regard to statement (2), if we reduce the absurd assumption of stocks for two years in advance to the point where it begins to take on some meaning, it signifies that the commodity market is overstocked. This would cause a fall in prices. Less would have to be paid for a bale of cotton. This would by no means justify the conclusion that money for the purchase of a bale of cotton is more easily borrowed. This depends on the state of the money market. If money can be borrowed more easily, it is only because commercial credit is in a state requiring it to make less use than usual of bank credit. The commodities glutting the market are either means of subsistence or means of production. The low price of both increases the industrial capitalist's profit. Why should it depress the interest rate, unless it be through the antithesis, rather than the identity, between the abundance of industrial capital and the demand for money accommodation? Circumstances are such that the merchant and the industrial capitalist can more easily advance credit to one another; owing to this facilitation of commercial credit, both industrialist as well as merchant need less bank credit; hence the interest rate can be low. This low interest rate has nothing to do with the influx in precious metal, although both may run parallel to each other, and the same causes bringing about low prices of imported articles may also produce a surplus of imported precious metal. If the import market were really glutted, it would prove that a decrease in the demand for imported articles had taken place, and this would be inexplicable at low prices, unless it were attributed to a contraction of domestic industrial production; but this, again, would be inexplicable, so long as there is excessive importing at low prices. A mass of absurdities — in order to prove that a fall in prices = a fall in the interest rate. Both may simultaneously exist side by side. But if they do, it will be a reflection of the opposition in the directions of the movement of industrial and the movement of loanable money capital. It will not be a reflection of their identity.

In regard to statement (3), it is hard to understand even after this exposition why money interest should be low when commodities are available in abundance. If commodities are cheap, then I may need only £1,000 instead of the previous £2,000 to buy a definite quantity. But perhaps I nevertheless invest £2,000, and thus buy twice the quantity which I could have bought formerly. In this way, I expand my business by advancing the same capital, which I may have to borrow. I buy £2,000 worth of commodities, the same as before. My demand on the money market therefore remains the same, even though my demand on the commodity market rises with the fall in commodity prices. But if this demand for commodities should decrease, that is, if production should not expand with the fall in commodity prices, an event which would contradict all the laws of the *Economist*, then the demand for loanable money capital would decrease, although the profit would increase. But this increasing profit would create a demand for loan capital. Incidentally, a low level of commodity prices may be due to three causes. First, to lack of demand. In such a case, the interest rate is low because production is paralysed and not because commodities are cheap, for the low prices are but a reflection of that paralysis. Second, it may be due to supply exceeding demand. This may be the result of a glut on the market, etc., which leads to a crisis and may coincide with a high interest rate during the crisis itself; or, it may be the result of a fall in the value of commodities, so that the same demand can be satisfied at lower prices. Why should the interest rate fall in the last case? Because profits increase? If this were due to less money capital being required for obtaining the same productive or commodity capital, it would merely prove that profit and interest are inversely proportional to each other. In any case, the general statement of the *Economist* is false. Low money prices for commodities and a low interest rate do not necessarily go together. Otherwise, the interest rate would be lowest in the poorest countries, where money prices for produce are lowest, and highest in the richest countries, where money prices for agricultural products are highest. In general, the *Economist* admits: If the value of money falls, it exerts no influence on the interest rate. £100 bring £105 the same as ever. If the £100 are worth less, so are the £5 interest. This relation is not affected by the appreciation or depreciation of the original sum. Considered from the point of view of value, a definite quantity of commodities is equal to a definite sum of money. If this value increases, it is equal to a larger sum of money. The opposite is true when it falls. If the value is equal to 2,000, then 5% = 100; if it is equal to 1,000, then 5% = 50. But this does not alter the interest rate in any way. The rational part of this matter is merely that greater money accommodation is required when it takes £2,000 to sell the same quantity of commodities than when only £1,000 are required. But this merely shows that profit and interest are here inversely proportional to each other. For the lower the prices of the components of constant and variable capital, the higher the profit and the lower the interest. But the opposite can also be and is often the case. For instance, cotton may be cheap because no demand exists for yarn and fabrics; and cotton may be relatively expensive because a large profit in the cotton industry creates a great demand for it. On the other hand, the profits of industrialists may be high precisely because the price of cotton is low. Hubbard's table proves that the interest rate and the prices of commodities execute completely independent movements, whereas the movements of the interest rate adhere closely to those of the metal reserve and the rates of exchange.[a]

The *Economist* states:

"Whenever, therefore, commodities are abundant, the interest of money must be low."

Precisely the opposite obtains during crises. Commodities are superabundant, inconvertible into money, and therefore the interest rate is high; in another phase of the cycle the demand for commodities is great and therefore quick returns are made, but at the same time, prices of commodities are rising and because of the quick returns the interest rate is low.

"When they //the commodities// are scarce, the interest of money must be high."

The opposite is again true in the slack period following a crisis. Commodities are scarce, absolutely speaking, not with reference to demand; and the interest rate is low.

---

[a] See this volume, pp. 546-47.

In regard to statement (4), it is pretty evident that an owner of commodities, provided he can sell the latter at all, will get rid of them at a lower price when the market is glutted than he would when there is a prospect of the existing supply becoming rapidly exhausted. But why the interest rate should fall because of that is not so clear.

If the market is glutted with imported commodities, the interest rate may rise as a result of an increased demand on the part of the owners for loan capital, in order to avoid dumping their commodities on the market. The interest rate may fall, because the fluidity of commercial credit may keep the demand for bank credit relatively low.

———————

The *Economist*[a] mentions the rapid effect on the rates of exchange in 1847 of the raising of the interest rate and other circumstances exerting pressure on the money market. But it should be borne in mind that the gold drain continued until the end of April in spite of the change in the rates of exchange; a turn did not take place here until early May.

On January 1, 1847, the metal reserve of the Bank was £15,066,691; the interest rate $3\frac{1}{2}$%; three months' rates of exchange on Paris 25.75; on Hamburg 13.10; on Amsterdam $12.3\frac{1}{4}$. On March 5, the metal reserve had fallen to £11,595,535; the discount had risen to 4%; the rate of exchange fell to $25.67\frac{1}{2}$ on Paris; $13.9\frac{1}{4}$ on Hamburg; and $12.2\frac{1}{2}$ on Amsterdam. The drain of gold continued.

See the following table:

1847	Bullion Reserve of the Bank of England (£)	Money Market	Highest Three-Month Rates		
			Paris	Hamburg	Amsterdam
March 20	11,231,630	Bank disc. 4%	$25.67^1/_2$	$13,9^3/_4$	$12.2^1/_2$
April 3	10,246,410	,, ,, 5%	25.80	13.10	$12.3^1/_2$
April 10	9,867,053	Money very scarce . . .	25.90	$13.10^1/_2$	$12.4^1/_2$
April 17	9,329,941	Bank disc. 5.5%	$26.02^1/_2$	$13.10^3/_4$	$12.5^1/_2$
April 24	9,213,890	Pressure	26.05	13.12	12.6
May 1	9,337,716	Increasing pressure . . .	26.15	$13.12^3/_4$	$12.6^1/_2$
May 8	9,588,759	Highest pressure	$26.27^1/_2$	$13.15^1/_2$	$12.7^3/_4$

———————

[a] The foregoing table is given in the article "The Present Crisis and the Bank Bill", *The Economist*, No. 208, August 21, 1847.

In 1847, the total export of precious metal from England amounted to £8,602,597.

Of this to the United States . .	£3,226,411
France	£2,479,892
Hanse towns . . .	£ 958,781
Holland	£ 247,743

In spite of the change in the rates at the end of March, the drain of
gold continued for another full month, probably to the United States.

"We thus see" //says the *Economist*, 1847, p. 954// "how rapid and striking was the
effect of a rise in the rate of interest, and the pressure which ensued in correcting an
adverse exchange, and in turning the tide of bullion back to this country. This effect
was produced entirely independent of the balance of trade. A higher rate of interest
caused a lower price of securities, both foreign and English, and induced large purchases to be made on foreign account, which increased the amount of bills to be drawn
from this country, while, on the other hand, the high rate of interest and the difficulty
of obtaining money was such that the demand of those bills fell off, while their amount
increased.... For the same cause orders for imports were countermanded, and investments of English funds abroad were realised and brought home for employment here.
Thus, for example, we read in the *Rio de Janeiro Price Current* of the 10th May, 'Exchange
//on England// has experienced a further decline, principally caused by a pressure
on the market for remittance of the proceeds of large sales of //Brazilian// government
stock, on English account.'[a] Capital belonging to this country, which has been invested
in public and other securities abroad, when the interest was very low here, was thus
again brought back when the interest became high."

ENGLAND'S BALANCE OF TRADE

India alone has to pay 5 million in tribute for "good government",
interest and dividends on British capital, etc., not counting the sums
sent home annually by officials as savings from their salaries, or by
English merchants as part of their profit to be invested in England.
Every British colony continually has to make large remittances for
the same reason. Most of the banks in Australia, the West Indies, and
Canada, have been founded with English capital, and the dividends
are payable in England. In the same way, England owns many foreign securities — European, North American and South American —
on which it draws interest. In addition to this it has interests in
foreign railways, canals, mines, etc., with corresponding dividends.
Remittance on all these items is made almost exclusively in products

---

[a] Ibid.

over and above the amount of English exports. On the other hand, what is sent from England to owners of English securities abroad and for consumption by Englishmen abroad, is insignificant in comparison.

The question, so far as it concerns the balance of trade and the rates of exchange, is "at any particular moment one of time".

"Practically speaking ... England gives long credits upon her exports, while the imports are paid for in ready money. At particular moments this difference of practice has a considerable effect upon the exchanges. At a time when our exports are very considerably increasing, e. g., 1850, a continual increase of investment of British capital must be going on ... in this way remittances of 1850 may be made against goods exported in 1849. But if the exports of 1850 exceed those of 1849 by more than 6 million, the practical effect must be that more money is sent abroad, to this amount, than returned in the same year. And in this way an effect is produced on the rates of exchange and the rate of interest. When, on the contrary, our trade is depressed after a commercial crisis, and when our exports are much reduced, the remittances due for the past years of larger exports greatly exceed the value of our imports; the exchanges become correspondingly in our favour, capital rapidly accumulates at home, and the rate of interest becomes less." (*Economist*, January 11, 1851.[a])

The foreign rates of exchange can change:

1) In consequence of the immediate balance of payments, no matter what the cause — a purely mercantile one, or capital investment abroad, or government expenditures for wars, etc., in so far as cash payments thereby are made to foreign countries.

2) In consequence of money depreciation — whether metal or paper — in a particular country. This is purely nominal. If £1 should represent only half as much money as formerly, it would naturally be counted as 12.5 francs instead of 25 francs.

3) When it is a matter of a rate of exchange between countries, of which one uses silver and the other gold as "money", the rate of exchange depends upon the relative fluctuations of the value of these two metals, since these necessarily alter the parity between them. This is illustrated by the rates of exchange in 1850; they were unfavourable to England, although that country's export rose enormously. Yet no drain of gold took place. This was a result of a momentary rise in the value of silver as against gold. (See *Economist*, November 30, 1850.[b])

Parity for the rate of exchange of £1 is: Paris, 25 francs 20 cent.;

***

[a] See "The Balance of Trade. England with the World". - [b] See "The Remarkable Phenomena of the Foreign Exchanges."

Hamburg, 13 marks banko 10.5 shillings; Amsterdam, 11 florins 97 cent. To the extent that the Paris rate of exchange exceeds 25.20 francs, it becomes more favourable to the English debtor of France, or the buyer of French commodities. In both cases he needs fewer pounds sterling in order to accomplish his purpose.— In remoter countries, where precious metal is not easily obtained when bills of exchange are scarce and insufficient for remittances to be made to England, the natural effect is to drive up the prices of such products as are generally shipped to England since a greater demand arises for them, in order to send them to England in place of bills of exchange; this is often the case in India.

An unfavourable rate of exchange, or even a drain of gold, can take place when there is a great abundance of money in England, the interest rate is low and the price for securities is high.

In the course of 1848 England received large quantities of silver from India, since good bills of exchange were rare and mediocre ones were not readily accepted in consequence of the crisis of 1847 and the general lack of credit in business with India. All this silver had barely arrived before it found its way to the continent, where the revolution led to the formation of many hoards. The bulk of the same silver made the trip back to India in 1850, since the rate of exchange now made this profitable.

———

The monetary system is essentially a Catholic institution, the credit system essentially Protestant. "THE SCOTCH HATE GOLD." In the form of paper the monetary existence of commodities is only a social one. It is *Faith* that brings salvation.[a] Faith in money value as the immanent spirit of commodities, faith in the mode of production and its pre-destined order, faith in the individual agents of production as mere personifications of self-expanding capital. But the credit system does not emancipate itself from the basis of the monetary system any more than Protestantism has emancipated itself from the foundations of Catholicism.

———

[a] Mark 16:16.

Chapter XXXVI

PRECAPITALIST RELATIONSHIPS

Interest-bearing capital, or, as we may call it in its antiquated form, usurer's capital, belongs together with its twin brother, merchant's capital, to the antediluvian forms of capital, which long precede the capitalist mode of production and are to be found in the most diverse economic formations of society.

The existence of usurer's capital requires that at least a portion of products should be transformed into commodities, and that money should have developed in its various functions along with trade in commodities.

The development of usurer's capital is bound up with the development of merchant's capital and especially that of money-dealing capital. In ancient Rome, beginning with the last years of the Republic, when manufacturing stood far below its average level of development in the ancient world, merchant's capital, money-dealing capital, and usurer's capital developed to their highest point within the ancient form.

We have seen that hoarding necessarily appears along with money. But the professional hoarder does not become important until he is transformed into a usurer.

The merchant borrows money in order to make a profit with it, in order to use it as capital, that is, to expend it. Hence in earlier forms of society the money lender stands in the same relation to him as to the modern capitalist. This specific relation was also experienced by the Catholic universities.

"The universities of Alcalá, Salamanca, Ingolstadt, Freiburg in Breisgau, Mayence, Cologne, Trèves, one after another recognised the legality of interest for commercial loans. The first five of these approbations were deposited in the archives of the Consulate of the city of Lyons and published in the appendix to the *Traité de l'usure et des intérêts*, by Bruyset-Ponthus, Lyons." (M. Augier, *Le Crédit public, etc.*, Paris, 1842, p. 206.)

In all the forms in which slave economy (not the patriarchal kind, but that of later Grecian and Roman times) serves as a means of amassing wealth, where money therefore is a means of appropriating the labour of others through the purchase of slaves, land, etc., money can be expanded as capital, i. e., bear interest, for the very reason that it can be so invested.

The characteristic forms, however, in which usurer's capital exists in periods antedating capitalist production are of two kinds. I purposely say characteristic forms. The same forms repeat themselves on the basis of capitalist production, but as mere subordinate forms. They are then no longer the forms which determine the character of interest-bearing capital. These two forms are: *first*, usury by lending money to extravagant members of the upper classes, particularly landowners; *secondly*, usury by lending money to small producers who possess their own conditions of labour — this includes the artisan, but mainly the peasant, since particularly under precapitalist conditions, in so far as they permit of small independent individual producers, the peasant class necessarily constitutes the overwhelming majority of them.

Both the ruin of rich landowners through usury and the impoverishment of the small producers lead to the formation and concentration of large amounts of money capital. But to what extent this process does away with the old mode of production, as happened in modern Europe, and whether it puts the capitalist mode of production in its stead, depends entirely upon the stage of historical development and the attendant circumstances.

Usurer's capital as the characteristic form of interest-bearing capital corresponds to the predominance of small-scale production of the self-employed peasant and small master craftsman. When the labourer is confronted by the conditions of labour and by the product of labour in the shape of capital, as under the developed capitalist mode of production, he has no occasion to borrow any money as a producer. When he does any money borrowing, he does so, for instance, at the pawnshop to secure personal necessities. But wherever the labourer is the owner, whether actual or nominal, of his conditions of labour and his product, he stands as a producer in relation to the money lender's capital, which confronts him as usurer's capital. Newman expresses the matter insipidly when he says the banker is respected, while the usurer is hated and despised, because the banker lends to the rich, whereas the usurer lends to the poor. (F. W. Newman, *Lectures on Pol. Econ.*, London, 1851, p. 44). He overlooks the fact that a difference between two modes of social production and their corresponding social orders lies at the heart of the matter and that the situation cannot be explained by the distinction between rich and poor. Moreover, the usury which sucks dry the small producer goes hand in hand with the usury which sucks dry the rich owner of a large estate. As soon as the usury of the Roman patricians had completely ruined the Roman plebeians, the small peasants, this form of exploitation came to an end and a pure slave economy replaced the small-peasant economy.

In the form of interest, the entire surplus above the barest means of subsistence (the amount that later becomes wages of the producers) can be consumed by usury (this later assumes the form of profit and ground rent), and hence it is highly absurd to compare the level of *this* interest, which assimilates *all* the surplus value excepting the share claimed by the state, with the level of the modern interest rate, where interest constitutes at least normally only a part of the surplus value. Such a comparison overlooks that the wage worker produces and gives to the capitalist who employs him, profit, interest and ground rent, i. e., the entire surplus value. Carey makes this absurd comparison in order to show how advantageous the development of capital, and the fall in the interest rate that accompanies it, are for the labourer.[57] Furthermore, while the usurer, not content with squeezing the surplus labour out of his victim, gradually acquires possession even of his very conditions of labour, land, house, etc., and is continually engaged in thus expropriating him, it is again forgotten that, on the other hand, this complete expropriation of the labourer from his conditions of labour is not a result which the capitalist mode of production seeks to achieve, but rather the established prerequisite for its point of departure. The wage slave, just like the real slave, cannot become a creditor's slave due to his position — at least in his capacity as producer; the wage slave, it is true, can become a creditor's slave in his capacity as consumer. Usurer's capital in the form whereby it indeed appropriates all of the surplus labour of the direct producers, without altering the mode of production; whereby the ownership or possession by the producers of the conditions of labour — and small-scale production corresponding to this — is its essential prerequisite; whereby, in other words, capital does not directly subordinate labour to itself, and does not, therefore, confront it as industrial capital — this usurer's capital impoverishes the mode of production, paralyses the productive forces instead of developing them, and at the same time perpetuates the miserable conditions in which the social productivity of labour is not developed at the expense of labour itself, as in the capitalist mode of production.

Usury thus exerts, on the one hand, an undermining and destructive influence on ancient and feudal wealth and ancient and feudal property.[a] On the other hand, it undermines and ruins small-peasant and small-burgher production, in short, all forms in which the producer still appears as the owner of his means of production. Under the developed capitalist mode of production, the labourer is not the owner of the conditions of production, i. e., the field which he cultivates, the raw materials which he processes, etc. But under this system estrangement of the producer from the conditions of production reflects an actual revolution in the mode of production itself. The isolated labourers are brought together in large workshops for the purpose of carrying out separate but interconnected activities; the tool becomes a machine. The mode of production itself no longer permits the dispersion of the instruments of production associated with small property; nor does it permit the isolation of the labourer himself. Under the capitalist mode of production usury can no longer separate the producer from his conditions of production, for they have already been separated.

Usury centralises money wealth where the means of production are dispersed. It does not alter the mode of production, but attaches itself firmly to it like a parasite and makes it wretched. It sucks out its blood, enervates it and compels reproduction to proceed under ever more pitiable conditions. Hence the popular hatred against usurers, which was most pronounced in the ancient world where ownership of the conditions of production by the producer himself was at the same time the basis for political status, the independence of the citizen.

To the extent that slavery prevails, or in so far as the surplus product is consumed by the feudal lord and his retinue, while either the slave-owner or the feudal lord fall into the clutches of the usurer, the mode of production still remains the same; it only becomes harder on the labourer. The indebted slave-holder or feudal lord becomes more oppressive because he is himself more oppressed. Or he finally makes way for the usurer, who becomes a landed proprietor or a slave-holder himself, like the knights in ancient Rome. The place of the old exploiter, whose exploitation was more or less patriarchal because it was largely a means of political power, is taken by a hard, money-mad parvenu. But the mode of production itself is not altered thereby.

Usury has a revolutionary effect in all precapitalist modes of pro-

---

[a] The passage beginning with this paragraph and up to the quotation from Hüllmann, is to be compared with *The Economic Manuscript of 1861-63*. See present edition, Vol. 32, pp. 534-41.

duction only in so far as it destroys and dissolves those forms of property on whose solid foundation and continual reproduction in the same form the political organisation is based. Under Asian forms, usury can continue a long time, without producing anything more than economic decay and political corruption. Only where and when the other prerequisites of the capitalist mode of production are present does usury become one of the means assisting in establishment of the new mode of production by ruining the feudal lord and small-scale producer, on the one hand, and centralising the conditions of labour into capital, on the other.

In the Middle Ages, no country had a general rate of interest. The Church forbade, from the outset, all lending at interest. Laws and courts offered little protection for loans. The interest rate was so much the higher in individual cases. The limited circulation of money, the need to make most payments in cash, compelled people to borrow money, and all the more so when the exchange business was still undeveloped. Therefore wide divergences in interest rates and in the concept of usury. In Charlemagne's time, it was considered usurious to charge 100%. In Lindau on Lake Constance, local burghers took $216\frac{2}{3}$ % in 1344. In Zurich, the City Council fixed the legal interest rate at $43\frac{1}{3}$ %. In Italy, 40% had to be paid sometimes, although the usual rate from the 12th to the 14th century did not exceed 20%. Verona decreed that $12\frac{1}{2}$ % should be the legal rate. Frederick II fixed the rate at 10%, but only for Jews. He did not wish to speak for Christians. In Rhenish Germany, 10% was the usual rate as early as the 13th century (Hüllmann, *Geschichte des Städtewesens*, II, S. 55-57).

Usurer's capital employs the method of exploitation characteristic of capital yet without the latter's mode of production. This condition also repeats itself within bourgeois economy, in backward branches of industry or in those branches which resist the transition to the modern mode of production.[a] For instance, if we wish to compare the English interest rate with the Indian, we should not take the interest rate of the Bank of England, but rather, e. g., that charged by lenders of small machinery to small producers in domestic industry.

Usury, in contradistinction to consuming wealth, is historically important, inasmuch as it is in itself a process generating capital. Usurer's capital and merchant's wealth promote the formation of moneyed wealth independent of landed property. The less products assume the character of commodities, and the less intensively and extensively exchange value has taken hold of production, the more does money appear as actual wealth as such, as wealth in general — in contrast to its limited representation in use values. This is the basis of hoarding. Aside from money as world money and as hoard, it is, in particular, the form of means of payment whereby it appears as

[a] Ibid., p. 535.

the absolute form of commodities. And it is especially its function as a means of payment which develops interest and thereby money capital. What squandering and corrupting wealth desires is money as such, money as a means of buying everything (also as a means of paying debts). The small producer needs money above all for making payments. (The transformation of services and taxes in kind to landlords and the state into money rent and money taxes plays a great role here.) In either case, money is needed as such. On the other hand, it is in usury that hoarding first becomes reality and that the hoarder fulfils his dream. What is sought from the owner of a hoard is not capital, but money as such; but by means of interest he transforms this hoard of money into capital, that is, into a means of appropriating surplus labour in part or in its entirety, and similarly of securing a hold on a part of the conditions of production themselves, even though they may nominally remain the property of others. Usury lives in the pores of production, as it were, just as the gods of Epicurus lived in the space between worlds. Money is so much harder to obtain, the less the commodity form constitutes the general form of products. Hence the usurer knows no other barrier but the capacity of those who need money to pay or to resist. In small-peasant and small-burgher production money serves as a means of purchase, mainly, whenever the conditions of production of the labourer (who is still predominantly their owner under these modes of production) are lost to him either by accident or through extraordinary upheavals, or at least are not replaced in the normal course of reproduction. Means of subsistence and raw materials constitute an essential part of these conditions of production. If these become more expensive, it may make it impossible to replace them out of the returns for the product, just as ordinary crop failures may prevent the peasant from replacing his seed in kind. The same wars through which the Roman patricians ruined the plebeians by compelling them to serve as soldiers and which prevented them from reproducing their conditions of labour, and therefore made paupers of them (and pauperisation, the crippling or loss of the conditions of reproduction is here the predominant form) — these same wars filled the store-rooms and coffers of the patricians with looted copper, the money of that time. Instead of directly giving plebeians the necessary commodities, i. e., grain, horses, and cattle, they loaned them this copper for which they had no use themselves, and took advantage of this situation to exact enormous usurious interest, thereby turning the plebeians into their debtor slaves. During the reign of Charlemagne, the Frankish peasants were likewise ruined by wars, so that they faced no choice but to become serfs instead of debtors. In the Roman Empire, as is known, extreme hunger frequently resulted in the sale of children and also in free men selling themselves as slaves to the rich. So much for general turning-points. In individual cases the maintenance or loss of the conditions of production on the part of small producers depends on a thousand contingencies, and every one of these contingencies or losses signifies impoverishment and becomes a crevice into which a parasitic usurer may creep. The mere death of his cow may render the small peasant incapable of renewing his reproduction on its former scale. He then falls into the clutches of the usurer, and once in the usurer's power he can never extricate himself.

The really important and characteristic domain of the usurer, however, is the function of money as a means of payment. Every payment of money, ground rent, tribute, tax, etc., which becomes due on a certain date, carries with it the need to secure money for such a purpose. Hence from the days of ancient Rome to those of modern times, wholesale usury relies upon tax collectors, *fermiers généraux, receveurs généraux*. Then, there develops with commerce and the generalisation of commodity production the separation, in time, of purchase and payment. The money has to be paid on a definite date. How this can lead to circumstances in which the money capitalist and usurer, even nowadays, merge into one is shown by modern money crises. This same usury, however, becomes one of the principal means of further developing the necessity for money as a means of payment — by driving the producer ever more deeply into debt and destroying his usual means of payment, since the burden of interest alone makes his normal reproduction impossible. At this point, usury sprouts up out of money as a means of payment and extends this function of money as its very own domain.

The credit system develops as a reaction against usury. But this should not be misunderstood, nor by any means interpreted in the manner of the ancient writers, the church fathers, Luther or the early socialists. It signifies no more and no less than the subordination of interest-bearing capital to the conditions and requirements of the capitalist mode of production.

On the whole, interest-bearing capital under the modern credit system is adapted to the conditions of capitalist production. Usury as such does not only continue to exist, but is even freed, among nations with a developed capitalist production, from the fetters imposed upon it by all previous legislation. Interest-bearing capital retains the form of usurer's capital in relation to persons or classes, or in circumstances where borrowing does not, nor can, take place in the sense corresponding to the capitalist mode of production; where borrowing takes place as a result of individual need, as at the pawnshop; where money is borrowed by wealthy spendthrifts for the purpose of squandering; or where the producer is a non-capitalist producer, such as a small farmer or craftsman, who is thus still, as the immediate producer, the owner of his own conditions of production; finally where the capitalist producer himself operates on such a small scale that he resembles those self-employed producers.

What distinguishes interest-bearing capital — in so far as it is an essential element of the capitalist mode of production — from usurer's capital is by no means the nature or character of this capital itself. It is merely the altered conditions under which it operates, and consequently also the totally transformed character of the borrower who confronts the money lender. Even when a man without fortune receives credit in his capacity of industrialist or merchant, it occurs with the expectation that he will function as capitalist and appropriate unpaid labour with the borrowed capital. He receives credit in his capacity of potential capitalist. The circumstance that a man without fortune but possessing energy, solidity, ability and business acumen may become a capitalist in this manner — and the commercial value of each individual is pretty accurately estimated under the capitalist mode of production — is greatly admired by apologists of the capitalist system. Although this circumstance continually brings an unwelcome number of new soldiers of fortune into the field and into competition with the already existing individual capitalists, it also reinforces the supremacy of capital itself, expands its base and enables it to recruit ever new forces for itself out of the substratum of society. In a similar way, the circumstance that the Catholic Church in the Middle Ages formed its hierarchy out of the best brains in the land, regardless of their estate, birth or fortune, was one of the principal means of consolidating ecclesiastical rule and suppressing the laity. The more a ruling class is able to assimilate the foremost minds of a ruled class, the more stable and dangerous becomes its rule.

The initiators of the modern credit system take as their point of departure not an anathema against interest-bearing capital in general, but, on the contrary, its explicit recognition.

We are not referring here to such reactions against usury which attempted to protect the poor against it, like the *Monts-de-piété* (1350 in Sarlins in Franche-Comté, later in Perugia and Savona in Italy, 1400 and 1479).[58] These are noteworthy mainly because they reveal the irony of history, which turns pious wishes into their very opposite during the process of realisation. According to a moderate estimate, the English working class pays 100% to the pawnshops, the modern successors of *Monts-de-piété*.[21] We are also not referring to the credit fantasies of such men as Dr. Hugh Chamberleyne or John Briscoe, who attempted during the last decade of the 17th century to emancipate the English aristocracy from usury by means of a farmers' bank using paper money based on real estate.[22]

The credit associations established in the 12th and 14th centuries in Venice and Genoa arose from the need for marine commerce and the wholesale trade based on it to emancipate themselves from the domination of outmoded usury and the monopolisation of the money business. While the actual banks founded in those city-republics assumed simultaneously the shape of public credit institutions from which the state received loans on future tax revenues, it should not be forgotten that the merchants founding those associations were themselves prominent citizens of those states and as much interested in emancipating their government as they were in emancipating

---

[21] "It is by frequent fluctuations within the month, and by pawning one article to relieve another, where a small sum is obtained, that the premium for money becomes so excessive. There are about 240 licensed pawnbrokers in the metropolis, and nearly 1,450 in the country. The capital employed is supposed somewhat to exceed a million pounds sterling; and this capital is turned round thrice in the course of a year, and yields each time about $33\frac{1}{2}$ per cent on an average; according to which calculation, the inferior orders of society in England pay about one million a year for the use of a temporary loan, exclusive of what they lose by goods being forfeited" (J. D. Tuckett, *A History of the Past and Present State of the Labouring Population*, London, 1846, I, p. 114).

[22] Even in the titles of their works [a] they state as their principal purpose "the general good of the landed men, the great increase of the value of land, the exemption of the nobility, gentry, etc., from taxes, enlarging their yearly estates, etc." Only the usurers would stand to lose, those worst enemies of the nation who had done more injury to the nobility and yeomanry than an army of invasion from France could have done.

---

[a] See H. Chamberlayne, *A Proposal by Dr. Hugh Chamberlayne in Essex Street, for a Bank of Secure Current Credit to be Founded upon Land...*, [London], 1695; and J. Briscoe, *A Discourse on the Late Funds of the Million, Lottery-Act, and Bank of England*, London, 1696.

themselves from the exactions of usurers,[23] and at the same time in getting tighter and more secure control over the state. Hence, when the Bank of England was to be established, the Tories also protested:

> "Banks are republican institutions. Flourishing banks existed in Venice, Genoa, Amsterdam, and Hamburg. But who ever heard of a Bank of France or Spain?"

The Bank of Amsterdam, in 1609, was not epoch-making in the development of the modern credit system any more than that of Hamburg in 1619. It was purely a bank for deposits. The cheques issued by the bank were indeed merely receipts for the deposited coined and uncoined precious metal, and circulated only with the endorsement of the acceptors. But in Holland commercial credit and dealing in money developed hand in hand with commerce and manufacture, and interest-bearing capital was subordinated to industrial and commercial capital by the course of development itself. This could already be seen in the low interest rate. Holland, however, was considered in the 17th century the model of economic development, as England is now. The monopoly of old-style usury, based on poverty, collapsed in that country of its own weight.

During the entire 18th century there is the cry, with Holland referred to as an example, for a compulsory reduction of the rate of interest (and legislation acts accordingly), in order to subordinate interest-bearing capital to commercial and industrial capital, instead of the reverse. The main spokesman for this movement is Sir Josiah Child, the father of ordinary English private banking. He declaims against the monopoly of usurers in much the same way as the wholesale clothing manufacturers, Moses & Son, do when leading the fight against the monopoly of "private tailors". This same Josiah Child is simultaneously the father of English stock-jobbing. Thus, this

---

[23] "The rich goldsmith" (the precursor of the banker), "for example, made Charles II of England pay twenty and thirty per cent for accommodation. A business so profitable, induced the goldsmith 'more and more to become lender to the King, to anticipate all the revenue, to take every grant of Parliament into pawn as soon as it was given; also to outvie each other in buying and taking to pawn BILLS, ORDERS, and TALLIES, so that, in effect, all the revenue passed through their hands'" (John Francis, *History of the Bank of England*, London, 1848, I, p. 31). "The erection of a bank had been suggested several times before that. It was at last a necessity" (l. c., p. 38). "The bank was a necessity for the government itself, sucked dry by usurers, in order to obtain money at a reasonable rate, on the security of parliamentary grants" (l. c., pp. 59, 60).

autocrat of the East India Company defends its monopoly in the name of free trade. Versus Thomas Manley (INTEREST OF MONEY MISTAKEN)⁵⁹ he says:

"As the champion of the timid and trembling band of usurers he erects his main batteries at that point which I have declared to be the weakest ... he denies point-blank that the low rate of interest is the cause of wealth and vows that it is merely its effect." (*Traités sur le Commerce*, etc., 1669, trad. Amsterdam et Berlin, 1754.) ª "If it is commerce that enriches a country, and if a lowering of interest increases commerce, then a lowering of interest or a restriction of usury is doubtless a fruitful primary cause of the wealth of a nation. It is not at all absurd to say that the same thing may be simultaneously a cause under certain circumstances, and an effect under others" (1. c., p. 155). "The egg is the cause of the hen, and the hen is the cause of the egg. The lowering of interest may cause an increase of wealth, and the increase of wealth may cause a still greater reduction of interest" (1. c., p. 156). "I am the defender of industry and my opponent defends laziness and sloth" (p. 179).

This violent battle against usury, this demand for the subordination of interest-bearing capital to industrial capital, is but the herald of the organic creations that establish these prerequisites of capitalist production in the modern banking system, which on the one hand robs usurer's capital of its monopoly by concentrating all idle money reserves and throwing them on the money market, and on the other hand limits the monopoly of the precious metal itself by creating credit money.

The same opposition to usury, the demand for the emancipation of commerce, industry and the state from usury, which are observed here in the case of Child, will be found in all writings on banking in England during the last third of the 17th and the early 18th centuries. We also find colossal illusions about the miraculous effects of credit, abolition of the monopoly of precious metal, its displacement by paper, etc. The Scotsman William Paterson, founder of the Bank of England and the Bank of Scotland, is by all odds Law the First.⁶⁰

Against the Bank of England "all goldsmiths and pawnbrokers set up a howl of rage". (Macaulay, *History of England*, IV, p. 499.)

"During the first ten years the Bank had to struggle with great difficulties; great foreign feuds; its notes were only accepted far below their nominal value ... the goldsmiths" (in whose hands the trade in precious metals served as a basis of a primitive

---

ª 1. c., p. 120.

banking business) "were jealous of the Bank, because their business was diminished, their discounts were lowered, their transactions with the government had passed to their opponents" (J. Francis, 1. c., p. 73).[a]

Even before the establishment of the Bank of England a plan was proposed in 1683 for a National BANK OF CREDIT, which had for its purpose, among others,

"that tradesmen, when they have a considerable quantity of goods, may, by the help of this bank, deposit their goods, by raising a credit on their own dead stock, employ their servants, and increase their trade, till they get a good market instead of selling them at a loss".[b]

After many endeavours this BANK OF CREDIT was established in Devonshire House on Bishopsgate Street. It made loans to industrialists and merchants on the security of deposited goods to the amount of three-quarters of their value, in the form of bills of exchange. In order to make these bills of exchange capable of circulating, a number of people in each branch of business were organised into a society, from which every possessor of such bills would be able to obtain goods with the same facility as if he were to offer them cash payment. This bank's business did not flourish. Its machinery was too complicated, and the risk too great in case of a commodity depreciation.

If we go by the actual content of those records which accompany and theoretically promote the formation of the modern credit system in England, we shall not find anything in them but — as one of its conditions — the demand for a subordination of interest-bearing capital and of loanable means of production in general to the capitalist mode of production. On the other hand, if we simply cling to the phraseology, we shall be frequently surprised by the agreement — including the mode of expression — with the illusions of the followers of Saint-Simon about banking and credit.

Just as in the writings of the physiocrats the *cultivateur* does not stand for the actual tiller of the soil, but for the big farmer, so the *travailleur* with Saint-Simon, and continuing on through his disciples, does not stand for the labourer, but for the industrial and commercial capitalist.

"*Un travailleur a besoin d'aides, de seconds, d'ouvriers; il les cherche intelligents,*

---

[a] The quotation is paraphrased. - [b] J. Francis, *History of the Bank of England...* Vol. I, p. 40.

habiles, dévoués; il les met à l'oeuvre, et leurs travaux sont productifs."[a] (*Religion saint-simonienne. Économie politique et Politique*, Paris, 1831, p. 104.)

In fact, one should bear in mind that only in his last work, *Le Nouveau christianisme*, Saint-Simon speaks directly for the working class and declares their emancipation to be the goal of his efforts. All his former writings are, indeed, mere encomiums of modern bourgeois society in contrast to the feudal order, or of industrialists and bankers in contrast to marshals and juristic law manufacturers of the Napoleonic era. What a difference compared with the contemporaneous writings of Owen![24] For the followers of Saint-Simon, the industrial capitalist likewise remains the *travailleur par excellence*, as the above-quoted passage indicates. After reading their writings critically, one will not be surprised that their credit and bank fantasies materialised in the *Crédit mobilier*, founded by an ex-follower of Saint-Simon, Emile Péreire.[61] This form, incidentally, could become dominant only in a country like France, where neither the credit system nor large-scale industry had reached the modern level of development. This was not at all possible in England and America.— The embryo of *Crédit mobilier* is already contained in the following passages from *Doctrine de St. Simon. Exposition. Première année, 1828-29,* 3me éd., Paris, 1831. It is understandable that bankers can lend money more cheaply than the capitalists and private usurers. These bankers are, therefore,

"able to supply tools to the industrialists far more cheaply, that is, at *lower interest*, than the real estate owners and capitalists, who may be more easily mistaken in their choice of borrowers" (p. 202).

[24] Marx would surely have modified this passage considerably, had he reworked his manuscript. It was inspired by the role of the ex-followers of Saint-Simon under France's Second Empire, where, just at the time that Marx wrote the above, the world-redeeming credit fantasies of this school, through the irony of history, were being realised in the form of a swindle on a scale never seen before. Later Marx spoke only with admiration of the genius and encyclopaedic mind of Saint-Simon. When in his earlier works the latter ignores the antithesis between the bourgeoisie and the proletariat which was just then coming into existence in France, when he includes among the *travailleurs* that part of the bourgeoisie which was active in production, this corresponds to Fourier's conception of attempting to reconcile capital and labour and is explained by the economic and political situation of France in those days. The fact that Owen was more far-sighted in this respect is due to his different environment, for he lived in a period of industrial revolution and of acutely sharpening class antagonisms.— *F. E.*

---

[a] "A *travailleur* needs helpers, supporters, *labourers*; he looks for such as are intelligent, able, devoted; he puts them to work, and their labour is productive."

But the authors themselves add in a footnote:

"The advantage that would accrue from the mediation of bankers between the idle rich and the *travailleurs* is often counterbalanced, or even cancelled, by the opportunities offered in our disorganised society to egoism, which may manifest itself in various forms of fraud and charlatanism. The bankers often worm their way between the *travailleurs* and idle rich for the purpose of exploiting both to the detriment of society."

Travailleur here means *capitaliste industriel*. Incidentally, it is wrong to regard the means at the command of the modern banking system merely as the means of idle people. In the first place, it is the portion of capital which industrialists and merchants temporarily hold in the form of idle money, as a money reserve or as capital to be invested. Hence it is idle capital, but not capital of the idle. In the second place, it is the portion of all revenue and savings in general which is to be temporarily or permanently accumulated. Both are essential to the nature of the banking system.

But it should always be borne in mind that, in the first place, money — in the form of precious metal — remains the foundation from which the credit system, by its very nature, can *never* detach itself. Secondly, that the credit system presupposes the monopoly of social means of production by private persons (in the form of capital and landed property), that it is itself, on the one hand, an immanent form of the capitalist mode of production, and, on the other, a driving force in its development to its highest and ultimate form.

The banking system, so far as its formal organisation and centralisation is concerned, is the most artificial and most developed product turned out by the capitalist mode of production, a fact already expressed in 1697 in *Some Thoughts of the Interests of England*. This accounts for the immense power of an institution such as the Bank of England over commerce and industry, although their actual movements remain completely beyond its province and it is passive toward them. The banking system possesses indeed the form of universal book-keeping and distribution of the means of production on a social scale, but solely the form. We have seen that the average profit of the individual capitalist, or of every individual capital, is determined not by the surplus labour appropriated at first hand by each capital, but by the quantity of total surplus labour appropriated by the total capital, from which each individual capital receives its dividend only proportional to its aliquot part of the total capital. This social character of capital is first promoted and wholly realised through the full development of the credit and banking system. On the other hand this goes farther. It places all the available and even potential capital of society that is not yet actively employed at the disposal of the industrial and commercial capitalists so that neither the lenders nor users of this capital are its owners or producers. It thus does away with the private character of capital and thus contains in itself, but only in itself, the abolition of capital itself. By means of the banking system the distribution of capital as a special business, a social function, is taken out of the hands of the private capitalists and usurers. But at the same time, banking and credit thus become the most potent means of driving capitalist production beyond its own limits, and one of the most effective vehicles of crises and swindle.

The banking system shows, furthermore, by substituting various forms of circulating credit in place of money, that money is in reality nothing but a particular expression of the social character of labour and its products, which, however, as antithetical to the basis of private production, must always appear in the last analysis as a thing, a special commodity, alongside other commodities.

Finally, there is no doubt that the credit system will serve as a powerful lever during the transition from the capitalist mode of production to the mode of production of associated labour; but only as one element in connection with other great organic revolutions of the mode of production itself. On the other hand, the illusions concerning the miraculous power of the credit and banking system, in the socialist sense, arise from a complete lack of familiarity with the capitalist mode of production and the credit system as one of its forms. As soon as the means of production cease being transformed into capital (which also includes the abolition of private property in land), credit as such no longer has any meaning. This, incidentally, was even understood by the followers of Saint-Simon. On the other hand, as long as the capitalist mode of production continues to exist, interest-bearing capital, as one of its forms, also continues to exist and constitutes in fact the basis of its credit system. Only that sensational writer, Proudhon, who wanted to perpetuate commodity production and abolish money,[25]

[25] Karl Marx, *Misère de la Philosophie*, Bruxelles et Paris, 1847. [a]—Karl Marx, *Kritik der Polit. Oekonomie*, S. 64.[b]

[a] See present edition, Vol. 6, pp. 105-212. - [b] Ibid, Vol. 29, p. 323.

was capable of dreaming up the monstrous *crédit gratuit*,[62] the ostensible realisation of the pious wish of the petty-bourgeois estate.

In *Religion saint-simonienne. Économie politique et Politique*, we read on page 45:

"Credit serves the purpose, in a society in which some own the instruments of industry without the ability or will to employ them, and where other industrious people have no instruments of labour, of transferring these instruments in the easiest manner possible from the hands of the former, their owners, to the hands of the others who know how to use them. Note that this definition regards credit as a result of the way in which *property* is constituted."

Therefore, credit disappears with this constitution of property. We read, furthermore, on page 98, that the present banks

"consider it their business to follow the movement initiated by transactions taking place outside of their domain, but not themselves to provide an impulse to this movement; in other words, the banks perform the role of capitalists in relation to the *travailleurs*, whom they loan money".

The notion that the banks themselves should take over the management and distinguish themselves

"through the number and usefulness of their managed establishments and of promoted works" (p. 101)

contains the *Crédit mobilier* in embryo. In the same way, Charles Pecqueur demands that the banks (which the followers of Saint-Simon call a *Système général des banques*) "should rule production". Pecqueur is essentially a follower of Saint-Simon, but much more radical. He wants

"the credit institution ... to control the entire movement of national production."—"Try to create a national credit institution, which shall advance the wherewithal to needy people of talent and merit, without, however, forcibly tying these borrowers together through close solidarity in production and consumption, but on the contrary enabling them to determine their own exchange and production. In this way, you will only accomplish what the private banks already accomplish now, that is, anarchy, disproportion between production and consumption, the sudden ruin of one person, and the sudden enrichment of another; so that your institution will never get any farther than producing a certain amount of benefits for one person, corresponding to an equivalent amount of misfortune to be endured by another ... and you will have only provided the wage labourers assisted by you with the means to complete with one another just as their capitalist masters now do" (C. Pecqueur, *Théorie nouvelle d'économie soc. et pol.*, Paris, 1842, p. 434).[a]

---

[a] l. c., pp. 433-34.

We have seen that merchant's capital and interest-bearing capital are the oldest forms of capital. But it is in the nature of things that interest-bearing capital assumes in popular conception the form of capital *par excellence*. In merchant's capital there takes place the work of middleman, no matter whether considered as cheating, labour, or anything else. But in the case of interest-bearing capital the self-reproducing character of capital, the self-expanding value, the production of surplus value, appears purely as an occult property. This accounts for the fact that even some political economists, particularly in countries where industrial capital is not yet fully developed, as in France, cling to interest-bearing capital as the fundamental form of capital and regard ground rent, for example, merely as a modified form of it, since the loan form also predominates here. In this way, the internal organisation of the capitalist mode of production is completely misunderstood, and the fact is entirely overlooked that land, like capital, is loaned only to capitalists. Of course, means of production in kind, such as machines and business offices, can also be loaned instead of money. But they then represent a definite sum of money, and the fact that in addition to interest a part is paid for wear and tear is due to their use value, i.e., the specific natural form of these elements of capital. The decisive factor here is again whether they are loaned to direct producers, which would presuppose the non-existence of the capitalist mode of production — at least in the sphere in which this occurs — or whether they are loaned to industrial capitalists, which is precisely the assumption based upon the capitalist mode of production. It is still more irrelevant and meaningless to drag the lending of houses, etc., for individual use into this discussion. That the working class is also swindled in this form, and to an enormous extent, is self-evident; but this is also done by the retail dealer, who sells means of subsistence to the worker. This is secondary exploitation, which runs parallel to the primary exploitation taking place in the production process itself. The distinction between selling and loaning is quite immaterial in this case and merely formal, and, as already indicated,[a] cannot appear as essential to anyone, unless he be wholly unfamiliar with the actual nature of the problem.

----

[a] See this volume, pp. 345-48.

Usury, like commerce, exploits a given mode of production. It does not create it, but is related to it outwardly. Usury tries to maintain it directly, so as to exploit it ever anew; it is conservative and makes this mode of production only more pitiable. The less elements of production enter into the production process as commodities, and emerge from it as commodities, the more does their origination from money appear as a separate act. The more insignificant the role played by circulation in the social reproduction, the more usury flourishes.

That money wealth develops as a special kind of wealth, means in respect to usurer's capital that it possesses all its claims in the form of money claims. It develops that much more in a given country, the more the main body of production is limited to natural services, etc., that is, to use values.

Usury is a powerful lever in developing the preconditions for industrial capital in so far as it plays the double role, first, building up, in general, an independent money wealth alongside that of the merchant, and, secondly, appropriating the conditions of labour, that is, ruining the owners of the old conditions of labour.

INTEREST IN THE MIDDLE AGES

"In the Middle Ages the population was purely agricultural. Under such a government as was the feudal system there can be but little traffic, and hence but little profit. Hence the laws against usury were justified in the Middle Ages. Besides, in an agricultural country a person seldom wants to borrow money except he be reduced to poverty or distress.... In the reign of Henry VIII, interest was limited to 10 per cent. James I reduced it to 8 per cent. ... Charles II reduced it to 6 per cent; in the reign of Queen Anne, it was reduced to 5 per cent.... In those times, the lenders ... had, in fact, though not a legal, yet an actual monopoly, and hence it was necessary that they, like other monopolists, should be placed under restraint. In our times, it is the rate of profit which regulates the rate of interest. In those times, it was the rate of interest which regulated the rate of profit. If the money lender charged a high rate of interest to the merchant, the merchant must have charged a higher rate of profit on his goods. Hence, a large sum of money would be taken from the pockets of the purchasers to be put into the pockets of the money lenders" (Gilbart, *The History and Princ. of Banking*, pp. 164, 165).

"I have been told that 10 gulden are now taken annually at every Leipzig Fair,[63] that is, 30 on each hundred; some add the Neuenburg Fair, thus making 40 per hundred; whether that is so, I don't know. For shame! What will be the infernal outcome of this?... Whoever now has 100 florins at Leipzig, takes 40 annually, which is the same as devouring one peasant or burgher each year. If one has 1,000 florins, he takes 400 annually, which means devouring a knight or a rich nobleman per year. If one has 10,000 florins, he takes 4,000 per year, which means devouring a rich count each year. If one has 100,000 florins, as the big merchants must possess, he takes 40,000 annually, which means devouring one affluent prince each year. If one has 1,000,000 florins, he takes 400,000 annually, which means devouring one mighty king every year. And he does not risk either his person or his wares, does not work, sits near his fire-place and roasts apples; so might a lowly robber sit at home and devour a whole world in ten years." (Quoted from *Bücher vom Kaufhandel und Wucher* vom Jahre 1524, Luther's *Werke*, Wittenberg, 1589, Teil 6.[a])

"Fifteen years ago I took pen in hand against usury, when it had spread so alarmingly that I could scarcely hope for any improvement. Since then it has become so arrogant that it deigns not to be classed as vice, sin or shame, but achieves praise as pure virtue and honour, as though it were performing a great favour and Christian service for the people. What will help deliver us now that shame has turned into honour and vice into virtue?" (*An die Pfarrherrn wider den Wucher zu predigen*, Wittenberg, 1540.)

––––––––––

"Jews, Lombards, usurers and extortioners were our first bankers, our primitive traffickers in money, their character little short of infamous.... They were joined by London goldsmiths. As a body ... our primitive bankers ... were a very bad set, they were gripping usurers, iron-hearted extortioners." (D. Hardcastle, *Banks and Bankers*, 2nd ed., London, 1843, pp. 19, 20.)

"The example shown by Venice" (in establishing a bank) "was thus quickly imitated; all sea-coast towns, and in general all towns which had earned fame through their independence and commerce, founded their first banks. The return voyage of their ships, which often was of long duration, inevitably led to the custom of lending on credit. This was further intensified by the discovery of America and the ensuing trade with that continent." (This is the main point.) "The chartering of ships made large loans necessary—a procedure already obtaining in ancient Athens and Greece. In 1308, the Hanse town of Bruges possessed an insurance company" (M. Augier, l. c., pp. 202, 203).

To what extent the granting of loans to landowners, and thus to the pleasure-seeking wealthy in general, still prevailed in the last third of the 17th century, even in England, before the development of modern credit, may be seen, among others, in the works of Sir Dudley North. He was not only one of the first English merchants, but also one of the most prominent theoretical economists of his time: [64]

"The moneys employed at interest in this nation, are not near the tenth part; disposed to trading people, wherewith to manage their trades; but are for the most part lent for the supplying of luxury, and to support the expense of persons, who though great owners of lands, yet spend faster than their lands bring in; and being loath to sell, choose rather to mortgage their estates" (*Discourses upon Trade*, London, 1691, pp. 6, 7).

Poland in the 18th century:

"Warsaw carried on a large bustling business in bills of exchange which, however, had as its principal basis and aim the usury of its bankers. In order to secure money, which they could lend to spendthrift gentry at 8% and more, they sought and obtained

––––––––––

[a] S. 312-13.

abroad open exchange credit, that is, credit that had no commodity trade as its basis, but which the foreign drawee continued to accept as long as the returns from these manipulations did not fail to come in. However, they paid heavily for this through bankruptcies of men like Tepper and other highly respected Warsaw bankers" (J. G. Büsch, *Theoretisch-praktische Darstellung der Handlung, etc.*, 3rd ed., Hamburg, 1808, Vol. II, pp. 232, 233).

ADVANTAGES DERIVED BY THE CHURCH FROM THE PROHIBITION OF INTEREST

"Taking interest had been interdicted by the Church. But selling property for the purpose of finding succour in distress had not been forbidden. It had not even been prohibited to transfer property to the money lender as security for a certain term, until a debtor repaid his loan, leaving the money lender free to enjoy the usufruct of the property as a reward for his abstinence from his money.... The Church itself, and its associated communes and *pia corpora*,[a] derived much profit from this practice, particularly during the crusades. This brought a very large portion of national wealth into possession of the so-called 'dead hand',[65] all the more so because the Jews were barred from engaging in such usury, the possession of such fixed liens not being concealable.... Without the ban on interest churches and cloisters would never have become so affluent" (1. c., p. 55).

---

[a] pious corporations

Part VI

TRANSFORMATION OF SURPLUS PROFIT INTO GROUND RENT

Chapter XXXVII

INTRODUCTION

The analysis of landed property in its various historical forms is beyond the scope of this work.[66] We shall be concerned with it only in so far as a portion of the surplus value produced by capital falls to the share of the landowner. We assume, then, that agriculture is dominated by the capitalist mode of production, just as manufacture is; in other words, that agriculture is carried on by capitalists who differ from other capitalists primarily in the manner in which their capital, and the wage labour set in motion by this capital, are invested. So far as we are concerned, the farmer produces wheat, etc., in much the same way as the manufacturer produces yarn or machines. The assumption that the capitalist mode of production has encompassed agriculture implies that it rules over all spheres of production and bourgeois society, i.e., that its prerequisites, such as free competition among capitals, the possibility of transferring the latter from one production sphere to another, and a uniform level of the average profit, etc., are fully matured. The form of landed property which we shall consider here is a specifically historical one, a form *transformed* through the influence of capital and of the capitalist mode of production, either of feudal landownership, or of small-peasant agriculture as a means of livelihood, in which the *possession* of the land constitutes one of the prerequisites of production for the direct producer, and in which his *ownership* of land appears as the most advantageous condition for the prosperity of *his* mode of production. Just as the capitalist mode of production in general is based on the expropriation of the conditions of labour from the labourers, so does it in agriculture presuppose the expropriation of the rural labourers from the land and their subordination to a capitalist, who carries on agriculture for the sake of profit. Thus, for the purpose of our analysis, the objection that other forms of landed property and of agriculture have existed, or still exist, is quite irrelevant. Such an objection can only apply to those economists who treat the capitalist mode of production in agriculture, and the form of landed property corresponding to it, not as historical but rather as eternal categories.[67]

For our purposes it is necessary to study the modern form of landed property, because our task is to consider the specific conditions of production and circulation which arise from the investment of capital in agriculture. Without this, our analysis of capital would not be complete. We therefore confine ourselves exclusively to the investment of capital in agriculture itself, that is, in producing the principal agricultural crop which feeds a given people. We can use wheat for this purpose, because it is the principal means of subsistence in modern capitalistically developed nations. (Or, instead of agriculture, we can use mining because the laws are the same for both.)

One of the big contributions of Adam Smith was to have shown that ground rent for capital invested in the production of such agricultural products as flax and dye-stuffs, and in independent cattle-raising, etc., is determined by the ground rent obtained from capital invested in the production of the principal article of subsistence.[a] In fact, no further progress has been made in this regard since then. Any limitations or additions would belong in an independent study of landed property, not here.[68] Hence, we shall not speak of landed property *ex professo* — in so far as it does not refer to land destined for wheat production — but shall merely refer to it on occasion by way of illustration.

It should be noted for the sake of completeness that we also include water, etc., in the term land, in so far as it belongs to someone as an accessory to the land.

Landed property is based on the monopoly by certain persons over definite portions of the globe, as exclusive spheres of their private will to the exclusion of all others.[26] With this in mind, the problem is to ascertain the economic value, that is, the realisation of this monopoly

---

[26] Nothing could be more comical than Hegel's development of private landed property. According to this, man as an individual must endow his will with reality as the soul of external nature, and must therefore take possession of this nature and make

---

[a] A. Smith, *An Inquiry into the Nature and Causes of the Wealth of Nations*, London, 1776, pp. 182-202.

on the basis of capitalist production. With the legal power of these persons to use or misuse certain portions of the globe, nothing is decided. The use of this power depends wholly upon economic conditions, which are independent of their will. The legal view itself only means that the landowner can do with the land what every owner of commodities can do with his commodities. And this view, this legal view of free private ownership of land, arises in the ancient world only with the dissolution of the organic order of society, and in the modern world only with the development of capitalist production. It has been imported by Europeans to Asia only here and there. In the section dealing with primitive accumulation (Buch I, Kap. XXIV [b]), we saw that this mode of production presupposes, on the one hand, the separation of the direct producers from their position as mere ac-

---

it his private property. If this were the destiny of the "*individual*", of man as an individual, it would follow that every human being must be a landowner, in order to become a real individual. Free private ownership of land, a very recent product, is, according to Hegel, not a definite social relation, but a relation of man as an individual to "nature", "an absolute right of man to appropriate all things" (Hegel, *Philosophie des Rechts*, Berlin, 1840, S. 79). This much, at least, is evident: the individual cannot maintain himself as a landowner by his mere "will" against the will of another individual, who likewise wants to become a real individual by virtue of the same strip of land. It definitely requires something other than goodwill. Furthermore, it is absolutely impossible to determine where the "individual" draws the line for realising his will—whether this will requires for its realisation a whole country, or whether it requires a whole group of countries by whose appropriation "the supremacy of my will over the thing can be manifested".[a] Here Hegel comes to a complete impasse. "The appropriation is of a very particular kind; I do not take possession of more than I touch with my body; but it is clear, on the other hand, that external things are more extensive that I can grasp. By thus having possession of such a thing, some other is thereby connected to it. I carry out the act of appropriation by means of my hand, but its scope can be extended" (p. 90). But this other thing is again linked with still another, and so the boundary within which my will, as the soul, can pour into the soil, disappears. "When I possess something, my mind at once passes over to the idea that not only this property in my immediate possession, but what is associated with it is also mine. Here positive right must decide, for nothing more can be deduced from the concept" (p. 91). This is an extraordinarily naïve admission "of the concept", and proves that this concept which makes the blunder at the very outset of regarding as absolute a very definite legal view of landed property—belonging to bourgeois society—understands "nothing" of the actual nature of this landed property. This contains at the same time the admission that "positive right" can, and must, alter its determinations as the requirements of social, i. e., economic, development change.

---

[a] Hegel, *Grundlinien der Philosophie des Rechts*, S. 80. - [b] English edition: Part VIII (see present edition, Vol. 35, pp. 704-61).

cessories to the land (in the form of vassals, serfs, slaves, etc.), and, on the other hand, the expropriation of the mass of the people from the land. To this extent the monopoly of landed property is a historical premise, and continues to remain the basis of the capitalist mode of production, just as in all previous modes of production which are based on the exploitation of the masses in one form or another. But the form of landed property with which the incipient capitalist mode of production is confronted does not suit it. It first creates for itself the form required by subordinating agriculture to capital. It thus transforms feudal landed property, clan property, small-peasant property in mark communes — no matter how divergent their juristic forms may be — into the economic form corresponding to the requirements of this mode of production. One of the major results of the capitalist mode of production is that, on the one hand, it transforms agriculture from a mere empirical and mechanical self-perpetuating process employed by the least developed part of society into the conscious scientific application of agronomy, in so far as this is at all feasible under conditions of private property[27]; that it completely divorces landed

---

[27] Very conservative agricultural chemists, such as Johnston, admit that a really rational agriculture is confronted everywhere with insurmountable barriers stemming from private property.[a] So do writers who are *ex professo* advocates of the monopoly of private property in the world, for instance, Charles Comte in his two-volume work,[b] which has as its special aim the defence of private property. "A nation," he says, "cannot attain to the degree of prosperity and power compatible with its nature, unless every portion of the soil nourishing it is assigned to that purpose which agrees best with the general interest. In order to give to its wealth a strong development, one sole and above all highly enlightened will should, if possible, take it upon itself to assign each piece of its domain its task and make every piece contribute to the prosperity of all others. But the existence of such a will ... would be incompatible with the division of the land into private plots ...and with the authority guaranteed each owner to dispose of his property in an almost absolute manner."[c] Johnston, Comte, and others, only have in mind the necessity of tilling the land of a certain country as a whole, when they speak of a contradiction between property and a rational system of agronomy. But the dependence of the cultivation of particular agricultural products upon the fluctuations of market prices, and the continual changes in this cultivation with these price fluctuations — the whole spirit of capitalist production, which is directed toward the immediate gain of money — are in contradiction to agriculture, which has to minister to the entire range of permanent necessities of life required by the chain of successive generations. A striking illustration of this is furnished by the forests, which are only rarely managed in a way more or less corresponding to the interests of society as a whole, i. e., when they are not private property, but subject to the control of the state.

---

[a] J. Johnston, *Notes on North America. Agricultural, Economical and Social*, Vol. I, Edinburgh and London, 1851. - [b] *Traité de la propriété*, Tome 1, Paris, 1834. - [c] Ibid., p. 228.

property from the relations of dominion and servitude, on the one hand, and, on the other, totally separates land as a condition of labour from landed property and landowner—for whom the land merely represents a certain money assessment which he collects by virtue of his monopoly from the industrial capitalist, the tenant farmer; it dissolves the connection between landownership and the land so thoroughly that the landowner may spend his whole life in Constantinople, while his estates lie in Scotland. Landed property thus receives its purely economic form by discarding all its former political and social embellishments and associations, in brief all those traditional accessories, which are denounced, as we shall see later, as useless and absurd superfluities by the industrial capitalists themselves, as well as their theoretical spokesmen, in the heat of their struggle with landed property. The rationalising of agriculture, on the one hand, which makes it for the first time capable of operating on a social scale, and the reduction *ad absurdum* of property in land, on the other, are the great achievements of the capitalist mode of production. Like all of its other historical advances, it also attained these by first completely impoverishing the direct producers.

Before we proceed to the problem itself, several more preliminary remarks are necessary to avoid misunderstanding.

The prerequisites for the capitalist mode of production therefore are the following: The actual tillers of the soil are wage labourers employed by a capitalist, the tenant farmer who is engaged in agriculture merely as a particular field of exploitation for capital, as investment for his capital in a particular sphere of production. This capitalist farmer pays the landowner, the owner of the land exploited by him, a sum of money at definite periods fixed by contract, for instance, annually (just as the borrower of money capital pays a fixed interest), for the right to invest his capital in this specific sphere of production. This sum of money is called ground rent, no matter whether it is paid for agricultural land, building lots, mines, fishing grounds, or forests, etc. It is paid for the entire time for which the landowner has contracted to rent his land to the tenant farmer. Ground rent, therefore, is here that form in which property in land is realised economically, that is, produces value. Here, then, we have all three classes—wage labourers, industrial capitalists, and landowners—constituting together, and in their mutual opposition, the framework of modern society.

Capital may be fixed in the land, incorporated in it either in a transitory manner, as through improvements of a chemical nature, fertilisation, etc., or more permanently, as in drainage canals, irrigation works, levelling, farm buildings, etc. Elsewhere I have called the capital thus applied to land *la terre-capital*.[28] It belongs to the category of fixed capital. The interest on capital incorporated in the land and the improvements thus made in it as an instrument of production can constitute a part of the rent paid by the farmer to the landowner,[29] but it does not constitute the actual ground rent, which is paid for the use of the land as such — be it in a natural or cultivated state. In a systematic treatment of landed property, which is not within our scope, this part of the landowner's revenue would have to be discussed at length.[66] But a few words about it will suffice here. The more transitory capital investments, which accompany the ordinary production processes in agriculture, are all made without exception by the farmer. These investments, like cultivation proper in general, improve the land,[30] increase its output, and transform the land from mere material into land-capital when the cultivation is carried on more or less rationally, i. e., when it is not reduced to a brutal spoliation of the soil, as was in vogue, e. g., among the former slave-holders in the United States; however, the gentlemen landowners secure themselves against such practice by contract. A cultivated field is worth more than an uncultivated one of the same natural quality. The more permanent fixed capital investments, which are incorporated in the soil and used up in a longer period of time, are also in the main, and in some spheres often exclusively, made by the farmer. But as soon as the time stipulated by contract has expired — and this is one of the reasons why with the development of capitalist production the

---

[28] *Misère de la Philosophie*.[a] There I have made a distinction between *terre-matière* and *terre-capital*. "The very fact of applying further outlays of capital to land already transformed into means of production increases land as capital without adding anything to land as matter, that is, to the extent of the land.... Land as capital is no more eternal than any other capital... Land as capital is fixed capital; but fixed capital gets used up just as much as circulating capital."

[29] I say "can" because under certain circumstances this interest is regulated by the law of ground rent and, therefore, can disappear, as in the case of competition between virgin lands of great natural fertility.

[30] See James Anderson and Carey.[b]

---

[a] See present edition, Vol. 6, p. 205. - [b] J. Anderson, *A Calm Investigation of the Circumstances that Have Led to the Present Scarcity of Grain in Britain*, pp. 35-36, 38; H. Ch. Carey, *The Past, the Present, and the Future*, pp. 129-31.

landowners seek to shorten the contract period as much as possible — the improvements incorporated in the soil become the property of the landowner as an inseparable feature of the substance, the land. In the new contract made by the landowner he adds the interest for capital incorporated in the land to the ground rent itself. And he does this whether he now leases the land to the farmer who made these improvements or to some other farmer. His rent is thus inflated; and should he wish to sell his land (we shall see immediately how its price is determined), its value is now higher. He sells not merely the land but the improved land, the capital incorporated in the land for which he paid nothing. Quite aside from the movements of ground rent itself, here lies one of the secrets of the increasing enrichment of landowners, the continuous inflation of their rents, and the constantly growing money value of their estates along with progress in economic development. Thus they pocket a product of social development created without their help — *fruges consumere nati*.[a] But this is at the same time one of the greatest obstacles to a rational development of agriculture, for the tenant farmer avoids all improvements and outlays for which he cannot expect complete returns during the term of his lease. We find this situation denounced as such an obstacle again and again, not only in the 18th century by James Anderson, the actual discoverer of the modern theory of rent[b] — who was also a practical farmer and an advanced agronomist for his time — but also in our own day by opponents of the present constitution of landed property in England.

A. A. Walton, in his *History of the Landed Tenures of Great Britain and Ireland*, London, 1865, says on this score (pp. 96, 97):

"All the efforts of the numerous agricultural associations throughout the country must fail to produce any very extensive or really appreciable results in the real advancement of agricultural improvement, so long as such improvements mean in a far higher degree increased value to the estate and rent-roll of the landlord, than bettering the condition of the tenant farmer or the labourer. The farmers, generally, are as well aware as either the landlord or his agent, or even the president of the Agricultural Association, that good drainage, plenty of manure, and good management, combined with the increased employment of labour, to thoroughly cleanse and work the land, will produce wonderful results both in improvement and production. To do all this, however, considerable outlay is required, and the farmers are also aware, that however much they may improve the land or enhance its value, the landlords will, in

---

[a] Horace, *Epistles*, Book I, 2, 27. - [b] On J. Anderson's theory of rent see present edition, Vol. 31, pp. 344-46, 351-54, 371-76.

the long run, reap the principal benefit, in higher rents and the increased value of their estates.... They are shrewd enough to observe what those orators" (landowners and their agents speaking at agricultural festivities), "by some singular inadvertence, omit to tell them — namely, that the lion's share of any improvements they may make is sure to go into the pockets of the landlords in the long run.... However much the former tenant may have improved the farm, his successor will find that the landlord will always increase the rent in proportion to the increased value of the land from former improvements."

In agriculture proper this process does not yet appear quite as plainly as when the land is used for building purposes. By far the largest portion of land used in England for building purposes but not sold as a FREEHOLD is leased by the landowners for 99 years or, if possible, for a shorter term. After the lapse of this period the buildings fall into the hands of the landowner together with the land itself.

"They" (the tenants) "are bound to deliver up the house at the expiration of the lease, in good tenantable condition, to the great landlord, after having paid an exorbitant ground rent up to the expiration of the lease. No sooner is the lease expired, than the agent or surveyor will come and examine your house, and see that you put it into good repair, and then take possession of it, and annex it to his lord's domains.... The fact is, if this system is permitted to be in full operation for any considerable period longer, the whole of the house property in the kingdom will be in the hands of the great landlords, as well as the land. The whole of the West End of London, north and south from Temple Bar,[69] may be said to belong to about half a dozen great landlords, all let at enormous rents, and where the leases have not quite expired they are fast falling due. The same may be said either more or less of every town in the kingdom. Nor does this grasping system of exclusion and monopoly stop even here. Nearly the whole of the dock accommodation in our seaport towns is by the same process of usurpation in the hands of the great leviathans of the land" (l. c., p. 93).[a]

It is evident in these circumstances that when the census for England and Wales in 1861 gives the total population as 20,066,224 and the number of landlords as 36,032, the proportion of owners to the number of houses and to population would look completely different if the large owners were placed on one side and the small ones on the other.

This illustration of ownership in buildings is important. In the first place, it clearly shows the difference between actual ground rent and interest on fixed capital incorporated in the land, which may constitute an addition to ground rent. Interest on buildings, like that on capital incorporated in the land by the tenant in agriculture, falls into the hands of the industrial capitalist, the building speculator,

---

[a] Pp. 92-93.

or the tenant, so long as the lease lasts, and has in itself nothing to do with ground rent, which must be paid on stated dates annually for the use of the land. Secondly, it shows that capital incorporated in the land by others ultimately passes into the hands of the landlord together with the land, and that the interest for it inflates his rent.

Some writers, acting either as spokesmen of landed property and taking up the cudgels against the attacks of bourgeois economists, or in an endeavour to transform the capitalist system of production from a system of contradictions into one of "harmonies", like Carey, have tried to represent ground rent, the specific economic expression of landed property, as identical with interest.[a] This would eliminate the opposition between landlords and capitalists. The opposite method was employed in the early stages of capitalist production. In those days, landed property was still regarded by popular conception as the pristine and respectable form of private property, while interest on capital was decried as usury. Dudley North, Locke and others, therefore, represented interest on capital as a form analogous to ground rent,[70] just as Turgot deduced the justification for interest from the existence of ground rent.[b] — Aside from the fact that ground rent may, and does, exist in its pure form without any addition for interest on capital incorporated in the land, those more recent writers forget that, in this way, the landlord not only receives interest on other persons' capital that costs him nothing, but also pockets this capital of others without recompense. The justification of landed property, like that of all other forms of property corresponding to a certain mode of production, is that the mode of production itself is a transient historical necessity, and this includes the relations of production and exchange which stem from it. It is true, as we shall see later, that landed property differs from other kinds of property in that it appears superfluous and harmful at a certain stage of development, even from the point of view of the capitalist mode of production.[c]

Ground rent may in another form be confused with interest and thereby its specific character overlooked. Ground rent assumes the form of a certain sum of money, which the landlord draws annually by leasing a certain plot on our planet. We have seen that every

[a] H. Ch. Carey, *Principles of Political Economy*. Part the first, pp. 129-30. -
[b] A. R. J. Turgot, *Réflexions sur la formation et la distribution des richesses*, §§ 73, 85. -
[c] See this volume, pp. 798-800.

particular sum of money may be capitalised, that is, considered as the interest on an imaginary capital. For instance, if the average rate of interest is 5%, then an annual ground rent of £200 may be regarded as interest on a capital of £4,000. Ground rent so capitalised constitutes the purchase price or value of the land, a category which like the price of labour is *prima facie* irrational, since the earth is not the product of labour and therefore has no value. But on the other hand, a real relation in production is concealed behind this irrational form. If a capitalist buys land yielding a rent of £200 annually and pays £4,000 for it, then he draws the average annual interest of 5% on his capital of £4,000, just as if he had invested this capital in interest-bearing papers or loaned it directly at 5% interest. It is the expansion of a capital of £4,000 at 5%. On this assumption, he would recover the purchase price of his estate through its revenues in twenty years. In England, therefore, the purchase price of land is calculated in so many YEARS' PURCHASE which is merely another way of expressing the capitalisation of ground rent. It is in fact the purchase price — not of the land, but of the ground rent yielded by it — calculated in accordance with the usual interest rate. But this capitalisation of rent assumes the existence of rent, while rent cannot inversely be derived and explained from its own capitalisation. Its existence, independent of its sale, is rather the starting-point for the inquiry.

It follows, then, that the price of land may rise or fall inversely as the interest rate rises or falls if we assume ground rent to be a constant magnitude. If the ordinary interest rate should fall from 5% to 4%, then the annual ground rent of £200 would represent the annual realisation from a capital of £5,000 instead of £4,000. The price of the same piece of land would thus have risen from £4,000 to £5,000, or from 20 years' to 25 YEARS' PURCHASE. The converse would take place in the opposite case. This is a movement of the price of land which is independent of the movement of ground rent itself and regulated only by the interest rate. But as we have seen that the rate of profit has a tendency to fall in the course of social progress, and, therefore, the interest rate has the same tendency, so far as it is regulated by the rate of profit; and that, furthermore, the interest rate shows a tendency to fall in consequence of the growth of loanable capital, apart from the influence of the rate of profit, it follows that the price of land has a tendency to rise, even independently of the movement of ground rent and the prices of the products of the land, of which rent constitutes a part.

The confusion of ground rent itself with the interest form which it assumes for the buyer of the land—a confusion resulting from complete lack of familiarity with the nature of ground rent—must necessarily lead to the most absurd conclusions. Since landed property is considered in all ancient countries as a particularly genteel form of property, and its purchase also as an eminently safe capital investment, the interest rate at which ground rent is bought is generally lower than that of other long-term investments of capital, so that a buyer of real estate draws, for instance, only 4% on his purchase price, whereas he would draw 5% for the same capital in other investments. In other words, he pays more capital for ground rent than he would for the same annual amount of income from other investments. This leads Mr. Thiers to conclude in his generally very poor work on *La Propriété*[a] (a reprint of his speech in the French National Assembly in 1848 directed against Proudhon)[71] that ground rent is low, whereas it merely proves that its purchase price is high.

The fact that capitalised ground rent appears as the price or value of land, so that land, therefore, is bought and sold like any other commodity, serves some apologists as a justification for landed property since the buyer pays an equivalent for it, the same as for other commodities; and the major portion of landed property has changed hands in this way. The same reason in that case would also serve to justify slavery, since the returns from the labour of the slave, whom the slave-holder has bought, merely represent the interest on the capital invested in this purchase. To derive a justification for the existence of ground rent from its sale and purchase means in general to justify its existence by its existence.

As important as it may be for a scientific analysis of ground rent—that is, the independent and specific economic form of landed property on the basis of the capitalist mode of production—to study it in its pure form free of all distorting and obfuscating irrelevancies, it is just as important for an understanding of the practical effects of landed property—even for a theoretical comprehension of a multitude of facts which contradict the concept and nature of ground rent and yet appear as modes of existence of ground rent—to learn the sources which give rise to such muddling in theory.

---

[a] L. A. Thiers, *Rapport du citoyen Thiers, précédé de la proposition du citoyen Proudhon relative à l'impôt sur le revenu, et suivi de son discours prononcé à l'Assemblée nationale, le 31 juillet 1848*, Paris, 1848.

In practice, naturally, everything appears as ground rent that is paid as lease money by tenant to landlord for the right to cultivate the soil. No matter what the composition of this tribute and no matter what its sources, it has this in common with the actual ground rent — that the monopoly of the so-called landed proprietor of a portion of our planet enables him to levy such tribute and impose such an assessment. It has this in common with the actual ground rent — that it determines the price of land, which, as we have indicated earlier, is nothing but the capitalised income from the lease of the land.

We have already seen that interest for the capital incorporated in the land may constitute such an extraneous component of ground rent, a component which must become a continually growing extra charge on the total rent of a country as economic development progresses. But aside from this interest, it is possible that the lease money may conceal in part, and in certain cases in its entirety, i. e., in complete absence of the actual ground rent — when the land is, therefore, actually worthless — a deduction from the average profit or from the normal wages, or both. This portion, whether of profit or wages, appears here as ground rent, because instead of falling to the industrial capitalist or the wage worker, as would normally be the case, it is paid to the landlord in the form of lease money. Economically speaking, neither the one nor the other of these portions constitutes ground rent; but, in practice, it constitutes the landlord's revenue, an economic realisation of his monopoly, much as actual ground rent, and it has just as determining an influence on land prices.

We are not speaking now of conditions in which ground rent, the manner of expressing landed property in the capitalist mode of production, formally exists without the existence of the capitalist mode of production itself, i. e., without the tenant himself being an industrial capitalist, nor the type of his management being a capitalist one. Such is the case, e. g., in *Ireland*. The tenant there is generally a small farmer. What he pays to the landlord in the form of rent frequently absorbs not merely a part of his profit, that is, his own surplus labour (to which he is entitled as possessor of his own instruments of labour), but also a part of his normal wage, which he would otherwise receive for the same amount of labour. Besides, the landlord, who does nothing at all for the improvement of the land, also expropriates his small capital, which the tenant for the most part incorporates in the land through his own labour. This is precisely what a usurer would do under similar circumstances, with just the difference that the usurer would at least risk his own capital in the operation. This continual plunder is the core of the dispute over the Irish Tenancy Rights Bill. The main purpose of this Bill is to compel the landlord when ordering his tenant off the land to indemnify the latter for his improvements on the land, or for his capital incorporated in the land.[72] Palmerston used to wave this demand aside with the cynical answer:

"The House of Commons is a house of landed proprietors."

Nor are we referring to exceptional circumstances in which the landlord may enforce a high rental — even in countries with capitalist production — that stands in no relation to the yield from the soil. Of such a nature, for example, is the leasing of small patches of land to labourers in English factory districts, either as small gardens or for amateur spare-time farming (Reports of Inspectors of Factories).

We are referring to ground rent in countries with developed capitalist production. Among English tenants, for instance, there are a number of small capitalists who are destined and compelled by education, training, tradition, competition, and other circumstances to invest their capital as tenants in agriculture. They are forced to be satisfied with less than the average profit, and to turn over part of it to the landlords as rent. This is the only condition under which they are permitted to invest their capital in the land, in agriculture. Since landlords everywhere exert considerable, and in England even overwhelming, influence on legislation, they are able to exploit this situation for the purpose of victimising the entire class of tenants. For instance, the Corn Laws of 1815[73] — a bread tax, admittedly imposed upon the country to secure for the idle landlords a continuation of their abnormally increased rentals during the anti-Jacobin war[74] — had indeed the effect, excluding cases of a few extraordinarily rich harvests, of maintaining prices of agricultural products above the level to which they would have fallen had corn imports been unrestricted. But they did not have the effect of maintaining prices at the level decreed by the law-making landlords to serve as normal prices in such manner as to constitute the legal limit for imports of foreign corn. But the leaseholds were contracted in an atmosphere created by these normal prices. As soon as the illusion was dispelled, a new law was passed, containing new normal prices, which were as much the impotent expression of a greedy landlord's fantasy as the old ones. In this way, tenants were defrauded from 1815 up to the thirties. Hence the standing problem of AGRICULTURAL DISTRESS during this entire period. Hence the expropriation and the ruin of a whole generation of tenants during this period and their replacement by a new class of capitalists.[31]

A much more general and important fact, however, is the depression of the actual farm labourer's wage below its normal average, so that part of it is deducted to become part of the lease money and thus, in the guise of ground rent, it flows into the pocket of the landlord rather than the labourer. This is, for example, quite generally the case in England and Scotland, with the exception of a few favourably situated counties. The inquiries into the level of wages by the parliamentary investigating committees,[75] which were appointed before the passage of the Corn Laws in England — so far the most valuable and almost unexploited contributions to the history of wages in the 19th century, and at the same time a pillory erected for themselves by the English aristocracy and bourgeoisie — proved convincingly and beyond a doubt that the high rates of rent, and the corresponding rise in land prices during the anti-Jocobin war, were due in part to no other cause but deductions from wages and their depression to a level that was even below the physical minimum requirement; in other words, to part of the normal wage being handed over to the landlords. Various circumstances, such as the depreciation of money and the manipulation of the Poor Laws in the agricultural districts,[76] had made this operation possible at a time when the incomes of the tenants were enormously increasing and the landlords were amassing fabulous riches. Indeed, one of the main arguments of both tenants and landlords for the introduction of duties on corn was that it was physically impossible to depress farm labourers' wages any lower. This state of affairs has not significantly changed, and in England, as in all European countries, a portion of the normal wage is absorbed by ground rent just as ever. When Count Shaftesbury, then Lord Ashley, one of the philanthropic aristocrats, was so extraordinarily moved by the condition of English factory operatives and acted as

---

[31] See the Anti-Corn Law Prize Essays.[a] However, the Corn Laws always kept prices at an artificially higher level. For the better placed tenants this was favourable. They profited from the passivity in which the protective duties kept the great mass of tenants who relied, with or without good reason, on the exceptional average price.

---

[a] *The Three Prize Essays on Agriculture and the Corn Law.* Manchester-London, 1842.

their spokesman in Parliament during the agitation for a ten-hour day, the spokesmen of the industrialists took their revenge by publishing wage statistics of agricultural labourers in the villages belonging to him (see Buch I, Kap. XXIII, 5, e[a]) ("The British Agricultural Proletariat"), which clearly showed that a portion of the ground rent of this philanthropist consisted merely of loot filched for him by his tenants out of the wages of agricultural labourers. This publication is also interesting for the fact that its revelations may bravely take their place beside the worst exposures made by the committees in 1814 and 1815.[b] As soon as circumstances force a temporary increase in the wage of agricultural labourers a cry goes up from the tenant farmers that raising wages to the normal level, as done in other branches of industry, would be impossible and would ruin them, unless ground rent were reduced at the same time. Therein lies the confession that under the head of ground rent there is a deduction of the labourers' wages which is handed over to the landlords. For instance, from 1849 to 1859 the wages of agricultural labourers rose in England through a combination of momentous events: the exodus from Ireland, which cut off the supply of agricultural labourers coming from there; an extraordinary absorption of the agricultural population by factories; a war-time demand for soldiers; an exceptionally large emigration to Australia and the United States (California), and other circumstances which need not be dwelt upon here. At the same time, average prices of grain fell by more than 16% during this period, with the exception of the poor agricultural years 1854 to 1856. The tenant farmers clamoured for a reduction in rents. They were successful in individual cases, but on the whole failed to achieve this demand. They had recourse to a decrease in production costs, among other things by the mass introduction of steam-engines and new machinery, which to some extent replaced horses and pushed them out of the economy, but also brought about, in part, an artificial overpopulation by throwing agricultural day labourers out of work, and thereby caused a new drop in wages. And this took place in spite of the overall relative decrease in agricultural population during that decade as compared with the growth of total population, and in spite of an absolute decrease in agricultural population in

---

[a] English edition: Ch. XXV, 5, e (see present edition, Vol. 35, pp. 665-88). - [b] The reference is to The House of Lords investigating committees which made inquiries into the level of wages.

some purely agricultural districts.[32] Thus Fawcett, then professor of political economy at Cambridge, who died in 1884 while Postmaster General, stated at the Social Science Congress on October 12, 1865:[78]

"The labourers were beginning to emigrate, and the farmers were already beginning to complain that they would not be able to pay such high rents as they have been accustomed to pay, because labour was becoming dearer in consequence of emigration."

Here, then, high ground rent is directly identified with low wages. And in so far as the level of land prices is determined by this circumstance — increasing rent — a rise in the value of land is identical with a depreciation of labour, the high price of land is identical with the low price of labour.

The same is true of France.

"The rental rises because the prices of bread, wine, meat, vegetables and fruit rise, on the one hand, while, on the other hand, the price of labour remains unchanged. If the older people examine the accounts of their fathers, taking us back about 100 years, they will find that the price of a day's labour in rural France was the same as it is now. The price of meat has trebled since then.... Who is the victim of this revolution? Is it the rich man, who is the proprietor of an estate, or the poor man who works it?... The increase in rental is evidence of a public disaster" (*Du Mécanisme de la Société en France et en Angleterre*, by M. Rubichon, 2nd ed., Paris, 1837, p. 101).

Illustrations of rent representing deductions, on the one hand, from average profit and, on the other, from average wages:

Morton,[b] real estate agent and agricultural mechanic who was previously quoted, states that it has been observed in many localities that rent for large estates is lower than for small ones because

"the competition is usually greater for the latter than for the former, and as few small farmers are able to turn their attention to any other business than that of farming, their anxiety to get a suitable occupation leads them in many instances to give more rent than their judgement can approve of" (John L. Morton, *The Resources of Estates*, London, 1858, p. 116).

However, this difference is supposed to be gradually disappearing in England; this he attributes largely to the emigration precisely

---

[32] John Ch. Morton, *The Forces Used in Agriculture*. Lecture read in the London SOCIETY OF ARTS,[77] in 1859,[a] was based upon authentic documents collected from about 100 tenants in 12 Scottish and 35 English counties.

---

[a] Under the title: "On the Forces Used in Agriculture". - [b] Here Marx quotes John Lockart Morton and not John Chalmers Morton who was quoted above.

of the class of small tenants. The same Morton illustrates with an example in which clearly the wage of the tenant himself, and even more surely that of his labourers, suffers a deduction for ground rent. This takes place in the case of leaseholds with less than 70 to 80 acres (30-34 ha.) where a two-horse plough cannot be maintained.

"Unless the tenant works with his own hands as laboriously as any labourer, his farm will not keep him. If he entrusts the performance of his work to workmen while he continues merely to observe them, the chances are, that at no distant period, he will find he is unable to pay his rent" (l. c., p. 118).

Morton concludes, therefore, that unless the tenants of a certain locality are very poor, the leaseholds should not be smaller than 70 acres, so that the tenants may keep two or three horses.

Extraordinary sagacity on the part of Monsieur Léonce de Lavergne, *Membre de l'Institut et de la Société Centrale d'Agriculture.*[79] In his *Economie Rurale de l'Angleterre* (quoted from the English translation, London, 1855), he makes the following comparison of the annual advantage derived from cattle which is employed in France but not in England where it is replaced by horses (p. 42):

FRANCE:	Milk	£4 million	ENGLAND:	Milk	£16 million
	Meat	£16 million		Meat	£20 million
	Labour	£8 million		Labour	—
		£28 million			£36 million

But the greater total for England is obtained here because according to his own testimony milk is twice as expensive in England as in France whereas he assumes the same prices for meat in both countries (p. 35); therefore, English milk production shrinks to £8 million and the total to £28 million, which is the same as in France. It is indeed rather too much when Mr. Lavergne allows the quantities and price differences to enter simultaneously into his calculations so that when England produces certain articles more dearly than France, this appears to be an advantage of English agriculture, whereas at best it signifies a larger profit for the tenants and landlords.

That Mr. Lavergne is not only familiar with the economic achievements of English agriculture, but also subscribes to the prejudices of the English tenants and landlords, is shown on page 48:

"One great drawback attends cereals generally ... they exhaust the soil which bears them."

Not only does Mr. Lavergne believe that other plants do not do so, but also believes that fodder crops and root crops enrich the soil:

"Forage plants derive from the atmosphere the principal elements of their growth, while they give to the soil more than they take from it; thus both directly and by their conversion into animal manure contributing in two ways to repair the mischief done by cereals and exhausting crops generally; one principle, therefore, is that they should at least alternate with these crops; in this consists the Norfolk rotation" (pp. 50, 51).

No wonder that Mr. Lavergne, who believes these English rustic fairy-tales, also believes that the wages of English farm labourers have lost their former abnormality since the duties on corn have been lifted. (See what has been previously said on this point. Buch I, Kap. XXIII, 5, pp. 701 to 729.[a]) But let us also listen to Mr. John Bright's speech in Birmingham, December 13, 1865. After mentioning the 5 million families entirely unrepresented in Parliament, he continues:

"There is among them one million, or rather more than one million, in the United Kingdom who are classed in the unfortunate list of paupers. There is another million just above pauperism, but always in peril lest they should become paupers. Their condition and prospects are not more favourable than that. Now look at the ignorant and lower strata of this portion of the community. Look to their abject condition, to their poverty, to their suffering, to their utter hopelessness of any good. Why, in the United States—even in the Southern States during the reign of slavery—every Negro had an idea that there was a day of jubilee for him. But to these people—to this class of the lowest strata in this country—I am here to state that there is neither the belief of anything better nor scarcely an aspiration after it. Have you read a paragraph which lately appeared in the newspapers about John Cross, a Dorsetshire labourer? He worked six days in the week, had an excellent character from his employer for whom he had worked twenty-four years at the rate of eight shillings per week. John Cross had a family of seven children to provide for out of these wages in his hovel—for a feeble wife and an infant child. He took—legally, I believe he stole—a wooden hurdle of the value of sixpence. For this offence he was tried before the magistrates and sentenced to 14 or 20 days' imprisonment.... I can tell you that many thousands of cases like that of John Cross are to be found throughout the country, and especially in the south, and that their condition is such that hitherto the most anxious investigator has been unable to solve the mystery as to how they keep body and soul together. Now cast your eye over the country and look at these five million of families and the desperate condition of this strata of them. Is it not true that the unenfranchised nation may be said to toil and toil and knowing almost no rest? Compare it with the ruling class—but if I do I shall be charged with communism.... But compare this great toiling and unenfranchised nation with the section who may be considered the governing classes. Look at its wealth; look at its ostentation—look at its luxury. Behold its weariness—for there is weariness amongst them, but it is the weariness of satiety—and see how they rush from place to place, as it were, to discover some new pleasure" (*Morning Star*, December 14, 1865).

---

[a] English edition: Ch. XXV, 5 (see present edition, Vol. 35, pp. 642-703).

It is shown in what follows how surplus labour, and consequently surplus product, is generally confused with ground rent — that qualitatively and quantitatively specifically determined, at least on the basis of the capitalist mode of production, part of the surplus product.[a] The natural basis of surplus labour in general, that is, a natural prerequisite without which such labour cannot be performed, is that Nature must supply — in the form of animal or vegetable products of the land, in fisheries, etc.— the necessary means of subsistence under conditions of an expenditure of labour which does not consume the entire working day. This natural productivity of agricultural labour (which includes here the labour of simple gathering, hunting, fishing and cattle-raising) is the basis of all surplus labour, as all labour is primarily and initially directed toward the appropriation and production of food. (Animals also supply at the same time skins for warmth in colder climates; also cave-dwellings, etc.)

The same confusion between surplus product and ground rent is found differently expressed by Mr. Dove.[b] Originally agricultural and industrial labour were not separated; the latter was an adjunct of the former. The surplus labour and the surplus product of the land-cultivating tribe, house commune, or family included both agricultural and industrial labour. Both went hand in hand. Hunting, fishing and agriculture were impossible without suitable tools. Weaving, spinning, etc., were first carried on as an agrarian side line.

We have previously shown that just as the labour of an individual workman breaks up into necessary and surplus labour, the aggregate labour of the working class may be so divided that the portion which produces the total means of subsistence for the working class (including the means of production required for this purpose) performs the necessary labour for the whole of society. The labour performed by the remainder of the working class may then be regarded as surplus labour. But the necessary labour consists by no means only of agricultural labour, but also of that labour which produces all other products necessarily included in the average consumption of the labourer. Furthermore, from the social standpoint, some perform only necessary labour because others perform only surplus labour, and vice versa. It is but a division of labour between them. The same holds for the division of labour between agricultural and industrial

---

[a] See this volume, pp. 768-76. - [b] P. E. Dove, *The Elements of Political Science*, pp. 264, 273.

labourers in general. The purely industrial character of labour, on the one hand, corresponds to the purely agricultural character on the other. This purely agricultural labour is by no means natural, but is rather a product — and a very modern one at that, which has not yet been achieved everywhere — of social development — and corresponds to a very definite stage of the development of production. Just as a portion of agricultural labour is objectified in products which either minister only to luxury or serve as raw materials in industry, but by no means serve as food, let alone as food for the masses, so on the other hand a portion of industrial labour is objectified in products which serve as necessary means of consumption for both agricultural and non-agricultural labourers. It is a mistake, from a social point of view, to regard this industrial labour as surplus labour. It is, in part, as much necessary labour as the necessary portion of the agricultural labour. It is also but a form rendered independent of a part of industrial labour which was formerly naturally connected with agricultural labour, a necessary mutual supplement to the specifically agricultural labour now separated from it. (From a purely material point of view, 500 mechanical weavers, e. g., produce surplus fabrics to a far greater degree, that is, more than is required for their own clothing.)

Finally, it should be borne in mind in considering the forms of manifestation of ground rent, that is, the lease money paid under the heading of ground rent to the landlord for the use of the land for purposes of production or consumption, that the price of things which have in themselves no value, i. e., are not the product of labour, such as land, or which at least cannot be reproduced by labour, such as antiques and works of art by certain masters, etc., may be determined by many fortuitous combinations. In order to sell a thing, nothing more is required than its capacity to be monopolised and alienated.

———

There are three main errors to be avoided in studying ground rent, and which obscure its analysis.

1) Confusing the various forms of rent pertaining to different stages of development of the social production process.

Whatever the specific form of rent may be, all types have this in common: the appropriation of rent is that economic form in which landed property is realised, and ground rent, in turn, presupposes the existence of landed property, the ownership of certain portions of our planet by certain individuals. The owner may be an individual representing the community, as in Asia, Egypt, etc.; or this landed property may be merely incidental to the ownership of the immediate producers themselves by some individuals as under slavery or serfdom; or it may be a purely private ownership of Nature by non-producers, a mere title to land; or, finally, it may be a relationship to the land which, as in the case of colonists and small peasants owning land, seems to be directly included — in the isolated and not socially developed labour — in the appropriation and production of the products of particular plots of land by the direct producers.

This *common element* in the various forms of rent, namely that of being the economic realisation of landed property, of legal fiction by grace of which certain individuals have an exclusive right to certain parts of our planet — makes it possible for the differences to escape detection.

2) All ground rent is surplus value, the product of surplus labour. In its undeveloped form as rent in kind it is still directly the surplus product itself. Hence, the mistaken idea that the rent corresponding to the capitalist mode of production — which is always a surplus over and above profit, i. e., above a value portion of commodities which itself consists of surplus value (surplus labour) — that this special and specific component of surplus value is explained by merely explaining the general conditions for the existence of surplus value and profit in general. These conditions are: the direct producers must work beyond the time necessary for reproducing their own labour power, for their own reproduction. They must perform surplus labour in general. This is the subjective condition. The objective condition is that they must be *able* to perform surplus labour. The natural conditions must be such that a *part* of their available labour time suffices for their reproduction and self-maintenance as producers, that the production of their necessary means of subsistence shall not consume their whole labour power. The fertility of Nature establishes a limit here, a starting-point, a basis. On the other hand, the development of the social productive power of their labour forms the other limit. Examined more closely, since the production of means of subsistence is the very first condition of their existence and of all production in general, labour used in this production, that is, agricultural labour in the broadest economic sense, must be fruitful enough so as not to absorb the entire available labour time in the production of means of subsistence for the direct producers, that is, agricultural surplus labour and there-

fore agricultural surplus product must be possible. Developed further, the total agricultural labour, both necessary and surplus labour, of a segment of society must suffice to produce the necessary subsistence for the whole of society, that is, for non-agricultural labourers too. This means therefore that the major division of labour between agricultural and industrial labourers must be possible; and similarly between tillers of the soil producing means of subsistence and those producing raw materials. Although the labour of the direct producers of means of subsistence breaks up into necessary and surplus labour as far as they themselves are concerned, it represents from the social standpoint only the necessary labour required to produce the means of subsistence. Incidentally, the same is true for all division of labour within society as a whole, as distinct from the division of labour within individual workshops. It is the labour necessary for the production of particular articles, for the satisfaction of some particular need of society for these particular articles. If this division is proportional, then the products of various groups are sold at their values (at a later stage of development they are sold at their prices of production), or at prices which are certain modifications of these values or prices of production determined by general laws. It is indeed the effect of the law of value, not with reference to individual commodities or articles, but to each total product of the particular social spheres of production made independent by the division of labour; so that not only is no more than the necessary labour time used up for each specific commodity, but only the necessary proportional quantity of the total social labour time is used up in the various groups. For the condition remains that the commodity represents use value. But if the use value of individual commodities depends on whether they satisfy a particular need then the use value of the mass of the social product depends on whether it satisfies the quantitatively definite social need for each particular kind of product in an adequate manner, and whether the labour is therefore proportionately distributed among the different spheres of production in keeping with these social needs, which are quantitatively circumscribed. (This point is to be noted in connection with the distribution of capital among the various spheres of production.) The social need, that is, the use value on a social scale, appears here as a determining factor for the amount of total social labour time which is expended in various specific spheres of production. But it is merely the same law which is already applied in the case of single commodities, namely, that the use value of a commodity is the basis of its exchange value and thus of its value. This point has a bearing upon the relationship between necessary and surplus labour only in so far as a violation of this proportion makes it impossible to realise the value of the commodity and thus the surplus value contained in it. For instance, let us assume that proportionally too much cotton goods have been produced, although only the labour time necessary under the prevailing conditions is incorporated in this total cloth production. But in general too much social labour has been expended in this particular line; in other words, a portion of this product is useless. The whole of it is therefore sold solely as if it had been produced in the necessary proportion. This quantitative limit to the quota of social labour time available for the various particular spheres of production is but a more developed expression of the law of value in general, although the necessary labour time assumes a different meaning here. Only just so much of it is required for the satisfaction of social needs. The limitation occurring here is due to the use value. Society can use only so much of its total labour time for this particular kind of product under prevailing conditions of production.[a] But the subjective and objective conditions of surplus labour and surplus value in general have nothing to do with the particular form of either the profit or the rent. These conditions apply to surplus value as such, no matter what special form it may assume. Hence they do not explain ground rent.

3) It is precisely in the economic realisation of landed property, in the development of ground rent, that the following characteristic peculiarity comes to the fore, namely that its amount is by no means determined by the actions of its recipient, but rather by the independent development of social labour in which the recipient takes no part. It may easily happen, therefore, that something is regarded as a peculiarity of rent (and of the product of agriculture in general), which is really a common feature of all branches of production and all their products where the basis is commodity production — and, in particular, capitalist production, which is in its entirety commodity production.

The amount of ground rent (and with it the value of land) grows with social development as a result of the total social labour. On the one hand, this leads to an expansion of the market and of the demand for products of the soil, and, on the other, it stimulates the demand

---

[a] See present edition, Vol. 28, p. 332.

for land itself, which is a prerequisite of competitive production in all lines of business activity, even those which are not agricultural. More exactly — if one considers only the actual agricultural rent — rent, and thereby the value of the land, develops with the market for the products of the soil, and thus with the increase in the non-agricultural population, with its need and demand partly for means of subsistence and partly for raw materials. It is in the nature of the capitalist mode of production to continually reduce the agricultural population as compared with the non-agricultural, because in industry (in the strict sense) the increase of constant capital in relation to variable capital goes hand in hand with an absolute increase, though relative decrease, in variable capital; on the other hand, in agriculture the variable capital required for the exploitation of a certain plot of land decreases absolutely; it can thus only increase to the extent that new land is taken into cultivation, but this again requires as a prerequisite a still greater growth of the non-agricultural population.

In fact, we are not dealing here with a characteristic peculiarity of agriculture and its products. On the contrary, the same applies to all other branches of production and products where the basis is commodity production and its absolute form, capitalist production.

These products are commodities, or use values, which have an exchange value that is to be realised, to be converted into money, only in so far as other commodities form an equivalent for them, that is, other products confront them as commodities and values; thus, in so far as they are not produced as immediate means of subsistence for the producers themselves, but as commodities, as products which become use values only by their transformation into exchange values (money), by their alienation. The market for these commodities develops through the social division of labour; the division of productive labour mutually transforms their respective products into commodities, into equivalents for each other, making them mutually serve as markets. This is in no way peculiar to agricultural products.

Rent can develop as money rent only on the basis of commodity production, in particular capitalist production, and it develops to the same extent that agricultural production becomes commodity production, that is, to the same extent that non-agricultural production develops independently of agricultural production, for to that degree the agricultural product becomes commodity, exchange value, and value. In so far as commodity production and thus the production of value develops with capitalist production so does the production of surplus value and surplus product. But in the same proportion as the latter develops, landed property acquires the capacity of capturing an ever-increasing portion of this surplus value by means of its land monopoly and thereby, of raising the value of its rent and the price of the land itself. The capitalist still performs an active function in the development of this surplus value and surplus product. But the landowner need only appropriate the growing share in the surplus product and the surplus value, without having contributed anything to this growth. This is the characteristic peculiarity of his position, and not the fact that the value of the products of the land, and thus of the land itself, increases to the degree that the market for them expands, the demand grows and with it the world of commodities which confronts the products of the land — in other words, the mass of non-agricultural commodity producers and non-agricultural commodity production. But since this takes place without any action on his part, it appears to him as something unique that the mass of value, the mass of surplus value, and the transformation of a portion of surplus value into ground rent should depend upon the social production process, on the development of commodity production in general. For this reason, Dove, for instance, tries to evolve rent from this. He says that rent does not depend upon the mass of the agricultural product, but upon its value [a]; however, this depends upon the mass and productivity of the non-agricultural population. But it is also true of every other product that it can only develop as a commodity partly as the mass and partly as the variety of other commodities, which form equivalents for it, increase. This has already been demonstrated in connection with the general presentation of value. [b] On the one hand, the exchangeability of a product in general depends on the multiplicity of commodities existing in addition to it. On the other hand, on it depends in particular the quantity in which this product can be produced as a commodity.

No producer, whether industrial or agricultural, when considered by himself alone, produces value or commodities. His product becomes a value and a commodity only in the context of definite social interrelations. In the first place, in so far as it appears as the expression of social labour, hence in so far as the individual producer's labour time counts as a part of the social labour time in general; and, second-

---

[a] P. E. Dove, *The Elements of Political Science*, p. 279. - [b] See present edition, Vol. 29, pp. 280-81.

ly, this social character of his labour appears impressed upon his product through its pecuniary character and through its general exchangeability determined by its price.

Therefore, if, on the one hand, surplus value or, still more narrowly, the surplus product in general is explained instead of rent, the mistake is made, on the other hand, of ascribing exclusively to agricultural products a characteristic which belongs to all products in their capacity as commodities and values. This is vulgarised still more by those who pass from the general determination of value over to the *realisation* of the value of a specific commodity. Every commodity can realise its value only in the process of circulation, and whether it realises its value, or to what extent it does so, depends on prevailing market conditions.

It is not a singularity of ground rent, then, that agricultural products develop into, and as, values, i. e., that they confront other commodities as commodities, and that non-agricultural products confront them as commodities; or that they develop as specific expressions of social labour. The singularity of ground rent is rather that together with the conditions in which agricultural products develop as values (commodities), and together with the conditions in which their values are realised, there also grows the power of landed property to appropriate an increasing portion of these values, which were created without its assistance; and so an increasing portion of surplus value is transformed into ground rent.

Chapter XXXVIII
DIFFERENTIAL RENT: GENERAL REMARKS

In the analysis of ground rent we shall begin with the assumption that products paying such a rent, products in which a portion of the surplus value, and therefore also a portion of the total price, resolves itself into ground rent, i. e., that agricultural as well as mining products are sold at their prices of production like all other commodities. (It suffices for our purposes to confine ourselves to agricultural and mining products.) In other words, their selling prices are made up of the elements of their cost (the value of consumed constant and variable capital) plus a profit determined by the general rate of profit and calculated on the total advanced capital, whether consumed or not. We assume, then, that average selling prices of these products are equal to their prices of production. The question now arises how it is possible for ground rent to develop under these conditions, i. e., how it is possible for a portion of the profit to become transformed into ground rent, so that a portion of the commodity price falls to the landlord.

In order to demonstrate the general character of this form of ground rent, let us assume that most of the factories of a certain country derive their power from steam-engines, while a smaller number derive it from natural waterfalls. Let us further assume that the price of production in the former amounts to 115 for a quantity of commodities which have consumed a capital of 100. The 15% profit is calculated not solely on the consumed capital of 100, but on the total capital employed in the production of this commodity value. We have previously shown[a] that this price of production is not determined by the individual cost price of every single industrial producer, but by the average cost price of the commodity under average conditions of capital in the entire sphere of production. It is, in fact, the market price of production, the average market price as distinct from its oscillations. It is in general in the form of the market price, and, furthermore, in the form of the regulating market price, or market price of production, that the nature of the value of commodities asserts itself, its determination not by the labour time necessary in the case of any individual producer for the production of a certain quantity of commodities, or of some individual commodity, but by the socially necessary labour time; that is, by the labour time, required for the production of the socially necessary total quantity of commodity varieties on the market under the existing average conditions of social production.

As definite numerical proportions are immaterial in this case, we shall assume furthermore that the cost price in factories run on water power is only 90 instead of 100. Since the regulating market price of production of this quantity of commodities = 115, with a profit of 15%, the manufacturers who operate their machines on water power will also sell their commodities at 115, i. e., the average price regulating the market price. Their profit would then be 25 instead of 15; the regulating price of production would allow them a surplus profit of 10% not because they sell their commodities above the price of

---

production, but because they sell them at the price of production, because their commodities are produced, or their capital operates, under exceptionally favourable conditions, i. e., under conditions which are more favourable than the average prevailing in this sphere.

Two things become evident at once:

First, the surplus profit of the producers who use a natural waterfall as motive power is, to begin with, in the same class with all surplus profit (and we have already analysed this category when discussing prices of production)[a] which is not the fortuitous result of transactions in the circulation process, of the fortuitous fluctuations in market prices. This surplus profit, then, is likewise equal to the difference between the individual price of production of these favoured producers and the general social price of production regulating the market in this entire production sphere. This difference is equal to the excess of the general price of production of the commodities over their individual price of production. The two regulating limits of this excess are, on the one hand, the individual cost price, and thus the individual price of production, and, on the other hand, the general price of production. The value of commodities produced with water power is smaller because a smaller total quantity of labour is required for their production, i. e., less labour — in an objectified form — enters into the constant capital as part of the latter. The labour employed here is more productive, its individual productive power is greater than that employed in the majority of factories of the same kind. Its greater productive power is shown in the fact that in order to produce the same quantity of commodities, it requires a smaller quantity of constant capital, a smaller quantity of objectified labour, than the other. It also requires less living labour, because the water-wheel need not be heated. This greater individual productive power of employed labour reduces the value, but also the cost price and thereby the price of production of the commodity. For the industrial capitalist this expresses itself in a lower cost price for his commodities. He has to pay for less objectified labour, and also less wages for less living labour power employed. Since the cost price of his commodities is lower, his individual price of production is also lower. His cost price is 90 instead of 100. His individual price of production would therefore be only $103\frac{1}{2}$ instead of 115 ($100:115 = 90:103\frac{1}{2}$). The difference between his individual price of production and the general price of production

---

[a] See this volume, pp. 196-97.

is limited by the difference between his individual cost price and the general cost price. This is one of the magnitudes which form the limits to his surplus profit. The other is the magnitude of the general price of production into which the general rate of profit enters as one of the regulating factors. Were coal to become cheaper, the difference between his individual cost price and the general cost price would decrease, and with it his surplus profit. Should he be compelled to sell his commodities at their individual value, or at the price of production determined by their individual value, then the difference would disappear. It is, on the one hand, a result of the fact that the commodities are sold at their general market price, the price brought about by the equalisation of individual prices through competition, and, on the other, a result of the fact that the greater individual productive power of labour set in motion by him does not benefit the labourer, but the employer, as does all productive power of labour; that it appears as the productive power of capital.

Since the level of the general price of production is one of the limits of this surplus profit, the level of the general rate of profit being one of its factors, this surplus profit can only arise from the difference between the general and the individual price of production, and consequently from the difference between the general and the individual rate of profit. An excess above this difference presupposes the sale of products above, not at, the price of production regulated by the market.

Secondly, thus far, the surplus profit of the manufacturer using natural water power instead of steam does not differ in any way from any other surplus profit. All normal surplus profit, that is, all surplus profit not due to fortuitous sales or market price fluctuations is determined by the difference between the individual price of production of the commodities of a particular capital and the general price of production, which regulates the market prices of the commodities produced by the capital in this sphere of production in general, or, in other words, the market prices of commodities of the total capital invested in this sphere of production.

But now we come to the difference.

To what circumstance does the manufacturer in the present case owe his surplus profit, the surplus resulting for him personally from the price of production regulated by the general rate of profit?

He owes it in the first instance to a natural force — the motive power of the waterfall — which is found readily available in Nature and is not itself a product of labour like the coal which transforms water into steam. The coal, therefore, has value, must be paid for by an equivalent, and has a cost. The waterfall is a natural production agent in the production of which no labour enters.

But this is not all. The manufacturer who operates with steam also employs natural forces which cost him nothing yet make the labour more productive and increase the surplus value and thereby the profit, inasmuch as they thus cheapen the manufacture of the means of subsistence required for the labourers. These natural forces are thus quite as much monopolised by capital as the social natural forces of labour arising from co-operation, division of labour, etc. The manufacturer pays for coal, but not for the capacity of water to alter its physical state, to turn into steam, not for the elasticity of the steam, etc. This monopolisation of natural forces, that is, of the increase in labour power produced by them, is common to all capital operating with steam-engines. It may increase that portion of the product of labour which represents surplus value in relation to that portion which is transformed into wages. In so far as it does this, it raises the general rate of profit, but it does not create any surplus profit, for this consists precisely of the excess of individual profit over average profit. The fact that the application of a natural force, a waterfall, creates surplus profit in this case, cannot therefore be due solely to the circumstance that the increased productive power of labour here results from the application of a natural force. Other modifying circumstances are necessary.

Conversely. The mere application of natural forces in industry may influence the level of the general rate of profit because it affects the quantity of labour required to produce the necessary means of subsistence. But in itself it does not create any deviation from the general rate of profit, and this is precisely the point in which we are interested here. Furthermore, the surplus profit which some individual capital otherwise realises in a particular sphere of production — for deviations of the rates of profit in various spheres of production are continually balanced out into an average rate — is due, aside from purely fortuitous deviations, to a reduction in cost price, in production costs. This reduction arises either from the fact that capital is used in greater than average quantities, so that the *faux frais*ᵃ of production are reduced, while the general causes increasing the productive power of

___
ᵃ unproductive costs

labour (co-operation, division of labour, etc.) can become effective to a higher degree, with more intensity, because their field of activity has become larger; or it may arise from the fact that, aside from the amount of functioning capital, better methods of labour, new inventions, improved machinery, chemical manufacturing secrets, etc., in short, new and improved, better than average means of production and methods of production are used. The reduction in cost price and the surplus profit arising from it are here the result of the manner in which the functioning capital is invested. They result either from the fact that the capital is concentrated in the hands of one person in extraordinarily large quantities (a condition that is cancelled out as soon as equal magnitudes of capital are used on the average), or from the fact that a certain magnitude of capital functions in a particularly productive manner (a condition that disappears as soon as the exceptional method of production becomes general or is surpassed by a still more developed one).

The cause of the surplus profit, then, arises here from the capital itself (which includes the labour set in motion by it) whether it be due to the greater magnitude of capital employed or to its more efficient application; and, as a matter of fact, there is no particular reason why all capital in the same production sphere should not be invested in the same manner. On the contrary, the competition between capitals tends to cancel these differences more and more. The determination of value by the socially necessary labour time asserts itself through the cheapening of commodities and the compulsion to produce commodities under the same favourable conditions. But matters are different with the surplus profit of a manufacturer who makes use of the waterfall. The increased productive power of the labour used by him comes neither from the capital and labour itself, nor from the mere application of some natural force different from capital and labour but incorporated in the capital. It arises from the greater natural productive power of labour bound up with the application of a force of Nature, but not a force of Nature that is at the command of all capital in the same sphere of production, as for example the elasticity of steam. In other words, its application is not to be taken for granted whenever capital is generally invested in this sphere of production. On the contrary, it is a monopolisable force of Nature which, like the waterfall, is only at the command of those who have at their disposal particular portions of the earth and its appurtenances. It is by no means within the power of capital to call into existence this natural premise for a greater productive power of labour in the same manner as any capital may transform water into steam. It is found only locally in Nature and, wherever it does not exist, it cannot be established by a definite investment of capital. It is not bound to goods which labour can produce, such as machines and coal, but to specific natural conditions prevailing in certain portions of land. Those manufacturers who own waterfalls exclude those who do not from using this natural force, because land, and particularly land endowed with water power, is scarce. This does not prevent the amount of water power available for industrial purposes from being increased, even though the number of natural waterfalls in a given country is limited. The waterfall may be harnessed by man in order to fully exploit its motive force. If such exists, the water-wheel may be improved so as to make use of as much of the water power as possible; where the ordinary wheel is not suitable for the water supply, turbines may be used, etc. The possession of this natural force constitutes a monopoly in the hands of its owner; it is a condition for an increase in the productive power of the invested capital that cannot be established by the production process of the capital itself [33]; this natural force, which can be monopolised in this manner, is always bound to the land. Such a natural force does not belong to the general conditions of the sphere of production in question, nor to those conditions of the latter which may be generally established.

Now let us assume that the waterfalls, along with the land to which they belong, are held by individuals who are regarded as owners of these portions of the earth, i. e., who are landowners. These owners prevent the investment of capital in the waterfalls and their exploitation by capital. They can permit or forbid such utilisation. But a waterfall cannot be created by capital out of itself. Therefore, the surplus profit which arises from the employment of this waterfall is not due to capital, but to the utilisation of a natural force which can be monopolised, and has been monopolised, by capital. Under these circumstances, the surplus profit is transformed into ground rent, that is, it falls into possession of the owner of a waterfall. If the manufacturer pays the owner of a waterfall £10 annually, then his profit is £15, that

[33] Concerning extra profit, see the *Inquiry* (against Malthus).[a]

---

[a] Reference to *An Inquiry into Those Principles, Respecting the Nature of Demand and the Necessity of Consumption, lately advocated by Mr. Malthus*, London, 1821.

is, 15% on the £100 which then make up his cost of production; and he is just as well or possibly better off than all other capitalists in his sphere of production who operate with steam. It would not alter matters one bit if the capitalist himself should be the owner of a waterfall. He would, in such a case, pocket as before the surplus profit of £10 in his capacity as waterfall owner, and not in his capacity as capitalist; and precisely because this surplus does not stem from his capital as such, but rather from the control of a limited natural force distinct from his capital which can be monopolised, is it transformed into ground rent.

First, it is evident that this rent is always a differential rent, for it does not enter as a determining factor into the general production price of commodities, but rather is based on it. It invariably arises from the difference between the individual production price of a particular capital having command over the monopolised natural force and the general production price of the total capital invested in the sphere of production concerned.

Secondly, this ground rent does not arise from the absolute increase in the productive power of employed capital, or labour appropriated by it, since this can only reduce the value of commodities; it is due to the greater relative fruitfulness of specific separate capitals invested in a certain production sphere, as compared with investments of capital which are excluded from these exceptional and natural conditions favouring productive power. For instance, if the use of steam should offer overwhelming advantages not offered by the use of water power, despite the fact that coal has value and the water power has not, and if these advantages more than compensated for the expense, then, the water power would not be used and could not produce any surplus profit, and therefore could not produce any rent.

Thirdly, the natural force is not the source of surplus profit, but only its natural basis, because this natural basis permits an exceptional increase in the productive power of labour. In the same way, use value is in general the bearer of exchange value, but not its cause. If the same use value could be obtained without labour, it would have no exchange value, yet it would retain, as before, the same natural usefulness as use value. On the other hand, nothing can have exchange value unless it has use value, i. e., unless it is a natural bearer of labour. Were it not for the fact that the various values are averaged out into prices of production, and the various individual prices of production into a general price of production regulating the market, the mere increase in the productive power of labour through utilisation of the waterfall would merely lower the price of commodities produced with the aid of this waterfall, without increasing the share of profit contained in these commodities. Similarly, on the other hand, this increased productive power of labour itself would not be converted into surplus value were it not for the fact that capital appropriates the natural and social productive power of the labour used by it as its own.

Fourthly, the private ownership of the waterfall in itself has nothing to do with the creation of the surplus value (profit) portion, and therefore, of the price of the commodity in general, which is produced by means of the waterfall. This surplus profit would also exist if landed property did not exist; for instance, if the land on which the waterfall is situated were used by the manufacturer as unclaimed land. Hence landed property does not create the portion of value which is transformed into surplus profit, but merely enables the landowner, the owner of the waterfall, to coax this surplus profit out of the pocket of the manufacturer and into his own. It is not the cause of the creation of such surplus profit, but is the cause of its transformation into the form of ground rent, and therefore of the appropriation of this portion of the profit, or commodity price, by the owner of the land or waterfall.

Fifthly, it is evident that the price of the waterfall, that is, the price which the landowner would receive were he to sell it to a third party or even to the manufacturer himself, does not immediately enter into the production price of the commodities, although it does enter into the individual cost price of the manufacturer; because the rent arises here from the price of production of similar commodities produced by steam machinery, and this price is regulated independently of the waterfall. Furthermore, this price of the waterfall on the whole is an irrational expression, but behind it is hidden a real economic relationship. The waterfall, like land in general, and like any natural force, has no value because it does not represent any objectified labour, and therefore, it has no price, which is normally no more than the expression of value in money terms. Where there is no value, there is also *eo ipso* nothing to be expressed in money. This price is nothing more than the capitalised rent. Landed property enables the owner to appropriate the difference between the individual profit and average profit. The profit thus acquired, which is renewed every year, may be capitalised, and appears then as the price of the natural force itself.

If the surplus profit realised by the manufacturer using the waterfall amounts to £10 per year, and the average interest is 5%, then these £10 represent the annual interest on a capital of £200 and the capitalisation of the annual £10 which the waterfall enables its owner to appropriate from the manufacturer, appears then as the capital value of the waterfall itself. That it is not the waterfall itself which has value, but that its price is a mere reflection of the appropriated surplus profit capitalistically calculated, becomes at once evident from the fact that the price of £200 represents merely the product obtained by multiplying a surplus profit of £10 by 20 years, whereas, other conditions remaining equal, the same waterfall will enable its owner to appropriate these £10 every year for an indefinite number of years — 30 years, 100 years, or x years; and, whereas, on the other hand, should some new method of production not applicable with water power reduce the cost price of commodities produced by steam machinery from £100 to £90, the surplus profit, and thereby the rent, and thus the price of the waterfall, would disappear.

Now that we have described the general concept of differential rent, we shall pass on to its consideration in agriculture proper. What applies to agriculture will also apply on the whole to mining.

Chapter XXXIX

FIRST FORM OF DIFFERENTIAL RENT
(DIFFERENTIAL RENT I)

Ricardo is quite right in the following observations:

"RENT IS ALWAYS THE DIFFERENCE BETWEEN THE PRODUCE OBTAINED BY THE EMPLOYMENT OF TWO EQUAL QUANTITIES OF CAPITAL AND LABOUR" (*Principles*, p. 59).[a]

//He means differential rent, for he assumes that no other rent but differential rent exists.//

He should have added, "on equal areas of land" in so far as it is a matter of ground rent and not surplus profit in general.

In other words, surplus profit, if normal and not due to accidental occurrences in the circulation process, is always produced as a difference between the products of two equal quantities of capital and labour, and this surplus profit is transformed into ground rent when

---

[a] A reference to: *On the Principles of Political Economy, and Taxation*, London, 1821.

two equal quantities of capital and labour are employed on equal areas of land with unequal results. Moreover, it is by no means absolutely necessary for this surplus profit to arise from the unequal results of equal quantities of invested capital. The various investments may also employ unequal quantities of capital. Indeed, this is generally the case. But equal proportions, for instance £100 of each, produce unequal results; that is, their rates of profit are different. This is the general prerequisite for the existence of surplus profit in any sphere of capital investment. The second prerequisite is the transformation of this surplus profit into the form of ground rent (of rent in general as a form distinct from profit); it must be investigated in each case: when, how, under what conditions this transformation takes place.

Ricardo is also right in the following observation, provided it is limited to differential rent:

"WHATEVER DIMINISHES THE INEQUALITY IN THE PRODUCE OBTAINED ON THE SAME OR ON NEW LAND, TENDS TO LOWER RENT, AND WHATEVER INCREASES THAT INEQUALITY, NECESSARILY PRODUCES AN OPPOSITE EFFECT AND TENDS TO RAISE IT" (p. 74).

However, among these causes are not merely the general ones (fertility and location), but also 1) the distribution of taxes, depending on whether it operates uniformly or not; the latter is always the case when, as in England, it is not centralised and when the tax is levied on land, not on rent; 2) the inequalities arising from a difference in agricultural development in different parts of the country, since this line of production, owing to its traditional character, evens out with more difficulty than manufacture; and 3) the inequality in distribution of capital among tenants. Since the invasion of agriculture by the capitalist mode of production, transformation of independently producing peasants into wage-workers, is in fact the last conquest of this mode of production, these inequalities are greater here than in any other line of production.

Having made these preliminary remarks, I will first present a brief summary of the characteristic features of my analysis in contradistinction to that of Ricardo, etc.

———

We shall first consider the unequal results of equal quantities of capital applied to different plots of land of equal size; or, in the case of unequal size, results calculated on the basis of equal areas.

The two general causes of these unequal results — quite independent of capital — are: 1) *Fertility*. (With reference to this first point, it will be necessary to discuss what is meant by natural fertility of land and what diverse factors are involved.) 2) The *location* of the land. This is a decisive factor in the case of colonies and in general determines the sequence in which plots of land can be cultivated. Furthermore, it is evident that these two different causes of differential rent—fertility and location—may work in opposite directions. A certain plot of land may be very favourably located and yet be very poor in fertility, and vice versa. This circumstance is important, for it explains how it is possible that bringing into cultivation the land of a certain country may equally well proceed from the better to the worse land as vice versa. Finally, it is clear that the progress of social production in general has, on the one hand, the effect of evening out differences due to location as a cause of differential rent, by creating local markets and improving locations through establishing communication and transportation facilities; on the other hand, it increases the differences in individual locations of plots of land by separating agriculture from manufacture and by forming large centres of production, on the one hand, while relatively isolating agricultural districts, on the other.

For the present, however, we shall leave this point concerning location out of consideration and confine ourselves to natural fertility. Aside from climatic factors, etc., the difference in natural fertility depends on the difference in the chemical composition of the top soil, that is, on its different plant nutrition content. However, assuming the chemical composition and natural fertility in this respect to be the same for two plots of land, the actual effective fertility differs depending on whether these elements of plant nutrition are in a form which may be more or less easily assimilated and immediately utilised for nourishing the crops. Hence, it will depend partly upon chemical and partly upon mechanical developments in agriculture to what extent the same natural fertility may be made available on plots of land of similar natural fertility. Fertility, although an objective property of the soil, always implies an economic relation, a relation to the existing chemical and mechanical level of development in agriculture, and, therefore, changes with this level of development. Whether by chemical means (such as the use of certain liquid fertilisers on stiff clay soil and calcination of heavy clayey soils) or mechanical means (such as special ploughs for heavy soils), the obstacles which made a soil of equal fertility actually less fertile can be eliminated (drainage also belongs under this head). Or even the sequence in types of soils taken under cultivation may be changed thereby, as was the case, for instance, with light sandy soil and heavy clayey soil at a certain period of development in English agriculture. This shows once again that historically, in the sequence of soils taken under cultivation, one may pass over from more fertile to less fertile soils as well as vice versa. The same results may be obtained by an artificially created improvement in soil composition or by a mere change in agricultural methods. Finally, the same result may be brought about by a change in the hierarchical arrangement of the soil types due to different conditions of the subsoil, as soon as the latter likewise begins to be tilled and turned over into top layers. This is in part dependent on the employment of new agricultural methods (such as the cultivation of fodder grass) and in part on the employment of mechanical means which either turn the subsoil over into top layers, mix it with top soil, or cultivate the subsoil without turning it up.

All these influences upon the differential fertility of various plots of land are such that from the standpoint of economic fertility the level of the productive power of labour, in this case the capacity of agriculture to make the natural soil fertility immediately exploitable — a capacity which differs in various periods of development — is as much a factor in so-called natural soil fertility as its chemical composition and other natural properties.

We assume, then, the existence of a particular stage of development in agriculture. We assume furthermore that the hierarchical arrangement of soil types accords with this stage of development, as is, of course, always the case for simultaneous capital investments on different plots of land. Differential rent may then form either an ascending or a descending sequence, for although the sequence is given for the totality of actually cultivated plots of land, a series of movements leading to its formation has invariably taken place.

Let us assume the existence of four kinds of soil: A, B, C, D. Let us furthermore assume the price of one quarter of wheat = £3, or 60 shillings. Since the rent is solely differential rent, this price of 60 shillings per quarter for the worst soil is equal to the price of production,[80] that is, equal to the capital plus average profit.

Let A be this worst soil, which yields 1 quarter = 60 shillings for each 50 shillings spent; hence the profit amounts to 10 shillings, or 20%.

Let B yield 2 quarters = 120 shillings for the same expenditure. This would mean 70 shillings of profit, or a surplus profit of 60 shillings.

Let C yield 3 quarters = 180 shillings for the same expenditure; total profit = 130 shillings; surplus profit = 120 shillings.

Let D yield 4 quarters = 240 shillings = 180 shillings of surplus profit.

We would then have the following sequence:

TABLE I

Type of Soil	Product		Capital Advanced	Profit		Rent	
	Quarters	Shillings		Quarters	Shillings	Quarters	Shillings
A	1	60	50	$^1/_6$	10	—	—
B	2	120	50	$1^1/_6$	70	1	60
C	3	180	50	$2^1/_6$	130	2	120
D	4	240	50	$3^1/_6$	190	3	180
Total. . .	10 qrs	600sh.				6 qrs	360sh.

The respective rents are: D = 190sh.— 10sh., or the difference between D and A; C = 130sh.— 10sh., or the difference between C and A; B = 70sh.— 10sh., or the difference between B and A; and the total rent for B, C, D = 6 quarters = 360 shillings, equal to the sum of the differences between D and A, C and A, B and A.

This sequence, which represents a given product in a given condition may, considered abstractly (we have already offered the reasons why this may be the case in reality), descend from D to A, from fertile to less and less fertile soil, or rise from A to D, from relatively poor to more and more fertile soil, or, finally, may fluctuate, i. e., now rising, now descending — for instance from D to C, from C to A, and from A to B.

The process in the case of a descending sequence was as follows: The price of a quarter of wheat rose gradually from, say, 15 shillings to 60 shillings. As soon as the 4 quarters produced by D (we may consider these 4 quarters as so many million quarters) no longer sufficed, the price of wheat rose to a point where the supply shortage could be produced by C. That is to say, the price of wheat must have risen to 20 shillings per quarter. When it had risen to 30 shillings per quarter, B could be taken under cultivation, and when it reached 60 shillings A could be taken under cultivation; and the capital invested did not have to content itself with a rate of profit lower than 20%. In this manner, a rent was established for D, first of 5 shillings per quarter = 20 shillings for the 4 quarters produced by it; then of 15 shillings per quarter = 60 shillings, then of 45 shillings per quarter = 180 shillings for 4 quarters.

If the rate of profit of D originally was similarly = 20%, then its total profit on 4 quarters of wheat was also but 10 shillings, but this represented more grain when the price was 15 shillings than it does when the price is 60 shillings. But since the grain enters into the reproduction of labour power, and part of each quarter has to make good some portion of wages and another constant capital, the surplus value under these conditions was higher, and thus other things being equal the rate of profit too. (The matter of the rate of profit will have to be specially analysed, and in greater detail.)

On the other hand, if the sequence were in the reverse order, that is, if the process initiated from A, then the price of wheat at first would rise above 60 shillings per quarter when new land would have to be taken under cultivation. But since the necessary supply would be produced by B, a supply of 2 quarters, the price would fall to 60 shillings again; for B produced wheat at a cost of 30 shillings per quarter, but sold it at 60 shillings because his supply just sufficed to cover the demand. Thus a rent was formed, first of 60 shillings for B, and in the same way for C and D; it is assumed throughout that the market price remained at 60 shillings, although C and D produced wheat having an actual value of 20 and 15 shillings per quarter respectively, because the supply of the one quarter produced by A was needed as much as ever to satisfy the total demand. In this case, the increase in demand above supply, which was first satisfied by A, then by A and B, would not have made it possible to cultivate B, C and D successively, but would merely have caused a general extension of the sphere of cultivation, and the more fertile lands might only later come under cultivation.

In the first sequence, an increase in price would raise the rent and decrease the rate of profit. Such a decrease might be entirely or partially checked by counteracting circumstances. This point will have to be treated later in more detail. It should not be forgotten that the general rate of profit is not determined uniformly in *all* spheres of production by the surplus value. It is not the agricultural profit which determines industrial profit, but vice versa.[81] But of this more anon.

In the second sequence the rate of profit on invested capital would remain the same. The amount of profit would be represented by less grain; but the relative price of grain, compared with that of other commodities, would have risen. However, the increase in profit wherever such an increase takes place, becomes separated from the profit in the form of rent, instead of flowing into the pockets of the capitalist tenant farmer and appearing as a growing profit. The price of grain, however, would remain unchanged under the conditions assumed here.

The development and growth of differential rent would remain the same for fixed as well as for increasing prices, and for a continuous progression from worse to better soils as well as for a continuous retrogression from better to worse soils.

Thus far we have assumed: 1) that the price rises in one sequence and remains stationary in the other; 2) that there is a continuous progression from better to worse soil, or from worse to better soil.

But now let us assume that the demand for grain rises from its original figure of 10 to 17 quarters; furthermore, that the worst soil A is displaced by another soil A, which produces $1\frac{1}{3}$ quarters at a price of production of 60 shillings (50sh. cost plus 10sh. for 20% profit), so that its price of production per quarter = 45 shillings; or, perhaps, the old soil A may have improved through continuous rational cultivation, or be cultivated more productively at the same cost, for instance through the introduction of clover, etc., so that its output with the investment of capital rises to $1\frac{1}{3}$ quarters. Let us also assume that soil types B, C and D yield the same output as previously, but that new soil types have been introduced, for instance, A' with a fertility lying between A and B, and also B' and B" with a fertility between B and C. We should then observe the following phenomena:

First: The price of production of a quarter of wheat, or its regulating market price, falls from 60 shillings to 45 shillings, or by 25%.

Second: The cultivation proceeds simultaneously from more fertile to less fertile soil, and from less fertile to more fertile soil. Soil A' is more fertile than A, but less fertile than the hitherto cultivated soils B, C and D. B' and B" are more fertile than A, A' and B, but less fertile than C and D. The sequence thus proceeds in crisscross fashion. Cultivation does not proceed to soil absolutely less fertile than A, etc., but to relatively less fertile soil with respect to the hitherto most fertile soil types C and D; on the other hand, cultivation does not proceed to soil absolutely more fertile, but to relatively more fertile soil with respect to the hitherto least fertile soil A, or A and B.

Thirdly: The rent on B falls; likewise the rent on C and D; but the total rental in grain rises from 6 quarters to $7\frac{2}{3}$; the amount of cultivated and rent-yielding land increases, and the amount of produce rises from 10 quarters to 17. The profit, although it remains the same for A, rises if expressed in grain, but the rate of profit itself might rise, because the relative surplus value does. In this case, the wage, i. e., the investment of variable capital and therefore the total outlay, is reduced because of the cheapening of means of subsistence. This total rental expressed in money falls from 360 shillings to 345 shillings.

Let us draw up the new sequence. //Table II.//

TABLE II

Type of Soil	Product		Capital Invested	Profit		Rent		Price of Production per Quarter
	Quarters	Shillings		Quarters	Shillings	Quarters	Shillings	
A	$1^1/_3$	60	50	$^2/_9$	10	—	—	45 sh.
A′	$1^2/_3$	75	50	$^5/_9$	25	$^1/_3$	15	36 sh.
B	2	90	50	$^8/_9$	40	$^2/_3$	30	30 sh.
B′	$2^1/_3$	105	50	$1^2/_9$	55	1	45	$25^5/_7$ sh.
B″	$2^2/_3$	120	50	$1^5/_9$	70	$1^1/_3$	60	$22^1/_2$ sh.
C	3	135	50	$1^8/_9$	85	$1^2/_3$	75	20 sh.
D	4	180	50	$2^8/_9$	130	$2^2/_3$	120	15 sh.
Total...	17					$7^2/_3$	345	

Finally, if only soil types A, B, C and D were cultivated as before, but their productiveness rose in such a way that A produced 2 quarters instead of 1 quarter, B — 4 quarters instead of 2, C — 7 quarters instead of 3, and D — 10 quarters instead of 4, so that the same causes affect the various types of soil differently, the total production increases from 10 quarters to 23. Assuming that demand absorbs these 23 quarters through an increase in population and a fall in prices, we should obtain the following result:

TABLE III

Type of Soil	Product		Capital Invested	Price of Production per Quarter	Profit		Rent	
	Quarters	Shillings			Quarters	Shillings	Quarters	Shillings
A	2	60	50	30	$^1/_3$	10	0	0
B	4	120	50	15	$2^1/_3$	70	2	60
C	7	210	50	$8^4/_7$	$5^1/_3$	160	5	150
D	10	300	50	6	$8^1/_3$	250	8	240
Total...	23						15	450

The numerical proportions in this and in other tables are chosen at random but the assumptions are quite rational.

The first and principal assumption is that an improvement in agriculture acts differently upon different soils, and in this case affects the best types of soil, C and D, more than types A and B. Experience has shown that this is generally the case, although the opposite may also take place. If the improvement affected the poorer soils more than the better ones, rent on the latter would have fallen instead of risen.— But in our table, we have assumed that the absolute growth in fertility of all soil types is simultaneously accompanied by an increase in greater relative fertility of the better soil types, C and D; this means an increase in the difference between the product at the same capital investment, and thus an increase in differential rent.

The second assumption is that total demand keeps pace with the increase in the total product. *First*, one need not imagine such an increase coming about abruptly, but rather gradually — until sequence III is established. *Secondly*, it is not true that the consumption of necessities of life does not increase as they become cheaper. The abolition of the Corn Laws [73] in England proved the reverse to be the case (see Newman[a]); the opposite view stems solely from the fact that large and sudden differences in harvests, which are mere results of weather, bring about at one time an extraordinary fall, at another an extraordinary rise, in grain prices. While in such a case the sudden and short-lived reduction in price does not have time to exert its full effect upon the extension of consumption, the opposite is true when a reduction arises from the lowering of the regulating price of production itself, i. e., is of a long-term nature. *Thirdly*, a part of the grain may be consumed in the form of brandy or beer; and the increasing consumption of both of these items is by no means confined within narrow limits. *Fourthly*, the matter depends in part upon the increase in population and in part on the fact that the country may be grain-exporting, as England still was long after the middle of the 18th century, so that the demand is not solely regulated within the confines of national consumption. *Finally*, the increase and the cheapness of wheat production may result in making wheat, instead of rye or oats, the principal article of consumption for the masses, so that the demand for it may grow if only for this reason, just as the opposite may take place when production decreases and prices rise.— Thus, under these assump-

---

[a] F. W. Newman, *Lectures on Political Economy*, p. 158.

tions, and with the previously selected ratios, sequence III yields the result that the price per quarter falls from 60 to 30 shillings, that is, by 50%; that production, compared to sequence I, increases from 10 to 23 quarters, i. e., by 130%; that the rent remains fixed for soil B, increases by 25%[a] for C, and by $33\frac{1}{3}$%[b] for D; and that the total rental increases from £18 to £22$\frac{1}{2}$,[c] i. e., by 25%.[d]

A comparison of these three tables (whereby sequence I is to be taken twice, rising from A to D, and descending from D to A), which may be considered either as given gradations under some stage of society, for instance, as existing side by side in three different countries, or as succeeding one another in different periods of development within the same country, shows:

1) The sequence, when complete, whatever the course of its formative process may have been, invariably appears as being in a descending line; for when analysing rent the point of departure will always be land yielding the maximum rent, and only finally do we come to land yielding no rent.

2) The price of production on the worst soil, i. e., which yields no rent, is always the one regulating the market price, although the latter in Table I, if its sequence were formed in an ascending line, only remained fixed because better and better soil was constantly drawn into cultivation. In such a case, the price of grain produced on the best soil is a regulating one in so far as it depends upon the quantity produced on such soil to what extent soil type A remains the regulator. If B, C and D should produce more than demand requires, A would cease to be the regulator. Storch has this point in mind when he adopts the best soil type as the regulating one.[e] In this manner, the American price of grain regulates the English price.

3) Differential rent arises from differences in the natural fertility of the soil which is given for every given stage of agricultural development (leaving aside for the present the question of location); in other words, from the limited area of the best land, and from the circumstance that equal amounts of capital must be invested on unequal types of soil, so that an unequal product results from the same amount of capital.

---

[a] In the 1894 German edition this reads: doubles. - [b] Ibid.: more than doubles. - [c] Ibid.: 22. - [d] Ibid.: 22^1/$_9$%. - [e] H. Storch, *Cours d'économie politique, ou Exposition des principes qui déterminent la prospérité des nations*, Tome II, pp. 78-79. See also this volume, p. 182.

4) The existence of a differential rent and of a graduated differential rent can develop equally well in a descending sequence, which proceeds from better to worse soils, as in an ascending one, which progresses in the opposite direction from worse to better soils; or it may be brought about in checkered fashion by alternating movements. (Sequence I may be formed by proceeding from D to A, or from A to D; sequence II comprises both types of movement.)

5) Depending on its mode of formation, differential rent may develop along with a stationary, rising or falling price of the products of the land. In the case of a falling price, total production and total rental may rise, and rent may develop on hitherto rentless land, even though the worst soil A may have been displaced by a better one or may itself have improved, and even though the rent may decrease on other land which is better, or even the best (Table II); this process may also be connected with a fall in total rent (in money). Finally, at a time when prices fall on account of a general improvement in cultivation, so that the product of the worst soil and its price decrease, the rent on some of the better soils may remain the same, or may fall, while it may rise on the best ones. Nevertheless, the differential rent of every soil, compared with the worst soil, depends, if the difference in quantity of products is given, upon the price, say, of a quarter of wheat. But when the price is given, differential rent depends upon the magnitude of the difference in quantity of products, and if with an increasing absolute fertility of all soils that of the better ones grows relatively more than that of the worse ones, the magnitude of this difference grows proportionately. In this way (Table I), when the price is 60 shillings, the rent on D is determined by its differential product as compared with A; in other words, by the surplus of 3 quarters. The rent is therefore = 3 × 60 = 180 shillings. But in Table III, where the price = 30 shillings, the rent is determined by the quantity of surplus product of D as compared with A = 8 quarters; we therefore obtain 8 × 30 = 240 shillings.

This takes care of the first false assumption regarding differential rent—still found among West, Malthus, and Ricardo—namely, that it necessarily presupposes a movement toward worse and worse soil, or an ever-decreasing fertility of the soil.[82] It can be formed, as we have seen, with a movement toward better and better soil; it can be formed when a better soil takes the lowest position that was formerly occupied by the worst soil; it can be connected with a progressive improvement in agriculture. The precondition is merely the inequality of different kinds of soil. So far as the increase in productivity is concerned, it assumes that the increase in absolute fertility of the total area does not eliminate this inequality, but either increases it, leaves it unchanged, or merely reduces it.

From the beginning to the middle of the 18th century, England's grain prices constantly fell in spite of the falling prices of gold and silver, while at the same time (viewing this entire period as a whole) there was an increase in rent, in the over-all amount of rent, in the area of cultivated land, in agricultural production, and in population. This corresponds to Table I taken in conjunction with Table II in an ascending line, but in such a way that the worst land A is either improved or eliminated from the grain-producing area; however, this does not mean that it was not used for other agricultural or industrial purposes.

From the early 19th century (date to be specified more precisely) until 1815 there is a constant rise in grain prices, accompanied by a steady increase in rent, in the over-all amount of rent, in the area of cultivated land, in agricultural production, and in population. This corresponds to Table I in a descending line. (Cite some sources here on the cultivation of inferior land in that period.)

In Petty's and Davenant's time, farmers and landowners complained about improvements and the bringing into cultivation of new land; the rent on better lands decreased, and the total amount of rent increased through the extension of the area of land yielding rent.

(These three points should be illustrated later by further quotations; likewise the difference in fertility of various cultivated sections of land in a particular country.)

Regarding differential rent in general, it is to be noted that the market value is always above the total price of production of the total quantity of products. As an example, let us take Table I. Ten quarters of total product are sold for 600 shillings because the market price is determined by the price of production of A, which amounts to 60 shillings per quarter. But the actual price of production is:

A	1 qr = 60 sh.	1 qr = 60 sh.
B	2 qrs = 60 sh.	1 qr = 30 sh.
C	3 qrs = 60 sh.	1 qr = 20 sh.
D	4 qrs = 60 sh.	1 qr = 15 sh.

10 qrs = 240 sh. Average
1 qr = 24 sh.

The actual price of production of these 10 quarters is 240 shillings; but they are sold for 600 shillings, i. e., at 250% of the price of production. The actual average price for 1 quarter is 24 shillings; the market price is 60 shillings, i. e., also 250% of the production price.

This is determination by market value as it asserts itself on the basis of the capitalist mode of production through competition; the latter creates a false social value. This arises from the law of market value, to which the products of the soil are subject. The determination of the market value of products, including therefore agricultural products, is a social act, albeit a socially unconscious and unintentional one. It is based necessarily upon the exchange value of the product, not upon the soil and the differences in its fertility. If we suppose the capitalist form of society to be abolished and society organised as a conscious and planned association, then the 10 quarters would represent a quantity of independent labour time equal to that contained in 240 shillings. Society would not then buy this agricultural product at two and a half times the actual labour time embodied in it and the basis for a class of landowners would thus be destroyed. This would have the same effect as a reduction in price of the product to the same amount resulting from foreign imports. While it is, therefore, true that, by retaining the present mode of production, but assuming that the differential rent is paid to the state, prices of agricultural products would, everything else being equal, remain the same, it is equally wrong to say that the value of the products would remain the same if capitalist production were superseded by association. The identity of the market price for commodities of the same kind is the manner whereby the social character of value asserts itself on the basis of the capitalist mode of production and, in general, any production based on the exchange of commodities between *individuals*. What society overpays for agricultural products in its capacity of consumer, what is a minus in the realisation of its labour time in agricultural production, is now a plus for a portion of society, for the landlords.

A second circumstance, important for the analysis to be given under II in the next chapter, is the following:

It is not merely a matter of rent per acre, or per hectare, nor generally of a difference between the price of production and the market price, nor between the individual and the general price of production per acre, but it is also a question of how many acres of each type of soil are under cultivation. The point of importance here relates directly only to the magnitude of the rental, that is, the total rent of the entire cultivated area; but it serves us at the same time as a stepping-stone to the consideration of a rise in the *rate of rent* although there is no rise in prices, nor increase in the differences in relative fertility of the various types of soil if prices fall. We had above:

TABLE I

Type of Soil	Acres	Price of Production	Product	Rent in Grain	Rent in Money
A	1	£3	1 qr	0	0
B	1	£3	2 qrs	1 qr	£3
C	1	£3	3 qrs	2 qrs	£6
D	1	£3	4 qrs	3 qrs	£9
Total	4 acres		10 qrs	6 qrs	£18

Now let us assume that the number of cultivated acres is doubled in every category. We then have:

TABLE Ia

Type of Soil	Acres	Price of Production	Product	Rent in Grain	Rent in Money
A	2	£6	2 qrs	0	0
B	2	£6	4 qrs	2 qrs	£6
C	2	£6	6 qrs	4 qrs	£12
D	2	£6	8 qrs	6 qrs	£18
Total	8 acres		20 qrs	12 qrs	£36

Let us assume two more cases. Suppose in the first case production expands on the two poorest types of soil in the following manner:

TABLE Ib

| Type of Soil | Acres | Price of Production | | Product | Rent in Grain | Rent in Money |
		Per Acre	Total			
A	4	£3	£12	4 qrs	0	0
B	4	£3	£12	8 qrs	4 qrs	£12
C	2	£3	£6	6 qrs	4 qrs	£12
D	2	£3	£6	8 qrs	6 qrs	£18
Total	12 acres		£36	26 qrs	14 qrs	£42

and, finally, let us assume an unequal expansion of production and cultivated area for the four soil categories:

TABLE Ic

Type of Soil	Acres	Price of Production		Product	Rent in Grain	Rent in Money
		Per Acre	Total			
A	1	£3	£3	1 qr	0	0
B	2	£3	£6	4 qrs	2 qrs	£6
C	5	£3	£15	15 qrs	10 qrs	£30
D	4	£3	£12	16 qrs	12 qrs	£36
Total	12 acres		£36	36 qrs	24 qrs	£72

In the first place, the rent per acre remains the same in all these cases — I, Ia, Ib and Ic — for, in fact, the result of the same investment of capital per acre of the same soil type has remained unchanged. We have only assumed what is true of any country at any given moment; namely, that various soil types exist in definite ratios to the total cultivated area. And we also assumed what is always true of any two countries being compared, or of the same country at different periods, namely, that the proportions in which the total cultivated area is distributed among the different soil types vary.

In comparing Ia with I we see that if the area under cultivation in all four categories increases in the same proportion a doubling of the cultivated acreage doubles the total production, and that the same applies to the rent in grain and money.

However, if we compare Ib and then Ic with I, we see that in both cases a tripling of the area under cultivation occurs. It increases in both cases from 4 acres to 12, but in Ib classes A and B contribute most to the increase, with A yielding no rent and B yielding the smallest amount of differential rent. Thus, out of the 8 newly cultivated acres, A and B account for 3 each, i e., 6 together, whereas C and D account for 1 each, i. e., 2 together. In other words, three-quarters of the increase is accounted for by A and B, and only one-quarter by C and D. With this premise, in Ib compared with I the trebled area of cultivation does not result in a trebled product, for the product does not increase from 10 to 30, but only to 26. On the other hand, since a considerable part of the increase concerns A, which does not yield any rent, and since the major part of the increase on better soils concerns B, the rent in grain rises only from 6 to 14 quarters, and the rent in money from £18 to £42.

But if we compare Ic with I, where the land yielding no rent does not increase in area and the land yielding a minimum rent increases but slightly, while C and D account for the major part of the increase, we find that when the cultivated area is trebled production increases from 10 to 36 quarters, i. e., to more than three times its original amount. The rent in grain increases from 6 to 24 quarters or to four times its original amount; and similarly money rent, from £18 to £72.

In all these cases it is in the nature of things that the price of the agricultural product remains unchanged. The total rental increases in all cases with the extension of cultivation, unless it takes place exclusively on the worst soil, which does not yield any rent. But this increase varies. Should this extension involve the better soil types and the total output, consequently, increase not merely in proportion to the extension of the area, but rather more rapidly, then the rent in grain and money increases to the same extent. Should it be the worst soil, and the types of soil close to it, that are principally involved in the extension (whereby it is assumed that the worst soil represents a constant type), the total rental does not increase in proportion to the extension of cultivation. Thus, given two countries in which soil A, yielding no rent, is of the same quality, the rental is inversely proportional to the aliquot part represented by the worst soil and the inferior soil types in the total area under cultivation, and therefore inversely proportional to the output, assuming equal capital investments on equal total land areas. A relationship between the quantity of the worst and the quantity of the better cultivated land in the total land area of a given country thus has an opposite influence on the total rental than the relationship between the quality of the worst cultivated land and the quality of the better and best has on the rent per acre and — other circumstances remaining the same — on the total rental. Confusion between these two points has given rise to all kinds of erroneous objections raised against differential rent.

The total rental, then, increases by the mere extension of cultivation, and by the consequent greater investment of capital and labour in the land.

But the most important point is this: Although it is our assumption that the ratio of rents per acre for the various kinds of soil remains the same, and therefore also the rate of rent considered with reference to capital invested in each acre, yet the following is to be observed: If we compare Ia with I, the case in which the number of cultivated acres and the capital invested in them have been proportionately increased, we find that as the total production has increased proportionately to the expanded cultivated area, i. e., as both have been doubled, so has the rental. It has risen from £18 to £36, just as the number of acres has risen from 4 to 8.

If we take the total area of 4 acres, we find that the total rental amounted to £18 and thus the average rent, including the land which does not yield any rent is £4 $\frac{1}{2}$. Such a calculation might be made, say, by a landlord owning all 4 acres; and in this way the average rent is statistically computed for a whole country. The total rental of £18 is obtained by the investment of a capital of £10. We call the ratio of these two figures the rate of rent; in the present case it is therefore 180%.

The same rate of rent obtains in Ia, where 8 instead of 4 acres are cultivated, but all types of land have contributed to the increase in the same proportion. The total rental of £36 yields for 8 acres and an invested capital of £20 an average rent of £4$\frac{1}{2}$ per acre and a rate of rent of 180%.

But if we consider Ib, where the increase has taken place mainly upon two inferior categories of soil, we obtain a rent of £42 for 12 acres, or an average rent of £3 $\frac{1}{2}$ per acre. The total invested capital is £30, and therefore the rate of rent = 140%. The average rent per acre has thus decreased by £1, and the rate of rent has fallen from 180 to 140%. Here then we have a rise in the total rental from £18 to £42, but a drop in the average rent calculated per acre as well as on the basis of capital; the drop takes place parallel to an increase in production, but not proportionately. This occurs even though the rent for all types of soil, calculated per acre as well as on the basis of capital outlay, remains the same. This occurs because three-quarters of the increase is accounted for by soil A, which does not yield any rent, and soil B, which yields only minimum rent.

If the total extension in Case Ib had taken place solely on soil A, we should have 9 acres on A, 1 acre on B, 1 acre on C and 1 acre on D. The total rental would be £18, the same as before; the average rent for the 12 acres therefore would be £1$\frac{1}{2}$ per acre; and a rent of £18 on an invested capital of £30 would give a rate of rent of 60%. The average rent, calculated per acre as well as on the basis of the invested capital, would have greatly decreased, while the total rental would not have increased.

Finally, let us compare Ic with I and Ib. Compared with I, the area has been trebled, and also the invested capital. The total rental is £72 for 12 acres, or £6 per acre — as against £$4\frac{1}{2}$ in Case I. The rate of rent on the invested capital (£72:£30) is 240% instead of 180%. The total output has risen from 10 to 36 quarters.

Compared with Ib, where the total number of cultivated acres, the invested capital, and the differences between the cultivated soil types are the same, but the distribution different, the output is 36 quarters instead of 26 quarters, the average rent per acre is £6 instead of £$3\frac{1}{2}$, and the rate of rent with reference to the same total advanced capital is 240% instead of 140%.

No matter whether we regard the various conditions in tables Ia, Ib and Ic as existing simultaneously side by side in different countries, or as existing successively in the same country, we come to the following conclusions: So long as the price of grain remains unchanged because the yield on the worst, rentless soil remains the same; so long as the difference in the fertility of the various cultivated types of soil remains the same; so long the respective outputs remain the same, hence, given equal capital investments on equal aliquot parts (acres) of cultivated area in every type of soil; so long as the ratio, therefore, between the rents per acre on each category of soil is constant, and the rate of rent on the capital invested in each plot of the same kind of soil is constant: *First*, the rental constantly increases with the extension of cultivated area and with the consequent increased capital investment, except for the case where the entire increase is accounted for by rentless land. *Secondly*, the average rent per acre (total rental divided by the total number of cultivated acres) as well as the average rate of rent (total rental divided by the invested total capital) may vary very considerably; and, indeed, both change in the same direction, but in different proportions to each other. If we leave out of consideration the case in which the expansion takes place only on the rentless soil A, we find that the average rent per acre and the average rate of rent on the capital invested in agriculture depend on the proportions which the various classes of soil constitute in the total cultivated area; or, what amounts to the same thing, on the distribution of the total employed capital among the kinds of soil of varying fertility. Whether much or little land is cultivated, and whether the total rental is therefore larger or smaller (with the exception of the case in which the expansion is confined to A), the average rent per acre, or the average rate of rent on the invested capital, remains the same as long as the proportions of the various categories of soil in the total cultivated area remain unchanged. In spite of an increase, even a very considerable one, in the total rental with the extension of cultivation and expansion of capital investment, the average rent per acre and the average rate of rent on capital decrease when the extension of rentless land, and land yielding only little differential rent, is greater than the extension of the superior one yielding greater rent. Conversely, the average rent per acre and the average rate of rent on capital increase proportionately to the extent that better land constitutes a relatively greater part of the total area and therefore employs a relatively greater share of the invested capital.

Hence, if we consider the average rent per acre, or hectare, of the total cultivated land, as is generally done in statistical works, in comparing either different countries in the same period, or different periods in the same country, we find that the average level of rent per acre, and consequently total rental, corresponds to a certain extent (although by no means identical, but rather a more rapidly increasing extent) to the absolute, not to the relative, fertility of the soil in a given country; that is, to the average amount of produce which it yields from the same area. For the larger the share of superior soils in the total cultivated area, the greater the output for equal capital investments on equally large areas of land; and the higher the average rent per acre. In the reverse case the opposite takes place. Thus, rent does not appear to be determined by the ratio of differential fertility, but by the absolute fertility, and the law of differential rent appears invalid. For this reason certain phenomena are disputed, or an attempt is made to explain them by non-existing differences in average prices of grain and in the differential fertility of cultivated land, whereas such phenomena are merely due to the fact that the ratio of the total rental to the total area of cultivated land or to the total capital invested in the land — as long as the fertility of the rentless soil remains the same and therefore the prices of production, and the differences between the various kinds of soil remain unchanged — is determined not merely by the rent per acre or the rate of rent on capital, but quite as much by the relative number of acres of each type of soil in the total number of cultivated acres; or, what amounts to the same thing, by the distribution of the total invested capital among the various types of soil. Curiously enough, this fact has been completely overlooked thus far. At any rate, we see (and this is important for our further analysis) that the relative level of the average rent per acre, and the average rate of rent (or the ratio of the total rental to the total capital invested in the land), may rise or fall by merely extensively expanding cultivation, as long as prices remain the same, the differential fertilities of the various soils remain unaltered, and the rent per acre, or rate of rent for capital invested per acre in every type of soil actually yielding rent, i. e., for all capital actually yielding rent, remains unchanged.

––––––––

It is necessary to make the following additional points with reference to the form of differential rent considered under heading I; they also apply in part to differential rent II:

First, it was seen that the average rent per acre, or the average rate of rent on capital, may increase with an extension of cultivation when prices are stationary and the differential fertility of the cultivated plots of land remains unaltered. As soon as all the land in a given country has been appropriated, and investments of capital in land, cultivation, and population have reached a definite level — all given conditions as soon as the capitalist mode of production becomes the prevailing one and also encompasses agriculture — the price of uncultivated land of varying quality (merely assuming differential rent to exist) is determined by the price of the cultivated plots of land of the same quality and equivalent location. The price is the same — after deducting the cost of bringing the new land into cultivation — even though this land does not yield any rent. The price of the land is, indeed, nothing but the capitalised rent. But even in the case of cultivated land, the price pays only for future rents, as, for instance, when the prevalent interest rate is 5% and the rent for twenty years is paid at one time in advance. When land is sold, it is sold as land yielding rent, and the prospective character of the rent (which is here considered as a product of the soil, but it only seems to be that) does not distinguish the uncultivated from the cultivated land. The price of the uncultivated land, like its rent — the price of which represents the contracted form of the latter — is quite illusory as long as the land is not actually used. But it is thus determined *a priori* and is realised as soon as a purchaser is found. Hence, while the actual average rent in a given country is determined by its actual average annual rental and the relation of the latter to the total cultivated area, the price of the uncultivated land is determined by the price of the cultivated land, and is therefore but a reflection of the capital invested in the cultivated land and the results obtained therefrom. Since all land with the exception of the worst yields rent (and this rent, as we shall see under the head of differential rent II, increases with the quantity of capital and corresponding intensity of cultivation), the nominal price of uncultivated plots of land is thus formed, and they thus become commodities, a source of wealth for their owners. This explains at the same time, why the price of land increases in a whole region, even in the uncultivated part (Opdyke[a]). Land speculation, for instance, in the United States, is based solely on this reflection thrown by capital and labour on uncultivated land.

Secondly, progress in extending cultivated land generally takes place either toward inferior soil or on the various given types of soil in varying proportions depending on the manner in which they are met. Progress to inferior soil is naturally never made voluntarily, but can only result from rising prices, assuming a capitalist mode of production, and can only result from necessity under any other mode of production. However, this is not absolutely so. Poor soil may be preferred to a relatively better soil on account of location, which is of decisive importance for every extension of cultivation in young countries; furthermore, even though the soil formation in a certain region may generally be classified as fertile, it may nevertheless consist of a motley confusion of better and worse soils, so that the inferior soil may have to be cultivated if only because it is found in the immediate vicinity of the superior soil. If inferior soil is surrounded by superior soil, then the latter gives it the advantage of location in comparison with more fertile soil which is not yet, or is about to become, part of the cultivated area.

Thus, the State of Michigan was one of the first Western States to become an exporter of grain. Yet its soil on the whole is poor. But its proximity to the State of New York and its water-ways via the Lakes and Erie Canal initially gave it the advantage over the States endowed by Nature with more fertile soil, but situated farther to the West. The example of this State, as compared with the State of New York, also demonstrates the transition from superior to inferior soil. The soil of the State of New York, particularly its western part, is incomparably more fertile, especially for the cultivation of wheat. This fertile soil was transformed into infertile soil by rapacious methods of cultivation, and now the soil of Michigan appeared as the more fertile.

---

[a] Reference to G. Opdyke, *A Treatise on Political Economy*.

"In 1838, wheaten flour was shipped at Buffalo for the West; and the wheat-region of New York, with that of Upper Canada, were the main sources of its supply. Now, after only twelve years, an enormous supply of wheat and flour is brought from the West, along Lake Erie, and shipped upon the Erie Canal for the East, at Buffalo and the adjoining port of Blackrock... The effect of these large arrivals from the Western States — which were unnaturally stimulated during the years of European famine ... has been to render wheat less valuable in western New York, to make the wheat culture less remunerative, and to turn the attention of the New York farmers more to grazing and dairy husbandry, fruit culture, and other branches of rural economy, in which they think the North-West will be unable so directly to compete with them" (J. W. Johnston, *Notes on North America*, London, 1851, I, p. 222[a]).

Thirdly, it is a mistaken assumption that the land in colonies and, in general, in young countries which can export grain at cheaper prices, must of necessity be of greater natural fertility. The grain is not only sold below its value in such cases, but below its price of production, i. e., below the price of production determined by the average rate of profit in the older countries.

The fact that we, as Johnston says (p. 223),

"are accustomed to attach the idea of great natural productiveness and of boundless tracts of rich land, to those new States from which come the large supplies of wheat that are annually poured into the port of Buffalo,"

is primarily the result of economic conditions. The entire population of such an area as Michigan, for instance, is at first almost exclusively engaged in farming, and particularly in producing agricultural mass products, which alone can be exchanged for industrial products and tropical goods. Its entire surplus production appears, therefore, in the form of grain. This from the outset sets apart the colonial states founded on the basis of the modern world market from those of earlier, particularly ancient, times. They receive through the world market finished products, such as clothing and tools which they would have to produce themselves under other circumstances. Only on such a basis were the Southern States of the Union enabled to make cotton their staple crop. The division of labour on the world market makes this possible. Hence, if they *seem* to have a large surplus production considering their youth and relatively small population, this is not so much due to the fertility of their soil, nor the fruitfulness of their labour, but rather to the one-sided form of their lalour, and therefore of the surplus produce in which such labour is incorporated.

---

[a] l. c., pp. 222-23.

Furthermore, a relatively inferior soil which is newly cultivated and never before touched by civilisation provided the climatic conditions are then not completely unfavourable, has accumulated a great deal of plant food that is easily assimilated — at least in the upper layers of the soil — so that it will yield crops for a long time without the application of fertilisers and even with very superficial cultivation. The western prairies have the additional advantage of hardly requiring any clearing expenses since Nature has made them arable.[33a] In less fertile areas of this kind, the surplus is not produced as a result of the high fertility of the soil, i. e., the yield per acre, but as a result of the large acreage which may be superficially cultivated, since such land costs the cultivator nothing, or next to nothing as compared with older countries. This is the case, for instance, where share cropping exists, as in parts of New York, Michigan, Canada, etc. A family superficially cultivates, say, 100 acres, and although the output per acre is not large, the output from 100 acres yields a considerable surplus for sale. In addition to this, cattle may be grazed on natural pastures at almost no cost, without requiring artificial grass meadows. It is the quantity of the land, not its quality, which is decisive here. The possibility of such superficial cultivation is naturally more or less rapidly exhausted, namely, in inverse proportion to the fertility of the new soil and in direct proportion to the export of its products.

"And yet such a country will give excellent first crops, even of wheat, and will supply to those who skim the first cream off the country, a large surplus of this grain to send to market" (l.c., p. 224).

Property relations in countries with maturer civilisations, with their determination of the price of uncultivated soil by that of the cultivated, etc., make such an extensive economy impossible.

[33a] //It is precisely the rapidly growing cultivation of such prairie or steppe regions which of late has turned the renowned statement of Malthus, that "the population is a burden upon the means of subsistence",[a] into ridicule, and produced in its stead the agrarian lament that agriculture, and with it Germany, will be ruined, unless the means of subsistence which are a burden upon the population are forcibly kept away from them. The cultivation of these steppes, prairies, pampas, llanos, etc., is nevertheless only in its beginning; its revolutionising effect on European agriculture will, therefore, make itself felt in the future even more so than hitherto.— F. E.//

---

[a] [T. R. Malthus], *An Essay on the Principles of Population*.

That this soil, therefore, need not be exceedingly rich, as Ricardo imagines, nor that soils of equal fertility need be cultivated, may be seen from the following: In the State of Michigan 465,900 acres were planted in 1848 to wheat which yielded 4,739,300 bushels, or an average of $10\frac{1}{5}$ bushels per acre; after deducting seed grain, this leaves less than 9 bushels per acre. Of the 29 counties of this State, 2 produced an average of 7 bushels, 3 an average of 8 bushels, 2—9, 7—10, 6—11, 3—12, 4—13 bushels, and only one county produced an average of 16 bushels, and another 18 bushels per acre (l.c., p. 225).

For practical cultivation higher soil fertility coincides with greater capability of immediate exploitation of such fertility. The latter may be greater in a naturally poor soil than in a naturally rich one; but it is the kind of soil which a colonist will take up first, and must take up when capital is wanting.

Finally, the extension of cultivation to larger areas — aside from the case just mentioned, in which recourse must be had to soil inferior than that cultivated hitherto — to the various kinds of soil from A to D, thus, for instance, the cultivation of larger tracts of B and C does not by any means presuppose a previous rise in grain prices any more than the preceding annual expansion of cotton spinning, for instance, requires a constant rise in yarn prices. Although a considerable rise or fall in market prices affects the volume of production, nevertheless, regardless of it there is in agriculture (just as in all other capitalistically operated branches of production) a continuous relative overproduction, in itself identical with accumulation, even at those average prices whose level has neither a retarding nor exceptionally stimulating effect on production. Under other modes of production this relative overproduction is effected directly by the population increase, and in colonies by steady immigration. The demand increases constantly, and, in anticipation of this, new capital is continually invested in new land, although this varies with the circumstances for different agricultural products. It is the formation of new capitals which in itself brings this about. But so far as the individual capitalist is concerned, he measures the volume of his production by that of his available capital, to the extent that he can still control it himself. His aim is to capture as big a portion as possible of the market. Should there be any overproduction, he will not take the blame upon himself, but places it upon his competitors. The individual capitalist may expand his production by appropriating a larger aliquot share of the existing market or by expanding the market itself.

Thus far we have considered differential rent only as the result of varying productivity of equal amounts of capital invested in equal areas of land of different fertility, so that differential rent was determined by the difference between the yield from the capital invested in the worst, rentless soil and that from the capital invested in superior soil. We had side by side capitals invested in different plots of land, so that every new investment of capital signified a more extensive cultivation of the soil, an expansion of cultivated area. In the last analysis, however, differential rent was by its nature merely the result of the different productivity of equal capitals invested in land. But can it make any difference if capitals of different productivity are invested successively in the same plot of land or side by side in different plots of land, provided the results are the same?

To begin with, there is no denying that, in so far as the formation of surplus profit is concerned, it is immaterial whether £3 in production price per acre of A yield 1 qr, so that £3 is the price of production and the regulating market price of 1 qr, while £3 in production price per acre of B yield 2 qrs, and thereby £3 of surplus profit, similarly, £3 in production price per acre of C yield 3 qrs and £6 of surplus profit, and, finally, £3 in production price per acre of D yield 4 qrs and £9 of surplus profit; or whether the same result is achieved by applying these £12 in production price, or £10 of capital, with the same success in the same sequence upon one and the same acre. It is in both cases a capital of £10, whose value portions of £$2\frac{1}{2}$ each are successively invested — whether in four acres of varying fertility side by side, or successively in one and the same acre of land — and because of their varying outputs, one portion yields no surplus profit, whereas the other portions yield surplus profit proportionate to their difference in yield with respect to rentless investment.

The surplus profits and the various rates of surplus profit for the different value portions of capital are formed in the same manner in both cases. And the rent is nothing but a form of this surplus profit, which constitutes its substance. But at any rate, in the second method, there are some difficulties concerning the transformation of surplus profit into rent, this change of form, which includes the transfer of surplus profit from the capitalist tenant farmer to the landowner.

This accounts for the obstinate resistance of English tenant farmers to official agricultural statistics. And it accounts for their struggle against the landlords over the determination of actual results derived from their capital investments (Morton). For rent is fixed when land is leased, and after that the surplus profit arising from successive investments of capital flows into the pockets of the tenant as long as the lease lasts. This is why the tenants have fought for long leases, and, on the other hand, due to the greater power of the LANDLORDS, an increase in the number of TENANCIES AT WILL has taken place, i. e., leases which can be cancelled annually.

It is therefore evident from the very outset that, even if immaterial for the law of formation of surplus profit, it makes a considerable difference for the transformation of surplus profit into ground rent whether equal capitals are invested side by side in equal areas of land with unequal results, or whether they are invested successively in the same land. The latter method confines this transformation, on the one hand, within narrower limits, on the other hand, within more variable limits. For this reason, the work of the tax-assessor, as Morton shows in his *Resources of Estates*, becomes a very important, complicated and difficult profession in countries practising intensive cultivation (and, economically speaking, we mean nothing more by intensive cultivation than the concentration of capital upon the same plot rather than its distribution among several adjoining pieces of land). If soil improvements are of a more permanent nature the artificially increased differential fertility of the soil coincides with its natural differential fertility as soon as the lease expires, and therefore the assessment of the rent corresponds to the determination of the rent on plots of different fertilities in general. On the other hand, in so far as the formation of surplus profit is determined by the magnitude of operating capital, the amount of rent for a certain amount of operating capital is added to the average rent of the country and thus provision is made for the new tenant to command sufficient capital to continue cultivation in the same intensive manner.

———————

In the study of differential rent II, the following points are still to be emphasised.

First, its basis and point of departure, not just historically, but also in so far as concerns its movement at any given period of time, is differential rent I, that is, the simultaneous cultivation side by side of soils of unequal fertility and location; in other words, the simultaneous application, side by side, of unequal portions of the total agricultural capital upon plots of land of unequal quality.

Historically this is self-evident. In the colonies, colonists have but little capital to invest; the principal production agents are labour and land. Every individual head of family seeks for himself and his kin an independent field of employment alongside his fellow-colonists. This must generally be the case in agriculture proper even under precapitalist modes of production. In the case of sheep-herding and cattle-raising, in general, as independent lines of production, exploitation of the soil is more or less common and extensive from the very outset. The capitalist mode of production has for its point of departure former modes of production in which the means of production were, in fact or legally, the property of the tiller himself, in a word, a handicraft-like pursuit of agriculture. It is in the nature of things that the latter gives way but gradually to the concentration of the means of production and their transformation into capital, as against direct producers transformed into wage labourers. In so far as the capitalist mode of production is manifested here typically, it occurs at first particularly in sheep-herding and cattle-raising. But it is thus manifested not in a concentration of capital upon a relatively small area of land, but in production on a larger scale, economising in the expense of keeping horses, and in other production costs; but, in fact, not by investing more capital in the same land. Furthermore, in accordance with the natural laws of field husbandry, capital—used here, at the same time, in the sense of means of production already produced—becomes the decisive element in soil cultivation when cultivation has reached a certain level of development and the soil has been correspondingly exhausted. So long as the tilled area is small in comparison with the untilled, and so long as the soil strength has not been exhausted (and this is the case when cattle-raising and meat consumption prevail in the period before agriculture proper and plant nutrition have become dominant), the new developing mode of production is opposed to peasant production mainly in the extensiveness of the land being tilled at the expense of a capitalist, in other words, again in the extensive application of capital to larger areas of land. It should therefore be remembered from the outset that differential rent I is the historical basis which serves as a point of departure. On the other hand, the movement of differential rent II at any given moment occurs only within a sphere which is itself but the variegated basis of differential rent I.

Secondly, in the differential rent in form II, the differences in distribution of capital (and ability to obtain credit) among tenants are added to the differences in fertility. In manufacture proper, each line of business rapidly develops its own minimum volume of business and a corresponding minimum of capital, below which no individual business can be conducted successfully. In the same way, each line of business develops a normal average amount of capital above this minimum, which the bulk of producers should, and do, command. A larger volume of capital can produce extra profit; a smaller volume does not so much as yield the average profit. The capitalist mode of production spreads in agriculture but slowly and unevenly, as may be observed in England, the classic land of the capitalist mode of production in agriculture. In so far as the free importation of grain does not exist, or its effect is but limited because its volume is small, producers working inferior soil, and thus under worse than average conditions of production, determine the market price. A larger portion of the total mass of capital invested in husbandry, and in general available to it, is in their hands.

It is true that the peasant, for example, expends much labour on his small plot of land. But it is labour isolated from objective social and material conditions of productivity, labour robbed and stripped of these conditions.

This circumstance enables the actual capitalist tenant farmers to appropriate a portion of surplus profit — a fact which would not obtain, at least so far as this point is concerned, if the capitalist mode of production were as evenly developed in agriculture as in manufacture.

Let us first consider just the formation of surplus profit with differential rent II, without for the present bothering about the conditions under which the transformation of this surplus profit into ground rent may take place.

It is then evident that differential rent II is merely differently expressed differential rent I, but identical to it in substance. The variation in fertility of various soil types exerts its influence in the case of differential rent I only in so far as unequal results are attained by capitals invested in the soil, i. e., the amount of products obtained either with respect to equal magnitudes of capital, or proportionate amounts. Whether this inequality takes place for various capitals invested successively in the same land or for capitals invested in several plots of differing soil type — this can change nothing in the difference in fertility nor in its product and can therefore change nothing in the formation of differential rent for the more productively invested portions of capital. It is still the soil which, now as before, shows different fertility with the same investment of capital, save that here the same soil performs for a capital successively invested in different portions what various kinds of soil do in the case of differential rent I for different equal portions of social capital invested in them.

If the same capital of £10, which is shown in Table I[a] to be invested in the form of independent capitals of £2$\frac{1}{2}$ each by various tenants in each acre of the four soil types A, B, C and D, were instead successively invested in one and the same acre D, so that the first investment yielded 4 qrs, the second 3, the third 2, and the fourth 1 qr (or in the reverse order), then the price of the quarter furnished by the least productive capital, namely = £3, would not yield any differential rent, but would determine the price of production, so long as the supply of wheat whose price of production is £3 were needed. And since our assumption is that the capitalist mode of production prevails, so that the price of £3 includes the average profit made by a capital of £2$\frac{1}{2}$ generally, the other three portions of £2$\frac{1}{2}$ each will yield surplus profit in accordance with the difference in output, since this output is not sold at its own price of production, but at the price of production of the least productive investment of £2$\frac{1}{2}$; the latter investment does not yield any rent and the price of its products is determined by the general law of prices of production. The formation of surplus profit would be the same as in Table I.

Once again it is seen here that differential rent II presupposes differential rent I. The minimum output obtained from a capital of £2$\frac{1}{2}$, i. e., from the worst soil, is here assumed to be 1 qr. Assumed, also, is that aside from the £2$\frac{1}{2}$ which yield him 4 qrs and for which he pays a differential rent of 3 qrs, the tenant operating with soil type D invests in this same soil £2$\frac{1}{2}$ which yield him only 1 qr, like the same capital upon the worst soil A. This would be an investment of capital which does not yield rent, since it returns to him only average profit. There would be no surplus profit which could be transformed into rent. On the other hand, this decreasing yield of the second investment of capital in D would have no influence on the rate of profit. It would be the same as though £2$\frac{1}{2}$ had been invested anew in an additional acre of soil type A, a circumstance which would in no way af-

---

fect the surplus profit and, therefore, the differential rent of soils A, B, C and D. But for the tenant, this additional investment of $£2\frac{1}{2}$ in D would have been quite as profitable as, in accordance with our assumption, the investment of the original $£2\frac{1}{2}$ per acre of D, although the latter yields 4 qrs. Furthermore, if two other investments of $£2\frac{1}{2}$ each should yield an additional output of 3 qrs and 2 qrs respectively, a decrease would have taken place again compared with the output from the investment of $£2\frac{1}{2}$ in D, which yielded 4 qrs, i. e., a surplus profit of 3 qrs. But it would be merely a decrease in the amount of surplus profit, and would not affect either the average profit or the regulating price of production. The latter would be the case only if the additional production yielding this decreasing surplus profit made the production upon A superfluous, and threw acre A out of cultivation. In this case, the decreasing productiveness of the additional investment of capital in acre D would be accompanied by a fall in the price of production, for instance, from $£3$ to $£1\frac{1}{2}$, if acre B would become the rentless soil and regulator of the market price.

The output from D would now be $= 4 + 1 + 3 + 2 = 10$ qrs whereas formerly it was $= 4$ qrs. But the price per quarter as regulated by B would have fallen to $£1\frac{1}{2}$. The difference between D and B would be $= 10 - 2 = 8$ qrs, at $£1\frac{1}{2}$ per quarter $= £12$, whereas the money rent from D was previously $= £9$. This should be noted. Calculated per acre, the magnitude of rent would have risen by $33\frac{1}{3}\%$ in spite of the decreasing rate of surplus profit on the two additional capitals of $£2\frac{1}{2}$ each.

We see from this to what highly complicated combinations differential rent in general, and in form II coupled with form I, in particular, may give rise, whereas Ricardo, for instance, treats it very one-sidedly and as though it were a simple matter. As in the above case, a fall in the regulating market price and at the same time rise in rent from fertile soils may take place so that both the absolute product and the absolute surplus product increase. (In differential rent I, in descending order, the relative surplus product and thus the rent per acre may increase, although the absolute surplus product per acre remains constant or even decreases.) But at the same time, productiveness of the investments of capital made successively in the same soil decreases, although a large portion of them falls to the more fertile soils. From a certain point of view — as concerns both output and prices of production — the productivity of labour has risen. But from another point of view, it has decreased because the rate of surplus profit and the surplus product per acre decrease for the various investments of capital in the same land.

Differential rent II, with decreasing productiveness of successive investments of capital, would necessarily be accompanied by a rise in price of production and an absolute decrease in productivity only if investments of capital could be made in none but the worst soil A. If an acre of A, which with an investment of capital of £$2\frac{1}{2}$ yielded 1 qr at a price of production of £3, should only yield a total of $1\frac{1}{2}$ qrs with an additional outlay of £$2\frac{1}{2}$, i e., a total investment of £5, then the price of production of this $1\frac{1}{2}$ qrs = £6, or that of 1 qr = £4. Every decrease in productivity with a growing investment of capital would here mean a relative decrease in output per acre, whereas upon superior soils it would only signify a decrease in the additional surplus product.

But by the nature of things, with the development of intensive cultivation, i. e., with successive investments of capital in the same soil, this will take place more advantageously, or to a greater extent on better soils. (We are not referring to permanent improvements by which a hitherto useless soil is converted into useful soil.) The decreasing productiveness of successive investments of capital must, therefore, have principally the effect indicated above. The better soil is selected because it affords the best promise that capital invested in it will be profitable, since it contains the most natural elements of fertility, which need but be utilised.

When, after the abolition of the Corn Laws, cultivation in England became still more intensive, a great deal of former wheat land was devoted to other purposes, particularly cattle pastures, while the fertile land best suited for wheat was drained and otherwise improved. The capital for wheat cultivation was thus concentrated in a more limited area.

In this case — and all possible surplus rates between the greatest surplus product of the best soil and the output of rentless soil A coincide here with an absolute, rather than a relative, increase in surplus product per acre — the newly formed surplus profit (potential rent) does not represent a portion of a former average profit transformed into rent (a portion of the output in which the average profit formerly was expressed) but an additional surplus profit, which is transformed out of this form into rent.

On the other hand, only in the case where the demand for grain increased to such an extent that the market price rose above the price of production of A, so that the surplus product of A, B, or any other kind of soil could be supplied only at a price higher than £3 would the decrease in yield from an additional investment of capital in any of the soil types A, B, C and D be accompanied by a rise in the price of production and the regulating market price. In so far as this lasted for a lengthy period of time without resulting in the cultivation of additional soil A (of at least the quality of A), or without a cheaper supply resulting from other circumstances, wages would rise in consequence of the increase in the price of bread, everything else being equal, and the rate of profit would fall accordingly. In this case, it would be immaterial, whether the increased demand were satisfied by bringing under cultivation soil of inferior quality than A, or by additional investments of capital, in any of the four types of soil. Differential rent would then increase together with a falling rate of profit.

This one case, in which the decreasing productiveness of subsequent additional capitals invested in already cultivated soils may lead to an increase in the price of production, a fall in the rate of profit, and the formation of higher differential rent—for the latter would increase under the given circumstances upon all kinds of soil just as though soil of inferior quality than A were regulating the market price—has been labelled by Ricardo as the only case, the normal case—to which he reduces the entire formation of differential rent II.

This would also be the case if only type A soil were cultivated and successive investments of capital in it were not accompanied by a proportional increase in produce.

Here then, in the case of differential rent II, one completely loses sight of differential rent I.

Except for this case, in which the supply from the cultivated soils is either insufficient and the market price thus continually higher than the price of production until new additional soil of inferior quality is taken under cultivation or until the total product from the additional capital invested in various kinds of soil can be supplied only at a higher price of production than that hitherto prevailing—except for this case, the proportional drop in productivity of the additional capitals leaves the regulating price of production and the rate of profit unchanged. For the rest, three more cases are possible:

a) If the additional capital invested in any one of the types of soil A, B, C or D yields only the rate of profit determined by the price of production of A, then no surplus profit, and therefore no potential rent, is formed, any more than there would be if additional type A soil had been cultivated.

b) If the additional capital yields a larger product, new surplus profit (potential rent) is, of course, formed provided the regulating price remains the same. This is not necessarily the case; it is not the case, in particular, when this additional production throws soil A out of cultivation and thus out of the sequence of competing soils. In this case, the regulating price of production falls. If this were accompanied by a fall in wages, or if the cheaper product were to enter into the constant capital as one of its elements, the rate of profit would rise. If the increased productivity of the additional capital had taken place upon the best soils C and D, it would depend entirely upon the degree of increased productivity and the amount of additional new capital to what extent the formation of increased surplus profit (and thus increased rent) would be associated with the fall in prices and the rise in the rate of profit. The latter may also rise without a fall in wages, through a cheapening of the elements of constant capital.

c) If the additional investment of capital takes place with decreasing surplus profit, but in such manner that the yield from this investment still leaves a surplus above the yield from the same capital invested in A, a new formation of surplus profit takes place under all circumstances, unless the increased supply excludes soil A from cultivation. This may take place simultaneously upon D, C, B and A. But, on the other hand, if the worst soil A is squeezed out of cultivation, then the regulating price of production falls and it will depend upon the relation between the reduced price of 1 qr and the increased number of quarters forming surplus profit whether the surplus profit expressed in money, and consequently the differential rent, rises or falls. But at any rate, it is noteworthy here that with decreasing surplus profit from successive investments of capital the price of production may fall, instead of rising, which it seemingly should do at first sight.

These additional investments of capital with decreasing surplus yields correspond entirely to the case in which, e. g., four new independent capitals of £$2\frac{1}{2}$ each would be invested in soils with fertility between A and B, B and C, C and D, and yielding $1\frac{1}{2}$, $2\frac{1}{3}$, $2\frac{2}{3}$, and 3 qrs respectively. Surplus profit (potential rent) would take shape on all these soils for all four additional capitals, although the rate of surplus profit, compared with that for the same investment of capital on the correspondingly better soil, would have decreased. And it would be quite immaterial whether these four capitals were invested in D, etc., or distributed between D and A.

We now come to an essential difference between the two forms of differential rent.

Under differential rent I, with constant price of production and constant differences, the average rent per acre, or the average rate of rent on capital, may increase together with the rental. But the average is a mere abstraction. The actual amount of rent, calculated per acre or with respect to capital, remains the same here.

On the other hand, under the same conditions, the amount of rent calculated per acre may increase although the rate of rent, measured relative to invested capital, remains the same.

Let us assume that production is doubled by the investment of £5 instead of £$2\frac{1}{2}$ in each of the soils A, B, C and D, i. e., a total of £20 instead of £10, and that the relative fertility remains unchanged. This would be tantamount to cultivating 2 instead of 1 acre of each of these kinds of soil at the same cost. The rate of profit would remain the same; also its relation to surplus profit or rent. But if A were now to yield 2 qrs, B—4, C—6, and D, 8, the price of production would nevertheless remain £3 per quarter because this increase is not due to doubled fertility with the same capital, but to the same proportional fertility with a doubled capital. The two quarters of A would now cost £6 just as 1 qr cost £3 before. The profit would have doubled on all four soils, but only because the invested capital was doubled. In the same proportion, however, the rent would also have been doubled; it would be 2 qrs for B instead of 1, 4 qrs for C instead of 2, and 6 for D instead of 3; and correspondingly, the money rent for B, C and D would now be £6, £12, and £18 respectively. Like the yield per acre, the rent in money per acre would be doubled, and, consequently, also the price of the land whereby this money rent is capitalised. Calculated in this manner, the amount of rent in grain and money increases, and thus the price of land, because the standard used in its computation, i. e., the acre, is an area of constant magnitude. On the other hand, calculated as rate of rent on invested capital, there is no change in the proportional amount of rent. The total rental of 36 is to the invested capital of 20 as the rental of 18 is to the invested capital of 10. The same holds true for the ratio of money rent from each type of soil to the capital invested in it; for instance, in C, £12 rent is to £5 capital as £6 rent was formerly to £$2\frac{1}{2}$ capital. No new differences arise here between the invested capitals, but new surplus profits do, merely because the additional capital is invested in one of the rent-bearing soils, or in all of them, with the same proportional yield as previously. If this double investment took place, for example, only in C, the differential rent between C, B and D, calculated with respect to capital, would remain the same: for when the amount of rent obtained from C is doubled, so is the invested capital.

This shows that the amount of rent in produce and money per acre, and therefore the price of land, may rise, while the price of production, the rate of profit, and the differences remain unchanged (and therefore the rate of surplus profit or of rent, calculated with respect to capital, remains unchanged).

The same may take place with decreasing rates of surplus profit, and therefore of rent, that is, with decreasing productivity of the additional investments of capital that still yield rent. If the second investments of capital of $£2\frac{1}{2}$ had not doubled the output, but B had yielded only $3\frac{1}{2}$ qrs, C—5 qrs, and D—7 qrs, then the differential rent for the second $£2\frac{1}{2}$ of capital in B would be only $\frac{1}{2}$ qr instead of 1, on C—1 qr instead of 2 and on D—2 qrs instead of 3. The proportions between rent and capital for the two successive investments would then be as follows:

	First Investment				Second Investment		
B:	Rent £3,	Capital	£2¹/₂	Rent	£1¹/₂,	Capital	£2¹/₂
C:	" £6,	"	£2¹/₂	"	£3,	"	£2¹/₂
D:	" £9,	"	£2¹/₂	"	£6,	"	£2¹/₂

In spite of this decreased rate of relative productivity of capital, and thus of the surplus profit calculated on capital, the rent in grain and money would have increased on B from 1 to $1\frac{1}{2}$ qrs (from £3 to $£4\frac{1}{2}$, on C— from 2 to 3 qrs (from £6 to £9), and on D—from 3 to 5 qrs (from £9 to £15). In this case, the differences for the additional capitals, compared with the capital invested in A, would have decreased, the price of production would have remained the same, but the rent per acre, and consequently the price of land per acre, would have risen.

The combinations of differential rent II, which presupposes differential rent I as its basis, will now be taken up.

Chapter XLI

DIFFERENTIAL RENT II.— FIRST CASE:
CONSTANT PRICE OF PRODUCTION

The assumption here implies that the market price is regulated as before by the capital invested in the worst soil A.

I. If the additional capital invested in any one of the rent-bearing soils — B, C, D — produces only as much as the same capital upon soil A, i. e., if it yields only the average profit at the regulating price of production, but no surplus profit, then the effect upon the rent is nil. Everything remains as before. It is the same as though an arbitrary number of acres of A quality, i. e., of the worst soil, has been added to the cultivated area.

II. The additional capitals yield additional produce proportional to their magnitude on every one of the various soils; in other words, the volume of production grows according to the specific fertility of each soil type — in proportion to the magnitude of the additional capital. In Chapter XXXIX, we started with the following Table I:

Type of Soil	Acres	Capi-tal £	Profit £	Price of Prod. £	Out-put Qrs	Selling Price £	Pro-ceeds £	Rent Qrs	Rent £	Rate of Surplus Profit
A	1	$2^1/_2$	$^1/_2$	3	1	3	3	0	0	0
B	1	$2^1/_2$	$^1/_2$	3	2	3	6	1	3	120%
C	1	$2^1/_2$	$^1/_2$	3	3	3	9	2	6	240%
D	1	$2^1/_2$	$^1/_2$	3	4	3	12	3	9	360%
Total ..	4	10		12	10		30	6	18	

This is now transformed into:

TABLE II

Type of Soil	Acres	Capital £	Profit £	Price of Prod. £	Out-put Qrs	Selling Price £	Pro-ceeds £	Rent Qrs	Rent £	Rate of Surplus Profit
A	1	$2^1/_2 + 2^1/_2 = 5$	1	6	2	3	6	0	0	
B	1	$2^1/_2 + 2^1/_2 = 5$	1	6	4	3	12	2	6	120%
C	1	$2^1/_2 + 2^1/_2 = 5$	1	6	6	3	18	4	12	240%
D	1	$2^1/_2 + 2^1/_2 = 5$	1	6	8	3	24	6	18	360%
	4	20			20		60	12	36	

It is not necessary in this case that the investment of capital be doubled in all soils, as in the table. The law is the same so long as additional capital is invested in one, or several, of the rent-bearing soils, no matter in what proportion. It is only necessary that production should increase upon every soil in the same ratio as the capital. The rent increases here merely in consequence of an increased investment of capital in the soil, and in proportion to this increase. This increase in produce and rent in consequence of, and proportionately to, the increased outlay of capital is just the same as regards the quantity of produce and rent, as when the cultivated area of the rent-bearing plots of land of the same quality had been increased and taken under cultivation with the same outlay of capital as that previously invested in the same types of soils. In the case of Table II, for instance, the result would remain the same, if the additional capital of $£2\frac{1}{2}$ per acre were invested in an additional acre of B, C and D.

Furthermore, this assumption does not imply a more productive investment of capital, but only an outlay of more capital upon the same area with the same success as before.

All relative proportions remain the same here. Of course, if we do not consider the proportional differences, but consider the purely arithmetic ones, then the differential rent may change upon the various soils. Let us assume, for instance, that additional capital has been invested only in B and D. The difference between D and A is then = 7 qrs whereas previously it was = 3; the difference between B and A = 3 qrs, whereas previously it was = 1; that between C and B = −1, whereas previously it was = +1, etc. But this arithmetic difference, which is decisive in differential rent I in so far as it expresses the difference in productivity with equal investment of capital, is here quite immaterial, because it is merely a consequence of different additional investments of capital, or of no additional investments, while the difference for each equal portion of capital upon the various plots of land remains unchanged.

III. The additional capitals yield surplus produce and thus form surplus profit, but at a decreasing rate, not in proportion to their increase.

In the case of this third assumption, it is again immaterial whether the additional second investments of capital are uniformly distributed among the various soils or not; whether the decreasing production of surplus profit takes place proportionately or not; whether the additional investments of capital are all in the same rent-bearing type of

TABLE III

Type of Soil	Acres	Capital £	Pro-fit £	Price of Prod. £	Output Qrs	Sel-ling Price £	Pro-ceeds £	Rent		Rate of Surplus Profit
								Qrs	£	
A	1	$2^1/_2$	$^1/_2$	3	1	3	3	0	0	0
B	1	$2^1/_2 + 2^1/_2 = 5$	1	6	$2 + 1^1/_2 = 3^1/_2$	3	$10^1/_2$	$1^1/_2$	$4^1/_2$	90%
C	1	$2^1/_2 + 2^1/_2 = 5$	1	6	$3 + 2 = 5$	3	15	3	9	180%
D	1	$2^1/_2 + 2^1/_2 = 5$	1	6	$4 + 3^1/_2 = 7^1/_2$	3	$22^1/_2$	$5^1/_2$	$16^1/_2$	330%
		$17^1/_2$	$3^1/_2$	21	17		51	10	30	

soil, or whether they are distributed equally or unequally among rent-bearing plots of land of varying quality. All these circumstances are immaterial for the law that is to be developed. The only assumption is that additional investments of capital yield surplus profit upon any one of the rent-bearing soils, but in decreasing proportion to the amount of the increase in capital. The limits of this decrease, in the table before us, are between 4 quarters = £12, the output from the first outlay of capital on the best soil D, and 1 quarter = £3, the output from the same outlay of capital in the worst soil A. The output from the best soil in case of the investment of capital I constitutes the top limit, and the output from the same outlay of capital in the worst soil A, which yields neither rent nor surplus profit, is the bottom limit of output, which successive investments of capital yield upon any of the soil types producing surplus profit with decreasing productivity of successive investments of capital. Just as assumption II corresponds to the case in which new plots of the same quality are added from the better soils to the cultivated area, in which the quantity of any one of the cultivated soils is increased, so assumption III corresponds to the case in which additional plots are cultivated whose various degrees of fertility are distributed among soils ranging from D to A, i. e., from the best to the worst soils. If the successive outlays of capital are made exclusively in soil D, they may include the existing differences between D and A, then differences between D and C, and likewise between D and B. If they are all made in soil C, then only differences between C and A, and C and B; if exclusively in B, then only differences between B and A.

But this is the law: the rent increases absolutely upon all these soils, even if not in proportion to the additional capital invested.

The rate of surplus profit, considering both the additional capital and the total capital invested in the soil, decreases; but the absolute magnitude of the surplus profit increases; just as the decreasing rate of profit on capital in general is, in the main, accompanied by an increase in the absolute amount of profit. Thus the average surplus profit of a capital invested in B = 90% on the capital, whereas it was = 120% for the first outlay of capital. But the total surplus profit increases from 1 qr to $1\frac{1}{2}$ qrs, or from £3 to £$4\frac{1}{2}$. The total rent — considered by itself rather than in relation to the doubled magnitude of the advanced capital — has risen absolutely. The differences in rents from various soils and their relative proportions may vary here; but this variation in differences is a consequence, not cause, of the increase in rents in relation to one another.

IV. The case in which additional investments of capital in the better soils yield more produce than the original ones requires no further analysis. It goes without saying that under this assumption the rent per acre will increase, and proportionately more than the additional capital, no matter in which kind of soil the outlay has been made. In this case, the additional investment of capital is accompanied by improvements. This includes the cases in which an additional outlay of less capital produces the same or a greater effect than an additional outlay of more capital did formerly. This case is not quite identical with the former one, and the distinction is important in all investments of capital. For instance, if 100 yields a profit of 10, and 200 employed in a certain form yields a profit of 40, then the profit has risen from 10% to 20%, and to that extent it is the same as though 50 employed in a more effective form yields a profit of 10 instead of 5. We assume here that the profit is associated with a proportional increase in output. But the difference is that I must double the capital in the one case, whereas in the other, the effect I produce is doubled with the capital employed hitherto. It is by no means the same whether I produce: 1) the same output as before with half as much living and objectified labour, or 2) twice the output as before with the same labour, or 3) four times the former output with twice the labour. In the first case, labour — in a living or objectified form — is released, and may be employed otherwise; the power to dispose of capital and labour increases. The release of capital (and labour) is in itself an augmentation of wealth; it has exactly the same effect as though this additional capital has been obtained by accumulation, but it saves the labour of accumulation.

Assume that a capital of 100 has produced an output of ten metres. The 100 includes constant capital, living labour and profit. Thus a metre costs 10. Now, if I can produce 20 metres with the same capital of 100, then a metre costs 5. If, on the other hand, I can produce 10 metres with a capital of 50, then a metre likewise costs 5, and should the former supply of commodities suffice a capital of 50 is released. If I have to invest a capital of 200 in order to produce 40 metres, then a metre also costs 5. The determination of value, and also the price, does not permit any difference to be discerned here; no more than the amount of output proportional to the advance of capital. But in the first case, capital is released; in the second case additional capital is saved to be used perhaps to double production if necessary; in the third case, the increased output can only be obtained by augmenting the advanced capital, although not in the same proportion as when the increased output was to have been supplied by the old productive power. (This belongs in Part I.)

From the viewpoint of capitalist production, the employment of constant capital is always cheaper than that of variable capital, not as regards increasing the surplus value, but rather as regards reducing the cost price — and saving of costs even in the element creating surplus value, in labour, performs this service for the capitalist and makes profit for him so long as the regulating price of production remains the same. This presupposes, in fact, the development of credit and an abundance of loan capital corresponding to the capitalist mode of production. On the one hand, I employ £100 additional constant capital, if £100 is the output of five labourers during the year; on the other hand, £100 in variable capital. If the rate of surplus value = 100%, then the value created by the five labourers = £200; on the other hand, the value of £100 constant capital = £100 and as capital it is perhaps = £105, if the interest rate = 5%. The same sums of money express very different values, from the viewpoint of the output they produce, depending on whether they are advanced to production as magnitudes of value of constant or of variable capital. Furthermore, as regards the cost of the commodities from the viewpoint of the capitalist, there is also this difference, that of the £100 constant capital only the wear and tear enters into the value of the commodity in so far as this money is invested in fixed capital, whereas the £100 invested in wages must be completely reproduced in the commodity.

In the case of colonists, and independent small producers in general, who have no access to capital at all or only at high interest rates, that part of the output which represents wages is their revenue, whereas for the capitalist it constitutes an advance of capital. The former, therefore, regards this expenditure of labour as the indispensable prerequisite for the labour product, which is the thing that interests him above all. But, as regards his surplus labour, after deducting the necessary labour, it is evidently realised in the surplus product; and as soon as he can sell the latter, or use it for himself, he looks upon it as something that cost him nothing, because it cost him no objectified labour. It is only the expenditure of the latter which appears to him as alienation of wealth. Of course, he tries to sell as high as possible; but even a sale below value and below the capitalist price of production still appears to him as profit, unless this profit is anticipated by debts, mortgages, etc. For the capitalist, on the other hand, the investment of both variable and constant capital represents an advance of capital. The relatively larger advance of the latter reduces the cost price, and in fact the value of the commodities, everything else being equal. Hence, although profit arises only from surplus labour, consequently only from the employment of variable capital, it may still seem to the individual capitalist that living labour is the most expensive element in his price of production which should be reduced to a minimum before all else. This is but a capitalistically distorted form of the fact that the relatively greater use of congealed labour, as compared with living labour, signifies an increase in the productivity of social labour and a greater social wealth. From the viewpoint of competition, everything appears thus distorted and turned topsy-turvy.

Assuming prices of production to remain unchanged, the additional investments of capital in the better soils, that is, in all soils from B upward, may be made with unaltered, increasing, or decreasing productivity. For soil A this would only be possible under the conditions assumed by us, if productivity remains the same — whereby the land continues to yield no rent — and also if productivity increases; a portion of the capital invested in A would then yield rent, while the remainder would not. But it would be impossible if productivity on A were to decrease, for then the price of production would not remain unchanged, but would rise. Yet in all these cases, i. e., whether the surplus product yielded by the additional investments is proportional to the latter or is greater or smaller than this proportion — whether, therefore, the rate of surplus profit on the capital remains constant, rises or falls when this capital increases, the surplus product and the corresponding surplus profit per acre increases, and hence also the potential rent in grain and money. The growth in the mere quantity of surplus profit or rent, calculated per acre, that is, an increasing quantity calculated on the basis of some constant unit — in the present case on a definite quantity of land such as an acre or a hectare — expresses itself as an increasing ratio. Hence the magnitude of the rent, calculated per acre, increases under such circumstances simply in consequence of the increase in the capital invested in the land. This takes place, to be sure, assuming the prices of production remain the same, and, on the other hand, regardless of whether the productivity of the additional capital remains unaltered, or whether it decreases or increases. The latter circumstances modify the range in which the magnitude of rent per acre increases but not the existence of this increase itself. This is a phenomenon peculiar to differential rent II, and distinguishing it from differential rent I. If the additional investments of capital were made successively in space, side by side in new additional soil of corresponding quality, rather than successively in time in the same soil, the quantity of the rental would have increased, and, as previously shown, so would the average rent from the total cultivated area, but not the magnitude of the rent per acre. Given the same result so far as quantity and value of total production and surplus product are concerned, the concentration of capital upon a smaller area of land increases the amount of rent per acre, whereas under the same conditions, its dispersion over a larger area, all other conditions being equal, does not produce this effect. But the more the capitalist mode of production develops, the more does the concentration of capital upon the same area of land develop, and, therefore, the more does the rent, calculated per acre, increase. Consequently, given two countries in which the prices of production are identical, the differences in soil type are identical, and the same amount of capital is invested — but in the one country more in the form of successive outlays upon a limited area of land, whereas in the other more in the form of co-ordinated outlays upon a larger area — then the rent per acre, and thereby the price of land, would be higher in the first country and lower in the second, although the total rent would be the same for both countries. The difference in magnitude of rent could thus not be explained here to be a result of a difference in the natural fertility of the various soils, nor a result of a difference in the quantity of employed labour, but solely a result of different ways in which the capital is invested.

When we refer to surplus product here, this should always be understood to mean that aliquot part of the output which represents surplus profit. Ordinarily, we mean by excess product or surplus product that portion of the output which represents the total surplus value, or in some cases that portion which represents the average profit. The specific meaning which this term assumes in the case of rent-bearing capital gives rise to misunderstanding, as previously pointed out.[a]

Chapter XLII

DIFFERENTIAL RENT II.— SECOND CASE:
FALLING PRICE OF PRODUCTION

The price of production may fall when additional investments of capital take place with an unaltered, falling or rising rate of productivity.

I. Productivity of the additional investment of capital remains the same

In this case, the assumption, therefore, is that the output increases proportionally to the capital invested in the various soils and in accordance with their respective qualities. This means for constant differences in soils that the surplus product increases in proportion to the increased investment of capital. This case, then, excludes any additional investment of capital in soil A which might affect the differential rent. For this soil, the rate of surplus profit = 0; thus, it remains = 0 since we have assumed that the productiveness of the additional capital, and therefore the rate of surplus profit, remain the same.

But under these conditions the regulating price of production can only fall, because it is the price of production of the next best soil, of B, or any better soil than A, rather than that of A, which becomes the regulator; so that the capital is withdrawn from A, or perhaps from A and B if the price of production of C should become the regulating one, and thus all soil inferior to C would be eliminated from the competition among grain-producing soils. The prerequisite for this is, under the assumed conditions, that the additional yield from the

---

[a] See this volume, pp. 627-33.

additional investments of capital satisfy the demand, so that the output from the inferior soil A, etc., become superfluous for the re-establishment of a full supply.

Thus, let us take, for instance, Table II, but in such a way that 18 qrs instead of 20 satisfy the demand. Soil A would drop out; B and its price of production of 30 shillings per quarter would become regulating. The differential rent then assumes the following form:

TABLE IV

Type of Soil	Acres	Capital £	Profit £	Price of Production £	Output Qrs	Selling Price per qr £	Proceeds £	Rent in Grain Qrs	Rent in Money £	Rate of Surplus Profit
B	1	5	1	6	4	1¹/₂	6	0	0	0
C	1	5	1	6	6	1¹/₂	9	2	3	60%
D	1	5	1	6	8	1¹/₂	12	4	6	120%
Total	3	15	3	18	18		27	6	9	

Compared with Table II, the total rent would hence have fallen from £36 to £9, and in grain from 12 qrs to 6 qrs; total output would have fallen only by 2 qrs, from 20 to 18. The rate of surplus profit calculated on the capital would have fallen to one-third, i. e., from 180% to 60%.[a] Thus, the fall in the price of production is accompanied here by a decrease of the rent in grain and money.

Compared with Table I, there is merely a decrease in money rent; the rent in grain is in both cases 6 qrs; but in the one case it = £18, and in the other £9. For soil C, the rent in grain, compared with Table I, has remained the same. In fact, it is owing to the additional production resulting from the uniformly acting additional capital that the yield from A has been excluded from the market, and thereby soil A has been eliminated as a competing producing agent, and it is owing to this fact that a new differential rent I has been formed in which the better soil B plays the same role as did formerly the inferior soil A. Consequently, on the one hand, the rent from B has disappeared; on the other hand, nothing has been altered in the differences

---

[a] In the 1894 German edition "one-half, from 180% to 90%".

between B, C and D by the investment of additional capital — in accordance with our assumption. For this reason, that part of the output which is transformed into rent is reduced.

If the above result — the satisfaction of the demand with A excluded — had been accomplished, perchance, by the investment of more than double the capital in C or D, or in both, then the matter would assume a different aspect. For example, if the third investment of capital were made in C:

TABLE IVa

Type of Soil	Acres	Capital $£$	Profit $£$	Price of Production $£$	Output Qrs	Selling Price $£$	Proceeds $£$	Rent in Grain Qrs	Rent in Money $£$	Rate of Surplus Profit
B	1	5	1	6	4	$1^1/_2$	6	0	0	0
C	1	$7^1/_2$	$1^1/_2$	9	9	$1^1/_2$	$13^1/_2$	3	$4^1/_2$	60%
D	1	5	1	6	8	$1^1/_2$	12	4	6	120%
Total	3	$17^1/_2$	$3^1/_2$	21	21		$31^1/_2$	7	$10^1/_2$	

In this case, compared with Table IV, the output from C has risen from 6 to 9 qrs, the surplus product from 2 to 3 qrs, and the money rent from £3 to £$4^1/_2$. Compared with Table II, where the latter was £12, and Table I, where it was £6, the money rent has, on the other hand, decreased. The total rental in grain = 7 qrs and has fallen compared with Table II (12 qrs) and risen compared with Table I (6 qrs); in money (£$10^1/_2$) it has fallen compared with both (£18 and £36).

If the third investment of capital of £$2^1/_2$ had been employed on soil B, it would indeed have altered the quantity of production, but would not have affected the rent, since, according to our assumption, the successive investments do not produce any differences upon the same soil and soil B does not yield any rent.

If we assume, on the other hand, that the third investment of capital takes place upon D instead of C, we have the following:

Type of Soil	Acres	Capital £	Profit £	Price of Production £	Output Qrs	Selling Price £	Proceeds £	Rent		Rate of Surplus Profit
								Qrs	£	
B	1	5	1	6	4	$1^1/_2$	6	0	0	0
C	1	5	1	6	6	$1^1/_2$	9	2	3	60%
D	1	$7^1/_2$	$1^1/_2$	9	12	$1^1/_2$	18	6	9	120%
Total	3	$17^1/_2$	$3^1/_2$	21	22		33	8	12	

Here the total product = 22 qrs, more than double that of Table I, although the invested capital = only £$17^1/_2$ as against £10, that is, not twice the amount. The total product is also larger by 2 qrs than that of Table II, although the advanced capital in the latter is larger — namely, £20.

Compared with Table I, the rent in grain from soil D has increased from 3 to 6 qrs, whereas the money rent, £9, has remained the same. Compared with Table II, the grain rent from D is the same, namely, 6 qrs, but the money rent has fallen from £18 to £9.

Comparing the total rents, the grain rent from Table IVb = 8 qrs is larger than that from Table I = 6 qrs and than that from Table IVa = 7 qrs; but it is smaller than that from Table II = 12 qrs. The money rent from Table IVb = £12 is larger than that from Table IVa = £$10^1/_2$, and smaller than that from Table I = £18 and that from Table II = £36.

In order that the total rental may, under the conditions of Table IVb (with the elimination of rent from B), be equal to that of Table I, we need £6 more of surplus product, that is, 4 qrs at £$1^1/_2$, which is the new price of production. We then have a total rental of £18 again as in Table I. The magnitude of the required additional capital will vary according to whether we invest it in C or D, or divide it between the two.

On C, £5 capital yields 2 qrs of surplus product; consequently, £10 additional capital yields 4 qrs of additional surplus product. On D, £5 additional capital would suffice to produce 4 qrs of additional grain rent under the conditions assumed here, namely that the productivity of the additional investments of capital remains the same. We should then obtain the following results:

TABLE IVc

Type of Soil	Acres	Capital £	Profit £	Price of Production £	Output Qrs	Selling Price £	Proceeds £	Rent		Rate of Surplus Profit
								Qrs	£	
B	1	5	1	6	4	1¹/₂	6	0	0	0
C	1	15	3	18	18	1¹/₂	27	6	9	60%
D	1	7¹/₂	1¹/₂	9	12	1¹/₂	18	6	9	120%
Total	3	27¹/₂	5¹/₂	33	34		51	12	18	

TABLE IVd

Type of Soil	Acres	Capital £	Profit £	Price of Production £	Output Qrs	Selling Price £	Proceeds £	Rent		Rate of Surplus Profit
								Qrs	£	
B	1	5	1	6	4	1¹/₂	6	0	0	0
C	1	5	1	6	6	1¹/₂	9	2	3	60%
D	1	12¹/₂	2¹/₂	15	20	1¹/₂	30	10	15	120%
Total	3	22¹/₂	4¹/₂	27	30		45	12	18	

The total money rental would be exactly one-half of what it was in Table II, where the additional capitals were invested at constant prices of production.

The most important thing is to compare the above tables with Table I.

We find that while the price of production has fallen by one-half, i. e., from 60 shillings to 30 shillings per quarter, the total money rental has remained the same, namely = £18, and the grain rent has correspondingly doubled from 6 to 12 qrs. Upon B the rent has disappeared; upon C the money rent has risen by one-half in IVc, but has fallen by one-half in IVd; upon D in IVc, it has remained the same, = £9, and has risen from £9 to £15 in IVd. The production has risen from 10 to 34 qrs in IVc, and to 30 qrs in IVd; the profit from £2 to £5¹/₂ in IVc and to £4¹/₂ in IVd. The total investment of capital has risen in the one case from £10 to £27¹/₂, and in the other from £10 to £22¹/₂;

i. e., in both cases it has more than doubled. The rate of rent, that is, the rent calculated on the advanced capital, is in all tables from IV to IVd everywhere the same for each kind of soil — which was already implied in the assumption that the rate of productivity for the two successive investments of capital remains the same for each soil type. But compared with Table I this rate has fallen, both for the average of all kinds of soil and for each one of them individually. In Table I it was $= 180\%$ on an average, whereas in IVc it $= \frac{18}{27^{1}/_{2}} \times 100 = 65^{5}/_{11}\%$ and in IVd it $= \frac{18}{22^{1}/_{2}} \times 100 = 80\%$. The average money rent per acre has risen. Formerly, in Table I, its average was £$4^{1}/_{2}$ per acre from all four acres, whereas in IVc and IVd it is £6 per acre upon the 3 acres. Its average upon the rent-bearing land was formerly £6, whereas now it is £9 per acre. Hence the money value of the rent per acre has risen and now represents twice as much grain as it did formerly; but the 12 qrs of grain rent are now less than one-half of the total output of 34 and 30^{a} qrs respectively, whereas in Table I the 6 qrs represent $\frac{3}{5}$ the total output of 10 qrs. Consequently, although the rent as an aliquot part of the total output has fallen, and has also fallen when calculated on the invested capital, its money value calculated per acre has risen, and still more its value as a product. If we take soil D in Table IVd, we find that the price of production corresponding to the capital outlay here $=$ £15, of which £$12^{1}/_{2}$ is invested capital. The money rent $=$ £15. In Table I, for the same soil D, the price of production was $=$ £3, the invested capital $=$ £$2^{1}/_{2}$ and the money rent $=$ £9; that is, the latter was three times the price of production and almost four times the capital. In Table IVd, the money rent for D, £15, is exactly equal to the price of production and larger than the capital by only $\frac{1}{5}$. Nevertheless, the money rent per acre is $\frac{2}{3}$ larger, namely, £15 instead of £9. In Table I, the grain rent of 3 qrs $= \frac{3}{4}$ of the total product of 4 qrs; in Table IVd it is 10 qrs, or one-half the total product (20 qrs) per acre of D. This shows that the money value and grain value of the rent per acre may rise, although it constitutes a smaller aliquot part of the total yield and has fallen in proportion to the advanced capital.

The value of the total product in Table I $=$ £30, the rent $=$ £18, or more than one-half of it. The value of the total product in IVd $=$ £45, of which the rent $=$ £18, or less than one-half.

---

^{a} In the 1894 German edition "33 and 27".

Now, the reason why in spite of the fall in price by £1^1/$_2$ per quarter, i. e., a fall of 50%, and in spite of the reduction in competing soil from 4 to 3 acres, the total money rent remains the same and the total grain rent is doubled, while, calculated per acre, both the grain rent and money rent rise, is that more quarters of surplus product are produced. The price of grain falls by 50%, and the surplus product increases by 100%. But in order to obtain this result, the total production under the conditions assumed by us must be trebled, and the investment of capital in the superior soils must be more than doubled. At what rate the latter must increase depends in the first place upon the distribution of additional capital investments among the better and best soils, always assuming that the productivity of the capital invested in each soil type increases proportionately to its magnitude.

If the fall in price of production were smaller, less additional capital would be required to produce the same money rent. If the supply required to throw soil A out of cultivation — and this depends not merely upon the output per acre of A, but also upon the share held by A in the entire cultivated area — thus, if the supply required for this purpose were larger, and thereby also the amount of additional invested capital required in soils better than A, then, other circumstances remaining the same, the money and grain rents would have increased still more, although soil B would have ceased yielding money and grain rents.

If the capital eliminated from A had been = £5, the tables to be compared for this case would be tables II and IVd. The total product would have increased from 20 to 30 qrs. The money rent would be only half as large, or £18 instead of £36; the grain rent would be the same, namely = 12 qrs.

If a total product of 44 qrs = £66 could be produced upon D with a capital = £27^1/$_2$ — corresponding to the old rate for D, 4 qrs per £2^1/$_2$ capital — then the total rental would once more reach the level attained in Table II, and the table would appear as follows:

Type of Soil	Capital £	Output Qrs	Grain Rent Qrs	Money Rent £
B	5	4	0	0
C	5	6	2	3
D	27^1/$_2$	44	22	33
Total	37^1/$_2$	54	24	36

The total production would be 54 qrs as against 20 qrs in Table II, and the money rent would be the same, = £36. But the total capital would be £37¹/₂, whereas in Table II it was = 20. The total advanced capital would be double almost, while production would be nearly treble; the grain rent would be double and the money rent would remain the same. Hence, if the price falls — while productivity remains the same — as a result of the investment of additional money capital in the better soils which yield rent, that is, all soils better than A, then the total capital has a tendency not to increase at the same rate as production and grain rent; thus the increase in grain rent may compensate for the loss in money rent due to the falling price. The same law also manifests itself in that the advanced capital must be proportionately larger as more is invested in C than D, i. e., in soils yielding less rent rather than in soils yielding more rent. The point is simply this: in order that the money rent may remain the same or rise, a definite additional quantity of surplus product must be produced, and the greater the fertility of the soils yielding surplus product, the less capital this requires. If the difference between B and C, and C and D, were still greater, still less additional capital would be required. The specific proportion is determined by 1) the ratio of fall in price, in other words, by the difference between soil B, which does not yield rent now, and soil A, which formerly was the soil not yielding rent; 2) the ratio of the differences between the soils better than B upwards; 3) the amount of newly invested additional capital, and 4) its distribution among the soils of varying quality.

In fact, we see that this law merely expresses what was already ascertained in the first case: When the price of production is given, no matter what its magnitude, the rent may increase as a result of additional capital investment. For owing to the elimination of A, we now have a new differential rent I with B as the worst soil and £1¹/₂ per quarter as the new price of production. This applies to Table IV as well as to Table II. It is the same law, except that our point of departure is soil B instead of A, and our price of production is taken as £1¹/₂ instead of £3.

The important thing here is this: To the extent that so much and so much additional capital was necessary in order to withdraw the capital from soil A and create the supply without it, we find that this may be accompanied by an unaltered, rising, or falling rent per acre, if not from all plots of land then at least from some, and so far as the average of the cultivated plots is concerned. We have seen that grain rent and money rent do not maintain a uniform relation to one another. It is merely due to tradition that grain rent is still of any importance in economics. One might demonstrate equally well that, e. g., a manufacturer can buy much more of his yarn with his profit of £5 than he could formerly with a profit of £10. It shows at any rate, that messieurs landlords, when they are simultaneously owners or shareholders in manufacturing establishments, sugar refineries, distilleries, etc., may in their capacity as producers of their own raw materials still make a considerable profit when the money rent is falling.[34]

II. Decreasing rate of productivity of the additional capital

This introduces nothing new into the problem, in so far as the price of production may also fall in this case, as in the case just considered, only when additional investments of capital in better soils than A render the output from A superfluous and the capital is therefore withdrawn from A, or A is employed for the production of other products. This case has been exhaustively discussed above. It was shown that the rent in grain and money per acre may increase, decrease, or remain unchanged.

For convenience in making comparisons we reproduce the following table:

TABLE I

Type of Soil	Acres	Capital £	Profit £	Price of Production per Qr	Output Qrs	Grain Rent Qrs	Money Rent Qrs	Rate of Surplus Profit
A	1	$2^1/_2$	$^1/_2$	3	1	0	0	0
B	1	$2^1/_2$	$^1/_2$	$1^1/_2$	2	1	3	120%
C	1	$2^1/_2$	$^1/_2$	1	3	2	6	240%
D	1	$2^1/_2$	$^1/_2$	$^3/_4$	4	3	9	360%
Total	4	10			10	6	18	180% average

[34] The above tables IVa to IVd had to be recalculated due to an error in computation which ran through all of them. While this did not affect the theoretical conclusions drawn from these tables, it introduced, in part, quite monstrous numerical values for production per acre. Even these are not objectionable in principle. For all relief and topographical maps it is customary to choose a much larger scale for the vertical than for the horizontal. Nevertheless, should anyone feel that his agrarian feelings have been injured thereby, he is at liberty to multiply the number of acres by any numerical value that will satisfy him. One might also choose 10, 12, 14, 16 bushels (8 bushels = 1 quarter)

Now let us assume that a quantity of 16 qrs [a] supplied by **B, C,** and **D** at a decreasing rate of productivity suffices to exclude **A** from cultivation. In such case, Table III is transformed into the following:

TABLE V

Type of Soil	Acres	Investment of Capital £	Profit £	Output Qrs	Selling Price £	Proceeds £	Grain Rent Qrs	Money Rent £	Rate of Surplus Profit
B	1	$2^1/_2 + 2^1/_2$	1	$2 + 1^1/_2 = 3^1/_2$	$1^5/_7$	6	0	0	0
C	1	$2^1/_2 + 2^1/_2$	1	$3 + 2 = 5$	$1^5/_7$	$8^4/_7$	$1^1/_2$	$2^4/_7$	$51^3/_7\%$ [b]
D	1	$2^1/_2 + 2^1/_2$	1	$4 + 3^1/_2 = 7^1/_2$	$1^5/_7$	$12^6/_7$	4	$6^6/_7$	$137^1/_7\%$ [c]
Total	3	15		16		$27^3/_7$	$5^1/_2$	$9^3/_7$	$94^2/_7\%$ [d] average

Here, at a decreasing rate of productivity of the additional capital, and a varying decrease for the various soil types, the regulating price of production has fallen from £3 to £$1^5/_7$. The investment of capital has risen by one-half—from £10 to £15. The money rent has fallen by almost one-half—from 18 to £$9^3/_7$, but the grain rent has fallen by only $\frac{1}{12}$ —from 6 qrs to $5\frac{1}{2}$ qrs. The total output has risen from 10 to 16, or by 60%. The grain rent constitutes a little more than one-third of the total product. The advanced capital is to the money rent as $15:9\frac{3}{7}$, whereas formerly this ratio was 10:18.

III. Rising rate of productivity of the additional capital

This differs from Variant I at the beginning of this chapter, where the price of production falls while the rate of productivity remains the same, merely in that when a given amount of additional produce is required to exclude soil A this occurs here more quickly.

The effect may vary in accordance with the distribution of investments among the various soils for a falling, as well as an increasing,

per acre in Table I instead of 1, 2, 3, 4 quarters, and the derived numerical values in the other tables would remain within the limits of probability; it will be found that the result, i. e., the ratio of rent increase to capital increase, is exactly the same. This has been done in the tables included by the editor in the next chapter.— *F. E.*

---

[a] In Table III. - [b] In the 1894 German edition "$51^2/_5$". - [c] Ibid.: "$137^1/_5$". - [d] Ibid.: "$94^3/_{10}\%$". Here, as well as in tables VI, VII, VIII, IX and X the land which yields no rent is left out of consideration.

productivity of the additional capital investments. In so far as this varying effect balances out the differences, or accentuates them, the differential rent of the better soils, and thereby the total rental too, will fall or rise, as was already the case in differential rent I. In other respects, everything depends upon the magnitude of the land area and capital excluded together with A, and upon the relative magnitude of advanced capital required with a rising productivity in order to produce the additional output to meet the demand.

The only point worth while analysing here, and which really takes us back to the investigation of the way in which this differential profit is transformed into differential rent, is the following:

In the first case, where the price of production remains the same the additional capital which may be invested in soil A does not affect the differential rent as such, since soil A, as before, does not yield any rent, the price of its produce remains the same, and it continues to regulate the market.

In the second case, Variant I, where the price of production falls while the rate of productivity remains the same, soil A will necessarily be excluded, and still more so in Variant II (falling price of production with falling rate of productivity), since otherwise the additional capital invested is soil A would have had to raise the price of production. But here, in Variant III of the second case, where the price of production falls because the productivity of the additional capital rises, this additional capital may under certain circumstances be invested in soil A as well as in the better soils.

Let us assume that when invested in soil A an additional capital of $£2\frac{1}{2}$ produces $1\frac{1}{5}$ qrs instead of 1 qr.

TABLE VI

Type of Soil	Acres	Capital £	Profit £	Price of Production £	Output Qrs	Selling Price £	Proceeds £	Rent Qrs	Rent £	Rate of Surplus Profit
A	1	$2^1/_2 + 2^1/_2 = 5$	1	6	$1 + 1^1/_5 = 2^1/_5$	$2^8/_{11}$	6	0	0	0
B	1	$2^1/_2 + 2^1/_2 = 5$	1	6	$2 + 2^2/_5 = 4^2/_5$	$2^8/_{11}$	12	$2^1/_5$	6	120%
C	1	$2^1/_2 + 2^1/_2 = 5$	1	6	$3 + 3^3/_5 = 6^3/_5$	$2^8/_{11}$	18	$4^2/_5$	12	240%
D	1	$2^1/_2 + 2^1/_2 = 5$	1	6	$4 + 4^4/_5 = 8^4/_5$	$2^8/_{11}$	24	$6^3/_5$	18	360%
	4	20	4	24	22		60	$13^1/_5$	36	240%

Aside from being compared with the basic Table I, this table should be compared with Table II, where a two-fold investment of capital is associated with a constant productivity, proportional to the investment of capital.

In accordance with our assumption, the regulating price of production falls. If it were to remain constant, $= £3$, then the worst soil A, which used to yield no rent with an investment of only $£2\frac{1}{2}$, would now yield rent without worse soil being brought under cultivation. This would have occurred due to an increase in the productivity of this soil, but only for a part of the capital, not for the original capital invested. The first $£3$ of production price yield 1 qr; the second yield $1\frac{1}{5}$ qrs; but the entire output of $2\frac{1}{5}$ qrs is now sold at its average price. Since the rate of productivity increases with the additional investment of capital, this presupposes an improvement. The latter may consist of a general increase in capital invested per acre (more fertiliser, more mechanised labour, etc.), or it may be that only through this additional capital it is at all possible to bring about a qualitatively different more productive investment of the capital. In both cases, the investment of $£5$ of capital per acre yields an output of $2\frac{1}{5}$ qrs, whereas the investment of one-half of this capital, i. e., $£2\frac{1}{2}$, yields only 1 qr of produce. The produce from soil A could, regardless of transient market conditions, only continue to be sold at a higher price of production instead of at the new average price, as long as a considerable area of type A soil continued to be cultivated with a capital of only $£2\frac{1}{2}$ per acre. But as soon as the new relation of $£5$ of capital per acre, and thereby the improved management, becomes universal, the regulating price of production would have to fall to $£2\frac{8}{11}$. The difference between the two portions of capital would disappear, and then, in fact, the cultivation of an acre of soil A with a capital of only $£2\frac{1}{2}$ would be abnormal, i. e., would not correspond to the new conditions of production. It would then no longer be a difference between the yields from different portions of capital invested in the same acre, but between a sufficient and an insufficient total investment of capital per acre. This shows, *first of all*, that insufficient capital in the hands of a large number of tenant farmers (it must be a large number, for a small number would simply be compelled to sell below their price of production) produces the same effect as a differentiation of the soils themselves in a descending line. The inferior cultivation of inferior soil increases the rent from superior soils; it may even lead to rent being yielded from better cultivated soil of equally poor quality, which would otherwise not be yielded. It shows, *secondly*, that differential rent, in so far as it arises from successive investments of capital in the same total area, resolves itself in reality into an average, in which the effects of the various investments of capital are no longer recognisable and distinguishable, and therefore do not result in rent being yielded from the worst soil, but rather: 1) make the average price of the total yield for, say, an acre of A, the new regulating price and 2) appear as alteration in the total quantity of capital per acre required under the new conditions for the adequate cultivation of the soil; and in which the individual successive investments of capital, as well as their respective effects, will appear indistinguishably blended together. It is exactly the same with the individual differential rents from the superior soils. In each case, they are determined by the difference between the average output from the soil in question and the output from the worst soil at the increased capital investment — which has now become normal.

No soil yields any produce without an investment of capital. This is the case even for simple differential rent, differential rent I; when it is said that one acre of soil A, which regulates the price of production, yields so much and so much produce at such and such a price, and that superior soils B, C and D yield so much differential produce, and therefore so much and so much money rent at the regulating price of production, it is always assumed that a definite amount of capital is invested which, under the prevailing conditions of production, is considered normal. In the same way, a certain minimum capital is required for every individual branch of industry in order that the commodities may be produced at their price of production.

If this minimum is altered as a result of succesive investments of capital associated with improvements on the same soil, it occurs gradually. So long as certain number of acres, say, of A, do not receive this additional working capital, a rent is produced upon the better cultivated acres of A due to the unaltered price of production, and the rent from all superior soils, B, C and D, is increased. But as soon as the new method of cultivation has become general enough to be the normal one, the price of production falls; the rent from the superior plots declines again, and that portion of soil A that does not possess the working capital, which has now become the average, must sell its produce below its individual price of production, i. e., below the average profit.

In the case of a falling price of production, this also occurs even with decreasing productivity of the additional capital — as soon as the required total product is supplied, in consequence of increased investment of capital, by the superior soils, and thus, e. g., the working capital is withdrawn from A, i. e., A no longer competes in the production of this particular product, e. g., wheat. The quantity of capital which is now required, on an average, to be invested in the better soil B, the new regulator, now becomes normal: and when one speaks of the varying fertility of plots of land, it is assumed that this new normal quantity of capital per acre is employed.

On the other hand, it is evident that this average investment of capital, say, in England, of £8 per acre prior to 1848, and £12 subsequent to that year, will constitute the standard in concluding leases. For the farmer expending more than this, the surplus profit is not transformed into rent for the duration of the contract. Whether this takes place after expiration of the contract or not will depend upon the competition among the farmers who are in a position to make the same extra capital advance. We are not referring here to such permanent soil improvements that continue to provide the increased output with the same or even with a decreasing outlay of capital. Such improvements, although products of capital, have the same effect as natural differences in the quality of the land.

We see, then, that a factor comes into consideration in the case of differential rent II which does not appear in the case of differential rent I as such, since the latter can continue to exist independently of any change in the normal investment of capital per acre. It is, on the one hand, the blurring of results from various investments, of capital in regulating soil A, whose output now simply appears as a normal average output per acre. It is, on the other hand, the change in the normal minimum, or in the average magnitude of invested capital per acre, so that this change appears as a property of the soil. It is, finally, the difference in the manner of transforming surplus profit into the form of rent.

Table VI shows, furthermore, compared with tables I and II, that the grain rent has more than doubled in relation to I, and has increased by $1\frac{1}{5}$ qrs in relation to II; while the money rent has doubled in relation to I, but has not changed in relation to II. It would have increased considerably if (other conditions remaining the same) more of the additional capital had been allocated to the superior soils, or if on the other hand the effect of the additional capital on A had been less appreciable, and thus the regulating average price per quarter from A had been higher.

If the increase in fertility by means of additional capital should produce varying results for the various soils, this would produce a change in their differential rents.

In any case, it has been shown that the rent per acre, for instance with a doubled investment of capital, may not only double, but may more than double—while the price of production falls in consequence of an increased rate of productivity of the additional capital invested, i. e., when this productivity grows at a higher rate than the advanced capital. But it may also fall if the price of production should fall much lower as a result of a more rapid increase in productiveness of soil A.

Let us assume that the additional investments of capital, for instance in B and C, do not increase the productivity at the same rate as they do for A, so that the proportional differences decrease for B and C and the increase in output does not make up for the fall in price. Then, compared with Table II, the rent from D would remain unchanged, and that from B and C would fall.

TABLE VIa

Type of Soil	Acres	Capital £	Profit £	Output per Acre Qrs	Selling Price £	Proceeds £	Grain Rent Qrs	Money Rent £
A	1	$2^1/_2 + 2^1/_2 = 5$	1	$1 + 3 = 4$	$1^1/_2$	6	0	0
B	1	$2^1/_2 + 2^1/_2 = 5$	1	$2 + 2^1/_2 = 4^1/_2$	$1^1/_2$	$6^3/_4$	$^1/_2$	$^3/_4$
C	1	$2^1/_2 + 2^1/_2 = 5$	1	$3 + 5 = 8$	$1^1/_2$	12	4	6
D	1	$2^1/_2 + 2^1/_2 = 5$	1	$4 + 12 = 16$	$1^1/_2$	24	12	18
Total	4	20		$32^1/_2$			$16^1/_2$	$24^3/_4$

Finally, the money rent would rise if more additional capital were invested in the superior soils with the same proportional increase in fertility than in A, or if the additional investments of capital in the superior soils were effective at an increasing rate of productivity. In both cases the differences would increase.

The money rent falls when the improvement due to additional investment of capital reduces the differences completely or in part, and affects A more than B and C. The smaller the increase in productivity of the superior soils, the more it falls. It depends upon the extent of inequality produced, whether the grain rent shall rise, fall or remain stationary.

The money rent rises, and similarly the grain rent, either when — the proportional difference in additional fertility of the various soils remaining unaltered — more capital is invested in the rent-bearing soils than in rentless soil A, and more in soils yielding higher rent than in those yielding lower rents; or when the fertility — the additional capital remaining equal — increases more on the better and best soils than on A, i. e., the money and grain rents rise in proportion to this increase in fertility of the better soils above that of the poorer ones.

But under all circumstances, there is a relative rise in rent when increased productive power is the result of an addition of capital, and not merely the result of increased fertility with unaltered investment of capital. This is the absolute point of view, which shows that here, as in all former cases, the rent and increased rent per acre (as in the case of differential rent I on the entire cultivated area — the magnitude of the average rental) are the result of an increased investment of capital in land, no matter whether this capital functions with a constant rate of productivity at constant or decreasing prices or with a decreasing rate of productivity at constant or falling prices, or with an increasing rate of productivity at falling prices. For our assumption: constant prices with a constant, falling, or rising rate of productivity of the additional capital, and falling prices with a constant, falling, or rising rate of productivity, resolves itself into: a constant rate of productivity of the additional capital at constant or falling prices, a falling rate of productivity at constant or falling prices, and a rising rate of productivity at constant and falling prices. Although the rent may remain stationary, or may fall, in all these cases, it would fall more if the additional investment of capital, other circumstances remaining the same, were not a prerequisite for the increased fertility. The additional capital, then, is always the cause for the relatively high rent, although absolutely it may have decreased.

Chapter XLIII

DIFFERENTIAL RENT II.—THIRD CASE:
RISING PRICE OF PRODUCTION

//A rising price of production presupposes that the productivity of the poorest quality land yielding no rent decreases. The assumed regulating price of production cannot rise above £3 per quarter unless the £2$\frac{1}{2}$ invested in soil A produce less than 1 qr, or the £5 — less than 2 qrs, or unless an even poorer soil than A has to be taken under cultivation.

For constant, or even increasing, productivity of the second investment of capital this would only be possible if the productivity of the first investment of capital of £2$\frac{1}{2}$ had decreased. This case occurs often enough. For instance, when with superficial ploughing the exhausted top soil yields ever smaller crops, under the old method of cultivation, and then the subsoil, turned up through deeper ploughing, produces better crops than before with more rational cultivation. But, strictly speaking, this special case does not apply here. The decrease in productivity of the *first* £2$\frac{1}{2}$ of invested capital signifies for the superior soils, even when the conditions are assumed to be analogous there, a decrease in differential rent I; yet here we are considering only differential rent II. But since this special case cannot occur without presupposing the existence of differential rent II, and represents in fact the reaction of a modification of differential rent I upon II, we shall give an illustration of it.

The money rent and proceeds are the same as in Table II. The increased regulating price of production makes good what has been lost in quantity of produce; since this price and the quantity of produce are inversely proportional, it is evident that their mathematical product will remain the same.

TABLE VII

Type of Soil	Acres	Invested Capital £	Profit £	Price of Production £	Output Qrs	Selling Price £	Proceeds £	Grain Rent Qrs	Money Rent £	Rate of Rent
A	1	2$^1/_2$ + 2$^1/_2$	1	6	$^1/_2$ + 1$^1/_4$ = 1$^3/_4$	3$^3/_7$	6	0	0	0
B	1	2$^1/_2$ + 2$^1/_2$	1	6	1 + 2$^1/_2$ = 3$^1/_2$	3$^3/_7$	12	1$^3/_4$	6	120%
C	1	2$^1/_2$ + 2$^1/_2$	1	6	1$^1/_2$ + 3$^3/_4$ = 5$^1/_4$	3$^3/_7$	18	3$^1/_2$	12	240%
D	1	2$^1/_2$ + 2$^1/_2$	1	6	2 + 5 = 7	3$^3/_7$	24	5$^1/_4$	18	360%
		20			17$^1/_2$		60	10$^1/_2$	36	240%

In the above case, it was assumed that the productive power of the second investment of capital was greater than the original productivity of the first investment. Nothing changes if we assume the second investment to have only the same productivity as the first, as shown in the following table:

TABLE VIII

Type of Soil	Acres	Invested Capital £	Profit £	Price of Prod. £	Output Qrs	Selling Price £	Proceeds £	Rent in Grain Qrs	Rent in Money £	Rate of Surplus Profit
A	1	$2^1/_2 + 2^1/_2 = 5$	1	6	$^1/_2 + 1 = 1^1/_2$	4	6	0	0	0
B	1	$2^1/_2 + 2^1/_2 = 5$	1	6	$1 + 2 = 3$	4	12	$1^1/_2$	6	120%
C	1	$2^1/_2 + 2^1/_2 = 5$	1	6	$1^1/_2 + 3 = 4^1/_2$	4	18	3	12	240%
D	1	$2^1/_2 + 2^1/_2 = 5$	1	6	$2 + 4 = 6$	4	24	$4^1/_2$	18	360%
		20			15		60	9	36	240%

Here, too, the price of production rising at the same rate compensates in full for the decrease in productivity in the case of yield as well as money rent.

The third case appears in its pure form only when the productivity of the second investment of capital declines, while that of the first remains constant — which was always assumed in the first and second cases. Here differential rent I is not affected, i. e., the change affects only that part which arises from differential rent II. We shall give two illustrations: in the first we assume that the productivity of the second investment of capital has been reduced to $\frac{1}{2}$, in the second to $\frac{3}{4}$.

TABLE IX

Type of Soil	Acres	Invested Capital £	Profit £	Price of Prod. £	Output Qrs	Selling Price £	Proceeds £	Rent in Grain Qrs	Rent in Money £	Rate of Rent
A	1	$2^1/_2 + 2^1/_2 = 5$	1	6	$1 + ^1/_2 = 1^1/_2$	4	6	0	0	0
B	1	$2^1/_2 + 2^1/_2 = 5$	1	6	$2 + 1 = 3$	4	12	1	6	120%
C	1	$2^1/_2 + 2^1/_2 = 5$	1	6	$3 + 1^1/_2 = 4^1/_2$	4	18	3	12	240%
D	1	$2^1/_2 + 2^1/_2 = 5$	1	6	$4 + 2 = 6$	4	24	$4^1/_2$	18	360%
		20			15		60	9	36	240%

Table IX is the same as Table VIII, except for the fact that the decrease in productivity in VIII occurs for the first, and in IX for the second investment of capital.

TABLE X

Type of Soil	Acres	Invested Capital £	Profit £	Price of Prod. £	Output Qrs	Selling Price £	Proceeds £	Rent in Grain Qrs	Rent in Money £	Rate of Rent
A	1	$2^1/_2 + 2^1/_2 = 5$	1	6	$1 + {}^1/_4 = 1^1/_4$	$4^4/_5$	6	0	0	0
B	1	$2^1/_2 + 2^1/_2 = 5$	1	6	$2 + {}^1/_2 = 2^1/_2$	$4^4/_5$	12	$1^1/_4$	6	120%
C	1	$2^1/_2 + 2^1/_2 = 5$	1	6	$3 + {}^3/_4 = 3^3/_4$	$4^4/_5$	18	$2^1/_2$	12	240%
D	1	$2^1/_2 + 2^1/_2 = 5$	1	6	$4 + 1 = 5$	$4^4/_5$	24	$3^3/_4$	18	360%
		20		24	$12^1/_2$		60	$7^1/_2$	36	240%

In this table, too, the total proceeds, the money rent and rate of rent remain the same as in tables II, VII and VIII, because produce and selling price are again inversely proportional, while the invested capital remains the same.

But how do matters stand in the other possible case when the price of production rises, namely, in the case of a poor quality soil not worth cultivating until then that is taken under cultivation?

Let us suppose that a soil of this sort, which we shall designate by a, enters into competition. Then the hitherto rentless soil A would yield rent, and the foregoing tables VII, VIII and X would assume the following forms:

TABLE VIIa

Type of Soil	Acres	Capital £	Profit £	Price of Prod. £	Output Qrs	Selling Price £	Proceeds £	Rent Qrs	Rent £	Increase
a	1	5	1	6	$1^1/_2$	4	6	0	0	0
A	1	$2^1/_2 + 2^1/_2$	1	6	${}^1/_2 + 1^1/_4 = 1^3/_4$	4	7	${}^1/_4$	1	1
B	1	$2^1/_2 + 2^1/_2$	1	6	$1 + 2^1/_2 = 3^1/_2$	4	14	2	8	$1 + 7$
C	1	$2^1/_2 + 2^1/_2$	1	6	$1^1/_2 + 3^3/_4 = 5^1/_4$	4	21	$3^3/_4$	15	$1 + 2 \times 7$
D	1	$2^1/_2 + 2^1/_2$	1	6	$2 + 5 = 7$	4	28	$5^1/_2$	22	$1 + 3 \times 7$
				30	19		76	$11^1/_2$	46	

TABLE VIIIa

Type of Soil	Acres	Capital £	Profit £	Price of Prod. £	Output Qrs	Selling Price £	Proceeds £	Rent Qrs	Rent £	Increase
a	1	5	1	6	$1^1/_4$	$4^4/_5$	6	0	0	0
A	1	$2^1/_2 + 2^1/_2$	1	6	$^1/_2 + 1 = 1^1/_2$	$4^4/_5$	$7^1/_5$	$^1/_4$	$1^1/_5$	$1^1/_5$
B	1	$2^1/_2 + 2^1/_2$	1	6	$1 + 2 = 3$	$4^4/_5$	$14^2/_5$	$1^3/_4$	$8^2/_5$	$1^1/_5 + 7^1/_5$
C	1	$2^1/_2 + 2^1/_2$	1	6	$1^1/_2 + 3 = 4^1/_2$	$4^4/_5$	$21^3/_5$	$3^1/_4$	$15^3/_5$	$1^1/_5 + 2 \times 7^1/_5$
D	1	$2^1/_2 + 2^1/_2$	1	6	$2 + 4 = 6$	$4^4/_5$	$28^4/_5$	$4^3/_4$	$22^4/_5$	$1^1/_5 + 3 \times 7^1/_5$
	5			30	$16^1/_4$		78	10	48	

TABLE Xa

Type of Soil	Acres	Capital £	Profit £	Price of Prod. £	Output Qrs	Selling Price £	Proceeds £	Rent Qrs	Rent £	Increase
a	1	5	1	6	$1^1/_8$	$5^1/_3$	6	0	0	0
A	1	$2^1/_2 + 2^1/_2$	1	6	$1 + ^1/_4 = 1^1/_4$	$5^1/_3$	$6^2/_3$	$^1/_8$	$^2/_3$	$^2/_3$
B	1	$2^1/_2 + 2^1/_2$	1	6	$2 + ^1/_2 = 2^1/_2$	$5^1/_3$	$13^1/_3$	$1^3/_8$	$7^1/_3$	$^2/_3 + 6^2/_3$
C	1	$2^1/_2 + 2^1/_2$	1	6	$3 + ^3/_4 = 3^3/_4$	$5^1/_3$	20	$2^5/_8$	14	$^2/_3 + 2 \times 6^2/_3$
D	1	$2^1/_2 + 2^1/_2$	1	6	$4 + 1 = 5$	$5^1/_3$	$26^2/_3$	$3^7/_8$	$20^2/_3$	$^2/_3 + 3 \times 6^2/_3$
				30	$13^5/_8$		$72^2/_3$	8	$43^2/_3$	

By interpolating soil a there arises a new differential rent I; upon this new basis, differential rent II likewise develops in an altered form. Soil a has different fertility in each of the above three tables; the sequence of proportionally increasing fertilities begins only with soil A. The sequence of rising rents also behaves similarly. The rent of the worst rent-bearing soil, previously rentless, is a constant which is simply added to all higher rents; only after deducting this constant does the sequence of differences clearly become evident for the higher rents, and similarly its parallel in the fertility sequence of the different soils. In all the tables, the fertilities from A to D are related as $1 : 2 : 3 : 4$, and correspondingly the rents:

in VIIa, as $1 : (1 + 7) : (1 + 2 \times 7) : (1 + 3 \times 7)$,

in VIIIa, as $1\frac{1}{5}:(1\frac{1}{5}+7\frac{1}{5}):(1\frac{1}{5}+2\times7\frac{1}{5}):(1\frac{1}{5}+3\times7\frac{1}{5})$,
and in Xa, as $\frac{2}{3}:(\frac{2}{3}+6\frac{2}{3}):(\frac{2}{3}+2\times6\frac{2}{3}):(\frac{2}{3}+3\times6\frac{2}{3})$.

In brief, if the rent from A = n, and the rent from the soil of next higher fertility = n + m, then the sequence is as follows: n : (n + m) : : (n + 2m) : (n + 3m), etc.— *F. E.*//

//Since the foregoing third case had not been elaborated in the manuscript—only the title is there—it was the task of the editor to fill in the gap, as above, to the best of his ability. However, in addition, it still remains for him to draw the general conclusions from the entire foregoing analysis of differential rent II, consisting of three principal cases and nine subcases. The illustrations presented in the manuscript, however, do not suit this purpose very well. In the first place, they compare plots of land whose yields for equal areas are related as 1:2:3:4; i. e., differences, which exaggerate greatly from the very first, and which lead to utterly monstrous numerical values in the further development of the assumptions and calculations made upon this basis. Secondly, they create a completely erroneous impression. If for degrees of fertility related as 1:2:3:4, etc., rents are obtained in the sequence 0:1:2:3, etc., one feels tempted to derive the second sequence from the first, and to explain the doubling, tripling, etc., of rents by the doubling, tripling, etc., of the total yields. But this would be wholly incorrect. The rents are related as 0:1:2:3:4 even when the degrees of fertility are related as n : (n + 1) : (n + 2) : (n + 3) : : (n + 4). The rents are not related as the *degrees* of fertility, but as the *differences* of fertility—beginning with the rentless soil as the zero point.

The original tables had to be offered to illustrate the text. But in order to obtain a perceptual basis for the following results of the investigation, I present below a new series of tables in which the yields are indicated in bushels ($\frac{1}{8}$ quarter, or 36.35 litres) and shillings (= marks).

The first of these, Table XI, corresponds to the former Table I. It shows the yields and rents for soils of five different qualities, A to E, with a *first* capital investment of 50 shillings, which added to 10 shillings profit = 60 shillings total price of production per acre. The yields in grain are made low: 10, 12, 14, 16, 18 bushels per acre. The resulting regulating price of production is 6 shillings per bushel.

The following 13 tables correspond to the three cases of differential rent II treated in this and the two preceding chapters with an *addi-*

tional invested capital of 50 shillings per acre in the same soil with constant, falling and rising prices of production. Each of these cases, in turn, is presented as it takes shape for: 1) constant, 2) falling, and 3) rising productivity of the second investment of capital in relation to the first. This yields a few other variants, which are especially useful for illustration purposes.

For case I: Constant price of production — we have:

Variant 1: Productivity of the second investment of capital remains the same (Table XII).

2: Productivity declines. This can take place only when no second investment of capital is made in soil A, i.e., in such a way that

a) soil B likewise yields no rent (Table XIII) or

b) soil B does not become completely rentless (Table XIV).

Variant 3: Productivity increases (Table XV). This case likewise excludes a second investment of capital in soil A.

For case II. Falling price of production — we have:

Variant 1: Productivity of the second investment of capital remains the same (Table XVI).

2: Productivity declines (Table XVII). These two variants require that soil A be eliminated from competition, and that soil B become rentless and regulate the price of production.

3: Productivity increases (Table XVIII). Here soil A remains the regulator.

For case III: Rising price of production — two eventualities are possible: soil A may remain rentless and continue to regulate the price, or poorer soil than A enters into competition and regulates the price, in which case A yields rent.

First eventuality: Soil A remains the regulator.

Variant 1: Productivity of the second investment remains the same (Table XIX). This is admissible under the conditions assumed by us, provided the productivity of the first investment decreases.

2: Productivity of the second investment decreases (Table XX). This does not exclude the possibility that the first investment may retain the same productivity.

3: Productivity of the second investment increases (Table XXI). This, again, presupposes falling productivity of the first investment.

Second eventuality: An inferior quality soil (designated as a) enters into competition; soil A yields rent.
Variant 1: Productivity of the second investment remains the same (Table XXII).
Variant 2: Productivity declines (Table XXIII).
        3: Productivity increases (Table XXIV).
These three variants conform to the general conditions of the problem and require no further comment.
The tables now follow:

TABLE XI

Type of Soil	Price of Production Sh.	Output Bushels	Selling Price Sh.	Proceeds Sh.	Rent Sh.	Rent Increase
A	60	10	6	60	0	0
B	60	12	6	72	12	12
C	60	14	6	84	24	2×12
D	60	16	6	96	36	3×12
E	60	18	6	108	48	4×12
					120	10×12

For second capital invested in the same soil.
First Case: Price of production remains unaltered.
Variant 1: Productivity of the second investment of capital remains the same.

TABLE XII

Type of Soil	Price of Production Sh.	Output Bushels	Selling Price Sh.	Proceeds Sh.	Rent Sh.	Rent Increase
A	$60 + 60 = 120$	$10 + 10 = 20$	6	120	0	0
B	$60 + 60 = 120$	$12 + 12 = 24$	6	144	24	24
C	$60 + 60 = 120$	$14 + 14 = 28$	6	168	48	2×24
D	$60 + 60 = 120$	$16 + 16 = 32$	6	192	72	3×24
E	$60 + 60 = 120$	$18 + 18 = 36$	6	216	96	4×24
					240	10×24

Variant 2: Productivity of the second investment of capital declines; no second investment in soil A.

1) Soil B ceases to yield rent.

TABLE XIII

Type of Soil	Price of Production Sh.	Output Bushels	Selling Price Sh.	Proceeds Sh.	Rent Sh.	Rent Increase
A	60	10	6	60	0	0
B	$60 + 60 = 120$	$12 + 8 = 20$	6	120	0	0
C	$60 + 60 = 120$	$14 + 9^1/_3 = 23^1/_3$	6	140	20	20
D	$60 + 60 = 120$	$16 + 10^2/_3 = 26^2/_3$	6	160	40	2×20
E	$60 + 60 = 120$	$18 + 12 = 30$	6	180	60	3×20
					120	6×20

2) Soil B does not become completely rentless.

TABLE XIV

Type of Soil	Price of Production Sh.	Output Bushels	Selling Price Sh.	Proceeds Sh.	Rent Sh.	Rent Increase
A	60	10	6	60	0	0
B	$60 + 60 = 120$	$12 + 9 = 21$	6	126	6	6
C	$60 + 60 = 120$	$14 + 10^1/_2 = 24^1/_2$	6	147	27	$6 + 21$
D	$60 + 60 = 120$	$16 + 12 = 28$	6	168	48	$6 + 2 \times 21$
E	$60 + 60 = 120$	$18 + 13^1/_2 = 31^1/_2$	6	189	69	$6 + 3 \times 21$
					150	$4 \times 6 + 6 \times 21$

Variant 3: Productivity of the second investment of capital increases; here, too, no second investment in soil A.

TABLE XV

Type of Soil	Price of Production Sh.	Output Bushels	Selling Price Sh.	Proceeds Sh.	Rent Sh.	Rent Increase
A	60	10	6	60	0	0
B	$60 + 60 = 120$	$12 + 15 = 27$	6	162	42	42
C	$60 + 60 = 120$	$14 + 17^1/_2 = 31^1/_2$	6	189	69	$42 + 27$
D	$60 + 60 = 120$	$16 + 20 = 36$	6	216	96	$42 + 2 \times 27$
E	$60 + 60 = 120$	$18 + 22^1/_2 = 40^1/_2$	6	243	123	$42 + 3 \times 27$
					330	$4 \times 42 + 6 \times 27$

Second Case: Price of production declines.
Variant 1: Productivity of the second investment of capital remains
the same. Soil A is excluded from competition and soil B
becomes rentless.

TABLE XVI

Type of Soil	Price of Production	Output Bushels	Selling Price Sh.	Proceeds Sh.	Rent Sh.	Rent Increase
B	60 + 60 = 120	12 + 12 = 24	5	120	0	0
C	60 + 60 = 120	14 + 14 = 28	5	140	20	20
D	60 + 60 = 120	16 + 16 = 32	5	160	40	2 × 20
E	60 + 60 = 120	18 + 18 = 36	5	180	60	3 × 20
					120	6 × 20

Variant 2: Productivity of the second investment of capital declines;
soil A is excluded from competition and soil B becomes
rentless.

TABLE XVII

Type of Soil	Price of Production Sh.	Output Bushels	Selling Price Sh.	Proceeds Sh.	Rent Sh.	Rent Increase
B	60 + 60 = 120	12 + 9 = 21	$5^5/_7$	120	0	0
C	60 + 60 = 120	14 + 10$^1/_2$ = 24$^1/_2$	$5^5/_7$	140	20	20
D	60 + 60 = 120	16 + 12 = 28	$5^5/_7$	160	40	2 × 20
E	60 + 60 = 120	18 + 13$^1/_2$ = 31$^1/_2$	$5^5/_7$	180	60	3 × 20
					120	6 × 20

Variant 3: Productivity of the second investment of capital increases; soil A remains in competition; soil B yields
rent. [See Table XVIII on p. 709.]
Third Case: Price of production rises.
A) Soil A remains rentless and continues to regulate the price.
Variant 1: Productivity of the second investment of capital remains
the same: this requires decreasing productivity of the first
investment of capital.

TABLE XVIII

Type of Soil	Price of Production Sh.	Output Bushels	Selling Price Sh.	Proceeds Sh.	Rent Sh.	Rent Increase
A	60 + 60 = 120	10 + 15 = 25	$4^4/_5$	120	0	0
B	60 + 60 = 120	12 + 18 = 30	$4^4/_5$	144	24	24
C	60 + 60 = 120	14 + 21 = 35	$4^4/_5$	168	48	2 × 24
D	60 + 60 = 120	16 + 24 = 40	$4^4/_5$	192	72	3 × 24
E	60 + 60 = 120	18 + 27 = 45	$4^4/_5$	216	96	4 × 24
					240	10 × 24

TABLE XIX

Type of Soil	Price of Production Sh.	Output Bushels[a]	Selling Price Sh.	Proceeds Sh.	Rent Sh.	Rent Increase
A	60 + 60 = 120	$7^1/_2 + 10 = 17^1/_2$	$6^6/_7$	120	0	0
B	60 + 60 = 120	$9 + 12 = 21$	$6^6/_7$	144	24	24
C	60 + 60 = 120	$10^1/_2 + 14 = 24^1/_2$	$6^6/_7$	168	48	2 × 24
D	60 + 60 = 120	$12 + 16 = 28$	$6^6/_7$	192	72	3 × 24
E	60 + 60 = 120	$13^1/_2 + 18 = 31^1/_2$	$6^6/_7$	216	96	4 × 24
					240	10 × 24

Variant 2: Productivity of the second investment of capital decreases; which does not exclude constant productivity of the first investment.

TABLE XX

Type of Soil	Price of Production Sh.	Output Bushels	Selling Price Sh.	Proceeds Sh.	Rent Sh.	Rent Increase
A	60 + 60 = 120	10 + 5 = 15	8	120	0	0
B	60 + 60 = 120	12 + 6 = 18	8	144	24	24
C	60 + 60 = 120	14 + 7 = 21	8	168	48	2 × 24
D	60 + 60 = 120	16 + 8 = 24	8	192	72	3 × 24
E	60 + 60 = 120	18 + 9 = 27	8	216	96	4 × 24
					240	10 × 24

[a] In the 1894 German edition figures from Table XXI were erroneously inserted under this head.

Variant 3: Productivity of the second investment of capital rises; under the assumed conditions this presupposes declining productivity of the first investment.

TABLE XXI

Type of Soil	Price of Production Sh.	Output Bushels	Selling Price Sh.	Proceeds Sh.	Rent Sh.	Rent Increase
A	60 + 60 = 120	5 + 12$^1/_2$ = 17$^1/_2$	6$^6/_7$	120	0	0
B	60 + 60 = 120	6 + 15 = 21	6$^6/_7$	144	24	24
C	60 + 60 = 120	7 + 17$^1/_2$ = 24$^1/_2$	6$^6/_7$	168	48	2 × 24
D	60 + 60 = 120	8 + 20 = 28	6$^6/_7$	192	72	3 × 24
E	60 + 60 = 120	9 + 22$^1/_2$ = 31$^1/_2$	6$^6/_7$	216	96	4 × 24
					240	10 × 24

B) An inferior soil (designated as a) becomes the price regulator and soil A thus yields rent. This makes admissible for all variants constant productivity of the second investment.

Variant 1: Productivity of the second investment of capital remains the same.

TABLE XXII

Type of Soil	Price of Production Sh.	Output Bushels	Selling Price Sh.	Proceeds Sh.	Rent Sh.	Rent Increase
a	120	16	7$^1/_2$	120	0	0
A	60 + 60 = 120	10 + 10 = 20	7$^1/_2$	150	30	30
B	60 + 60 = 120	12 + 12 = 24	7$^1/_2$	180	60	2 × 30
C	60 + 60 = 120	14 + 14 = 28	7$^1/_2$	210	90	3 × 30
D	60 + 60 = 120	16 + 16 = 32	7$^1/_2$	240	120	4 × 30
E	60 + 60 = 120	18 + 18 = 36	7$^1/_2$	270	150	5 × 30
					450	15 × 30

Variant 2: Productivity of the second investment of capital declines. [See Table XXIII on p. 711.]

Variant 3: Productivity of the second investment increases. [See Table XXIV on p. 711.]

These tables lead to the following conclusions:

In the first place, the sequence of rents behaves exactly as the sequence of fertility differences — taking the rentless regulating soil as

TABLE XXIII

Type of Soil	Price of Production Sh.	Output Bushels	Selling Price Sh.	Proceeds Sh.	Rent Sh.	Rent Increase
a	120	15	8	120	0	0
A	$60 + 60 = 120$	$10 + 7^1/_2 = 17^1/_2$	8	140	20	20
B	$60 + 60 = 120$	$12 + 9 = 21$	8	168	48	$20 + 28$
C	$60 + 60 = 120$	$14 + 10^1/_2 = 24^1/_2$	8	196	76	$20 + 2 \times 28$
D	$60 + 60 = 120$	$16 + 12 = 28$	8	224	104	$20 + 3 \times 28$
E	$60 + 60 = 120$	$18 + 13^1/_2 = 31^1/_2$	8	252	132	$20 + 4 \times 28$
					380	$5 \times 20 + 10 \times 28$

TABLE XXIV

Type of Soil	Price of Production Sh.	Output Bushels	Selling Price Sh.	Proceeds Sh.	Rent Sh.	Rent Increase
a	120	16	$7^1/_2$	120	0	0
A	$60 + 60 = 120$	$10 + 12^1/_2 = 22^1/_2$	$7^1/_2$	$168^3/_4$	$48^3/_4$	$15 + 33^3/_4$
B	$60 + 60 = 120$	$12 + 15 = 27$	$7^1/_2$	$202^1/_2$	$82^1/_2$	$15 + 2 \times 33^3/_4$
C	$60 + 60 = 120$	$14 + 17^1/_2 = 31^1/_2$	$7^1/_2$	$236^1/_4$	$116^1/_4$	$15 + 3 \times 33^3/_4$
D	$60 + 60 = 120$	$16 + 20 = 36$	$7^1/_2$	270	150	$15 + 4 \times 33^3/_4$
E	$60 + 60 = 120$	$18 + 22^1/_2 = 40^1/_2$	$7^1/_2$	$303^3/_4$	$183^3/_4$	$15 + 5 \times 33^3/_4$
					$581^1/_4$	$5 \times 15 + 15 \times 33^3/_4$

the zero point. It is not the absolute yield, but only the differences in yield which are the factors determining rent. Whether the various soils yield 1, 2, 3, 4, 5 bushels, or whether they yield 11, 12, 13, 14, 15 bushels per acre, the rents in both cases form the sequence 0, 1, 2, 3, 4 bushels, or their equivalent in money.

But far more important is the result with respect to the total rent yields for repeated investment of capital in the same land.

In five out of the thirteen analysed cases, the total rent *doubles* when the investment of capital is doubled; instead of 10 × 12 shillings it becomes 10 × 24 shillings = 240 shillings. These cases are:

Case I, constant price, variant 1: corresponding production rise (Table XII).

Case II, falling price, variant 3: increasing production rise (Table XVIII).

Case III, increasing price, first eventuality (where soil A remains the regulator), in all three variants (tables XIX, XX and XXI).

In four cases the rent *more than doubles*, namely:

Case I, variant 3, constant price, but increasing production rise (Table XV). The total rent climbs to 330 shillings.

Case III, second eventuality (where soil A yields rent), in all three variants (Table XXII, rent = $15 \times 30 = 450$ shillings; Table XXIII, rent = $5 \times 20 + 10 \times 28 = 380$ shillings; Table XXIV, rent = $5 \times 15 + 15 \times 33^3/_4 = 581^1/_4$ shillings).

In one case the rent *rises*, but not to twice the amount yielded by the first investment of capital.

Case I, constant price, variant 2: falling productivity of the second investment, under conditions whereby B does not become completely rentless (Table XIV, rent = $4 \times 6 + 6 \times 21 = 150$ shillings).

Finally, only in three cases does the total rent remain at the same level with a second investment — for all soils taken together — as with the first investment (Table XI); these are the cases in which soil A is excluded from competition and B becomes the regulator and thereby rentless soil. Thus, the rent for B not only vanishes but is also deducted from every succeeding term of the rent sequence; the result is thus determined. These cases are:

Case I, variant 2, when the conditions are such that soil A is excluded (Table XIII). The total rent is 6×20, or $10 \times 12 = 120$, as in Table XI.

Case II, variants 1 and 2. Here soil A is necessarily excluded in accordance with the assumptions (tables XVI and XVII) and the total rent is again $6 \times 20 = 10 \times 12 = 120$ shillings.

Thus, this means: In the great majority of all possible cases the rent rises — per acre of rent-bearing land as well as particularly in its total amount — as a result of an increased investment of capital in the land. Only in three out of the thirteen analysed cases does its total remain unaltered. These are the cases in which the lowest quality soil — hitherto the regulator and rentless — is eliminated from competition and the next quality soil takes its place, i. e., becomes rentless. But even in these cases, the rents upon the superior soils rise in comparison with the rents due to the first capital investment; when the rent for C falls from 24 to 20, then those for D and E rise from 36 and 48 to 40 and 60 shillings respectively.

A fall in the total rents below the level for the first investment of capital (Table XI) would be possible only if soil B as well as soil A were to be excluded from competition and soil C were to become regulating and rentless.

Thus, the more capital is invested in the land, and the higher the development of agriculture and civilisation in general in a given country, the more rents rise per acre as well as in total amount, and the more immense becomes the tribute paid by society to the big landowners in the form of surplus profits — so long as the various soils, once taken under cultivation, are all able to continue competing.

This law accounts for the amazing vitality of the class of big landlords. No social class lives so sumptuously, no other class claims the right it does to traditional luxury in keeping with its "estate," regardless of where the money for this purpose may be derived, and no other class piles debt upon debt so light-heartedly. And yet it always lands again on its feet — thanks to the capital invested by other people in the land, which yields it a rent, completely out of proportion to the profits reaped therefrom by the capitalist.

However, the same law also explains why the vitality of the big landlord is gradually being exhausted.

When the English corn duties were abolished in 1846, the English manufacturers believed that they had thereby turned the landowning aristocracy into paupers. Instead, they became richer than ever. How did this occur? Very simply. In the first place, the farmers were now compelled by contract to invest £12 per acre annually instead of £8. And secondly, the landlords, being strongly represented in the Lower House too, granted themselves a large government subsidy for drainage projects and other permanent improvements on their land. Since no total displacement of the poorest soil took place, but rather, at worst, it became employed for other purposes — and mostly only temporarily — rents rose in proportion to the increased investment of capital, and the landed aristocracy consequently was better off than ever before.

But everything is transitory. Transoceanic steamships and the railways of North and South America and India enabled some very singular tracts of land to compete in European grain markets. These were, on the one hand, the North American prairies and the Argentine pampas — plains cleared for the plough by Nature itself, and virgin soil which offered rich harvests for years to come even with primitive cultivation and without fertilisers. And, on the other hand, there were the land holdings of Russian and Indian communist communities which had to sell a portion of their produce, and a constantly increasing one at that, for the purpose of obtaining money for taxes wrung from them — frequently by means of torture — by a ruthless and despotic state. These products were sold without regard to price of production, they were sold at the price which the dealer offered, because the peasant perforce needed money without fail when taxes became due. And in face of this competition — coming from virgin plains as well as from Russian and Indian peasants ground down by taxation — the European tenant farmer and peasant could not prevail at the old rents. A portion of the land in Europe fell decisively out of competition as regards grain cultivation, and rents fell everywhere; our second case, variant 2 — falling prices and falling productivity of the additional investment of capital — became the rule for Europe; and therefore the lament of farmers from Scotland to Italy and from southern France to East Prussia. Fortunately, the plains are far from being entirely brought under cultivation; there are enough left to ruin all the big landlords of Europe and the small ones into the bargain.— F. E.//

———

The headings under which rent should be analysed are:
A. Differential rent.
1) Conception of differential rent. Water-power as an illustration. Transition to agricultural rent proper.
2) Differential rent I, arising from the varying fertility of various plots of land.
3) Differential rent II, arising from successive investments of capital in the same land. Differential rent II should be analysed:
a) with a stationary,
b) falling,
c) and rising price of production.
And also
d) transformation of surplus profit into rent.
4) Influence of this rent upon the rate of profit.
B. Absolute rent.
C. The price of land.
D. Final remarks concerning ground rent.

———

Overall conclusions to be drawn from the consideration of differential rent in general are the following:

First, the formation of surplus profit may take place in various ways. On the one hand, based on differential rent I, that is, on the investment of the entire agricultural capital in land consisting of soils of varying fertility. Or, in the form of differential rent II, based on the varying differential productivity of successive investments of capital in the same land, i. e., a greater productivity — expressed, e. g., in quarters of wheat — than is secured with the same investment of capital in the worst land — rentless, but which regulates the price of production. But no matter how this surplus profit may arise, its transformation into rent, i. e., its transfer from farmer to landlord, always presupposes that the various actual individual production prices of the partial outputs of the individual successive investments of capital (i. e., independent of the general price of production by which the market is regulated) have previously been reduced to an individual average price of production. The excess of the general regulating production price of the output per acre over this individual average production price constitutes and is a measure of the rent per acre. In the case of differential rent I, the differential results are in themselves distinguishable because they take place upon different portions of land — distinct from one another and existing side by side — given an investment of capital per acre and a degree of cultivation considered normal. In the case of differential rent II, they must first be made distinguishable; they must in fact be transformed back into differential rent I, and this can only take place in the indicated way. For example, let us take Table III, S. 226.[a]

Soil B yields for the first invested capital of £$2\frac{1}{2}$—2 quarters per acre, and for the second investment of equal magnitude — $1\frac{1}{2}$ quarters; together — $3\frac{1}{2}$ quarters from the same acre. It is not possible to distinguish which part of these $3\frac{1}{2}$ quarters is a product of invested capital I and which part a product of invested capital II, for it is all grown upon the same soil. In fact, the $3\frac{1}{2}$ quarters is the yield from the total capital of £5; and the actual fact of the matter is simply this: a capital of £$2\frac{1}{2}$ yielded 2 quarters, and a capital of £5 yielded $3\frac{1}{2}$ quarters rather than 4 quarters. The situation would be just the same

---

[a] See this volume, p. 679.

if the £5 yielded 4 quarters, i. e., if the yield from both investments of capital were equal; similarly, if the yield were even 5 quarters, i. e., if the second investment of capital were to yield a surplus of 1 quarter. The price of production of the first 2 quarters is £$1\frac{1}{2}$ per quarter, and that of the second $1\frac{1}{2}$ quarters is £2 per quarter. Consequently the $3\frac{1}{2}$ quarters together cost £6. This is the individual price of production of the total product, and, on the average, amounts to £1 $14\frac{2}{7}$ sh. per quarter, i. e., approximately £$1\frac{3}{4}$. With the general price of production determined by soil A, namely £3, this results in a surplus profit of £$1\frac{1}{4}$ per quarter, and thus for the $3\frac{1}{2}$ quarters, a total of £$4\frac{3}{8}$. At the average price of production of B this corresponds to about $1\frac{1}{2}$ quarters. In other words, the surplus profit from B is represented by an aliquot portion of the output from B, i. e., by the $1\frac{1}{2}$ quarters, which express the rent in terms of grain, and which sell — in accordance with the general price of production — for £$4\frac{1}{2}$. But on the other hand, the excess product from an acre of B over that from an acre of A does not automatically represent surplus profit, and thereby surplus product. According to our assumption, an acre of B yields $3\frac{1}{2}$ quarters, whereas an acre of A yields only 1 quarter. Excess product from B is, therefore, $2\frac{1}{2}$ quarters but the surplus product is only $1\frac{1}{2}$ quarters; for the capital invested in B is twice that invested in A, and thus its price of production is double. If an investment of £5 were also to take place in A, and the rate of productivity were to remain the same, then the output would be 2 quarters instead of 1 quarter, and it would then be seen that the actual surplus product is determined by comparing $3\frac{1}{2}$ with 2, not $3\frac{1}{2}$ with 1; i. e., it is only $1\frac{1}{2}$ quarters, not $2\frac{1}{2}$ quarters. Furthermore, if a third investment of capital, amounting to £$2\frac{1}{2}$, were made in B, and this were to yield only 1 quarter — this quarter would then cost £3 as in A — its selling price of £3 would only cover the price of production, would provide only the average profit, but no surplus profit, and would thus yield nothing that could be transformed into rent. The comparison of the output per acre from any given soil type with the output per acre from soil A does not show whether it is the output from an equal or from a larger investment of capital, nor whether the additional output only covers the price of production or is due to greater productivity of the additional capital.

Secondly, assuming a decreasing rate of productivity for the additional investments of capital whose limit, so far as the new formation of surplus profit is concerned, is that investment of capital which just covers the price of production, i.e., which produces a quarter as dearly as the same investment of capital in an acre of soil A, namely, at £3, according to our assumption—it follows from what has just been said: that the limit, where the total investment of capital in an acre of B would no longer yield any rent, is reached when the individual average production price of output per acre of B would rise to the price of production per acre of A.

If only investments of capital are made in B that yield the price of production, i.e., yield no surplus profit nor new rent, then this indeed raises the individual average price of production per quarter, but does not affect the surplus profit, and eventually the rent, formed by previous investments of capital. For the average price of production always remains below that of A, and when the price excess per quarter decreases, the number of quarters increases proportionately, so that the total excess in price remains unaltered.

In the case assumed, the first two investments of capital in B amounting to £5 yield $3\frac{1}{2}$ quarters, thus according to our assumption $1\frac{1}{2}$ quarters of rent = £$4\frac{1}{2}$. Now, if a third investment of £$2\frac{1}{2}$ is made, but one which yields only an additional quarter, then the total price of production (including 20% profit) of the $4\frac{1}{2}$ quarters = £9; thus the average price per quarter = £2. The average price of production per quarter upon B has thus risen from £$1\frac{5}{7}$ to £2, and the surplus profit per quarter, compared with the regulating price of A, has fallen from £$1\frac{2}{7}$ to £1. But $1 \times 4\frac{1}{2} = £4\frac{1}{2}$ just as formerly $1\frac{2}{7} \times 3\frac{1}{2} = £4\frac{1}{2}$.

Let us assume that a fourth and fifth additional investment of capital, amounting to £$2\frac{1}{2}$ each, are made in B, which do no more than produce a quarter at its general price of production. The total product per acre would then be $6\frac{1}{2}$ quarters and their price of production £15. The average price of production per quarter for B would have risen again—from £2 to £$2\frac{4}{13}$—and the surplus profit per quarter, compared with the regulating price of production of A, would have dropped again—from £1 to £$\frac{9}{13}$. But these £$\frac{9}{13}$ would now have to be calculated upon the basis of $6\frac{1}{2}$ quarters instead of $4\frac{1}{2}$ quarters. And $\frac{9}{13} \times 6\frac{1}{2} = 1 \times 4\frac{1}{2} = £4\frac{1}{2}$.

It follows from this, firstly, that no increase in the regulating price of production is necessary under these circumstances, in order to make possible additional investments of capital in the rent-bearing soil—even to the point where the additional capital completely ceases to produce surplus profit and continues to yield only the average profit. It follows furthermore that the total surplus profit per acre remains the same here, no matter how much surplus profit per quarter may decrease; this decrease is always balanced by a corresponding increase in the number of quarters produced per acre. In order that the average price of production might reach the level of the general price of production (hence £3 for soil B), it is necessary that supplementary investments be made whose output has a higher price of production than the regulating one of £3. But we shall see that this alone does not suffice without further ado to raise the average price of production per quarter of B to the general price of production of £3.

Let us assume that soil B produced:

1) $3\frac{1}{2}$ quarters whose price of production is, as before, £6, i. e., two investments of capital amounting to £$2\frac{1}{2}$ each both yielding surplus profit, but of decreasing amount.

2) 1 quarter at £3; an investment of capital in which the individual price of production is equal to the regulating price of production.

3) 1 quarter at £4; an investment of capital in which the individual price of production is higher by 33% [a] than the regulating price.

We should then have $5\frac{1}{2}$ quarters per acre for £13 with an investment of a capital of £$10\frac{7}{10}$ [b]; this is four times the original invested capital, but not quite three times the output of the first investment of capital.

$5\frac{1}{2}$ quarters at £13 gives an average price of production of £$2\frac{4}{11}$ per quarter, i. e., an excess of £$\frac{7}{11}$ per quarter, assuming the regulating price of production of £3. This excess may be transformed into rent. $5\frac{1}{2}$ quarters sold at the regulating price of production of £3 yield £$16\frac{1}{2}$. After deducting the production price of £13, a surplus profit, or rent, of £$3\frac{1}{2}$ remains, which, calculated at the present average price of production per quarter of B, that is, at £$2\frac{4}{11}$ per quarter, represents $1\frac{25}{52}$ [c] quarters. The money rent would be lower by £1

---

[a] In the 1894 German edition "25%". - [b] Ibid., "10". - [c] Ibid., "1⁵/₇₂".

and the grain rent by about $\frac{1}{2}$ quarter, but in spite of the fact that the fourth additional investment of capital in B not only fails to yield surplus profit, but yields less than the average profit, surplus profit, and rent still continue to exist. Let us assume that, in addition to investment 3), investment 2) also produces at a price exceeding the regulating price of production. Then the total production is: $3\frac{1}{2}$ quarters for £6 + 2 quarters for £8; total $5\frac{1}{2}$ quarters for £14 production price. The average price of production per quarter would be £$2\frac{6}{11}$ and would leave an excess of £$\frac{5}{11}$. The $5\frac{1}{2}$ quarters, sold at £3, give £$16\frac{1}{2}$; deducting the £14 production price leaves £$2\frac{1}{2}$ for rent. At the present average price of production upon B, this would be equivalent to $\frac{55}{56}$ of a quarter. In other words, rent is still yielded although less than before.

This shows, at any rate, that with additional investments of capital in the better soils whose output costs more than the regulating price of production the rent does not disappear—at least not within the bounds of admissible practice—although it must decrease. It will decrease in proportion, on the one hand, to the aliquot part formed by this less productive capital in the total investment of capital, and on the other hand, in proportion to the decrease in its productiveness. The average price of its produce would still lie below the regulating price and would thus still permit surplus profit to be formed that could be transformed into rent.

Let us now assume that, as a result of four successive investments of capital (£$2\frac{1}{2}$; £$2\frac{1}{2}$, £5 and £5) with decreasing productivity, the average price per quarter of B coincides with the general price of production.

Capital £	Profit £	Output Qrs	Price of Production		Selling Price £	Proceeds £	Surplus for Rent	
			per Qr £	Total £			Qrs	£
1)	$2^1/_2$	$^1/_2$	2	$1^1/_2$	3	3	6	1	3
2)	$2^1/_2$	$^1/_2$	$1^1/_2$	2	3	3	$4^1/_2$	$^1/_2$	$1^1/_2$
3)	5	1	$1^1/_2$	4	6	3	$4^1/_2$	$-^1/_2$	$-1^1/_2$
4)	5	1	1	6	6	3	3	-1	-3
	15	3	6		18		18	0	0

The farmer, in this case, sells every quarter at its individual price of production, and consequently the total number of quarters at their average price of production per quarter, which coincides with the regulating price of £3. Hence he still makes a profit of 20% = £3 upon his capital of £15. But the rent is gone. What has become of the excess in this equalisation of the individual prices of production per quarter with the general price of production?

The surplus profit from the first £$2\frac{1}{2}$ was £3, from the second £$2\frac{1}{2}$ it was £$1\frac{1}{2}$; total surplus profit from $\frac{1}{3}$ of the invested capital, that is, from £5 = £$4\frac{1}{2}$ = 90%.

In the case of investment 3), the £5 not only fails to yield surplus profit, but its output of $1\frac{1}{2}$ quarters, sold at the general price of production, gives a deficit of £$1\frac{1}{2}$. Finally, in the case of investment 4), which likewise amounts to £5, its output of 1 quarter, sold at the general price of production, gives a deficit of £3. Both investments of capital together thus give a deficit of £$4\frac{1}{2}$, which is equal to the surplus profit of £$4\frac{1}{2}$, realised from investments 1) and 2).

The surplus profit and deficit balance out. Therefore the rent disappears. In fact, this is possible only because the elements of surplus value, which formed surplus profit or rent, now enter into the formation of the average profit. The farmer makes this average profit of £3 on £15, or 20%, at the expense of the rent.

The equalisation of the individual average price of production of B to the general price of production of A, which regulates the market price, presupposes that the difference of the individual price of the produce from the first investments of capital below the regulating price is more and more compensated and finally balanced out by the difference of the price of the produce from the subsequent investments of capital above the regulating price. What appears as surplus profit, so long as the produce from the first investments of capital is sold by itself, thus gradually becomes part of its average price of production, and thereby enters into the formation of the average profit, until it is finally completely absorbed by it.

If only £5 are invested in B instead of £15 and the additional $2\frac{1}{2}$ quarters of the last table are produced by taking $2\frac{1}{2}$ new acres of A under cultivation with an investment of £$2\frac{1}{2}$ per acre, then the additional invested capital would amount to only £$6\frac{1}{4}$, i. e., the total investment in A and B for the production of these 6 quarters would be only $£11\frac{1}{4}$, instead of $£15$, and their total price of production, including profit, $£13\frac{1}{2}$. The 6 quarters would still be sold for $£18$, but the investment of capital would have decreased by $£3\frac{3}{4}$, and the rent from B would be $£4\frac{1}{2}$ per acre, as before. It would be different if the production of the additional $2\frac{1}{2}$ quarters required that a soil inferior to A, for instance, A_{-1} and A_{-2}, be taken under cultivation, so that the price of production per quarter would be: for $1\frac{1}{2}$ quarters on soil $A_{-1} = £4$, and for the last quarter on soil $A_{-2} = £6$. In this case, $£6$ would be the regulating price of production per quarter. The $3\frac{1}{2}$ quarters from B would then be sold for $£21$ instead of $£10\frac{1}{2}$, which would mean a rent of $£15$ instead of $£4\frac{1}{2}$, or, a rent in grain of $2\frac{1}{2}$ quarters instead of $1\frac{1}{2}$ quarters. Similarly, a quarter on A would now yield a rent of $£3 = \frac{1}{2}$ quarter.

Before discussing this point further, another observation:

The average price of a quarter from B is equalised, i. e., coincides with the general production price of $£3$ per quarter, regulated by A, as soon as that portion of the total capital which produces the excess of $1\frac{1}{2}$ quarters is balanced by that portion of the total capital which produces the deficit of $1\frac{1}{2}$ quarters. How soon this equalisation is effected, or how much capital with underproductiveness must be invested in B for this purpose, will depend, assuming the surplus productivity of the first investments of capital to be given, upon the relative underproductiveness of the later investments compared with an investment of the same amount in the worst, regulating soil A, or upon the individual price of production of their produce, compared with the regulating price.

The following conclusions can now be drawn from the foregoing:

First: So long as the additional capitals are invested in the same land with surplus productivity, even if the surplus productivity is decreasing, the absolute rent per acre in grain and money increases, although it decreases relatively, in proportion to the advanced capital (in other words, the rate of surplus profit or rent). The limit is established here by that additional capital which yields only the average profit, or for whose produce the individual price of production coincides with the general price of production. The price of production remains the same under these circumstances, unless the production from the poorer soils becomes superfluous as a result of increased supply. Even when the price is falling, these additional capitals may within certain limits still produce surplus profit, though less of it.

Secondly: The investment of additional capital yielding only the average profit, whose surplus productivity therefore $= 0$, does not alter in any way the amount of the existing surplus profit, and consequently of rent. The individual average price per quarter increases thereby upon the superior soils; the excess per quarter decreases, but the number of quarters which contain this decreased excess increases, so that the mathematical product remains the same.

Thirdly: Additional investments of capital, the produce of which has an individual price of production exceeding the regulating price — the surplus productivity is therefore not merely $= 0$, but less than zero, or a negative quantity, that is, less than the productivity of an equal investment of capital in the regulating soil A — bring the individual average price of production of the total output from the superior soil closer and closer to the general price of production, i. e., reduce more and more the difference between them which constitutes the surplus profit, or rent. An increasingly greater part of what constituted surplus profit or rent enters into the formation of the average profit. But nevertheless, the total capital invested in an acre of B continues to yield surplus profit, although the latter decreases as the amount of capital with underproductiveness increases and to the extent of this underproductiveness. The rent, with increasing capital and increasing production, in this case decreases absolutely per acre, not merely relatively with reference to the increasing magnitude of the invested capital, as in the second case.

The rent can be eliminated only when the individual average price of production of the total output from the better soil B coincides with the regulating price, so that the entire surplus profit from the first more productive investments of capital is consumed in the formation of average profit.

The minimum limit of the drop in rent per acre is that point at which it disappears. But this point does not occur as soon as the additional investments of capital are underproductive, but rather as soon as the additional investment of underproductive capital becomes so large in magnitude that its effect is to cancel the overproductiveness of the first investments of capital, so that the productiveness of the total invested capital becomes the same as that of the capital invested in

A, and the individual average price per quarter of B becomes therefore the same as that per quarter of A.

In this case too, the regulating price of production, £3 per quarter, would remain the same, although the rent had disappeared. Only beyond this point would the price of production have to rise in consequence of an increase either in the extent of underproductiveness of the additional capital or in the magnitude of the additional capital of equal underproductiveness. For instance, if, in the above table (S. 265 [a]) $2\frac{1}{2}$ quarters were produced instead of $1\frac{1}{2}$ quarters upon the same soil at £4 per quarter, we would have had a total of 7 quarters for £22 price of production; a quarter would have cost $£3\frac{1}{7}$; it would thus be $£\frac{1}{7}$ above the general price of production, and the latter would therefore have to rise.

For a long time, then, additional capital with underproductiveness, or even increasing underproductiveness, might be invested until the individual average price per quarter from the best soils became equal to the general price of production, until the excess of the latter over the former—and thereby the surplus profit and the rent—entirely disappeared.

And even then, the disappearance of rent from the better soils would only signify that the individual average price of their produce coincides with the general price of production, so that an increase in the latter would not yet be required.

In the above illustration, upon better soil B—which is however the lowest in the sequence of better or rent-bearing soils—$3\frac{1}{2}$ quarters were produced by a capital of £5 with surplus productiveness and $2\frac{1}{2}$ quarters by a capital of £10 with underproductiveness, i. e., a total of 6 quarters; $\frac{5}{12}$ of this total is thus produced by the latter portions of capital with underproductiveness. And it is only at this point that the individual average price of production of the 6 quarters rises to £3 per quarter and thus coincides with the general price of production.

Under the law of landed property, however, the latter $2\frac{1}{2}$ quarters could not have been produced in this way at £3 per quarter, except when they could be produced upon $2\frac{1}{2}$ new acres of soil A. The case

---

[a] See this volume, p. 719.

in which the additional capital produces only at the general price of production, would have constituted the limit. Beyond this point, the additional investment of capital in the same land would have had to cease.

Indeed, if the farmer once pays $£4\frac{1}{2}$ rent for the first two investments of capital, he must continue to pay it, and every investment of capital which produced a quarter for more than $£3$ [a] would result in a deduction from his profit. The equalisation of the individual average price, in the case of underproductiveness, is thereby prevented.

Let us take this case in the previous illustration, where the price of production for soil A, $£3$ per quarter, regulates the price for B.

Capital $£$	Profit $£$	Price of Production $£$	Output Qrs	Price of Production per Qr $£$	Selling Price		Surplus Profit $£$	Loss $£$
					per Qr $£$	Total $£$		
$2\frac{1}{2}$	$\frac{1}{2}$	3	2	$1\frac{1}{2}$	3	6	3	—
$2\frac{1}{2}$	$\frac{1}{2}$	3	$1\frac{1}{2}$	2	3	$4\frac{1}{2}$	$1\frac{1}{2}$	—
5	1	6	$1\frac{1}{2}$	4[b]	3	$4\frac{1}{2}$	—	$1\frac{1}{2}$
5	1	6	1	6	3	3	—	3
15	3	18				18	$4\frac{1}{2}$	$4\frac{1}{2}$

The price of production for the $3\frac{1}{2}$ quarters in the first two investments of capital is likewise $£3$ per quarter for the farmer, since he has to pay a rent of $£4\frac{1}{2}$; thus the difference between his individual price of production and the general price of production is not pocketed by him. For him, then, the excess in produce price for the first two investments of capital cannot serve to balance out the deficit incurred by the produce in the third and fourth investments of capital.

The $1\frac{1}{2}$ quarters from investment 3) cost the farmer $£6$, profit included; but at the regulating price of $£3$ per quarter, he can sell them for only $£4\frac{1}{2}$. In other words, he would not only lose his whole profit, but $£\frac{1}{2}$, or 10% of his invested capital of $£5$, over and above it. The loss of profit and capital in the case of investment 3) would amount to $£1\frac{1}{2}$, and in the case of investment 4) to $£3$, i. e., a total of $£4\frac{1}{2}$, or just as much as the rent from the better investments of cap-

---

[a] In the 1894 German edition: "for less than $£3$". - [b] In the 1894 German edition: "3".

ital; the individual price of production for the latter, however, cannot take part in equalising the individual average price of production of the total product from B, because the excess is paid out as rent to a third party.

If it were necessary, to meet the demand, to produce the additional $1\frac{1}{2}$ quarters by the third investment of capital the regulating market price would have to rise to £4 per quarter. In consequence of this rise in the regulating market price, the rent from B would rise for the first and second investments, and rent would be formed upon A.

Thus although differential rent is but a formal transformation of surplus profit into rent, and property in land merely enables the owner in this case to transfer the surplus profit of the farmer to himself, we find nevertheless that successive investment of capital in the same land, or, what amounts to the same thing, the increase in capital invested in the same land, reaches its limit far more rapidly when the rate of productivity of the capital decreases and the regulating price remains the same; in fact a more or less artificial barrier is reached as a consequence of the mere formal transformation of surplus profit into ground rent, which is the result of landed property. The rise in the general price of production, which becomes necessary here within more narrow limits than otherwise, is in this case not merely the cause of the increase in differential rent, but the existence of differential rent as rent is at the same time the reason for the earlier and more rapid rise in the general price of production—in order to ensure thereby the increased supply of produce that has become necessary.

The following should furthermore be noted:

By an additional investment of capital in soil B, the regulating price could not, as above, rise to £4 if soil A were to supply the additional produce below £4 by a second investment of capital, or if new and worse soil than A, whose price of production were indeed higher than £3 but lower than £4, were to enter into competition. We see, then, that differential rent I and differential rent II, while the first is the basis of the second, serve simultaneously as limits for one another, whereby now a successive investment of capital in the same land, now an investment of capital side by side in new additional land, is made. In like manner they limit each other in other cases; for instance, when better soil is taken up.

Chapter XLIV

DIFFERENTIAL RENT
ALSO ON THE WORST CULTIVATED SOIL

Let us assume the demand for grain is rising, and the supply can only result from successive investments of capital under conditions of underproductiveness in the rent-bearing soils, or by additional investment of capital, also with decreasing productivity, in soil A, or by the investment of capital in new lands of inferior quality than A.

Let us take soil B as representative of the rent-bearing soils.

The additional investment of capital demands an increase in the market price above the hitherto regulating price of production of £3 per quarter, in order to make possible the increased production upon B of one quarter (which may here stand for one million quarters, just as every acre may stand for one million acres). Increased output may also be yielded by soils C and D, etc., the soils bearing the highest rent, but only with decreasing surplus productiveness; but it is assumed that the quarter from B is necessary in order to meet the demand. If this quarter is more cheaply produced by investing more capital in B than with the same addition of capital to A, or by descending to soil A₋₁, which may, e. g., require £4 to produce a quarter, whereas the addition to capital A might do so for £3¾, then the additional capital on B will regulate the market price.

A produces a quarter for £3, as heretofore. Similarly B, as before, produces a total of $3\frac{1}{2}$ quarters at an individual price of production of £6 for its total output. Now, if an additional £4 of production price (including profit) becomes necessary on B in order to produce an additional quarter, whereas it could have been produced on A for £3¾, then it would naturally be produced on A, rather than on B. Let us assume, then, that it can be produced on B with the additional price of production of $£3\frac{1}{2}$. In this case, $£3\frac{1}{2}$ would become the regulating price for the entire output. B would now sell its present output of $4\frac{1}{2}$ quarters for $£15\frac{3}{4}$. Of this £6 is the price of production for the first $3\frac{1}{2}$ quarters and the $£3\frac{1}{2}$ for the last quarter, i. e., a total of $£9\frac{1}{2}$. This leaves a surplus profit for rent = $£6\frac{1}{4}$ as against the former $£4\frac{1}{2}$. In this case, an acre of A would also yield a rent of $£\frac{1}{2}$; but it would not be the worst soil A, but rather the better soil B that would regulate the price of production of $£3\frac{1}{2}$. Of course, we assume here that new soil of quality A and equally favourable location as that hitherto cultivated is not available, but that either a second investment of capital in the already cultivated plot A at a higher price of production, or the cultivation of an even poorer soil A.₋₁, is required. As soon as differential rent II comes into force through successive investments of capital, the limits of the rising price of production may be regulated by better soil; and the worst soil, the basis of differential rent I, may also yield rent. Thus, even barely with a differential rent, all cultivated land would yield rent. We would then have the following two tables, where by price of production we mean the sum of the invested capital plus 20% profit; in other words, on every $£2\frac{1}{2}$ of capital $£\frac{1}{2}$ of profit or a total of $£3$.

Type of Soil	Acres	Price of Production £	Output Qrs	Selling Price £	Proceeds £	Grain Rent Qrs	Money Rent £
A	1	3	1	3	3	0	0
B	1	6	$3\frac{1}{2}$	3	$10\frac{1}{2}$	$1\frac{1}{2}$	$4\frac{1}{2}$
C	1	6	$5\frac{1}{2}$	3	$16\frac{1}{2}$	$3\frac{1}{2}$	$10\frac{1}{2}$
D	1	6	$7\frac{1}{2}$	3	$22\frac{1}{2}$	$5\frac{1}{2}$	$16\frac{1}{2}$
Total	4	21	$17\frac{1}{2}$		$52\frac{1}{2}$	$10\frac{1}{2}$	$31\frac{1}{2}$

This is the state of affairs before the new capital of $£3\frac{1}{2}$, which yields only one quarter, is invested in B. After this investment, the situation looks as follows:

Type of Soil	Acres	Price of Production £	Output Qrs	Selling Price £	Proceeds £	Grain Rent Qrs	Money Rent £
A	1	3	1	$3\frac{1}{2}$	$3\frac{1}{2}$	$\frac{1}{7}$	$\frac{1}{2}$
B	1	$9\frac{1}{2}$	$4\frac{1}{2}$	$3\frac{1}{2}$	$15\frac{3}{4}$	$1\frac{11}{14}$	$6\frac{1}{4}$
C	1	6	$5\frac{1}{2}$	$3\frac{1}{2}$	$19\frac{1}{4}$	$3\frac{11}{14}$	$13\frac{1}{4}$
D	1	6	$7\frac{1}{2}$	$3\frac{1}{2}$	$26\frac{1}{4}$	$5\frac{11}{14}$	$20\frac{1}{4}$
Total	4	$24\frac{1}{2}$	$18\frac{1}{2}$		$64\frac{3}{4}$	$11\frac{1}{2}$	$40\frac{1}{4}$

//This, again, is not quite correctly calculated. First of all, the cost of the $4\frac{1}{2}$ qrs for farmer B is $£9\frac{1}{2}$ in price of production and, secondly, $£4\frac{1}{2}$ in rent, i.e., a total of $£14$; average per quarter = $= £3\frac{1}{9}$. This average price of his total production thus becomes the regulating market price. Thus, the rent on A would amount to $£\frac{1}{9}$ instead of $£\frac{1}{2}$, and that on B would remain $£4\frac{1}{2}$ as heretofore; $4\frac{1}{2}$ qrs at $£3\frac{1}{9} = £14$ and, if we deduct $£9\frac{1}{2}$ in price of production, $£4\frac{1}{2}$ remain for surplus profit. We see, then, that in spite of the required change in numerical values this illustration shows how, by means of differential rent II, better soil, already yielding rent, may regulate the price and thus transform *all* soil, even hitherto rentless, into rentbearing soil.— *F. E.*//

The grain rent must rise as soon as the ragulating price of production of the grain rises, i. e., as soon as the price of production of a quarter of grain from the regulating soil, or the regulating invested capital in one of the various soil types, rises. It is the same as though all soils had become less productive and produced, e. g., only $\frac{5}{7}$ quarter instead of 1 quarter with every new investment of $£2\frac{1}{2}$. Whatever else they produce in grain with the same investment of capital is transformed into surplus product, which represents the surplus profit and therefore the rent. Assuming the rate of profit remains the same, the farmer can buy less grain with his profit. The rate of profit may remain the same if wages do not rise — either because they are depressed to the physical minimum i. e., below the normal value of labour power; or because the other articles of consumption needed by the labourer and supplied by manufacture have become relatively cheaper; or because the working day has become longer or more intensive, so that the rate of profit in nonagricultural lines of production, which, however, regulates the agricultural profit, has remained the same or has risen; or, finally, because more constant and less variable capital is employed in agriculture, even though the amount of capital invested is the same.

We have thus considered the first method by which rent may arise on the hitherto worst soil A without taking still worse soil under cultivation; that is, rent may arise from the difference between its individual, hitherto regulating, price of production and the new, higher price of production, whereby the last additional capital employed under conditions of underproductiveness upon the better soil supplies the necessary additional produce.

If the additional produce had to be supplied by soil A$_{-1}$, which cannot produce a quarter for less than $£4$, then the rent per acre of A would have risen to $£1$. But, in this case, soil A$_{-1}$ would have taken the place of A as the worst cultivated soil, and the latter would have moved into the lowest position in the sequence of rent-bearing soils. Differential rent I would have changed. This case, then, is not included in the consideration of differential rent II, which arises from the varying productiveness of successive investments of capital in the same piece of land.

But aside from this, differential rent may arise on soil A in two other ways.

With the price unchanged—any given price, even a lower one compared to former ones—when the additional investment of capital results in surplus productiveness, which *prima facie*, and up to a certain point must always be the case precisely on the worst soil.

Secondly, however, when the productiveness of successive investments of capital in soil A decreases.

It is assumed in both cases that the increased production is required to meet demand.

But from the point of view of differential rent, a peculiar difficulty arises here owing to the previously developed law—according to which it is always the individual average price of production per quarter for the total production (or the total outlay of capital) which acts as the determining factor. In the case of soil A, however, there is not, as in the cases of the better soils, another price of production which limits for new investments of capital the equalisation of the individual with the general price of production. For the individual price of production of A is precisely the general price of production regulating the market price.

Let us assume:

1) *When the productive power of successive investments of capital is increasing*, 1 acre of A will produce 3 qrs instead of 2 qrs given an investment of £5—corresponding to a price of production of £6. The first investment of £2$\frac{1}{2}$ yielded 1 qr, the second—2 qrs. In this case, a price of production of £6 will yield 3 qrs, so that the average cost of a quarter will be £2; i. e., if the 3 qrs are sold at £2 per quarter, then A, as heretofore, does not yield any rent, but only the basis of differential rent II has been altered; the regulating price of production is now £2 instead of £3; a capital of £2$\frac{1}{2}$ now produces an average of 1$\frac{1}{2}$ qrs on the worst soil, instead of 1 qr, and now this is the official productivity for all better soils given an investment of £2$\frac{1}{2}$. From now on, a portion of their former surplus product enters into the formation of their necessary output, just as a portion of their surplus profit enters into forming the average profit.

On the other hand, if the calculation is made upon the basis of better soils, where the average calculation does not alter the absolute surplus at all, because for them the general price of production is the limit for the investment of capital, then a quarter from the first investment of capital costs £3 and the 2 qrs from the second investment cost only £$1\frac{1}{2}$ each. This would thereby give rise to a grain rent of 1 qr and a money rent of £3 on A, but the 3 qrs would be sold for the old price of £9. If a third investment of £$2\frac{1}{2}$ were made under conditions of the same productiveness as the second investment, then the total would be 5 qrs for a price of production of £9. If the individual average price of production of A should remain the regulating price, then a quarter would now be sold at £$1\frac{4}{5}$. The average price would have fallen once more — not through a new rise in productiveness of the third investment of capital, but merely through the addition of a new investment of capital having the same additional productiveness as the second. Instead of raising the rent as on the rent-bearing soils, the successive investments of capital in soil A of higher, but constant productiveness would proportionally lower the price of production and thereby, everything else being equal, the differential rent on all other soils. On the other hand, if the first investment of capital which produces 1 qr at a price of production of £3 should in itself remain regulating, then 5 qrs would be sold for £15, and the differential rent of the later investments of capital in soil A would amount to £6. The additional capital per acre of soil A, however it is applied, would be an improvement in this case, and would make the original portion of capital more productive. It would be ridiculous to say that $\frac{1}{3}$ of the capital had produced 1 qr and the other $\frac{2}{3}$ — 4 qrs. For £9 per acre would always produce 5 qrs, while £3 would produce only 1 qr. Whether or not a rent would arise here, whether or not a surplus profit would be derived, would depend wholly upon the circumstances. Normally the regulating price of production would have to fall. This would be the case, if this improved but more expensive cultivation of soil A should occur only because it also takes place on the better soils, in other words, if a general revolution in agriculture should occur; so that when we now refer to the natural fertility of soil A, it is assumed that it is worked with £6 or £9 instead of £3. This would particularly apply if the bulk of cultivated acres of soil A, which furnish the main supply of a given country, should employ this new method. But if the improvement should at first extend only to a small area of A, then this better cultivated portion would yield a surplus profit, which the landlord would be quick to transform wholly or in part into rent, and to fix in the form of rent. In this way — if the demand kept pace with the increasing supply — as more and more of soil A began to employ the new method of cultivation, rent might be gradually formed on all soil of quality A, and the surplus productivity might be eliminated wholly or in part, depending on market conditions. The equalisation of the price of production of A to the average price of its produce obtained under conditions of increased outlay of capital might thus be prevented by fixing the surplus profit of this increased investment of capital in the form of rent. Thus, as was previously seen to be the case for the better soils when the productive power of the additional capital decreased, it would again be the transformation of surplus profit into ground rent, i. e., the intervention of property in land, which would raise the price of production, instead of the differential rent merely being the result of the difference between the individual and the general price of production. It would prevent, in the case of soil A, the coincidence of both prices because it would interfere with the regulation of the price of production by the average price of production on A; it would thus maintain a higher price of production than necessary and thereby create rent. Even if grain were freely imported from abroad, the same result could be brought about or perpetuated by compelling farmers to use soil capable of competing in grain cultivation without yielding rent, at the price of production regulated from abroad, for other purposes, e. g., pasturage, so that only rent-bearing soils would be used for grain cultivation, i. e., only soils whose individual average price of production per quarter were below that determined from abroad. On the whole, it is to be assumed that in the given case, the price of production will fall, but not to the level of its average; it will be higher than the average, but below the price of production of the worst cultivated soil A, so that the competition from new soil A is limited.

2) *When the productive power of additional capitals is decreasing.*

Let us assume that soil A$_{-1}$ requires £4 to produce the additional quarter, whereas soil A produces it for £3$\frac{3}{4}$, i. e., more cheaply, but still £$\frac{3}{4}$ more dearly than the quarter produced by its first investment of capital. In this case, the total price of the two quarters produced upon A would = £6$\frac{3}{4}$; thus the average price per quarter = £3$\frac{3}{8}$. The price of production would rise, but only by £$\frac{3}{8}$, whereas it would rise by another £$\frac{3}{8}$, or to £3$\frac{3}{4}$, if the additional capital were invested in new land which produced at £3$\frac{3}{4}$, and it would thus bring about a proportional increase in all other differential rents.

The price of production of $£3\frac{3}{8}$ per quarter for A would thus be equalised to its average price of production with an increased investment of capital, and would be the regulating price; thus, it would not yield any rent, since it would not produce any surplus profit.

However, if this quarter, produced by the second investment of capital, were sold for $£3\frac{3}{4}$, soil A would now yield a rent of $£\frac{3}{4}$, and indeed, on all acres of A in which no additional investment of capital had taken place and which thus would still produce at $£3$ per quarter. So long as any uncultivated field of A remain, the price could rise only temporarily to $£3\frac{3}{4}$. Competition from new fields of A would hold the price of production at $£3$ until all land of type A, whose favourable location enables it to produce a quarter at less than $£3\frac{3}{4}$, would be exhausted. This is then what we would assume, although the landlord, so long as an acre of land yields rent, will not let a tenant farmer have another acre rent-free.

It would again depend to what extent a second investment of capital in the available soil A had become general, whether the price of production is equalised at the average price or whether the individual price of production of the second investment of capital becomes regulating at $£3\frac{3}{4}$. The latter occurs only when the landowner has sufficient time until demand is satisfied to fix as rent the surplus profit derived at the price of $£3\frac{3}{4}$ per qr.

Concerning decreasing productiveness of the soil with successive investments of capital, see Liebig.[83] We have observed that the successive decrease in surplus productive power of invested capital invariably increases the rent per acre, so long as the price of production remains constant, and that this may occur even with a falling price of production.

But, in general, the following is to be noted.

From the standpoint of the capitalist mode of production, a relative increase in the price of products always takes place when these products cannot be secured unless an expenditure or payment not previously made is incurred. For by the replacement of capital consumed in production we mean only the replacement of values represented by certain means of production. Natural elements entering as agents into production, and which cost nothing, no matter what role they play in production, do not enter as components of capital, but as a free gift of Nature to capital, that is, as a free gift of Nature's productive power to labour, which, however, appears as the productive power of capital, as all other productivity under the capitalist mode of production. Therefore, if such a natural power, which originally costs nothing, takes part in production, it does not enter into the determination of price, so long as the product which it helped to produce suffices to meet the demand. But if in the course of development, a larger output is demanded than that which can be supplied with the help of this natural power, i. e., if this additional output must be created without the help of this natural power, or by assisting it with human labour power, then a new additional element enters into capital. A relatively larger investment of capital is thus required in order to secure the same output. All other circumstances remaining the same, a rise in the price of production takes place.

———

(From a notebook "begun in mid-February 1876". [a])

Differential rent and rent as mere interest on capital incorporated in the soil.

The so-called permanent improvements — which change the physical, and, in part, also the chemical conditions of the soil by means of operations requiring an expenditure of capital, and which may be regarded as an incorporation of capital in the soil — nearly all amount to giving a particular piece of land in a certain limited locality such properties as are naturally possessed by some other piece of land elsewhere, sometimes quite near by. One piece of land is naturally level, another has to be levelled; one possesses natural drainage, another requires artificial drainage; one is endowed by Nature with a deep layer of top soil, another needs artificial deepening; one clay soil is naturally mixed with the proper amount of sand, another has to be treated to obtain this proportion; one meadow is naturally irrigated or covered with layers of silt, another requires labour to obtain this condition, or, in the language of bourgeois economics, it requires capital.

It is indeed a truly amusing theory, whereby here, in the case of one piece of land whose comparative advantages have been acquired, rent is interest, whereas in the case of another piece of land which possesses these advantages naturally, it is not interest.[b] (In fact, this is so

———

[a] Inserted by Engels. - [b] See this volume, p. 616.

distorted in practice that since rent really coincides in the one case with interest, in the other cases, where this is positively not the case, it must be called interest, it is falsely also called interest.) However, land yields rent after capital is invested not because capital is invested, but because the invested capital makes this land more productive than it formerly was. Assuming that all the land of a given country requires this investment of capital, every piece of land which has not received it must first pass through this stage, and the rent (interest yielded in the given case) borne by land already provided with investment of capital constitutes differential rent just as though it naturally possessed this advantage and the other land had first to acquire it artificially.

This rent too, which may be resolved into interest, becomes pure differential rent as soon as the invested capital is redeemed. Otherwise, one and the same capital would have to exist twice as capital.

———

A most amusing phenomenon is that all opponents of Ricardo who oppose the idea that value determination is based exclusively on labour rather than regarding differential rent as arising from differences in soil, point out that here Nature rather than labour determines value; but at the same time they credit this determination to the location of the land, or—and to an even greater extent—the interest on capital put into the land during its cultivation. The same labour produces the same value in a product created during a given period of time; but the magnitude or quantum of this product, and consequently also the portion of value associated with some aliquot part of this product, depends for a given quantity of labour solely upon the quantum of product, and the latter, in turn, depends upon the productivity of the given quantum of labour rather than the absolute magnitude of this quantum. It is immaterial whether this productivity is due to Nature or to society. Only in the case when the productivity itself costs labour, and consequently capital, does it increase the price of production by a new element—which Nature by itself does not do.

Chapter XLV

ABSOLUTE GROUND RENT

In the analysis of differential rent we proceeded from the assumption that the worst soil does not pay any ground rent; or, to put it more generally, only such land pays ground rent whose product has an individual price of production below the price of production regulating the market, so that in this manner a surplus profit arises which is transformed into rent. It is to be noted, to begin with, that the law of differential rent as such is entirely independent of the correctness or incorrectness of this assumption.

Let us call the general price of production, by which the market is regulated, P. Then, P coincides with the individual price of production of the output of the worst soil A; i. e., its price pays for the constant and variable capital consumed in production plus the average profit (= profit of enterprise plus interest).

The rent in this case is equal to zero. The individual price of production of the next better soil B is $= P'$, and $P > P'$; that is, P pays for more than the actual price of production of the product of soil B. Let us now assume that $P - P' = d$; d, the excess of P over P', is therefore the surplus profit which the farmer of soil type B realises. This d is converted into rent, which must be paid to the landlord. Let P'' be the actual price of production of the third type of soil C, and $P - P'' = 2d$; then this 2d is converted into rent; similarly, let P''' be the individual price of production of the fourth type of soil D, and $P - P''' = 3d$, which is converted into ground rent, etc. Now let us assume the premiss for soil A, that rent $= 0$ and therefore the price of its product $= P + 0$, is erroneous. Assume rather that it, too, yields rent $= r$. In that case, two different conclusions follow.

First: The price of the product of soil A would not be regulated by the price of production on the latter, but would include an excess above this price, i. e., would be $= P + r$. Because assuming the capitalist mode of production to be functioning normally, that is, assuming that the excess r which the farmer pays to the landlord represents neither a deduction from wages nor from the average profit of capital, the farmer can only pay it by selling the product above its price of production, thus, yielding him surplus profit if he did not have to turn over this excess to the landlord in the form of rent. The regulating market price of the total output on the market derived from all soils would then not be the price of production which capital generally yields in all spheres of production, i. e., a price equal to costs plus average profit, but rather the price of production plus the rent, $P + r$, and not P. For the price of the product of soil A represents generally the limit of the regulating general market price, i. e., the price at which the total product can be supplied, and to that extent it regulates the price of this total product.

But *secondly*: Although the general price of agricultural products would in this case be significantly modified, the law of differential rent would nevertheless in no way lose its force. For if the price of the product of soil A, and thereby the general market price $= P + r$, the price for soils B, C, D, etc., would likewise $= P + r$. But since $P - P' = d$ for soil B, then $(P + r) - (P' + r)$ would likewise $= d$, and $P - P'' = (P + r) - (P'' + r) = 2d$ for soil C; and finally $P - P''' = (P + r) - (P''' + r) = 3d$ for soil D, etc. Thus the differential rent would be the same as before and would be regulated by the same law, although the rent would include an element independent of this law and would show a general increase together with the price of the agricultural product. It follows, then, that no matter what the case may be as regards the rent of the least fertile soils, the law of differential rent is not only independent of it, but that the only manner of grasping differential rent in keeping with its character is to let the rent on soil $A = 0$. Whether this actually $= 0$ or > 0 is immaterial so far as the differential rent is concerned, and, in fact, does not come into consideration.

The law of differential rent, then, is independent of the results of the following study.

If we were now to inquire more deeply into the basis of the assumption that the product of the worst soil A does not yield any rent, the answer would of necessity be as follows: If the market price of the agricultural product, say grain, attains that level where an additional investment of capital in soil A results in the usual price of production, i. e., the usual average profit on the capital is yielded, then this condition suffices for investing the additional capital in soil A. In other words, this condition is sufficient for the capitalist to invest new capital yielding the usual profit and to employ it in the normal manner.

It should be noted here that in this case, too, the market price must be higher than the price of production of A. For as soon as the additional supply is created, it is evident that the relation between supply and demand becomes altered. Formerly the supply was insufficient. Now it is sufficient. Hence the price must fall. In order to fall, it must have been higher than the price of production of A. But due to the fact that soil A newly taken under cultivation is less fertile, the price does not fall again as low as when the price of production of soil B regulated the market. The price of production of A constitutes the limit, not for the temporary but for the relatively permanent rise of the market price. On the other hand, if the new soil taken under cultivation is more fertile than the hitherto regulating soil A, and yet only suffices to meet the increased demand, then the market price remains unchanged. The investigation of the question whether the poorest type of soil yields rent, however, coincides in this case too with our present inquiry, for here too the assumption that soil A does not yield any rent would be explained by the fact that the market price is sufficient for the capitalist farmer to exactly cover, with this price, the invested capital plus the average profit; in brief, it would be explained by the fact that the market price yields him the price of production of his commodities.

At any rate, the capitalist farmer can cultivate soil A under these conditions, inasmuch as he, as capitalist, has such power of decision. The prerequisite for the normal expansion of capital in soil A is now present. But from the premiss that the farmer can now invest capital in soil A under average conditions for the expansion of capital, even if he did not have to pay any rent, it nowise follows that this land, belonging to category A, is now at the disposal of the farmer without further ado. The fact that the tenant farmer could realise the usual profit on his capital did he not have to pay any rent, is by no means a basis for the landlord to lend his land gratis to the farmer and to become so philanthropic as to grant *crédit gratuit* for the sake of a business friendship. Such an assumption would mean the abstraction of landed property, the elimination of landownership, and it is precisely the existence of the latter that constitutes a limitation to the investment of capital and the free expansion of capital in the land. This limitation does not at all disappear before the simple reflection of the farmer that the level of grain prices would enable him to realise the usual profit from the investment of his capital in the exploitation of soil A did he not have to pay any rent; in other words, if he could proceed in effect as though landed property did not exist. But differential rent presupposes the existence of a monopoly in landownership, landed property as a limitation to capital, for without it surplus profit would not be transformed into ground rent nor fall to the share of the landlord instead of the farmer. And landed property as a limitation continues to exist even when rent in the form of differential rent disappears, i. e., on soil A. If we consider the cases in a country with capitalist production, where the investment of capital in the land can take place without payment of rent, we shall find that they are all based on a *de facto* abolition of landed property, if not also the legal abolition; this, however, can only take place under very specific circumstances which are by their very nature accidental.

First: When the landlord is himself a capitalist, or the capitalist is himself a landlord. In this case he may *himself manage* his land as soon as market price has risen sufficiently to enable him to get, from what is now soil A, the price of production, that is, replacement of capital plus average profit. But why? Because for him landed property does not constitute an obstacle to the investment of his capital. He can treat his land simply as an element of Nature and therefore be guided solely by considerations of expansion of his capital, by capitalist considerations. Such cases occur in practice, but only as exceptions. Just as capitalist cultivation of the soil presupposes the separation of functioning capital from landed property, so does it as a rule exclude self-management of landed property. It is immediately evident that this case is a purely accidental one. If the increased demand for grain requires the cultivation of a larger area of soil type A than is in the hands of self-managing proprietors, in other words, if a part of it must be rented to be at all cultivated, then this hypothetical lifting [a] of the limitation created by landed property to the investment of capital at once collapses. It is an absurd contradiction to start out with the differentiation under the capitalist mode of production between capital and land, farmers and landlords, and then to turn round and assume that landlords, as a rule, manage their own land wherever and whenever capital would not draw rent from the cultivation of the soil if landed property were not separate and distinct from it. (See the passage by Adam Smith concerning mining rent, quoted below.[b]) This abolition of landed property is fortuitous. It may or may not occur.

Secondly: In the total area of a leasehold there may be certain pieces which do not yield any rent at the existing level of market prices, so that they are in fact loaned gratis; but the landlord does not look upon it in that light, because he sees the total rental of the leased land, not the specific rent of the individual component plots. In this case, as regards the rentless component plots of the leasehold, landed property as a limitation to the investment of capital is eliminated for the farmer; and this, indeed, by contract with the landlord himself. But he does not pay rent for these plots merely because he pays rent

---

[a] In the 1894 German edition "Auffassung"; corrected after Marx's manuscript. - [b] See this volume, p. 761.

for the land associated with them. A combination is here presupposed whereby poorer soil A does not have to be resorted to as a distinctly new field of production in order to produce the deficit supply, but rather whereby it merely constitutes an inseparable part of the better land. But the case to be investigated is precisely that in which certain pieces of land of soil type A must be independently managed, i. e., for the conditions generally prevailing under the capitalist mode of production, they must be independently leased.

Thirdly: A farmer may invest additional capital in the same leasehold even if the additional product secured in this manner yields him only the price of production at the prevailing market prices, i. e., provides him with the usual profit but does not enable him to pay any additional rent. He thus pays ground rent with one portion of the capital invested in the land, but not with the other. How little this assumption helps to solve the problem, however, is seen from the following: If the market price (and the fertility of the soil) enables him to obtain an additional yield with his additional capital, which, as in the case of the old capital, yields a surplus profit in addition to the price of production, he is able to pocket this surplus profit so long as his lease does not expire. But why? Because the limitation placed by landed property on the investment of his capital in land has been eliminated for the duration of the lease. But the simple fact that additional soil of poorer quality must be independently cleared and independently leased in order for him to secure this surplus profit proves irrefutably that the investment of additional capital in the old soil no longer suffices to produce the required increased supply. One assumption excludes the other. It is true that now one might say: The rent on the worst soil A is itself differential rent — whether the comparison is made with respect to the land cultivated by the owner himself (this occurs, however, as a purely chance exception) or with respect to the additional investment of capital in the old leaseholds which do not yield any rent. However, this would be 1) a differential rent which does not arise from the difference in fertility of the various categories of soil, and which therefore would *not* presuppose that soil A does not yield any rent and its produce sells at the price of production; and 2) the circumstance whether additional investments of capital in the same leasehold yield rent or not is just as irrelevant to the question as to whether the new soil of class A to be taken under cultivation pays rent or not, as it is irrelevant to, say, the establishment of a new and independent manufacturing business whether another manufacturer in the same line invests a portion of his capital in inter-est-bearing papers because he cannot use all of it in his business, or whether he makes certain improvements which do not yield him the full profit, but nevertheless do yield more than interest. This is of sec-ondary importance to him. The additional new establishments, on the other hand, must yield the average profit and are organised in the hope of obtaining this average profit. It is true, to be sure, that the additional investments of capital in the old leaseholds and the addi-tional cultivation of new land of soil type A mutually restrict one an-other. The limit, up to which additional capital may be invested in the same leasehold under less favourable conditions of production, is determined by the competing new investments in soil A; on the other hand, the rent which this category of soil can yield is limited by the competing additional investments of capital in the old leaseholds.

But all this dubious subterfuge does not solve the problem, which, simply stated, is this: Assume the market price of grain (which in this inquiry stands for products of the soil in general) to be sufficient to permit taking portions of soil A under cultivation and that the capital invested in these new fields could return the price of production of the produce, i. e., replace capital plus average profit. Thus assume that conditions exist for the normal expansion of capital on soil A. Is this sufficient? Can this capital then really be invested? Or must the mar-ket price rise to the point where even the worst soil A yields rent? In other words, does the landowner's monopoly hinder the investment of capital which would not be the case from the purely capitalist stand-point in the absence of this monopoly? It follows from the way in which the question itself is posed that if, e. g., additional capitals are invested in the old leaseholds, yielding the average profit at the given market price, but no rent, this circumstance in no way answers the question whether capital may now really be invested in soil A, which also yields the average profits but no rent. But this is precisely the question before us. The fact that additional investments of capital not yielding any rent do not satisfy the demand is proved by the necessity of taking new land of soil type A under cultivation. Just two alterna-tives are possible if the additional cultivation of soil A takes place only in so far as it yields rent, that is, yields more than the price of produc-tion. Either the market price must be such that even the last addi-tional investments of capital in the old leaseholds yield surplus profit, whether pocketed by the farmer or by the landlord. This rise in price and this surplus profit from the last additional investments of capital would then result from the fact that soil A cannot be cultivated without yielding rent. For if the price of production were sufficient for cultivation to take place, merely yielding average profit, the price would not have risen so high, and competition from new plots would have been felt as soon as they just yielded this price of production. Competing with the additional investments in old leaseholds not yielding any rent would then be investments in soil A, which likewise do not yield any rent.— Or, the last investments in the old leaseholds do not yield any rent, but nevertheless the market price has risen sufficiently to make it possible for soil A to be taken under cultivation and to yield rent. In this case, the additional investment of capital not yielding any rent was only possible because soil A cannot be cultivated until the market price permits it to pay rent. Without this condition, its cultivation would have already begun at a lower price level; and those later investments of capital in the old leaseholds, which require the high market price in order to yield the usual profit without rent, could not have taken place. At the high market price, it is true, they yield only the average profit. At a lower market price, which would have become the regulating price of production from the time soil A came under cultivation, they would thus not have yielded this average profit, i. e., the investments would thus not have taken place at all under such conditions. In this way, the rent from soil A would indeed constitute differential rent compared with the investments in the old leaseholds not yielding any rent. But that such differential rent is formed on the land areas of A is but a consequence of the fact that the latter are not at all available to cultivation, unless they yield rent; i. e., that the necessity for this rent exists, which, in itself, is not determined by any differences in soil types, and which constitutes the barrier to possible investment of additional capitals in the old leaseholds. In either case, the rent from soil A would not be simply a consequence of the rise in grain prices, but, conversely, the fact that the worst soil must yield rent in order to make its cultivation at all possible, would be the cause for the rise in the grain price to the point where this condition may be fulfilled.

Differential rent has the peculiarity that landed property here merely intercepts the surplus profit which would otherwise flow into the pocket of the farmer, and which the latter may actually pocket under certain circumstances during the period of his lease. Landed property is here merely the cause for transferring a portion of the commodity price which arises without the property having anything to do with it (indeed, in consequence of the fact that the price of production which regulates the market price is determined by competition) and which resolves itself into surplus profit—the cause for transferring this portion of the price from one person to another, from the capitalist to the landlord. But landed property is not the cause which *creates* this portion of the price, or the rise in price upon which this portion of the price is premised. On the other hand, if the worst soil A cannot be cultivated—although its cultivation would yield the price of production—until it produces something in excess of the price of production, rent, then landed property is the creative cause of *this* rise in price. *Landed property itself has created rent.* This fact is not altered, if, as in the second case mentioned, the rent now paid on soil A constitutes differential rent compared with the last additional investment of capital in old leaseholds, which pay only the price of production. For the circumstance that soil A cannot be cultivated until the regulating market price has risen high enough to permit rent to be yielded from soil A—only this circumstance is the basis here for the fact that the market price rises to a point which enables the last investments in the old leaseholds to yield, indeed, only their price of production, but a price of production which, at the same time, yields rent on soil A. The fact that the latter has to pay rent at all is, in this case, the cause for the differential rent between soil A and the last investments in the old leaseholds.

When stating, in general, that soil A does not pay any rent—assuming the price of grain is regulated by the price of production—we mean rent in the categorical sense of the word. If the farmer pays "lease money" which constitutes a deduction from the normal wages of his labourers, or from his own normal average profit, he does not pay rent, i. e., an independent component of the price of his commodities distinct from wages and profit. We have already indicated that this continually takes place in practice. In so far as the wages of the agricultural labourers in a given country are, in general, depressed below the normal average level of wages, so that a deduction from wages, a part of the wages, as a general rule enters into rent, this does not constitute an exceptional case for the farmer cultivating the worst soil. In the same price of production which makes cultivation of the worst soil possible these low wages already form a constituent element, and the sale of the product at the price of production does not therefore enable the farmer cultivating this soil to pay any rent. The landlord can also lease his land to some labourer, who may be satisfied to pay to the former in the form of rent, all or the largest part of that which he realises in the selling price over and above the wages. In all these cases, however, no real rent is paid in spite of the fact that lease money is paid. But wherever conditions correspond to those under the capitalist mode of production, rent and lease money must coincide. Yet it is precisely this normal condition which must be analysed here.

Since even the cases considered above — where, under the capitalist mode of production, investments of capital in the land may actually take place without yielding rent — do not contribute to the solution of our problem, so much less does reference to colonial conditions. The criterion establishing a colony as a colony — we are referring here only to true agricultural colonies — is not merely the prevailing vast area of fertile land in a natural state. It is rather the circumstance that this land has not been appropriated, has not been subjected to private ownership. Herein lies the enormous difference, as regards the land, between old countries and colonies: the legal or actual nonexistence of landed property, as Wakefield [35] correctly remarks, and as Mirabeau *père*, the physiocrat, and other elder economists, had discovered long before him. It is quite immaterial here whether the colonists simply appropriate the land, or whether they actually pay to the state, in the form of a nominal land price, a fee for a valid legal title to the land. It is also immaterial that the colonists already settled there may be the legal owners of the land. In fact, landed property constitutes no limitation here to the investment of capital — and also of labour without capital; the appropriation of some of the land by the colonists already established there does not prevent the newcomers from employing their capital or their labour upon new land. Therefore, when it is necessary to investigate the influence of landed property upon the prices of products of the land and upon rent — in those cases where landed property restricts land as an investment sphere of capital — it is highly absurd to speak of free bourgeois colonies where, in agriculture, neither the capitalist mode of production exists, nor the form of landed property corresponding to it — which, in fact, does not exist at all. Ricardo, e. g., does so in his

[35] Wakefield, *England and America*, London, 1833. Compare also *Das Kapital*, Buch I, Kap. XXV.[a]

---

[a] English edition: Ch. XXXIII (see present edition, Vol. 35, pp. 751-61).

chapter on ground rent.[a] In the preface he states that he intends to investigate the effect of the appropriation of land upon the value of the products of the soil, and directly thereafter he takes the colonies as an illustration, whereby he assumes that the land exists in a relatively elementary form and that its exploitation is not limited by the monopoly of landed property.

The mere legal ownership of land does not create any ground rent for the owner. But it does, indeed, give him the power to withdraw his land from exploitation until economic conditions permit him to utilise it in such a manner as to yield him an excess, be it used for actual agricultural or other production purposes, such as buildings, etc. He cannot increase or decrease the absolute magnitude of this sphere, but he can change the quantity of land placed on the market. Hence, as Fourier already observed, it is a characteristic fact that in all civilised countries a comparatively appreciable portion of land always remains uncultivated.

Thus, assuming the demand requires that new land be taken under cultivation, whose soil, let us say, is less fertile than that hitherto cultivated — will the landlord lease it for nothing, just because the market price of the product of the land has risen sufficiently to return to the farmer the price of production, and thereby the usual profit, on his investment in this land? By no means. The investment of capital must yield him rent. He does not lease his land until he can be paid lease money for it. Therefore, the market price must rise to a point above the price of production, i. e., to $P + r$, so that rent can be paid to the landlord. Since according to our assumption, landed property does not yield anything until it is leased, is economically valueless until then, a small rise in the market price above the price of production suffices to bring the new land of poorest quality on the market.

The following question now arises: Does it follow from the fact that the worst soil yields ground rent which cannot be derived from any difference in fertility that the price of the product of the land is necessarily a monopoly price in the usual sense, or a price into which the rent enters like a tax, with the sole distinction that the landlord levies the tax instead of the state? It goes without saying that this tax has its specific economic limits. It is limited by additional investments of capital in the old leaseholds, by competition from products of the land coming from abroad — assuming their import is unrestricted — by

---

[a] D. Ricardo, *On the Principles of Political Economy, and Taxation*, Ch. II.

competition among the landlords themselves, and finally by the needs of the consumers and their ability to pay. But this is not the question here. The point is whether the rent paid on the worst soil enters into the price of the products of this soil — which price regulates the general market price according to our assumption — in the same way as a tax placed on a commodity enters into its price, i. e., as an element that is independent of the value of the commodity.

This, by no means, necessarily follows, and the contention that it does has been made only because the distinction between the value of commodities and their price of production has heretofore not been understood. We have seen that the price of production of a commodity is not at all identical with its value, although the prices of production of commodities, considered in their totality, are regulated only by their total value, and although the movement of production prices of various kinds of commodities, all other circumstances being equal, is determined exclusively by the movement of their values. It has been shown that the price of production of a commodity may lie above or below its value, and coincides with its value only by way of exception. Hence, the fact that products of the land are sold above their price of production does not at all prove that they are sold above their value; just as the fact that products of industry, on the average, are sold at their price of production does not prove that they are sold at their value. It is possible for agricultural products to be sold above their price of production and below their value, while, on the other hand, many industrial products yield the price of production only because they are sold above their value.

The relation of the price of production of a commodity to its value is determined solely by the ratio of the variable part of the capital with which the commodity is produced to its constant part, or by the organic composition of the capital producing it. If the composition of the capital in a given sphere of production is lower than that of the average social capital, i. e., if its variable portion, which is used for wages, is larger in its relation to the constant portion, used for the material conditions of labour, than is the case in the average social capital, then the value of its product must lie above the price of production. In other words, because such capital employs more living labour, it produces more surplus value, and therefore more profit, assuming equal exploitation of labour, than an equally large aliquot portion of the social average capital. The value of its product, therefore, is above the price of production, since this price of production is equal to capital replacement plus average profit, and the average profit is lower than the profit produced in this commodity. The surplus value produced by the average social capital is less than the surplus value produced by a capital of this lower composition. The opposite is the case when the capital invested in a certain sphere of production is of a higher composition than the social average capital. The value of commodities produced by it lies below their price of production, which is generally the case with products of the most developed industries.

If the capital in a certain sphere of production is of a lower composition than the average social capital, then this is, in the first place, merely another way of saying that the productive power of the social labour in this particular sphere of production is below the average; for the level of productive power attained is manifested in the relative preponderance of constant over variable capital, or in the continual decrease — for the given capital — of the portion used for wages. On the other hand, if the capital in a certain sphere of production is of a higher composition, then this reflects a development of productive power that is above the average.

Leaving aside actual works of art, whose consideration by their very nature is excluded from our discussion, it is self-evident, moreover, that different spheres of production require different proportions of constant and variable capital in accordance with their specific technical features, and that living labour must play a bigger role in some, and smaller in others. For instance, in the extractive industries, which must be clearly distinguished from agriculture, raw material as an element of constant capital is wholly absent, and even auxiliary material rarely plays an important role. In the mining industry, however, the other part of constant capital, i. e., fixed capital, plays an important role. Nevertheless, here too, progress may be measured by the relative increase of constant capital in relation to variable capital.

If the composition of capital in agriculture proper is lower than that of the average social capital, then, *prima facie*, this expresses the fact that in countries with developed production agriculture has not progressed to the same extent as the processing industries. Such a fact could be explained — aside from all other circumstances, including in part decisive economic ones — by the earlier and more rapid development of the mechanical sciences, and in particular their application compared with the later and in part quite recent development of chemistry, geology and physiology, and again, in particular, their application to agriculture. Incidentally, it is an indubitable and long-known fact [36] that the progress of agriculture itself is constantly expressed by a relative growth of constant capital as compared with variable capital. Whether the composition of agricultural capital is lower than that of the average social capital in a specific country where capitalist production prevails, for instance England, is a question which can only be decided statistically, and for our purposes it is superfluous to go into it in detail. In any case, it is theoretically established that the value of agricultural products can be higher than their price of production only on this assumption. In other words, a capital of a certain size in agriculture produces more surplus value, or what amounts to the same, sets in motion and commands more surplus labour (and with it employs more living labour generally) than a capital of the same size of average social composition.

This assumption, then, suffices for that form of rent which we are analysing here, and which can obtain only so long as this assumption holds good. Wherever this assumption no longer holds, the corresponding form of rent likewise no longer holds.

However, the mere existence of an excess in the value of agricultural products over their price of production would not in itself suffice to explain the existence of a ground rent which is independent of differences in fertility of various soil types and in successive investments of capital on the same land — a rent, in short, which is to be clearly distinguished in concept from differential rent and which we may therefore call *absolute rent*. Quite a number of manufactured products are characterised by the fact that their value is higher than their price of production, without thereby yielding any excess above the average profit, or a surplus profit, which could be converted into rent. Conversely, the existence and concept of price of production and general rate of profit, which it implies, rest upon the fact that individual commodities are not sold at their value. Prices of production arise from an equalisation of the values of commodities. After replacing the respective capital values used up in the various spheres of production, this distributes the entire surplus value, not in proportion to the amount produced in the individual spheres of production and thus incorporat-

---

[36] See Dombasle [a] and R. Jones. [b]

---

[a] Apparently this refers to M. Dombasle, *Annales agricoles de Roville, ou Mélanges d'agriculture, d'économie rurale et de législation agricole*, Paris, 1824-37. - [b] *An Essay on the Distribution of Wealth, and on the Sources of Taxation*, Part I, *Rent*, London, 1831, p. 227.

ed in their commodities, but in proportion to the magnitude of advanced capitals. Only in this manner do average profit and price of production arise, whose characteristic element the former is. It is the perpetual tendency of capitals to bring about through competition this equalisation in the distribution of surplus value produced by the total capital, and to overcome all obstacles to this equalisation. Hence it is their tendency to tolerate only such surplus profits as arise, under all circumstances, not from the difference between the values and prices of production of commodities but rather from the difference between the general price of production governing the market and the individual prices of production differing from it; surplus profits which obtain within a certain sphere of production, therefore, and not between two different spheres, and thus do not affect the general prices of production of the various spheres, i. e., the general rate of profit, but rather presuppose the transformation of values into prices of production and a general rate of profit. This supposition rests, however, as previously discussed,[a] upon the constantly changing proportional distribution of the total social capital among the various spheres of production, upon the perpetual inflow and outflow of capitals, upon their transferability from one sphere to another, in short, upon their free movement between the various spheres of production, which represent so many available fields of investment for the independent components of the total social capital. The premiss in this case is that no barrier, or just an accidental and temporary barrier, interferes with the competition of capitals — for instance, in a sphere of production, in which the commodity values are higher than the prices of production or where the surplus value produced exceeds the average profit — to reduce the value to the price of production and thereby proportionally distribute the excess surplus value of this sphere of production among all spheres exploited by capital. But if the reverse occurs, if capital meets an alien force which it can but partially, or not at all, overcome, and which limits its investment in certain spheres, admitting it only under conditions which wholly or partly exclude that general equalisation of surplus value to an average profit, then it is evident that the excess of the value of commodities in such spheres of production over their price of production would give rise to a surplus profit, which could be converted into rent and as such made independent with respect to profit. Such an alien force

---

[a] See this volume, pp. 194-95.

and barrier are presented by landed property, when confronting capital in its endeavour to invest in land; such a force is the landlord vis-à-vis the capitalist.

Landed property is here the barrier which does not permit any new investment of capital in hitherto uncultivated or unrented land without levying a tax, or in other words, without demanding a rent, although the land to be newly brought under cultivation may belong to a category which does not yield any differential rent and which, were it not for landed property, could have been cultivated even at a small increase in market price, so that the regulating market price would have netted to the cultivator of this worst soil solely his price of production. But owing to the barrier raised by landed property, the market price must rise to a level at which the land can yield an excess over the price of production, i. e., yield a rent. However, since the value of the commodities produced by agricultural capital is higher than their price of production, according to our assumption, this rent (save for one case which we shall discuss forthwith) forms the excess of value over the price of production, or a part of it. Whether the rent equals the entire difference between the value and price of production, or only a greater or lesser part of it, will depend wholly on the relation between supply and demand and on the area of land newly taken under cultivation. So long as the rent does not equal the excess of the value of agricultural products over their price of production, a portion of this excess will always enter into the general equalisation and proportional distribution of all surplus value among the various individual capitals. As soon as the rent does equal the excess of the value over the price of production, this entire portion of surplus value over and above the average profit will be withdrawn from this equalisation. But whether this absolute rent equals the whole excess of value over the price of production, or just a part of it, the agricultural products will always be sold at a monopoly price, not because their price exceeds their value, but because it equals their value, or because their price is lower than their value but higher than their price of production. Their monopoly would consist in the fact that, unlike other products of industry whose value is higher than the general price of production, they are not levelled out to the price of production. Since one portion of the value, as well as of price of production, is an actually given constant, namely the cost price, representing the capital $= k$ used up in production, their difference consists in the other, the variable portion, the surplus value, which equals p, the profit, in the price of production, i. e., equals the total surplus value calculated on the social capital and on every individual capital as an aliquot part of the social capital; but which in the value of commodities equals the actual surplus value created by this particular capital, and forms an integral part of the commodity values produced by this capital. If the value of commodities is higher than their price of production, then the price of production $= k + p$, and the value $= k + p + d$, so that $p + d =$ the surplus value contained therein. The difference between the value and the price of production, therefore, $= d$, the excess of surplus value created by this capital over the surplus value allocated to it through the general rate of profit. It follows from this that the price of agricultural products may lie higher than their price of production, without reaching their value. It follows, furthermore, that a permanent increase in the price of agricultural products may take place up to a certain point, before their price reaches their value. It follows likewise that the excess in the value of agricultural products over their price of production can become a determining element of their general market price solely as a consequence of the monopoly in landed property. It follows, finally, that in this case the increase in the price of the product is not the cause of rent, but rather that rent is the cause of the increase in the price of the product. If the price of the product from a unit area of the worst soil $= P + r$, then all differential rents will rise by corresponding multiples of r, since the assumption is that $P + r$ becomes the regulating market price.

If the average composition of the nonagricultural social capital were $= 85_c + 15_v$, and the rate of surplus value $= 100\%$, then the price of production would $= 115$. If the composition of the agricultural capital were $= 75_c + 25_v$, and the rate of surplus value were the same, then the value of the product and the regulating market price would $= 125$. If the agricultural and the nonagricultural product should be equalised to the same average price (we assume for the sake of brevity the total capital in both lines of production to be equal), then the total surplus value would $= 40$, or 20%, on the 200 of capital. The product of the one as well as the other would be sold at 120. In an equalisation into prices of production, the average market prices of the nonagricultural product would thus lie above, and those of the agricultural product below, their value. If the agricultural products were sold at their full value, they would be higher by 5, and the industrial products lower by 5, then they are in the equalisation. If market conditions do not permit the sale of the agricultural products at their full value, to the full surplus above the price of production, then the effect lies between the two extremes; the industrial products are sold somewhat above their value, and the agricultural products somewhat above their price of production.

Although landed property may drive the price of agricultural produce above its price of production, it does not depend on this, but rather on the general state of the market, to what degree market price exceeds the price of production and approaches the value, and to what extent therefore the surplus value created in agriculture over and above the given average profit shall either be transformed into rent or enter into the general equalisation of the surplus value to average profit. At any rate this absolute rent arising out of the excess of value over the price of production is but a portion of the agricultural surplus value, a conversion of this surplus value into rent, its being filched by the landlord; just as the differential rent arises out of the conversion of surplus profit into rent, its being filched by the landlord under a generally regulating price of production. These two forms of rent are the only normal ones. Apart from them the rent can be based only upon an actual monopoly price, which is determined neither by price of production nor by value of commodities, but by the buyers' needs and ability to pay. Its analysis belongs under the theory of competition, where the actual movement of market prices is considered.

If all the land suitable for agriculture in a certain country were leased — assuming the capitalist mode of production and normal conditions to be general — there would not be any land not paying rent; but there might be some capitals, certain parts of capitals invested in land, that might not yield any rent. For as soon as the land has been rented, landed property ceases to act as an absolute barrier against the investment of necessary capital. Still, it continues to act as a relative barrier even after that, in so far as the reversion to the landlord of the capital incorporated in the land circumscribes the activity of the tenant within very definite limits. Only in this case all rent would be transformed into differential rent, although this would not be a differential rent determined by any difference in soil fertility, but rather by the difference between the surplus profits arising from the last investments of capital in a particular soil type and the rent paid for the lease of the worst quality land. Landed property acts as an absolute barrier only to the extent that the landlord exacts a tribute for making land at all accessible to the investment of capital. When such access has been gained, he can no longer set any absolute limits to the size of any investment of capital in a given plot of land. In general, housing construction meets a barrier in the ownership by a third party of the land upon which the houses are to be built. But, once this land has been leased for the purpose of housing construction, it depends upon the tenant whether he will build a large or a small house.

If the average composition of agricultural capital were equal to, or higher than, that of the average social capital, then absolute rent— again in the sense just described—would disappear; i. e., rent which differs equally from differential rent as well as that based upon an actual monopoly price. The value of agricultural produce, then, would not lie above its price of production, and the agricultural capital would not set any more labour in motion, and therefore would also not realise any more surplus labour than the nonagricultural capital. The same would take place, were the composition of agricultural capital to become equal to that of the average social capital with the progress of cultivation.

It seems to be a contradiction, at first glance, to assume that, on the one hand, the composition of agricultural capital rises, in other words, that its constant component increases with respect to its variable, and, on the other hand, that the price of the agricultural product should rise high enough to permit rent to be yielded by new and worse soil than that previously cultivated, a rent which in this case could originate only from an excess of market price over the value and price of production, in short, a rent derived solely from a monopoly price of the product.

It is necessary to make a distinction here.

In the first place, it was noted in considering the manner in which rate of profit is formed, that capitals, which have the same composition technologically speaking, i. e., which set equivalent amounts of labour in motion relative to machinery and raw materials, may nonetheless have different compositions owing to different values of the constant portions of these capitals. The raw materials or machinery may be dearer in one case than in another. For the same quantity of labour to be set in motion (and this would be required, according to our assumption, to work up the same mass of raw materials), a larger capital would have to be advanced in the one case than in the other, since the same amount of labour cannot be set in motion with, say, a capital of 100 if the cost of raw material, which must be covered out of the 100, is 40 in one case and 20 in another. But it would become immediately evident that these two capitals are of the same technical composition, as soon as the price of the dearer raw material fell to the level of the cheaper one. The value ratio between variable and constant capital would have become the same in that case, although no change had taken place in the technical proportions between the living labour and the mass and nature of the conditions of labour employed by this capital. On the other hand, a capital of lower organic composition could assume the appearance of being in the same class with one of a higher organic composition, merely from a rise in the value of its constant portions, solely from the viewpoint of its value composition. Suppose one capital $= 60_c + 40_v$, because it employs much machinery and raw material compared to living labour power, and another capital $= 40_c + 60_v$, because it employs much living labour (60%), little machinery (e. g., 10%) and compared to labour power less and cheaper raw material (e. g., 30%). Then a simple rise in the value of raw and auxiliary materials from 30 to 80 could equalise the composition, so that now the second capital would consist of 80 raw material and 60 labour power for 10 in machines, or $90_c + 60_v$, which, in percentages, would also $= 60_c + 40_v$, with no change having taken place in the technical composition. In other words, capitals of equal organic composition may be of different value composition, and capitals with identical percentages of value composition may show varying degrees of organic composition and thus express different stages in the development of the social productive power of labour. The mere circumstance, then, that agricultural capital might be on the general level of value composition, would not prove that the social productivity of labour is equally developed in it. It would merely show that its own product, which again forms a part of its conditions of production, is dearer, or that auxiliary materials, such as fertiliser, which used to be close by, must now be brought from afar, etc.

But aside from this, the peculiar nature of agriculture must be taken into account.

Suppose labour-saving machinery, chemical aids, etc., are more extensively used in agriculture, and that therefore constant capital increases technically, not merely in value, but also in mass, as compared with the mass of employed labour power, then in agriculture (as in mining) it is not only a matter of the social, but also of the natural, productivity of labour which depends on the natural conditions of labour. It is possible for the increase of social productive power in agriculture to barely compensate, or not even compensate, for the decrease in natural power— this compensation will nevertheless be effective only for a short time— so that despite technical development there, no cheapening of the product occurs, but only a still greater increase in price is averted. It is also possible that the absolute mass of products decreases with rising grain prices, while the relative surplus product increases; namely, in the case of a relative increase in constant capital which consists chiefly of machinery or animals requiring only replacement of wear and tear, and with a corresponding decrease in variable capital which is expended in wages requiring constant replacement in full out of the product.

Moreover, it is also possible that with progress in agriculture only a moderate rise in market price above the average is necessary, in order to cultivate and draw a rent from poorer soil, which would have required a greater rise in market price if technical aids were less developed.

The fact that in larger-scale cattle-raising, for example, the mass of employed labour power is very small compared with constant capital as represented in cattle itself, could be taken to refute the assertion that more labour power, on a percentage basis, is set in motion by agricultural capital than by the average social capital outside of agriculture. But it should be noted here that we have taken as determining for rent analysis that portion of agricultural capital which produces the principal plant foodstuffs providing the chief means of subsistence among civilised nations. Adam Smith— and this is one of his merits — has already demonstrated that a quite different determination of prices is to be observed in cattle-raising, and, for that matter, generally for capitals invested in land which are not engaged in raising the principal means of subsistence, e. g., grain. Namely in that case the price is determined in such a way that the price of the product of the land — which is used for cattle-raising, say as an artificial pasture, but which could just as easily have been transformed into cornfields of a certain quality — must rise high enough to produce the same rent as on arable land of the same quality. In other words, the rent of cornfields becomes a determining element in the price of cattle, and for this reason Ramsay has justly remarked that the price of cattle is in this manner artificially raised by the rent, by the economic expression of landed property, in short, through landed property.[a]

"By the extension of cultivation the unimproved wilds become insufficient to sup-

---

[a] G. Ramsay, *An Essay on the Distribution of Wealth*, pp. 278-79.

ply the demand for butcher's meat. A great part of the cultivated lands must be employed in rearing and fattening cattle, of which the price, therefore, must be sufficient to pay, not only the labour necessary for tending them, but the rent which the landlord and the profit which the farmer could have drawn from such land, employed in tillage. The cattle bred upon the most uncultivated moors, when brought to the same market, are, in proportion to their weight or goodness, sold at the same price as those which are reared upon the most improved land. The proprietors of those moors profit by it, and raise the rent of their land in proportion to the price of their cattle" (Adam Smith, Book I, Ch. XI, Part 1.[a])

In this case, likewise, as distinct from grain rent, the differential rent is in favour of the worst soil.

Absolute rent explains some phenomena, which, at first sight, seem to make merely a monopoly price responsible for the rent. To go on with Adam Smith's example, take the owner of some Norwegian forest, for instance, which exists independent of human activity, i. e., it is not a product of silviculture. If the proprietor of this forest receives a rent from a capitalist who has the timber felled, perhaps in consequence of a demand from England, or if this owner has the timber felled himself acting in the capacity of capitalist, then a greater or smaller amount of rent will accrue to him in timber, apart from the profit on invested capital. This appears to be a pure monopoly charge derived from a pure product of Nature. But, as a matter of fact, the capital here consists almost exclusively of a variable component expended in labour, and thus sets more surplus labour in motion than another capital of the same size. The value of the timber, then, contains a greater surplus of unpaid labour, or surplus value, than that of a product of a capital of a higher organic composition. For this reason the average profit can be derived from this timber, and a considerable surplus in the form of rent can fall to the share of the owner of the forest. Conversely, it may be assumed that, owing to the ease with which timber-felling may be extended, in other words, its production rapidly increased, the demand must rise very considerably for the price of timber to equal its value, and thereby for the entire surplus of unpaid labour (over and above that portion which falls to the capitalist as average profit) to accrue to the owner in the form of rent.

We have assumed that the land newly brought under cultivation is of still inferior quality than the worst previously cultivated. If it is better, it yields a differential rent. But here we are analysing precisely the case wherein rent does not appear as a differential rent. There are

---

[a] See *An Inquiry into the Nature and Causes of the Wealth of Nations*, Vol. 1, p. 185.

only two cases possible: The newly cultivated soil is either inferior to, or just as good as the previously cultivated soil. If inferior, then the matter has already been analysed. It remains only to analyse the case in which it is just as good.

As already developed in our analysis of differential rent, the progress of cultivation may just as well bring equally good, or even better soils under the plough as worse soil.

First. Because in differential rent (or any rent in general, since even in the case of nondifferential rent the question always arises whether, on the one hand, the soil fertility in general, and, on the other hand, its location, admit of its cultivation at the regulating market price so as to yield a profit and rent) two conditions work in opposing directions, now cancelling one another, now alternately exerting the determining influence. The rise in market price — provided the cost price of cultivation has not fallen, i. e., no technical progress has given a new impetus to further cultivation — may bring under cultivation more fertile soil formerly excluded from competition by virtue of its location. Or it may so enhance the advantage of the location of the inferior soil that its lesser fertility is counterbalanced by it. Or, without any rise in market price the location may bring better soils into competition through improvement in means of communication, as can be observed on a large scale in the prairie States of North America. In countries of older civilisation the same also takes place constantly if not to the same extent as in the colonies, where, as Wakefield correctly observes, location is decisive.[a] To sum up, then, the contradictory influences of location and fertility, and the variableness of the location factor, which is continually counterbalanced and perpetually passes through progressive changes tending towards equalisation, alternately carry equally good, better or worse land areas into new competition with the older ones under cultivation.

Secondly. With the development of natural science and agronomy the soil fertility is also changed by changing the means through which the soil constituents may be rendered immediately serviceable. In this way, light soil types in France and in the eastern counties of England, which were regarded as inferior at one time, have recently risen to first place. (See Passy.[b]) On the other hand, soil considered inferior

---

a [E. G. Wakefield] *England and America. A Comparison of the Social and Political State of Both Nations*, Vol. I, pp. 214-15. - b H. Passy, *Rente du sol*. In: Dictionnaire de l'économie politique, Tome II, p. 515.

not for bad chemical composition but for certain mechanical and physical obstacles that hindered its cultivation, is converted into good land as soon as means to overcome these obstacles have been discovered.

Thirdly. In all ancient civilisations, old historical and traditional relations, for instance, in the form of state-owned lands, communal lands, etc., have purely arbitrarily withheld from cultivation large tracts of land, which only return to it little by little. The succession in which they are brought under cultivation depends neither upon their good quality nor siting, but upon wholly external circumstances. In tracing the history of English communal lands turned successively into private property through the ENCLOSURE BILLS and brought under the plough, nothing would be more ridiculous than the fantastic idea that a modern agricultural chemist, such as Liebig, had indicated the selection of land in this succession, designating certain fields for cultivation owing to chemical properties and excluding others. What was more decisive in this case was the opportunity which makes the thief; the more or less plausible legalistic subterfuges of the big landlords to justify their appropriation.

Fourthly. Apart from the fact that the stage of development reached at any time by the population and capital increase sets certain limits, even though elastic, to the extension of cultivation, and apart from chance effects which temporarily influence the market price — such as a series of good or bad seasons — the extension of agriculture over a larger area depends on the overall state of the capital market and business conditions in a country. In periods of stringency it will not suffice for uncultivated soil to yield the tenant an average profit — no matter whether he pays any rent or not — in order that additional capital be invested in agriculture. In other periods when there is a plethora of capital, it will pour into agriculture even without a rise in market price if only other normal conditions are present. Better soil than hitherto cultivated would in fact be excluded from competition solely on the basis of unfavourable location, or if hitherto insurmountable obstacles to its employment existed, or through chance. For this reason we should only concern ourselves with soils which are just as good as those last cultivated. However, there still exists the difference in cost of clearing for cultivation between the new soil and the one last cultivated. And it depends upon the level of market prices and credit conditions whether this will be undertaken or not. As soon as this soil then actually enters into competition, the market price will fall once more to its former level, assuming other conditions to be equal, and the new soil will then yield the same rent as the corresponding old soil. The assumption that it does not yield any rent is proved by its advocates by assuming precisely what they are called upon to prove, namely that the last soil did not yield any rent. One might prove in the same manner that houses which were the last built do not yield any rent for the building outside of house rent proper, even though they are leased. In fact, however, they do yield rent even before yielding any house rent, when they frequently remain vacant for a long period. Just as successive investments of capital in a certain piece of land may bring a proportional surplus and thereby the same rent as the first investment, so fields of the same quality as those last cultivated may bring the same proceeds for the same cost. Otherwise it would be altogether inexplicable how fields of the same quality are ever brought successively under cultivation; it seems that either it would be necessary to take all together, or rather not a single one of them, in order not to bring all the remaining ones into competition. The landlord is always ready to draw a rent, i. e., to receive something for nothing. But capital requires certain conditions to fulfil his wish. Competition between pieces of land does not, therefore, depend upon the landlord desiring them to compete, but upon the capital existing which seeks to compete with other capitals in the new fields.

To the extent that the agricultural rent proper is purely a monopoly price, the latter can only be small, just as the absolute rent can only be small here under normal conditions whatever the excess of the product's value over its price of production. The essence of absolute rent, therefore, consists in this: Given the same rate of surplus value, or degree of labour exploitation, equally large capitals in various spheres of production produce different amounts of surplus value, in accordance with their varying average composition. In industry these various masses of surplus value are equalised into an average profit and distributed uniformly among the individual capitals as aliquot parts of the social capital. Landed property hinders such an equalisation among capitals invested in land, whenever production requires land for either agriculture or extraction of raw materials, and takes hold of a portion of the surplus value, which would otherwise take part in equalising to the general rate of profit. The rent, then, forms a portion of the value, or, more specifically, surplus value, of commodities, and instead of falling into the lap of the capitalists, who have extracted it from their labourers, it falls to the share of the landlords, who extract it from the capitalists. It is hereby assumed that the agricultural capital sets more labour in motion than an equally large portion of nonagricultural capital. How far the discrepancy goes, or whether it exists at all, depends upon the relative development of agriculture as compared with industry. It is in the nature of the case that this difference must decrease with the progress of agriculture, unless the proportionate decrease of variable as compared with constant capital is still greater in the case of industrial than in the case of agricultural capital.

This absolute rent plays an even more important role in the extractive industry proper, where one element of constant capital, raw material, is wholly lacking and where, excluding those lines in which capital consisting of machinery and other fixed capital is very considerable, by far the lowest composition of capital prevails. Precisely here, where the rent appears entirely attributable to a monopoly price, unusually favourable market conditions are necessary for commodities to be sold at their value, or for rent to equal the entire excess of a commodity's surplus value over its price of production. This applies, for instance, to rent from fisheries, stone quarries, natural forests, etc. [37]

Chapter XLVI

BUILDING SITE RENT. RENT IN MINING.
PRICE OF LAND

Wherever rent exists at all, differential rent appears at all times, and is governed by the same laws, as agricultural differential rent. Wherever natural forces can be monopolised and guarantee a surplus profit to the industrial capitalist using them, be it waterfalls, rich mines, waters teeming with fish, or a favourably located building site, there the person who by virtue of title to a portion of the globe has become the proprietor of these natural objects will wrest this surplus profit from functioning capital in the form of rent. Adam Smith has

---

[37] Ricardo deals with this very superficially. See the passage directed against Adam Smith concerning forest rent in Norway, at the very beginning of Chapter II, in *Principles*.[a]

---

[a] See *On the Principles of Political Economy and Taxation*, pp. 53-54.

set forth, as concerns land for building purposes, that the basis of its rent, like that of all nonagricultural land, is regulated by agricultural rent proper (Book I, Ch. XI, 2 and 3).[a] This rent is distinguished, in the first place, by the preponderant influence exerted here by location upon differential rent (very significant, e. g., in vineyards and building sites in large cities); secondly, by the palpable and complete passiveness of the owner, whose sole activity consists (especially in mines) in exploiting the progress of social development, toward which he contributes nothing and for which he risks nothing, unlike the industrial capitalist; and finally by the prevalence of monopoly prices in many cases, particularly through the most shameless exploitation of poverty (for poverty is more lucrative for house rent than the mines of Potosi[84] ever were for Spain[38]), and the monstrous power wielded by landed property, when united hand in hand with industrial capital, enables it to be used against labourers engaged in their wage struggle as a means of practically expelling them from the earth as a dwelling place.[39] One part of society thus exacts tribute from another for the permission to inhabit the earth, as landed property in general assigns the landlord the privilege of exploiting the terrestrial body, the bowels of the earth, the air, and thereby the maintenance and development of life. Not only the population increase and with it the growing demand for shelter, but also the development of fixed capital, which is either incorporated in land, or takes root in it and is based upon it, such as all industrial buildings, railways, warehouses, factory buildings, docks, etc., necessarily increase the building rent. A confusion of house-rent, in so far as it constitutes interest and amortisation on capital invested in a house, and rent for the mere land, is not possible in this case, even with all the goodwill of a person like Carey, particularly when landlord and building speculator are different persons, as is true in England. Two elements should be considered here: on the one hand, the exploitation of the earth for the purpose of reproduction or extraction; on the other hand, the space required as an element of all production and all human activity. And

---

[38] Laing, Newman.[b]
[39] Crowlington Strike. Engels, *Lage der arbeitenden Klasse in England*, S. 307.[c]

---

[a] See A. Smith, *An Inquiry into the Nature and Causes of the Wealth of Nations*, London, 1776. - [b] S. Laing, *National Distress; its Causes and Remedies*, London, 1844; F. W. Newman, *Lectures on Political Economy*, London, 1857. - [c] See present edition, Vol. 4, pp. 543-44.

property in land demands its tribute in both senses. The demand for building sites raises the value of land as space and foundation, while thereby the demand for elements of the terrestrial body serving as building material grows simultaneously. [40]

That it is the ground rent, and not the house, which forms the actual object of building speculation in rapidly growing cities, especially where construction is carried on as an industry, e. g., in London, has already been illustrated in Book II, Chapter XII, S. 215, 216, in the testimony of a big building speculator in London, Edward Capps, given before the Select Committee on Bank Acts of 1857. He stated there, No. 5435:

"I think a man who wishes to rise in the world can hardly expect to rise by following out a FAIR TRADE ...it is necessary for him to add speculative building to it, and that must be done not on a small scale; ...for the builder makes very little profit out of the buildings themselves; he makes the principal part of the profit out of the improved ground rents. Perhaps he takes a piece of ground, and agrees to give £300 a year for it; by laying it out with care, and putting certain descriptions of buildings upon it, he may succeed in making £400 or £450 a year out of it, and his profit would be the increased ground rent of £100 or £150 a year, rather than the profit of the buildings which ..., in many instances, he scarcely looks at at all."

And parenthetically it should not be forgotten that after the lapse of the lease, generally at the end of 99 years, the land with all its buildings and its ground rent—usually increased in the interim twice or three times, reverts from the building speculator or his legal successor to the original last landlord.

Mining rent proper is determined in the same way as agricultural rent.

"There are some mines, of which the produce is barely sufficient to pay the labour and replace, together with its ordinary profits, the stock employed in working them. They afford some profit to the undertaker of the work, but no rent to the landlord. They can be wrought advantageously by nobody but the landlord, who, being himself the undertaker of the work, gets the ordinary profit of the capital which he employs in it. Many coalmines in Scotland are wrought in this manner, and can be wrought in no other. The landlord will allow nobody else to work them without paying some rent, and nobody can afford to pay any" (Adam Smith, Book I, Ch. XI, 2).[b]

[40] "The paving of the streets of London has enabled the owners of some barren rocks on the coast of Scotland to draw a rent from what never afforded any before." Adam Smith, Book I, Chapter XI, 2.[a]

---

[a] See *An Inquiry into the Nature and Causes of the Wealth of Nations*. Vol. 1, pp. 204-05. - [b] Ibid., p. 207.

It must be distinguished, whether the rent springs from a monopoly price, because a monopoly price of the product or the land exists independently of it, or whether the products are sold at a monopoly price, because a rent exists. When we refer to a monopoly price, we mean in general a price determined only by the purchasers' eagerness to buy and ability to pay, independent of the price determined by the general price of production, as well as by the value of the products. A vineyard producing wine of very extraordinary quality which can be produced only in relatively small quantities yields a monopoly price. The wine-grower would realise a considerable surplus profit from this monopoly price, whose excess over the value of the product would be wholly determined by the means and fondness of the discriminating wine-drinker. This surplus profit, which accrues from a monopoly price, is converted into rent and in this form falls into the lap of the landlord, thanks to his title to this piece of the globe endowed with singular properties. Here, then, the monopoly price creates the rent. On the other hand, the rent would create a monopoly price if grain were sold not merely above its price of production, but also above its value, owing to the limits set by landed property to the investment of capital in uncultivated land without payment of rent. That it is only the title of a number of persons to the possession of the globe enabling them to appropriate to themselves as tribute a portion of the surplus labour of society and furthermore to a constantly increasing extent with the development of production, is concealed by the fact that the capitalised rent, i. e., precisely this capitalised tribute, appears as the price of land, which may therefore be sold like any other article of commerce. The buyer, therefore, does not feel that his title to the rent is obtained gratis, and without the labour, risk, and spirit of enterprise of the capitalist, but rather that he has paid for it with an equivalent. To the buyer, as previously indicated, the rent appears merely as interest on the capital with which he has purchased the land and consequently his title to the rent. In the same way, the slaveholder considers a Negro, whom he has purchased, as his property, not because the institution of slavery as such entitles him to that Negro, but because he has acquired him like any other commodity, through sale and purchase. But the title itself is simply transferred, and not created by the sale. The title must exist before it can be sold, and a series of sales can no more create this title through continued repetition than a single sale can. What created it in the first place were the production relations. As soon as these have reached a point where they must shed their skin, the material source of the title, justified economically and historically and arising from the process which creates social life, falls by the wayside, along with all transactions based upon it. From the standpoint of a higher economic form of society, private ownership of the globe by single individuals will appear quite as absurd as private ownership of one man by another. Even a whole society, a nation, or even all simultaneously existing societies taken together, are not the owners of the globe. They are only its possessors, its usufructuaries, and, like *boni patres familias*, they must hand it down to succeeding generations in an improved condition.

In the following analysis of the price of land we leave out of consideration all fluctuations of competition, all land speculation, and also small landed property, in which land forms the principal instrument of producers and must, therefore, be bought by them at any price.

I. The price of land may rise without the rent rising, namely:

1) by a mere fall in interest rate, which causes the rent to be sold more dearly, and thereby the capitalised rent, or price of land, rises;

2) because the interest on capital incorporated in the land rises.

II. The price of land may rise, because the rent increases.

The rent may increase, because the price of the product of the land rises, in which case the rate of differential rent always rises, whether the rent on the worst cultivated soil be large, small or nonexistent. By rate we mean the ratio of that portion of surplus value converted into rent to the invested capital which produces the agricultural product. This differs from the ratio of surplus product to total product, for the total product does not comprise the entire invested capital, namely, the fixed capital, which continues to exist alongside the product. On the other hand, it covers the fact that on soils yielding differential rent an increasing portion of the product is transformed into an excess of surplus product. The increase in price of agricultural product of the worst soil first creates rent and thereby the price of land.

The rent, however, may also increase without a rise in price of the agricultural product. This price may remain constant, or even decrease.

If the price remains constant, the rent can grow only (apart from monopoly prices) because, on the one hand, given the same amount of capital invested in the old lands, new lands of better quality are cultivated, which merely suffice, however, to cover the increased demand, so that the regulating market price remains unchanged. In this case, the price of the old lands does not rise, but the price of the newly cultivated lands rises above that of the old ones.

Or, on the other hand, the rent rises because the mass of capital exploiting the land increases, assuming that the relative productivity and market price remain the same. Although the rent thus remains the same compared with the invested capital, still its mass, for instance, may be doubled, because the capital itself has doubled. Since no fall in price has occurred, the second investment of capital yields a surplus profit just as well as the first, and it likewise is transformed into rent after the expiration of the lease. The mass of rent rises here, because the mass of capital producing a rent increases. The contention that various successive investments of capital in the same piece of land can produce rent only in so far as their yield is unequal, so that a differential rent thus arises, is reduced to the contention that when two capitals of £1,000 each are invested in two fields of equal productivity, only one of them can produce a rent, although both fields belong to a better soil type, which produces differential rent. (The mass of rental, the total rent of a country, grows therefore with the mass of capital invested, without the price of the individual pieces of land, or the rate of rent, or even the mass of rent on individual pieces of land, necessarily increasing; the amount of rental grows in this case with the extension of cultivation over a wider area. This may even be combined with a decrease in rent on individual holdings.) Otherwise, this contention would lead to the other, namely, that the investment of capital in two different pieces of land existing side by side follows different laws than the successive investment of capital in the same plot, whereas differential rent is derived precisely from the identity of the law in both cases, from the increased productiveness of capital invested either in the same field or in different fields. The only modification which exists here and is overlooked is that successive investments of capital, when applied to different pieces of land, meet the barrier of landed property, which is not the case with successive investments of capital in the same piece of land. This accounts for the opposing tendencies by which these two different forms of investment curb each other in practice. No difference in capital ever appears here. If the composition of the capital remains the same, and similarly the rate of surplus value, the rate of profit remains unaltered, so that the mass of profit is doubled when the capital is doubled. In like manner the rate of rent remains the same under the assumed conditions. If a capital of £1,000 produces a rent of x, then a capital of £2,000, under the assumed conditions, produces a rent of 2X. But calculated with reference to the area of land, which has remained unaltered, since, according to our assumption, the doubled capital operates in the same field, the level of rent has also risen as a consequence of its increase in mass. The same acre which yielded a rent of £2, now yields £4. [41]

The relation of a portion of the surplus value, of money rent — for money is the independent expression of value — to the land is in itself absurd and irrational; for the magnitudes which are here measured by one another are incommensurable — a particular use value, a piece of land of so many and so many square feet, on the one hand, and value, especially surplus value, on the other. This expresses in fact nothing more than that, under the given conditions, the ownership of so many square feet of land enables the landowner to wrest a certain quantity of unpaid labour, which the capital wallowing in these square feet like a hog in potatoes has realised. //Written in the manuscript here in brackets, but crossed out, is the name "Liebig".// But *prima facie* the expression is the same as if one desired to speak of the relation of a five-pound note to the diameter of the earth. However, the reconciliation of irrational forms in which certain economic relations appear and assert themselves in practice does not concern the active agents of these relations in their everyday life. And since they are accustomed to move about in such relations, they find noth-

---

[41] It is one of the merits of Rodbertus whose important work on rent [a] we shall discuss in Book IV[7] to have developed this point. He commits the one error, however, of assuming, in the first place, that as regards capital an increase in profit is always expressed by an increase in capital, so that the ratio remains the same when the mass of profit increases. But this is erroneous, since the rate of profit may increase, given a changed composition of capital, even if the exploitation of labour remains the same, precisely because the proportional value of the constant portion of capital compared with its variable portion falls. Secondly, he commits the mistake of dealing with the ratio of money rent to a quantitatively definite piece of land, e. g., an acre, as though it had been the general premiss of classical economics in its analysis of the rise or fall of rent. This, again, is erroneous. Classical economics always treats the rate of rent, in so far as it considers rent in its natural form, with reference to the product, and in so far as it considers rent as money rent, with reference to the advanced capital, because these are in fact the rational expressions.

---

[a] The reference is to Rodbertus, *Sociale Briefe an von Kirchmann*, Dritter Brief: Widerlegung der Ricardo'schen Lehre von der Grundrente und Begründung einer neuen Rententheorie, Berlin, 1851.

ing strange therein. A complete contradiction offers not the least mystery to them. They feel as much at home as a fish in water among manifestations which are separated from their internal connections and absurd when isolated by themselves. What Hegel says with reference to certain mathematical formulas applies here: that which seems irrational to ordinary common sense is rational, and that which seems rational to it is itself irrational.[a]

When considered in connection with the land area itself, a rise in the mass of rent is thus expressed in the same way as a rise in the rate of rent, and hence the embarrassment experienced when the conditions which would explain the one case are lacking in the other.

The price of land, however, may also rise even when the price of the agricultural product decreases.

In this case, the differential rent, and with it the price of the better lands, may have risen, owing to further differentiations. Or, if this is not the case, the price of the agricultural product may have fallen by virtue of greater labour productive power but in such a manner that the increased production more than counterbalances this. Let us assume that one quarter cost 60 shillings. Now, if the same acre, with the same capital, should produce two quarters instead of one, and the price of one quarter should fall to 40 shillings, then two quarters would cost 80 shillings, so that the value of the product of the same capital invested in the same acre would have risen by one-third, despite the fall in price per quarter by one-third. How this is possible without selling the product above its price of production or above its value, has been developed in the analysis of differential rent. As a matter of fact it is possible only in two ways. Either bad soil is excluded from competition, but the price of the better soil increases with the increase in differential rent, i. e., the general improvement affects the various soil types differently. Or, the same price of production (and the same value, if absolute rent is paid) expresses itself on the worst soil through a larger mass of products, when labour productivity has become greater. The product represents the same value as before, but the price of its aliquot parts has fallen, while their number has increased. This is impossible when the same capital has been employed; for in this case the same value always expresses itself through any portion of the product. It is possible, however, when additional capital has

---

[a] Hegel, *Encyclopädie der philosophischen Wissenschaften im Grundrisse*, 1. Teil, *Die Logik*. In: *Werke*, Band 6, Berlin, 1840, S. 404.

been expended for gypsum, guano, etc., in short, for improvements the effects of which extend over several years. The stipulation is that the price of an individual quarter falls, but not to the same extent as the number of quarters increases.

III. These different conditions under which rent may rise, and with it the price of land in general, or of particular kinds of land, may partly compete, or partly exclude one another, and can only act alternately. But it follows from the foregoing that the consequence of a rise in the price of land does not necessarily signify also a rise in rent, or that a rise in rent, which always brings with it a rise in the price of land, is not necessarily contingent upon an increase in the agricultural product. [42)]

———

Rather than tracing to their origin the real natural causes leading to an exhaustion of the soil, which, incidentally, were unknown to all economists writing on differential rent owing to the level of agricultural chemistry in their day, the shallow conception was seized upon that any amount of capital cannot be invested in a limited area of land; as the *Edinburgh Review*,[a] for instance, argued against Richard Jones that all of England cannot be fed through the cultivation of Soho Square. If this be considered a special disadvantage of agriculture, precisely the opposite is true. It is possible to invest capital here successively with fruitful results, because the soil itself serves as an instrument of production, which is not the case with a factory, or holds only to a limited extent, since it serves only as a foundation, as a place and a space providing a basis of operations. It is true that, compared with scattered handicrafts, large-scale industry may concentrate much production in a small area. Nevertheless a definite amount of space is always required at any given level of productivity, and the construction of tall buildings also has its practical limitations. Beyond this any expansion of production also demands an extension of land area. The fixed capital invested in machinery, etc., does not improve through use, but on the contrary, wears out. New inventions may indeed permit some improvement in this respect, but with any given

———

[42)] Concerning the actual fall in the price of land when rent rises, see Passy.

———

[a] See a review on R. Jones' book, *An Essay on the Distribution of Wealth and on the Sources of Taxation*. In: *The Edinburgh Review*, Tome LIV, August-December 1831, pp. 94-95.

development in productive power, machines will always deteriorate. If productive power is rapidly developed, all of the old machinery must be replaced by the more advantageous; in other words, it is lost. The soil, however, if properly treated, improves all the time. The advantage of the soil, permitting successive investments of capital to bring gains without loss of previous investments, implies the possibility of differences in yield from these successive investments of capital.

Chapter XLVII

GENESIS OF CAPITALIST GROUND RENT

I. INTRODUCTORY REMARKS

We must clarify in our minds wherein lies the real difficulty in analysing ground rent from the viewpoint of modern economics, as the theoretical expression of the capitalist mode of production. Even many of the more modern writers have not as yet grasped this, as evidenced by each renewed attempt to "newly" explain ground rent. The novelty almost invariably consists in a relapse into long out-of-date views. The difficulty is not to explain the surplus product produced by agricultural capital and its corresponding surplus value in general. This question is solved in the analysis of the surplus value produced by all productive capital, in whatever sphere it may be invested. The difficulty consists rather in showing the source of the excess of surplus value paid the landlord by capital invested in land in the form of ground rent, after equalisation of the surplus value to the average profit among the various capitals, after the various capitals have shared in the total surplus value produced by the social capital in all spheres of production in proportion to their relative size; in other words, the source subsequent to this equalisation and the apparently already completed distribution of all surplus value which, in general, is to be distributed. Quite apart from the practical motives, which prodded modern economists as spokesmen of industrial capital against landed property to investigate this question — motives which we shall point out more clearly in the chapter on history of ground rent — the question was of paramount interest to them as theorists. To admit that the appearance of rent for capital invested in agriculture is due to some particular effect produced by the sphere of investment itself, due to singular qualities of the earth's crust itself, is tantamount to giving up the conception of value as such, thus tantamount to abandoning all attempts at a scientific understanding of this field. Even the simple observation that rent is paid out of the price of agricultural produce — which takes place even where rent is paid in kind if the farmer is to recover his price of production — showed the absurdity of attempting to explain the excess of this price over the ordinary price of production; in other words, to explain the relative dearness of agricultural products on the basis of the excess of natural productivity of agricultural production over the productivity of other lines of production. For the reverse is true: the more productive labour is, the cheaper is every aliquot part of its product, because so much greater is the mass of use values incorporating the same quantity of labour, i. e., the same value.

The whole difficulty in analysing rent, therefore, consists in explaining the excess of agricultural profit over the average profit, not the surplus value, but the excess of surplus value characteristic of this sphere of production; in other words, not the "net product", but the excess of this net product over the net product of other branches of industry. The average profit itself is a product formed under very definite historical production relations by the movement of social processes, a product which, as we have seen, requires very complex adjustment. To be able to speak at all of an excess over the average profit, this average profit itself must already be established as a standard and as a regulator of production in general as is the case under capitalist production. For this reason in social formations where it is not capital which performs the function of enforcing all surplus labour and appropriating directly all surplus value and where therefore capital has not yet completely, or only sporadically, brought social labour under its control there can be no talk of rent in the modern sense, a rent consisting of a surplus over the average profit, i. e., over and above the proportional share of each individual capital in the surplus value produced by the total social capital. It reflects naïveté, e. g., of a person like Passy (see below), when he speaks of rent in primitive society as an excess over profit[a] — a historically defined social form of surplus value, but which, according to Passy, might almost as well exist without any society.

For the older economists, who in general merely begin analysing the capitalist mode of production, still undeveloped in their day, the

---

[a] H. Passy, *Rente du sol*. In: Dictionnaire de l'économie politique, Tome II, p. 511.

analysis of rent offers either no difficulty at all, or only a difficulty of a completely different kind. Petty, Cantillon, and in general those writers who are closer to feudal times, assume ground rent to be the normal form of surplus value in general,[a] whereas profit to them is still amorphously combined with wages, or at best appears to be a portion of surplus value extorted by the capitalist from the land-lord. These writers thus take as their point of departure a situation where, in the first place, the agricultural population still constitutes the overwhelming majority of the nation, and, secondly, the landlord still appears as the person appropriating at first hand the surplus la-bour of the direct producers by virtue of his monopoly of landed pro-perty, where landed property, therefore, still appears as the main condition of production. For these writers the question could not yet be posed, which, inversely, seeks to investigate from the viewpoint of capitalist production how landed property manages to wrest back again from capital a portion of the surplus value produced by it (that is, filched by it from the direct producers) and already appropriated directly.

The *physiocrats* are troubled by difficulties of another nature. As the actually first systematic spokesmen of capital, they attempt to analyse the nature of surplus value in general. For them, this analysis coin-cides with the analysis of rent, the only form of surplus value which they recognise. Therefore, they consider rent-yielding, or agricultural, capital to be the only capital producing surplus value, and the agri-cultural labour set in motion by it, the only labour producing surplus value, which from a capitalist viewpoint is quite properly considered the only productive labour. They are quite right in considering the creation of surplus value as decisive. Apart from other merits to be set forth in Book IV,[7] they deserve credit primarily for going back from merchant's capital, which functions solely in the sphere of circulation, to productive capital, in opposition to the mercantile system, which, with its crude realism, constitutes the actual vulgar economy of that period, pushing into the background in favour of its own practical in-terests the beginnings of scientific analysis made by Petty and his suc-cessors. In this critique of the mercantile system, incidentally, only its conceptions of capital and surplus value are dealt with. It has already been indicated previously that the monetary system correctly pro-

---

[a] [Petty,] *A Treatise of Taxes and Contributions*, pp. 23-24; [Richard Cantillon,] *Essai sur la nature du commerce en général*, Amsterdam, 1756.

claims production for the world market and the transformation of the output into commodities, and thus into money, as the prerequisite and condition of capitalist production.[a] In this system's further development into the mercantile system, it is no longer the transformation of commodity value into money, but the creation of surplus value which is decisive—but from the meaningless viewpoint of the circulation sphere and, at the same time, in such manner that this surplus value is represented as surplus money, as the balance of trade surplus. At the same time, however, the characteristic feature of the interested merchants and manufacturers of that period, which is in keeping with the stage of capitalist development represented by them, is that the transformation of feudal agricultural societies into industrial ones and the corresponding industrial struggle of nations on the world market depends on an accelerated development of capital, which is not to be arrived at along the so-called natural path, but rather by means of coercive measures. It makes a tremendous difference whether national capital is gradually and slowly transformed into industrial capital, or whether this development is accelerated by means of a tax which they impose through protective duties mainly upon landowners, middle and small peasants, and handicraftsmen, by way of accelerated expropriation of the independent direct producers, and through the violently accelerated accumulation and concentration of capital, in short by means of the accelerated establishment of conditions of capitalist production. It simultaneously makes an enormous difference in the capitalist and industrial exploitation of the natural national productive power. Hence the national character of the mercantile system is not merely a phrase on the lips of its spokesmen. Under the pretext of concern solely for the wealth of the nation and the resources of the state, they, in fact, pronounce the interests of the capitalist class and the amassing of riches in general to be the ultimate aim of the state, and thus proclaim bourgeois society in place of the old divine state. But at the same time they are consciously aware that the development of the interests of capital and of the capitalist class, of capitalist production, forms the foundation of national power and national ascendancy in modern society.

The physiocrats, furthermore, are correct in stating that in fact all production of surplus value, and thus all development of capital, has for its natural basis the productivity of agricultural labour. If man

---

[a] See present edition, Vol. 29, pp. 389-90.

were not capable of producing in one working day more means of subsistence, which signifies in the strictest sense more agricultural products than every labourer needs for his own reproduction, if the daily expenditure of his entire labour power sufficed merely to produce the means of subsistence indispensable for his own individual requirements, then one could not speak at all either of surplus product or surplus value. An agricultural labour productivity exceeding the individual requirements of the labourer is the basis of all societies, and is above all the basis of capitalist production, which disengages a constantly increasing portion of society from the production of basic foodstuffs and transforms them into "FREE HANDS", as Steuart[a] has it, making them available for exploitation in other spheres.

But what can be said of more recent writers on economics, such as Daire, Passy, etc., who parrot the most primitive conceptions concerning the natural conditions of surplus labour and thereby surplus value in general, in the twilight of classical economy, indeed on its very death-bed, and who imagine that they are thus propounding something new and striking on ground rent[b] long after this ground rent has been investigated as a special form and become a specific portion of surplus value? It is particularly characteristic of vulgar economy that it echoes what was new, original, profound and justified during a specific outgrown stage of development, in a period when it has turned platitudinous, stale, and false. It thus confesses its complete ignorance of the problems which concerned classical economy. It confounds them with questions that could only have been posed on a lower level of development of bourgeois society. The same holds true of its incessant and self-complacent rumination of the physiocratic phrases concerning free trade. These phrases have long since lost all theoretical interest, no matter how much they may engage the practical attention of this or that state.

In natural economy proper, when no part of the agricultural product, or but a very insignificant portion, enters into the process of circulation, and then only a relatively small portion of that part of the product which represents the landlord's revenue, as, e. g., in many Roman latifundia, or upon the villas of Charlemagne,[85] or more or

---

[a] J. Steuart, *An Inquiry into the Principles of Political Œconomy*, Vol. I, Dublin, 1770, p. 396. - [b] E. Daire, *Introduction sur la doctrine des physiocrates*. In: *Physiocrates*, Première partie, Paris, 1846; H. Passy, *Rente du sol*. In: Dictionnaire de l'économie politique, Tome II, p. 511.

less during the entire Middle Ages (see Vinçard, *Histoire du travail*), the product and surplus product of the large estates consists by no means purely of products of agricultural labour. It encompasses equally well the products of industrial labour. Domestic handicrafts and manufacturing labour, as secondary occupations of agriculture, which forms the basis, are the prerequisite of that mode of production upon which natural economy rests—in European antiquity and the Middle Ages as well as in the present-day Indian community, in which the traditional organisation has not yet been destroyed. The capitalist mode of production completely abolishes this relationship; a process which may be studied on a large scale particularly in England during the last third of the 18th century. Thinkers like Herrenschwand, who had grown up in more or less semi-feudal societies, still consider, e. g., as late as the close of the 18th century, this separation of manufacture from agriculture as a foolhardy social adventure, as an unthinkably risky mode of existence. And even in the agricultural economies of antiquity showing the greatest analogy to capitalist agriculture, namely Carthage and Rome, the similarity to a plantation economy is greater than to a form corresponding to the really capitalist mode of exploitation. [42a] A formal analogy, which, simultaneously, however, turns out to be completely illusory in all essential points to a person familiar with the capitalist mode of production, who does not, like Herr Mommsen, [43] discover a capitalist mode of production in every monetary economy, is not to be found at all in continental Italy during antiquity, but at best only in Sicily, since this island served Rome as an agricultural tributary so that its agriculture was aimed chiefly at export. Farmers in the modern sense existed there.

[42a] Adam Smith emphasises how, in his time (and this applies also to the plantations in tropical and subtropical countries in our own day), rent and profit were not yet divorced from one another,[a] for the landlord was simultaneously a capitalist, just as Cato, for instance, was on his estates. But this separation is precisely the prerequisite for the capitalist mode of production, to whose conception the basis of slavery moreover stands in direct contradiction.

[43] Herr Mommsen, in his "Römische Geschichte", by no means uses the term capitalist in the sense employed by modern economics and modern society, but rather in the manner of popular conception, such as still continues to thrive, though not in England or America, but nevertheless on the European continent, as an ancient tradition reflecting bygone conditions.

---

[a] A. Smith, *An Inquiry into the Nature and Causes of the Wealth of Nations*, Vol. 1, p. 44.

An erroneous conception of the nature of rent is based upon the fact that rent in kind, partly as tithes to the church and partly as a curiosity perpetuated by long-established contracts, has been dragged over into modern times from the natural economy of the Middle Ages, completely in contradiction to the conditions of the capitalist mode of production. It thereby creates the impression that rent does not arise from the price of the agricultural product, but from its mass, thus not from social conditions, but from the earth. We have previously shown that although surplus value is manifested in a surplus product the converse does not hold that a surplus product, representing a mere increase in the mass of product, constitutes surplus value. It may represent a minus quantity in value. Otherwise the cotton industry of 1860, compared with that of 1840, would show an enormous surplus value, whereas on the contrary the price of the yarn has fallen. Rent may increase enormously as a result of a succession of crop failures, because the price of grain rises, although this surplus value appears as an absolutely decreasing mass of dearer wheat. Conversely, the rent may fall in consequence of a succession of bountiful years, because the price falls although the reduced rent appears as a greater mass of cheaper wheat. As regards rent in kind, it should be noted now that, in the first place, it is a mere tradition carried over from an obsolete mode of production and managing to prolong its existence as a survival. Its contradiction to the capitalist mode of production is shown by its disappearance of itself from private contracts, and its being forcibly shaken off as an anachronism, wherever legislation was able to intervene as in the case of church tithes in England. [86] Secondly, however, where rent in kind persisted on the basis of capitalist production, it was no more, and could be no more, than an expression of money rent in medieval garb. Wheat, for instance, is quoted at 40 shillings per quarter. One portion of this wheat must replace the wages contained therein, and must be sold to become available for renewed expenditure. Another portion must be sold to pay its proportionate share of taxes. Seed and even a portion of fertiliser enter as commodities into the process of reproduction, wherever the capitalist mode of production and with it division of social labour are developed, i. e., they must be purchased for replacement purposes; and therefore another portion of this quarter must be sold to obtain money for this. In so far as they need not be bought as actual commodities, but are taken out of the product itself in kind, in order to enter into its reproduction anew as conditions of production — as occurs not only in agriculture, but in many other lines of production producing constant capital — they figure in the books as money of account and are deducted as elements of the cost price. The wear and tear of machinery, and of fixed capital in general, must be made good in money. And finally comes profit, which is calculated on this sum, expressed as costs either in actual money or in money of account. This profit is represented by a definite portion of the gross product, which is determined by its price. And the excess portion which then remains forms rent. If the rent in kind stipulated by contract is greater than this remainder determined by the price, then it does not constitute rent, but a deduction from profit. Owing to this possibility alone, rent in kind is an obsolete form, in so far as it does not reflect the price of the product, but may be greater or smaller than the real rent, and thus may comprise not only a deduction from profit, but also from those elements required for capital replacement. In fact, this rent in kind, so far as it is rent not merely in name but also in essence, is exclusively determined by the excess of the price of the product over its price of production. Only it presupposes that this variable is a constant magnitude. But it is such a comforting reflection that the product *in natura* should suffice, first, to maintain the labourer, secondly, to leave the capitalist tenant farmer more food than he needs, and finally, that the remainder should constitute the natural rent. Quite like a manufacturer producing 200,000 yards of cotton goods. These yards of goods not only suffice to chothe his labourers; to clothe his wife, all his offspring and himself abundantly; but also leave over enough cotton for sale, in addition to paying an enormous rent in terms of cotton goods. It is all so simple! Deduct the price of production from 200,000 yards of cotton goods, and an excess of cotton goods must remain for rent. But it is indeed a naïve conception to deduct the price of production of, say, £10,000 from 200,000 yards of cotton goods, without knowing the selling price, to deduct money from cotton goods, to deduct an exchange value from a use value as such, and thus to determine the excess of yards of cotton goods over pounds sterling. It is worse than squaring the circle, which is at least based upon the conception that there is a limit at which straight lines and curves imperceptibly flow together. But such is the prescription of M. Passy. Deduct money from cotton goods, before the cotton goods have been converted into money, either in one's mind or in reality! What remains is the rent, which, however, is to be grasped *naturaliter* (see, for instance,

Karl Arnd[a]) and not by deviltries of sophistry. The entire restoration of natural rent is finally reduced to this foolishness, the deduction of the price of production from so many and so many bushels of wheat, and the subtraction of a sum of money from a cubic measure.

II. LABOUR RENT

If we consider ground rent in its simplest form, that of *labour rent*, where the direct producer, using instruments of labour (plough, cattle, etc.) which actually or legally belong to him, cultivates soil actually owned by him during part of the week, and works during the remaining days upon the estate of the feudal lord without any compensation from the feudal lord, the situation here is still quite clear, for in this case rent and surplus value are identical. Rent, not profit, is the form here through which unpaid surplus labour expresses itself. To what extent the labourer (A SELF-SUSTAINING SERF) can secure in this case an excess above his indispensable necessities of life, i. e., an excess above that which we would call wages under the capitalist mode of production, depends, other circumstances remaining unchanged, upon the proportion in which his labour time is divided into labour time for himself and enforced labour time for his feudal lord. This excess above the indispensable requirements of life, the germ of what appears as profit under the capitalist mode of production, is therefore wholly determined by the amount of ground rent, which in this case is not only directly unpaid surplus labour, but also appears as such. It is unpaid surplus labour for the "owner" of the means of production, which here coincide with the land, and so far as they differ from it, are mere accessories to it. That the product of the serf must here suffice to reproduce his conditions of labour, in addition to his subsistence, is a circumstance which remains the same under all modes of production. For it is not the result of their specific form, but a natural requisite of all continuous and reproductive labour in general, of any continuing production, which is always simultaneously reproduction, i. e., including reproduction of its own operating conditions. It is furthermore evident that in all forms in which the direct labourer remains the "possessor" of the means of production and labour condi-

---

[a] K. Arnd, *Die naturgemässe Volkswirtschaft, gegenüber dem Monopoliengeiste und dem Communismus*, S. 461-62.

tions necessary for the production of his own means of subsistence, the property relationship must simultaneously appear as a direct relation of lordship and servitude, so that the direct producer is not free; a lack of freedom which may be reduced from serfdom with enforced labour to a mere tributary relationship. The direct producer, according to our assumption, is to be found here in possession of his own means of production, the necessary material labour conditions required for the realisation of his labour and the production of his means of subsistence. He conducts his agricultural activity and the rural home industries connected with it independently. This independence is not undermined by the circumstance that the small peasants may form among themselves a more or less natural production community, as they do in India, since it is here merely a question of independence from the nominal lord of the manor. Under such conditions the surplus labour for the nominal owner of the land can only be extorted from them by other than economic pressure, whatever the form assumed may be. [44] This differs from slave or plantation economy in that the slave works under alien conditions of production and not independently. Thus, conditions of personal dependence are requisite, a lack of personal freedom, no matter to what extent, and being tied to the soil as its accessory, bondage in the true sense of the word. Should the direct producers not be confronted by a private landowner, but rather, as in Asia, under direct subordination to a state which stands over them as their landlord and simultaneously as sovereign, then rent and taxes coincide, or rather, there exists no tax which differs from this form of ground rent. Under such circumstances, there need exist no stronger political or economic pressure than that common to all subjects to that state. The state is then the supreme lord. Sovereignty here consists in the ownership of land concentrated on a national scale. But, on the other hand, no private ownership of land exists, although there is both private and common possession and use of land.

The specific economic form, in which unpaid surplus labour is pumped out of direct producers, determines the relationship of rulers

---

[44] Following the conquest of a country, the immediate aim of a conqueror was also to convert its people to his own use. Cf. Linguet. [a] See also Möser. [b]

---

[a] [N. Linguet,] *Théorie des loix civiles, ou Principes fondamentaux de la société*, Tomes I-II, Londres, 1767. - [b] J. Möser, *Osnabrückische Geschichte*, I. Theil, Berlin und Stettin, 1780.

and ruled, as it grows directly out of production itself and, in turn, re-
acts upon it as a determining element. Upon this, however, is founded
the entire formation of the economic community which grows up out
of the production relations themselves, thereby simultaneously its
specific political form. It is always the direct relationship of the
owners of the conditions of production to the direct producers —
a relation always naturally corresponding to a definite stage in the
development of the methods of labour and thereby its social productivity — which reveals the innermost secret, the hidden basis of the entire social structure, and with it the political form of the relation of sovereignty and dependence, in short, the corresponding specific form
of the state. This does not prevent the same economic basis — the same
from the standpoint of its main conditions — due to innumerable
different empirical circumstances, natural environment, racial relations, external historical influences, etc., from showing infinite variations and gradations in appearance, which can be ascertained only by
analysis of the empirically given circumstances.

So much is evident with respect to labour rent, the simplest and
most primitive form of rent: Rent is here the primeval form of surplus
value and coincides with it. But this identity of surplus value with unpaid labour of others need not be analysed here, because it still exists
in its visible, palpable form, since the labour of the direct producer for
himself is still separated in space and time from his labour for the
landlord, and the latter appears directly in the brutal form of enforced labour for a third person. In the same way the "attribute" possessed by the soil to produce rent is here reduced to a tangibly open
secret, for the disposition to furnish rent here also includes human labour power bound to the soil, and the property relation which compels the owner of labour power to drive it on and activate it beyond
such measure as is required to satisfy his own indispensable needs.
Rent consists directly in the appropriation of this surplus expenditure
of labour power by the landlord; for the direct producer pays him no
additional rent. Here, where surplus value and rent are not only
identical but where surplus value has the tangible form of surplus
labour, the natural conditions or limits of rent, being those of surplus
value in general, are plainly clear. The direct producer must 1)
possess enough labour power, and 2) the natural conditions of his
labour, above all the soil cultivated by him, must be productive
enough, in a word, the natural productivity of his labour must be big
enough to give him the possibility of retaining some surplus labour

over and above that required for the satisfaction of his own indispensable needs. It is not this possibility which creates the rent, but rather compulsion which turns this possibility into reality. But the possibility itself is conditioned by subjective and objective natural circumstances. And here too lies nothing at all mysterious. Should labour power be minute, and the natural conditions of labour scanty, then the surplus labour is small, but in such a case so are the wants of the producers on the one hand and the relative number of exploiters of surplus labour on the other, and finally so is the surplus product, whereby this barely productive surplus labour is realised for those few exploiting landowners.

Finally, labour rent in itself implies that, all other circumstances remaining equal, it will depend wholly upon the relative amount of surplus labour, or enforced labour, to what extent the direct producer shall be enabled to improve his own condition, to acquire wealth, to produce an excess over and above his indispensable means of subsistence, or, if we wish to anticipate the capitalist mode of expression, whether he shall be able to produce a profit for himself, and how much of a profit, i. e., an excess over his wages which have been produced by himself. Rent here is the normal, all-absorbing, so to say legitimate form of surplus labour, and far from being excess over profit, which means in this case being above any other excess over wages, it is rather that the amount of such profit, and even its very existence, depends, other circumstances being equal, upon the amount of rent, i. e., the enforced surplus labour to be surrendered to the landowners.

Since the direct producer is not the owner, but only a possessor, and since all his surplus labour *de jure* actually belongs to the landlord, some historians have expressed astonishment that it should be at all possible for those subject to enforced labour, or serfs, to acquire any independent property, or relatively speaking, wealth, under such circumstances. However, it is evident that tradition must play a dominant role in the primitive and undeveloped circumstances on which these social production relations and the corresponding mode of production are based. It is furthermore clear that here as always it is in the interest of the ruling section of society to sanction the existing order as law and to legally establish its limits given through usage and tradition. Apart from all else, this, by the way, comes about of itself as soon as the constant reproduction of the basis of the existing order and its fundamental relations assumes a regulated and orderly form in the course of time. And such regulation and order are themselves indispensable elements of any mode of production, if it is to assume social stability and independence from mere chance and arbitrariness. These are precisely the form of its social stability and therefore its relative freedom from mere arbitrariness and mere chance. Under backward conditions of the production process as well as the corresponding social relations, it achieves this form by mere repetition of their very reproduction. If this has continued on for some time, it entrenches itself as custom and tradition and is finally sanctioned as an explicit law. However, since the form of this surplus labour, enforced labour, is based upon the imperfect development of all social productive powers and the crudeness of the methods of labour itself, it will naturally absorb a relatively much smaller portion of the direct producer's total labour than under developed modes of production, particularly the capitalist mode of production. Take it, for instance, that the enforced labour for the landlord originally amounted to two days per week. These two days of enforced labour per week are thereby fixed, are a constant magnitude, legally regulated by prescriptive or written law. But the productivity of the remaining days of the week, which are at the disposal of the direct producer himself, is a variable magnitude, which must develop in the course of his experience, just as the new wants he acquires, and just as the expansion of the market for his product and the increasing assurance with which he disposes of this portion of his labour power will spur him on to a greater exertion of his labour power, whereby it should not be forgotten that the employment of his labour power is by no means confined to agriculture, but includes rural home industry. The possibility is here presented for definite economic development taking place, depending, of course, upon favourable circumstances, inborn racial characteristics, etc.

III. RENT IN KIND

The transformation of labour rent into rent in kind changes nothing from the economic standpoint in the nature of ground rent. The latter consists, in the forms considered here, in that rent is the sole prevailing and normal form of surplus value, or surplus labour. This is further expressed in the fact that it is the only surplus labour, or the only surplus product, which the direct producer, who is in *possession* of the labour conditions needed for his own reproduction, must give up to the *owner* of the land, which in this situation is the all-embracing condition of labour. And, furthermore, that land is the only condition of labour which confronts the direct producer as alien property, independent of him, and personified by the landlord. To whatever extent rent in kind is the prevailing and dominant form of ground rent, it is furthermore always more or less accompanied by survivals of the earlier form, i. e., of rent paid directly in labour, corvée labour, no matter whether the landlord be a private person or the state. Rent in kind presupposes a higher stage of civilisation for the direct producer, i. e., a higher level of development of his labour and of society in general. And it is distinct from the preceding form in that surplus labour needs no longer be performed in its natural form, thus no longer under the direct supervision and compulsion of the landlord or his representatives: the direct producer is driven rather by force of circumstances than by direct coercion, through legal enactment rather than the whip, to perform it on his own responsibility. Surplus production, in the sense of production beyond the indispensable needs of the direct producer, and within the field of production actually belonging to him, upon the land exploited by himself instead of, as earlier, upon the nearby lord's estate beyond his own land, has already become a self-understood rule here. In this relation the direct producer more or less disposes of his entire labour time, although, as previously, a part of this labour time, at first practically the entire surplus portion of it, belongs to the landlord without compensation; except that the landlord no longer directly receives this surplus labour in its natural form, but rather in the products' natural form in which it is realised. The burdensome, and according to the way in which enforced labour is regulated, more or less disturbing interruption by work for the landlord (see Buch I, Kap. VIII, 2, "Manufacturer and Boyard"[a]) stops wherever rent in kind appears in pure form, or at least it is reduced to a few short intervals during the year, when a continuation of some corvée labour side by side with rent in kind takes place. The labour of the producer for himself and his labour for the landlord are no longer palpably separated by time and space. This rent in kind, in its pure form, while it may drag fragments along into more highly developed modes of production and production relations, still presupposes for its existence a natural economy, i. e., that the conditions of the economy are either wholly or for the overwhelming part produced by the

---

[a] English edition: Ch. X. See present edition, Vol. 35, pp. 243-51.

economy itself, directly replaced and reproduced out of its gross product. It furthermore presupposes the combination of rural home industry with agriculture. The surplus product, which forms the rent, is the product of this combined agricultural and industrial family labour, no matter whether rent in kind contains more or less of the industrial product, as is often the case in the Middle Ages, or whether it is paid only in the form of actual products of the land. In this form of rent it is by no means necessary for rent in kind, which represents the surplus labour, to fully exhaust the entire surplus labour of the rural family. Compared with labour rent, the producer rather has more room for action to gain time for surplus labour whose product shall belong to himself, as well as the product of his labour which satisfies his indispensable needs. Similarly, this form will give rise to greater differences in the economic position of the individual direct producers. At least the possibility for such a differentiation exists, and the possibility for the direct producer to have in turn acquired the means to exploit other labourers directly. This, however, does not concern us here, since we are dealing with rent in kind in its pure form; just as in general we cannot enter into the endless variety of combinations wherein the various forms of rent may be united, adulterated and amalgamated. The form of rent in kind, by being bound to a definite type of product and production itself and through its indispensable combination of agriculture and domestic industry, through its almost complete self-sufficiency whereby the peasant family supports itself through its independence from the market and the movement of production and history of that section of society lying outside of its sphere, in short owing to the character of natural economy in general, this form is quite adapted to furnishing the basis for stationary social conditions as we see, e.g., in Asia. Here, as in the earlier form of labour rent, ground rent is the normal form of surplus value, and thus of surplus labour, i.e., of the entire excess labour which the direct producer must perform gratis, hence actually under compulsion although this compulsion no longer confronts him in the old brutal form—for the benefit of the owner of his essential condition of labour, the land. The profit, if by erroneously anticipating we may thus call that portion of the direct producer's labour excess over his necessary labour, which he retains for himself, has so little to do with determining rent in kind, that this profit, on the contrary, grows up behind the back of rent and finds its natural limit in the size of rent in kind. The latter may assume dimensions which seriously imperil reproduction of the conditions of labour, the means of production themselves, rendering the expansion of production more or less impossible and reducing the direct producers to the physical minimum of means of subsistence. This is particularly the case, when this form is met with and exploited by a conquering commercial nation, e. g., the English in India.

IV. MONEY RENT

By money rent—as distinct from industrial and commercial ground rent based upon the capitalist mode of production, which is but an excess over average profit—we here mean the ground rent which arises from a mere change in form of rent in kind, just as the latter in turn is but a modification of labour rent. The direct producer here turns over instead of the product, its price to the landlord (who may be either the state or a private individual). An excess of products in their natural form no longer suffices; it must be converted from its natural form into money form. Although the direct producer still continues to produce at least the greater part of his means of subsistence himself, a certain portion of this product must now be converted into commodities, must be produced as commodities. The character of the entire mode of production is thus more or less changed. It loses its independence, its detachment from social connection. The ratio of cost of production, which now comprises greater or lesser expenditures of money, becomes decisive; at any rate, the excess of that portion of gross product to be converted into money over that portion which must serve, on the one hand, as means of reproduction again, and, on the other, as means of direct subsistence, assumes a determining role. However, the basis of this type of rent, although approaching its dissolution, remains the same as that of rent in kind, which constitutes its point of departure. The direct producer as before is still possessor of the land, either through inheritance or some other traditional right, and must perform for his lord, as owner of his most essential condition of production, excess corvée labour, that is, unpaid labour for which no equivalent is returned, in the form of a surplus product transformed into money. Ownership of the conditions of labour as distinct from land, such as agricultural implements and other goods and chattels, is transformed into the property of the direct producer even under the earlier forms of rent, first in fact, and then also legally, and even more so is this the precondition for the form of money rent. The transformation of rent in kind into money rent, taking place first sporadically and then on a more or less national scale, presupposes a considerable development of commerce, of urban industry, of commodity production in general, and thereby of money circulation. It furthermore assumes a market price for products, and that they be sold at prices roughly approximating their values, which need not at all be the case under earlier forms. In Eastern Europe we may still partly observe this transformation taking place under our very eyes. How unfeasible it can be without a certain development of social labour productivity is proved by various unsuccessful attempts to carry it through under the Roman Empire, and by relapses into natural rent after seeking to convert at least the state tax portion of this rent into money rent. The same transitional difficulties are evidenced, e. g., in prerevolutionary France, when money rent was combined with and adulterated by, survivals of its earlier forms.

Money rent, as a transmuted form of rent in kind, and in antithesis to it, is, nevertheless, the final form, and simultaneously the form of dissolution of the type of ground rent which we have heretofore considered, namely ground rent as the normal form of surplus value and of the unpaid surplus labour to be performed for the owner of the conditions of production. In its pure form, this rent, like labour rent and rent in kind, represents no excess over profit. It absorbs the profit, as it is understood. In so far as profit arises beside it practically as a separate portion of excess labour, money rent like rent in its earlier forms still constitutes the normal limit of such embryonic profit, which can only develop in relation to the possibilities of exploitation, be it of one's own excess labour or that of another, which remains after the performance of the surplus labour represented by money rent. Should any profit actually arise along with this rent, then this profit does not constitute the limit of rent, but rather conversely, the rent is the limit of the profit. However, as already indicated, money rent is simultaneously the form of dissolution of the ground rent considered thus far, coinciding *prima facie* with surplus value and surplus labour, i. e., ground rent as the normal and dominant form of surplus value.

In its further development money rent must lead—aside from all intermediate forms, e. g., the small peasant tenant farmer—either to the transformation of land into peasants' freehold, or to the form corresponding to the capitalist mode of production, that is, to rent paid by the capitalist tenant farmer.

With money rent prevailing, the traditional and customary legal relationship between landlord and subjects who possess and cultivate a part of the land, is necessarily turned into a pure money relationship fixed contractually in accordance with the rules of positive law. The possessor engaged in cultivation thus becomes virtually a mere tenant. This transformation serves on the one hand, provided other general production relations permit, to expropriate more and more the old peasant possessors and to substitute capitalist tenants in their stead. On the other hand, it leads to the former possessor buying himself free from his rent obligation and to his transformation into an independent peasant with complete ownership of the land he tills. The transformation of rent in kind into money rent is furthermore not only inevitably accompanied, but even anticipated, by the formation of a class of propertyless day labourers, who hire themselves out for money. During their genesis, when this new class appears but sporadically, the custom necessarily develops among the more prosperous peasants subject to rent payments of exploiting agricultural wage labourers for their own account, much as in feudal times, when the more well-to-do peasant serfs themselves also held serfs. In this way, they gradually acquire the possibility of accumulating a certain amount of wealth and themselves becoming transformed into future capitalists. The old self-employed possessors of land themselves thus give rise to a nursery school for capitalist tenants, whose development is conditioned by the general development of capitalist production beyond the bounds of the countryside. This class shoots up very rapidly when particularly favourable circumstances come to its aid, as in England in the 16th century, where the then progressive depreciation of money enriched them under the customary long leases at the expense of the landlords.

Furthermore: as soon as rent assumes the form of money rent, and thereby the relationship between rent-paying peasant and landlord becomes a relationship fixed by contract — a development which is only possible generally when the world market, commerce and manufacture have reached a certain relatively high level — the leasing of land to capitalists inevitably also makes its appearance. The latter hitherto stood beyond the rural limits and now carry over to the countryside and agriculture the capital acquired in the cities and with it the capitalist mode of operation developed — i. e., creating a product as a mere commodity and solely as a means of appropriating surplus value. This form can become the general rule only in those countries which dominate the world market in the period of transition from the feudal to the capitalist mode of production. When the capitalist tenant farmer steps in between landlord and actual tiller of the soil, all relations which arose out of the old rural mode of production are torn asunder. The farmer becomes the actual commander of these agricultural labourers and the actual exploiter of their surplus labour, whereas the landlord maintains a direct relationship, and indeed simply a money and contractual relationship, solely with this capitalist tenant. Thus, the nature of rent is also transformed, not merely in fact and by chance, as occurred in part even under earlier forms, but normally, in its recognised and prevailing form. From the normal form of surplus value and surplus labour, it descends to a mere excess of this surplus labour over that portion of it appropriated by the exploiting capitalist in the form of profit; just as the total surplus labour, profit and excess over profit, is extracted directly by him, collected in the form of the total surplus product, and turned into cash. It is only the excess portion of this surplus value which is extracted by him from the agricultural labourer by direct exploitation, by means of his capital, which he turns over to the landlord as rent. How much or how little he turns over to the latter depends, on the average, upon the limits set by the average profit which is realised by capital in the nonagricultural spheres of production, and by the prices of nonagricultural production regulated by this average profit. From a normal form of surplus value and surplus labour, rent has now become transformed into an excess over that portion of the surplus labour claimed in advance by capital as its legitimate and normal share, and characteristic of this particular sphere of production, the agricultural sphere of production. Profit, instead of rent, has now become the normal form of surplus value and rent still exists solely as a form, not of surplus value in general, but of one of its offshoots, surplus profit, which assumes an independent form under particular circumstances. It is not necessary to elaborate the manner in which a gradual transformation in the mode of production itself corresponds to this transformation. This already follows from the fact that it is normal for the capitalist tenant farmer to produce agricultural products as commodities, and that, while formerly only the excess over his means of subsistence was converted into commodities, now but a relatively insignificant part of these commodities is directly used by him as means of subsistence. It is no longer the land, but rather capital, which has now brought even agricultural labour under its direct sway and productiveness.

The average profit and the price of production regulated thereby are formed outside of relations in the countryside and within the sphere of urban trade and manufacture. The profit of the rent-paying peasant does not enter into it as an equalising factor, for his relation to the landlord is not a capitalist one. In so far as he makes profit, i. e., realises an excess above his necessary means of subsistence, either by his own labour or through exploiting other people's labour, it is done behind the back of the normal relationship, and other circumstances being equal, the size of this profit does not determine rent, but on the contrary, it is determined by the rent as its limit. The high rate of profit in the Middle Ages is not entirely due to the low composition of capital, in which the variable component invested in wages predominates. It is due to swindling on the land, the appropriation of a portion of the landlord's rent and of the income of his vassals. If the countryside exploits the town politically in the Middle Ages, wherever feudalism has not been broken down by exceptional urban development — as in Italy, the town, on the other hand, exploits the land economically everywhere and without exception, through its monopoly prices, its system of taxation, its guild organisation, its direct commercial fraudulence and its usury.

One might imagine that the mere appearance of the capitalist farmer in agricultural production would prove that the price of agricultural products, which from time immemorial have paid rent in one form or another, must be higher, at least at the time of this appearance, than the prices of production of manufacture whether it be because the price of such agricultural products has reached a monopoly price level, or has risen as high as the value of the agricultural products, and their value actually is above the price of production regulated by the average profit. For were this not so, the capitalist farmer could not at all realise, at the existing prices of agricultural produce, first the average profit out of the price of these products, and then pay out of the same price an excess above this profit in the form of rent. One might conclude from this that the general rate of profit, which guides the capitalist farmer in his contract with the landlord, has been formed without including rent, and, therefore, as soon as it assumes a regulating role in agricultural production, it finds this excess at hand and pays it to the landlord. It is in this traditional manner that, for instance, Herr Rodbertus explains the matter. But:

First. This appearance of capital as an independent and leading force in agriculture does not take place all at once and generally, but gradually and in particular lines of production. It encompasses at first, not agriculture proper, but such branches of production as cattle-breeding, especially sheep-raising, whose principal product, wool, offers at the early stages a constant excess of market price over price of production during the rise of industry, and this does not level out until later. Thus in England during the 16th century.

Secondly. Since this capitalist production appears at first but sporadically, the assumption cannot be disputed that it first extends only to such land categories as are able, through their particular fertility, or their exceptionally favourable location, to generally pay a differential rent.

Thirdly. Let us even assume that at the time this mode of production appeared — and this indeed presupposes an increasing preponderance of urban demand — the prices of agricultural products were higher than the price of production, as was doubtless the case in England during the last third of the 17th century. Nevertheless, as soon as this mode of production has somewhat extricated itself from the mere subordination of agriculture to capital, and as soon as agricultural improvement and the reduction of production costs, which necessarily accompany its development, have taken place, the balance will be restored by a reaction, a fall in the price of agricultural produce, as happened in England in the first half of the 18th century.

Rent, thus, as an excess over the average profit cannot be explained in this traditional way. Whatever may be the existing historical circumstances at the time rent first appears, once it has struck root it cannot exist except under the modern conditions earlier described.

Finally, it should be noted in the transformation of rent in kind into money rent that along with it capitalised rent, or the price of land, and thus its alienability and alienation become essential factors, and that thereby not only can the former peasant subject to payment of rent be transformed into an independent peasant proprietor, but also urban and other moneyed people can buy real estate in order to lease it either to peasants or capitalists and thus enjoy rent as a form of interest on their capital so invested; that, therefore, this circumstance likewise facilitates the transformation of the former mode of exploitation, the relation between owner and actual cultivator of the land, and of rent itself.

V. MÉTAYAGE AND PEASANT PROPRIETORSHIP
OF LAND PARCELS

We have now arrived at the end of our elaboration of ground rent.
In all these forms of ground rent, whether labour rent, rent in kind, or money rent (as merely a changed form of rent in kind), the one paying rent is always supposed to be the actual cultivator and possessor of the land, whose unpaid surplus labour passes directly into the hands of the landlord. Even in the last form, money rent in so far as it is "pure", i. e., merely a changed form of rent in kind — this is not only possible, but actually takes place.

As a transitory form from the original form of rent to capitalist rent, we may consider the metayer system, or share-cropping, under which the manager (farmer) furnishes labour (his own or another's), and also a portion of working capital, and the landlord furnishes, aside from land, another portion of working capital (e. g., cattle), and the product is divided between sharecropper and landlord in definite proportions which vary from country to country. On the one hand, the farmer here lacks sufficient capital required for complete capitalist management. On the other hand, the share here appropriated by the landlord does not bear the pure form of rent. It may actually include interest on the capital advanced by him and an excess rent. It may also absorb practically the entire surplus labour of the farmer, or leave him a greater or smaller portion of this surplus labour. But, essentially, rent no longer appears here as the normal form of surplus value in general. On the one hand, the sharecropper, whether he employs his own or another's labour, is to lay claim to a portion of the product not in his capacity as labourer, but as possessor of part of the instruments of labour, as his own capitalist. On the other hand, the landlord claims his share not exclusively on the basis of his landownership, but also as lender of capital.[44a]

A survival of the old communal ownership of land, which had endured after the transition to independent peasant farming, e. g., in Poland and Rumania, served there as a subterfuge for effecting a transition to the lower forms of ground rent. A portion of the land

[44a] Cf. Buret, Tocqueville, Sismondi.[a]

---

[a] Cf. E. Buret, *Cours d'économie politique*, Bruxelles, 1842; A. de Tocqueville, *L'ancien régime et la révolution*, Paris, 1856; J. C. L. Simonde de Sismondi, *Nouveaux principes d'économie politique*, seconde édition, Tome I, Paris, 1827.

belongs to the individual peasant and is tilled independently by him. Another portion is tilled in common and creates a surplus product, which serves partly to cover community expenses, partly as a reserve in cases of crop failure, etc. These last two parts of the surplus product, and ultimately the entire surplus product including the land upon which it has been grown, are more and more usurped by state officials and private individuals, and thus the originally free peasant proprietors, whose obligation to till this land in common is maintained, are transformed into vassals subject either to corvée labour or rent in kind, while the usurpers of common land are transformed into owners, not only of the usurped common lands, but even the very lands of the peasants themselves.

We need not further investigate slave economy proper (which likewise passes through a metamorphosis from the patriarchal system mainly for home use to the plantation system for the world market) nor the management of estates under which the landlords themselves are independent cultivators, possessing all instruments of production, and exploiting the labour of free or unfree bondsmen, who are paid either in kind or money. Landlord and owner of the instruments of production, and thus the direct exploiter of labourers included among these elements of production, are in this case one and the same person. Rent and profit likewise coincide then, there occurring no separation of the different forms of surplus value. The entire surplus labour of the labourers, which is manifested here in the surplus product, is extracted from them directly by the owner of all instruments of production, to which belong the land and, under the original form of slavery, the immediate producers themselves. Where the capitalist outlook prevails, as on American plantations, this entire surplus value is regarded as profit; where neither the capitalist mode of production itself exists, nor the corresponding outlook has been transferred from capitalist countries, it appears as rent. At any rate, this form presents no difficulties. The income of the landlord, whatever it may be called, the available surplus product appropriated by him, is here the normal and prevailing form, whereby the entire unpaid surplus labour is directly appropriated, and landed property forms the basis of such appropriation.

Further, *proprietorship of land parcels*. The peasant here is simultaneously the free owner of his land, which appears as his principal instrument of production, the indispensable field of employment for his labour and his capital. No lease money is paid under this form.

Rent, therefore, does not appear as a separate form of surplus value, although in countries in which otherwise the capitalist mode of production is developed, it appears as a surplus profit compared with other lines of production; but as surplus profit which, like all proceeds of his labour in general, accrues to the peasant.

This form of landed property presupposes, as in the earlier older forms, that the rural population greatly predominates numerically over the town population, so that, even if the capitalist mode of production otherwise prevails, it is but relatively little developed, and thus also in the other lines of production the concentration of capital is restricted to narrow limits and a fragmentation of capital predominates. In the nature of things, the greater portion of agricultural produce must be consumed as direct means of subsistence by the producers themselves, the peasants, and only the excess above that will find its way as commodities into urban commerce. No matter how the average market price of agricultural products may here be regulated, differential rent, an excess portion of commodity prices from superior or more favourably located land, must evidently exist here as much as under the capitalist mode of production. This differential rent exists, even where this form appears under social conditions, under which no general market price has as yet been developed; it appears then in the excess surplus product. Only then it flows into the pockets of the peasant whose labour is realised under more favourable natural conditions. The assumption here is generally to be made that no absolute rent exists, i. e., that the worst soil does not pay any rent — precisely under this form where the price of land enters as a factor in the peasant's actual cost of production whether because in the course of this form's further development either the price of land has been computed at a certain money value, in dividing up an inheritance, or, during the constant change in ownership of an entire estate, or of its component parts, the land has been bought by the cultivator himself, largely by raising money on mortgage; and, therefore, where the price of land, representing nothing more than capitalised rent, is a factor assumed in advance, and where rent thus seems to exist independently of any differentiation in fertility and location of the land. For, absolute rent presupposes either realised excess in product value above its price of production, or a monopoly price exceeding the value of the product. But since agriculture here is carried on largely as cultivation for direct subsistence, and the land exists as an indispensable field of employment for the labour and capital of the majority of the population, the regulating market price of the product will reach its value only under extraordinary circumstances. But this value will, generally, be higher than its price of production owing to the preponderant element of living labour, although this excess of value over price of production will in turn be limited by the low composition even of non-agricultural capital in countries with an economy composed predominantly of land parcels. For the peasant owning a parcel, the limit of exploitation is not set by the average profit of capital, in so far as he is a small capitalist; nor, on the other hand, by the necessity of rent, in so far as he is a landowner. The absolute limit for him as a small capitalist is no more than the wages he pays to himself, after deducting his actual costs. So long as the price of the product covers these wages, he will cultivate his land, and often at wages down to a physical minimum. As for his capacity as land proprietor, the barrier of ownership is eliminated for him, since it can make itself felt only vis-à-vis a capital (including labour) separated from landownership, by erecting an obstacle to the investment of capital. It is true, to be sure, that interest on the price of land — which generally has to be paid to still another individual, the mortgage creditor — is a barrier. But this interest can be paid precisely out of that portion of surplus labour which would constitute profit under capitalist conditions. The rent anticipated in the price of land and in the interest paid for it can therefore be nothing but a portion of the peasant's capitalised surplus labour over and above the labour indispensable for his subsistence, without this surplus labour being realised in a part of the commodity value equal to the entire average profit, and still less in an excess above the surplus labour realised in the average profit, i. e., in a surplus profit. The rent may be a deduction from the average profit, or even the only portion of it which is realised. For the peasant parcel holder to cultivate his land, or to buy land for cultivation, it is therefore not necessary, as under the normal capitalist mode of production, that the market price of the agricultural products rise high enough to afford him the average profit, and still less a fixed excess above this average profit in the form of rent. It is not necessary, therefore, that the market price rise either up to the value or the price of production of his product. This is one of the reasons why grain prices are lower in countries with predominant small peasant land proprietorship than in countries with a capitalist mode of production. One portion of the surplus labour of the peasants, who work under the least favourable conditions, is bestowed gratis upon society and does not at all enter into the regulation of price of production or into the creation of value in general. This lower price is consequently a result of the producers' poverty and by no means of their labour productivity.

This form of free self-managing peasant proprietorship of land parcels as the prevailing, normal form constitutes, on the one hand, the economic foundation of society during the best periods of classical antiquity, and on the other hand, it is found among modern nations as one of the forms arising from the dissolution of feudal landownership. Thus, the YEOMANRY in England,[87] the peasantry in Sweden, the French and West German peasants. We do not include colonies here, since the independent peasant there develops under different conditions.

The free ownership of the self-managing peasant is evidently the most normal form of landed property for small-scale operation, i. e., for a mode of production, in which possession of the land is a prerequisite for the labourer's ownership of the product of his own labour, and in which the cultivator, be he free owner or vassal, always must produce his own means of subsistence independently, as an isolated labourer with his family. Ownership of the land is as necessary for full development of his mode of production as ownership of tools is for free development of handicraft production. Here is the basis for the development of personal independence. It is a necessary transitional stage for the development of agriculture itself. The causes which bring about its downfall show its limitations. These are: Destruction of rural domestic industry, which forms its normal supplement as a result of the development of large-scale industry; a gradual impoverishment and exhaustion of the soil subjected to this cultivation; usurpation by big landowners of the common lands, which constitute the second supplement of the management of land parcels everywhere and which alone enable it to raise cattle; competition, either of the plantation system or large-scale capitalist agriculture. Improvements in agriculture, which on the one hand cause a fall in agricultural prices and, on the other, require greater outlays and more extensive material conditions of production, also contribute towards this, as in England during the first half of the 18th century.

Proprietorship of land parcels by its very nature excludes the development of social productive forces of labour, social forms of labour, social concentration of capital, large-scale cattle-raising, and the progressive application of science.

Usury and a taxation system must impoverish it everywhere. The expenditure of capital in the price of the land withdraws this capital from cultivation. An infinite fragmentation of means of production, and isolation of the producers themselves. Monstrous waste of human energy. Progressive deterioration of conditions of production and increased prices of means of production — an inevitable law of proprietorship of parcels. Calamity of seasonal abundance for this mode of production.[45]

One of the specific evils of small-scale agriculture where it is combined with free landownership arises from the cultivator's investing capital in the purchase of land. (The same applies also to the transitory form, in which the big landowner invests capital, first, to buy land, and second, to manage it as his own tenant farmer.) Owing to the changeable nature which the land here assumes as a mere commodity, the changes of ownership increase,[46] so that the land, from the peasant's viewpoint, enters anew as an investment of capital with each successive generation and division of estates, i. e., it becomes land purchased by him. The price of land here forms a weighty element of the individual unproductive costs of production or cost price of the product for the individual producer.

The price of land is nothing but capitalised and therefore anticipated rent. If capitalist methods are employed by agriculture, so that the landlord receives only rent, and the farmer pays nothing for land except this annual rent, then it is evident that the capital invested by the landowner himself in purchasing the land constitutes indeed an interest-bearing investment of capital for him, but has absolutely nothing to do with capital invested in agriculture itself. It forms neither a part of the fixed, nor of the circulating, capital employed here[47]; it

[45] See the speech from the throne of the King of France in Tooke.[a]

[46] See Mounier and Rubichon.[b]

[47] Dr. H. Maron (*Extensiv oder Intensiv?*)//no further information given about this pamphlet// starts from the false assumption of the adversaries he opposes. He assumes that capital invested in the purchase of land is "investment capital", and then engages in a controversy about the respective definitions of investment capital and working capital, that is, fixed and circulating capital. His wholly amateurish conceptions of capital in general, which may be excused incidentally in one who is not an economist in

[a] Th. Tooke, W. Newmarch, *A History of Prices, and of the State of the Circulation, during the Nine Years 1848-56*, Vol. VI, London, 1857, pp. 29-30. - [b] L. Mounier, *De l'agriculture en France*, Paris, 1846; M. Rubichon, *Du mécanisme de la société en France et en Angleterre*, Paris, 1837.

merely secures for the buyer a claim to receive annual rent, but has absolutely nothing to do with the production of the rent itself. The buyer of land just pays his capital out to the one who sells the land, and the seller in return relinquishes his ownership of the land. Thus this capital no longer exists as the capital of the purchaser; he no longer has it; therefore it does not belong to the capital which he can invest in any way in the land itself. Whether he bought the land dear or cheap, or whether he received it for nothing, alters nothing in the capital invested by the farmer in his establishment, and changes nothing in the rent, but merely alters the question whether it appears to him as interest or not, or as higher or lower interest respectively.

Take, for instance, the slave economy. The price paid for a slave is nothing but the anticipated and capitalised surplus value or profit to be wrung out of the slave. But the capital paid for the purchase of a slave does not belong to the capital by means of which profit, surplus labour, is extracted from him. On the contrary. It is capital which the slaveholder has parted with, it is a deduction from the capital which he has available for actual production. It has ceased to exist for him, just as capital invested in purchasing land has ceased to exist for agriculture. The best proof of this is that it does not reappear for the slaveholder or the landowner except when he, in turn, sells his slaves or land. But then the same situation prevails for the buyer. The fact that he has bought the slave does not enable him to exploit the slave without further ado. He is only able to do so when he invests some additional capital in the slave economy itself.

The same capital does not exist twice, once in the hands of the seller, and a second time in the hands of the buyer of the land. It passes from the hands of the buyer to those of the seller, and there the matter ends. The buyer now no longer has capital, but in its stead a piece of land. The circumstance that the rent produced by a real investment of capital in this land is calculated by the new landowner as interest on capital which he has not invested in the land, but given away to acquire the land, does not in the least alter the economic nature of the land factor, any more than the circumstance that someone has paid £1,000 for 3% consols has anything to do with the capital out of whose revenue the interest on the national debt is paid.

view of the state of German political economy, conceal from him that this capital is neither investment nor working capital, any more than the capital which someone invests at the Stock Exchange in purchasing stocks or government securities, and which, for him, represents a personal investment of capital, is "invested" in any branch of production.

In fact, the money expended in purchasing land, like that in purchasing government bonds, is merely capital *in itself*, just as any value sum is capital in itself, potential capital, on the basis of the capitalist mode of production. What is paid for land, like that for government bonds or any other purchased commodity, is a sum of money. This is capital in itself, because it can be converted into capital. It depends upon the use put to it by the seller whether the money obtained by him is really transformed into capital or not. For the buyer, it can never again function as such, no more than any other money which he has definitely paid out. It figures in his accounts as interest-bearing capital, because he considers the income, received as rent from the land or as interest on state indebtedness, as interest on the money which the purchase of the claim to this revenue has cost him. He can only realise it as capital through resale. But then another, the new buyer, enters the same relationship maintained by the former, and the money thus expended cannot be transformed into actual capital for the expender through any change of hands.

In the case of small landed property the illusion is fostered still more that land itself possesses value and thus enters as capital into the price of production of the product, much as machines or raw materials. But we have seen that rent, and therefore capitalised rent, the price of land, can enter as a determining factor into the price of agricultural products in only two cases. First, when as a consequence of the composition of agricultural capital—a capital which has nothing to do with the capital invested in purchasing land—the value of the products of the soil is higher than their price of production, and market conditions enable the landlord to realise this difference. Second, when there is a monopoly price. And both are least of all the case under the management of land parcels and small landownership because precisely here production to a large extent satisfies the producers' own wants and is carried on independently of regulation by the average rate of profit. Even where cultivation of land parcels is conducted upon leased land, the lease money comprises, far more so than under any other conditions, a portion of the profit and even a deduction from wages; this money is then only a nominal rent, not rent as an independent category as opposed to wages and profit.

The expenditure of money capital for the purchase of land, then, is not an investment of agricultural capital. It is a decrease *pro tanto* in the capital which small peasants can employ in their own sphere of production. It reduces *pro tanto* the size of their means of production and thereby narrows the economic basis of reproduction. It subjects the small peasant to the money-lender, since credit proper occurs but rarely in this sphere in general. It is a hindrance to agriculture, even where such purchase takes place in the case of large estates. It contradicts in fact the capitalist mode of production, which is on the whole indifferent to whether the landowner is in debt, no matter whether he has inherited or purchased his estate. The nature of management of the leased estate itself is not altered whether the landowner pockets the rent himself or whether he must pay it out to the holder of his mortgage.

We have seen that, in the case of a given ground rent, the price of land is regulated by the interest rate. If the rate is low, then the price of land is high, and vice versa. Normally, then, a high price of land and a low interest rate should go hand in hand, so that if the peasant paid a high price for the land in consequence of a low interest rate, the same low rate of interest should also secure his working capital for him on easy credit terms. But in reality, things turn out differently when peasant proprietorship of land parcels is the prevailing form. In the first place, the general laws of credit are not adapted to the farmer, since these laws presuppose a capitalist as the producer. Secondly, where proprietorship of land parcels predominates — we are not referring to colonies here — and the small peasant constitutes the backbone of the nation, the formation of capital, i. e., social reproduction, is relatively weak, and still weaker is the formation of loanable money capital, in the sense previously elaborated. This presupposes the concentration and existence of a class of idle rich capitalists (Massie).[a] Thirdly, here where the ownership of the land is a necessary condition for the existence of most producers, and an indispensable field of investment for their capital, the price of land is raised independently of the interest rate, and often in inverse ratio to it, through the preponderance of the demand for landed property over its supply. Land sold in parcels brings a far higher price in such a case than when sold in large tracts, because here the number of small buyers is large and that of large buyers is small (Bandes Noires,[88] Rubichon[b]; Newman[c]). For all these reasons, the price of land rises here with a relatively high rate of interest. The relatively low interest, which the peasant derives

---

[a] J. Massie, *An Essay on the Governing Causes of the Natural Rate of Interest*, London, 1750, pp. 23-24. - [b] See this volume, p. 794. - [c] F. W. Newman, *Lectures on Political Economy*, London, 1851, pp. 180-81.

here from the outlay of capital for the purchase of land (Mounier,[a]) corresponds here, on the other side, to the high usurious interest rate which he himself has to pay to his mortgage creditors. The Irish system bears out the same thing, only in another form.

The price of land, this element foreign to production in itself, may therefore rise here to such a point that it makes production impossible (Dombasle[b]).

The fact that the price of land plays such a role, that purchase and sale, the circulation of land as a commodity, develops to this degree, is practically a result of the development of the capitalist mode of production in so far as a commodity is here the general form of all products and all instruments of production. On the other hand, this development takes place only where the capitalist mode of production has a limited development and does not unfold all of its peculiarities, because this rests precisely upon the fact that agriculture is no longer, or not yet, subject to the capitalist mode of production, but rather to one handed down from extinct forms of society. The disadvantages of the capitalist mode of production, with its dependence of the producer upon the money price of his product, coincide here therefore with the disadvantage occasioned by the imperfect development of the capitalist mode of production. The peasant turns merchant and industrialist without the conditions enabling him to produce his products as commodities.

The conflict between the price of land as an element in the producers' cost price and no element in the price of production of the product (even though the rent enters as a determining factor into the price of the agricultural product, the capitalised rent, which is advanced for 20 years or more, by no means enters as a determinant) is but one of the forms manifesting the general contradiction between private landownership and a rational agriculture, the normal social utilisation of the soil. But on the other hand, private landownership, and thereby expropriation of the direct producers from the land — private landownership by the one, which implies lack of ownership by others — is the basis of the capitalist mode of production.

Here, in small-scale agriculture, the price of land, a form and result of private landownership, appears as a barrier to production itself.

---

[a] L. Mounier, *De l'agriculture en France*, Paris, 1846. - [b] C. J. Dombasle de, *Annales agricoles de Roville ou mélanges d'agriculture, d'économie rurale et de législation agricole*, Paris, 1824-37.

In large-scale agriculture, and large estates operating on a capitalist basis, ownership likewise acts as a barrier, because it limits the tenant farmer in his productive investment of capital, which in the final analysis benefits not him, but the landlord. In both forms, exploitation and squandering of the vitality of the soil (apart from making exploitation dependent upon the accidental and unequal circumstances of individual producers rather than the attained level of social development) takes the place of conscious rational cultivation of the soil as eternal communal property, an inalienable condition for the existence and reproduction of a chain of successive generations of the human race. In the case of small property, this results from the lack of means and knowledge of applying the social labour productive power. In the case of large property, it results from the exploitation of such means for the most rapid enrichment of farmer and proprietor. In the case of both through dependence on the market price.

All critique of small landed property resolves itself in the final analysis into a criticism of private ownership as a barrier and hindrance to agriculture. And similarly all countercriticism of large landed property. In either case, of course, we leave aside all secondary political considerations. This barrier and hindrance, which are erected by all private landed property vis-à-vis agricultural production and the rational cultivation, maintenance and improvement of the soil itself, develop on both sides merely in different forms, and in wrangling over the specific forms of this evil its ultimate cause is forgotten.

Small landed property presupposes that the overwhelming majority of the population is rural, and that not social, but isolated labour predominates; and that, therefore, under such conditions wealth and development of reproduction, both of its material and spiritual prerequisites, are out of the question, and thereby also the prerequisites for rational cultivation. On the other hand, large landed property reduces the agricultural population to a constantly falling minimum, and confronts it with a constantly growing industrial population crowded together in large cities. It thereby creates conditions which cause an irreparable break in the coherence of social interchange prescribed by the natural laws of life. As a result, the vitality of the soil is squandered, and this prodigality is carried by commerce far beyond the borders of a particular state (Liebig).[a]

---

[a] Liebig, *Die Chemie in ihrer Anwendung auf Agricultur und Physiologie.*

While small landed property creates a class of barbarians standing halfway outside of society, a class combining all the crudeness of primitive forms of society with all the anguish and misery of civilised countries, large landed property undermines labour power in the last region, where its prime energy seeks refuge and stores up its strength as a reserve fund for the regeneration of the vital force of nations — on the land itself. Large-scale industry and large-scale mechanised agriculture work together. If originally distinguished by the fact that the former lays waste and destroys principally labour power, hence the natural force of human beings, whereas the latter more directly exhausts and ruins the natural vitality of the soil, they join hands in the further course of development in that the industrial system in the countryside also enervates the labourers, and industry and commerce on their part supply agriculture with the means for exhausting the soil.

Part VII

REVENUES AND THEIR SOURCES

Chapter XLVIII

THE TRINITY FORMULA

I [48)

Capital — profit (profit of enterprise plus interest), land — ground rent, labour — wages, this is the trinity formula which comprises all the secrets of the social production process.

Furthermore, since as previously[a] demonstrated interest appears as the specific characteristic product of capital and profit of enterprise on the contrary appears as wages independent of capital, the above trinity formula reduces itself more specifically to the following:

Capital — interest, land — ground rent, labour — wages, where profit, the specific characteristic form of surplus value belonging to the capitalist mode of production, is fortunately eliminated.

On closer examination of this economic trinity, we find the following:

First, the alleged sources of the annually available wealth belong to widely dissimilar spheres and are not at all analogous with one another. They have about the same relation to each other as lawyer's fees, red beets and music.

Capital, land, labour! However, capital is not a thing, but rather a definite social production relation, belonging to a definite historical formation of society, which is manifested in a thing and lends this thing a specific social character. Capital is not the sum of the material and produced means of production. Capital is rather the means of

---

[48)] The following three fragments were found in different parts of the manuscript for Part VI.— *F. E.*

---

[a] See this volume, Part 1, Ch. XXIII.

production transformed into capital, which in themselves are no more capital than gold or silver in itself is money. It is the means of production monopolised by a certain section of society, confronting living labour power as products and working conditions rendered independent of this very labour power, which are personified through this antithesis in capital. It is not merely the products of labourers turned into independent powers, products as rulers and buyers of their producers, but rather also the social forces and the future ... //? illegible// [a] form of this labour, which confront the labourers as properties of their products. Here, then, we have a definite and, at first glance, very mystical, social form of one of the factors in a historically produced social production process.

And now alongside of this we have the land, inorganic nature as such, *rudis indigestaque moles*,[b] in all its primeval wildness. Value is labour. Therefore surplus value cannot be earth. Absolute fertility of the soil effects nothing more than the following: a certain quantity of labour produces a certain product — in accordance with the natural fertility of the soil. The difference in soil fertility causes the same quantities of labour and capital, hence the same value, to be manifested in different quantities of agricultural products; that is, causes these products to have different individual values. The equalisation of these individual values into market values is responsible for the fact that the

"ADVANTAGES OF FERTILE OVER INFERIOR SOIL ... ARE TRANSFERRED FROM THE CULTIVATOR OR CONSUMER TO THE LANDLORD" (Ricardo, *Principles*, p. 62).

And finally, as third party[c] in this union, a mere ghost — "the" Labour, which is no more than an abstraction and taken by itself does not exist at all, or, if we take ... //illegible//,[d] the productive activity of human beings in general, by which they promote the interchange with Nature, divested not only of every social form and well-defined character, but even in its bare natural existence, independent of society, removed from all societies, and as an expression and confirmation of life which the still nonsocial man in general has in common with the one who is in any way social.

---

[a] A later collation with the manuscript showed that the text reads as follows: "die Gesellschaftlichen Kräfte und Zusammenhängende Form dieser Arbeit" (the social forces of their labour and socialised form of this labour). - [b] Ovid, *Metamorphoses*, Book I, 7. - [c] F. Schiller, "Die Bürgschaft". - [d] As has been established by later reading of the manuscript, it reads here: "wenn wir das Gemeinte nehmen" (if we take that which is behind it).

II

Capital — interest; landed property, private ownership of the Earth, and, to be sure, modern and corresponding to the capitalist mode of production — rent; wage labour — wages. The connection between the sources of revenue is supposed to be represented in this form. Wage labour and landed property, like capital, are historically determined social forms; one of labour, the other of monopolised terrestrial globe, and indeed both forms corresponding to capital and belonging to the same economic formation of society.

The first striking thing about this formula is that side by side with capital, with this form of an element of production belonging to a definite mode of production, to a definite historical form of social process of production, side by side with an element of production amalgamated with and represented by a definite social form are indiscriminately placed: the land on the one hand and labour on the other, two elements of the real labour process, which in this material form are common to all modes of production, which are the material elements of every process of production and have nothing to do with its social form.

Secondly. In the formula: capital — interest, land — ground rent, labour — wages, capital, land and labour appear respectively as sources of interest (instead of profit), ground rent and wages, as their products, or fruits; the former are the basis, the latter the consequence, the former are the cause, the latter the effect; and indeed, in such a manner that each individual source is related to its product as to that which is ejected and produced by it. All the proceeds, interest (instead of profit), rent, and wages, are three components of the value of the products, i. e., generally speaking, components of value or expressed in money, certain money components, price components. The formula: capital — interest is now indeed the most meaningless formula of capital, but still one of its formulas. But how should land create value, i. e., a socially defined quantity of labour, and moreover that particular portion of the value of its own products which forms the rent? Land, e. g., takes part as an agent of production in creating a use value, a material product, wheat. But it has nothing to do with the production of the *value of wheat*. In so far as value is represented by wheat, the latter is merely considered as a definite quantity of objectified social labour, regardless of the particular substance in which this labour is manifested or of the particular use value of this substance. This nowise contradicts that 1) other circumstances being equal, the cheapness or dearness of wheat depends upon the productivity of the soil. The productivity of agricultural labour is dependent on natural conditions, and the same quantity of labour is represented by more or fewer products, use values, in accordance with such productivity. How large the quantity of labour represented in one bushel of wheat depends upon the number of bushels yielded by the same quantity of labour. It depends, in this case, upon the soil productivity in what quantities of product the value shall be manifested. But this value is given, independent of this distribution. Value is represented in use value; and use value is a prerequisite for the creation of value; but it is folly to create an antithesis by placing a use value, like land, on one side and on the other side value, and a particular portion of value at that. 2) ...//here the manuscript breaks off//.

III

Vulgar economy actually does no more than interpret, systematise and defend in doctrinaire fashion the conception of the agents of bourgeois production who are entrapped in bourgeois production relations. It should not astonish us, then, that vulgar economy feels particularly at home in the estranged outward appearances of economic relations in which these *prima facie* absurd and perfect contradictions appear and that these relations seem the more self-evident the more their internal relationships are concealed from it, although they are understandable to the popular mind. But all science would be superfluous if the outward appearance and the essence of things directly coincided. Thus, vulgar economy has not the slightest suspicion that the trinity which it takes as its point of departure, namely, land — rent, capital — interest, labour — wages or the price of labour, are *prima facie* three impossible combinations. First we have the use value *land*, which has no value, and the exchange value *rent*: so that a social relation conceived as a thing is made proportional to Nature, i. e., two incommensurable magnitudes are supposed to stand in a given ratio to one another. Then *capital — interest*. If capital is conceived as a certain sum of values represented independently by money, then it is *prima facie* nonsense to say that a certain value should be worth more than it is worth. It is precisely in the form: capital — interest that all intermediate links are eliminated, and capital is reduced to its most general formula, which therefore in itself is also inexplicable and absurd. The vulgar economist prefers the formula capital — interest, with its occult quality of making a value unequal to itself, to the formula capital — profit, precisely for the reason that this already more nearly approaches actual capitalist relations. Then again, driven by the disturbing thought that 4 is not 5 and that 100 taler cannot possibly be 110 taler, he flees from capital as value to the material substance of capital; to its use value as a condition of production of labour, to machinery, raw materials, etc. Thus, he is able once more to substitute in place of the first incomprehensible relation, whereby 4 = 5, a wholly incommensurable one between a use value, a thing on one side, and a definite social production relation, surplus value, on the other, as in the case of landed property. As soon as the vulgar economist arrives at this incommensurable relation, everything becomes clear to him, and he no longer feels the need for further thought. For he has arrived precisely at the "rational" in bourgeois conception. Finally, *labour — wages*, or price of labour, is an expression, as shown in Book I, which *prima facie* contradicts the conception of value as well as of price — the latter generally being but a definite expression of value. And "price of labour" is just as irrational as a yellow logarithm. But here the vulgar economist is all the more satisfied, because he has gained the profound insight of the bourgeois, namely, that he pays money for labour, and since precisely the contradiction between the formula and the conception of value relieves him from all obligation to understand the latter.

——————

We [49] have seen that the capitalist process of production is a historically determined form of the social process of production in general. The latter is as much a production process of material conditions of human life as a process taking place under specific historical and economic production relations, producing and reproducing these production relations themselves, and thereby also the bearers of this process, their material conditions of existence and their mutual relations, i. e., their particular socio-economic form. For the aggregate of these relations, in which the agents of this production stand with respect to Nature and to one another, and in which they produce, is precisely society, considered from the standpoint of its economic

[49] Beginning of Chapter XLVIII according to the manuscript.— *F. E.*

structure. Like all its predecessors, the capitalist process of production proceeds under definite material conditions, which are, however, simultaneously the bearers of definite social relations entered into by individuals in the process of reproducing their life. Those conditions, like these relations, are on the one hand prerequisites, on the other hand results and creations of the capitalist process of production; they are produced and reproduced by it. We saw also that capital — and the capitalist is merely capital personified and functions in the process of production solely as the agent of capital — in its corresponding social process of production, pumps a definite quantity of surplus labour out of the direct producers, or labourers; capital obtains this surplus labour without an equivalent, and in essence it always remains forced labour — no matter how much it may seem to result from free contractual agreement. This surplus labour appears as surplus value, and this surplus value exists as a surplus product. Surplus labour in general, as labour performed over and above the given requirements, must always remain. In the capitalist as well as in the slave system, etc., it merely assumes an antagonistic form and is supplemented by complete idleness of a stratum of society. A definite quantity of surplus labour is required as insurance against accidents, and by the necessary and progressive expansion of the process of reproduction in keeping with the development of the needs and the growth of population, which is called accumulation from the viewpoint of the capitalist. It is one of the civilising aspects of capital that it enforces this surplus labour in a manner and under conditions which are more advantageous to the development of the productive forces, social relations, and the creation of the elements for a new and higher form than under the preceding forms of slavery, serfdom, etc. Thus it gives rise to a stage, on the one hand, in which coercion and monopolisation of social development (including its material and intellectual advantages) by one portion of society at the expense of the other are eliminated; on the other hand, it creates the material means and embryonic conditions, making it possible in a higher form of society to combine this surplus labour with a greater reduction of time devoted to material labour in general. For, depending on the development of labour productivity, surplus labour may be large in a small total working day, and relatively small in a large total working day. If the necessary labour time $= 3$ and the surplus labour $= 3$, then the total working day $= 6$ and the rate of surplus labour $= 100\%$. If the necessary labour $= 9$ and the surplus labour $= 3$, then the total working day = 12 and the rate of surplus labour only = $33\frac{1}{3}$ %. In that case, it depends upon the labour productivity how much use value shall be produced in a definite time, hence also in a definite surplus labour time. The actual wealth of society, and the possibility of constantly expanding its reproduction process, therefore, do not depend upon the duration of surplus labour, but upon its productivity and the more or less copious conditions of production under which it is performed. In fact, the realm of freedom actually begins only where labour which is determined by necessity and mundane considerations ceases; thus in the very nature of things it lies beyond the sphere of actual material production. Just as the savage must wrestle with Nature to satisfy his wants, to maintain and reproduce life, so must civilised man, and he must do so in all social formations and under all possible modes of production. With his development this realm of physical necessity expands as a result of his wants; but, at the same time, the forces of production which satisfy these wants also increase. Freedom in this field can only consist in socialised man, the associated producers, rationally regulating their interchange with Nature, bringing it under their common control, instead of being ruled by it as by the blind forces of Nature; and achieving this with the least expenditure of energy and under conditions most favourable to, and worthy of, their human nature. But it nonetheless still remains a realm of necessity. Beyond it begins that development of human energy which is an end in itself, the true realm of freedom, which, however, can blossom forth only with this realm of necessity as its basis. The shortening of the working day is its basic prerequisite.

In a capitalist society, this surplus value, or this surplus product (leaving aside chance fluctuations in its distribution and considering only its regulating law, its standardising limits), is divided among capitalists as dividends proportionate to the share of the social capital each holds. In this form surplus value appears as average profit which falls to the share of capital, an average profit which in turn divides into profit of enterprise and interest, and which under these two categories may fall into the laps of different kinds of capitalists. This appropriation and distribution of surplus value, or surplus product, on the part of capital, however, has its barrier in landed property. Just as the operating capitalist pumps surplus labour, and thereby surplus value and surplus product in the form of profit, out of the labourer, so the landlord in turn pumps a portion of this surplus value, or surplus product, out of the capitalist in the form of rent in accordance with the laws already elaborated.

Hence, when speaking here of profit as that portion of surplus value falling to the share of capital, we mean average profit (equal to profit of enterprise plus interest) which is already limited by the deduction of rent from the aggregate profit (identical in mass with aggregate surplus value); the deduction of rent is assumed. Profit of capital (profit of enterprise plus interest) and ground rent are thus no more than particular components of surplus value, categories by which surplus value is differentiated depending on whether it falls to the share of capital or landed property, headings which in no whit however alter its nature. Added together, these form the sum of social surplus value. Capital pumps the surplus labour, which is represented by surplus value and surplus product, directly out of the labourers. Thus, in this sense, it may be regarded as the producer of surplus value. Landed property has nothing to do with the actual process of production. Its role is confined to transferring a portion of the produced surplus value from the pockets of capital to its own. However, the landlord plays a role in the capitalist process of production not merely through the pressure he exerts upon capital, nor merely because large landed property is a prerequisite and condition of capitalist production since it is a prerequisite and condition of the expropriation of the labourer from the conditions of labour, but particularly because he appears as the personification of one of the most essential conditions of production.

Finally, the labourer in the capacity of owner and seller of his individual labour power receives a portion of the product under the label of wages, in which that portion of his labour appears which we call necessary labour, i. e., that required for the maintenance and reproduction of this labour power, be the conditions of this maintenance and reproduction scanty or bountiful, favourable or unfavourable.

Whatever may be the disparity of these relations in other respects, they all have this in common: Capital yields a profit year after year to the capitalist, land a ground rent to the landlord, and labour power, under normal conditions and so long as it remains useful labour power, a wage to the labourer. These three portions of total value annually produced, and the corresponding portions of the annually created total product (leaving aside for the present any consideration of accumulation), may be annually consumed by their respective owners, without exhausting the source of their reproduction. They are like the annually consumable fruits of a perennial tree, or rather three trees; they form the annual incomes of three classes, capitalist, landowner and labourer, revenues distributed by the functioning capitalist in his capacity as direct extorter of surplus labour and employer of labour in general. Thus, capital appears to the capitalist, land to the landlord, and labour power, or rather labour itself, to the labourer (since he actually sells labour power only as it is manifested, and since the price of labour power, as previously shown, inevitably appears as the prices of labour under the capitalist mode of production), as three different sources of their specific revenues, namely, profit, ground rent and wages. They are really so in the sense that capital is a perennial pumping-machine of surplus labour for the capitalist, land a perennial magnet for the landlord, attracting a portion of the surplus value pumped out by capital, and finally, labour the constantly self-renewing condition and ever self-renewing means of acquiring under the title of wages a portion of the value created by the labourer and thus a part of the social product measured by this portion of value, i. e., the necessities of life. They are so, furthermore, in the sense that capital fixes a portion of the value and thereby of the product of the annual labour in the form of profit; landed property fixes another portion in the form of rent; and wage labour fixes a third portion in the form of wages, and precisely by this transformation converts them into revenues of the capitalist, landowner, and labourer, without, however, creating the substance itself which is transformed into these various categories. The distribution rather presupposes the existence of this substance, namely, the total value of the annual product which is nothing but objectified social labour. Nevertheless, it is not in this form that the matter appears to the agents of production, the bearers of the various functions in the production process, but rather in a distorted form. Why this takes place will be developed in the further course of our analysis. Capital, landed property and labour appear to those agents of production as three different, independent sources, from which as such there arise three different components of the annually produced value—and thereby the product in which it exists; thus, from which there arise not merely the different forms of this value as revenues falling to the share of particular factors in the social process of production, but from which this value itself arises, and thereby the substance of these forms of revenue.

//Here one folio sheet of the manuscript is missing.// [89]

... Differential rent is bound up with the relative soil fertility, in other words, with properties arising from the soil as such. But, in the first place, in so far as it is based upon the different individual values of the products of different soil types, it is but the determination just mentioned; secondly, in so far as it is based upon the regulating general market value, which differs from these individual values, it is a social law carried through by means of competition, which has to do neither with the soil nor the different degrees of its fertility.

It might seem as if a rational relation were expressed at least in "labour — wages". But this is no more the case than with "land — ground rent". In so far as labour is value-creating, and is manifested in the value of commodities, it has nothing to do with the distribution of this value among various categories. In so far as it has the specifically social character of wage labour, it is not value-creating. It has already been shown in general that wages of labour, or price of labour, is but an irrational expression for the value, or price of labour power; and the specific social conditions, under which this labour power is sold, have nothing to do with labour as a general agent in production. Labour is also objectified in that value component of a commodity which as wages forms the price of labour power; it creates this portion just as much as the other portions of the product; but it is objectified in this portion no more and no differently than in the portions forming rent or profit. And, in general, when we establish labour as value-creating, we do not consider it in its concrete form as a condition of production, but in its social delimitation which differs from that of wage labour.

Even the expression "capital — profit" is incorrect here. If capital is viewed in the only relation in which it produces surplus value, namely, its relation to the labourer whereby it extorts surplus labour by compulsion exerted upon labour power, i.e., the wage labourer, then this surplus value comprises, outside of profit (profit of enterprise plus interest), also rent, in short, the entire undivided surplus value. Here, on the other hand, as a source of revenue, it is placed only in relation to that portion falling to the share of the capitalist. This is not the surplus value which it extracts generally but only that portion which it extracts for the capitalist. Still more does all connection vanish no sooner the formula is transformed into "capital — interest".

If we at first considered the disparity of the above three sources, we now note that their products, their offshoots, or revenues, on the other hand, all belong to the same sphere, that of value. However, this is compensated for (this relation not only between incommensurable magnitudes, but also between wholly unlike, mutually unrelated, and noncomparable things) in that capital, like land and labour, is simply considered as a material substance, that is, simply as a produced means of production, and thus is abstracted both as a relation to the labourer and as value.

Thirdly, if understood in this way, the formula, capital — interest (profit), land — rent, labour — wages, presents a uniform and symmetrical incongruity. In fact, since wage labour does not appear as a socially determined form of labour, but rather all labour appears by its nature as wage labour (thus appearing to those in the grip of capitalist production relations), the definite specific social forms assumed by the objective conditions of labour — the produced means of production and the land — with respect to wage labour (just as they, in turn, conversely presuppose wage labour), directly coincide with the material existence of these conditions of labour or with the form possessed by them generally in the actual labour process, independent of its concrete historically determined social form, or indeed independent of *any* social form. The changed form of the conditions of labour, i. e., alienated from labour and confronting it independently, whereby the produced means of production are thus transformed into capital, and the land into monopolised land, or landed property — this form belonging to a definite historical period thereby coincides with the existence and function of the produced means of production and of the land in the process of production in general. These means of production are in themselves capital by nature; capital is merely an "economic appellation" for these means of production; and so, in itself land is by nature the earth monopolised by a certain number of landowners. Just as products confront the producer as an independent force in capital and capitalists — who actually are but the personification of capital — so land becomes personified in the landlord and likewise gets on its hind legs to demand, as an independent force, its share of the product created with its help. Thus, not the land receives its due portion of the product for the restoration and improvement of its productivity, but instead the landlord takes a share of this product to chaffer away or squander. It is clear that capital presupposes labour as wage labour. But it is just as clear that if labour as wage labour is taken as the point of departure, so that the identity of labour in general with wage labour appears to be self-evident, then

capital and monopolised land must also appear as the natural form of
the conditions of labour in relation to labour in general. To be capital, then, appears as the natural form of the means of labour and
thereby as the purely real character arising from their function in the
labour process in general. Capital and produced means of production
thus become identical terms. Similarly, land and land monopolised
through private ownership become identical. The means of labour as
such, which are by nature capital, thus become the source of profit,
much as the land as such becomes the source of rent.

Labour as such, in its simple capacity as purposive productive activity, relates to the means of production, not in their social determin-
ate form, but rather in their concrete substance, as material and
means of labour; the latter likewise are distinguished from one another merely materially, as use values, i. e., the land as unproduced, the
others as produced, means of labour. If, then, labour coincides with
wage labour, so does the particular social form in which the conditions of labour confront labour coincide with their material existence.
The means of labour as such are then capital, and the land as such is
landed property. The formal independence of these conditions of labour in relation to labour, the unique form of this independence with
respect to wage labour, is then a property inseparable from them as
things, as material conditions of production, an inherent, immanent,
intrinsic character of them as elements of production. Their definite
social character in the process of capitalist production bearing the
stamp of a definite historical epoch is a natural, and intrinsic substantive character belonging to them, as it were, from time immemorial,
as elements of the production process. Therefore, the respective part
played by the earth as the original field of activity of labour, as the
realm of forces of Nature, as the pre-existing arsenal of all objects of
labour, and the other respective part played by the produced means
of production (instruments, raw materials, etc.) in the general process
of production, must seem to be expressed in the respective shares
claimed by them as capital and landed property, i. e., which fall to the
share of their social representatives in the form of profit (interest) and
rent, like to the labourer— the part his labour plays in the process of
production is expressed in wages. Rent, profit and wages thus seem to
grow out of the role played by the land, produced means of production, and labour in the simple labour process, even when we consider
this labour process as one carried on merely between man and Nature, leaving aside any historical determination. It is merely the same

thing again, in another form, when it is argued: the product in which a wage labourer's labour for himself is manifested, his proceeds or revenue, is simply wages, the portion of value (and thereby the social product measured by this value) which his wages represent. Thus, if wage labour coincides with labour generally, then so do wages with the produce of labour, and the value portion representing wages with the value created by labour generally. But in this way the other portions of value, profit and rent, also appear independent with respect to wages, and must arise from sources of their own, which are specifically different and independent of labour; they must arise from the participating elements of production, to the share of whose owners they fall; i. e., profit arises from the means of production, the material elements of capital, and rent arises from the land, or Nature, as represented by the landlord (Roscher).[a]

Landed property, capital and wage labour are thus transformed from sources of revenue — in the sense that capital attracts to the capitalist, in the form of profit, a portion of the surplus value extracted by him from labour, that monopoly in land attracts for the landlord another portion in the form of rent; and that labour grants the labourer the remaining portion of value in the form of wages — from sources by means of which one portion of value is transformed into the form of profit, another into the form of rent, and a third into the form of wages — into actual sources from which these value portions and respective portions of the product in which they exist, or for which they are exchangeable, arise themselves, and from which, therefore, in the final analysis, the value of the product itself arises.[50]

In the case of the simplest categories of the capitalist mode of production, and even of commodity production, in the case of commodities and money, we have already pointed out the mystifying character that transforms the social relations, for which the material elements of wealth serve as bearers in production, into properties of these things themselves (commodities) and still more pronouncedly transforms

---

[50] Wages, profit, and rent are the three original sources of all revenue, as well as of all exchangeable value (A. Smith).[b][90] — It is thus that the causes of material production are at the same time the sources of the original revenues which exist (Storch, I, p. 259).[c]

[a] W. Roscher, *System der Volkswirtschaft*, Band I, Stuttgart und Augsburg, 1858. -
[b] A. Smith, *An Inquiry into the Nature and Causes of the Wealth of Nations*, Vol. I, p. 63. -
[c] See *Cours d'économie politique etc.* Quoted in French.

the production relation itself into a thing (money). All forms of society, in so far as they reach the stage of commodity production and money circulation, take part in this perversion. But under the capitalist mode of production and in the case of capital, which forms its dominant category, its determining production relation, this enchanted and perverted world develops still more. If one considers capital, to begin with, in the actual process of production as a means of extracting surplus labour, then this relationship is still very simple, and the actual connection impresses itself upon the bearers of this process, the capitalists themselves, and remains in their consciousness. The violent struggle over the limits of the working day demonstrates this strikingly. But even within this nonmediated sphere, the sphere of direct action between labour and capital, matters do not rest in this simplicity. With the development of relative surplus value in the actual specifically capitalist mode of production, whereby the productive powers of social labour are developed, these productive powers and the social interrelations of labour in the direct labour process seem transferred from labour to capital. Capital thus becomes a very mystic being since all of labour's social productive forces appear to be due to capital, rather than labour as such, and seem to issue from the womb of capital itself. Then the process of circulation intervenes, with its changes of substance and form, on which all parts of capital, even agricultural capital, devolve to the same degree that the specifically capitalist mode of production develops. This is a sphere where the relations under which value is originally produced are pushed completely into the background. In the direct process of production the capitalist already acts simultaneously as producer of commodities and manager of commodity production. Hence this process of production appears to him by no means simply as a process of producing surplus value. But whatever may be the surplus value extorted by capital in the actual production process and appearing in commodities, the value and surplus value contained in the commodities must first be realised in the circulation process. And both the restitution of the values advanced in production and, particularly, the surplus value contained in the commodities seem not merely to be realised in the circulation, but actually to arise from it; an appearance which is especially reinforced by two circumstances: first, the profit made in selling depends on cheating, deceit, inside knowledge, skill and a thousand favourable market opportunities; and then by the circumstance that added here to labour time is a second determining element — time of circulation. This acts, in fact, only as a negative barrier against the formation of value and surplus value, but it has the appearance of being as positive a basis as labour itself and of introducing a determining element that is independent of labour and resulting from the nature of capital. In Book II we naturally had to present this sphere of circulation merely with reference to the form determinations which it created and to demonstrate the further development of the structure of capital taking place in this sphere. But in reality this sphere is the sphere of competition, which, considered in each individual case, is dominated by chance; where, then, the inner law, which prevails in these accidents and regulates them, is only visible when these accidents are grouped together in large numbers, where it remains, therefore, invisible and unintelligible to the individual agents in production. But furthermore: the actual process of production, as a unity of the direct production process and the circulation process, gives rise to new formations, in which the vein of internal connections is increasingly lost, the production relations are rendered independent of one another, and the component values become ossified into forms independent of one another.

The conversion of surplus value into profit, as we have seen, is determined as much by the process of circulation as by the process of production. Surplus value, in the form of profit, is no longer related back to that portion of capital invested in labour from which it arises, but to the total capital. The rate of profit is regulated by laws of its own, which permit, or even require, it to change while the rate of surplus value remains unaltered. All this obscures more and more the true nature of surplus value and thus the actual mechanism of capital. Still more is this achieved through the transformation of profit into average profit and of values into prices of production, into the regulating averages of market prices. A complicated social process intervenes here, the equalisation process of capitals, which divorces the relative average prices of the commodities from their values, as well as the average profits in the various spheres of production (quite aside from the individual investments of capital in each particular sphere of production) from the actual exploitation of labour by the particular capitals. Not only does it appear so, but it is true in fact that the average price of commodities differs from their value, thus from the labour realised in them, and the average profit of a particular capital differs from the surplus value which this capital has extracted from the labourers employed by it. The value of commodities appears, directly, solely in the influence of fluctuating productivity of labour upon the fall and rise of the prices of production, upon their movement and not upon their ultimate limits. Profit seems to be determined only secondarily by direct exploitation of labour, in so far as the latter permits the capitalist to realise a profit deviating from the average profit at the regulating market prices, which apparently prevail independent of such exploitation. Normal average profits themselves seem immanent in capital and independent of exploitation; abnormal exploitation, or even average exploitation under favourable, exceptional conditions, seems to determine only the deviations from average profit, not this profit itself. The division of profit into profit of enterprise and interest (not to mention the intervention of commercial profit and profit from money dealing, which are founded upon circulation and appear to arise completely from it, and not from the process of production itself) consummates the individualisation of the form of surplus value, the ossification of its form as opposed to its substance, its essence. One portion of profit, as opposed to the other, separates itself entirely from the relationship of capital as such and appears as arising not out of the function of exploiting wage labour, but out of the wage labour of the capitalist himself. In contrast thereto, interest then seems to be independent both of the labourer's wage labour and the capitalist's own labour, and to arise from capital as its own independent source. If capital originally appeared on the surface of circulation as a fetishism of capital, as a value-creating value, so it now appears again in the form of interest-bearing capital, as in its most estranged and characteristic form. Wherefore also the formula capital — interest, as the third to land — rent and labour — wages, is much more consistent than capital — profit, since in profit there still remains a recollection of its origin, which is not only extinguished in interest, but is also placed in a form thoroughly antithetical to this origin.

Finally, capital as an independent source of surplus value is joined by landed property, which acts as a barrier to average profit and transfers a portion of surplus value to a class that neither works itself, nor directly exploits labour, nor can find morally edifying rationalisations, as in the case of interest-bearing capital, e. g., risk and sacrifice of lending capital to others. Since here a part of the surplus value seems to be bound up directly with a natural element, the land, rather than with social relations, the form of mutual estrangement and ossification of the various parts of surplus value is completed, the inner connection completely disrupted, and its source entirely buried, precisely because the relations of production, which are bound to the various material elements of the production process, have been rendered mutually independent.

In capital — profit, or still better capital — interest, land — rent, labour — wages, in this economic trinity represented as the connection between the component parts of value and wealth in general and its sources, we have the complete mystification of the capitalist mode of production, the conversion of social relations into things, the direct coalescence of the material production relations with their historical and social determination. It is an enchanted, perverted, topsy-turvy world, in which Monsieur le Capital and Madame la Terre do their ghost-walking as social characters and at the same time directly as mere things. It is the great merit of classical economy to have destroyed this false appearance and illusion, this mutual independence and ossification of the various social elements of wealth, this personification of things and conversion of production relations into entities, this religion of everyday life. It did so by reducing interest to a portion of profit, and rent to the surplus above average profit, so that both of them converge in surplus value; and by representing the process of circulation as a mere metamorphosis of forms, and finally reducing value and surplus value of commodities to labour in the direct production process. Nevertheless even the best spokesmen of classical economy remain more or less in the grip of the world of illusion which their criticism had dissolved, as cannot be otherwise from a bourgeois standpoint, and thus they all fall more or less into inconsistencies, half-truths and unsolved contradictions. On the other hand, it is just as natural for the actual agents of production to feel completely at home in these estranged and irrational forms of capital — interest, land — rent, labour — wages, since these are precisely the forms of illusion in which they move about and find their daily occupation. It is therefore just as natural that vulgar economy, which is no more than a didactic, more or less dogmatic, translation of everyday conceptions of the actual agents of production, and which arranges them in a certain rational order, should see precisely in this trinity, which is devoid of all inner connection, the natural and indubitable lofty basis for its shallow pompousness. This formula simultaneously corresponds to the interests of the ruling classes by proclaiming the physical necessity and eternal justification of their sources of revenue and elevating them to a dogma.

In our description of how production relations are converted into entities and rendered independent in relation to the agents of production, we leave aside the manner in which the interrelations, due to the world market, its conjunctures, movements of market prices, periods of credit, industrial and commercial cycles, alternations of prosperity and crisis, appear to them as overwhelming natural laws that irresistibly enforce their will over them, and confront them as blind necessity. We leave this aside because the actual movement of competition belongs beyond our scope,[1] and we need present only the inner organisation of the capitalist mode of production, in its ideal average, as it were.

In preceding forms of society this economic mystification arose principally with respect to money and interest-bearing capital. In the nature of things it is excluded, in the first place, where production for the use value, for immediate personal requirements, predominates; and secondly, where slavery or serfdom form the broad foundation of social production, as in antiquity and during the Middle Ages. Here, the domination of the producers by the conditions of production is concealed by the relations of dominion and servitude, which appear and are evident as the direct motive power of the process of production. In early communal societies in which primitive communism prevailed, and even in the ancient communal towns, it was this communal society itself with its conditions which appeared as the basis of production, and its reproduction appeared as its ultimate purpose. Even in the medieval guild system neither capital nor labour appear untrammelled, but their relations are rather defined by the corporate rules, and by the same associated relations, and corresponding conceptions of professional duty, craftsmanship, etc. Only when the capitalist mode of production [a]—

Chapter XLIX

CONCERNING THE ANALYSIS
OF THE PROCESS OF PRODUCTION

For the purposes of the following analysis we may leave out of consideration the distinction between price of production and value, since this distinction disappears altogether when, as here, the value of

---

[a] The manuscript breaks off here.

the total annual product of labour is considered, i. e., the product of the total social capital.

Profit (profit of enterprise plus interest) and rent are nothing but peculiar forms assumed by particular parts of the surplus value of commodities. The magnitude of surplus value is the limit of the total size of the parts into which it may be divided. Average profit plus rent are, therefore, equal to the surplus value. It is possible for part of the surplus labour, and thus surplus value, contained in the commodities, not to take part directly in the equalisation of an average profit, so that part of the commodity value is not expressed at all in its price. But first, this is balanced either by the fact that the rate of profit increases, when the commodities sold below their value form an element of the constant capital, or by profit and rent being represented by a larger product, when commodities sold below their value enter into the portion of value consumed as revenue in the form of articles for individual consumption. Secondly, this is eliminated in the average movement. At any rate, even if a portion of surplus value not expressed in the price of the commodity is lost for the price formation, the sum of average profit plus rent in its normal form can never be larger than the total surplus value, although it may be smaller. Its normal form presupposes wages corresponding to the value of labour power. Even monopoly rent, in so far as it is not a deduction from wages, i. e., does not constitute a special category, must always indirectly be a part of the surplus value. If it is not part of the price excess above the price of production of the commodity itself, of which it is a constituent part (as in differential rent), or an excess portion of the surplus value of the commodity itself, of which it is a constituent part, above that portion of its own surplus value measured by the average profit (as in absolute rent), it is at least part of the surplus value of other commodities, i. e., of commodities which are exchanged for this commodity having a monopoly price. The sum of average profit plus ground rent can never be greater than the magnitude of which they are components and which exists before this division. It is therefore immaterial for our discussion whether the entire surplus value of the commodities, i. e., all the surplus labour contained in the commodities, is realised in their price or not. The surplus labour is not entirely realised if only for the reason that due to a continual change in the amount of labour socially necessary to produce a certain commodity, resulting from the constant change in the productiveness of labour, some commodities are always produced under abnormal conditions and must, therefore, be sold below their individual value. At any rate, profit plus rent equal the total realised surplus value (surplus labour), and for purposes of this discussion the realised surplus value may be equated to all surplus value; for profit and rent are realised surplus value, or, generally speaking, the surplus value which passes into the prices of commodities, thus in practice all the surplus value forming a constituent part of this price.

On the other hand, wages, which form the third specific form of revenue, are always equal to the variable component part of capital, i. e., the component part which is laid out in purchasing living labour power, paying labourers rather than in means of labour. (The labour which is paid in the expenditure of revenue is itself paid in wages, profit, or rent, and therefore does not form any value portion of commodities by which it is paid. Hence it is not considered in the analysis of commodity value and of the component parts into which it is divided.) It is the objectification of that portion of the total working day of the labourer in which the value of variable capital and thus the price of labour is reproduced; that portion of commodity value in which the labourer reproduces the value of his own labour power, or the price of his labour. The total working day of the labourer is divided into two parts. One portion in which he performs the amount of labour necessary to reproduce the value of his own means of subsistence; the paid portion of his total labour, the portion necessary for his own maintenance and reproduction. The entire remaining portion of the working day, the entire excess quantity of labour performed above the value of the labour realised in his wages, is surplus labour, unpaid labour, represented in the surplus value of his total commodity production (and thus in an excess quantity of commodities), surplus value which in turn is divided into differently named parts, into profit (profit of enterprise plus interest) and rent.

The entire value portion of commodites, then, in which the total labour of the labourers added during one day, or one year, is realised, the total value of the annual product, created by this labour, is divided into the value of wages, into profit and into rent. For this total labour is divided into necessary labour, by which the labourer creates that value portion of the product with which he is himself paid, that is, his wages, and into unpaid surplus labour, by which he creates that value portion of the product which represents surplus value and which is later divided into profit and rent. Aside from this labour, the labourer performs no labour, and aside from the total value of the product, which assumes the forms of wages, profit and rent, he creates no value. The value of the annual product, in which the new labour added by the labourer during the year is incorporated, is equal to the wage, or the value of the variable capital plus the surplus value, which in turn is divided into the forms of profit and rent.

The entire value portion of the annual product, then, which the labourer creates in the course of the year, is expressed in the annual value sum of the three revenues, the value of wages, profit, and rent. Evidently, therefore, the value of the constant portion of capital is not reproduced in the annually created value of product, for the wages are only equal to the value of the variable portion of capital advanced in production, and rent and profit are only equal to the surplus value, the excess of value produced above the total value of advanced capital, which equals the value of the constant capital plus the value of the variable capital.

It is completely irrelevant to the problem to be solved here that a portion of the surplus value converted into the form of profit and rent is not consumed as revenue, but is accumulated. That portion which is saved up as an accumulation fund serves to create new, additional capital, but not to replace the old capital, be it the component part of old capital laid out for labour power or for means of labour. We may therefore assume here, for the sake of simplicity, that the revenue passes wholly into individual consumption. The difficulty is twofold. On the one hand, the value of the annual product, in which the revenues, wages, profit and rent, are consumed, contains a portion of value equal to the portion of value of constant capital used up in it. It contains this portion of value in addition to that portion which resolves itself into wages and that which resolves itself into profit and rent. Its value is therefore = wages + profit + rent + C (its constant portion of value). How can an annually produced value, which only = wages + profit + rent, buy a product the value of which = (wages + profit + rent) + C? How can the annually produced value buy a product which has a higher value than its own?

On the other hand, if we leave aside that portion of constant capital which did not pass over into the product, and which therefore continues to exist, although with reduced value, as before the annual production of commodities; in other words, temporarily leaving out of consideration the employed, but not consumed, fixed capital, then the constant portion of advanced capital is seen to have been wholly transferred to the new product in the form of raw and auxiliary materials, whereas a part of the means of labour has been wholly consumed and another part only partially, and thus only a part of its value has been consumed in production. This entire portion of constant capital consumed in production must be replaced in kind. Assuming all other circumstances, particularly the productive power of labour, to remain unchanged, this portion requires the same amount of labour for its replacement as before, i. e., it must be replaced by an equivalent value. If not, then reproduction itself cannot take place on the former scale. But who is obliged to perform this labour, and who does perform it?

As to the first difficulty: Who is obliged to pay for the constant portion of value contained in the product, and with what? — It is assumed that the value of constant capital consumed in production reappears as a part of the value of the product. This does not contradict the assumptions of the second difficulty. For it has already been demonstrated in Book I (Kap. V) ("The Labour Process and the Process of Producing Surplus Value") how the old value remains simultaneously preserved in the product through the mere addition of new labour, although this does not reproduce the old value and does no more than add to it, creates merely additional value; but that this results from labour, not in so far as it is value-creating, i. e., labour in general, but in its function as definite productive labour. Therefore, no additional labour was necessary to preserve the value of the constant portion in the product in which the revenue, i. e., the entire value created during the year, is expended. But to be sure, new additional labour is required to replace the value and use value of constant capital consumed during the preceding year, without the replacement of which no reproduction at all is possible.

All newly added labour is represented in the value newly created during the year, and this in turn is divided into the three revenues: wages, profit and rent.— Thus, on the one hand, no excess social labour remains for the replacement of the consumed constant capital, which must be replaced partially in kind and according to its value, and partially merely according to its value (for pure wear and tear of fixed capital). On the other hand, the value annually created by labour, divided into wages, profit and rent, and to be expended in this form, appears not to suffice to pay for, or buy, the constant portion of capital, which must be contained, outside their own value, in the annual product.

It is seen that the problem presented here has already been solved in the consideration of reproduction of the total social capital — Book II, Part III. We return to it here, in the first place, because surplus value had not been developed there in its revenue forms: profit (profit of enterprise plus interest) and rent, and could not, therefore, be treated in these forms; and then, also because precisely in the form of wages, profit and rent there is contained an incredible blunder in analysis, which pervades all political economy since Adam Smith.

We divided all capital there into two big classes: Class I, producing means of production, and Class II, producing articles of individual consumption. The fact that certain products may serve equally well both for personal consumption and as means of production (a horse, grain, etc.) does not invalidate the absolute correctness of this division in any way. It is actually no hypothesis, but merely an expression of fact. Take the annual product of a country. One portion of the product, whatever its ability to serve as means of production, passes over into individual consumption. It is the product for which wages, profit and rent are expended. This product is the product of a definite department of the social capital. It is possible that this same capital may also produce products belonging to Class I. In so far as it does so, it is not the portion of this capital consumed in the products of Class II, products belonging actually to individual consumption, which supplies the productively consumed products belonging to Class I. This entire product II, which passes into individual consumption, and for which therefore the revenue is spent, is the existent form of the capital consumed in it plus the produced surplus. It is thus the product of a capital invested solely in the production of articles of consumption. And in the same way Department I of the annual product, which serves as means of reproduction — raw materials and instruments of labour — whatever capacity this product may otherwise possess *naturaliter* to serve as means of consumption, is the product of a capital invested solely in the production of means of production. By far the greater part of products forming constant capital exists also materially in a form in which it cannot pass into individual consumption. In so far as this could be done, e. g., in so far as a farmer could eat his seed-corn, butcher his draught animals, etc., the economic barrier works the same for him as if this portion did not exist in consumable form.

As already indicated, we leave out of consideration in both classes the fixed portion of constant capital, which continues to exist in kind and, so far as its value is concerned, independently of the annual product of both classes.

In Class II, for the products of which wages, profit and rent are expended, in short, the revenues consumed, the product itself consists of three components so far as its value is concerned. One component is equal to the value of the constant portion of capital consumed in production; a second component is equal to the value of the variable advanced capital laid out in wages; finally, a third component is equal to the produced surplus value, thus = profit + rent. The first component of the product of Class II, the value of the constant portion of capital, can be consumed neither by the capitalist of Class II, nor by the labourers of this class, nor by the landowners. It forms no part of their revenues, but must be replaced in kind and must be sold for this to occur. On the other hand, the other two components of this product are equal to the value of the revenues created in this class, = wages + profit + rent.

In Class I the product consists of the same constituents, as regards form. But that part which here forms revenue, wages + profit + rent, in short, the variable portion of capital + surplus value, is not consumed here in the natural form of products of this Class I, but in products of Class II. The value of the revenues of Class I must, therefore, be consumed in that portion of products of Class II which forms the constant capital of II to be replaced. The portion of the product of Class II which must replace its constant capital is consumed in its natural form by the labourers, capitalists and landlords of Class I. They spend their revenue for this product of II. On the other hand, the product of I, to the extent that it represents a revenue of Class I, is productively consumed in its natural form by Class II, whose constant capital it replaces in kind. Finally, the used-up constant portion of capital of Class I is replaced out of the very products of this class, which consist precisely of means of labour, raw and auxiliary materials, etc., partly through exchange by capitalists of I among themselves, partly so that some of these capitalists can directly use their own product once more as means of production.

Let us take the previous scheme (Book II, Chapter XX, II) for simple reproduction:

$$\left.\begin{array}{l} \text{I. } 4{,}000_c + 1{,}000_v + 1{,}000_s = 6{,}000 \\ \text{II. } 2{,}000_c + \ \ \ 500_v + \ \ \ 500_s = 3{,}000 \end{array}\right\} = 9{,}000.$$

According to this, the producers and landlords of II consume $500_v + 500_s = 1{,}000$ as revenue; $2{,}000_c$ remains to be replaced. This is consumed by the labourers, capitalists and those who draw rent from I, whose income $= 1{,}000_v + 1{,}000_s = 2{,}000$. The consumed product of II is consumed as revenue by I, and the portion of the revenue of I representing an unconsumable product is consumed as constant capital by II. It remains then to account for the $4{,}000_c$ of I. This is replaced out of the product of I itself, which $= 6{,}000$, or rather $= 6{,}000 - 2{,}000$; for these $2{,}000$ have already been converted into constant capital for II. It should be noted, of course, that these numbers have been chosen arbitrarily, and so the relation between the value of the revenues of I and the value of the constant capital of II appears arbitrary. It is evident, however, that so far as the process of reproduction is normal and takes place under otherwise equal circumstances, i. e., leaving aside the accumulation, the sum of the values of wages, profit and rent in Class I must equal the value of the constant portion of capital of Class II. Otherwise either Class II will not be able to replace its constant capital, or Class I will not be able to convert its revenue from unconsumable into consumable form.

Thus, the value of the annual commodity product, just like the value of the commodity product produced by some particular investment of capital, and like the value of any individual commodity, resolves itself into two component parts: A, which replaces the value of the advanced constant capital, and B, which is represented in the form of revenue — wages, profit and rent. The latter component part of value, B, is counterposed to the former A, in so far as A, under otherwise equal circumstances: 1) never assumes the form of revenue and 2) always flows back in the form of capital, and indeed constant capital. The other component, B, however, carries within itself, in turn, an antithesis. Profit and rent have this in common with wages: all three are forms of revenue. Nevertheless they differ essentially in that profit and rent represent surplus value, i. e., unpaid labour, whereas wages represent paid labour. The portion of the value of the product which represents wages expended thus replaces wages, and, under the conditions assumed by us, where reproduction takes place on the same scale and under the same conditions, is again reconverted into wages, flows back first as variable capital, as a component of the capital that must be advanced anew for reproduction. This portion has a two-fold function. It exists first in the form of capital and is exchanged as such for labour power. In the hands of the labourer, it is transformed into revenue which he draws out of the sale of his labour power, is converted as revenue into means of subsistence and consumed. This double process is revealed through the mediation of money circulation. The variable capital is advanced in money, paid out as wages. This is its first function as capital. It is exchanged for labour power and transformed into the manifestation of this labour power, into labour. This is the process as regards the capitalist. Secondly, however: with this money the labourers buy a part of the commodities produced by them, which is measured by this money, and is consumed by them as revenue. If we imagine the circulation of money to be eliminated, then a part of the labourer's product is in the hands of the capitalist in the form of available capital. He advances this part as capital, gives it to the labourer for new labour power, while the labourer consumes it as revenue directly or indirectly through exchange for other commodities. That portion of the value of the product, then, which is destined in the course of reproduction to be converted into wages, into revenue for the labourers, first flows back into the hands of the capitalist in the form of capital, or more accurately variable capital. It is an essential requirement that it should flow back in this form in order for labour as wage labour, the means of production as capital, and the process of production itself as a capitalist process, to be continually reproduced anew.

In order to avoid unnecessary difficulty, one should distinguish gross output and net output from gross income and net income.

The gross output, or gross product, is the total reproduced product. With the exception of the employed but not consumed portion of fixed capital, the value of the gross output, or gross product, equals the value of capital advanced and consumed in production, that is, constant and variable capital plus surplus value, which resolves itself into profit and rent. Or, if we consider the product of the total social capital instead of that of an individual capital, the gross output equals the material elements forming the constant and variable capital, plus the material elements of the surplus product in which profit and rent are represented.

The gross income is that portion of value and that portion of the gross product measured by it which remains after deducting that portion of value and that portion of the product of total production measured by it which replaces the constant capital advanced and consumed in production. The gross income, then, is equal to wages (or the portion of the product destined to again become the income of the labourer) + profit + rent. The net income, on the other hand, is the surplus value, and thus the surplus product, which remains after deducting wages, and which, in fact, thus represents the surplus value realised by capital and to be divided with the landlord, and the surplus product measured by it.

Thus, we saw that the value of each individual commodity and the value of the total commodity product of each individual capital is divided into two parts: one replaces only constant capital, and the other, although a fraction of it flows back as variable capital — thus also flows back in the *form* of capital — nevertheless is destined to be wholly transformed into gross income, and to assume the form of wages, profit and rent, the sum of which makes up the gross income. Furthermore, we saw that the same is true of the value of the annual total product of a society. A difference between the product of the individual capitalist and that of society exists only in so far as: from the standpoint of the individual capitalist the net income differs from the gross income, for the latter includes the wages, whereas the former excludes them. Viewing the income of the whole society, national income consists of wages plus profit plus rent, thus, of the gross income. But even this is an abstraction to the extent that the entire society, on the basis of capitalist production, bases itself on the capitalist standpoint and thereby considers only the income resolved into profit and rent as net income.

On the other hand, the fantasy of men like Say, to the effect that the entire yield, the entire gross output, resolves itself into the net income of the nation or cannot be distinguished from it, that this distinction therefore disappears from the national viewpoint, is but the inevitable and ultimate expression of the absurd dogma pervading political economy since Adam Smith, that in the final analysis the value of commodities resolves itself completely into income, into wages, profit and rent.[51]

---

[51] Ricardo makes the following very apt comment on thoughtless Say: "Of net produce and gross produce, M. Say speaks as follows: 'The whole value produced is the gross produce; this value, after deducting from it the cost of production, is the net produce' (Vol. II, p. 491).[a] There can, then, be no net produce, because the cost of

[a] J. B. Say, *Traité d'économie politique*, Paris, 1819.

To comprehend, in the case of each individual capitalist, that a portion of his product must be transformed again into capital (even aside from the expansion of reproduction, or accumulation), indeed not only into variable capital, which is destined to again become in its turn income for the labourers, thus a form of revenue, but also into constant capital, which can never be transformed into revenue— such discernment is naturally extraordinarily easy. The simplest observation of the process of production shows this clearly. The difficulty first begins as soon as the process of production is viewed as a whole. The value of the entire portion of the product which is consumed as revenue in the form of wages, profit and rent (it is entirely immaterial whether the consumption is individual or productive), indeed, completely resolves itself under analysis into the sum of values consisting of wages plus profit plus rent, that is, into the total value of the three revenues, although the value of this portion of the product, just like that which does not enter into revenue, contains a value portion = C, equal to the value of the constant capital contained in these portions, and thus *prima facie* cannot be limited by the value of the revenue. This circumstance which, on the one hand, is a practically irrefutable fact, on the other hand, an equally undeniable theoretical contradiction, presents a difficulty which is most easily circumvented by the assertion that commodity value contains another portion of value, merely appearing to differ, from the standpoint of the individual capitalist, from the portion existing in the form of revenue. The phrase: that which appears as revenue for one constitutes capital for another, relieves one of the necessity for any further reflection. But how, then, the old capital can be replaced when the value of the entire product is consumable in the form of revenue; and how the value of the product of each individual capital can be equal to the value sum of the three revenues plus C, constant capital, whereas the sum of the values of the products of all capitals is equal to the value sum of

production, according to M. Say, consists of rent, wages and profits. On page 508 he says: 'The value of a product, the value of a productive service, the value of the cost of production, are all, then, similar values, whenever things are left to their natural course.' Take a whole from a whole, and nothing remains" (Ricardo, *Principles*, Chapter XXXII, p. 512, Note). — By the way we shall see later that Ricardo nowhere refuted Smith's false analysis of commodity price, its reduction to the sum of the values of the revenues. He does not bother with it, and accepts its correctness so far in his analysis that he "abstracts" from the constant portion of the value of commodities. He also falls back into the same way of looking at things from time to time.

the three revenues plus 0 — this appears, of course, as an insoluble
riddle and must be solved by declaring that the analysis is completely
incapable of unravelling the simple elements of price, and must be
content to go around in a vicious circle making a spurious advance
ad infinitum. Thus, that which appears as constant capital may be
resolved into wages, profit and rent, but the commodity values in
which wages, profit and rent appear, are determined in their turn by
wages, profit and rent, and so forth *ad infinitum*.[52]

The fundamentally erroneous dogma to the effect that the value
of commodities in the last analysis may be resolved into wages +
profit + rent also expresses itself in the proposition that the consumer
must ultimately pay for the total value of the total product; or also
that money circulation between producers and consumers must ultimately be equal to the money circulation between the producers
themselves (Tooke[b]); all these propositions are as false as the axiom
upon which they are based.

The difficulties, which lead to this erroneous and *prima facie* absurd
analysis, are briefly these:

1) The fundamental relationship of constant and variable capital,
hence also the nature of surplus value, and thereby the entire basis of
the capitalist mode of production, are not understood. The value of
each partial product of capital, each individual commodity, contains

[52] "In every society the price of every commodity finally resolves itself into some
one or other, or all of those three parts" viz., wages, profits, rent ... "A fourth part, it
may perhaps be thought, is necessary for replacing the stock of the farmer or for compensating the wear and tear of his labouring cattle, and other instruments of husbandry. But it must be considered that the price of any instrument of husbandry, such as
a labouring horse, is itself made up of the same three parts: the rent of the land upon
which he is reared, the labour of tending and rearing him, and the profits of the farmer,
who advances both the rent of his land and the wages of his labour. Though the price of
the corn, therefore, may pay the price as well as the maintenance of the horse, the
whole price still resolves itself either immediately or ultimately into the same three
parts of rent, labour" meaning wages "and profit." (Adam Smith.) [a] We shall show later
on how Adam Smith himself feels the inconsistency and insufficiency of this subterfuge,
for it is nothing but a subterfuge on his part to send us from Pontius to Pilate while
nowhere does he indicate the real investment of capital, in which case the price of
the product resolves itself ULTIMATELY into these three parts, without any further *prog-
ressus*.

[a] *An Inquiry into the Nature and Causes of the Wealth of Nations*, Vol. 1, pp. 60-61. -
[b] Th. Tooke, *An Inquiry into the Currency Principle* p. 36.

a portion of value = constant capital, a portion of value = variable capital (transformed into wages for labourers), and a portion of value = surplus value (later split into profit and rent). Thus, how is it possible for the labourer with his wages, the capitalist with his profit, the landlord with his rent, to be able to buy commodities, each of which contains not only one of these constituent elements, but all three of them; and how is it possible for the sum of the values of wages, profit and rent, that is, the three sources of revenue together, to be able to buy the commodities which go to make up the total consumption of the recipients of these incomes—commodities containing an additional component of value, namely constant capital, outside these three components of value? How should they buy a value of four with a value of three? [53]

[53] Proudhon exposes his inability to grasp this in the ignorant formulation: *l'ouvrier ne peut pas racheter son propre produit*,[a] because the interest which is added to the *prix-de-revient* [b] is contained in the product.[c] But how does M. Eugène Forcade teach him to know better? "If Proudhon's objection were correct, it would strike not only the profits of capital, but would eliminate the possibility even of industry. If the labourer is compelled to pay 100 for each article for which he has received only 80, if his wages can buy back only the value which he has put into a product, it could be said that the labourer cannot buy back anything, that wages cannot pay for anything. In fact, there is always something more than the wages of the labourer contained in the cost price, and always more than the profits of enterprise in the selling price, for instance, the price of raw materials, often paid to foreign countries. ... Proudhon has forgotten about the continual growth of national capital; he has forgotten that this growth refers to all labourers, whether in an enterprise or in handicrafts." (*Revue des deux Mondes*, 1848, Tome 24, p. 998-99.) [d] Here we have the optimism of bourgeois thoughtlessness in the form of sagacity that most corresponds to it. M. Forcade first believes that the labourer could not live did he not receive a higher value than that which he produces, whereas conversely the capitalist mode of production could not exist were he really to receive all the value which he produces. Secondly, he correctly generalises the difficulty, which Proudhon expressed only from a narrow viewpoint. The price of commodities contains not only an excess over wages, but also over profit, namely, the constant portion of value. According to Proudhon's reasoning, then, the capitalist too could not buy back the commodities with his profit. And how does Forcade solve this riddle? By means of a meaningless phrase: the growth of capital. Thus the continual growth of capital is also supposed to be substantiated, among other things, in that the analysis of commodity prices, which is impossible for the political economist as regards a capital of 100, becomes superfluous in the case of a capital of 10,000. What would be said of a chemist,

[a] the labourer cannot buy back his own product - [b] cost price - [c] P.J. Proudhon, *Qu'est-ce que la propriété? ou Recherches sur le principe du droit et du gouvernement*, pp. 201-02. - [d] E. Forcade, *La Guerre du socialisme. II. L'économie politique révolutionnaire et sociale*, pp. 998-99. Quoted partly in French, partly in German.

We presented our analysis in Book II, Part III.

2) The method is not grasped whereby labour, in adding a new value, preserves the old value in a new form without producing this old value anew.

3) The pattern of the process of reproduction is not understood — how it appears not from the standpoint of individual capital, but rather from that of the total capital; the difficulty is not understood how it is that the product in which wages and surplus value, in short, the entire value produced by all the labour newly added during the year, is realised, replaces the constant part of its value and yet at the same time resolves itself into value limited solely by the revenues; and furthermore how it is that the constant capital consumed in production can be replaced in substance and value by new capital, although the total sum of newly added labour is realised only in wages and surplus value, and is fully represented in the sum of the values of both. It is precisely here that the main difficulty lies, in the analysis of reproduction and the relations of its various component parts, both as concerns their material character and their value relationships.

4) To these difficulties is added still another, which increases even more as soon as the various component parts of surplus value appear in the form of mutually independent revenues. This difficulty consists in the definite designations of revenue and capital interchanging, and altering their position, so that they seem to be merely relative determinations from the point of view of the individual capitalist and to disappear when the total process of production is viewed as a whole. For instance, the revenue of the labourers and capitalists of Class I, which produces constant capital, replaces in value and substance the constant capital of the capitalists of Class II, which produces articles of consumption. One may, therefore, squeeze out of the dilemma by remonstrating that what is revenue for one is capital for another and that these designations thus have nothing to do with the actual peculiarities of the value components of commodities. Furthermore: com-

who, on being asked How is it that the product of the soil contains more carbon than the soil? would answer: It comes from the continual increase in agricultural production. The well-meaning desire to discover in the bourgeois world the best of all possible worlds replaces in vulgar economy all need for love of truth and inclination for scientific investigation.[a]

---

[a] See also present edition, Vol. 30, pp. 345-46.

modities which are ultimately destined to form the substantive elements of revenue expenditure, that is, articles of consumption, pass
through various stages during the year, e. g., woollen yarn, cloth. In
one stage they form a portion of constant capital, in the other they are
consumed individually, and thus pass wholly into the revenue. One
may therefore imagine along with Adam Smith that constant capital
is but an apparent element of commodity value, which disappears in
the total pattern. Thus, a further exchange takes place of variable
capital for revenue. The labourer buys with his wages that portion of
commodities which form his revenue. In this way he simultaneously
replaces for the capitalist the money form of variable capital. Finally:
one portion of products which form constant capital is replaced in
kind or through exchange by the producers of constant capital themselves; a process with which the consumers have nothing to do. When
this is overlooked the impression is created that the revenue of consumers replaces the entire product, i. e., including the constant portion
of value.

5) Aside from the confusion which the transformation of values
into prices of production brings about, another arises due to the
transformation of surplus value into different, special, mutually independent forms of revenue applying to the various elements of production, i. e., into profit and rent. It is forgotten that the fact that the
values of commodities are the basis, and that the division of these commodity values into distinct constituent parts, and the further development of these constituents of value into forms of revenue, their conversion into relations of various owners of different factors of production to these individual components of value, their distribution
among these owners according to definite categories and titles, itself
alters nothing in value determination and its law. Just as little is the
law of value changed by the circumstance that the equalisation of
profit, i. e., the distribution of the total surplus value among the various capitals, and the obstacles which landed property partially (in
absolute rent) puts in the way of this equalisation, bring about a di-
vergence between the regulating average prices and the individual
values of commodities. This again affects merely the addition of surplus value to the various commodity prices, but does not abolish surplus value itself, nor the total value of commodities as the source of
these various component parts of price.

This is the *quid pro quo* which we shall consider in the next chapter,
and which is inevitably linked with the illusion that value arises out of

its own component parts. And namely, the various component values of the commodity acquire independent forms as revenues, and as such revenues they are related back to the particular material elements of production as their sources of origin instead of to the value of the commodity as their source. They are actually related back to those sources—however, not as components of value, but rather as revenues, as components of value falling to the share of these particular categories of agents in production: the labourer, the capitalist and the landlord. But then one might fancy that these constituents of value, rather than arising out of the division of commodity value, conversely form it instead only through their combination, which leads to the pretty and vicious circle, whereby the value of commodities arises out of the sum of the values of wages, profit and rent, and the value of wages, profit and rent, in its turn, is determined by the value of commodities, etc.[54]

[54] "The circulating capital invested in materials, raw materials and finished goods is itself composed of goods, the necessary price of which is formed of the same elements; so that, viewing the total goods in one country, it would mean duplication to count this portion of circulating capital among the elements of the necessary price." (Storch, *Cours d'économie politique*, II, p. 140.)—By these elements of circulating capital Storch means the constant portion of the value (fixed capital is merely circulating in a different form). "It is true that the wages of the labourer, like that portion of profit of enterprise which consists of wages, if we consider them as a part of the means of subsistence, also consist of goods bought at current prices and which likewise comprise wages, interest on capital, ground rent and profit of enterprise.... This observation merely serves to prove that it is impossible to resolve the necessary price into its simplest elements." (Ibid., Note.) [a]—In his *Considérations sur la nature du revenu national* (Paris, 1824), Storch indeed realises in his controversy with Say to what absurdity the erroneous analysis of commodity value leads—when it resolves value into mere revenues. He correctly points out the folly of such results—not from the viewpoint of the individual capitalist, but from that of a nation—but himself goes no step further in his analysis of the *prix nécessaire* from that presented in his *Cours*, that it is impossible to resolve it into its actual elements, without resolving it into a spurious advance *ad infinitum*. "It is evident that the value of the annual product is divided partly into capitals and partly into profits, and that each one of these portions of value of the annual product regularly goes to buy the products needed by the nation, as much to preserve its capital as to renew its consumption fund (pp. 134, 135).... Can it" (a self-employed peasant family) "live in its barns or stables, eat its seed and forage, clothe itself with its draught cattle, dispense with its agricultural implements? According to the thesis of M. Say one must answer all these questions in the affirmative (pp. 135, 136).... If it is admitted that the revenue of a nation is equal to its gross product, i. e., if no capital has to be deducted from it, then it must also be admitted that a nation can spend the entire value of its

[a] Here and below cited in French.

Considering reproduction in its normal state, only a part of newly added labour is employed for production, and thus for replacement of constant capital; precisely that part which replaces the constant capital used up in the production of articles of consumption, of material elements of revenue. This is balanced by the fact that this constant portion of Class II costs no additional labour. But, now, this constant capital (looking upon the total process of reproduction, in which then the above-mentioned equalisation of Classes I and II is included), not representing a product of newly added labour, although this product could not be created without it — this constant capital, in the process of reproduction, considered from the standpoint of substance, is exposed to certain accidents and dangers which could decimate it. (Furthermore, however, considered from the point of view of value as well, it may be depreciated through a change in the productive power of labour; but this refers only to the individual capitalist.) Accordingly, a portion of the profit, therefore of surplus value and thereby also surplus product, in which (as concerns value) only newly added labour is represented, serves as an insurance fund. And it matters not whether this insurance fund is managed by insurance companies as a separate business or not. This is the sole portion of revenue which is neither consumed as such nor serves necessarily as a fund for accumulation. Whether it actually serves as such, or covers merely a loss in reproduction, depends upon chance. This is also the only portion of surplus value and surplus product, and thus of surplus labour, which would continue to exist, outside of that portion serving for accumulation, and hence expansion of the process of reproduction, even after the abolition of the capitalist mode of production. This, of course, presupposes that the portion regularly consumed by direct producers does not remain limited to its present minimum. Apart from surplus labour for those who on account of age are not yet, or no longer, able to take part in production, all labour to support those who do not work would cease. If we think back to the beginnings of society, we find no produced means of production, hence no constant capital, the value of which could pass into the product, and which, in reproduction on the same scale, would have to be replaced in kind out of the product and to a degree measured by its value. But Nature there directly provides the means of subsistence, which need not first be pro-

annual product unproductively without impairing its future income in the least (147). The products which constitute the capital of a nation are not consumable" (p. 150).

duced. Nature thereby also gives to the savage who has but few wants
to satisfy the time, not to use the as yet nonexistent means of production in new production, but to transform, alongside the labour required to appropriate naturally existing means of subsistence, other
products of Nature into means of production: bows, stone knives, boats,
etc. This process among savages, considered merely from the substantive side, corresponds to the reconversion of surplus labour into new
capital. In the process of accumulation, the conversion of such products of excess labour into capital obtains continually; and the circumstance that all new capital arises out of profit, rent, or other forms
of revenue, i. e., out of surplus labour, leads to the mistaken idea that
all value of commodities arises from some revenue. This reconversion
of profit into capital shows rather upon closer analysis that, conversely, the additional labour—which is always represented in the form
of revenue—does not serve for the maintenance, or reproduction
respectively, of the old capital value, but for the creation of new excess capital so far as it is not consumed as revenue.

The whole difficulty arises from the fact that all newly added labour, in so far as the value created by it is not resolved into wages, appears as profit—interpreted here as a form of surplus value in general—i. e., as a value which costs the capitalist nothing and which, of
course, therefore does not have to replace for him anything advanced,
any capital whatever. This value thus exists in the form of available
additional wealth, in short, from the viewpoint of the individual capitalist, in the form of his revenue. But this newly created value can just
as well be consumed productively as individually, equally well as capital or revenue. As a consequence of its natural form, some of it must
be productively consumed. It is, therefore, evident that the annually
added labour creates capital as well as revenue; as becomes evident in
the process of accumulation. However, the portion of labour power
employed in the creation of new capital (thus analogous to that portion of the working day employed by a savage, not for acquiring subsistence, but to fashion tools with which to acquire his subsistence)
becomes invisible in that the entire product of surplus labour first appears in the form of profit; a designation which indeed has nothing to
do with this surplus product itself, but refers merely to the individual
relation of the capitalist to the surplus value pocketed by him. In fact,
the surplus value created by the labourer is divided into revenue and
capital; i. e., into articles of consumption and additional means of
production. But former constant capital taken over from the previous

year (leaving aside the portion impaired and thus *pro tanto* destroyed, thus so far as it does not have to be reproduced—and such disturbances in the process of reproduction fall under insurance) is not reproduced as concerns value by the newly added labour.

We see, furthermore, that a portion of the newly added labour is continually absorbed in the reproduction and replacement of consumed constant capital, although this newly added labour resolves itself solely into revenue, into wages, profit and rent. But it is thereby overlooked 1) that one value portion of the product of this labour is *no* product of this new additional labour, but rather pre-existing and consumed constant capital; that the portion of the product in which this part of value appears is thus also not transformed into revenue, but replaces the means of production of this constant capital in kind; 2) that the portion of value in which this newly added labour actually appears is not consumed as revenue in kind, but replaces the constant capital in another sphere, where it is transformed into a natural form, in which it may be consumed as revenue, but which in its turn is again not entirely a product of newly added labour.

In so far as reproduction obtains on the same scale, every consumed element of constant capital must be replaced in kind by a new specimen of the same kind, if not in quantity and form, then at least in effectiveness. If the productive power of labour remains the same, then this replacement in kind implies replacing the same value which the constant capital had in its old form. But should the productive power of labour increase, so that the same material elements may be reproduced with less labour, then a smaller portion of the value of the product can completely replace the constant part in kind. The excess may then be employed to form new additional capital or a larger portion of the product may be given the form of articles of consumption, or the surplus labour may be reduced. On the other hand, should the productive power of labour decrease, then a larger portion of the product must be used for the replacement of the former capital, and the surplus product decreases.

The reconversion of profit, or generally of any form of surplus value, into capital shows—leaving aside the historically defined economic form and considering it merely as the simple formation of new means of production—that the situation still prevails whereby the labourer performs labour to produce means of production beyond the labour for acquiring his immediate means of subsistence. Transformation of profit into capital is no more than employing a portion of excess labour to form new, additional means of production. That this takes place in the shape of a transformation of profit into capital signifies merely that it is the capitalist rather than the labourer who disposes of excess labour. That this excess labour must first pass through a stage in which it appears as revenue (whereas, e. g., in the case of a savage it appears as excess labour directly destined for the production of means of production) means simply that this labour, or its product, is appropriated by the nonworker. However, what is actually transformed into capital is not profit as such. Transformation of surplus value into capital signifies merely that the surplus value and surplus product are not consumed individually as revenue by the capitalist. But, what is actually so transformed is value, objectified labour, or the product in which this value is directly manifested, or for which it is exchanged after having been previously transformed into money. And when the profit is transformed back into capital, this definite form of surplus value, or profit, does not form the source of the new capital. The surplus value is thereby merely changed from one form into another. But it is not this change of form which turns it into capital. It is the commodity and its value which now function as capital. However, that the value of the commodity is not paid for — and only by this means does it become surplus value — is quite irrelevant for the objectification of labour, the value itself.

The misunderstanding is expressed in various forms. For instance, that the commodities which compose the constant capital also contain elements of wages, profit and rent. Or, on the other hand, that what is revenue for the one is capital for another, and that therefore these are but subjective relations. Thus the yarn of the SPINNER contains a portion of value representing profit for him. Should the weaver buy the yarn, he realises the profit of the SPINNER, but for himself this yarn is merely a part of his constant capital.

Aside from the previous remarks made concerning the relations between revenue and capital, the following is to be noted: That which, as regards value, passes along with the yarn as a constituent element into the capital of the weaver, is the value of the yarn. In what manner the parts of this value have been resolved for the SPINNER himself into capital and revenue, or, in other words, into paid and unpaid labour, is completely irrelevant for the value determination of the commodity itself (aside from modifications through the average profit). Back of this still lurks the idea that the profit, or surplus value in general, is an excess above the value of the commodity, which can only be made by an extra charge, mutual cheating, or gain through selling. When the price of production is paid, or even the value of the commodity, the component values of the commodity which appear to the seller in the form of revenue are naturally also paid. Monopoly prices, of course, are not referred to here.

Secondly, it is quite correct to say that the component parts of commodities which make up the constant capital, like any other commodity value, may be reduced to portions of value which resolve themselves for the producers and the owners of the means of production into wages, profit and rent. This is merely a capitalist form of expression for the fact that all commodity value is but the measure of the socially necessary labour contained in a commodity. But it has already been shown in Book I that this nowise prevents the commodity product of any capital from being split into separate parts, of which one represents exclusively the constant portion of capital, another the variable portion of capital, and a third solely surplus value.

Storch expresses the opinion of many others when he says:

"The saleable products which make up the national revenue must be considered in political economy in two different ways: relative to individuals as values, and relative to the nation as goods; for the revenue of a nation is not appraised, like that of an individual, by its value, but by its utility or by the wants which it can satisfy." (*Consid. sur le revenu national*, p. 19.)[a]

In the first place, it is a false abstraction to regard a nation whose mode of production is based upon value, and furthermore is capitalistically organised, as an aggregate body working merely for the satisfaction of the national wants.

Secondly, after the abolition of the capitalist mode of production, but still retaining social production, the determination of value continues to prevail in the sense that the regulation of labour time and the distribution of social labour among the various production groups, ultimately the bookkeeping encompassing all this, become more essential than ever.

---

[a] The reference is to *Considérations sur la nature du revenu national*. Cited in French.

Chapter L

ILLUSIONS CREATED BY COMPETITION

It has been shown that the value of commodities, or the price of production regulated by their total value, resolves itself into:

1) A portion of value replacing constant capital, or representing past labour, which was used up in the form of means of production in making the commodity; in a word, the value, or price, which these means of production carried into the production process of the commodities. We are not referring at all here to individual commodities, but to commodity capital, that is, the form in which the product of the capital during a definite period of time, say a year, manifests itself; the individual commodity forms one element of commodity capital, which, moreover, so far as its value is concerned, resolves itself into the same analogous constituents.

2) The portion of value representing variable capital, which measures the income of the labourer and is transformed into wages for him; i. e., the labourer has reproduced these wages in this variable portion of value; in short, the portion of value which represents the paid portion of new labour added to the above constant portion in the production of the commodities.

3) Surplus value, i. e., the portion of value of the commodity product in which the unpaid labour, or surplus labour, is incorporated. This last portion of value, in its turn, assumes the independent forms which are at the same time forms of revenue: the forms of profit on capital (interest on capital as such and profit of enterprise on capital as functioning capital) and ground rent, which is claimed by the owner of the land participating in the production process. The components 2) and 3), that is, the portion of value which always assumes the revenue forms of wages (of course only after the latter have first gone through the form of variable capital), profit and rent, is distinguished from the constant component 1) by the fact that in it is embodied that entire value in which the new additional labour added to the constant part, to the means of production of the commodities, is objectified. Now, apart from the constant portion, it is correct to say that the value of a commodity, i. e., to the extent that it represents newly added labour, continually resolves itself into three parts, which constitute three forms of revenue, namely, wages, profit and rent, [55] the res-

[55] In breaking down the value added to the constant portion of capital into wages,

pective magnitudes of whose value, that is, the aliquot portions which they constitute in the total value, are determined by various specific laws developed above. But, it would be a mistake to state the converse, namely, that the value of wages, rate of profit and rate of rent form independent constituent elements of value, whose synthesis gives rise to the value of commodities, apart from the constant component; in other words, it would be a mistake to say that they are constituent components of the value of commodities, or of the price of production. [56]

The difference is easily seen.

Let us assume that the value of the product of a capital of 500 is equal to $400_c + 100_v + 150_s = 650$; let the 150_s, in turn, be divided into 75 profit + 75 rent. We will also assume, in order to forestall useless difficulties, that this is a capital of average composition, so that its price of production and its value coincide; this coincidence always takes place whenever the product of such an individual capital may be considered as the product of some portion — corresponding to its magnitude — of the total capital.

Here wages, measured by variable capital, form 20% of the advanced capital; surplus value, calculated on the total capital, forms 30%, namely 15% profit and 15% rent. The entire value component of the commodity representing the newly added labour is equal to

profit and ground rent, it goes without saying that these are portions of value. One may, indeed, conceive of them as existing in the direct product in which this value appears, i. e., in the direct product produced by labourers and capitalists in some particular sphere of production — for instance, yarn produced in the spinning industry. But in fact they do not materialise in this product any more or any less than in any other commodity, in any other component of the material wealth having the same value. And in practice wages are indeed paid in money, that is, in the pure expression of value, likewise interest and rent. For the capitalist, the transformation of his product into the pure expression of value is indeed very important; in the distribution itself this transformation is already assumed. Whether these values are reconverted into the same product, the same commodity, out of whose production they arose, whether the labourer buys back a part of the product directly produced by himself or buys the product of some other labour of a different kind, has nothing to do with the matter itself. Herr Rodbertus quite unnecessarily flies into a passion about this.[a]

[56]* "It will be sufficient to remark that the same general rule which regulates the value of raw produce and manufactured commodities is applicable also to the metals; their value depending not on the rate of profits, nor on the rate of wages, nor on the rent paid for mines, but on the total quantity of labour necessary to obtain the metal and to bring it to market."* (Ricardo, *Principles*, Ch. III, p. 77.)

───────────

[a] Cf. also criticism of Rodbertus on this question given in the *Economic Manuscripts of 1861-63* (present edition, Vol. 31, pp. 376-86).

$100_v + 150_s = 250$. Its magnitude does not depend upon its division into wages, profit and rent. We see from the relation of these parts to each other that labour power, which is paid with 100 in money, say £100, has supplied a quantity of labour represented by money to the amount of £250. We see from this that the labourer performed $1\frac{1}{2}$ times as much surplus labour as he did labour for himself. If the working day = 10 hours, then he worked 4 hours for himself and 6 hours for the capitalist. Therefore, the labour of the labourers paid with £100 is expressed in a money value of £250. Apart from this value of £250, there is nothing to divide between labourer and capitalist, between capitalist and landlord. It is the total value newly added to the value of the means of production, i. e., 400. The specific commodity value of 250 thus produced and determined by the quantity of labour objectified in it constitutes the limit, therefore, for the dividends which the labourer, capitalist and landlord will be able to draw from this value in the form of revenue — wages, profit and rent.

Let us assume that a capital of the same organic composition, that is, the same proportion between employed living labour power and constant capital set in motion, is compelled to pay £150 instead of £100 for the same labour power which sets in motion the constant capital of 400. And let us further assume that profit and rent share in the surplus value in different proportions. Since we have assumed that the variable capital of £150 sets the same quantity of labour in motion as did the variable capital of £100, the newly produced value would = 250, as before, and the value of the total product would be 650, also as before, but we would then have $400_c + 150_v + 100_s$; and these 100_s would divide, say, into 45 profit and 55 rent. The proportion in which the newly produced total value would be distributed as wages, profit and rent would now be very different; similarly, the magnitude of the advanced total capital would be different, although it only sets the same total quantity of labour in motion. Wages would amount to $27\frac{3}{11}$ %, profit — $8\frac{2}{11}$ %, and rent — 10% of the advanced capital; thus, the total surplus value would be somewhat over 18%.

As a result of the increase in wages, the unpaid portion of total labour would be different and thereby the surplus value too. If the working day contained 10 hours, the labourer would have worked 6 hours for himself and only 4 hours for the capitalist. The proportions of profit and rent would also be different; the reduced surplus value would be divided in a different proportion between the capitalist and the landlord. Finally, since the value of the constant capital would have remained the same and the value of the advanced variable capital would have risen, the reduced surplus value would express itself in a still more reduced rate of gross profit, by which we mean in this case the ratio of the total surplus value to the total advanced capital.

The change in the value of wages, in the rate of profit, and in the rate of rent, whatever the effect of the laws regulating the proportions of these parts to each other, could only move within the limits set by the newly produced commodity value of 250. An exception could only take place if rent should be based on a monopoly price. This would nowise alter the law, but merely complicate the analysis. For if we consider only the product itself in this case, then only the division of surplus value would be different. But if we consider its relative value as compared with other commodities, then we should find solely this difference — that a portion of the surplus value had been transferred from them to this particular commodity.

To recapitulate:

Value of the Product	New Value	Rate of Surplus Value	Rate of Gross Profit
First Case: $400_c + 100_v + 150_s = 650$	250	150%	30%
Second Case: $400_c + 150_v + 100_s = 650$	250	$66^2/_3\%$	$18^2/_{11}\%$

In the first place, the surplus value falls one-third of what it was, i. e., from 150 to 100. The rate of profit falls by a little more than one-third, i. e., from 30% to 18%, because the reduced surplus value must be calculated on an increased total advanced capital. But it by no means falls in the same proportion as the rate of surplus value. The latter falls from $\frac{150}{100}$ to $\frac{100}{150}$, that is, from 150% to $66\frac{2}{3}\%$, whereas the rate of profit only falls from $\frac{150}{500}$ to $\frac{100}{550}$, or from 30% to $18\frac{2}{11}\%$. The rate of profit, then, falls proportionately more than the mass of surplus value, but less than the rate of surplus value. We find, furthermore, that value, as well as mass of products, remains the same, so long as the same quantity of labour is employed, although the advanced capital has increased due to the augmentation of its variable component. This increase in advanced capital would indeed be very much felt by a capitalist undertaking a new enterprise. But considering reproduction as a whole, augmentation of the variable capital merely means that a larger portion of the value newly created by newly added labour is converted into wages, and thus, in the first place, into variable capital instead of into surplus value and surplus product. The value of the product thus remains the same, because it is limited on the one hand by the value of the constant capital = 400, and on the other by the number 250, in which the newly added labour is represented. Both, however, remain unaltered. This product would, as before, represent the same amount of use value in the same magnitude of value, to the extent that it would itself again enter into the constant capital; thus, the same mass of elements of constant capital would retain the same value. The matter would be different if wages were to rise not because the labourer received a larger share of his own labour, but if he received a larger portion of his own labour because the labour productivity had decreased. In this case, the total value in which the same labour, paid and unpaid, would be incorporated, would remain the same. But the mass of products in which this quantity of labour would be incorporated would have decreased so that the price of each aliquot portion of this product would rise, because each portion would contain more labour. The increased wages of 150 would not represent any more product than the wages of 100 did before; the reduced surplus value of 100 would represent merely $\frac{2}{3}$ of the former product, i. e., $66\frac{2}{3}$ % of the mass of use values formerly represented by 100. In this case, the constant capital would also become dearer to the extent that this product would enter into it. However, this would not be the result of the increase in wages, but rather the increase in wages would be a result of the increase in the price of commodities and a result of the diminished productivity of the same quantity of labour. It appears here as though the increase in wages had made the product dearer; however, this increase is not the cause, but rather the result, of a change in the value of the commodities, due to the decreased productivity of labour.

On the other hand, all other circumstances remaining the same, i. e., if the same quantity of employed labour is still represented by 250, then, if the value of the means of production employed should rise or fall, the value of the same quantity of products would rise or fall by the same magnitude. $450_c + 100_v + 150_s$ gives a product value = = 700; but $350_c + 100_v + 150_s$ gives a value for the same quantity of products of only 600, as against a former 650. Hence if the advanced capital, set in motion by the same quantity of labour, increases or decreases, then the value of the product rises or falls, other circumstances remaining the same, if the increase or decrease in advanced capital is due to a change in the magnitude of the value of the constant portion of capital. On the other hand, the value of the product remains unchanged if the increase or decrease in advanced capital is caused by a change in the magnitude of the value of the variable portion of capital, assuming the labour productivity remains the same. In the case of the constant capital, the increase or decrease in its value is not compensated for by any opposite movement. But in the case of the variable capital, assuming the labour productivity remains the same, an increase or decrease in its value is compensated for by the opposite movement on the part of the surplus value, so that the value of the variable capital plus the surplus value, i. e., the value newly added by labour to the means of production and newly incorporated in the product, remains the same.

But if the increase or decrease in the value of the variable capital or wages is due to a rise or fall in the price of commodities, i. e., a decrease or increase in the productive power of the labour employed by this investment of capital, then the value of the product is affected. But the rise or fall in wages in this case is not a cause, but merely an effect.

On the other hand, assuming the constant capital in the above illustration to remain $= 400_c$, if the change from $100_v + 150_s$ to $150_v + 100_s$, i. e., the increase in variable capital, should be due to a decrease in the productive power of labour, not in this particular branch of industry, say, cotton spinning, but perhaps in agriculture which provides the labourer's foodstuffs, i. e., due to a rise in the price of these foodstuffs, then the value of the product would remain unchanged. The value of 650 would still be represented by the same quantity of cotton yarn.

It follows, furthermore, from the above: If the decrease in the expenditure of constant capital is due to economies, etc., in lines of production whose products enter into the labourer's consumption, then this, just like the direct increase in the productivity of the employed labour itself, may lead to a decrease in wages due to a cheapening of the means of subsistence of the labourer, and may lead, therefore, to an increase in the surplus value; so that the rate of profit in this case would grow for two reasons, namely, on the one hand, because the value of the constant capital decreases, and on the other hand, because the surplus value increases. In our consideration of the transformation of surplus value into profit, we assumed that wages do not fall, but remain constant, because there we had to investigate the fluctuations in the rate of profit, independent of the changes in the rate of surplus value. Moreover, the laws developed there are general ones, and also apply to investments of capital whose products do not enter into the labourer's consumption, whereby changes in the value of the product, therefore, are without influence upon the wages.

———

Thus, the separation and resolution of new value annually added by new labour to the means of production, or to the constant part of capital, into the various forms of revenue, viz., wages, profit and rent, do not at all alter the limits of the value itself, the total value to be distributed among these various categories; any more than a change in the mutual relations of these individual parts can change their total, this given magnitude of value. The given number 100 always remains the same, whether it is divided into 50 + 50, or into 20 + 70 + 10, or into 40 + 30 + 30. The portion of the value of the product which is resolved into these revenues is determined just like the constant portion of the value of capital, by the value of the commodities, i. e., by the quantity of labour objectified in them in each case. Given first, then, is the quantity of value of commodities to be divided among wages, profit and rent; in other words, the absolute limit of the sum of the portions of value of these commodities. Secondly, as concerns the individual categories themselves, their average and regulating limits are likewise given. Wages form the basis in this limitation. They are regulated on the one hand by a natural law; their lower limit is determined by the physical minimum of means of subsistence required by the labourer for the conservation of his labour power and for its reproduction; i. e., by a definite quantity of commodities. The value of these commodities is determined by the labour time required for their reproduction; and thus by the portion of new labour added to the means of production, or by the portion of each working day required by the labourer for the production and reproduction of an equivalent for the value of these necessary means of subsistence. For instance, if his average daily means of subsistence have a value = 6 hours of average labour, then he must work on an average six hours per day for himself. The actual value of his labour power deviates from this physical minimum; it differs according to climate and level of social development; it depends not merely upon the physical, but also upon the historically developed social needs, which become second nature. But in every country, at a given time, this regulating average wage is a given magnitude. The value of all other revenue thus has its limit. It is always equal to the value in which the total working day (which coincides in the present case with the average working day, since it comprises the total quantity of labour set in motion by the total social capital) is incorporated minus the portion of the working day incorporated in wages. Its limit is therefore determined by the limit of the value in which the unpaid labour is expressed, that is, by the quantity of this unpaid labour. While the portion of the working day which is required by the labourer for the reproduction of the value of his wages finds its ultimate limit in the physical minimum of wages, the other portion of the working day, in which surplus labour is incorporated, and thus the portion of value representing surplus value, finds its limit in the physical maximum of the working day, i. e., in the total quantity of daily labour time during which the labourer can, in general, be active and still preserve and reproduce his labour power. Since we are here concerned with the distribution of the value which represents the total labour newly added per year, the working day may be regarded here as a constant magnitude, and is assumed as such, no matter how much or how little it may deviate from its physical maximum. The absolute limit of the portion of value which forms surplus value, and which resolves itself into profit and ground rent, is thus given. It is determined by the excess of the unpaid portion of the working day over its paid portion, i. e., by the portion of the value of the total product in which this surplus labour exists. If we call the surplus value thus limited and calculated on the advanced total capital — the profit, as I have done, then this profit, so far as its absolute magnitude is concerned, is equal to the surplus value and, therefore, its limits are just as much determined by law as the latter. On the other hand, the level of the rate of profit is likewise a magnitude held within certain specific limits determined by the value of commodities. It is the ratio of the total surplus value to the total social capital advanced in production. If this capital = 500 (say millions) and the surplus value = 100, then 20% constitutes the absolute limit of the rate of profit. The distribution of the social profit according to this rate among the capitals invested in the various spheres of production creates prices of production which deviate from the values of commodities and which are the real regulating average market prices. But this deviation abolishes neither the determination of prices by values nor the regular limits of profit. Instead of the value of a commodity being equal to the capital consumed in its production plus the surplus value contained in it, its price of production is now equal to the capital, c, consumed in its production plus the surplus value falling to its share as a result of the general rate of profit, for instance 20% on the capital advanced in its production, counting both the consumed and the merely employed capital. But this additional amount of 20% is itself determined by the surplus value created by the total social capital and its relation to the value of this capital; and for this reason it is 20% and not 10 or 100. The transformation of values into prices of production, then, does not remove the limits on profit, but merely alters its distribution among the various particular capitals which make up the social capital, i. e., it distributes it uniformly among them in the proportion in which they form parts of the value of this total capital. The market prices rise above and fall below these regulating prices of production, but these fluctuations mutually balance each other. If one examines price lists over a more or less long period of time, and if one disregards those cases in which the actual value of commodities is altered by a change in the productivity of labour, and likewise those cases in which the process of production has been disturbed by natural or social accidents, one will be surprised, in the first place, by the relatively narrow limits of the deviations, and, secondly, by the regularity of their mutual compensation. The same domination of the regulating averages will be found here that Quetelet pointed out in the case of social phenomena. If the equalisation of the values of commodities into prices of production does not meet any obstacles, then the rent resolves itself into differential rent, i. e., it is limited to the equalisation of the surplus profits which would be given to some capitalists by the regulating prices of production and which are now appropriated by the landlord. Here, then, rent has its definite limit of value in the deviations of the individual rates of profit, which are caused by the regulation of prices of production by the general rate of profit. If landed property obstructs equalisation of the values of commodities into prices of production, and appropriates absolute rent, then the latter is limited by the excess of the value of the agricultural products over their price of production, i. e., by the excess of the surplus value contained in them over the rate of profit assigned to the capitals by the general rate of profit. This difference, then, forms the limit of the rent, which, as before, is but a definite portion of the given surplus value contained in the commodities.

Finally, if equalisation of surplus value into average profit meets with obstacles in the various spheres of production in the form of artificial or natural monopolies, and particularly monopoly in landed property, so that a monopoly price becomes possible, which rises above the price of production and above the value of the commodities affected by such a monopoly, then the limits imposed by the value of the commodities would not thereby be removed. The monopoly price of certain commodities would merely transfer a portion of the profit of the other commodity producers to the commodities having the monopoly price. A local disturbance in the distribution of the surplus value among the various spheres of production would indirectly take place, but it would leave the limit of this surplus value itself unaltered. Should the commodity having the monopoly price enter into the necessary consumption of the labourer, it would increase the wage and thereby reduce the surplus value, assuming the labourer receives the value of his labour power as before. It could depress wages below the value of labour power, but only to the extent that the former exceed the limit of their physical minimum. In this case the monopoly price would be paid by a deduction from real wages (i. e., the quantity of use values received by the labourer for the same quantity of labour) and from the profit of the other capitalists. The limits within which the monopoly price would affect the normal regulation of the prices of commodities would be firmly fixed and accurately calculable.

Thus just as the division of the newly added value of commodities, and, in general, value resolvable into revenue, finds its given and regulating limits in the relation between necessary and surplus labour, wages and surplus value, so does the division of surplus value itself into profit and ground rent find its limits in the laws regulating the equalisation of the rate of profit. As regards the division into interest and profit of enterprise, the average profit itself forms the limit for both taken together. It furnishes the given magnitude of value which they may split among themselves and which alone can be so divided. The specific ratio of this division is here fortuitous, i. e., it is determined exclusively by conditions of competition. Whereas in other cases the balancing of supply and demand is equivalent to elimination of the deviations in market prices from their regulating average prices, i. e., elimination of the influence of competition, it is here the only determinant. But why? Because the same production factor, capital, has to divide its share of the surplus value between two owners of the same production factor. But the fact that there is no definite, regular limit here for the division of the average profit does not remove its limit as part of commodity value; just as the fact that two partners in

a certain business divide their profit unequally due to different external circumstances does not affect the limits of this profit in any way.

Hence, although the portion of the commodity value in which the
new labour added to the value of the means of production is incorporated is divided into various parts, which in the form of revenue
assume mutually independent forms, this is no reason for now considering wages, profit and ground rent as the constituent elements
which, in combination or taken all together, are the source of the
regulating price (NATURAL PRICE, *prix necessaire*) of the commodities
themselves; so that it is not the commodity value, after deducting the
constant portion of value, which would be the original unit that divides into these three parts, but rather, conversely, the price of each of
these three parts would be independently determined, and the price
of the commodities would then be formed by adding these three independent magnitudes together. In reality, the commodity value is the
magnitude which precedes the sum of the total values of wages, profit
and rent, regardless of the relative magnitudes of the latter. In the
above erroneous conception, wages, profit and rent are three independent magnitudes of value, whose total magnitude produces, limits
and determines the magnitude of the commodity value.

In the first place it is evident that if wages, profit and rent were
to form the price of commodities, this would apply as much to the
constant portion of the commodity value as to the other portion, in
which variable capital and surplus value are incorporated. Thus, this
constant portion may here be left entirely out of consideration, since
the value of the commodities of which it is composed would likewise
resolve itself into the sum of the values of wages, profit and rent. As
already noted, this conception, then, denies the very existence of such
a constant portion of value.

It is furthermore evident that value loses all meaning here. Only
the conception of price still remains, in the sense that a certain
amount of money is paid to the owner of labour power, capital and
land. But what is money? Money is not a thing, but a definite form of
value, hence, value is again presupposed. Let us say, then, that a definite amount of gold or silver is paid for these elements of production,
or that it is mentally equated to them. But gold and silver (and the
enlightened economist is proud of this discovery) are themselves commodities like all other commodities. The price of gold and silver is
therefore likewise determined by wages, profit and rent. Hence we
cannot determine wages, profit and rent by equating them to a cer-

tain amount of gold and silver, for the value of this gold and silver, by means of which they should be evaluated as in their equivalent, should be first determined precisely by them, independently of gold and silver, i. e., independently of the value of any commodity, which value is precisely the product of the above three factors. Thus, to say that the value of wages, profit and rent consists in their being equivalent to a certain quantity of gold and silver, would merely be saying that they are equal to a certain quantity of wages, profit and rent.

Take wages first. For it is necessary to make labour the point of departure, even in this view of the matter. How, then, is the regulating price of wages determined, the price about which its market prices oscillate?

Let us say that it is determined by the supply and demand of labour power. But what sort of labour power demand is this? It is a demand made by capital. The demand for labour is therefore tantamount to the supply of capital. In order to speak of a supply of capital, we should know above all what capital is. Of what does capital consist? If we take its simplest aspect, it consists of money and commodities. But money is merely a commodity form. Capital, then, consists of commodities. But the value of commodities, according to our assumption, is determined, in the first instance, by the price of the labour producing the commodities, by wages. Wages are here presupposed and are treated as a constituent element of the price of commodities. This price then should be determined by the ratio of available labour to capital. The price of the capital itself is equal to the price of the commodities of which it is composed. The demand by capital for labour is equal to the supply of capital. And the supply of capital is equal to the supply of a quantity of commodities of given price, and this price is regulated in the first place by the price of labour, and the price of labour in turn is equal to that portion of the commodity price constituting the variable capital, which is granted to the labourer in exchange for his labour; and the price of the commodities constituting this variable capital is again determined, in turn, primarily by the price of labour; for it is determined by the prices of wages, profit and rent. In order to determine wages, we cannot, therefore, presuppose capital, for the value of the capital is itself determined in part by wages.

Moreover, dragging competition into this problem does not help at all. Competition makes the market prices of labour rise or fall. But suppose supply and demand of labour are balanced. How are wages then determined? By competition. But we have just assumed that competition ceases to act as a determinant, that its influence is cancelled due to equilibrium between its two mutually opposing forces. Indeed, it is precisely the natural price of wages that we wish to find, i. e., the price of labour that is not regulated by competition, but which, on the contrary, regulates the latter.

Nothing remains but to determine the necessary price of labour by the necessary means of subsistence of the labourer. But these means of subsistence are commodities, which have a price. The price of labour is therefore determined by the price of the necessary means of subsistence and the price of the means of subsistence, like that of all other commodities, is determined primarily by the price of labour. Therefore, the price of labour determined by the price of the means of subsistence is determined by the price of labour. The price of labour is determined by itself. In other words, we do not know how the price of labour is determined. Labour in this case has a price in general, because it is considered as a commodity. In order, therefore, to speak of the price of labour, we must know what price in general is. But we do not learn at all in this way what price in general is.

Nevertheless, let us assume that the necessary price of labour is determined in this agreeable manner. Then how is the average profit determined, the profit of every capital under normal conditions, which constitutes the second element in the price of commodities? The average profit must be determined by an average rate of profit; how is this rate determined? By competition among the capitalists? But the competition already presupposes the existence of profit. It presupposes various rates of profit, and thus various profits — either in the same or in different branches of production. Competition can influence the rate of profit only to the extent that it affects the prices of commodities. Competition can only make the producers within the same sphere of production sell their commodities at the same prices, and make them sell their commodities in different spheres of production at prices which will give them the same profit, the same proportional addition to the price of commodities which has already been partially determined by wages. Hence competition can only equalise inequalities in the rate of profit. In order to equalise unequal rates of profit, profit must exist as an element in the price of commodities. Competition does not create it. It lowers or raises its level, but does not create the level which is established when equalisation has been achieved. And when we speak of a necessary rate of profit, what we wish to know is precisely the rate of profit independent of the movements of competition, which in turn regulates competition itself. The average rate of profit sets in when there is an equilibrium of forces among the competing capitalists. Competition may establish this equilibrium but not the rate of profit which makes its appearance with this equilibrium.When this equilibrium is established, why is the general rate of profit now 10, or 20, or 100%? Because of competition? No, on the contrary, competition has eliminated the causes producing deviations from 10, 20, or 100%. It has brought about a commodity price whereby every capital yields the same profit in proportion to its magnitude. The magnitude of this profit itself, however, is independent of competition. The latter merely reduces, again and again, all deviations to this magnitude. One person competes with another, and competition compels him to sell his commodities at the same price as the other. But why is this price 10 or 20 or 100?

Thus, nothing remains but to declare rate of profit, and therefore profit, to be in some unaccountable manner a definite extra charge added to the price of commodities, which up to this point was determined by wages. The only thing that competition tells us is that this rate of profit must be a given magnitude. But we knew this before —when we dealt with general rate of profit and "necessary price" of profit.

It is quite unnecessary to wade through this absurd process anew in the case of ground rent. One can see without doing this that, when carried out more or less consistently, it makes profit and rent merely appear as definite extra charges added by unaccountable laws to the price of commodities, a price primarily determined by wages. In short, competition has to shoulder the responsibility of explaining all the meaningless ideas of the economists, whereas it should rather be the economists who explain competition.

Now, disregarding here the illusion of a profit and rent being created by circulation, i. e., price components arising through sale — and circulation can never give what it did not first receive — the matter simply amounts to this:

Let the price of a commodity determined by wages = 100; let the rate of profit be 10% of wages, and the rent 15% of wages. Then the price of the commodity determined by the sum of wages, profit and rent = 125. This additional 25 cannot arise from the sale of the commodity. For all who sell one another commodities sell at 125 that which costs 100 in wages; which is the same as if they had all sold at

100. Thus, the operation must be considered independently of the circulation process.

If the three share the commodity itself, which now costs 125 — and it does not alter matters any if the capitalist first sells at 125, and then pays 100 to the labourer, 10 to himself, and 15 to the landlord — the labourer receives $\frac{4}{5}$ = 100 of the value and of the product. The capitalist receives $\frac{2}{25}$ of the value and of the product, and the landlord $\frac{3}{25}$. Since the capitalist sells at 125 instead of 100, he gives the labourer only $\frac{4}{5}$ of the product incorporating the latter's labour. Thus, it would be just the same as if he had given 80 to the labourer and retained 20 — of which 8 would fall to his share and 12 to the landlord. In this case he would have sold the commodity at its value, since in fact the additions to the price represent increases that are independent of the value of the commodity, which under the assumption made above is determined by the value of wages. This, in a roundabout way, amounts to saying that according to this conception the term "wages," here 100, means the value of the product, i. e., the sum of money in which this definite quantity of labour is represented; but that this value in turn differs from the real wage and therefore leaves a surplus. But here the surplus is realised by a nominal addition to the price. Hence, if wages were equal to 110 instead of 100, the profit would have to be = 11 and the ground rent = $16\frac{1}{2}$, so that the price of the commodity would = $137\frac{1}{2}$. This would leave the proportions unaltered. But since the division would always be obtained by way of a nominal addition of definite percentages to wages, the price would rise and fall with the wages. Wages are here first set equal to the value of the commodity, and then divorced from it again. In fact, however, this amounts to saying in a roundabout and irrational way that the value of the commodity is determined by the quantity of labour contained in it, whereas the value of wages is determined by the price of the necessary means of subsistence, and the excess of value above the wages forms profit and rent.

The splitting of the value of commodities after subtracting the value of the means of production consumed in their creation; the splitting of this given quantity of value, determined by the quantity of labour objectified in the produced commodities, into three component parts, which assume, as wages, profit and rent, independent and mutually unrelated forms of revenue — this splitting appears in a perverted form on the surface of capitalist production, and consequently in the minds of those captivated by the latter.

Let the total value of a certain commodity = 300, of which 200 is the value of the means of production, or elements of constant capital, consumed in its production. This leaves 100 as the amount of new value added to the commodity during its process of production. This new value of 100 is all that is available for division among the three forms of revenue. If we let wages = x, profit = y and ground rent = z, then the sum of x + y + z will always = 100 in our case. But to the industrialists, merchants and bankers, and to the vulgar economists, this appears quite different. For them, the value of the commodity, after subtracting the value of the means of production consumed by it, is not given = 100, this 100 then being divided into x, y and z. But rather, the price of the commodity simply consists of the value of wages, the value of profit and the value of rent, which magnitudes are determined independently of the value of the commodity and of each other, so that x, y and z are each given and determined independently, and only from the sum of these magnitudes, which may be smaller or larger than 100, is the magnitude of the value of the commodity itself obtained by adding these component values together. This *quid pro quo* is inevitable because:

First: The component parts of the value of a commodity appear as independent revenues in relation to one another, and as such are related to three very dissimilar production factors, namely labour, capital and land, and therefore they seem to arise from the latter. Ownership of labour power, capital and land is the cause for these various component values of commodities falling to the share of the respective owners, and thus transforming themselves into revenue for them. But the value does not arise from a transformation into revenue; it must rather exist before it can be converted into revenue, before it can assume this form. The illusion that the opposite is true is strengthened all the more as the determination of the relative magnitudes of these three components in relation to one another follows different laws, whose connection with, and limitation by, the value of the commodities themselves nowise appear on the surface.

Secondly: We have seen[a] that a general rise or fall in wages, by causing a movement of the general rate of profit in the opposite direction — other circumstances remaining the same — changes the prices of production of the various commodities, i. e., raises some and lowers

---

[a] See this volume, pp. 198-202.

others, depending on the average composition of capital in the respective spheres of production. Thus, experience shows here that in some spheres of production, at any rate, the average price of a commodity rises because wages have risen, and falls because wages have fallen. But "experience" does not show that the value of commodities, which is independent of wages, secretly regulates these changes. However, if the rise in wages is local, if it only takes place in particular spheres of production as a result of special circumstances, then a corresponding nominal rise in the prices of these commodities may occur. This rise in the relative value of one kind of commodity in relation to the others, for which wages have remained unchanged, is then merely a reaction against the local disturbance in the uniform distribution of surplus value among the various spheres of production, a means of equalising the particular rates of profit into the general rate. "Experience" shows in this case that wages again determine the price. Thus, in both of these cases experience shows that wages determine the prices of commodities. But "experience" does not show the hidden cause of this interrelation. Furthermore: The average price of labour, i. e., the value of labour power, is determined by the production price of the necessary means of subsistence. If the latter rises or falls, the former rises or falls accordingly. Thus, experience again shows the existence or a connection between wages and the price of commodities. But the cause may appear as an effect, and the effect as a cause, which is also the case in the movements of market prices, where a rise of wages above their average corresponds to the rise of market prices above the prices of production during periods of prosperity, and the subsequent fall of wages below their average corresponds to a fall of market prices below the prices of production. To the dependence of prices of production upon the values of commodities *prima facie* there would always have to correspond, apart from the oscillatory movements of market prices, the experience that whenever wages rise the rate of profit falls, and vice versa. But we have seen[a] that the rate of profit may be determined by movements in the value of constant capital, independently of the movements of wages; so that wages and rate of profit, instead of moving in opposite directions, may move in the same direction, may rise or fall together. If the rate of surplus value were to directly coincide with the rate of profit, this

---

[a] See this volume, pp. 106-23.

would not be possible. Similarly if wages should rise as a result of a
rise in the prices of the means of subsistence, the rate of profit may remain the same, or even rise, due to greater intensity of labour or prolongation of the working day. All these experiences bear out the illusion created by the independent and distorted form of the component
values, namely, that either wages alone, or wages and profit together,
determine the value of commodities. Once such an illusion appears
with respect to wages, once the price of labour and the value created
by labour seem to coincide, the same automatically applies to profit
and rent. Their prices, i. e., their money expression, must then be
regulated independently of labour and of the value created by the
latter.

Thirdly: Let us assume that according to direct experience the values of a commodity, or the prices of production — which merely
appear to be independent of the values — always coincide with the
market prices of the commodity rather than merely prevailing as the
regulating average prices by constant compensation of the continual
fluctuations in market price. Let us assume, furthermore, that reproduction always takes place under the same unaltered conditions, i. e.,
labour productivity remains constant in all elements of capital. Finally, let us assume that the component value of the commodity product,
which is formed in every sphere of production by the addition of
a new quantity of labour — i. e., a newly produced value — to the value of the means of production, always splits into constant proportions of wages, profit and rent, so that the wage actually paid always
directly coincides with the value of labour power, the profit actually
realised — with the portion of the total surplus value which falls to
the share of every independently functioning part of the total capital
by virtue of the average rate of profit, and the actual rent is always
limited by the bounds within which ground rent on this basis is normally confined. In a word, let us assume that the division of the socially produced values and the regulation of the prices of production
takes place on a capitalist basis, but that competition is eliminated.

Thus, under these assumptions, namely, if the value of commodities were constant and appeared so, if the component value of the commodity product which resolves itself into revenues were to remain
a constant magnitude and always appeared as such, and finally, if
this given and constant component value always split into constant
proportions of wages, profit and rent — even under these assumptions, the real movement would necessarily appear in a distorted

form; not as the splitting of a previously given magnitude of value into three parts which assume mutually independent forms of revenue, but, on the contrary, as the formation of this magnitude of value from the sum of the independent and separately determined, each by itself, constituent elements — wages, profit and ground rent. This illusion would necessarily arise, because in the actual movement of individual capitals, and the commodities produced by them, not the value of commodities would appear to be a precondition of its splitting but, conversely, the components into which it is split function as a precondition of the value of the commodities. In the first place, we have seen that to every capitalist the cost price of his commodities appears as a given magnitude and continually appears as such in the actual price of production. The cost price, however, is equal to the value of the constant capital, the advanced means of production, plus the value of labour power, which, however, appears to the agent of production in the irrational form of the price of labour, so that wages simultaneously appear as revenue of the labourer. The average price of labour is a given magnitude, because the value of labour power, like that of any other commodity, is determined by the necessary labour time required for its reproduction. But as concerns that portion of the value of commodities which is embodied in wages, it does not arise from the fact that it assumes this form of wages, that the capitalist advances to the labourer his share of his own product in the form of wages, but from the fact that the labourer produces an equivalent for his wages, i. e., that a portion of his daily or annual labour produces the value contained in the price of his labour power. But wages are stipulated by contract, before their corresponding value equivalent has been produced. As an element of price, whose magnitude is given before the commodity and its value have been produced, as a constituent part of the cost price, wages thereby do not appear as a portion which detaches itself in independent form from the total value of the commodity, but rather, conversely, as a given magnitude, which predetermines this value, i. e., as a creator of price and value. A role similar to that of wages in the cost price of commodities is played by the average profit in their price of production, for the price of production is equal to cost price plus average profit on the advanced capital. This average profit figures practically, in the mind and calculation of the capitalist himself, as a regulating element, not merely in so far as it determines the transfer of capitals from one sphere of investment into another, but also in all sales and contracts which embrace a process of reproduction extending over long periods. But so far as it figures in this manner, it is a pre-existent magnitude, which is in fact independent of the value and surplus value produced in any particular sphere of production, and thus even more so in the case of any individual investment of capital in any sphere of production. Rather than appearing as a result of a splitting of value, it manifests itself much more as a magnitude independent of the value of the produced commodities, as pre-existing in the process of production of commodities and itself determining the average price of the commodities, i. e., as a creator of value. Indeed, the surplus value, owing to the separation of its various portions into mutually, completely unrelated forms, appears in still more concrete form as a prerequisite for creating commodity value. A part of the average profit in the form of interest confronts the functioning capitalist independently as an assumed element in the production of commodities and of their value. No matter how much the magnitude of the interest fluctuates, at each moment and for every capitalist it is a given magnitude entering into the cost price of the commodities produced by him as individual capitalist. The same role is played by ground rent in the form of lease money fixed by contract for the agricultural capitalist, and in the form of rent for business premises in the case of other entrepreneurs. These portions into which surplus value is split, being given as elements of cost price for the individual capitalist, appear conversely therefore as creators of surplus value; creators of a portion of the price of commodities, just as wages create the other. The secret wherefore these products of the splitting of commodity value constantly appear as prerequisites for the formation of value itself is simply this, that the capitalist mode of production, like any other, does not merely constantly reproduce the material product, but also the social and economic relations, the characteristic economic forms of its creation. Its result, therefore, appears just as constantly presupposed by it, as its presuppositions appear as its results. And it is this continual reproduction of the same relations which the individual capitalist anticipates as self-evident, as an indubitable fact. So long as the capitalist mode of production persists as such, a portion of the newly added labour continually resolves itself into wages, another into profit (interest and profit of enterprise), and a third into rent. In contracts between the owners of various agencies of production this is always assumed, and this assumption is correct, however much the relative proportions may fluctuate in individual cases. The definite form in which the parts of value confront each other is presupposed because it is continually reproduced and it is continually reproduced because it is continually presupposed.

To be sure, experience and appearance now also demonstrate that market prices, in whose influence the capitalist actually sees the only determination of value, are by no means dependent upon such anticipation, so far as their magnitude is concerned; that they do not correspond to whether the interest or rent were set high or low. But the market prices are constant only in their variation, and their average over longer periods results precisely in the respective averages of wages, profit and rent as the constant magnitudes, and therefore, in the last analysis, those dominating the market prices.

On the other hand, it seems plain on reflection that if wages, profit and rent are creators of value since they seem to be presupposed in the production of value, and are assumed by the individual capitalist in his cost price and price of production, then the constant portion, whose value enters as given into the production of every commodity, is also a creator of value. But the constant portion of capital is no more than a sum of commodities and, therefore, of commodity values. Thus we should arrive at the absurd tautology that commodity value is the creator and cause of commodity value.

However, if the capitalist were at all interested in reflecting about this — and his reflections as capitalist are dictated exclusively by his interests and self-interested motives — experience would show him that the product which he himself produces enters into other spheres of production as a constant portion of capital, and that products of these other production spheres enter into his own product as constant portions of capital. Since the additional value, so far as his new production is concerned, seems to be formed, from his point of view, by the magnitudes of wages, profit and rent, then this also holds good for the constant portion consisting of the products of other capitalists. And thus, the price of the constant portion of capital, and thereby the total value of the commodities, reduces itself in the final analysis, although in a manner which is somewhat unaccountable, to a sum of values resulting from the addition of independent creators of value — wages, profit and rent — which are regulated according to different laws and arise from different sources.

Fourthly: Whether the commodities are sold at their values or not, and hence the determination of value itself, is quite immaterial for the individual capitalist. It is, from the very outset, a process that takes place behind his back and is controlled by the force of circumstances independent of himself, because it is not the values, but the divergent prices of production, which form the regulating average prices in every sphere of production. The determination of value as such interests and has a determining effect on the individual capitalist and the capital in each particular sphere of production only in so far as the reduced or increased quantity of labour required to produce commodities, as a consequence of a rise or fall in productive power of labour, enables him in one instance to make an extra profit, at the prevailing market prices, and compels him in another to raise the price of his commodities, because more wages, more constant capital, and thus more interest, fall upon each portion of the product, or individual commodity. It interests him only in so far as it raises or lowers the cost of production of commodities for himself, thus only in so far as it makes his position exceptional.

On the other hand, wages, interest and rent appear to him as regulating limits not only of the price at which he can realise the profit of enterprise, the portion of profit falling to his share as functioning capitalist, but also at which he must generally be able to sell his commodities, if continued reproduction is to take place. It is quite immaterial to him whether or not he realises, through sale, the value and surplus value incorporated in his commodities, provided only that he makes the customary, or larger, profit of enterprise at given prices, over and above his individual cost price determined by wages, interest and rent. Apart from the constant portion of capital — wages, interest and rent appear to him, therefore, as the limiting and thereby productive determining elements of the commodity price. Should he succeed, e. g., in depressing wages below the value of labour power, i. e., below its normal level, in obtaining capital at a lower interest rate, and in paying less lease money than the normal amount for rent, then it is completely irrelevant to him whether he sells his product below its value, or even below the general price of production, thereby giving away gratis a portion of the surplus labour contained in the commodities. This also applies to the constant portion of capital. If an industrialist, e. g., can buy his raw material below its price of production, then this buffers him against loss, even should he sell it in the finished product under its price of production. His profit of enterprise may remain the same, or even increase, if only the excess of the commodity price over its elements, which must be paid, replaced by an equivalent, remains the same or increases. But aside from the value of the means of production which enter into the production of his commodities as a given price magnitude, it is precisely wages, interest and rent which enter into this production as limiting and regulating price magnitudes. Consequently they appear to him as the elements determining the price of the commodities. Profit of enterprise, from this standpoint, seems to be either determined by the excess of market prices, dependent upon accidental conditions of competition, over the immanent value of commodities determined by the above-mentioned elements of price; or, to the extent that this profit itself exerts a determining influence upon market prices, it seems itself, in turn, dependent upon the competition between buyers and sellers.

In the competition of individual capitalists among themselves as well as in the competition on the world market, it is the given and assumed magnitudes of wages, interest and rent which enter into the calculation as constant and regulating magnitudes; constant not in the sense of being unalterable magnitudes, but in the sense that they are given in each individual case and constitute the constant limit for the continually fluctuating market prices. For instance, in competition on the world market it is solely a question of whether commodities can be sold advantageously with existing wages, interest and rent at, or below, existing general market prices, i. e., realising a corresponding profit of enterprise. If wages and the price of land are low in one country, while interest on capital is high, because the capitalist mode of production has not been developed generally, whereas in another country wages and the price of land are nominally high, while interest on capital is low, then the capitalist employs more labour and land in the one country, and in the other relatively more capital. These factors enter into calculation as determining elements in so far as competition between these two capitalists is possible. Here, then, experience shows theoretically, and the self-interested calculation of the capitalist shows practically, that the prices of commodities are determined by wages, interest and rent, by the price of labour, capital and land, and that these elements of price are indeed the regulating constituent factors of price.

Of course, there always remains an element here which is not assumed, but which results from the market price of commodities, namely, the excess above the cost price formed by the addition of the aforementioned elements: wages, interest and rent. This fourth element seems to be determined by competition in each individual case, and in the average case by the average profit, which in its turn is regulated by this same competition, only over longer periods.

Fifthly: On the basis of the capitalist mode of production, it becomes so much a matter of course to split up the value, in which newly added labour is represented, into the forms of revenue, of wages, profit and ground rent, that this method is applied (leaving aside earlier stages of history, from which we gave illustrations in our study of ground rent) even where the preconditions for these forms of revenue are missing. That is, all is subsumed by analogy under these forms of revenue.

When an independent labourer — let us take a small farmer, since all three forms of revenue may here be applied — works for himself and sells his own product, he is first considered as his own employer (capitalist), who makes use of himself as a labourer, and second as his own landlord, who makes use of himself as his own tenant. To himself as wage worker he pays wages, to himself as capitalist he gives the profit, and to himself as landlord he pays rent. Assuming the capitalist mode of production and the relations corresponding to it to be the general basis of society, this subsumption is correct, in so far as it is not thanks to his labour, but to his ownership of means of production — which have assumed here the general form of capital — that he is in a position to appropriate his own surplus labour. And furthermore, to the extent that he produces his product as commodities, and thus depends upon its price (and even if not, this price is calculable), the quantity of surplus labour which he can realise depends not on its own magnitude, but on the general rate of profit; and likewise any eventual excess above the amount of surplus value determined by the general rate of profit is, in turn, not determined by the quantity of labour performed by him, but can be appropriated by him only because he is owner of the land. Since such a form of production not corresponding to the capitalist mode of production may thus be subsumed under its forms of revenue — and to a certain extent not incorrectly — the illusion is all the more strengthened that capitalist relations are the natural relations of every mode of production.

Of course, if wages are reduced to their general basis, namely, to that portion of the product of the producer's own labour which passes over into the individual consumption of the labourer; if we relieve this portion of its capitalist limitations and extend it to that volume of consumption which is permitted, on the one hand, by the existing productivity of society (that is, the social productivity of his own individual labour as actually social), and which, on the other hand, the full development of the individuality requires; if, furthermore, we reduce the surplus labour and surplus product to that measure which is required under prevailing conditions of production of society, on the one side to create an insurance and reserve fund, and on the other to constantly expand reproduction to the extent dictated by social needs; finally, if we include in No. 1 the necessary labour, and in No. 2 the surplus labour, the quantity of labour which must always be performed by the able-bodied in behalf of the immature or incapacitated members of society, i. e., if we strip both wages and surplus value, both necessary and surplus labour, of their specifically capitalist character, then certainly there remain not these forms, but merely their rudiments, which are common to all social modes of production.

Moreover, this method of subsumption was also characteristic of previous dominant modes of production, e. g., feudalism. Production relations which nowise corresponded to it, standing entirely beyond it, were subsumed under feudal relations, e. g., in England, the TENURES IN COMMON SOCAGE (as distinct from TENURES ON KNIGHT'S SERVICE), which comprised merely monetary obligations and were feudal in name only.

Chapter LI

DISTRIBUTION RELATIONS
AND PRODUCTION RELATIONS

The new value added by the annual newly added labour — and thus also that portion of the annual product in which this value is represented and which may be drawn out of the total output and separated from it — is thus split into three parts, which assume three different forms of revenue, into forms which express one portion of this value as belonging or falling to the share of the owner of labour power, another portion to the owner of capital, and a third portion to the owner of landed property. These, then, are relations, or forms of distribution, for they express the relations under which the newly produced total value is distributed among the owners of the various production agents.

From the common viewpoint these distribution relations appear as natural relations, as relations arising directly from the nature of all social production, from the laws of human production in general. It cannot, indeed, be denied that precapitalist societies disclose other modes of distribution, but the latter are interpreted as undeveloped, unperfected and disguised, not reduced to their purest expression and their highest form and differently shaded modes of the natural distribution relations.

The only correct aspect of this conception is: Assuming some form of social production to exist (e. g., primitive Indian communities, or the more ingeniously developed communism of the Peruvians), a distinction can always be made between that portion of labour whose product is directly consumed individually by the producers and their families and — aside from the part which is productively consumed — that portion of labour which is invariably surplus labour, whose product serves constantly to satisfy the general social needs, no matter how this surplus product may be divided, and no matter who may function as representative of these social needs. Thus, the identity of the various modes of distribution amounts merely to this: they are identical if we abstract from their differences and specific forms and keep in mind only their unity as distinct from their dissimilarity.

A more advanced, more critical mind, however, admits the historically developed character of distribution relations, [56 a)] but nevertheless clings all the more tenaciously to the unchanging character of production relations themselves, arising from human nature and thus independent of all historical development.

On the other hand, scientific analysis of the capitalist mode of production demonstrates the contrary, that it is a mode of production of a special kind, with specific historical features; that, like any other specific mode of production, it presupposes a given level of the social productive forces and their forms of development as its historical precondition: a precondition which is itself the historical result and product of a preceding process, and from which the new mode of production proceeds as its given basis; that the production relations corresponding to this specific, historically determined mode of production — relations which human beings enter into during the process of social life, in the creation of their social life — possess a specific, historical and transitory character; and, finally, that the distribution relations essentially coincident with these production relations are their opposite side, so that both share the same historically transitory character.

[56 a)] J. Stuart Mill, *Some Unsettled Questions in Political Economy*, London, 1844.[a]

---

[a] The reference is to *Essays on Some Unsettled Questions of Political Economy*, Essay II, pp. 47-74.

In the study of distribution relations, the initial point of departure is the alleged fact that the annual product is apportioned among wages, profit and rent. But if so expressed, it is a misstatement. The product is apportioned on one side to capital, on the other to revenue. One of these revenues, wages, itself constantly assumes only the form of revenue, revenue of the labourer, after it has first confronted this labourer in the *form of capital*. The confrontation of produced conditions of labour and of the products of labour generally, as capital, with the direct producers implies from the outset a definite social character of the material conditions of labour in relation to the labourers, and thereby a definite relationship into which they enter with the owners of the conditions of production and among themselves during production itself. The transformation of these conditions of labour into capital implies in turn the expropriation of the direct producers from the land, and thus a definite form of landed property.

If one portion of the product were not transformed into capital, the other would not assume the forms of wages, profit and rent.

On the other hand, if the capitalist mode of production presupposes this definite social form of the conditions of production, so does it reproduce it continually. It produces not merely the material products, but reproduces continually the production relations in which the former are produced, and thereby also the corresponding distribution relations.

It may be said, of course, that capital itself (and landed property which it includes as its antithesis) already presupposes a distribution: the expropriation of the labourer from the conditions of labour, the concentration of these conditions in the hands of a minority of individuals, the exclusive ownership of land by other individuals, in short, all the relations which have been described in the part dealing with primitive accumulation (Buch I, Kap. XXIV). But this distribution differs altogether from what is understood by distribution relations when the latter are endowed with a historical character in contradistinction to production relations. What is meant thereby are the various titles to that portion of the product which goes into individual consumption. The aforementioned distribution relations, on the contrary, are the basis of special social functions performed within the production relations by certain of their agents, as opposed to the direct producers. They imbue the conditions of production themselves and their representatives with a specific social quality.

They determine the entire character and the entire movement of production.

Capitalist production is distinguished from the outset by two characteristic features.

First. It produces its products as commodities. The fact that it produces commodities does not differentiate it from other modes of production; but rather the fact that being a commodity is the dominant and determining characteristic of its products. This implies, first and foremost, that the labourer himself comes forward merely as a seller of commodities, and thus as a free wage labourer, so that labour appears in general as wage labour. In view of what has already been said, it is superfluous to demonstrate anew that the relation between capital and wage labour determines the entire character of the mode of production. The principal agents of this mode of production itself, the capitalist and the wage labourer, are as such merely embodiments, personifications of capital and wage labour; definite social characteristics stamped upon individuals by the process of social production; the products of these definite social production relations.

The characteristic 1) of the product as a commodity, and 2) of the commodity as a product of capital, already implies all circulation relations, i. e., a definite social process through which the products must pass and in which they assume definite social characteristics; it likewise implies definite relations of the production agents, by which the value expansion of their product and its reconversion, either into means of subsistence or into means of production, are determined. But even apart from this, the entire determination of value and the regulation of the total production by value results from the above two characteristics of the product as a commodity, or of the commodity as a capitalistically produced commodity. In this entirely specific form of value, labour prevails on the one hand solely as social labour; on the other hand, the distribution of this social labour and the mutual supplementing and interchanging of its products, the subordination under, and introduction into, the social mechanism, are left to the accidental and mutually nullifying motives of individual capitalist producers. Since these latter confront one another only as commodity owners, and everyone seeks to sell his commodity as dearly as possible (apparently even guided in the regulation of production itself solely by his own free will), the inner law enforces itself only through their competition, their mutual pressure upon each other, whereby the deviations are mutually cancelled. Only as an inner law, vis-à-vis the individual agents, as a blind law of Nature, does the law of value exert its influence here and maintain the social equilibrium of production amidst its accidental fluctuations.

Furthermore, already implicit in the commodity, and even more so in the commodity as a product of capital, is the objectification of the social features of production and the personification of the material foundations of production, which characterise the entire capitalist mode of production.

The *second* distinctive feature of the capitalist mode of production is the production of surplus value as the direct aim and determining motive of production. Capital produces essentially capital, and does so only to the extent that it produces surplus value. We have seen in our discussion of relative surplus value, and further in considering the transformation of surplus value into profit, how a mode of production peculiar to the capitalist period is founded hereon — a special form of development of the social productive powers of labour, but confronting the labourer as powers of capital rendered independent, and standing in direct opposition therefore to the labourer's own development. Production for value and surplus value implies, as has been shown in the course of our analysis, the constantly operating tendency to reduce the labour time necessary for the production of a commodity, i. e., its value, below the actually prevailing social average. The pressure to reduce cost price to its minimum becomes the strongest lever for raising the social productive power of labour, which, however, appears here only as a continual increase in the productiveness of capital.

The authority assumed by the capitalist as the personification of capital in the direct process of production, the social function performed by him in his capacity as manager and ruler of production, is essentially different from the authority exercised on the basis of production by means of slaves, serfs, etc.

Whereas, on the basis of capitalist production, the mass of direct producers is confronted by the social character of their production in the form of strictly regulating authority and a social mechanism of the labour process organised as a complete hierarchy — this authority reaching its bearers, however, only as the personification of the conditions of labour in contrast to labour, and not as political or theocratic rulers as under earlier modes of production — among the bearers of this authority, the capitalists themselves, who confront one another only as commodity owners, there reigns complete anarchy within which the social interrelations of production assert themselves only as an overwhelming natural law in relation to individual free will.

Only because labour pre-exists in the form of wage labour, and the means of production in the form of capital—i. e., solely because of this specific social form of these two essential production agents—does a part of the value (product) appear as surplus value and this surplus value as profit (rent), as the gain of the capitalist, as additional available wealth belonging to him. But only because this surplus value thus appears as *his profit* do the additional means of production, which are intended for the expansion of reproduction, and which constitute a part of this profit, present themselves as new additional capital, and the expansion of the process of reproduction in general as a process of capitalist accumulation.

Although the form of labour as wage labour is decisive for the form of the entire process and the specific mode of production itself, it is not wage labour which determines value. In the determination of value, it is a question of social labour time in general, the quantity of labour which society generally has at its disposal, and whose relative absorption by the various products determines, as it were, their respective social importance. The definite form in which the social labour time prevails as decisive in the determination of the value of commodities is of course connected with the form of labour as wage labour and with the corresponding form of the means of production as capital, in so far as solely on this basis does commodity production become the general form of production.

Let us moreover consider the so-called distribution relations themselves. The wage presupposes wage labour, and profit—capital. These definite forms of distribution thus presuppose definite social characteristics of production conditions, and definite social relations of production agents. The specific distribution relations are thus merely the expression of the specific historical production relations.

And now let us consider profit. This specific form of surplus value is the precondition for the fact that the new creation of means of production takes place in the form of capitalist production; thus, a relation dominating reproduction, although it seems to the individual capitalist as if he could in reality consume his entire profit as revenue. However, he thereby meets barriers even in the form of insurance and reserve funds, laws of competition, etc., which hamper him and prove to him in practice that profit is not a mere distribution category of the individually consumable product. The entire process of capitalist production is furthermore regulated by the prices of the products. But the regulating prices of production are themselves in turn regulated by the equalisation of the rate of profit and its corresponding distribution of capital among the various social spheres of production. Profit, then, appears here as the main factor, not of the distribution of products, but of their production itself, as a factor in the distribution of capitals and labour itself among the various spheres of production. The division of profit into profit of enterprise and interest appears as the distribution of the same revenue. But it arises, to begin with, from the development of capital as a self-expanding value, a creator of surplus value, i. e., from this specific social form of the prevailing process of production. It evolves credit and credit institutions out of itself, and thereby the form of production. As interest, etc., the ostensible distribution forms enter into the price as determining production factors.

Ground rent might seem to be a mere form of distribution, because landed property as such does not perform any, or at least any normal, function in the process of production itself. But the circumstance that 1) rent is limited to the excess above the average profit, and that 2) the landlord is reduced from the manager and master of the process of production and of the entire process of social life to the position of mere lessor of land, usurer in land and mere collector of rent, is a specific historical result of the capitalist mode of production. The fact that the earth received the form of landed property is a historical precondition for this. The fact that landed property assumes forms which permit the capitalist mode of operation in agriculture is a product of the specific character of this mode of production. The income of the landlord may be called rent, even under other forms of society. But it differs essentially from rent as it appears in this mode of production.

The so-called distribution relations, then, correspond to and arise from historically determined specific social forms of the process of production and mutual relations entered into by men in the reproduction process of human life. The historical character of these distribution relations is the historical character of production relations, of which they express merely one aspect. Capitalist distribution differs from those forms of distribution which arise from other modes of production, and every form of distribution disappears with the specific form of production from which it is descended and to which it corresponds.

The view which regards only distribution relations as historical, but not production relations, is, on the one hand, solely the view of the initial, but still timid criticism of bourgeois economy. On the other hand, it rests on the confusion and identification of the process of social production with the simple labour process, such as might even be performed by an abnormally isolated human being without any social assistance. To the extent that the labour process is solely a process between man and Nature, its simple elements remain common to all social forms of development. But each specific historical form of this process further develops its material foundations and social forms. Whenever a certain stage of maturity has been reached, the specific historical form is discarded and makes way for a higher one. The moment of arrival of such a crisis is disclosed by the depth and breadth attained by the contradictions and antagonisms between the distribution relations, and thus the specific historical form of their corresponding production relations, on the one hand, and the productive forces, the production powers and the development of their agencies, on the other hand. A conflict then ensues between the material development of production and its social form. [57]

Chapter LII

CLASSES

The owners merely of labour power, owners of capital, and landowners, whose respective sources of income are wages, profit and ground rent, in other words, wage labourers, capitalists and landowners, constitute then three big classes of modern society based upon the capitalist mode of production.

In England, modern society is indisputably most highly and classically developed in economic structure. Nevertheless, even here the stratification of classes does not appear in its pure form. Middle and intermediate strata even here obliterate lines of demarcation everywhere (although incomparably less in rural districts than in the cities). However, this is immaterial for our analysis. We have seen that the continual tendency and law of development of the capitalist mode

[57] See the work on *COMPETITION AND CO-OPERATION* (1832?).[a]

---

[a] This refers apparently to *A Prize Essay on the Competitive Merits of Competition and Cooperation*, London, 1834.

of production is more and more to divorce the means of production from labour, and more and more to concentrate the scattered means of production into large groups, thereby transforming labour into wage labour and the means of production into capital. And to this tendency, on the other hand, corresponds the independent separation of landed property from capital and labour, [58] or the transformation of all landed property into the form of landed property corresponding to the capitalist mode of production.

The first question to be answered is this: What constitutes a class? — and the reply to this follows naturally from the reply to another question, namely: What makes wage labourers, capitalists and landlords constitute the three great social classes?

At first glance — the identity of revenues and sources of revenue. There are three great social groups whose members, the individuals forming them, live on wages, profit and ground rent respectively, on the realisation of their labour power, their capital, and their landed property.

However, from this standpoint, physicians and officials, e. g., would also constitute two classes, for they belong to two distinct social groups, the members of each of these groups receiving their revenue from one and the same source. The same would also be true of the infinite fragmentation of interest and rank into which the division of social labour splits labourers as well as capitalists and landlords — the latter, e. g., into owners of vineyards, farm owners, owners of forests, mine owners and owners of fisheries.

//Here the manuscript breaks off.//

[58] F. List remarks correctly: "The prevalence of a self-sufficient economy on large estates demonstrates solely the lack of civilisation, means of communication, domestic trades and wealthy cities. It is to be encountered, therefore, throughout Russia, Poland, Hungary and Mecklenburg. Formerly, it was also prevalent in England; with the advance of trades and commerce, however, this was replaced by the breaking up into middle estates and the leasing of land." (*Die Ackerverfassung, die Zwergwirtschaft und die Auswanderung*, 1842, p. 10.)

F. ENGELS

SUPPLEMENT
TO *CAPITAL*,
VOLUME THREE [91]

Written by F. Engels in May - June 1895

Introduction and the first article were first published in the journal *Die Neue Zeit*, Bd. I., No. 1, 1895-96. The second article was first published in Russian in the journal *Bolshevik*, No. 23-24, 1932

Published according to the manuscript

Collated with *Die Neue Zeit* text

Translated from the German

The third book of *Capital* is receiving many and various interpretations ever since it has been subject to public judgement. It was not to be otherwise expected. In publishing it, what I was chiefly concerned with was to produce as authentic a text as possible, to demonstrate the new results obtained by Marx in Marx's own words as far as possible, to intervene myself only where absolutely unavoidable, and even then to leave the reader in no doubt as to who was talking to him. This has been deprecated. It has been said that I should have converted the material available to me into a systematically written book, *en faire un livre*, as the French say; in other words, sacrifice the authenticity of the text to the reader's convenience. But this was not how I conceived my task. I lacked all justification for such a revision, a man like Marx has the right to be heard himself, to pass on his scientific discoveries to posterity in the full genuineness of his own presentation. Moreover, I had no desire thus to infringe — as it must seem to me — upon the legacy of so pre-eminent a man; it would have meant to me a breach of faith. And third, it would have been quite useless. For the people who cannot or do not want to read, who, even in Volume I, took more trouble to understand it wrongly than was necessary to understand it correctly — for such people it is altogether useless to put oneself out in any way. But for those who are interested in a real understanding, the original text itself was precisely the most important thing; for them my recasting would have had at most the value of a commentary, and, what is more, a commentary on something unpublished and inaccessible. The original text would have had to be referred to at the first controversy, and at the second and third its publication *in extenso* would have become quite unavoidable.

Such controversies are a matter of course in a work that contains so much that is new, and in a hastily sketched and partly incomplete first draft to boot. And here my intervention, of course, can be of use: to eliminate difficulties in understanding, to bring more to the fore important aspects whose significance is not strikingly enough evident in the text, and to make some important additions to the text written in 1865 to fit the state of affairs in 1895. Indeed, there are already two points which seem to me to require a brief discussion.

I

LAW OF VALUE AND RATE OF PROFIT

It was to be expected that the solution of the apparent contradiction between these two factors would lead to debates just as much after the publication of Marx's text as before it. Some were prepared for a complete miracle and find themselves disappointed because they see a simple, rational, prosaically-sober solution of the contradiction instead of the hocus-pocus they had expected. Most joyfully disappointed of course is the well-known, illustrious Loria. He has at last found the Archimedian fulcrum from which even a gnome of his calibre can lift the solidly built gigantic Marxian structure into the air and explode it. What! he declaims indignantly. Is that supposed to be a solution? That is pure mystification! When the economists speak of value, they mean value that is actually established in exchange.

> "No economist with any trace of sense has ever concerned himself or will ever want to concern himself with a value which commodities do not sell for *and never can sell for* (*nè possono vendersi mai*).... In asserting that the value for which commodities *never* sell is proportional to the labour they contain, what does Marx do except repeat in an inverted form the thesis of the orthodox economists, that the value for which commodities sell is *not* proportional to the labour expended on them?... Matters are not helped by Marx's saying that despite the divergency of individual prices from individual values the total price of all commodities always coincides with their total value, or the amount of labour contained in the totality of the commodities. For inasmuch as value is nothing more than the exchange ratio between one commodity and another, the very concept of a total value is an absurdity, nonsense ... a *contradictio in adjecto*...." [a]

At the very beginning of the book, he argues, Marx says that exchange can equate two commodities only by virtue of a similar and

---

[a] contradiction in definition

equally large element contained in them, namely, the equal amount of labour. And now he most solemnly repudiates himself by asserting that commodities exchange with one another in a totally different ratio than that of the amount of labour contained in them.

"Was there ever such an utter *reductio ad absurdum*, such complete theoretical bankruptcy? Was ever scientific suicide committed with greater pomp and more solemnity!" (*Nuova Antologia*, Feb. 1, 1895, pp. 477-78, 479.)

We see our Loria is more than happy. Wasn't he right in treating Marx as one of his own, as an ordinary charlatan? There you see it — Marx sneers at his public just like Loria; he lives on mystifications just like the most insignificant Italian professor of economics. But, whereas Dulcamara[a] can afford that because he knows his trade, the clumsy Northerner, Marx, commits nothing but ineptitudes, writes nonsense and absurdities, so that there is finally nothing left for him but solemn suicide.

Let us save for later the statement that commodities have never been sold, nor can even be sold, at the values determined by labour. Let us deal here merely with Mr. Loria's assurance that

"value is nothing more than the exchange ratio between one commodity and another," and that therefore "the very concept of a total value of commodities is an absurdity, nonsense...."

The ratio in which two commodities are exchanged for each other, their value, is therefore something purely accidental, stuck on to the commodities from the outside, which can be one thing today and something else tomorrow. Whether a metric hundredweight of wheat is exchanged for a gramme or a kilogramme of gold does not in the least depend upon conditions inherent in that wheat or gold, but upon circumstances totally foreign to both. For otherwise these conditions would also have to assert themselves in the exchange, dominate the latter on the whole, and also have an independent existence apart from exchange, so that one could speak of a total value of commodities. That is nonsense, says the illustrious Loria. No matter in what ratio two commodities may be exchanged for each other, that is their value — and that's all there is to it. Hence value is identical with price, and every commodity has as many values as the prices it can get. And price is determined by supply and demand; and anyone asking any more questions is a fool to expect an answer.

---

[a] Charlatan in *L'Elisir d'Amore*, comic opera by Donizetti.

But there is a little hitch to the matter. In the normal state, supply and demand balance. Therefore, let us divide all the commodities in the world into two halves, the supply group and the equally large demand group. Let us assume that each represents a price of 1,000,000 million marks, francs, pounds sterling, or what you will. According to elementary arithmetic that makes a price or value of 2,000,000 million. Nonsense, absurd, says Mr. Loria. The two groups together may represent a price of 2,000,000 million. But it is otherwise with value. If we say price: 1,000 + 1,000 = 2,000. But if we say value: 1,000 + + 1,000 = 0. At least in this case, where the totality of commodities is involved. For here the commodities of each of the two groups are worth 1,000,000 million only because each of the two can and will give this sum for the commodities of the other. But if we unite the totality of the commodities of both groups in the hands of a third person, the first has no value in his hand any longer, nor the second, and the third certainly not — in the end no one has anything. And again we marvel at the superiority with which our southern Cagliostro[a] has manhandled the concept of value in such a fashion that not the slightest trace of it has been left. This is the acme of vulgar economics![1]

---

[1] Somewhat later, the same gentleman "well-known through his fame"[b] (to use Heine's phrase) also felt himself compelled to reply to my preface to Volume III — after it was published in Italian in the first number of *Rassegna* in 1895. The reply is printed in the *Riforma Sociale* of February 25, 1895. After having lavished upon me the inevitable (and therefore doubly repulsive) adulation, he states that he never thought of filching for himself Marx's credit for the materialist conception of history. He acknowledged it as early as 1885 — to wit, quite incidentally in a magazine article. But in return he passes over it in silence all the more stubbornly precisely where it is due, that is, in his book on the subject, where Marx is mentioned for the first time on page 129, and then merely in connection with small landed property in France. And now he bravely declares that Marx is not at all the originator of this theory; if Aristotle had not already suggested it, Harrington undoubtedly proclaimed it as early as 1656, and it had been developed by a Pleiad of historians, politicians, jurists and economists long before Marx. All of which is to be read in the French edition of Loria's book. In short, the perfect plagiarist. After I have made it impossible for him to brag any more with plagiarisms from Marx, he boldly maintains that Marx adorns himself with borrowed plumes just as he himself does. From my other attacks, Loria takes up the one that, according to him, Marx never planned to write a second or indeed a third volume of *Capital*. "And now Engels replies triumphantly by throwing the second and third volumes at me ... excellent! And I am so pleased with these volumes, to which I owe so much intellectual enjoyment, that never was a victory so dear to me as today this defeat is — if

---

[a] An Italian alchemist and charlatan. His real name is Guiseppe Balsamo.-
[b] H. Heine, *Ritter Olaf*.

First page of Engels' manuscript
"Law of Value and Rate of Profit"

In Braun's *Archiv für soziale Gesetzgebung*, Vol. VII, No. 4, Werner Sombart gives an outline of the Marxian system which, taken all in all, is excellent. It is the first time that a German university professor succeeds on the whole in seeing in Marx's writings what Marx really says, stating that the criticism of the Marxian system cannot consist of a refutation —

"LET THE POLITICAL CAREERIST DEAL WITH THAT"

— but merely in a further development. Sombart, too, deals with our subject, as is to be expected. He investigates the importance of value in the Marxian system, and arrives at the following results: Value is not manifest in the exchange relation of capitalistically produced commodities; it does not live in the consciousness of the agents of capitalist production; it is not an empirical, but a mental, a logical fact; the concept of value in its material definiteness in Marx is nothing but the economic expression for the fact of the social productive power of labour as the basis of economic existence; in the final analysis the law of value dominates economic processes in a capitalist economic system, and for this economic system quite generally has the following content: the value of commodities is the specific and historical form in which the productive power of labour, in the last analysis dominating all economic processes, asserts itself as a determining factor.— So says Sombart; it cannot be said that this conception of the

it really is a defeat. But is it actually? Is it really true that Marx wrote, with the intention of publication, this mixture of disconnected notes that Engels, with pious friendship, has compiled? Is it really permissible to assume that Marx ... confided the coronation of his work and his system to these pages? Is it indeed certain that Marx would have published that chapter on the average rate of profit, in which the solution, promised for so many years, is reduced to the most dismal mystification, to the most vulgar playing with phrases? It is at least permissible to doubt it.... That proves, it seems to me, that Marx, after publishing his magnificent (*splendido*) book, did not intend to provide it with a successor, or else wanted to leave the completion of the gigantic work to his heirs, outside his own responsibility."

So it is written on p. 267. Heine could not speak any more contemptuously of his philistine German public than in the words: "The author finally gets used to his public as if it were a reasonable being." [a] What must the illustrious Loria think his public is?

In conclusion, another load of praise comes pouring down on my unlucky self. In this our Sganarelle [b] puts himself on a par with Balaam, who came to curse but whose lips bubbled forth "words of blessing and love" [92] against his will. For the good Balaam was distinguished by the fact that he rode upon an ass that was more intelligent than its master. This time Balaam evidently left his ass at home.

---

[a] H. Heine, afterword to *Romancero*. - [b] A character from Molière's *Don Juan*.

significance of the law of value for the capitalist form of production is wrong. But it does seem to me to be too broad, and susceptible of a narrower, more precise formulation; in my opinion it by no means exhausts the entire significance of the law of value for the economic stages of society's development dominated by this law.

There is a likewise excellent article by Conrad Schmidt on the third volume of *Capital* in Braun's *Sozialpolitisches Centralblatt*, February 25, 1895, No. 22. Especially to be emphasised here is the proof of how the Marxian derivation of average profit from surplus value for the first time gives an answer to the question not even posed by economics up to now: how the magnitude of this average rate of profit is determined, and how it comes about that it is, say, 10 or 15% and not 50 or 100%. Since we know that the surplus value first appropriated by the industrial capitalist is the sole and exclusive source from which profit and rent flow, this question solves itself. This passage of Schmidt's article might be directly written for economists *à la* Loria, if it were not labour in vain to open the eyes of those who do not want to see.

Schmidt, too, has his formal misgivings regarding the law of value. He calls it a scientific *hypothesis*, set up to explain the actual exchange process, which proves to be the necessary theoretical starting-point, illuminating and indispensable, even in respect of the phenomena of competitive prices which seem in absolute contradiction to it. According to him, without the law of value all theoretical insight into the economic machinery of capitalist reality ceases. And in a private letter that he permits me to quote, Schmidt declares the law of value within the capitalist form of production to be a pure, although theoretically necessary, fiction. [93]— This view, however, is quite incorrect in my opinion. The law of value has a far greater and more definite significance for capitalist production than of a mere hypothesis, not to mention a fiction, even though a necessary one.

Sombart, as well as Schmidt—I mention the illustrious Loria merely as an amusing vulgar-economic foil—does not make sufficient allowance for the fact that we are dealing here not only with a purely logical process but with a historical process and its explanatory reflection in thought, the logical pursuance of its inner connections.

The decisive passage is to be found in Marx, Buch III, I, S. 154[a]: "The whole difficulty arises from the fact that commodities are not

---

[a] See this volume, p. 174.

exchanged simply as *commodities*, but as *products of capitals*, which claim participation in the total amount of surplus value, proportional to their magnitude, or equal if they are of equal magnitude."

To illustrate this difference, it is supposed that the workers are in possession of their means of production, that they work on the average for equally long periods of time and with equal intensity, and exchange their commodities with one another directly. Then, in one day, two workers would have added by their labour an equal amount of new value to their products, but the product of each would have different value, depending on the labour already embodied in the means of production. This latter part of the value would represent the constant capital of capitalist economy, while that part of the newly added value employed for the worker's means of subsistence would represent the variable capital, and the portion of the new value still remaining would represent the surplus value, which in this case would belong to the worker. Thus, after deducting the amount to replace the "constant" part of value only advanced by them, both workers would get equal values; but the ratio of the part representing surplus value to the value of the means of production — which would correspond to the capitalist rate of profit — would be different in each case. But since each of them gets the value of the means of production replaced through the exchange, this would be a wholly immaterial circumstance.

"The exchange of commodities at their values, or approximately at their values, thus requires a *much lower stage* than their exchange at their prices of production, which requires a definite level of capitalist development.... Apart from the domination of prices and price movement by the law of value, it is quite appropriate to regard the values of commodities as not only *theoretically* but also *historically prius* to the prices of production. This applies to conditions *in which the labourer owns his means of production*, and this is the condition of the landowning farmer living off his own labour and the craftsman, in the ancient as well as in the modern world. This agrees also with the view we expressed previously, that the evolution of products into commodities arises through exchange between different communities, not between the members of the same community. It holds not only for this primitive condition, but also for subsequent conditions, based on slavery and serfdom, and for the guild organisation of handicrafts, so long as the means of production involved in each branch of production can be transferred from one sphere to another only with difficulty and therefore the various spheres of production are related to one another, within certain limits, as foreign countries or communist communities" (Marx, Buch III, I, S. 155, 156).[a]

Had Marx had an opportunity to go over the third volume once more, he would doubtless have extended this passage considerably. As it stands it gives only a sketchy outline of what is to be said on the point in question. Let us therefore examine it somewhat closer.

We all know that at the beginnings of society products are consumed by the producers themselves, and that these producers are spontaneously organised in more or less communistic communities; that the exchange of the surplus of these products with strangers, which ushers in the conversion of products into commodities, is of a later date; that it takes place at first only between individual communities of different tribes, but later also prevails within the community, and contributes considerably to the latter's dissolution into bigger or smaller family groups. But even after this dissolution, the exchanging family heads remain working peasants, who produce almost all they require with the aid of their families on their own farmsteads, and get only a slight portion of the required necessities from the outside in exchange for surplus products of their own. The family is engaged not only in agriculture and livestock-raising; it also works their products up into finished articles of consumption; now and then it even does its own milling with the hand-mill; it bakes bread, spins, dyes, weaves flax and wool, tans leather; builds and repairs wooden buildings, makes tools and utensils, and not infrequently does joinery and blacksmithing; so that the family or family group is in the main self-sufficient.

The little that such a family had to obtain by barter or buy from outsiders, even up to the beginning of the 19th century in Germany, consisted principally of the objects of handicraft production, that is, such things the nature of whose manufacture was by no means unknown to the peasant, and which he did not produce himself only because he lacked the raw material or because the purchased article was much better or very much cheaper. Hence the peasant of the Middle Ages knew fairly accurately the labour time required for the manufacture of the articles obtained by him in barter. The smith and the cartwright of the village worked under his eyes; likewise the tailor

---

[a] See this volume, pp. 175-76.

and shoemaker, who in my youth still paid their visits to our Rhine peasants, one after another, turning the homemade materials into shoes and clothing. The peasants, as well as the people from whom they bought, were themselves workers; the exchanged articles were each one's own products. What had they expended in making these products? Labour and labour alone: to replace tools, to produce the raw material, and to process it they spent nothing but their own labour power; how then could they exchange these products of theirs for those of other labouring producers otherwise than in the ratio of the labour expended on them? Not only was the labour time spent on these products the only suitable measure for the quantitative determination of the values to be exchanged: no other was at all possible. Or is it believed that the peasant and the artisan were so stupid as to give up the product of ten hours' labour of one person for that of a single hour's labour of another? No other exchange is possible in the whole period of peasant natural economy than that in which the exchanged quantities of commodities tend to be measured more and more according to the amounts of labour embodied in them. From the moment money penetrates into this mode of economy, the tendency towards adaptation to the law of value (in the Marxian formulation, *nota bene!*) grows more pronounced on the one hand, while on the other it is already interrupted by the interference of usurers' capital and fleecing by taxation; the periods for which prices, on the average, approach to within a negligible margin of values begin to grow longer.

The same holds good for exchange between peasant products and those of the urban artisans. At the beginning this barter takes place directly, without the medium of the merchant — on the cities' market days, when the peasant sells and makes his purchases. Here too, not only does the peasant know the artisan's working conditions, but the latter knows those of the peasant as well. For the artisan is himself still a bit of a peasant; he not only has a vegetable and fruit garden, but very often also has a small piece of land, one or two cows, pigs, poultry, etc. People in the Middle Ages were thus able to check up with considerable accuracy on each other's production costs for raw material, auxiliary material, and labour time — at least in respect of articles of daily general use.

But how, in this barter on the basis of quantity of labour, was the latter to be calculated, even if only indirectly and relatively, for products requiring longer labour, interrupted at irregular intervals, and uncertain in yield — e.g., grain or cattle? And among people, to boot, who could not calculate? Obviously only by means of a lengthy process of zigzag approximation, often feeling the way here and there in the dark, and, as is usual, learning only through mistakes. But each one's necessity for covering his outlay on the whole always helped to return to the right direction; and the small number of kinds of articles in circulation, as well as the often century-long stable nature of their production, facilitated the attaining of this goal. And that it by no means took so long for the relative amount of value of these products to be fixed fairly closely is already proved by the fact that cattle, the commodity for which this appears to be most difficult because of the long time of production of the individual head, became the first rather generally accepted money commodity. To accomplish this, the value of cattle, its exchange ratio to a large number of other commodities, must already have attained a relatively unusual stabilisation, acknowledged without contradiction in the territories of many tribes. And the people of that time were certainly clever enough — both the cattle-breeders and their customers — not to give away the labour time expended by them without an equivalent in barter. On the contrary, the closer people are to the primitive state of commodity production — the Russians and Orientals for example — the more time do they still waste today, in order to squeeze out, through long tenacious bargaining, the full compensation for their labour time expended on a product.

Starting with this determination of value by labour time, the whole of commodity production developed, and with it the multifarious relations in which the various aspects of the law of value assert themselves, as described in the first part of Volume I of *Capital*; that is, in particular, the conditions under which labour alone is value-creating. These are conditions which assert themselves without entering the consciousness of the participants and can themselves be abstracted from daily practice only through laborious theoretical investigation; which act, therefore, like natural laws, as Marx proved to follow necessarily from the nature of commodity production. The most important and most incisive advance was the transition to metallic money, the consequence of which, however, was that the determination of value by labour time was no longer visible upon the surface of commodity exchange. From the practical point of view, money became the decisive measure of value, all the more as the commodities entering trade became more varied, the more they came from distant countries, and the less, therefore, the labour time necessary for their production could be checked. Money itself usually came first from foreign parts; even when precious metals were obtained within the country, the peasant and artisan were partly unable to estimate approximately the labour employed therein, and partly their own consciousness of the value-measuring property of labour had been fairly well dimmed by the habit of reckoning with money; in the popular mind money began to represent absolute value.

In a word: the Marxian law of value holds generally, as far as economic laws are valid at all, for the whole period of simple commodity production, that is, up to the time when the latter suffers a modification through the appearance of the capitalist form of production. Up to that time prices gravitate towards the values fixed according to the Marxian law and oscillate around those values, so that the more fully simple commodity production develops, the more the average prices over long periods uninterrupted by external violent disturbances coincide with values within a negligible margin. Thus the Marxian law of value has general economic validity for a period lasting from the beginning of exchange, which transforms products into commodities, down to the 15th century of the present era. But the exchange of commodities dates from a time before all written history, which in Egypt goes back to at least 2500 B. C., and perhaps 5000 B. C., and in Babylon to 4000 B. C., perhaps 6000 B. C.; thus the law of value has prevailed during a period of from five to seven thousand years. And now let us admire the thoroughness of Mr. Loria, who calls the value generally and directly valid during this period, a value at which commodities are never sold nor can ever be sold, and with which no economist having a spark of common sense would ever occupy himself!

We have not spoken of the merchant up to now. We could save the consideration of his intervention for now, when we pass to the transformation of simple into capitalist commodity production. The merchant was the revolutionary element in this society where everything else was stable—stable, as it were, through inheritance; where the peasant obtained not only his hide of land but his status as a freehold proprietor, as a free or enthralled quit-rent peasant or serf, and the urban artisan his trade and his guild privileges by inheritance and almost inalienably, and each of them, in addition, his customers, his market, as well as his skill, trained from childhood for the inherited craft. Into this world then entered the merchant with whom its revolution was to start. But not as a conscious revolutionary; on the

contrary, as flesh of its flesh, bone of its bone. The merchant of the
Middle Ages was by no means an individualist; he was essentially an
associate like all his contemporaries. The mark association, grown out
of primitive communism, prevailed in the countryside. Each peasant
originally had an equal hide, with equal pieces of land of each quality, and a corresponding, equal share in the rights of the mark. After
the mark had become a closed association and no new hides were allocated any longer, subdivision of the hides occurred through inheritance, etc., with corresponding subdivisions of the common rights in
the mark; but the full hide remained the unit, so that there were half,
quarter and eighth-hides with half, quarter and eighth-rights in the
mark. All later productive associations, particularly the guilds in the
cities, whose statutes were nothing but the application of the mark constitution to a craft privilege instead of to a restricted area of land,
followed the pattern of the mark association. The central point of the
whole organisation was the equal participation of every member in
the privileges and produce assured to the guild, as is strikingly expressed in the 1527 license of the Elberfeld and Barmen yarn trade.
(Thun: *Industrie am Niederrhein*, Vol. II, p. 164 ff.) The same holds true
of the mine guilds, where each share participated equally and was also divisible, together with its rights and obligations, like the hide of
the mark member. And the same holds good in no less degree of the
merchant companies, which initiated overseas trade. The Venetians
and the Genoese in the harbour of Alexandria or Constantinople,
each "nation" in its own *fondaco* — dwelling, inn, warehouse, exhibi-
tion and salesrooms, together with central offices — formed complete
trade associations; they were closed to competitors and customers;
they sold at prices fixed among themselves; their commodities had
a definite quality guaranteed by public inspection and often by
a stamp; they deliberated in common on the prices to be paid by the
natives for their products, etc. Nor did the Hanseatic merchants act
otherwise on the German Bridge (Tydske Bryggen) in Bergen, Norway; the same held true of their Dutch and English competitors. Woe
to the man who sold under the price or bought above the price! The
boycott that struck him meant at that time inevitable ruin, not counting the direct penalties imposed by the association upon the guilty.
And even closer associations were founded for definite purposes, such
as the Maona of Genoa in the 14th and 15th centuries, for years the
ruler of the alum mines of Phocaea in Asia Minor, as well as of
the Island of Chios; furthermore the great Ravensberg Trading

Company, which dealt with Italy and Spain since the end of the 14th century, founding branches in those countries; the German company of the Augsburgers: Fugger, Welser, Vöhlin, Höchstetter, etc.; that of the Nürnbergers: Hirschvogel and others, which participated with a capital of 66,000 ducats and three ships in the 1505-06 Portuguese expedition to India, making a net profit of 150%, according to others, 175% (Heyd: *Levantehandel*, II, 524)[a]; and a large number of other companies, "Monopolia", over which Luther waxes so indignant.

Here for the first time we meet with a profit and a rate of profit. The merchant's efforts are deliberately and consciously aimed at making this rate of profit equal for all participants. The Venetians in the Levant, and the Hanseatics in the North, each paid the same prices for his commodities as his neighbour; his transport charges were the same, he got the same prices for his goods and bought return cargo for the same prices as every other merchant of his "nation". Thus the rate of profit was equal for all. In the big trading companies the allocation of profit *pro rata* of the paid-in capital share is as much a matter of course as the participation in mark rights *pro rata* of the entitled hide share, or as the mining profit *pro rata* of the mining share. The equal rate of profit, which in its fully developed form is one of the final results of capitalist production, thus manifests itself here in its simplest form as one of the points from which capital started historically, as a direct offshoot in fact of the mark association, which in turn is a direct offshoot of primitive communism.

This original rate of profit was necessarily very high. The business was very risky not only because of widespread piracy; the competing nations also permitted themselves all sorts of acts of violence when the opportunity arose; finally, sales and marketing conditions were based upon licenses granted by foreign princes, which were broken or revoked often enough. Hence, the profit had to include a high insurance premium. Then turnover was slow, the handling of transactions protracted, and in the best periods, which, admittedly, were seldom of long duration, the business was a monopoly trade with monopoly profit. The very high interest rates prevailing at the time, which always had to be lower on the whole than the percentage of usual commercial profit, also prove that the rate of profit was on the average very high.

---

[a] The reference is to *Geschichte des Levantehandels im Mittelalter*.

But this high rate of profit, equal for all participants and obtained through joint labour of the community, held only locally within the associations, that is, in this case the "nation". Venetians, Genoese, Hanseatics, and Dutchmen each had a special rate of profit, and at the beginning more or less for each individual market area as well. Equalisation of these different company profit rates took place in the opposite way through competition. First, the profit rates of the different markets for one and the same nation. If Alexandria offered more profit for Venetian goods than Cyprus, Constantinople or Trebizond, the Venetians would start more capital moving towards Alexandria, withdrawing it from trade with the other markets. Then the gradual equalisation of profit rates among the different nations, exporting the same or similar goods to the same markets, had to follow, and some of these nations were very often squeezed to the wall and disappeared from the scene. But this process was being continually interrupted by political events, just as all Levantine trade collapsed owing to the Mongolian and Turkish invasions; the great geographic-commercial discoveries after 1492 [94] only accelerated this decline and then made it final.

The sudden expansion of the market area that followed and the revolution in communications connected with it, introduced no essential change at first in the nature of trade operations. At the beginning, co-operative companies also dominated trade with India and America. But in the first place, bigger nations stood behind these companies. In trade with America, the whole of great united Spain took the place of the Catalonians trading with the Levant; alongside it two great countries like England and France; and even Holland and Portugal, the smallest, were still at least as large and strong as Venice, the greatest and strongest trading nation of the preceding period. This gave the travelling merchant, the MERCHANT ADVENTURER of the 16th and 17th centuries, a backing that made the company, which protected its companions with arms also, more and more superfluous, and its expenses an outright burden. Moreover, the wealth in a single hand grew considerably faster, so that single merchants soon could invest as large sums in an enterprise as formerly an entire company. The trading companies, wherever still existent, were usually converted into armed corporations, which conquered and monopolistically exploited whole newly discovered countries under the protection and the sovereignty of the mother country. But the more colonies were founded in the new areas, largely by the state, the more did company trade recede before that of the individual merchant, and the equalisation of the profit rate became therewith more and more a matter of competition exclusively.

Up to now we have become acquainted with a rate of profit only for merchant capital. For only merchant and usurers' capital had existed up to that time; industrial capital was yet to be developed. Production was still predominantly in the hands of workers owning their own means of production, whose work therefore yielded no surplus value to any capital. If they had to surrender a part of the product to third parties without compensation, it was in the form of tribute to feudal lords. Merchant capital, therefore, could only make its profit, at least at the beginning, out of the foreign buyers of domestic products, or the domestic buyers of foreign products; only toward the end of this period — for Italy, that is, with the decline of Levantine trade — were foreign competition and the difficulty of marketing able to compel the handicraft producers of export commodities to sell the commodity under its value to the exporting merchant. And thus we find here that commodities are sold at their values, on the average, in the domestic retail trade of individual producers with one another, but, for the reasons given, not in international trade as a rule. Quite the opposite of the present-day world, where the production prices hold good in international and wholesale trade, while the formation of prices in urban retail trade is governed by quite other rates of profit. So that the meat of an ox, for example, experiences today a greater rise in price on its way from the London wholesaler to the individual London consumer than from the wholesaler in Chicago, including transport, to the London wholesaler.

The instrument that gradually brought about this revolution in price formation was industrial capital. Rudiments of the latter had been formed as early as the Middle Ages, in three fields — shipping, mining and textiles. Shipping on the scale practised by the Italian and Hanseatic maritime republics was impossible without sailors, i. e., wage labourers (whose wage relationship may have been concealed under association forms with profit-sharing), or without oarsmen — wage labourers or slaves — for the galleys of that day. The guilds in the ore mines, originally associated workers, had already been converted in almost every case into stock companies for exploiting the deposits by means of wage labourers. And in the textile industry the merchant had begun to place the petty master-weaver directly in his service, by supplying him with yarn and having it made into cloth for his account in return for a fixed wage, in short, by himself changing from a mere buyer into a so-called *contractor*.

Here we have the first beginning of the formation of capitalist surplus value. We can ignore the mining guilds as closed monopoly corporations. With regard to the shipowners it is obvious that their profit had to be at least as high as the customary one in the country, plus an extra increment for insurance, depreciation of ships, etc. But how were matters with the textile contractors, who first brought commodities, directly manufactured for capitalist account, into the market and into competition with the commodities of the same sort made for handicraft account?

Merchant capital's rate of profit was at hand to start with. Likewise, it had already been equalised to an approximate average rate, at least for the locality in question. Now what could induce the merchant to take on the extra business of a contractor? Only one thing: the prospect of greater profit at the same selling price as the others. And he had this prospect. By taking the petty master into his service, he broke through the traditional bonds of production within which the producer sold his finished product and nothing else. The merchant capitalist bought the labour power, which still owned its production instruments but no longer the raw material. By thus guaranteeing the weaver regular employment, he could depress the weaver's wage to such a degree that a part of the labour time furnished remained unpaid for. The contractor thus became an appropriator of surplus value over and above his commercial profit. Admittedly, he had to employ additional capital to buy yarn, etc., and leave it in the weaver's hands until the article for which he formerly had to pay the full price only upon purchasing it was finished. But, in the first place, he had already used extra capital in most cases for advances to the weaver, who as a rule submitted to the new production conditions only under the pressure of debt. And secondly, apart from that, the calculation took the following form:

Assume that our merchant operates his export business with a capital of 30,000 ducats, sequins, pounds sterling or whatever the case may be. Of that, say, 10,000 are engaged in the purchase of domestic goods, whereas 20,000 are used in the overseas market. Say the capital is turned over once in two years. Annual turnover = 15,000. Now our merchant wants to become a contractor, to have cloth woven for his own account. How much additional capital must he invest? Let us assume that the production time of the piece of cloth, such as he sells, averages two months, which is certainly very high. Let us further assume that he has to pay for everything in cash. Hence he must advance enough capital to supply his weavers with yarn for two months. Since his turnover is 15,000 a year he buys cloth for 2,500 in two months. Let us say that 2,000 of that represents the value of yarn, and 500 weavers' wages; then our merchant requires an additional capital of 2,000. We assume that the surplus value he appropriates from the weaver by the new method totals only 5 per cent of the value of the cloth, which constitutes the certainly very modest surplus-value rate of 25 per cent. ($2,000c + 500v + 125s$; $s' = \frac{125}{500} = 25\%$; $p' = \frac{125}{2,500} = 5\%$.) Our man then makes an extra profit of 750 on his annual turnover of 15,000, and has thus got his additional capital back in $2\frac{2}{3}$ years.

But in order to accelerate his sales and hence his turnover, thus making the same profit with the same capital in a shorter period of time, and hence a greater profit in the same time, he will donate a small portion of his surplus value to the buyer — he will sell cheaper than his competitors. The latter will also gradually be converted into contractors, and then the extra profit for all of them will be reduced to the ordinary profit, or even to a lower profit on the capital that has been increased for all of them. The equality of the profit rate is re-established, although possibly on another level, by a part of the surplus value made at home being turned over to the foreign buyers.

The next step in the subjugation of industry by capital takes place through the introduction of manufacture. This, too, enables the manufacturer, who is most often his own export trader in the 17th and 18th centuries — generally in Germany down to 1850, and still today here and there — to produce cheaper than his old-fashioned competitor, the handicraftsman. The same process is repeated; the surplus value appropriated by the manufacturing capitalist enables him (or the export merchant who shares with him) to sell cheaper than his competitors, until the general introduction of the new mode of production, when equalisation again takes place. The already existing mercantile rate of profit, even if it is levelled out only locally, remains the Procrustean bed in which the excessive industrial surplus value is lopped off without mercy.

If manufacture sprang ahead by cheapening its products, this is even more true of modern industry, which forces the production costs of commodities lower and lower through its repeated revolutions in production, relentlessly eliminating all former modes of production.

It is large-scale industry, too, that thus finally conquers the domestic market for capital, puts an end to the small-scale production and natural economy of the self-sufficient peasant family, eliminates direct exchange between small producers, and places the entire nation in the service of capital. Likewise, it equalises the profit rate of the different commercial and industrial branches of business into *one* general rate of profit, and finally ensures industry the position of power due to it in this equalisation by eliminating most of the obstacles formerly hindering the transfer of capital from one branch to another. Thereby the conversion of values into production prices is accomplished for all exchange as a whole. This conversion therefore proceeds according to objective laws, without the consciousness or the intent of the participants. Theoretically there is no difficulty at all in the fact that competition reduces to the general level profits which exceed the general rate, thus again depriving the first industrial appropriator of the surplus value exceeding the average. All the more so in practice, however, for the spheres of production with excessive surplus value, with high variable and low constant capital, i. e., with low capital composition, are by their very nature the ones that are last and least completely subjected to capitalist production, especially agriculture. On the other hand, the rise of production prices above commodity values, which is required to raise the below-average surplus value, contained in the products of the spheres of high capital composition, to the level of the average rate of profit, appears to be extremely difficult theoretically, but is soonest and most easily effected in practice, as we have seen. For when commodities of this class are first produced capitalistically and enter capitalist commerce, they compete with commodities of the same nature produced by precapitalist methods and hence dearer. Thus, even if the capitalist producer renounces a part of the surplus value, he can still obtain the rate of profit prevailing in his locality, which originally had no direct connection with surplus value because it had arisen from merchant capital long before there was any capitalist production at all, and therefore before an industrial rate of profit was possible.

II

THE STOCK EXCHANGE

1. The position of the stock exchange in capitalist production in

general is clear from Vol. III, Part 5, especially Chapter.ª But since 1865, when the book was written, a change has taken place which today assigns a considerably increased and constantly growing role to the stock exchange, and which, as it develops, tends to concentrate all production, industrial as well as agricultural, and all commerce, the means of communication as well as the functions of exchange, in the hands of stock exchange operators, so that the stock exchange becomes the most prominent representative of capitalist production itself.

2. In 1865 the stock exchange was still a *secondary* element in the capitalist system. Government bonds represented the bulk of exchange securities, and even their sum-total was still relatively small. Besides, there were joint-stock banks, predominant on the continent and in America, and just beginning to absorb the aristocratic private banks in England, but still relatively insignificant *en masse*. Railway shares were still relatively weak compared to the present time. There were still only few directly productive establishments in stock company form — and, like the banks, most of all in the *poorer* countries: Germany, Austria, America, etc. The "minister's eye" was still an unconquered superstition.

At that time, the stock exchange was still a place where the capitalists took away each other's accumulated capital, and which directly concerned the workers only as new proof of the demoralising general effect of capitalist economy and as confirmation of the Calvinist doctrine that predestination (alias chance) decides, even in this life, blessedness and damnation, wealth, i. e., enjoyment and power, and poverty, i. e., privation and servitude.

3. Now it is otherwise. Since the crisis of 1866 accumulation has proceeded with ever-increasing rapidity, so that in no industrial country, least of all in England, could the expansion of production keep up with that of accumulation, or the accumulation of the individual capitalist be completely utilised in the enlargement of his own business; English cotton industry as early as 1845; the railway swindles. But with this accumulation the number of *rentiers*, people who were fed up with the regular tension in business and therefore wanted merely to amuse themselves or to follow a mild pursuit as directors or governors of companies, also rose. And third, in order to facilitate the investment of this mass floating around as money capital, new legal

---

ª In the MS., Engels left a blank for the chapter number to be entered. Chapter XXVII, "The Role of Credit in Capitalist Production", apparently was intended.

forms of limited liability companies were established wherever that had not yet been done, and the liability of the shareholder, formerly unlimited, was also reduced $\pm$ [a] (joint-stock companies in Germany, 1890. Subscription 40 per cent!).

4. Thereafter, gradual conversion of industry into stock companies. One branch after another suffers this fate. First iron, where giant plants are now necessary (before that, mines, where not already organised on shares). Then the chemical industry, likewise machinery plants. On the continent, the textile industry; in England, only in a few areas in Lancashire (Oldham Spinning Mill, Burnley Weaving Mill, etc., tailor co-operatives, but this is only a preliminary stage which will again fall into the MASTERS' hands at the next crisis), breweries (the American ones sold a few years ago to English capital, then Guinness, Bass, Allsopp). Then the trusts, which create gigantic enterprises under common management (such as United Alkali). The ordinary individual firm is + & + [b] only a preliminary stage to bring the business to the point where it is big enough to be "founded".

Likewise in trade: Leafs, Parsons, Morleys, Morrison, Dillon — all founded. The same in retail stores by now, and not merely under the cloak of co-operation *à la* "STORES".

Likewise banks and other credit establishments even in England. A tremendous number of new banks, all shares DELIMITED. Even old banks like [c] ..., etc., are converted, with seven private shareholders, into LIMITED companies.

5. The same in the field of agriculture. The enormously expanded banks, especially in Germany under all sorts of bureaucratic names, more and more the holders of mortgages; with their shares the actual higher ownership of landed property is transferred to the stock exchange, and this is even more true when the farms fall into the creditors' hands. Here the agricultural revolution of prairie cultivation is very impressive; if it continues, the time can be foreseen when England's and France's land will also be in the hands of the stock exchange.

6. Now all foreign investments in the form of shares. To mention England alone: American railways, North and South (consult the STOCK-LIST), Goldberger, etc.

---

[a] more or less - [b] more and more - [c] Illegible. It would seem to be "Glyn & Co."— the name of a bank.

7. Then colonisation. Today this is purely a subsidiary of the stock exchange, in whose interests the European powers divided Africa a few years ago, and the French conquered Tunis and Tonkin. Africa leased directly to companies (Niger, South Africa, German South-West and East Africa), and Mashonaland and Natal seized by Rhodes for the stock exchange.

NOTES
AND
INDEXES

NOTES

[1] Volume III of *Capital*, edited by Frederick Engels and published in Hamburg in November 1894, concludes the theoretical part of Marx's main economic writing.

Both the economic theory itself and the structure of *Capital*, Book III included, were the product of many years of study. In his work on the manuscript of Book III Marx evidently followed the plan which he had drawn up when writing the Economic Manuscript of 1857-58, and which he sets out in a letter to Engels dated April 2, 1858: "*Capital* falls into 4 sections. a) Capital *en général*... b) *Competition*, or the interaction of many capitals. c) *Credit*, where capital, as against individual capitals, is shown to be a universal element. d) *Share capital* as the most perfected form (turning into communism) together with all its contradictions" (see present edition, Vol. 40, p. 298). In the course of his further study, however, Marx concentrated on the first point dealing with "capital in general", and was to set forth the problems of the process of production of capital, the process of its circulation, and the unity of the two, or capital and profit (interest) (ibid., p. 287).

"The Draft Plan of the Chapter on Capital", drawn up after the completion of the Economic Manuscript of 1857-58, listed the problems to be examined in the section "Capital and Profit" (ibid., Vol. 29, p. 516).

The next stage in Marx's economic studies was the manuscript of 1861-63 in which he scientifically substantiated the theory of average profit and price of production, and also formulated the doctrine of special forms of surplus value — industrial profit, rent, interest, etc.

In December 1862, basing himself on the new results of his studies, Marx wrote down in Notebook XVIII a detailed plan of Part III, or Section III, of *Capital*, according to which the future book was to have the following chapters:

"1) Conversion of surplus value into profit. Rate of profit as distinguished from rate of surplus value.

"2) Conversion of profit into average profit. Formation of the general rate of profit. Transformation of values into prices of production.

"3) Adam Smith's and Ricardo's theories on profit and prices of production.

"4) *Rent*. (Illustration of the difference between value and price of production.)

"5) History of the so-called Ricardian law of rent.

"6) Law of the fall of the rate of profit. Adam Smith, Ricardo, Carey.

"7) Theories of profit. Query: whether Sismondi and Malthus should also be included in the *Theories of Surplus Value*.

"8) Division of profit into industrial profit and interest. Mercantile capital. Money capital.

"9) Revenue AND ITS SOURCES. The question of the relation between the processes of production and distribution also to be included here.

"10) REFLUX movements of money in the process of capitalist production as a whole.

"11) Vulgar economy.

"12) *Conclusion. "Capital and wage labour"* (ibid., Vol. 33, pp. 346-47).

This plan served, in fact, as the basis for the manuscript of the third book. A comparison of the text of this manuscript and the exposition of the same issues in the Economic Manuscript of 1861-63 shows that Marx not only made use of certain fundamental ideas set out in this manuscript, but included in the text whole passages from it (see respective footnotes).

As early as July 1863, having finished the Economic Manuscript of 1861-63 (see present edition, vols 30-34), Marx turned to his plans concerning *Capital*. His aim, as formulated on May 29, 1863, was "to make a *fair copy* of the political economy for the printers (and give it a final polish)" (ibid., Vol. 41, p. 474). Marx began preparing Book I and continued working on it till the summer of 1864. Of this manuscript only "Chapter Six. Results of the Direct Production Process" has survived in full (ibid., Vol. 34. pp. 355-466). Marx already envisaged *Capital* as consisting of four books and he wrote about this to Ludwig Kugelmann on October 13, 1866 (ibid., Vol. 42, p. 328).

At the end of summer, 1864, Marx finished work on Book I of *Capital* and immediately began Book III. In the first half of 1865, however, he interrupted his work on Book III in order to write the first draft of Book II. The only full manuscript version of Book III had been written by early 1866.

Engels started to prepare this manuscript for the printers at the end of February 1885, as is seen from his correspondence, and continued working on it almost to the end of his life. It was Engels' great service to prepare for the printers and publish Volume III of Marx's *Capital*.—5, 112, 119, 211, 223, 234, 236, 310, 397, 818.

² As early as 1865, when working on the manuscript Marx planned to have *Capital* translated into English (see Marx's letter to Engels of July 31, 1865; present edition, Vol. 42, p. 173). Reporter Peter Fox, a member of the British labour movement, was to help him find a publisher. However, he died in 1869, and nothing was settled. The English translation of Volume I of *Capital*, edited by Engels, appeared after Marx's death, in January 1887 (ibid., Vol. 35). The translation was done by Samuel Moore and Edward Aveling between mid-1883 and March 1886; Eleanor Marx-Aveling assisted in preparing the translation for the press.— 5

³ Since the late 1860s Marx repeatedly asked his correspondents to send him materials on landed property in various countries (see present edition, Vol. 43, pp. 61 and 412). He also informed them that he intended to use this new material to supplement the section on ground rent. Having received numerous statistical reference books and other publications on landed property in Russia from Nikolai Danielson, in particular, and having made a thorough study of them, Marx wrote to his Russian correspondent on December 12, 1872: "In Volume II of *Capital* I shall, in the section on landed property, deal in great detail with the Russian form" (ibid., Vol. 44, p. 457). This passage, among other excerpts from Marx's letters to him, was quoted by Danielson in his letter to Engels of August 25 (September 6), 1885. He thought they

could be used in the preface to Volume III of *Capital*. See also Engels' letter to Danielson of June 3, 1885 (ibid., Vol. 47, p. 294).—10

⁴ Cf. the contents of Book III of *Capital* as set forth by Marx in his letter to Engels of April 30, 1868 (ibid., Vol. 43, pp. 21-25).—10

⁵ A reference to: 1) *First Report from the Secret Committee on Commercial Distress; with the minutes of evidence.* Ordered, by the House of Commons, to be printed, 8 June 1848; 2) *Report from the Secret Committee of the House of Lords, Appointed to Inquire into the Causes of the Distress which has for some time prevailed among the commercial classes, and how far it has been affected by the laws for regulating the issue of banknotes payable on demand.* Together with the minutes of evidence and an appendix. Ordered, by the House of Commons, to be printed, 28 July 1848. [Reprinted 1857.]—11

⁶ A reference to: *Report from the Select Committee on Bank Acts; together with the proceedings of the Committee, minutes of evidence, appendix and index.* Ordered, by the House of Commons, to be printed, 30 July 1857; and: *Report from the Select Committee on the Bank Acts; together with the proceedings of the Committee, minutes of evidence, appendix and index.* Ordered, by the House of Commons, to be printed, 1 July 1858.—11

⁷ Marx first mentioned Book IV, which deals with the history of the theory of surplus value, in "Chapter Six. Results of the Direct Production Process", which has survived from the draft version of Book I of *Capital* (ibid., Vol. 34, p. 454), and also in his letter to Ludwig Kugelmann of October 13, 1866 (ibid., Vol. 42, p. 328).

Engels did not have time to realise his intention to publish *Theories of Surplus Value* as Volume IV of *Capital*. It was first published by Karl Kautsky between 1905 and 1910. In the present edition it is published as part of the Economic Manuscript of 1861-63 (see vols 30-34).—11, 168, 765, 770

⁸ The economic *theory of marginal utility* appeared in the 1870s. According to this theory, the value of a commodity is determined by its "marginal utility", that is, by the subjective evaluation of the utility of the commodity which satisfies the least urgent need of a buyer.—13

⁹ The *Fabians*—members of the English reformist *Fabian Society* founded by middle-class intellectuals in 1884; among its leaders were Sidney and Beatrice Webb. The Society was named after the Roman general of the 3rd century B. C., Quintus Fabius Maximus, surnamed Cunctator ("the delayer") for his cautious tactics in the war against Hannibal.

The Fabians believed that the transition from capitalism to socialism was possible through gradual minor reforms in society. In 1900 the Fabian Society affiliated to the Labour Party.—13

¹⁰ Wilhelm Lexis dealt with this problem in his "Kritische Erörterungen über die Währungsfrage" published in *Jahrbuch für Gesetzgebung. Verwaltung und Volkswirthschaft im Deutschen Reich*, 5 Jg., 1. Heft, Leipzig, 1881, S. 87-132.

Bimetallism (or double standard)—a monetary system in which gold and silver are a legal universal equivalent and the basis of national money circulation (the 16th-19th cent).—14, 319

¹¹ In the French edition of Volume I of *Capital* used by Loria, this chapter corresponds to Chapter IX: "Rate and Mass of Surplus Value" of the German edition. In the present edition it is Chapter XI (see Vol. 35).—19

¹² According to the views prevalent in chemistry in the 18th century, combustion was attributed to the presence in combustible bodies of a particular substance— phlogiston—which separates from them in burning. As it was known, however, that metals increased in weight during prolonged heating in the air, the supporters of the phlogistic theory sought to ascribe to phlogiston a negative weight. This theory was proved untenable by the French physicist Antoine Lavoisier who explained the process of combustion as the combination of the burning substance with oxygen.

Engels deals with the phlogistic theory also in the Preface to Volume II of *Capital* (see Vol. 36, p. 19).—43

¹³ In January 1849 Proudhon attempted to found a *People's Bank* in order to promote a peaceful transition to *socialism*, which, for him, consisted in the liquidation of loan interest and the introduction of exchange without money with the producer receiving full equivalent of his labour revenue. This bank went bankrupt in two months. Marx gave a detailed critical analysis of Proudhon's views in *The Poverty of Philosophy. Answer to the "Philosophy of Poverty" by M. Proudhon* and *Outlines of the Critique of Political Economy* (see present edition, Vol. 6, pp. 105-212 and Vol. 28, pp. 352-54 respectively).—44

¹⁴ See G. Ramsay, *An Essay on the Distribution of Wealth*, Edinburgh, London, 1836, pp. 23-24, 49 and 183-84; T. R. Malthus, *Principles of Political Economy*, London, 1836, p. 268; N. W. Senior, *Letters on the Factory Act*, London, 1837, pp. 11-17; R. Torrens, *An Essay on the Production of Wealth*, London, 1821, pp. 344-49. Cf. K. Marx, Economic Manuscript of 1861-63 (present edition, Vol. 33, pp. 72-73). —48

¹⁵ Marx had already made a critical analysis of Malthus' views in the Economic Manuscript of 1861-63 (see present edition, Vol. 32, pp. 209-58). According to the plan of Part III of *Capital*, drawn up in December 1862, Malthus' theory was to be examined in one of the historico-critical chapters (see Note 1). In the course of writing *Capital* Marx decided to transfer these chapters to Volume IV (see Note 7).—51

¹⁶ Engels has in mind Wilhelm Lexis' review of Volume II of *Capital* published in *Jahrbücher für Nationalökonomie und Statistik*, Neue Folge, 11. Band, Jena, 1885, S. 458-59.—80

¹⁷ In 1844, workers in the town of Rochdale (Lancashire industrial region) who had been influenced by Owen's ideas took the initiative in organising a consumers' co-operative, the Rochdale Equitable Pioneers' Society, which became the prototype for workers' cooperatives in England and other countries. Workers' cooperatives often combined productive functions with their activities as consumer co-operative societies.—89

¹⁸ Marx took the quotation from a review of this Report in *The Westminster Review*, Vol. 38, 1842, p. 102.—91

¹⁹ *Killing No Murder* was the title of a pamphlet that appeared in England in 1657. Its author, Edward Sexby, stated that it was a patriotic duty that Lord Protector Oliver Cromwell, a hated and cruel tyrant, be assassinated.—93

²⁰ The *Court of Queen's Bench* is one of the high courts in England; in the nineteenth century (up to 1873) it was an independent supreme court for criminal and civil cases, competent to review the decisions of lower judicial bodies.—93

²¹ The reference is to *An Act for the Further Amendment of the Laws Relating to Labour in Factories* (12 and 20 Victoria, Chapter 38) of June 30 1856. See also K. Marx, "Condition of Factory Laborers" (present edition, Vol. 15, pp. 251-54).—94

²² High import duties on agricultural produce were imposed by the Corn Laws (first introduced in the fifteenth century) in the interests of the landowners in order to maintain high prices on the home market. See also Note 73.—109, 325

²³ The *Ten Hours' Bill*, passed by the British Parliament on June 8, 1847, applied only to adolescents and women and was ignored by many manufacturers.

In February 1850 the Court of Chancery (one of Britain's high courts) acquitted a number of manufacturers accused of infringing the Ten Hours' Bill. This ruling caused protests from the workers. On August 5, 1850, Parliament passed a new Bill which stipulated a 10¹/₂-hour working day for women and adolescents and fixed the beginning and end of the working day.

On more details on this Bill see present edition, Vol. 35, p. 297 and Vol. 10, pp. 271-76, 288-300.—109

²⁴ See Ch. Babbage, *Traité sur l'économie des machines et des manufactures*, Paris, 1833, pp. 377-78. Cf. K. Marx, Economic Manuscript of 1861-63 (present edition, Vol. 33, p. 350) and *Capital* (ibid., Vol. 35, p. 394).—115

²⁵ See H. C. Carey, *Principles of Political Economy*, Philadelphia, 1837. Cf. K. Marx, *Outlines of the Critique of Political Economy* (present edition, Vol. 29, p. 138).—115

²⁶ On the *cotton shortage* caused by the American Civil War of 1861-65 see K. Marx, "The British Cotton Trade" and "On the Cotton Crisis" (present edition, Vol. 19, pp. 17-20 and 160-62).—122

²⁷ On the *Relief Committees* see K. Marx, "Workers' Distress in England" (present edition, Vol. 19, pp. 239-42).—133

²⁸ *Ateliers nationaux* (national ateliers, workshops) were instituted by the Provisional Government immediately after the February revolution of 1848. By this means the government sought to discredit Louis Blanc's ideas on the "Organisation of Labour" in the eyes of the workers and, at the same time, to utilise those employed in the national workshops, organised on military lines, against the revolutionary proletariat. Revolutionary ideas, however, continued to gain ground in the national workshops. The government took steps to reduce the number of workers employed in them, to transfer a large number to public works in the provinces, and finally to liquidate the workshops. This precipitated a proletarian uprising in Paris in June 1848. After its suppression, the Cavaignac Government issued a decree on July 3 disbanding the national workshops.

For the assessment of the national workshops see K. Marx, *The Class Struggles in France, 1848 to 1850* (present edition, Vol. 10, p. 63).—135

²⁹ The *settlement laws* existed in England from 1662. They actually deprived farm labourers of their right to move from one place to another. Being a component part of the poor laws, they stipulated the return of farm labourers to the place of their birth or permanent residence by court decision. Restricting the labourers' freedom of movement, the legislation thus enabled employers to cut their wages to the minimum.—174, 181

³⁰ These views are to be found in D. Ricardo, *On the Principles of Political Economy, and Taxation*, 3rd ed., London, 1821, pp. 60-61 and H. Storch, *Cours d'économie*

politique..., tome II, St.-Pétersbourg, 1815, pp. 78-79. Cf. K. Marx, Economic Manuscript of 1861-63 (present edition, Vol. 31, pp. 326-34).—182

[31] Th. Corbet, *An Inquiry into the Causes and Modes of the Wealth of Individuals...*, London, 1841, pp. 42-44. Cf. K. Marx, Economic Manuscript of 1861-63 (present edition, Vol. 33, p. 243).—182

[32] Marx analysed Ricardo's views on the relation of wages, profit and price of production in the Economic Manuscript of 1861-63 (present edition, Vol. 32, pp. 52-103). That he intended to devote a special chapter to Ricardo is seen from the plan of Part III of *Capital* drawn up in December 1862 (see Note 1).—202

[33] The reference is to the general law of capitalist accumulation formulated by Marx in Volume I of *Capital* (present edition, Vol. 35, p. 639).—220

[34] Marx had already critically analysed Smith's views in the Economic Manuscript of 1861-63 (present edition, Vol. 31, pp. 439-57 and Vol. 33, pp. 92-93, 103, 108-09). According to the plan of Part III of *Capital*, drawn up in December 1862, Smith's law of the fall of the rate of profit was to be examined in Chapter 6 (see Note 1). In the course of writing *Capital*, Marx decided to transfer historico-critical chapters to Volume IV (see Note 7).—223

[35] *Profit upon alienation* or *profit upon expropriation* is a concept formulated by James Steuart in *An Inquiry into the Principles of Political Oeconomy* (Vol. I, London, 1805, p. 244) which Marx cited and analysed in the Economic Manuscript of 1861-63 (present edition, Vol. 30, pp. 351-52).—229, 327

[36] The Dutch East India Company, founded in 1602, had a monopoly of trade with the Orient and played an important role in Holland's colonial expansion, particularly in the Indian Ocean. It carried on a bitter competitive struggle against the British East India Company. In 1798 the Dutch East India Company was abolished and the whole of its property transferred to the Batavian Republic, which was virtually a French possession.—305, 327

[37] The ancient philosopher Epicurus believed in an infinity of worlds, each originating and existing according to its own natural laws. The gods, though he believed in them, he saw as being outside and between the worlds, and not exerting any influence on either the development of the universe, or human life.—328

[38] Marx is referring to the greatly reduced importance of Genoa, Venice and other North Italian cities in transit commerce at the end of the fifteenth century following the great geographical discoveries of the time: the discovery of Cuba, Haiti and the Bahama Islands, the continent of North America, the sea route to India round the Cape and, finally, the continent of South America.—331

[39] Marx ironically calls Karl Arnd "the philosopher of the dog tax" because, in a special paragraph of his book (§ 88, pp. 420-21), he advocated this tax.—361

[40] In order to prevent a growth in the national debt, William Pitt the Younger, then British Prime Minister, introduced in 1786 a sinking fund, i. e., a scheme whereby a certain portion of public revenues was used every year to purchase state promissory notes. However, the war with France (1793-1802) was accompanied by a sharp increase in the national debt. The imbalance between revenues and expenditure led, first, to a limit on the issue of banknotes, and in 1797 to the enactment of a law relieving the Bank of England of the obligation to accept banknotes. Marx wrote in detail about Pitt's sinking fund laws in the article "Mr. Disraeli's Budget" published

in the *New-York Daily Tribune*, No. 5318, May 7, 1858 (present edition, Vol. 15, pp. 512-14); cf. K. Marx, Economic Manuscript of 1861-63 (ibid., Vol. 33, pp. 222-24).—392

41 Josiah Child's book was first published in London in 1668 as a small pamphlet. In 1669-70 he wrote ten additional chapters, and the book was republished many times.—394

42 Five Chinese cities (Canton, Shanghai, Amoy, Ninbo and Fuchou) were opened to English trade by the Nanking Treaty imposed on China in 1842 as a result of the so-called first Opium War, which Britain had been waging against China since 1839.—405

43 Marx means the champions of the *Currency Principle*—one of the schools of the quantity theory of money widely subscribed to in Britain in the first half of the nineteenth century. According to this theory, the value and price of commodities are determined by the quantity of money in circulation, and economic crises are caused mainly by violations of the laws of money circulation. The proponents of the quantity theory sought to maintain the stability of money circulation by means of obligatory gold backing of banknotes.

   Marx showed the untenability of the currency principle in *A Contribution to the Critique of Political Economy* (present edition, Vol. 29, pp. 412-15).—415

44 The reference is to the coalition wars of the European states against revolutionary and Napoleonic France lasting from 1792 to 1815.

   The Crimean War of 1853-56 was a war between Russia and a coalition of Britain, France, Turkey and the Kingdom of Sardinia (Piedmont).—421

45 Engels is referring to the great swindle connected with the bribery of French statesmen, officials and the press by the Panama Canal joint-stock company, founded in France on the initiative of Ferdinand de Lesseps, an engineer and businessman, in 1879. The Company went bankrupt at the end of 1888. This caused widescale ruin among small shareholders and numerous bankruptcies.—437

46 Here Marx has in mind bourgeois political economists, primarily Adam Smith, who regarded money circulating in the form of gold and silver as the most indifferent and useless form of capital.—461

47 Marx is presumably referring to Chapter II of W. Petty's *Verbum Sapiently, or an Account of the Wealth and Expences of England and the Method of Raising Taxes in the Most Equal Manner*, London, 1691, and particularly the statement: "Whereas the Stock of the Kingdom yielding but 15 Millions of proceeds, is worth 250 Millions; then the People who yield 25, are worth $416^2/_3$ Millions."—463

48 A reference to the *Bank Charter Act* (An Act to Regulate the Issue of Banknotes, and for Giving to the Governor and Company of the Bank of England Certain Privileges for a Limited Period) which was introduced by Robert Peel on July 19, 1844. It provided for the division of the Bank of England into two separate departments, each with its own cash account—the Banking Department, dealing exclusively with credit operations, and the Issue Department, issuing banknotes.

   The Act was repeatedly infringed by the government itself, particularly during the 1847 and 1857 monetary crises. Marx analysed the content and significance of the Act of 1844 in a series of articles written for the *New-York Daily Tribune* in 1857 and 1858 (present edition, vols 15 and 16).—474, 538, 545

⁴⁹ A reference to the money reform in Russia. In 1895-97 gold monometallism and free exchange of paper money for gold were introduced in the country. The issue of banknotes by the State Bank was limited: it could issue banknotes up to the value of 600 million rubles with no less than half the sum backed by gold, and banknotes issued in excess of that sum had to be backed by gold to the full.

The transition to the gold standard contributed to the development of the country's industry and trade and stimulated the import of foreign capital.—521

⁵⁰ The *Bank Restriction Act*, passed in 1797, established a compulsory rate of exchange and rescinded the exchange of banknotes for gold. The exchange was enacted again in 1819 and completely restored in 1821.—528

⁵¹ The reference is to the case of Davidson, who was accused of swindles with bills of exchange. This case was described in S. Laing's *New Series of the Great City Frauds of Cole, Davidson, & Gordon*, London [1869].

Assizes — periodical sessions of the higher courts formerly held in every English county for the trial of civil and criminal cases.—532

⁵² The reference is to the *Birmingham school* of "little shilling men", founded by the Birmingham banker Thomas Attwood. Its propounders supported a project for reducing the gold content of the money unit in England—"the project of the little shilling". At the same time they opposed the government measures to curtail the amount of money in circulation. In fact the policy of currency devaluation served the interests of the Treasury and big businessmen, who were the main recipients of all possible credits, because it enabled state and private debts to be redeemed in devalued money. On this school see also K. Marx, *A Contribution to the Critique of Political Economy* (present edition, Vol. 29, pp. 319-20).—535, 555

⁵³ The *British East India Company* was founded at the beginning of the seventeenth century. It had a monopoly of trade with the East Indies and played a decisive part in establishing the British colonial empire. The Company was liquidated in 1858, during the popular Indian uprising of 1857-59.—536

⁵⁴ That Marx intended to do this is seen from his plan of the economic manuscript in the letter to Engels of April 2, 1858, where he enumerated four sections, one of which was to deal with credit. See Note 1.—545

⁵⁵ The reference is to the popular unrest in several provinces of China. In the mid-1850 this grew into a peasant war that resulted in the insurgents establishing a state of their own over a considerable part of China's territory. The state was called Taiping Tango (hence the name of the movement — the Taiping uprising). The Taiping uprising lasted till 1864.—548

⁵⁶ Marx stresses the importance of the Russian goldmines that, alongside those in California, augmented the gold reserves of the European banks. In Notebook V on economic issues written in January 1851 Marx noted a considerable growth in the output of gold in Russia between 1840 and 1848.

The value of Russian gold extracted in 1850 was £4 million, that of Californian gold — £10 million.—560

⁵⁷ Marx criticised Carey's unhistorical approach. Carey compared the rate of interest at the early stages of capitalism with the level of this interest under developed capitalism — in the economic manuscripts of 1857-58 and of 1861-63 (present edition, Vol. 29, p. 227 and Vol. 34, pp. 118-19 respectively).—590

⁵⁸ *Monts-de-piété* or *montes de pièta*—loan offices or pawnshops set up in Western Europe to counterbalance usury. In the fifteenth century the King of France Louis XI granted the Lombards the right to give loans on the security of property at a legalised rate of interest. *Monts-de-piété*, however, failed to protect poor people from usurers.—596

⁵⁹ Marx is inaccurate here. Thomas Manley did not write the anonymous treatise *Interest of Money Mistaken* published in London in 1668. He was one of the authors of another treatise similar in content and published in 1669. The author of this particular treatise is not known.—598

⁶⁰ This refers to John Law, the Scottish economist and financier, who sought to implement in France his financial projects based on the erroneous idea that a state can increase the country's wealth by issuing banknotes without security. In 1716 Law founded a private bank that, in 1718, was turned into a state bank. In addition to implementing the unlimited emission of banknotes, Law withdrew metallic money from circulation and supported various speculative undertakings. The controversy aroused by Law's activities culminated, at the end of 1720, in the final collapse of the bank and "Law's system".—598

⁶¹ The *Crédit mobilier* (Société générale du Crédit mobilier)—a big French joint-stock bank founded by the Péreire brothers in 1852. It was notorious for its speculation. The Crédit mobilier took an active part in building railways and setting up industrial enterprises. It went bankrupt in 1867.—600

⁶² Proudhon expounded this theory in *Gratuité du crédit. Discussion entre M. Fr. Bastiat et M. Proudhon*, Paris, 1850. Cf. also present edition, Vol. 29, pp. 219-22.—603

⁶³ A reference to a 100-gulden loan with interest payable in three instalments at the Leipzig Fair: New Year, Easter (spring) and at Michaelmas (autumn).—605

⁶⁴ Marx examined Sir Dudley North's views in the Economic Manuscript of 1861-63 (present edition, Vol. 34, pp. 272-74).—606

⁶⁵ A reference to the *mortmain*—the right of the medieval feudal lord to inherit the property of the dead serf peasant. Since the property and the land of the dead peasant usually went to his heirs, the latter were obliged to pay a specially onerous fee for it to the lord.—607

⁶⁶ Marx planned to expound the results of his economic research in six books: 1) On capital, 2) Landed property, 3) Wage labour, 4) The State, 5) International trade, 6) World market. He wrote about this in his letters to Ferdinand Lassalle of February 22 and to Engels of April 2, 1858 (present edition, Vol. 40, pp. 270 and 298). Thus problems of landed property were to be examined in a separate book. Marx intended to supplement the section on ground rent with the material on landed property in various countries, Russia in particular (see Note 3). Engels also mentions this in his preface. Marx's plans, however, remained unfulfilled.—608, 613

⁶⁷ The reference is primarily to David Ricardo's theory of rent. Marx criticised it as being unhistorical in his work *The Poverty of Philosophy. Answer to the "Philosophy of Poverty" by M. Proudhon* (present edition, Vol. 6, pp. 201-03).—609

⁶⁸ See Note 66 and Marx's remarks on this point in the Economic Manuscript of 1861-63 (present edition, Vol. 31, pp. 563-66 and Vol. 34, pp. 265-66).—609

⁶⁹ *Temple Bar*—stone gates built in the fourteenth century at the west end of the Fleet Street in London.—615

⁷⁰ Marx made a detailed analysis of John Locke's and Dudley North's views in the Economic Manuscript of 1861-63 (present edition, Vol. 34, pp. 85-88 and 272-74). A description of Turgot's views is to be found in Vol. 30, pp. 366-67 and Vol. 32, p. 476.—616

⁷¹ In his speech on July 26, 1848 in the National Assembly, Thiers opposed the proposals to reform credit and taxation which Proudhon had submitted to the Assembly's finance committee. After Proudhon's speech of July 31, 1848, Thiers published his own speech in a separate pamphlet as an attack on his opponent. See also K. Marx, "On Proudhon", present edition, Vol. 20, p. 31.—618

⁷² A reference to the debate in the House of Commons (June 24, 1853) on the Bill on Irish landlords and tenants introduced by the Aberdeen Ministry.

The government hoped to normalise relations between landlords and tenants by granting the latter certain rights and thereby mitigating the agrarian struggle in the country. After more than two years of debates Parliament rejected the Bill.

For details see K. Marx, "The Indian Question.— Irish Tenant Right" (present edition, Vol. 12, pp. 157-62).—620

⁷³ On Corn Laws see Note 22.

In 1815 a law was passed prohibiting grain imports when grain prices in England fell below 80 shillings per quarter. In 1822 the law was modified slightly, and in 1828 a sliding scale was introduced — a system of raising or lowering tariffs in proportion to the fall or rise of grain prices on the home market. The industrial bourgeoisie who opposed the Corn Laws under the slogan of free trade secured their repeal in 1846.—620, 650

⁷⁴ A reference to the wars waged by Britain against the French Republic and Napoleonic Empire in 1793-1815.— 620

⁷⁵ A reference to the Blue Books: *Report from the Select Committee on Petitions Relating to the Corn Laws of this Kingdom: together with the minutes of evidence, and an appendix of accounts.* Ordered, by the House of Commons, to be printed, 26 July 1814; *Reports Respecting Grain, and the Corn Laws: viz.: First and Second Reports from the Lords Committee, appointed to enquire into the state of the growth, commerce, and consumption of grain, and all laws relating thereto.* Ordered, by the House of Commons, to be printed, 23 November 1814.

The *Blue Books* — periodical collections of documents of the British Parliament and Foreign Office. The first were published in the seventeenth century.—621

⁷⁶ According to the Poor Laws, which were introduced in England in the sixteenth century and remained in force at the beginning of the nineteenth century, a special tax to support the poor was collected in each parish. The parishioners unable to provide for themselves and their families received support through the poor-box.— 621

⁷⁷ The *Society of Arts and Trades* — a cultural and philanthropic society founded in 1754. The Society tried to prevent the development of the mass strike movement in Britain and sought to play the part of arbitrator between workers and employers. Marx ironically called it the "Society of Arts and Tricks".— 623

⁷⁸ The reference is to the Congress of the *National Association for the Promotion of Social Sciences*, an educational and philanthropic society founded in 1857.— 623

⁷⁹ This refers to *l'Institut de France*—France's highest scientific and art centre, which included the Académie Française.—624

⁸⁰ Here and below Marx uses the term *Produktionkosten* in the meaning of price of production.—645

⁸¹ Marx made this proposition when he criticised Ricardo's views in the Economic Manuscript of 1861-63 (present edition, Vol. 32, pp. 99-101 and 288-89).—647

⁸² A reference to: [E. West,] *Essay on the Application of Capital to Land, with observations shewing the impolicy of any great restriction of the importation of corn..*, London, 1815; Th. R. Malthus, *Principles of Political Economy Considered with a View to Their Practical Application*, London, 1820 and *An Inquiry into the Nature and Progress of Rent, and the Principles by which it is Regulated*, London, 1815; D. Ricardo, *On the Principles of Political Economy, and Taxation*, 3rd ed., London, 1821, Ch. II.—652

⁸³ This notebook, written by Marx in 1865-66, when he was working on the manuscript of Volume III of *Capital*, contains extracts from J. Liebig's books: *Herr Dr. Emil Wolff in Hohenheim und die Agrikultur Chemie*, 1855; *Die Chemie in ihrer Anwendung auf Agricultur und Physiologie*, 1862; *Einleitung in die Naturgezetze des Feldbaues*, 1862. —732

⁸⁴ *Potosi*—a town in the south of Bolivia. It was founded by the Spanish conquistadors in 1547, after the discovery there of rich silver deposits two years earlier. In the second half of the eighteenth century the deposits were exhausted and the town gradually fell into decline.— 760

⁸⁵ The reference is to the economic organisation, established in about 800 A. D. on the vast estates owned by Charlemagne. Special attention was given to more effective control over the fulfilment of numerous obligations imposed on the peasants working on such estates, as well as to the preservation of the estates themselves and of profits received from them.— 772

⁸⁶ The reference is to the so-called *Tithe Commutation Acts* of 1836-60, which replaced Church tithe in kind by money payments for land.— 774

⁸⁷ *Yeomen*—English freeholders who had largely disappeared by approximately the mid-18th century partly as a result of the primitive accumulation of capital, which took the form of communal land enclosure and its appropriation by the landlords. The Yeomen were excellent archers and, before the spread of firearms, usually formed the main force of the English troops. Yeomen were superseded by small tenant farmers.—793

⁸⁸ *Bandes Noires*—special mounted detachments which appeared in the fourteenth century at European courts and fought under black banners. In the nineteenth century this name was applied in France to the associations of profiteers who bought up large estates and resold them in smaller plots because the demand and price for them were higher.—797

⁸⁹ Engels is inaccurate here. A perusal of the manuscript of Volume III of *Capital* showed that Marx planned to arrange the three fragments which Engels placed at the beginning of Chapter XLVIII in the following order: fragment III was to be first, then the text marked by Engels as the beginning of the chapter; fragments I and II should follow a page now missing from the manuscript (see this volume, p. 809).—809

[90] Marx set out a detailed analysis of Smith's view of wages, profit and ground rent as sources of value in Volume II of *Capital* and in the Economic Manuscript of 1861-63 (present edition, Vol. 36 and Vol. 30, pp. 398-99).—813

[91] This work was written after the publication of Volume III of *Capital*. Engels wrote to Karl Kautsky on May 21, 1895 (present edition, Vol. 49) that he intended to have the supplement to Volume III of *Capital* published in the *Neue Zeit* as two articles. The first of them, "The Law of Value and the Rate of Profit", was occasioned by the polemic in economic literature over "the contradiction" between volumes I and III of *Capital*. For the second article he sketched a draft plan of 7 points dealing with the main problems to be discussed.—873

[92] According to the biblical legend (Numbers 22-24), Balak, King of Moab, asked Balaam to curse the children of Israel. However, told only to say the words God put in his mouth, Balaam blessed them instead.— 881

[93] The reference is to Conrad Schmidt's letter of March 1, 1895. Engels analysed the propositions it contained in his reply of March 12, 1895 (present edition, Vol. 49). — 882

[94] The reference is primarily to Christopher Columbus' expeditions which opened up the continent of America and the West India islands: the Bahamas, the Antilles and other islands in the Caribbean Sea.—890

NAME INDEX

INDEX OF LITERARY AND MYTHOLOGICAL NAMES

INDEX OF QUOTED
AND MENTIONED LITERATURE

WORKS BY KARL MARX AND FREDERICK ENGELS

Marx, Karl

Capital. A Critique of Political Economy. Volume I. Book One: *The Process of Production of Capital* (present edition, Vol. 35)
— Das Kapital. Kritik der politischen Oekonomie. Erster Band. Buch I: Der Produktionsprocess des Kapitals. Hamburg, 1867.—7
— Idem. Zweite verbesserte Auflage. Hamburg, 1872.—10, 31, 38, 41, 43, 44, 53-54, 77-79, 86, 96, 97, 133, 141, 159, 229, 261
— Idem. Dritte vermehrte Auflage. Hamburg, 1883.—10, 31, 38, 41, 43, 44, 53-54, 77-79, 86, 96, 97, 133, 141, 145, 159, 229, 261
— Idem. Vierte durchgesehene Auflage. Hamburg, 1890.—485, 519-21, 567, 610, 622, 625, 632, 781, 805, 808, 809-10, 822, 837-38, 865
— *Capital: A Critical Analysis of Capitalist Production.* Translated from the Third German Edition by Samuel Moore and Edward Aveling and edited by Frederick Engels. London, 1887.—5

Capital. A Critique of Political Economy. Volume II. Book Two. *The Process of Circulation of Capital* (present edition, Vol. 36)
— Das Kapital. Kritik der politischen Oekonomie von Karl Marx. Zweiter Band. Buch II: Der Circulationsprocess des Kapitals. Hrsg. von F. Engels. Hamburg, 1885.—7, 20, 27, 37, 54, 74-78, 79, 119, 266, 267, 279, 287, 300, 303, 340, 442, 479, 528, 557, 626, 761, 823, 824-25

Capital. A Critique of Political Economy. Volume III. Book Three: *The Process of Capitalist Production as a Whole.* Edited by Frederick Engels (this volume)
— Das Kapital. Kritik der politischen Oekonomie. Dritter Band. Buch III: Der Gesammtprocess der kapitalistischen Produktion. Hrsg. von Friedrich Engels. Hamburg, 1894.—5, 6, 7, 10, 464, 487, 489, 500, 509, 527, 571, 583, 604, 616, 626, 633, 634-35, 651, 670, 683-84, 715, 723, 733, 738, 748, 797, 801, 854, 855, 882-83, 884

A Contribution to the Critique of Political Economy. Part One (present edition, Vol. 29, pp. 257-417)
— Zur Kritik der politischen Oekonomie. Erstes Heft. Berlin, 1859.—169, 173, 174, 315, 323-24, 343, 428, 445, 451-52, 542, 543, 545, 555-56, 602-03, 632, 771

Economic Manuscript of 1861-63. A Contribution to the Critique of Political Economy (present edition, vols 30-34).—11
— Zur Kritik der politischen Ökonomie (Manuskript 1861-1863)
— Vol. 30.—91, 231, 391, 831
— Vol. 31.—138, 141, 178, 201, 241, 614, 840
— Vol. 32.—49, 116, 223, 229, 236, 238, 240, 242, 244, 247, 253, 255, 322, 329, 335, 342, 343, 345, 346, 347, 354, 366, 367, 373, 379, 380, 381, 385, 387, 389, 390, 391, 396, 591, 592, 593
— Vol. 33.—45, 46, 47, 48, 52, 84, 86, 90, 92, 96, 99, 140, 150, 158, 165, 169, 170, 207, 210, 230, 231, 240, 246, 249, 255, 258, 259, 263, 264, 265, 266, 273, 275, 276, 278, 279, 281, 285, 286, 288, 291, 293, 297, 299, 300, 302, 306, 315, 317, 321, 322, 326, 327, 328, 334, 355, 384, 392, 394, 395
— Vol. 34.—103, 213, 217, 227, 229, 231, 249, 306, 331, 374, 375, 605

The Poverty of Philosophy. Answer to the "Philosophy of Poverty" by M. Proudhon (present edition, Vol. 6, pp. 105-212)
— Misère de la philosophie. Réponse à la philosophie de la misère de M. Proudhon. Paris-Bruxelles, 1847.—602, 613

Outlines of the Critique of Political Economy (Economic Manuscripts of 1857-58) (present edition, vols 28-29)
— Grundrisse der Kritik der politischen Ökonomie [manuscript].—188-89, 242-43, 248-49, 450-51

Engels, Frederick

The Condition of the Working-Class in England. From Personal Observation and Authentic Sources (present edition, Vol. 4, pp. 295-596)
— Die Lage der arbeitenden Klasse in England nach eigner Anschauung und authentischen Quellen. Leipzig, 1845.—760

Preface [to the first English edition of *Capital*, Volume I] (present edition, Vol. 35, pp. 30-36)
— Preface. In: K. Marx, *Capital: A Critical Analysis of Capitalist Production.* London, 1887.—488-89

Supplement to "Capital", Volume Three. I. Law of Value and Rate of Profit (this volume, pp. 875-94)
— Ergänzung und Nachtrag zum III. Buche des "Kapital". 1. Wertgesetz und Profitrate. In: *Die Neue Zeit*, Bd. 1, Nr. 1-2, 1895-96.—16

WORKS BY DIFFERENT AUTHORS

[Anderson, A.] *An Historical and Chronological Deduction of the Origin of Commerce, from the Earliest Accounts to the Present Time. Containing, an history of the great commercial interests of the British Empire.* With an appendix. In two volumes. Vol. 2. London, 1764.—331

Anderson, J. *A Calm Investigation of the Circumstances that Have Led to the Present Scarcity of Grain in Britain: suggesting the means of alleviating that evil, and of preventing the recurrence of such a calamity in future.* (Written December 1800.) 2nd ed., London, 1801.—613

Aristoteles. *De republica libri VIII.* In: *Aristotelis Opera* ex recensione Immanuelis Bekkeri. Accedunt Indices Sylburgiani. Tomus X. Oxonii, 1837.—383

Arnd, K. *Die naturgemässe Volkswirthschaft, gegenüber dem Monopoliengeiste und dem Communismus, mit einem Rückblicke auf die einschlagende Literatur.* Hanau, 1845.—361, 776

Augier, M. *Du Crédit public et de son histoire depuis les temps anciens jusqu'à nos jours.* Paris, 1842.—588, 606

Babbage Ch. *Traité sur l'économie des machines et des manufactures.* Paris, 1833.—106, 115

Balzac, Honoré de. *Les paysans.*—43

Bastiat, F., Proudhon, P. J. *Gratuité du crédit. Discussion entre M. Fr. Bastiat et M. Proudhon.* Paris, 1850.—343-45, 602-03

Baynes [J.] *The Cotton Trade.* Two Lectures ... by Mr. Alderman Baynes ... Blackburn, London, 1857. Quoted from: *Reports of the Inspectors of Factories ... for the Half Year Ending 31st October 1858.* London, 1858.—124

Bell, G. M. *The Philosophy of Joint Stock Banking.* London, 1840.—542

Bellers, J. *Essays About the Poor, Manufactures, Trade, Plantations, and Immorality.* London, 1699.—285

Bible
The Old Testament
  Ezekiel.—329
  Isaiah.—329
The New Testament
  Mark.—587

Bosanquet, J. W. *Metallic, Paper, and Credit Currency, and the Means of Regulating their Quantity and Value.* London, 1842.—368, 398

Briscoe J. *A Discourse on the Late Funds of the Million-Act, Lottery-Act, and Bank of England. Shewing, that they are injurious to the nobility and gentry, and ruinous to the trade of the nation. Together with proposals for the supplying their Majesties with money on easy terms, exempting the nobility, gentry &c. from taxes, enlarging their yearly estates, and enriching all the subjects in the Kingdom, by a national land-bank. Humbly offered and submitted to the consideration of the Lords spiritual and temporal, and Commons in Parliament assembled.* 3rd ed., with an appendix. London, 1696.—596

Buret, E. *Cours d'économie politique.* Bruxelles, 1842.—

Büsch, J. G. *Theoretisch-praktische Darstellung der Handlung in ihren mannichfaltigen Geschäften.* Bd. II. 3. Ausgabe. Hamburg, 1808.—606-07

Cairnes, J. E. *The Slave Power: Its Character, Career, & Probable Designs: Being an attempt to explain the real issues involved in the American contest.* London, 1862.—381, 382

[Cantillon, R.] *Essai sur la nature du commerce en général.* In: *Discours politiques.* Tome III. Amsterdam, 1756.—770

Carey, H. C. *Principles of Political Economy. Part the first: Of the Laws of the Production and Distribution of Wealth.* Philadelphia, 1837.—115, 606
— *Principles of Social Science.* In 3 vols. Vol. 3. Philadelphia, London, Paris, 1859.—396

922 Index of Quoted and Mentioned Literature

— *The Past, the Present, and the Future.* Philadelphia, 1848.—613

Chalmers, Th. *On Political Economy in Connexion with the Moral State and Moral Prospects of Society.* Second edition. Glasgow, 1832.—244, 439

Chamberlayne, H. *A Proposal for a Bank of Secure Current Credit to be Founded upon Land, in Order to the General Good of Landed Men, to the Great Increase of the Value of Land, and the no Less Benefit of Trade and Commerce.* [London,] 1695.—596

Cherbuliez, A. *Richesse ou pauvreté. Exposition des causes et des effets de la distribution actuelle des richesses sociales.* Paris, 1841.— 158

Child, J. *Traités sur le commerce et sur les avantages qui résultent de la réduction de l'interest de l'argent, avec un petit traité contre l'usure;* par Thomas Culpeper. Trad. de l'anglois. Amsterdam et Berlin, 1754.— 394, 598

Comte, Ch. *Traité de la propriété.* Tomes I-II. Paris, 1834.— 611

Coquelin, Ch. *Du Crédit et des banques dans l'industrie.* In: *Revue des deux Mondes.* 4e serie. T. 31. Paris, 1842.— 399

Corbet, Th. *An Inquiry into the Causes and Modes of the Wealth of Individuals; or the principles of trade and speculation explained.* In two parts. London, 1841.— 165, 170, 182, 207, 305-06

The Currency Theory Reviewed; in a Letter to the Scottish People on the Menaced Interference by Government with the Existing System of Banking in Scotland. By a Banker in England. Edinburgh, 1854.— 404, 412, 433, 472, 517

Daire, E. *Introduction sur la doctrine des physiocrates.* In: *Physiocrates.* Avec une introduction et des commentaires par E. Daire. Première partie. Paris, 1846.— 772

Doctrine de Saint-Simon. Exposition. Première année. 1828-1829. Troisième édition. Paris, 1831.— 600

Dombasle, M. de. *Annales agricoles de Roville, ou Mélanges d'agriculture, de'économie rurale, et de législation agricole.* 1e-8e et dernière livraison, supplément. Paris, 1824-1837.— 747

Dove, P. E. *The Elements of Political Economy.* Edinburgh, 1854.— 626, 632

Dureau de la Malle, [A. J. C. A.] *Économie politique des Romains.* Tome première, Paris, 1840.— 105

[Enfantin, B. P.] *Religion saint-simonienne. Économie politique et Politique,* Paris, 1831. — 600, 603

[Evans, D. M.] *The City, or the Physiology of London Business; with sketches on change, and at the coffee houses.* London, 1845.— 388

Feller, F. E. and Odermann, K. G. *Das Ganze der kaufmännischen Arithmetik. Für Handels-, Real- und Gewerbschulen, so wie zum Selbstunterricht für Geschäftsmänner überhaupt.* Siebente Auflage. Leipzig 1859.— 312

Fireman, P. *Kritik der Marx'schen Werttheorie.* In: *Jahrbücher für Nationalökonomie und Statistik...* 3. Folge, Bd. 3, Jena, 1892.— 16-17, 23

Forcade, E. *La Guerre du socialisme. II. L'économie politique révolutionnaire et sociale.* In: *Revue des deux Mondes,* nouvelle série, tome XXIV. Paris, 1848.— 830

Francis, J. *History of the Bank of England, Its Times and Traditions.* Third edition. Vol. I. London, 1848.—597-99

Fullarton, J. *On the Regulation of Currencies; being an examination of the principles, on which it is proposed to restrict, within certain fixed limits, the future issues on credit of the Bank of England, and of the other banking establishments throughout the country.* 2nd ed., with corr. and add. London, 1845.—402, 446-52, 457

Gilbart, J. W. *The History and Principles of Banking.* London, 1834.—337, 358, 402-04, 605
— *An Inquiry into the Causes of the Pressure on the Money Market during the Year 1839.* London, 1840.—536-37, 540-41

Goethe, J. W. von. *Faust.* Der Tragödie erster Teil.—391

[Greg, R. H.] *The Factory Question, considered in relation to its effects on the health and morals of those employed in factories. And the "Ten Hour's Bill", in relation to its effects upon the manufactures of England, and those of foreign countries.* London, 1837. Quoted from: *Reports of the Inspectors of Factories ... for the Half Year ending 31st October 1848 ...* London, 1849.—109

Hamilton, R. *An Inquiry Concerning the Rise and Progress, the Redemption and Present State, and the Management, of the National Debt of Great Britain.* Second edition, enlarged. Edinburgh, 1814.—392

Hardcastle, D. *Banks and Bankers.* Second edition. London, 1843.—541, 606

Hegel, G. W. F. *Encyclopädie der philosophischen Wissenschaften im Grundrisse.* Theil I. *Die Logik.* In: *Werke.* Band VI. Berlin, 1840.—766
— *Grundlinien der Philosophie des Rechts.* In: *Werke.* Band VIII. Berlin, 1840. —609-10

Heyd, W. *Geschichte des Levantehandels im Mittelalter.* Band II. Stuttgart, 1879.—889

[Hodgskin, Th.] *Labour Defended Against the Claims of Capital; or, the Unproductiveness of Capital Proved. With reference to the present combinations amongst journeymen.* By a Labourer. London, 1825.—387, 396

Horace (Quintus Horatius Flaccus). *Epistolae.*—201, 614

Hubbard, J. G. *The Currency and the Country.* London, 1843.—412-13

Hüllmann, K. *Staedtewesen des Mittelalters.* Th. 1-2. Bonn, 1826-1827.—316, 318, 592

Hume, D. *Of Interest.* In: *Essays and Treatises on Several Subjects.* In two volumes. A new edition. Vol. I, containing essays, moral, political and literary. London, 1764.—374

An Inquiry into Those Principles, Respecting the Nature of Demand and the Necessity of Consumption, Lately Advocated by Mr. Malthus, from Which It Is Concluded, that Taxation and the Maintenance of Unproductive Consumers Can Be Conducive to the Progress of Wealth. London, 1821.—193, 639

Interest of Money Mistaken, or a Treatise, proving, that the abatement of interest is the effect and not the cause of the riches of a nation, and that six per cent is a proportionable interest to the present condition of this Kingdom. London, 1668.—598

Johnston, J. F. W. *Notes on North America, Agricultural, Economical, and Social.* Vol. 1. Edinburgh and London, 1851.— 611, 663-64

Jones, R. *An Introductory Lecture on Political Economy Delivered at King's College, London, 27th February 1833. To which is added a syllabus of a course of lectures on the wages of labour.* London, 1833.— 265
— *An Essay on the Distribution of Wealth, and on the Sources of Taxation.* Part I: Rent. London, 1831.— 747

Kiesselbach, W. *Der Gang des Welthandels und die Entwicklung des europäischen Völkerlebens im Mittelalter.* Stuttgart, 1860.— 325

Kinnear, J. G. *The Crisis and the Currency: with a comparison between the English and Scotch systems of banking.* London, 1847.— 440, 523

Laing, Samuel. *National Distress; its Causes and Remedies.* London, 1844.— 760

Laing, Seton. *A New Series of the Great City Frauds of Cole, Davidson & Gordon.* Fifth edition, London [1869].— 532

Lavergne, L. de. *The Rural Economy of England, Scotland, and Ireland.* Translated from the French. Edinburgh and London, 1855.— 624-25

Leatham, W. *Letters on the Currency, addressed to Charles Wood, Esq. M. P. ... and ascertaining for the first time, on true principles, the amount of inland and foreign bills of exchange in circulation for several consecutive years, and out at one time.* Second edition with corrections and additions. London, 1840.— 398

Lexis, W. *Kritische Erörterungen über die Währungsfrage.* In: *Jahrbuch für Gesetzgebung, Verwaltung und Volkswirthschaft im Deutschen Reich ...* Hrsg. von Gustav Schmoller. 5. Jg., 1.Heft. Leipzig, 1881.— 14
— *Die Marx'sche Kapitaltheorie.* In: *Jahrbücher für Nationalökonomie und Statistik.* Gegr. von Bruno Hildebrand, hrsg. von Johannes Conrad. Neue Folge, 11. Bd. Jena, 1885.— 12-13

Liebig, J. von. *Die Chemie in ihrer Anwendung auf Agricultur und Physiologie.* In zwei Theilen. Siebente Auflage. Theil I: *Der chemische Proceß der Ernährung der Vegetabilien.* Braunschweig, 1862.— 732, 799

[Linguet, S. N. H.] *Théorie des loix civiles, ou Principes fondamentaux de la société.* Tomes I-II. Londres, 1767.— 88, 777

List, F. *Die Ackerverfassung, die Zwergwirthschaft und die Auswanderung.* Stuttgart, Tübingen, 1842.— 871

Loria, A. *Les Bases économiques de la constitution soziale.* Deuxième édition. Paris, 1893.— 19
— *Die Durchschnittsprofitrate auf Grundlage des Marx'schen Wertgesetzes.* Von Dr. Conrad Schmidt. Stuttgart, 1889. In: *Jahrbücher für Nationalökonomie und Statistik.* Neue Folge, Bd. 20, Jena, 1890.— 19, 20
— *Karl Marx.* In: *Nuova Antologia di Scienze, Lettere ed Arti.* Roma, Seconda serie, Vol. 38, Nr. 7, 1 April 1883.— 19
— *L'opera postuma di Carlo Marx.* In: *Nuova Antologia. Rivista di Scienze, Lettere ed Arti.* Roma, Terza serie. Vol. 55, Nr. 3, 1 Febbraio 1895.— 876-81
— *La teoria economica della costituzione politica.* Roma, Torino, Firenze, 1886.— 19

Luther, M. *An die Pfarrherrn wider den Wucher zu predigen.* Vermanung, Wittemberg, 1540. In: *Der sechste Teil der Bücher des Ehrnwirdigen Herrn Doctoris Martini Lutheri ...*

Wittembergk, 1589.—345, 391-92, 605-06
— *Von Kauffshandlung und Wucher.* In: *Der sechste Teil der Bücher des Ehrnwirdigen Herrn Doctoris Martini Lutheri...* Wittembergk, 1589.—329

Luzac, E. *Hollands Rijkdom ...* Deel 3. Leyden, 1782. Quoted from: Simon Vissering, *Handboek van praktische staathuishoudkunde.* Deel 1. Amsterdam 1860-61.—317

[Luxenberg, A.] *Bemerkung zu dem Aufsätze des Herrn Stiebeling: Über den Einfluß der Verdichtung des Kapitals auf den Lohn und die Ausbeutung der Arbeit.* In: *Die Neue Zeit,* Nr. 3, 1887.—22

Macaulay, Th. B. *The History of England from the Accession of James the Second.* Vol. IV. London, 1855.—599

Malthus, T. R. *Definitions in Political Economy, preceded by an inquiry into the rules which ought to guide political economists in the definition and use of their terms; with remarks on the deviation from these rules in their writings.* London, 1827.—41
— A new edition, with a preface, notes and supplementary remarks by John Cazenove. London, 1853.—43
— (anon.) *An Essay on the Principle of Population, as It Affects the Future Improvement of Society, with remarks on the speculations of Mr. Godwin, M. Condorcet, and other writers.* London, 1798.—393, 664
— *An Inquiry into the Nature and Progress of Rent, and the Principles by which it is Regulated.* London, 1815.—652
— *Principles of Political Economy Considered with a View to Their Practical Application.* London, 1820.—190
— *Principles of Political Economy ...* Second edition, with considerable additions from the author's own manuscript and an original memoir. London, 1836.—40, 48, 169, 197, 652

Maron, H. *Extensiv oder Intensiv? Ein Kapitel aus der land-wirthschaftlichen Betriebslehre.* Oppeln, 1859.—794

[Massie, J.] *An Essay on the Governing Causes of the Natural Rate of Interest; wherein the sentiments of Sir William Petty and Mr. Locke, on that head, are considered.* London, 1750. —331, 351, 357, 360, 363, 374

Mill, J. St. *Essays on Some Unsettled Questions of Political Economy.* London, 1844 —864
— *Principles of Political Economy with Some of Their Applications to Social Philosophy.* Second edition. In two volumes. Vol. I, London, 1849.—387, 396

Mommsen, Th. *Römische Geschichte.* Zweite Auflage. Bd. I-III. Bd. I, Berlin, 1856. —325, 383, 773

Morton, J. Ch. *On the Forces Used in Agriculture.* In: *The Journal of the Society of Arts.* Vol. VII, 9 December 1859.—623

Morton J. L. *The Resources of Estates: Being a treatise on the agricultural improvement and general management of landed property.* London, 1858.—623, 624, 667

Möser, J. *Osnabrückische Geschichte.* Theil I. Berlin, Stettin, 1780.—777

Mounier, L. *De l'agriculture en France, d'après les documents officiels, avec des remarques par Rubichon.* Tomes 1-2. Paris, 1846.—794, 798

Müller, A. H. *Die Elemente der Staatskunst. Oeffentliche Vorlesungen vor Sr. Durchlaucht dem Prinzen Bernhard von Sachsen-Weimar und einer Versammlung von Staatsmännern und Diplomaten, im Winter von 1808 auf 1809, zu Dresden, gehalten.* Dritter Theil. Berlin, 1809.— 355, 395

Newman, F. W. *Lectures on Political Economy.* London, 1851.— 589

Newman, S. P. *Elements of Political Economy.* Andover and New York, 1835.— 278

[North, D.] *Discourses upon Trade; principally directed to the cases of the interest, coynage, clipping, increase of money.* London, 1691.— 606

Observations on Certain Verbal Disputes in Political Economy, particularly relating to value, and to demand and supply. London, 1821.— 182, 190

Opdyke, G. *A Treatise on Political Economy.* New York, 1851.— 361, 662

Passy, H. *Rente du sol.* In: *Dictionnaire de l'économie politique.* Tome II. Paris, 1854.— 756, 769, 772

Pecqueur, C. *Théorie nouvelle d'économie sociale et politique, ou Études sur l'organisation des sociétés.* Paris, 1842.— 603

[Petty, W.] *A Treatise of Taxes & Contributions. Shewing the nature and measures of crown-lands, assessments, customs, poll-moneys, lotteries, benevolence, penalties, monopolies, offices, tythes, raising of coins, hearth-money, excise, etc. With several intersperst discourses and digressions concerning wars, the church, universities, rents and purchases, usury and exchange, banks and lombards, registries for conveyances, beggars, ensurance, exportation of money, wool, free-ports, coins, housing, liberty of conscience, etc. The same being frequently applied to the present state and affairs of Ireland.* London, 1667.— 770

Poppe, J. H. M. *Geschichte der Technologie seit der Wiederherstellung der Wissenschaften bis an das Ende des achtzehnten Jahrhunderts.* Bd. I. Göttingen, 1807.— 334

Price, R. *An Appeal to the Public, on the Subject of the National Debt.* London, 1772.— 392

— *Observations on Reversionary Payments; on Schemes for Providing Annuities for Widows, and for Persons in Old Age; on the Method of Calculating the Values of Assurances on Lives; and on the National Debt.* 2nd ed. London, 1772.— 393

Proudhon, P. J. *Gratuité du crédit.* See: Bastiat, Fr. *Gratuité du crédit. Discussion entre M. Fr. Bastiat et M. Proudhon.*— 343-45, 602-03

— *Qu'est-ce que la propriété? ou Recherches sur le principe du droit et du gouvernement.* Paris, 1841.— 830

Terence (Publius Terentius Afer), *Andria,* Act I, Scene 1.— 223

Quételet, A. *Sur l'homme et le développement de ses facultés, ou Essai de physique sociale.* Tomes I-II. Paris. 1835.— 847

Ramsay, G. *An Essay on the Distribution of Wealth.* Edinburgh, 1846.— 43, 48, 278, 359, 360, 376, 377, 754

Reden, F. W. von. *Vergleichende Kultur-Statistik der Geburts- und Bevölkerungsverhältnisse der Groß-Staaten Europa's.* Berlin, 1848.— 464

Ricardo, D. *On the Principles of Political Economy, and Taxation.* Third edition. London, 1821.— 108, 116, 178, 182, 201, 236, 238, 322, 642-43, 652, 759, 802, 828, 840

— *Principles of Political Economy, and Taxation.* In: *The Works of D. Ricardo.* With a notice of the life and writings of the author, by J. R. MacCulloch. 2nd. ed. London, 1852.— 69, 222, 236

Rodbertus [-Jagetzow, J. K.] *Sociale Briefe an von Kirchmann.* Dritter Brief: Widerlegung der Ricardo'schen Lehre von der Grundrente und Begründung einer neuen Rententheorie. Berlin, 1851.— 138, 765, 787, 840

Roscher, W. *Die Grundlagen der Nationalökonomie. Ein Hand- und Lesebuch für Geschäftsmänner und Studierende.* Dritte, vermehrte und verbesserte Auflage. Stuttgart, Augsburg, 1858. In: Roscher W. *System der Volkswirthschaft.* Erster Band. Stuttgart, Augsburg, 1858.— 223, 306, 322, 396, 813

[Roy, H.] *The Theory of the Exchanges. The Bank Charter Act of 1844. The Abuse of the Metallic Principle to Depreciation.* Parliament mirrored in debate, supplemental to *The Stock Exchange and the Repeal of Sir J. Barnard's Act.* London, 1864.— 359, 361

Rubichon, M. *Du Mécanisme de la société en France et en Angleterre.* Nouvelle édition. Paris, 1837.— 623, 794, 797

Saint-Simon, C. H. *Nouveau christianisme. Dialogues entre un conservateur et un novateur.* 1er dialogue. Paris, 1825.— 600

Say, J. B. *Traité d'économie politique, ou simple exposition de la manière dont se forment, se distribuent et se consomment les richesses.* 3e éd. T. 1. Paris, 1817.— 278

— *Traité d'économie politique, ou simple exposition de la manière dont se forment, se distribuent et se consomment les* richesses. 4e éd. T. 2. Paris, 1819.— 828

Schmidt, C. *Der dritte Band des "Kapital".* In: *Sozialpolitisches Centralblatt,* 25. Februar 1895.— 882

— *Die Durchschnittsprofitrate auf Grundlage les Marx'schen Werthgesetzes.* Stuttgart, 1889.— 14, 16

— *Die Durchschnittsprofitrate und das Marx'sche Werthgesetz.* In: *Neue Zeit,* Revue des geistigen und öffentlichen Lebens ... 11. Jg. Nr. 3, 4. Stuttgart, 1893.— 15, 18, 20

Senior, N. W. *Letters on the Factory Act, as It Affects the Cotton Manufacture. To which are appended, a letter to Mr. Senior from L. Horner, and minutes of a conversation between Mr. E. Ashworth, Mr. Thomson and Mr. Senior.* London, 1837-40.— 38, 48

Sismondi, J. C. L. Simonde de. *Nouveaux principes d'économie politique, ou de la richesse dans ses rapports avec la population.* Seconde édition. Tomes I-II. Paris, 1827.— 475, 789

Smith, A. *An Inquiry into the Nature and Causes of the Wealth of Nations.* In two volumes. Vol. I. London, 1776.— 236, 327, 381, 471, 609, 773, 813, 828

— *Recherches sur la nature et les causes de la richesse des nations.* Traduction nouvelle, avec des notes et observations; par German Garnier. T. I. Paris 1802.— 141

Sombart, W. *Zur Kritik des ökonomischen Systems von Karl Marx.* In: *Archiv für soziale Gesetzgebung und Statistik.* Band VII, Berlin, 1894.— 881

Some Thoughts of the Interest of England. By a Lover of Commerce. London, 1697.— 601

Steuart, J. *An Inquiry into the Principles of Political Oeconomy.* In three volumes. Vol. I. Dublin, 1770.— 772

— *An Inquiry into the Principles of Political Oeconomy* ... In: *The Works, Political, Metaphysical, and Chronological* ... *Now first collected by General Sir James Steuart Bart, his son, from his father's corrected copies, to which are subjoined anecdotes of the author. In six volumes. Vol. I, London, 1805.*— 228, 327

— *Recherche des principes de l'économie politique, ou essai sur la science de la police intérieure des nations libres* ... Paris, 1789.— 362

Stiebeling, G. *Das Werthgesetz und die Profit-Rate.* Leichtfaßliche Auseinandersetzung einiger wissenschaftlichen Fragen. Mit einem polemischen Vorwort. New York, [1890].— 22-23

Storch, H. *Considérations sur la nature du revenu national.* Paris, 1824.— 833, 838
— *Cours d'économie politique, ou Exposition des principes qui déterminent la prospérité des nations.* Tomes I-II. St.-Pétersbourg, 1815.— 182, 651, 813, 833

Thiers, A. *Rapport du citoyen Thiers, précédé de la proposition du citoyen Proudhon relative à l'impôt sur le revenu, et suivi de son discours prononcé à l'Assemblée nationale, le 31 juillet 1848.* Paris, 1848.— 618

Thun, A. *Die Industrie am Niederrhein und ihre Arbeiter.* Theil II. *Die Industrie des bergischen Landes.* Leipzig, 1879.— 888

Tocqueville, A. *L'ancien régime et la révolution.* Paris, 1856.— 789

Tooke, Th. *A History of Prices, and of the State of the Circulation, from 1793 to 1837; preceded by a brief sketch of the state of the corn trade in the last two centuries.* In 2 vols. Vol. 2. London, 1838.— 368

— *A History of Prices, and of the State of the Circulation, from 1839 to 1847 inclusive: with a general review of the currency question, and remarks on the operation of the Act 7 & 8 Vict. c. 32. Being a continuation of the history of prices from 1793 to 1839.* London, 1848.— 358

— *An Inquiry into the Currency Principle; the connection of the currency with prices, and the expediency of a separation of issue from banking.* Second edition. London, 1844.— 353, 369, 399, 401, 436, 439, 829

Tooke, Th., Newmarch, W. *A History of Prices, and of the State of the Circulation, during the Nine Years 1848-1856.* In two volumes; forming the 5th and 6th volumes of the *History of Prices from 1792 to the Present Time.* Vol. VI. London, 1857.— 794

Torrens, R. *An Essay on the Production of Wealth; with an appendix, in which the principles of political economy are applied to the actual circumstances of this country.* London, 1821.— 43, 48, 108
— *On the Operation of the Bank Charter Act of 1844, as it Affects Commercial Credit.* Second edition. London, 1847.— 352

Tuckett, J. D. *A History of the Past and Present State of the Labouring Population, Including the Progress of Agriculture, Manufactures and Commerce.* In two volumes. Vol. I. London, 1846.— 596

Ure, A. *Philosophie des manufactures ou économie industrielle de la fabrication du coton, de la laine, du lin et de la soie, avec la description des diverses machines employeés dans les ateliers anglais.* Paris, 1836.— 84, 106, 384

Verri, P. *Meditazioni sulla Economia Politica ... con Annatazioni di Gian-Rinaldo Carli.* In: *Scrittori Classici Italiani di Economia Politica.* Parte moderna. Tomo XV. Milano, 1804.—278

Vinçard, P. *Histoire du travail et des travailleurs en France.* T. I-II. Paris, 1845.—773

Vissering, S. *Handboek van praktische Staathuishoudkunde.* Deel 1. Amsterdam, 1860-61. —316, 318

[Wakefield, E. G.] *England and America. A Comparison of the Social and Political State of Both Nations.* In two volumes. London, 1833.—743, 756

Walton, A. *History of the Landed Tenures of Great Britain and Ireland, from the Norman Conquest to the Present Time, Dedicated to the People of the United Kingdom.* London, 1865. —604-05

[West, E.] *Essay on the Application of Capital to Land, with observations shewing the impolicy of any great restriction of the importation of corn, and that the bounty of 1688 did not lower the price of it.* By a fellow of University College, Oxford. London, 1815.—240, 652

Wolf, J. *Das Rätsel der Durchschnittsprofitrate bei Marx.* In: *Jahrbücher für Nationalökonomie und Statistik.* Gegr. von Bruno Hildebrand. Hrsg. von J. Conrad. Dritte Folge, Bd. II. Jena, 1891.—17

— *Sozialismus und kapitalistische Gesellschaftsordnung. Kritische Würdigung beider als Grundlegung einer Sozialpolitik.* Stuttgart, 1892.—21

DOCUMENTS

An Act for Inspection of Coal Mines in Great Britain. [14 August 1850]. In: *A Collection of the public general statutes passed in the thirteenth and fourteenth year of the reign of Her Majestry Queen Victoria: Being the third session of the fifteenth Parliament of the United Kingdom of Great Britain and Ireland.* London, 1850.—91.

An Act for Vesting Certain Sums in Commissioners, at the end of every quarter of a year, to be by them applied to the reduction of the national debt. (Anno vicesimo sexto Georgii III regis.) Paris, 1808.—394

An Act for the Further Amendment of the Laws Relating to Labour in Factories [30th June 1856]. In: *The Statutes of the United Kingdom of Great Britain and Ireland, 12 & 20 Victoria, 1856.* London, 1856.—93

An Act to Amend the Laws Relating to Labour in Factories. [6th June 1844.] In: *The Statutes of the United Kingdom of Great Britain and Ireland, 7 & 8 Victoria, 1844.* London, 1844. —92

Coal Mine Accidents. Abstract of Return to an Address of the Honourable the House of Commons, dated 3 May 1861, etc. Ordered, by the H. of C., to be printed, 6 February 1862. —91

First Report from the Secret Committee on Commercial Distress; with the minutes of evidence. Ordered, by the House of Commons, to be printed, 8 June 1848 [London, 1848]. —410, 413-14, 450, 468, 472-73, 484-85, 486

First Report from the Select Committee of the House of Lords on the Sweating System; together with the proceedings of the committee, minutes of evidence, and appendix. Ordered, by the House of Commons, to be printed, 11 August 1888.— 333

First Report of the Children's Employment Commissioners in Mines and Collieries. Presented to both Houses of Parliament, by command of Her Majesty. 21 April 1841. [London, 1842].— 91

Public Health. Sixth Report of the Medical Officer of the Privy Council. With appendix. 1863. Presented pursuant to Act of Parliament. London, 1864. — 94-99

Report from the Secret Committee of the House of Lords, Appointed to Inquire into the Causes of the Distress which has for some time prevailed among the commercial classes, and how far it has been affected by the laws for regulating the issue of banknotes payable on demand. Together with the minutes of evidence and an appendix. Ordered, by the House of Commons, to be printed, 28 July 1848. [Reprinted 1857.] — 11, 410, 411, 508-09, 521-22, 523, 524-25, 535-36, 540, 548, 549, 553-54, 555, 556, 557-58, 559, 563-64

Report from the Select Committee on Bank Acts; together with the proceedings of the Committee, minutes of evidence, appendix and index. Ordered, by the House of Commons, to be printed, 30 July 1857.— 410, 411, 414-15, 417, 419, 420, 421, 422, 423, 424, 427-32, 445-46, 483, 492, 494, 499, 507, 508-09, 517, 518, 520, 523, 525, 526, 529-36, 537, 538, 540, 546, 547, 551, 553, 555-56, 557, 559, 560, 562, 565, 566, 567, 569, 570-71, 573, 574-79

Report from the Select Committee on the Bank Acts; together with the proceedings of the Committee, minutes of evidence, appendix and index. Ordered, by the House of Commons, to be printed, 1 July 1858.— 11, 474, 483, 495, 497, 520, 521-22, 560

Report from the Select Committee on Petitions Relating to the Corn Laws of this Kingdom: together with the minutes of evidence, and an appendix of accounts. Ordered, by the House of Commons, to be printed, 26 July 1814.— 620-21

Reports of the Inspectors of Factories to Her Majesty's Principal Secretary of State for the Home Department.— 620
— *for the Half Year Ending 31st October 1845.* London, 1846.— 125
— *for the Half Year Ending 31st October 1846.* London, 1847.— 125, 126
— *for the Half Year Ending 31st October 1847.* London, 1848.— 126
— *for the Half Year Ending 31st October 1848.* London, 1849.— 81, 109
— *for the Half Year Ending 30th April 1849.* London, 1849.— 127
— *for the Half Year Ending 31st October 1849.* London, 1850.— 127
— *for the Half Year Ending 30th April 1850.* London, 1850.— 127
— *for the Half Year Ending 31st October 1850.* London, 1851.— 124, 127-28
— *for the Half Year Ending 30th April 1851.* London, 1851.— 124
— *for the Half Year Ending 31st October 1852.* London, 1853.— 99-102
— *for the Half Year Ending 30th April 1853.* London, 1853.— 128
— *for the Half Year Ending 31st October 1853.* London, 1854.— 128
— *for the Half Year Ending 30th April 1854.* London, 1854.— 128
— *for the Half Year Ending 31st October 1855.* London, 1856.— 92
— *for the Half Year Ending 31st October 1858.* London, 1859.— 81, 123-25
— *for the Half Year Ending 30th April 1859.* London, 1859.— 128
— *for the Half Year Ending 31st October 1859.* London, 1860.— 128
— *for the Half Year Ending 30th April 1860.* London, 1860.— 128

— *for the Half Year Ending 31st October 1860.* London, 1861.— 129
— *for the Half Year Ending 30th April 1861.* London, 1861.— 94, 129, 130
— *for the Half Year Ending 31st October 1861.* London, 1862.— 82, 129, 130
— *for the Half Year Ending 30th April 1862.* London, 1862.— 94, 104, 130-31
— *for the Half Year Ending 31st October 1862.* London, 1863.— 92, 104, 129, 131
— *for the Half Year Ending 30th April 1863.* London, 1863.— 131
— *for the Half Year Ending 31st October 1863.* London, 1864.— 92, 102, 103, 104, 111, 129, 130-36
— *for the Half Year Ending 30th April 1864.* London, 1864.— 129-30, 135

Reports Respecting Grain, and the Corn Laws; viz.: First and Second Reports from the Lords Committees, appointed to enquire into the state of the growth, commerce, and consumption of grain, and all laws relating thereto. Ordered, by the House of Commons, to be printed, 23 November 1814.— 620-21

ANONYMOUS ARTICLES AND REPORTS PUBLISHED
IN PERIODIC EDITIONS

The Economist, No. 217, October 23, 1847: *The Scotch Bank Bill — 1845.*— 558
— No. 221, November 20, 1847: *The Changed Distribution of Capital.*— 497
— No. 224, December 11, 1847: *Conformity of Convertible Notes with a Metallic Currency.*— 568
— No. 379, November 30, 1850: *The Remarkable Phenomena of the Foreign Exchanges.* — 586
— No. 386, January 11, 1851: *The Balance of Trade. England with the World.*— 586

The Edinburgh Review or Critical Journal; for August-December, 1831. Review of the book: R. Jones, *An Essay on the Distribution of Wealth and on the Sources of Taxation.*— 767

INDEX OF PERIODICALS

SUBJECT INDEX
(to volumes 35-37)

200-06, 226, 238-39, 240-41, 302-
04, 312, 335-37, 509-10, 587-88,
590-91, 614, 616
— starting-point and premises of—
35, 157, 178-81, 326-27, 339-40,
358, 570-71, 619, 705, 706, 748-51,
759; 37, 195, 589, 590, 609, 610,
611
— contradictions of—35, 8, 15, 19-20,
122-23, 186, 295-97, 336-37, 361-
62, 410-11, 435, 443-45, 446-50,
464-65, 480-83, 503-04, 506-07,
509, 530, 639-40, 651-52, 749-50;
36, 315-16; 37, 89-90, 121-22, 243-
44, 247-48, 249, 255, 256, 257, 262,
263, 265, 284, 285-86, 567-68, 569
— and feudalism—35, 706
— historical necessity of—35, 339-40,
516-17
— as a passing historical phase—35,
10-11, 14-15, 34, 489, 581, 587-88,
748-51
— purchase and sale of labour power
as a basic condition of—36, 20-21,
36, 42-43, 81-82, 88-89, 121-22,
343, 351, 383-84
— and separation of labour power
from means of production—36, 38
— and commodity production—36,
42, 115, 121, 494-95, 499-500; 37,
179, 180, 181
— labourers and means of production
as factors of production—36, 40-41
— and revolutionisation of economic
structure of society—36, 42, 62-63
— compelling motive of—36, 63-65,
74-75, 84-85, 102, 124-25, 157,
349, 383-84, 444, 502-03
— vulgar political economy on capitalist process of production—36,
73
— and technique—36, 42, 62-63, 83-
84, 112, 172-73
— continuity of capitalist production—36, 107-08, 110, 280-81
— and evolution of agricultural labourer into wage labourer—36,
121-22

— mode of production and mode of
exchange—36, 121-22
— and market—36, 154-55; 37, 111,
265
— anarchy of production and waste of
productive forces—36, 174-75,
315-16, 468-69
— crisis and abnormal conditions of
process of production—36, 317-18
— unproductive expenses (faux frais)
of—36, 135, 140, 142-43, 152-53,
344
— and credit—36, 344
— and condition of working class—
36, 409-10
— and foreign trade—36, 469-70
— method of analysing—36, 508, 509
— as a synthesis of the processes of
production and circulation—37,
28, 45, 813, 814
— its distinction from the mode of
production based on slavery—37,
33
— and economy of constant capital—
37, 87-88, 89
— and development of the productive
power of labour—37, 88-89, 256,
257, 258, 265
— and social character of production—37, 91-92, 93, 191, 265, 567-
68, 569
— as immediately preceding the socialist mode of production—37,
92, 434-35
— classes under capitalist mode of
production—37, 194, 851-52, 853
— and the process of accumulation—
37, 215, 216, 217, 264, 265
— and relative overpopulation—37,
216, 220, 227, 235
— production of surplus value and
profit as purpose of—37, 239-40,
241, 242, 243, 244, 250, 255, 256,
863-64
— historical character of—37, 240,
256, 257, 258, 262, 614, 615, 801,
802, 866
— barriers of production under—37,
248-49, 256, 257, 262, 505

— and methods to reduce time of turnover in agriculture — *36*, 243-45
— changes in amount of — *36*, 258
— turnover of constant and variable
part of — *36*, 293-94
— and the cost price — *37*, 34, 37-38
— and value of the commodity product — *37*, 109-10
— and development of the productive
forces of labour — *37*, 258
— loan of — *37*, 341-43
Circulation
— and the metamorphoses of commodities — *35*, 114-16, 118-22
— simple circulation — *35*, 167-69
— difference from the direct exchange
of products — *35*, 121-23
— identity of sale and purchase — *35*,
122-23
— and capitalism — *35*, 157, 356-58
— of money — *35*, 124-28, 130-31,
144-45, 146, 149-50; *36*, 413, 477
— production of commodities and circulation of commodities — *36*, 39
— of surplus value and capital value — *36*, 48, 50, 73-74
— of capital as part of general circulation of commodities — *36*, 65-66,
75-76
— of surplus value in simple reproduction — *36*, 71-72, 73, 75-77
— and formation of a fund for purchase and payment — *36*, 82-83
— money capital and speed of — *36*,
114
— of industrial capital and world
market — *36*, 115
— amount of money required for —
36, 118, 284, 323, 327, 329-30, 339,
343
— as a phase of reproduction process — *36*, 30-31, 132-33, 349; *37*,
278-79, 288, 813, 814
— and formation of supply — *36*, 147,
148, 151
— improvement in means of transportation and time of — *36*, 252, 253
— credit and metallic circulation —
36, 499-500

— seeming derivation of surplus value
from circulation — *37*, 43-44, 47,
137, 814
— time of circulation — *37*, 47, 74-75,
84, 278-79, 301, 814
— and the value of commodities — *37*,
279
See also *Exchange*
Civil War in America — *35*, 9, 292, 296,
305-06, 424, 436, 437, 574, 760
Clan — *35*, 718-20
Classes
— capitalist reproduction as reproduction of class of wage labourers
and class of capitalists — *36*, 39,
378, 390-91, 414-15
— exploitation of working class under
capitalism — *36*, 43, 353, 509, 515-
16
— industrial capital and class antagonism between capitalists and wage
labourers — *36*, 62-63
— working class and crises of overproduction — *36*, 316-17, 409-10
See also *Capitalist; Peasantry*
Classical bourgeois political economy
— general definition of — *35*, 14, 91,
440, 533, 537, 541, 562, 606, 611-
12
— analysis of economic categories and
processes — *35*, 30-34, 56-57, 90-91,
154-55, 159, 177, 180-82, 214-15,
310-12, 353, 359, 366-67, 390-91,
510, 517-18, 520-25, 537-40, 541,
584-87, 590-92, 595, 602, 604-05,
609-10, 616-17, 625-26
— Ricardo on the correlation of the
prices of production and values of
commodities — *37*, 177-79
— Ricardo on the ground rent — *37*,
182, 642-43, 671, 673, 743-44, 758
— Ricardo on the influence of foreign
trade on the general rate of profit — *37*, 236-37
— Ricardo on the rate of profit — *37*,
239, 240, 241
— Newman on the correlation of commerce and industry — *37*, 278

D

G

- production relations under— *37*, 762, 818, 867
- and the slave's labour conditions— *37*, 776-77
- price of slaves— *37*, 795
- antagonistic form of surplus labour in the slave system— *37*, 806

Slave trade— *35*, 272-73, 740, 746-48

Small landed property
- form of landed property for small-scale operation— *37*, 608, 793
- causes of decay of small-scale landed property— *37*, 793
- and the development of productive power of labour— *37*, 793
- and price of land— *37*, 794, 796, 797, 798-99
- illusions created by— *37*, 796
- and exploitation of land— *37*, 798-99, 800

See also *Peasant proprietorship of land parcels*

Small landowner— *37*, 785, 788, 789, 790, 791, 792

Small producer, small production— *37*, 174, 175-76, 214, 331, 332, 333, 608, 681-82, 776, 777, 778, 779, 780, 781, 782, 784-85, 793, 796-98, 881, 883

Social product
- two departments of— *36*, 366, 393-95
- replacement of value and substance of component parts of— *36*, 391-92, 393
- composition of— *36*, 428-30
- as capital and as revenue— *36*, 435

Socialised production— see *Communist society*

Socialism— see *Communism; Communist mode of production*

Socialist revolution— *35*, 16, 35, 491, 504-07, 749-51; *37*, 263, 438

Socially necessary labour time
- definition of— *35*, 49, 82, 220-21, 329-30, 551-52
- as substance of value— *35*, 49, 55-56, 82-83, 196-97, 198-99, 205-07, 220-21, 321-24
- and competition— *35*, 350

Society
- its wealth— *37*, 354, 437-38, 568, 807
- its economic and political structure— *37*, 778-79, 805

Socio-economic formation
- character of its development— *35*, 10
- division of labour in different formations of society— *35*, 364-65
- reproduction, simple and on an extended scale in different formations— *35*, 594
- form of surplus value as a distinguishing feature of antagonistic social formations— *35*, 226-28, 243-45
- capitalist relations as the product of the downfall of previous forms of society— *35*, 179-81
- significance of means of labour for the investigation of extinct economic forms of society— *35*, 189-90
- instruments of labour as a distinguishing feature of social formations— *35*, 188-89

Spain— *35*, 35, 515, 739, 747

Speculation— *35*, 160-61, 202, 219-20, 275, 589, 660-61, 742-43, 759-60

State
- the weapon of capital— *35*, 276, 290-91, 314, 367-68, 610-11, 641-42, 726-31, 739-40
- state "regulation" of economic life— *35*, 246-48, 276-78, 283-302, 303-05, 492-98, 502-05, 562
- and import and export of precious metal— *37*, 318
- as owner of the surplus product in the precapitalist societies— *37*, 328
- national debt— *37*, 392-93, 394, 462, 463, 523-24
- government bonds— *37*, 400-01, 406, 455, 456, 467, 475, 476, 500-01, 795
- and differential rent— *37*, 654
- as a landowner— *37*, 779

See also *Factory legislation*